Encyclopedia of Indian Religions

Series Editor
Arvind Sharma

K.T.S. Sarao • Jeffery D. Long
Editors

Buddhism and Jainism

Volume 2

M–Z

With 187 Figures and 1 Table

Springer

Editors
K.T.S. Sarao
University of Delhi, Department of Buddhist Studies
Delhi, India

Jeffery D. Long
Elizabethtown College, Department of Religious Studies
Elizabethtown, USA

ISBN 978-94-024-0851-5 ISBN 978-94-024-0852-2 (eBook)
ISBN 978-94-024-0853-9 (print and electronic bundle)
DOI 10.1007/978-94-024-0852-2

Library of Congress Control Number: 2016953015

Printed on acid-free paper

This Springer imprint is published by Springer Nature
The registered company is Springer Science+Business Media B.V.
The registered company address is: Van Godewijckstraat 30, 3311 GX Dordrecht, The Netherlands

Preface

This encyclopedia is the result of a massive and coordinated international effort among scholars of Indian religions to develop a useful resource for researchers engaged in the investigation of these traditions. This effort has involved the collaboration and cooperation of research scholars from across the globe, tapping into disciplines as varied as linguistics, sociology, anthropology, history, theology, and philosophy. It is a work that has been years in the making and all of us who have been involved are pleased to see it moving to its final fruition.

The two traditions that form the topic of this particular volume, the Buddhist and Jain traditions, are of special importance to anyone who wants to understand the religious heritage and landscape of India. There is a certain logic to placing these two in a volume together. Both are what are known as *Śramaṇa* or "striving" traditions. This is the name by which ascetics of northern India in the first millennium BCE referred to themselves. It differentiates one who achieves the heights of spiritual realization through personal effort from those who are held to have achieved these heights through birth – the claim that some members of the *Brāhmaṇa* or Brahmin class made for themselves during the same period. There were Brahmins (by birth) who were also Śramaṇas, some of whose teachings can be found in the *Upaniṣads*, or late Vedic writings also composed in the first millennium BCE. But among those Śramaṇa traditions that differentiated themselves from Vedic or Brahminical schools of thought, the two that survive to the present day are Buddhism and Jainism.

As Śramaṇa traditions, Buddhism and Jainism share many of the same ideological views and assumptions. There is, of course, as already mentioned, the emphasis on one's own effort in the attainment of spiritual realization. And there is also the assumption that such realization leads to liberation from the cycle of karma and rebirth. In both of these traditions, those who have achieved perfect awakening, perfect awareness – the Buddhas in the case of Buddhism, the Jinas in Jainism – stand even above the Gods and Goddesses in the esteem in which they are held. Unlike the deities – who, for all the grandeur, remain nonetheless bound to the cycle of rebirth – these beings have managed to disentangle the threads of saṃsāra and are now free from the suffering which living in the material world inevitably brings.

The Buddhist and Jain terms defined in this volume do not form a comprehensive list (which would be far beyond the scope even of an ambitious encyclopedia such as this one). They do, however, provide an excellent starting point for research scholars who are seeking a deeper understanding of key topics connected with these two traditions. And we are proud to say that the information presented represents the latest in our scholarly understanding of these traditions, the cutting edge of our available knowledge.

We are proud to be involved with this project, which we now humbly offer to the world.

Delhi, India
Elizabethtown, USA
February, 2017

Professor K.T.S. Sarao
Professor Jeffery D. Long
Volume Editors

Series Editor

Arvind Sharma Formerly of the I.A.S., Arvind Sharma (b.1940) is the Birks Professor of Comparative Religion in the School of Religious Studies at McGill University in Montreal, Canada. He has also taught at various universities in Australia and the United States and has published extensively in the fields of comparative religion and Indology. He is currently the general editor of *Encyclopedia of Indian Religions* (Springer, 2017) and his forthcoming works include *Orientalism Two, Our Civilization*, and *How to Read the Manusmṛti*.

About the Editors

K.T.S. Sarao was born in a remote village in Sangrur district of Punjab (India) where he received his initial school education. After doing his pre-university from Panjab University, he joined the University of Delhi from where he received the degrees of Bachelor of Arts (Honors in History with Economics), Master of Arts (History), Master of Philosophy (Chinese and Japanese Studies), and Doctor of Philosophy (Indian Buddhism). He was awarded the prestigious Commonwealth Scholarship in 1985 to study at the University of Cambridge from where he received his second Doctor of Philosophy (Pāli and Buddhist Archeology) in 1989. He began his teaching career in 1981 at Delhi University's KM College where he taught history for about 12 years. In 1993, he joined the Department of Buddhist Studies, Delhi University, as a reader (associate professor) in Indian Buddhism and Pāli. In 1995, he was appointed to a professorial chair in Buddhist Studies at Delhi University. In his capacity as a professor, he has also been working as a member of the Delhi University Court since 1993. Besides having worked as head of the Department of Buddhist Studies, Delhi University, he has also sat on the governing bodies of different colleges of Delhi University. Professor Sarao has also been a member of the Governing Committee of the Central University of Tibetan Studies (Sarnath) and the Academic Council of the Jaina Visvabharati University (Ladnun). He has also been a visiting fellow/professor at Dongguk University (South Korea), Chung-Hwa Institute of Buddhist Studies (Taiwan), Sorbonne (France), Cambridge University (UK),

Visvabharati (India), and PS Royal Buddhist University (Cambodia). He has written 16 books and published more than 150 research papers and articles. Some of his important books are *The Origin and Nature of Ancient Indian Buddhism* (1989), *Urban Centres and Urbanisation as Reflected in the Pāli Vinaya and Sutta Piṭakas* (1990), *Pilgrimage to Kailash: The Indian Route* (2009), *The Dhammapada: A Translator's Guide* (2009), and *The Decline of Indian Buddhism: A Fresh Perspective* (2012). He has successfully supervised 53 Ph.D. theses and over 70 M.Phil. dissertations. The Preah Sihanouk Royal Buddhist University, Phnom Penh (Cambodia), conferred on him the degree of D.Litt. (Honoris Causa) in 2011. He takes keen interest in mountainous trekking, religious pluralism, and interfaith dialogue.

Jeffery D. Long is Professor of Religion and Asian Studies at Elizabethtown College, where he has taught since receiving his Ph.D. in the Philosophy of Religions from the University of Chicago Divinity School in the year 2000. Long is the editor of three books: *A Vision for Hinduism* (2007), *Jainism: An Introduction* (2009), and *The Historical Dictionary of Hinduism* (2011). He is currently working on a two-volume introduction to Indian philosophy, including a textbook and a reader of primary sources. His other publications include over four dozen articles and reviews in various edited volumes and scholarly journals, including *Prabuddha Bharata*, the *Journal of Vaishnava Studies*, the *Journal of Religion*, and the *Journal of the American Academy of Religion*. He has taught in the International Summer School for Jain Studies in New Delhi, India, lectured at the Siddhachalam Jain Tirth, in Blairstown, New Jersey, and in April 2013, he delivered the inaugural Virchand Gandhi lecture in Jain studies at the Claremont School of Theology. Most recently, he spoke at the International Conference on Science and Jain Philosophy, held at the Indian Institute of Technology in Mumbai, India.

Contributors

Bhikkhu Anālayo Center for Buddhist Studies, University of Hamburg, Balve, Germany

Michael Anderson Claremont School of Theology, Claremont Lincoln University, Claremont, CA, USA

James B. Apple Department of Religious Studies, University of Calgary, Calgary, AB, Canada

Ana Bajželj Department of Philosophy, Faculty of Arts, University of Ljubljana, Ljubljana, Slovenia

Polonsky Academy, The Van Leer Jerusalem Institute, Jerusalem, Israel

A. W. Barber Department of Communication and Culture, University of Calgary, Calgary, AB, Canada

Claudine Bautze-Picron Centre National de la Recherche Scientifique (CNRS), UMR 7528 'Mondes Iranien et Indien', Paris, France

Radha Madhav Bharadwaj Department of History, Deen Dayal Upadhyaya College, University of Delhi, Karampura, New Delhi, India

Whitny M. Braun Center for Jain Studies, Claremont Lincoln University, Claremont, CA, USA

Sean Butler Claremont Graduate University, Claremont, CA, USA

Madhumita Chattopadhyay Department of Philosophy, Jadavpur University, Kolkata, West Bengal, India

Angraj Chaudhary Vipassana Research Institute, Dhammagiri, Igatpuri, Nashik, Maharashtra, India

Mangala Ramchandra Chinchore Department of Philosophy, Centre for Studies in Classical Indian Buddhist Philosophy and Culture, University of Pune, Pune, Maharashtra, India

Gregory M. Clines Committee on the Study of Religion, Harvard University, Cambridge, MA, USA

Mahinda Deegalle Department of Humanities, Colgate University, New York, USA

Bath Spa University, UK

K. L. Dhammajoti Centre of Buddhist Studies, The University of Hong Kong, Hong Kong, China

Brianne Donaldson Claremont School of Theology, Claremont, CA, USA

William Edelglass Philosophy and Environmental Studies, Marlboro College, Marlboro, VT, USA

Joseph P. Elacqua Center for Language and Learning Development, Mohawk Valley Community College, Utica, NY, USA

Matthew Zaro Fisher Claremont Graduate University and the Center for Jain Studies at Claremont Lincoln University, Claremont, CA, USA

Peter Gilks International College of I-Shou University, Kaohsiung, Taiwan

Pradeep P. Gokhale Department of Philosophy, University of Pune, Pune, Maharashtra, India

Dr. B. R. Ambedkar Chair, Central University of Tibetan Studies, Varanasi, Uttar Pradesh, India

Siyaram Mishra Haldhar Department of Buddhist Studies, University of Delhi, Delhi, India

Georgios T. Halkias Oxford Centre of Buddhist Studies, Oxford, UK

Robert Harding Faculty of Asian and Middle Eastern Studies, University of Cambridge, Cambridge, UK

Jens-Uwe Hartmann Institut für Indologie und Tibetologie, University of Munich, Munich, Germany

Jackie Ho Department of Interdisciplinary Studies, University of Calgary Room 3168, Professional Faculties Building, Calgary, AB, Canada

Christopher Hrynkow Department of Religion and Culture, Saint Thomas More College, University of Saskatchewan, Saskatoon, SK, Canada

Pankaj Jain Department of Anthropology, Department of Philosophy and Religion, University of North Texas, Denton, TX, USA

Jordan Johnson School of Historical, Philosophical, and Religious Studies, Arizona State University, Tempe, AZ, USA

Klaus Karttunen Department of World Cultures, University of Helsinki, Helsinki, Finland

Y. Karunadasa University of Kelaniya, Kelaniya, Sri Lanka

Centre of Buddhist Studies, The University of Hong Kong, Hong Kong, China

Kai Ana Makanoe Kaikaulaokaweilaha Kaululaau Department of Philosophy, University of Bristol, Bristol, UK

Department of Philosophy, California State University, Los Angeles, CA, USA

Amy Paris Langenberg Religion and Women's Studies, Auburn University, Auburn, AL, USA

Der-Huey Lee Research Center for Buddhist Education, Peking University, Beijing, China

Department of Philosophy, Chinese Culture University, Taipei, Taiwan

Keith A. Leitich Department of Business and Social Science, Pierce College Puyallup, Puyallup, WA, USA

William Magee UMA Institute of Tibetan Studies, Charlottesville, VA, USA

Tibetan Studies, Dharma Drum Buddhist College, Taipei County, Taiwan, China

Walter Menezes Department of Humanities and Social Sciences, Indian Institute of Technology Bombay, Mumbai, Maharashtra, India

Vakul Mittal Indian Buddhism, Lucknow, UP, India

Pankaj Mohan Faculty of International Korean Studies, The Academy of Korean Studies, Gyeonggi-do, South Korea

Asha Mukherjee Department of Philosophy and Religion, Visva-Bharati Central University, Santiniketan, WB, India

Hari Shankar Prasad Department of Philosophy, University of Delhi, New Delhi, Delhi, India

Leonard C. D. C. Priestley Department of East Asian Studies and Centre for South Asian Studies, University of Toronto, Richmond Hill, ON, Canada

Christopher S. Queen Division of Continuing Education, Harvard University, Cambridge, MA, USA

Ram Kumar Rana Department of Buddhist Studies, Faculty of Arts, University of Delhi, Delhi, India

Rajesh Ranjan Department of Pali, Nava Nalanda Mahaviihara (Deemed to be University), Nalanda, Bihar, India

Anamika Roy Department of Ancient History, Culture and Archaeology, University of Allahabad, Allahabad, India

K. Sankarnarayan K.J. Somaiya Centre for Buddhist Studies, Mumbai, India

K. T. S. Sarao Department of Buddhist Studies, University of Delhi, Delhi, India

Kanika Sarao Department of History, University of Delhi, Delhi, DL, India

Burkhard Scherer Department of Theology and Religious Studies, Canterbury Christ Church University, Canterbury, Kent, UK

Rolf Scheuermann Cultural Transfers and Cross-Contacts in the Himalayan Borderlands, Institute for South Asian, Tibetan and Buddhist Studies, University of Vienna, Vienna, Austria

Wm. Andrew Schwartz Claremont Graduate University, Claremont, CA, USA

C. D. Sebastian Department of Humanities and Social Sciences, Indian Institute of Technology Bombay, Mumbai, India

Anita Sharma Department of East Asian Studies, University of Delhi, Delhi, India

Anand Singh School of Buddhist Studies and Civilization, Gautam Buddha University, Greater Noida, UP, India

Institute of Management Sciences, University of Lucknow, Lucknow, UP, India

Arvind Kumar Singh Department of Buddhist Studies, Faculty of Arts, University of Delhi, Delhi, India

School of Buddhist Studies and Civilization, Gautam Buddha University, Greater Noida, Uttar Pradesh, India

Jagbir Singh Department of Buddhist Studies, University of Delhi, Delhi, India

Jaya Singh Department of Applied Science and Humanities, I.T.S. Engineering College, Greater Noida Gautam Buddh Technical University, Lucknow, Ghaziabad, UP, India

Renuka Singh Department of Sociology, Centre for the Study of Social Systems, School of Social Sciences, Jawaharlal Nehru University, New Delhi, India

Sanjay Kr. Singh Department of Buddhist Studies, University of Delhi, Delhi, India

Daniel Stender Hamburg, Germany

Eiji Suhara School of International Letters and Cultures, Arizona State University, Tempe, AZ, USA

Kanoko Tanaka Komazawa University, Tokyo, Japan

Shanker Thapa Faculty of Buddhist Studies, Lumbini Buddhist University, Lumbini Rupandehi, Nepal

Sau Lin Tong Department of Cultural and Religious Studies, The Chinese University of Hong Kong, Hong Kong, China

Stephanie Varnon-Hughes Claremont Lincoln University, Claremont, CA, USA

Chapla Verma Department of Philosophy and Religion, American Public University, Charles Town, WV, USA

Sophorntavy Vorng Department of Religious Diversity, Max Planck Institute for the Study of Religious and Ethnic Diversity, Göttingen, Niedersachsen, Germany

Sean Ward The School of the Art Institute of Chicago, Chicago, IL, USA

Sarah Whylly Religion Department, Florida State University, Tallahassee, FL, USA

Charles Willemen International Buddhist College, Songkhla, Thailand

Serinity Young Department of Classical, Middle Eastern, and Asian Languages and Cultures, Queens College, Flushing, NY, USA

Anthropology Department, American Museum of Natural History, New York, NY, USA

M

Madhupurī

▶ Mathurā

Madhurā

▶ Mathurā

Madhyama Āgama

▶ Majjhima Nikāya

Madhyamā Pratipad

▶ Middle Way (Buddhism)

Mādhyamika

William Magee
UMA Institute of Tibetan Studies, Charlottesville, VA, USA
Tibetan Studies, Dharma Drum Buddhist College, Taipei County, Taiwan, China

Synonyms

Proponents of non-nature; Proponents of the middle way

Definition

Mādhyamika is a Buddhist system of tenets (or a proponent of those tenets) propounding a middle free from the extremes of permanence (that phenomena ultimately exist) and annihilation (that phenomena do not exist even conventionally). Mādhyamikas propound the nonexistence of a nature – true establishment – and assert that phenomena are established as dependent arisings.

Introduction

A person who is a Mādhyamika (in English, a proponent of the Middle Way School) is a proponent of the Great Vehicle (see the entry on "▶ Mahāyāna") Buddhist tenet system called Mādhyamika, considered by many to be the highest expression of Buddhist philosophical thought. A Buddhist tenet system is differentiated from non-Buddhist tenet systems by adhering to the well-known four seals that certify a philosophical position as Buddhist: all compounded things are impermanent, all contaminated things are suffering, all phenomena are selfless, and nirvana is peace.

Later doxographers in Tibet (see the entry on "▶ Tibet") identified four schools of Buddhist tenets: the Great Exposition School (see the entry on "▶ Vaibhāṣika"), the Sūtra School (see the entry on "▶ Sautrāntika"), the Mind Only School (see the entry on "▶ Yogācāra"), and Mādhyamika (the Middle Way School). Each

K.T.S. Sarao, J.D. Long (eds.), *Buddhism and Jainism*, Encyclopedia of Indian Religions,
DOI 10.1007/978-94-024-0852-2

system attempts to describe how phenomena exist, avoiding the two extremes of permanence and nonexistence and thereby occupying a philosophical middle, the ideal Buddhist philosophical position.

In general, holding to an extreme of permanence implies that one's philosophical view has deviated from reality toward a belief in an overly substantial mode of existence. Holding to an extreme of nonexistence implies that phenomena do not exist. Since nihilistic beliefs prompt unethical behavior, they are considered to be particularly dangerous wrong views, leading to rebirth in unfortunate circumstances. From a Buddhist perspective, only a middle between these extremes describes reality, wherein there is the possibility of causes functioning to produce effects.

The actual definitions of the middle and the extremes vary with each tenet system. Unlike other tenet systems, the Mādhyamika equates the extreme of permanence with true existence. True existence refers to inherent existence or own-being (svabhāva). In this system which denies the existence of true existence, each material and mental phenomenon in the universe is said to exist conventionally as a mere designation. Things do not exist by way of their own entity. When searched for among their bases of designation (their parts and so forth) all that can be found of them are terms and names (see the section on "Ultimate Analysis"). While things exist conventionally as names, their ultimate truth is an *emptiness of an inherently existent nature that is truly established* (see the entry on "► Śūnyatā"). An inherently existent nature truly established does not exist, but is only imagined to exist by an innate ignorance conceiving of a self.

The Mādhyamika view involves the negation of inherent existence: emptiness. Although emptiness is a mere absence of inherent existence, the negation does not preclude causes and effects which are like the creations of a magician, appearing to be inherently existent but actually not inherently existent. Thus, the Mādhyamika view includes a negative aspect – the absence of inherent existence – and a positive aspect – a presentation of conventional phenomena which are like illusions.

Emptiness is often asserted to be a negative phenomenon. It is negative because it is an absence of inherent existence that is cognized through the elimination of an object-to-be-negated (inherent existence). Within being a negative, emptiness is said by followers of the Prāsaṅgika-Mādhyamika school (the most influential of the Mādhyamika divisions) to be a non-affirming negative because nothing remains following the refutation of the object-to-be-negated.

Negatives can be divided into affirming negatives and non-affirming negatives. An affirming negative leaves something after the elimination. For instance, the affirming negative "the fat Devadatta does not eat during the day" affirms that he eats during the night. Unlike an affirming negative, a non-affirming negative leaves nothing after the negation. Emptiness for the Prāsaṅgika-Mādhyamika school is a non-affirming negative because it is a mere elimination of inherent existence in a thing. Without inherent existence, phenomena are relegated to the status of mere imputations onto their bases of imputation.

Phenomena that are mere imputations fulfill the criteria of existing, according to the Mādhyamika School. They exist even though their final mode of existence is emptiness of inherent existence. Proponents of Mādhyamika are also called proponents of non-entityness because they propound that phenomena have no entityness, that is, no true establishment or own-being.

It is said that the innate ignorance that conceives of inherent existence traps beings in cyclic existence. The process of acquiring the wisdom necessary to overcome ignorance is often described as having three aspects: hearing, thinking, and meditating. The Mādhyamika tradition claims that it is helpful to consult the great commentaries, to study logic and other ancillary topics, generate an inferential cognition of emptiness, and pursue this inference in meditation until one's realization becomes a direct perception of emptiness. The Mādhyamika School holds that realization of emptiness yields the wisdom that acts as an antidote to the ignorance that is the root of cyclic existence. With the realization of emptiness, one is released from ignorance, anger, and attachment, the causes of rebirth in cyclic existence. Finally, Mādhyamikas assert that complete familiarity with emptiness leads to the omniscient consciousness of enlightenment.

Perfection of Wisdom Sūtras

The central tenets of the Mādhyamika School are derived from the Prajñāparamitā (Perfection of Wisdom) Sūtras. Little is known about the origins and development of the Prajñāparamitā Sūtras. Buddhist tradition ascribes them to the Buddha, but some scholars place their composition at a various later dates. Conze gives a range from 100 B.C.E. to 1200 C.E. and places the *Eight Thousand Stanza Perfection of Wisdom Sūtra* as the oldest of the texts. Lancaster confirms this in his report that the *Eight Thousand Stanza Perfection of Wisdom Sūtra* was the first of the Mahāyāna Sūtras to appear in China, around 180 C.E.

Emptiness and inherent existence are the subject matter of numerous passages in the Perfection of Wisdom Sūtras. The *Eight Thousand Stanza Perfection of Wisdom Sūtra* brings up nature in its discussion of the emptiness of the five aggregates. It states:

> Subhuti, since the five aggregates are without nature, they have a nature of emptiness.

The five aggregates are often spoken of in Perfection of Wisdom Sūtras in terms of being empty, and this passage states that their emptiness is due to their lack of nature. The passage speaks of nature in two contradictory senses: the imagined nature that the aggregates do not possess but appear to possess is inherent existence. This is mentioned in the phrase: "the five aggregates are without nature." Their emptiness of inherent existence, which is their reality nature, is also referred to as "they have a nature of emptiness."

The *Eight Thousand Stanza Perfection of Wisdom Sūtra* shows the early usage of "nature" in two contradictory senses of the reality nature and the inherent nature. The Perfection of Wisdom Sūtras are also a source for the assertion that emptiness itself is devoid of nature.

Nāgārjuna

Although the Buddha himself first propounded emptiness in the Perfection of Wisdom Sūtras, Nāgārjuna is held to be the founder of the Mādhyamika School because he composed the Six Collections of Reasonings for the sake of determining the definitive emptiness by way of many reasonings.

Nāgārjuna propagated Great Vehicle teachings two millennia ago at Nālandā Monastic University in Magadha. Little is known of his life or times except for the extensive mythology surrounding him, complete with numerous prophesies of his birth from both sūtra and tantra literature. Even without historical data, the existence of such an extensive mythology clearly indicates the importance for the Mahāyāna of this early treatise author.

Nāgārjuna is considered by his followers to have expressed the essence of the Perfection of Wisdom Sūtras in his seven treatises:

1. Fundamental Treatise called "Wisdom" (dbu ma'i bstan bcos/dbu ma rtsa ba'i tshig le'ur byas pa shes rab ces bya ba, madhyamakaśāstra/prajñānāmamūlamadhyamakakārikā)
2. Essay on the Mind of Enlightenment (byang chub sems kyi 'grel pa, bodhicittavivaraṇa)
3. Refutation of Objections (rtsod pa bzlog pa'i tshig le'ur byas pa, vigrahavyāvartanīkārikā)
4. Seventy Stanzas on Emptiness (stong pa nyid bdun cu pa'i tshig le'ur byas pa, śūnyatāsaptatikārikā)
5. Sixty Stanzas of Reasoning (rigs pa drug cu pa'i tshig le'ur byas pa, yuktiṣaṣṭikākārikā)
6. Treatise called "The Finely Woven" (zhib mo rnam par 'thag pa zhes bya ba'i mdo, vaidalyasūtranāma)
7. Precious Garland of Advice for the King (rgyal po la gtam bya rin po che'i phreng ba, rājaparikathāratnāvalī)

From among these, Nāgārjuna's *Treatise on the Middle* is the central treatise of the Mādhyamika tradition. Tibetan exegetes usually approach Nāgārjuna's *Treatise* through Chandrakīrti's

Clear Words commentary. Chandrakīrti describes the purpose of Nāgārjuna's treatise as being a hermeneutical one, to determine the interpretable and the definitive among passages of scripture through providing examples of ultimate analysis proving that phenomena are empty of true establishment. Although the purpose of the *Treatise* is to determine the interpretable and the definitive among passages of scripture, the subject matter of the *Treatise* is extensive, covering many topics regarding emptiness and other topics. For instance, besides emptiness, the *Treatise* discusses the Four Noble Truths, actions and their effects, the Three Jewels, and so forth. However, the main subject matter is the proof of emptiness through ultimate analysis.

Ultimate Analysis

For students of Mādhyamika, one of the most valued aspects of the *Treatise on the Middle* is Nāgārjuna's investigative method. Perhaps Nāgārjuna's most important innovation is the employment of ultimate analysis to determine the ontological status of things. Unlike conventional analysis – which inquires into what something is – ultimate analysis inquires into how something exists by searching for a findable mode of subsistence. Such analysis seeks an inherently existent essence or nature through examining objects or events for evidence of inherent existence. Thus, the sphere of ultimate analysis is limited to determining the presence or absence of inherent existence.

In practice, ultimate analysis finds nothing. This non-finding of a findable mode of subsistence confirms the absence of such a mode (which would be inherent existence) and thus the presence of the emptiness of inherent existence. Not everyone agrees that this is Nāgārjuna's intention in his *Treatise*, but for those who do agree, the important point is that ultimate analysis is engaged in a search for inherent existence or persuasive evidence of inherent existence, and not just existence in general. Since nothing has inherent existence (described as independent existence by Nāgārjuna and his followers), ultimate analysis always finds just nothing. This non-finding of inherent existence is variously interpreted, but is often asserted by Mādhyamika practitioners to be the finding of its absence, the emptiness of inherent existence. In the face of the ultimate analyses of Nāgārjuna, the non-finding of inherent existence is the finding of emptiness.

Thus, Mādhyamikas are saying that unenlightened beings live in a world of entities that appear to exist by way of their own nature, and yet are merely imputations. All these entities function and yet are empty of inherent existence. Things that exist conventionally, such as tables, jars, mental events, and so forth, are all said to be conventional truths.

Ultimate analysis shows that each phenomena also has an ultimate truth, an emptiness of inherent existence. The conventional truth, the table, and the ultimate truth, the emptiness of the table, are related as one entity, but different isolates (i.e., things that exist as one entity but can be isolated by thought, such as a pot and its impermanence). In this way there are two truths for each phenomenon.

Emptiness is also empty. However, it is said to be an ultimate rather than a conventional truth because it exists the way it appears to an ultimate consciousness. An ultimate consciousness does not cognize conventionalities but instead realizes emptiness: it has the absence of inherent existence as its object. According to some Tibetan meditation systems, ultimate consciousnesses can be conceptual or nonconceptual. A nonconceptual ultimate consciousness is a meditative equipoise directly realizing emptiness. A conceptual ultimate consciousness realizes emptiness through a conceptual image. Since emptiness is a slightly hidden phenomenon (like impermanence), it can be brought to mind indirectly at first through an inference and then, eventually, directly in meditation. Because all emptinesses are generically similar, perception of the emptiness of any phenomenon leads to a realization of the emptiness of all phenomena. This is important for Mādhyamika soteriological theories, since it means that the meditator need not realize the emptiness of all things in order to be released from ignorance: the realization of the emptiness of one thing (such as the self of the person) is all that is required to remove ignorant misconceptions of other things.

Just as there exist ultimate and conventional consciousnesses capable of certifying the two truths for a phenomenon, so too there are conventional and ultimate analyses. Conventional analysis is any type of logical process that inquires into conventionalities to determine facts. Conventional analysis is performed when inquiring into the facts of ordinary matters: taxes, the weather, and so forth. According to Tibetan scholars, confusion sometimes arises when one mistakes an ultimate analysis for a conventional analysis; at such times it seems a paradox has been identified, for instance, the question, "If a tree falls in the forest and there is no one to hear, does it make a sound?" This often-asked question may in fact be inquiring into the mode of subsistence of sound, since it is trying to determine whether sound is dependent on ears and so forth. Therefore, it may be an ultimate analysis. Similarly, the commonly discussed "paradox" of Zeno, regarding the impossibility of Achilles catching the tortoise (since the distance between them must be halved ad infinitum), may also be considered ultimate analysis by Tibetan proponents of Mādhyamika.

A basic premise of ultimate analysis is that inherent existence, if it existed, would always be findable. This is because inherent existence as defined by Nāgārjuna is independent of causes, parts, and imputation. In discussing a classic tetralemma posed by Nāgārjuna regarding the impossibility of inherently existent production from self, other, both self and other, or causelessly, Chandrakīrti and later Tibetan exegetes expand on Nāgārjuna's thinking (see the entry on "▶ Nāgārjuna"). In their commentarial literature on the *Treatise*, they assert that if a thing has inherent existence it must be immutable, it must not depend on another, it must always be existent or nonexistent, it must be substantially existent, it must be vividly observable separately from all other phenomena, it must have one unchanging entity, and it must be simultaneous with its causes and conditions, and so forth. Their position is that something with inherent existence would have a mode of subsistence that would make it a solid, visible, findable entity. If a thing cannot be found under analysis than it must not be inherently existent; it must be empty of inherent existence and have some other mode of subsistence: in short, it must be a dependent arising, an entity that is merely imputed in dependence on its parts.

In chapter two of the *Treatise on the Middle*, titled "An Analysis of Going and Coming," Nāgārjuna uses ultimate analysis to examine motion for evidence of inherent existence. In one section of this entry Nāgārjuna examines the path beneath the person walking. He divides the road into three parts relative to the person's foot: the not yet gone over, the already gone over, and the currently being gone over. There is no fourth possibility.

First Nāgārjuna looks at the not yet gone over. Certainly there is no motion to be found there, since the walker has not yet arrived at that part of the road. Regarding the already gone over, there is no motion on that part of the road either, since the walker has moved on from there. The only place left to find motion is on the currently being gone over. But Nāgārjuna points out the difficulty of finding motion there. If one asserts that the motion is under the heel, then the toe of the walker is on the not yet gone over part of the road (and there is no motion on the not yet gone over part). If one asserts that the motion is at the toe, then the heel of the walker is on the already gone over part of the road (and there is no motion on the already gone over part). If one says that the motion is beneath the foot as a whole, that is ignoring the obvious fact that there is no foot separate from its various parts: toe, heel, and middle.

Since inherently existent motion would have to exist from its own side and not be dependent on imputation, this analysis reveals an absence of inherently existent motion. For some interpreters, this means that Nāgārjuna has proven that there is no motion at all. However, according to other (especially the Tibetan Ge-luk) exegetes, it is important to understand that motion exists, since the walker indeed gets from point A to point B. But they assert that the motion is merely imputed: a name given to its parts. It is conventionally existent, lacking inherent existence.

Although the Mādhyamika School makes the point that things are unfindable under analysis, it also asserts this position to be compatible with cause and effect. Many are puzzled at how the Mādhyamika School can assert the existence of a world of merely imputed entities in which specific causes lead to their own discrete effects. If all is imputation, cannot anything be anything? The answer given is usually that all things existing as imputations does not mean that anything can be anything, but rather that phenomena exist interdependently with mind. Because they exist interdependently with mind they do not have inherent, independent existence. Instead, things exist dependently. Lacking the inherent existence they would have with independence, things exist only conventionally. From the Mādhyamika standpoint, only conventionally existent phenomena possess the fluidity necessary to be effects and to produce causes. All other modes of subsistence involving true existence are too solid for causality to operate. Similarly, nonexistent entities also cannot produce effects.

Divisions of Mādhyamika

The two main sub-schools of the Mādhyamika system are the Svātantrika and Prāsaṅgika Mādhyamika. These terms do not appear in Indian texts but are adduced by Tibetan doxographers. They state that the split occurred in the sixth century when Bhāvaviveka, in his *Lamp for (Nāgārjuna's) Wisdom* (*prajñāpradīpa*), criticized Buddhapālita's *Commentary* (see the entry on "▸ Buddhapālita") for its use of logical consequences (*prāsaṅga*) (see the entry on "▸ Bhāvaviveka"). Among other criticisms of Buddhapālita, Bhāvaviveka asserted that a philosophical argument must be stated as an "autonomous syllogism" (*svātantraprayoga*). In response, Chandrakīrti rejected Bhāvaviveka's argument. He stated in his *Clear Words,* that it is unsuitable for a Mādhyamika to use autonomous syllogisms. Because of this, Chandrakīrti is considered by many to be the founder of Prāsaṅgika. In this way the Svātantrika and Prāsaṅgika schools became differentiated from each other.

A further division appeared in the eighth century, when Shāntarakṣhita incorporated elements of the Yogācāra system (see entry on "▸ Yogācāra") into that of Bhāvaviveka. Shāntarakṣhita later traveled to Tibet and taught his Mādhyamika system there, where it came to be known as the Yogācāra-Svātantrika-Mādhyamika in contradistinction to Bhāvaviveka's Sautrāntika-Svātantrika-Mādhyamika.

From the point of view of Tibetan doxographers, the primary difference between the Svātantrika and Prāsaṅgika systems is not whether they employ *prāsaṅga* or not, but in the subtlety of their view of emptiness. The Svātantrika view is that phenomena are established by way of their own character conventionally but not ultimately. The Prāsaṅgika view is that phenomena are not established by way of their own character even conventionally.

Mādhyamika in Tibet

From among the two Great Vehicle philosophical systems originating in India – Mādhyamika and Yogācāra – most Tibetan lineages favored the Mādhyamika. Inspired by the presence of Shāntarakṣhita (c. 725–784) and Kamalashīla (c. 740–797), and then reinvigorated by Atisha after a period of anti-Buddhist sentiment, Mādhyamika became the dominant philosophical system of Tibetan Buddhism.

Kamalashīla was one of the great pandits of Nālandā Monastery in Northern India. He journeyed to Tibet at the request of the king and founded Samye (*bsam yas*), the first Tibetan Buddhist monastery, where the first Tibetan Buddhist monks were ordained. His compendium of philosophical systems, the *Tattvasamgraha*, serves as a model for later Tibetan presentations of tenets (*grub mtha'*). Shāntarakṣhita's student Kamalashīla also made the journey to Tibet, where legend has it he was victorious in a debate at Samye with a Chinese monk named Hva-shang Mahāyāna. At stake in this debate was whether meditation on emptiness had content or whether it focused on nothingness. Kamalashīla took the side of content and his victory had a profound effect on later Tibetans who asserted a gradual path to enlightenment as opposed to a sudden path. Kamalashīla is the author of a commentary on the *Tattvasamgraha* and other works on Mādhyamika practice and view, such as the *Madhyamakaloka*.

Following a period of Buddhist persecution by the Tibetan king Lang-dar-ma (*glang dar ma*), the Indian pandit Atisha arrived in Tibet in 1041. Atisha founded the Sang-pu Monastery and the Ka-dam-pa (*bka' gdam pa*) lineage. The Ka-dam-pa lineage stressed a gradual path to enlightenment, and its founder's most influential text, the *Lamp for the Path to Enlightenment* (*bodhipathapradipa*), presented Buddhist practices organized in stages according to the capacities of three types of beings: those who wish for high status in future lives, those who desire a solitary peace, and those who aspire to the bodhisattva ideal of leading all sentient beings to enlightenment. This organizing principle and the literary genre of stages of the path texts was further developed in the fourteenth and fifteenth centuries by Tsong-kha-pa.

Early Tibetan proponents of Mādhyamika (*dbu ma pa*) include Ngok Lotsawa (*rnog lo tsa ba*), Cha-pa-cho-gyi-senge (*phyva pa chos kyi seng ge*), and Nyi-ma-drak (*nyi ma grags*). Since Nāgārjuna's *Treatise* is terse, Tibetan exegetes preferred not to approach it without a commentary. These scholars introduced the commentarial works of Chandrakīrti into Tibet, and from then on Chandrakīrti's commentaries on Nāgārjuna remained the most influential among those who considered Nāgārjunian emptiness of inherent existence to be the final ultimate.

In the twelfth century, a competing interpretation of the Indian commentaries was put forward by Dol-po Shay-rab-gyal-tsen (*dol po pa shes rab rgyal mtshan*, 1292–1361), the founder of the Jo-nang lineage. Dol-po asserted an inherently existent Buddha within all beings. Since this Buddha is empty of being anything other than itself, it is called an "Other Emptiness." According to this system, phenomena do not exist at all, but the Other Emptiness is not a phenomenon: it is the noumenon which exists by way of its own nature. Dol-po Shay-rab-gyal-tsen felt this type of emptiness to be the actual meaning of the sūtras and commentaries of Indian Buddhism and that it was the most profound ultimate. Dol-po, who came upon this interpretation in a vision, relegated the "self-emptiness" of Nāgārjuna (or as he called it, "empty empty") to a provisional position. One of Dol-po's innovations was to mix sūtra and tantra texts into one system, with the Kālachakra Tantra elevated into the position of being the chief mode of progressing on the path. He rejected traditional interpretations of Mādhyamika and referred to his own system as Great Mādhyamika (*dbu ma chen po*).

Many Tibetan Mādhyamikas before the fourteenth century, including Dol-po, stressed nihilistic interpretations of the emptiness propounded by Nāgārjuna and Chandrakīrti. In the fourteenth and fifteenth centuries, Tsong-kha-pa Lo-sang-drak-pa (*tsong kha pa blo bzang grags pa*, 1359–1417), father of the Tibetan Ge-luk (*dge lugs*) lineage, established a logically structured, methodical approach to establishing a Prāsaṅgika-Mādhyamika view that upholds conventional existence and conventionally existent causes and effects, while rejecting any sort of existence that is established by way of its own nature. Tsong-kha-pa's disciples founded the Ge-luk lineage, which due to the political power of its Dalai Lamas eventually became the dominant lineage in Tibetan Buddhism.

Tsong-kha-pa upholds conventionally existent phenomena by distinguishing two separate spheres of awareness: ultimate consciousnesses and conventional consciousnesses. These consciousnesses certify the existence of objects in their spheres (emptinesses and all other phenomena, respectively) by means of valid cognition. Valid cognitions, which yield incontrovertible knowledge, can be either inferences that occur in dependence on a correct sign or direct perceptions. In this way, Tsong-kha-pa explains why an ultimate analysis of a pot, which finds nothing, does not deny the existence of the pot (which is a conventional phenomena and not within its sphere) but only denies the inherent existence of the pot.

Since Tsong-kha-pa asserts that conceptual inferential consciousnesses can behold emptiness incontrovertibly, by means of a correct sign or reason, he based a large part of his meditational structure on identifying emptiness through reasoning. He called this approach the Path of Reasoning.

Tsong-kha-pa wrote numerous treatises in his lifetime, but among his most important works on the Mādhyamika view are:

> Explanation of (Nāgārjuna's) "Treatise on the Middle": Ocean of Reasoning/Great Commentary on (Nāgārjuna's) "Treatise on the Middle" (dbu ma rtsa ba'i tshig le'ur byas pa shes rab ces bya ba'i rnam bshad rigs pa'i rgya mtsho/rtsa shes tik chen);
>
> Extensive Explanation of (Chandrakīrti's) "Supplement to (Nāgārjuna's) 'Treatise on the Middle'": Illumination of the Thought (dbu ma la 'jug pa'i rgya cher bshad pa dgongs pa rab gsal);
>
> Great Exposition of the Stages of the Path/Stages of the Path to Enlightenment Thoroughly Teaching All the Stages of Practice of the Three Types of Beings (lam rim chen mo; skyes bu gsum gyi rnyams su blang ba'i rim pa thams cad tshang bar ston pa'i byang chub lam gyi rim pa).
>
> The Essence of Good Explanations, Treatise Discriminating the Interpretable and the Definitive (drang ba dang nges pa'i don rnam par phye ba'i bstan bcos legs bshad snying po).

Tsong-kha-pa's disquisitions on Mādhyamika all have a "political" agenda as well as a soteriological goal: the refutation of nihilistic interpretations of Nāgārjuna (especially the Other Emptiness of Dol-po) and the establishment of his own interpretation of the "self-emptiness" found in Nāgārjuna's texts as the most profound Buddhist ultimate.

Interpretations of Mādhyamika

Just as there were a variety of interpretations of Mādhyamika in Tibet, so modern scholars of Mādhyamika find they do not agree on the meaning of Nāgārjuna's texts. Tibetan and non-Tibetan interpretations can be conveniently categorized with reference to Tsong-kha-pa's schema of variant interpretations, which finds all interpretations that do not accord with his own either "too broad" or "too narrow" (in the sense of insufficient). "Too broad" interpretations of Mādhyamika negate existence itself, and not merely inherent existence. "Too narrow" interpretations negate something that is, in Tsong-kha-pa's opinion, not inherent existence and therefore not subtle enough to destroy all traces of the ignorance that binds creatures to the round of rebirth.

"Too broad" interpretations, according to Tsong-kha-pa's system, are those which are nihilistic. They assert that Nāgārjuna's ultimate analyses reveal that phenomena do not exist. Tsong-kha-pa's explanation is that such analyses do not reveal that things do not exist, but merely reveal that things do not inherently exist. Instead of being nonexistent, according to Tsong-kha-pa, phenomena are certified existent by valid cognitions. This explanation has been widely criticized in Tibet by such authors as Tak-tsang (*stag tshang lo tsa ba shes rab rin chen*), Go-ram-pa (*go ram pa*), and Gendun Cho-pel (*dge 'dun chos 'phel*), who feel that a consciousness that is revealed to be mistaken about the appearance of a phenomenon cannot also be considered valid in the sense of incontrovertible.

"Too narrow" interpretations of Nāgārjuna include Svātantrika-Mādhyamikas as well as modern theorists who see Mādhyamika as a critique of language and conceptuality. These modern interpretations are often attempts to align Nāgārjuna's theories with those of European philosophers. Numerous more traditional "insufficient interpretations" view Mādhyamika as an attack on Hindu philosophical assertions or see it as a sophisticated method for refuting all philosophical theses. It is no wonder that this last interpretation is very common in Tibetan and modern philosophical circles since Nāgārjuna and Āryadeva both have statements to the effect that they have no theses, systems of thought, or positions. However, Tsong-kha-pa feels that these statements require interpretation. He ammends these statements to the effect that they have no theses, systems of thought, or positions involving inherent existence.

Cross-References

- ▶ Bhāvaviveka
- ▶ Buddhapālita
- ▶ Mahāyāna
- ▶ Nāgārjuna
- ▶ Sautrāntika
- ▶ Śūnyatā
- ▶ Tibet
- ▶ Vaibhāṣika
- ▶ Yogācāra

References

1. Conze E (1973) The perfection of wisdom in eight thousand lines and its verse summary. Four Seasons Foundation, Berkeley
2. Garfield JL (1994) The fundamental wisdom of the middle way. Oxford University Press, Oxford
3. Hayes RP (1994) Nāgārjuna's appeal. Lond: J Indian Philos 22:229–378
4. Hopkins J (1998) Buddhist advice for living & liberation: Nagarjuna's precious garland. Snow Lion, Ithaca
5. Hopkins J (1996) Meditation on emptiness. Wisdom, London
6. Lancaster L (1975) The oldest Mahayana Sūtra: its significance for the study of Buddhist development. Eastern Buddh 8
7. Lopez DS (1987) A study of Svatantrika. Snow Lion, Ithaca
8. Magee W (2004) Expressing the fallacy from the viewpoint of a pervader: Nāgārjuna and the putative consequences of Svabhāva. Chung-Hwa Buddh J 17
9. Magee W (2000) The nature of things: emptiness and essence in the Geluk World. Snow Lion, Ithaca
10. Murti TRV (1980) The central philosophy of Buddhism. Unwin, London
11. Napper E (1989) Dependent arising and emptiness. Wisdom, London
12. Newland G (1994) The two truths. Snow Lion, Ithaca
13. Robinson RH (1972) Did Nagarjuna really refute all philosophical views? Philos East West 22
14. Ruegg DS (1963) The Jo Nan Pas: a school of Buddhist ontologists, according to the Grub Mtha' Sel Gyi Me Lon. J Am Orient Soc
15. Ruegg DS (1981) The literature of the Madhyamaka School of philosophy in India. Otto Harrassowitz, Wiesbaden
16. Stearns CR (1996) The Buddha from Dolpo: a study of the life and thought of the Tibetan master Dolpopa Sherab Gyaltsen. State University of New York Press, Albany
17. Williams P (1989) Mahayana Buddhism. Routledge, London

Magadha

K. T. S. Sarao
Department of Buddhist Studies, University of Delhi, Delhi, India

Synonyms

Modern South Bihar

Definition

An important kingdom in ancient India.

Magadha was one of the 16 *mahājanapadas* (states) at the time of the Buddha. According to Buddhaghosa, it got its name from a tribe of khattiyas called *Magadhā* ([1], p. 135f). Initially, Rājagaha (Sk: Rājagṛha) was its capital which was later shifted to Pāṭaliputta (Sk: Pāṭaliputra). The core of the state was the area of modern Bihar south of the Gaṅgā. In most of the pre-Buddhist Brāhmaṇical texts, Magadha was considered as outside the pale of Āriyan and Brāhmaṇical culture and was, therefore, looked down upon by Brāhmaṇical writers. At the time of the Buddha, the kingdom of Magadha was bounded on the south by the Vindhyā mountains, on the west by the river Sona, on the north by the Gaṅgā, and on the east by the river Campā, the state of Aṅga being beyond the Campā ([2], Vol. iv, p. 454). Sona formed the boundary between Magadha and the Licchavi Confederacy, and both the states evidently had equal rights over the river. According to one of the Jātakas, the state of Magadha was initially under the suzerainty of Aṅga ([2], Vol. vi, p. 272). In the Buddha's day, Magadha and Aṅga together consisted of 80,000 villages ([3], p. 179) and had a circumference of about 300 leagues ([4], p. 148). The cornfields of Magadha were rich and fertile ([5], vs. 208), and Magadha was known for a special kind of garlic ([6], p. 920). During the early Buddhist period, Magadha was an important political and commercial center, and was visited by people from all

M

parts of northern India in search of commerce and of learning. In *Sārattha-ppakāsinī* the commentary of the *Saṃyutta Nikāya*, it has been mentioned that the people of Aṅga and Magadha had a practice of performing a sacrifice annually to god Mahābrahmā, in which a fire was kindled with 60 cartloads of firewood. These people held the belief that anything cast into the sacrificial fire would bring a thousand-fold reward ([7], p. 269).

Apart from the Buddhist and Jaina texts, the ancient kingdom of Magadha is mentioned in the *Rāmāyaṇa*, the *Mahābhārata*, and the *Purāṇas*. The earliest reference to the Magadha people occurs in the *Atharvaveda*. Magadha was the cradle of two of India's major religions, Jainism and Buddhism ([3], p. 5), and it was from here that they spread to different parts of the Indian subcontinent. The Buddha's chief disciples, Sāriputta and Moggallāna, were natives of Magadha. Two of India's greatest empires, the Mauryan Empire (c. 221–185 B.C.E.) and the Gupta Empire (c. 219–540 C.E.), originated from Magadha. However, the information available on the early rulers of Magadha is very scanty. According to the Purāṇas, the Magadha empire was established by the Bṛhadratha, who was the sixth in line from Emperor Kuru of the Bharata dynasty. The Bṛhadrathas were succeeded by the Pradyotas who in turn were followed by the Haryanka dynasty. It appears that Magadha was ruled by the Haryanka dynasty for some 200 years, its most important kings being Bimbisāra and Ajātasattu (Sk: Ajātaśatru), both of whom were contemporaries of the Buddha. Bimbisāra was responsible for expanding the boundaries of his kingdom through matrimonial alliances and conquest. The states of Aṅga and Kāśī became part of Magadha during his reign. Bimbisāra was murdered by his son, Prince Ajātaśatru. Under Ajātaśatru, the dynasty reached its largest extent. Ajātasattu succeeded in annexing Kosala with the help of the Licchavis, and later after several attempts, he succeeded also in annexing the Licchavi Confederacy to his empire ([8], pp. 73f, 86). Under Bimbisāra and Ajātasattu, Magadha rose to such political eminence that for several centuries the history of northern India was practically the history of Magadha.

The Haryanka dynasty was overthrown by the Śiṣunāga dynasty. The last ruler of Śiṣunāga dynasty, Kāḷāśoka, was assassinated by Mahāpadma Nanda, the first of the so-called Nine Nandas (Mahāpadma and his eight sons). The Nanda dynasty is said to have ruled for about 100 years. Around 321 B.C.E., the Nanda dynasty was ended by Candragupta who became the first king of the great Mauryan dynasty. Candragupta's grandson, King Aśoka, was one of India's most powerful and famous emperors.

The Śuṅga dynasty was established in 185 B.C.E. when king Bṛhadratha, the last of the Mauryan rulers, was assassinated by his commander in chief, Puṣyamitra Śuṅga, who then ascended the throne. The Śuṅga dynasty was replaced by the Kaṇva dynasty which ruled over Magadha from 71 B.C.E. to 26 B.C.E. Following the collapse of the Kaṇva dynasty, the Śātavāhana dynasty of the Andhra kingdom replaced the Magadha kingdom as the most powerful Indian state. However, Magadha regained its older glory under the Gupta dynasty which ruled from c. 219 to 550 C.E. The Gupta Empire was marked by extensive achievements in science, technology, literature, art, and philosophy. The Gupta period is particularly known for having produced scholars such as Kālidāsa, Āryabhaṭa, Varāhamihira, Viṣṇu Śarma, and Vātsyāyana who made great advancements in many academic fields.

Cross-References

- ▶ Ajātasattu
- ▶ Ambapālī
- ▶ Aśoka
- ▶ Bimbisāra
- ▶ Pasenadi
- ▶ Puṣyamitra Śuṅga
- ▶ Rājagaha (Pāli)

References

1. Smith H (ed) (1916) Sutta-Nipāta commentary being Paramatthajotikā II, vol 1. Pali Text Society, London

2. Fausböll V (ed) (1977–1897) The Jātakas, 7 vols. Trübner, London
3. Oldenberg H (ed) (1979) The Vinaya Piṭakaṃ, vol 1. Pali Text Society, London
4. Rhys Davids TW, Carpentier JE, Stede W (1886) The Sumaṅgala-Vilāsinī: Buddhaghosa's commentary on the Dīgha Nikāya, vol 1. Pali Text Society, London
5. Hermann O, Pischel R (1990) The Theragāthā, second edition with appendices by K. R. Norman & L. Alsdorf. Oxford, Pali Text Society
6. Takakusu J, Nagai M (1954) Samantapāsādikā: Buddhaghosa's commentary on the Vinaya Piṭaka, vol 4. Pali Text Society, London
7. Woodward FL (1929) The Sārattha-ppakāsinī, Buddhaghosa's commentary on the Saṃyutta Nikāya, vol 1. Pali Text Society, London
8. Rhys Davids TW, Carpenter JE (1901) The Dīgha Nikāya, vol 2. Pali Text Society, London
9. Law BC (1946) The Magadhas in ancient India. Royal Asiatic Society, London
10. Rhys Davids TW (1903) Buddhist India. G.P. Putnam's Sons, New York
11. Sinha BP (1977) Dynastic history of Magadha. Abhinav Publications, New Delhi

Magic (Buddhism)

Serinity Young
Department of Classical, Middle Eastern, and Asian Languages and Cultures, Queens College, Flushing, NY, USA
Anthropology Department, American Museum of Natural History, New York, NY, USA

Synonyms

Magico-religious practices

Definition

Phenomena that goes beyond what is understand able in terms of the natural world.

Early Buddhism

Buddhism has its share of so-called magico-religious practices as both magic and religion partake of the supernatural, that is, phenomena, practices, and individuals that go beyond what is understandable in terms of the natural world. Buddhist ideas about magic go back to the supernatural acts of the historical Buddha. The importance of these ideas can be gauged from the fact that certain of the Buddha's miraculous or magical acts are commemorated at four of the eight major Buddhist pilgrimage sites of northern India. First is Śravastī, where he performed the Twin Miracle. The details surrounding this event reveal the Buddha's complex attitude toward the miraculous. According to the *Dhammapad-Aṭṭhakathā* ([1], xiv.2; 3.35–47), the fullest version of this story, a layman suspended a bowl high off the ground and challenged anyone who claimed to be an arhat (an enlightened one) to prove it by flying up and taking the bowl. Six non-Buddhist teachers tried and failed, but when the Buddhist monk Piṇḍola learned of this challenge to the Buddha's teachings, he succeeded in flying up to get it. After the Buddha heard about this, he made the rule forbidding the nuns and monks the exercise of supernatural powers in front of householders. (*Vinaya*, *Culla Vagga*, v.8:ii, contains this rule embedded in a much briefer story.) The six non-Buddhists thought that this rule would also apply to the Buddha so they challenged him to a magic display, which he accepted. The contest was held at Śravastī, where several of the Buddha's disciples, both female and male, offered to perform miracles in his place, but the Buddha declined their offers of assistance. These exchanges signify the belief in the acquisition of supernatural powers by the Buddha's followers. In response to the challenge of the non-Buddhists, the Buddha rose up in the air with fire rising from his shoulders and water pouring from his lower body. The six challengers and many other witnesses were said to have been converted to Buddhism by this act. Afterwards, the Buddha ascended to Trāyastriṃśa Heaven to preach to his dead mother and where he remained for three months. Seemingly, it is all right for the Buddha to publicly perform miracles, but not for his disciples.

The second pilgrimage site to commemorate a miracle of the Buddha is at Sāṃkāśya, where he descended from Trāyastriṃśa Heaven

M

accompanied by the gods Indra and Brahma. This miracle is also recorded in the *Dhammapad-Aṭṭha-kathā* ([1], xiv.2; 3.52–54) and it also led to the conversion of the many people who witnessed it. The third pilgrimage site connected to the performance of a miracle by the Buddha is Rajgir, where he tamed a rampaging elephant by simply holding up his hand, and the fourth is Vaiśali, where he received an offering of honey from a monkey.

The other four pilgrimage sites commemorate his birth, enlightenment, first sermon, and death. In the Mahāyāna tradition, these are referred to as and understood to be the places where the Buddha performed the eight great illusions (*māyā*) that enabled him to preach the dharma, such as being born. These pilgrimage sites, and consequently, these miraculous events or illusions, became one of the major themes in Buddhist art in the heartland of Buddhism during the fourth to the twelfth century ([2], pp. 32–46).

Of further interest, Aśvaghhoṣa's epic, the *Saundarananda*, is about the Buddha's use of the supernatural power of flying to convert his handsome half brother Nanda. Nanda and his beautiful wife Sundarī are madly in love. Indeed, they are so involved with each other that they do not hear the Buddha arrive to beg for alms. Nanda is terribly upset about this failure of hospitality and respect for his older brother, so he set out after the Buddha. In this way, he ends up among the monks, as a monk, but such a reluctant one. Nanda never ceases to long for his beautiful wife. In an attempt to free Nanda from her charms, the Buddha flies with him up to Trāyastriṃśa Heaven where they see divine women, the *apsaras*, Indra's celestial courtesans. Nanda develops an ardent desire for the *apsaras* and, returning to earth, devotes himself to ascetic practices in order to ultimately reach this heaven and those divine women ([3], 264ff). Slowly, he comes to understand that even heavenly pleasures are empty and vain, so he retires into the forest and becomes an arhat. The point is that Nanda's enlightenment is stimulated by the Buddha's miraculous ability to fly and to enter other realms, a power the Buddha used out of compassion to convert his brother.

As mentioned, several of the Buddha's disciples were known for their supernatural powers, which are based on *iddhi* (Skt., *iddhi*, later *siddhi*). *Iddhi* is a fruit (*phala*) of enlightenment that gives one the ability to fly, to pass through walls, become invisible, and shape-shift – in short, it plays havoc with physical form which Buddhists consider to be illusory and changeable. *Iddhi* is one of the five, sometimes six, classes of higher knowledge, *abhiñña* (Skt. *abhijña*). Two others are the ability to recall past lives and the ability to know the minds of others ([4], pp. 99–117). These powers are similar to those possessed by other ancient Indian *ṛṣi*s.

So, despite the Buddha's injunction to his disciples against displaying these powers to householders, the belief in these powers is at the core of Buddhist thought, which interprets the Buddha's many supernatural acts as based on his compassionate wish to lead people to enlightenment, and his followers modeled themselves on his behavior. Once enlightenment is achieved, supernormal powers are gained, but they are only to be used out of compassion for people who do not believe in the teachings of the Buddha ([5], pp. 51).

A later example of magical powers comes from the second-century C.E. Buddhist biography of Emperor Aśoka, the *Aśokāvadāna*, in which supernatural power plays a central role in Aśoka's conversion to Buddhism. The was brought about by the Buddhist monk Samudra, who inadvertently wandered into a prison Aśoka had built and from which no one was allowed to leave. By witnessing the horrible tortures that await him before his execution, Samudra realized the Buddhist truth of suffering and during the night attained enlightenment. The next day, he is sentenced to be boiled alive, but he enters a meditative trance that prevents the cauldron from getting hot, and when the executioner looks in the cauldron, he sees Samudra seated on a lotus. The executioner immediately sent word to Aśoka who came to see for himself. With his newly gained supernatural knowledge, Samudra realized the time had come for Aśoka's conversion and he began to perform his *iddhi*s. Just like the Buddha, he flew into the air where he remained while water pours from half his body and fire from the other half. Aśoka asked who he was and Samudra explained he was a follower of the Buddha and that the Buddha had predicted Aśoka's reign and that he would redistribute the Buddha's relics throughout the land. Aśoka converts and agrees to distribute the relics, after which Samudra leaves without giving him any further teaching ([6], pp. 73–76).

What is of particular interest in this Buddhist tale is the idea that the most important and influential layman in Buddhist history, Emperor Aśoka, was converted by a supernatural display, not by the teachings of the Buddha. This is shown in the next scene where Aśoka gives the very un-Buddhist order to have the executioner burned to death. The rest of the story will deal with Aśoka's gradual awakening to the dharma through the wisdom and supernatural powers of his teacher Upagupta, but this is not part of his conversion.

Mahāyna Buddhism

One of the earliest and most influential Mahāyāna texts is the *Lotus Sutra* (*Saddharma-puṇḍarīka*), the setting of which immediately takes one out of the realm of everyday occurrences into a realm that transcends ordinary concepts of time, space, and possibility where miraculous events are common. In the center of this realm, the historical Buddha Śākyamuni sits in his supernatural aspect, surrounded by gods, demons, and other heavenly and earthly beings as he preaches. On the first page, it states that arhats possess the five *abhijñas*; in chapter 3, the Buddha says it is through his *abhijñas* that he saves people as do the bodhisattvas once they have reached the state of not sliding back ([7], p. 89). In chapter 20, the Buddha and another worthy demonstrate their magical powers by extending their tongues into another world. Rays issued from their tongues and from those rays issued hundreds of thousands of bodhisattvas. In chapter 21, the Buddha gives *dhāranī*s, magical or sacred words that offer protection against demons, sorcerers, ghosts, and so forth, as do the four guardians of the directions. Finally, chapter 24 lists the many miraculous protections the celestial bodhisattva Avaloklitеśvara offers to those who call upon him, such as protection from fire, drowning, executioners, robbers, and enemies. He can even bring children to devoted parents. Avalokiteśvara is said to be versed in magic and therefore offers protection from the magic of sorcerers and witches. In other words, Buddhist magic is said to be stronger than any other magic. Further, miraculous events are ubiquitous in most Mahāyāna sutras.

Bodhisattvas are the ideal beings of Mahāyāna Buddhism and miraculous events performed out of compassion, their leading virtue, are often associated with them. Due to the decline of Buddhism in India, many now lost Sanskrit Buddhist texts were preserved in Tibetan. For example, a short biography of Śāntideva, the eighth-century author of the pivotal Mahāyāna text, *Entering the Path of Enlightenment* (*Bodhicharyāvatara*), is contained in a Tibetan collection of biographies of Indian Buddhists pandits translated by Lobsang N. Tsonawa. The *Bodhicharyāvatara* is a classical guide to becoming a bodhisattva. Significantly, this short biography describes Śāntideva's rich visionary life and the miracles he performed out of compassion, such as replacing the lost eye of a king, flying, and creating food for starving people. He also competed in a context of magical skills with a non-Buddhist, who he defeated by creating a destructive wind and then restoring everything the wind had overturned, which led to the conversion of many people ([8], pp. 60–62). Similar stories are told about the other pandits in this collection.

The Mahāsiddhas

Especially well known for the power of *siddhi* are the 84 mahāsiddhas, 80 male and 4 female wandering tantric yogis who flourished in northern India between the eighth and twelfth centuries and who deeply influenced Tantric Buddhism. Tantra's origins were outside the great monastic institutions of the period; it began and flourished among wandering yogis from a wide range of social backgrounds, though eventually tantra became part of the monastic curriculum. Mahāsiddha biographies compiled by Abhayadatta, between the end of the eleventh century and the beginning of the twelfth, reveal the magical powers these siddhas possessed. For instance, there is Virūpa, who had the power to stop the sun in the sky, Maṇibhadrā and others who could fly, and Nāgārjuna who could control demons and create apparitions ([9], pp. 27–32, 208–210, 75–80).

The *siddhi* of creating apparitions forms the heart of another biography preserved in Tibetan, that of the long-suffering Tilopa and his guru Nāropa, who created endless apparitions that caused Tilopa great pain and suffering. When Nāropa would ask him if he was happy, Tilopa would reply that he was suffering because he could not get beyond dualistic thinking – he had not yet reached enlightenment (e.g., [10], p. 53). This and other biographies reveal that *siddhi*s were still employed as a teaching device – something to get people's attention and push them into a state of higher awareness.

Interestingly, the antinomian practices of Tantric Buddhism and Tantric Hinduism reify ideas about women as polluters and utilize them for the benefit of men by advocating contact with menstrual blood and sexual intercourse as a path to supernatural power. Further, they positively incorporate the pan-Indian connections between women and magic in the figure of the *ḍākinī*, who can confer *siddhi*. *Ḍākinī*s are the divine and semidivine initiatory females who are so prominent in the lives of mahāsiddhas and other tantric practitioners, although they are sometimes actual historical women who initiate adepts, awaken their consciousness, and instill them with supernormal powers. On rare occasions, the term is used to describe a highly advanced, living female practitioner. *Ḍākinī* was translated into Tibetan as mkha' 'gro ma, which means "sky goer" – they cross over between realms, as between the divine and the mundane. Being initiatory goddesses, they have important salvational roles and they also represent wisdom (*prajñā*), which they can bestow along with *siddhi*s. They do this through dreams, visions, or sudden appearances in various forms: as old disgusting women, or as dogs, or as young beautiful women, and so on. Indian mahāsiddhas who constantly interacted with *ḍākinī*s were Kāṇhapa, Bhikṣana, Kantalipa, Udhilipa, and Nāropa, among others.

*Ḍākinı*s are comparable to *yakśī*s, ancient Indian tree goddesses, in their ability to grant boons, to bestow blessings. The great alchemist and mahāsiddha Nāgārjuna was said to have propitiated numerous *yakśī*s in order to obtain power over the elements, and they acted as his consorts ([9], pp. 76–77). Iconographically, *ḍākinī*s are usually depicted like *yakśī*s in early Buddhism, as voluptuous, mostly nude though bejeweled women.

In conclusion, Buddhist magic existed from the earliest days of the historical Buddha and through the rise of Mahāyāna and Tantric Buddhism, yet it clearly drew on indigenous beliefs and practices.

Cross-References

▶ Aśvaghoṣa
▶ *Iddhi*

References

1. Helmer Smith (ed) (1925) Dhammapad-Aṭṭha-kathā. Pali Text Society, Oxford. Translated by Eugene Watson Burlingame (1921, 1999) Buddhist legends. Pali Text Society, New Delhi
2. Huntington JC (1987) Pilgrimage as image: the cult of the Astamahāprātihārya, Part I. Orientations 18(4)
3. Aśvaghoṣa (1999) Saundarananda Mahākāvya of Ācārya Aśvaghoṣa with Tibetan and Hindi translations (trans: Jamspal ĀSL) Central Institute of Higher Tibetan Studies, Sarnath. Translated by Johnston EH (1932) The Saundarananda or Nanda the fair. Oxford University Press, Oxford.
4. Katz N (1982) Buddhist images of human perfection. Motilal Banarsidass, Delhi
5. Ray RA (1994) Buddhist saints in India: a study in Buddhist values and orientations. Oxford University Press, New York/Oxford
6. Strong JS (1983) The legend of King Aśoka. Princeton University Press, Princeton
7. Kern H (trans) (1963, 1884) Saddharma-puṇḍarıka or the lotus of the true law. Dover, New York
8. Tsonawa LN (trans) (1985) Indian Buddhists Pandits from "The Jewel Garland of Buddhist History". Library of Tibetan Books & Archives, New Delhi
9. Abhayadatta (1979) The Caturaśīti-siddha-pravṛtti. In: Buddha's lions: the lives of the eighty-four Siddhas (trans: Robinson JB). Dharma Publishing, Berkeley
10. Guenther HV (trans) (1963) The life and teaching of Nāropa. Oxford University Press, Oxford

Magico-religious Practices

▶ Magic (Buddhism)

Mahābodhī

▶ Bodhagayā

Mahābodhi Taru

▶ *Bodhi Tree*

Mahākāla/Dravyakāla

▶ Time (Buddhism)

Mahākassapa

▶ Kassapa

Mahākassapa Thera

▶ Kassapa

Mahākāśyapa

▶ Kassapa

Mahāmaudglyāyana

▶ Moggallāna

Mahāmeru

▶ Meru (Buddhism)

Mahāmoggallāna

▶ Moggallāna

Mahāneru

▶ Meru (Buddhism)

Mahānidāna

▶ Lalitavistara

Mahāpajāpatī

▶ Pajāpati Gotamī

Mahā-Pakaraṇa

▶ Paṭṭhāna

Mahāprajāpatī

▶ Pajāpati Gotamī

Mahāprajāpatī Gautamī

▶ Pajāpati Gotamī

M

Mahāsāṅghika

Charles Willemen
International Buddhist College, Songkhla, Thailand

Definition

Mahāsāṅghikas are "Those of the Great Saṅgha, Order, Community." Mahāsāṅghika is a school resulting from the first and fundamental split in the Buddhist order, fourth century B.C. The other group is known as Sthaviravāda.

The very first division in the Buddhist order resulted in two branches: Mahāsāṅghikas, those of the Great Community, and Sthaviras, Elders [1, 3–5]. The so-called second council in Vaiśālī did not result in a division, but shortly afterward, during the reign of Mahāpadma Nanda in Pāṭaliputra, the split occurred, ca. 340 B.C. The majority was called Mahāsāṅghika. A well-known tradition claims that the discord was all about five points concerning the characteristics of an arhat, a worthy one. The *bhikṣu*, monk, Mahādeva maintained that an arhat, subject to temptation, is subject to retrogression from his level of attainment, might have a residue of ignorance, has doubts, gains knowledge through another's help, and enters upon the path by means of an exclamation such as "*Duḥkha* (suffering)!". So, the arhat was inferior to the bodhisattva. Some sources furthermore see a Mahādeva at the origin of later discord in Mahāsāṅghika circles in Andhra.

The Mahāsāṅghika *Śāriputraparipṛcchā, Questions of Śāriputra*, which only exists in a Chinese translation of the Eastern Jin (317–420 A.D.), Taishō ed.1465, makes it clear that the oldest *vinaya* is the one of the Mahāsāṅghikas, and that the Sthaviras just wanted to add to the rules. W. Pachow's comparative study of 1955 of the *Prātimokṣa* rules, the monastic code of precepts, of the different schools, confirms this information. The so-called third council, ca. 250 B.C., during Aśoka's reign (ca. 264–227 B.C.) in Pāṭaliputra, was a Sthaviravāda council, known only in the Theravāda tradition. Because of the considerable influence of the Theravāda tradition, which considers the Mahāsāṅghikas as lax, many scholars have relied on its views.

The complete Mahāsāṅghika *vinaya* exists in Chinese translation, Taishō ed.1425, of 416–418 A.D., by Buddhabhadra and, mainly, Faxian. Faxian had obtained the Indian original copy during his stay in Pāṭaliputra [5, 7, 9].

It is now common knowledge that *vinaya*, not any doctrinal view, is the basis for any schism in the *saṅgha*, order, in India. Doctrinal views may result in a separate group within a school, *nikāya*, but not in a schism. The first schism, however, has determined the further development of Buddhism in India, and beyond. Mahāsāṅghikas spread out from Magadha via Mathurā to the Gandharan area, even to Bactria [2], the westernmost part of the Gandharan cultural area. From Gandhāra they spread to Hotan (Khotan). It must be remembered that they were not the only school which spread along this route. Mahāsāṅghikas were also in Avanti, the area of Mahākātyāyana, and they spread to India's southeastern area, to Andhra [10, 11]. This last area was overwhelmingly Mahāsāṅghika. Nāgārjuna's Madhyamaka was a Mahāsāṅghika group in that area. The Gandharan area, especially its western part, was mainly Sarvāstivāda, also before Kaniṣka's Sarvāstivāda synod ca. 170 A.D. in Kaśmīra. Sarvāstivādins say that "everything," all factors, *dharmas*, exist. They develop knowledge, *jñāna*, and strive for arhatship. The plan for their expositions is often based on the four noble truths. The rival Mahāsāṅghikas develop wisdom, *prajñā* insight into the emptiness of factors, *dharmas*. They develop the bodhisattva ideal and want *anuttarasamyaksaṃbodhi* unsurpassed right awakenment, of a Buddha. Arhatship is considered a lesser ideal. The plan for their expositions is rather based on the six perfections, *pāramitās*. The antagonism between the two great branches can be seen in the Gandharan area. Part of the oldest part(s) of the *Aṣṭasāhasrikāprajñāpāramitāsūtra*, the oldest *prajñāpāramitā*, perfection of wisdom, text, which was translated in Chinese in the second century A.D. in Luoyang, may have been composed in the first century B.C. in the Gandharan area [6, 9]. This text teaches about the role of wisdom in *yogācāra*, the practice of yoga, as opposed to the development of knowledge in Sarvāstivāda *yogācāra*. When ca. 200 A.D. the Sanskrit Vaibhāṣika "orthodoxy" was established in the North, in Kaśmīra, Nāgārjuna organized a Mādhyamika group in Andhra. The rivalry between Sarvāstivādins and Mahāsāṅghikas was constant, but they also adopted useful and successful practices of their rivals in their respective *yogācāra*, meditative practice [13].

In this context one may think of Harivarman's (Sautrāntika Sarvāstivādin influenced by Mahāsāṅghika ideas) *(Jñānakāya) Prodbhūtopadeśa*, Taishō ed.1646, better known in the past as *Tattvasiddhiśāstra* or *Satyasiddhiśāstra* (ca. 300 A.D.); Kumārajīva's conversion from Sarvāstivāda to Nāgārjuna's Madhyamaka (end of fourth century); Aśvaghoṣa (ca. 100 A.D.), a Sarvāstivādin influenced by Mahāsāṅghika ideas; and numerous *Yogācārabhūmis*, meditation manuals.

Mahāsāṅghikas are essential in the development of the so-called Mahāyāna movement, as is generally acknowledged. As the result of the Mahāsāṅghika-Sarvāstivāda rivalry and dynamics, Sthaviravāda schools such as the Dharmaguptakas, but mainly Sautrāntika Sarvāstivāda groups, played a very important role too (Asaṅga's Yogācāra group; most probably Pure Land Buddhism).

Mahāsāṅghikas are said to have had a *Tripiṭaka*, but also a fourth *Kṣudrakapiṭaka*, containing *vaipulyasūtras*, newly developed (Mahāyāna) *sūtras*. They even seem to have had a *Dhāraṇīpiṭaka*. *Dhāraṇīs* in this case are mnemotechnical means, used by expounders of the doctrine (*dharmabhāṇakas*), preachers. Excellent preachers may be called bodhisattvas, a common phenomenon in East Asia.

Sectarian Development

Mahāsāṅghikas first split into two groups, ca. 300 B.C., in Pāṭaliputra: Ekavyāvahārikas, who expound "a single (transcendent) utterance," and Kukkuṭikas (also called Gokulikas), most likely from the Kukkuṭārāma in Pāṭaliputra. The first group became known as Lokottaravāda, "proclaiming transcendency." They were in northern India and in the Gandharan cultural area, not in the South [1]. The *Mahāvastu*, a biography of the Buddha, is part of their *vinaya* [8]. *Prajñāpāramitā* literature is linked with Lokottaravāda views. They held that Buddha transcends human limitations, that there are many Buddhas in all of the ten directions and at all times. The Kukkuṭikas ca. 250 B.C. split into Bahuśrutīyas, "learned ones," and Prajñaptivādins, "nominalists," those who offer provisional designations, who hold that any statement is just conventional [1, 4, 5, 12]. The first group, which spread to the northwestern area and also to Andhra, was quite influenced by Sarvāstivāda (Sautrāntika) *abhidharma*. The second group mainly spread to southern India. Mahāsāṅghikas had *Peṭakopadeśas*, explanatory discourses about the *(Sūtra) Piṭaka*. Mahākātyāyana, the famous preacher from Avanti, was the ultimate authority. Maybe ca. 200 B.C. the Caitikas or Caityas, those who worship at shrines (*caitya*), appear. They supposedly withdrew from the area of the Ganges to Andhra, where they founded Buddhist centers, for example, in Amarāvatī. The Caitikas, first century A.D. (?), formed two groups, Pūrvaśailas (or Uttaraśailas) and Aparaśailas, in the mountains to the East and to the West of Dhānyakaṭaka (Amarāvatī). Xuanzang (seventh century) informs about the past glory of these two groups. Two more groups, Rājagirika and Siddhārthika, are distinguished within the Caitikas in the third and fourth centuries. They were known to Buddhaghosa (ca. 370–450 A.D.), who was very well informed about the region of Andhra.

Cross-References

- Arahant
- Aṣṭasāhasrikāprajñāpāramitā
- Aśvaghoṣa
- Buddhaghosa
- Buddhist Councils
- Faxian (337–422 C.E.)
- Gandhara
- Nāgārjuna
- Prajñāpāramitā
- Sarvāstivāda

► Sautrāntika
► Sthaviravāda
► Sukhāvatī

References

1. Bareau A (1955) Les sectes bouddhiques du petit véhicule. École Française d'Extrême-Orient, Saigon
2. Braarvig J et al (eds) (2000) Buddhist manuscripts in the schøyen collection, vol I. Hermes, Oslo
3. Cox C (2004) Mainstream Buddhist schools. In: Buswell R (ed) Encyclopedia of Buddhism. Macmillan Reference USA, New York, pp 501–507
4. Dutt N (latest reprint 2007) Buddhist sects in India. Motilal Banarsidass, Delhi
5. Gómez L (2005) Mahāsāṃghika. In: Jones L (ed) Encyclopedia of religion, 2nd edn. Macmillan Reference USA, Gale Virtual Reference Library, Detroit
6. Hirakawa A (1st ed 1990 Hawaii; Indian ed 1993) A history of Indian Buddhism (trans: Groner P). Motilal Banarsidass, Delhi
7. Hirakawa A (1982) Monastic discipline for the Buddhist nuns, an English translation of the Chinese text of the Mahāsāṃghika-Bhikṣuṇī-Vinaya. Kashi Prasad Jayaswal Research Institute, Patna
8. Jones J (1st ed 1930; 3 vols 1949–1956) The Mahāvastu. Luzac, London
9. Lamotte É (1988) History of Indian Buddhism: from the origins to the Śaka era (trans: Sara Webb-Boin). Université Catholique de Louvain, Institut Orientaliste, Louvain-La-Neuve
10. Matsuda J (1925) Origins and doctrines of early Indian Buddhist schools. Asia Major 2:1–78
11. Prebish Ch, Nattier J (1977) Mahāsāṅghika origins. The beginnings of Buddhist sectarianism. Hist Relig 16:237–272
12. Tsukamoto K (2004) The cycle of the formation of the schismatic doctrines. BDK English Tripiṭaka. Numata Center for Buddhist Translation and Research, Berkeley
13. Willemen C (2008) Kumārajīva's explanatory discourse about abhidharmic literature. J Int Coll Postgrad Buddh Stud 12:27–83

Mahāvairocana

► Vairocana

Mahāvasin Vihāra

► Nāgārjunakoṇḍa

Mahāyāna

K. T. S. Sarao
Department of Buddhist Studies, University of Delhi, Delhi, India

Synonyms

Great vehicle

Definition

One of the two major schools of Buddhism prominent in North Asia, including China, Mongolia, Tibet, Korea, and Japan.

Introduction

Buddhism is generally divided into two *yānas* – Hīnayāna and Mahāyāna. The term *Hīnayāna* is usually applied to early Buddhism which began with the nirvāṇa of Buddha. Mahāyāna branched out of Hīnayāna though it traces its ultimate authority to Buddha himself. The usual explanation offered for prefixing *mahā* (superior, big, great) and *hīna* (inferior, small, low) to *yāna* (vehicle) is that the former takes a practitioner to the highest goal of buddhahood as accomplished by Siddhārtha Gautama himself, while the latter takes a person only to the stage of an arahant, which is considered, in many ways, inferior to that of a buddha. Further, as maintained by Asaṅga, the Mahāyānists never seek their own salvation first. They take the vow that they will attain *bodhi* only after they have done all that is necessary for making all the other beings attain the goal. As compared to this, the Hīnayānists seek their own salvation first which, according to Asaṅga, is selfish, and therefore he justifies the use of the prefix *hīna* for them and *mahā* for his own *yāna* (see [12], p. 8). As Mahāyāna popularized the concept of a bodhisattva (literally *an enlightened being* or *a potential buddha*) whose salient features are compassion and kindness and also promoted the *pūjā* (devotional worship) of bodhisattvas such as Mañjuśrī, Avalokiteśvara, and Maitreya, Mahāyāna is also sometimes, and perhaps more accurately, called *Bodhisattvayāna*. Indian Mahāyāna Buddhism consisted primarily of two schools, viz., the Madhyamaka/Mādhyamika (*middle way*) School founded by Nāgārjuna and the Yogācāra (*consciousness only*) School founded by Asaṅga and Vasubandhu.

Origin

The background to the origin of Mahāyāna Buddhism and the exact location and date of its origin are not clear. It appcars that Mahāyāna Buddhism grew as a full-fledged sect over a period of time at different places. It is noteworthy that most of the features of Mahāyāna can be shown to have their roots in early Buddhism. Although in Pāli Tipiṭaka Buddha is largely depicted as an historical and ordinary human being, at some places in the same Tipiṭaka, the terms *rūpa-kāya* and *dhamma-kāya* are used, and he is also identified with the Dhamma (Sk: Dharma). Even the roots of the doctrine of the identity of Buddha and the Dharma can be traced in the *Tisaraṇa* (Sk: *Triś araṇa*) formula. According to Theravāda Buddhism, Gotama (Sk: Gautama) Buddha completely ceased to exist from the moment he attained Nibbāna (Sk: Nirvāṇa). The chain of cause and effect (Pāli: *paṭiccasamuppāda*; Sk: *pratītyasamutpāda*) which constituted his body and mind came to a complete halt; the aggregate of the elements of being (Pāli: *khandhas*; Sk: *skandhas*) which made up his human personality was fully dissolved leaving only Nirvāṇa in which there is no person or individual. However, the implication of the formula *Buddhaṃ śaraṇaṃ gacchāmi* is that Buddha still exists in some sense and protects those who take shelter in him. Thus the *Triśaraṇa* formula carried in its womb the Trikāya doctrine of Mahāyāna. It implies that though Buddha in his earthly form may well have ceased to exist the moment he attained Nirvāṇa, the Dharmakāya (i.e., Buddha in the form of Dharma) is still in existence. For instance, it has been stated in the *Milindapañha* that though Buddha had passed away completely in Nirvāṇa, he still exists in his Dharma. Similarly, the theory of twofold truth of the Mahāyānists can be traced in the Tipiṭaka. For instance, Buddha is stated to have said in the *Saṃyutta Nikāya* that the truth that what he had revealed is much less than what he had not revealed ([6], Vol. vi, p. 31).

The germs of the Mahāyānist doctrine of bhakti can also be traced in the Theravādin virtue of *saddhā* (Sk: *śradhā*). Earliest Buddhism accepts the existence of gods, both small and great, though as finite beings subject to the functioning of the saṃsāra. Further, it may be said that Buddha's decision, despite initial hesitation, to preach out of sheer compassion, may well have formed the basis for the development of the concept of compassionate bodhisattvas and devotion to them. Moreover, in the Pāli Tipiṭaka, there is no dearth of references either to the usefulness of worship offerings to Buddha or the *pūjā* of the stūpas and the relics. The stūpa was viewed by the laity as symbolizing not only the memory of Buddha but also the very presence of his personage. In other words, the stūpa stood as a symbol of Buddha's divine existence through the presence of his body relics (*dhātu*) in it and in the prayers that were offered to the stūpa itself; all sorts of boons, both spiritual and secular, were solicited. This clearly was a giant leap from the idea of Buddha who had become completely extinct to that of a living lord who bestowed on his devotees a wide variety of boons ([4], p. 185). The same could be said about Buddha's transcendental character as he is mentioned as a transcendental (Pāli: *lokottara*; Sk: *lokottara*) person in the late Pāli texts (e.g., [1], pp. 505, 1093, 1446). Similarly, it can be said about the doctrine of Śūnyatā as there are many references in the Pāli Tipiṭaka to Śūnyatā (Pāli: Suññatā) (e.g., [6], Vol. ii, p. 267; [9], Vol. ii, p. 304).

One explanation of the origins of the Mahāyāna is that during the Second Buddhist Council, a major division (*mahābheda*) took place in the saṃgha. One group that kept to the teachings of the elders (Sk: Sthavira; Pāli: Thera) took the name of Sthaviravāda (Pāli: Theravāda) and the second group being bigger in size became known as the Mahāsāṃghika (great assembly). It has been sometimes suggested that in southern India the Mahāsāṃghika assembly developed two views which became distinctive features of Mahāyāna. First, Buddha was transcendental and not just a historical person. Second, he used skillful means (Sk: *upayakauśalya*; Pāli: *upāyakosala*) for the purposes of teaching the subtle aspects of *buddhavacana* (teachings of Buddha). Thus, it seems that the Mahāsāṃghika School through its liberal attitude and some of its special theories provided the nest of Mahāyāna Buddhism (see [2], p. 121).

It has also been suggested that the origins of Mahāyāna lay in the development of written texts. For instance, it has been suggested by Gombrich that so long as Buddhist tradition was transmitted orally, it was not possible to have much variation in the tradition because huge bodies of monks would have been needed for the preservation of the variant doctrines. However, once the discourses began to be written down, it became possible to preserve a wider variation in doctrinal viewpoints, and this resulted in the rise of the Mahāyāna traditions (see [7]).

There were also many external factors that provided a very unique character to Mahāyāna. For instance, when Mahāyāna was slowly evolving (c. 300 BCE. to 100 CE), it came into contact with several foreign people such as the Greeks, Parthians, Śakas, and Kuṣāṇas, and in all probability, it found it quite helpful to mold itself to the exigencies of the situation while dealing with these foreigners. Further, the Mahāyāna doctrine of *bhakti* appears to have been strongly influenced by Brāhmaṇical Hinduism. The different *devas* (deities) that surrounded Buddha in the Pāli Tipiṭaka were mere accessories, and their removal would not have affected his teachings if they were all removed. However, doctrinal importance of the different bodhisattvas in Mahāyāna became so pivotal that their absence would result in the collapse of the entire Mahāyāna structure.

Chief Characteristics of Mahāyāna

For the purposes of imparting legitimacy to their religion, the Mahāyānists advocated the doctrine of twofold truth in the *buddhavacana*: the conventional truth (*saṃvṛtisatya*) meant for ordinary people and the absolute truth (*parmārthasatya*) meant for the highly evolved ones. Hīnayāna, according to them, is concerned with the conventional truth, whereas Mahāyāna is concerned with the absolute truth. Mahāyāna sūtras also give a philosophical explanation of the two *yānas*. According to them, there are two veils (*āvaraṇas*) that shield the truth: the veil of impurities (*kleśāvaraṇa*) and the veil of ignorance (*jñeyāvaraṇa*). The *kleśāvaraṇa* can be removed through adherence to the ethical rules and practice of meditation. The Mahāyānists believe that the Hīnayānists are taught only the means of the removal of *kleśāvaraṇa*, and hence they can get rid themselves only of impurities leading to the realization of just *pudgalaśūnyatā* (emptiness of a self; nonexistence of individuality) and arhatship. As compared to this, the Mahāyānists are taught the means of the removal of both *kleśā varaṇa* and *jñeyāvaraṇa*. Consequently, they become free from impurities as well as ignorance and realize both *pudgala-śūnyatā* and *dharmaśū nyatā* (emptiness of phenomena; nonexistence of objective world), resulting in buddhahood.

The main difference between the two rests on the interpretation of *śūnyatā* or *anātman*. Whereas the Hīnayānists understand *śūnyatā* or *anātman* as the nonexistence of any real substance as *ātman* or individuality, i.e., *pudgalaśūnyatā*, the Mahāyānists take it to be not only the nonexistence of individuality (*pudgalaśūnyatā*) but also that of the objective world (*dharmaśūnyatā*). In other words, according to the Mahāyānists, the truth is *śūnyatā* of both *pudgalaśūnyatā* and *dharmaśūnyatā*. This *śūnyatā* is without any attribute, negation of being and nonbeing, or *tathatā* (the state of thusness) or *dharmadhātu* (totality of phenomenal manifestations which is identical with Nirvāṇa or Buddha). Thus, *śūnyatā* is the truth, eternal, and indescribable. Further, Mahāyāna contains a rich cosmology, with a plurality of buddhas and bodhisattvas with their abodes in different worlds and buddha realms. The doctrine of *Trikāya* supports these constructions, making Buddha himself a transcendental figure who, in fact, is "an omnipotent divinity endowed with numerous supernatural attributes and qualities... almost as an omnipotent and almighty godhead" ([8], pp. 1, 85).

In respect of the saṃgha life, the outstanding difference between the two systems exists in the relative importance assigned to ordination into the saṃgha and observance of the Vinaya. From the Mahāyāna perspective, all the sentient beings have the potential to attain the *summum bonum*, i.e., buddhahood. It is attainable by all, who cultivate the *bodhicitta* (mind directed toward *bodhi*, enlightenment of the mind), and everyone who does so is a "buddha in waiting" (*bodhisattva*). In the later history of saṃgha in India, both Theravāda and Mahāyāna traditions existed alongside each other. Moreover, the existence of Mahāyānist monks in the saṃgha, to whom monkhood itself was not a necessary precondition for the pursuit of a spiritual career, was neither disruptive nor productive of any revolutionary change ([4], p. 170).

Out of its emphasis on *Bhakti* (devotion) as fundamental in the religion, the Mahāyāna evolved an elaborate ritualism of *pūjā* but bypassed the ancient Vinaya. Mahāyāna texts such as the *Śūraṅgama Sūtra* consider the Vinaya as helpful in the cultivation of a specific type of mind qualities rather than following a set of rules of discipline. Still the Mahāyānists did not go so far as to do away with the rules. It is only that they did not consider them as absolutely binding. To them, the Vinaya had a use and significance different from what the Theravāda conceived: its *raison d'être* was to lead the devotee's mind to a state most favorable to cultivation of the higher wisdom. Interestingly, it is also worth noticing that through the breadth and depth of India, there were a large number of *vihāras* which were not exclusive to any specific sect and where monks owing allegiance to different sects lived harmoniously. In fact, coexistence of different sects in a saṃgha seems to have been the normal practice ([4], p. 216). As mentioned by Parmārtha, a Buddhist sect known as the Kaulikas strongly believed that the real teachings of Buddha were not the Vinaya, but the Abhidhamma, and that "a Bhikkhu may or may not have three robes for covering his body; may or may not reside in a monastery; and may or may not have his meal within the time-limit" (see [3], pp. 15–64).

Central to Mahāyāna ideology is the idea of the bodhisattva, one who seeks to become a buddha. As compared to Theravādin perspective, which limits the designation of bodhisattva to Gautama Buddha in his previous births, Mahāyāna teaches that anyone can aspire to accomplish *bodhi* and thereby become a bodhisattva. In the Mahāyāna tradition, the emphasis is less on nirvāṇa and more on *prajñā*. In Mahāyāna, *bodhi* consists in understanding the true nature of reality which is to be understood through *prajñā* (wisdom) and actualized through *karuṇā* (compassion). Mahāyānists feel that since no individual has an *ātman* (self), there is no real difference between them and others. The upshot of this is that they do not see any difference between their own liberation and that of the others.

Though the standard model of kamma (Sk: karma) in Buddhism decrees that only one's actions can influence one's future, inscriptional evidence from the early historic period of Indian history indicates that there existed the concept of transference of merit. This idea of transference of merit was originally used to transfer merit to one's dead forefathers leading to their salvation. However, the use of merit toward acquiring *prajñā* ultimately leading to *bodhi*, in place of using accumulated merit for improving future rebirths within *saṃsāra*, was innovated by Mahāyāna. The growth of this type of cosmology led to a major shift away from the idea of Buddha Śākyamuni being the sole source of salvation to the view of there being many other sources. Consequently, an assortment of deities, ranging from bodhisattvas such as Avalokiteśvara to buddhas such as Amitābha, became fashionable within Mahāyāna.

Crucial to the Mahāyāna salvific vision is the doctrine of skillful means (*upāya*). Motivated by compassion and guided by wisdom and insight, buddhas and bodhisattvas wish to lead ordinary beings to liberation. Their individually appropriate methods are beyond ordinary comprehension and may even seem deceptive, but they are justified by the superior insight of these saviors.

The most famous examples of this idea are given in parables from the Saddharmapuṇḍarīka Sūtra (*Lotus Sūtra*); they have served as influential models for later elaborations, particularly in popular literature.

The Indian Mahāyāna developed two principal philosophical schools: Madhyamaka and Yogācāra which flourished in India from the third-fourth century CE till about the twelfth century CE. According to Madhyamaka (middle way), founded by Nāgārjuna (second to third centuries CE), all phenomena are without essence (*svabhāva*) as they are dependently co-arisen. Madhyamaka is a systematization of the Prajñāpāramitā scriptures, where it is emphasized that the doctrine of wisdom (*prajñā*) is the most important of the six perfections (*pāramitās*) that the bodhisattva needs to cultivate. The other five *pāramitās* are *dāna* (generosity), *sī la* (virtuous conduct), *kṣanti* (forbearance), *vīrya* (vigor), and dhyāna (meditative contemplation). The Yogācāra (practice of yoga), also known as Vijñānavāda (consciousness only) and *cittamātra* (mind only), was founded by the half brothers Vasubandhu and Asaṅga. It synthesized Abhidharmic modes of analyzing mental processes with the Madhyamaka notion of emptiness. Besides Madhyamaka and Yogācāra, other philosophical traditions, such as a Yogācāra–Madhyamaka fusion, a Tathāgatagarbha (Buddha nature) tradition which emphasizes the inherent seed of bodhi in all beings and a school of logic and epistemology (*pramāṇa*), have also been recognized by modern scholars.

Cross-References

- Asaṅga
- Avalokiteśvara
- Bodhi
- Bodhisattva
- Buddhist Councils
- Dharma
- Khandha
- Mādhyamika
- Mañjuśrī
- Nāgārjuna
- Nirvāṇa
- Pāramitās
- Paṭiccasamuppāda
- Saddharmapuṇḍrīka Sūtra
- Saṃgha
- Saṃsāra
- Saṃyutta Nikāya
- Śūnyatā
- Tathāgatagarbha
- Tipiṭaka
- Tri-kāya
- Vijñānavāda
- Yogācāra

References

1. Bapat PV, Vadekar RD (eds) (1940) The Dhammasaṅgaṇi. The Bhandarkar Research Institute, Poona
2. Conze E (1951) Buddhism: its essence and development. Philosophical Library, New York
3. Demiéville P (1931) L'origine des sectes bouddhiques d'après Paramārtha. Mélanges chinois et bouddique, vol I. L'Institut Belge de Hautes Études Chinoises, Bruxelles, pp 15–64
4. Drewes D (2010) Early Indian Mahāyāna Buddhism. Relig Compass 4.2:55–65, 66–74
5. Dutt S (1988) Buddhist monks and monasteries of India: their history and their contribution to Indian culture. Motilal Banarsidass, Delhi, reprint
6. Feer ML (1884–1898) The Saṃyutta Nikāya, 5 vols. Pali Text Society, London
7. Gombrich PF (1990) How the Mahāyāna began. In: Skorupski T (ed) The Buddhist forum: seminar papers 1987–1988. School of Oriental and African Studies, London, pp 21–30
8. Guang X (2005) The three bodies of the Buddha: the origin and development of the Trikāya theory. Routledge Curzon, Oxford
9. Oldenberg H (1879–1883) The Vinaya Piṭakaṃ, 5 vols. Pali Text Society, London
10. Pande GC (1993) Studies in Mahāyāna. Central Institute of Higher Tibetan Studies, Sarnath
11. Sangharakshita B (1987) A survey of Buddhism, 6th totally revised edition. Tharpa Publications, London
12. Śāstrī YS (1989) Mahāyānasūtrālaṅkāra of Asaṅga: a study of Vijñānavāda Buddhism. Sri Satguru Publications, Delhi
13. Schopen G (2003) Mahāyāna. In: Buswell RE (ed) Encyclopedia of Buddhism. Macmillan, Indianapolis, pp 492–499
14. Suzuki DT (1907) Outlines of Mahāyāna Buddhism. Luzac and Company, London
15. Williams P (2009) Mahāyāna Buddhism: the doctrinal foundations, 2nd edn. Routledge, London

Mahāyāna Laṅkāvatāra Sūtra

▶ Laṅkāvatāra Sūtra

Mainstream Buddhism

▶ Theravāda

Majjhima Nikāya

K. T. S. Sarao
Department of Buddhist Studies, University of Delhi, Delhi, India

Synonyms

Collection of Middle Length Discourses; Madhyama Āgama; Majjhima Saṅgīti; The Book of the Middle Length Sayings

Definition

The second of the five divisions of the Pāli *Sutta Piṭaka.*

The *Majjhima Nikāya* is a Buddhist scripture, the second of the five *nikāyas* (collections) in the *Sutta Piṭaka*, which is one of the "three baskets" that constitute the Pāli *Tipiṭaka* of Theravāda Buddhism. In English, it is known as the "Collection of Middle Length Discourses" or "Middle Collection." It consists of 152 *suttas* (Sk: *sūtras* discourses) by the Buddha and his chief disciples, which together constitute a comprehensive body of Buddhist teaching (*Buddhavacana*), concerning all aspects of the Buddhism. The 152 suttas are grouped into three books (*paṇṇāsas*) called *Mahāpaṇṇāsa* (first 50 suttas), *Majjhimapaṇṇāsa* (sutta nos. 51–100), and *Uparipaṇṇāsa* (sutta nos. 101–152). Each of these three books is subdivided into groups of ten *suttas.* Occasionally, these *suttas* are also clustered into pairs called *Cūḷa* (small) and *Mahā* (great) *suttas*. At the First Saṅgīti (council) that took place at Rājagaha 3 months after the death of the Buddha, the job of memorizing the *Majjhima Nikāya* and of transmitting it further intact was assigned to the "school" of Sāriputta ([1], Vol. i, p. 15). Buddhaghosa wrote a commentary to the *Majjhima Nikāya*, which is called the *Papañcasūdanī*, and Sāriputta of Ceylon wrote its *ṭīkā*, the *Līnatthappakāsinī*. The *Majjhima Nikāya* is also called the *Majjhima Saṅgīti* ([2], Vol. i, p. 2). It has been prophesied in the *Papañcasūdanī* that when the *Sāsana* (Buddhism) disappears, the *Majjhima Nikāya* shall predecease the *Dīgha Nikāya* ([2], Vol. ii, p. 881).

The *Majjhima Nikāya* corresponds to the *Madhyama Āgama* found in the *Sūtra Piṭakas* of various Sanskrit-based early Buddhist schools, fragments of which are extant in Sanskrit. Portions of the Sarvāstivāda *Madhyama Āgama* also survive in Tibetan translation. A complete translation of the *Madhyama Āgama* of the Sarvāstivāda school was done by Saṃghadeva in the Eastern Jin dynasty in 397–398 C.E. This translation is known as the *Zhōng Ahánjīng* (Taishō 26) and contains 222 *sūtras* [3].

The *Majjhima Nikāya* deals with almost all the important tenets of Buddhism, and light has been thrown not only on the life of the Buddhist monks and nuns but also on subjects such as Brāhmaṇical *yajñas* (sacrifices), different forms of asceticism, the relation of the Buddha to the Nigaṇṭhas (Jainas), the four noble truths, the doctrine of kamma, refutation of the self (*attā*), and different modes of meditation, and the social and political conditions prevalent at that time have all been discussed in this *Nikāya* ([4], p. 116). Some interesting details relating to the life of the Buddha are also available in the *Majjhima Nikāya*. For instance, the *Mahāsaccakasuttana* (no. 36) contains the well-known legend of the Bodhisatta meditating as a child under a Jambu tree. The *Ariyapariyesanasuttanta* (no. 26) talks about the Buddha's teachers Āḷāra Kālāma and Udaka Rāmaputta.

In some of the *suttas* of the *Majjhima Nikāya*, it has been stated that the particular dialogue took place after the Mahāparinibbāna. This indicates

M

that these *suttas* are younger than those in the *Dīgha Nikāya* ([5], p. 34). For instance, the *Bakkulasuttanta* (no.124) mentions that Bakkula, who was regarded as the fittest among all the monks, entered Nibbāna 80 years after joining the saṃgha. It seems that he must have survived the Buddha by half a century, a fact that has drawn the attention of the author of the *Papañcasūdanī*, who points out that this *sutta* was recited only during the Second Buddhist Council, i.e., a 100 years after the Mahāparinibbāna. This comment of the commentator is of great consequence for the history of the Pāli Tipiṭaka, for it indicates that even the Theravādin tradition admits to later additions ([5], p. 34).

Views of the Buddha on some intricate matters have also been spelled out in some of the *suttas* of the *Majjhima Nikāya*. For instance, in *Channovāda Suttanta* (no. 144), the Buddha's view on suicide has been expressed. In this *sutta*, seriously ill monk Channa has been mentioned as expressing a desire to commit suicide but is advised against such an action by Sāriputta and Mahācunda. However, when the matter is reported to the Buddha, he does not object to the suicide as only the craving for rebirth should be overcome. The *Dhātuvibhaṅga Suttanta* (no. 140) talks about the possibility of a person entering Nibbāna without having to become a fully ordained monk. Here, in this *sutta*, the story of a novice Pukkusāti, who met the Buddha by chance, is related. This novice met the Buddha without knowing him as he had received his *pabbajjā* from another monk. After being taught by the Buddha, he recognized him and requested for the *upasampadā*. But he died before bowl and robe were made available. Still the Buddha announced that Pukkusāti had entered Nibbāna even without having become a fully ordained monk. The content of the *Majjhima Nikāya* shows a greater variety of topics than does the *Dīgha Nikāya*. Only the major debates are absent in the *Majjhima Nikāya*, though discussions with heretics do occur. For instance, in the *Upālisuttanta* (no. 56) and the *Kukkuravatikasuttanta* (no. 57), description of strange ascetical practices has been given. It was suggested by Franke and Manné that the *Majjhima Nikāya* might have been used to instruct converts to Buddhism ([6], p. 1102; [7], pp. 71, 78).

Cross-References

- ▶ Bodhisatta
- ▶ Dhamma
- ▶ Dīgha Nikāya
- ▶ Four Noble Truths
- ▶ Kamma
- ▶ Rājagaha (Pāli)
- ▶ Sāriputta
- ▶ Sutta Piṭaka
- ▶ Theravāda
- ▶ Vinaya

References

1. Rhys Davids TW, Carpentier JE, Stede W (eds) (1886–1932) The Sumaṅgala-Vilāsinī: Buddhaghosa's commentary on the Dīgha NikÈya, 3 vols. PTS, London
2. Woods JH, Kosambi D, Horner IB (eds) (1922–1938) Papañcasūdanī: Majjhimanikāyaṭṭhakathā of Buddhaghosācariya, 5 vols. Pali Text Society, London
3. Keown D (2004) A dictionary of Buddhism. Oxford University Press, Oxford
4. Law BC (1983) A history of Pāli Literature, reprint, vol 1. Indological Book House, Delhi
5. von Hinüber O (1996) A handbook of Pāli literature. Walter de Gruyter, Berlin
6. Franke RO (1978) Klein Schriften, 2 vols. Franz Steiner Verlag, Wiesbaden
7. Manné J (1990) Categories of Sutta in the Pāli Nikāyas and their implications for our appreciation of the Buddhist Teaching and Literature. J Pali Text Soc 15:29–87
8. Feer ML (1884–1898) The Saṃyutta Nikāya, 5 vols. Pali Text Society, London
9. Jayawardhana S (1993) Handbook of Pāli literature. Karunaratne, Colombo
10. Law BC (1930) Chronology of the Pāli canon. Ann Bhandarkar Orient Res Inst (Poona) 12(Pt 2):171–201
11. Muller C (ed) Digital Dictionary of Buddhism. http://www.buddhism-dict.net/ddb/
12. Rhys Davids CAF, Thera SS, Woodward FL (trans) (1917–1930) The book of the Kindred sayings, 5 vols. Pali Text Society, London
13. Webb R (1975) An analysis of the Pāli canon. Buddhist Publication Society, Kandy

Majjhimā Paṭipadā

▶ Middle Way (Buddhism)

Majjhima Saṅgīti

▶ Majjhima Nikāya

Majjhimā-Paṭipadā

Mangala Ramchandra Chinchore
Department of Philosophy, Centre for Studies in Classical Indian Buddhist Philosophy and Culture, University of Pune, Pune, Maharashtra, India

Synonyms

Majjhimā-paṭipadā (in Pāli)/(Sk. *Madhyamā-pratipat*) translated as Middle-way/path.

Definition

Duḥkha-nirodha-gāminī-pratipat (a way to control/destroy pain and suffering), known as *Aṣṭāṅgika-mārga* (Eightfold path) in Early Buddhism, part of the first sermon given by the Buddha known as the *Dhamma-cakka-pabattana-sutta* (Turning the Wheel of *Dhamma*), path of non-extremism.

Majjhimā-patipada Alternative to Extremities

Majjhimā-paṭipadā (in Pāli)/*Madhyamā-pratipat* (in Sanskrit) (translated as Middle-way) traditionally is known as the path discovered by Gautama the Buddha. After realization of the ultimate truth/enlightenment (*Bodhi*), Buddha gave the first sermon at Sārnātha, known as the "Turning the Wheel of *Dhamma*" (*Dhamma-cakka-pabattana-sutta*), to his five contemporary ascetic disciples. He described them the features of proper modes of life, which he himself adopted and motivated others to choose as the best alternative, and then they became disciples of him.

The then society consisted of two types of people, one, common man who was thinking that bodily pleasure is the ultimate joy (like *Cārvākas*) and upheld indulgence into sensualism (Sk. *Kāmeśukāmasukhāllika*). Buddha pointed out it to be low, ignoble, vulgar, unworthy, and useless. The Buddha was indeed showing a way to become free from *Duḥkha,* but obviously not by prescribing immorality and licentiousness. On the other side, there were many knowledgeable (like *Vedic/Upaniṣadic)* and spiritual practitioners (like *Sāṁkhyas*), who were engaged in sacrifices, rites, and rituals, and upheld that body is impure. For removing physical impurity and/or keeping self (Sk. *Átman*) intact in clean-body, penance by self-mortification (Sk. *Átmaklamathānuyoga*), (like Jainas), is essential. But according to the Buddha that too is ultimately painful, pessimistic, unworthy, and useless.

In the *Dhamma-cakka-pabattana-sutta* (*Saṁyutta-Nikāya*) [1], he explained the redundancy of the prevalent modes of living – culminating at the end in extremism of self-mortification or self-indulgence, hedonism or asceticism, agnosticism or skepticism, craving for existence (Sk. *Bhava*) or nonexistence (Sk. *Vibhava*).

It is stated in the *Mahāsaccaka-sutta* (*Majjhima-Nikāya*) [2] that he was not able to reach the goal by following the then available paths, realized their futility, and hence he rejected them all. They did not give him peace and satisfaction. It was because his contemporaries were committed to specific positions dogmatically, and were not able to comprehend the facts of life and nature of the ultimate truth, that is, pain and suffering (Sk. *Duḥkha*). However, he warns to be aware and suggests the possible alternative to live life properly, namely, the middle-way (Sk. *Madhyamā-pratipad*), which is also known as

Eightfold path (Sk. *Aṣṭāṅgika-mārga*). It is a path that gives vision/insight, leads to peace of mind, and enables to develop wisdom and ability to mitigate suffering.

In the *Aṅguttara-Nikāya* [3] experience of the Buddha himself is illustrated. When he was a prince, he was provided excessive luxuries to obtain sensuous pleasure. Similarly when he became homeless and was wandering in search of spiritual truth, he followed the traditional modes of ascetic austerities for self-realization by mortifying body, and hence torturing it wrongly. Everyone attempts to become free from pain and suffering (Sk. *Duḥkha*), but the way chosen should not be overloaded by restrictions and extremities. Buddha's attempt at articulating the middle-way is to maintain a balance, a kind of transcendence (and not synthesis).

The Buddha being free from all kinds of commitments was able to experience facts as they are, think discursively, and contemplate independently in an innovative way to realize the dynamic nature of truth. What he felt, realized, sensed cannot be uniformly repeated and/or held to be identical with others. That is the reason why Buddha was insisting on self-experimentation and discovery of truth independently. The Buddha advises to become a guide unto oneself (Pāli - *Attāno padīpo bhava*) and suggests to adopt a new alternative. He, perhaps, intended to make one self-reliant and preserve autonomy for making one confident to confront facts of life, without committing apriorily to some or the other kind of "ism" (Pāli - *Diṭṭhi*/Sk. *Dṛṣṭi*) – perspective.

Majjhimā-paṭipadā is a doctrine, which consists of two words: "*Majjhimā*" (middle), which connotes avoiding the "*Antas*" (extremes), keeping balance, remaining moderate. "*Paṭipadā*" implies a practising way or following a path. When the word "*Anta*" (ends) is used, it means that there are minimally two extremes; since (logically speaking) two is the smallest number denoting many. This can be witnessed by the denial of his six (more than two) contemporary ascetics-monks (Sk. *Śramaṇas*).

Middle (Sk. "*Madhya*") connotes/indicates equidistance and/or avoidance of eccentricity or excessiveness of any kind. It is not strict bipolarity and perhaps, the way in which modern interpreters hold the dialectic mode of thinking. Reality/life does not strictly consist of antinomies, but has variety/plurality of different kinds, and opposition is just one kind of it. "*Madhya*" is a mode of analyzing the dynamic nature of reality, including human life. While opposing singularity as well as multiplicity, it seems, the central focus of attention is not on the number and form of polarities in philosophical reflections, but on the fundamental commitments, which should not be eccentric. Further, path ensures that it is being practiced having specific direction and does not remain a theoretical consideration or a mere conceptual analysis.

"*Madhyamā*" is an attribute of the word "*Pratipad*" (path/way of life). While living life at every moment one has to confront problems, find out solutions to them, resolve/dissolve them, and if they are not solved one has to leave them or change perspective to look at problems or else accept them as part of life (Sk. *Duḥkha-nirodha*). It is a struggle not only for existence and survival, but also for developing and liberating oneself to grow progressively. Middle-path is neither a highly sophisticated technique, nor a superficial/mechanical method. It is a simple and natural action-oriented plan of life, which can be adopted by all even by the illiterates. It is a path of awakening and peace.

Solutions cannot be readily available, and occasions/happenings/events cannot be apriorily predicted/determined in life. One has to make decisions using one's own discretionary power ex-tempo, depending upon problem/s confronted. There is neither authoritative guide, like supernatural God, nor text/s or tradition/s, like *Vedas*, nor even standard procedures led down permanently relevant to be practiced. The issue of prescriptions/injunctions or prohibitions/restrictions cannot be decided eternally once and for all. It differs, taking into various considerations contextually, determining the meaning or content and criterion of rightness and well-being, based on moral considerations. One has to decide what is right and what is wrong contextually, using general parameters merely as directives. That is why "*Madhya*" means negation of any kind of extremity and equidistancing oneself from limitations, by discovering a new framework, transcending the lacuna of the earlier prevalent ones. Later on, this was interpreted as contextual-relativism by the followers of Buddhism.

In the *Sacca-vibhaṅga-sutta* [3] it is told that Buddha was attempting to explain the nature of life and the world, which is susceptible to pain and suffering (*Duḥkha*). While explaining nature of the *Cattāri Ariya Saccāni* (Four Noble Truths), in two contexts the word "*Majjha*" (middle) is mentioned:

(a) Why *Duḥkha* arises in human life? – Where the analysis of *Duḥkha-samudaya* in terms of the *Dvādaśa-nidānas* occurs. While referring to the Middle-path, Buddha explained to Kaccāyana, "The World, in general, inclines to two views: existence or non-existence (Pāli - *atthitā ca natthitā ca*), *Sāssatavāda/Śaśvatavāda* (eternalism of materialist kind, or spiritualist, or even transcendental one) or *Ucchedavāda* (nihilism of mechanical kind, or dialectical). But for he who, with the highest wisdom, sees the up-rising of the world as it really is, realizes that truth is beyond them. In both, I was under the wrong impression that existence is substantial." However, existence cannot be defined in terms of "is, is not, synthesis of both and rejection of all." It is erroneous way to describe the ultimate truth by using (four) normal categories of understanding the phenomenal existence. From this, one should not hastily conclude that truth is mystical and be skeptical about existence of the ultimate reality. Rather, it is beyond the limits of rational modes of thinking, and cannot be explained in terms of conventional modes of expression restrictively. To explain it in a particular way is losing its dynamicity and making it absolute/fixed, which the Buddha was trying to avoid/deny.
(b) Yet, in another context while explaining how to bring pain and suffering (Sk. *Duḥkha*) to an end,that is, *Duḥkha-nirodha-gāminī-pratipad* (a way to control/destroy/mitigate pain and suffering) reference to the *Majjhimā-paṭipadā* occurs.

In the *Saṁyutta-Nikāya, Kaccāyana-sutta* [4], it is stated that Buddha realized the meaning of "*Majjha*" (middle), when he was sitting on Nirañjanā (which later on came to be known as river Falgu) river-bank, in his 6th year of practicing severe austerities (Sk. *Tapas*). Suddenly, he happened to hear a musician teaching his student how to play the *Vīṅā* (a type of Indian string-instrument), while passing in a boat. The teacher instructed his student that tightening of strings of the *Vīṅā* too much will cause them to snap, and leaving them too loose will cease to produce a harmonious sound.

It is this incidence which, perhaps, provided him a clue to realize the meaning of "skillful-art to keep balance of means" in practice, and he articulated the "middle-path." He understood the importance of the "insightful way in life" and stipulated some "indicators giving direction" toward tranquility and peaceful living, known as the Eightfold path (Sk. *Aṣṭāṅgika-mārga*). Pain and suffering (*Duḥkha*) arises in human life, because one clings/craves for substantial things and beings, and misunderstands them as essential ones. For preserving/sustaining existence, namely, mundane pleasure and joy, or else methods for getting supermundane eternal/spiritual happiness, one generally prefers such modes leaning toward eternality and substantiality. Unfortunately, that is done at the cost of or neglecting the importance of the present precious moments of life.

"*Madhya*" (balance) is the back-bone of "*Saṁyak*" (right/proper/moderate) in the Eightfold path (*Aṣṭāṅgika-mārga*), and hence it (*Aṣṭāṅgika-mārga*) is also known as the middle-way (*Majjhimā-paṭipadā*). It is helpful and mandatory for all kinds of followers to emancipate from suffering, irrespective of the difference between *Sādhujana* – ordained monks and nuns (Pāli - *Bhikkhu-Bhikkhuṇī*), and laity/householders (Pāli - *Puthujana*) – men and women.

In early Buddhism, ethical aspect of the Eightfold path (*Aṣṭāṅgika-mārga*) was insisted to be practiced by all, and it is understood in the larger frame of the four noble truths, as explained in the *Dhamma-cakka-pabattana-sutta*. The Eightfold path (*Aṣṭāṅgika-mārga*) was explained concurrently in both the forms – right (Pāli - *sacca*) and

M

wrong (Pāli - *micchā*) – in order to make the followers aware of the wrong direction to be avoided and conversely proper direction to be adopted and followed.

Later on, *Mahāyāna* Buddhists explained the term "*Madhya*" (middle) in relation to metaphysical aspect of it. For them, interdependence (Sk. *Pratītya-samutpāda*), perhaps, is a mode of discovering truth conventionally experienced, and it becomes a central point of the focus. For, it is in the context of *Dvādaśa-nidānas,* proper diagnosis of *Duḥkha,* and moderate modes of getting freedom from it are to be used. So, explaining the nature of existence is the starting point of realizing truth. Thus, really speaking, in all the four truths, while interpreting and comprehending their meaning, "*Madhya*" is pertinent and relevant.

In order to highlight the meaninglessness of the conventional reality (Sk. *Saṁvṛtti/Vyavahāra-sat*), its vacuous nature and emptiness (Sk. *Śūnyatā*) should be highlighted and refuted. To realize the nature of comprehension, as devoid of truth, is itself a way to realize and emancipate (Sk. *Nirvāṇa*). For *Mahāyānists* in general and *Mādhyamikas* in particular, the mode of philosophisation – comprehension and understanding – is the central point of attention. They seem to be presuming that life can be lived rightly by following the ethical path laid down by the Buddha. Instead of emphasizing on the Eightfold path (*Aṣṭāṅgika-mārga*) advocated by *Hīnayāna*, as a new form of *Madhyamā-pratipad* the *Pāramitās* are highlighted by both *Mādhyamikas* and *Yogācārins*. It is because mere practice is too restrictive and personalized, and hence is not enough to realize the ultimate truth. Additionally, it requires to be supplemented by correct methods of philosophisation – practice needs to be supported by theoretical framework of understanding as well. Thus, for the realization of emancipation (Sk. *Nirvāṇa*), proper understanding of Interdependence (*Pratītya-samutpāda*), Emptiness (*Śnyatā*), and the Middle-path (*Madhyamā-pratipad*) is required.

In the *Hīnayāna* tradition too, following the middle-path (*Majjhimā-paṭipadā*) is just a beginning or entering into Buddhist stream of life, that is, the *Sotāpatti/Śrotāpanna* (stream-entering), the first stage of emancipation (Pāli - *Nibbāna*/Sk. *Nirvāṅa*). It is a stage where one starts realizing one's own ignorance (Sk. *Avidyā*) and futility of craving (Sk. *Tṛṣṅā*). It is an attempt to eradicate illusion of the eternality of self (Pāli - *Sakkāya-diṭṭhi*/Sk. *Satkāya-dṛṣṭi*), vacuousness of doubt and hair-splitting analysis (Pāli - *Vicīkiccā*/Sk. *Vicīkitsā*), and undertaking critical examination of indulgence into wrong/illicit rites and ceremonies (Pali-*Silabbata-parāmassa*/Sk. *Śīlavrata-parāmarśa*). It gives hope that one can become entitled to/deserving (*Arhat*) for emancipation (Pāli - *Nibbāna*) in this life and world. Thus, one follows a way not only to become free from pain and suffering (*Duḥkha*), but to lead toward enlightenment (Sk. *Bodhi*) also, and finally emancipation (Sk. *Nirvāṅa*).

Cross-References

- *Aṣṭāṅgamārga*
- *Avidyā*
- *Bodhi*
- Buddha (Concept)
- *Cattāri Ariya Saccāni*
- *Dhamma*
- *Dhammacakkappavattana-sutta*
- *Duḥkha*
- *Duhkha – Unpleasant*
- *Hīnayāna*
- *Madhyamā Pratipad*
- *Mahāyāna*
- *Majjhimā-paṭipadā* (in Pāli)
- *Nirvāṇa*
- *Pāramitā*
- *Pratītya Samutpāda*
- *Śramaṇa*
- *Sotāpanna*
- *Śūnya*
- *Uccheda-vāda*
- *Yogācāra*

References

1. (1995) Saṁyutta-Nikāya, Dhamma-cakka-pabattana-sutta and Kaccāyana-sutta, 12, 15, 17, 35, 48. Tipiṭaka,

Chaṭṭha Saṅgāyana edn (CD-ROM Version-3). Vipassana Research Institute, Igatpuri
2. (1995) Majjhima-Nikāya, Mahāsaccaka-sutta, 36. Tipiṭaka, Chaṭṭha Saṅgāyana edn (CD-ROM Version-3). Vipassana Research Institute, Igatpuri
3. (1995) Aṅguttara-Nikāya, Sacca-vibhaṅga-sutta. Tipiṭaka, Chaṭṭha Saṅgāyana edn (CD-ROM Version-3). Vipassana Research Institute, Igatpuri
4. (1995) Kaccayana-sutta; Samyutta-Nikaya. Tipiṭaka, Chaṭṭha Saṅgāyana edn (CD-ROM Version-3). Vipassana Research Institute, Igatpuri

Manas

► Mind (Buddhism)

Manas Sarovar

► Mānasarovara (Buddhism)

Manasarovar

► Anotatta
► Mānasarovara (Buddhism)

Mānasārovara

► Anotatta

Mānasarovara (Buddhism)

K. T. S. Sarao
Department of Buddhist Studies, University of Delhi, Delhi, India

Synonyms

Anavatapta; Anotatta; Lake Manas; Manas Sarovar; Manasarovar; Mapham Yutso; Tso Rimpoche

Definition

A fresh water lake located in Tibet which is sacred to the Hindus, Buddhists, Jains, and Bönpas.

Lake Mānasarovara, along with Mount Kailash and lake Rākṣas/Rākas, is located in the western Tibetan plateau between the Gurla Mandhata mountain in the southeast and Kunlun mountain in the northwest. The name *mānasarovara*, i.e., *manas* ("mind" or "consciousness") + *sarovara* (lake) means "Lake of Consciousness and Enlightenment." According to a legend mentioned in the *Rāmāyaṇa*, this lake was created by the mind of Brahmā at the request of ascetics who needed a water source for their daily religious ablutions. The Tibetan name for Mānasarovara is *Mapham Yutso* which means the "Unconquerable Turquoise Lake." It is also known as *Tso Rimpoche* (Precious Lake) to the Tibetans. This holiest of lakes of the world, located 36 km southeast of Mount Kailash, is like a giant magic mirror. Situated at a height of 14,900 ft from the sea level, it is perhaps the highest fresh water lake on earth.

Buddhists consider Mānasarovara as the earthly manifestation of lake Anavatapta (Pāli: Anotatta), where Queen Māyā, the Buddha's mother, had been taken in her dream to be bathed before conceiving the great being. The Buddhist texts talk of the Buddha often going to Anavatapta for his ablutions and then proceeding to Uttarakuru for alms, returning to have his meal and to meditate on its banks. Buddhist texts also talk of many buddhas, pratyeka buddhas, arahants, *devas*, and *yakṣas* bathing and/or sporting on its banks. Four channels open out of the lake in the direction of the four quarters viz., Sīhamukha, Hatthimukha, Assamukha, and Usabhamukha. Four rivers, viz., Brahmaputra, Karnali, Indus, and Sutlej are said to flow from these channels.

Mānasarovara is considered a personification of purity and someone taking a dip or drinking its water is believed to be cleansed of all sins, being awarded after death with a place in the heavenly abode of Lord Śiva (Śivaloka). According to ancient Buddhist cosmological view, Anavatapta lies at the center of the world and would be the last to dry up at the end of the world. As the light of both the sun and the moon never falls directly on the water of this lake but only in reflection, its water stays perpetually cool. Buddhist texts also mention that as the name *anavatapta* means *free from heat*, the waters of the lake are considered as having the quality of soothing the fires that torment beings.

Though some scholars believe that the practice of pilgrimage began in Tibet at the earliest in the seventh century C.E. with the arrival of Buddhism from India, it is almost certain that Indians have been visiting Mānasarovara as pilgrims since 1000 B.C.E., if not earlier. It must be noted that in those early centuries, Tibet did not exist in as much isolation as is generally believed and Indian and Tibetan cultures have been enriching each other since prehistoric times. Thu, it has been suggested that there may have been links between Brāhmaṇical-Hinduism and the early Tibetan faith, Bön. Such links may well have been stimulated by the presence of gold and other precious metals in the Kailash-Mānasarovara region.

With a circumference of 91 km and a maximum depth of 230 ft, this lake is viewed as an eight-

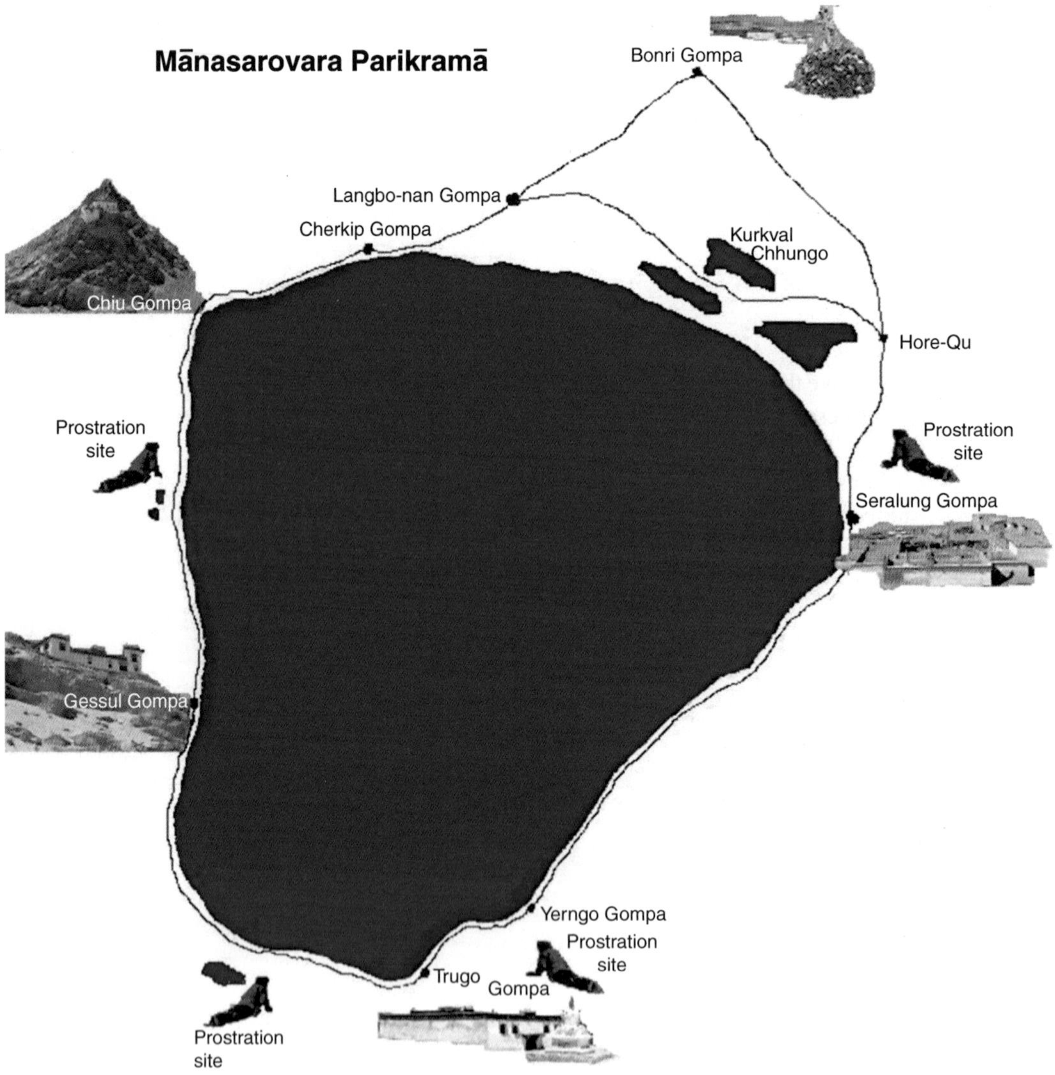

Mānasarovara (Buddhism), Fig. 1 The Mānasarovara Parikramā route

petalled lotus or a maṇḍala-square with four doors to the cardinal directions. A person who has the wisdom eye can see on its eastern shore *jambuvrikṣa*, the tree of life. The Buddha blesses this lake and sits along with his 500 bodhisattvas (enlightened beings) on lotus flowers blooming in it. For the shamans, the holy water from the lake purifies the pollution of being born from a human womb. A ritual bath in the lake endows a shaman with divine wisdom enabling him to work as a mediator between the worlds of gods and humans. Thus, he can interpret *devavāṇi* (godly speech) to his lay devotees, thereby solving their dilemmas.

In modern times, those pilgrims who perform the complete *parikramā* (circumambulation) of Mānasarovara on foot take 3–4 days (Fig. 1). Indian pilgrims generally do the *parikramā* in cars and buses. In the pre 1959 period the *parikramā* included a visit to each of the eight gompas (monasteries) located around it: Chiu, Charyip (Cherkip), Langbo-nan (Langpona), Bonri, Seralung, Yerngo (Nyego), Trugo (Thugolho/Trus), and Gossul. However, now only Chiu, Seralung, and Trugo are visited by the pilgrims.

Its disc is shaped like the sun and represents the power of consciousness, and is a symbol of good fortune and fertility. But just as consciousness is balanced by unconsciousness, Mānasarovara is matched by the conch-shaped Rākas Tal to the west. It is the abode of the mountain god, Gombo Beng, the great guardian of Tantrism. This god is sometimes identified with Rāvaṇa, the demon king of Lanka, who once was a serious devotee of Śiva. An historical issue which arises, concerns Mānasarovara which, at least in recent times, has been considered auspicious, in contrast to Rākas Tal, envisaged as inauspicious. It has been suggested that this is a comparatively recent understanding, and that the early Buddhist pilgrims who reached the region via the Satluj identified Rākas Tal as Lake Anavatapta. He argues that later Hindu pilgrims identified Mānasarovara as the auspicious lake due to its location on the right-hand side of the mountain in the view of the pilgrims coming from the south. Others have suggested the possibility that initially only one lake existed.

Cross-References

▶ Kailash

References

1. Allen C (1982) A mountain in Tibet: the search for Mount Kailas and the sources of the great rivers of Asia. André Deutsch, London
2. Buffetrille K (1998) Reflections on pilgrimages to sacred mountains, lakes and caves. In: McKay A (ed) Pilgrimage in Tibet. Curzon Press, Richmond Surrey, pp 18–34
3. Hamsa BS (n.d.) The holy mountain: being the story of a pilgrimage to Lake Manas and of initiation on Mount Kailash in Tibet. Faber and Faber, London.
4. Johnson R, Moran K (1989) Tibet's sacred mountain of Tibet: the extraordinary pilgrimage to Mount Kailas. Park Street Press, Rochester
5. Pranavananda S (1949) Kailās-Mānasarovar. S.P. League, Calcutta
6. Sarao KTS (2009) Pilgrimage to Kailash: the Indian route. Aryan Books International, Delhi

Mañjughoṣa

▶ Mañjuśrī

Manjushri

▶ Mañjuśrī

Mañjuśrī

James B. Apple
Department of Religious Studies, University of Calgary, Calgary, AB, Canada

Synonyms

Kumāra; Mañjughoṣa; Manjushri; Mañjuvajra; Vādirājā; Vādisiṃha; Vāgīśvara

Definition

Bodhisattva of wisdom in Mahāyāna forms of Buddhism.

Mañjuśrī, which means "Gentle Glory" or "Sweet Splendor," is the personification of discriminative awareness (*prajñā*) and one of the oldest and most important bodhisattvas within Mahāyāna forms of Buddhism. Mañjuśrī, as a distinguished bodhisattva, is associated with wisdom and eloquent speech, and his alternative names, such as Mañjughoṣa, Mañjusvara, Vādirājā, and Vāgīśvara, indicate this relation. He is also renowned through his epithet *kumārabhūta* ("being a youth" or "being a crown prince"), which signifies youth, royalty, and chastity.

Mañjuśrī's historical beginnings as a figure remain obscure and scholars have postulated his cultural formation as being influenced by Pañcaśikha ([1], pp. 66–70), the king of Gandharvas, as well as the eternally youthful Brahmā Sanatkumāra ([2], pp. 6–8). Mañjuśrī begins to appear in Mahāyāna Buddhist texts from the second century C.E., as his presence is attested in six of nine sūtra translations preserved in Chinese from the time of the Indo-Scythian translator Lokakṣema (ca. 168–189 C.E.) ([3], p. 163). Among these texts, the *Lokānuvartanā sūtra* distinguishes Mañjuśrī as a key interlocutor with the Buddha and the *Drumakinnararājaparipṛcchā sūtra* ranks him next to the Buddha as a spiritual friend (*kalyāṇamitra*). The *Ajātaśatru-kaukṛtya-vinodana sūtra* provides Mañjuśrī with his earliest starring role as spiritual mentor to the Magadhan King Ajātaśatru. In this sūtra, the Buddha explains how countless other Buddhas in the past were Mañjuśrī's disciples in the past, and that in the future he will instigate innumerable Buddhas to attain awakening ([4], p. 183). Although associated with wisdom, Mañjuśrī does not appear in the earliest Perfection of Wisdom literature. Early Mahāyāna sūtras among Lokakṣema's corpus portray Mañjuśrī as an interlocutor with Buddhas and bodhisattvas, as a promoter of Mahāyāna texts, as a spiritual friend (*kalyāṇamitra*), and as a converter of beings to the *bodhisattva* path leading to Buddhahood.

In subsequent centuries, Mañjuśrī appears as an extraordinary bodhisattva who teaches and guides beings in over 100 Mahāyāna sūtras. His appearance in numerous sūtras translated into Chinese by Dharmarakṣa (230–308 C.E.) testifies to his increasing prominence in the third and fourth centuries. The *Avaivartikacakra sūtra* mentions that Mañjuśrī is foremost among myriads of bodhisattvas. Mañjuśrī is enumerated first among bodhisattvas in the *Saddharmapuṇḍarīka sūtra* and is depicted as having served innumerable Buddhas in the past. The 12th chapter of the *Saddharmapuṇḍarīka sūtra* tells of Mañjuśrī's 8-year-old Nāga princess disciple and the countless beings of the chthonic Nāga kingdom who he led and inspired [5]. In the *Mañjuśrīvikrīḍita sūtra* he converts a prostitute to the Mahāyāna path. In the *Ratnakāraṇḍa sūtra* Mañjuśrī's exposition of the Buddhist dharma so overwhelms the followers of the Jain teacher Satyaka Nirgranthaputra that they prostrate before him and praise Śākyamuni Buddha [6]. In the *Gandavyūha sūtra*, Mañjuśrī is presented as one of the chief bodhisattva attendants of Vairocana Buddha and the first of 52 teachers that the spiritual aspirant Sudhana encounters in his journey to awakening. Mañjuśrī famously occupies a pivotal role in the *Vimalakīrti-nirdeśa-sūtra* where he is the only bodhisattva capable of entering into dialog with the lay bodhisattva Vimalakīrti and thereby propels the unfolding of the text's profound teachings on emptiness (*śūnyatā*) [7]. By the third to fourth century, Mañjuśrī is depicted as being equivalent to a Buddha and having his own buddha-field in the *Aṅgulimālīya* and *Mañjuś rībuddhakṣetraguṇavyūha sūtras* ([2], p. 32). In addition to these texts, a number of later Mahāyāna sūtras contain Mañjuśrī's name in their title, such as the *Mañjuśrīparipṛcchā, Mañjuśrīnirdeśa* and *Mañjuśrīvikurāṇaparivarta* ([8], p. 3). All of this literary evidence indicates that Mañjuśrī was seen as a primary spokesperson for Mahāyāna views of the path, whose rhetorical eloquence exemplified subtle teachings on non-duality and emptiness. He served as a symbol of authority and legitmacy for Mahāyāna teachings to supersede mainstream

Buddhist teachings and eventually came to embody the discriminative awareness of inconceivable Buddhahood.

Buddhist scholars are traditionally represented throughout the medieval period of Indian Buddhist scholasticism, from the fifth to the tenth century, as invoking Mañjuśrī for inspiration and empowerment to authenticate their technical digests. Madhyamaka scholars, such as Nāgārjuna, Āryadeva, and Buddhapālita, as well as Yogācāra masters like Vasubandhu often provide opening salutations in their texts that supplicate and praise Mañjuśrī. Later in Tibet, kings such as Khri-srong lde-btsan (ca. 740–798) and scholars such as Sa-skya Paṇḍita Kun-dga' rgyal-mtshan (1182–1251) and Tsong-kha-pa blo-bzang grags-pa (1357–1419) would be considered emanations and embodiments of Mañjuśrī [6].

The literary evidence for the veneration of Mañjuśrī after the fall of the Gupta empire in the sixth century increases with the advent of the Vajrayāna or tantric phase of Buddhism under the socioeconomic influences of the South Asian Pāla dynasty (750–1150 C.E.). During the Pāla dynastic period, devotional and ritual texts outlining the worship of Mañjuśrī began to appear in great numbers. Likewise, archeological evidence for the iconographical portrayal of Mañjuśrī, preserved in bronze and stone representations, suggests that he was worshipped in the great monastic complexes of Bengal and Bihar. Iconographical evidence for the representation of Mañjuśrī in India is not clearly attested before the sixth century. The increase of tantric Buddhist ritual works for the worship of Mañjuśrī is attested by the large numbers (41) of visualization instruction manuals, or *sādhana*s, devoted to him in the collection called the *Sādhana-mālā* ([2], p. 25). Texts such as the late seventh-century *Āryamañjuśrīnamāṣṭaśatakam* and *Mañjuśrīmūlakalpa* illustrate Mañjuśrī's importance as a figure of wisdom and devotion. From the eighth to the twelfth century in South Asia, the *Mañjuśrīnāmasaṃgīti* emerged as the central focus for the veneration of Mañjuśrī among Buddhist monks and laypeople. In this text, Mañjuśrī is portrayed as the wisdom or non-dual awakened awareness (*jñāna*) embodied by every Buddha. Mañjuśrī is therefore referred to in this text and its commentaries as Mañjuśrī the "Knowledge-Being" (Mañjuśrī-jñānasattva) [9]. The *Mañjuśrīnāmasaṃgīti* was the root text of over 22 commentaries and over 130 related works, surpassing any other Buddhist tantric text related to Mañjuśrī ([2], p. 33). Mañjuśrī is most often depicted as a youthful, 16-year-old crown prince sitting on a lotus throne. He holds the flaming sword of wisdom in his right hand which signifies the discriminative awareness that cuts through the ignorance which binds beings in the cycle of suffering and rebirth. A story from the *Susṭhitamati-devaputra-paripṛcchā* appears to be the earliest account for Mañjuśrī's iconographic affiliation with a sword representing wisdom ([2], p. 14). His left hand upholds a text from the perfection of wisdom (*prajñāpāramitā*), the source of his embodiment as discriminative awareness. Later Indian scholars such as Dharmamitra (ca. 800–850) and Atiśa, particularly in his autocommentary to the *Bodhipatha-pradīpa* (c. 1042 C.E.), consider Mañjuśrī as the progenitor of the lineage of profound view (*gambhīra*) that cognizes *śūnyatā*, having its foundation in the human realm beginning with Nāgārjuna ([10], p. 23). Atiśa will also explain in his *Ratnakaraṇ-ḍodghaṭa-madhyamakopadeśa* that Ārya Mañjuśrī is a primordial buddha (ādibuddha) and the Gnostic mind of all Buddhas [11]. The worship of Mañjuśrī as an object of meditation and devotion spread beyond South Asia into Central and East Asia. Mañjuśrī worship became an important Buddhist cult during the Tang dynasty in China, and, by the end of the seventh century, there was a well established cult of Mañjuśrī at Wutai Shan [12]. In Tibet, from the eighth century onward, Mañjuśrī became identified with political figures and religious scholars. In Nepal, Mañjuśrī accounts for Mañjuśrī's creation of the Kathmandu valley and subsequent establishment of Buddhism. In sum, Mañjuśrī is an important bodhisattva in all Mahāyāna Buddhist traditions and lineages and continues to be worshipped throughout the world.

Cross-References

- ► Bodhisattva
- ► Mahāyāna
- ► Prajñāpāramitā
- ► Wisdom (Buddhism)

References

1. Lalou M (1930) Iconographie des étoffes peintes-paṭa-dans le Mañjuśrīmūlakalpa. Libraire Orientaliste Paul Geuthner, Paris
2. Tribe A (1999) Mañjuśrī: origins, role and significance, parts I, II, III. West Buddh Rev 1(2)
3. Harrison PM (2000) Mañjuśrī and the cult of the celestial bodhisattvas. Chung-Hwa Buddh J 13.2:157–193
4. Harrison PM (2004) How the Buddha became a bodhisattva. In: Lopez DS (ed) Buddhist scriptures. Penguin, New York, pp 172–184
5. Hurvitz L (2009) Scripture of the lotus blossom of the fine dharma (the lotus Sūtra). Columbia University Press, New York
6. Harrington L (2002) A view of Mañjuśrī: wisdom and its crown prince in Pāla-period India. PhD thesis, Columbia University Press
7. Thurman RAF (1976) The holy teaching of Vimalakīrti: a Mahāyāna scripture. The Pennsylvania State University Press, University Park
8. Wayman A (1985) Chanting the names of Mañjuśrī: the Mañjuśrī-nāma-saṃgīti, Sanskrit and Tibetan texts. Shambala, Boston
9. Davidson RM (1981) The litany of names of Mañjuśrī. Text and translation of the Mañjuśrīnāmasaṃgīti. In: Strickmann (ed) Tantric and Taoist studies (R.A. Stein Festschrift). Melanges Chinois et Bouddhiques, vol XX–XXI. Institut Belge des Hautes Etudes Chinoises, Brussels, pp 1–69
10. Apple JB (2008) Stairway to Nirvāṇa: a study of the twenty Saṃghas based on the works of Tsong kha pa. State University of New York Press, Albany
11. Apple JB (2010) Atiśa's open basket of jewels: a middle way vision in late phase Indian Vajrayāna. Indian Int J Buddh Stud 11:117–198
12. Birnbaum R (1983) Studies on the mysteries of Mañjuśrī: a group of East Asian Maṇḍalas and their traditional symbolism. Society for the Study of Chinese Religions, Boulder

Mañjuvajra

► Mañjuśrī

Mantra

Kanoko Tanaka
Komazawa University, Tokyo, Japan

Synonyms

Dhāraṇī; Pranidhāna; Satya vacana; Vidya

Definition

Mantra is the Sanskrit term for "sacred utterance (having the power to realize whatever he may wish)." The word is derived from the root "man-" meaning "think" (also in *manas*, "mind") and "-tra" as a suffix meaning "vehicle," "tool," and "instrument." In Avestan, it is called "monθra."

Therefore, the most important must be the purpose of uttering the *mantra*, not "the vehicle of thought" itself. Man is responsible for what she/he should realize by using the tool of *mantra* because it is believed that her/his wish will be fulfilled without fail once it is uttered. Therefore, the word *mantra* can be translated as "satya vacana" (true words) which translators in China also described the same in Chinese characters (pronounced *Shingon* in Japanese, known as the proper name for the esoteric Shingon sect; *Shingon-shū* of Japanese Buddhism established by *Kūkai*, 774–835).

In Vedic tradition, *mantra* tends to be utilized for fulfilling many kinds of desires of this life, and *brāhmaṇas* (Vedic priests who exercise their privilege to make use of the verbal power from *Brahman* identified with *ātman*) try to control even the will of gods. In Buddhist context, on the other hand, the power of *mantra* is used *not only* for protecting himself against all kinds of *kleśa* (worldly and selfish desires arising from his own "mind," which are basically comprised of three kinds of poison: *lobha* (greed toward desirable objects), *dveśa* (anger against undesirable objects), and *moha* (foolish ignorance of the true state of causation)) and attaining *bodhi* (Buddhahood as the final goal of all the Buddhists; the perfect awakening about the phenomenal world where the living beings suffer from taking rebirth according to the law of *saṃsāra*) *but also* for the purpose of relieving and saving living beings (*sattva*) from their sufferings and guiding them toward the spiritual stage of Buddhahood.

In Mahāyāna Buddhism, the altruistic vows (*pranidhāna*) made by a *bodhisattva* (a person who seeks for *bodhi* or Buddhahood for the sake of saving all the living beings among sufferings of life in this phenomenal world) also can be regarded as a sort of *mantra* in the broadest meaning because he will never wish to attain Buddhahood without completing all of the items that were sworn in the beginning. The most famous example must be the 48 vows of the Bodhisattva Dharmākara who later became the Amitābha Buddha and established the Pure Land in the West. Chanting "Ṇamo Amitābha Buddha" is a kind of *Buddha anusmṛti* or *Buddha manasikāra* (imaging, memorizing, and keeping the Buddha firmly in one's mind), which may also look like a *mantra*, but in Pure Land Buddhism, this chanting would rather show one's sincere gratitude toward the Amitābha Buddha who let him take rebirth in the ideal land for training himself to attain Buddhahood, because it is regarded as very much difficult for a human being to reach the Pure Land only by his own efforts. Therefore, "Ṇamo Amitābha Buddha" does not mean "please save me," but may imply the Buddhist way of expressing his rapture: "Thank you so much for having saved me already in this life. You promised to guide me *there* in your Land." As it were, "Ṇamo..." in this case is the *mantra* already fulfilled which has the power to relieve one's mind from all the sufferings during his lifetime.

By virtue of the Buddha (or the bodhisattva) himself, the act of salvation can be fulfilled. This kind of thoughts naturally developed into the worship of the Buddhist *sūtra* itself whose virtues should be shared to everyone reciting and transcribing its text regarded as the collection of sacred *mantras*.

Among a number of Early Mahāyāna *sūtras*, the *Prajñāpāramitā-hṛdaya-sūtra* (or the *Saddharmapuṇḍarīka sūtra*) may be one of the most well-known examples of endowing the great benefits of chanting *mantras* in the form of a sūtra, by virtue of a Bodhisattva's *prajñā pāramitā* (the perfect attainment of Buddhist wisdom *seeing* everything *as it is*, according to the law of causation).

In this *sūtra*, the Avalokiteśvara Bodhisattva, who is believed to have already attained the Buddhahood long, long ago but dare not become a Buddha for the purpose of acting his salvation in this world, is preaching toward Śāriputra (who is known as one of the greatest disciples of the Buddha Śākyamuṇi versed in learning and practicing the *prajñā*) about the wisdom (*prajñā*) of *śū nyatā* (observing that everything in the phenomenal world is dependent upon causation, there can be no permanent ego as a substance). The nature of *mantra* in this sūtra can be shown in the last few lines:

1. tasmāj jñātavyam prajñāpāramitā *mahāmantromahāvidyāmantro'nuttaramantro 'samasamamantraḥ* sarvaduḥkhapraśamanaḥ satyam amithyatvāt.
2. prajñāpāramitāyām ukto *mantraḥ*. tad yathā: gate gate pāragate pārasaṃgate bodhi svāhā.

Trial translation in the context of this entry:

1. ...Therefore, it is necessary to recognize as follows: prajñāpāramitā is the great *mantra* (true word), and the *mantra* based upon the great vidyā (wisdom and knowledge to dispel the darkness of delusion), and the *mantra* that is supreme, and the incomparable *mantra*, and the (true) word of relieving all the sufferings, and (it is the word of) truth (having the power of fulfilling every wish) that will never commit any fault.
2. The magic words as the *mantra* (true word) identical to prajñāpāramitā are as follows: Going, going, going over the other shore (of *bodhi*, the perfect Awakening) and reaching *there* to perfection. May the Awakening be auspicious!

"The *mantra* based upon the great vidyā" is just like a medicine to remove three kinds of poison (*lobha*, *dveśa*, and *moha*) from one's mind when he utters it and fully understands its true meaning.

This poison is called "kleśa" as a whole, meaning "one's misunderstanding toward this phenomenal world." Unawakened people are in ignorance of their own selfishness to prevent them from realizing the true nature of this life. Once they have realized it completely, the stage of their minds (called "prajñāpāramitā") will guide them to the best way of living a full life without any sufferings.

"The *mantra* that is supreme" is believed as the best way of relieving human beings from the world of *saṃsāra* and encouraging them to make a good contribution toward the *same* world from another standpoint of the Awakened One, being so far from the realm of "kleśa" or delusion.

"The incomparable *mantra*" is promising a candidate for "prajñāpāramitā" to reach the final goal equal to the ideal stage of Buddhahood.

"The (true) word of relieving all the sufferings" actually relieves one's sufferings of the present time and will certainly remove all the karmic habits causing much more sufferings in the future.

Known from the Sanskrit text shown above, the word "vidyā" is synonymous with "mantra" as well as "dhāraṇī" (literally meaning "memory power") which are generally regarded as magic formulas whose pronunciations in Sanskrit and their meanings are difficult to be understood by common people and even specialists of the Buddhist community. This kind of difficulty is easily connected with the next stage of Buddhist thoughts that *mantra* must be a mysterious and symbolic instrument to condense the essence of the Buddha's Awakening (bodhi) when uttering one in the most effective way of performing an esoteric rituals.

Thus, the Esoteric, Vajrayāna, or Tantric forms of Buddhism, evolved from Mahāyāna, established the method of unifying oneself with the Mahāvairocana Buddha (the Great Sun Buddha or the cosmic Buddha) who is a personification of the Buddha Dharma itself (dharmakāya) having the workings of *body*, *speech*, and *mind* ("three secrets") whose real natures are too much immeasurable and mysterious to understand. (In the Exoteric or non-Esoteric Buddhism, the dharmakāya originally means "an accumulation of the Buddha dharma" which can never be personified.) The Esoteric Buddhists believe that one's own speech (*mantra*), sacred hand gestures (*mudrā*), and sacred envisioning (*maṇḍala*) would become similar to those of the Mahāvairocana Buddha whose "three secrets" should finally enter into the believer himself. This kind of mysterious possession is called "adhiṣṭhāna," meaning "corresponding with each other." Among the "three secrets," *mantra* is the most powerful factor of embodying the wisdom of the Buddha's Awakening to enlighten the darkness of *avidyā* (not seeing everything as it is, but seeing it from a selfish and biased viewpoint with a jaundiced eye).

Quite different from the ultimate purpose of Buddhist practice, *mantra* may be often regarded just as magic words fulfilling one's worldly wishes (good fortune and prosperity in lifetime) at the time of performing *homa* (esoteric rituals of burning small pieces of fragrant wood on the altar to invoke divine help). It is almost throwing back to the Vedic *homa* pursuing all kinds of desires of this world.

Probably, those who are familiar to Buddhist cultures have ever heard the sounds of the *mantra* symbolizing the sacred wisdom of the Avalokiteśvara Bodhisattva: "Om mani padme hum" (hail to the jewel cherished in the lotus flower), chanted by Tibetan Buddhists. They just try to purify their own minds with the repetition of this *mantra* without having any more desires causing spiritual troubles and pains. The magnificent figure of Mount Kailash (6,656 m) also reminds pilgrims of the true path of human life; every moment, their voices of *mantra* are blown away by the wind from the Himalayas.

Mantra is not a mere magic spell, but a guide to the goal of one's life. And she/he does not always find out "mantra" only from Pāli and Sanskrit texts of some Buddhist scriptures but also consciously and unconsciously *regard* everyday greetings and blessing toward all others *as* a sort of "mantra": "How are you ?," "Are you all right ?," "Have a good day!" and so on. When you go out, you may say to your mother: "See you!" She will say "See you later. Take care!" Only if you could go home safely, you would say to her: "Hello, Mom!

I'm home." And she may say "Welcome (home)!" or any other words of relief, especially when you have safely returned from a distant place. Without being supported by such a daily conversation between the two, human beings very easily lose their peaceful minds. By using merciful, humane, and good words to each other every day, they can feel happy, take care of others, and naturally protect themselves against evil thought, evil speech, and evil conduct. This is nothing but an effect of "mantra" on human minds just as discoursed in Buddhist scriptures. By nature, Buddhist "mantras" are not a specific thing to be uttered at the time of rituals, although quite a few people tend to regard them as the tools of fulfilling their personal and selfish desires.

Being versed in psychology, the Buddha Śākyamuṇi himself is actually chanting a sort of "mantra." For example, *Suttanipāta* 147 says: "No matter who they are; visible beings and invisible beings, those who are living far away and nearby, those who have already been born and wish to be born from now on, May all living beings (*sabbe satta*) be happy!" He uttered this in verse in order that people may easily memorize and try to chant it day and night. Whenever they recite "May all living beings be happy!" in their minds, it will purify their own minds, make them truly happy, and generate the power of making others happy. In this sense, the words of the Buddha in verse can be regarded as "mantras." He uttered his words only when they were helpful to listeners; otherwise, he used to keep silence. That is why the term "muṇi" of "Śākyamuṇi" means "the person who wisely keeps silence in readiness for answering any question from all others in suffering (the unenlightened; the unawakened)." In this way, it is important to see "mantra" practically and universally, without giving a stereotyped definition.

References

1. Mizuno K (1980) The Beginnings of Buddhism. Kosei Publishing, Tokyo
2. Alper HP (1989) Mantra. State University of New York Press, Albany
3. Hirakawa A (1990) A History of Indian Buddhism from Śākyamuṇi to early Mahāyāna. Motilal Banarsidass, Delhi
4. Abe R (1999) The Weaving of Mantra: Kūkai and the construction of esoteric Buddhist discourses. Colombia University Press, New York
5. Gyatso T, the 14th Dalai Lama, Yuko Miyasaka (tr) (2002) Essence of the Heart Sūtra. Shunjusha, Tokyo (Japanese version)
6. Miyamoto K (2004) What is the Prajñā-pāramitā-hṛdya-Sūtra ? From Buddha to Mahāyāna. Shunjusha, Tokyo (Japanese version)

Mantranaya

▸ Vajrayāna (Buddhism)

Mantrayāna

▸ Vajrayāna (Buddhism)

Mapham Yutso

▸ Mānasarovara (Buddhism)

Māra

Bhikkhu Anālayo
Center for Buddhist Studies, University of Hamburg, Balve, Germany

Definition

Māra, the "Evil One," is the god of temptation in Buddhism.

Māra in Buddhism

Māra, whose name literally stands for death or for what brings death, is conceived of in the Buddhist tradition as a celestial being, *deva*, dwelling in the highest heaven of the sensual realm. His function in Buddhist texts is to act as an antagonist to the Buddha and his disciples, advocating enjoyment of sensual pleasures instead of renunciation and striving for liberation. Hence, the task of defeating Māra and going beyond his reach of power is a recurrent theme in early Buddhist discourse.

In his role as a tempter, Māra approaches the Buddha-to-be in an attempt to impede the bodhisattva Gotama's progress to awakening by recommending the acquisition of merits and the performance of fire sacrifice instead of striving for liberation ([1], 426ff). Later tradition presents a more dramatic version of this encounter. At the head of a frightening army, Māra attacks the bodhisattva, who calls to witness the goddess earth for his right to remain on the seat where he is to win awakening. This scene has become a favorite theme in iconographic representations.

In the early Buddhist discourses, Māra has not yet assumed such a belligerent attitude. He is, however, thought to be able to exert power over ordinary people. Thus, he influences the inhabitants of a village to abuse Buddhist monks ([2], Vol. I, p. 334) or those of another village not to give alms to the Buddha ([3], Vol. I, p. 114). He also confuses the mind of the Buddha's attendant ([4], Vol. II, p. 104) and prevents a group of religious wanderers, *paribbājaka*, from becoming followers of the Buddha ([4], Vol. III, p. 57). He has similar power over some of the gods, as he gets a god to speak according to his design ([3], Vol. I, p. 67) and on another occasion brings the whole assembly of Brahmā under his influence ([2], Vol. I, p. 327).

Throughout two subdivisions of the canonical collections of discourses, the *Mārasaṃyutta* and the *Bhikkhunīsaṃyutta* ([3], Vol. I, p. 103ff), Māra is shown in his various attempts to disturb and unsettle the Buddha and his disciples. At times he does so in disguise, taking on a frightful appearance, such as a great elephant or a huge snake, or else he creates a loud noise nearby by shattering some rocks. Such attempts to frighten the Buddha meet with no success, as a fully awakened one is beyond fear.

Other episodes report Māra engaging in a discussion with the Buddha, trying to arouse doubts in the Buddha about his attainment of liberation, challenging him for taking a nap after a night spent in meditation practice, or trying to tempt him with the suggestion that he should exercise worldly dominion. Another trial of the Buddha involves Māra's daughters, who assume various beautiful shapes in order to lure the Buddha into sensual desire.

Some episodes report how Māra tries to create a disturbance when the Buddha is delivering teachings to his disciples. In several discourses, Māra accosts Buddhist nuns who are meditating in solitude, trying to confuse them with doctrinal arguments or tempting them to give up their life of renunciation and indulge in sensual pleasures instead. In all these instances, however, he is unable to achieve his purposes. Each time, he is recognized for whom he is and thereon has to vanish in discomfiture.

This appears to be an invariable pattern, where Māra has to disappear as soon as he is recognized by those he attempts to disturb. Especially remarkable are those episodes where Māra attempts to lure arahant nuns with sensuality and tries to frighten the Buddha or to challenge the Buddha's awakening. Such attempts are from the outset doomed to failure, as according to early Buddhist doctrine an arahant has forever eradicated sensual desire as well as fear, and a Buddha is endowed with the certain knowledge – reckoned an intrepidity, *vesārajja* – of being fully awakened.

Such episodes make it clear that Māra does not always function as the personification of inner defilements in the sense of acting out internal struggles. Rather, these tales interpret challenges the Buddha and the nuns had to face in contemporary society as the work of Māra. The didactic function of such tales would thus be to provide an example of how such challenges should be faced. In this way, any external threat or challenge can be interpreted as a challenge by Māra, and the proper attitude is to remain balanced by recognizing it as such.

Māra also takes part in the events that lead up to the Buddha's passing away. Soon after the

Buddha's awakening, Māra had already attempted to convince the Buddha that he should pass away right away. The report goes that the Buddha refused, indicating that he would first ensure that his teaching was well established, in the sense that his monastic and lay followers of both genders were capable of teaching in their turn ([4], Vol. II, p. 104). However, when Māra makes the same request again at a later time, once the Buddha has become old and his teaching has become well established, the Buddha acquiesces and relinquishes his life principle, even though he would have been able to continue living considerably longer.

In other words, challenges by Māra do not only require facing the personal difficulties a disciple may experience in his or her progress toward awakening, but according to this text it seems as if Māra can also be countered by ensuring the continuity of the Buddha's teaching. By continuing to spread the Buddha's message of liberation even after he has passed away – death being one of the shades of meaning inherent in the term *māra* – the disciples continue with the task of not allowing Māra to get the upper hand, thereby keeping open the path to the deathless, *amata*, the Buddha had discovered.

Mara in its early Buddhist use does not refer only to the individual Māra that lived at the time of the Buddha, but rather to a role that throughout the past – and presumably also in the future – is taken up by a succession of individuals. Thus, one of the chief disciples of the Buddha, an arahant by the name of Mahāmoggallāna, had in a past life been a Māra himself ([2], Vol. I, p. 333).

Besides this usage by way of a particular role taken up by a succession of individual gods, the term Māra can also acquire a general sense, where it stands for the six senses – the five physical senses together with the mind – and their corresponding objects ([3], Vol. IV, p. 38), or else refer to the five aggregates that according to early Buddhism are the main constituents of an individual ([3], Vol. III, p. 189), namely, bodily form, feeling, perception, volitional formations, and consciousness.

In later Theravāda tradition ([5], p. 211), references to Māra are analyzed into five different aspects, in the sense that the term Māra can stand representative for:

- Defilements, *kilesa*
- The five aggregates
- Karmic formations, *abhisaṅkhāra*
- The god Māra
- Death

Four of the manifestations of Māra in the above set – Māra as defilements, aggregates, god, and death – are also mentioned in several other texts, such as the *Lalitavistara* ([6], p. 224) or the *Mahāvastu* ([7], Vol. III, p. 281). According to the 26th tale in the *Divyāvadāna*, Māra is eventually tamed and converted by the arhat Upagupta.

References

1. Andersen D, Smith H (ed) (1913) The Sutta-nipāta. Pali Text Society, London (references are by stanza)
2. Trenckner V, Chalmers R (eds) (1888–1896) The Majjhima Nikāya, 3 vols. Pali Text Society, London
3. Feer L (ed) (1888–1898) The Saṃyutta Nikāya, 5 vols. Pali Text Society, Oxford
4. Carpenter JE, Rhys Davids TW (eds) (1890–1911) The Dīgha Nikāya, 3 vols. Pali Text Society, London
5. Rhys Davids CAF (ed) (1920) The Visuddhimagga of Buddhaghosa. Pali Text Society, London
6. Lefmann S (1902) Lalita Vistara, Leben und Lehre des Çâkya-Buddha. Verlag der Buchhandlung des Waisenhauses, Halle
7. Senart É (1897) Le Mahāvastu, Texte Sanscrit Publié pour la Première Fois et Accompagné d'Introductions et d'un Commentaire. Imprimerie Nationale, Paris
8. Bloss LW (1978) The taming of Māra: witnessing to the Buddha's virtues. Hist Relig 17:156–176
9. Boyd JW (1975) Satan and Māra, Christian and Buddhist symbols of evil. Brill, Leiden
10. Guruge AWP (1997) The Buddha's encounters with Māra the Tempter, their representation in literature and art. BPS, Kandy
11. Karetzky PE (1982) Māra Buddhist deity of death and desire. East West 32:147–155
12. Ling TO (1962) Buddhism and the mythology of evil. A study in Theravāda Buddhism. Allen & Unwin, London
13. Malandra GH (1981) Māra's army: text and image in early Indian art. East West 31:121–130
14. Strong J (1992) The legend and Cult of Upagupta, Sanskrit Buddhism in North India and Southeast Asia. Princeton University Press, Princeton
15. Wayman A (1959) Studies in Yama and Māra. Indo-Iranian J 3(2):112–131

Marriage (Buddhism)

Madhumita Chattopadhyay
Department of Philosophy, Jadavpur University, Kolkata, West Bengal, India

Synonyms

Conjugal bond; Wedding

Definition

Condition of man and woman legally (socially) united for the purpose of living together and procreating lawful offspring.

Buddhist Account of Marriage

Buddhism is well known to the whole world as a religion striving to attain a stage of enlightenment which can be attained only when one can overcome the fetters of worldly existence or *saṁsāra.* Naturally it seems that such a religion would give importance only on celibacy. But that is not the true essence of Lord Buddha's teachings. Lord Buddha did not want to confine his religion to only one group of people like the monks and nuns who form a very small class among the whole population, the majority being constituted by the householders (*upāsaka* and *upāsikā*) who lead a family life. He looked deeper into the nature of man and tried to find out what should be the religious duty for such family persons in the society. He recognized the sexual element in human nature as the most deep-rooted instinct which cannot be ignored or condemned and which is present among both men and women. So naturally the question arises as to how this aspect of human nature can be dealt with in a proper way for the benefit of the whole society. There are three possible alternatives – (1) People can live dependent on their sexuality in a righteous way which can generate worldly pleasure and happiness in a righteous manner; (2) they can live dependent on all the abuses and perversions of sexuality arising out of greed and hatred, as a result of which there will be pain and suffering; and (3) they may live neither dependent on it nor ignore this basic instinct. They can keep themselves free of dependence on such instinct. Obviously the second alternative cannot be accepted and the third alternative is also not tenable, since men and women are naturally drawn toward each other by the deep instinct to retain their generation and to have worldly pleasure. So the first alternative alone stands, and that leads to the question what is noble and religious in that life. Lord Buddha, as is usual in his teachings, did not prescribe anything regarding the age of marriage, nor marriage ritual, nor did he say anything about monogamy or polygamy. He only taught that each member of the society has a part to play and the nobility of the part played is measured by the player's avoiding harm to others, not stealing, not committing any adultery, and not lying and that these ethical qualities constitute the nobility. Men and women both are equally important for a society and so the relationship between them should be one which can grow freely without any sort of fear. It is a mutual understanding which creates security along with truthfulness. Marriage is a partnership relation where happiness and success are based on the mutual understanding of the values of both. Both should be absolutely faithful to each other. Lord Buddha advised that from the moment of marriage the husband should look at all women other than his wife as mother, sister, or daughter according to their age. Marriage is a partnership in which each of the partners performs his/her specific duties to fulfill the aims of the partnership. The husband hands over full authority to the wife in her own sphere of work. It is the duty of the husband to earn, to secure the family, and protect his livelihood and reputation. He should seek to please and beautify his wife, to give her open and affectionate signs of his care and admiration. On the other hand, for the woman there is also a down-to-earth basis to married life. The wife particularly has the duty of creating a pleasing and hospitable home. While the husband's duty is to earn for the family, the wife has a major part to play in organizing the economic welfare of the family. She has to be chaste and faithful to her husband and protect the sincerity and confidence of the marriage. Thus Buddha looked into marriage from a very pure and practical standpoint, namely, what can make a marriage work successfully, irrespective of age, class, race, etc. He specified five ways by which a husband is to behave with his wife – (1) by honor, (2) by respect, (3) by faithfulness, (4) by handing over authority to her, and (5) by giving her ornaments. On the other hand, the wife being so cared of by her husband has to show her compassion toward him in five ways – (1) by doing her work well, (2) by showing hospitality to her husband and his relatives, (3) by being faithful, (4) by saving what he earns, and (5) by exhibiting skill and diligence in all her duties. Sometimes Buddha has compared the wife with the sacrificial fire and holds that just as a priest treats the sacrificial fire with utmost care, similarly the husband should treat his wife with care. Her life and well-being are his only reasons for existence. By looking after her, by honoring her, by protecting her from all dangers, and esteeming her, he is able to perform his major role. For the wife also Buddha has recommended some roles. First, she must look after her husband with loving sympathy and in this respect her role will be like that of a mother. Secondly, she must show respect toward him and honor him quietly, in this respect her role is like that of a younger sister. Thirdly, she has the role of a best friend to her husband – she must be glad to see him and be with him at all moments of pleasure and sorrow. Finally she must be as obedient and loyal to her husband as a faithful servant is to his master. In short, both the husband and the wife should be compassionate to each other. As in other relationships, in the case of marital relationship also, the key concept is compassion according to Buddha. By this what is emphasized is that the married life is a unique balance of enlightened self-interest and unselfish devotion. Every action, physical, mental, or verbal, is performed with the aim of the welfare of the other. Successful marriage grows from mutual understanding of each other and from true loyalty. It involves a response to many needs and not mere physical satisfaction. It is a protection from loneliness and is a safeguard of one's family tradition. Through the performance of different roles, each partner gets strength from the other and provides support and appreciation to the other. So there should be no question of superiority and inferiority between the husband and the wife. Superiority is to be found in generosity, loyalty, and dedication to the noble path. In short, a marriage relationship is one of religious partnership, and according to Lord Buddha, the religiosity consists not in anything ritual, any custom, or in any rule; it is rather an opportunity bestowed on each other to develop virtue and understanding. When people of the society are able to lead their marital life in such a peaceful disciplined manner, the well-being of the society will automatically follow.

A cursory glance may be taken as to how the notion of marriage was actually practiced in the Buddhist society. In the Buddhist society, three types of marriage were prevalent – (1) marriage arranged by the guardians, (2) marriage selected by the girl herself, generally known as *svayamvara*, and (3) marriage proceeding entirely out of love without any ceremonies and without consulting relatives, which generally is held secretly and this marriage is called *gandharva-vivāha*. In the Indian tradition, though a maiden and a lover could unite themselves through love, the usual course was for the father to select the girl's husband and arrange for her marriage. But as in the Buddhist society women attained more independence than before, the responsibility of the father to select a suitable groom for his daughter became not so important, and the girls themselves came to have more voice in this regard. In the Jātaka there is the story of princess Kaṇhā who requested her mother to persuade her father to arrange an assembly of noble persons, from whom she could choose someone as her husband. Such a system is known as *svayaṁvara*; in such a system a number of eligible suitors desiring to marry the princess are assembled and the princess could select publicly among those suitors, her husband. After making the choice, the girl would utter the words *gaṇhāmi* meaning "I accept him as my husband." However, it would be wrong to think that this *svayaṁvara* marriage was the only type of marriage prevalent in Buddhist society. Following the general Indian tradition, the parents wishing a happy married life for their daughter usually thought it proper to exercise their parental control over the selection of the husband. In the commentary on the *Therīgāthā* the phrase "giving their daughter in marriage" occurs quite often. In arranging such marriage the parents tried their best to retain the status and reputation of the family. At the same time attempts were made to get their daughter married to person of equal status and of the same caste. In the same text there is the story of Isidāsī who was the daughter of a virtuous and rich merchant; she was given in marriage to one who was of the same status and who was the son of another merchant. Uttarā, the daughter of the chief Commander of the king of Saurāṣṭra, was married to a person of equal status. Such stories are very common in Buddhist literature. Even boys are spoken of as marrying with the consent of their parents and parents seem sometimes to have proposed a certain alliance for their sons. In Buddhist literature there are ample cases where the parents did not take the initiative to find a suitable husband for their daughter but the suitors approached them and proclaimed their desire to get married with their daughter. And sometimes, it so happened that the proud father turned down their request on the ground that he was not worthy of his daughter. But at the same time it is to be remembered that there was no such hard and fast rule in the Buddhist society that the equality of status is to be maintained at the time of marriage. In the texts like *Therīgāthā* or *Mahāvaṁsa* there are several instances as evidences. For instance, Pasendi, the king of Kośala, was married to Mallikā who was the daughter of a maid servant and the king accepted her as his wife and took her to his kingdom. King Aśoka also married a girl called Devī who was the daughter of a merchant and she became the mother of his children Sanghamitrā and Mahendra who were sent to Sri Lanka to preach Buddhism. Similarly, when Kisā Gotamī, the daughter of a very poor family, was married to the son of a rich merchant, the equality of status was not maintained. In the *Divyāvadāna* the story of Śārdulakarṇa, the son of a lower caste, a Caṇḍāla, being married to the daughter of a Brāhmaṇa is told. But stories are also found in the same texts where the parents had taken precautionary measures to protect the reputation of the family and the daughters were kept in close doors in their parent's house out of the fear that their daughter might elope with some undesirable persons. And, in spite of all protections often the basic instinct of the daughter led her to find out ways to move out with her beloved and get married. In the Jātakas there is the story of a girl who was nurtured in a very conservative manner and kept completely ignorant of worldly matters. One day when she looked down from an upper storey upon the street, she saw a hunchback. From her nurse she heard that in the cow tribe a hunch denotes royalty; by analogy she regarded this man to be of royal status and fell in love with him. Then she disguised herself and collected the best of her belongings and set off with him. Her madness of youth and lust for a man led her to ignore the dictates of her parents and not to waste any time to obtain their sanction.

Apart from these three types of marriage, sometimes a man would steal a girl by force or by alluring her through some attractive gifts and marry her. In the Aśoka Jātaka there is the story that the king of Kośala defeated the king of Benares in a battle and stole his queen; later on he married her and made her the chief queen. In the Takka Jātaka, another story of marrying a girl after stealing by force is mentioned. The chief of a gang of robbers once stole a village girl and gave her the status of his wife.

No age was actually prescribed as the appropriate age of marriage for a girl. But probably girls got married at the age between 16 and 20. Visākhā, for example, was married when she was 16 years old. In the commentaries on the *Dhammapada* and the *Therīgāthā* stories of Bhaddā Kuṇḍalakesā, Selā, Ālavikan, and Sumedhā are told. These girls were unmarried even at the age of 16. These stories indicate that the girls usually got married at an age higher than that of child marriage. Another evidence against child marriage may be cited from the story of Ghoṣaka. Ghoṣaka, a rich merchant, when asked by a king to get his daughter Sāmāvatī married to him, turned down the request of the king saying that the householders do not give marriage of young daughters out of the fear that they might be maltreated and ill-used. But it cannot be conclusively said that child marriage was totally absent in the Buddhist society. For in the *Saṁyutta Nikāya*, it has been told that one of the woes that a woman did suffer as distinguished from a man is that she has to go to her husband's family leaving behind her parents and other relatives at a "tender" age. Though what is meant by "tender age" has not been made very clear, but commentary holds that it indicates an age between 12 and 20. One illuminating reference in support of marriage below the age of 12 is recorded in the *Bhikkhuṇi-vibhanga*, where a girl of less than 12 was ordained by the alms-women. She was said to be a bride and stayed with her husband. That the custom of child marriage was not totally unknown is evident from a passage of the *Milindapañhā* where two persons were arguing with each other as to who can be a proper husband. In course of such argument, one man mentioned "the little girl, the mere child," whom his rival chose as his wife, cannot be considered as the same person whom he chose when she was grown up. On the basis of all this, what can be said is that though in the early days of Buddhism girls were not given in marriage at a very early age below 10, the custom of child marriage became popular in the later days of Buddhism.

The arrangement of a marriage bond was a strictly family affair. No astrologer was called in to approve the union. An auspicious day was selected for the celebration. For marriage the general convention was that the groom had to go to the house of the bride. There the wedding ceremony was performed without the intervention of any priest and was a purely civil or domestic affair. There were no rites, no rituals, no oath-taking, no oblation, and no sort of superstition. There were only festivities and feasting at the house of the bride, and such festivals sometimes continued for more than 1 or 2 days according to the means of her parents. Sometimes gifts were offered to the poor people. When the festivities were over, the newly married girl would leave for her in-law's house with her husband, in accordance with the joint family set up, customary in those days.

After marriage when the bride starts her journey to her in-law's house, she is given the following advices by her parents:

1. Do not bring outside the fire which lies within the house. The significance is that the girl should not disclose the secret discussions made within the family by her in-laws to anyone outside the family.
2. Do not bring inside the house any fire from outside. This means that what is being discussed by the servants, should not be disclosed to any family members for that may create disputes.
3. If you desire to lend money to anyone, give loans to those who can repay.
4. Never lend money to anyone who does not repay.
5. Give donations to persons irrespective of whether they can repay or not. That is, if any poor relative or friend needs some help at the moment of distress, it is a duty to help them, without taking into consideration whether they will be able to repay it in future or not.
6. Sit happily. That is, if any elderly relative enters the room, the bride should stand up and will remain so till they are seated.
7. Eat happily. That is, she should take her meal only after serving her respected in-laws and her husband and being sure that they are satisfied.
8. Sleep happily. The bride should perform her duties toward her in-laws, specially father-in-law and mother-in-law, and then should go to sleep.
9. Take care of the fire. That is, she should take care of her father-in-law and mother-in-law properly just as one does while handling fire.
10. Have devotion for the family deities. If any monk comes to the house as a guest, he must be treated with due respect. She must satisfy him with proper food and drink.

These advices indicate that the girl is given instruction by her parents to adjust herself well with all the relatives in the in-law's house. She must behave as an indispensable member of the family caring always for everyone and showing regards to others which they deserve and try her best to retain the status and tradition of the family. By showing her modesty and respect to her parents-in-law and by the performance of her duties to them, she would become a model to other women.

Generally, the practice of taking dowry at the time of marriage was not popular in the Buddhist society, but it was expected that the father would present their daughter jewelry, clothes, and sometimes money. In the case of very rich persons, some more items could be added. In the commentary on the *Dhammapada* it is said that at the time of marriage of Visākhā her father presented her with 500 pieces of gold, silver, and copper dishes; a huge quantity of husked rice; plowshares and other implements; 1,500 female slaves; a great herd of cattle; and a magnificent creeper. Anāthapiṇḍaka also gave splendid presents to his daughter at the time of marriage and sent her in great state to her in-law's house. When Mahākośala, who was the father of Pasendi, the king of Kośala, arranged the marriage of his daughter Kosala-devī with king Bimbisāra, he gave her a village in Kāsī as bath-money. Similarly, Pasendi also at the time of the marriage of his daughter Bajirā with Ajātasatru had presented another village in Kāśī as gift. There was also a custom to receive gifts from the guests during marriage. However, that the convention of paying bride-money was not totally absent in the Buddhist society can be inferred from a sentence found in the *Milindapañhā*. The sentence says "The little girl, the mere child, whom you chose in marriage and paid a price for, is one; the girl grown up to full age, whom I chose in marriage and paid a price for is another." The sentence indicates that the custom of paying bride-price was not unpopular in later days of Buddhism.

However, it was not essential for women to get married to save her self-respect or the reputation of the family. It was not considered a disgrace to a woman to remain unmarried as it was during the Smṛti period. In the early days of Buddhism such unmarried girls would go unabused, contented, and had a respectable position at their home spending their time caring for their parents, younger brothers, and sisters. Lots of unmarried women joined the Order of Bhikkhuṇis. In spite of the respect and reputation they received from their family members, they could not suppress their inner feeling of disappointment of not being able to find a husband and they became jealous of other women who were able to fulfill the traditional role of a wife and a mother. This can be inferred from the story of Sumanā, the youngest daughter of Anāthapiṇḍaka, in the commentary on the *Dhammapada*. There it is stated that she was very much disappointed at her failure to get a husband for her. The status of the unmarried woman also changed in the later days of Buddhism. For example, during the time when *Milindapañhā* was composed, a woman without a husband was considered to be among the ten sorts of individuals who are despised, undesirable, and thought shameful and were looked down upon. Her status was the same as a weak creature, as one who has no character or reputation. This indicates that with the passing of time, the upliftment of status which Buddha wanted to bring for the women, gradually decreased.

In the Buddhist time the general practice of marriage was monogamous. But there was no hard and fast rule in this regard and the practice of polygamy was not condemned. In fact, for the people of the upper class like the kings or the nobles and the rich persons, it was a customary right to have more than one wife and there was no limit to the number of wives that a man might have. But the evidences show that in most cases, except few exceptional ones, most ordinary persons used to have only one wife. The custom of having more than one wife prevailed mostly among the wealthy class, among the kings, the nobles and the merchants. Thus Pasendi had five wives, and Bimbisāra has been reported in the *Mahāvagga* to have 500 wives. The commentary on the *Dhammapada* mentions three brothers who were all prosperous merchants to have respectively two, four, and eight wives. Evidence also is found in the Buddhist literature of a wealthy person, a millionaire, having a single wife. The usual reason for taking a second wife was the barrenness of the first wife. The public opinion prevalent in the Buddhist time as in the Vedic days was that a family cannot sustain without a child. So when a wife was found to be incapable of giving birth to a child, the husband decided to remarry. But there were other reasons also; for example, if the chastity of the wife was in doubt, the husband did remarry. Polyandry, on the other hand, was in all probability absent in the society. Even if it existed, it was a rather rare event. There is the mention of only a single case in the *Jātaka*, namely, in the Kuṇāla Jātaka where the princess Kāṇhā decided to have five husbands at the same time.

The custom of divorce was prevalent at that time also, though it was not legalized. Example may be cited of Isidāsī, who had to return twice to her parental house by being rejected and disliked by her two husbands. She married twice, but on each occasion she was unable to satisfy her husband and so each of them had expelled her out of the house. So remarrying a second person after divorcing the first husband is a modern outlook and this is not found mentioned in any other case like this. In the Ucchanga Jātaka there is the story of a woman whose husband, son, and brother were put to prison. She requested the king several times for their release. Her requests were turned down; then she began to cry. Moved by her tears the king decided to release only one of them and asked her opinion regarding whom she wants to have free. Then the lady asked for the release of her brother on the ground that since she is alive, it is possible for her to get another husband and another son, but as her parents are dead it will not be possible to get another brother. From her argument it can be inferred that in those days marrying a person even when her husband was alive, was not blameworthy.

Even remarriage of widows was not unpopular in the Buddhist society. In the text *Mahāvaṁsa*, the episode is stated of king Khallaṭāṇga who was defeated and killed by his army chief. In revenge, the youngest brother of the king killed the army chief and accepted the wife of the king Khallaṭāṇga as his wife.

Though in the teachings of Lord Buddha, an ideal position was given to the wife in the married life, equal to the position of the husband, like all ideals it yielded infinite variations. In a practical situation, the wife was often considered as the "*pāda-paricārikā*," as serving on one's feet, a symbol of the most utter humility. This makes it clear that her prestige was kept in check. She was still considered to be inferior and a possession of the husband and was never considered fit for getting independence. If one looks at the list of ten wives mentioned in the Vinaya, one will find that in the Buddhist society, some wives were regarded as slaves while there were those to be enjoyed or made use of occasionally (*bhoga-vāsinī*). Since the husband considered the wives to be his possession, he could give her to others, if he so desired. For example, in the *Avadānakalpalatā*, Kṣemendra tells us the story of king Śrīsena, whose wife was Jayaprabhā. He offered Jayaprabhā as a gift to his *guru*. Similar is the story of king Maṇicud who donated his wife, queen Padmāvatī, for the service of the old sage Marīci.

All these indicate that though Lord Buddha considered marriage to be a very noble and virtuous relationship based on mutual love and respect for each other, this ideal situation got changed as days rolled on. In later days women were not given that respectable position, but had to submit to male domination.

Cross-References

- ▶ Festivals (Buddhism)
- ▶ Gender (Buddhism)
- ▶ Homosexuality (Buddhism)
- ▶ Sociology (Buddhism)
- ▶ Thera- and Therīgāthā
- ▶ Upāsaka
- ▶ Women (Buddhism)

References

1. Cowell EB (ed) (1997) The Jātakas or stories of the Buddha's former birth. Low Price Publications, Delhi, Reprint
2. Geiger W (1980) The Mahāvaṃsa or the Great Chronicle of Ceylon. Pali Text Society, London

3. Horner IB (1990) Women under primitive Buddhism. Motilal Banarsidass, Delhi, Indian Reprint
4. Janes K (1989) The social face of Buddhism. Wisdom, London
5. Musaeus-Higgins M (2005) Jātakamālā or a Garland of birth stories. Low Price Publications, Delhi, Indian Reprint
6. Max Műller F (trans) (1998) The Dhammapada, sacred books of the east series. Motilal Banarsidass, Delhi, Indian Reprint
7. Paul DY (1979) Women in Buddhism: images of the feminine in Mahāyāna tradition. Asian Humanities Press, California
8. Rhys Davids CAF (trans) (2005) The book of the kindred sayings (Saṁyutta Nikāya), Parts 1–5, Motilal Banarsidass, Delhi, Indian Reprint
9. Rhys Davids CAF, Norman KR (1989) Poems of Early Buddhist Nuns (Therīgāthā). Pali Text Society, London
10. Rhys Davids TW (trans) (1995) The questions of King Milinda, sacred books of the east series, vol 36, Pts I & II. Motilal Banarsidass, Delhi, Indian Reprint
11. Strong JS (2008) The legend of King Aśoka: a study and translation of the Aśokāvadāna, Motilal Banarsidass, Delhi
12. Vaidya PL (ed) (1959) Divyāvadāna. Mithila Institute of Post-Graduate Studies and Research in Sanskrit Learning, Darbhanga
13. Vaidya PL (ed) (1989) Avadāna-kalpalatā of Kṣemendra, vol 1. Mithila Institute of Post-Graduate Studies and Research in Sanskrit Learning, Darbhanga
14. Willis J (ed) (1989) Feminine ground: essays on women and Tibet. Snow Lion Publications, Ithaca

Materialism (Buddhism)

Ana Bajželj
Department of Philosophy, Faculty of Arts, University of Ljubljana, Ljubljana, Slovenia
Polonsky Academy, The Van Leer Jerusalem Institute, Jerusalem, Israel

Synonyms

Annihilationism; Cārvāka; Lokāyata; Uccheda-vāda

Definition

Materialism was one of the many Indian traditions, in the context of which Buddhism emerged and the position of which it refuted. The Buddha regarded his doctrine to be the middle way between the extremes of eternalism and annihilationism. The first extreme refers to the Upaniṣadic view that the self survives the death of the body, whereas the second extreme, which is linked to annihilationism, refers to the view that the self is destroyed along with the destruction of the body. The most prominent group of annihilationists were probably the materialists who equated the self with the gross material body. This tradition rejected the religious paradigm of its contemporaries and thus refuted the ideas of rebirth, karma, and nirvāṇa.

Buddhism and Materialism

The Buddha described his doctrine as the middle way (Skt. madhyamā pratipad) between extremes. Practically, this was considered to be the middle path between indulging in sensual pleasures on the one hand and observing strict austerities on the other. When applied to the view of reality, the middle way implied surpassing two extreme positions, namely, eternalism (Skt. śāśvata-vāda) on the one hand and annihilationism (Skt. uccheda-vāda) on the other. Eternalism accepted the existence of the immutable self (Skt. ātman) that continues to be even after the death of the body. This view applies to the Vedic tradition and its philosophical streams. In contrast to this, the latter position of annihilationism declared the self to perish with the physical death. The range of annihilationist views recorded in the Buddhist sources is quite vast and varies from the acceptance of the changeless self which does not survive the death of the body to the refutation of the very notion of the self. The diverse positions of annihilationism are put forward in the Brahmajāla-sutta that outlines seven different annihilationist views on the self, which despite quite divergent takes on the nature of the self all claim it to be destroyed with the death of the body. These seven understand the self to be (1) composed of gross matter, (2–3) composed of subtle matter, and (4–7) immaterial and formless. The materialists were a group of individuals that adhered to the first view of the self being made of gross matter. Accordingly, they maintained that there is nothing that remains after the death of the body and the dispersion of the material elements. The materialist view therefore rejected the idea of rebirth and with it the notion of karmic retribution as well as the possibility of nirvāṇa.

Amongst the six different teachers, whose doctrines the Buddha described in the Sāmaññaphala-sutta as unsatisfactory, Ajita Kesakambali was the most prominent representative of the materialist position. He taught that a person consists of four great elements, namely, earth, water, fire, and air. According to his teaching, when a person dies, earthly components return to earth, fluid to water, heat to fire, and wind to air, while the sense faculties pass into space. Consequently, there is no permanent ātman that would continue to exist in afterlife. For Ajita Kesakambali, the notion of acts having good and bad consequences is equally flawed, for everyone, the fool and the wise, no matter what the nature of one's past actions might be, perishes upon physical death. Therefore, according to Sāmaññaphala-sutta Ajita Kesakambali considered the idea of repayment in another life to be an empty lie. It must be pointed out, however, that information on Ajita Kesakambali is only available through secondary references of his opponents; the accounts of his position are thus inevitably biased.

The teachings of Ajita Kesakambali are often mentioned in relation to the school of thought that came to be known as Lokāyata. In his study on ancient Indian materialism Debiprasad Chattopadhyaya proposes that the traditions of Tantra, Sāṃkhya, and Lokāyata were all varieties of materialism [1]. He relates the Tantric tradition to the early agricultural society, in which the parallel between the human body and the cosmos was recognized. In this context, the intercourse between a man and a woman, representing life, was deemed to contribute to the fertility of the land.

Despite Sāṃkhya being later categorized as one of the Brahmanical schools of thought (Skt. darśana), Chattopadhyaya argues that its early tradition was a form of materialism. According to his theory, Sāṃkhya held prakṛti or matter to be the primary principle that evolved from an undifferentiated to a manifested state. Chattopadhyaya considers the multiplicity of consciousness principles or puruṣas to have been fairly unimportant in the early development of this tradition and suggests that they were introduced as an additional element to the original 24-element materialist scheme of reality.

Lokāyata was an Indian tradition that was most unambiguously materialist in nature. Its origin is occasionally attributed to the legendary Bṛhaspati whose sūtras are referred to in secondary sources but have not been preserved. The name of the school derives from the word "loka," meaning "the world" and referring to the doctrine that only the empirical world exists. The adherents of this tradition proposed a specific epistemological position in relation to their ontology, accepting perception (Skt. pratyakṣa) as the sole valid means of knowledge (Skt. pramāṇa). Refuting inference (Skt. anumāna), analogy (Skt. upamāna), and verbal testimony (Skt. śabda) as unreliable, they concluded that it is impossible to prove the existence of the soul, life after death, and karmic retribution. Therefore, according to Lokāyata, all an individual is, is a composition of the four elements (earth, water, fire, and air). Even one's consciousness is a product of this temporary makeup and thus has a material origin. Another name that has been attributed to this materialist tradition is Cārvāka, a term possibly stemming from a name of a sage or the verbal root √carv-, to eat or chew. The latter explanation is related to the frequent accounts of materialists as uninhibited hedonists. However, since these sorts of descriptions are found in secondary sources that are aimed at refuting the opponents' viewpoint, they may be understood as attempts to degrade a position that may well have been very popular with the people. None of the original texts of the Lokāyata tradition have been preserved, with the possible exception of Jayarāśi Bhaṭṭa's Tattvopaplavasiṃha.

Buddhism considers the materialist position to be a wrong view, that is, one of the ten unwholesome courses of action, which has a greater potential than anything else to lead to a particularly unfortunate birth, that is, as an animal or a hell-being. In other words, as a wrong view, the materialist position is bound to lead away from liberation and result in suffering. The Buddha thus rejected this extreme position and instead proposed that despite the nonexistence of ātman, the recurrent afterlives continue to be produced through ignorance, craving, and karmic fruition. He explained this continuity by introducing a temporal model of empirical conditionality which systematically points out the factors that lead to the arising of unsatisfactoriness and further rebirths. This scheme is referred to as pratītya-samutpāda or the scheme of dependent origination. The Buddhist doctrine of karmically generated selfless continuation in the cycle of rebirths that is aimed at liberation from it therefore rejects the materialist position of no afterlife, no karmic retribution, and no nirvāṇa.

Cross-References

- ▶ Ajita Keśakambali
- ▶ Anattā (Buddhism)
- ▶ Atheism (Buddhism)
- ▶ Ātman
- ▶ Causality (Buddhism)
- ▶ Death (Buddhism)
- ▶ Eschatology (Buddhism)
- ▶ Kamma
- ▶ Karma
- ▶ Khandha
- ▶ Liberation (Buddhism)
- ▶ Majjhimā Paṭipadā
- ▶ Middle Way (Buddhism)
- ▶ Paṭicca Samuppāda
- ▶ Person (Buddhism)
- ▶ Philosophy (Buddhism)
- ▶ Psychology (Buddhism)
- ▶ Reality (Buddhism)
- ▶ Rebirth (Buddhism)
- ▶ Relativity (Buddhism)
- ▶ Science (Buddhism)
- ▶ Soul

References

1. Chattopadhyaya D (1985) Lokāyata: a study in ancient materialism. People's Publishing House, New Delhi
2. Daksinaranjan S (1957) A short history of Indian materialism. The Book Company, Calcutta
3. Dasgupta S (1955) A history of Indian philosophy, vol V. Cambridge University Press, Cambridge
4. Mittal KK (1974) Materialism in Indian thought. Munihiram Manoharlal, New Delhi

Mathurā

Anand Singh
School of Buddhist Studies and Civilization, Gautam Buddha University, Greater Noida, UP, India
Institute of Management Sciences, University of Lucknow, Lucknow, UP, India

Synonyms

Gundāvana; *Klisoboras*; Madhupurī; Madhurā; Śūraśena; Suryapura; Uttara Madhurā; *Vraja* Veranjā

Definition

Mathurā, a city of great antiquity, is situated in the upper Gangā Valley. Buddhist literature praised it as a famous center of trade and art. The *Mahābhārata* speaks of this place as birthplace of Lord Krishna. In early period, Mathurā was known for Buddhism and their school of art [22].

Introduction

Mathurā lies in the upper Gangā Valley as an integral part of the Yamunā basin between the latitude 27°14′N to 27°58′N and longitude 77°17′E to 78°12′E. Some regions of Mathurā, which extend in the arid zone, are less fertile than the doab of the middle Gangā Valley [13]. The *Harivaṃsa Purāna* says it is a prosperous country with many pasture lands which nurtured people [12]. Fa-hien mentions the kingdom of *Ma-teou-lo* (Mathurā) is situated on the banks of the river *Po-na* (Yamunā). He says that

Mathurā has 20 *saṃghārāmas* with 3,000 monks residing in it and Buddhism is in prosperous state in this country. He further says that people of this city killed no living creature. They do not drink intoxicating liquor, and with the exception of *Cāṇḍalas*, they eat neither garlic nor onions [1]. Hiuen-tsang says it is a great country with Mathurā as a capital extending 833 miles (5,000 *li*) in circuit. Cunningham says that it might include the modern districts of Mathurā, Bharatpur, Dholpur, Alvar, and a part of Gwalior [7].

Origin of Names

In the literary texts, Mathurā is known as Madhurā, Suryapura, Madhupurī, Śūraśena, and *Vraja*. Śūraśena was its most popular name and was included in the 16 *mahājanpadas* with Mathurā as capital [14]. Mathurā is also known as Uttara Madhurā, probably to distinguish it from a city of the same name in the South India [9]. The *Ghata Jātaka* speaks of Maha Sāgara as the king of Uttara Madhurā [8]. Pliny speaks of it as Methoras [16]. In the Jaina literature, Mathurā is known as Saurapura or Suryapura [10]. The *Rāmāyana* calls it Madhupurī, the abode of Madhu and the father of Lavanya, and it is also known as *Vraja* and *Gokula* [14].

History of Mathurā

Since 1000 B.C.E. onward, the Aryan bands started penetrating the Gangā Valley and the process of cultural assimilation and colonization followed. There is clear evidence of eastward migration of the Aryans from Sarasvatī valley to establish settlements, clear forests, and to cultivate the freshly cleared land. The *Śatpatha Brāhmana* mentions Videgha Mādhava with his priest Rāhugana carried sacred fire to eastward after leaving Sarasvatī valley and moving down to Gangā-Yamunā doab until he reached Sadānirā [24]. During this period, urbanization started here and Śūraśena *mahājanpada* with Mathurā as its capital came into existence. The Yadus were ruling in the *Vraja* region and were divided into several clans like Vitihotras and Satvatas. The Satvatas were further divided into Daivavridha, Andhaka, Mahābhoja, and Vriśnis [14]. The *Śatpatha Brāhmana* describes the defeat of the Satvatas by the Bhāratas who took away their sacred fire of Aśvamedha sacrifice [24]. The *Arthasaśtra* says Vriśnis as the *saṃgha* or a republic [21]. Megasthenes mentions Mathurā as a stronghold of Heraklese (Vāsudeva) worshipping [16]. The descendant of the Andhakas was Kaṃsa who was killed by his maternal nephew Krishna. When Jarāsandha, the king of Magadha came to know of it, he was annoyed with Krishna. Due to this fear, the Vriśnis left Mathurā and migrated to Dwarakā [11]. Arrian mentions two great cities *Metoras* and *Klisoboras* and the navigable river *Jobares* flowed their territories [4]. Pliny mentions river Yamunā as *Jomaes* which passed between the towns of *Methora* and *Klisobora* [16]. The city of *Klisobora* has been identified as Vrindāvana, the grove of *kadamba* trees (basil forests) famous for the Krishna's dalliance with the *gopis* (milkmaids) [17].

Śūraśena is one of the *aryajanpada* lying south of the Kurus and to the east of the Matsyas [10]. In the Śaka and Kushāna age, it was in a flourishing stage. From Kankalī Tīlā of Mathurā, the inscriptions of Indo-Scythian kings Kaṇiṣka, Vasiṣka, Huviṣka, and Vāsudeva have been discovered. The coins of Appolodates, Menander, are also found. An elephant capital of the time of Huviṣka with several sculptured pillars of Buddhist railings of large size and few portions of their rails are also found [6]. The lion capital inscription of the Śaka ruler Rajvula is found from Mathurā written in the *kharosthi* script that mentions a Buddhist vihāra built by his chief queen [23]. The excavation of Katrā shows a broken Buddhist railing pillar, a statue of Mahāmāyā standing under *sāla* tree, and an inscription of the Gupta period giving the genealogical records from Śri Gupta to Samudragupta. Another inscription found in the excavation on the base of a statue of Śakyabikkhu mentions the Yaśa vihāra of Mathurā [6].

Mathurā was also a trade center in the early age. The mercantile communities like *vanika*, *sresthi*, *sārthavāha*, *gandhikas*, *suvarnakāras*, *lohakāras*, *kumbhakāras*, *manikāras*, and *kalvalas* are mentioned in the contemporary literature. Kautilya speaks of thriving cotton industry of Mathura [21]. The cotton of Mathurā was known as *sātaka*. The Buddhist literature gives a good account of the route from Mathurā to Rājagaha. From Mathurā, this route proceeded to Veranjā, Soreyya, Sankissa, Kanyakubja, and finally reached Prayāga [15]. Pliny also mentions route connecting Mathurā. A highway from Caspian sea to mouth of the Ganges via Alexandria of the Aria (Heart), Prophthasia of Drangae (Seistan), the city of Arachosei (Alexandria in Kandhar), Hortospana (Kabul), Paucolatis (Puskalavati), Takṣasilā, Iomana (Mathura), Prayāga, and Palibrotha has been described by him [16]. The epigraphic records of the age of Śakas, Kushanas, Gupta, and post Gupta period gave vivid accounts of trading activities of Mathurā and its people. Since early medieval age, its prosperity started declining due to emergence of feudalism.

Depiction of Mathurā in Buddhist Literature

The expansion of Buddhism in Mathurā started during the age of the Buddha. *The Aṅguttara Nikāya* says that once the Buddha was journeying from Mathurā to Veranjā and took shelter under the tree in Mathurā to preach a congregation of the lay followers [18], the Buddha saw Mathurā with a distinct disfavor. It is said when the Buddha reached Mathurā, the presiding mother Goddess of the city, taking his arrival as an impediment in her worship, stood naked before him. The Buddha admonished her by saying that it did not suit a virtuous woman to do so [3]. The Buddha has mentioned the five demerits of Mathurā, namely, the banks of rivers being flooded, the countryside full of thorns and pegs, sandy and rocky land, people eating in the last quarter of the night, and the presence of many women [4]. In Mathurā, the Buddha also subdued the Yakṣa Gardabha who devoured children and the Yakṣis Alika, Benda, Maghā, and Tiṃisika [4]. Mahākaccāna was instrumental in spreading of Buddhism in Mathurā. Avantiputta, the king of Mathurā, visited him and enquired about the superiority of the brahmanas over other varnas. The *Madhura Sutta* gives description of this. Mahākaccāna confers that wealth can be gained by all, not only the brahmanas. A brahmana can experience the result of his actions both good and bad in this world and in the next, just as the members of the other *varnas*. A brahmana can seek more homage on account of his *varna* [19]. The Sarvāstivādin and Mahāsaṃghika were two dominant sects of Buddhism in Mathurā in the Śaka and Kuṣāna age. Fahien mentions prosperity of Buddhist establishments [1]. Hiuen-tsang speaks about the *saṃghārāmas* and monks residing in it and says that Buddhism had to compete with other sects like Vaiśnavism, and subsequently, Buddhism declined in Mathurā region [14].

Mathurā School of Art

In the beginning of the Christian era, Mathurā school of art became active and produced remarkable statues of the Buddha, the Jaina *tirthānkaras*, and Hindu Gods and Goddesses which earned for her the enviable position in the art world of contemporary India, but the Buddha images of Mathurā are exclusive. The unmistakable identity of all Mathurā Buddhist sculptures is the spotted red sandstone from Sikrī [14]. During archaeological explorations, a sizable number of statues, *āyagpattas*, stone railings, and stūpas are discovered showing the excellence of the Mathurā art. Some of the important archaeological sites are [6]:

1. The ruins of Katrā at the southern side of the district jail
2. Kankalī Tīlā about half a mile south from Katrā
3. Chaubarā mound one mile and a quarter to the southwest of Katrā

In the Mat shrine on the mound Tokri Tīlā, the colossal images of Kaniṣka and Wima Kadphisis clad in Scythic dress are found indicating *daivakula* tradition of the Kuṣānas [6].

Some of the important features of Mathura school of art are [5]:

1. The *saṃghati* of the Buddha in Mathurā school shows ridgelike parallel folds on the drapery,

and the drapery folds near neck are loosely held on both sides.
2. The trough of the *saṃghati* assumes a curvilinear form which provides "U"-shaped loop at the bottom.
3. Mathurā Buddha is columnar and statuesque. He is taller and massive, and these features imbibed from the early yakṣa model.
4. The Uśnīśa is taller, and the halo is very ornate in Mathurā.

Though majority representations are Buddhist, some Jaina remains are also visible. The ruins of a Jaina shrine dating back to the pre-Christian era and a large number of dedicatory inscriptions engraved on the images of Jinas, *āyagapattas*, and arches dating from the first two centuries of Christian era are found in Mathurā. The references of the teachers of the donors, their *kula*, *gotra, śā khā*, etc. are also mentioned in it. The earliest Jaina inscription of Mathurā has been assigned to the middle of the second century B.C.E. It records the donation of ornamental arch for the Jaina temple by the lay follower Uttaradaśaka, son of Vachhi and disciple of ascetic Mahārakhita [2]. Another inscription from Mathurā mentions worshipping of the *arhat* Vardhamāna by Amohinī, Kochhi, the wife of Pāla who was son of Hariti, and together with her sons Palaghosha, Pothaghosha, Dhanaghosha, etc. [2]. The Jaina *āyagapatta* is an ornamental slab or tablet of homage bearing the portrait of *tirthānkaras* or other Jaina symbols. One such *āyagpatta* was set up by Svayaśa, the wife of dancer Phaguyaśa. It gives an impressive view of a Jaina stupa surrounded by a circumambulatory path with a railing [20]. The *toranas* have also been excavated in Mathurā. The *toranas* generally show the veneration of holy symbols and *tirthānkaras* by the lay followers and divinities. In one *torana* of Mathurā, a relief depicts paying homage by two *suparnas* to *tirthānkara* [20].

The Mathura school of art not only exported the Buddha statues to various parts of the Indian subcontinent but also influenced the Sārnāth school of art which created wonderful images of the Buddha in the age of imperial Guptas.

Cross-References

- ▶ Bodhisattva
- ▶ Gandhara
- ▶ Mahāsāṅghika
- ▶ Stūpa
- ▶ Yakṣa

References

1. Beal S (1869, reprint 2005) Travels of Fa-hien and Sung-yun from China to India. D.K. Printworld, New Delhi
2. Burgess J, Fuhrer A (1892–1894) Epigraphia Indica, vol II. Archaeological Survey of India, New Delhi
3. Chandra M (1977) Trade & trade routes in ancient India. Abhinav Prakashan, New Delhi
4. Chinnok EJ (1893) (ed) Arrian anabasis Indica. George Bell Press, London
5. Coomarswamy AK (1965) History of Indian & Indonesian art. Dover publications, New York
6. Cunningham A (1873) Report of Archaeological Survey of India, vol III. ASI, New Delhi
7. Cunningham A (2006, reprint) The ancient geography of India (the Buddhist period). Low Price Publication, New Delhi
8. Fausbal V (ed) (1877–1897) Jātakas, 7 vols. PTS, London
9. Hardy E (ed) (1901) Vimānavatthu. Pali Text Society, London
10. Jain JC (1947) Life in ancient India as depicted in Jaina canons. New Book Company, Bombay
11. Kinjawadekar R (ed) (1929–1933) Mahābhārata. Poona Press, Poona
12. Kinjawadekar R (ed) (1936) Harivamsa Purana. Chitrashala Press, Poona
13. Lal M (1987–1988) Population distribution and its movement during the first and second millennia B.C. in the gangetic divide and upper ganga plain, Puratattva. Indian Archaeological Society, New Delhi
14. Majumdar RC (1951) The age of imperial unity. Bhartiya Vidya Bhavan, Bombay
15. Malasekera GP (2007, reprint) Dictionary of Palī proper names. MLBD, New Delhi
16. Mayhoff C (ed) (1892–1909) Pliny, Naturalis Historia. Teubner, Leipzig
17. Mcrindle JW (ed) (1877) Ancient India as described by Megasthenes and Arrian. Oxford university, London
18. Morris R, Hardy E (1885–1900) Aṅguttar Nikāya. Pali Text Society, London
19. Rhys Davids TW (1881) Majjhima Nikāya. SBE, Oxford/London
20. Shah CJ (1932, reprint 2007) Jainism in North India. D.K. Printworld, New Delhi

21. Shamsastri R (ed) (1919) Arthaśāstra of Kautilya. Wesleyan Mission Press, Mysore
22. Singh A (2005) Tourism in ancient India. Serial Publication, New Delhi
23. Sircar DC (1942) Select inscriptions bearing on Indian history & civilization, vol I. Calcutta
24. Weber A (ed) (1882–1900) Śatapatha Brāhamana. SBE, Oxford

Maudgalyāyana

▶ Moggallāna

Meditation

▶ Ānāpānasati
▶ Dhyāna/Jhāna
▶ Mysticism (Buddhism)

Medium of Motion

▶ Dharma (Jainism)

Memorization, Remembrance, Recollection, Reminiscence, Recall

▶ Memory (Buddhism)

Memory (Buddhism)

Kanoko Tanaka
Komazawa University, Tokyo, Japan

Synonyms

Dhāraṇī, Smṛti; Memorization, Remembrance, Recollection, Reminiscence, Recall

Definition

Memory is an ability to *store*, *retain*, and *recall* what has been memorized so far:

All kinds of thoughts, speech, and activities in the history of human beings could not have been carried out properly without having the neural system of the *hippocampus*, a major component of the brain which has developed much more successfully than that of any other mammals on the earth, where information and experiences in human life should be stored in a proper process of *encoding* (registering some received information), *storage* (creating a permanent or temporal record of the received information), and *retrieval* (recalling the stored information whenever needed, in response to some cue for use).

As far as the history of Buddhism is concerned, it is desirable for a Buddhist to develop one's *memory power* in order to recall any time what is taught in the sūtras and put it into practice in the midst of one's daily life. Oblivion should be avoided no matter how much it may cost, for the sake of living a good Buddhist life and transmitting the heritage of Buddhism from one to other generations in the future.

1. As far as the Buddha Śākyamuṇi's physical features are concerned, all of his disciples did not try to memorize them properly because he taught as follows when Ānanda, who had been always at his side, grieved bitterly at the fact that the Buddha, his great master, was about to start his journey to the realm of death (the perfect goal of nirvāṇa; *parinirvāṇa*) : "Be ye islands unto yourselves. Take the self as your refuge. Take yourselves to no external refuge. Hold fast to the *dharma* as an island" (*Dīgha-nikāya* 16). The Buddha should deserve to be respected by other people only because his *dharma* is honorable. Therefore, it is natural that nobody tried to engrave or paint any image of the Buddha in his life time and even after his death, until the first Buddha image was created for some reasons around the first or second century, A.D. The physical features of the Buddha image are full of imaginative elements based on a legendary theory to tell about how

great persons visually looked like, in spite of the fact that the *historical* Buddha himself was nothing but a monk tonsured just as his own disciple. That is, the emergence of Buddha image in the history of Indian Buddhism was the beginning of *creating the memory* of the Buddha which came to be yearned for by those who were eager to see *him* in person. It is quite interesting that Buddhist people in later periods believed without any doubt that the *Buddha image*, far from the ordinary figure of human beings, was a true and real *memory* of the Buddha himself. This may be one of the best example of showing "*Memory and Oblivion*."

2. Then, how the teachings of the Buddha Śākyamuṇi, which should be regarded as the essence of the dharma, were memorized and edited by his disciples after he had passed away?

   For the first time, under the leadership of Mahākāśyapa, they came together at a cave situated just outside the walled city of Rājagṛha, the capital of Magadha, and mutually recited all of the Buddha's sermons and precepts (vinaya) memorized by Ānanda (in charge of sermons) and Upāli (in charge of precepts) in order to reconfirm and establish the true form of Buddha Dharma.

   From ancient times in India, they never try to transcribe the sacred words of a great religious leader for the purpose of engraving them deeply in their own minds. Modern people may think much of the written scriptures, but ancient and even modern Indians tend to regard *oral tradition* as much more important than a written language which is not yet a part of one's nature as long as he cannot recall and recite it from *memory* at any time. Reciting valuable teachings by heart should be the best attitude of a truly active follower of a religious leader who is living an altruistic life.

   Therefore, Mahākāśyapa positively held the convention of "*saṃgīti*" meaning "*to sing together.*" Just as the word "*Saṃgīta*" (song) is one of the most popular names of Indian females, it is not very special for Indian people to memorize sacred sūtras of their own sects. By singing the verses of the sūtras, they can find it easy to memorize and recall them. The famous phrase "evaṃ mayā śrutam" (Thus I heard from the Buddha; Thus said the Buddha) is the beginning of so many Buddhist scriptures, for the purpose of authorizing their contents; "This is not a pseudo, but a real theory of the Buddha himself." Written form of Buddhist scriptures (sūtras) appeared for the first time in the history of Buddhism around the first century B.C. at a Saṃgha in Śrī Lanka. Monks used "*pattra*," a sort of long-shaped leaf, for inscribing the sūtra, hoping that it will remain forever even among the war and other disasters to destroy their community anytime. However, they never cease polishing up their *memory power* in order to transmit *orally* the Buddha Dharma from one generation to another.

3. For example, *dhāraṇī* originally means the power of storing everything that is learnt from the Buddha Dharma. By memorizing one item of the teachings, it is getting easier to recall many other items, because *one* reminds him of the *others* through the act of association in his mind. *Dhāraṇī* is such an art of *mnemonics* to help a Buddhist not to do evil but to do good in accordance with the Buddha Dharma. "*Mantra*" is often called "*dhāraṇī*," but "*mantra*" tends to be shorter than "*dhāraṇī*." "*Mantra*" has a specific meaning to suggest the *verbal power* to realize what is uttered, without fail. On the other hand, "*dhāraṇī*" points to the *memory power* itself.
4. The word "*smṛti*" also can be translated as "*memory*": "not to forget what one has ever experienced in the past days." In Buddhist context, good experiences (e.g., to realize how life is transient and how potential at the same time, only if one try to live a positive life within the time limited) should be the best object of meditation. In this case, the act of concentrating one's mind upon the object is nothing but a *smṛti*. Moreover, the act of chanting the Buddha's name, visualizing the Buddha image, and contemplating the virtues of the Buddha is called "*Buddhanusmṛti*" especially regarded as the most important in the Pure Land Buddhism.

5. Memorizing one's past faults and sins must be essential for a human being who can recall them as clearly as possible, feel shame at what were done in the past, confess all of them, and seek after forgiveness. Without having the *memory power* he will not be able to take the responsibility of atoning his past faults and sins in the best way and should fail to relieve his mind from a guilty conscience. Oblivion may release a man from a sense of guilt, but he does not deserve to take part in the social life again, but has to be punished in a proper way. Even in the lifetime of the Buddha Śākyamuṇi who taught how to avoid doing wrong and evil, his disciples were not perfect to observe the rules of the Saṃgha (the community of monks or nuns). By the kind advice from King Biṃbisāra of Magadha who told the Buddha that it was very much helpful to adopt non-Buddhist rituals of *uposadha* for improving the moral life of Buddhists, the Buddhist own *uposadha* (the function of coming together twice a month, on the days of a new moon and a full moon, reconfirming the rules of the Saṃgha, confessing one's sin, and forgiving one another) had started in due course.

   From the viewpoint of a sinner, not only "*kṣama*" (craving for others' forgiveness with patience) but also "*āpatti-pratideśana*" (confessing and purifying one's sin) should be necessary for taking a new step of his life for the right direction of Buddhist goal (bodhi; the perfect Awakenings). Those who may still recall his sins are also desirable to tolerate what he did in the past. *Memories* both of a sinner and a person who was troubled with the sinner's deeds may finally reconcile to each other: Such a situation as this can be seen from ancient to modern generations. This is one of good examples of the *memory power* useful for preserving morality of the human life.
6. Ontologically speaking, it is well known that Buddhist philosophy always positively denies the substantial entity named "the eternal soul" which most of the non-Buddhist people need to believe as the essence of human existence. One of the reasons should come from Buddhist thoughts that a human being (and even any other kind of living beings) is organically composed of the physical, verbal, and mental *karma* changing every moment according to the present conditions of his own mind and the environment all around him. It is neither substantial nor unchanging. But such a karmic way of living a life is believed to preserve the effective power to be taken over beyond this life and should cause the natures of the next life, following the law of causation, without being intervened by God or any other kind of supernatural beings. Such a theory as this has several versions among the schools of Nikāya Buddhism just as Sarvāstivādins, Sautrantikas, etc., whose thinking of *karma* probably through the practice of meditation later evolved into the thoughts of the Mahāyāna Mādhyamika and Yogacāra schools that good, bad, and morally neutral karma, just as the seeds (*bījā*) deeply kept in one's mind, should sprout as a result when the time is ripe according to some conditions.

   The issues of *karma* stated above may be a sort of "*karmic memory*" kept through the past, the present, and the future life of one's own, no matter whether he may not memorize his past days very well owing to some problems of the hippocampus, one of the most essential system of storing memory *only* through the medium of cellular tissues of neuron. The *karmic memory* in Buddhist philosophy, on the other hand, will never be lost as long as all of the effects of his *karma* should not be dissolved by attaining the stage of nirvāṇa or mokṣa: the state of mind successful in eliminating every cause of one's sufferings (*kleśa*) or so-called *three poisons* of lust (rāga), hatred (dveṣa), and delusion (moha). Thus, medical science and religious philosophy are on different levels.
7. Regarding the issues of (5), "*abhijñāna*" (special abilities or wisdom to be obtained by the experiences of deep meditation reaching the state of eliminating every *kleśa* arisen so far) deserves referring here. One of the six kinds of *abhijñāna* is known as the abilities of knowing everything about one's own and others' own previous lives. Ordinary people cannot remember anything about their karmic existences of

the past, but "ārhat" (those who have obtained the *abhijñāna* for altruistic purposes) is believed to see everything when meeting everyone. It is a sort of beneficial *memory power* as the result of accumulating good deeds of previous lives, not the supernatural abilities whose origin is quite unknown and mysterious.

Cross-References

▶ Mantra

References

1. Masutani F (1957) A Comparative Study of Buddhism and Christianity. Bukkyo Dendo Kyokai, Tokyo
2. Hirakawa A (1993) A History of Indian Buddhism. Motilal Banarsidass, Delhi
3. Tanaka K (1998) Absence of the Buddha Image in Early Buddhist Art-Toward its Significance in Comparative Religion. D.K.Printworld (P) Ltd, New Delhi
4. Tanaka K (1999) The "Empty Throne" in early Buddhist art and its sacred memory left behind after the emergence of the Buddha image. In: Wessel R, Jeroen S (eds) Memory and oblivion: Proceedings of the XXIXth International Congress of the History of Art held in Amsterdam, 1–7 September 1996. Kluwer Academic Publishers, The Netherlands, pp 619–624

Menses

▶ Menstruation (Buddhism)

Menstruation (Buddhism)

Amy Paris Langenberg
Religion and Women's Studies, Auburn University, Auburn, AL, USA

Synonyms

Female bleeding; Menses; Periodic bleeding

Definition

The periodic discharge of blood and other tissues from the uterus/womb that occurs among sexually mature women who are neither pregnant nor menopausal.

Introduction

In many South and Southeast Asian Buddhist countries, women are refused entry at certain shrines and temples due to menstrual and birth impurity. This seemingly un-Buddhist anxiety about female blood has piqued the interest of researchers, as Buddhist texts contain very few specific prohibitions regarding the menstruating woman's qualifications to practice the dharma [3, 11, 15]. A not uncommon interpretation of temple purity laws fingers *brāhmaṇa* or other local religious influences [15]. But, while unarguably in dialogue with *brāhmaṇa* culture from early on, South Asian Buddhists also developed their own special interpretations of the female reproductive body, many of which emphasize its fundamental impurity. A look at classical Indian Buddhist sources, in particular the *Vinaya*, reveals several distinctive interpretations of menstruation.

Menstrual Blood in Sūtra, Abhidharma, Tantra, and Buddhist Hagiography

The issue of female blood does not receive the sort of focused attention in classical sources that it does in, for instance, *brāhmaṇa* dharma texts, or East Asian apocryphal *sūtras* concerning the blood-bowl hell, but references to menstruation do reliably occur within certain Indian Buddhist contexts. Starting with the early discourses, timely menstruation is always listed as a necessary condition for the conception of new human life. For instance, according to the Pāli *Mahātaṇhāsankhaya Sutta*, an early discourse that uses events of the human life cycle to flesh out, as it were, the doctrine of dependent arising, the mother must be "a menstruating woman" (*utunī*) in order for conception to occur.

Here, the term likely connotes a sexually mature and fertile woman who has not reached menopause, rather than a woman who is actively bleeding. *Avadānas* contain many instances of the same bit of medical wisdom, though the context is somewhat different. In these Buddhist narratives, the reader/auditor is often reminded that if he wishes for the birth of son, he must abandon his fruitless pleadings at the altar of local fertility gods and rely instead on the Buddha's understanding of conception. Later Buddhist embryological texts such as the *Garbhāvakrānti-sūtra* even discuss in detail the causes and symptoms of healthy or unhealthy menstruation [10].

In abhidharma texts such as Vasubandhu's *Abhidharmakośabhāṣya*, the bloody effluvia of the womb are regularly mentioned as an aspect of birth suffering (*janmaduḥkha*). Birth and rebirth is undesirable, at least in part because the womb brims with repulsive female fluids [1, 19]. Conversely, spiritual elevation is sometimes associated with an escape from female blood. For instance, in several important hagiographies, the Bodhisattva, whose unusual experience of birth marks his specialness, is said to have been born untainted by the womb's fluids [2, 13, 17]. The women of Akṣobhya's buddha-field – Abhirati, one of the few buddha-fields in which women appear at all – are so superior that they neither menstruate nor experience pain during childbirth [4, 12].

The language of disgust is often harnessed to the task of generating aversion (*saṃvega*) in Buddhist discussions of birth and female sexuality. Uterine blood is one item in a list of bodily fluids (pus, urine, feces, etc.) that render the female body a repulsive site of degradation. In Tantric ritual contexts, by contrast, female blood is recognized as a power substance and endowed with liberative qualities. The yoginī's possession of female blood is an essential part of her value as a yogic partner. The list of 22 esoteric signs (*sandhyā-bhāṣā*) glossed in the *Hevajra-tantra* includes, for instance, the word *sihlaka* (frankincense), which corresponds to blood, evidence of the importance of this substance in esoteric communal ritual. In its descriptions of yogic practice, *Caṇḍamahāroṣaṇa-tantra*, a text of the *yoginī* class, encourages the practitioner to actually sip the menstrual fluids issuing from his female partner's body [20]. Demonstrating a more subtle approach, the *Kālacakra* tantric initiation imaginatively engages the generative power of female fluids in its mimicry of human gestation.

Menstrual Regulations in the Vinaya

Medieval tantric inversions aside, the association of female blood with spiritual inferiority is a basic aspect of Indian Buddhist views on menstruation. How might this view play out in Buddhist-inflected society? How was menstruation managed, controlled, and infused with social meaning in ancient Indian Buddhist communities? For this, it is best to turn to *Vinaya*, or Buddhist monastic law. While they vary in detail, the sectarian Buddhist *Vinayas* all contain one or more of the following: (1) a rule requiring nuns to wear a menstrual cloth, (2) a rule forbidding nuns to keep communally owned menstrual cloths beyond a certain period of time, and (3) a rule barring women from the community who menstruate either too much or not at all [5, 6, 9, 16, 18]. For instance, a rule (*prāyaścittika* 144) from the Mūlasarvāstivāda *Bhikṣuṇī Prātimokṣasūtra* (nun's disciplinary code) ordains that when a nun does not keep a special garment to conceal her menstrual flow, it is an offense requiring expiation. Tibetan translators have rendered the term for this special garment "a cover for sorrow." The commentary for this rule provides a fuller context and a possible clue about the reasons for the Tibetan translators' interesting word choice. Here, the rebellious nun Sthūlanandā (literally, "Fat Stupid Nandā") fails to wear her menstrual cloth when she goes into the town of Śrāvastī to beg alms. She is menstruating, and blood runs freely down her legs, attracting the attention of brahmins and householders. When they ask her about the blood, she rudely suggests they ask their female relatives to explain what it is. The ensuing public umbrage forces the Buddha to issue a precept absolutely requiring all nuns to keep a menstrual cloth. Even then, the obdurate Sthūlanandā objects, saying that the menstrual cloth merely conceals the sorrow of women, something which, presumably, she would prefer to put on display.

Another passage about Sthūlanandā from the procedural section of the Mūlasarvāstivāda nuns' *Vinaya* states that "not being without passion because of the (moral) deficiency of their previous actions, from time to time nuns bled from their genitals." Because of this, their lower garments became "unseemly, full of flies, and not attractive." The nuns washed and dyed them but it happened repeatedly. Again, the Lord advised the nuns to "keep" a special garment for concealing the menstrual blood. In this episode, Sthūlanandā raises no protests against the menstrual cloth but again suffers a mishap in town when it falls to the ground in front of a group of inquisitive children. The lord then advises the nuns to tie their menstrual cloths with a string to their waists so as to avoid such difficulties.

In an autocommentary on his important digest of the Mūlasarvāstivāda *vinaya* tradition (the *Vinayasūtra*), Guṇaprabha clusters the rule regarding nuns keeping a menstrual cloth with two other rules and labels the cluster in a revealing way. Nuns, he says, must keep a special garment for concealing the menstrual flow and tie it with a string. They must wash and dye it from time to time. They must also keep a bathing robe. They may not have their soiled clothing washed by a washerman (but must do it themselves). These rules, he says, all pertain to concealing or guarding the *bhaga*, or female sexual organ. Guṇaprabha's grouping together of ordinances that "guard the female sexual organs" of nuns suggests that such rules may have been an expression of anxiety about the monastic *bhaga*, which along with all of its products and functions, was to be concealed, contained, and protected in public settings [8].

Some of the sectarian *Vinayas* also include passages forbidding the ordination of women who either menstruate too much, or not at all. The woman who continuously menstruates is forbidden, the text implies, because her lower garment is always soiled and attracts flies. The woman who has no menstrual blood at all and does not menstruate is also forbidden, apparently because her condition encourages her to take on airs and behave arrogantly toward her elders and betters. Several of the *vinaya* texts cited here interpret the correlation between female blood and spiritual inferiority mentioned above quite directly. They assume that cessation of desire results in cessation of menstruation. An ordinary unenlightened woman who happens not to menstruate for some other reason is therefore in a position to claim spiritual attainments she does not possess and may tease older more accomplished nuns who still menstruate. Such a woman is therefore barred from the nuns' community.

Brāhmaṇa Influence?

Taken together, *vinaya* sources indicate that while the nuns' menstrual cloth was clearly a hygienic aid to nuns, it was also instituted in response to dominant social mores regarding menstrual blood. For instance, a rule (*pācittiya* 47) from the Pāli *Vinaya* references what appears to be a menstrual garment to be worn in public houses in order to signal compliance with such mores [6, 7]. The Mahāsāṅghika-lokottaravādin *Bhikṣuṇī-vinaya* contains a rule (*prakīrṇaka* 16) forbidding nuns to wash their menstrual cloths at public bathing places (*tīrthas*) after other bathers complain that "This entire place has been made impure by [their] blood" [16]. These passages suggest that menstruating nuns' use of legally mandated items in a closely regulated manner was for the purpose of signaling to the larger lay community their status as properly respectful and observant menstruating women.

In creating rules regarding nuns' menstruation, Buddhist lawgivers may well have drawn selectively from common menstrual practices, especially *brāhmaṇa* household ritual. They did not, however, actually replace their own views of female impurity with *brāhmaṇa* views. For the authors of *brāhmaṇa* household law, the menstruating wife occupies a temporary state of impurity and is briefly exiled from the daily life of the family, but the freshly bathed, shampooed, coiffed, anointed, and sexually available wife is considered pure. Although Buddhists and scholars of Buddhism have tended to attribute Buddhist notions of female impurity to the powerful influence of purity-obsessed Brahmin culture, this ascription is not borne out very well by the textual evidence. Indeed, it is quite remarkable how much the early dharma literature discusses not the impurity of women, but their inherent purity. Baudhāyana is not alone among *brāhmaṇa* lawgivers in asserting that "Women have an unparalleled means of purification and they never become sullied, for month after month their menstrual flow washes away their sins" [14]. Classical Indian Buddhist texts, on the other hand, tend to view the benighted female embodiment as a state of permanent moral, if not ritual, impurity and the female womb through which all humans pass as the original source of a type of pervasive bodily loathsomeness that is impossible to cleanse with *brāhmaṇa* techniques like bathing or penance. As noted above, contact with or possession of female blood is linked to lower moral status across Buddhist literature. A number of *vinaya* texts on menstruation also articulate a clear connection between the moral degeneracy of women, past and present, and the fact that they leak impurities once a month. Thus, what is a temporary and easily remedied state of impurity in the early dharma literature, one reflective of a generalized past sin disconnected from the deeds of any particular woman, is generally regarded in canonical Buddhist contexts as a permanent and highly personal state in which impurity has penetrated far into the mind.

To the extent that early monastic lawgivers did mimic *brāhmaṇa* religious law by isolating female blood from public bathing places, and legally regulating women's menstrual procedures, they probably did so not out of concerns about *brāhmaṇa* style ritual impurity, but to normalize lay-nun interactions and protect monastic harmony. Despite mainstream Buddhist objections to many *brāhmaṇa* views regarding purity and the body, it was simply unthinkable in the ritual-social environment of ancient India for a mixed-sex religious community dependent on alms to forgo construction of a policy regarding menstruation. Whatever their understanding of female impurity, everyone seemed to agree that *bhagas*, particularly those associated with ascetic women, were a potential source of moral degeneration and impropriety, and required careful husbandry [8]. Indeed, in most religious cultures, celibate or otherwise, female bodies have been considered too important and powerful to simply leave unregulated. Menstrual rules are a part of this overall regulatory program. By instituting formal rules, monastic lawyers were thus able to provide menstruating Buddhist nuns with a set of chaste, respectable, and suitably feminine behaviors both inside and outside of the nunnery.

Cross-References

- ▶ Bhikkhunī
- ▶ Gender (Buddhism)
- ▶ Nuns (Buddhism)
- ▶ Women (Buddhism)

References

1. Faure B (2003) The power of Denial: Buddhism, purity, and gender. Princeton University Press, Princeton
2. Goswami B (2001) Lalitavistara. The Asiatic Society, Kolkota
3. Gutschow K (2004) Being a Buddhist nun: the struggle for enlightenment in the Himalayas. Harvard University Press, Cambridge
4. Harrison P (1987) Who gets to ride in the great vehicle? Self-image and identity among the followers of the early Mahāyāna. J Int Assoc Buddh Stud 10:67–89
5. Heirmann A (2002) The discipline in four parts. Rules for nuns according to the Dharmaguptakavinaya. Motilal Banarsidass, Delhi
6. Horner IB (1949) The book of the discipline: Vinayapitaka. Luzac, London
7. Hüsken U (2001) Pure or clean? Tradit South Asian Med 6:85–96
8. Jyväsjärvi MJ (2011) Fragile virtue: women's monastic practice in early medieval India. Harvard University Dissertation, Cambridge
9. Kabilsingh C (1998) The Bhikkhunī Pātimokkha of the six schools. Sri Satguru, Delhi
10. Kritzer R (2009) Life in the womb: conception and gestation in Buddhist scripture and classical Indian medical literature. In: Sasson V, Law JM (eds)

Imagining the fetus: the unborn in myth, religion, and culture. Oxford University Press, Oxford/New York
11. Makley CE (2005) The body of a nun: nunhood and gender in contemporary amdo. In: Gyatso J, Havnevik H (eds) Women in Tibet. Columbia University Press, New York
12. Nattier J (2009) Gender and hierarchy in the lotus Sūtra. In: Teiser S, Stone J (eds) Readings of the lotus Sūtra. Columbia University Press, New York
13. Ohnuma R (2012) Ties that bind: maternal imagery and discourse in Indian Buddhism. Oxford University Press, New York
14. Olivelle P (2003) Dharmasūtras: the law codes of Āpastamba, Gautama, Baudhāyana, and Vasiṣṭha. Motilal Banarsidass, Delhi
15. Prapapornpipat K (2008) Visible and invisible obstacles facing the Bhikkhuṇī movement in Thailand. In: Tsomo KL (ed) Buddhist women in a global multicultural community. Sukhi Hotu, Petaling Jaya
16. Roth G (1970) Bhikṣuṇī-Vinaya: including Bhikṣuṇī-prakīrṇaka and a summary of the Bhikṣu-Prakīrṇaka of the Ārya-Mahāsāṃghika-Lokottaravadin. K.P. Jayaswal Research Institute, Patna
17. Sasson V (2009) A womb with a view: the Buddha's final fetal experience. In: Sasson V, Law J (eds) Imagining the fetus: the unborn in myth, religion, and culture. Oxford University Press, Oxford/New York
18. Tsomo KL (1996) Sisters in solitude: two traditions of Buddhist monastic ethics for women. SUNY Press, Albany
19. de la Vallée Poussin L, Pruden LM (1988) Abhidharmakośabhāṣyam. Asian Humanities Press, Berkeley
20. White DG (2003) Kiss of the Yoginī: tantric sex in its South Asian contexts. University of Chicago Press, Chicago

Mental Cultivation

▶ *Bhāvanā*

Mercy Killing

▶ Euthanasia

Meru

▶ Kailash

Meru (Buddhism)

K. T. S. Sarao
Department of Buddhist Studies, University of Delhi, Delhi, India

Synonyms

Hemameru; Mahāmeru; Mahāneru; Mount Meru; Neru; Sineru; Sumeru

Definition

A mountain forming the center of the world in the Buddhist cosmology.

Mt. Meru, the king of mountains, which forms the center of the world (*axis mundi*) in the Buddhist cosmology, is known by various names such as Hemameru, Mahāmeru, Mahāneru, Neru, Sineru, and Sumeru. It is said to have been formed out of various precious metals manifesting itself spontaneously resembling the hub of a waterwheel, its eastern part being made out of silver, the southern part out of lapis lazuli, the western part out of ruby, and the northern part from gold. Buddhist texts, including the Aṅguttara Nikāya, the Dhammapada-aṭṭhakathā, the Paramatthajotikā, the Samantapāsādikā, the Visuddhimagga, and Vasubandhu's Abhidharmakośabhāṣyam, mention its depth, height, and width as 80,000 (according to some texts 80,000) yojanas (approximately 4.5–7.5 miles). It is shaped like an hourglass, with its middle being half of its top and base. In the Buddhist cosmology, Meru's square base is surrounded by a square moat-like ocean, which is in turn surrounded by a ring wall of mountains, which is in turn surrounded by a sea, each diminishing in width and height from the one closer to Meru. There are seven enchanting lakes and seven surrounding golden mountain walls, until one comes to the vast outer sea which forms most of the surface of the world, in which the known continents are merely small islands. The seven golden mountains are Yugaṃdhara, Īṣādhara, Karavīka (Sk: Khadiraka), Sudassana (Sk: Sudarśana), Assakanna (Sk: Aśvakarṇa), Vinataka, and Nemindhara measuring 40,000, 20,000, 10,000, 5,000, 2,500, 1,250, and 625 miles, respectively, in height. The continents of Uttarakuru, Jambudvīpa, Pūrvavideha, and Aparagodānīya are located respectively to the north, south, east, and west of Mt. Meru. Jumbudvīpa, the known world, is mentioned as the most excellent among these four continents.

In the Buddhist cosmology, the Tāvatiṃsa (Sk: Trāyastriṃśa), the divine abode, is located on the top of Mt. Meru, which is the highest plane in direct physical contact with the earth. The next 40,000 yojanas below the Tāvatiṃsa consist of steep precipice, tapering inward like an upturned mountain until it is reduced to 20,000 yojanas square at a height of 40,000 yojanas from the sea level. From here downward, Meru begins to get enlarged again, going down in four terraced ledges, each wider than the one above. The first terrace forms the "heavenly abode" of the Four Great Kings (*deva mahārājā*) and is divided into four parts which respectively face north, south, east and west. Each section is ruled by one of the Four Great Kings, who faces outward toward the quarter of the world that he administers. The Sun and Moon also circumambulate Meru at an altitude of 40,000 yojanas in a clockwise direction. The alteration of day and night is based upon this rotation. Thus, when the Sun is to the north of Meru, the full shadow of the mountain falls over the continent of Jambudvīpa, and it is midnight there; at the same time, it is noon in the opposing northern continent of Uttarakuru, dawn in the eastern continent of Pūrvavideha, and dusk in the western continent of Aparagodānīya. However, half a day later, when the Sun moves to the south, it is noon in Jambudvīpa, dusk in Pūrvavideha, dawn in Aparagodānīya, and midnight in Uttarakuru. The next three terraces down the slopes of Meru are each twice as longer and broader. They comprise the followers of the Four Great Kings, namely, *yakṣas*, *gandharvas*, *nāgas*, and *kumbhāṇḍas*. In the center of the Tāvatiṃsa is located the palace of Śakra, the "Most Victorious Mansion," produced out of sundry costly metals. In the middle of Mt. Meru are located the four great islands (*Mahādīpā*) with their 2,000 smaller islands (*cūḷadīpā*). At its foot (according to some texts in its inner caverns) is situated the Asurabhavana (Residence of the Demons) whose dimensions are 10,000 yojanas. In the commentaries of both the *Dhammapada* and the *Sutta-Nipāta*, it has been mentioned that the Asurabhavana was not originally there but came into existence through the power of the Asuras when they were pushed down from the Tāvatiṃsa by the Devas (demigods).

Meru is considered to be the center of not only the physical world but also the metaphysical and spiritual worlds. Many well-known temples have been erected as symbolic representations of Mt. Meru. When the Buddha went to Tāvatiṃsa, he covered the entire distance of 6,800,000 yojanas from the earth till there in three strides. He put his right foot down on the top of Yugandhara, his left on Meru, and the next step brought him to Tāvatiṃsa. Meru is often used in the Buddhist texts as a metaphor and a simile for size, extreme difficulty, and stability, its chief characteristic being its unshakability (*suṭṭhuṭhapita*), size, and imperturbability. Each "world system," known as Cakkavāḷa (Sk: Cakravāda) in Buddhist cosmology, has its own Meru and its end. Thus, a time comes when even Meru is destroyed.

Cross-References

▶ The Buddha of Healing

References

1. Andersen D, Smith H (eds) (1913) The Sutta-Nipāta. Pali Text Society, London
2. Cowell ED, Neil RA (eds) (1886) The Divyāvadāna. Cambridge University Press, Cambridge
3. Fausböll V (ed) (1877–1897) The Jātakas, 7 vols. Trübner, London
4. Feer ML (ed) (1884–1898) The Saṃyutta Nikāya, 5 vols. Pali Text Society, London
5. Geiger W, Rickmers, M (trans) (1929–1930) The Cūḷavaṃsa: being the more recent part of the Mahāvaṃsa, 2 vols. Pali Text Society, London

6. Morris R, Hardy E (eds) (1885–1900) The Aṅguttara Nikāya, 5 vols. Pali Text Society, London
7. Norman HC (ed) (1906) The commentary on the Dhammapada, 4 vols. Pali Text Society, London
8. Pruden LM (trans) (1988) Abhidharmakośabhāṣyam, 4 vols. Asian Humanities, Berkeley
9. Smith H (ed) (1916–1918) Sutta-Nipāta commentary being Paramatthajotikā II, 3 vols. Pali Text Society, London
10. Sorensen PK (1994) Tibetan Buddhist historiography: the mirror illuminating the Royal Genealogies. Harrassowitz Verlag, Wiesbaden
11. Takakusu J, Nagai M (eds) (1947–1975) Samantapāsādikā: Buddhaghosa's commentary on the Vinaya Piṭaka, 8 vols. (including index by H. Kopp). Pali Text Society, London
12. Trenckner V, Chalmers R (eds) (1888–1896) The Majjhima Nikāya, 3 vols. Pali Text Society, London
13. Warren HC, Kosambi D (eds) (1951) The Visuddhimagga of Buddhaghosācāriya, vol 41, Harvard oriental series. Harvard University Press, Cambridge, MA

Metaphysical Idealism (Buddhism)

▶ Idealism (Buddhism)

Metta

K. Sankarnarayan
K.J. Somaiya Centre for Buddhist Studies, Mumbai, India

Synonyms

Affectionate; Amity; Benevolent; Friendship; Kind; Love; Loving-kindness

Definition of *Metta*

The very definition of *metta* (loving-kindness) between one and the other is like the blend of the milk and water which cannot be separated (*khirodakibhuta*) ([7], Vol. I.4.1.326) and to have the eye of affection toward every being (*annamannam piyacakkhuhi sampasanta viharama ti*) ([7], Vol. I.4.1.326). The concepts of *metta* (loving-kindness) and *karuna* (empathy/compassion) are the two corner stone of the teachings of the Buddha. *Metta* is one of the foremost among the four sublime or divine abode (*brahmavihara*) or "best modes of life" or dwelling with Brahma ([6], Pt.II), viz, *metta* (loving-kindness), *karuna* (compassion), *mudita* (altruistic joy), and *upekkha* (equanimity). Without the first and the foremost of the divine abode, one will be unable to reach the divine abode of the path of enlightenment.

Brahmavihara: This is known as ([9], Vol. III.Pt.2..10.2.1.987) *Ariyan* way (*ariyavihara*) or the best of ways or divine ways (*brahmavihara*) or the Tathagata's way of life (*Tathagata vihara*). The Exposition of the Divine States ([13], Vol. I.9.240 *brahmavihara niddesa, mettabhavana*) are love (*metta*), empathy (*karuna*), altruistic joy (*mudita*), and equanimity (*upekkha/upeksa*) which are set forth immediately after the subjects of meditation on the recollections, should first, having cut off the obstacles, taken up the subject of meditation, on the evils of hate and the advantages of forbearance (*khanti* or *ksanti*). Thus, the development of love (*mettabhavana*) begins and the feeling of hatred is withdrawn from the mind. One should develop "love" for oneself first (*pathamam attanam mettaya pharitva*) and never toward others whether friends or dear ones, etc., since one is one's own master ([3], Ch. XII.v.160). Thus, one should diffuse oneself with love and be free from *dukkha* (misery) reminding of affectionate expressions and other causes of love and tender feeling, used by one who is dear, affectionate, and respected by him and the virtue, learning, and other causes of reverence possessed by such one, be his teacher or like his teacher, and keep reminding himself of the welfare. This would take away the enmity within him with all emancipation of will (*ceto-vimutti*) through love (*metta*) which does reflect on others with full of love and affection ([9], Vol. I.Pt.2.9 4.226). Thus, to practice a heart of love (*metta cittam*) all through the day even if it was as light as one pull at the cow's udder ([10], tr. Pt.II, p. 177), this practice will become a vehicle (*yanikata*) and a base, will take his stand on it firmly (*vatthuta*), and stores up

M

(*paricita*) thoroughly (*susamarata*). Feeling of love by acts of speech (*mettam vacikammam*), by acts of thought (*mettam manokammam*), and by acts of body (*mettam kayakammam*) help live all together on friendly terms and harmonious as milk and water blend, regarding one another with an eye of affection ([7], Vol. I.4.1.326).

Developing Loving-Kindness (*Mettabhavana*/*Mettasahagatena*): Getting rid of all defilements beholds the self purified of all evil unskilled states; when one beholds the self freed, delight is born; rapture is born from delight; when in rapture, the body is impassible; when the body is impassible, it experiences joy; being joyful, the mind is concentrated. Thus, one dwells having suffused the first quarter with the mind of friendliness, likewise the second, the third, and the fourth, in every way he dwells with the mind of friendliness, loving-kindness (*mettasahagatena cetasa, averena pharitva viharati* – [7], Vol. I. 4., 10.438). While staying at Jetavana near Savatthi, the lord addressed Rahula ([7], Vol. II.2.2.120) to develop (*bhavana*) the development that is "friendliness" (*mettabhavana*) by which malevolence will be rid of. It is also pointed out that to have boundless freedom of mind is to have the mind of friendliness ([7], Vol. III.3.7.230); thus, for the development of mindfulness, the development of friendliness is important ([7], Vol. III.2.8. 147).

The Importance of "Loving-Kindness": The importance of "loving-kindness" is emphasized as whatever grounds there are for making merit productive of a future birth; all these do not equal a 16th part of the mind release of loving-kindness. The mind release of loving-kindness surpasses them and shines forth, bright and brilliant ([6], 1.3.22). "For one who mindfully develops boundless loving-kindness, seeing the destruction of clinging, the fetters are worn away" ([6], I.1.7.27, tr.; Vol. XLVII, p. 15). The Buddha points out three "fires" – the fire of lust (*raga*), the fire of hatred (*dosa*), and the fire of delusion (*moha*); the fire of hatred is to be distinguished by loving-kindness (*dosaggim pana mettaya*) ([6], 3.5.4. 93).

Thus, with the heart and mind filled with loving-kindness, abundant, expansive, limitless, and free from enmity and ill will, just as a mighty trumpeter makes himself heard without difficulty in all four directions, even so, of all things that have shape our life, there is not one that he passes by or leaves aside, but regards them all with a heart set free through deep-felt loving-kindness ([4], Vol. I. 13.556).

The Attitude Toward All Living Beings with the Loving-Kindness: ([11], 1.8 metta sutta) One having developed loving-kindness (*metta*) should be capable, straight, and upright and speak gently without any conceit ([11], 1.8.v.143); contended and easy to support with calmness and zealous without being greedy ([11], v.144); and make all around him happy with his loving-kindness ([11], v.145); all means all creatures moving or still without exception, small or great; they should be treated all alike with loving-kindness (*Sn*.v.146); one having developed loving-kindness should make everyone around happy whether they are seen or unseen, whether they live nearby or far-off ([11], v.147); loving-kindness should avoid humiliating or despising and should avoid getting angry at any cost toward everyone ([11], v.148).

The attitude toward others should be like a mother toward her only child who is to be protected with unbound loving-kindness ([11], v.149); should cultivate unbound loving-kindness toward all the world, above and below and across without any impediment, without enmity, and without rivalry ([11], v.149); should not subscribe wrong views, but should be endowed with insight and virtue as the result of unbound loving-kindness ([11], v.152).

In the "Exposition of the Divine States" ([13], Vol. I.9.1.240 – *Brahmaviharaniddeso*) loving-kindness is given the first place. Besides, it is explained toward whom loving-kindness should not be developed ([14], tr. The Path of Purification, Pt.II. IX.1. pp. 340–360). But the foremost is to love oneself ([14], p. 341) with a heart full of love and speak with kind loving words pervade far reaching (mettaya), grown great, and beyond measure, without enmity and without ill will. This is in the context of one who has reached ecstasy by the *Jhanas* ([14], p. 354); one who lives with such heart full of love toward all living beings and nonhuman beings "Devas guard him" as parents guard their son ([13], Vol. I.9.1. 258 – *devata rakkhanti puttamiva matapitaro*; [14], pp. 360–361); fire, poison, and sword come not near him ([13], Vol. I.9.1 – *nassa aggi va sattham va kamati*) – the body of him who lives in love fire does not burn, etc.; one who lives in loving-kindness concentrates his mind quickly ([13], Vol. I.9, 258 – *cittam samadhiayati*); his complexion is serene – has calm countenance, like a ripe palm about to fall from stalk (*mukhavanno vippasidati bandhana pavuttam talapakkam*); he dies undeluded – the death of him who lives in loving-kindness knows no delusion; without delusion he dies as though falling into sleep (*asammulho kalangkaroti.. sammohamaranam.... niddam okkamanto*).

Who Is a *Kalyana Mitta*? ([1], Vol. II.Pt.2. *devatavagga* 7. *mittasutta* 3.): A spiritual friendship ([9], Vol. III.Pt.1.1.6.1; 7.1; 8.1): One who is involved in such a relationship is known as a "good friend," "virtuous friend," "noble friend," or "admirable friend." The good friend means the giver of a subject of meditation; one who is adorable, revered, and lovable; a counselor; a patient listener; a speaker of discourses deep, and one who would not apply himself to useless ends; (*piyo garu, bhavaniyo, vatta ca vacankkhamo gambiranca katham katta, ... evamadi gunasamannagatam ... kalyanamittam* – [13], Vol. I.3.42). Those whose conduct in deed, word, and thought is virtuous; for them, self is friend. Nevertheless, for them, self is a dear friend because that is which a friend would do to a friend, even that are they themselves doing to the self. Therefore, for them the self is a dear friend. A friend who is righteous, an intimate who expands the Ariyan Eightfold Path with right views based on detachment. This is the method by which one has to understand how the whole of holy life consists in friendship, in association, and in intimacy with what is lovely ([9], Vol.I.Pt.1. 3.2.8.129; [9], Vol. III.Pt.1.1.2.2). He is the spiritual friend who is possessed of systematic attention and who cultivates the seven limbs of wisdom that is mindfulness ([9], Vol. III.Pt.I.2.5.10.231).

Cross-References

- ▶ Brahmavihāra
- ▶ *Caga* – Generosity

References

1. (1995) Angutta Nikaya. Vipassana Research Institute (VRI), Igatpuri
2. The gradual saying (Woodward FL, tr. Pt. I. 2000, Pt. II, 2001.& V, 1996); (Hare EM, tr. Pt. III. 2001 & Pt. IV 2001). Pali Text Society (PTS), Oxford/London
3. Kalupahana DJ (text & tr.) (2008) Dhammapada. Buddhist Cultural Centre, Dehiwala, Sri Lanka
4. (1995) Digha Nikaya. VRI
5. (tr) (1995) The dialogues of the Buddha, vol. II & III. Sacred Books of the Buddhists
6. (1998) Itivuttaka Pali. VRI
7. (1995) Majjhima Nikaya. VRI
8. Horner IB (1999) Middle length sayings (tr. Pt. I., 2000, Pt. III). PTS
9. (1994) Samyutta Nikaya. VRI
10. Kindred Sayings (Rhys Davids, tr. Pt.I, 1999 & Pt.II. 2002, Woodward FL, tr. Pt. III. 1995, & IV.1996 & V.1997). PTS
11. Bapat PV (ed) (1990) Suttanipata. Bibliotheca Indo-Buddhica, No.75. Sri Satguru, Delhi
12. Norman KR (tr) (2001) The group of discourses, 2nd edn. PTS
13. (1998) Visuddhimagga, of Buddhaghosa, Pt.I & II. VRI
14. Pe Maung Tin (tr) (2003) The path of purification, I, II, III. PTS

M

Middle Way (Buddhism)

Ana Bajželj
Department of Philosophy, Faculty of Arts, University of Ljubljana, Ljubljana, Slovenia
Polonsky Academy, The Van Leer Jerusalem Institute, Jerusalem, Israel

Abbreviations

S Saṃyutta Nikāya

Synonyms

Madhyamā pratipad; Majjhimā paṭipadā; Pratītya samutpāda; Paṭicca samuppāda; Śūnyatā

Definition

The expression "middle way" refers to the Buddhist understanding of practical life, avoiding the extremes of self-denial and self-indulgence, as well as the view of reality that avoids the extreme positions of eternalism and annihilationism.

The Buddhist Understanding of the Middle Path

The notion of the middle way refers to the Buddha's resistance to unconditionally accept any extreme ways of practice or theoretical viewpoints. The Buddha described himself as a vibhajyavādin (one who asserts propositions conditionally) rather than an ekāntavādin (on who maintains one absolute position). The middle path generally refers to the avoidance of two extremes of practical life, namely, indulgence in sensual pleasures on the one hand and severe asceticism on the other. According to the religious biography, the Buddha was supposed to have lived a very comfortable and affluent life before renunciation. However, upon seeing a sick man, an old man, a dead man, and an ascetic, he decided to give up this pleasurable life of a householder and become a wandering ascetic, searching for a release from unsatisfactoriness (duḥkha). He undertook different techniques, amongst which he particularly applied himself to the practice of strict austerities. After living in this manner for several years and being dissatisfied with the methods of other renounciates, he quietly sat under a tree, straining neither physically nor mentally. It was there that he attained enlightenment (nirvāṇa). In his first teaching that followed this experience, recorded in the discourse titled The Setting in Motion of the Wheel of the Dharma or the Dharmacakrapravartana sūtra (S V 421–423), the Buddha talked about the realization of the path to enlightenment, which lies in the middle way that avoids both practical extremes of pleasurable life and self-mortification. This practical middle path, which is the way to the attainment of nirvāṇa, is separated into eight sections which together bear the name of the noble eightfold path. This eight-part practical instruction is what constitutes the last of the four noble truths (catvāri āryasatyāni) by means of which the Buddha described the nature of reality. Its subdivisions are (1) right view (samyagdṛṣṭi), (2) right intention (samyaksaṃkalpa), (3) right speech (samyagvācā), (4) right action (samyakkarmanta), (5) right livelihood (samyagājīva), (6) right effort (samyagvyāyāma), (7) right mindfulness (samyaksmṛti), and (8) right concentration (samyaksamādhi). These eight are not to be taken as successive components but rather as complementary factors on the path to liberation. They can further be assembled into three units of wisdom (prajñā; 1, 2), morality (śīla; 3–5), and meditative cultivation (samādhi; 6–8).

Another way of understanding the middle way of Buddhism is to see it as the middle path between the position that proposes the existence of a changeless essence of all things on the one hand and the position that life ends with the death of the body on the other. The first view is referred to as the extreme of eternalism (śāśvatavāda) and primarily concerns the Vedic schools of thought. The second view is referred to as the extreme of annihilationism (ucchedavāda) and applies to the Indian materialist tradition that pronounced a purely material existence of beings and discarded the Indian religious paradigm, including the notions of karma and saṃsāra. The Buddhist way amid the two extremes is the rejection of the idea of an eternal independent self and the simultaneous acceptance of the theory of rebirth. There is, therefore, no persistent agent that is subject to rebirth, however, the continuity of life, death, and rebirth is still brought about through ignorance, craving, and karmic fruition. According to the Buddhist doctrine, all that a person is, is a continuous flux of aggregates (skandha) or bundles of phenomena of which there are five, that is, form (rūpa), feelings (vedanā), cognition (saṃjña), volitions (saṃskāra), and consciousness (vijñāṇa). These are transient and operate in dynamic conditionality. They are not supported by any permanent substratum. This aspect of the Buddhist teaching is termed the doctrine of no-self (anātman). The five aggregates represent the static model of the experience of beings. The temporal scheme of this experience is represented with a 12-link chain of relations, which is referred to as dependent origination (pratītya samutpāda). It is occasionally also translated as dependent arising or origination-in-dependence, all translations referring to the same idea that there is not a single phenomenon that arises without being conditioned by something else other than itself. The early Buddhist theory utilized this model in order to explain the arising of unsatisfactoriness and the selfless karmic continuity within saṃsāra. Besides proposing the middle position between eternalism and annihilationism, this causal chain also represents the middle way between two theories of causation, namely, self-causation on the one hand and external causation on the other. The 12 interdependent links (nidāna) of the sequence are (1) ignorance (avidyā), (2) volitions (saṃskāra), (3) consciousness (vijñāna), (4) name-form (nāma-rūpa), (5) six sense spheres (ṣadāyatana), (6) contact (sparśa), (7) feelings (vedanā), (8) craving (tṛṣṇā), (9) grasping (upādāna), (10) becoming (bhava), (11) birth (jāti), and (12) old age and death (jarāmaraṇa). This model demonstrates how the mechanism of conditionality operates. If "A" comes into existence because of "B" then the cessation of "B" leads to the cessation of "A." Likewise, reversing the causal chain that leads to it results in the cessation of unsatisfactoriness. The model of dependent origination thus manages to evade absolute identity as well as absolute difference between successive lives, as every existence comes about in relation to its condition and additionally, the conditions that led to the arising of this currently operational conditioning factor. This also applies to the continuity during an individual life, as all the experiential events are selfless, yet dependent on other aspects of experience in order to arise. The Buddhist approach toward selfless empirical continuity in saṃsāra, therefore, represents the middle way between the idea that the "person" in the next existence or instant is exactly the same as the one in the previous one on the one hand and the idea that the two are completely different on the other.

More specifically, the notion of the middle way refers to one of the Mahāyāna Buddhist schools, namely, Mādhyamika (lit. middling) or school of the "middle way." The founder of this tradition is thought to be Nāgārjuna, a Buddhist monk who lived in the second century C.E. Nāgārjuna universalized the model of dependent origination to form a general scheme of relativity and maintained that every single event is essentially embedded in the nexus of causal relations. In other words, every element of existence is conditioned and, accordingly, there is not a single event in reality that occurs accidentally. Nāgārjuna termed this lack of independent existence emptiness (śūnyatā). Everything is empty as it is not self-maintained, including the notion of emptiness itself. Emptiness as the ultimate truth of the relativity of all things is again considered to be the middle way between the extremes of eternalism and annihilationism.

Adherents of another branch of Mahāyāna Buddhism, namely, Yogācāra or Vijñāṇavāda disagreed with this interpretation of the middle way as emptiness. For them the idea that not one single element of reality is independently existent, implied nihilism. Opposing this, they introduced consciousness (vijñāna) as the only primary existent and a substratum for all other phenomenal events. The adherents of Yogācāra maintained that what is normally thought to be a dualistic world of subjects and objects is merely a fabrication projected onto the way things truly are. Further, they argued that even for the absence of subject-object dichotomies to exist, there needs to be something that is lacking in them. They deemed this something to be a continuously changing flow of consciousness. Based on this they developed a model of three aspects, describing the relationship between consciousness and the phenomenal misapprehension. The first aspect is the "constructed aspect" (parikalpitasvabhāva) and refers to the understanding of the world as divided into subjects and objects, a polarization that is incorrect. The second aspect is the "dependent aspect" (paratantrasvabhāva), referring to the Mādhyamika understanding of reality. The third aspect is the "perfected aspect" (parinișpannasvabhāva). This relates to the Yogācara understanding of reality, in which there is, as noted, one inherently existing thing, namely, the flux of consciousness, which is empty of dualistic constructs. As this approach denies the illusory constructs but retains the scheme of conditional dependency, the Yogācārins consider it to be the true middle way between not negating enough and negating too much.

M

Cross-References

- ▶ Anattā (Buddhism)
- ▶ Aryasacca
- ▶ Causality (Buddhism)
- ▶ Craving
- ▶ Dhamma/Dharma (Buddhist)
- ▶ Dukkha
- ▶ Enlightenment
- ▶ Eschatology (Buddhism)
- ▶ Idealism (Buddhism)
- ▶ Insight
- ▶ Kamma
- ▶ Karma
- ▶ Khandha
- ▶ Mādhyamika
- ▶ Mahāyāna
- ▶ Majjhimā Paṭipadā
- ▶ Materialism (Buddhism)
- ▶ Nāgārjuna
- ▶ Nāma-Rūpa
- ▶ Paṭicca Samuppāda
- ▶ Philosophy (Buddhism)
- ▶ Psychology (Buddhism)
- ▶ Reality (Buddhism)
- ▶ Rebirth (Buddhism)
- ▶ Relativity (Buddhism)
- ▶ Renunciation
- ▶ Saṃkhāra
- ▶ Saṃskāra
- ▶ Sārnāth
- ▶ Soul
- ▶ Śūnyatā
- ▶ Śūnya
- ▶ Vijñāna
- ▶ Vijñānavāda
- ▶ Yogācāra

References

1. Berger DL (2001) The special meaning of the middle way: the Mādhyamika critique of Indian ontologies of identity and difference. J Dharma 26:282–310
2. Bucknell RS (1999) Conditioned arising evolves: variation and change in textual accounts of the Paṭicca-samuppāda doctrine. J Int Assoc Buddh Stud 22:311–342
3. Burton D (1999) Emptiness appraised: a critical study of Nāgārjuna's philosophy. Curzon, Richmond, Surrey
4. Burton D (2001) Is Madhyamaka Buddhism really the middle way? Emptiness and the problem of Nihilism. Contemp Buddh 2(2):177–190
5. de La Vallee Poussin L (1928) Notes on (1) *śūnyatā* and (2) the middle path. Indian Hist Q 4:161–168
6. Garfield J (1995) The fundamental wisdom of the middle way: Nāgārjuna's Mūlamadhyamakākarikā. Oxford University Press, Oxford/New York
7. Gómez LO (1976) Proto-Mādhyamika in the Pāli Canon. Philos East West 26(2):137–165
8. Harris IC (1991) The continuity of Madhyamaka and Yogācāra in Indian Mahāyāna Buddhism. E. J. Brill, Leiden/New York
9. Huntington CW (2003) The emptiness of emptiness. an introduction to early Indian Mādhyamika. Motilal Banarsidass, Delhi
10. Kalupahana D (1986) The philosophy of the middle way Mūlamadhyamakakārikā. State University of New York Press, Albany
11. Karunadasa Y (1987) Anattā as via media. Sri Lanka J Buddh Stud 1:1–9
12. King R (1994) Early Yogācāra and its relationship with the Madhyamaka School. Philos East West 44(4):659–686
13. Law BC (1937) Formulation of Pratītyasamutpāda. J Roy Asiat Soc GB Irel 2:287–292
14. Priest G (2009) The structure of emptiness. Philos East West 59:467–480
15. Tatia N (1995) The non-absolutistic view and the middle way (*anekānta* and *madhyamā pratipad*). Indian Int J Buddh Stud 5(1):1–21
16. Van An D (1963) On the middle way in Yogācāra Buddhism. J Indian Buddh Stud 21:329–335
17. Williams DM (1974) The translation and interpretation of the twelve terms in the Paṭiccasamuppāda. Numen 21:35–63, Fasc. 1
18. Williams P (1991) On the interpretation of Madhyamaka thought. J Indian Philos 19:191–218

Migadāya

▶ Sārnāth

Mikkyō

▶ Vajrayāna (Buddhism)

Military

► Warfare (Buddhism)

Mind (Buddhism)

Bhikkhu Anālayo
Center for Buddhist Studies, University of Hamburg, Balve, Germany

Synonyms

Citta; *Manas*

Definition

Understanding the nature of the mind and successfully cultivating it are central concerns of the Buddhist teachings. Hence, the mind is investigated and analyzed in various ways in the Buddhist texts.

Mind in Buddhism

The importance given to the mind in Buddhist thought is reflected in a discourse that records an encounter between the Buddha and a Jain ascetic ([1], Vol. I, p. 372). The discourse reports that, while the Jain upheld the self-evident position at first sight that bodily action is weightier than verbal or mental action, the Buddha countered that for him mental action was the weightiest type of action. Behind this position stands the importance given to volition in Buddhist thought as the central driving force behind any action manifesting at the mental, verbal, or physical level.

The same primacy given to the mind has also found a poetic expression in the twin stanzas that open the *Dhammapada* collection, according to which mind is the forerunner of all things ([2], 1–2). The whole world is in fact led by mind, which is the one thing that has everything else under its control ([3], Vol. I, p. 39).

The complexity of the analysis of the mind undertaken in the early Buddhist texts is also reflected in the use of different terms to refer to the mind. Three such Pāli terms are *citta*, *mano*, and *viññāṇa*. Although at times these three occur together as near synonyms ([4], Vol. I, p. 21), taken on their own each of them conveys a slightly different nuance.

Citta stands for the mind as the center of subjective experience, in particular in the sense of signifying the activity of the will and what could perhaps best be gathered under the header of emotion. *Mano* represents mind as a mode of action distinct from verbal and bodily action and as the sixth of the senses, where – besides the five physical senses of eye, ear, nose, tongue, and body – it covers the activity of thought and reflection. *Viññāṇa* refers to being conscious by way of any of the senses and denotes the stream of consciousness that sustains personal continuity during a single life and through subsequent rebirths. *Viññāṇa* is also part of the analysis of an individual into five aggregates, *khandha*. While the first of these five stands for the physical body, the remaining four represent different aspects of the mind. These are, besides *viññāṇa* as consciousness, feeling, perception, and volitional formations.

The perspective consistently adopted in early Buddhism in regard to each of these manifestations of the mind is that, even though the existence of the mind as a process is never questioned, to presume that any unchanging substance or self can be found within the mind is considered a thoroughly mistaken notion. What is commonly referred to as "mind," then, should be understood with wisdom as being merely a conditioned and impermanent process of mental events. From an early Buddhist perspective, the existence of such a mental flux is all that is required to account for continuity throughout life and from one life to another, for the margin of personal freedom to take decisions amid a complex set of conditionings of the mind, and for the karmic retribution that is inexorably linked to the ethical quality of any such decision taken.

M

The quality of this mental flux thus depends on one's own past volitional activities. One important principle here is that what one frequently thinks about will in turn lead to a corresponding inclination of the mind ([1], Vol. I, p. 115). Hence, the degree to which one's mind is at present under the influence of defilements reflects of one's own past interests and concerns. While the mind might naturally be undefiled and even luminous ([5], Vol. I, p. 10), only too often its actual condition is one of being overcome by various detrimental influences.

This situation is the reason Buddhist teachings give considerable importance to mental cultivation, *bhāvanā*. The prevalence of such concern in the early Buddhist teachings has found its expression in various categories that identify mental states or factors that are either detrimental to one's mental well-being or else beneficial for mental culture.

Certain detrimental influences on the mind are subsumed under the heading of the "influxes" or "taints," *āsava*. Usually occurring as a set of three, with sometimes the influx of views, *diṭṭhāsava*, added as a fourth, the standard listing speaks of the influxes of sensuality, of (desire for continued) existence, and of ignorance, respectively, *kāmāsava*, *bhavāsava*, and *avijjāsava*.

Another set of injurious factors are the *anusaya*s, "underlying tendencies" that lurk in the mind and cause the arising of unwholesome mental states. A standard set of seven such *anusaya*s covers sensual desire, irritation, views, doubt, conceit, lust for existence, and ignorance.

In the context of meditation practice proper, the five hindrances, *nīvaraṇa*, are identified as particularly harmful. These are sensual desire, ill will, sloth-and-torpor, restlessness-and-worry, and doubt, which "hinder" and obstruct the development of deep concentration and insight.

Beneficial mental qualities that stand in opposition to the five hindrances are the seven factors of awakening, *bojjhaṅga*. These comprise mindfulness, investigation of phenomena, energy, joy, tranquility, concentration, and equanimity. Another beneficial set comes under the topic of the faculties, *indriya*, or the powers, *bala*, which comprise confidence or faith, energy, mindfulness, concentration, and wisdom.

The basic distinction that underlies these categories, a distinction that runs like a red thread through the whole of the early Buddhist teachings on the nature of the mind, is the differentiation between what is wholesome or skillful, *kusala*, and what is unwholesome or unskillful. The injunction to remove the unwholesome and develop what is wholesome in a way provides a succinct summary of what cultivation of the mind in early Buddhism is concerned with. For achieving this aim, the development of the two complementary mental qualities of tranquility, *samatha*, and insight, *vipassanā*, is particularly called for.

With the development of Abhidharma thought, the analysis of the mind in the Buddhist traditions becomes more detailed and a range of mental states and mental factors are identified. As part of this development, the impermanent nature of the mind is given special emphasis, leading to the theory of momentariness. This somewhat radical conception of the impermanent nature of the mind, which proposes that each mind moment disappears as soon as it has appeared, would then have stimulated further developments in order to account for mental continuity. In the southern Buddhist tradition this was achieved through the concept of the *bhavaṅga*, the subliminal consciousness, whereas within some of the northern Buddhist traditions the concept of the *ālaya-vijñāṇa*, the store consciousness, can be seen to fulfill a similar function. Perhaps in opposition to what was perceived as a tendency toward substantialism among some Abhidharma philosophers, eventually the notion arose that reality in its ultimate sense is "mind only."

The early Buddhist position, however, consistently maintains a middle position according to which, even though mind is of prime importance, reality is not grounded in mind alone. Similarly, while mind is seen as nothing apart from or above an ever-changing process of mental flux, the early Buddhist conception of the mind does allow for continuity throughout the cycle of rebirths, for the effect of mental conditioning on decision making, and for karmic retribution, without needing to introduce additional concepts for this purpose.

Concern with the mind in early Buddhism is, in fact, above all pragmatic, in the sense of having the prescriptive function of showing the path to the liberation of the mind, without attempting an exhaustive descriptive treatment of the mind in all its possible modes, functions, and manifestations. This pragmatic concern is summed up succinctly in a verse in the following manner:

> Not doing any evil,
> Undertaking what is wholesome,
> Cleansing one's own mind,
> This is the teaching of Buddhas ([2], 183).

Cross-References

▶ Ālaya-vijñāna
▶ Bhāvanā
▶ Meditation
▶ Nāma-rūpa
▶ Viññāṇa

References

1. Trenckner V, Chalmers R (eds) (1888–1896) The Majjhima Nikāya, 3 vols. Pali Text Society, London
2. von Hinüber O, Norman KR (eds) (1994) The Dhammapada. Pali Text Society, London (references are by stanza)
3. Feer L (ed) (1888–1898) The Saṃyutta Nikāya, 5 vols. Pali Text Society, Oxford
4. Carpenter JE, Rhys Davids TW (eds) (1890–1911) The Dīgha Nikāya, 3 vols. Pali Text Society, London
5. Morris R, Hardy E (eds) (1885–1900) The Aṅguttara Nikāya, 5 vols. Pali Text Society, London
6. Ergardt JT (1986) Man and his destiny, the release of the mind. A study of citta in relation to dhamma in some ancient Indian texts. Brill, Leiden
7. Griffiths PJ (1991) On being mindless: Buddhist meditation and the mind-body problem. Open Court, Illinois
8. Hamilton S (1996) Identity and experience, the constitution of the human being according to early Buddhism. Luzac Oriental, London
9. Harvey P (1993) The mind-body relationship in Pāli Buddhism, a philosophical investigation. Asian Philos 3(1):29–41
10. Johansson REA (1965) Citta, mano, Viññāṇa – a psychosemantic investigation. Univ Ceylon Rev 23(1/2):165–215
11. Minh Thanh T (2001) The mind in early Buddhism. Munshiram Manoharlal, Delhi

Mind Reading

▶ Abhiññā

Mind-Only

▶ Vijñānavāda

Mixed Āgama

▶ Saṃyutta Nikāya

Modern South Bihar

▶ Magadha

Moggallāna

K. T. S. Sarao
Department of Buddhist Studies, University of Delhi, Delhi, India

Synonyms

Kolita; Mahāmaudglyāyana; Mahāmoggallāna; Maudgalyāyana

Definition

Chief disciple of the Buddha and best known for the possession of psychic powers and preaching skills.

Moggallāna was born in a village called Kolitagāma near Rājagaha. His mother was a brāhmaṇa woman called Moggalī (Moggallānī) and his father was the chief householder of Kolitagāma. Moggallāna was also called Kolita after the name of his village. According to the *Buddhavaṃsa*, Moggallāna's body was of the color of the blue lotus or the rain cloud. He was older than the Buddha and was born on the same day as Sāriputta. Both Moggallāna and Sāriputta belonged to rich families and were childhood friends, their families having maintained an unbroken friendship for seven generations. Once after having watched a mime play, the two friends realized that the world is impermanent and, hence, decided to give up the lives of householders. Initially, they became the disciples of Sañjaya Belaṭṭhiputta, one of the six famous heretical teachers of the Buddha's time. However, having found no satisfaction under him or many other teachers, they wandered unsatisfied all over India. Later, promising that whoever first found what they were looking for would tell the other, they parted company.

While wandering about in Rājagaha, Sāriputta met the Buddhist monk Assaji who converted him to Buddhism. He became a *sotāpanna* (entered the stream to enlightenment) after hearing from Assaji a stanza on *Paṭiccasamuppāda* (Sk: *pratītyasamutpāda*, *Dependent Arising*). Thereafter, he found Moggallāna and repeated before him the stanza that he heard from Assaji. Moggallāna also became a *sotāpanna*. Then the two decided to pay a visit to the Buddha at Veḷuvana. They also requested Sañjaya, their former teacher, to accompany them. But he refused. However, 250 disciples of Sañjaya joined them and were ordained by the Buddha. Except Sāriputta and Moggallāna, they all attained arahantship. Moggallāna went to the Magadhan village of Kallavāla where he tried unsuccessfully for 6 days. However, on the seventh day after his ordination, the Buddha after having known through clairvoyance, appeared before him and exhorted him to try ardently. Consequently, he succeeded in attaining arahantship.

On the day that Sāriputta and Moggallāna were ordained, the Buddha declared them to be his chief disciples. Some monks were upset at the newcomers being shown such an honor. But the Buddha pointed out that they deserved this due to their dedication and resolve in their previous lives. The Buddha also pointed out that the other monks should follow the examples of these two ideal disciples. In the *Saccavibhaṅga Sutta* of the *Majjhima Nikāya* the Buddha thus distinguishes them from the others by saying that: "Sāriputta trains in the fruits of conversion, Moggallāna trains in the highest good. Sāriputta can teach and clarify the Four Noble Truths; Moggallāna, on the other hand, teaches by his psychic marvel."

According to the Pāli texts, Moggallāna's supremacy lay in his possession of *iddhi* (Sk: *ṛddhi*; psychic power). Through the use of his psychic power, he could produce not only a living shape as many times as he wished but could also metamorphose himself into any shape at will. He is also said to have stated that he could squash Mt. Meru like a kidney bean. When the Buddhist Order did not receive alms in Verañjā, Moggallāna made an offer to turn the earth upside down, so that they could use the crux of the earth as food. Once with his great toe he shook the monastic residence of Migāramātupāsāda so severely that he terrified into silence those monks inside it who had been making a nuisance of themselves by indulging in noisy and frivolous talk. At another time, when Moggallāna visited Sakka to know if he had benefited from the Buddha's teaching, he found him far too vainglorious and conceited. Thus, he rattled his palace so hard that his hair stood on end with fright and his vanity vanished. According to the *Paramattha-Dīpanī*, the commentary of the *Theragāthā*, Moggallāna's best show of *iddhi*, was the taming of the Nāga Nandopananda, a feat which no other monk could have attained. Without having to enter any specific state of mind, Moggallāna could see *petas* (Sk: *pretas*) and other spirits not visible to normal human eyes. He would often visit different worlds to bring news regarding them to the Buddha. There is a collection of stories relating to such visits in the *Vimānavatthu*.

Though Moggallāna's supremacy lay in the possession of *iddhi*, in wisdom, too, he was rated only second to Sāriputta. Along with Sāriputta, Moggallāna could answer questions which were beyond the capability of all other monks. He was well known for his eloquent sermons some of which were attended even by various *devas* (gods) including Sakka, king of the *devas*. The Buddha is said to have personally complimented

Moggallāna for his powers of preaching. When the Buddha went to preach the *Abhidhamma* in Tāvatiṃsa, it was Moggallāna to whom he gave the responsibility of preaching to people during his absence. He took every task assigned by the Buddha seriously and thus, the Buddha often employed him as a messenger to deliver important messages. Above all, Moggallāna was entrusted by the Buddha with the task of looking after matters relating to the welfare of monks. The Buddha placed great faith in him and Sāriputta for the purposes of keeping the Buddhist Order pure.

When Devadatta created a schism in the Buddhist Order and went away with 500 of the monks to Gayāsīsa, the Buddha entrusted the task to Sāriputta and Moggallāna of winning those monks back. They did so successfully. It was quite usual for Sāriputta and Moggallāna to travel together at the head of the monks. When Rāhula, the Buddha's son, was ordained, Sāriputta was his preceptor and Moggallāna his teacher. Both Moggallāna and Sāriputta not only deeply cared about each other but also had great mutual admiration. Sāriputta's verses (nos. 1179–81) in praise of Moggallāna and Moggallāna's in praise of Sāriputta (nos. 1176–78) in the *Theragāthā* are a good example of their respect and admiration for each other. Their love for the Buddha was their strongest bond and whenever they were away from him, they were able to converse with him through extrasensory means.

Moggallāna died before the Buddha and 2 weeks after Sāriputta. According to the Pāli texts, his death resulted from a plot by the Niganṭhas (Jainas). Moggallāna used to visit various worlds and return with the news that whereas the Buddha's followers were reborn in happy worlds, the followers of the Niganṭhas were reborn in unhappy worlds. Apparently as a result of such statements by Moggallāna, the number of the followers of the Niganṭhas got reduced significantly. Thus, they hired criminals to kill Moggallāna. These criminals surrounded Moggallāna's cell, but he, aware of their intentions, managed to escape through the keyhole six times. However, on the seventh occasion, they succeeded on catching him. They beat him up severely, crushing his bones and leaving him for dead. Having recovered consciousness, he dragged himself to the Buddha with great effort, took his leave, and passed into *nibbāna* (Sk: *nirvāṇa*). According to the Jātaka account, his cremation was performed with much honor. The Buddha is said to have got his mortal remains collected and a stūpa was erected over his relics in Veḷuvana. The importance of Moggallāna in Theravāda Buddhism can be measured from the fact that he is connected with different characters in as many as 27 Jātakas.

Cross-References

▶ Abhidhamma Piṭaka
▶ Buddhavaṃsa
▶ Iddhi
▶ Jātaka
▶ Jhāna
▶ Kapilavatthu
▶ Meru
▶ Paṭiccasamuppāda
▶ Pātimokkha
▶ Rāhula
▶ Sāriputta
▶ Thera- and Therīgāthā
▶ Vimānavatthu

References

1. Fausböll V (ed) (1977–1897) The Jātaka, 6 vols. Luzac, London
2. Feer ML (ed) (1884–1889) The Saṃyutta Nikāya, 5 vols. Pali Text Society, London
3. Hecker H (1994) Maha-Moggallana. Buddhist Publication Society, Kandy
4. Jayawickrama NA (1974) Buddhavaṃsa and Cariyāpiṭaka, new edn. Pali Text Society, London
5. Norman HC (1906) The commentary on the Dhammapada, 4 vols. Pali Text Society, London
6. Ñyānaponika T, Hecker H (2003) Great disciples of the Buddha: their lives, their works, their legacy. Wisdom, Boston
7. Oldenberg H, Pischel R (1990) The Thera- and Therīgāthā (with Appendices by K.R. Norman & L. Alsdorf), 2nd edn. Pali Text Society, Oxford
8. Olderberg H (ed) (1879–1883) The Vinaya Piṭakaṃ, 5 vols. Pali Text Society, London

M

9. Trenckner V, Chalmers R (eds) (1888–1896) The Majjhima Nikāya, 3 vols. Pali Text Society, London
10. Woodward FL (ed) (1940–1959) Paramattha-Dīpanī: Theragāthā-Aṭṭhakathā, the commentary of Dhammapālācariya, 3 vols. Pali Text Society, London

Moha

► Kilesa (Kleśa)

Mokṣa

► Heaven (Jainism)

Moksha

► Ahiṃsā (Jainism)
► Karma (Jainism)

Molinī

► Vārāṇasī (Buddhism)

Monastery

► Vihāra

Mother of the Buddhas

► *Prajñāpāramitā*

Mount Meru

► Meru (Buddhism)

Muditā

K. T. S. Sarao
Department of Buddhist Studies, University of Delhi, Delhi, India

Synonyms

Altruistic joy; Appreciative joy; Sympathetic joy

Definition

Muditā is the sympathetic joy that arises from delighting in other people's well-being.

Muditā is the sympathetic joy that comes from appreciating the well-being and success of other people rather than resenting it. In its broadest sense, *muditā* consists of a wholesome attitude of exultation in the well-being of all sentient beings. In the Pāli texts, it is often mentioned as part of the triumvirate, *mettā* (loving kindness), *karuṇā* (compassion), and *muditā*. It is also one of the four sublime states *(brahmavihāras*) or the four immeasurables (Skt: *apramāṇa*, Pāli: *appamaññā*) consisting of *mettā*, *karuṇā*, *muditā*, and *upekkhā* (Skt: *upekṣā*; equanimity) and is traditionally considered as the most difficult to nurture. The traditional paradigmatic instance of this mental-state is the outlook of a parent observing the accomplishments of a child. This is not to be confused with vainness because a person feeling muditā ought not to draw any monetary or other personal benefits from the accomplishments of others. Through muditā-meditation one not only cultivates sympathetic joy but also counters the bitterness that one often feels at the accomplishments of others. The deeper one gets into it, the better one becomes in one's own plentiful joy and the easier it then becomes to take delight in the happiness of others. As pointed out by the Buddha in the *Dīgha Nikāya*, "a disciple dwells pervading the entire world everywhere and equally with his heart filled with sympathetic joy, abundant, grown great, measureless, free from enmity and free from distress."

Though *muditā* has not received as much attention in the Buddhist literature as *mettā* and *karuṇā*, its cultivation is a prerequisite for the cultivation of *mettā* and *karuṇā*. It is comparatively easier for one to be compassionate or friendly in circumstances requiring them than cherishing a spur-of-the-moment feeling of shared joy outside the confines of one's kinsfolk and friends. Mostly one needs to make a conscious effort to identify oneself with the joys and successes of other people. However, one's ability to do so has its origins in one's psyche which may be even deeper than one's reactions related to compassion. For instance, one definitely wants to be happy, with or without good reason, but at the same time gives it precedence over the shared grief of compassion. As humans are gregarious by nature, such a tendency already provides them with familiarity to some extent with shared emotions and joy, though generally at a much lower level than in the present context. Moreover, human beings also have a natural tendency for mutual assistance and cooperation. Furthermore, it is also true that happiness gives birth to happiness and selfless joy can emanate from it easily. Undoubtedly, the negative impulses in humans, such as jealousy and aggression, are far more visible than their positive inclinations toward social service, mutual assistance, and altruistic appreciation of the accomplishments of fellow human beings. However, as all these positive qualities lie hidden in human beings and are rarely cultivated, it is only proper to appeal to them and stimulate them. "If it were impossible to cultivate the good, I would not tell you to do so," said the Buddha. If this potential for unselfish joy is widely and methodically encouraged and cultivated, beginning with kids and continued with grown-ups, the seeds of muditā can give birth to many virtues such as magnanimity, tolerance, generosity, friendliness, and compassion. When unselfish joy grows, many evil tendencies in the human heart such as jealousy, ill-will, coldheartedness, and miserliness will come under complete control, if not disappear altogether. Unselfish joy can, indeed, act as a powerful catalyst in activating hidden forces of the good in the human heart. Envy and jealousy, which are the chief opponents of muditā, can not only corrupt one's character but also the social relationships at many levels of one's life. Thus, it is important to cultivate muditā as the antidote to envy and jealousy.

Muditā is also central to the stimulation of charity and social work. Muditā also prevents compassionate action from being tainted by a patronizing attitude which often either hurts or drives away the receiver. Moreover, when *karuṇā* and muditā go together, the chances of the deeds of service turning into dead routine become far less. Furthermore, *arati* (which may be translated variously as discontent, aversion, indifference, listlessness, and boredom), the distant enemy of muditā, can be overpowered through a cooperation of *karuṇā* and muditā. In one who helps and gives, the joy that one finds in such an action increases the blessings provided by these wholesome actions. Consequently, unselfishness becomes ever more natural to one.

Appraisal of accomplishment is the forerunner to muditā, and its appreciation a constituent of muditā. Finding the good in other people and learning to identify and appreciate what good there is, is what is implicitly denoted by muditā. Spur-of-the-moment and genuine participation in the moments of glory of others is conceivable only when the virtue of muditā is nurtured to its full potential. Deriving genuine joy at the good fortune of others is indeed a rare quality. The virtue of muditā may best be seen at work in the joy of parents over the success of their children. The same may be seen in the sincere delight that teachers derive at the accomplishments of their students, especially when the fear of the younger overtaking the older is always looming large.

Cross-References

- ▶ Brahmavihāra
- ▶ Karuṇā
- ▶ Metta

References

1. Andersen D, Smith H (eds) (1984) The Sutta-Nipāta, reprint. Pali Text Society, London

M

2. Feer ML (ed) (1884–1898) The Saṃyutta Nikāya, 5 vols. Pali Text Society, London
3. Morris R, Hardy E (eds) (1885–1900) The Aṅguttara Nikāya (1885–1900), 5 vols. Pali Text Society, London
4. Rhys Davids TW, Carpentier JE, Stede W (eds) (1886–1932) The Sumaṅgala-Vilāsinī: Buddhaghosa's commentary on the Dīgha Nikāya, 3 vols. Pali Text Society, London
5. Rhys Davids TW, Rhys Davids CAF (trans) (1899, 1910, 1957) Dialogues of the Buddha, reprints, 3 vols. Sacred Books of the Buddhists, London
6. Rhys Davids TW, Carpenter JE (eds) (1890–1911) The Dīgha Nikāya. Pali Text Society, London
7. Smith H (ed) (1916–1918) Sutta-Nipāta commentary being Paramatthajotikā II, 3 vols. Pali Text Society, London
8. Trenckner V (ed) (1880) The Milindapañho. Williams and Norgate, London

Munificence

▶ Dāna (Buddhism)

Mystic

▶ Mysticism (Buddhism)

Mystical Experience

▶ Mysticism (Buddhism)

Mysticism (Buddhism)

Sean Ward
The School of the Art Institute of Chicago, Chicago, IL, USA

Synonyms

Cessation; Emptiness; Enlightenment; Esoteric; Ineffable; Meditation; Mystic; Mystical experience; Non-dualistic; Occultism; Philosophy; Revelation; Secret; Spiritualism; Yoga

Definition

Mysticism

Practices and systems of thought within a doctrinal and ritual context aimed at the spiritual apprehension of knowledge remote to the intellect, gained only through a mystical experience and/or intuition. Mysticism is seen as an intimate and disciplined search for salvation, union, or liberation with the absolute or God. It is considered a direct experience of this absolute or God through learned techniques that are an uneasy fit into traditional notions of religious belief [1, 2].

Locating Mysticism in Indian Buddhism

Mysticism

At the core of all religion, mysticism can be found. It is derived from a documented vivid personal experience and is usually established in religions through a founder who had such an experience. As long as participants of a religion continue to regard and believe in a transcendent reality, a religion's longevity is maintained past their origins. This gives members a way to communicate these beliefs as a translation of these direct experiences [1, 6]. Because mysticism is commonly associated with ineffability, linguistic formulation tends to be seen as inexact and a mystic's experience to be indescribable. Thus, secrecy of the mind is commonly referred to. The multiplicity of uses, experiences, and interpretations makes a single definition of the term ineffectual. "A desire for unity with God" is seen as the familiar definition applied to the concept trying to incapsulate its meaning, but this is misleading because not all mystics across traditions would summarize their pursuit in this way, e.g., Buddhism has no God to become unified with. There is the denial of a "self" existing in Buddhism making a unification between self and God (unio mystica) impossible and the term mysticism an anachronism [10]. To assist in understanding the full scope of mysticism, scholars have tried to broaden some characteristics that run throughout. Beyond a unification of self with the One or God, it involves a uniting of vision and perception directly through objects with the One. Another characteristic concerns the development of an inner life in relation to the One, a striving for an ultimate truth of reality and the universe. It also offers the religious principle of the sacred, feelings of contentment, and euphoria which can be categorized under inexpressible or inarticulable feelings [5].

Mystical Experience

In order to better understand the definition of mysticism, the mystical experience needs to be described. Mystical experiences are defined and contextualized in reflection of the doctrine practiced. As described above, the general activity of mystical experiences is the apprehension of a transcendent realm that is beyond or within the self. It is difficult to have a criterion that scholars, mystics, and practitioners of religion can agree to [3]. Examples of trying to establish a distinguishing criterion can be found in the work of R.C. Zaehner and Paul Griffiths. Zaehner and Griffiths each describe three types of the mystical experience, where if the presence of one of these markers is detected, it could be said to be a mystical experience. For R.C. Zaehner, it is the panenhenic, monistic, and theistic experience. The panenhenic experience puts the focus not on the unity with an inner self but about creating a comprehensive feeling of connection and accordance with the physical world around. The monistic represents the sublimation of space and time as an undifferentiated transcending experience. Lastly, theistic experience is defined as a duality within the experience of the subject that is having the experience and the experience itself [3, 12]. Griffiths' three types are hinged upon the state of consciousness: pure, unmediated, and nondualistic. A pure consciousness event has no phenomenological conditions, is not shaped by the surrounding culture or concepts, and may be both unmediated and nondualistic. In the unmediated, the emphasis is on the condition of separation from context and the experience, reducing outside influence, whereas the nondualistic is founded on the inseparable subject from the object of experience. Under Griffiths attributes, pure, unmediated, and nondualistic are concomitant and can help make up the mystical experience through various configurations of the three [9].

Mysticism in Buddhism

There is no corpus of mystical texts in Indian Buddhism or Buddhism in general for that matter. Mysticism tends to be seen not as a negligible or heretical aspect but as a thing that permeates its doctrine and practice since early Buddhism and its various adaptions throughout the world. It is difficult to maintain a singular definition as both relevant and all encompassing regarding both mysticism and the mystical experience. There is continued debate and scholarly work done on the linguistic, conceptual, and meaning of mysticism in the area of study of world religions. The etymological foundation of mysticism gives little clarity to the term's enduring ambiguous definition, experience, and practice [1, 6].

There is much debate whether Buddhism is inherently mystical or not. The concern being that if mysticism penetrates its teachings, the Buddha's sacred biography and related practice, how could it be considered mystical. Mysticism in this sense can be defined as a form of religious life originating in mystical experiences with the struggle of linguistically trying to interpret them. The practice of Buddhism is initiated through doctrinal teachings as a way to build upon what could be described as mystical experiences. If Buddhism is considered to be based in pure mysticism, then these mystical events are given little translation from their origin of experience into a doctrinal foundation. This creates uncertainty regarding the importance of a written doctrine when encountering mystical experiences [9].

There is no precise nature or equivalent form in human experience for these mystical experiences. It is the mythological concept of nirvana that expresses the intention of Buddhism and the penetration of mysticism in its doctrines. There are no absolute interpretations given, and any explanations only point toward the event or knowledge of mysticism which is left being deciphered through intuition. Experience is given precedent over concept or theory and leaves faith as the principal element [4].

Context for Mysticism

Parallel to the debate over Buddhism being essentially mystical, there are scholars that see early Buddhism as a philosophically minded position of disconcertion practicing a discipline of enlightenment. In time, this opposition and refusal became debased delivering Buddhism as a popular religion. Another viewpoint is that Buddhism was originally a popular religious movement following the Buddha's writings while a monastic elite diverted, transforming it into an ascetic practice. A third group states that in the earliest phase of the known history of Buddhism, it included both an ascetic and commoner ingredient while maintaining a confluence of philosophy and popular ideas [6, 7].

It is has been difficult to estimate the place of mysticism in the present. The syncretistic practice of Buddhism and the adaption of various cultures have left the Buddhist tradition as being more locally self-defined. The process of acculturation began in the sixth century in India and continues to create distinct cultural forms of Buddhism. Symbols and specific rituals mark these practices in the cultures of China, Japan, Korea, Tibet, Sri Lanka, and Southeast Asia. In India, royal and popular support in the northeast under the Pala dynasty from the eighth to the twelfth century gave Buddhism some prosperity but faced aggressive criticism [2].

Experiences of Mysticism in Buddhism

From its beginning, the Buddhist tradition has incorporated a strain of mystical experiencing that has influenced its philosophy. There is no way of knowing exactly what the Buddha actually experienced but the earliest reports communicate a mystical experience that has been interpreted as a state of cessation and as an experience of emptiness. These are only two experiences of a multitude of interpretations and examples of the Buddha's teachings, practice of meditation, and form of mysticism in Buddhism.

The Experience of Emptiness

Nagarjuna's Mulamadhyamakakarika offers the state of emptiness to describe the experience and the path to enlightenment in Buddhism. Giving Buddhism a mystical direction from its origins, faced with its negative terms – nonattainment, nonassertion, and nonrelieance. Typically, the paths to emptiness vary; through the practice of confrontational paradoxical thoughts in instruction or as in Yogacara Buddhism, thoughts are seen as free of their subject and their subject is not dependent on these thoughts as objects. Rather than logic or metaphysics, emptiness is pursued in a factual attainment in Yogacara [1, 6].

Emptiness is more comparable to forgetting, a lack of response to the external world. In order to allow the mind to forget, mystics use meditation techniques to prime the mind. Mystics have revealed that forgetting embraces the forgetting of specific religious tradition. This leaves a cross-cultural phenomenon where the individual experience creates no distinction between subject and object. This is considered a pure consciousness event, where the content of this might contain characteristics of specific traditions, but the overall structure is inclusive.

State of Cessation

Cessation is considered as an important element of nirvana. The state of cessation in Buddhism relates to the ending of thoughts and feeling, not an ending to vital organic functions such as organs or heat. It is usually associated with being in a trance, where sense perception and the formation of concepts have ceased. Some scholars see cessation not defined as a pure consciousness event like the experience of emptiness because it is assumed that the subject is considered to be in a "mindless" state, while others challenge this notion because it would be difficult to explain a subject's resuscitation from this condition where all mental activity has ended.

In Mahayana, this debate was addressed with the concept of "dlaya- vijfidna." Where when a person is experiencing a state of cessation, his or her consciousness, vijfidna, does not escape the body because dlayavijfidna (presence) remains.

It is difficult to decipher whether this is in direct relationship to an actual experience or is a theory. The early Mahayana was affected by mystical experience and saw its role as a component of wisdom that rises above language and ordinary variety of thought.

This experience of cessation tends to be described as ineffable where the mental representations are indescribable by the subject. If a person is free from mental activity, points of view, and concepts; there is a loss of perceived diverse forms since they have vanished with the subject's perception. Consciousness being empty of mental representations does not mean the subject is unconscious. In early Buddhism, practitioners had difficulty communicating these experiences linguistically. The principal objective of early Buddhism being this mystical experience of cessation, where a specific quality is uncertain, is closely tied to what came to be known as nirvana. The element of cessation became a fundamental part of nirvana though many writings stress an intellectual aspect which came to be the presiding characteristic [8, 10].

Nirvana as Enlightenment and a Form of Mysticism

Nirvana is believed to be an enlightened view of the world. It is considered an ultimate reality and as a permanent state which is reached by an ineffable mystical experience where language and thinking is transcended. Through various interpretations of the experience, a meaning can be formed allowing a reception of a new understanding of a person's being-in-the-world [9].

By intuition, nirvana is to be understood; the doctrine and its ultimate reality are conceived as the mystical trend experienced in Buddhism [11]. Those that adopted doctrines (e.g., Sthiramati and Nagarjuna) in the history of Buddhism that this form of mysticism resides, believe that the ultimate truth of the universe and of the Buddha cannot be known through the intellect but through unrecognized knowledge inherent within the truth itself. It is along the bodhisattva's path to Buddhahood that this knowledge is attained and handed down by the Buddha in the sutras. The sutras do not dictate the way but situate themselves as a preparation or guide to such revelations [8].

Cross-References

▶ God (Buddhism)

References

1. Akira H (2007) A history of Indian Buddhism: from Sakyamuni to early Mahayana. Motilal Banarsidass, Delhi
2. Bowker J (ed) (1997) The Oxford dictionary of world religions. Oxford University Press, New York
3. Fischer-Schreiber I (1994) Buddhism & Taoism. In: Schuhmacher S, Woerner G (eds) The encyclopedia of eastern philosophy and religion, 3rd edn. Shambhala Publishing, Boston
4. Griffiths PJ (1993) The problem of pure consciousness, mysticism and philosophy. Oxford University Press, New York/London
5. Guiley RE (1991) Harper's encyclopedia of mystical & paranormal experience. HarperCollins, San Francisco
6. Hallisey C, Reynolds FE (1998) Buddhism. In: Macmillan information now encyclopedia: world religions, 2nd edn. Simon and Schuster Macmillan, New York
7. Johnson WL, Robinson RH (1982) The Buddhist religion: a historical introduction. Wadsworth, California
8. Nakamura H (2007) Indian Buddhism: a survey with bibliographical notes. Motilal Banarsidass, Delhi
9. Pyysiainen I (1993) Beyond language and reason: mysticism in Indian Buddhism. Vammalan, Helsinki
10. Smith JZ (ed) (1995) The HarperCollins dictionary of religion. HarperCollins, San Francisco
11. Warder AK (1997) Indian Buddhism. Motilal Banarsidass, Delhi
12. Zaehner RC (1961) Mysticism, sacred and profane. Oxford University Press, New York

N

Nāgārjuna

Burkhard Scherer
Department of Theology and Religious Studies, Canterbury Christ Church University, Canterbury, Kent, UK

Synonyms

Klu sgrub (Tibetan); Long shu (Chinese); Ryūmō (Japanese)

Definition

Buddhist philosopher of the second century Common Era; author of the Mūlamadhyamakakārikā.

Introduction

The Buddhist philosopher Nāgārjuna lived most probably in the second century C.E. (Common Era). He is the author of, among others, the Mūlamadhyamakakārikā and the Śūnyatasaptatikarika.

Nāgārjuna is generally acknowledged as the founder of the Mādhyamika Philosophy of Mahāyāna Buddhism, which consolidates the Path of Emptiness (Śūnyatāvāda) expounded in the early Perfection of Wisdom (Prajñāpāramitā) Sūtras.

Life and Legends

The historical Nāgārjuna lived between the first and third centuries C.E. in Central/South India. Nāgārjuna's connections to the Sātavāhana kings are key factors for dating and locating him ([1]; [2], p. 261). A Sātavāhana king is the addressee of the Ratnavalı (Precious Garland) and the Suhṛllekha (Letter to a Friend), two popular philosophical works ascribed to and most probably authored by Nāgārjuna. Nāgārjuna was very likely a late-second-century or early-third-century Buddhist monk who lived, for at least a portion of his career, in a Pūrvaśailya, Aparaśailya, or Caityaka monastery in the area of Andhra ([3], pp. 86–88).

In the Indo-Tibetan hagiographical tradition, numerous legends ornate the life of Nāgārjuna. Works such as the eleventh century *Caturaśītisiddhapravṛtti by Abhayadattaśrī or Tibetan dharma chronicles (chos 'byung) such as those by Bu ston and Tārānātha claim that Nāgārjuna lived 400 years after the Buddha's passing. According to the legends, Nāgārjuna's knowledge and usage of the elixir of life extended his life span to 600 years. His activities concentrated in the southern regions of India, where he shared this magic with his patron king. Eventually, the crown prince waiting to ascend the throne resorted to murderous ambitions in order to get the elixir and his father out of the way; he succeeded in finding the only way to kill Nāgārjuna: by cutting off his head with a blade of grass.

K.T.S. Sarao, J.D. Long (eds.), *Buddhism and Jainism*, Encyclopedia of Indian Religions,
DOI 10.1007/978-94-024-0852-2

Nāgārjuna's name "Arjuna (hero) among the Nāgas" points to the popular myth, which recounts how he supposedly retrieved the profound Perfection of Wisdom teachings in their complete 100,000-verse version from the Nāga realm at the bottom of the ocean. Indo-Tibetan art depicts Nāgārjuna in front of a divine cobra (nāga) halo.

Much scholarship has been devoted to separating facts from myth [1, 3]. It has generally been accepted that Nāgārjuna's longevity serves to disguise the existence of different scholars bearing the name "Nāgārjuna," the early one being the Mādhyamika philosopher, the latter one (or even two) being a tantric master or alchemist. As for Nāgārjuna the philosopher, it suffices to identify him simply as the author of the Mūlamadhyamakakārikā (MMK) and the Śūnyatāsaptatikārikā (ŚS).

Works

The authenticity of the majority of works ascribed to Nāgārjuna has been drawn into question using philosophical and stylistic compatibility with the MMK and the ŚS as the litmus test. Lindtner ([4], pp. 10–17) has suggested a canon of 13 authentic Nāgārjunian works, although suspicion has also been raised concerning some texts in Lindtner's canon, that is, numbers VIII–XI below:

I. Mūlamadhyamakakārikā (MMK)
Sanskrit edition by de La Vallée Poussin, St. Petersburg 1913; de Jong, Adyar Madras 1977; *translations*: Kalupahana 1986 [5]; Wood 1994 [6]; McCagney 1997 [7].

II. Śūnyatāsaptati (ŚS)
Tibetan edition and translation by Lindtner [4]; Tola and Dragonetti 1995 [8].

III. Vigrahavyāvartanī
Sanskrit/Tibetan edition by Lindtner [4]; translations by Wood [6] and Westerhoff [9].

IV. Vaidalyaprakaraṇa
Tibetan edition and translation by Tola and Dragonetti [8].

V. *Vyavahārasiddhi
Fragment; Tibetan edition by Lindtner [4].

VI. Yuktiṣaṣṭikā
Tibetan edition by Lindtner [4]; edition and translation by Tola and Dragonetti [8].

VII. Catuḥstava
Sanskrit edition by Tucci 1932 (Vols. II and IV) and Lindtner ([4], Vols. I, III); edited and translated by Tola and Dragonetti [8]).

VIII. Ratnāvalī
Sanskrit, Tibetan, and Chinese edition by Michael Hahn, Bonn 1982; translated from the Tibetan by Jeffrey Hopkins 1975/1998 (see [10]). On the question of authenticity, see [2] and [3] (pp. 271–278).

IX. Pratītyasamutpādahṛdayakārikā
Sanskrit edition by Gokhale 1940; Tibetan edition and translation by Jamieson [11] 2000. Authenticity denied by Dragonetti [12].

X. Sūtrasamuccaya
Tibetan edition by Pāsadika, Copenhagen 1989.

XI. Bodhicittavivaraṇa
Tibetan edition and translation by Lindtner [4]; authenticity denied by Ruegg, Williams, and Dragonetti [12].

XII. Suhṛllekha ("Letter to a Friend")
Tibetan edition by Pema Tenzin, CIHTS Sarnath 2002; translation by the Padmakara Translation Group [13].

XIII. *Bodhisaṃbhāra
Tibetan edition and translation by Lindtner [4].

Philosophy

The point of departure within Nāgārjuna's MMK and ŚS is the 12 nidānas (chains) of the pratītyasamutpāda (dependent origination) as explained, for example, in the Kaccāyānagotta Sutta (Saṃyuttanikāya xxii 15). Hence, as Kalupahana argues, Nāgārjuna's philosophy carefully moves within the frame of early Buddhist philosophy [5]. Nāgārjuna stresses the absence of intrinsic existence not only of the Self but also of all conditioned phenomena. Following on from the Prajñāpāramitā teachings, he points to the preliminary nature of all phenomena and philosophical concepts including key Buddhist tenets using śūnyatā (emptiness, openness) as a function of deconstruction, rather than a static ontological concept [10, 14].

Hence in his works, Nāgārjuna refutes mainly the wrong views on an alleged essence (svabhāva) of phenomena while avoiding positive statements on the nature of reality: all phenomena are empty of intrinsic, independent existence; all phenomena lack a permanent essence. His philosophy is referred to as "middle" (madhyamaka) doctrine, clearly pointing to early Buddhist teachings, in which both the assertion of nonreality (nāstidṛṣṭi, nihilism; ucchedadṛṣṭi, annihilationism) and the assertion of reality (astidṛṣṭi, essentialism, substantialism; śāśvatādṛṣṭi eternalism) are refuted. Conditioned reality neither exists ontologically nor in a nihilistic sense: The experienced conditioned reality is the fluid process of karma. Despite this affirmation of the middle, Indian philosophers of the Nyāyā-Vaiśesika, Vedānta, and Sāṃkhya schools, as well as rival Buddhist philosophers and modern scholars – Bournof, Jacobi, Walleser, de La Vallée Poussin, and Lamotte, and more recently Wood [6] and Burton [15] – frequently align Mādhyamika philosophy with nihilism. Also, Nāgārjuna's notion of emptiness has been criticized as self-refuting ([16], pp. 66–68). Non-nihilistic readings of Nāgārjuna are put forward by scholars including Stcherbatsky, Murti, and Ruegg, and more recently Eckel [17], Silburn, Vivenza [18], Westerhoff [19], and Scherer [10, 14]. Contemporary non-nihilistic interpretations of Nāgārjuna hold either that the nature of ultimate reality is beyond conceptualizations or "that the very idea of a final ontology is incoherent" ([20], p. 864).

Cross-References

- Mādhyamika
- Philosophy (Buddhism)
- Prajñāpāramitā
- Reality (Buddhism)

References

1. Mabbet I (1998) The problem of the historical Nagarjuna revisited. JAOS 118(3):332–346
2. Walser J (2002) Nāgārjuna and the Ratnāvalī: new ways to date an old philosopher. JIABS 25:209–262
3. Walser J (2005) Nāgārjuna in context: Mahāyāna Buddhism and early Indian culture. Columbia University Press, New York
4. Lindtner C (1982) Nagarjuniana: studies in the writings and philosophy of Nāgārjuna. Akademisk Forlag, Copenhagen
5. Kalupahana D (1986) Mūlamadhyamakakārikā of Nāgārjuna: the philosophy of the middle way. SUNY Press, Albany
6. Wood T (1994) Nāgārjunian disputations: a philosophical journey through an Indian looking-glass. University of Hawaii Press, Honolulu
7. McCagney N (1997) Nāgārjuna and the philosophy of openness. Rowman & Littlefield, Oxford
8. Tola F, Dragonetti C (1995) On Voidness: a study on Buddhist nihilism. Motilal, Delhi
9. Westerhof J (2010) The dispeller of disputes: Nāgārjuna's Vigrahavyāvartanī. Oxford University Press, Oxford
10. Scherer B (2012) Nāgārjuna on temporary happiness and liberation: readings of the Ratnāvalī in India, Tibet and China. In: Sharma A (ed) Buddhism in East Asia: traditions, changes, and challenge. Motilal, Delhi, pp. 131–144
11. Jamieson R (2000) Nāgārjuna's verses on the great vehicle and the heart of dependent origination. Peter Lang, New York
12. Dragonetti C (1986) On Śuddhamati's Pratītyasamutpādahṛdayakārikā and on Bodhicittavivaraṇa. WZKS 30:110–122
13. Padmakara Translation Group (2005) Nāgārjuna's letter to a friend. Snow Lion, Ithaca
14. Scherer B (2009) Karma: the transformations of a Buddhist conundrum. In: Chetyrova L et al (eds) Vajrayana Buddhism in Russia. Unlimited Space, St. Petersburg, pp 259–270
15. Burton D (1999) Emptiness appraised. Routledge, London
16. Ganeri J (2001) Philosophy in classical India. Routledge, London
17. Eckel M (1992) To see the Buddha: a philosopher's quest for the meaning of emptiness. Princeton University Press, Princeton
18. Vivenza J-M (2001) Nāgārjuna et la doctrine de la vacuité. Albin Michel, Paris
19. Westerhoff J (2009) Nāgārjuna's Madhyamaka: a philosophical introduction. Oxford University Press, Oxford
20. Siderits M (2010) Review of Westerhoff, J (2009). Mind 119(475):864–867

Nāgārjunakoṇḍa

Anand Singh
School of Buddhist Studies and Civilization, Gautam Buddha University, Greater Noida, UP, India
Institute of Management Sciences, University of Lucknow, Lucknow, UP, India

Synonyms

Mahāvasin vihāra; *Nallamalai*; *Śrīparvata*; *Vijayapuri*

Definition

Nāgārjunakoṇḍa is a Buddhist site situated about 20 km from Macherla in Guntur district of Andhra Pradesh, India. The site is named after the great Mahāyāna expert Nāgārjuna who founded the *Madhyamika* School of philosophy [5].

Introduction

Nāgārjunakoṇḍa is situated on latitude 16°31′N and longitude 79°14′E on the right bank of river Krishna in Paland subdivision of Guntur district of Andhra Pradesh, India. It is about 166 km to the south east of Hyderabad, the capital of Andhra Pradesh, and about 147 km away from Guntur town. Nāgārjunakoṇḍa is encircled by Nāllamallai hills on three sides and the western as well as some northern areas are enclosed by the river Krishna. The entire place was surrounded by the dense *paśu vemula* forest. The area is named after the great Buddhist philosopher Nāgārjuna who resided on one of its hills popularly known as Śriparvata. During an archeological excavation a number of stūpas, apsidal temples, and vihāras such as Dharnī vihāra, Kumāra Nandi vihāra, Mahisāsaka vihāra, Bahuśrutiya vihāra, and temples like Nodagīśvara, Kārtikeya, etc., were found [3].

Origin of the Names

Nāgārjunakoṇḍa was named after the *Sūnyavāda* philosopher Nāgārjuna. He was born at Vidarbha in a Brāhmana family. He was an authoritative exponent of the doctrine of existence and non-existence, i.e., *Śūnyatā* or *Tathatā*. He was a staunch disciplinarian and is said to have expelled from the *samgha* a large number of monks who broke the discipline in the observance of the Vinaya rules. He became the head of the *saṃgha* at Nālandā [4]. In his last phase of life he retired to the Nāgārjuna hills at Śriparvata. This place is also known as Vijaypurī, the capital of Ikṣavāku dynasty founded by Śāntamūla (Chāmtamūla). The *Purānas* call them Śriparvatiya Andhras who ruled from Vijayapurī situated in the Nāgārjunakoṇḍa, valley in the Nāllamalur range [4]. An inscription of king Virapurusadatta of the Ikṣavāku dynasty calls him as *Śriparvatadhipati* whose capital was Vijaypurī. The Nāgārjunakoṇḍa inscriptions are mostly records of benefactions of some royal female members of the Virapurusadatta family in favor of *Mahacetiya* of Nāgārjunakoṇḍa lying in the vicinity of Vijyapuri, the Ikṣavāku capital.

History of Nāgārjunakoṇḍa

The history of Nāgārjunakoṇḍa started taking shape during the age of the Sātvahanas. The discovery of coins belonging to Gautamiputra Śātakarni, Vasishthiputra Pulumavi, and Yajna Śri Śātkarni and an inscription of Gautamiputra Vijaya Śātakarni of his sixth regnal year show hold of the Sātvahanas over Nāgārjunakoṇḍa [13]. It has been presumed that Vijyapurī was founded by Vijaya Śātkarni [8]. The Tibetan tradition says the Sātvahanas were the great patrons of Nāgārjuna and built a *mahācetiya* and a *mahāvihāra* in honor of the revered teacher [14]. The Nāgārjunakoṇḍa came into prominence only after annexation of some parts of the valley from the Sātvahanas by Vasishthiputra Chantumula, the founder of the Ikṣavākus. The Ikṣavākus ruled for 75 years (225–300 C.E.).

During the reign of second Ikṣavāku king Virapurusadatta [12] and his son Ehuvala Camtamula, Buddhism became prosperous. The kings and their queens, *upāsikas*, *upāsakas*, *bikkhus*, and *bikkhunis* and some of the monks from distant places like Śri Lanka contributed for the development of Buddhism in Nāgārjunakoṇḍa which made it a great center of Buddhist learning.

The archeological as well as literary evidences show that the monastic complex of Nāgārjunakoṇḍa developed in the third to fourth centuries C.E. The copper plate inscription of Śri Mūla Raja, of fifth century C.E., issued from Kondavidu mentions Navakamikka, a resident of Aparaśaila vihāra [2]. It shows that the Buddhist stūpas and mahāvihāras were flourishing in this age. But in the time of Rudrapurusadatta, the Ikṣavākus were overthrown by the Pallavas. They were great patrons of Brahmanism and caused serious damage to Buddhism in Śriparvata [11]. After this invasion Buddhists might have existed for sometime in the valley but a lack of patronage gave jolt to all architectural activities in Śriparvata. With the loss of political and economic importance the structure fell into ruins and silted up by the flood waters and encroached by the forest.

It seems that the Vajrayāna Buddhism had its origin in the Valley of Nāgārjunakoṇḍa under influence of Nāgārjuna. From Nāgārjunakoṇḍa a mutilated image of Hariti showing Vajrayāna features has been found. The Goddess is shown seated with her legs dangling and wearing griddle, wristlets, and anklets [6]. An inscription in Brahmī character is also found from here showing *akṣyanivi*, a perpetual grant to light the lamp in devotion of the Buddha [13].

In modern age Nāgārjunakoṇḍa was accidently discovered in February 1920 by a local school teacher. On his information S. R. Saraswati visited the place to examine the mound. A. H. Longhurst for the first time excavated the site between 1927 and 1931 to expose the hidden structure under the mound. T. N. Ramchandran re-excavated it during 1930–1940 and after that a majority of vihāras and stūpas were unearthed [15]. An extensive survey was conducted between 1954 and 1960 by R. Subrahmanyam to explore the antiquities submerged under the water of Nāgārjunasagar dam. Subrahmanyam has explored more than a 100 sites ranging from the prehistoric age to the medieval age. The prominent Buddhist structures were restored on the top of the hill and a museum was constructed here to preserve all the antiquities.

Objects of Worship at Nāgārjunakoṇḍa

During excavations 32 stūpas were discovered belonging to Theravāda, Aparaśaila, and Bahuśrutiya schools. These stūpas can be classified into wheel-shaped and rubble stūpas. The Theravādins were supposed to be the first who constructed the stūpas and vihāras in Nāgārjunakoṇḍa, immediately followed by the Aparamahāvinseliyas [1]. It has also been accepted that the wheel-shaped stūpas which belonged to Aparamahāvinaseliyas reflect an advance over the rubble stūpas of the Theravādins [8]. A large number of brick-built stūpas of various sizes have been scattered in the valley of Nāgārjunakoṇḍa. Most of the stūpas are built on large and high platforms. The majority of the stūpas have a typical Andhra style wheel-based architecture and only few stūpas are built of rubble generally without spokes but some of them with *āyaka* platforms [8]. The wheel-based architecture is supposed to be an advanced type of stūpa with a certain ideological and technical significance. The wheel suggests the *dhammacakkapavattana* and the spokes may stand for the teaching of Buddha. It seems that most of the sects of the valley were orthodox and hence their stūpas were not ornamented. Only the Aparaśailas embraced a popular view and carved out beautiful sculptures in their vihāras and stūpas. The stūpas were invariably coated with a plaster of lime and some of them encased with limestone slabs.

The direct evidence of the stone railings in the stūpas are absent in Nāgārjunakoṇḍa. Longhurst opines that the *mahāstūpa* of Nāgārjunakoṇḍa was provided with the railing of wood on a supporting brick foundation. The discovery of 30 pieces of lime stone beams resembling the crossbars of the railing suggests existence of such structure [3].

Theravāda Stūpas

In Nāgārjunakoṇḍa nine Buddhist monuments have been attributed to the Theravādins. Out of nine, three structures are supported by the inscriptions and the remaining six are identified on the basis of their architectural features [8]. The earliest epigraphic reference is dated to the fourteenth regnal year, i.e., 245 C.E. of the king Sri Virapurusadatta, which mentions the Sihalavihāra on Culadhammagiri. The inscription says about maintenance and the addition of certain features in the existing stūpas [9]. Sihalavihāra on Chula-Dhammagiri was a large complex with a stūpa, vihāra, and *cetiya*. The main stūpa of the complex was built with a spherical rim made of bricks. The inner core of the stūpa was filled with the rubble. The *āyaka* pillars are absent in this stūpa because the monks of Śri Lanka did not adopt wheel-shaped structures as well as *āyaka* for their stūpas.

The other inscription gives information of establishments to the Mahisāsaka sect constructed in the eleventh regnal year of Ehuvala Camtamula by his sister Kadabaksiri, the queen of the king of Vanavasi. [9]. The Mahisāsakas were a branch of Theravāda and an orthodox sect. They had a large following in Śri Lanka, and in India their main center was in Vanavasi in the South. Their vihāras had generally two stūpas, one with a solid structure and small projections, so small that they could not accommodate the *āyaka* pillars. The second stūpa was wheel based with a hub and eight spokes – *āyaka* platform [8].

The third group belongs to the Mahāvihāravasins who were mainly from Śri Lanka [9]. Their main stūpa was built with a solid brick structure on a raised platform with two votive stūpas on its southern side. The monks of this vihāra were said to have propagated Buddhism in Kandhara, Yavana country, Vanavasa, and Śri Lanka [4].

The six more clusters of vihāras and stūpas have been identified as structure of Theravādins on basis of their architectural attributes. Generally these stūpas were built on a large platform with a brick-built circular rim and their core was filled with rubble. Sometimes the stūpa was approached on two sides by a flight of steps and the vihāras consisted of four wings with a *mandapa* in the center [8].

Bahuśrutiya Stūpas

The Bahuśrutiya, the most popular sect of Nāgārjunakoṇḍa, was probably named after the founder of the sect Bahuśruta [8]. They were lenient and tried to reconcile the differences between Theravāda and Mahāsaṃghika but were unsuccessful in their effort. The largest establishment in Nāgārjunakoṇḍa belongs to them, situated in the northern part of the valley. The majority of structure were either renovated or constructed during the reign of the third Ikṣavāku king Ehuvala Camtamūla, Mahadevī Bhattidevī, the wife of Mathariputta Virapurusadatta, and the mother of Ehuvala and the whole complex is known as Devī vihāra [10]. The main stūpa has been built on wheel plan in the west of the vihāra establishment. The wheel has two circular rims connected by 12 spokes. The inner circle is connected with the hub by eight spokes. The stūpa has *āyaka* platforms in all four directions. Two apsidal temples are also found near the stūpa.

The second Bahuśrutiya structure is situated in the northeast part of the valley. This sacred complex has a six-spoke stūpa with a diameter of 8.5 m with *āyaka* platforms at four cardinal points but without any *āyaka* pillars. The third complex is lying adjacent to the second complex. Its stūpa is without spokes and was constructed on a square platform. The steps were provided to reach the stūpa from the western side of the platform. At the eastern side of the stūpa two *cetiyagrahas* facing each other were built [8].

Aparamahāvinaseliya Stūpas

The Aparaśailas were known as Aparamahāvinaseliya in the inscriptions granted to them. Their five sacred complexes are known with the *mahācetiya* in the center of the Valley. The main stūpa of the Aparaśaila is supposed to be the earliest in Nāgārjunakoṇḍa. H. Sarcar says that it was built in the sixth regnal year (246 C.E.) of Virapurusadatta of the Ikṣavāku dynasty [8]. But A. H. Longhurst has ascertained that the stūpa existed even before the Ikṣavāku rule and only *āyaka* platforms were added in this age [3]. This was also attested by epigraphic records that the *āyaka* pillars were built by the princess of the Ikṣavāku family in the reign of Śri Virapurusadatta [4]. This stūpa is the largest in Nāgārjunakoṇḍa with diameter of 27.7 m. It has three concentric circles, connected with each other by the cross and railing walls which have divided the space into 40 chambers. The *āyaka vedica* is built in each cardinal directions surmounted by the *āyaka* pillars [3]. Probably the stūpa had a railing that stood on the brick foundation and the *torana* was built by extending the railing outward [3]. In its evolved stage the dome of the stūpa was plastered indicating that the early stage had only a plain structure. The relics have also been discovered in one of the outer chamber of the stūpa where a fragment of bone was placed in a small round gold reliquary kept in a silver casket together with some gold flowers, pearls, garnets, and crystals [3].

Some other stūpas and vihāras are placed on square platforms and had *āyaka vedicas* with the *āyaka pillars*. The drums of the few stūpas are encased with carved limestone slabs as a good number of bas-relief sculptures have been discovered [7].

Votive Stūpas

The votive stūpas are *samkalpit* made in devotion by the monks as well as the lay-followers. These stūpas of various sizes are built around the main stūpa. Sometimes a separate platform was made to accommodate them [8]. All the votive stūpas of Nāgārjunakoṇḍa are constructed with solid core and without an *āyaka* platform.

Some of the stūpas were decorated with *Svastika* symbols. These *Svastikas* are carved in the center of the base but not visible from the base. The relevance of this symbol is still not known. It seems that it was signifying the religious ideology rather than an architectural attribute.

Cross-References

- ▶ Mahāyāna
- ▶ Stūpa
- ▶ Theravāda
- ▶ Vihāra

References

1. Geiger W (1905) Mahāvaṃsa. Leipzig Press, Leipzig
2. Krishnasastri VV (1922) Three grants of Prithvi Sri Mularaja from Kodavidu. Hyderabad
3. Longhurst AH (1936) The story of the Stūpa. Ceylon Government Press, Colombo
4. Majumdar RC (1954) (ed) The age of imperial unity. Bhartiya Vidya Bhavan Press, Bombay
5. Radhakrishanan S (1958) The cultural heritage of India, vol I. Ramkrishna Mission Press, Calcutta
6. Rama K (1994) Buddhist art of Nāgārjunakoṇḍa. Sundeep Prakashan, New Delhi
7. Ramchandran TN (1953) Nāgārjunakoṇḍa, Memoirs of Archaeological Survey of India, vol 77. Delhi
8. Sarkar H, Mishra BN (1966) Nāgārjunakoṇḍa, Archaeological Survey of India, Goodearth, New Delhi
9. Sastri H (1929–1930) (ed) Epigraphia Indica, vol XX. Archcological Survcy of India, Ncw Dclhi
10. Sastri H (1931–1932) (ed) Epigraphia Indica, vol XXI. Archaeological Survey of India, New Delhi
11. Sircar DC, Chhabra BC (1957–1858) (ed) Epigraphia Indica, vol XXXII. Archaeological Survey of India, New Delhi
12. Sircar DC (1959–1960) (ed) Epigraphia Indica, vol XXXIII. Archaeological Survey of India, New Delhi
13. Sircar DC (1961–1962) (ed) Epigraphia Indica, vol XXXIV. Archaeological Survey of India, New Delhi
14. Sivaramamurti C (1942) Amravati sculptures in the Madras Government Museum Bulletin, vol IV. Madras
15. Subramanyam R (1975) Nāgārjunakoṇḍa, Memoirs of Archaeological Survey of India, vol 75. Archaeological Survey of India, New Delhi

Nāgasena

K. T. S. Sarao
Department of Buddhist Studies, University of Delhi, Delhi, India

Definition

An Indian Buddhist monk who lived in circa second century B.C.E.

Nāgasena was an Indian Buddhist monk who is known for his discussions with King Milinda, the Bactrian Indo-Greek king Menandros/Menander (also spelled as Menadra or Minedra). King Menander ruled in the Kabul-Gandhāra region and is said to have travelled to Sāgala to have a debate with Nāgasena. Sāgala is now identified with the modern city of Sialkot in Pakistan. According to the *Milindapañha*, King Milinda was unhappy with, or rather disparaging toward, Buddhist scholars of his time as none of them could satisfactorily answer his queries. To solve this problem, many leading arahants led by Assagutta along with god Sakka approached a god called Mahāsena to help them by performing the explicit task of dissipating King Milinda's doubts. Mahāsena at that time had been living in Tāvatiṃsa (the Buddhist Heaven of the Thirty-Three). Consequently, Mahāsena gave his consent to make this sacrifice in line with the Bodhisattva ideal to be born as a human on earth so that he could dispel Milinda's doubts and hence promote the principles of the Dharma ([4], pp. 10–11).

He was born in the house of brāhmaṇa Soṇuttara in Kajaṅgala ([4], p. 11). Kajaṅgala was either a town (*nagara*) or a city-state (*janapada*) that formed the eastern boundary of Majjhimadesa ([7], i.197; [3], i.49) and is sometimes identified with Kankjol located 18 miles to the south of Rajmahal in Bihar ([1], pp. 548–549). But according to the Chinese version of the *Milindapañha*, he was from Kashmir ([9], p. 26). He entered the saṃgha (Buddhist Order) under Rohaṇa, later studied under Assagutta at the Vattaniya monastery, and attained the first fruit of emancipation (*sotāpanna*) ([4], pp. 11–13). Thereafter, he was sent to Pāṭaliputra (modern Patna in the Indian province of Bihar), where he studied under monk Dhammarakkhita, and attained arhatship. Subsequently, Nāgasena went to the Saṃkheyya monastery in Sāgala where his momentous dialogue with Milinda took place ([4], 14ff).

Talking about the past lives of Nāgasena and Milinda, the *Milindapañha* ([4], 4ff) mentions that at the time of Kassapa Buddha, they were a monk and novice, respectively, in a monastery located on the banks of the Gaṅgā. On not obeying the monk to remove a heap of rubbish, the novice was hit by the monk with the handle of a broom. Crying and throwing the rubbish, the novice took a vow to be successively reborn until attaining nibbāna and becoming a person of great might and glory. On hearing the novice, the monk also took a vow to be successively reborn until attaining nibbāna and becoming a monk prompt in answering all questions of the novice. Five hundred years after the nibbāna of the Buddha, the novice was born as King Milinda in Sāgala. To answer his questions, the monk was born as Nāgasena.

Nāgasena is depicted in the *Milindapañha* as a monk with unusual qualities who "is shown as astute and able, a ready talker of vast learning and with an immense fund of similes at his command… (who)… also performed… the seemingly incredible feat of mastering the whole of the Abhidhamma Piṭaka after only one exposition of it by Rohana, his preceptor" ([4], xxvi–xxvii). According to a legend told in late medieval Pāli texts, the *Jinakālamālī* and the *Sāsanavaṃsa,* Nāgasena had an ardent wish to make an image of the Buddha which at a future date would illumine the ruling dynasties of Kamboja, Pagan, and Thailand. This resulted in the making of the famous Emerald Buddha which is now popularly worshipped in parts of Southeast Asia (see [4], xxvii).

The sermon, as recorded in the *Milindapañha*, is a compilation of the doctrines of Hīnayāna School where a detailed account of the conversation that took place between Nāgasena and King Milinda is given. King Milinda placed 82 dilemmas before Nāgasena and the latter responded to each of them to the complete satisfaction of the king. At the conclusion of the dialogue, King Milinda appears to have taken shelter in the Triple Gem (*Tisaraṇa*). He also had a monastery built which he named Milindavihāra and gifted to Nāgasena.

Nothing is known of Nāgasena after his lengthy dialogue with the king. The reason for this appears to be that he had been brought into the world of the humans for the sake of the Dharma. After he had completed his job, historical focus appears to have shifted away from him. Despite this, he left behind a method of elucidating the Buddhavacana (teaching of Buddha) which became the blueprint of later exposition. As pointed out by Horner, his refined intermingling of metaphysics and ethics, argument and example, created a module of suitable discourse and an inspiration to practice the Dharma ([4], xxvii). Interestingly, Nāgasena's teacher Assagutta's name appears only in the Pāli commentaries. The names of other teachers, Rohana and Dhammarakkhita, are mentioned only in the *Jinakālamālī* and nowhere else in the Pāli literature. In this regard, Horner has pointed out that "the virtual restriction to *Milindapañha* of so many potentially important figures does not tend to place them in an authentic historical setting" ([4], xxvii).

Cross-References

▶ Abhidhamma Piṭaka
▶ Arahant
▶ Bodhisattva
▶ Dharma
▶ Sagga
▶ Saṃgha

References

1. Cunningham A (1871) The ancient geography of India, I. Trübner, London, Shastri SM (rev and ed) (1924) Chuckervertty, Calcutta
2. Demieville P (1924) Les versions chinoises du Milindapañha. Bull l'Ecole française d'Extreme-Orient XXIV:1–259
3. Fausböll V (ed) (1977–1897) The Jātakas, vol 6. Trübner, London
4. Horner IB (1963–1964) Milinda's questions, vol 2. Luzac, London
5. Little S (1992) The Arhats in China and Tibet. Artibus Asiae 52(3/4):255–281
6. Malalasekera GP (1935) Dictionary of Pali proper names, vol 1, Reprint. Oriental Reprint, New Delhi, 1983
7. Oldenberg H (ed) (1879–1883) The Vinaya Piṭakaṃ, vol 5. Pali Text Society, London
8. Schober J (1997) Sacred biographies in the Buddhist traditions of Southeast Asia. University of Hawai'i Press, Hawai'i
9. Xing G (2005) The concept of the Buddha. Routledge Curzon, London

Nālandā

K. T. S. Sarao
Department of Buddhist Studies, University of Delhi, Delhi, India

Definition

Ancient Indian town and a famous university.

Located about 90 km to the southeast of Patna in Bihar, Nālandā was a center of higher learning from about the fifth century C.E. till the thirteenth century C.E. The ruins of the ancient city of Nālandā have been located about 7 miles each to the southwest of Bihar Sharif and north-northwest Rājagīr. Early Buddhist texts mention Nālandā as an influential, wealthy, and prosperous city (*nagara*), which was crowded and thickly populated ([14], i.377; [11], i.211). The Buddha often stayed here at the Pāvārikambavana during his visits ([14], i.371). This city was connected through a road to both Rājagaha and Pāṭaliputta ([11], ii.81, 84; [8], p. 287). A *cetiya* (sepulchral cairn) known as Bahuputta is said to have been located between Rājagaha and Nālandā ([4], ii.220) which were one *yojana* (about 7 miles) apart ([12], i.35). Once at the Buddha's time, this city is said to have suffered from a severe famine ([4], v.322).

As initially Nālandā was a Jaina stronghold, it remained relatively unknown compared with other Buddhist sites until the Gupta dynasty ([10], p. 59). When the Chinese pilgrim, Faxian, visited Nālandā toward the beginning of the fifth century C.E., he did not see anything of Buddhist importance here. But when Xuanzang visited it in the second quarter of the seventh century, it had become internationally famous and it seems that its rise to fame happened sometime after Faxian's visit ([10], p. 59). The famous University of Nālandā was established in the first half of the fifth century C.E. during the reign of King Śakrāditya of the Gupta Dynasty ([3], p. 329). Xuanzang reported about 10,000 students and 1,511 teachers. When Yijing, another Chinese Buddhist monk, visited here in 673–695 C.E.,

Nālandā, Fig. 1 Ancient Nālandā

there were eight colleges with 300 rooms and 3,500 students. Apart from the Gupta kings, Nālandā University was patronized by King Harṣa and the Pālas ([3], p. 329). At the time of King Harṣa, the university is reported to have owned 200 villages that had been given to it as grants.

The history of ancient Nālandā University may broadly be divided into two parts (see [3], p. 344):

1. The period of growth, development, and maturity from the sixth to the ninth century C.E., when it followed overwhelmingly liberal traditions inherited from the Gupta period
2. The period of gradual decline and ultimate oblivion from the ninth to the thirteenth century C.E. when the tantric developments within Buddhism had become quite pronounced in eastern India

According to Hwui-Li, the author of *The Life of Xuanzang*, Nālandā was held in contempt by some Theravādins for its emphasis on philosophy of the Mahāyāna School ([6], p. 171). Vajrayāna appears to have made its appearance at Nālandā by about the mid-seventh century C.E. but was probably not accepted as a mainstream school until the ninth century C.E. Some orthodox Sri Lankan monks are reported to have destroyed the Vajrayāna scriptures and images in Buddhist establishments ([7], pp. 185–191, 369). However, by the Pāla period, secular and Brāhmaṇical-Hindu courses were being taught alongside with Buddhist ones at Nālandā (Fig. 1).

Nālandā was one of the world's first residential universities with dormitories for students. The building was considered an architectural masterpiece and was marked by a lofty wall and one gate. It had eight separate compounds and ten temples, along with many other meditation halls and classrooms located in the midst of lakes and parks. The subjects taught here covered a wide range of learning. During its golden days, the university attracted scholars and students from as far away as Tibet, China, Korea, Japan, Indonesia, Turkey, Greece, and Greater Persia. Some of the famous Buddhist scholars who had either studied or taught at Nālandā were Nāgārjuna, Dinnāga, Candrakīrti, Śīlabhadra, Dharmakīrti, Jinamitra, Śāntarakṣita, Padmasambhava, Xuanzang, Vajrabhodhi, Amoghavajra, Nāropa, Atiśa, and Rāhulaśrībhadra. The title *acāriya* (equivalent to modern doctorate) was conferred upon those of outstanding academic achievements and who had mastered the five sciences, i.e., grammar and philology, medicine, logic, metaphysics, and fine arts ([3], p. 323). "During its long and memorable lifespan Nālandā, though functioned primarily as a Buddhist university, also accommodated and trained countless individuals from diverse backgrounds including Buddhist and non-Buddhist, the novice and wise, the young and aged, the religious and secular, Indians and foreigners alike" ([10], p. 59).

The library at Nālandā University was an immense complex where students and teachers produced copies of texts meticulously. Called the Dharmagaṅgā, or Piety Mart, it consisted of three large buildings: the Ratnasāgara, the Ratnadadhi, and the Ratnarañjaka. The Ratnadadhi, meaning the Ocean of Gems, was nine stories high and housed the most sacred manuscripts including the Prajñāpāramitā Sūtra and the Guhyasamāja ([2], p. 4). According to the *Bhāskara Saṃhitā*, the library was housed in a "finely built stone building" and each manuscript was covered with cloth, tied, and kept on shelves. The librarian was not only responsible for maintaining the materials but also for guiding readers in their studies ([9], p. 4). The exact number of volumes of the Nālandā University Library is not known but it is estimated to have been in the hundreds of thousands. Apart from religious texts, the library collected manuscripts on subjects such as grammar, logic, literature, astrology, astronomy, and medicine. The library of Nālandā University followed a cataloging scheme which was possibly based on a text classification scheme developed by the great Sanskrit linguist Pāṇinī ([9], p. 4).

Nālandā University was ransacked by Bakhtiyar Khilji, a general of Qutb-ud-din Aibak, in 1193. The Persian historian Minhaj al-Siraj, in his chronicle the *Tabaqat-i-Nasiri*, reports that thousands of monks were burned alive and an equal number beheaded. The "smoke from the burning manuscripts hung for days like a dark pall over the low hills" ([13], p. 188). The last abbot of Nālandā, Śākyaśrībhadra, fled to Tibet in 1204. According to a Tibetan legend, the university and library were reportedly repaired shortly after by Muditabhadra, a Buddhist sage. When the Tibetan monk Dharmasvāmin visited Nālandā in 1,235, he found it damaged and plundered with a 90-year-old teacher, Rāhula Śrībhadra, instructing a class of about 70 students. Unfortunately, the library was again burned by Tīrthaka mendicants ([2], p. 28). Whatever remained of the extremely enervated Buddhist community, it appears to have struggle with scarce resources until about 1,400 when Chagalarāja was reportedly the last king to have patronized Nālandā ([7], pp. 206–213).

The excavations conducted at Nālandā so far have mainly concentrated on the monastic area where nothing prior to the Guptas has been found ([1], 1925–1926, 100–107; 1926–1927, 127–35; 1928–1929, 85–87; [5], 1975–1976, 8–9; 1976–1977, 13; 1977–1978, 16; 1978–1979, 67; 1979–1980, 14; 1981–1982, 12). Majority of the structural remains date from the Pāla period, though a number of them have an earlier nucleus. The total area covered by the ruins is more than 2 × 1 miles (1,280 acres.)

Cross-References

- ▶ Candrakīrti
- ▶ Faxian (337–422 C.E.)
- ▶ Mahāyāna
- ▶ Nāgārjuna
- ▶ Prajñāpāramitā-Hṛdaya Sūtra
- ▶ Rājagaha (Pāli)
- ▶ Xuanzang (Hieun-Tsang)

References

1. Annual report of the archaeological survey of India. Government of India, New Delhi
2. Datta BK (1970) Libraries and librarianship of ancient and medieval India. Atma Ram, Delhi
3. Dutt S (1962) Buddhist monks and monasteries of India: their history and contribution to Indian culture. George Allen and Unwin, London
4. Feer ML (ed) (1884–1898) The Saṃyutta Nikāya, vol 5. Pali Text Society, London
5. Indian archaeology: a review. Journal of the Archaeological Survey of India, New Delhi
6. Joshi L (1967) Studies in the Buddhistic culture of India. Motilal Banarsidass, Delhi
7. Misra BN (1998) Nālandā, vol 1. Munshiram Manoharlal Publishers, New Delhi

8. Oldenberg H (ed) (1879–1883) The Vinaya Piṭakaṃ, vol 5. Pali Text Society, London
9. Patel J, Kumar K (2001) Libraries and librarianship in India. Greenwood Press, Westport
10. Phuoc LH (2012) Buddhist architecture. Kindle edition, Grafikol
11. Rhys Davids TW, Carpentier JE (eds) (1890–1911) The Dīgha Nikāya, vol 3. Pali Text Society, London
12. Rhys Davids TW, Carpentier JE, Stede W (eds) (1886–1932) The Sumaṅgala-Vilāsinī: Buddhaghosa's commentary on the Dīgha Nikāya, vol 3. PTS, London
13. Sen GE (1964) The story of early Indian civilization. Orient Longmans, Delhi
14. Trenckner V, Chalmers R (eds) (1888–1896) The Majjhima Nikāya, vol 3. Pali Text Society, London

Nallamalai

▶ Nāgārjunakoṇḍa

Nāma-rūpa

Bhikkhu Anālayo
Center for Buddhist Studies, University of Hamburg, Balve, Germany

Synonyms

Name-and-form

Definition

Nāma-rūpa has two related but slightly distinct meanings. In one sense, the term refers to "name-and-form" as the fourth of the twelve links in the standard presentation in Buddhist texts of dependent arising, *paṭicca samuppāda*. Alternatively, *nāma-rūpa* can also stand for "mind-and-matter."

Mind and Matter

The sense of *nāma-rūpa* as "mind-and-matter" is evident in the historically later commentarial conception of *nāma-rūpa-pariccheda-ñāṇa*, the "knowledge of delimitating mind-and-matter." This knowledge corresponds to the third of seven stages of mental purification that form the scaffolding of a central manual of the Theravāda tradition, the *Visuddhimagga* ([1], p. 587). Knowledge of delimitating mind-and-matter goes hand in hand with the "knowledge of discerning conditions," *paccaya-pariggaha-ñāṇa*.

Together these two knowledges represent the insight that what subjectively is seen as a compact "I" at the core of experience is in reality made up of different components – in particular of material and mental parts – which interrelate with each other by way of conditionality. This understanding, which corresponds to the purification of views in a scheme of seven purifications, is a basic requirement for the development of insight. Based on this understanding, the development of insight by contemplating the impermanent, unsatisfactory, and not-self nature of all aspects of subjective experience takes place.

To appreciate the meaning of knowledge of delimitating mind-and-matter, it needs noting that the two terms *nāma* and *rūpa* are grouped together. This is the case when *nāma-rūpa* has the sense of "mind-and-matter" in the context of the commentarial scheme of insight knowledges as well as when it carries the meaning of "name-and-form" in the context of dependent arising, *paṭicca samuppāda*. This grouping together reflects the fact that early Buddhism does not pin body against mind. Instead, the two are seen as interdependent and closely related phenomena.

Name and Form

The other sense of *nāma-rūpa* as "name-and-form" is relevant to the early Buddhist doctrine of dependent arising, *paṭicca samuppāda*, which in its standard formulation has ignorance as its beginning point and via a series of intermittent links leads up to the genesis of *dukkha* – a term whose meaning ranges from barely noticeable dissatisfaction to outright suffering as inherent features of human existence. The whole series of links of the dependent arising of *dukkha* proceeds through the following steps, each of which forms a condition for the next one:

- Ignorance
- Volitional formations
- Consciousness
- Name-and-form
- Six senses
- Contact
- Feeling
- Craving
- Clinging
- Becoming
- Birth
- Old age and death

In this series of conditionally related links, *nāma-rūpa* stands between consciousness and the six senses. According to the standard definition of *nāma-rūpa* in relation to this series of links, *rūpa* stands for materiality by way of the four great elements ([2], Vol. I, p. 53). These four great elements are earth, water, fire, and wind, which according to tradition stand representative for the four material qualities of solidity, cohesion, temperature, and motion. In short, *rūpa* thus stands for the experience of matter.

Nāma, on the other hand, comprises the mental aspects of feeling, *vedanā*, perception, *saññā*, volition, *cetanā*, contact, *phassa*, and attention, *manasikāra*. This definition is significant insofar as here *nāma* does not comprise the whole of the mind. Consciousness, being a condition for *nāma-rūpa* in the series of conditionally related links of dependent arising, *paṭicca samuppāda*, is itself not part of what it conditions: *nāma-rūpa*. This difference needs to be clearly noted, since, as mentioned above, the expression *nāma-rūpa* can elsewhere refer to mind-and-matter, with *nāma* including consciousness and thereby representing the mind in its entirety. The *Visuddhimagga* in fact shows clear awareness of these two distinct usages, as it indicates that, in the context of dependent arising, *nāma* stands only for the three aggregates of feeling, perception, and volitional formations ([1], p. 558), different from the way the same work understands the implications of *nāma* in the context of *nāma-rūpa-pariccheda-ñāṇa*.

In the context of dependent arising, then, *nāma* stands only for those mental activities that are experienced by consciousness. These are, according to the above definition, feeling, perception volition, contact, and attention. In this way, this definition of *nāma* assembles those particular mental factors that are required for the coming into being of a "name" in its basic sense. Contact and attention provide the first input of a previously unknown object. This object is then felt and perceived, and eventually something will be done with it. The whole complex of mental operations that in this way takes place finds its conjunction in the "name" under which the hitherto unknown object will be remembered and conceptualized.

This sense of naming is also evident in a closer examination of *nāma-rūpa* provided in another discourse, which indicates that in the absence of *nāma* there would be no "designation contact," *adhivacana-samphassa* ([3], Vol. II, p. 62). Similarly, in the absence of *rūpa* there would be no "resistance contact," *paṭigha-samphassa*. In other words, *nāma* is responsible for conceptual designation in the sense of identification or "naming," whereas *rūpa* provides the input of resistance in the sense of experienced materiality.

The range of *nāma-rūpa* – as the conceptual and apparitional aspects of an object (using the term "apparitional" for the entire physical appearance of the object, not only for its visual impact) – encompasses the whole gamut of what is present to consciousness. This can be seen in one discourse which explicitly speaks of "this body and external name-and-form" ([4], Vol. II, p. 24), where *nāma-rūpa* appears to represent the entire field of experience available to consciousness.

In iconic representations of the twelve links of dependent arising, *nāma-rūpa* is at times represented by a blind person and a cripple. The cripple cannot walk, but needs to be carried by the blind person. The blind person cannot see, but needs to be told the proper direction by the cripple. Comparable to these two, *nāma* and *rūpa* cooperate to bring about what is experienced by consciousness.

In this way, *nāma-rūpa* depends on consciousness, in the sense that the conceptual and apparitional aspects of an object require consciousness in order to be experienced. In turn, consciousness depends on name-and-form as that which provides the content of what is experienced by consciousness.

This relationship between name-and-form and consciousness is comparable to two bundles of reeds that lean against each other ([4], Vol. II, p. 114). When one is removed, the other will fall as well. The reciprocal conditioning of name-and-form and consciousness was apparently part of the pre-awakening development of insight of the bodhisattva Gotama, the Buddha-to-be ([4], Vol. II, p. 104). His realization of this relationship is described in the following way: "Consciousness revolves around and does not go beyond name-and-form. It is to this extent that one may be born, become old, die, pass away, and be reborn, that is, when conditioned by name-and-form there is consciousness and conditioned by consciousness there is name-and-form."

The reciprocal conditioning of consciousness and name-and-form ([3], Vol. II, p. 56), highlighted in this way, presents a basic matrix of experience, which from an early Buddhist perspective turns out to be an interaction of contact by way of resistance and designation with consciousness as that which experiences such contact. It is the interplay of these two aspects – consciousness on the one side and name-and-form on the other – that makes up the "world" of experience.

The repercussions of this continuous interplay finds its expression in a dictum, according to which living beings who are entrenched in name-and-form hold it to be real to such an extent that they come to conceive as a self what is devoid of a self ([5], 756).

Another aspect of the same situation is the role played by craving. A simile presents this theme by identifying name as one end and form as the other, while consciousness stands in the middle. In this setting, craving is the seamstress that keeps it all together ([6], Vol. III, p. 400).

The solution to this predicament is to eradicate all craving for *nāma-rūpa* ([4], Vol. I, p. 12). What according to early Buddhist thought lies beyond the reciprocal conditioning of *nāma-rūpa* and consciousness, then, is the experience of Nirvāṇa. As a verse sums up:

> Where water, earth,
> fire and wind do not gain a footing,
> here the streams turn back and the whirlpool no longer revolves,
> here name-and-form ceases entirely ([4], Vol. I, p. 15).

Cross-References

- ▶ Mind (Buddhism)
- ▶ Vijñāna
- ▶ Viññāṇa

References

1. Rhys Davids CAF (ed) (1920) The Visuddhimagga of Buddhaghosa. Pali Text Society, London
2. Trenckner V, Chalmers R (eds) (1888–1896) The Majjhima Nikāya, 3 vols. Pali Text Society, London
3. Carpenter JE, Rhys Davids TW (eds) (1890–1911) The Dīgha Nikāya, 3 vols. Pali Text Society, London
4. Feer L (ed) (1888–1898) The Saṃyutta Nikāya, 5 vols. Pali Text Society, Oxford
5. Andersen D, Smith H (ed) (1913) The Sutta-nipāta. Pali Text Society, London (references are by stanza)
6. Morris R, Hardy E (eds) (1885–1900) The Aṅguttara Nikāya, 5 vols. Pali Text Society, London
7. Hamilton S (1996) Nāmarūpa. In id. Identity and experience, the constitution of the human being according to early Buddhism. Luzac Oriental, London, pp 121–137
8. Ñāṇananda (1985) The Vortical interplay – consciousness versus name-and-form. In: id. The magic of the mind. BPS, Kandy, pp 25–33
9. Reat NR (1987) Some fundamental concepts of Buddhist psychology. Religion 17:15–28
10. Wayman A (1982/1984) A study of the Vedāntic and Buddhist theory of Nāma-Rūpa. In: Hercus LA (ed) Indological and Buddhist studies. Delhi, Sri Satguru, pp 617–642

Namaskāra Mantra

▶ Ṇamōkarā Mantra

Name-and-Form

▶ *Nāma-rūpa*

Ṇamōkarā Mantra

Brianne Donaldson
Claremont School of Theology, Claremont, CA, USA

Synonyms

Namaskāra mantra; Navakār Mahā-mantra; Navkār mantra; Pañca namaskāra mantra

Definition

An ancient Prākrit homage to the five types of illumined personages worthy of reverence in the Jain worldview.

Daily Practice

The fivefold salutation (pañca namaskāra) of the Ṇamōkarā mantra is the most recited in Jain devotional practices. It honors the five revered personalities (parameṣṭins) in the Jain mokṣa-mārga:

Ṇamo arahaṃtāṇaṃ – I honor the Arhats (those illumined Jinas or Tīrthaṇkaras).
Ṇamo siddhāṇaṃ – I honor the siddhas (those who have achieved mokṣa).
Ṇamo āyariyāṇaṃ – I honor the Ācāryas (the Jain spiritual leaders).
Ṇamo uvajjhāyāṇaṃ – I honor the Upādhyāyas (the Jain spiritual teachers).
Ṇamo loe savva-sāhūṇaṃ – I honor the monks and nuns of the world.

To these five lines, the Mūrtipūjaka Śvetāmbara Jains add ([6], p. 115):

Eso pañca ṇamokkāro savva-pāvappaṇāsaṇo
maṃgalāṇaṃ ca savvesiṃ paḍhamaṃ havai maṃgalam

This fivefold salutation destroys bad karma and obstacles. And among all auspicious statements, it is the first and foremost.

This mantra offers benefit to those who hear it, but more so for those who speak it ([4], p. 46). It is both an outward veneration and the cultivation of noble qualities within the Self ([7], p. 241). Its recitation is thought to offer protection, give success, destroy karma, and cure illnesses ([3], p. 95). Because of its condensed power, it subsumes other mantras and practices and functions as a replacement for sacrifice ([4], p. 82). Jains recite this mantra in all liturgies, ascetic initiations, and before any important act. Devout Jains recite the mantra in order to eliminate pride and ego and to reflect on one's personal vows and the deepening of those commitments toward new vows ([2], p. 199).

History

Like the Jain scriptures, the five salutations are considered to be without beginning or author, potentially transmitted from the tīrthaṇkaras through their gaṇadharas. The origin of the mantra is unknown, but the Arhats and siddhas are mentioned in an inscription of King Khāravela (circa 150 B.C.E.) and textual evidence supports Vīrasena's claims (eighth century C.E.) that it was expanded to five homages in the Digambara *Ṣaṭkhaṇḍāgama* (ca. second century C.E.), though it is unclear whether the alleged author Puṣpadanta composed it or merely inserted it. The Śvetambara *Bhagavatī Sūtra* begins with a fivefold homage to the Brāhmī script and scriptures rather than ascetics, and the mantra is also found at the beginning of the Śvetambara *Prajñāpanā Sūtra*, though some suspect it was a later interpolation ([8], p. 153).

Story and Symbol

The mantra is a transformational tool in many Jain stories ([1], p. 82). The medieval tale of Śrīpāl and Mayṇasundarī features the mantra as part of the extensive Navpad Oḷī fast that cured not only Śrīpāl's leprosy but hundreds of other lepers as well ([4], p. 82). The mantra is often linked to the Navpad (nine post) yantra which is the visual representation of the five salutations, plus the Three

Jewels of right perception, knowledge, and action, along with a fourth aspiration of right austerity. This yantra is venerated in the Navpad pūjā, the Siddhacakra mahāpūjā, and the ritual fasts of Navpad Oḷi and Āyambil Oḷī ([4], p. 200 n. 2).

Cross-References

► Arhat (Sanskrit)
► Moksha
► Prākrit

References

1. Dundas P (2002) The Jains, 2nd edn. Routledge, New York
2. Jaini P (2001) The Jaina path of purification. Motilal Banarsidass, Delhi
3. Kelting MW (2001) Singing to the Jinas: Jain laywomen, Maṇḍaḷ singing, and the negotiations of Jain devotion. Oxford University Press, New York
4. Kelting MW (2009) Heroic wives: rituals, stories, and the virtues of Jain wifehood. Oxford University Press, New York
5. Kumar S (1987) Song of the soul: an introduction to the Ṇamōkar Mantra. Siddhachalam Publishers, Blairstown
6. Long J (2009) Jainism: an introduction. I. B. Tauris, New York
7. Titze K (2001) Jainism: a pictorial guide to the religion of non-violence. Motilal Banarsidass, Delhi
8. Wiley K (2010) The A to Z of Jainism. Scarecrow Press, Lanham

Napumsaka

► Homosexuality (Jainism)

Napumsakaveda

► Homosexuality (Jainism)

Naraka

► Hell (Buddhism)

Nāthadeva

► Avalokiteśvara

Nature Worship (Buddhism)

Christopher Hrynkow
Department of Religion and Culture, Saint Thomas More College, University of Saskatchewan, Saskatoon, SK, Canada

Synonyms

Bio-spiritual practices in Buddhism; Buddhist animism; Buddhist veneration of the natural world

Definition

The veneration of elements of the natural world, the cosmos, or natural phenomena by Buddhists.

Buddhist Nature Worship and Bio-spirituality

Nature worship is associated with the veneration of animals, plants, geological forms, the cosmos, and geophysical phenomena like the wind and earthquakes. Religious studies scholarship, both implicitly and explicitly, has often been categorized as a more primitive animist spiritual practice as opposed to a "true" religion. This dichotomy has been most marked in Western-influenced scholarship. However, with an emerging focus on non-formal religious practices and consciousness of the problematic nature of the Earth crisis, there is a growing corpus of literature dealing with issues at the intersection of religion and ecology. In particular, there is increasing interest in practices and teachings that accord spiritual value to nonhuman elements of the natural world.

Buddhism and Buddhist themes figure prominently in these scholarly writings.

Buddhism can offer fertile soil for cultivating a bio-spiritual ecological ethic. One of the most obvious places to look for animist worldviews within the religion are practices associated with trees. Religious tree worship preceded the genesis of Buddhism in India. As it sprung its own branches and roots, Buddhism adapted select tree-centered spiritual practices in a syncretistic manner. Of particular importance in this regard are that trees are associated with the life of the Buddha. The sal tree species is venerated as a result of its connection to both the birth and death of the Buddha. The Asoka tree and plaksha tree are considered sacred due their importance in Siddhārtha Gautama's birth [1]. He later achieved enlightenment under a pipal tree, which then became known as the Bodhi tree. The descendant of the original tree remains on the site in Bodh Gaya, Bihar, which is the most central of the four main pilgrimage sites associated with the life of the Buddha. As a result of its close association with the enlightenment moment and its importance in other Indian religious traditions, the tree species, a wild fig, was giving the name *Ficus religiosa*. In general, large and old trees are particularly revered in Buddhism. Explicitly acknowledging pre-Buddhist animist roots to the veneration of trees, Buddhist scholar Lila de Silva nonetheless strongly asserts that the veneration of trees does not violate the belief system of Buddhism [2].

Due to these associations with sacredness combined with the spiritual importance of forest-dwelling and meditation in natural surroundings, Buddhists monks are forbidden to cut down trees. One story connected to this tradition speaks of a monk who cut a branch of a tree long ago only to have the spirit of the tree complain to Buddha. Other plants are also granted respect and strict Buddhists tend to be vegetarians and may avoid eating seeds so as to allow plants to continue in their life force. Considered to have a particularly strong life force, the lotus flower is another scared plant, said to have sprung up in the first steps of the Buddha taken immediately after his birth. For Buddhists, all animals also have spirits and have the opportunity to someday gain enlightenment, making them worthy of respect [3]. The worldview growing from these understandings serves to engender a deep vision on interconnectedness based on the Buddha's teaching that humans share kinship with other species on a continuum of life [4]. A recurring image in Buddhist teaching that reinforces the understanding of such a deep connectivity is Mahayana Buddhism's rendering of Indra's Net, an infinitely massive web with a multi-faced jewel at each point of connection, which reflects all the other jewels in the net [5]. For those who venerate the Buddha, the possibility that he might take on animal form within this reality of connectivity in order to teach or be present in a particular context further encourages reverence for life [4].

The Buddha also explained in his teachings that he enjoyed his animal lives as much as his human lives. In many senses, Buddhist duties extend to other members of the natural world, as exemplified by the figure of the bodhisattva who comes back in compassion to help other sentient beings reach enlightenment [4]. Even for the individual seeking enlightenment, as noted by eighth century Indian Buddhist scholar, Shantideva, the wilderness, uncontrolled by humanity, is considered the place, even above a monastery or a town, which best fostered religious insights [6]. In short, the immanence of the sacred permeates the natural world in Buddhist spirituality, which, as a result, tends toward an animistic recognition of the Buddha-nature present in all things.

Such animist practices and teachings are often interesting from a phenomenological and ethnographical perspective. In addition, if the historian of religions Thomas Berry's insight that the human is derivative and the earth is primary [7] is taken seriously, then the (re)enchantment of the world accompanying animist worldviews is not primitive but, rather, is progressive in a significant and practical sense in this world. These teachings and practices help to accord a form of moral worth to nonhuman elements of the natural world. In this regard, humans are counseled by Buddhist teachings to live like a bee drinking nectar and bringing life to the flower through pollination without destroying that which sustains its bodily being

[4]. According to a Buddhist-influenced Berryite perspective, adopting such an attitude toward faithful living helps to ensure that the intertwined human and Earth projects succeed [7]. In the end, fostering that dual success may prove to be the ultimate value of animist-oriented Buddhist nature spiritualities.

Cross-References

▶ Bodhi Tree
▶ Pilgrimage (Buddhism)

References

1. Randhawa MS (1964) The cult of tress and tree-worship in Buddhist-Hindu sculpture. All India Fine Arts and Crafts Society, New Delhi
2. Kabilsigh C (1987) How Buddhism can help protect nature. In: Davies S (ed) Tree of life: Buddhism and protection of nature. Buddhist Perception of Nature Project, Hong Kong
3. de Silva L (1992) The Hills wherein my soul delights. In: Batchelor M, Kerry B (eds) Buddhism and ecology, World Wide Fund for Nature Series. Cassel, London
4. Cain C (2009) Down to earth: religious paths toward custodianship of nature. University Press of America, Lanham
5. Batchelor S (1992) The sands of the Ganges: notes towards a Buddhist ecological philosophy. In: Batchelor M, Kerry B (eds) Buddhism and ecology, World Wide Fund for Nature Series. Cassel, London
6. Batchelor M (1992) Even the stones smile. In: Batchelor M, Kerry B (eds) Buddhism and ecology, World Wide Fund for Nature Series. Cassel, London
7. Berry T (2009) The Sacred Universe: earth, spirituality, and religion in the twenty-first century. Columbia University Press, New York

Navakār Mahā-Mantra

▶ Ṇamōkarā Mantra

Navayāna

▶ Engaged Buddhism

Navkār Mantra

▶ Ṇamōkarā Mantra

Nayavāda

▶ Relativity (Jainism)

Neru

▶ Meru (Buddhism)

Nigoda

Michael Anderson
Claremont School of Theology, Claremont
Lincoln University, Claremont, CA, USA

Synonyms

Sadharana

Definition

Submicroscopic, undifferentiated, colonial creatures.

Introduction

Foundational to Jain cosmology and ethics is the *jīva*, or soul. Unique to Jainism is the idea that there are innumerable souls that suffuse all of reality ([1], p. 149). As an individual *jīva* progresses toward liberation, it is born and reborn into new embodiments based on its karmic burden. These embodiments stem from the rebirth destinies (*gatis*), which is divided into four categories: human beings (*manusyas*), heavenly beings (*devas*), hell beings (*narakis*), and animals and plants (*tiryanca*) ([2], p. 39). The latter category of animals and plants is described as "the lowest of possible destinies" and is characterized as possessing "extremely gross sensory activity and pervasive ignorance" ([3], p. 109). This group is further divided into several subgroups based on sensory capacity, of which the lowest form is the *nigoda*.

Classifying the *Nigoda*

The *nigoda* is a type of *ekendriyas*, "single-sense beings whose whole awareness is limited to the tactile mode" ([4], p. 126). However, they are quite dissimilar from other one-sensed beings. For instance, Padmanabh Jaini describes that the category of *ekendriyas* is composed of four types of elemental bodies and *vanaspati* (plant bodies). The latter is divided further into *pratyeka* and *nigoda*. Elemental bodies and *pratyeka* are defined as having "a rudimentary body for some soul" and "an entire plant-body 'to themselves' (i.e., one plant/one soul)," respectively ([4], pp. 126–127). The dissimilarity is due to the fact that *nigoda* exists "at so low a level that they do not even possess an individual body, but rather exist as a part of a cluster or 'ball' (*goluka*) or organisms of the same type" ([4], p. 127). Elemental bodies and plant bodies are one to one; meanwhile, the *nigoda* exists in a colony of tiny, undifferentiated creatures.

Indeed, the *nigoda* is a form of vegetal life that is "characterized by innumerable souls sharing a common body" ([2], p. 39). Kristi Wiley explains that "[t]he body of a *nigoda* is formed by the operation of the common body-making karma (*sadharana sarira nama karma*), and such bodies are called 'group souled' (*samanya*)" ([2], p. 54). Once the body is formed, it lives for an incredibly long period of time; however, the souls born within it live for but a fraction of a second before they die and are reborn again within it. Ellison Banks Findly explains how these beings are found in every part of the universe, much like elemental bodies; however, they are distinguished in that they can "inhabit such places as the tissues of plant, animal and human hosts, and are said to contract and expand, 'as the requirements may be, to fit in with the corporeal frames'" ([5], p. 118). Illustrating this further, Findly describes all the space of the world as "closely packed with [*nigoda*] like a box filled with powder" ([5], p. 118).

Jaini points out, however, that two types of souls exist within *nigoda*. The first, *itara-nigodas* (also known as *caturgati nigoda* or *vyavaharika nigoda*), are those who "have at some time been in higher states [of embodiment] but have fallen back" ([4], p. 127). This is illustrated by the story of Makkhali Gośāla, the leader of the Ājīvika sect of Indian philosophy. The story states that Gośāla committed a deed so terrible that he was reborn as a *nigoda*. This deed was "the ultimate heresy," in that he said that "knowledge was in no way efficacious in terms of the possibility of attaining *mokṣa*" ([4], p. 127). The second type of soul is the *nitya-nigoda*, "those which have *never yet* been out of *nigoda* existence" ([4], p 127). The unique Śvetambara term for this type of soul is *avyavaharika nigoda*, which means those that are "'not susceptible of specific designation'" ([4], p. 128). These souls have never experienced individual embodiment; rather, they have only experienced reality within the colonial body of a *nigoda*.

N

Karmic Discontinuities

Jaini raises the issue of two unforeseen consequences with the idea of certain souls always having been *nigodas*. First, he asks what happens with the fact that as souls experience "departure" via *mokṣa*, why has not the universe been emptied of living souls? The response is the very fact of the *nitya-nigoda* prevents this; indeed, the *nitya-nigoda* are "infinite (*anantananta*) in number" and thus "provide an inexhaustible reservoir of souls" ([4], p. 128). However, this leads to the second consequence: "that there is in fact a definite beginning and end to *samsara*, and that a soul's progress from the former to the latter seems in many respects to mirror the very evolution of consciousness itself" ([4], p. 129).

It is argued that Jains do not wish to view "[o]ne-sensed beings... as primitive forms of life whose souls are in the initial stages of a progressive linear evolutionary development into two-sensed life-forms, and so forth" ([2], p. 40). This, as Jaini suggests, "flies in the face of their cherished belief in cyclic, beginningless operation of karma" ([4], p. 129). One way Jains have challenged this is by claiming some stories of "groups of souls sometimes leav[ing] *nigoda* existence and proceed[ing] directly to the human destiny, from which, with no further rebirths, they attain to *siddha*-hood" ([4], p. 129). Jaini speculates that the issue of the *nigoda* could suggest the doctrine of karma being a "later" development to an already "well-developed theoretical framework describing the operation of the universe" ([4], p. 129).

Challenging Ahimsa, Considering Ecology

The submicroscopic *nigoda* radically challenges the principle of *ahimsa*, or nonviolence. As Jeffery Long explains, "[f]or human beings, the very act of being alive involves the destruction of such tiny life forms. Eating, digesting food, breathing, sitting, and moving about: all involve the destruction of *nigodas* on a massive scale" ([6], p. 100). It is said that *nigodas* "especially [concentrate] in the flesh of human beings and animals as well as in certain roots and bulbs" ([4], p. 127). These creatures also are prevalent in other substances, such as "liquor or honey" or anything else "where fermentation or sweetness is present" ([3], p. 168). Thus, it is obvious to see how certain Jain dietary practices developed, as this would lead to the death of innumerable souls. Additionally, the sheer presence of *nigodas* offers a rationale for the limited movement and use of the *muhpatti* by some Jain ascetics. Ahimsa, it seems, requires a well-cultivated "*nigoda* consciousness."

Indeed, this "*nigoda* consciousness" is critical, especially when one takes into consideration Anne Vallely's exploration of the creative understanding of *nigoda* and *ahimsa* by Jains affected by diaspora. She describes how "[t]he traditional Jain concern for the smallest of life-forms (individual *nigodas*) has been transformed into a general concern for 'the environment' and is expressed within a discourse of ecology" ([7], p. 206). This new interpretation highlights what Vallely suggests as a Jain consideration of nature as a "'moral theater,'" and "[r]ather than being trivial, it is the harm done to these small life-forms (each endowed with a soul) that is the primary cause of our karmic bondage" ([7], p. 215).

The *nigodas* are of critical importance to Jain cosmology and ethics. Over time, Jains have been able to specify with technical detail the exact natures and classifications of *nigoda* in relation to other one-sensed beings but also between different types of souls that exist within a *nigoda*. However, that does not mean that they do not come without their challenges. Indeed, while the system accepts *nigodas* in their microscopic abundance, they challenge both the understanding of karma and *ahimsa*.

Cross-References

▶ Ahimsa
▶ Ecology (Buddhism)
▶ Jīva
▶ Karma (Jainism)
▶ Saṃsāra

References

1. Chapple CK (2006) Jainism and ecology: transformation of tradition. In: Gottlieb RS (ed) The Oxford handbook of religion and ecology. Oxford University Press, Oxford, pp 147–159
2. Wiley KL (2002) The nature of nature: Jain perspectives on the natural world. In: Chapple CK (ed) Jainism and ecology: nonviolence in the web of life. Harvard University Press, Cambridge, pp 35–39
3. Jaini PS (1998) The Jaina path of purification. Motilal Banarsidass, Delhi
4. Jaini PS (2000) Collected papers on Jaina studies. Motilal Banarsidass, Delhi
5. Findly EB (1996) Plant lives: borderline beings in Indian traditions. Motilal Banarsidass, Delhi

6. Long JD (2009) Jainism: an introduction. I.B. Tauris, London
7. Vallely A (2002) From liberation to ecology: ethical discourse among orthodox and diaspora Jains. In: Chapple CK (ed) Jainism and ecology: nonviolence in the web of life. Harvard University Press, Cambridge, pp 193–216

Nikāya Buddhism

▶ Theravāda

Niraya

▶ Hell (Buddhism)

Nirīśvaravāda

▶ Atheism (Buddhism)

Nirukta

▶ Commentarial Literature

Nirvana

▶ Heaven (Jainism)

Nirvāṇa

▶ Parinirvāṇa

Niyati

▶ Fate (Buddhism)

Noble Truths

▶ Aryasacca

No-Ego

▶ Anattā (Buddhism)

Non-dualistic

▶ Mysticism (Buddhism)

Nonliving Substance

▶ Ajīva

Non-returner

▶ *Anāgāmin*

Non-sentient Substance

▶ Ajīva

Non-soul

▶ Ajīva

Nonviolence

▶ Ahiṃsā (Buddhism)

N

Northwestern Prakrit

► Kharoṣṭhī Script

No-Self

► Anattā (Buddhism)

No-Soul

► Anattā (Buddhism)

No-Soul (Buddhism)

► Anattā (Buddhism)

Nothing

► Śūnya

Nothingness

► Śūnyatā

Nuns (Buddhism)

► Bhikkhunī

Nyāya-śāstra

► Logic (Buddhism)

O

Objective Idealism

► Idealism (Buddhism)

Occultism

► Mysticism (Buddhism)

Offering

► Dāna (Buddhism)

Ogha

► Āsavas (Āśravas)

Old Age (Buddhism)

► *Jarā-maraṇa*

Old Age and Death

► *Jarā-maraṇa*

Omniscience

Pradeep P. Gokhale
Department of Philosophy, University of Pune, Pune, Maharashtra, India
Dr. B. R. Ambedkar Chair, Central University of Tibetan Studies, Varanasi, Uttar Pradesh, India

Synonyms

Sarvajñatā, sabbaññutā (Pali); *Savvaṇṇutā* (Ardhamāgadhī)

Definition

Omniscience means knowledge of everything, direct awareness of everything, or capacity to know everything. By "everything" is meant either each and every thing or everything worth knowing. Omniscience as a quantity is said to belong to God, or to a liberated being.

The Concept of Omniscience in Indian Philosophy

"Omniscience" means knowledge of everything. Religions and philosophical systems which accept God as the creator, sustainer, and destroyer of the universe accept Him as omniscient because knowledge of everything is required for

K.T.S. Sarao, J.D. Long (eds.), *Buddhism and Jainism*, Encyclopedia of Indian Religions,
DOI 10.1007/978-94-024-0852-2

controlling everything. But religions or religious-philosophical systems which do not accept creator God also tend to accept certain authority as omniscient. In Indian philosophy, *Patañjali's* Yoga accepts a special type of *puruṣa* which it calls *īś vara* and regards omniscience as its characteristic. *Īśvara* of Yoga is not creator God but the ideal self. Hence, *īśvara* becomes a mark of perfection in Yoga. In Jainism too a liberated self is regarded as omniscient. In fact, omniscience is regarded as the intrinsic characteristic of every *jīva* which becomes manifest at the time of liberation according to Jainism. Some systems accept founders of the systems and/or emancipated persons in general as omniscient. Accordingly, Kapila (*Sāṅkhya*), Gautama the Buddha (Buddhism), and *Mahāvīra* and other *tīrthaṁkaras* (Jainism) are accepted as omniscient by the respective systems. Generally, all the religious-philosophical systems of Indian philosophy accept omniscience as a possibility or actuality in some form or the other with the notable exception of Pūrvamīmaṁsā which explicitly rejects the authority of the so-called omniscient being.

The Sanskrit term used for omniscient being is *sarvajña* (*sabbaññu* in Pāli, *savvaṇṇu* in Ardhamāgadhī), which means "one who knows everything." However, what exactly is meant by the expression "knowing everything" in the context of these different systems is not always clear and it does not always mean the same thing either. Hence, before considering the arguments for and against omniscience, it is necessary to consider different connotations the term assumes in different contexts.

"Knowing Everything": Episodic or Dispositional

The verb "know" is often used in dispositional sense, where it does not refer to the actual state of consciousness, but the capacity to bring relevant facts to one's awareness or capacity to answer certain questions correctly. Sometimes, the verb is used in episodic sense when it refers to the actual state of consciousness. Accordingly, one can distinguish between two senses of "omniscience": "Omniscience" in episodic sense would mean the state of consciousness in which one is simultaneously aware of each and every fact. "Omniscience" in dispositional sense would mean one's capacity to bring any fact to awareness as and when required. In *Milindapañho* (IV.1.19) [1], Milinda asks a question to Nāgasena about Buddha's omniscience. Nāgasena answers the question by bringing out the dispositional nature of Buddha's omniscience. "The omniscience of the blessed one was dependent on reflection. If he did reflect, he knew whatever he wanted to know." Jaina conception of omniscience on the other hand is episodic. Liberated *jīva* is said to have *kevalajñāna* in the sense that he was supposed to be simultaneously and directly aware of all that is the case, independently of any reflection or inquiry.

"Knowing Everything": Knowing All Essences or All Details

In a *Chhanogya Upaniṣad* dialogue (*Prapāṭhaka* 6) Śvetaketu asks his father about the instruction following which unheard becomes heard, unthought becomes thought, and unknown becomes known. The answer takes the form of an inquiry into essential or universal factors. For example, it is said then that by knowing one earthen body everything earthen becomes known. Here, a distinction is made between what is real (*satya*) and what is transient and nominal (*vācārambhaṇam vikāro nāmadheyam*). So knowledge of universal or essential aspects of the world is regarded as "knowledge of everything." In the ultimate analysis *sat* ("real") is regarded as the essence of everything and is called Brahman. Knowledge of accidental features is not regarded as knowledge proper.

Treating knowledge of essences as the knowledge of everything can be called an essentialist approach to omniscience. Different schools of Indian philosophy share this approach though they may not deny the status of knowledge to the knowledge of changing details. For instance, knowing all the seven *padārthas* (Nyāya-

Vaiśeşika), 25 tattvas (*sāṅkhya*), five *skandhas* (Early Buddhism), everything as consciousness and momentary (Yogācāra Buddhism), everything as *śūnya* (Mādhyamika Buddhism) would amount to "knowing everything" in the respective systems. Knower of everything in this sense is called *saṅkşiptasarvajña* or *sankşepasarvajña* ("knowing everything in nutshell") in *Tattvasaṅgraha* (verses 3131–3134). But he cannot be called omniscient in the strict sense of the term. Omniscience in the strict sense would involve not only the knowledge of all essences, but knowledge of all details; it should involve the knowledge of essential as well as accidental properties of all the things. Jainas advocate this notion of omniscience and claim that a liberated *Jīva* is omniscient in this sense.

Knowing Everything Important or Knowing Each and Every Thing Important as well as Unimportant

Sometimes the notion of omniscience is conditioned or guided by moral or soteriological considerations. The omniscient person according to this notion knows everything which one ought to know or which is conducive to liberation. In a dominant tradition of Buddhism, the Buddha is regarded as omniscient in this sense. Dharmakīrti says in *Pramāṇavārtika* (verses I.32–35):

> A knowledgeable person is searched by the people for following in practice what he has said, because they are afraid of being deceived, if they act according to the instructions of an ignorant person.
>
> So one should consider the knowledge of the authority about what ought to be done. What is the use of his knowledge about the number of insects?
>
> One who knows the nature of what should be avoided, what should be accepted and the means of avoiding or accepting that, should be regarded as the authority, not the knower if everything.
>
> Whether he has the vision of remote objects or not he should have vision of the right things. If a person with remote sensing is the authority, then come on, let us adore the vultures.

This spirit of emphasizing "knowledge of whatever is important" continues in Buddhism after Dharmakīrti with greater or less extent and then the Buddha is regarded as omniscient in this revised sense. Ratnakīti in his essay "*Sarvajñasiddhi*" distinguishes between *upayuktasarvajña* (knower of every useful thing) and *Sarvasarvajña* (knower of each and every thing) and focuses on the proof of the former. In Jainism, in contrast, the general tendency has been to understand omniscience as the knowledge of each and every thing.

There are important exceptions to this general trend in Jainism. For instance, Kandakunda distinguishes between omniscience from conventional point of view and that from decisive point of view (*vyavahāranaya* and *niścayanaya*). Former according to him is "knowledge of each and every thing," but latter is "knowledge of the self." That is because knowledge of the self is the most important thing for liberation according to him. Another Jaina scholar, Yogīndu has a similar view.

Negative and Positive Aspects of *Sarvajñatā*

Sometimes an omniscient is described not with a specific and positive way, but in a negative way, namely, "Nothing is unknown to him," "Nothing is hidden from him" where it is not possible to enumerate as to what exactly such a person knows. In the negative sense, the term s*arvajñatā* is understood as the complete absence of ignorance. Ignorance here is understood as a positive element or a material element which obstructs or obscures soul's capacity to know. When the soul's capacity to know gets obscured, it is regarded as the state of bondage. When the soul becomes free from this state, its unlimited capacity for knowledge becomes manifest. And this itself is described as s*arvajñatā*. What exactly is meant by *sarva* (everything) here may not be clear. This state of the soul could even be the state of pure consciousness (consciousness without content). Here, the concept of omniscience and the concept of emancipatory knowledge seem to overlap with each other. Sometimes, in the mainstream Jainism, for instance, the meaning of "*sarva*" in "s*arvajña*" is clear where it means all substances with all their past, present, and future modes.

Controversy in India Over the Doctrine of Omniscience

The peculiarity of the debate on omniscience in Indian philosophy is that it is not a debate between a religious approach and an antireligious approach, but it is largely a debate between or among different religious approaches. Those who defend the doctrine of omniscience do so in one religious framework, but those who oppose the doctrine do so in another religious framework. Pūrvamīmāṁsakas, like Kumārilabhaṭṭa, vehemently criticized the Buddhist and Jaina doctrines of omniscience as baseless and dogmatic, but they themselves adhered to an equally dogmatic doctrine of impersonal and eternal authority called Vedas. In fact, the view of the nonreligious school called Lokāyata was that both the parties in this debate are equally dogmatic Mīmāṁsakas while criticizing the doctrine of omniscience were primarily concerned with the question whether the rules regarding duties and obligations can be derived from the intuitive insights of some authoritative persons or they should be derived from the impersonal and eternal source called Vedas. The issue has moral and social implications. Mīmāṁsakas are the advocates of the rigid social order involving ritualism of sacrifices and hierarchy of *varṇas* and castes. Buddhists and Jainas were opposed to this social order and the Buddha or Mahāvīra who advocated an egalitarian code of conduct and the nonritualistic, spiritual path to emancipation became their authority. In order to establish their authoritative status they went to the extent of regarding these authorities as all-knowing. Hence, the debate between impersonality (*apauruṣeyatva*) of Vedas on the one hand and omniscience (*sarvajñatā*) of the Buddha of Mahāvīra on the other is the scholastic manifestation of the debate between two different approaches to life – Brahmanical and Śrāmaṇic. Though the other schools like Sāṅkhya, Yoga, and *Vedānta* uphold the doctrine of *sarvajñatā* in some form, the major parties in the controversy over *sarvajñatā* are three: *Pūrvamīmāṁsā*, Buddhism, and Jainism. Now the salient features of the debate on *sarvajñatā* will be presented in three steps:

1. Kumārila's objections against the doctrine of omniscience
2. Buddhist explanation and defense of the doctrine
3. Jaina explanation and defense of the doctrine

Kumārila's Objections Against the Doctrine of Omniscience

Kumārila raises his objections against the doctrine of omniscience in general and also with particular reference to Buddhism and Jainism, in *Ślokavārtika* (second chapter, verses 111–151) [2]. Kumārila is not against omniscience in a secondary sense, provided it involves knowledge of *dharma* derived from the Vedas. Accordingly, somebody may be called omniscient if he knows different kinds of truths by different means to knowledge (Kumārila accepts in all six means to knowledge) and knows as a part of it what is right and what is wrong from the Vedas. But Kumārila is against the idea of omniscience advocated by Buddhists and Jainas according to whom the so-called omniscient being knows everything by a single means to knowledge – by extraordinary perception or divine vision. Kumārila's arguments against omniscience can be summarized by dividing them into three groups:

(a) General objections against omniscience
(b) Specific arguments against the Buddhist conception
(c) Specific arguments against the Jaina conception

General Objections Against Omniscience

1. Specific types of objects can be known by specific *pramāṇas* only. No single *pramāṇa* is capable of knowing all types of objects. For instance, perception is never capable of knowing future objects and inference is not capable of knowing objects for which there is no reason. This objection challenges the epistemological possibility of omniscience.

2. An omniscient being cannot be known by perception, nor can his existence be inferred.
3. Nonexistence of omniscient being can be proved by inference (for instance, "Buddha was not omniscient because he was a person, like you and me").
4. Omniscient being cannot be established by an authoritative text (*āgama*) because if the so-called authoritative text is authored by the omniscient being himself, then the argument will be circular. If the text is authored by some other person, how can it be authentic?
5. The eternal text (Vedas) does not contain a statement about an omniscient being. If there is such a statement, it is mere eulogy (*arthavāda*), because if such a statement is accepted as true, then the status of Vedas themselves will be secondary and nonexternal.
6. If an eternal text is accepted, omniscient being will be superfluous because right conduct can be known from the text itself. In addition to the above, another important objection is generally attributed to Kumārila: "If the Buddha is omniscient, where is the certainty that Kapila is not omniscient? And if both are omniscient, how is there difference of opinion between them?"

Kumārila's Specific Objections Against the Buddhist Conception

Buddhists, as Kumārila understands them, regard the Buddha as omniscient in the sense of being the authority for *Dharma*. They prove him as the authority for *Dharma* on the basis of his reliability proved in empirical matters. Secondly, Buddhists regard the omniscient being to be free from passions. Kumārila raises various objections against this conception; the major ones are the following:

1. If the Buddha as the authority with regard to *Dharma* is established on the basis of his authoritative character in empirical matters, then the authoritative character of the Buddha will be other-dependent or extrinsic ("*pāratantrya*"). For Kumārila other-dependent authority is not real authority. This objection is an off-shoot of Kumārila's view of intrinsic authenticity (*svataḥ prāmāṇya*).
2. The one who wants to prove the Buddha as omniscient, one has to be oneself omniscient. In this way, there should be many omniscient beings in order there to be a single omniscient being.
3. If an omniscient being is free from passions then he will be without any voluntary activity. Since teaching *Dharma* is a voluntary activity, *Dharma* cannot be taught by an omniscient being.

Kumārila's Specific Objections Against the Jaina Conception

Kumārila specifically mentions the Jaina conception of omniscience according to which *jīva* has the knowledge of all objects such as subtle, past, etc., independently of sense organs. This is a stricter and wider concept of omniscience and naturally all the objections stated hitherto (general objections and objections against the Buddhist conception) will be applicable to it. Kumārila raises two additional objections especially against the Jaina conception.

1. The existence of an omniscient being cannot be proved in Jainism without the authenticity of their *āgamas*, but the authenticity of their *āgamas* cannot be proved without acceptance of an omniscient being.
2. Jaina concept of "omniscient being" has no instance in today's world.

Buddhist and Jaina Defense of the Doctrine

Though Buddhist and Jaina conceptions of omniscience differ considerably, they have some common features and a common form of proof. The common aspects of the Buddhist and Jaina defense may be stated as follows:

1. Omniscience for both involves moral purity, passionlessness. Both of them claim that there is no contradiction between the act of speaking that belongs to the omniscient being and his passionless or desireless character.

2. Mīmāṁsā criticism sometimes presupposes two theses:
   (a) That of intrinsic authenticity (*svataḥ prāmāṇya*) of knowledge.
   (b) That of the eternal, impersonal, and authentic character of the Vedas. These presuppositions of *Mīmāṁsākas* are criticized vehemently by Jainas and Buddhists which give the scope for their proof of noneternal, yet authentic character of their *Āgamas* and also that of their "omniscient" authors whose authenticity can be proved extrinsically.
3. Though in Jainism and Buddhism the authenticity of their Texts seems to be derived from the omniscience of their authors and vice versa, in order to avoid obvious circularity, these systems present independent inferences in order to prove the existence of an omniscient being as they conceive of him.

As has been shown before, many orthodox systems too accept omniscience. But since these systems are generally in a compromising position with Pūrvamīmāṁsā on the matters such as authenticity of the Vedas, Vedic ritualism, and hierarchical social order, the debate between Mīmāṁsākas and these systems does not take a serious form. For Buddhists and Jainas, however, the controversy with Pūrvamīmāṁsā becomes serious because they are strongly against of Pūrvamīmāṁsā on the above matters. One finds therefore long chapters and essays written by the scholars belonging to these two schools defending their doctrine of omniscience. On the Buddhist side the major scholars who present and defend the doctrine are Dharmakīrti, Śāntarakṣita, Kamalaśīla, Jñānaśrīmitra, and Ratnakīrti. (*Jñānaśrīmitra's* original essay "*Sarvajñasiddhi*" is not available. Ratnakīrti's essay with the same title is claimed by the author to be a summary of *Jñānaśrīmitra's* essay.)

On Jaina side there are a host of scholars such as Samantabhandra, Haribhadra, Akalaṅka, Vidyānanda, and Prabhācandra. A brief and synoptic survey of the Jaina and Buddhist defense will now be made in what follows.

Buddhist Defense of the Idea of Omniscience

Buddhists in their proof of the omniscient being generally follow Dharmakīrti's line that the Buddha is omniscient not in the sense of the knower of all details, but in the sense of knower of all that is important from the point of view of the cessation of sufferings. Another conception of omniscience they sometimes uphold is that of "knowledge of everything as momentary and unsubstantial." Śāntarakṣita in the last chapter of *Tattvasaṅgraha* [3] discusses the doctrine in detail. In his counterattack against Mīmāṁsā approach he shows how nonexistence of an omniscient being cannot be established through non-apprehension (anupalabadhi) as *pramāṇa*. Moreover, it cannot be established by the one who is himself non-omniscient. While explaining the epistemological possibility of omniscience in the Buddhist framework, Śāntarakṣita gives explanation from Sauṭrāntika as well as Yogācāra point of view. From the former, it will be included in Yogic perception (yogijñāna) through which one can know past, present, and future objects vividly, and in this sense, directly. From the latter it will be a kind of mental perception and unlike sensory perception which is restricted by the nature of the object, is capable of congnizing all types of objects.

Ratnakīrti, as indicated earlier, distinguishes between "knower of every useful thing" and knower of each and every thing. For defending the existence of the former, Ratnakīrti presents and defends the following argument:

(Statement of *Vyāpti*:) Whatever is the mental phenomenon accompanied by a devoted, uninterrupted, and prolonged practice is worthy of manifestation.

(Positive instance:) Like the figure of a woman for her lover.

(Property bearer:) The consciousness of the four noble truths

(Reason property:) is the mental phenomenon accompanied by devoted, uninterrupted, and prolonged practice.

(Conclusion: therefore it is worthy of manifestation.)

Through the explanation and justification of this argument Ratnakīrti tries to show that the four noble truths must be manifest to someone [4].

Jaina Defense of the Doctrine of Omniscience

Though while answering Mīmāṁsā criticism of omniscience the arguments of Jainas and Buddhists are by and large similar, while explaining and defending their own conceptions they naturally become different because of the peculiarities of these conceptions.

Majority of Jaina scholars accept their religious epoch-makers (*tīrthaṅkaras*) and also liberated *jīvas* as omniscient in the literal sense – that is, knowers of all essential as well as accidental aspects of everything, important as well as unimportant. They define omniscience as the direct knowledge of all substances with all their past, present, and future modes. Every soul (*jīva*) according to them has intrinsic capacity for infinite knowledge (*anatajñāna*), which is also called absolute knowledge (*kevalajñāna*). It is direct knowledge in the sense that it is not mediated by sense organs or even mind (*manas*). This intrinsic capacity in ordinary *jīvas* is obscured by the *kārmic* particles known as *jñānāvaraṇīya* (knowledge obscuring) *karma*. In fact, any knowledge is possible only due to destruction or subsidence of the respective type of *jñānāvaraṇīya karma*. With the help of intensive austerity and spiritual practice it is possible to destroy or remove forever all types of knowledge-obscuring karmas from the *jīva*. In such a state, the intrinsic capacity of the soul to know everything becomes manifest. This type of knowledge is called *kevalajñāna*. This notion of *jīva* according to which knowledge is intrinsic and knowledge-obscuring karma is extrinsic to it itself becomes a basis for the possibility of omniscience. In their epistemology Jainas deny contact (*sannikarṣa*) theory of perception, and particularly with regard to extraordinary perception which they call "perception in the ultimate sense" (*pāramārthika pratyakṣa*) Jainas claim that such a perception occurs without any mediation of sense organs or mind. It occurs simply out of *jīva's* intrinsic capacity subject to the destruction or subsidence of the relevant *jñānāvaraṇīya karma*. Hence, *kevalajñāna* becomes epistemologically possible for them because no contact is needed between *jīva* and objects whether the objects are proximate or remote, whether they are past, present, or future.

In support of the above basic framework Jaina scholars present some arguments for strengthening the case for the existence of the omniscient being. For instance:

1. Samantabhadra claimed that the existence of an omniscient being is established from the fact that to some beings invisible things like atoms, things, or persons remote in time and place become known as objects of direct cognition.
2. The scholars like Akalaṅka, Hemacandra, and Malliṣeṇa claim that astronomy and the occult sciences which give correct information about future events and supersensible objects is a clear indication of the possibility of an omniscient being [5].

It is clear that though the above arguments create a logical space in which existence of an omniscient being is conceivable, they do not give sufficiently strong evidence for his existence.

On the other hand there are considerations which seem to go against the existence of an omniscient being in its extreme sense. For instance:

1. An omniscient being is supposed to know directly all the past, present, and future modes of all substances. But direct knowledge by its very nature can have only present modes as its objects. Past and future modes, by their very nature, are not present. Hence, omniscience as direct knowledge becomes impossible.
2. Knowledge by its very nature is about something. This "about-ness" indicates a relation. Hence, direct knowledge seems to presuppose a certain contact/connection of *jīva* with the object. But Jainas hold that knowledge which is direct in the strict sense of the term does not involve any contact (*sannikarṣa*) of *jīva* with the object. How they can explain "about-ness" of the omniscient knowledge would be a problem.

The above problems occur also because Jainas are accepting omniscience in episodic sense and not in dispositional sense.

In so far as the notion of an omniscient being in mitigated sense is concerned – such as "knower of everything important," "knower of the essence of everything," etc. – the question pertains to the idea of an extraordinary reliable person accepted by different systems in one way or the other. It so happens that the extraordinary reliable persons accepted by different systems have mutually contrary perceptions of reality. Whose perception is veridical and whose is illusory cannot be decided by referring it back to the so-called reliable persons themselves (because it will amount to begging the question), but it can probably be done by bringing in other evidences. In the latter case, the authority of the reliable person becomes superfluous. *Mīmāṁsākas* seem to be right in raising this point. This, however, does not make their case for "impersonal eternal authoritative text" stronger.

Cross-References

► Knowledge (Buddhism)

References

1. Rhys Davids TW (Tr) (2003) The questions of king Milinda. Motilal Banafsidass, Delhi
2. Dvārikādcsaśāstrī S (ed) (1978) Ślokavavārittika of Śrī Kumārilabhaṭṭa with the commentary Nyāyarathckara of Śrī pārthasārathi Miśra. Tara, Varanasi
3. Shastri SD (ed) (1968) "*Atīndriyārthadarśiparīkṣā*". Tattvasaṅgraha of Ācārya Shāntarakṣita with the commentary 'Pañjikā' of shri kamalashī, vol 2. Bauddha Bharati, Varanasi, pp 987–1130
4. Thakur A (ed) (1975) "*Sarvajñasiddhiḥ*". Ratnakīrtinibandhāvaliḥ (Buddhist Nyāya works of Ratnakīrti). Kashi Prasad Jayaswal Research Institute, Patna, pp 1–31
5. Singh RJ (1974) The Jaina concept of omniscience. L. D. Institute on Indology, Ahmedabad, 9

Once-Returner

► *Sakadāgāmin*

Oral Transmission

Bhikkhu Anālayo
Center for Buddhist Studies, University of Hamburg, Balve, Germany

Synonyms

Anuśrava (Sanskrit); *Anussava* (Pāli)

Definition

Oral transmission in the sense of verbally passing on teachings "from mouth to ear" was the main means at the disposition of the early Buddhists in order to preserve their teachings for later generations.

Oral Transmission in Early Buddhism

In the absence of the use of writing for maintaining a textual tradition, the early Buddhists relied on oral means of transmission for passing on to posterity the discourses that had been delivered by the Buddha and his disciples. In doing so, the early Buddhists would have followed the example set by the Vedic oral transmission, where recitation of texts appears to have been carried out over successive generations with an impressive degree of precision. Unlike their Vedic predecessors, however, the Buddhist reciters involved in oral transmission had not necessarily been trained in memorization skills from their early youth onward and thus needed to employ various means to ensure the correct handing of their texts.

One of these means is the use of repetition, where similar situations are described with the help of standardized pericopes that are adjusted to the particular situation with the most minimal change necessary. Repetition is also used when presenting doctrinal items, where distinctions between a positive and a negative description employ nearly the same terms and expressions, only differing in the use of a negation. These features make the early Buddhist textual material somewhat tedious to read in modern translation, although the effect of repetition would have had quite a different impact in the oral setting of ancient India.

Another oral feature is the use of a principle referred to under the name "waxing syllables." This principle is applied to a string of synonyms, which are often employed in order to safeguard against loss, since a series of similar words stands much greater chance of being remembered than a single word. At the same time, the basic message leaves a deeper impression on the listening audience. The terms in such a string of synonyms are then usually arranged according to the principle of "waxing syllables." That is, words with fewer syllables come first and are followed by words with an equal or higher number of syllables; hence, this pattern is referred to with the term "waxing syllables."

One out of many examples would be a recurrent description of someone being afraid, which reads like this: *bhīto saṃviggo lomahaṭṭhajāto*. The three terms have basically the same meaning and are arranged according to their respective syllable count of two, three, and six syllables. In an oral setting, the recitation of such a string of terms arranged according to the principle of waxing syllables creates a crescendo effect and leaves a somewhat rhythmic impression, which is then easily remembered.

Such features clearly reflect a concern among the early Buddhist reciters for verbatim oral repetition. In fact the fortnightly recital of the code of rules to be undertaken in any monastic setting – perhaps one of the most evident and frequent instances of early Buddhist oral recitation – would have required precise recall of the text in question. In this respect, the early Buddhist oral tradition differs from oral literature of an epic or narrative type, where improvisation and innovation are typical and even required aspects of the oral performance. While such literature is freely re-created every time it is told, the early Buddhist oral tradition was concerned with the exact preservation of material considered to be sacred, for which free improvisation is not appropriate. Besides, the so-called councils or communal recitations, *saṅgīti*, clearly point to the practice of group recital which would have left no scope for free improvisation.

Oral transmission continued even after the texts were committed to writing. Thus, the Chinese pilgrim Fǎxiǎn reports that when he went to India at the end of the fourth century in order to search for *Vinaya* manuscripts to be brought back to China for translation, he found that the texts were still passed on by oral means (Taishō, Vol. 51, p. 864b). This goes to show that the purpose of oral transmission goes beyond the mere preservation of the texts.

The discourses in fact report that at times a monk would recite something to himself, while being alone and in seclusion ([7], Vol. I, p. 209). The same is also recorded for the Buddha ([7], Vol. II, p.74). Since the discourse recited by the Buddha involves a rather basic aspect of his own teachings, it seems less probable that this episode depicts an instance of oral rehearsing of texts. Instead, it suggests that oral recitation can at times have a meditative function. In fact, a listing of occasions when liberation can happen indicates that, if previous practice has sufficiently matured the mind, the decisive breakthrough to realization can happen when one is engaged in the oral recitation of a text ([3], Vol. III, p. 241).

In sum, formal aspects like repetition, the use of pericopes, and the application of the principle of waxing syllables to strings of synonyms testify to the nature of early Buddhist oral transmission as attempting the accurate verbatim preservation of texts. Alongside such concerns, however, oral transmission appears to have been an integral part of the overall soteriological project of mental cultivation, *bhāvanā*.

O

Cross-References

▶ Bhāvanā
▶ Tipiṭaka

References

1. Allon M (1997) Style and function: a study of the dominant stylistic features of the prose portions of Pāli canonical sutta texts and their mnemonic function.

International Institute for Buddhist Studies of the International College for Advanced Buddhist Studies, Tokyo
2. Anālayo Bh (2007) Oral dimensions of Pāli discourses: pericopes, other mnemonic techniques, and the oral performance context. Can J Buddh Stud 3:5–33
3. Carpenter JE, Rhys Davids TW (eds) (1890–1911) The Dīgha Nikāya, 3 vols. Pali Text Society, London
4. Collins S (1992) Notes on some oral aspects of Pāli literature. Indo-Iranian J 35:121–135
5. Cousins LS (1983) Pali oral literature. In: Denwood P (ed) Buddhist studies: ancient and modern. Curzon, London, pp 1–11
6. Coward H (1986) Oral and written texts in Buddhism. Adyar Libr Bull 50:299–313
7. Feer L (ed) (1888–1898) The Saṃyutta Nikāya, 5 vols. Pali Text Society, Oxford
8. Wynne A (2004) The oral transmission of early Buddhist literature. J Int Assoc Buddh Stud 27(1):97–127

Ordination

Angraj Chaudhary
Vipassana Research Institute, Dhammagiri, Igatpuri, Nashik, Maharashtra, India

Synonyms

Renunciation

Definition

Ordination means renouncing home literally and figuratively for a homeless life and accepting the life of an ascetic or a monk.

Causes of Ordination, Formula to Ordain and Persons Eligible for It

Ordination means "going forth" from home to a homeless life. It also means adopting the life of an ascetic or a monk. The Pali word for ordination is *pabbajjā* (Sanskrit *pravrajyā*). It is derived from *pa+vraj* (*to go*), which means going out from home not only in the literal sense but also in the figurative sense. In the latter sense it means to detach oneself from worldly affairs. When one experiences suffering in life, finds that the world is too much with him and he burns with the fires of *rāga* (craving) *dosa* (aversion) and *moha* (ignorance) he wants to free himself from burning passions and live the life of a monk with only a few wants. He wants peace and harmony. This becomes his main motive to become a monk. The adoption of the life of a monk is to make efforts to root out the cause of suffering and experience peace and tranquillity.

When a person decides to leave home for a homeless life and adopt the life of a monk or an ascetic he has to undergo a ceremony called *pabbajjā* (ordination ceremony). In the Theravāda tradition one seeking ordination is first ordained as a novice (*sāmaṇera*). After some years he is given higher ordination called *upasampadā* if he is found fit by the senior monks.

In the beginning the Buddha used to ordain persons willing to be monks by pronouncing these words:- *Ehi bhikkhu, svākkhāto dhammo, cara brahmacariyaṃ sammādukkhassa antakiriyāya'ti* ([1], p. 16). i.e., "Come, monks, well proclaimed is the dhamma. Live the noble life for the complete ending of suffering.")

The next stage of ordination came when 60 *arahants* went to different parts of India to spread the teachings of the Buddha. When people heard his teachings some of them wanted to leave home for a homeless life and become monks. So they had to be brought to the Buddha for the purpose of being ordained by him as in the beginning they thought it was the Buddha who could ordain people. This meant long journeys and fatigue for those willing to become monks. So the Buddha authorized the monks to ordain them and he explained the manner they should do it.

The person seeking ordination must first shave his hair and beard and then put on saffron or yellow robes. Then adjusting his robe on the left shoulder he should pay homage to the bhikkhus. He should then squat or if he cannot squat, he should kneel before them with hands raised and palms together. Then he should say *Buddhaṃ saraṇaṃ gacchāmi* (I take refuge in the Buddha), *Dhammaṃ saraṇaṃ gacchāmi* (I take refuge in the Dhamma) and *Saṅghaṃ saraṇam gacchāmi*

(I take refuge in the Saṅgha-the Order of monks). This should be repeated three times.

This was the short formula to ordain people in the beginning. But then as the number of people seeking ordination increased and many undeserving and unsuitable persons began to come, more restrictions were imposed.

At present a person seeking ordination as a novice (*sāmaṇera*) has to take ten precepts besides taking the three refuges.

When a *sāmaṇera* is admitted to the Order he is expected to observe the following ten precepts (*sikkhāpadāni*). They are:- *Pāṇātipātā veramaṇī sikkhāpadaṃ samādiyāmi, adinnādānā veramaṇī... abrahmacariyā veramaṇī ... musāvādā veramaṇī...surāmerayamajjappamādaṭṭhānā veramaṇī ... vikālabhojanā veramaṇī ... naccagītavāditavisūkadassanā veramaṇī... mālāgandhavilepanadhāraṇavibhūsanaṭṭhānā veramaṇī ... uccāsayanamahāsayanā veramaṇī... jātarūparajatapaṭiggahaṇā veramaṇī sikkhāpadaṃ samādiyāmi* ([1], p. 105). i.e., "I undertake to abstain from killing, stealing, sexual misconduct, lying and from intoxicants, from eating at the wrong time, from dancing, singing, music and worldly entertainments, from wearing garlands, from using perfumes and cosmetics from wearing jewellery and other bodily adornments, from using high and luxurious beds and from accepting gold and silver." He is also expected to study the Dhamma and Vinaya from his elders. He should attend to senior monks and do his duties towards them. And lastly he should make himself eligible for higher ordination (*upsampadā*).

A *sāmaṇera* is not expected to observe the rainy retreat but a bhikkhu is supposed to live at one place during the rainy season.

Before one seeks admission into the order as a *samaṇera* he reflects: "Household life is crowded and dusty; life gone forth is wide open, it is not easy, while living in a home, to lead the holy life utterly perfect and pure as a polished shell." ([2], p. 272; and see *Cūlahatthipadopama Sutta* for its Pali equivalent – *Sambādho gharāvāso rajopatho, abbhokāso pabbajjā. Nayidaṃ sukaraṃ agāraṃ ajjhāvasatā ekantaparipuṇṇaṃ ekantaparisuddhaṃ saṅkhalikhitaṃ brahmacariyaṃ carituṃ. Yaṃnūnāhaṃ kesamassuṃ ohāretvā kāsāyāni vatthāni acchādetvā agārasmā anagāriyaṃ pabbajeyya'nti* ([3], I. 239).

Thus reflecting he gives up his property and relatives considering them as obstacles in his spiritual journey. The usual formula to give up is, "*Appaṃ vā bhogakkhandhaṃ mahantaṃ vā bhogakkhandhaṃ pahāya appaṃ vā ñātiparivaṭṭaṃ mahantaṃ vā ñātiparivaṭṭaṃ pahāya* (21.240) i.e., abandoning a small or a large fortune, abandoning a small or a large circle of relatives *kesamassuṃ ohāretvā kāsāyāni vatthāni acchādetvā agārasmā anagāriyaṃ pabbajati*" ([3], I. 240) i.e., he shaves off his hair and beard, wears a yellow robe and leaves home for a homeless life. The ceremony of ordination is performed by the senior monks when he approaches them with a request to ordain him.

Unless he develops detachment from worldly things, unless he reduces his desires, it cannot be expected of him to make progress on the spiritual path.

It is said in the *Dhammapada*: "Hard it is to go forth, from home to homelessness, To take delight in it is hard."

Duppabbajjaṃ durabhiramaṃ,...// [4], verse 302

Therefore unless one realizes at the experiential level the burning and suffering caused by thoughts of sensuality (*kilesa kāma*) and objects of sense (*vatthu kāma*) it is difficult to become disenchanted with the world.

The Buddha wanted sincere and genuine persons to seek ordination. The thought of leaving home should come from deep within. It should not be sudden and based on certain painful circumstance in life. Keeping this in mind the Buddha allowed monks to disrobe if they are not fit for it i.e., if they cannot lead a virtuous life – a life disciplined by the rules of Vinaya prescribed by the Buddha.

If one renounces home sincerely and honestly he cannot be called an escapist. He does not lead an indolent life, he does not become a parasite on society but he works hard in his life and does a lot for the people around him. He presents his ideal character as he is free from greed and aversion or he has less of them. He lives a disciplined and restrained life. Thus he becomes an example to the people. He is not selfish. He does not care about only himself but he cares about others also. He develops altruistic behaviour and thinks of doing good to others. An ideal bhikkhu is like a bee, which collects honey from the flowers without harming their color and fragrance.

Yathā'pi bhamaro puppham̧, vaṇṇagandham̧ aheṭhayam̧/

Paleti rasam'ādāya, evam̧ gāme munī care// [4], verse 49.

Are all persons eligible to seek ordination? The answer is an emphatic "No." In the Vinaya Piṭaka there are rules framed by the Buddha as to who is eligible and who is not, for ordination. Persons suffering from leprosy, boils, asthma, and epilepsy are not eligible for ordination. Why? Because they cannot work hard which is the prerequisite of leading a meaningful spiritual life. A being other than human being, a female (later she was thought to be eligible for ordination), a man in debt, one in military service are also not eligible for ordination. Why were the last two not allowed? Because the Buddha thought that a man in debt wants to be ordained because of his intention to escape from his obligation to pay off the debt. He did not allow a man in military service to be ordained because of his intention to live an easy life, not a life of hardship. The Buddha was a practical man. Had he allowed persons in military service to be ordained who would defend the country in the event of an attack by the enemy? If all soldiers of a country want to be ordained will it not be an easy victim to the enemy?

One who has not taken permission from his parents is also ineligible for ordination. Why? Because in that case the parents might not think good of the monk who ordains him. One who is not 20 years old, one who does not have an alms-bowl and robes are also not eligible for ordination.

From the restrictions imposed by the Buddha it is clear that he allowed only genuine persons to be ordained, not those who had some ulterior motives. One in debt wanted to be ordained because he did not want to pay off the debt and one in military service wanted to be ordained because he wanted to shirk the hard duty of a military personnel as said above. One in his teens wanted to be ordained because his parents might have chided him for some of his faults.

When the senior monks are satisfied with a sāmaṇera's answers to questions put by them then only he receives ordination.

Cross-References

▶ Renunciation

References

1. Mahāvagga (Vinaya Piṭaka. V.R.I. Dhammagiri (1998) Unless otherwise mentioned, all books referred to here are published by V.R.I. Dhammagiri, in 1998)
2. Bhikkhu Ñāṇamoli, Bhikkhu Bodhi (Trs) (1995) The Middle Length Discourses of the Buddha. Wisdom Publications, Boston
3. Majjhima Nikāya
4. Dhammapada, verse nos are given

Ornament of Clear Realization

▶ Abhisamayālam̧kāra

Orthodox Buddhism

▶ Theravāda

Outcast

▶ Caṇḍāla (Buddhism)

P

Pacceka-Buddha

► Pratyeka-Buddha

Padma

► Padmasambhava

Padmakara

► Padmasambhava

Padmasambhava

Georgios T. Halkias
Oxford Centre of Buddhist Studies, Oxford, UK

Abbreviations

Tib. Tibetan

Synonyms

Great Ācārya; Guru Rinpoche; Lotus guru; Padma; Padmakara

Definition

Lotus-born (Tibetan: *padma 'byung gnas*).

The Precious Guru

The Indian master Padmasambhava is one of the most renowned and revered figures in Tibet's religious history. Across the Tibetan cultural world he is nostalgically referred to as *Guru Rinpoche* ("precious Teacher") and figures prominently in pilgrimage narratives, monastic dances and Buddhist histories. He is held in special veneration by adherents of the Old School of Tibetan Buddhism (Nyingma) for concealing Buddhist teachings in several mediums, including the mind of his disciples, and predicting their discovery for the benefit of future generations (Fig. 1).

Tibet's Golden Age

Padmasambhava is credited with the transmission of Tantric Buddhism in Tibet and the Himalayas and with visionary Tantric teachings promulgated in his name. He is celebrated as a "second Buddha" for attending to the spiritual and temporal well-being of the Tibetans, but the life of this wandering ascetic is yet to be substantiated by historical research and it has even been proposed that he never lived. This is an unwarranted conclusion, and literary evidence show that his legend

K.T.S. Sarao, J.D. Long (eds.), *Buddhism and Jainism*, Encyclopedia of Indian Religions,
DOI 10.1007/978-94-024-0852-2

Padmasambhava, Fig. 1 Statue of Padmasambhava (Photograph by Georgios Halkias)

circulated not long after the collapse of the Tibetan Empire in 842 C.E. culminating in his apotheosis in the twelfth century [1]. His first complete hagiography is attributed to Yeshe Tsogyal, his principal female Tibetan disciple [2]. The *Copper Temple Biography* (*Zangs gling ma*) was redacted by Nyangral Nyima Özer (1136–1204), an alleged reincarnation of the Tibetan Emperor Trisong Detsen (755-c. 794). For the Nyingma, Nyima Özer is the first "Treasure King" of five chief disciples prophesied by Padmasambhava to take rebirth in this world in order to rediscover and propagate his hidden Buddhist teachings known as *treasures* (Tib. *gter-ma*). *The Copper Temple Biography* incorporates earlier material recycled in later Padma hagiographies, which numbered, by the mid-sixteenth century, to at least 50 [3].

The importation of Indian Buddhism to Tibet is a historical event of great importance for the formulation of Tibetan ethnic and cultural identity. Central to Tibet's Golden Age in the eighth century is an epic story of religious conversion featuring the Dharma-Ruler (Tib. *chos-rgyal*) Trisong Detsen who commissioned learned Buddhist teachers from India, like the Buddhist monk Śāntarakṣita (725–788), to visit Central Tibet and assist in establishing Buddhism as the official religion of the empire. According to Tibetan religious histories Śāntarakṣita encountered hostility from local factions to his plans to built Tibet's first monastic compound at Samye and persuaded Trisong Detsen to dispatch a royal mission and invite the *siddha* Padmasambhava to assist him with his task. Padmasambhava's arrival in Tibet is linked with the ritual consecration of Samye around 779, and with the spread of Tantric rituals, teachings, and erection of *stūpas*. The Tibetan Emperor was apparently so impressed with the Guru's spiritual power and charisma to neutralize local and supernatural forces opposing the spread of Buddhism that he, along with other members of the aristocracy, became one of his 25 main disciples. In appreciation, he offered him Yeshe Tsogyal, one of his court ladies, as his Tantric consort. According to some sources Padmasambhava stayed in Tibet for 56 years, while for others soon after the foundation of Samye he was accused for practicing magic and was forced to leave. It is said that he was unable to finish teaching Trisong Detsen and he assigned his disciple, the translator Vairocana, to complete this task. The Bön tradition offers an alternative biography in which the sage Drenpa Namkha had two sons – Tsewang Rigzin who continued his father's work as a Bönpo missionary and Padmasambhava who established the lineage of the Nyingma School [4]. The legendary embellishment of these references suggests Tibetan strategies for indigenizing Indian Tantrism, a process fundamental to the foundation of the Nyingma School [5], and competition between Tibet's pre-Buddhist religious traditions and the earliest strands of Indo-Tibetan Buddhism in the empire.

Sacred Lands and Pilgrimage Cultures

In Oḍḍiyāna (Tib. U-rgyan), located by Tibetologists in Swat Valley (Pakistan), there was King Indrabodhi who had no successors to the throne. One day, while on a journey with his minister, he found a little boy by Lake Dhanakosha whom he regarded as an answer to his prayers. He named him Padmakara, the Lotus Born, and raised him as his son and crown prince. However, like Buddha Śākyamuni before him, the child's unusual spiritual constitution led him to renounce his noble bride Prabhadhari and the life and pleasures of the court. Against the King's wishes, he pursued the life of an itinerant ascetic, following Buddhist teachers, meditating at different places, and attaining complete liberation and mastery of the phenomenal world. It is believed that Padmasambhava attained the "Great Transference" and resides in an immortal rainbow-body at the Palace of Lotus Light in the Glorious Copper-Coloured Mountain (Tib. *Zangs-mdog dpal-ri*). From his Pure Land populated by "*rākṣasas*," located in the island of Chamara (south India) or south-west of Tibet, he sends countless emanations to benefit sentient beings.

Padmasambhava's life and works are shrouded in extraordinary tales and symbolic narratives [6]. He appears in various places and in various forms, speaks different languages, fights and binds indigenous demons and performs extraordinary feats, like the transformation of barren lands into irrigation fields – an enterprise that suggests technical knowledge of water management brought to Tibet from his native land. According to another popular tale, he resurrects Trisong Detsen's daughter, Princess Pema Sel who had prematurely died at the age of 8 and transmits to her the esoteric precepts of the teachings known as the "Great Perfection," or Dzogchen.

A popular theme relates his name to his spontaneous birth from a lotus floating in Lake Dhanakosha. Birth from a lotus is an Indian religious motif symbolizing immaculate origins and spiritual purity. These Pure Land associations are further reinforced in narratives that portray him as an enlightened emanation of Buddha Amitābha at the physical level. For the Nyingma and Kagyud Schools of Tibetan Buddhism the trinity of Amitābha, Padmasambhava, and Avalokiteśvara is regarded as the three aspects or bodies of a single Buddha.

There are many sacred places and pilgrimage sites (caves, hermitages, mountains, valleys, lakes, and so forth) associated with Padmasambhava in Tibet, Nepal, Bhutan, and the Indian Himalayan regions of Ladakh, Sikkim, Himachal Pradesh, and Arunachal Pradesh. Many of them are linked to episodes from his legendary life, like the Lake Rewalsar (Tib. Tso-Pema) in Himachal Pradesh formed around the pyre set by the King of Zahor to punish Padmasambhava for courting his daughter, princess Mandāravā. The great majority of Tibetan sacred sites claim to have been places where the Tantric master meditated, like the Crystal Cave at Yarlung valley and Bumthang in Bhutan where he subjugated local spirits converting them into guardians of the Buddhist faith. The famous "Tiger's Nest" hermitage at Paro is a site of national pride for the people of Bhutan and derives its sanctity from Padmasambhava's miraculous visit on the back of a tigress. Another popular pilgrimage site is the Maratika cave in northern Nepal where he and his Tantric consort Mandāravā meditated on Buddha Amitāyus and attained the *siddhi* of immortality. There are numerous formations on rocks and caves identified as either self-arisen signs of the Lotus Guru or physical imprints left by his body, hands, and feet, while from time to time visionaries search for "pure lands" hidden in the Himalayan valleys (Tib. *sbas-yul*) that have been previously revealed or prophesied by Padmasambhava as sacred places of refuge and meditation.

Visionary Literature

While the Nyingma School adheres to Indian Tantric teachings shared by all Schools of Tibetan Buddhism, their Buddhist canon is altogether distinctive for preserving a large corpus of

Padmasambhava, Fig. 2 Mural of Padmasambhava with consorts (Photograph by Georgios Halkias)

esoteric teachings (*treasures*) attributed to Padmasambhava who predicted the suitable time of their disclosure, the persons who would reveal them, and the destined recipients who would be holders of Treasure lineages. The act of concealing and revealing *treasures* is associated with the blissful synergy of a Tantric consort and there are ample references of Padmasambhava practicing sexual yoga with a number of female companions. The princess Mandāravā of Zahor and Yeshe Tsogyal of Tibet commonly figure in Treasure lore as enlightened holders of the Buddha's teachings (Fig. 2).

In addition to several Padma hagiographies, like *The Testimony of Padmasambhava* (*Padma bka'thang*) redacted by Orgyen Lingpa in the fourteenth century, there are Tantric cycles and individual ritual works revealed by treasure-finders and attributed to Padmasambhava. Among these we find: *The Liberation by Hearing in the Intermediate State* (*Bar do thos grol*) known as the "Tibetan Book of the Dead" rediscovered by Karma Lingpa in the fourteenth century [7]; *The Gradual Path of the Wisdom Essence* (*Zhal gdams lam rim ye shes snying po)*, instructions on the gradual path to enlightenment revealed in the nineteenth century by Chokgyur Lingpa [8]; *The Innermost Spirituality of the Ḍākinī* (*Mkha' gro snying thig*), a set of 17 esoteric Tantras from the "Great Perfection" taught to Pema Sel [9]; the Tantras of the wrathful deity of Vajrakīla [10], and so forth. *The Rosary of Esoteric Views* (*Manngag ltaba'i phrengba*) deals with different paths and vehicles and is the only text attributed to the Lotus Guru that has been handed down as an oral tradition and not as a *treasure* text. Liturgical practices commemorating Padmasambhava are usually done on the tenth lunar day and often include, the *Seven-Line Supplication to Padmasambhava*, one of the best-known invocation prayers in the Tibetan world that ends with an abridged version of Padmasambhava's mantra in Sanskrit *Oṃ Āḥ Hūṃ Vajra Guru Padma Siddhi Hūṃ*.

Padmasambhava, Fig. 3 Procession of the "Guru's Eight Aspects." Monastic festival, Kungri, India 2007 (Photograph by Georgios Halkias)

Iconography

Representations of Padmasambhava, sited on a lotus, feature in many statues, paintings, murals, prayer-flags, and amulets. He is the subject of many Tibetan paintings (*thangka*), such as those depicting his buddha-field, the Glorious Copper-Coloured Mountain where he is usually flanked by Mandāravā and Yeshe Tsogyal, or those representing his lineage, his eight manifestations, or his disciples. In his "primary form" he is distinguished for his wide-open eyes and penetrating gaze, a characteristic of a particular meditation technique, holding a five-pronged *vajra* (thunderbolt) in his right hand and in his left a skull-cup containing a long-life vase filled with the nectar of longevity, and a trident-topped *khaṭvāṅga* with three severed heads. These aspects clearly link him to the Kāpālika traditions in India. He commonly wears a five-petalled lotus hat with a vulture's feather on top and he is usually seated with his two feet in the royal posture. There are eight different forms or manifestations representing facets of his life and spiritual accomplishments: Pema Gyalpo (Lotus King) in royal attire adorned with a crown of gold, earrings, and necklace and holding a double-sided drum in his right hand and a gold mirror in his left; Nyima Ozer (Ray of the Sun) shown at times as a naked ascetic in a loincloth and holding a *khaṭvāṅga* which points toward the sun; Loden Chokse (Supreme Knowledge Holder) in princely clothes beating a hand-drum with his right hand and holding a skull-cup filled with *amrita* with his left; Pema Jungne (Padmasambhava) often sited on a lotus, dressed in the three robes of a Buddhist monk and holding a *vajra* in his right hand and a skull-cup in his left; Shakya Senge (Lion of the Shakya) represented in the form of a Buddha dressed in monastic robes. His right hand displays the earth-touching gesture and his left supports a begging-bowl; Senge Dradok (Roaring Lion) in a dark-blue fierce form holding a *vajra* in one hand and a scorpion, or making a subjugating gesture in the other. He sits on a demon wearing a skull-crown and a tiger-skin loincloth; Dorje Drolo in red wrathful appearance riding on a fierce tigress. He brandishes a *vajra* in his right hand and a ritual dagger in his left; and Orgyen Dorje Chang (Vajra bearer of Oḍḍiyāna) depicted in sexual union with Yeshe Tsogyal. He is of dark blue color and holds a *vajra* and a hand-bell crossed at his heart, while his white naked consort raises a skull-bowl filled with nectar. In memory of Padmasambhava's ritual dance of Vajrakīla enacted at the consecration of Samye, there are annual festivals (Tib. 'cham) staged throughout monasteries in India, Nepal, Bhutan and Tibet where masked dancers also perform the "Guru's Eight Aspects" [11] (Fig. 3).

Cross-References

- ▶ Amitābha
- ▶ Buddha (Concept)
- ▶ Demon
- ▶ Enlightenment (Buddhism)
- ▶ Folklore (Buddhism)
- ▶ Magic (Buddhism)
- ▶ Mantra
- ▶ Monastery
- ▶ Mysticism (Buddhism)
- ▶ Pilgrimage (Buddhism)
- ▶ Politics (Buddhism)
- ▶ Revelation
- ▶ Sacred Biography (Buddhism)
- ▶ Tantra
- ▶ Tibet

References

1. Dalton J (2004) The early development of the Padmasambhava legend in Tibet: a study of IOL Tib J 644 and Pelliot tibétain 307. J Am Orient Soc 124:759–772
2. Kunsang E (tr) (1993) The lotus-born: the life story of Padmasambhava. Recorded by Yeshe Tsogyal. Shambhala, Boston
3. Blondeau AM (1979) Analysis of the biographies of Padmasambhava according to Tibetan tradition: classification of sources. In: Aris M et al (eds) Tibetan studies in honor of Hugh Richardson. Aris and Phillips, Warminster
4. Blondeau AM (1988) mKhyen-brtse'i dbang-po: la biographie de Padmasambhava selon la tradition du bsGrags-pa Bon, et ses sources. In: Gnoli G et al (eds) Orientalia Iosephi Tucci Memoriae Dicata. Istituto Italiano per il Medio ed Estremo Oriente, Rome
5. Mayer R, Cantwell C (2008) Enduring myths: smrang, rabs and ritual in the Dunhuang texts on Padmasambhava. Revue d'Etudes Tibétaines 15:289–312
6. Zangpo N (2002) Guru Rinpoche: his life and times. Snow Lion, Ithaca
7. Lopez D (2011) The Tibetan book of the dead: a biography. Princeton University Press, Princeton
8. Rinpoche D (2007) Great perfection: outer and inner preliminaries. Snow Lion, Ithaca
9. Kunsang E (tr) (1999) The light of wisdom, vol I. Ranjung Yeshe, Hong Kong
10. Boord MJ (2002) A bolt of lightning from the blue: the vast commentary of Vajrakīla that clearly defines the essential points. Edition Khordong, Berlin
11. Cantwell C (1995) The dance of the guru's eight aspects. Tibet J XX:47–63

Pagoda

▶ Cetiya

Painful

▶ Dukkha

Pajāpatī

▶ Pajāpati Gotamī

Pajāpati Gotamī

K. T. S. Sarao
Department of Buddhist Studies, University of Delhi, Delhi, India

Synonyms

Mahāpajāpatī; Mahāprajāpatī Gautamī; Mahāprajāpatī; Pajāpatī; Prâjapati Gautami; Prajāpatī Gautamī; Prajāpatī

Definition

Stepmother of the Buddha, first Buddhist nun, and an eminent Therī.

Pajāpatī Gotamī, also known as Mahāpajāpatī Gotamī (Sk: Mahāprajāpatī Gautamī), is widely regarded as the first woman to request ordination from the Buddha and hence the progenitor of the order of Buddhist nuns (bhikkhunī saṃgha). She was both the Buddha's maternal aunt and adoptive mother, raising him after the death of her sister, Queen Māyā/Mahāmāyā, the Buddha's birth mother. She was born at Devadaha; Daṇḍapāṇi and Suppabuddha were her brothers, and Mahāmāyā was her elder sister ([5], Vol. xviii, p. 7f). However, according to the *Apadāna*, she was the daughter of Añjana Sakka and his wife Sulakkhanā ([6], Vol. ii, p. 538). The *Mahāvastu* says her father was Añjana and her mother Yasodharā ([4], Vol. ii, p. 18). At the time of her birth, an astrologer predicted that Mahāpajāpatī Gotamī would have great leadership qualities, and hence she was named *Mahāpajāpatī* (leader of a large assembly). Gotamī was her clan name ([11], Vol. ii, p. 774; [14], Vol. i, p. 1001). Both she and her elder sister Mahāmāyā were married to King Suddhodana, leader of the Śākyas. When Mahāmāyā died 7 days after giving birth to Siddhattha (the future Buddha), Mahapajapati put her own children Nanda and Sundarī Nandā in the care of nurses and personally took over the responsibility of nursing Siddhattha.

When after attaining enlightenment, the Buddha visited Kapilavatthu, Mahāpajāpati began to practice the dhamma and achieved the stage of a stream enterer (*sotāpanna*). When her husband, Suddhodana, died, she decided to request ordination. Her opportunity came when the Buddha visited Kapilavatthu to settle a dispute between the Sākiyans and the Koḷiyans over sharing the waters of the river Rohiṇī. After settling the dispute, the Buddha preached the *Kalahavivāda Sutta*, and 500 young Sākiyan men joined the saṃgha. Their wives, led by Pajāpatī, went to the Buddha and requested to be ordained. According to tradition, she thrice requested the Buddha's permission to join the saṃgha but was refused each time. Finally, she cut her hair, put on the robes of a nun, and, accompanied by 500 Śākyan women, walked to Vesālī. Upon arrival, she approached Ānanda, the Buddha's personal attendant and one of his principal disciples. He approached the Buddha on Mahāpajāpatī's behalf and the Buddha in response to his query affirmed that women are qualified to achieve the final fruit of the dhamma (i.e., nirvāṇa) and granted her request. However, the Buddha is said to have stipulated eight important rules (*garudhammā*) as the condition for Mahāpajāpatī's admission to the saṃgha. These rules were ([3], Vol. V, pp. 354–355):

1. A nun who has been ordained (even) for a century must greet respectfully, rise up from her seat, salute with joined palms, do proper homage to a monk ordained but that day. And this rule is to be honored, respected, revered, venerated, and never to be transgressed during her life.
2. A nun must not spend the rains (*vassāvāsa*) in a residence where there is no monk.
3. Every half-month, a nun should desire two things from the bhikkhu saṃgha: the asking (as to the date) of the Observance (uposatha) day, and the coming for the exhortation.
4. After the rains, a nun must invite (criticism both from) the bhikkhu saṃgha and the bhikkhunī saṃgha on any of three grounds: what they have seen, what they have heard, and what they have suspected.
5. A nun, offending against an important rule, must undergo penance (*mānatta*) for half a month before both saṃghas.
6. When, as a probationer, she has trained in the six rules (*sikkhamānā*) for 2 years, she should seek ordination from both saṃghas.
7. A monk must not be abused or reviled in any way by a nun.
8. From today, admonition of monks by nuns is forbidden, but the admonition of nuns by monks is not forbidden. This rule, too, is to be honored, respected, revered, venerated, and never to be transgressed during her life.

Later some nuns raised doubts about the procedure adopted in Pajāpatī's ordination and refused to hold the *uposatha* with her. However, the Buddha announced that he himself had ordained her and that everything was proper ([8], Vol. iv, p. 149). After her ordination, Pajāpatī came to the Buddha and worshipped him. The Buddha preached to her and gave her a subject for meditation. Besides being the first Buddhist

P

nun and leader of the Bhikkhunī Saṃgha since its inception, she attained the six higher knowledges and supernormal powers. Once at an assembly of monks and nuns in Jetavana, the Buddha declared Pajāpatī chief of those who had experience (*rattaññūnam*) ([7], Vol. i, p. 25). She often served as a trusted intermediary in communications between the *bhikkhunī* and the Buddha.

In her past life, at Padumuttara Buddha's time, Mahāpajāpatī was born in Haṃsavatī. In this birth on hearing the Buddha assign the foremost place in experience to a nun, she resolved to gain similar recognition herself, doing many good deeds to that end. After many births, she was born at Vārāṇasī when she served five Paccekabuddhas. After that, she was born in a village near Vārāṇasī, and ministered to 500 Paccekabuddhas ([6], Vol. ii, p. 529ff; [11], Vol. i, p. 185f.; [15], p. 140ff). It is said that once Pajāpatī made a wonderfully elaborate robe made of marvelous material for the Buddha. But the Buddha declined to accept it and recommended that it be given to the saṃgha. Mahāpajāpatī was highly disappointed. When Ānanda apprised the Buddha of her disappointment, the latter explained that he had done so not only for the greater benefit of Mahāpajāpatī but also to set this as an example for the future benefactors of the saṃgha ([14], Vol. ii, p. 1001ff). That the Buddha had great love for her is reflected in an example when she lay ill. As there were no monks to visit her and preach to her, this being against the rule, the Buddha made an amendment in the rule and went personally to preach to her ([10], Vol. iv, p. 56). Mahāpajāpatī's name appears several times in the Jātakas ([2], Vol. ii, p. 202, Vol. iii, p. 182, Vol. vi, p. 481). In the later part of her life, she attained arhanthood, as is recorded in her own verse, in the *Therīgāthā*: "cessation has been attained by me" ([9], p. 158). She died at Vesālī at the ripe age of 120. On realizing that her life was coming to an end, she took leave of the Buddha and died after performing various miracles. It has been pointed out in the texts that in terms of marvels which went with her funeral rites, they were second only to those of the Buddha.

Six verses uttered by Mahāpajāpatī form part of the *Therīgāthā* ([9], pp. 157–162). Her accomplishments have always inspired women and within the male-dominated social context of her age, she became a quintessential example of a woman's potential for spiritual achievement and leadership.

Cross-References

- ▶ Arahant
- ▶ Bhikkhunī
- ▶ Jātaka
- ▶ Mahāpajāpatī
- ▶ Pacceka-Buddha
- ▶ Saṃgha
- ▶ Thera- and Therīgāthā

References

1. Blackstone KR (1998) Women in the footsteps of the Buddha: struggle for liberation in the Therīgāthā. Curzon Press, Richmond
2. Fausböll V (ed) (1977–1897) The Jātaka, 6 vols. Luzac, London
3. Horner IB (tr) (1951) The book of discipline, vol 5. Pali Text Society, London
4. Jones JJ (trans) (1949–1956) The Mahāvastu, Sacred books of the east, 3 vols (16, 18, 19). Luzac, London
5. Law BC (ed and tr) (1958) The chronicle of the Island of Ceylon or the Dīpavaṃsa. Ceylon Hist J (Colombo) 7:1–266
6. Lilley ME (ed) (2000) Apadāna, 2 vols. Pali Text Society, London
7. Morris R, Hardy E (eds) (1885–1900) The Aṅguttara Nikāya, 5 vols. Pali Text Society, London
8. Norman HC (ed) (1906) The commentary of the Dhammapada, 4 vols. Pali Text Society, London
9. Norman KR (tr) (1991) The elders' verses. II: Therīgāthā. Pali Text Society, Oxford
10. Olderberg H (ed) (1879–1883) The Vinaya Piṭakaṃ, 5 vols. Pali Text Society, London
11. Walleser H, Kopp H (eds) (1924–1956) Manorathapūraṇī: Buddhaghosa's Commentary on the Aṅguttara Nikāya. 5 vols. Pali Text Society, London
12. Walters JS (1994) The Buddha's mother's story. Hist Relig 33:350–379
13. Walters JS (1995) Gotamī's story. In: Lopez DS Jr (ed) Buddhism in practice. Princeton University Press, Princeton, pp 113–138
14. Woods JH, Kosambi D, Horner IB (eds) (1922–1938) Papañcasūdanī: Majjhimanikāyaṭṭhakathā of Buddhaghosācariya, 5 vols. Pali Text Society, London

15. Woodward FL, Hardy E, Muller E, Barua DL et al (eds) (1891–1977) Paramatthadīpanī, Dhammapālācariya's commentary on the Therīgāthā, the Vimānavatthu. Pali Text Society, London

Pakudha Kātyāyana

Mangala Ramchandra Chinchore
Department of Philosophy, Centre for Studies in Classical Indian Buddhist Philosophy and Culture, University of Pune, Pune, Maharashtra, India

Definition

Ājīvaka, holder of *Akṛtatāvāda*, one of the six well-known *Śrāmaṇic* thinkers, learned, well-known ascetics, and acclaimed contemporary philosophers,

Akṛtatāvādī Buddhas' Opponent

It is a fact that the Buddha did not emerge in a vacuum, but had some intellectual background on which he taught the truth of life and the world in a novel way. His prevalent background and contextual framework enables one to know the significant contribution of the Buddha. One gets clarity in understanding by contrast to the alternative theories in circulation in ancient India. When one searches for his contemporary prominent thinkers to understand that historical context and situation in order to situate the Buddha, the name of Pakudha Kaccāyana (Sk. Prakṛudha-Kātyāyana) is traceable prominently. In the *Praś ṇopaniṣad* and the *Sāmaññaphala-sutta* (i.e., the second *sutta*) of the *Dīgha-Nikaya*, one is told that he was the senior most among philosophers (*titthiyā/tirthyāḥ)* contemporary with Gautama Buddha [1].

Prakṛudha Kātyāyana seems to be *Ājīvaka* and upholder of *Akutavāda* (Sk. *Akṛtatāvāda*) (nonaction theory). According to him, the world is constituted of the seven eternal substances, namely, *Pṛthivi-kāya* (earth), *Āpa-kāya* (water), *Tejas-kāya* (fire), *Vāyu-kāya* (air), *Sukha* (joy/happiness), *Duḥkha* (unhappiness/suffering), and *Ātman*/*Jīva* (self/consciousness). Out of these elementary substances, the first four are visible and material, whereas the last three are invisible and spiritual. They are by nature different, and hence plurality (*Anekavāda*) is embedded into the very nature of the universe. It is this which makes Prakṛudha Kātyāyana *Anekāṁtavādī* (pluralist). They are eternal substances and remain unaffected in any composition. "*Akṛta*" means "not being made," similar to "doing nothing," "without effect."

Basically all of them are not created (Sk. *Anirmita*), impossible to be done away with (Sk. *Avadhya*), steady/changeless (Sk. *Kūṭastha*), static (Sk. *Staṁbhavat*), immovable (Sk. *Acala*), cannot be harmed or get annihilated (Sk. *Ahanya*), and cannot undergo modification/transformation/alteration (Sk. *Avikārī*) by anything like happiness or unhappiness (Sk. *Sukha-Duḥkha*). They do not interact among themselves and are in-affective. Rather as the seven constitutive elementary substances of the world are not liable to change, nothing made out of it also changes and obviously is eternal, that is, *Śāśtvata-vāda* (doctrine of eternality and stability). Change is superficial and not real [2]. Change is just mechanical movement, and there is no difference in the external world of things and human beings with regard to change. Both are movements/actions (Sk. *Kriyā*) and predetermined by the laws of nature, which are beyond human control. Human beings are merely passive recipients of whatever happens in the world – inner or outer.

Further, any action does not bear effect – good or bad. Obviously one should not bother about the results and consequences of actions performed; that is how he denies moral causality. Even if one kills somebody with a knife, it goes into the hollow and cannot kill/destroy any eternal substance. That is why, in the world, there is no need of an agent (like God) to destroy, kill, listen, speak, know, or make others know. There is no essential relation between action and retribution of its fruits. Consequently, morality in an individual or social life is not required. One does not live

P

according to one's will, leave apart doing something purposively and intending to respond in a particular way. One is helpless, as things are beyond control. Such helplessness obviously leads to fatalism (Sk. *Daivāda*). So do not do anything, because nothing is going to happen. Even if one performs or not, it is not going to produce any effect, and ultimately it will not affect one's life.

Death is mere dissolution of bound into unbound bodily/physical eternal substances. Pleasure (Sk. *Sukha*) creates attachment of self to body. Suffering/unhappiness (Sk. *Duḥkha*) is separation or detachment. If the goal of life is happiness, then enjoy as per your will licentiously. Self (Sk. *Ātman*) is mentioned as an independent spiritual substance, because of which there is consciousness (Sk. *Cetanā*) to experience bodily pleasure. He asserted complete freedom, insisted on the natural way of life (Sk. *Yadṛcchāvāda*), and promoted spontaneity (Sk. *Svabhāva*) [3].

Truly speaking, in the *Sāmaññaphala-sutta* of the *Dīgha-Nikāya*, one does not find any passage directly stating views of Prakṛudha Kātyāyana, but only the criticism of Prakṛudha Kātyāyana by the Buddha is seen [4]. It is obvious because the Buddha himself was not interested in criticism and debate. Though what the Buddha taught was indirectly a blow to and rejection of all such contemporary views. He was not intending to establish his own views, nor was he interested to oppose that of others. Rather he was interested in teaching to live independently of the prevalent dogmas and insisted on practicing morality in a novel way.

The Buddha's teaching, especially his doctrine of *Anattā* (Sk. *Anātmatā*) (non-substantiality) and *Aniccā* (Sk. *Anityatā*) (impermanence), is a kind of criticism of Prakṛudha Kātyāyana's *Akṛtatāvāda* (nonaction theory). Buddhist theory of *Anātmatā – Pudgala-nairātmya* (non-eternality of self/soul) and *Dharma-nairātmya* (non-eternality of nature/elements/features) – is a denial of all kinds of substances irrespective of the consideration whether they are material or spiritual. Obviously, eternality of the seven substances including *Ātman* or *Jīva* is rejected. Similarly, according to the Buddha, everything is subject to change (Sk. *Anitya*) and there is no predetermination – causal or purposive. What one experiences is only interrelatedness – *Pratītya-samutpāda*.

One thing is clear that man cannot live without action; rather action is the indicator of liveliness. Naturally, *Akarma-vāda* (not to do action) cannot be advocated by anybody. After doing action (Sk. *Kriyā*) only, the question of whether it is performed with or without volition (mechanically) arises. In other words, whether it produces intended results or not is a point of debate. With reference to the human world at least, motives and intentions are involved behind actions, and minimally sometimes at least they do reap the fruits intended. Otherwise nobody would have purposively performed actions and have desired for their effects to be fructified in life.

Further, the entire universe is not completely predetermined by causal laws of nature or fully governed as per dictates of the will of an agent – human or divine. Hence, it is not the knife but the person using the knife [5] to be held responsible for using it properly or wrongly, and that brings in the significant role of morality in human life. To hold that man who is misusing the knife should not be punished or held guilty is to promote immorality. Consequently, the society will be irresponsible and may lead to chaos. It is social licentiousness and propagation of immorality by Prakṛudha Kātyāyana's *Akṛtatāvāda* which was rejected and criticized by the Buddha, for *Akṛtatāvāda* goes against proper organization of society and rule-governed life. Morality is essential to bring in peace. There is a difference between mechanical movements (*Kriyā*) and voluntary actions (Sk. *Karma*). Human beings have intentions and motives (Sk. *Hetu*); they are not machines. Volitions make one responsible and moral. There is indeed a need of morality, accountability, and allocation of responsibility.

Moreover, the Buddha advocated the eightfold path (Sk. *Aṣṭāṅgika-mārga*), which is based on intentional efforts for the development of character (Sk. *Śīla*). Hence, actions do lead to results and the effect of an action is presumed. In Buddhism, right and wrong actions (Pali *Kusala/Akusala-Kamma*) play a vital role. The Buddha was not interested in creating chaos in the society, but intended to bring in change through morality, in order to establish peace by a new world-order. It was essential to make people responsible and maintain social order by advocating rules and regulations (*Vinaya*). With an alternative set of ideas, he desired to motivate people in the right direction. Doing action in the right way is essential to organize and transform society morally. Thus, there is an indirect criticism of the *Akṛtatāvāda* of Prakṛudha Kātyāyana by the Buddha.

Cross-References

- ▶ Anattā (Buddhism)
- ▶ *Anicca*
- ▶ *Aṣṭāṅgamārga*
- ▶ *Cetanā*
- ▶ *Dīgha Nikāya*
- ▶ *Duḥkha*
- ▶ *Karma*
- ▶ *Kusala*
- ▶ *Pratītya Samutpāda*
- ▶ *Puḍgala (Puggala)*
- ▶ *Śīla*
- ▶ *Sukha*
- ▶ *Vinaya*

References

1. Kasyapa BJ (ed) (1961) Dīgha-Nikāya. Pali Text Publication Board, Bihar Govt, Nalanda
2. Walsh M (1995) The long discourse of the Buddha: a translation of the Dīgha-Nikāya (1. *Brahmajāla-sutta* – pp 67–90 and 2. *Sāmaññaphala-sutta* – pp 91–109). Wisdom, Boston
3. Winternitz M (1993) *Sāmaññaphala-sutta* (i.e. the second *sutta*) of the *Dīgha-Nikāya*. In: History of Indian literature, vol II. Motilal Banarsidass, Delhi, pp 36, 191
4. Warder AK (2000) Indian Buddhism, 3rd edn. Motilal Banarsidass, Delhi, pp 38–41
5. Thomas EJ (tr) (1935) Early Buddhist scriptures. Kegan Paul, London

Palace of Indra

▶ Amaravati

Pāli

Sanjay Kr. Singh
Department of Buddhist Studies, University of Delhi, Delhi, India

Definition

The language of Theravādin Buddhist texts.

Introduction

The word *Pāli* means "a scriptural text." However, western scholars have used the term to mean the language in which those scriptures were written. Hence, over a period of time, the word has come to mean as "the language of the Buddhist scriptures." This meaning can be said to be a slight extension of the original use of the word.

Pali refers to that ancient language in which canonical works and commentaries could be found thereon, in addition to several other writings of the Southern Buddhists, that is, those belonging to the countries of modern Myanmar, Sri Lanka, and Thailand. In fact, these are the only works of Hīnayāna Buddhism that exist today.

Many centuries ago, Hīnayāna Buddhists also wrote their scriptures in languages other than Pāli. However, with the early extinction of Buddhism from India, all those non-Pāli texts were lost. Since, Pāli at that time was the language for writing scriptures for most Buddhists throughout India – both northern and southern – it would be incorrect to term Pāli as the language of Hīnayāna Buddhism or Southern Buddhism.

As a Middle Indic or Middle Indo-Aryan language, Pāli is sometimes grouped in the Prakrit languages. Most of the features of the Pāli language seem to be borrowed from other Middle Indo-Aryan languages, and hence, its actual origin is not known. The main idea or core of the Pāli language is from the vernaculars used in west and west-central India and is different from the vernacular language used by the Buddha, who hailed from the north and northeastern part of India.

P

Buddha's own language was neither Pāli nor Māgadhī, as claimed by several historians, and both Pāli and Māgadhī differ from each other in many parameters.

It is said that the Buddha permitted his disciples to learn and teach his preaching in their own languages. So, initially Buddhism spread in various local languages, as the followers were from different parts of the country. And when the process of compiling canon of scriptures began few centuries after the death of the Buddha, some of those local dialects were able to influence the language of the scriptures, thus forming a dialectical mixture. While it is difficult to accurately determine the period when the language to be used in the writings of scriptures was finalized, it is very likely that the first canon was written between the third and the first centuries B.C.E.

The linguistic tradition must have been fixed during that time with rules and practices laid down. As the Pāli canonical texts and their commentaries began to be written, they were exported to Ceylon and became a part of their Hīnayāna Buddhism or Southern Buddhism. When the Indian subcontinent was invaded by Muslim and Arab rulers, Pāli became extinct along with Buddhism and was preserved only in the countries that are today referred to as Southern Buddhist countries.

Tipiṭaka is the collective name given to the canonical texts and their commentaries in Pāli language. Besides Sri Lanka, these texts are currently preserved in Myanmar and Thailand, where they were carried from the ancient Ceylon. Tradition says they originated in India and were carried to Ceylon by Emperor Asoka's son Mahinda in the third-century B.C.E.

During the time of Buddha, Sanskrit was already a language of the learned and not readily comprehensible by common masses. Hence, the Buddha wanted to have another language as a medium to spread his teachings. Due to the Buddha's preference for non-Sanskrit local vernaculars, several Middle Indo-Aryan vernaculars prevailing at that time were used by his followers to spread his teachings. With the passage of time, many different linguistic versions of the Buddha's teachings evolved. These words and sermons of the Buddha in different languages were preserved at the evolving centers of Buddhist learning, which in turn added to their prestige.

Since none of the different linguistic versions was unmixed, some of the dialect versions were adopted by the great learning centers through the wandering teachers. The multiplicity of dialects, all enjoying equal acceptance, is what makes it difficult to assign a place of origin to Pāli.

The Buddha preached in Kosala (modern Ayodhyā in Uttar Pradesh of India) and Magadha (modern Patna and Gaya districts in Bihar of India). In Ceylon, the language of Magadha, for reasons not well-known, was referred to as Pāli, considered to be the synonym of Māgadhī.

Pāli scriptures have three chronological dialects. First is the "gāthās" or verses of the canon. The other two are the canonical prose and postcanonical prose. There is also postcanonical verse in which older and younger forms are found to be mixed indiscriminately. Neither of these dialects has close relation with Māgadhī Prakrit, but some Māgadhī-like forms are definitely found in the Pāli works. However, grammarians consider such forms to be borrowings from the Māgadhī dialect, first into various non-Māgadhī dialects, and later on, through them into Pāli. Some grammarians have suggested Takṣaśilā (modern Taxila), a great place for learning in ancient times, and Ujjayini (modern Ujjain) to be the places where Pāli initially developed as a language.

Features of Pāli language

A Middle Indo-Aryan language, Pāli is closest to Old Indo-Aryan language, that is, Vedic and Sanskrit. In general, it has the same type of relationship with Old Indo-Aryan language as all other Middle Indo-Aryan languages have. However, it is not easy to derive it completely from any of the well-documented older dialects. Hence, it is probable that the basis of Pali might be some other Old Indo-Aryan dialect. For instance, the enclitic third personal pronoun in Pāli *se* is found in Avestan *se*, Old Persian *saiy*, but not in Vedic or Sanskrit.

In Pāli phonology, Sanskrit vowel ṛ is represented by *a*, *i*, or *u*. And the long diphthongs *ai* and *au* coalesce with *e* and *o*. Normally, long vowels get shortened in close syllables and are present only in open syllables, which results in two new vowels in Pāli, short *e* and *o*, for example, *oṭṭha-* "lip"; Sanskrit *oṣṭha*. Moreover, single Sanskrit consonants nearly remain unchanged, except that *d* and *dh* become *l* and *lh*, respectively (as in the ṛgveda), and the three sibilants coalesce as *s*. Also, consonant clusters normally get simplified and assimilated as two consonants only, for example, *tikkh a-* "sharp"; Sanskrit *tīkṣna*, *aggi-* "fire"; Sanskrit *agni* and *satta* "seven"; Sanskrit *sapta*. All final consonants disappear, for example, *vijju* "lightning"; Sanskrit *vidyut*.

Talking about nouns in Pali, the declension seems to have been simplified compared to that of Sanskrit, for example, the dual number is lost and the eight-case system is reduced. The dative almost completely gets coalesced with the genitive. In the commonest declension, that in *a*, it does not denote direction of motion and a few less common meanings. In the *a-* declension, the instrumental plural ends in *-ehi* (e.g., *dhammehi*), deriving from a form like Vedic *-ebhis* rather than from Sanskrit *-ais*. In all declensions, the dative plural gets coalesced with the genitive plural and the ablative plural with the instrumental plural. In addition, stems ending in consonants are usually converted to vowel declension types, either by addition of a vowel after the consonant, for example, Sanskrit *āpad-* "misfortune" is represented by *āpada-* or by loss of final consonants of the stems.

In the Pali verb system, changes are even greater than in that of the noun. In the younger dialect than in the older, the middle voice is generally obsolescent. There are active endings instead of middle in the passive system. There is almost no perfect tense. The past tense is an amalgam of aorist and flawed forms, which have complicated rules for the appearance or nonappearance of the prefix *a-*. The optative is, however, found in Pali. There are also traces of the Vedic subjunctive in the old dialect.

Several of the verbs of the many types of the present Sanskrit system are found in the commonest type which has a suffix *-a-*, the thematic type. There has also been a spread of a type with suffix *-e-*, which derives from Sanskrit denominative verbs with suffix *-aya-*, for example, *maññeti* "he thinks" as well as *maññati*; Sanskrit *manyate*, Pāli *katheti*; Sanskrit *kathayati* "he tells," and *vadeti* "he says" as well as the old type *vadati*. Although some verbs retain a few historically correct forms, in addition to the new ones, in the future or the past participle or elsewhere, the present stem usually tends to spread through all other parts of the verb system. An example of this can be seen in forms of the verb meaning "to drink," which in Sanskrit has a reduplicated present *pibati* "he drinks," but future *pāsyati* "he will drink" and gerund *pītva* "having drunk"; in Pāli corresponding forms are *pivati*, *pivissati* (and *pāssati*), *and pivitvā* (and *pītvā*), and there are past forms *pivāsim* "I drank" and *apivi* "he drank."

Pāli Literature

Majority of the existing older literature in Pāli language is collected in the *Tipiṭaka Pāli*, the canon of the Theravada school of Buddhism. Although Theravada claimed to be the only orthodox tradition, actually it was only one of a number of schools that gradually became separated when Buddhism began to be propagated over northern India after the *Nibbāna* (Pāli; Sanskrit, *Nirvāṇa*) of the Buddha.

The Theravada school of Buddhism was originally located in central and western India. During the fifth to third-century B.C.E., this school seems to have orally rehearsed its canon in the region's local dialect as per the Buddha's command that his disciples should preach his teachings in their own language rather than in Sanskrit. Comparing with other canons, one learns that the Pāli canon mainly consists of a common source of teaching that is ascribed to the Buddha. There might have been minor modifications, and some secondary texts would have been appended.

The compositions of around the second-century B.C.E. are the significant latest additions to the compositions. Owing to the common similarity with the older texts of other schools,

P

including their contents, it can be assumed that the Pāli canon is essentially the literature of the empire of Magadha and the middle Ganges basin during the sixth to fourth centuries B.C.E., with a later extension to the west.

It is assumed that some time before the fifth-century C.E., the language of the canon came to be treated as the Buddha's own language or the northeastern dialect of Māgadhī. As a result, Pāli emerged as the standard and international language of Theravada Buddhism. Pāli, as a literary language, flourished in India till the Turk invasion, especially in south India till the fourteenth-century C.E.

Pāli was introduced in Ceylon by the third-century B.C.E., from where it spread to Burma by the eleventh-century C.E. Pāli was in use till the twentieth century in Cambodia, Vietnam, Laos, and Thailand. In Indonesia too, it existed in about the eleventh-century C.E. In Ceylon, the Pāli canon was written during the first-century B.C.E. due to the need to put orally transmitted teachings of the Buddha from further misinterpretations. Literature after that period was all completely written.

Divisions of the Tipiṭaka

The *Tipiṭaka*, meaning "Threefold Basket" (Sanskrit, *Tripiṭaka*), consists of three parts: *Vinaya Piṭaka*, *Sutta Piṭaka*, and *Abhidhamma Piṭaka*. *Vinaya Piṭaka* is an elaboration of 227 rules of the Buddhist monastic discipline. It includes explanation of the founding of each rule by the Buddha. It also briefly discusses the Buddha's life, his founding of the order, and a record of events in the order down to the first great schism. It was written around c. 386 B.C.E. Content-wise, it is mainly legalistic, though it has a few incidental narratives of literary merit, besides much matter of sociological interest.

Sutta Piṭaka, the second of the *Tipiṭaka*, consists of doctrines (*dhammā*) of Buddhism developed in dialogues (*sutta* or *suttanta*), stories, and poems. The dialogues contain discussions on philosophical and metaphysical topics like the nature of the universe, the presence of a soul, free will, causation, immortality, ethics, transmigration, and the deity. It also contains discussion on the good life, including the unsatisfactory nature of the pursuit of transient worldly happiness, self-possession, harmless living, the Buddhist way of renunciation, self-control, wisdom, and meditation leading to detachment, *upekkhā*, and the state in which *nibbāna* or Enlightenment can be attained.

Here, the Buddha is depicted as a traveler to different parts of eastern India where he engages in dialogues. It is given in direct speech in an incisive and lively style on meeting with wandering philosophers, kings, priests, ascetics, nobles, and other people from various professions in the towns and cities. For those people who have not renounced their life and become a wanderer, good friendship and social virtues are suggested for increasing the happiness of the individual as well as the society. In these discourses, humor exists, for instance, when the Buddha narrates tales to portray the degeneration of the society resulting from the attempts of a king to do away with crime in his own manner, in utter disregard of external law (dhammā).

Another instance is of a deity, who claims to have created the universe and says he is omniscient and omnipresent but is mainly concerned with protecting his own ignorance before the other inhabitants of heaven. The longer dialects are considered to be the best and are collected separately in the Dīgha-nikāya (collection of long dialogues), which is supposed to be the most ancient and authentic part of the Sutta, due to the fluency and richness of the language and also because of the originality and the variety of its episodes.

At times, short poems or verses occur in the dialogues. It may be a spontaneous verse (udāna) uttered under the inspiration of some experience or incident. It is usually told with metaphorical reference to Buddhist teachings. Sometimes, it may be a brief summary of Buddhist doctrine. There is a dialogue that is said to have been added later by Buddha's disciple Ānanda. This dialogue has several incidental verses in elaborate lyric meters that vividly describe the qualities of the Buddha. There is yet another dialogue that contains few inquisitive verses from common folklore about the guardian spirits of the four parts of the earth, one of whom rules over a utopian territory that has neither work nor property.

The *Dīgha-nikāya*, along with three other *Nikāyas* – the *Majjhima* (medium length), *Saṃyutta* (classified), and *Aṅguttara* (enumerating) – form the Four *Nikāyas*, which are interlocking but not quite uniform.

A fifth *nikāya*, called the *Khuddaka-nikāya* (collection of minor texts), is a collection of the poetry of the canon, except as noted above and the songs (*geyya*) in the first section of the *Saṃyutta*. This probably started as a collection of poems by followers of the Buddha, including few short dialogues attributed to the Buddha himself. Although the Buddha recommended the hearing of songs, he is believed to have disapproved poetic compositions as a worldly means of earning a livelihood. Hence, initially the official version of the doctrine may not have included the *Khuddaka* texts.

The discourses of the Buddha were abounding with stories, similes, and some verses that give a lead to the poetic presentation of *dhamma*. The *Khuddaka* texts were perhaps greatly expanded down to at least the third-century B.C.E., and new genres were used for the propagation of Buddhist philosophical teachings.

Pāli poetry may be divided into lyric and epic. In a lyric, around 30 different meters are used. There prevails a great variety of rhythmical patterns and musical words. In an epic, there is a single narrative meter that has a very flexible line, and monotony is avoided. While the old meters were narrative and permitted variation of rhythm except in the final cadence, Pāli meters are quantitative.

In the old or archaic meters, the variation was possible by substituting a short syllable for a long one and was based on the number of syllables in a line. While in the Pāli lyric meters, two short syllables are exactly equal to one long. Sometimes, the two short syllables are substituted for one long.

Majority of Pāli lyric meters have a musical phrase as a basis and possess a structure that was unknown to Indian poetry in the fifth-century B.C.E. Along with certain features of style, content, vocabulary, and figures of speech, these new meters of Pāli poetry are the prototypes of those of the *kāvya* literature in Sanskrit, Prakrit, Apabhraṃśa, and classical Hindi. Some dramatic dialogues in verse that imply some kind of performance have been adduced as proof concerning the growth of the Indian drama during this period.

The best examples of Pāli epic poetry are found in the *Khuddaka*, in its longer stories, the *Jātaka*. Some stories are common to both the *Dīgha* and the *Jātaka*. The *Dīgha* contains a few *Jātakas*, that is, stories of the Buddha's births or incarnations in prose. However, an epic narrative (*akkhāna*) could be either in prose or verse. Later on, these two forms diverged greatly from their basic well-known tradition of storytelling and became the *kāvya* and verse *mahākāvya* (epic).

Several *Jātaka* pieces have too few verses to narrate a story. These give only the climax or most significant speech or the moral of a once well-known story. However, in certain cases, the complete story is preserved in ancient form in the *Dīgha* or elsewhere. The *Jātaka* is a significant treasury of ancient folktales, with only a layer of Buddhist ethics. These possess rich data on ancient society.

The *Khuddaka* also includes four inferior narrative books in verse. These were compiled as edifying material for routine preaching, for instance, the lives of Buddhas, *Buddhavaṃsa*, and legends of monks and nuns, *Apadāna*. Moreover, there are the lyric anthologies, which are the work of several hundred authors, both men and women. There is also the *Dhammapada*, *Suttanipāta*, *Theragāthā*, and *Therīgāthā*, which (except the *Dhammapada*) contain the ballads and some short epic episodes. In addition to five other miscellaneous books, the *Khuddaka* includes also an extensive philosophical compendium (*Paṭisaṃbhidāmagga*) similar to the *Abhidhamma* books.

The *Abhidhamma Piṭaka* is a collection of treatises that systematically elaborate the Buddhist philosophy in accordance with Theravada teaching. While the *Sutta* is the most interesting of these divisions, as it contains the largest and earliest texts, the *Abhidhamma* is a secondary systematization of the doctrines of the *Sutta*.

The *Abhidhamma* originated as an explanation and elaboration of certain lists and summaries of points of doctrine called *Mātikā* (notes). Majority of the *mātikās* in the *Abhidhamma* and much of their explanations are found scattered in the *Sutta*. The basic list is promulgated in the *Dīgha* account of the Buddha's instructions to the monks before his *Nibbana*. It consists of the *Vibhaṅga*, the *Dhammasaṅgaṇi* and *Dhātukathā*, the *Puggalapaññatti*, the *Kathāvatthu*, and the *Yamaka*. The *Vibhaṅga* is the basic synopsis of *mātikās* and explanations. The *Dhammasaṅgaṇi* and *Dhātukathā* are primarily cross-classifications of points of doctrine on ethics, psychology, physics, etc., leading to a synthetic system of natural and moral philosophy. The *Puggalapaññatti* enumerates types of characters. The *Kathāvatthu* consists of polemic on points disputed with other schools of Buddhism and exemplifies early techniques of debate and logic. The *Yamaka* is a manual of exercises in formal logic. The *Paṭṭhāna* is a grandiose elaboration of a general theory of causality synthesized from elements of causal theory in the *Sutta* and *Vibhaṅga*. The causal theories were fundamental to the early Buddhist doctrine about the nature of the universe and of man's predicament in it.

Later Pāli Literature

It is found in the historical novel (*akkhāyikā*), the *Milindapañha*, in which it begins with a long *Dīgha* style dialogue. Gradually, the work seems to have grown by large additions to important points of perhaps the first-century B.C.E. At around the same period, theoretical works on exegesis like *Netti* and *Peṭakopadesa* were written. Both these works were Indian. The earliest existing grammar of Kaccāyana is also an Indian work.

The Mahāvihāra (Great Monastery) in Anuradhapura, the ancient capital of Ceylon, became the main center of Theravada learning in the fifth-century C.E. In India, new languages were adopted by new movements and schools of Buddhism, eclipsing the Theravada school that followed the canon in the ancient Pāli.

In order to interpret the canon, the Sinhalese translated oral commentarial (*Aṭṭhakathā*) traditions into the ancient Sinhalese language from the third-century B.C.E. onward. This commentary got comprehensively completed by around 100 C.E. Successive writers in Ceylon compiled the *Dīpavaṃsa* or the "History of the Island" in Pāli (verse form) by the fourth-century C.E.

Indian Buddhists getting education at Anuradhapura in Ceylon translated the essential parts of the Sinhalese commentary into Pāli language in the fifth-century C.E. Then a person by name Buddhaghosa wrote an introductory account of the whole range of Sinhalese doctrine called the *Visuddhimagga*. He also wrote commentaries on the *Vinaya*, *Abhidhamma*, Four *Nikāyas*, and two *Khuddaka* texts. Subsequently, commentaries on the remaining *Khuddaka* books and the *Netti* were written by Dhammapāla, Buddhadatta, Upasena, Mahānāma, and the anonymous authors of the *Apadāna Commentary*, *Jātaka Commentary*, which includes full stories for all the *Jātakas*, and *Dhammapada Commentary*, which possess more than 400 illustrative stories.

At the beginning of the sixth-century C.E., *Mahāvaṃsa* (Great History), a verse chronicle based on the *Dīpavaṃsa*, was written by Mahānāma. It was unified in treatment and much more polished in style compared to the *Dīpavaṃsa*. It, in fact, marked the beginning of a new phase in Pāli literature, referred to as the later *kāvya*, which is not continuous with the old Pāli *kāvya* in the canon, the direct successors of which were in Sanskrit and Prakrit. It derives its style after old Pāli *kāvya* had undergone several centuries of refinement at the hands of various successors.

The aim of the *Mahāvaṃsa*, according to Mahānāma, was to inspire good people with religious emotion. Like the *Dīpavaṃsa*, Mahānāma's chronicle narrates the history of Buddhism from the Buddha's complete Enlightenment to the third-century B.C.E. in India and the fourth-century C.E. in Ceylon. Mahānāma is influenced by the conventions of an epic *kavya*, and he interrupts his annals to celebrate the deeds of Devānaṃpiyatissa (third-century B.C.E.) and Vaṭṭagāmani (first-century B.C.E.). These two great Sinhalese kings were primarily responsible for the introduction and firm establishment of Buddhism in Ceylon.

In Ceylon, Vaṭṭagāmani is regarded as a national hero who freed his country from Tamil rule. Later poets in Ceylon wrote supplements to the *Mahāvaṃsa*, which are often called *Cūlavaṃsa* or "Little History." The first and longest *Cūlavaṃsa* was written by Dhammakitti in the thirteenth-century C.E. It centers on the epic treatment of Parakkamabāhu I (twelfth-century C.E.). The last supplement covers up to the arrival of English in Ceylon.

The mode of chronicle epic was adopted for writing the histories of various countries of Southeast Asia as well as for writing other narratives, especially the life of the Buddha. Some such writings were the Medhankara's *Jinacarita* written in Ceylon in the thirteenth century and the anonymous *Mālālaṅkāra* written in Burma in the eighteenth century. The *Buddhālaṅkāra* of Sīlavaṃsa (Burma; fifteenth century) narrates the popular story of the Buddha's previous incarnation as Sumedha, when he first resolved to become a Buddha.

There are many other books that deal with certain other aspects of religious history. The prose (*Mahā*) *Bodhivaṃsa* by Upatissa (c. 970 C.E.) on the bringing of a cutting of the Buddha's enlightenment tree to Ceylon is of great stylistic interest. It displays much of the vocabulary of contemporary Sanskrit *kāvya* assimilated to Pāli. In Dhammakitti's *Dāṭhāvaṃsa* (Ceylon, c. 1200) on the Tooth Relic, the style of the true Sanskrit *mahākāvya* with its several cantos in different meters, often of lyric origin, is exemplified. Then, there are twentieth-century *mahākāvyas* such as Medhānanda's *Jinavaṃsadīpa* (published 1917 in Ceylon) on the life of the Buddha. Other noted biographies include Mahāmaṅgala's *Buddhaghosuppatti*, considered to be a popular religious novel on the life of the saint, and the learned Ñanābhivaṃsa's *Rājādhirājavilāsini* (Burma; eighteenth century) which celebrates the deeds of the contemporary king of Burma, Bodopayā.

The *Pajjāmadhu* of Buddhappiya, an Indian monk living in Ceylon in thirteenth century, describing the Buddha epitomizes the later lyric *kāvya*. The *Telakatāhagāthā* on renunciation, recited by a monk thrown into a cauldron of boiling oil, who miraculously remains alive for a time because of his innocence also illustrates the later lyric *kāvya*. The much longer *Samantakūṭavaṇṇanā* of Vedeha (Ceylon; thirteenth century) is on the borderline of epic and lyric. It describes the Buddha's life and mythical visits to Ceylon, culminating with his visit to its highest peak, the Adam's peak. Vedeha remarkably describes the Sinhalese scenery in his work.

The *Jinālaṅkāra* of Buddharakkhita (Ceylon; twelfth century) on the life of the Buddha represents the genre of *citrakavya*, or poem displaying virtuosity in wordplay and in the mere technicalities of *kāvya* composition as an end in themselves. In late twelfth century, Ānanda wrote *Saddhammopāyana*, a simple but effective didactic poem in 19 cantos. It urges the reader to seize the opportunity of following the Buddhist way. A fine example of his art is the description of the sufferings of animals, especially as beasts of burden.

The anonymous thirteenth-century *attanagaluvihāravaṃsa* (history of the *attanagalu* monastery) is a *kāvya* in mixed prose and verse (a *campu*). In it, Pāli prose has been given a very elaborate and significant treatment, imitating the style of the Sanskrit novels of Bāṇa. Vedeha's *Rasavāhini* is another outstanding collection of popular old stories.

However, much of the old Sinhalese literature remains untranslated. Pāli commentaries written after the eighth century were provided with subcommentaries (*ṭīkā*) which explained the words therein and thus ended up elaborating the exposition of the basic canonical texts. All *ṭīkās* are more technical than the commentaries and as such provide a sufficient basis for modern lexicography. The earliest cycle of *ṭīkās*, of the eighth or ninth centuries, consists of Dhammapāla's work on the Four *Nikāyas* and the *Jātaka*, Vajirabuddhi's on the *Vinaya*, and Ānanda's on the *Abhidhamma*. Dhammapāla, a pupil of Ānanda, wrote a subcommentary on his teacher's *ṭīkā*.

In the twelfth century, Kassapa in south India wrote a succinct *Vinaya ṭīkā* which might be more

P

easily assimilated by his pupils. At around the same time, Sāriputta in Ceylon wrote detailed *ṭīkās* on the *Vinaya* and the *Four Nikāyas*. In addition, there is a cycle of undated *ṭikas* on the *Khuddaka* and many *ṭīkās* on such treatises (commentaries) as the *Visuddhimagga*. A "new" *Dīgha ṭīkā* was also written in Burma in the eighteenth or nineteenth century. Still, exegesis neither came to an end with the Pāli versions of the commentaries nor with the numerous handbooks on various aspects of philosophy and the discipline.

Cross-References

▶ Dhammapāla
▶ Hīnayāna
▶ Jātaka
▶ Prākrit
▶ Tipiṭaka
▶ Visuddhimagga

References

1. Bapat PV (1971) 2500 years of Buddhism. Publication Division, Govt. of India Delhi
2. Geiger W (1993) Pali literature and language, reprint (Eng. trans: Ghosh B). Munshiram Manoharlal, New Delhi
3. Hazra KL (1994) Pali language and literature. Munshiram Manoharlal, New Delhi
4. Law BC (1974) A history of Pali literature, vol I & II. Indological Book House, Delhi
5. Norman KR (ed) (2000) Pali grammar. Pali Text Society, Oxford
6. Winternitz M (1977) A history of Indian literature, reprint, vol II. Munshiram Manoharlal, New Delhi

Pañca Namaskāra Mantra

▶ Ṇamōkarā Mantra

Pañcasila

▶ Warfare (Buddhism)

Pañca-Sīla

▶ *Pañcaśīla*

Pañcaśīla

Mangala Ramchandra Chinchore
Department of Philosophy, Centre for Studies in Classical Indian Buddhist Philosophy and Culture, University of Pune, Pune, Maharashtra, India

Synonyms

Pañca-Sīla (in Pali); *Pañca-śīla* (in Sk.) (Five-precepts)

Definition

Samyak-Karmānta (right-action) for all followers of Buddhism, vows/promises are made to develop moral character, ideal personality, and virtues for both ordained *Bhikṣu-Bhikṣuṇī* (monks-nuns) and *Upāsakas-Upāsikās* (lay-men-women). Prayer of everyday practitioners. Core of Buddhist way of life.

Minimum Duties and Responsibilities to Become a Man

Pañca-śīla (Five-precepts) is a concept, which occurs in the context of Eightfold-path (Sk. *Aṣṭāṅgika-mārga*) in general, and right-action (*Samyak-Karmānta*) in particular [1]. The Eightfold-path (Sk. *Aṣṭāṅgika-mārga*) is nothing else but a way to mitigate/control/destroy pain and suffering (Sk. *Duḥkha-nirodha-gāminī-pratipad*), discovered by Gautama, the Buddha, and taught to his then prevalent disciples [2]. They are vows/promises, which enable anybody to develop *Śīla* – moral character, ideal personality, and virtues facilitating convenience in practical life. There are basic five points of training oneself to be observed by all practitioners of Buddhism, irrespective of the difference between ordained monks-nuns (Sk. *Bhikṣu-Bhikṣuṇī*) on the one hand, and all lay-disciples men-women (Sk. *Upāsakas-Upāsikās*) on the other. They are precepts/vows/promises that are often recited after the three-refuges (Sk. *Tri-śaraṇas*), viz. the Buddha, the teaching (Pali-*Dhamma*), and the community of followers of Buddhism (Sk. *Saṁgha*) [3]. They are not imperatives, prescription/prohibitions, or rules laid down by the eternal authority, but modes of training facilitative to practice Buddhist way of life. By taking these five vows and/or voluntary promises, one on the one hand refrains or abandons evil tendencies prevalent and likely to predominate in one self, but by observing these promises given by one's own conviction on the other hand, one attempts to develop virtues, which leads to perfection. They are conducive to and facilitative to any lay-person, who desires to follow and practice the Buddhist way of life.

The five percepts/vows/promises are:

1. *Pāṇātipāta veramani, sikkhāpadaṁ samādiyāmi/* which is generally translated as "I undertake the first vow, to refrain from destroying life of the living creatures." It connotes that a disciple can be considered as the noble one provided, she/he does not perform any act of taking away the life of not only human beings but also of any sentient being. It is an act which I myself will not do, nor can anybody force me to do, or further still if somebody else is doing anything of that kind I shall never associate myself in any way with it. It is a promise not only to abandon the habit (if at all it is already there), or at present an act to be undertaken, or refrain from doing the act in future. One has to be cautious, careful, and use one's own conscience about the act/s one performs, and see to it that they do not create any harm to oneself and others. To put it in other words, I do not have any right to kill myself, or any sentient being in the world. It is an oath that one should not totally annihilate any living creature, which will completely destroy the species. In doing so, one makes himself/herself and others free from danger, animosity, and oppression to all sentient beings. By doing this, one gains freedom from one's own inner cruelty.

   Here it is worth to note that the word "*Atipāta*" means excess or extreme kind of destruction [4], which clearly shows that the Buddha and following him all the Buddhists were aware that it is impossible to practice nonviolence radically and abstain oneself from killing. While living either knowingly but most unwillingly, or else even unknowingly and unintentionally one does violence to oneself and others – human beings or other living organism and various kinds of species [5]. It is done in order to survive, sustain, and exist, and further progress but that too is morally wrong. Hence, to pretend to claim that one is following complete nonviolence in practice is either bluffing or it is just a matter of hypocrisy, formality, and superficiality. Instead of pretending and boasting, it is better to be truthful to oneself at least, and hence the word deliberately is used "*Atipāta*," which means killing in excess is to be avoided, that is factually practicable and significant, a promise given by the Buddhist followers.
2. *Adinnādanā veramaṇi, sikkhāpadaṁ samādiyami/* which is usually translated as "I undertake the second vow, to refrain from taking that which is not given." It means, whatever I do not possess, if I claim it to be mine even though it is not given to me, it is morally wrong and I should refrain myself from such an act at any cost. I shall teach myself and others that whatever is given alone should be accepted. I do not have any right to encroach upon someone else's possessions, with or without his/her permission.

   One should abandon from taking away what is not given (which means stealing – either by force or by not obviously noticeable modes). The disciple of Buddhism can be considered as a noble one, provided one promises that she/he will abstain from taking away what is not given – at present or in future, small or big, concretely in the form of objects or in an abstract way. In doing so, one makes oneself free from danger, animosity, and oppression to all sentient beings. And thereby one gains freedom from one's own inner instinct of possession by stealing.
3. *Kāmesu micchācāra veramani, sikkhāpadaṁ samādiyāmi/* which is generally translated as

"I undertake the third vow to refrain from sexual misconduct." It connotes that I promise not to succumb to illicit sex. The disciple of Buddhism can be considered as a noble one, provided one promises that she/he will abstain from sexual misconduct [6]. By promising and practicing it, one gives freedom to others from danger, animosity, and oppression to all sentient beings of (different/same) sex. By taking this vow, one gains limitless freedom from one's own sexual instinct. It is an oath abiding by social, moral, and religious demands in one's own personal life as well. And hence the word "*Micchācāra*" (misconduct) in this context needs to be carefully paid attention to, especially in contrast to another word which often occurs in Buddhist literature "*Sadācāra*" (good-conduct) [7]. It is not allowing to cross the boundaries permitted – by nature and culture. If it is within permissible limits, there is no objection by society and religion. But excessive indulgence, rape, and unlawful sexual pleasure, etc., and such type of behavior physically, mentally/emotionally, or even verbally is to be refrained from and avoided or better to be controlled at any cost. One should not do it by oneself and should refrain from helping others indulging in it.

4. *Musāvāda veramani, sikkhāpadaṁ samādiyāmi*/ which is often translated as "I undertake the fourth vow, to refrain from incorrect/wrong/lie-speech." The disciple of Buddhism can be considered as a noble one, provided one promises that she/he will abstain from lying, abusing, speaking harsh words, etc. It is a promise that one will abandon, if it is already there and in future refrain from lying, slander, using harsh words, frivolous talk, abusive words, chattering, etc., which are illustrations of evil speech. It is not only I will follow, but I will teach and persuade others to follow. That will make one free from danger, animosity, and oppression to all sentient beings. In getting freedom from wrong speech, one gains sweetness of heart, entertains agreeable ideas, and comprehends truth beneficial to all.

   Here it is worth to note that neither the Buddha nor his followers are prescribing complete silence, but what is said should not be non-sensical, false, evil, or wrong. Excess and absence both are to be avoided, by any follower of Buddhism is an oath undertaken willingly by oneself and to be taught to all fellow beings, is a promise given by disciple of Buddhism. I myself will not do it, nor allow others to do it, is a precept to be observed in practice at present and in future.

5. *Surāmerayamajjā pamādatthāna veramani, sikkhāpadam samādiyāmi/* which is translated commonly as "I undertake the fifth precept to refrain from intoxicating drinks and drugs, which lead to carelessness." It connotes that the disciple of Buddhism can be considered as a noble one, provided one promises to abstain from intoxicants, flesh, and poisonous drinks, which defile body, mind and harbor evil modes of behavior. In doing so one becomes free from danger, animosity, and oppressing to all sentient beings. And in return gains control over one's own overwhelming instincts and excesses of passions.

All these above-mentioned five promises made by the disciple if practiced consensuously and consistently, they in return bring in virtues, which are of great value – to oneself and society at large – traditionally observed since ancient times preserving originality of the Buddhist way of life. They have a long standing and are maintained in unadulterated form right from the beginning till the end – that is not open to suspicion at present or in future will never be open to suspicion, and will not be mistaken/misunderstood by any person, who is knowledgeable, who can contemplate, and is a priest.

Cross-References

- ► Alcoholic Drinks and Drinking (Buddhism)
- ► *Aṣṭāṅgamārga*
- ► *Dhamma*
- ► Duhkha – Unpleasant
- ► *Karma*
- ► Nonviolence
- ► *Saṅgha*
- ► *Tṛṣṇā*
- ► *Upāsaka*

References

1. (1995) *Sāmaññaphala-Sutta* (*Dīgha-Nikāya-II*), *Tipiṭaka*, *Chaṭṭha Saṇgāyana* edition (CD-ROM Version-3). Vipassana Research Institute, Igatpuri
2. Kasyapa BJ (ed) (1961) *Dīgha-Nikāya*. Pali Text Publication Board, Bihar Govt, Nalanda
3. (1995) *Dīgha-Nikāya-I*, *Tipiṭaka*, *Chaṭṭha Saṇgāyana* edition (CD-ROM Version-3). Vipassana Research Institute, Igatpuri
4. Chinchore MR (2006) Conception of *Ahiṁsā* in Buddhism: a critical note. Annals of the Bhandarkar Oriental Research Institute, Pune, pp 103–109
5. Warder AK (2000) Indian Buddhism, 3rd edn. Motilal Banarsidass, Delhi, p 185
6. (1995) *Majjhima-Nikāya*, *Tipiṭaka*, *Chaṭṭha Saṇgāyana* edition (CD-ROM Version-3).Vipassana Research Institute, Igatpuri
7. Vaidya PL (ed) (1961) *Śāntīdeva's Bodhicaryāvatāra* (with *Pañjikā* of Prajñakaramati). Mithila Institute, Darbhanga

Pañca-Śīla

▶ *Pañcaśīla*

Pañcaśīla

▶ Ethics (Buddhism)

Paññā

Angraj Chaudhary
Vipassana Research Institute, Dhammagiri, Igatpuri, Nashik, Maharashtra, India

Synonyms

Insight; Knowledge (Sikhism); Knowledge; Prajñā; Understanding; Wisdom

Definition

Paññā is understanding or wisdom gained at the experiential level, not at the intellectual level.

Paññā is translated into English as understanding, knowledge, wisdom, and insight. But knowledge is different from understanding. Understanding is wisdom and insight, because they come from one's experience. But as far as knowledge is concerned, it is based on understanding but it is not experience. It is based on experience. In one of his essays, Aldous Huxley has brought out the difference between knowledge and understanding. "Understanding can only be talked about, and that very inadequately, it cannot be passed on, it can never be shared. There can, of course, be knowledge of such an understanding, and this knowledge may be passed on. But we must always remember that knowledge of understanding is not the same thing as understanding, which is the raw material of that knowledge. It is different from understanding as the doctor's prescription for penicillin is different from penicillin. Understanding is as rare as emeralds, and so is highly prized. The knowers would dearly love to be understanders; but either their stock of knowledge does not include the knowledge of what to do in order to be understanders, or else they know theoretically what they ought to do, but go on doing the opposite all the same. In either case they cherish the comforting delusion that knowledge, and above all pseudo knowledge are understanding" [1].

Huxley's "understanding" comes very close to "direct experience," which is prajñā. Prajñā is made up of prefix "*pra*," which means *pratyakṣa* ("direct") and "*jñā*" means "to experience." So *prajñā* means direct knowledge, that is, knowledge at the experiential level. One can know that *rasamalai* (a variety of Indian sweet) is sweet by eating and tasting it, not by hearing somebody say that it is sweet. And how can one differentiate between one kind of sweetness and another kind of sweetness without tasting them? Understanding is like tasting, not imagining nor intellectualizing.

The *paññā* that the Buddha talks about is born out of one's own experience. The purer the experience the clearer and sharper is the *paññā* and the experience of a person can be pure when he is free from defilements. According to the Buddha, defilements can be removed by observing *sīla*

P

(precepts). That is why it has been said that wisdom is purified by morality. The following quotation from the *Soṇadaṇḍa Sutta* brings out the characteristics of *paññā*.

> *Sīlaparidhotā paññā, paññāparidhotaṃ sīlaṃ. Yattha sīlaṃ tattha paññā, yattha paññā tattha sīlaṃ. Sīlavato paññā, paññavato sīlaṃ.* ([2], Vol. I, p. 108)

"For wisdom is purified by morality, and morality is purified by wisdom: where one is, the other is, the moral man has wisdom and the wise man has morality, and the combination of morality and wisdom is called the highest thing in the world" ([3], p. 131).

In the *Mūlapariyāya Sutta*, the Buddha has shown that only a virtuous man can have understanding, wisdom, or insight and a wise man *is* virtuous. Of the three kinds of people, namely, *puthujjana* (a worldling), *sekkha* (a learner), and an Arhant, a Buddha or a Tathāgata, the last has developed complete understanding because he is virtuous.

In the *Aṭṭhakathā* of this *sutta*, it has been shown that complete understanding or comprehension (*pariññā*) consists of three stages, namely, *ñāta pariññā, tīraṇa pariññā*, and *pahāna pariññā* ([4], Vol. I, p. 32) *Ñāta pariññā* is a stage at which one becomes thoroughly familiar with an object, say, the earth (*pathavī*), in terms of its characteristics (*lakkhaṇa*), its function (*rasa*), its manifestation (*paccupaṭṭhāna*), and its immediate cause (*padaṭṭhāna*), that is, one does not know only its characteristics, function, and how it manifests but also knows its immediate cause. *Tīraṇa pariññā* is a higher stage of comprehension at which one realizes that nothing is permanent. All that look permanent reveal their three characteristics of impermanence, suffering, and no-self. This is a stage at which a meditator penetrates into dhammas and knows their true nature. *Pahāna pariññā* is the highest stage at which one begins to practice what he knows, that is, one begins to live up to his understanding or wisdom. In other words, he gives up his attachment to worldly objects and becomes completely free from *rāga* (craving) for them.

Paññā, as said above, is to know thoroughly and comprehensively. What to know? To know penetratingly the nature and ingredient of something. (*Pajānātīti paññā, yathāsabhāvaṃ pakārehi paṭivijjhatīti attho.* See [5], Vol. 1, p. 108). *Paññā* pierces into the real nature of things (*nibbijjhatīti nibbedhikā paññā*, [4], Vol. III, p. 105). It also grasps the real nature of things completely. And every object has three characteristics, namely, impermanence, suffering, and no-self (*sammasanaṃ paññā. Sā maggasampayutta aniccādisammasana kiccaṃ sādheti niccasaññādi pajahanato*, see also [4], Vol. III, p. 160). When a mediator practicing Vipassana knows at the level of his experience that what looks stable and permanent is not so, but it is characterized by the three characteristics of impermanence, suffering, and no-self, then it is *paññā* or insight attained through Vipassana.

In the *Mahāvedalla Sutta*, Sariputta explains the purpose of *paññā* (wisdom). He says that "the purpose of wisdom is direct knowledge, its purpose is full understanding, its purpose is abandoning" ([6], p. 389).

From these quotations, it is clear that *paññā* is not intellect, which according to OED [7] is defined as "the faculty of reasoning and understanding."

Mrs. C. A. F. Rhys Davids arrives at almost the same conclusion, of course, after a deep analysis of some of the *suttas* where "*paññā*" occurs. She examines two *suttas*, one from the *Dīgha Nikāya* and the other from the *Majjhima Nikāya* and at one point she says that "it might be called intellect 'at a higher power'." But she says further: "Nevertheless, it is clear that the term did not stand for bare mental process of a certain degree of complexity, but that it also implied mental process as cultivated in accordance with a certain system of concepts objectively valid for all Buddhist adepts. Hence I think it best to reject such terms as reason, intellect, and understanding, and to choose wisdom, or science, or knowledge or philosophy. Only they must be understood in this connection as implying the body of learning as assimilated and applied by the intellect of a given individual" ([8], pp. 17–18).

What Mrs. Rhys Davids understands from "understanding" is not the same as Aldous Huxley understands from it. But I think both of them, one using the term "wisdom" and the other using the term "understanding" mean more or less the same thing. Cultivation of mind by a man living a virtuous life is necessary for having wisdom or understanding which does not only enable him to see through the three characteristics of the objects of the world but also enables him to become disenchanted and disillusioned with them, develop non-attachment, and become free from desire to have them. Thus, the *paññā* he develops enables him to abandon objects of attachment.

Thus, *paññā* according to both of them is experiential knowledge, which is gained by concentrating one's mind and observing what happens within. *Paññā* goes where intellect cannot go.

This *paññā*, therefore, is the best instrument to know the real characteristics of worldly objects. Sharpening the weapon of *paññā* one can cut down the roots of desires – the cause of suffering and attain a blissful state. *Paññā* enables one to go beyond the conventional truth (*sammuti sacca*) and attain the ultimate truth (*paramattha sacca*) where one experiences the three characteristics (impermanence, suffering, and not-self) of all objects of the world people hanker after. When one attains this knowledge he becomes disillusioned and develops non-attachment.

Three kinds of *paññā* ([9], Vol. II, p. 65) have been described by the Buddha. The first is *sutamayā paññā*, that is, knowledge gained by listening to others. The second is *cintāmayā paññā*, which one attains not by listening to others but by his own reasoning and reflection. And the third – *bhāvanāmayā paññā* – is the *paññā*, which one attains by his own experience.

According to the Buddha, the third kind of *paññā* is the most important of all as it enables one to realize the real nature of things. So long as one does not know the real nature of things he lives in darkness. One is attracted toward them and creates desires (*taṇhā*), which are the causes of his suffering. *Paññā* helps one know the real nature of objects clearly. As a result, he grows wise, he knows the transitory nature of all objects of the world, is not attached to them, and does not create and multiply his desires. Thus, *paññā* liberates one from suffering and also helps him come out of the cycle of birth and death.

Of the three *paññās, sutamayā, cintāmayā,* and *bhāvanāmayā*, the Buddha gives more importance to the last one than the first two because it is this *paññā*, which when developed enables one to be non-attached to worldly things, to give up desire – the cause of suffering and become liberated. It enables him to break the cycle of birth and death. It is by virtue of the cultivation of this *paññā* that one really comes to know why and where *taṇhā* (desire) arises and how and where it can be ended. Thus, it is this *paññā*, which explains how desire is created and how it can be eliminated.

What Is Necessary for Developing This Paññā?

For developing this *paññā*, the purity of mind is a *sine qua non* and this purity of mind cannot be attained without observing precepts. Only when five precepts like abstaining from killing, stealing, committing adultery, telling lies, etc., and from taking intoxicants are observed, defilements like aversion, greed, sensuality, pride, etc., can be rooted out. Under the influence of these defilements, man violates precepts.

Abstaining from intoxicants is the most important condition for mind to work properly. How can it work properly under the influence of intoxicating things? Concentration of mind cannot be achieved if it is under the influence of pollutants like greed, aversion, jealousy, etc. They are powerful distracting agents. Observation of precepts enables one to get rid of them.

Once the concentration of mind is attained, it is easy to see the nature of things clearly at the experiential level. Experience keeps a dear school. Even fools can learn in the school of experience. What does experience do? It enables one to see things arising and passing away the same way over and over again. Sensation, which is an important object of meditation when one practices vipassana, arises on one's body and passes away. Whatever its nature is, pleasant, unpleasant, or neutral, it keeps on changing, it does not last for ever. One experiences this again and again. Thus, one's *bhāvanāmayā paññā* develops and he realizes with its help that nothing in this world is permanent. Thus, the veil of the darkness of ignorance is rent and he develops non-attachment to things of the world to which he used to be attached when he did not know their true nature.

The beauty of this *paññā* is that like the first two it cannot be developed by a man who has defilements like craving and aversion. Freedom from defilements is the *sine qua non* for developing this *paññā*. Because physical and vocal actions follow one's volition, wholesome or unwholesome, only freedom from defilements will keep both these actions pure.

With this *paññā* developed one can prove the veracity of the Law of Dependent Origination and the Law of Impermanence – profound laws discovered and taught by the Buddha. With the help of the Law of Dependent Origination, he proved how suffering is caused and how it can be ended. With the help of the Law of Impermanence, he showed why one should give up attachment for worldly objects – attachment which causes desire – the root cause of suffering.

But persons who are not pure, in other words, who do not observe *sīla* and whose physical and vocal actions are not pure are not spiritually fit to develop this *paññā*, let alone understand its characteristics. The laboratory where the experiment of whether the Law of Impermanence and the Law of Dependent Origination are true or not can be made only in this fathom long body by a person who has a pure mind and whose conduct is good.

Thus, it becomes clear that whereas the first two *paññās* can be understood by anybody whether his mind is pure or not, *bhāvanāmayā paññā* can be developed and understood by persons who have cultivated mental purity. It can only be understood by those who have cultivated mindfulness and who with its help understand the impermanent nature of reality, that is, who have developed *sampajañña* and these two qualities cannot be expected in a person who does not observe virtue (*sīla*). The concept of *bhāvanāmayā paññā* and how to develop it, therefore, is an invaluable contribution by the Buddha to world culture.

Once a deity asked the Buddha a question. The question was

> *Anto jaṭā bahi jaṭā,jaṭāya jaṭitā pajā/*
> *Taṃ taṃ gotama pucchāmi, ko imaṃ vijaṭaye jaṭanti* ([9], p. 1)

The inner tangle and the outer tangle—
This generation is entangled in a tangle,
And so I ask of Gotam this question:
Who succeeds in disentangling this tangle? [7]

The Buddha's answer was:

> *Sīle patiṭṭhāya naro sapañño, cittaṃ paññaṃ ca bhāvayaṃ/*
> *Ātāpī nipako bhikkhu, so imaṃ vijaṭaye jaṭanti* ([9], p. 2)

When a wise man, established well in Virtue,
Develops Consciousness and Understanding,
Then as a bhikkhu ardent and sagacious
He succeeds in disentangling this tangle [7].

How this *paññā* can help one to disentangle the tangle becomes clear from what Buddhaghosa says as to who can disentangle the tangle:

> Just as a man, standing on the ground and taking up a well-sharpened knife might disentangle a great tangle of bamboos, so too he.... standing on the ground of virtue and taking up with the hand of protective-understanding exerted by the power of energy the knife of insight-understanding well sharpened on the stone of concentration, might disentangle, cut away and demolish all the tangle of craving.... ([7], p. 4)

Buddhaghosa wrote the Visuddhimaggo (The Path of Purification) and explained *sīla* (virtue), *samādhi* (concentration), and *paññā* (wisdom or understanding) in detail.

According to him, "it is knowing (*jānana*) in a particular mode separate from the modes of perceiving (*sañjānana*) and cognizing (*vijānana*). For though the state of knowing (*jānana-bhāva*) is equally present in perception (*saññā*), in consciousness (*viññāṇa*) and in understanding (*paññā*) nevertheless perception is only the mere perceiving of an object as say 'blue' or 'yellow'; it cannot bring about the penetration of its characteristics as impermanent, painful and not-self. Consciousness knows the object as blue or yellow, and it brings about the penetration of its characteristics; but it cannot bring about, by endeavouring the manifestation of the [supramundane] path. Understanding knows the object in the way already stated, it brings about the penetration of the characteristics and it brings about, by endeavouring, the manifestation of the path" ([7], p. 480).

He further brings out the difference between perception, consciousness, and understanding by giving the example of how different persons see a coin. A child sees it differently from a villager and both see it differently from a money changer. A child perceives a coin and sees its color, etc., its external characteristic, or its external form. A villager sees the coin and apprehends its characteristics. In other words he sees color and something more. He penetrates into it and is conscious of its characteristics. A money changer does not only see the mode of the coin, or its characteristics, but also reaches "the manifestation of the path."

Prajñā helps one to understand that tangles are *taṇhās* (desires), which cause our suffering. It also shows the path to end it. Suffering can be made extinct by annihilating desires. But how to annihilate desires?

If one could know how *jaṭās* are formed and how he is entangled both inside and outside by them and how he can disentangle them he will have developed *paññā* (intuition, wisdom, or understanding).

Right view of the Noble Eight-fold Path comes under *prajñā* (understanding).

Right view, as explained by Venerable Sariputta in the *Sammādiṭṭhi Sutta* of the *Majjhima Nikāya*, consists in knowing wholesome actions and their roots and unwholesome actions and their roots. It also means knowing nutriment (*āhāra*) its origin, its cessation, and the way leading to the cessation of nutriment.

Right view is also understanding suffering, its cause, its cessation, and the way leading to its cessation. "Birth is suffering; ageing is suffering, death is suffering; sorrow, lamentation pain, grief and despair are suffering; not to obtain what one wants is suffering; in short, the five aggregates affected by clinging are suffering. This is called suffering.

"And what is the origin of suffering? It is craving, which brings renewal of being, is accompanied by delight and lust, and delights in this and that; that is craving for sensual pleasures, craving for being and craving for non-being. This is called the origin of suffering.

And what is the cessation of suffering? It is the remainderless fading away and ceasing, the giving up, the relinquishing, letting go, and rejecting of that same craving. This is called the cessation of suffering.

And what is the way leading to the cessation of suffering? It is just the Noble Eightfold Path; that is right view. . .right concentration. This is called the way leading to the cessation of suffering" [6].

On being further asked by the monks Sariputta said that if one understands ageing and death, their origin, their cessation, and the way leading to their cessation; if one understands birth, its origin, its cessation, and the way leading to its cessation; if one understands being, its origin, its cessation, and the way leading to its cessation he develops right view. If he understands clinging, craving, feeling, contact, the sixfold base, mentality-materiality, consciousness, formations and ignorance – the 12 links of the Law of Dependent Origination in this fourfold way, he develops right view. If he understands taints, their origin, their cessation and the way leading to their cessation, he has developed right view.

The Path to Develop *Bhāvanāmayā Paññā*

The Buddha has explained in many of the *suttas* the training that one has to undergo in order to develop this *paññā*. This training is gradual and there are several steps leading to its culmination. With the help of a beautiful simile he has shown how this training is given to produce the right type of effect. In the *Gaṇakamoggallāna Sutta* he says that "when a clever horse trainer obtains a fine thoroughbred colt, he first makes him get used to wearing the bit, and afterwards trains him further" (See [6], p. 874), In the same way the Tathagata first disciplines a person to be tamed by asking him to be virtuous, "restrained with the restraint of the Pātimokkha" and asks him to be "perfect in conduct and resort and seeing fear in the slightest fault, train by undertaking the training precepts" (ibid.).

After he gets into the habit of observing precepts he is further asked to guard the doors of his sense faculties. Why? Because unless the doors are guarded well he will, because of the ingrained habit of mind, see a beautiful form or hear a melodious sound or smell a sweet perfume and so on and will go on desiring them and create more miseries for him. When the sense faculties are unguarded, unwholesome states of covetousness and grief are likely to invade him. So, the Buddha expressly asks him not to grasp at the sign of an object nor at its features. (*Nānunimittagāhī hohi, nānu vyañjanagāhī hohi.*) *Nimitta* means the object such as eye and *vyañjana* means detailed description of its features like the black eye, the eye like that of doe or lotus and so on. The same thing applies to all the objects of other sense faculties if they are left unguarded. Therefore, restraint of all sense faculties should be practiced.

After observing precepts and practicing restraint of the sense faculties the Buddha teaches him to become moderate in eating. Why? Because if one is not moderate in eating, one will fall prey to sloth and laziness. Food should be taken not for amusement nor for intoxication nor for the sake of physical beauty and attractiveness. It should be taken only for the continuance of body so that a holy life can be lived. It should also be taken for developing endurance so that he can terminate old feelings without arousing new feelings and be healthy and blameless.

The next quality which the Buddha asks to develop is wakefulness. Only when one is awake one will be able to purify one's mind of obstructive states. The next step of the training is to develop mindfulness (*sati*) and full awareness (*sampajañña*) which should be cultivated in all situations of life.

After he develops mindfulness and full awareness, he is disciplined further. He is asked to "resort to a secluded resting place: the forest, the root of a tree, a mountain, a ravine, a hillside cave, a charnel ground, a jungle thicket, an open space or a heap of straw" after returning from his almsround and having his meal he sits down cross-legged, keeping his body erect and establishing mindfulness before him. He then purifies his mind of five hindrances such as *kāmacchanda* (covetousness, sensuality), *byāpāda* (ill-will), *thīnamiddha* (sloth and torpor), *uddhaccakukkucca* (restlessness and remorse), and *vicikicchā* (doubt). After he has got rid of the five hindrances, he is fit to practice *jhāna.* He enters upon and abides in the first *rūpāvacara jhāna*, which "is accompanied by applied and sustained thought, with rapture and pleasure born of seclusion. With the stilling of applied and sustained thought, he enters upon and abides in the second *jhāna*, which has self-confidence and singleness of mind without applied and sustained thought, with rapture and pleasure born of concentration. With the fading away as well of rapture he abides in equanimity, and mindful and fully aware, still feeling pleasure with the body, he enters upon and abides in the third *jhāna*, on account of which noble ones announce: 'He has a pleasant abiding who has equanimity and is mindful.' With the abandoning of pleasure and pain, and with the previous disappearance of joy and grief, he enters upon and abides in the fourth *jhāna*, which has neither pain nor pleasure and purity of mindfulness due to equanimity" ([6], pp. 876–877).

Any body who trains himself like this purifies his mind of all defilements by observing *sīla.* He does not further create defilements by guarding the doors of his sense faculties perfectly. What is needed for guarding the doors of sense faculties is wakefulness, which can be cultivated by being moderate in eating food. Wakefulness leads him to develop mindfulness (*sati*) and full awareness (*sampajaññā).* When these qualities are developed he becomes fit for practicing *jhāna* to attain concentration of mind and with this concentrated mind he sees reality as it is. Knowing the impermanent nature of all the objects of the world he develops non-attachment (*nirveda*) to them and thus stops creating desires – the root cause of suffering. All this is done by having knowledge at the experiential level. Thus, *bhāvanāmayā paññā* goes a long way in ending his suffering. This *paññā* also enables him to see how and where suffering is caused and also enables him to know how and where it can be ended. The philosophy of the Buddha has an action plan. What he propounds can be practiced in life and its fruit can be achieved.

Buddhaghosa says almost the same thing as to how to develop *paññā.* He is quoted here in *extenso.*

> Now the things classed as aggregates, bases, elements, faculties, truths, dependent origination, etc., are the *soil* of this understanding, and the [first] two purifications, namely, Purification of Virtue, and Purification of Consciousness, are its *roots*, while the five purifications, namely, Purification of View, Purification by Overcoming doubt, Purification by Knowledge and Vision of What is the Path and What is not the Path, Purification by Knowledge and Vision of the Way, and Purification by Knowledge and Vision are the *trun*k. Consequently one who is perfecting these should first fortify his knowledge by learning and questioning about those things that are the 'soil' after he has perfected the two purifications that are the 'roots,' then he can develop the five purifications that are the 'trunk.' ([7], p. 488)

Developed *paññā*, according to Buddhaghosa, is like a big tree of which the roots are the two Purifications of Virtue and Consciousness. These roots are struck in the soil of aggregates, bases, elements, faculties, truths, etc., which draw sustenance from them and then grow into a big tree with five Purifications as its trunk.

When Buddhaghosa says that Purification of Virtue (*sīlavisuddhi*) and Purification of Consciousness (*cittavisuddhi*) are the roots of Understanding, he underlines the importance of both *sīla* and *samādhi.* Only a virtuous man can attain concentration of mind, which can enable him to see the real nature of reality. When he sees the reality as it is at the experiential level, he is on the way to develop non-attachment to the so-called attractive things because the darkness of ignorance is now over.

These two purifications, which are roots, derive their nourishment from the soil of aggregates, bases, elements, faculties, truths, dependent origination, and so on as said above. When they are studied in detail and their characteristics (*lakkhaṇa*), function (*rasa*), how they are manifested (*paccupaṭṭhāna*), and their immediate cause (*padaṭṭhana*) are known, it becomes clear that all things of the world are dependently originated.

When things are seen in such a way, then Purification of View (*diṭṭhi visuddhi*) is developed. This is followed by the development of Purification by Overcoming Doubt (*kaṅkhāvitaraṇa visuddhi*). Further progress is made and what is the Path and what is not the Path is known. Thus, Purification by Knowledge and Vision of "what is the Path" and "what is not the Path" (*maggāmaggañāṇadassana visuddhi*) is made. This is followed by the development of Purification by Knowledge and Vision of the Way (*paṭipadāñāṇadassanavisuddhi*) and finally Purification by Knowledge and Vision (*ñāṇadassanavisuddhi*) is developed.

This *paññā* is developed by practicing Vipassana. This is understanding based on direct experience. This *paññā* thus developed enables one to walk on the Noble Eightfold Path, cut all fetters that bind him to the wheel of birth and death, and also enables him to be liberated from suffering.

Cross-References

- Insight
- Knowledge (Buddhism)
- Knowledge (Sikhism)
- Wisdom (Buddhism)

References

1. Dharmasena CB (The Wheel no.39, Quoted from the Essay entitled Purification of View
2. Dīgha Nikāya (1998) (Unless otherwise mentioned all books referred to here are published by Vipassana Research Institute, Dhammagiri in 1998
3. Walshe M (tr) (1987) The Long Discourses of the Buddha. Wisdom, Boston
4. Pāthikavagga Ṭīkā
5. Sīlakkhandhavagga Abhinava Ṭīkā
6. Ñāṇamoli B, Bodhi B (trs) (1995) The Middle Length Discourses of the Buddha. Wisdom, Boston
7. Ñāṇamoli B (2001) The Path of Purification (Printed in Taiwan)
8. Rhys Davids CAF, Buddhist Psychology
9. Visuddhimaggo by Buddhaghosa
10. Majjhima Nikāya Aṭṭhakathā

Pāpa

► Evil (Buddhism)

Pāpa, Evil Action

► Sin (Buddhism)

Paramārtha

Charles Willemen
International Buddhist College, Songkhla, Thailand

Definition

Paramārtha (Chinese: Zhendi, 499–569) was, together with Kumārajīva and Xuanzang, one of the most influential translators of Sanskrit Buddhist texts in China.

Born Kulanātha in Ujjayinī, Avanti area, to a brahmin family, he eventually traveled to Funan (mainly Cambodia), where Buddhism prospered at the time. From there he went to Guangzhou, arriving in 546. He traveled on to Jiankang (Nanjing), capital of the Liang dynasty, in 548. Emperor Wu, a great patron of Buddhism, who had numerous exchanges with Funan, welcomed him, but the emperor was soon killed. Paramārtha then went to Jiangxi, and in 550 to Fuchun in Zhejiang, where his literary career seems to have begun. P. Demiéville has shown in 1929 that Paramārtha is the author of Taishō ed.1666, *Dasheng qi xin lun*. This text is also known as *Mahāyānaśraddhotpādaśāstra*, wrongly attributed to Aśvaghoṣa. Taishō ed.2033, known as Vasumitra's text about the different Buddhist schools, is most likely the work of Paramārtha. He apparently attributed some of his own shorter works to prominent figures linked with Kaniṣka's synod in Kaśmīra, end of the second century A.D. During the years 552–554 he was in Jiankang again, during emperor Yuan. After that he resumed his wandering life, to Yuzhang in Jiangxi, to Shixing in Guangdong. In 557–558 he was in Nankang in Jiangxi. Via Yuzhang he then arrived in Linquan in Jiangxi. In 562 he was in Jin'an in Fujian. From 562 on he was in Guangzhou again, where he passed away in February of 569. In 562 he actually managed to board a boat to return "home," but a storm blew the boat back to Guangzhou. He then translated the *She dasheng lun*, Taishō ed.1593, *Mahāyānasaṅgraha, Compendium of the Mahāyāna* attributed to Asaṅga (late fourth century). Paramārtha was often depressed, even suicidal. His last known attempt was in 568. His energy, however, was considerable. He is best known for his contribution to the development of the Yogācāra School in China [2]. He brought Sthiramati's *nirākāra* (without mode of activity) *cittamātra* (thought-only) from Valabhī to China. There we know this as the old *Cittamātra* School, before Kuiji (632–682), Xuanzang's disciple. Dharmapāla's (ca. 530–561) *sākāra* (having a mode of activity, Chinese: *faxiang*) *Vijñānavāda* (consciousness-only) in Nālandā was brought to China by Xuanzang (602–664). This became known as the new *Vijñānavāda*. Paramārtha brought out the *Dasheng weishi lun*, Taishō ed.1589, Vasubandhu's (ca. 350–430) *Viṃśatikā*, *Twenty Verses*, and also Vasubandhu's *Madhyāntavibhāga, On Distinguishing the Extremes from the Middle, Zhongbian fenbie lun*, Taishō ed.1599. He actually brought out a considerable number of texts. When he translated Vasubandhu's treatise, *Bhāṣya*, on Asaṅga's *Mahāyānasaṅgraha*, Taishō ed.1595, *She dasheng lun shi*, this text became the central text of a doctrinal *Shelun* (*Saṅgrahaśāstra*) School [3]. Xuanzang used this text for his own kind of Yogācāra. Paramārtha was not a mere translator. He sometimes added his own views [1]. For example, he posited a ninth level of consciousness, called *amalavijñāna*, immaculate consciousness. For him this level is the true source of all reality. It may be identified with the *Tathāgatagarbha*, Tathāgata-womb, the Buddha-nature inherent in all sentient beings, an idea not found in Xuanzang's *Faxiang*. But Xuanzang extensively used Paramārtha's work, often "correcting" the language. Paramārtha translated Vasubandhu's *Abhidharmakośabhāṣya, Jushe shi lun*, Taishō ed.1559, in 568. This text immediately replaced the Sautrāntika *abhidharma* of the doctrinal Abhidharma School, *Pitan Zong*, in South China. So, this text replaced Saṅghadeva's *Aṣṭagrantha, Ba jiandu lun*, Taishō ed.1543, and Saṅghavarman's *Miśrakābhidharmahṛdaya*, *Za epitan xin lun* Taishō ed.1552, first half of the fifth century. Paramārtha's text was studied in a "*Kośa*" School in the South, until Xuanzang brought out a new version of the *Kośabhāṣya* in Chang'an in 654, Taishō ed.1558, the beginning of a "new" *Kośa* School. The terminology of Xuanzang's version, although meant to be an improvement, has often misled later scholars. For example, an *abhidharma* with six feet, *zu, pāda*. The term for *pāda*: Xuanzang: foot, *zu*; Paramārtha: part, *fen*. The meaning of *zu*, "foot," actually is "part." Paramārtha's work laid the philosophical foundation in China for the so-called Yogācāra School, and also for Fazang's (ca. 736–838) *Huayan (Avataṃsaka)* School, for Zhiyi's (538–597) Tiantai School, and for *Chan* during the Sui and Tang dynasties.

Cross-References

► Asaṅga
► Tathāgatagarbha
► Vasubandhu
► Yogācāra

References

1. Boucher D (2004) Paramārtha. In: Buswell R (ed) Encyclopedia of Buddhism, vol II. Macmillan Reference USA, New York, pp 630–631
2. Miyakawa H (2005) Paramārtha. In: Jones L (ed) Encyclopedia of religion, 2nd edn. Macmillan Reference USA, Gale Virtual Reference Library, Detroit
3. Paul D (1984) Philosophy of mind in sixth-century China: Paramārtha's "Evolution of Consciousness". Stanford University Press, Stanford

Pāramitā

James B. Apple
Department of Religious Studies,
University of Calgary, Calgary, AB, Canada

Synonyms

Excellence; Perfection; Six perfections; Supremacy; Transcendental virtues; Virtues

Definition

The *pāramitās*, or perfections, are virtues that are fully developed by a bodhisattva (Buddha-in-training) to become a Buddha.

The *pāramitās* (Pāli, *pāramī*; Tibetan, *pha-rol-tu phyin-pa*; Chinese, *boluomi*; Japanese, *haramitsu*) are the virtues that are fully developed by a bodhisattva (Buddha-in-training) to become a Buddha. A number of Buddhist traditions acknowledge that the perfections are practiced through multiple lifetimes extending over aeons of time for the purpose of achieving full Buddhahood for the welfare of beings. The Sanskrit and Pāli noun *pāramitā* is derived from the adjective *parama*, meaning "high, complete, perfect." In this sense, *pāramitā* is an old noun denoting "the highest point" ([1], pp. 547, 548). The Theravāda has consistently understood the term in this way and has commonly used another derivative, *pāramī*, as a synonym. In contrast, Mahāyāna traditions have analyzed the term as consisting of two words, *pāram itā*, meaning "gone to the beyond," signifying its purport for progress in the bodhisattva path. The Chinese and Tibetan translations of the term *pāramitā* (*du* 度 and *pha-rol-tu phyin-pa*, respectively) reflect this latter understanding of its meaning. These interpretations may differ between mainstream Buddhist (*nikāya*) and Mahāyāna traditions, but the understandings they imply are found among most Buddhist schools. One representation saw the term as derived from *pāram* "other (side)" plus the past participle *ita* "gone" ([2], p. 153, n.35). This derivation is later preserved in the standard Tibetan translation *pha-rol-tu phyin-pa* "gone to the other shore." Other interpretations advocated that this etymology was misguided, and derived *pāramitā* from the term *parama* "excellent, supreme." The noun *pāramitā* is translated in early Chinese through "double translation" composed by *du wuji* 度無極, meaning "crossed over" (*du* 度) plus "unexcelled, limitless" (*wuji* 無極) which brings together both of the traditional etymologies ([2], p. 153). A number of Buddhist works provide semantic etymologies for *pāramitā*, etymologies which explain the meaning of the term rather than its linguistic origin, based on contextual underlying factors that a text is trying to advocate. The understanding of *pāramitā* in the sense of "to reach the other shore" generally conveys the idea that a perfection enables one to go from the realm of *saṃsāra*, the world of repeated rebirth and redeath, to the blissful realm of *nirvāṇa* [3].

The conception of the perfections as a set is not found in the earliest layers of Buddhist literature [4]. Rather, the perfections as a set of practices developed sometime before the Common Era as an alternative group of spiritual practices in conjunction with revised notions of Buddhahood as well as newly considered notions of what constitutes the path leading to Buddhahood. The *pāramitā*s furnished an arrangement of Buddhist thought and practice that focused on the ideal of the bodhisattva and how a bodhisattva was imagined to fulfill the immeasurable qualities and virtues necessary for the attainment of Buddhahood. The qualities of the *pāramitā*s and their outlines for practice were extensions of earlier mainstream Buddhist arrangements of practice, such as the three trainings (*triśīkṣa*) of morality (*śīla*), concentration (*samādhi*), and insight (*prajñā*), but were modified with the underlying ethos, aspirations, and commitments for attaining incomparable Buddhahood for the welfare of all beings.

The lists of perfections varied according to the genre of literature in which they appeared. What practices constituted the varied lists of perfections and how the perfections were conceived differed not only between groups but also between scholarly authors. The *pāramitā*s appear in Buddhist literature as a group in varying lists, but the lists of perfections are notoriously unfixed with six and ten perfections being the most common.

Perhaps the earliest genre of Buddhist literature in which the *pāramitā*s appear is the collections of *Jātakas*, the stories of the Buddha's previous lives. The *pāramitā*s in these stories provide major underlying themes such as self-sacrifice, ethical virtue, and patience that demonstrate the magnificent qualities developed by the Buddha in his previous lives by carrying out moral acts as a bodhisattva on the bodhisattva path. In the *Aviṣahya Jātaka*, for example, the bodhisattva cultivates the perfection of generosity (*dānapāramitā*) by donating alms to supplicants in spite of being reduced to poverty. The bodhisattva is a boy who refuses to steal, even after encouragement from his Brahmin teacher to do so, in the *Brāhmaṇa Jātaka*, to illustrate the cultivation of the perfection of morality (*śīlapāramitā*). In the *Kṣāntivādin Jātaka*, the bodhisattva is an ascetic who cultivates the perfection of forbearance (*kṣāntipāramitā*) by tolerating being violently disfigured by an angry king ([5], pp. 36, 37). Most Buddhist groups (*nikāya*) had collections of *Jātaka*s that differed in length and number. Buddhist groups and movements also understood the purport of the *Jātaka*s differently, with mainstream groups like the Theravāda seeing the perfections in the *Jātaka*s as qualities to be admired while Mahāyāna movements understood the perfections in the *Jātaka*s as models to emulate.

Theravāda Buddhist works, such as the *Cariyāpiṭaka*, arrange Jātaka tales based on a hierarchy of perfections. The Theravāda tradition recognizes ten perfections, although only eight are listed in the *Buddhāpadāna* and seven in the *Cariyāpiṭaka* [6]. In Theravāda traditions, the perfections provide Buddhists with a set of ideals to worship and venerate the Buddha as a model of incomparable spiritual significance and superiority. The ten perfections that have become commonly accepted among Theravāda traditions serve as guides to structuring the stories of the Buddha's previous lives, the Jātakas, and give evidence to the supremacy of the Buddha who has fulfilled these virtues in his awakening. The ten perfections in the Theravāda tradition are (1) generosity (*dāna*), (2) morality (*sīla*), (3) renunciation (*nekhamma*), (4) insight (*pañña*), (5) energy (*viriya*), (6) patience (*khanti*), (7) truthfulness (*sacca*), (8) resolution (*adhiṭṭhāna*), (9) loving kindness (*metta*), and (10) equanimity (*upekkhā*) [7].

A set of six perfections became common among some genres of mainstream Buddhist literature and developed into a standard list in a number of Mahāyāna sūtras. However, other lists of four, five, or seven also occurred. For instance, the *Māhavibhāṣa* of the Sarvāstivādin tradition defends a list of four perfections (*dāna*, *śīla*, *vīrya*, and *prajñā*), claiming that the other perfections are subsumed under these ([8], p. 184, n.25). The *Saddharmapuṇḍarīka-sūtra*, or "Lotus sūtra" recognizes a tradition with six perfections but also lists five perfections in some sections of the text. Likewise, the *Rāṣṭrapālaparipṛcchā-sūtra* provides lists of five or six but also provides lists at two places in the text which include seven or eight perfections. As modern scholarship has noted ([2], p. 53, n.36), aberrant lists of *pāramitās* may be found in the *Lalitavistara*, the larger *Sukhāvatīvyūha*, the *Vimalakīrtinirdeśa*, and the *Mahāvastu*. In time, a set of six perfections became standard in Mahāyāna sūtras. The six are (1) generosity (*dāna*), (2) morality (*śīla*), (3) patience (*kṣānti*), (4) vigor (*vīrya*), (5) concentration (*dhyāna*), and (6) wisdom (*prajñā*). This list was expanded to complement the ten stages (*bhūmi*) traversed by a bodhisattva in the course leading to full Buddhahood. The additional perfections were (7) skill-in-means (*upāya-kauś alya*), (8) resolution (*praṇidhāna*), (9) strength (*bala*), and (10) knowledge (*jñāna*) [9].

The perfections are discussed in varying ways in Mahāyāna sūtras and it is important to recognize the heterogeneous character of the presentation of perfections in early Mahāyāna discourses. The perfections as they appear in *sūtras* that become classified as Mahāyāna provide the themes and practices entailed in the bodhisattva ideal and constitute the practices a bodhisattva seeks to fulfill in carrying out their initial spiritual resolution (*bodhicitta*) and vows (*praṇidhāna*) to achieve Buddhahood for the welfare of all beings. The discussion of *pāramitās* found in the great and diverse variety of Mahāyāna sūtras generally appears in three different ways: those sūtras that center on the *pāramitās*, those which partially discuss the *pāramitās*, and *sūtras* that focus on a specific perfection. For instance, the *Ugraparipṛcchā* focuses on the perfection of generosity (dāna) and the *Upāliparipṛcchā* discusses morality (*śīla*) ([10], pp. 107–109). Sūtras which discuss the *pāramitās* as a set of six group them into subsets based on their overall orientation. For instance, the *Prajñāpāramitā* literature will group the six perfections into a subset of five which is supported by the overarching perfection of wisdom (*prajñāpāramitā*). Other *sūtras* outline the perfection into subsets that approach the *pāramitās* in terms of whether they constitute the equipment for merit (*puṇyasaṃbhāra*), usually including the perfections of *dāna*, *śīla*, and *kṣānti*, or the equipment of knowledge (*jñānasaṃbhāra*), usually including *dhyāna* and *prajñā*, with *vīrya* as a shared member between the equipment subsets ([11], pp. 63, 64).

In addition to Mahāyāna *sūtras*, a number of Indian Mahāyāna Buddhist *śāstras*, or technical digests, that have been preserved discuss the perfections directly. Nāgārjuna, considered to be one of the major figures for the rise of Mahāyāna traditions and famous for his articulation of the philosophy of emptiness (*śūnyatā*), composed two letters addressed to kings which advocate practicing the perfections on the bodhisattva path. Nāgārjuna's "Letter to a Friend" (*Suhṛllekha*, vs. 8) [12] and *Ratnāvalī* (iv.80), or "Precious Garland," [13] both mention the six perfections to be carried out by an aspiring bodhisattva. Maitreyanātha, a figure who is considered one of the founders of the Yogācāra tradition, elucidates the perfections in several works attributed to him that are preserved in Tibetan and Chinese. The *Ornament for Clear Realization* (*Abhisamayālaṃkāra*) and the *Ornament of the Mahāyāna Sūtras* (*Mahāyānasūtrālaṃkāra)* both have sections which discuss the perfections. The *Ornament for Clear Realization* (*Abhisamayālaṃkāra*) [15], an important technical digest that outlines the bodhisattva path, discusses the perfections throughout the text, and the 16th chapter of the *Ornament of the Mahāyāna Sūtras* [16] provides a summary on the six perfections. The *Mahāprajñāpāramitāśā stra*, an enormous commentary on the "Larger Prajñāpāramitā" composed in the fourth century, attributed to Nāgārjuna and preserved in Kumārajīva's Chinese translation, the *Dazhidulun* 大智度論, contains numerous chapters that extensively outline the perfections [17]. Āryaśūra (fourth century) composed his *Compendium of the Perfections* (*Pāramitāsamāsa*), a Sanskrit text in verse which outlines doctrines and practices for the six perfections [12]. Candrakīrti, an important seventh century Indian Buddhist thinker, composed his *Madhyamakāvatāra* which outlines the bodhisattva path in ten stages (bhūmi) based on the Daśabhūmika sūtra and correlates the stages with ten perfections leading to Buddhahood from a Madhyamaka perspective [9]. Śāntideva, a seventh century Indian Buddhist scholar-monk who is also considered a Madhyamaka philosopher, composed two major works that survive in Sanskrit, the *Bodhicaryāvatāra* ("Introduction to the Practice of Awakening") [17] and *Śikṣāsamuccaya* ("Compendium of Training") [18], which both discuss the Mahāyāna path of perfections. The *Bodhicaryāvatāra* is one of the earliest major Madhyamaka works to take the perfections of the bodhisattva as a focus for articulating the Mahāyāna path. The work outlines how the first five perfections are guided by and auxiliary to the sixth perfection, the perfection of wisdom (*prajñāpāramitā*).

The diversity of Mahāyāna Buddhist sources provided various and specific accounts of the perfections, and the perfections did not become systemematized into a set of six or ten until Mahāyāna movements became more developed. Even after Mahāyāna Buddhist movements became more popular in India, authors provided different accounts of the six or ten perfections, emphasizing distinctive points for their practice. Nevertheless, the characteristics of the six or ten perfections as found in Mahāyāna Buddhist literature share a number of general features. In general, the perfections were sequentially ordered in the Mahāyāna path to reflect a progressively developed cultivation of virtues leading to the goal of Buddhahood. According to Candrakīrti, the bodhisattva may simultaneously practice acts of generosity, morality, patience, and so forth, but they are mastered or perfected in a sequential order beginning with generosity (*dāna*) and culminating with awareness (*jñāna*) [9]. The perfections were infused with the spiritual intent for awakening (*bodhicitta*), the resolutions (*praṇidhāna*) to attain the goal for others, as well as the dedication or turning over (*pariṇāmana*) of the merit from one's cultivation of virtues for the benefit of all living beings in the course of reaching Buddhahood ([11], pp. 54, 55). The most common occurrence of the perfections among Mahāyāna sūtras was in a set of six, which have the following general characteristics.

The perfection of generosity (*dānapāramitā*) is often listed first and foremost among the perfections. Dāna means to give an ordinary gift, to give the gift of the dharma, or to give the gift of mental peace and tranquility to another. Dāna in Mahāyāna discourses serves as a symbol of self-sacrifice ([11], p. 70). The perfected act of giving is a statement of great compassion which indicated the dedication of a bodhisattva to others and a commitment for the sake of omniscience. The perfection of giving is based on the earlier models of giving found in mainstream Buddhist literature, particularly the *Jātaka*s. The story of Sadāprarudita in the *Aṣṭasāhasrikā prajñāpāramitā* reflects the importance of giving in the *Perfection of Wisdom* literature, as he gives away everything for the sake of highest awakening [19]. The multiple types of giving in Mahāyāna literature include *dharmadāna*, the gift of the teaching, and *āmiṣadāna*, material gifts. Mahāyāna sūtras also mention *abhayadāna*, the giving of fearlessness. Bodhisattvas seek to mentally renounce the body as well as thought of ownership. Sūtras often speak of the *dharmayajña* "dharma offering" to fulfill the perfection of giving [10]. Mahāyāna sūtras and technical digests will often describe the perfection of generosity as acts of giving that are perfected acts free of concept (*nirvikalpakapāramitā*) being triply pure (*trimaṇḍalapariśuddha*) in making no distinction between the thing given (*deya*), the donor (*dāyaka*), and the recipient (*pratigrāhaka*) [9]. Śāntideva sums up this perfection by stating that "the perfection of generosity is said to result from the mental attitude of relinquishing all that one has to people, together with the fruit of the act" [17].

The perfection of morality or ethical discipline (*śīlapāramitā*) is the attitude of abstention which refrains from harming others and, in turn, helping sentient beings by encouraging them to cultivate moral virtue. In this manner, bodhisattvas must purify their own conduct before installing others in practice. The *sūtras* primarily discuss the perfection of morality in relation to the ten virtuous paths of action (*daśakuśalapatha*), pure modes of conduct based on compassion and service to sentient beings ([11], p. 80). The ten modes of pure conduct were often combined with the five precepts (*pañcaśīla*) as a synthetic list of 11 moral precepts (*śikṣāpada*) ([2], pp. 107–111). The ten virtuous paths of action, as listed, for example, from the *Saddharmasmṛtyupasthāna sūtra* ([11], p. 81), consist of the following abstentions: abstention from taking life (*prāṇātighātād virati*), abstention from taking what was not given (*adattādānād virati*), abstention from wrong conduct regarding the passions (*kāmamithyācārād virati*), abstention from speaking falsehood (*mṛṣāvādāt prativirati*), abstention from calumny (*paiśunyāt prativarati*), abstention from harsh speech (*pāruṣyāt prativarati*), abstention from frivolous speech (*saṃbhinnapralāpāt prativirati*), abstention from covetousness (*abhidhyāyāḥ prativirati*), abstention from malice (*vyāpādāt prativirati*), and abstention from wrong views (*mithyādṛṣṭeḥ prativirati*). Later technical digests arrange the perfection of morality into three categories: the discipline of vows (*saṃvara–śīla*), the discipline of collecting virtuous dharmas (*kuś aladharmasaṃgrāhaka–śīla*), and the discipline of effecting the aims of sentient beings (*sattvārthakriyā–śīla*). The discipline of vows (*saṃvara-śīla*) is constituted by the ten virtuous paths of action. The discipline of collecting virtuous dharmas (*kuśaladharmasaṃgrāhaka–śīla*) seeks to increase virtuous qualities in the mind and not degenerate virtues already developed. The discipline of effecting the aims of sentient beings (*sattvārthakriyā–śīla*) focuses on welfare of living beings and accomplishing their aims in a suitable manner without wrongdoing [20]. Śīla as a perfection is not concerned only with one's own morality but focuses on the moral condition of the entire world ([11], p. 86).

The perfection of forbearance or patient endurance (*kṣāntipāramitā*) signifies cultivating a range of emotional and intellectual qualities to endure numerous types of hardship for the benefit of living beings. The *Pañcaviṃśatisāhasrikā prajñāpāramitā* mentions a twofold division of this perfection in terms of forbearance with regard to sentient beings (*sattvakṣānti*) and forbearance with regard to dharma (*dharmakṣānti*). Śāntideva notes in both his *Bodhicaryāvatāra* ([17], pp. 51–61) and *Śikṣāsamuccaya* [18], based on the *Dharmasaṅgīti Sūtra*, that *kṣānti* has three aspects: forbearance toward the endurance of suffering, forbearance in discerning the Dharma, and forbearance in the endurance of injuries from others (*kṣāntis trividhā dharmsaṅgītisūtre'bhihitā duḥkhādhivāsanakṣāntiḥ dharmanidhyānakṣāntiḥ parāpakāramarṣanakṣāntiś ceti/*). The perfection of forbearance is considered an interior mental quality that is developed within one's own mind and is not contingent upon changing other people's behavior or other external circumstances. The mental cultivation of the perfection of patient forbearance consists just in the perfect fulfillment of the mind's proficiency in ceasing one's own anger.

The fourth perfection, *vīrya*, may be translated as "energy," "striving," "exertion," "vigor," or "joyous perseverance." Śāntideva sums up *vīrya* as a perfection in his *Bodhicaryāvāra* (7.2) [17]: "What is *vīrya*? The endeavor to do what is skilful." *Vīryapāramitā* is the enthusiastic engagement in accumulating virtuous qualities and working for the welfare of all living beings. A number of Mahāyāna sūtras classify *vīrya* into two types: corporeal striving and mental striving ([11], pp. 93, 94). Mahāyāna scholastic texts, such as the *Bodhisattvabhūmi*, recognize three types of vīrya: armor-like exertion (*saṃnāhavīrya*), exertion which collects virtuous qualities (*kuś aladharmasaṃgrāhakavīrya*), and exertion carried out for the benefit of sentient beings (*sattvārthakriyāvīrya*) ([10], pp. 208, 209). *Vīrya* is devotion to courageous bodhisattva action, which aims at universal liberation, and is committed to working for the benefit of sentient beings. *Vīrya* strives for the strengthening of virtue and supports steadfastness to persevere in cultivating the other five perfections.

The fifth perfection, *dhyāna*, the perfection of meditative absorption or meditative stabilization, is a one-pointed state of mind, stabilized on virtue, that is able to fixate on an object of meditation without distraction ([21], pp. 206, 207). *Dhyāna* is therefore a technical term used by Buddhists to describe higher levels of consciousness that are attained through the practice of quiescence or *ś amatha* meditation ([17], p. 75). Bodhisattvas cultivate and master all forms of meditations, including liberations (*vimokṣa*), concentrations (*samādhi*), and attainments (*samāpatti*) ([22], p. 183). The discussion on *dhyānapāramitā* in Mahāyāna sūtras focuses on the ways in which meditative absorption may contribute to the actualization of the bodhisattva vow to be of benefit to sentient beings ([10], p. 217). The preliminary practices leading up to *dhyānapāramitā* build upon practices found in mainstream Buddhist meditative practices, and therefore Mahāyāna discourses on *dhyānapāramitā* center upon the mastery of supersory knowledge (*abhijñā*) and cognitive knowledge (*jñāna*). Through *dhyānapāramitā* the bodhisattva is said to attain five supersensory powers (*abhijñā*) that assist the bodhisattva in helping other beings and installing them in the practice of the six perfections. The five supersensory powers are the divine eye (*divyacakṣus*), the divine ear (*divyaśrota*), knowledge of others' thoughts (*paracitttajñāna*), remembrance of previous births (*pūrvanivāsānusmṛti*), and supernormal power (*ṛddhi*) ([11], pp. 99, 100).

The sixth perfection, *prajñā*, often translated as "wisdom" or "insight," is the analytical discernment that cognizes the ontological status of things. The acquirement of *prajñā* was considered essential to establish the other perfections of generosity, morality, patience, striving, and meditative absorption as actual "perfections." Prajñā as a perfection served as a guide for directing the other perfections toward Buddhahood, and the other perfections worked synergistically with prajñā to actualize awakening. *Prajñāpāramitā* was the insight or wisdom that constituted omniscient cognition (*sarvajñatā*) and was identified with the end itself, perfect awakening (*saṃbodhi*). *Prajñāpāramitā* was considered to be non-dual (*advaya*) awareness that was beyond all thought constructions (*vikalpa*) permeated with insight that was absolutely pure (*atyantaviśuddhi*), neither born nor extinguished (*anutpādānirodha*), and imperishable (*akṣaya*) ([23], pp. 159, 160). *Prajñāpāramitā* was generally regarded as exclusively teaching the realization of emptiness (*śūnyatā*), the reality of the essencelessness of things (*dharmanairatyma*) and of people (*pudgalanairatyma*). Buddhist sources provide multiple classifications for *prajñā*, including worldly (*laukika*) and supermundane (*lokottara*), along with a number of different forms of analysis and reasonings. Within Buddhist scholastic sources, *prajñā* as a perfection developed within a sequence of understanding, beginning with the discernment or wisdom acquired from hearing (*ś rutamāyi-prajñā*), leading to discernment or wisdom acquired from reflection (*cintamayā-prajñā*), that culminates in discernment or wisdom cultivated in meditation (*bhāvanāmayī-prajñā*) [24].

In the course of the development of Mahāyāna Buddhist literature, perfections were added to the list of six to complement the ten stages or levels (*bhūmi*) traversed by a bodhisattva on the way to Buddhahood. Four perfections – skilful means (*upāya-kauśalya*), resolution (*praṇidhāna*), power (*bala*), and knowledge (*jñāna*) – were added to establish a group of ten perfections (*daś apāramitā*). Skilful means (*upāya-kauśalya*) refers to the deft and proficient strategies or expedients that a bodhisattva utilizes to benefit sentient beings. *Praṇidhāna* refers to the vow or resolution that bodhisattvas make to save all living beings from *saṃsāra*. *Bala* refers to the strengths or powers of bodhisattvas to guide sentient beings in their practices. *Jñana-pāramitā* is the perfection of awareness or transcendental knowledge, and is the highest wisdom of a bodhisattva correlated with the tenth stage of practice [9].

The perfections were incorporated into the rituals and iconography of Tantric or Vajrayāna forms of Buddhism in the forms of feminine powers and forces ([25], pp. 323, 324). The *pāramitās* in Vajrayāna Buddhist literature were worshipped as deities (*pāramitādevī*) in human form with attributes of color and ornaments and their number was increased to 12, by adding *ratnapāramitā* ("jeweled perfection") and *vajrakarmapāramitā* to the list of ten found in Mahāyāna works [26].

Throughout the history of Buddhist forms of culture, the perfections have shaped the ideals and practices of those devoted to, or those seeking to emulate, Buddhas and bodhisattvas. The manner in which the perfections were understood in different Buddhist cultures, such as in Tibet or Southeast Asia, was dependent on the Buddhist literature that was accessible or acceptable to the particular culture and the interpretative attention given to that literature.

Cross-References

▶ Aṣṭasāhasrikāprajñāpāramitā
▶ Bodhisattva
▶ Mahāyāna
▶ Prajñāpāramitā
▶ Upāya

References

1. Thomas FW (1904) *Pāramitā* in Pali and Sanskrit books. J Roy Asiatic Soc 36:547–548
2. Nattier J (2003) A few good men: the Bodhisattva path according to the inquiry of Ugra (Ugraparipṛcchā). University of Hawaii Press, Honolulu
3. Dayal H (1970) The Bodhisattva doctrine in Buddhist Sanskrit literature. Motilal Banarsidass, Delhi
4. Hirakawa A (1973) The development of the six perfections. J Indian Buddh Stud 21(2):23–35
5. Ohnuma R (2007) Head, eyes, flesh, and blood: giving away the body in Indian Buddhist literature. Columbia University Press, New York
6. Horner IB (1975) The minor anthologies of the Pali canon. Part 3, chronicle of Buddhas = Buddhavamsa; and, basket of conduct = Cariyāpitaka. Distributed by Routledge and Kegan Paul, Pali Text Society, London
7. Dhammagavesi, Ven Pandita M (2002) Ten perfections: the ten virtues for those who seek enlightenment. Lankarama Vihara, Schofield
8. Boucher D (2008) Bodhisattvas of the forest and the formation of the Mahāyāna: a study and translation of the Rāṣṭrapālaparipṛcchā-sūtra. University of Hawaii Press, Honolulu
9. Huntington CW, Wangchen N, Candrakīrti (1989) The emptiness of emptiness: an introduction to early Indian Mādhyamika. University of Hawaii Press, Honolulu
10. Pagel U (1995) The Bodhisattvapiṭaka: its doctrines, practices and their positions in Mahāyāna literature. The Institute of Buddhist Studies, Tring
11. Meadows C, Āryaśūra (1986) Ārya-Śūra's compendium of the perfections: text, translation, and analysis of the Pāramitāsamāsa. Indica et Tibetica Verlag, Bonn
12. Klong-chen Ye-shes-rdo-rje, Nāgārjuna (2005) Nāgārjuna's letter to a friend: with commentary by Kangyur Rinpoche. Snow Lion, Ithaca
13. Nāgārjuna, Michael H (1982) Nāgārjuna's Ratnāvalī, vol 1. The basic texts. (Sanskrit, Tibetan, Chinese). Indica et Tibetica Verlag, Bonn
14. Sparham G (2006, trans) Abhisamayālaṃkāra with Vṛtti and Ālokā. First Abhisamaya, vol 1. Jain, Fremont
15. Asaṅga M, Robert AF, Thurman LJ, Vasubandhu (2004) The universal vehicle discourse literature = Mahāyānasūtrālaṁkāra. American Institute of Buddhist Studies, New York
16. Lamotte É (1944–1980) Le Traité de la Grande Vertu de Sagesse de Nāgārjuna. vols I–V. Institut Orientaliste, Louvain
17. Śāntideva KC, Skilton A (2008) The Bodhicaryāvatāra. Oxford University Press, Oxford
18. Śāntideva CB, Rouse WHD (2006) Śikṣāsamuccaya: a compendium of Buddhist doctrine. Motilal Banarsidass, Delhi
19. Conze E (1973) The perfection of wisdom in eight thousand lines & its verse summary. Four Seasons Foundation, Bolinas; distributed by Book People, Berkeley
20. Tatz M, Asaṅga, Tsoṅ-kha-pa Blo-bzaṅ-grags-pa (1986) Asaṅga's chapter on ethics with the commentary of Tsong-Kha-Pa, the basic path to awakening, the complete Bodhisattva. Edwin Mellen Press,Lewiston
21. Wogihara U (1971) Bodhisattvabhūmi: a statement of the whole course of the Bodhisattva: being the fifteenth section of the Yogācārabhūmi. Sankibo Buddhist Book Store, Tokyo
22. Braarvig J (1993) Akṣayamatinirdeśasūtra, vol 2, The tradition of imperishability in Buddhist thought. Solum Forlag, Oslo
23. Frauwallner E, Sangpo L (2010) The philosophy of Buddhism = die philosophie des Buddhismus. Motilal Banarsidass, New Delhi
24. Lamotte É (1944) Le Traité de la Grande Vertu de Sagesse de Nāgārjuna, vol I. Institut Orientaliste, Louvain

25. Bhattacharyya B (1958) The Indian Buddhist iconography. Firma K.L. Mukhopadhyay, Calcutta, pp 323–324
26. Bhattacharyya B, Mahāpaṇḍita Abhayākaragupta (1972) Niṣpannayogāvalī of Mahāpaṇḍita Abhayākaragupta. Oriental Institute, Baroda

Pāramitās

▶ Ethics (Buddhism)

Parātmasamatā

▶ Ethics (Buddhism)

Parinirvāṇa

Kanoko Tanaka
Komazawa University, Tokyo, Japan

Synonyms

Anupadhiśeṣa-nirvāṇa; Nirvāṇa

Definition

Skt.: parinirvāṇa, Pāli: parinibbāna. "Pari" means "full," "complete," "perfect," and so on. "Parinirvāṇa" (*pari* + *nirvāṇa*) can be understood as "Full Nirvāṇa." What makes the *nirvāṇa* "full"? The limited time of one's life will naturally complete the state of *nirvāṇa*, and the extinction of corporal remainder after death should complete the final stage of *nirvāṇa* perfectly free from the law of *saṃsāra* (= being born and dead endlessly in this world). However, this term does not refer merely to the *death* of the Buddha himself, as many wrongly discussed so far. Because during his lifetime, he had *already* completed the state of his mind called "nirvāṇa" (*nir* + *vāṇa*) meaning "fires" = *vāṇa* (of one's lust, anger, and delusion) which was "burnt out" or "blown out." Therefore, it is very sure that "parinirvāṇa" does not mean "completion of the *incomplete* nirvāṇa" but originally points to "the final stage of *nirvāṇa* at the end of lifetime" which should cause no more rebirths as the sources of suffering (= duḥkhāḥ). In this sense, both *nirvāṇa* and *parinirvāṇa* can be understood as the supreme state of the Buddha's own mind. In this way, the definition of parinirvāṇa can be done from many aspects.

According to the traditional thoughts of Indian religions, they are very much afraid of experiencing "death" again and again every time they take rebirths in this world. In Buddhist context, the best way of overcoming this problem is attaining the *nirvāṇa* in this life. When a brāhmaṇa named Udaya was much annoyed with Śramaṇa Gotama (= Śākyamuṇi Buddha) who visited his house to ask for alms *every* morning, the Buddha said to him: "... Again and again, you will go to (= take rebirth in) heaven, after giving alms again and again, ... Again and again, a human being gets tired, feels troubled and worries oneself. Again and again, a foolish man (= the unenlightened one) enters into the mother's womb (and continue his life of delusion). Again and again, he will be born and die. Again and again, dead bodies are brought to the grave. However, a man of rich wisdom gains the path never to return to his life of delusion and will never take rebirths any more..." (*Saṃyutta-nikāya, Sagātha-vagga* VII.2.2). Then, Udaya was immediately inspired by this sermon, felt so happy, and became a layman of the Gotama Buddha to the end of his life. This episode may suggest how the attainment of *parinirvāṇa* may be unusual and deserves to be memorized after coming ages. Probably this is one of the reasons why the Buddhists dared to build many stūpas, the semicircular containers of the Buddha's relics (= *buddha śarīra*) in India, in spite of the long-term tradition of cremating dead bodies (even of King Aśoka of the Mauryan dynasty, for instance) at the riverside.

The Buddha Śākyamuṇi often preached to his disciples: "Do not be neglect to complete your path leading to the goal (of *bodhi*)," to the end of his life. And he *himself* daily concentrated on the stage of *his own nirvāṇa* as carefully as possible during his lifetime, for the sake of making full use of his wisdom (= *prajñā*) and guiding the suffering people to the most comfortable state of mind (= *nirvāṇa*). As everyone's lifetime is not eternal but limited, even the duration of *his nirvāṇa* in this life will also come to an end some day. His disciples and laymen naturally praise *this nirvāṇa* by the term of "*parinirvāṇa*" in later periods.

At the age of 80, Śākyamuṇi Buddha became violently ill with diarrhea and hemorrhaging, just after taking the food (called "sūkara-maddava" in Pāli = a soft type of pork, or a variety of mushroom, for example, truffle found by a pig) offered by a blacksmith named Cunda at a Pāvā village. According to the *Mahāparinibbāna-suttanta*, the Buddha bravely continued to travel despite his serious illness, and finally arrived in Kuśinagara (Kuśinārā in Pāli), where he finally passed away (or entered *parinirvāṇa*) in a grove of sāla trees. Thinking of the remorseful Cunda, the Buddha kindly left him a message: "My friend, you will gain great benefits, because your offerings were the last food to be taken by the tathāgata (= 'Thus Come One' or a great person who completed his path) who has entered *nirvāṇa without corporal remainder* (= parinirvāṇa; anupadhiśeṣa-nirvāṇa-dhatu)." He uttered another verse, "Benefits will increase for givers. Hatred will never increase for those who may control his body and mind. A good person may abandon his evil deeds. He overcomes lust (rāga), anger (dveṣa), delusion (moha) and dissolved the chains of these three poisons." This utterance may prove that the Buddha could *perfectly* control his physical pains and kept calm in meditation to sympathize with a person (like Cunda) in sufferings. In this way, the state of nirvāṇa was originally *practical and perfect.* It was later called "*nirvāṇa with corporal remainder*" (= saupadhiśeṣa-nirvāṇa; nirvāṇa in this lifetime with his living body) according to Nikāya Buddhist doctrine, which was formulated by monks fond of *abhidharma* (= Studies of the Buddha dharma or the sūtras). They devoted themselves exclusively to the analysis of the Buddha dharma dogmatically, rather than practically, and thought as follows: "Even the Buddha did not attain the perfect *nirvāṇa* while living a life. He actually suffered from illness owing to his physical elements. Therefore, the true state of *nirvāṇa* can be attained just after death. The Buddha abandoned his physical body and could not be seen anywhere in this world in the form of a human being, but must have entered the realm of *parinirvāṇa* to exist eternally and unchangingly." This kind of thought about the nirvāṇa cannot be found anywhere in the teachings of early Buddhism. Ontologically *nirvāṇa* and *parinirvāṇa* are distinguishable, but the Buddha's teachings never contained any kind of ontology discussing the extinction of body and mind. The distorted theory of *nirvāṇa* may probably be influenced by non-Buddhist sects just as Jain philosophy where one's pure soul called "jīva" cannot be set free perfectly as long as one's body remains in lifetime, and the best way of attaining *nirvāṇa* is fasting to death, which is also the supreme practice of *ahiṃsā* (= non-killing or nonviolence toward living beings).

This view of nirvāṇa shown above was criticized by Mahāyāna Buddhists who positively sought for the final goal of Buddhist practice within this phenomenal world where they were able to live a good life full of energy for the sake of helping all others to attain the Buddhahood even before they may attain it for themselves, without yearning for their own release from *saṃsāra*, the cycle of birth, death, and rebirth. They are called "*bodhisattva*" in the altruistic context of Mahāyāna Buddhism.

In fact, the Buddha himself never responds to a metaphysical question made by his disciple named Māluṅkyāputta: "Whether the Buddha may continue to exist after death," according to the famous story of the *Cūḷa-Māluṅkyāputta-suttanta* (in the *Majjhima Nikāya* 7–63). He would rather concentrate on what may occur in a human mind according to the flow of time and how to control it in the best way toward the goal of nirvāṇa while living a life in the society. Otherwise, a man pierced by a poisoned arrow (= a metaphysical question) will never be saved while worrying about the origin and nature of the arrow rather than pulling it out.

Someone often says: "Buddhism is viewing only sufferings in this world. What a pessimistic religion!" Indeed, it may be true when taking up one of the basic doctrines as "sabbe saṅkhārā dukkhā" (Skt.: duḥkhāḥ sarva-saṁskārāḥ) meaning "For the unenlightened person, every aspect of the phenomenal world can be seen as sufferings through the medium of his body and mind." However, the same world as this can be seen as it is and even looks so fresh all the time of this life, only if he could blow off the fires of craving, hatred, and delusion which always generate rebirth-causing actions, and may enjoy a selfless and detached state of mind beyond sensory and vain pleasures. As the Awakened One never clings to anything, all the transient phenomena can be received naturally, as a matter of course. Therefore Buddhism is a religion to teach how to live a true life beyond any kind of bias toward the world around and the inner world of his own mind.

This is why Mahāyāna Buddhism tells about the great vehicle (= Mahāyāna) which may enable everyone to attain the Buddhahood during one's lifetime. In this context, the true practice of Buddhist doctrine must go beyond life and death, *saṃsāra* and even *nirvāṇa*, without distinguishing between the two, and should gain the perfect liberty of mind, continuing to live a life in this world. Such a *nirvāṇa* as this is often called "apratiṣṭhita-nirvāṇa" in the *Madhyāntavibhāga-bhāṣya*, whose practical value in everyone's daily life should be much higher than the metaphysical value of "*parinirvāṇa*" to be attained only by the Buddha himself.

Just as the Buddha himself said on his last journey moving northward to the direction of Kapilavastu, his own homeland entirely ruined by the conquest of Kosala: "Ānanda, there is no wonder that a human being should meet one's end," he truly passed away at the age of 80, inspiring others with his impressive personality, as if a big tree would die a natural death, falling down on the earth, calmly in silence. The term "*parinirvāṇa*" may deserve to be used for describing the peaceful end of his great life. Though the great, old, and big tree had already returned to dust (= even if the Buddha had been burnt to bones and ashes by cremation), so many fruits from his branches (= those who have learnt and mastered the Buddha-dharma) could actually spread over the lands of this world to take root into the soil. Thinking of the Buddha's *life* still remaining *in this way*, his *parinirvāṇa* reminds us of the following words: "I tell you the truth, unless a kernel of wheat falls to the ground and dies, it remains only a single seed. But if it dies, it produces many seeds" (John 12: 24), although the concept of "eternal life" after death cannot be the same between Buddhism and Christianity. However, it is sure that the Nikāya Buddhists *ontologically* came to regard the state of *nirvāṇa* as eternal and imperishable, which was named "asaṁskṛta-dharma." They believed that the Buddha must have existed in the realm of *parinirvāṇa* after leaving this world. Here it is worthy to take notice of the fact that this theory deviates from the original meaning of *parinirvāṇa* to be understood *only* through the Buddha's own experience of well-trained and the deepest meditation. *Parinirvāṇa* is not the ordinary death, but should be attained by the positive decision of the Awakened One who has already enjoyed the state of *nirvāṇa* in his life.

Then, how did the Buddha Śākyamuṇi enter *parinirvāṇa*? Of course, it was not in the same way as ordinary people have to pass away, anticipating more sufferings in the next birth. Just as he attained the Buddhahood in the fourth stage of *catur-dyāna* (= the four stages of meditation), he immediately entered *parinirvāṇa* after going through all the stages of high-grade meditation in the following manner: (1) starting from the first and lowest stage up to the highest stage (= nirodha-samāpatti), (2) returning from the highest stage down to the first stage, (3) starting afresh from the first stage up to the *catur-dyāna*, (4) finally entering the *parinirvāṇa* directly from the state of *catur-dyāna*, and (5) never coming to life any more. The very moment the Buddha had expired, it is said that a strong earthquake occurred and the thunder was rumbling over the heavens, according to the *Mahāparinibbāna-suttanta*.

One of his leading disciples named Anuruddha, who was also his own cousin from Śākya clan, composed a poem well known in later periods: "There was no more breathing in the great person whose mind resided in peace. The Sacred One far from all desires has expired, attaining the tranquility. He has endured (physical) pains with his brave mind. As if the light went out, *his mind* has (completely) been set free." This verse is telling about how his "ceto-vimutti" (= mind's perfect liberty) had reached a successful conclusion, *not* suggesting that he sometimes lost his peaceful mind while preserving the state of Buddhahood. Living a life as the finest expert in meditation, he never lost control of himself even at the time of entering the *parinirvāṇa*. Indeed, the *nirvāṇa* could be experienced as if the heat of the flames worrying his mind had been blown out. Whether he was sitting in a cross-legged position or lying down on his right side and with his head to the north just as seen in the sculptures and paintings of Buddhist art which described the scene of *Mahāparinirvāṇa* (= the great death of Śākyamuṇi Buddha), we have no authentic evidence. There is no literature on this issue, although the latter is too much popular in the legends of Buddha's life story. In case he expired in a cross-legged position, his disciples must have laid down his dead body for the preparation of a memorial ceremony to be held by the Malla tribe of Kuśinagara as the land of the *parinirvāṇa* and other lay believers from all directions who still find it difficult to control their minds toward heart-rending partings.

It is worthy of notice that the Buddha did *not* choose the meditation in the highest stage as the entrance of the end of his life, *but* returned to the *catur-dyāna* in the end. What is the reason? Because the stage of *catur-dyāna* was regarded as the ideal meditation full of the supreme wisdom which took a balance of "*śamatha*" and "*vipaś yanā*." The explanation on "*śamatha-vipaśyanā*" shall be given as follows, because it is also a good way of studying the nature of *parinirvāṇa*.

In Buddhism, calmness of human mind can be classified into four levels:

1. Kāma-dhātu-dyāna: This level of meditative calmness can be gained by ordinary people who always tend to look on everything in this phenomenal world with a prejudiced and self-willed mind working through five sense organs under the instinctive and irresistible desires. They can keep their minds very calm for a short time, but cannot be free from selfish desires (= kāma) as yet.
2. Rūpa-dhātu-dyāna (equal to the *vipaśyanā* meditation): When ceasing from looking everything with a jaundiced mind, he comes to see it just *as it is*, and to judge any kind of issues without fail. This is an insight meditation to concentrate his mind on one object and contemplate its meaning thoroughly, which can be divided into four levels (= *catur-dyāna*): the first (and lowest) dyāna, the second dyāna, the third dyāna, and the fourth (and the highest) dyāna. The last one is an ideal meditation because of keeping balance with the next step of meditation (= arūpa-dhātu-dyāna) which must be in the best and the most helpful condition of solving various problems of suffering people in this world. Therefore, the Buddha himself enjoyed *this fourth level* of meditation just after attaining the awakened experience for the first time under the sacred tree (named aśvattha, later called the *bodhi* tree) for the sake of thinking about how he should like to preach the essence of the Buddhahood to all others still in the unawakened state of mind.
3. Arūpa-dhātu-dyāna (equal to the *śamatha* meditation): In this meditation, the practitioner has no object of his concentration in the perfect serenity of mind. It is not a sleepy, faint, or trance-like condition, but a fully standby state of mind waiting for the time to make the most of his active wisdom (= prajñā), no matter what may happen at the next moment. As it were, this meditation may grasp all the objects around him at the same time. There is no obstacle of physical and material causes, but only the pure mind remains to work at his own free will. The arūpa-dhātu-dyāna is also divided into four levels which were regarded as the supreme by non-Buddhist sects.
4. Nirodha-samāpatti (peculiar to Buddhist meditation): This is the meditation of dissolving one's mind and all of its workings and entering the state of mindlessness that is thoughtlessly compared to the *nirvāṇa* without corporal remainder (= *parinirvāṇa*), but it aims at

building the ideal personality for contributing his wisdom to the peace and happiness of the society, which is very well proved by the 80 years' life of Śākyamuṇi Buddha.

At any rate, it is important to remember that the Awakened One (= the Buddha) did not go up to the nirodha-samāpatti but positively got down to the stage of *vipaśyanā* (= insight meditation) at the time of entering the *parinirvāṇa*. It may suggest us that the last moment of his life should be awakened to the full toward his consciousness of wisdom based on the Buddhahood (= bodhi), probably saying "Farewell" in his mind to everyone with whom he met and discussed on what is truth in this world. As he was fully conscious when dying, the voices of his disciples must have reached his ears. It is medically proved that one's auditory sense, among all other senses, can work in the clearest way until the dying hour. Therefore, it is wrong to regard the *parinirvāṇa* as self-defeating. It was not a mysterious experience, too. It was *just as* one of the rational and natural events of a human life. Even today, so many Buddhist people in the world are yearning for the peaceful and calm end of his long life. The unenlightened one has to take rebirths according to their own karmic causes, but he usually cares nothing for such a theory, but desires to live longer and die as painlessly as possible.

In spite of the facts discussed above, the concept of *parinirvāṇa* seems to have brought a terrible misunderstanding to the intelligentsia of European countries in the nineteenth century: Schopenhauer, Nietzsche, Hegel, etc. Each of them, according to their own viewpoints, earnestly read several books written by the orientalists and other writers who were still unskilled and immature to study Buddhist thoughts and could not translate the sūtras into French, German, and English in a proper way. Without having enough time to meet and discuss with Buddhist people about their faith, the Europeans jumped carelessly to the conclusion that Buddhists were nothing but the nihilists who ultimately have a faith in "anéantissement" (dissolution of one's soul; annihilation), probably just like a weak, faint, and even demential state of human existence, where there is no hope for one's resurrection and the eternal life, but only the extinction of his soul should be done. Such a misunderstanding as this may remind us of the theory made by Abhidharma traditions that the *nirvāṇa* without corporal remain (= *parinirvāṇa*) must be the supreme goal of a Buddhist practitioner. Both orientalists and philosophers of those days did not know very well about how the original forms of Indian Buddhism had been changed in various ways, and failed to grasp the essence of Buddhism. And, it is also sure that the Buddha Śākyamuṇi was not a scholar but a man of religion who never tried to give a clear definition of his own experience named *bodhi* so that foreign people in later periods may be able to understand it by getting over the cultural and religious differences between the two.

For the purpose of proving that the Buddha was never a nihilist, it is best to remember the law of causation (pratītya-samutpāda) to be discussed only in the range of phenomenal world where we live a life and can experience every moment all through our own sensory organs. Any kind of question about metaphysical, ontological, and supernatural issues was not a matter of concern to him. In this world, everything continues to exist, changing all the time. Even the so-called *soul* of a man is changing in accordance with his own physical, verbal, and mental karma which can be also classified into good, bad, and morally neutral karma. As Buddhist philosophers have been following the theory, "anātmanaḥ sarvadharmāḥ" (= everything of this world is not unchanging, and it is possible for everyone to change one's destiny with the purification of karmic life just from now on), they have never wished to use the term *soul* (*ātman*) which could be misunderstood as a metaphysical substance beyond human knowledge. However, they could not help recognizing *something like a soul* (called "*pudgala*" by Nikāya Buddhists) as the remaining power of one's karma to be taken over from this life to the next one, in order to take an ethical responsibility of reaping as one has sown.

Though the Buddha is believed to have dissolved all of his karmic remains leading to the *parinirvāṇa*, it does not mean that he ultimately aimed at attaining the state of "nothingness." Actually he often admonished that we should not be inclined to have *a threefold desire* (taṇhā; strong desires as if craving for water), for it is truly the cause of all sufferings (Skt.: duḥkha, Pāli: dukkha), classified as the first of the Four Noble Truth (duḥkha-āryasatya):

1. Kāma-taṇhā: Desires caused by the senses of eyes, ears, nose, tongue, and skin, or delusion worrying one's body and mind. It means that one should not indulge in such desires but had better watch all of them for keeping a peaceful mind. It is not a denial of human life itself.
2. Bhava-taṇhā: "Bhava," in this context, means "heavenly beings" superior to human beings in the world of saṃsāra. Taking a rebirth in the heaven blessed with long life and good pleasures was an object of yearning for non-Buddhist people. This type of life is still self-centered and full of earthly desires, and Buddhists do not wish to become such heavenly beings, but strive to attain the Buddhahood for altruistic purposes.
3. Vibhava-taṇhā: "Vibhava" means "nonexistence" and "nothingness." Among the contemporaries of Śākyamuṇi Buddha, there were not a few ascetics who regarded "nothingness" as the realm of ideal peace of one's soul (ātman) similar to the eternal sleep, and even recommended fasting to death. In Buddhism, this is also taken as self-centered to ignore one's own mission in this life.

   Before Śākyamuṇi became the Buddha, he saw this kind of people striving for "nothingness" and completely abandoned asceticism, decided to take foods offered by a young lady named Sujātā from Uruvelā to get back his physical strength, and finally reached the Awakened state of mind in the "śamatha-vipaśyanā" meditation already mentioned in the former paragraph of this article.
4. All of (1)–(3) are the extremes of "existence" and "nothingness." They are nothing but a delusion of human mind. Being detached from the two extremes is often called "madhyamā-pratipad." It is translated as "the middle path" in English, but we should not misunderstand it as "intentionally getting back on track at the middle path" because such adherence to "the middle path" is not *truly* "the middle path" any more. One after another, a human being is seized with all kinds of feelings every moment and is also captured by the ideal of Buddhism. Even after he may achieve one goal, it is advised that he should not hesitate to do away with an old method whenever facing a new situation, as if a raft must be left behind every time reaching ashore to rescue the drifters in the process of human life: birth, aging, illness, and passing away from this world. No attachments even to the Buddha and his teachings (Buddha-Dharma) are the most important for a Buddhist to gain the perfect liberty of mind, and to grasp the points of daily practice, just as told in the *Vajracchedikā-prajñāpāramitā-sūtra*, one of the early sūtras of Mahāyāna Buddhism.

On the basis of the argument mentioned above, the concept of "*parinirvāṇa*" evidently does not belong to the essential elements of Buddhism, but just admires the last moment of the Buddha's lifetime. It goes without saying that Buddhism is neither a pessimism nor a nihilism nor a faith in self-destruction, but it is always oriented toward the *present* life to be fully active every moment.

When someone asks whether the Buddha may continue to exist after the *parinirvāṇa*, there are several ways of response. Here are two examples for the moment:

1. Never to answer such a question, just like the Buddha himself made no answer. (See the former paragraph referring to the *Cūḷa-Māluṅkyāputta-suttanta* in the *Majjhima Nikāya* 7–63.)
2. Not to respond from a metaphysical viewpoint, but to explain from the aspect of causality by referring to the words of the *Prajñāpāramitā-hṛdaya-sūtra*: "anutpannā aniruddhā" meaning "All phenomena are always generated *not* from nothingness *but* from something causal, and they will never come to nothing and will never continue to exist without changing for

ever: In other words, all phenomena continue to exist forever, keep on changing every moment." This sort of idea on "*śūnyatā*" (Non-Substantiality) may look so abstract, unstable, and undependable for those who need to hold the steady support of their faith in Buddhism. Naturally Mahāyāna Buddhists in India had come to believe that the historical Buddha (= Śākyamuṇi) was an *avatāra* (= incarnation) of the eternal Dharma (= *nirmāna-kāya*), and eventually personified the Dharma itself (= *dharma-kāya*) which had been existing from everlasting and preaching forever. And the *sambhoga-kāya* like the Amitābha Buddha, who had already kept his vow to relieve all the people from sufferings, was described as the savior having the eternal life. Here we must be careful *not* to misunderstand these three kinds of *kāya* (= body of the Buddha) as substantial, but should interpret the eternal Dharma not ontologically but practically only for the purpose of living a better karmic life as long as one's karma may be positively changed in any way. In this sense, the state of "*parinirvāṇa*" can be regarded just as a temporal event of the vast stream of the great river named the Buddha-Dharma, although Śākyamuṇi Buddha as a human being certainly died at the age of 80 and was cremated at Kuśinagara. Here it is worthy to note that the Buddha-Dharma is not an invention of the Buddha himself but the eternal Law to be awakened by the great human being (to be called "Buddha," "the Awakened One"). The Law should continue to exist all the time, no matter whether the Buddha may appear in this world or not. However, the Law cannot be well realized by human beings, as long as the Buddha does not preach it to other people. Since there is an essential connection between the Buddha's life and the eternity of the Dharma itself, there is no wonder that Buddhists came to believe in the eternal life of the Buddha himself in later periods.

In fact, the historical event of *parinirvāṇa*, just after the death of the Buddha Śākyamuṇi, took the visual form of the "*stūpa*" built in commemoration of his great life and teachings. Though it contained his bones and ashes (= Buddha *śarīra*), the semicircular *stūpa* was worshipped as the living Buddha and the symbol of his Dharma rather than as a tomb around which people could only grieve for his death. Monks and nuns of the Buddhist community took the initiative in carrying out the plan to build many more *stūpas* under the patronage of contemporary dynasty (e.g., the Mauryan King Aśoka in the third century, B.C.), which can be proved by not a few inscriptions of donors who positively took part in the construction work of a *stūpa*, which were discovered in Sāñcī and Bhārhut, etc.

In the history of Indian Buddhism, the *parinirvāṇa* had become the *seeds* (= *bījā)* to sprout the eternal life of the Buddha-Dharma essential for the Buddhist faith to carry through generations. It is an accepted fact that Buddhists succeeded in sowing the *good* seed of activating their spiritual life, turning around the sayings; "As a man sows, so he shall reap" to briefly explain the law of causation. Above all, the sects of Mahāyāna Buddhism, as well as those of Nikāya Buddhism, strived to make their faith everlasting and gradually divinized and viewed the historical Buddha as superhuman. Thus the yearning for "eternity" and "divinity" is *also* found in the Buddhist thoughts, although its true meaning must reside in another realm of philosophy quite different from Christian faith in the "eternal life" and the "resurrection," for example.

In conclusion, scholars of Buddhism had better hold of many more aspects of "*parinirvāṇa*" thoughtfully in order to avoid misunderstanding its meaning: "As the term *parinirvāṇa* can be literally translated as the perfect dissolution of one's life free from the world of rebirth, Buddhism should be longing for death, after all" which may *still* happen to non-Buddhists who have never tried to study Buddhism in a proper way probably because they need to protect themselves from the realm of other religions so that their culture may not get into an identity crisis. Even if so, it must be an intellectual dishonesty for such people to look over the books on Buddhism of uneven quality and start making an image of Buddhism which is already distorted by their intentional or hasty value judgment toward Buddhist philosophy and culture which look so strange or mysterious to their own eyes.

Everyone cannot help thinking about others within the framework of his own standpoint, but he will be able to know more about the truth by taking time enough to approach it from multifaceted viewpoints. The original meaning of "*parinirvāṇa*" also can be evolved and deepened within the range of Buddhist thoughts streaming from the philosophy of Indian religions.

Cross-References

► Nirvāṇa
► Stūpa

References

1. Droit R-P (1997) Le Cult du Néant; Les Philosophes et le Bouddha. Editions du Seuil, Paris
2. Hirakawa A (1963) The Rise of Mahāyāna Buddhism and its Relationship to the Worship of Stūpas. Memoirs of the Research Department of the Toyo Bunko (The Oriental Library) No.22. The Toyo Bunko, Tokyo
3. Hirakawa A (1990) A History of Indian Buddhism. Motilal Banarsidass, Delhi
4. Mizuno K (1985) The Life of Śākyamuṇi Buddha (Shakuson no shougai). Shunjusha, Tokyo (Japanese edition)
5. Nakamura H (1980) Mahāparinibbāna-Suttanta. Iwanami Shoten, Tokyo (Japanese translation and commentary)
6. Rhys Davids TW, Estlin Carpenter J (eds) (1947) The Dīgha Nikāya. The Pāli Text Society, London
7. Tanaka K (2004, 2012) Comparative Religion – Many Views of "Life" on Earth– (Hikaku Shūkyougaku –Inochi no Tankyū –). Hokuju Shuppan, Tokyo (Japanese edition)

Parivrājaka

► Śramaṇa

Pārśva

► Pārśvanātha (Jainism)

Pārśvanātha (Jainism)

Gregory M. Clines
Committee on the Study of Religion, Harvard University, Cambridge, MA, USA

Synonyms

Pārśva

Definition

In Jainism, Pārśvanātha was the 23rd and penultimate Tīrthaṅkara (ford maker) of the current world age.

Introduction to Pārśvanātha

Along with the 24th Tīrthaṅkara, Vardhamāna Mahāvīra, Pārśvanātha is one of only two Tīrthaṅkaras believed to have been a historical individual. Scholarly consensus dates Pārśvanātha to sometime between the eighth and seventh centuries B.C.E. Scholars also believe the parents of Mahāvīra to have been lay followers of Pārśvanātha, and while the direct relationship between Pārśvanātha and Mahāvīra is difficult to trace (as will be shown below), it is widely believed that Mahāvīra originally took initiation within Pārśvanātha's ascetic lineage. In iconography, Pārśvanātha's emblem is the cobra or snake, his complexion is blue-black or blue-green, and his attendant deities are Dharaṇendra and Padmāvatī. Unlike icons of other Tīrthaṅkaras, which are for the most part identifiable only by either the emblems carved into the icon's base or the attendant deities who usually flank the Tīrthaṅkara, icons of Pārśvanātha are immediately recognizable by the snake-hood parasol that covers his head (explained in more detail below). According to copious Jain biographical literature, Pārśvanātha was born in Banāras to King Aśvasena and his wife, Queen Vāma. Pārśvanātha is one of only two Tīrthaṅkaras to

P

hail from Banāras, the other being the seventh of the present world age, Supārśvanātha. According to the eighth-century *Uttarapurāṇa* of the Digambara monk Guṇabhadra, Pārśvanātha was physically attractive, with an eternally youthful appearance and a body marked by auspicious signs, foreshadowing his future as either a great emperor (*cakravartin*) or religious ascetic. Guṇabhadra gives his height as nine *ratnis* (cubits), which translates roughly to 13½ ft. Pārśvanātha renounced the world at age 30, and his complete life span was 100 years. Along with 19 out of the 23 other Jain Tīrthaṅkaras of this world age, Pārśvanātha attained *nirvāṇa* (final liberation from the world of rebirth) on Mount Śikhar (also called Mount Sammeta) in the modern-day state of Jharkhand. Today, Mount Śikhar is a major pilgrimage site for both Digambara and Śvetāmbara Jains, though in recent years a dispute over control of the site has broken out between the two sects. Among modern-day Jains, Pārśvanātha is one of the most popular Tīrthaṅkaras in terms of being an object of worship and veneration. He is venerated as the Tīrthaṅkara who removes obstacles and is the most popular Tīrthaṅkara in terms of number of icons in temples throughout India. His attendant goddess, Padmāvatī, has also enjoyed popularity among Jain worshippers as being especially powerful and active in the world. This is especially true in Karnataka, where Padmāvatī has also come to be associated with Tīrthaṅkaras other than Pārśvanātha. Thought to be a curer of snakebites and a goddess of wealth and beauty, in Karnataka she is oftentimes worshipped independently on Fridays ([1], pp. 213–214).

The Previous Lives of Pārśva

Both the *Uttarapurāṇa* (*The Later Tale*) of Guṇabhadra and Hemacandra's *Triṣaṣṭiś alākāpuruṣacaritra* (*The Lives of Sixty-Three Illustrious Persons* [2, 3]) give extensive accounts of Pārśvanātha and his nine previous lives before being born to Queen Vāma and King Aśvasena. In the first accounted birth, the eventual Tīrthaṅkara is born as a Brahman named Marubhūti in the court of the righteous King Aravinda. He has one brother, named Kamaṭha, and both young men marry beautiful women. Though accomplished in the various arts of a Brahman, Marubhūti decides to renounce the world and take up religious mendicancy. His wife is unable to bear the celibate lifestyle forced upon her by her husband's renunciation, and she has an affair with her brother-in-law, Kamaṭha. When Marubhūti finds out about the affair, he informs the king, who then exiles Kamaṭha and parades him mockingly through the city riding an ass. Enraged, Kamaṭha goes to the forest and practices extreme asceticism. Marubhūti, now desirous of his brother's forgiveness for the pain he has caused him, goes to Kamaṭha. But when Marubhūti, bowing in front of his brother, asks for forgiveness, Kamaṭha, still angry over the embarrassment his brother has caused him, hurls a rock at Marubhūti's head, killing him.

Marubhūti is then reborn as an elephant wandering the forest. King Aravinda, who since Marubhūti's death has himself become a renunciant, eventually converts the elephant to the correct faith of Jainism, and the elephant becomes as devout a Jain layman as an elephant can be. Kamaṭha, upon dying, is reborn as a poisonous snake. Once, desirous of water from a nearby pond, the elephant Marubhūti becomes trapped in the thick mud on the bank. Kamaṭha, as the snake, is also by the pond and takes the opportunity to again kill his former brother, this time by biting him repeatedly with his extremely poisonous fangs. The elephant (again, who will eventually be born as Pārśva) is then reborn in one of the many Jain heavens, while the snake, upon his own death, is reborn in one of the many hells.

Upon completion of his time in heaven, the future Pārśva is reborn in the land of Tilakā as a Vidyādhara (semidivine demigod) prince named Karaṇavega. In time, he again decides to take renunciation and religious wandering. At the same time, Kamaṭha is again reborn as a snake, though this time a giant python. Again, Kamaṭha is responsible for the death of his former brother, this time by swallowing him whole while the prince is meditating. The Vidyādhara prince is then once again reborn in heaven, while the python, which later burns to death in a forest fire, is again reborn in hell.

At the end of his life in heaven, the future Pārśva descends and is reborn as Vajranābha, the son of King Vajravīrya. Again, Vajranābha rejects worldly pleasures and takes up a life of asceticism, wandering the Jvalana Mountain. Kamaṭha is also reborn on that mountain as a hunter named Kuraṅgaka. One day, Kuraṅgaka, dressed in tiger skins, stumbles upon Vajranābha practicing contemplation and, because of his enmity from previous births, shoots Vajranābha, killing him with a single arrow. Vajranābha is reborn as a god in the Graiveyika heaven, while Kuraṅgaka is reborn in the seventh level of hell.

In his eighth birth, Vajranābha falls from the Graiveyika heaven and enters into the womb of Sudarśanā, the wife of King Kuliśabāhu of Purāṇapura. Upon his birth, he is given the name Suvarṇabāhu among great joy and festivities. He eventually meets the Tīrthaṅkara Jagannātha, who convinces him to renounce the world. Again, Suvarṇabāhu finally meets his end while dedicated to asceticism at the hands (or literally paws) of his former brother, who has since been reborn as a vicious lion. In his penultimate round of rebirth, the future Pārśva is again reborn in the tenth level of heaven, while the lion Kamaṭha again descends into hell.

The Life of Pārśva

As mentioned before, Lord Pārśvanātha was born to King Aśvasena and his wife, Queen Vāma. Like all the Tīrthaṅkaras, Pārśvanātha was born into a Kṣatriya, or kingly caste, family. His name, "Pārśva," which literally means, "to the side," was given to him after his mother once saw a snake creeping at her side one night while she was still pregnant. As is the case with all Tīrthaṅkaras, Pārśva's mother saw a series of 14 dreams during her pregnancy that revealed the birth of either a great emperor (*cakravartin*) or a great ascetic. Though the specific dreams differ between Digambaras and Śvetāmbaras, one common list, in order, is as follows: an elephant, a bull, a lion, the goddess Śrī, a garland, the moon, the sun, a flag or banner, a water pot, a lotus lake, an ocean of milk, a divine palace, a heap of jewels, and a fire. Pārśva was born on the tenth day of the dark fortnight of the month of Pauṣ (mid-December to mid-January). Fifty-six goddesses helped Queen Vāma with the birth, and soon afterward the Kings of the Gods (Indras) brought the child to the top of Mount Meru for his postpartum bath and ablution (*abhiṣeka*). In time, Pārśva grew to become a magnificent child, handsome and adept at the martial arts. In adulthood, he defeated in battle King Yavana of Kaliṅga and married the princess Prabhāvatī. According to Hemacandra's *Triṣaṣṭiś alākāpuruṣacaritra*, Pārśva once saved a snake from a five-fire sacrifice being performed by Kaṭha, who was in fact Pārśva's former brother Kamaṭha [2, vol. 5, 392]. Upon his death, Kaṭha was reborn a demon named Meghamālin, while the snake whom Pārśva saved became a divine snake king named Dharaṇendra. According to Guṇabhadra's *Uttarapurāṇa*, Pārśva actually saved two snakes, a male and a female, from being cut by Kaṭha as he was unconsciously chopping wood for his fire sacrifice ([3], p. 22, verse 103).

Pārśva lived the life of a prince until age 30, when he was inspired to take renunciation upon seeing an image of his predecessor, Neminātha. As a wandering mendicant, Pārśva practiced extreme asceticism and fasting. Once, in an attempt to disrupt Pārśva from his meditation, the demon Meghamālin created a terrible storm that rained down upon the renunciant. Pārśva, unmoved, continued his practice. In the meantime, Dharaṇendra, the serpent king whom Pārśva had saved in his previous life, came to Pārśva's aid, shielding him from the onslaught with his seven hoods. Dharaṇendra then rebuked Meghamālin (who, again, is Kamaṭha) and finally convinced him to give up his wicked ways and take shelter with Lord Pārśva. It is because of this story that Pārśva icons always consist of him meditating underneath a seven-hooded snake parasol, making Pārśva icons instantly recognizable. In Guṇabhadra's version of the tale, both Dharaṇendra and his wife Padmāvatī help to shield Pārśva. They, in turn, are Pārśva's two assistant deities ([3], p. 28, verse 140).

Pārśva attained omniscience while seated under a *dhataki* tree in the city of his birth, Banāras, on the fourth day of the dark half of the month of Chaitra (March/April). He had, in total, spent 83 days as an ascetic before achieving omniscience and spent the next 69 years and 9 months preaching widely. According to the *Kalpa Sūtra*, at the time of his death, Pārśva had accrued a following of 164,000 male lay householders, 327,000 female lay disciples, 16,000 fellow ascetic monks, and 38,000 ascetic nuns ([4], p. 28). Both of his parents took initiation into his renunciant order. As mentioned previously, Pārśva attained final liberation from the world of rebirth on Mount Śikar at the age of 100. He died 83,750 years after his predecessor, Neminātha.

The Relationship of Pārśva and Mahāvīra

Pārśva lived approximately 250 years before his successor Mahāvīra, and the renunciant order founded by Pārśva was still active during Mahāvīra's time. Coupled with the fact that the *Ācārāṅga Sūtra* explains Mahāvīra's parents as being lay disciples of Pārśva, scholars agree that Mahāvīra probably originally renounced the world within Pārśva's ascetic lineage ([1], p. 30). In this light, Mahāvīra can be seen as a type of reformer within an older Jain religious tradition. This being the case, there is one major difference between the teachings of Pārśva and those of Mahāvīra. Pārśva taught a fourfold doctrine of asceticism which included abstention from violence, lying, stealing, and possession. Mahāvīra accepted these four vows and to them added one more: the vow of sexual abstinence (*brahmacārya*). Jain sources have attempted to reconcile this discrepancy between the teachings of Pārśva and Mahāvīra, as Jain dharma is considered to be eternal and universal. Tīrthaṅkaras are not considered to be formulators of Jain religious teachings, but rather messengers of its eternal, unchanging truth. If this is the case, then it is problematic that two Tīrthaṅkaras would teach different doctrines. One way of dealing with this problem has been to explain that sexual abstinence was included in Pārśva's teaching of nonpossession. Because Mahāvīra preached during a more morally delinquent time than did Pārśva, it was necessary for him to include for his followers an additional, specific vow prohibiting inappropriate sexual behavior. Followers of Pārśva, though, because of their moral uprightness, would have implicitly understood avoidance of sexual activity as a natural part of the vow of nonpossession. It is interesting to note that Ādinātha (also called Ṛṣabhadeva), the first of the 24 Tīrthaṅkaras, like Mahāvīra also preached a fivefold system of vows. This is because he was preaching the dharma to followers for the first time, and it was therefore difficult for them to understand and an explicit fifth vow was necessary to insure proper religious practice ([4], pp. 34–35). The intervening 22 Tīrthaṅkaras, though, between Ādinātha and Mahāvīra, all preached a fourfold religious doctrine.

One other difference between Pārśva and Mahāvīra concerns monks' attire in their respective lineages. Monks in Mahāvīra's lineage wandered naked, while those belonging to Pārśva's ascetic order wore clothes. Indeed, similar to the issue discussed above, Mahāvīra is directly linked with the first Tīrthaṅkara of this world age, Ādinātha, the monks of whose lineage were also said to renounce even basic clothing. Pārśva is included in the group of the 22 intervening Tīrthaṅkaras, in whose lineages the monks are all believed to have worn clothing.

Teasing out the exact relationship between Pārśva and Mahāvīra is an extremely difficult, if not impossible task. Biographies of Mahāvīra, for example, problematize the discussion above about Mahāvīra joining Pārśva's already extant ascetic lineage by asserting that he in fact renounced the world alone, accompanied only by gods. There is no information about his joining an already established lineage of monks. The *Viyāhapaṇṇatti*, the fifth Aṅga of the Jain canon, explains that while Mahāvīra spoke well of Pārśva, he acquired followers by converting monks from Pārśva's lineage, a conversion that included abandoning Pārśva's fourfold system of vows and formally adopting Mahāvīra's fivefold system ([1], p. 32). The history, then, of the relationship between the penultimate and final Tīrthaṅkaras of this world age is still a murky one, but what is undoubtedly true is that in the minds of most modern Jains, there exists a belief of some kind of link between the two men, who are both among the most popular of the 24 Tīrthaṅkaras.

Pārśvanātha Icons and Temples

Icons of the various Tīrthaṅkaras are usually identical, identifiable only through by the emblem usually carved into the base of the statue or by the individualized guardian deities associated with each Tīrthaṅkara. Icons of Pārśvanātha, though, are immediately recognizable from the seven-hooded cobra parasol that shields him. Only one other Tīrthaṅkara has enjoyed such individualized iconography: some early icons of Ādinatha are identifiable by shoulder-length hair. Though exact dating is difficult, there is evidence for very early Pārśvanātha icons. One, a standing bronze icon of Pārśvanātha that was found as part of a larger hoard of bronze statues in 1931 in Chausa, Bihar, has been dated by Shah to between the first century B.C.E. and the first century C.E. This date has been challenged, though, with other scholars assigning a date between the late third and early fourth centuries C.E. to the statues. Another Pārśvanātha statue, a 9-in. bronze that is currently featured as part of the collection at the Chhatrapati Shivaji Museum in Bombay, has also been dated to between 100 B.C.E. and the second century C.E. ([5], pp. 42–45).

Temples dedicated to Pārśvanātha are among the most popular and famous Jain temples in India, and indeed, geographically associated Pārśvanātha icons and temples play a major role in community and religious identity formation. One such example is the Śankheśvar Pārśvanātha Temple in the town of Śankheśvar, in northern Gujarat. The mythological story of the image in the temple begins in a previous time cycle, when the eighth Jina Dāmodara was asked by a Jain layman how he would attain salvation from the world. Dāmodara explained to the man, named Ashadhi, that he would be a pupil of Pārśvanātha during the next time cycle and would then attain liberation. At this point, a divine image of Śankheśvar Pārśvanātha appeared to Ashadhi, and he worshipped it for the rest of his life. Upon his death, Ashadhi ascended to heaven, along with the icon. The icon was also worshipped by Dharaṇendra and Padmāvatī, the king and queen of divine serpents. Later, during the present time cycle and the life of the 22nd Tīrthaṅkara, Neminātha, his cousin Krishna (famous as an avatar of Vishnu in Hindu traditions) fought a battle near Śankheśvar with Jarāsandha. At one point, Jarāsandha cast a spell that immobilized Krishna's army; to counteract the spell, Krishna performed a 3-day fast and worshipped Dharaṇendra. Pleased, Dharaṇendra gave the image of Śankheśvar Pārśvanātha to Krishna, who bathed the image and used to bathing water to sprinkle over his soldiers, in doing so curing their paralysis. Krishna went on to defeat Jarāsandha in battle and later installed the divine image in a temple.

In more recent history, the Śankheśvar Pārśvanātha icon can be traced back to the year 1099 C.E., when a man named Sajjana Shah, encouraged by a mendicant, built a Pārśvanātha temple in the town of Śankheśvar. Over the centuries the temple underwent numerous renovations but was eventually destroyed by the invading Muslim emperor Allauddin Khilji. The Pārśvanātha icon of the temple was saved from destruction but later lost. It was not until the seventeenth century that the icon was recovered. According to local history, a monk led a search for the image. Over a period of days, the monk saw a particular cow empty its udder of milk in the same spot every day. Digging up the spot revealed the icon! A new temple was built to house the icon in 1606 C.E., though it too was later destroyed, either by natural calamity or by military campaign. Finally, another temple, this one still standing, was built in 1704 C.E., and later renovated in 1910 C.E.

The Śankheśvar Pārśvanātha temple is an especially efficacious pilgrimage site to perform the *aththam tap*, the 3-day fast that Krishna performed in order to defeat Jarāsandha. Pilgrims have explained that while even a 1-day fast is difficult to perform in other places, the 3-day fast is easy at Śankheśvar because of the power of the icon. Pauṣ Tenth, the holiday celebrating the birth of Lord Pārśvanātha, is an especially popular time to come and fast. The temple is also famous for its especially efficacious shrine to Padmāvatī, Pārśvanātha's attendant goddess. While Tīrthaṅkaras are believed to be completely liberated from the world and unable to interact directly with human disciples, subsidiary deities like Padmāvatī are not liberated, and can therefore interact with petitioners in the world. Padmāvatī's shrine is oftentimes adorned with garlands of coconuts, a pan-Indian symbol for prosperity. Orthodox Jain teaching, though, is clear that no attendant god or goddess can be worshipped before the *Tīrthaṅkara* image. While Padmāvatī is therefore very popular among pilgrims, her worship is still secondary to that of Pārśvanātha ([6], pp. 65–68). The power of the Śankheśvar Pārśvanātha icon in Gujarat has led to replications of the icon being installed in temples throughout India, especially in areas where there is a sizeable Gujarati Jain presence. The Śankheśvar Pārśvanātha is just one example of a larger trend of "replication cults," in which especially powerful, place-specific icons are replicated and distributed outside of their original geographic area. These replicated icons form a bridge between the diasporic community and the original image, allowing followers to tap into the power of the original icon ([5], p. 186). Indeed, many of these replication cults take as their main icon some form of Pārśvanātha, serving as another testament to Pārśvanātha's popularity among the modern Jain laity.

Cross-References

▶ Dharma (Jainism)
▶ Heaven (Jainism)
▶ Jina
▶ Mount Meru
▶ Omniscience
▶ Rebirth
▶ Renunciation
▶ Saṃsāra
▶ Time (Jainism)
▶ Tīrthaṅkara (Jainism)
▶ Vārāṇasī (Buddhism)

References

1. Dundas P (2002) The Jains, 2nd edn. Routledge, London/New York
2. Triṣaṣṭiśalākāpuruṣacaritra (1962) The lives of sixty-three illustrious persons, 6 vols (trans: Johnson HM). Oriental Institute, Baroda (specifically volume 5)
3. Bollee W (2008) Acarya Gunabhadra's Parsvacaritam: life of Parsva. Hindi Granth Karyalay, Mumbai
4. von Glasenapp H (1999) Jainism: an Indian religion of salvation (trans: Shrotri SB). Motilal Banarsidass, Delhi
5. Cort JE (2010) Framing the Jina: narratives of icons and idols in Jain history. Oxford University Press, New York
6. Cort JE (1988) Pilgrimage to Shankheshvar Pārśvanātha. Cent Study World Relig Bull 14(1):63–72, Harvard Center for the Study of World Religions, Cambridge

Parva

▶ Uposatha

Pasenadi

K. T. S. Sarao
Department of Buddhist Studies, University of Delhi, Delhi, India

Synonyms

Agnidatta

Definition

King of Kosala and a contemporary of the Buddha.

Pasenadi was the king of Kosala and a contemporary of the Buddha. According to T. W. Rhys Davids, Pasenadi was his official title, and his personal name was Agnidatta ([7],

p. 10). He was the son of Mahākosala and was educated at Takkasilā. His father was so impressed with his qualities that he seems to have abdicated in Pasenadi's favor ([5], Vol. i, p. 338). He tried to put down bribery and corruption in his court, though he does not appear to have been very successful in his attempts ([12], Vol. i, p. 109f). As king, he enjoyed the company of wise men. Quite early in the Buddha's ministry, Pasenadi became his follower and close friend, and his devotion to the Buddha lasted till his death ([3], Vol. i, p. 69). According to Tibetan sources, Pasenadi's conversion was in the second year of the Buddha's ministry ([9], p. 49).

He is said to have guarded the reputation of both the Buddha and the Saṃgha very zealously and put down with a firm hand any attempt on the part of heretics to discredit them ([3], Vol. i, p. 153f; [12], Vol. ii, p. 529). Pasenadi was always ready to pay honor to those who had won the praise of the Buddha ([5], Vol. ii, p. 150ff; Vol. iii, p. 2ff; [11], Vol. ii, p. 100). Pasenadi enjoyed discussions on the Dhamma with the Buddha and leading Buddhist monks and nuns ([3], Vol. iv, p. 374ff; [11], Vol. ii, p. 118ff; Vol. ii, p. 125ff). He once saw some monks sporting in the river in a way that did not suit them, he ensured that the Buddha was made aware of it ([6], Vol. iv, p. 112). As a true Buddhist, he also extended his favors to other religious orders ([10], Vol. vi, p. 2). It is said that his alms-halls were always kept open to everyone desiring food or drink ([10], Vol. ii, p. 6). Pasenadi liked to be the foremost in gifts to the Buddha and the Saṃgha ([5], Vol. iii, p. 188ff).

Pasenadi's chief consort was Mallikā, daughter of a garland maker. He loved her dearly and trusted her judgment in all things. When in difficulty he consulted her, realizing that her wisdom was greater than his own ([3], Vol. i, p. 74). On one occasion, Pasenadi expressed to the Buddha his disappointment that Mallika should have borne him a daughter instead of a son, but the Buddha told him that daughter were equally good ([3], Vol. i, p. 83). Pasenadi had a sister, Sumanā, who became a nun and attained arahantship ([3], Vol. i, p. 97; [14], p. 22).

It has been told that the bowl out of which he ate was the size of a cartwheel ([12], Vol. i, p. 136). On one occasion, the Buddha is mentioned as telling him to eat less ([3], Vol. i, p. 81; [5], Vol. iii, p. 264f). He once tried to seduce a married woman by ordering her husband out of the town. But the king had a sleepless night and was advised by the Brāhmaṇas to order an animal sacrifice. But he abandoned the idea on the advice of the Buddha ([5], Vol. ii, p. 1ff; [12], Vol. i, p. 111). His devotion and attachment to the Buddha has formed the basis of many legends ([11], Vol. ii, p. 120). He frequently visited the Buddha and discussed various matters with him. When the Buddha went to Tāvatiṃsa, Pasenadi made an image of him in sandalwood so that he could honor him ([1], Vol. i, p. 1884: xliv). He is credited for having built monasteries for the Buddha, Pajāpatī Gotamī, and his teacher Bāvari ([1], Vol. ii, p. 1884: 2; [2], Vol. ii, p. 15; [5], Vol. iii, p. 241ff; [12], p. 580). He organized the celebrated almsgiving called *Asadisadāna* (incomparable) and gave four priceless gifts to the Buddha, namely, a white parasol, a couch, a stand, and a footstool ([5], Vol. iii, pp. 183–186). A Buddha is said to receive such gifts only once in his lifetime. Three *Jātakas*, namely, *Aditta*, *Dasabrāhmaṇa*, and *Sivi*, were preached in reference to *Asadisadāna*.

It has been pointed out in the sources that Pasenadi, in order to associate himself with the Buddha's family, sent word to the Sākiyan chiefs asking for the hand of one of their daughters. The Sākiyans considered it beneath their dignity to accede to such a request. However, as they did not want to displease Pasenadi, their overlord, they sent him the daughter of a slave woman. By her, Pasenadi had a son Viḍuḍabha. When Viḍuḍabha came to know of this, he vowed vengeance, and on becoming the king, he invaded the Sākiyan territory and massacred a large number of the Sākyans ([2], Vol. i, p. 133f.; Vol. iv, p. 144ff; [5], Vol. i, p. 339ff.). Brahmadatta, who entered the Saṃgha and became an arahant, was another son of Pasenadi ([13], Vol. i, p. 460). The *Dulva* says that Jeta, owner of Jetavana, was also Pasenadi's son ([9], p. 48).

Pasenadi died under tragic circumstances at the gates of Rājagaha, waiting for help from Ajātasattu against his son Viḍuḍabha who had captured the throne by deceit. Later, Ajātasattu performed the funeral rites over the king's body with great pomp ([2], Vol. iv, p. 150ff; [5], Vol. i, p. 353ff; [11], Vol. ii, p. 118). *Kosala Saṃyutta* of the *Saṃyutta Nikāya*, consisting of 25 anecdotes, is devoted to him. The *Anāgatavaṃsa* declared Pasenadi a Bodhisattva, who will be the fourth future Buddha ([4], p. 37).

Cross-References

- ▶ Dhamma
- ▶ Pajāpati Gotamī
- ▶ Rājagaha (Pāli)
- ▶ Saṃgha
- ▶ Takkasilā

References

1. Beal S (1884) Si-yu-ki: Buddhist record of the Western world, 2 vols. Trübner, London
2. Fausböll V (ed) (1877–1897) The Jātakas. Trübner, London
3. Feer ML (ed) (1884–1898) The Saṃyutta Nikāya, 5 vols. Text Society, London
4. Minayeff M (ed) (1886) Anāgata-vaṃsa. Journal of the Pali Text Society, London, pp 3–53
5. Norman HC (ed) (1906) The commentary on the Dhammapada, 4 vols. Pali Text Society, London
6. Oldenberg H (ed) (1879–1883) The Vinaya Piṭakaṃ, 5 vols. Pali Text Society, London
7. Rhys Davids TW (1903) Buddhist India. G.P. Putnam's Sons, New York
8. Rhys Davids TW, Carpenter JE (eds) (1890–1911) The Dīgha Nikāya, 3 vols. Pali Text Society, London
9. Rockhill WW (1884) The life of the Buddha and the early history of his order. Trübner, London
10. Steinthal P (ed) (1885) The Udāna. Pali Text Society, London
11. Trenckner V, Chalmers R (ed) (1888–1896) The Majjhima Nikāya, 3 vols. Pali Text Society, London
12. Woodward FL (ed) (1929–1937) The Sāratthappakāsinī, Buddhaghosa's commentary on the Saṃyutta Nikāya, 3 vols. Pali Text Society, London
13. Woodward FL (ed) (1940–1959) Paramattha-Dīpanī: Theragāthā-Aṭṭhakathā, the commentary of Dhammapālācariya, 3 vols. Pali Text Society, London
14. Woodward FL, Hardy E, Muller E, Barua DL et al (eds) (1891–1977) Paramatthadīpanī, Dhammapālācariya's commentary on the Therīgāthā, the Vimānavatthu. Pali Text Society, London

Passing Away

▶ Death (Buddhism)

Path of Analysis

▶ Paṭisambhidāmagga

Path of Discrimination

▶ Paṭisambhidāmagga

Paṭhavī

▶ Earth (Buddhism)

Paṭicca Samuppāda

▶ Middle Way (Buddhism)

Paṭiccasamuppāda

▶ Causality (Buddhism)

Pātimokkha

Rajesh Ranjan
Department of Pali, Nava Nalanda Mahaviihara (Deemed to be University), Nalanda, Bihar, India

Synonyms

Pāṭimokkha; Prātimokṣa

Definition

A name given to a collection of various precepts contained in the Vinaya, called *Vibhaṅga*, as they were recited in the fortnightly congregation of the Buddhist order (*Uposatha*) for the purpose of confession.

Introduction

The set of rules laid down to regulate the outward general behavior of the members of the Buddhist monastic order is known as *Pātimokkha*. It is so called because "It is the beginning, the mouth, the source so significant of all meritorious acts" (*ādimetam mukhametaṃ pamukhmetaṃ kusalānaṁ dhammānaṁ*) ([5]: 2.1, 4; pp. 106–143) which is further interpreted thus in the *Kaṅkhāvitaraṇī* – "one who leads meritorious life is relieved from the afflictions of purgatory lives and so also from self-censure" ([1]: 2).

Two *Pātimokkha*-s

With a view to facilitate a brief survey of the *dhammā* of the two *Pātimokkha*-s, the *Bhikkhu Pātimokkha* comprising 227 *dhammā* and the *Bhikkhunī Pātimokkha* containing 311, a section-wise list of their numbers, as given below, is desirable:

Section of the Pātimokkha	Bhikkhu Pātimokkha	Bhikkhunī Pātimokkha
1. Pārājikā dhammā (Defeat or expulsion)	04	08
2. Saṅghādisesā dhammā (Suspension)	13	17
3. Aniyatā dhammā (Indeterminates)	02	–
4. Nissaggiyā Pācittiya dhammā (Forfeiture)	30	30
5. Pācittiyā dhammā (Expiation)	92	166
6. Pāṭidesaniyā dhammā (Confession)	04	08
7. Sekhiyā dhammā (Rules of training)	75	75
8. Adhikaraṇasamathā dhammā (Ways of settling disputes)	07	07
	227	311

As all these *dhammā* pertain to noble conduct of the members of the saṃgha, a brief perusal is desirable in order to understand the purpose of their formulation.

First Section

To begin with, the first section of the *dhammā* consists of those offenses; after committing any which, the transgressor is defeated, i.e., becomes unfit for monk-life. Indulging in sexual intercourse, taking things not given, depriving any one of life, and speaking about one's superhuman attainments are such offenses which a monk or a nun must not commit. Besides, nuns have also to observe four more restraints annexed to one or other kind of sexual activities. Now it may, however, be opined in this context that the first three out of the four *dhammā* for monks and eight for nuns had been the principal constituents of the concept of sublime conduct (*pañcasīla*) followed by Indian society in general and those opting a life of homelessness in particular since time immemorial.

Second Section

The second section of the *dhammā* is named *Saṅghādisesa*. It is so named because a formal meeting of a competent order is required in the beginning (*ādi*) and so also at the end (*sesa*), i.e., at the time of imposing punishment upon the transgressor as well as when repealing it after the expiry of the period of punishment. The *dhammā* contained in this section are 13 for monks and 17 for nuns. Most of these are concerned with sexual activities but of less serious nature. The rest are as regards construction of a hut or monastery for one's own use, causing schism in a united *saṃgha*, supporting an irreligious monk and the like. The punishments prescribed for this group of offenses are *Mānatta* and *Parivāsa*. *Mānatta* is a kind of a fixed probation. As such the transgressor is debarred form the rights and privileges of the order for 6 days. Thus, more or less like the *Pārājika*, it is temporary suspension from the order. *Mānatta* is accompanied by *Parivāsa* if the transgressor concealed the offense intentionally. In such a case, it becomes almost impossible to ascertain the actual date of commission of the offense. As has already been said, all these offenses are requited with temporary withdrawal of the rights and privileges of the transgressor deserving as a full-fledged member of the Order.

Third Section

The third section of the *Bhikkhu Pātimokkha* is called *Aniyatā* (indeterminates) which contains only two *dhammā* as follows.

If a monk is seen by a trustworthy female lay-devotee seated with a woman in a secluded place:

(a) On a convenient sit, the monk commits an offense involving defeat, suspension, or expiation, if the monk acknowledges it himself.
(b) Convenient to say lewd words to that woman, the monk commits an offense involving suspension or expiation.

How much serious these two *dhammā* might have been, these involve an offense oscillating between defeat and suspension or expiation on the one hand and between suspension and expiation on the other. It appears, therefore, that these two *dhammā* should neither have been compiled under an independent section just after the second section, i.e., *Saṅghādisesa* nor before the fifth section, i.e., *Pācittiyā*, the section on expiation. Its proper and ideal place would have been at the end of the fifth section.

Nissaggiyā Pācittiyā Dhammā

Compiled in three groups, namely, *Cīvaravaggo*, *Elakavaggo*, and *Pattavaggo*, the *Nissaggiyā Pācittiyā dhammā* for monks are 30, each group containing ten *dhammā*. The *dhammā* contained in the first group are related to procurement, maintenance, and the use of cloth. So also the first seven *dhammā* of the second group are strictly concerned with procurement, maintenance, and use of silk and the remaining three restraining a monk from accepting money and its transaction in sale and purchase. The third group, *Pattavaggo* comprises, besides *dhammā* pertaining to bowl, *dhammā* as regards medicine, cloth, and other benefits of the order.

Despite the number of the *Nissaggiyā Pācittiyā dhammā* for nuns being the same as that for monks, i.e., 30, their arrangement in three groups is a bit different from them. They are as follows – (1) *Pattavaggo*, (2) *Cīvaravaggo*, and (3) *Jātaruparajatavaggo*. A perusal of the *dhammā* of the first two groups leads one to infer that the groups not only bear common titles but also their contents, with some necessary changes in wordings, are almost same. So far as the last group, *Jātaruparajata* group, is concerned, it is like the *dhammā* of the *Elakavaggo* of the *Nissaggiyā Pācittiyā* for monks. It is a conglomeration of miscellaneous *dhammā* as regards procurement of cloth and accepting money and its transaction.

Thus, the *dhammā* of this section pertaining to procurement, use, and storage of cloth are sufficient to opine that the procurement of cloth in those days was far more an arduous job than procurement of food stuff and other necessities of life. This justifies the punishment of expiation with forfeiture of the article in respect of which the offense is committed.

Pācittiyā Dhammā for Monks

Arranged in nine groups, each of 10 *dhammā* with the only exception of the eighth group which contains 13 *dhammā*, the *Pācittiyā dhammā* are altogether 92 for monks. These groups which are named on the basis of the first *dhammā* of the groups occur thus in the *Bhikkhu Pātimokkha* – (1) *Musāvādavaggo*, (2) *Bhūtagāmavaggo*, (3) *Bhikkhunovādavaggo*,

(4) *Bhojanavaggo*, (5) *Acelakavaggo*, (6) *Surāpānavaggo*, (7) *Sappāṇakavaggo*, (8) *Sahadhammikavaggo*, and (9) *Ratanavaggo*. In order to make the point explicit, the first group may be taken as an example. Though the maximum number of the *dhammā* of the group as it begins with restraining a monk from speaking a lie is concerning speech, the miscellaneous *dhammā* like restraining a monk from sharing a common cot with a woman and digging the earth himself or getting it done by anyone else are also contained in it. Thus, the title of the groups does not speak exactly the contents of the groups.

Pācittiyā Dhammā for Nuns

Similarly, the *Pācittiyā dhammā* for nuns, being 162 in number, are arranged in 16 groups and named after the first *dhammā* of each group. These *vaggas* are as noted below – (1) *Lasunavaggo*, (2) *Rattandhavago*, (3) *Maggavaggo*, (4) *Tuvaṭṭavaggo*, (5) *Cittāgāravaggo*, (6) *Ārāmavaggo*, (7) *Gabbhinīvaggo*, (8) *Kumārbhūtavaggo*, (9) *Chattāgāravaggo*, (10) *Musāvādavaggo*, (11) *Bhūtagāmavaggo*, (12) *Bhojanavaggo*, (13) *Carittavaggo*, (14) *Jotivaggo*, (15) *Diṭṭhivaggo*, and (16) *Dhammikavaggo*. All these groups, like the *Bhikkhu Pācittiyā dhammā*, are formed with 10 *dhammā* each, except the eighth and the ninth groups containing 13 *dhammā* each.

A comparative appraisal of the two sets of *dhammā* perused above leads us to construe that:

(a) The number of such *dhammā* in both the sets are not in round number, i.e., 92 and 162.
(b) The first group of *dhammā* of the *Pācittiyā* for monks is as regards false speech, whereas the first group of *dhammā* in case of nuns is pertaining to eating garlic, and these groups are accordingly named as *Musāvādavaggo* and *Lasunavaggo*.
(c) Out of 16 groups of the *Pācittiyā dhammā* for nuns, only 3 groups, i.e., vaggas 10, 11, and 12 share common titles with the first, second, and fourth groups of the *Pācittiyā dhammā* for monks, respectively, the first two groups (10th and 11th) possessing identical *dhammā* in toto and the last (12th) partially different.

Pāṭidesaniyā Dhammā

Pāṭidesaniyā dhammā are four for monks and eight for nuns. These are minor offenses which are requited with simple confession. The first two of the *Pāṭidesaniyā* are committed by a monk if he uses food, solid or soft, accepting with his own hand from the hand of a nun and on the direction of a nun to give rice or curry, respectively. The third is incurred by a monk if he accepts food from the families of learners (*sekhasammatani kulāni*) neither invited beforehand nor being ill. Likewise, the fourth is committed by a monk residing in a dangerous or frightening monastery not announced beforehand if he accepts food with his own hand being not ill.

It is interesting to note that, opposed to the *Pāṭidesaniyā dhammā* for monks, all of the eight *Pāṭidesaniyā dhammā* regarding nuns are pertaining to restriction on eating the eight dainties, namely, ghee (*sappi*), curd, oil, honey, butter, fish, meat, and milk by directing the donor to serve such articles of food. Most likely the purpose behind the imposition of such a restriction has not been taken into account anywhere in the Vinaya texts [3].

On the basis of the terminology of the *Sekhiyā dhammā*, the term *sekhiyā* may in brief be interpretated as "*sikkhā karaniyā' ti sekhiyā*," i.e., the custom or practice ought to be observed is *sekhiyā*. *Kaṅkhāvitaraṇī* explains it as follows – "*Ettha ca yasmā vattakhandhake vuttavattānipi tathā sikhitabbattā sekhiyāneva honti*" [1], i.e., these are so called because these are ought to be observed like the customs (*vattani*) laid down in the *Vattakhandhaka* (refers to the eighth *Khandhaka* of the *Cullavagga*; see [4]). Thus, *Sekhiyā dhammā* are rules regarding good manners enforced upon the members of the saṃgha, and therefore, not requited with any type of punishment.

Arranged in seven groups named after the first *dhammā* of the group, six groups from the beginning having 10 *dhammā* each and the last group 15 *dhammā*, the total number of such *dhammā* are thus 75 which are operative to the monks and nuns alike.

Adhikaraṇasamathā

The *Adhikaraṇasamathā* formed with two terms – *Adhikaraṇa* and *Samathā* – is the last section of the *Dhammā* of the *Pātimokkha*, the former term meaning a dispute and the latter conveying its settlement or disposal. Unlike the five sections of offenses proper along with their punishments and the last but one section, i.e., the *Sekhiyā* which lay down laws of good conduct to be observed, this section refers to four types of dispute together with seven ways of their disposal or settlement. A dispute may be caused because of four reasons, namely, *vivāda* (contention), *anuvāda* (censure), *āpatti* (offense), and *kicca* (the manner of putting up an agenda at formal meeting of the order). Named after their respective reasons of bringing about these disputes, these are named as below:

(a) *Vivādadhikaraṇa* (wrong representation of a legal matter)
(b) *Anuvādādhikaraṇa* (censure)
(c) *Āpattādhikaraṇa* (offense)
(d) *Kiccādhikaraṇa*[i] (the manner of putting up an agenda at formal meeting of the order)

An *adhikaraṇa* (a legal matter), to whatever category it may belong, is resolved by a duly appointed Saṅgha. The session of the Saṅgha is regulated by the rules of *Adhikaraṇasamathā*, i.e., ways of settlement of a dispute which are seven in number – *Sammukhavinaya* (a verdict in the presence), *Sativinaya* (a verdict of innocence), *Amulhavinaya* (a verdict of past insanity), *Paṭiññātakaraṇa* (a verdict to be carried out on acknowledgement), *Yebhuyyasikā* (the verdict of the majority), *Tasspāpiyyasikā* (a verdict for special depravity), and *Tiṇṇavāttharaka* (a verdict of covering up with grass).

In this regard, it is to be borne in mind that all the ways are not equally effective to the disposal of the disputes under reference. *Kaṅkhāvitaraṇī* specially makes a mention as to whichever way/ways would be operative to whichever dispute. The same may be produced in a tabular form as noted under:

(a) *Vivādādhikaraṇa* – *Sammukhavinaya, Yebhuyyasikā*
(b) *Anuvādādhikaraṇa* – *Sammukhavinaya, Sativinaya, Amulhavinaya, Tassapāpiyyasikaya*
(c) *Āpattādhikaraṇa* – *Sammukhavinaya, Paṭiññātakaraṇa, and Tiṇavatthāraka*
(d) *Kiccādhikaraṇa – Sammukhavinaya*

Conclusions

As remarked before, some of the aforesaid sections, for one reason or the other, seem unjustifiably included in the *Pātimokkha*. For instance, the offenses enlisted in the third section ought not to be treated as a separate section for they belong, according to the circumstances, to *Pārājika*, *Sanghādisesa*, or *Pācittiyā* section. Similarly, the restraints belonging to the seventh section, i.e., *Sekhiyā* can never come on the category of offenses as neither of the follies is retributed with any punishment or expiation. As such, Pachow aptly remarks that the violation of any of them by a Bhikkhu is not considered to be a criminal act but simply bad manners [2]. Likewise, the last section the *Adhikaraṇasamathā* gives different methods for the settlement of a disputed issue of the Order. Now what may be inferred is that out of the eight sections, only five, namely, *Pārājika*, *Saṅghādisesa*, *Nissaggiyā Pācittiyā*, *Pācittiyā*, and *Pāṭidesaniyā* are separate sections of what is called transgressions and expiations in the proper sense of the term.

There is another point that draws one's attention. The collective name of the first group of the Vinaya texts is *Vibhaṅga*, though the chronological history of formation of the Buddhist order is contained in the *Khandhaka* where information as regards the enlightenment of the Buddha under Bo-tree on the bank of the Nerañjara, the formation of the order of monks by turning the wheel of the *Dhammā* to the *Pañcavaggiyā*, his quondam colleagues at *Isipatana*, so on and so forth are vividly recorded. The *Vibhaṅga* consists of two closely connected texts, namely, *Bhikkhu Vibhaṅga* and *Bhikkhunī Vibhaṅga*. Both these texts are considered to be extensive treatises on the *Pātimokkha* rules giving the occasion for the formulation of each rule, with some explanation or illustration of various terms employed in the wording of the rules concerned. Some of such illustrations conform to the rule formulated, while some other form exception to them. These two texts, therefore, suitably called *Sutta Vibhaṅga*, very likely *Sutta* implying a rule and *Vibhaṅga* its exegetic delineation. It is important to note that these texts in the manuscripts are generally known as *Pārājika* and *Pācittiya*, respectively.

Similarly *Khandhaka* is the collective name of the second collection of the Vinaya texts which comprises two texts, the *Mahāvagga* and the *Cullavagga*. Out of these two texts, the former traces the history of the origins of the order of monks from its very inception, while the latter refers to the formation of the order of nuns. The *Mahāvagga* says that the Buddha, on the suggestion of the Magadhan king Bimbisāra, enjoined upon the monks to recite the Dhammā first which was instantaneously replaced by the lord himself with the recital of the *Pātimokkha*. Thus, the recital of the *Pātimokkha* which started with the formation of the order of monks persisted as an essential feature of the fortnightly gathering of monks (*Uposatha*) which was known as *Pātimokkhauddesa* or simply *Suttuddesa* as another epithet for it being *Pātimokkhasuttaṁ* as well. Opposed to it, as the order of nuns was constituted considerably late, the compilation of the *Bhikkhunī Pātimokkha* would have followed subsequently. Nevertheless, these are invariably referred to as *Ubhayāni Pātimokkhāni*, as if those were compiled simultaneously in quick succession.

In the light of the foregoing discussion, enjoining upon the monks to recite the *Pātimokkha* in their fortnightly congregation (*Uposatha*) at the very inception of the formation of the Order of monks, however, does not appear in consonance with the history of the formulation of the *Dhammā* of the *Pātimokkha* which were formulated by the lord himself after his sojourn at about seven different places beginning at Verañjā till his return therefrom to Vesālī via Payāgatittha and Vārāṇasī. The process, which began with the promulgation of *Pārājikā dhammā* at Vesali, persisted till the framing of *Sekhiyā dhammā* at Sāvatthi. So far as the place of formation of *Adhikaraṇasamathā dhammā* is concerned, the *Vibhaṅga* is mum. So also are *Samantapāsādikā* and *Kaṅkhāvitaraṇī*.

Cross-References

- ▶ Bimbisāra
- ▶ Saṃgha
- ▶ Uposatha

References

1. Maskel D (ed) (1981) Kaṅkhāvitaraṇī. Pali Text Society, London
2. Pachow W (1955) A comparative study of the Pātimokkha. Visvabharati, Santiniketan
3. Rhys Davids TW, Oldenberg H (trans) (1965) Vinaya texts, Part I. Motilal Banarsidass, Delhi
4. Tiwari M et al (eds) (1956) Cullavagga, Nalanda Devanāgarī Pāli series. Navanalanda Mahavihara, Nalanda
5. Tiwari M et al (eds) (1956) Mahāvagga, Nalanda Devanāgarī Pāli series. Navanalanda Mahavihara, Nalanda

Pāṭimokkha

▶ Pātimokkha

Paṭisambhidā

▶ Paṭisambhidāmagga

Paṭisambhidāmagga

K. T. S. Sarao
Department of Buddhist Studies,
University of Delhi, Delhi, India

Synonyms

Path of analysis; Path of discrimination; Paṭisambhidā; Way of comprehension

Definition

The Paṭisambhidāmagga is the 12th book of the Khuddaka Nikāya of the Sutta Piṭaka of Pāli Tipiṭaka.

The Paṭisambhidāmagga, twelfth book of the Khuddaka Nikāya, is the only Abhidhamma text that is part of the Khuddaka Nikāya. According to Hinüber, it has found its way into the Khuddaka Nikāya probably because it was composed rather late to be included in the Abhidhamma Piṭaka, which was already closed, while the end of the Khuddaka Nikāya always remained open for additions ([3], p. 60). In content, the Paṭisambhidāmagga is generally viewed as a supplement to the Vibhaṅga, and it has been suggested that it is most likely that before the development of the extant Abhidhamma Piṭaka, the Paṭisambhidāmagga existed as one of the Abhidhamma treatises. In the style of a true Abhidhamma text, its first *vagga* begins with a *mātikā* (table of contents) containing 73 different facets of *ñāṇa* (knowledge) and thereafter detailed elucidation on them. The second *vagga*, however, starts with a series of queries to be replied in the subsequent text, which, however, is not a dialogue. Like the Niddesa, the composition of the Paṭisambhidāmagga is ascribed to Sāriputta. It consists of 30 *kathās* (discussions or treatises) on different topics, of which the first, on knowledge, makes up about a third of the entire book. The book is divided into three *vaggas* (sections): Mahāvagga (Great Section), Yuganandhavagga (Coupling Section), and Paññāvagga (Knowledge Section). Each of these *vaggas* is further divided into ten *kathās*.

It has been suggested that the purpose of the Paṭisambhidāmagga may have been the first but not very successful attempt to systematize the Abhidhamma in the form of a handbook ([2], p. 126; [3], p. 60). If so, it could be a forerunner of both the Vimuttimagga and the Visuddhimagga ([3], p. 60). In contrast to these later texts, which are well organized and composed with great care, the Paṭisambhidāmagga appears rather to be patched together ([3], p. 60). According to the Dīpavaṃsa, the Paṭisambhidāmagga was rejected by the Mahāsaṃghikas at the Second Buddhist Council (V.37). According to Hinüber, as the Paṭisambhidāmagga gives an orthodox interpretation of canonical Theravāda literature, it is easy to understand why it could not possibly have been accepted by any other school ([3], p. 60). Not only is the treatment of the various subjects in the Paṭisambhidāmagga essentially scholastic in character, but whole passages are taken verbatim from the Vinaya Piṭaka, and the Dīgha, Aṅguttara, and Saṃyutta Nikāyas of the Sutta Piṭaka, while a general acquaintance with the early Buddhist legends is assumed (see [5], p. 285). However, according to Warder, the overall form of the book as well as the title suggest that at least the present arrangement of the discussions is not entirely casual and that the work sets out in systematic order the way to enlightenment ([10], p. 299).

The earliest portions of the Paṭisambhidāmagga were dated by A.K. Warder to between 237 B.C.E. and 100 B.C.E., with some additions possibly made as late as the fifth century C.E. ([10], pp. 299–302). However, according to Erich Frauwallner, the Paṭisambhidāmagga was most probably composed in the second century C.E. ([2], pp. 124–127). But L.S. Cousins disagrees with the late dating as it represents an earlier stage of development of thought than Theravāda canonical Abhidhamma treatises ([1], p. 155). According to Noa Ronkin, to judge from the Paṭisambhidāmagga's method of explaining the *dhammas*, it is in all likelihood "a transitional text residing somewhere in between the *suttas* and the *aṭṭhakathā*. It introduces new concepts and ideas that depart from the Nikāya outlook, while at the same time its method of explaining these concepts and ideas is not yet as consolidated as that of the commentaries, and ideas themselves are not fully worked out, or indeed are still latent" ([8], pp. 91–92).

According to J.P. McDermott, the most significant contribution of the Paṭisambhidāmagga is in its analysis of the four discriminations (I.I.416-433; II.VI) as well as the description of the Buddha's miracle of the double appearance (I.I.592-595) which appears to be the first such description in Pāli literature ([6], p. 219). A.K. Warder is of the view that the Paṭisambhidāmagga may be considered as a record of various discussions which had taken place in the Theravāda school, in which agreed doctrine, supplementary to what was found in the Tipiṭaka at that time, was noted and handed down ([10], p. 299). According to him, if the Buddha were to sit at some quiet place and write "a single book setting out his doctrine fully, then it might be thought he would have produced some such book as this... To answer the need in an age of highly organised 'monasteries' and 'schools' for a more academic type of textbook than the old Tipiṭaka Sutta, works such as the Paṭisambhidāmagga were compiled" ([10], p. 302). Thus, "What is really new in the... book is that a considerable step has been taken... towards a single all-embracing account in which, ideally, everything [the Buddha] was recorded to have said should find its proper place" ([10], p. 301–302).

A commentary of the Paṭisambhidāmagga, known as the Saddhammappakāsiṇī, was prepared by Mahānāma, a Sri Lankan Buddhist elder.

Cross-References

- ▶ Abhidhamma Piṭaka
- ▶ Khuddaka Nikāya
- ▶ Sāriputta
- ▶ Tipiṭaka
- ▶ Vibhaṅga
- ▶ Visuddhimagga

References

1. Cousins LS (1998) Review of Oskar von Hinüber's a handbook of Pāli literature, 1966, Walter de Gruyter, Berlin. Bull Sch Orient Afr Stud 61(1):155–156
2. Frauwallner E (1972) Abhidbarma-Studien IV. Der Abhidharma der anderen Schulen. Wien Z Kunde Süd-asiens 16:95–152
3. von Hinüber O (1996) A handbook of Pāli literature. Walter de Gruyter, Berlin
4. Joshi CV (trans) (1933–1947) The Saddhammappakāsinī: commentary on the Paṭisambhidāmagga, 3 vols. Pali Text Society, London
5. Law BC (1983) A history of Pali literature, reprint, vol 1. Indological Book House, Delhi
6. McDermott JP (1996) Paṭisambhidāmagga. In: Potter KH (ed) Encyclopedia of Indian philosophies, vol VII. Motilal Banarsidass, Delhi, pp 219–264
7. Ñaṇamoli B (trans) (1982) The path of discrimination (Paṭisambhidāmagga), with an intro. by A.K. Warder. Pali Text Society, London
8. Ronkin N (2005) Early Buddhist metaphysics: the making of a philosophical tradition. RoutledgeCurzon, London
9. Taylor AC (ed) (1979) Paṭisambhidāmagga [Combined vol]. Pali Text Society, London
10. Warder AK (2000) Indian Buddhism, 3rd rev edn. Motilal Banarsidass, Delhi
11. Winternitz M (1983) History of Indian literature (trans: Sarma VS), rev edn, vol 2. Motilal Banarsidass, Delhi

Paṭṭhāna

K. T. S. Sarao
Department of Buddhist Studies, University of Delhi, Delhi, India

Synonyms

Book of Causal Relationships; Book of Causes; Jñāna-prasthāna; Mahā-Pakaraṇa; Paṭṭhāna-Pakaraṇa

Definition

It is the last of the seven books of the Abhidhamma Piṭaka.

The Paṭṭhāna is the seventh and last book of the Abhidhamma Piṭaka. It may be described as "the book of causal relationships." It consists of three divisions, i.e., *Eka*, *Duka*, and *Tīka*. The whole of this book deals in great detail with the 22 *tīkas* (group of three's) and 100 couplets *dukas* (group of two's) with reference to the 24 *paccayas* or modes of relations which are assumed between phenomena (*dhammā*), psychological, and material: causal relationship, relationship of the subject and object, reciprocity, dependence, co-nascence, coexistence, contiguity, antecedence, and so on. The book primarily drives the point home that with the sole exception of Nirvāṇa which is absolute, there is nothing which is not relative in one way or another, i.e., which is not related to another thing in one of the 24 modes. Each reality in one's life can only arise because of a concurrence of various conditions which operate in a very complex way. These conditions are not abstractions but are functional in one's daily life all the time. What one takes for one's mind and one's body are mere elements which come into being because of the associated conditions. As pointed out by Hinüber, "It is easy to see that the number of possibilities that opens up here is almost limitless" ([1], p. 75).

The Paṭṭhāna is an enormous and by far the longest single text not only of the Abhidhamma Piṭaka but among all the texts of the Tipiṭaka. Its Commentary, the Pañcappakaraṇaṭṭhakathā, was apparently written by Buddhaghosa at the request of a monk known as Culla Buddhaghosa. The title the Paṭṭhāna is explained in this commentary as the basis for all the other Abhidhamma texts ([8]: 9.27) because the 24 *tīkas* and the 100 *dukas* are considered to be the *mātikā* (tabulated summaries) for all the Abhidhamma texts ([3]: 9.20–22; see [1], p. 75). However, as pointed out by Hinüber, this is contrary to the historical development ([1], p. 75).

The whole of the Paṭṭhāna is in its entirety devoted, first, to an investigation into the following 24 modes in which x is *paccaya* to y and, second, into demonstrating how, in material as well as psychological phenomena, every type of *paccaya* and groups of *paccayas* obtain (see [8], p. x):

1. Hetu (Condition, Causal Relation)
2. Ārammaṇa (Object (presented to mind))
3. Adhipati (Dominance)
4. Anantara (Contiguity)
5. Samanta (Immediate Contiguity)
6. Sahajāta (Co-nascence)
7. Aññamañña (Reciprocity)
8. Nissaya (Dependence)
9. Upanissaya (Sufficing dependence)
10. Purejāta (Antecedence)
11. Pacchājāta (Consequence)
12. Āsevana (Habitual recurrence)
13. Kamma (Action)
14. Vipāka (Result)
15. Āhāra (Support)
16. Indriya (Control, Faculty)
17. Jhāna
18. Magga (Path, Means)
19. Sampayutta (Association)
20. Vippayutta (Dissociation)
21. Atthi (Presence)
22. Natthi (Absence)
23. Vigata (Abeyance)
24. Avigata (Continuance)

Traditionally it has been assumed that apart from the 24 *Tīkas* and the 100 *Dukas* which were preached by the Buddha himself, another 42 *Dukas* were added by the Buddha's chief disciple, Sāriputta ([3]: 9.23–26; see [1], p. 75). Talking about the primary purpose behind the composition of the Paṭṭhāna, Hinüber has pointed out that it has been recognized in tradition that the Saṅgīti Suttanta (no. 33) and the Dasuttara Suttanta (no. 34) of the Dīgha Nikāya together with the Aṅguttara Nikāya form the basis of the Paṭṭhāna. "The text is thought to facilitate the use of the Suttantas for Abhidhamma specialists and this is the purpose usually ascribed to Paṭṭhāna by the tradition" ([3]: 9.27–29; see [1], p. 75).

The structure of Paṭṭhāna is not easy to follow and has not been examined sufficiently enough till date ([1], p. 75). Its "chapters are very difficult to understand, since they consist mostly of numerals. Since the enumeration chapters of the Paṭṭhāna list arithmetically the numbers ofanswers to each question, the exposition of this subject is very susceptible to presentation by charts" ([6], p. 107). C.A.F. Rhys Davids, while writing a general survey of the work on the Paṭṭhāna and other texts of the Abhidhamma Piṭaka by her and her colleagues spanning many years, said somewhat resignedly: "As we leave this house of cloistered lives, of a closed tradition, ofa past dominating presentand future, we have a sense of rooms, swept and garnished clean and tidy, of sealed windows, of drawn blinds, of no outlooktowards the dawn" ([9], p. 250). Despite her skepticism about the value of the Paṭṭhāna, a work of pure scholasticism and "being practically nothing more than a huge series of logical exercises in the correlating of terms, to be acquired, originally, by oral teaching" ([7], p. xi), C.A.F. Rhys Davids recommends that the Paṭṭhāna is "well worth the study of the historian of Buddhist ideas, and of logical and philosophical ideas in general. It is the one notable constructive contribution to knowledge in the Abhidhamma" ([7], p. v).

Cross-References

- ▶ Abhidhamma Piṭaka
- ▶ Aṅguttara Nikāya
- ▶ Buddhaghosa
- ▶ Dhammasaṅgaṇī
- ▶ Dīgha Nikāya
- ▶ Sāriputta
- ▶ Tipiṭaka

References

1. von Hinüber O (1996) A handbook of Pāli literature. Walter de Gruyter, Berlin
2. Law BC (1983) A history of Pāli literature, reprint, vol 1. Indological Book House, Delhi
3. Muller E (ed) (1979) The Atthasālinī: Buddhaghosa's commentary on the Dhammasaṅgṇī, rev edn. Pāli Text Society, London
4. Nārada U (trans) (1969, 1981) Conditional relations, 2 vols. Pāli Text Society, London
5. Nārada U (1979) Guide to conditional relations. Part I. Pāli Text Society, London
6. Norman KR (1983) A history of Indian literature: Pāli literature, vol VII, Fasc. 2. Otto Harrassowitz, Wiesbaden
7. Rhys Davids CAF (ed) (1906) The Dukapaṭṭhāna. Pāli Text Society, London
8. Rhys Davids CAF (ed) (1921, 1922, 1923). Tikapaṭṭhāna together with Buddhaghosa's Commentary from the Pañcappakaraṇaṭṭhakathā, 3 vols. Pāli Text Society, London
9. Rhys Davids CAF (1923) The Abhidhamma Piṭaka and commentaries. J R Asiatic Soc Great Britain Irel (New Ser) 55(2):243–250
10. Winternitz M (1983) History of Indian literature (trans: Sarma VS), rev edn., vol 2. Motilal Banarsidass, Delhi

Paṭṭhāna-Pakaraṇa

▶ Paṭṭhāna

Pausadha

▶ Uposatha

Perfect Wisdom

▶ *Prajñāpāramitā*

Perfection

▶ Pāramitā

Perfection of Insight

▶ *Prajñāpāramitā*

Perfection of Understanding

▶ *Prajñāpāramitā*

P

Perfection of Wisdom

▸ *Prajñāpāramitā*

Periodic Bleeding

▸ Menstruation (Buddhism)

Persecution (Buddhism)

K. T. S. Sarao
Department of Buddhist Studies, University of Delhi, Delhi, India

Definition

Did the Buddhists in India experience discrimination and harassment at the hands of Brāhmaṇical-Hindus and their kings?

Allegations of Persecution

It is alleged by some scholars that some of the ancient Indian kings and the brāhmaṇas as a priestly community despised the Buddhists and such a "hostile attitude was vigorously sustained till Buddhism was overpowered in India and disappeared from the land of its birth" ([25], p. 311). Some have even claimed that religious tolerance was alien to pre-British India and that there is sufficient actual or circumstantial evidence testifying to the destruction of monasteries by the brāhmaṇas and the creation by them of special militias aimed at intimidating the Buddhist monks and the laity ([49], pp. 1–36). Traditional doctrinal controversies between learned brāhmaṇas and Buddhist teachers, it is sometimes pointed out, turned into ordeals where the latter might be killed or exiled or obliged to convert. Attack on Aṅgulimāla by a frenzied mob, the murders of Moggallāna and Āryadeva, anti-Buddhist crusades of Kumārila Bhaṭṭa and Śaṃkarācārya, and an attempt by brāhmaṇas not only to burn the pavilion where Xuanzang was to be honored by king Harṣavardhana but also to kill pro-Buddhist Harṣavardhana himself ([6], p. 179) are given as important instances in support of such a hypothesis. The description of the Buddha in some of the Purāṇas as a grand seducer who brought the *asuras* to their ruin and the view in the *Yajñavalkya* that a bhikkhu in yellow robes is an ill omen are further quoted as examples of the contempt in which the Buddhists were held by the brāhmaṇas. Examples have also been cited of Brāhmaṇical temples which were originally Buddhist shrines [39]. Some scholars have also referred to "the philosophical plunder of Buddhism" by Brāhmaṇical-Hinduism which was accompanied by "mean-spirited ridicule" ([20], p. 11). Thus, it has been pointed out that it is not uncommon to find Buddhists being referred to as "outcastes" (*vasalaka*) and "devils/demons" (*daitya*, *dānava*) ([20], p. 10). Instances of the legacy of communal hatred against the Buddhists have also been cited from presented day practices in different parts of India. For instance, it has been pointed out that the modern Telugu words *lanja dibbalu*, which refer to mounds of earth containing Buddhist archaeological ruins, literally mean "prostitute hill" ([20], p. 10). Similarly, one is reminded of a practice at the Thiruvadigai temple in Cuddalore (Tamil Nadu) where apparently during the annual temple festival, the temple elephant knocks the Buddha sculpture, kept in one of the corners, thrice with its trunk to symbolize the victory of Śaivism over Buddhism ([1]: 2004).

Views Favoring Patronage and Support to Buddhism

As opposed to the above stated instance and views expressed in support of persecution of Buddhism, also there is no dearth of examples of brāhmaṇas and Brāhmaṇical-Hindu kings extending support in various forms, especially material support, to Buddhist institutions. If some brāhmaṇas were detractors of Buddhism, some of the best supporters of Buddhism were also brāhmaṇas. In fact, over a quarter of the Buddhist monks and nuns mentioned in the *Vinaya* and *Sutta Piṭaka* came from the Brāhmaṇa caste ([42], p. 69). Over 40% of the leading monks (*theras*) and nuns (*therīs*) mentioned in texts such as the Vinaya Piṭaka, Theragāthā, and Therīgāthā also belonged to the Brāhmaṇa caste ([42], p. 127). The Buddha made respectful reference to brāhmaṇas who observed their vows in contradistinction to those who were mere brāhmaṇas by birth, and he classed the worthy samaṇas with the Brāhmanas. The *Dhammapada* devotes a full chapter entitled *Brāhmaṇavagga* (vs. 383–423) detailing qualities of a Brāhmaṇa leaving no doubt that the word *Brāhmaṇa* was held in high esteem by the Buddha. "[I]n dozens of *Suttas*, meetings of brāhmaṇas and Buddha or his disciples and missionaries... almost always seem to be marked by courtesy on both sides. No meetings are recorded in the early Pāli texts or Brāhmaṇical texts about Śākyans condemning the tenets of ancient Brāhmaṇism or about brāhmaṇas censuring the Bauddha heterodoxy" ([26], Vol. V.II, p. 1004). As far as the Brāhmaṇical followers were concerned, to them, Buddhism was a mere sect within the Brāhmaṇical system. According to a tradition, Āryadeva, the pupil of Nāgārjuna, was murdered by one of the fanatical pupils of a teacher whom Āryadeva had defeated in a debate. Āryadeva had asked his disciples to forgive the killer. The murder of Moggallāna (supposedly committed at the behest of Niganṭhas), described only in the *Dhammapadaṭṭhakathā*, was an individual act of crime. Similarly, the assault on Aṅgulimāla had no religious motive behind it. As put by R. C. Mitra, "[t]he attitude of the Hindus might have graduated from cold to scorching contempt, but a policy of harrying the Buddhists out with fire and sword sounds like a myth" ([34], p. 20). "While isolated instances of actual violence by Hindu zealots doubtless did occur, these were probably not sufficient in number or impact to seriously cripple the groups towards which they were directed" ([22], p. 83). Though some aspects of the philosophy of Buddhism, especially its atheism and their dress or shaven-heads, may have often been the subjects of insensitive ridicule, it is not possible to find reliable evidence of any spirit of fanatical fury or fierce hatred in the sources. It was quite typical in India for holy persons to be surrounded by men and women of diverse religious backgrounds.

Critique of the Views Supporting Persecution

In connection with Xuanzang's story that the brāhmaṇas of Kanauja had set fire to the pavilion built for the reception of the Chinese pilgrim and that they even made an attempt on the life of the king, it may be said that king Harṣavardhana also hardly respected the principles of tolerance and liberty of speech. During the debate organized on the following day, he is said to have threatened to cut off the tongue of anyone who would dare oppose the distinguished guest ([6], p. 179). Similarly, the statement in the *Kerala-Utpatti* that the Buddhists were driven out of Kerala by Kumārila Bhaṭṭa does not appear to be correct. As pointed out by R. C. Mitra, "It appears very probable that the name of Kumārila, like that of the more eminent Saṃkara after him, was devised by later zealots as a plausible human agency with whom to associate the tradition of a heresy-hunt simply because these authors fashioned the new philosophy in vindication of orthodoxy which seemed to have knocked the bottom out of the Buddhist defence" ([34], p. 128). The writings of Kumārila do not reflect any anti-Buddhist frenzy. In fact, "he regards the Buddhist system of thought as authoritative... and... allows it the merit of having curbed extreme attachment to sensuous objects. He does not seem to be shocked by its opposition to the Veda, only he puts it in the same category with the Sāṃkhya, the Yoga, the Pañcarātra and the Pāśupata" ([34], p. 128). In the exposition of his own philosophy, Kumārila admits the validity of the Vijñānavāda doctrine and his respect for the Buddha only stops short of the recognition of the Avatārahood of the Buddha ([34], p. 129).

It cannot be denied that the archaeological records at Nāgārjunakoṇḍā appear to point toward destruction which is hard to explain as the vandalism of treasure seekers. The local tradition

P

ascribes the destruction of this place to Śaṃkarācārya, and the adjoining lands are still in the possession of those monks who owe allegiance to the Order of Śaṃkarācārya. However, apropos allegations of anti-Buddhist actions of Śaṃkarācārya, it may, on the whole, be said that spurious scandals are often an inevitable penalty of supreme eminence. The relationship of Śaṃkarācārya to Buddhism has been the subject of considerable debate since ancient times. If some have hailed him as the arch critic of Buddhism and the principal architect of its downfall in India, there have been others who have described him as a Buddhist in disguise (see [38], p. 255). When Śaṃkarācārya came north to the intellectual centers there, he borrowed many of the ideas that had been formulated by Buddhist philosophers of the past ([11], pp. 239–240). In his exposition that the world is an illusion, Śaṃkarācārya borrowed arguments from Mādhyamaka and Yogācāra, though he disagreed with them on some matters ([11], p. 248). Śaṃkarācārya was the spiritual grandson of Gauḍapāda. Gauḍapāda's ideas were "a synthesis of Vedantism and Buddhism" ([14], p. 3). In fact, Gauḍapāda's thinking often coincides so exactly with some aspects of Mahāyāna Buddhist philosophy that there are some who believe that he himself was a Buddhist. For instance, S. N. Dasgupta even thinks that since Gauḍapāda flourished after the advent of all the great Buddhist teachers, including Aśvaghoṣa, Nāgārjuna, Asaṅga, and Vasubandhu, "there is sufficient evidence in his kārikās for thinking that he was possibly himself a Buddhist, and considered that the teachings of the Upanishads tallied with those of Buddha" ([12], p. 423). Dasgupta further points out that "Gauḍapāda assimilated all the Buddhist Śūnyavāda and Vijñānavāda teachings, and thought that these held good of the ultimate truth preached by the Upaniṣads. It is immaterial whether he was a Hindu or a Buddhist, so long as we are sure that he had the highest respect for the Buddha and for the teachings which he believed to be his" ([12], p. 429). "Advaita-Vedanta of Śankara with its colorless Brahman contradicting all the empirical realities is in its turn the culmination of the evolution of the Upanishadic Buddhistic thought" ([13], p. 29). There is no doubt that he made efforts to fortify his kind of Brāhmaṇical-Hinduism by enrolling missionaries in its defense and organizing them into corporate monastic schools under the central direction of the Grand Abbot of Śringerī. But the legend of his having preached and led a bloody crusade against the Buddhists cannot be sustained. Called hidden Buddhist (*pracchana bauddha*) by some, Śaṃkarācārya may not have been exactly a bosom pal, still no special animosity is betrayed against the Buddhists in the writings attributed to him. It is also important to remember that Buddhism was in decline much before Śaṃkarācārya arrived on the scene. Moreover, Śaṃkarācārya refuted not just the Buddhists but also most of the other schools of Indian philosophy. But none of these other schools seems to have suffered any visible damage as a result. In any case, Tāranātha himself points out that both Kumārila and Śaṃkarācārya finally met their match in a Buddhist monk and were routed in the intellectual wrestling that ensued ([28], pp. 231–233).

In a well-documented study, it has been shown that over 40 important Buddhist thinkers from the eighth to the first quarter of the thirteenth century lived in India ([27], p. 166). However, during the same period, Brāhmaṇical-Hinduism had just about half a dozen thinkers of comparable repute. It seems that though these five centuries were a sun-set period for Buddhism, yet the few surviving Buddhist mahāvihāras due to the particular attention that they paid to academic and intellectual work, succeeded in producing quite a few thinkers of substance. However, compared to this, Brāhmaṇical-Hinduism during the same period appears to have been greatly agrarianized by the Bhakti Movement and was rather focusing on displacing Buddhism from the sociopolitical pedestal, leaving the path of wisdom (*jñānamārga*) almost entirely to Buddhism. "To have had not more than half a dozen thinkers during a period of almost 500 years does not speak very highly of Ācārya Śaṃkara's *Digvijaya*, so loudly proclaimed not only by his disciples but also others, in the Indian tradition" ([27], p. 166). Thus, it is difficult to believe that Śaṃkarācārya's views spread rapidly during his life time (c. 800

C.E.) with his far-flung *maṭhas* serving as radiation points. For instance, although Alberuni (fl. 1030) studied a mass of Sanskrit literature with access to learned brāhmaṇa informants, he makes no reference to Śaṃkarācārya ([19], pp. 78–88). If Śaṃkarācārya's views had not reached northern India in any strength by the eleventh century, they are, of course, likely to have spread more slowly, so as to obtain wide acceptance some time before the seventeenth century ([19], p. 79).

There Was No Continued and Organized Persecution

Religious persecution of a limited and temporary character was not really a *terra incognita*, particularly in the south. But Indian history does not bear out the fact of a continued and organized persecution as the state policy of a dynasty in a measure sufficient to exterminate an established faith. Had the Buddha been hated by the Brāhmaṇical society, the same society would not have accepted him as an incarnation of Viṣṇu. The *Garuḍa Purāṇa* (i.202) invokes the Buddha as an incarnation of Viṣṇu for the protection of the world from sinners and not for deluding *asuras* to their ruin as in the *Viṣṇu*, *Agni*, or other early Purāṇas. The *Varāha Purāṇa* also refers to the Buddha as an incarnation in no deprecating sense, but he is adored simply as the god of beauty (i.39–48). Superior contempt is the distinctively Hindu method of persecution. Purāṇas such as the *Viṣṇu*, *Vāyu*, and *Matsya* mention the Buddha as the grand seducer. The *Yajñavalkya* considers the sight of a monk with yellow robes as an execrable augury (i.273). But this kind of attitude was not always one sided, and some scholars have gone so far as to say that Buddhism was much more unfriendly toward Brāhmaṇical-Hinduism than the other way round. It is no secret that the Buddhists "criticized severely the doctrines of the Hindus, attacked their caste system, insulted the Hindu gods, and, in fact, did everything that is far from being friendly" ([5], p. 15). In fact, there is sufficient evidence to prove that the Buddhists tried to show different Brāhmaṇical deities in bad light. For instance, the Siddhas are expected to be served in heaven by Hari as gatekeeper. There are images in which Indra always serves to bear the parasol, and Gaṇeśa is at the feet of Vighnāṭaka ([8], pp. 62–163). However, such examples should not be stressed too far. It cannot be said with certainty that similes such as these smack of any sectarian disdain. They are more reflective of the period's peculiar fondness for grandiloquence and extravagant exaggeration than anything else.

The absence of one single truth in Brāhmaṇical-Hinduism created sufficient space for plurality of modes of faith in god and afterlife, including the denial of god's existence. Thus, the tolerance of divergent views is integral to Brāhmaṇical-Hinduism, and it may be said that in spite of some stray incidents resulting from the heat of sectarian rivalry here and there, there are no reliable examples of any purposive and sustained persecution much less a crusade. As pointed out by Murti, "polemic (*parapakṣanirākaraṇa*) is an integral part of each (Indian) system. It is an evidence of the maturity not only of one system, but of several contemporary ones from which it is differentiated. In spite of the heroic language used, polemics does not mean that rival systems are refuted out of existence; they are only differentiated from each other.... Philosophical schools have attained their fullness because of criticism and opposition" ([36], p. 8). Buddhism had neither been conceived by the Buddha as a proselytizing religion nor had it attained any numerical success to the extent that it may have posed any danger to the survival of Brāhmaṇical-Hinduism as a religion. The Buddhist challenge to thought was answered primarily on an intellectual plane, and on the whole, it is not easy to find any example of Brāhmaṇical hostility toward Buddhist lay supporters in India. Moreover, Indian Buddhism attempted to seek space within space rather than carving out its own space to the exclusion of others. In this sense, Buddhism did not pose any danger to Brāhmaṇical-Hinduism. However, Brāhmaṇical-brāhmaṇas as a priestly class did feel threatened by Buddhism from the time of king Aśoka onward when institutional Buddhism acquired the character of a pan-Indian religion with significant sociopolitical clout whereby the Buddha rose to the status of the most popular religious figure. The Brāhmaṇical-brāhmaṇas, as a priestly class with sociopolitical vested interest, came up with well-thought out two-pronged agenda for its own survival. One, they became designedly agreeable and assimilative toward those issues in Buddhist weltanschauung which had become socioreligiously commonsensical. A trend toward assimilation of Buddhism by Brāhmaṇical-Hinduism appears to have begun during the Gupta period. Kane has suggested that the Purāṇic practices and religious rites undermined the power and prestige of Buddhism and weaned away large sections of the supporters from the attractive features of Buddhism by securing to them in the reorientated Hindu faith the same benefits, social and spiritual, as promised by Buddhism ([26], Vol. V.II, pp. 913–914). In his opinion, the Purāṇas played a substantial role in bringing about the decline and disappearance of Buddhism by emphasizing and assimilating some of the principles and doctrines of the Buddha ([26], Vol. V.II, pp. 913–914). Slowly and steadily, the Buddha was assimilated into the pantheon of Viṣṇu, and the Bhakti Movement contributed significantly by providing a congenial environment for such a development. Secondly, began to, slowly and steadily, but systematically, subvert institutional Buddhism. As suggested by Ronald Inden, this is clearly visible in the shifting of the theories and political orientation of kingship from Buddhist to Vaiṣṇava and Śaiva rationales ([21], pp. 41–91). From the eighth century onward the Brāhmaṇical-Hindu gods, Viṣṇu and Śiva, usurped the place of the Buddha as the supreme, imperial deities ([21], p. 67). The Buddha lost his position to both Viṣṇu and Śiva as the *iṣṭa-devatā* of the royalty. In the end, the assimilation of the Buddha into Brāhmaṇical-Hinduism was so comprehensive that the Buddha lost all cultic veneration.

Puṣyamitra Śūṅga

A large number of Buddhist texts hold kings such as Puṣyamitra Śuṅga and Śaśāṅka particularly responsible for following deliberate and systematic policies of persecution against the followers of Buddhism. On the basis of the testimony of these texts, it has been alleged that the actions of these two kings particularly contributed toward the decline of Buddhism in India ([3], pp. 405–406; [5], p. 193; [9], pp. 166–167). Puṣyamitra Śuṅga (circa 184–148 B.C.E.) is generally regarded as the symbol and leader of the Brāhmaṇical revival that took place when the dynasty of the Mauryas, the alleged supporters of non-Brāhmaṇical faiths, was brought to an end by him. After seizing the throne, Puṣyamitra is alleged to have reestablished the sacrificial ceremonies of Vedic Brāhmaṇism ([18], p. 215). Haraprasad Sastri has pointed out that the various policies of Aśoka had destroyed the reputation of the brāhmaṇas and such actions, coming from a śūdra king, were particularly resented by the brāhmaṇas ([43], pp. 259–262). It is further alleged that Aśoka had acted against Brāhmaṇism by not only "showing up the false gods" who had been till then worshipped in Jambudvīpa but the propagation of Buddhism during the reign of the Mauryas had also disturbed the Brāhmaṇical social and religious order ([19], p. 258; [43], pp. 259–262). The end of the dynasty of the Mauryas at the hands of Puṣyamitra Śuṅga is seen as a victory of anti-Buddhist Brāhmaṇical forces which had been silently at work. Thus, it has been suggested that other than destroying Buddhist monasteries and stūpas and killing Buddhist monks, Puṣyamitra Śuṅga caused greater damage to Buddhism by letting unfavorable forces loose against it ([3], pp. 405–406; [9], pp. 166–167).

The different texts that talk about Puṣyamitra Śuṅga's anti-Buddhist activities, such as destroying Buddhist institutions and offering *dināra* gold coins as rewards for the heads of monks, are the *Divyāvadāna* (and its constituent, the *Aśokāvadāna*) ([35], pp. 133–135; [48], p. 282), the *Vibhāṣā* ([29], p. 387), the *Śāriputraparipṛcchā* ([29], pp. 389–391), the *Āryamañjuśrīmūlakalpa* ([24], pp. 18–19), and Tāranātha ([29], p. 121). On the basis of archaeological information available from Sāñcī stūpa, Ghositārāma of Kauśāmbī, and Deorkothar stupa, it has also been suggested that some of the destruction can be traced to Puṣyamitra Śuṅga from these places ([18], pp. 215–217; [32], p. 38; [33]).

Many Indologists have expressed skepticism about the truthfulness of the Buddhist legends alleging the persecution of Buddhism by Puṣyamitra Śuṅga ([15], p. 48; [23], pp. 257–265; [29], p. 392; [34], p. 125; [40], p. 355; [47], p. 200). Raychaudhury, for instance, points out that the ban on animal sacrifices did not necessarily entail antagonism toward the brāhmaṇas for the simple reason that the Brāhmaṇical literature itself stresses *ahiṃsā* and mentions the futility of laying great stress on sacrifices alone. Apropos the śūdra origin of the Mauryas, apart from the fact that the Mauryas are mentioned as kṣatriyas in the *Divyāvadāna*, Raychaudhury has pointed out that the *Purāṇa* statement that all kings succeeding Mahāpadma Nanda will be of śūdra origin implies that Nanda kings after Mahāpadma were śūdras and not the Mauryas because if it referred to succeeding dynasties, then even the Śuṅgas and Kaṇvas would have to be listed as śūdras ([40], p. 354). Some of the Mauryan officials were not only concerned specifically with safeguarding the rights and welfare of the brāhmaṇas, but some of the Mauryan kings themselves were also followers of Brāhmaṇism. Aśoka's frequent exhortations in his edicts for showing due respect to brāhmaṇas and śramaṇas hardly point to his being anti-Brāhmaṇical in outlook ([47], p. 200). Further, as pointed out by Lamotte, there are so many contradictions in the textual information that to judge from the documents, "Puṣyamitra must be acquitted through lack of proof" ([29], p. 392). Agreeing with Lamotte, D. Devahuti also feels that the account of Puṣyamitra's sudden destruction with all his army, after his promulgation at Śākala of a law promising *dīnāras* for the heads of Buddhist monks slain by his subjects, "is manifestly false" ([15], p. 48).

The testimony of the Buddhist legends also appears doubtful on various other counts. The earliest of the texts that mention these legends are chronologically far removed from the Śuṅgas. The traditional narrative in the *Divyāvadāna*, for instance, can at the earliest be dated to two centuries after Puṣyamitra's death. It is more likely that the *Divyāvadāna* legend is a Buddhist version of Puṣyamitra's attack on the Mauryas and reflects the fact that, with the declining influence of Buddhism at the Śuṅga imperial court, Buddhist monuments and institutions would naturally receive less royal attention. Moreover, the source itself in this instance being Buddhist would naturally exaggerate the wickedness of anti-Buddhists ([47], p. 200). Further, *dīnāra* coins (Roman *denarius* gold coins) were not prevalent at the time of the Śuṅgas. The earliest period during which these coins came into circulation in India was the first century C.E. Most interestingly, this legend of persecution in which a *dīnāra* is offered as an award for the head of a monk is first related in the *Aśokāvadāna* ([35], pp. 67–68) in connection with the persecution of the Jainas and the Ājīvikas by Aśoka and most clearly appears to be a fabrication. To say that Aśoka, whose devotion to all religious sects is undeniable through his edicts, persecuted the Nirgranthas or the Ājīvikas is simply absurd and so is the story of Puṣyamitra. Thus, "the carbon-copy allegation against Puṣyamitra may very reasonably be dismissed as sectarian propaganda" [16]. There is, in fact, no concrete evidence to show that any of the Mauryan kings discriminated against Brāhmaṇism. Aśoka, the most popular Mauryan king, did not appear to have any vulgar ambition of exalting his own religion "by showing up the false gods" of Brāhmaṇism. Thus, the hypothesis of a Brāhmaṇical persecution under Puṣyamitra loses much of its *raison d'être* ([34], p. 126; [40], p. 349).

The policy of Puṣyamitra appears to have been tolerant enough for the simple reason that if he were anti-Buddhist, he would have dismissed his Buddhist ministers. What is more, the court of Puṣyamitra's son was graced by Bhagavatī Kauśikī, a Buddhist nun. In addition to this, there is overwhelming evidence to show that Buddhism actually prospered during the reign of the Śuṅga kings. And it has actually been argued that archaeological evidence casts doubt on the claims made by Buddhist texts that the Śuṅgas persecuted the Buddhists ([47], p. 200). An

P

archaeological study of the celebrated stūpa at Sāñcī proves that it was enlarged and encased in its present covering during the Śuṅga period ([2], p. 160). The Aśokan pillar near it appears to have been willfully destroyed, but this event may have occurred at a much later date ([32], p. 90). The Bhārhut Buddhist Pillar Inscription of the time of the Śuṅgas actually records some additions to the Buddhist monuments "during the supremacy of the Śuṅgas" ([46], p. 87).

It may not be possible to deny the fact that Puṣyamitra showed no favor to the Buddhists, but it is not certain that he persecuted them. The only thing that can be said with certainty on the basis of the stories told in Buddhist texts about Puṣyamitra is that he might have withdrawn royal patronage from the Buddhist institutions ([18], pp. 210–211). This change of circumstance under his reign might have led to discontent among the Buddhists. It seems that as a consequence of this shifting of patronage from Buddhism to Brāhmaṇism, the Buddhists became politically active against him and sided with his enemies, the Indo-Greeks. "The Greek struggle with Puṣyamitra gave the Buddhists the prospect of renewed influence... What may be sensed is that strategic reasons made some Greeks the promoters of Buddhism and some Buddhists supporters of the Greeks" ([44], p. 141). This might have incited him to put them down with a heavy hand. Thus, if in some parts of Puṣyamitra's kingdom, a few monasteries were at all pillaged, it must be seen as a political move rather than a religious one. Moreover, in such cases, the complicity of the local governors also cannot be ruled out. Jayaswal has referred to another interesting aspect of the declaration made by Puṣyamitra ([23], p. 263). It was made at Śākala, the capital and base of Menander, setting a price of 100 *dīnāras* on the head of every Buddhist monk. The fact that such a fervid declaration was made not only at a place which was far removed from the center of the Śuṅga regime but also in the capital city of his archenemies, points to reasons motivated by political considerations. Thus, it would be fair to say that where the Buddhists did not or could not ally themselves with the invading Indo-Greeks, Puṣyamitra did not beleaguer them.

Śaśāṅka

The other king who is blamed for committing atrocities on Buddhists and Buddhist institutions is Śaśāṅka (circa 603–620 C.E.), a ruler from northwestern Bengal. Xuanzang, in his work Xiyuji, accuses Śaśāṅka of indulging in many acts of oppression against Buddhism ([30], pp. 142–143, 192, 226–227, 246, 249). Apart from this, *Āryamañjuśrīmūlakalpa* also supports the tradition of Śaśāṅka's hostility toward Buddhism ([24], pp. 49–50).

The evidence for the anti-Buddhist policy of Śaśāṅka has been evaluated by modern scholars quite vigorously. Some scholars have indicated that Śaśāṅka was one of the rare rulers of ancient India who followed a policy of persecution against the Buddhists, and thus, "it will not be justifiable to exculpate Śaśāṅka from his cruel actions" ([4], pp. 154–156; [10], p. 189). However, it has been suggested that to consider Śaśāṅka a persecutor of Buddhism would amount to simplistic understanding of history ([15], p. 48; [34], p. 127; [45], p. 259). The stories of persecution of Buddhism by Śaśāṅka cannot really be given credence without an independent testimony, because they rest upon "the sole evidence of Buddhist writers who cannot, by any means, be regarded as unbiased or unprejudiced, at least in any matter which either concerned Śaśāṅka or adversely affected Buddhism" ([31], p. 67). It is also pointed out in support of this opinion that the flourishing condition of Buddhism in the capital city of Śaśāṅka, as described by Xuanzang ([30], p. 303), is hardly compatible with the view that he was a religious bigot and a cruel persecutor of Buddhism. At the root of Śaśāṅka's ill feeling toward Buddhism was probably the fact that the Buddhists of these places in Magadha and elsewhere entered into some sort of conspiracy with Harṣavardhana against him, and therefore he wanted to punish them ([4], pp. 154–156). Moreover, as pointed out by B. P. Sinha, the Buddhists through their numerous monasteries and seats of learning exercised sufficient leverage in the politics of Magadha, and "[t]he uprooting of the Bodhi Tree may have been an economic move against the Buddhist hierarchy of Magadha, as presents from all over the Buddhist world were offered at the Bodhi Tree" ([45], pp. 259–260). The impressions of a foreign religious scholar like Xuanzang, perceiving in these acts of Śaśāṅka a deliberate policy to destroy Buddhism, are not surprising. Buddhist authors of later times, too, appear to have consciously or unconsciously seen religious fanaticism in the actions of Śaśāṅka. Thus, the motives of Śaśāṅka seem to have been both misunderstood and exaggerated, according to Sinha ([45], pp. 259–260). Moreover, as pointed out by Mitra, all of Śaśāṅka's persecuting acts being confined outside the limits of his own kingdom, it may be argued that his object was not so much to extirpate Buddhist heresy as to take the wind out of the sails of his own Buddhist subjects by destroying the sacred tree at Bodhagayā ([34], p. 127). Xuanzang's story has also been questioned by D. Devahuti who points out that the story of Śaśāṅka's death immediately after the desecration of the Buddha image is most suspect because it is just such an episode as Xuanzang would introduce in order to create effect. Moreover, Devahuti suspects that as the legend of Puṣyamitra was almost certainly known to Xuanzang, as it exists in more than one Chinese version, he had Puṣyamitra's fate in mind when he wrote of a similar curse on Śaśāṅka ([15], p. 48).

Cross-References

- ▶ Decline of Indian Buddhism
- ▶ Mādhyamika
- ▶ Mahāyāna
- ▶ Puṣyamitra Śuṅga
- ▶ Xuanzang (Hieun-Tsang)
- ▶ Yogācāra

References

1. Anand S (2004) The Bodhi's afterglow. Outlook India, 7 July
2. Archaeological Survey of India (1953) Ancient India: Bulletin of the Archaeological Survey of India, vol IX. New Delhi
3. Bagchi PC (1921) Decline of Buddhism and its causes. In: Sir Asutosh Mukerjee silver jubilee volumes, III. Calcutta University, Calcutta, pp 405–406
4. Basak RG (1967) The history of north-eastern India extending from the foundation of the Gupta Empire to the rise of the Pāla dynasty of Bengal: C.A.D. 320–760, 2nd rev & enl edn. Sambodhi Publications, Calcutta
5. Basham AL (1988) The vehicle of the thunderbolt and the decline of Buddhism in India. In: Embree AT (edited & revised) Sources of Indian tradition: from the beginning to 1800, 2nd edn, vol 2. Penguin Books
6. Beal S (tran) (1911) Life of Hieun-Tsiang by the Shaman Hwui Li. K. Paul, Trench & Trübner, London
7. Bhattacharyya B (1929) A peep into the later Buddhism. Ann Bhandarkar Orient Res Inst Poona 5(part III):1–24
8. Bhattacharyya B (1958) The Indian Buddhist iconography: mainly based on the Sādhanamālā and other cognate tantric texts of rituals, 2nd rev and enl edn. Firma K. Mukhopadhyay, Calcutta
9. Chakravartty G (1994) BJP-RSS and distortion of history. In: Lahiri P (ed) Selected writings on communalism. People's Publishing House, New Delhi, pp 161–172
10. Chatterji GS (1950) Harṣavardhana (in Hindi). Hiṇdustānī Ekaḍemī, Allahabad
11. Collins R (2000) The sociology of philosophies: a global theory of intellectual change. Harvard University Press, Cambridge, MA
12. Dasgupta SN (1922) A history of Indian philosophy, vol I. Cambridge University Press, Cambridge
13. Dasgupta SB (1962) Obscure religious cults, 2nd rev edn. Firma K. L. Mukhopadhyay, Calcutta
14. DasGupta RK (2003) Vedanta in Bengal. The Ramakrishna Mission, Kolkata
15. Devahuti D (1998) Harsha: a political study, third revised edn. Oxford University Press, New Delhi
16. Elst K (2007) Why Pushyamitra was more 'secular' than Ashoka? As seen on 20 April 2007. http://koenraadelst.bharatvani.org/print/articles/ayodhya/pushyamitra
17. Ghosh NN (1945) Did Puṣyamitra Śuṅga persecute the Buddhists? In: Bhandarkar DR et al (eds) B.C. Law, vol I. Bhandarkar Research Institute, Poona, pp 210–217
18. Ghoshal UN (1957) Studies in Indian History and Culture. Orient Longmans, Bombay
19. Habib I (1996) Medieval popular monotheism and its humanism: the historical setting. Soc Sci 21(3–4):78–88
20. Holt JC (2004) The Buddhist Viṣṇu: religious transformation, politics, and culture. Columbia University Press, New York
21. Inden RB (1998) Ritual, authority, and cycle time in Hindu kingship. In: Richards JF (ed) Kingship and authority in South Asia. Oxford University Press, New Delhi, pp 41–91

P

22. Jaini PS (1980) The disappearance of Buddhism and the survival of Jainism: a study in contrast. In: Narain AK (ed) Studies in history of Buddhism. B.R. Publishing Corporation, Delhi, pp 81–91
23. Jayaswal KP (1918) Revised notes on the Brahmin Empire. J Bihar Orissa Res Soc Patna IV(Pt III):257–265
24. Jayaswal KP (ed and trans) (1934) The text of the Mañju-śrī-mūlakalpa: an imperial history of India. Motilal Banarsidass, Lahore
25. Joshi LM (1977) Studies in the Buddhistic culture of India, 2nd rev edn. Motilal Banarsidass, Delhi
26. Kane PV (1993–1997) History of Dharmaśāstra, 3rd edn, 5 vols. Bhandarkar Research Institute, Pune
27. Krishna D (2001) Was Ācārya Śaṃkara responsible for the disappearance of Buddhist philosophy from India? In: New perspectives in Indian philosophy. Rawat Publications, Jaipur
28. Lama C, Chattopadhyaya A (trans) (1970) Tāranātha's history of Buddhism in India. Indian Institute of Advanced Study, Simla
29. Lamotte É (1988) History of Indian Buddhism: from the origins to the *ſaka* Era, tr. Sara Webb-Boin, Insitut Orientaliste, Louvain-la-Neuve
30. Li R (trans) (1996) The great Tang dynasty record of the western regions. Numata Center for Buddhist Translation and Research, Berkeley
31. Majumdar RC (1943) The history of Bengal, vol I. Dacca University, Dacca
32. Marshall JH (1955) A guide to Sanchi, 3rd edn. Manager of Publications, Delhi
33. Mishra PK (2001) Does newly excavated Buddhist temple provide a missing link? In: Archaeology. A Publication of the Archaeological Institute of America, April 2001. www.archaeology.org/online/news/deorkothar/. Accessed 15 Apr 2007.
34. Mitra RC (1954) The decline of Buddhism in India. Visva-Bharati, Santiniketan, Birbhum
35. Mukhopadhyaya S (ed) (1963) The Aśokāvadāna. Sahitya Akademi, New Delhi
36. Murti TRV (1996) The rise of philosophical schools. In: Coward HG (ed) Studies in Indian thought: collected papers of Prof. T.R.V. Murti. Motilal Banarsidass, Delhi, pp 1–16
37. Negi JS (1958) Groundwork of ancient Indian history. Allahabad University Press, Allahabad
38. Pande GC (1994) Life and thought of Śaṃkarācārya. Motilal Banarsidass, Delhi
39. Pillai SB (1976) Introduction to the study of temple art. Equator & Meridian, Thanjavur
40. Raychaudhury HC (1923) Political history of ancient India: from the accession of Parikshit to the extinction of the Gupta Dynasty. University of Calcutta, Calcutta
41. Rhys Davids TW (1896) Persecution of Buddhists in India. J Pāli Text Soc:87–92
42. Sarao KTS (1989) Origin and nature of ancient Indian Buddhism. Eastern Book Linkers, Delhi
43. Sastri H (1910) Causes of the dismemberment of the maurya empire. J Asiatic Soc Bengal Calcutta 4:259–262
44. Seldeslachts E (2007) Greece, the final frontier? The Westward spread of Buddhism. In: Heirman A, Bumbacher SP (eds) The spread of Buddhism. E.J. Brill, Leiden
45. Sinha BP (1954) The decline of the kingdom of Magadha (Cir. 455-1000 A.D.). Motilal Banarsidass, Bankipore
46. Sircar DC (ed) (1965) Select inscriptions bearing on Indian history and civilization, 2nd rev and enl edn, vol 1. University of Calcutta, Calcutta
47. Thapar R (1991) Aśoka and the decline of the Mauryas. Oxford University Press, New Delhi
48. Vaidya PL (ed) (1959) Divyāvadāna. Mithila Institute of Post-Graduate Studies and Research in Sanskrit Learning, Darbhanga
49. Verardi G (2003) Images of destruction, an enquiry into Hindu icons in their relations to Buddhism. In: Verardi G, Vita S (eds) Buddhist Asia 1: papers from the first conference of Buddhist studies held in Naples in May 2001, Kyoto. Italian School of Eastern Asian Studies, Kyoto, pp 1–36

Person

▶ Puḍgala (Puggala)

Person (Buddhism)

▶ Puḍgala (Puggala)

Personalists

▶ Pudgalavādins

Personhood

▶ Puḍgala (Puggala)

Petavatthu

K. T. S. Sarao
Department of Buddhist Studies, University of Delhi, Delhi, India

Definition

The Petavatthu is the seventh book of the Khuddaka Nikāya of the Sutta Piṭaka of Pāli Tipiṭaka.

The Petavatthu contains 51 stories in verse of persons who due to the consequences of their unwholesome deeds are reborn into the miserable realm (*yoni*) of the *petas* (Sk, *pretas*). A *peta* is a spirit/ghost of a dead person. It wanders about in the vicinity of the earth feeling hungry, restless, and tortured all the time. The only way for a *peta* to come out of such an existence is either by means of the offering of alms to monks or *dakkhiṇā* (Sk, *dakṣiṇā*, sacrificial gift) by his living relatives leading to his moving into a higher category of a *yakkha* (Sk, *yakṣa*) or after his exhaustion of the *kammaphala* (fruit of evil deeds), he may shift into another form of existence as a human or even a deva. According to the Sri Lankan chronicle the Mahāvaṃsa, the Petavatthu was taught by Mahinda to King Devānampiyatissa's queen Anulā and her companions on the day of his arrival in Anurādhapura ([2]: xiv.58). It has a commentary called the *Petavatthu Aṭṭhakathā* written by Dhammapāla.

The *vatthus* (stories) of the Petavatthu have been put together into four *vaggas* (chapters), viz., Uraga Vagga (12 stories), Ubbari Vagga (13 stories), Cūḷa Vagga (ten stories), and Mahā Vagga (16 stories). The primary focus of these stories is the functioning of the retributive karma and merit-making and merit transfer. The stories point out that giving alms to monks benefits those unhappy ghosts whose relatives indulge in the pious act of giving alms to the monks. If the living relatives of the ghosts do not provide help by offering *dakkhiṇā* in the form of material goods including food, clothes, and drinks, the ghosts suffer unremittingly of hunger and other deprivations. The importance of the Petavatthu, which is clearly addressed to the laity, lies in the fact that it is an important source for folk religion. In the popular form of Theravāda Buddhism, as illustrated in the stories of the Petavatthu, giving alms is considered as an important part of *petakicca* (duty towards the ghosts). The ordinary individual is not so much interested in nibbāna or fundamental realities as such but is seeker after good things of earthly life revolving around the basic needs and desire for the same in the next life. He believes that if he gives away generously of food and drink while during this earthly existence, he will be entitled to enjoy the same in the next life. The Petavatthu also appears to indicate that the needs of the *petas* are similar to those of human beings. However, a *peta* cannot directly take anything either voluntarily offered by his living relatives or for that matter by force or deceit. Only when a gift is made to a human being and its merit transferred to the *peta* can a *peta* receive its benefits. Interestingly, the *petas* of the Petavatthu are not any kind of evil spirits. As pointed out by B.C. Law, "the character of the *petas*... appears generally to have undergone a change for the better in their spirit life. Their hunger and thirst, their miseries and sufferings, the bitter experiences for past misconduct seem to have rubbed off their angularities, softened their temper, chastened their mind... One hardly finds them doing ill to others, they are too much pressed down with the burden of their own miseries to think of or to get any opportunity for doing mischief to others" ([7], pp. 262–263).

Though different portions of the Petavatthu belong to different periods, the text as a whole belongs to the youngest layer of the Pāli Tipiṭaka ([5], p. 51; [9], p. 96). The Pāli tradition itself considers some of the *vatthus* (stories) as young that were added to the collection only during the second council ([5], p. 51). Talking about the date of the Petavatthu, Winternitz points out that in the

Electronic supplementary material The online version of this chapter (doi:10.1007/978-94-024-0852-2_305) contains supplementary material, which is available to authorized users.

P

Petavatthu ([1]: IV.3) a king, Piṅgalaka by name, occurs, who, according to the Petavatthu aṭṭhakathā, ruled in Surat 200 years after the Buddha. Thus, even the commentator of a later time pushes this text to a period considerably removed from the time of the Buddha's life. Further, Winternitz points out that even if one admits that the notion of hell, as mentioned in the Petavatthu, had already existed in ancient Buddhism side by side with the arahant and nibbāna ideals, the Petavatthu cannot be considered to be very old (see [9], pp. 96–97). E. Hardy was of the opinion that the Petavatthu could have borrowed material useful for its purposes from other works of the Khuddaka Nikāya such as the Jātakas ([4], pp. 25–50), though, in Winternitz's opinion, the opposite of this could also be true ([9], p. 97 fn.1). B.C. Law has suggested that as there are allusions to King Aśoka in it, the Petavatthu, as we now have it, is a post-Mauryan or post-Aśokan compilation ([7], p. 37).

Commenting on the literary value of the Petavatthu, Winternitz finds it as "highly displeasing" and "fortunately not so voluminous" a work ([9], p. 96). The doctrine of Kamma is explained through examples "most inartistically" in the "stereotyped" small stories of the Petavatthu in which "what is poetical is only the metrical form" ([9], p. 96). However, according to B.C. Law, though some stories in the Petavatthu "may seem puerile and even absurd, [they] have served to restrain a believer in the words of the Buddha, from straying away from the path of virtue, in his body, or his word or his action and have made him practice charity and ahiṃsā towards all living creatures" ([7], pp. 262–263).

Cross-References

- ▶ Arahant
- ▶ Aśoka
- ▶ Jātaka
- ▶ Kamma
- ▶ Khuddaka Nikāya
- ▶ Tipiṭaka

References

1. Gehman HS (trans) (1974) Petavatthu: stories of the departed, the minor anthologies of the Pāli Canon, Part IV, new edn. Pali Text Society, London
2. Geiger W, Bode MH (trans) (1912) The Mahāvaṃsa or the Great Chronicle of Ceylon. Pali Text Society, London
3. Hardy E (ed) (1894) Petavatthu commentary Paramatthadīpanī IV. Pali Text Society, London
4. Hardy E (1899) Eine Buddhistische Bearbeitunge der Kṛṣṇa-Sage. Z Deutsch Morgenl Ges 53:25–50
5. von Hinüber O (1996) A handbook of Pāli literature. Walter de Gruyter, Berlin
6. Jayawickrama NA (ed) (1977) The Vimānavatthu and the Petavatthu, new edn. Pali Text Society, London
7. Law BC (1983) A history of Pali literature, reprint, vol 1. Indological Book House, Delhi
8. Masefield P, Jayawickrama NA (trans) (1989) Elucidation of the intrinsic meaning, so named the commentary on the Vimāna Stories. Pali Text Society, Oxford
9. Winternitz M (1983) History of Indian Literature (trans: Sarma VS) rev edn, vol 2. Motilal Banarsidass, Delhi

Philosophical Idealism (Buddhism)

▶ Idealism (Buddhism)

Philosophy

▶ Mysticism (Buddhism)

Philosophy (Buddhism)

Madhumita Chattopadhyay
Department of Philosophy, Jadavpur University, Kolkata, West Bengal, India

Synonyms

Basic tenets of Buddhism; Fundamental doctrines of Buddhism; Short overview of Buddhism

Definition

The basic doctrines preached by Lord Buddha regarding the nature of reality.

Buddhist Philosophy

Of the different schools of Indian philosophy which has gained popularity even in the twenty-first century throughout the different countries, Buddhism is the most important one. No other school has drawn attraction of so many people outside India. The simple reason for this is that Buddhism properly understood is a way of life and not a dogma which it has refused to become from the very beginning. That is why even after the lapse of so many years, its message is as pure and appealing today as it was more than 2,500 years ago.

Buddhism as a Religion: The different religions may be subdivided under two heads – one based on the revelation of a seer, a saint who is accepted as an authority and who is sent from the heavens for the welfare of mankind and the other is based on the teachings and doctrines regarding the fundamental facts of human life and existence. Buddhism as a religion is to be placed in the second category for nowhere in his teachings Buddha made any claim to be a spiritual *guru* deriving his authority from any external agency. He has regarded himself to be a guide, a ferryman who himself attaining the goal, wants to show others the way for such a destination. Properly speaking, Buddhism as a philosophical system is nothing but scheme of life which if followed properly would lead its adherents to spiritual happiness, which is the ultimate goal of all religions.

Social Background: Buddhism as a religion flourished at a time when the whole society was suffering from the disease of social discrimination among its members. In those days, performing rites and rituals was considered to be the only way to please the Gods and Goddesses for their favor and grace to avert evils and get the desired results. Only those belonging to the Brāhmaṇa class were eligible to perform such rites. Accordingly, they were thought of as the highest class or caste and the rest of the society people were divided into three other classes or castes in accordance with hierarchy, namely, the *kṣatriya*, the *vaiśya*, and the *śūdra*. The *śūdras* were considered to be the lowest among all and had to serve the other three higher castes. They were refused any right to study the Vedas or perform any sacrifice. Thus, there was a hierarchy prevalent in the society and this was completely determined by birth and not by other factors. In this background, when Lord Buddha came, the first thing he did was removal of this class discrimination among people. He showed that neither sacrifice nor total surrender to any transcendental deity is the way to liberation. Liberation is attainable through knowledge and this knowledge is open to all. This idea brought about a revolution in that societal setup and was at the root of the popularity of Buddhism.

The knowledge that Buddha regarded as the only way to liberation was not analytical knowledge. Logic and analysis did not play any significant role in Buddhism. The preference was always for practical techniques of self-transformation. They held that truth is not simply a matter of logic and reason; truth is a matter of realization which requires a great deal of inner upliftment beyond analytical reasoning. As such in Buddhist tradition, philosophy has been mainly meditative in character. Basic objective of the Buddhist teaching is to present before the people the means of shaping and conditioning one's own character so that by their own effort, they are able to attain a high level of psychological sophistication. Such sophistication will enable them to get rid of the evil roots like desire, intention, etc., which are responsible for the pains and sufferings of worldly existence. As such philosophy in the Buddhist tradition is considered from two aspects – *samatha* (calming) and *vipassana* (contemplation). Any concept which does not deal with such practical aspects of life is not considered to fall within philosophy in Buddhist tradition.

P

Texts of Buddhism: Generally, the teachings of Lord Buddha were oral in character; he used to deliver his teachings through conversation. And for this, he preferred to use the local dialect, namely, Pāli. Later on, they were recorded by his most intimate disciples in the form of three baskets, known as *Tripiṭakas*. These three canonical works are named *Vinaya-piṭaka, Sutta-piṭaka*, and *Abhidhamma-piṭaka*. Of these, the first deals chiefly with rules of conduct, the second contains sermons with parables, and the third deals with different philosophical problems. All these three contain information regarding the early philosophy of Buddhism.

Core Doctrines of Buddhism: The chief essence of Buddhist philosophical thinking has been identified by Mādhavācārya in his *Sarvadarśanasaṁgraha* [1] as "everything is suffering, everything is momentary and everything is free of permanent essence." That is, the doctrine of suffering, the doctrine of momentariness (*kṣaṇikatva*), and the doctrine of no-self (*nairātmya*) constitute the fundamental doctrines of Buddhism. Other issues discussed by the Buddhist thinkers are all related to these fundamental three. Since the main aim of Lord Buddha's teaching centered around the removal of suffering, it is better to start with the doctrine of four noble truths which deals mainly with suffering, its causes, and the cessation of suffering.

The Four Noble Truths (*Āryasatya*): The four noble truths are: (1) There is suffering. (2) There is a cause of suffering. (3) There is a cessation of suffering. (4) There is a way leading to the cessation of suffering [2]. There are several alternative senses for the use of the expression "Noble" [3]. These are: (1) The noble ones penetrate them and so they are regarded as noble. (2) The noble truths are the Noble One's truths. In Buddhism, the Perfect One is regarded as the Noble One. So the Truths taught by them are Noble. (3) They are noble because of the nobleness implied by their discovery. It is owing to the discovery of these truths that the Perfect One is fully enlightened. (4) The Noble Truths are noble because they are not unreal, not deceptive, not misleading. The real infallibility character constitutes the nobleness of these truths.

The first truth holds that life is full of misery and pain. Birth, old age, disease, death, sorrow, grief, wish, despair, in short all that is born of attachment is misery. The essential conditions of life, human and subhuman, are without exception full of misery. Apparently such a statement is thought to be wrong because of the presence of different sources of pleasure in human life. But for Buddha and also for some other Indian thinkers, such worldly pleasures are felt only by the short-sighted persons. The far-sighted persons can feel the transitoriness of such pleasure, the despair felt at their loss, and even before their loss, the constant anxiety of losing them makes such pleasures lose their charm and turn them into another type of suffering. So it cannot but be admitted that life is suffering. However, admission of suffering in all aspects of life does not turn Buddhism to be a pessimistic philosophy. The reason is that concern of Buddha was not simply the recognition of the presence of suffering in human life, but at the same time to find a remedy for it. This remedy cannot be found unless the causes of suffering are known. So the second noble truth is about the causes of suffering. The cause of human suffering has been explained by Buddha in the light of his doctrine of causation which is technically known as *Pratītyasamutpāda* or the doctrine of dependent origination. According to this doctrine, everything in this world is dependent on something else for its existence. So life's suffering, namely, old age, death, despair, etc. (known as *jarāmaraṇa*), occurs because there is birth (*jāti*). If a man was not born he would not suffer. Birth (*jāti*) again has its cause, namely, the desire to be born (*bhava*); it is a blind tendency, a predisposition to be born that gives rise to birth. This will to be born is due to the mental clinging (*upādāna*) or grasping the objects of the world. This clinging again is due to the thirst (*taṇhā*) or craving to enjoy the objects of the world. But man cannot have craving or thirst to enjoy the objects unless he had past experiences of the objects. So previous experience tinged with some pleasant feelings, known as *vedanā* in Buddhist philosophy, is the cause of the thirst. But such sense-experience could not occur unless there was sense-object contact (*sparśa*); such sense-object contact would not arise had there been the absence of the six sense organs (*ṣaḍāyatana*), namely, the five physical organs and one *manas* or internal organ. These sense organs are dependent for their existence on the mind-body organism (*nāmarūpa*) which constitutes the physical perceptible being of a man. But this organism could not develop in the mother's embryo without some initial consciousness (*vijñāna*). This initial consciousness can occur in the mother's embryo because of the impressions (*saṁskāra*) of past existences. The last state of the past life contains in a concentrated form the impressions of the past deeds done by him which are responsible for his rebirth in the present life. But such impressions are due to ignorance (*avidyā*). It is only because man does not have proper knowledge of the painful, transitory nature of objects that he wants to take birth again in this world. So all the sufferings of human beings are causally linked with some other factors and the root cause of all is ignorance. Since there are 12 links in the causal chain this is known as *dvādaśanidāna*; again as it provides an explanation of the existence in this world, it is known as *bhavacakra* or wheel of existence. Of these 12 links, ignorance (*avidyā*) and impression (*saṁskāra*) belong to the past life, while consciousness (*vijñāna*), mind-body organism (*nāmarūpa*), six sense organs (*ṣaḍāyatana*), contact (*sparśa*), feeling (*vedanā*), thirst (*taṇhā*), mental clinging (*upādāna*), and will to be born (*bhava*) belong to the present life; rebirth (*jāti*), old age, and other sufferings belong to the future life. Thus the *bhavacakra* or wheel of existence indicates that the present life is determined by the past life and the present life determines the future. It also implies that the cycle of birth and death does not presuppose a permanent self, nor does it depend upon the intervention of any transcendental deity.

The third noble truth holds that there is a cessation of suffering. The third noble truth actually follows from the second one. The second truth has identified the causes of suffering. So if these causes are eliminated, it will be possible to reach a stage which is completely free from all sufferings. Thus, the Buddhists point out that the cessation of suffering is a stage which can be attained in this very life if certain conditions are fulfilled. When one has been able to control one's passions completely and contemplated constantly on truth, one will be able to attain perfect wisdom which will enable him to overcome the fetters that bound one to this worldly existence. He will then be free or a liberated person. He is said to become an *Arhat*.

The Buddhists do not stop merely by pointing out that there is a stage free from suffering. They also have said that there is a way which can lead one to this stage. This is what the fourth noble truth says, namely, that there is a path to liberation and this path consists of eightfold steps, for which it is known as *aṣṭāngika mārga* or eightfold means. These eightfold means consists of the following eight things, namely, right views (*sammādiṭṭhi*), right resolve (*sammā sankappa*), right speech (*sammāvācā*), right conduct (*sammā kammanta*), right livelihood (*samma ajīva*), right effort (*sammā vāyāma*), right mindfulness (*sammā sati*), and right concentration (*sammā samādhi*). The essential point about this eightfold means is that this path gives importance to the harmonious cultivation of conduct (*śīla*), concentration (*samādhi*), and knowledge (*prajñā*). One starts with right views, a mere intellectual apprehension of the fourfold truths. But since old habits of thinking still continue, a conflict between the good and the bad occurs in his mind. The seven steps starting from right resolve, aim at resolving this conflict. Repeated contemplation of what is true and good, training of the will and emotion, ultimately enable the individual to attain a state in which thought, will, and emotion are all thoroughly cultured and purified in the light of truth. Perfect wisdom, perfect goodness, and perfect equanimity are attained at this stage, leading to the complete cessation of all kinds of suffering.

Doctrine of Causality: Basic to the analysis of the four noble truths stands the theory of causation. In fact, in the entire Buddhist framework, the theory of causation has a very important position. It is in terms of this theory that the doctrine of momentariness, their no-soul theory, their theory of reality, etc., have been developed. For them the real is that which can produce something (*arthakriyākāritvaṁ sat*). This capacity to produce something, in their language *arthakriyākāritva*, means nothing but the capacity to produce, to create. Again, it has been said that, that which is real is momentary. Therefore, it is evident that for any Buddhist, the doctrine of causation is the most fundamental one. This doctrine has the technical appellation *pratītyasamutpāda*. According to some, the expression *pratītyasamutpāda* [4] is comprised of two constituents – *pratītya* and *samutpāda.* Of them the first word *pratītya* is derived out of the prefix *prati* and the root "*i*" and the suffix *lyap.* The root "*i*" means to go and "*prati*" being a prefix has its potentiality of changing the meaning of the root. Therefore, in the present context, it is supposed to mean depending. The whole word *pratītya* means attainment by depending and *samutpāda* means origination. Therefore, the whole expression *pratītyasamutpāda* will mean the origination of existent objects depending on something, namely, the causes and the conditions. There is a second interpretation of the term according to which "*iti*" means "going" or destroying. That which passes through this going process or process of destruction is *itya*. *Prati* is used to mean *vīpsā* or repetition, that is, covering each case. Accordingly, the term *pratītya* will mean each object which can be destroyed; *samutpāda* means origination. Therefore, the entire term will signify the origination of objects destroyed as such. The Buddhist commentators prefer the first interpretation rather than the second one, as the use of the term *pratītya* in the sense of repetition does not apply to all cases. The real intention of the term *pratītyasamutpāda* is to signify the sense "being relative to something." So though the term *pratītyasamutpāda* is composed of two constituents, they are not to be taken in isolation; they rather form one single unit and convey the sense – (1) this being so, that arises (*asmin sati idaṁ bhavati*) or (2) this being produced that will be produced (*asyotpādād idam utpadyate*). In short, the Buddhists want to emphasize that nothing is produced at random, nor is the existent reality produced neither from a unique cause nor from a variety of causes. On the contrary, everything in the world has a relative character being dependent on something else for its origination. This view, as Buddha himself makes clear, avoids the two extremes, on the one hand eternalism or the theory that some entity exists eternally independent of everything else and nihilism that something existing can be annihilated. The doctrine of *pratītyasamutpāda* teaches us that everything that exists is dependent on something else for its existence and that thing in turn does not perish without leaving some effect. This doctrine is of so much importance in the whole Buddhist philosophy that Lord Buddha regards it as *dhamma* – "He who sees the *paṭiccasamuppāda* sees the *dhamma*, and he who sees the *dhamma* sees the *paṭiccasamuppāda*" [5].

Doctrine of Momentariness: Another important doctrine which constitutes the pillar-stone of Buddhist philosophy is the doctrine of momentariness or *kṣaṇikatva* also known as the doctrine of universal flux, namely, that everything in the universe is momentary, that is, is in a process of continual change. The transitoriness of all the objects of the world is admitted in the Upaniṣads also; but the Upaniṣads recognize that behind this constant change, there is a permanent reality. So change, though it is there, is not absolute. But the Buddhists deny this. They hold that all existence is momentary. Permanent existence, they argue, is a contradiction in terms. Their argument is based on their definition of existence (*sattā*). Existence is the causal efficiency to produce an action or an event. A seed, for example, causes the shoot and its capacity as a seed to produce the shoot must manifest itself at once. The Buddhists hold that a thing should be capable of producing something and yet should not produce it or do so only bit by bit is inconceivable. So, it has to be admitted that whatever capacity a thing has is at once and fully manifested; and since a thing exists only when it acts, it must be momentary. This causal efficiency is exercisable either in succession or simultaneity and as simultaneity and succession are incompatible with the notion of any permanent entity, causal efficiency is restricted to momentary entities alone. So, there cannot be any permanent entity in the universe, everything is momentary [6].

Doctrine of No-self: Another fundamental doctrine of Buddhist philosophy is the doctrine of no-self or *Nairātmyavāda*, according to which there is no self and persons are not ultimately real. In the *Anattalakkhanasutta* of *Mahāvagga*, it has been pointed out that the physical being, as well as the states of feeling, perceiving and thinking, volitions and activities, and even consciousness itself, is everchanging and impermanent, causing unrest or suffering. Hence, there cannot be an eternal permanent being called *ātmā* or *attā*. It is a mere conceit to say "I am this" or "This is mine." The *sakkāyadiṭṭhi* or the belief that individual existence is an absolute reality involving the existence of an eternal soul is often denounced as heresy. To speak of an individual called by such and such a name is mere convention. The doctrine of the Eternal as it is taught for instance in the *Kaṭhopaniṣad* or *Bhagavadgītā* or in the Sāṁkhya system cannot be admitted. The doctrine of *Ucchedavāda* or the doctrine of annihilation is also not justified. According to the Buddhists, all kinds of speculation and erroneous views about an eternal self are to be rejected. The self or ego in the conventional sense, however, is not denied. It is not denied that there is a self which thinks, speaks, feels, acts, and experiences the results of *karma* or actions in the course of rebirth. Only to believe that this self is an absolute reality, eternal, and everlasting is declared to be an utterly erroneous view. Hence, it is possible to speak in the conventional sense of knowing one's self or of controlling and restraining one's self and of man's being responsible for his own deeds. Though denying the continuity of an identical substance in man Buddha does not deny the continuity of the stream of successive states that compose his life. Life is an unbroken series of states: Each of these states depends on the condition just preceding and gives rise to the one just succeeding it. The continuity of the life-series thus can be explained in terms of the causal connection that exists among the different states. The Buddhists try to explain this continuity with the simile of a burning lamp. The flame of each moment is dependent on its own conditions and is different from the flame of another moment which is dependent on other conditions of its own. Yet there is an unbroken succession of the different flames. As from one flame another flame is lighted, there is a causal connection between the two. Similarly, the end-state of this life will cause the beginning of another state in the next life. Rebirth is therefore not transmigration that is passing of the same soul from one body to another, but is the occurrence of a new life by the present. The conception of soul or self is thus replaced here by an unbroken stream of consciousness. The present state of consciousness derives its character from the previous one and the future state of consciousness from the present state. Thus there is a continuous flow of consciousness from one birth to another or from childhood to old age in the same birth. Just as in a stream the water is continuously changing, still it is said that it is the same river, similarly each state of consciousness is different from the other, but the convention is to say that it is the same person. Memory, rebirth, and the notion of *karma* thus can be explained well in Buddhism even without admitting anything permanent [7].

Doctrine of Middle Path: The fundamental principle of Buddhist philosophy consists in the Middle Path which is the way to the realization of the ultimate end. This doctrine of Middle Path has both philosophical as well as ethical significance. Philosophically it meant avoidance of certain extreme assertions, which were present in Buddha's time, such as "the world is eternal," "the world is not eternal," "the soul is identical with the body," and "the soul is not identical with the body," etc. Ethically, it stood for the avoidance of extreme self-indulgence on the one hand and the extreme self-mortification on the other. The middle path is recommended not merely because it lies in the middle between worldly pleasures and ascetic self-torture but because there lies the right or perfect path for realizing the ideal in accordance with truth. Buddha explained the importance of the Middle Path with the help of the simile of a lute. Just as sweet notes can be obtained only when it is tuned neither too high nor too low, in the same way the goal is reached only when the two extremes are avoided. The Middle Path is the eightfold means (*aṣṭāngika mārga*), consisting of right understanding, right speech, right livelihood, right action, right exercise, right memory, right concentration, and right determination. This eightfold means is considered to provide a way of escape from suffering. The way includes all aspects of the seeker's training, physical, mental, and intellectual. Thus it is a threefold scheme of moral training, consisting of the practices of virtues and the avoidance of vices, the practice of meditation and the development of wisdom. It is by following the Middle Path that one can attain the ultimate aim of Buddhism [8].

Schools and Sects of Buddhism: Even during the lifetime of Buddha there were some people who did not accept his authority and tried to create divisions among his disciples by demanding more strict life for the aspirants of *Nirvāṇa*. Lord Buddha did not select anyone as the main proponent of his doctrine after his death, rather told his disciple Ānanda that the *dharma* and the *Vinaya* would be the supreme authority after his death. Since Buddha always used to preach his doctrines orally and those words were not recorded during his lifetime, so about a century after his death, differences arose among the monks about the actual words of Lord Buddha and their interpretation. Some monks made efforts to bring in relaxation of the stringent rules observed by the monks. The monks who deviated from the original practices were later called *Mahāsāṃghika*s while the orthodox monks were distinguished as the *Theravādins* (*Sthaviravādins*). This process of interpreting Buddha's teachings in a new way continued, and according to the difference in interpretation, there arose different sects. This went on multiplying till the number of sects became 18 in the second and third centuries after his passing away. Among the different sects, mention may be made of *Mahīsāsaka, Vātsīputrīya, Haimavata, Dharmaguptika, Kashyapīya, Sarvāstivādin, Bahuśrutīya, Caityaka*, and others, and all of them had different subsects [9]. The basic difference among all these sects and subsects was on ethico-religious issues as well as metaphysical speculations. However, the Buddhist and non-Buddhist thinkers mention the following as the main schools of Buddhism, namely, the *Sautrāntikas*, the *Vaibhāsikas*, the *Mādhyamikas*, and the *Yogācāras*. This classification into four schools was made mainly on the basis of two questions, one metaphysical concerning the existence of external objects and the other epistemological concerning the knowledge of those external objects. The questions may be formulated thus: (1) Is there any reality at all? (2) How can this reality be known? As regards the first question two answers are possible, namely, that there is an external reality independent of the mind and there is no reality independent of mind. Those who offer the first answer are known as the Realists. In Buddhist philosophy, the Vaibhāsikas and the Sautrāntikas are considered as realists. On the other hand, both the Yogācāra and the Mādhyamika schools of thinkers believe that there can be no object external to the mind. That is, both of them are supporters of Idealism. However, there is a difference between these two idealist schools of Buddhism. The Mādhyamikas hold that there is no reality, mental or nonmental. So ultimately it has to be said that everything is *śū nya*. On the other hand, the Yogācāras hold that only mind and its ideas alone are real. The nonmental or the material world is all devoid of reality. Since this school believes in the existence of *vijñāna*s, they are also known as *Vijñānavādin*s. As the Mādhyamika philosophers do not believe in the existence of anything neither mental nor nonmental, they are known as *Śūnyavādin*s. For those who believe in the reality of external objects, the question arises –how can this reality be known? This question can be answered in two ways – this external reality is directly known or this reality is known through inference. The Vaibhāsika thinkers believe that the external reality is directly perceived, but the Sautrāntikas believe that external objects are not directly perceived but are known through inference. Thus, there are four main schools representing four important philosophical standpoints.

On the basis of religious beliefs and practices, Buddhism is divided into two main schools known as *Hīnayāna* and *Mahāyāna*. These two schools differ from each other regarding the following fundamental points. First, the Hīnayāna school is conservative while the Mahāyāna school is catholic and progressive. Secondly, the former believes that Buddha was a human being who attained the state of enlightenment by his effort. As a human being, he was born and he also died. On the other hand, the Mahāyāna thinkers believe Lord Buddha as eternal, transcendental, and absolute, who can save all beings by his triple body. Thirdly, the former believes in one Buddha, the historical person while the latter believes in an infinite number of Bodhisattvas who take the vow to attain perfection and liberation of all. Lastly, the former aims at individual liberation while the latter admits that it is possible for all to attain liberation because all have Buddha-nature and desire for liberation. In spite of this difference, the two schools resemble on certain important points. First, both admit that enlightenment is the goal of Buddhism. Buddhism aims at removal of ignorance and achievement of enlightenment. Secondly, the world is without beginning or end. All phenomena are subject to the law of causation. There is no first cause. Thirdly, all is transitory, is in impermanent flow and flux. There is no being, only becoming. Fourthly, there is no permanent ego or self. Transmigration is due to karma. Actions in empirical life produce *karma.* Lastly, ignorance is the cause of suffering and such ignorance can be destroyed through following the Eightfold Noble Path and attaining the perfections (*pāramitā*).

Concluding Remarks: While winding up the whole discussion, a few points may be taken note of which have attracted the modern mind toward Buddhism throughout the world even after 2,550 years of his birth. The reason is that in spite of its religious aspect, Buddhism as a philosophy tackles the basic concerns of human beings in a manner which is intellectually acceptable to all scientific minded persons. The core doctrines of Buddhism are not at all exotic, nor are they influenced by cultural factors specific to any region. The Buddhists simply analyze and dismantle the mechanisms of happiness and suffering. Where does suffering come from, what are its causes, how can it be remedied? These are the basic worries of any human being. Through investigation and contemplation, Buddhism provides answer to all these questions. As such Buddhism has always been looked at as a rather unadulterated and straightforward doctrine capable of being accepted by any rational being with a critical bent of mind. To such a straightforward doctrine it has added a moral and spiritual dimension. This constitutes the basic reason for its popularity both as a religious and a philosophical movement.

Cross-References

▶ Abhidharma (Theravāda)
▶ Ahimsa
▶ Anattā (Buddhism)
▶ Anicca
▶ Ariya Saccāni
▶ Atheism (Buddhism)
▶ Avijjā
▶ Bodhicitta
▶ Bodhisattva
▶ Brahmavihāra
▶ Dhammapada
▶ Duḥkha
▶ Ethics (Buddhism)
▶ Evil (Buddhism)
▶ Good (Buddhism)
▶ Idealism (Buddhism)
▶ Jarā-maraṇa
▶ Justice
▶ Kamma
▶ Karuṇā
▶ Khandha
▶ Kilesa (Kleśa)
▶ Knowledge
▶ Liberation (Buddhism)
▶ Mādhyamika
▶ Mahāsāṅghika
▶ Mahāyāna
▶ Majjhimā Paṭipadā
▶ Memory (Buddhism)
▶ Middle Way (Buddhism)
▶ Nāgārjuna
▶ Pañcaśīla
▶ Paññā
▶ Paṭiccasamuppāda
▶ Prajñāpāramitā
▶ Psychology (Buddhism)
▶ Reality (Buddhism)
▶ Rebirth
▶ Saṃgha
▶ Saṃsāra

▶ Saṃskāra
▶ Sarvāstivāda
▶ Sautrāntika
▶ Sthaviravāda
▶ Tathāgata
▶ Truth (Buddhism)
▶ Vaibhāṣika
▶ Vasubandhu
▶ Yogācāra

References

1. Cowell EB, Gough AE (1997) Sarvadarśanasaṃgraha of Mādhavācārya: Sanskrit text-English translation-notes, 3rd edn. Parimal, Delhi
2. Hiriyanna M (2009) Outlines of Indian philosophy. Motilal Banarsidass, Delhi, Reprint
3. Ñāṇamoli B (1991) The path of purification: Visuddhimagga. Buddhist Publication Society, Kandy
4. Garfield JL (1995) The fundamental wisdom of the middle way. Oxford University Press, New York
5. Bapat PV (1997) 2500 years of Buddhism. Ministry of Information and Broadcasting, Government of India, Delhi
6. Mookerjee SK (1993) The Buddhist philosophy of universal flux. Motilal Banarsidass, Delhi, Reprint
7. Siderits M (2007) Buddhism as philosophy: an introduction. Ashgate, Great Britain
8. Stcherbatsky Th (1991) The central conception of Buddhism. Sri Satguru, Delhi, Indian Reprint
9. Dutta N (1970) Buddhist sects in India. Firma K.L. Mukhopadhyay, Calcutta

Phra Uppakhuta

▶ Upagupta

Pilgrimage (Buddhism)

K. T. S. Sarao
Department of Buddhist Studies, University of Delhi, Delhi, India

Synonyms

Dhammayātā; Dharmayātrā; Tīrthayātrā; Titthayātā

Definition

A devotional act of journeying to a sacred spot.

Introduction

Pilgrimage appears to have come into vogue in India earlier than elsewhere in the world and forms an integral part of all its major religious traditions. There are indications that the people of Indus civilization may have been practicing pilgrimage as early as 2500 B.C.E. Later, this practice was adopted by the different Indic religions, and Buddhism injected a new meaning into the institution of pilgrimage. After his Enlightenment at Bodhagayā, the Buddha spent the remaining 45 years of his earthly life in travel and advised his disciples to be wanderers. Within a short time after his death, lay devotees and members of the Order were making pilgrimages to the places associated with his life. Later, the stūpas (burial monuments) of prominent Buddhist personalities also became the centers of pilgrimage.

Aśoka's Contribution

Emperor Aśoka in the third century B.C.E. made significant contribution to the tradition of pilgrimage. His religious fervor coupled with the force of his imperial patronage initiated and sanctioned both a sacred geography and a pilgrimage practice in India. He mentions in his Rock Edict VIII that unlike the kings of the past who went on tours of pleasure, he decided to go on pilgrimages (*Dhammayātā*). Aśoka is also credited with popularizing relic worship through the redistribution of the Buddha's bodily relics, which were originally enshrined in eight stūpas. He is said to have built 84,000 stūpas called Dharmarājikas for this purpose. The stūpa with relics enshrined eventually became the central feature of virtually every Buddhist pilgrimage site within the Indian subcontinent. Other relics giving rise to pilgrimage sites, as historically recorded, are the Buddha's tooth relics, hair relics, begging bowl, and belt.

The most important places of pilgrimage directly associated with the Buddha are located in the Gaṅgā plains of northern India and southern Nepal, in the area which was known as Majjhimadesa (Sk. Madhyadeśa) at the Buddha's time. This is the region where Gautama Buddha lived and taught. In the *Mahāparinibbāna Suttanta* of the *Dīgha Nikāya*, the Buddha tells his chief disciple, Ānanda, that there are four places which a devout person should visit and look upon with reverence ([18], p. 153). These four places, which became known as the *Caturamahāprātihāṣryas* (the Four Great Wonders), are the following.

1. Lumbinī

Lumbinī (Nepal) was the place where Queen Maya gave birth to Siddhārtha Gautama. King Aśoka's Rummindei pillar inscription mentions him as having visited this place in c. 250 B.C.E. Apart from the pillar, this site now has many monasteries, a tank where the *nāgas* (water dragons) gave the Buddha his first holy bath, and the Māyādevī temple which stands on the exact spot where Siddhārtha was born.

2. Bodhagayā

This was the place where the buddha-to-be defeated Māra (māravijaya) and attained Enlightenment under the pipal tree (the bodhi tree in the present day Mahābodhi temple). As the most important Buddhist site, Bodhagayā is the primary pilgrimage destination for Buddhists. Extensively restored during the nineteenth century, the brick tower of the Mahābodhi temple overlooks Bodhagayā.

3. Sāranātha

Located on the outskirts of Vārāṇasī, Sāranātha is the place where the Buddha delivered his first sermon known as the Turning of the Wheel of the Dharma (*Dharmacakraparavartana*) at the Deer Park (Ṛṣipatana Mṛgadāva). The Dhamekh Stūpa that exists today was built from bricks during the fifth to sixth centuries C.E. and stands on the site of earlier structures.

4. Kusinārā

Kusinārā (Sk. Kuśinagara), capital of the Malla kingdom, was the place where the Buddha entered his final extinction (Mahāparinirvāṇa). The Mahāparinirvāṇa Stūpa marks the spot where the Buddha passed away. The temple contains a 6-m long statue of the Buddha in parinirvana posture (lying on one side).

In the later commentarial tradition, four other sites are also raised to a special status because Buddha had performed a certain miracle there. All the eight sites are collectively known as the *Aṣṭamahāprātihāryas* (the Eight Great Miracles). The last four of these eight places where certain miraculous events are reported to have occurred are as follows.

5. Sāvatthī

Sāvatthī (Sk. Śrāvastī) is the place of the "Illusion of the Twins" (*yamakaprātihārya*) or the "Great Illusion" (*mahāprātihārya*) where at the Jetavana monastery the Buddha showed his supernatural abilities in the performance of miracles. The Buddha spent much of his monastic life in Śrāvastī, the Buddha's main Rains Retreat where he gave discourses and engaged in debates.

6. Rājagaha

Rājagaha (Sk. Rājagṛha, present-day Rājgīr) is the place where the Buddha had subdued the wild elephant, Nālāgiri, through friendliness when Devadatta had plotted to get him killed. The Buddha spent several months meditating and preaching at Rajgir, converting Bimbisāra, the king of Magadha, and many others to Buddhism including Jīvaka (the king's physician), Śāriputra, and Maudgalyāyana who were to become important and influential disciples. Aśoka erected a pillar to mark his visit to Rājgīr, and accounts of the city, monasteries, and shrines appear in the journals of the Chinese pilgrims Faxian and Xuanzang.

7. Saṃkissā

Saṃkissā (Sk. Sāṃkāśya) is the place where the Buddha descended to Earth from the Trāyastriṃśa heaven (*devarohaṇa*) where he stayed for 3 months teaching his mother the Abhidharma. A shrine marked the spot where the Buddha's foot first touched the ground, and Aśoka also erected a pillar with an elephant capital to mark this holy place.

8. Vesālī

Vesālī (Sk. Vaiśālī) is the place where the Buddha had received an offering of honey from a monkey at the Monkey's Pond. Vaishali was the capital of the Vajjian Republic of ancient India. The Buddha made several visits to Vesālī for the purpose of preaching to the monastic community (saṃgha) and setting down many instructions and rules (*sūtras*).

Other than the above stated *aṣṭamahāprātihārya*, other important places of Buddhist pilgrimage are the following:

Kapilavatthu
Kapilavatthu (Sk. Kapilavastu) was the native city of the Buddha and royal capital of the Śākyas, where he spent the first 29 years of his life.
Sāñcī
Sāñcī (Sanchi) is a complex of monasteries, stupas, and temples dating from the third century B.C.E. to the eleventh century C.E. Although there is no known link to the Buddha, the relics of his two chief disciples, Śāriputra and Mudgalyāyana, together with the remains of later teachers were enshrined here.
Nālandā
The Buddha visited Nālandā many times, and Aśoka also came here to worship at the *caitya* of Sāriputra and ordered that a temple be constructed over the existing shrine. Nālandā became the most renowned monastic university in ancient India, allegedly accommodating 10,000 scholars and more than 1,000 teachers. It was an important destination for scholars who came to study the invaluable collection of manuscripts till the twelfth century.
Ajaṇṭā, Amarāvatī, Ellorā, and Nāgārjunakoṇḍa are the other important pilgrimage sites in India. In the Himalayas, particularly monasteries of Hemis, Alchi, Lamayuru, Chemrey, Shey, Spituk, and Thiksey in Ladakh; Rumtek, Enchey, Pemayangtse, Phensang, and Photong in Sikkim; Dhankar and Tabo in Himachal Pradesh; and Bomdila and Tawang in Arunachal Pradesh attract a large number of Buddhist pilgrims. McLeod Ganj (Dharamsala), the headquarters of H.H. Dalai Lama, is also now an important center of Buddhist pilgrimage.

Meaning of Pilgrimage

In India, pilgrimage is known as *tīrthayātrā* (Pāli *titthayātrā*). It means a devotional act of journeying (*yātrā*) to a sacred spot (*tīrtha*). The primary importance of a *tīrtha* lies in the fact that it is much more than a physical and topographical site. It is always a special point of the earth's surface endowed with a powerful mystique ([5], p. 3) and a focal point of energy imbued with sacred visions, spiritual dimensions, and healing powers. A *tīrtha* serves a two-way purpose by acting as a threshold between the earth (human world) and the heaven (the world of the gods). First, a *tīrtha* works as a gateway for the downward descent of various divine beings. These descending divinities are the well-known *avatāra*s and *bodhisattva*s. Second, a *tīrtha* acts as a door opened by an *avatāra* or a *bodhisattva* through which men and women may ascend in their prayers and rites. In other words, the full meaning of the term *tīrtha* is that it is a spiritual ford where heaven and earth meet and from where a spiritual person crosses the ocean of *Saṃsāra* (unending cycle of birth, death, and rebirth) and reaches the distant shore of *nirvāṇa* (Pāli *nibbāna*) or *mokṣa* depending upon his/her religious inclination. Thus, *tīrtha*s are perceived as sin-destroying localities ([3], p. 36). Thus, religiously speaking, pilgrimage is a transaction, an investment in the future ([15], p. 2).

Origin of Pilgrimage Centers

How did the various *tīrtha*s come into origin and grow into prominence? Since prehistoric times, Indians have viewed, among other things, water bodies, mountains, and river fords to be the abodes of divine beings and/or spirits. With the passage of time, different religious traditions developed various myths and legends through their association with these spots and with the great acts and appearances of various divine beings and/or spirits who had/have been dwelling there. Just as a field of the magnetic force is formed around a magnet, similarly there is formed a field of spiritual vibrations in those places where sages had lived and did *tapas* ([17], p. 5). Some of these divine beings and spirits also grew into great heroic characters. In other words, it may be said that a *tīrtha* is a place where one or more divinities or heroic personalities were born, died, or performed some superhuman deed, or a shrine where a particular deity had already signified it to be its pleasure to perform miracles. Saintly individuals who lead exemplary lives imbue their environments with holiness flowing from their spiritual practices. The devotees of these saintly personalities continue to derive spiritual inspiration even after their death. They do so by visiting those places which were associated with the saintly personalities. As time goes by, many folktales about the lives of these personalities metamorphose into legends, and sometimes even miracles are reported. Thus, more and more pilgrims are drawn to these spots from far and wide. Large gatherings of people throughout the year venerate Bodhgaya where the Buddha attained Enlightenment. It goes without saying that pilgrimage has permeated the lives of the Indian people to such an extent that it continues to affect the lives of most of them either directly or indirectly.

Salient Features of Pilgrimage

Most of the pilgrims take a short break, of a few days to a few weeks, from their normal daily affairs and return to those affairs following the completion of their pilgrimage. Others however, spend many years, perhaps all the remaining time of their lives, wandering to the thousands of sacred sites across India. These lifetime pilgrims generally fall into two distinct groups: first and quite visible, the sadhus (renunciatory ascetics) who are members of numerous different semi-monastic orders, and second, the elderly men and women who, having completed the responsibilities of raising and supporting children, have chosen to lead their final years visiting the shrines of the deities. At the shrines, pilgrims find not only free or inexpensive lodgings and food but also the companionship of other wandering pilgrims.

The most striking feature of pilgrimage as a physical act is the movement of pilgrim in earthly space. Of course, if the pilgrimage spot is closer to the residence of the pilgrim, the movement shall be short term and short distance. But it is perceived that the merit earned from the pilgrimage would be greater if the same pilgrimage spot is farther from the residence of the pilgrim and even better if it is littered with geographical features operating as physical obstructions. The various geographical features, besides bringing merit to the pilgrim, are viewed as providing protection by warding off hostile forces. Interestingly, the merit accrued from pilgrimage gets enhanced if besides the long distance and time taken, it involves undergoing and overcoming life-threatening situations. Thus, the arduous journey and the accompanying hardships and perils undergone by a pilgrim on the way bring correspondingly greater reward. In other words, the spiritual and physical endurance presented by the journey is perceived as directly proportional to merit-making and the alleviation of sin. Thus, mishaps, extremities of weather (including subzero temperatures, snow storms, bitter cold, and blazing sun), bad roads, devastating landslides, avalanches, flooding, torrential rains, turbulent rivers, swept away bridges, hunger and thirst, dangerous passes over high ranges, and occasional attacks by bandits and wild animals are generally seen as enhancing the value and merits of pilgrimage. Both the vitality and vulnerability of the traveler give the journey the character of an initiation. . . the self-inflicted pain to gain entrance into a new physical and metaphysical purification ([13], p. 99). In other words, natural and man-made hardships are perceived as instruments that help in cleansing the mind and the body of a pilgrim. Thus, for obvious reasons a genuine pilgrim is expected to choose a more prolonged and arduous route. In the classical Christian pilgrimage, hardships and ordeals suffered during pilgrimage were considered so important that sometimes pilgrims carried stones on their backs.

It is believed that death while on pilgrimage brings one the highest merit. Moreover, a pilgrim is also supposed to accept hardships uncomplainingly. Hence, walking is considered more meritorious than riding an animal or journeying in a vehicle to the holy spot. In other words, it is more like, say, scaling a mountain, where you would lose all the charm (read "merit" for pilgrimage) if you were dropped on top by helicopter than climbing in the usual fashion. Thus, it is not surprising that considerable distance and extremely difficult accessibility have played an important role in making shrines such as Mt Kailash classical pilgrimage destinations. H. Tichy, a German, met a bunch of emaciated Sri Lankans who had been traveling for over 3 years on their way to Mt Kailash ([15], p. 46). Of course, in the present times different types of facilities have made it much easier for pilgrims to reach the holy spots. Thus, if one were to compare the modern pilgrims with those of yesteryears, it may be said that with distances shortened by modern transportation, the commitment of pilgrims has correspondingly diminished. And so has the merit, it seems! The pilgrims of the past used to arrive slowly, traveling on foot from the farthest reaches of the region. Some used to prostrate all the way in a supreme act of devotion, measuring the entire holy path with the length of their bodies. Such a practice is known as *ṣaṣṭāṅga daṇḍa pradakṣiṇā* to the Indians, and the Tibetans call it *kiang khor* or *kiang chak*, that is, the method of successive prostration on the entire circuit, each prostration beginning where the preceding one ended. However, in the present times most of the pilgrims get themselves transported in vehicles like clothes in a suitcase, neither seeing nor hearing anything other than the noise of the vehicles carrying them to their destinations. In such a situation, spiritual interest gets a backseat, if not ignored altogether.

Moral and Ethical Aspect

Pilgrimage also has its moral and ethical aspect. Thus, during the period of the pilgrimage, a pilgrim is expected to perform austerities (*dhutaṅgas*), follow a code of conduct regarding food and dress, and perform various rituals including daily *upāsanā* and bath. Riding an animal on the way to the *tīrtha* or while performing the *parikramā* is considered a violation of the spirit of pilgrimage. Unless the pilgrim is physically infirm, riding an animal, it is believed, reduces the degree of merit. Most sources seem to agree that the animal gets a share in the merit earned by the pilgrim who rides it. A pilgrim is also expected to perform acts of charity. Indians are expected to avoid the use of leather garments and shoes. During and while preparing for the pilgrimage, the sadhus have to fast. At all the halting points on route to the shrine, the pilgrims are expected to rise early in the morning for the first *upāsanā*. Before going to sleep, they are also expected to offer the evening *upāsanā*. All pilgrims are expected to avoid liquor and refrain from eating meat as well as vegetables that smell, such as garlic and onions. But nowadays not many pilgrims observe such taboos.

Timing

Timing is an important, if not paramount, aspect of pilgrimage. Though some of the *tīrtha*s are visited by pilgrims throughout the year, visits on special days or occasions are supposed to carry more merit. Thus, paying a visit to a shrine on the day of a holy festival or in a particular year enhances the religious experience because on such occasions the concerned shrine is charged with greater divine significance and energy. Hence, it is believed that merit earned as a result of the Kailash pilgrimage performed during a *kumbh* or horse-year (for instance, the year 2002) is 12 times more than in another year. The holy shrines at Kailash and Manasarovar offer even greater indulgence or remission from sin if visited on the 15th of the 4th month, which is a very important day in the Buddhist calendar.

Ritual Bathing

Ritual bathing is an integral part of Indian pilgrimage though for the Tibetans it does not seem to hold much importance. Since prehistoric times, Indians have viewed water as containing purificatory qualities. Almost all Indian pilgrims make it a point to have a ritual bath in the freezing waters of Manasarovar. They believe that such a bath brings both spiritual and physical healing. The medicinal, magical, and supernatural properties of the waters of this lake are valued so much that almost all the returning pilgrims undergo enormous hardships in carrying home some quantity of the holy water. In fact, the most precious thing that pilgrims bring with them from a pilgrimage is the holy water for consumption and anointing.

Circumambulation

Parikramā is another important component of pilgrimage. It is a religious practice of high antiquity in India which is performed by passing clockwise around a person of reverence or holy object. It is called *pradakṣiṇā* (to go round keeping the object of reverence on the right). This practice is equally old in Tibet where it is known as *kora*. Unlike Hindus, Jainas, and Buddhists, the Tibetan Bönpos do the kora anticlockwise. For the Tibetan pilgrims, the ritual *kora* of Mt Kailash is the central activity of their pilgrimage. In strict contrast to this, for the Indian pilgrims the primary intention of their visit to a *tīrtha* is to venerate the sacred place and to receive the *darśan* of the deity. The term *darśan* means seeing and/or having a spiritual communion with a deity. This deity may be resident in the form of an image, statue, or icon in a temple's inner sanctum or in an open-air shrine. The image of the deity may be either an iconic or an aniconic form symbolizing the deity. In fact, in many well-known shrines, no statues of the deities are found but only aniconic blocks of stone or such other material. The rituals followed by the Tibetans while doing the *korā* are prostrations, offerings, and the recitation of *mantra*, during which they follow the instructions prescribed by the pilgrimage treatises. Failure to do the *parikramā* due to inclement weather or bad health is not really viewed by the Indian pilgrims as resulting in incomplete pilgrimage. Tibetan pilgrims believe that it is only by doing the *parikramā* of Mt Kailash that they could hope to attain spiritual purification leading to the ultimate liberation. Nonetheless, the potential for enlightenment, which, according to Buddhist belief, all sentient beings possess, is activated by the mere sight of Kailash.

The *Vinaya Piṭaka*, a Buddhist text of fifth century B.C.E., considers *parikramā*, prostrations, and making offerings during pilgrimage as spiritually significant. And if this is done on certain auspicious days, the merit thus gained is believed to be a hundred or even a thousand times greater. However, it may be interesting to ask if guides and porters earn individual merit and/or get a share in the merit earned by the pilgrim whose goods they transport on the *parikramā*. Porters, pony herders, and guides certainly do not go around the holy object with spirituality in mind. Same could be said of the adventure tourists. Some of the sources seem to give the impression that if reverence is lacking then nothing is gained by mere circling, and thus, a porter or a guide who does the *parikramā* for money does not get any merit from it. However, this does not seem to apply to the substitutes hired to perform the arduous journey for the indolent or the ill. In such a case, the religious merit earned is shared between the sponsor and he who actually walks along the path, provided, of course, the latter has undertaken the job as a pilgrim. But, to earn full merit, we are told, there can be no substitution.

Parikramā by prostration is a powerful way of showing devotion. It is believed that the merit earned through *parikramā* by prostration is many times more than the same done on foot. Pilgrims are not allowed to skip difficult parts, like frozen ground or streams. Interestingly, most religious traditions recognize proxy in pilgrimage. Where someone is unable to undertake the journey for reasons of illness, frailty, or otherwise he is permitted to arrange with someone else to perform the journey on his behalf. Thus, proxy pilgrims are sent. In some cases, Tibetans would carry a ribbon-decorated sheep as a proxy for a family member left behind. The Indo-Tibetan religious traditions also recognize a share in as well as transfer of merit earned through the performance of pilgrimage. Thus, Indian pilgrims perform *yajñas*, offer ritual giving (*dāna*), and take dips in the cold waters of the Manasarovar in the name of relatives and friends, both deceased and living.

Why Do People Go on Pilgrimage?

Though people of all religions go on pilgrimage to wipe out sins, many of them believe that the deity or deities who reside in the *tīrtha*s are able to fulfill their wishes. Thus, arduous journeys are undertaken to seek encouragement, solace, guidance, or inspiration. Many Indian pilgrims travel to their deities to ask for supernatural aid to end a spate of bad luck or for curing an illness. Others go to seek their deity's assistance in the fulfillment of long-held dreams. Some unmarried women go seeking a husband and the jobless a job. Some others go seeking a male heir. After securing a victory in an election or getting charge of a coveted ministry, many politicians in India are known to go on pilgrimage for thanksgiving. Some pilgrims go to discharge a religious obligation because of a prior vow to make a pilgrimage if the deity granted a wish. Some go on pilgrimage to say their thanks for the extra assistance that their deity rendered them in fulfilling wishes and dreams. Poverty appears to have been an important cause for inspiring pilgrimage. In times of hardship, the help or forgiveness of a deity is often invoked and a promise is made that a pilgrimage would be undertaken to the invoked god/goddess/saint's shrine for the favor. Thus, in the belief that various natural as well as unnatural calamities could be a physical manifestation of divine wrath, people go on pilgrimage to beg forgiveness or indeed to offer thanks for having come through difficulties.

Pilgrimage also carries penitential significance. A large number of people go on pilgrimage to seek forgiveness for a moral or ethical sin or legal crime. The purpose of penitential pilgrimage is for the salvation of transgressors even for salvation of the soul/being of their victims if the crime has been murder. This means that the resident deity is seen as having the power to grant forgiveness to pilgrims for their past, present, and future sins, thus saving them from torments in hell through a better rebirth or even a place in heaven. Many monks undertake the vows of abandonment by formally renouncing all ties and embracing pilgrimage as a full-time occupation. For such and other spiritual pilgrims, the rewards refer to the journey from ignorance to Enlightenment and culminating in liberation from the Saṃsāric cycle of birth, death, and rebirth.

In some cases, very different urges and incentives for pilgrimage seem to be at work. Thus, some pilgrims nowadays consider pilgrimage as an excuse for a spring excursion. It offers them the chance to get away from reality, break the routine, and to experience some level of freedom from domestic constraints, meet new people, and interact with new cultures. Apart from escapism, the experience of moving into an unfamiliar environment certainly inspires feelings of great anticipation and emotion among some pilgrims. Pilgrimage offers a chance for reflection and revaluation of life in a way not normally possible in domestic routine. Pilgrimage may also offer a quest for adventure and psychological healing, not to speak of spiritual purification. There are some places one goes not only to rest or to slow the march of time or to contemplate the power of nature but to make a pilgrimage into inner self. When you travel, you experience, in a very spiritual way, the act of rebirth. You confront completely new situations, the day passes more slowly, and on most journeys, you do not even understand the language the people speak... and you accept any small favor from the gods with great delight, as if it were an episode you would remember for the rest of your life [4]. Thus, whereas for some, pilgrimage is an inspiring and uplifting experience, for others it is introspective and humbling. The ever present dangers and struggles of modern life also seem to persuade quite a few persons to go on pilgrimage. However, pilgrimage is not always undertaken for the best of motives. Thus, even when begun in good faith, at times pilgrimage is known to have degraded into occasions of vice. In the pre-1959 period, bandits in western Tibet used to commit robberies and murder innocent people believing that in the end a few rounds of the holy Kailash would absolve them of all their ugly karma. In India, notorious gangsters and criminals are known to go on pilgrimage to evade arrest. Moreover, in the present times, the terms "pilgrim" and "pilgrimage" have come to acquire a somewhat devalued meaning and are often applied in a secular context. For example, fans of a political leader may choose to visit his grave and call it a pilgrimage!

Common masses have always believed that to receive or assist a pilgrim is to share in the merit and virtue of his journey. Thus, Hindu-Buddhist practices of charity (*maitrī, karuṇā*) and almsgiving (*bhikṣā*) invented a method of participating in the merits of a pilgrimage for those unable to take part in it. Thus, both secular and religious organizations providing support to pilgrims in various forms have existed in the Indo-Tibetan region since ancient times. For instance, inns came into existence in India as early as the third century B.C.E. Further, monastic institutions have always provided not only food and shelter to roving monks and nuns, but have also acted as open houses to all types and classes of pilgrims, including the poor and foreigners. Interestingly, pilgrims are also known to have indulged in merit-enhancing activities while on pilgrimage, for example, acting as postmen carrying letters from place to place as they went.

Pilgrimage holds significant economic importance as it gives boost to various commercial activities. The high mobility of people in the context of pilgrimage, the scale at which it takes place, as well as the vast distances covered by the pilgrims all contribute to the likelihood of trade. Thus, not only material and spiritual goals of many pilgrims coincided and still do, but *tīrtha*s and *maṇḍīs* (trading fairs) also often overlap. The economic existence of numerous lay travelers also revolves around business activities at pilgrimage sites. Many transporters, pony herders, horsemen, porters, and guides earn their livelihood by working for the pilgrims; thus, their avocation is a matter of interest to the government. There are others whose commercial enterprise means that they play a vital role in what could fairly be described as the pilgrimage industry, such as market vendors, souvenir sellers, hostel and hotel workers, transporters, and pony owners.

Cross-References

- ▶ Ajanta
- ▶ Amaravati
- ▶ Bhājā
- ▶ Bodhagayā
- ▶ Kailash
- ▶ Kapilavatthu
- ▶ Kārle
- ▶ Kusinārā
- ▶ Lumbinī
- ▶ Manasarovar
- ▶ Nālandā
- ▶ Rājagaha (Pāli)
- ▶ Sāñcī
- ▶ Sārnāth
- ▶ Sāvatthī
- ▶ Vesālī

References

1. Bharati SA (1963) Pilgrimage in the Indian tradition. Hist Relig 3(1):135–167
2. Buffetrille K (1998) Reflections on pilgrimages to sacred mountains, lakes and caves. In: McKay A (ed) Pilgrimage in Tibet. Curzon Press, Richmond, Surrey, pp 18–34
3. Chan V (1994) Tibet handbook: a pilgrimage guide. Moon, Chico
4. Coehlo P (1995) The pilgrimage, reprint. Harper, San Francisco
5. Dowman K (1988) The power-places of central Tibet: the Pilgrim's guide. Routeledge and Kegan Paul, London
6. Eck DL (1981) India's Tirthas: "Crossings" in sacred geography. Hist Relig 20.4
7. Ganhar JN (1973) Jammu shrines and pilgrimages. Ganhar, New Delhi
8. Hamsa BS (nd) The Holy mountain: being the story of a pilgrimage to Lake Manas and of initiation on Mount Kailash in Tibet. Faber and Faber, London
9. Hedin S (1925) My life as an explorer, reprint. Kodansha International, New York
10. Hopper S (2002) To be a pilgrim. Sutton Publishing, Phoenix Mill
11. Jha M (ed) (1985) Dimensions of pilgrimage: an anthropological perspective. Inter-India, New Delhi

P

12. Jha M (ed) (1995) Pilgrimage: concepts, themes, issues and methodology. Inter-India, New Delhi
13. Lemaire T (1970) Filosofie van het landscap. Ambo, Baarn
14. Madan TN (ed) (1981) Way of life: king, householder, renouncer, studies in honour of Louis Dumont. Vikas, New Delhi
15. McKay A (ed) (1998) Pilgrimage in Tibet. Curzon Press, Richmond, Surrey
16. Morinis EA (1984) Pilgrimage in the Hindu tradition. Oxford University Press, Delhi
17. Pranavananda S (1949) KailÈs-MÈnasarovar. S.P. League, Calcutta
18. Rhys Davids TW, Rhys Davids CAF (2000) The dialogues of the Buddha, vol 2. Motilal Banarsidass, Delhi, reprint
19. Sarao KTS (2009) Pilgrimage to Kailash: the Indian route. Aryan Books International, Delhi
20. Sarao KTS (2010) Urban centres and urbanisation as reflected in the Pāli Vinaya and Sutta Piṭakas, 3rd rev edn. Munshiram Manoharlal, New Delhi
21. Singh SP (1995) Origin and growth of the institution of pilgrimage. In: Dubey DP (ed) Pilgrimage studies: sacred places, sacred traditions. The Society of Pilgrimage Studies, Allahabad, pp 9–21
22. Snellgrove D (1981) Himalayan pilgrimage. Shambala, Boston
23. Thapar R (1981) The householder and the renouncer in the Brahmanical and Buddhist traditions. In: Madan TN (ed) Way of life: king, householder, renouncer, studies in honour of Louis Dumont. Vikas, New Delhi, pp 299–320
24. Turner V (1973) The center out there: Pilgrims' goal. Hist Relig 12:191–230

Pīlūzhénāfo

▸ Vairocana

Piṇḍolabhāradvāja

Angraj Chaudhary
Vipassana Research Institute, Dhammagiri, Igatpuri, Nashik, Maharashtra, India

Definition

Piṇḍola Bhāradvāja was the first among the Buddha's disciples to roar like a lion.

Piṇḍola Bhāradvāja is the Example of a Monk who worked hard with Phenomenal Sincerity to become an Arahant

Piṇḍola Bhāradvāja is the example of a monk who eventually became an arahant capable of answering any question put to him by any monk who had doubts about the path and the fruit [1]. His progress to arahanthood was very slow but sure. He became so confident of the Dhamma that he could roar like a lion. The Buddha declared him first among his disciples who could roar like a lion [2].

He also is the example of the qualitative change that he brought out in his life by walking on the Noble Eightfold Path. He was definitely very sincere and honest and he had the gift of working hard with phenomenal sincerity.

Piṇḍola Bhāradvā Had Joined the Buddha's Order Out of Greed

He had joined the Buddhist Order for gaining gifts and favors, which were given by people to the monks who had joined the Buddha's Order. He was very greedy, so greedy that his alms bowl made of dried gourd was larger than any monk's alms bowl.

He needed a bag to keep his alms bowl, which a monk was allowed to keep. But the Buddha did not allow him to have one until his alms bowl was worn down by the constant touch of his body [3].

Because he was very greedy and intemperate in diet, the Buddha remonstrated him. After this there was a great qualitative change in him. This is clear from what the Buddha says about him in his praise in the *Udāna*. Piṇḍola is a forest dweller, he eats what he gets in his alms bowl, he wears rag robes and has only three of them, he is contented with what he gets, and he is a real recluse who likes solitude, wants to be far away from the madding crowd, has ardent energy, practices hard ascetic life, and is given to higher thought [4].

The Buddha underlines other qualities of Piṇḍola Bhāradvāja. He said that Piṇḍola had greatly developed three faculties. They were the faculty of mindfulness, faculty of concentration, and faculty of wisdom [5].

That Piṇḍola had understood the teaching of the Buddha very thoroughly is clear from what he says to King Udena, who asked him why is it that young bhikkhus do not feel like enjoying sensual pleasures and lead a pure and holy life. The Buddha, according to Piṇḍola, is one who knows and sees, i.e., he has direct knowledge and he is fully enlightened. He teaches monks to regard women old enough to be their mothers as mothers, old enough to be their sisters as sisters, and old enough to be their daughters as daughters. They train their minds in this way to give up *rāga* (all kinds of desire) and, as a result, are able to lead a holy life. Besides he also asks them to review their bodies and meditate on the impurities there to develop nonattachment and also asks them to keep their sense faculties guarded so that evil unwholesome defilements of greed and aversion do not arise in them [6].

He was endowed with other qualities also. According to the *Apadāna*, he lived in a forest with predacious animals without fear. He achieved tranquillity, became free from the substratum of rebirth, and annihilated all his cankers or taints knowing them thoroughly. In other words, he had a direct knowledge of them with *bhāvanāmayā paññā*. He attained four *paṭisambhidās* [7] and eight *vimokkhas* [8]. He had also realized the six *abhiññās* (higher knowledges or apperceptions) [9].

The Buddha remonstrated Piṇḍola on two occasions: one when he was greedy for food and second when he performed a miracle to bring down a bowl made of sandalwood and placed on a high pole by a seṭṭhi of Rajagir by performing a miracle [10]. The Buddha was not happy as Piṇḍola had performed a miracle for getting a very cheap thing. He flew in the sky and had brought the bowl. It was like performing a miracle to cross a river in flood when one could do it by paying a few coins to the ferryman. The Buddha asked him not to perform such miracles for cheap things.

The Buddha was so unhappy about it that he asked the monks to ground the sandalwood alms bowl into sandal paste.

Piṇḍola was the son of King Uden's priest. His *gotta* was Bhāradvāja, so he was called Piṇḍola Bhāradvāja. Some commentator says that he was very greedy for food so he was called Piṇḍola [11]. But this does not sound logical. He must have been named as a child. So how could he have been named Piṇḍola at that age? It is possible that his name as a child would have been different and when people saw his greed for food he was given this name.

Piṇḍola used to take siesta in Udena's park at Kosambi. One day Uden's women who were there to wait upon him left Udena sleeping and went to Piṇḍola Bhāradvāja to listen to his preachings.

When Udena rose from his sleep, he found the women absent. When he saw that they were listening to Piṇḍola's preaching, he was very angry with him. He ordered his men to put a nest of red ants on his body to teach him a lesson. But Piṇḍola disappeared from there and returned to Sāvatth [12].

References

1. AA. 1.154 (Unless otherwise mentioned all books referred to here are published by Vipassana Research Institute, Dhammagiri in 1998)
2. S. Mahāvagga 3.299
3. Ud A p. 204; Also see DPPN, p 202
4. Meghiya vaggo, Piṇḍola Sutta, p 116
5. AA 1.155
6. S. Salāyatanasaṃyutta, 2.117
7. There are four paṭisambhidās viz. Attha paṭisambhidā (analytical knowledge of the true meaning), Dhamma paṭisambhidā (analytical knowledge of the Law). Nirutti paṭisambhidā (analytical knowledge of language) and Paṭibhāna paṭisambhidā (analytical knowledge of ready wit)
8. There are 8 vimokkhās namely four rūpāvacara jhānas and four arūpāvacara jhānas
9. Apadāna 1.47
10. Cv p. 229; Ap.A1.311; Therag A 1.265; Jat. A 4.235
11. Sāratthadīpanī Ṭīkā 3.351;AA1.153
12. S Salāyatana vagga A 3.38

Pipal

► *Bodhi Tree*

Pippali Kassapa

▶ Kassapa

Piṭakas

▶ Tipiṭaka

Pluralism (Buddhism)

K. T. S. Sarao
Department of Buddhist Studies, University of Delhi, Delhi, India

Synonyms

Interfaith dialogue; Religious diversity

Definition

A worldview that considers all religious belief systems as equally valid and promotes their harmonious coexistence.

Religious pluralism is a worldview that considers all religious belief systems as equally valid and promotes their harmonious coexistence. As each human being is endowed with uniqueness, variety is considered as healthy and desirable from the perspective of religious pluralism. Thus religious pluralism recognizes that one's religion is not the only and exclusive source of truth and it not only promotes commonness, cooperation, and better understanding between different religions but it also acknowledges the "otherness of others." The underlying spirit of religious pluralism is that it requires cooperation than competition between different religious belief systems. It also necessitates legal, social, and theological changes to overcome the causes that lead to conflicts between different religious systems on the one hand and between denominations within the religious systems on the other hand.

Occasionally, religious pluralism is used as a synonym for interfaith dialogue which refers to dialogical engagement between different religious communities for the purposes of reducing conflicts among them and to accomplish collectively agreed upon desirable objectives. Such an engagement requires that the aficionados of different religious systems adopt an attitude of inclusivism seeking an open-ended dialogue rather than having a mind-set of exclusivism whereby an attempt is made to proselytize followers of other religions. As pointed out by Hans Küng in his lecture on 31 March 2005 at the opening of the Exhibit on the World's Religions at Santa Clara University, "There will be no peace among the nations without peace among the religions. There will be no peace among the religions without dialogue among the religions."

Interestingly, nowadays some people challenge the desirability or even the possibility of belonging to just one religion for life, and it is not uncommon to come across people who feel happy belonging to more than one religious tradition. In fact, in East Asia, where boundaries between different religious traditions are more permeable, this has been happening for centuries. For instance, in Taiwan it is quite usual to see the same person owing allegiance to both a Dao and a Buddhist temple. Similarly, the practice of a Shinto wedding and Buddhist funeral in the same family is not considered unusual in Japan. In India, Jaina-Hindu weddings are quite common, and many Hindus do not consider it odd to visit Sikh, Buddhist, and Jain places of worship. In the West, a growing number of people these days feel perfectly at home practicing vipassanā and some even calling themselves as Christian-Buddhist.

Buddhists does not regard the existence of other religions as a hindrance to worldly progress and peace. Buddhism is a religion that not only follows the motto living and letting live but also promotes the ideal of happiness and welfare of maximum number of people (*bahujanahitāya bahujanasukhāya*, [9], Vol. I, p. 21). In the *Caṅkī Sutta* of the *Majjhima Nikāya*, the Buddha points out that "it is not proper for a wise man to who preserves truth to come to the definite conclusion: 'Only this is true, anything else is wrong'" ([6], p. 780). Similarly, in the *Sutta-Nipāta*, the Buddha says that "To be attached to one view and to look down upon others' views as inferior– this the wise men call a fetter" ([8], p. 798). Not only the inherent value of life itself but also the interdependence and reciprocity of human and other forms of life are a fundamental Buddhist belief. Thus, nature and humanity on the one hand and humans among themselves on the other are seen as mutually obligated to each other. A living entity can neither isolate itself from this causal nexus nor have an essence of its own. Buddhism also believes that all living beings are born again and again across species depending upon their karma and are hence interrelated inextricably. In other words, according to the Buddhist doctrines of *Dependent Arising* (*paṭiccasamuppāda*), Karma and Rebirth, harming any living being means harming oneself. Thus, from the Buddhist perspective all the humans, irrespective of the religious systems that they belong to, are kith and kin. As a modern Buddhist scholar has pointed out "Buddhism is not a religion which strengthens itself by persecuting others. Because it has loving-kindness as its basis, it can establish in strength the principle of Justice, Liberty and Equality to ensure peace and prosperity to all living beings" ([2], p. 262).

King Aśoka who ruled in India in the third century B.C.E. is a good example of a ruler who practiced religious pluralism in his policies. In his Major Rock Edict no. VII, he declares, "All faiths may exist in all places as all seek self-control and purity of mind." Further, in his Major Rock Edict no. XII, he says, "The Beloved of the Gods, the king Piyadassi, honors all faiths and both religioux and laymen. . . one should honor another man's sect, for by doing so one increases the influence of one's own faith and benefits that of the other man." The XIVth Dalai Lama, who has done a great deal of interfaith work throughout his life, believes that just as one food will not appeal to everybody, one religion or one set of beliefs will not satisfy everyone's needs. Therefore, it is greatly beneficial that a variety of different religions exist. According to him, "common aim of all religions, an aim that everyone must try to find, is to foster tolerance, altruism and love" (accessed on 04 Sept 2013 at http://art-tibet.org/buddhism.html).

Cross-References

▶ Aśoka
▶ Karma
▶ Paṭiccasamuppāda
▶ Rebirth

References

1. Kalupahana DJ (1976) Buddhist philosophy: a historical analysis. University Press of Hawaii, Honolulu
2. King WL (1984) In the hope of Nibbāna: an essay in Theravāda Buddhist ethics. Open Court Publishing, Lasalle
3. Murti TRV (1960) The central philosophy of Buddhism: a study of the Mādhyamika system, 2nd edn. Unwin Paperbacks, London, p 1980
4. Lamb C, Bryant MD (1999) Introduction. In: Lamb C, Bryant MD (eds) Religious conversion: contemporary practices and controversies. Cassell, London
5. Musser D, Sunderland D (2005) War or words: interreligious dialogue as an instrument of peace. The Pilgrim Press, Cleveland
6. Ñāṇamoli B, Bodhi B (eds) (1995) The middle length discourses of the Buddha: a new translation of the Majjhima Nikāya. Wisdom Publications, Boston
7. Nikam NA, McKeon R (eds and trans) (1959) The edicts of Asoka. University of Chicago Press, Chicago
8. Norman KR (1992) (trans) The group of discourses (Sutta-Nipāta), 2nd edn (trans: Introduction and notes). Pali Text Society, Oxford
9. Oldenberg H (ed) (1879–1883) The Vinaya Piṭaka, 5 vols. Pali Text Society, London
10. Smock D (ed) (2002) Interfaith dialogue and peacebuilding. US Institute of Peace Press, Washington, DC

Poems of Early Buddhist Monks

▶ Thera- and Therīgāthā

Poems of Early Buddhist Nuns

▶ Thera- and Therīgāthā

P

Points of Controversy

► Kathāvatthu

Politics (Buddhism)

Pankaj Mohan
Faculty of International Korean Studies, The Academy of Korean Studies, Gyeonggi-do, South Korea

Synonyms

Rājanīti

Definition

Buddhist view of kingship and the practice of conducting political affairs.

Introduction

At the turn of the twentieth century, Max Weber described Buddhism as a transcendental and apolitical system of belief. However, a close look at the history of Buddhism in India and beyond reveals that this faith was closely related to the political and social developments of the times. Rulers across Asia channeled the versatile resources of Buddhist symbolism to legitimize their political agenda and reinforce the sacred character of monarchical institution and besides, integrated Buddhism inextricably within their countries' political structures.

The rise of Buddhism in early India was linked to the formation of monarchical states and the emergence of urban centers. The age of the Buddha saw unprecedented changes in the material milieu of the northern India. Intensive agriculture with the use of iron implements and the consequent increase in surplus production led to urban growth. Buddhism recognized the new social reality: the patronage it enjoyed from urban elites such as the famous merchant Anāthapiṇḍaka who bought the park Jetavana for the Buddha suggests that Buddhism represented an alternative ideological mode to the primitive Brāhmaṇical norms and forged a close connection with new institutional formations which Brahmanism condemned and repudiated. The Brāhmaṇical tradition was critical of the urban spirit of the Gangetic valley of the sixth–fifth centuries B.C.E. understandably because such urban features as advanced agricultural technology specialized crafts and trade guilds and the new social elite who controlled them possessed the potential to disturb the lineage-based social order dominated by Brahmans. It is apparent that the Brāhmaṇical orthodoxy resisted the forces of social and political change in order to preserve its configurations of status and power, while Buddhism came to terms with them. It not only authenticated the enhanced social status of wealthy merchants but also accepted newly emergent occupational groups including courtesans and physicians.

The socially and politically engaged nature of early Buddhism is also attested in the support it received from the first aggressive monarchical states of Magadha and Kosala. King Ajātaśatru of Magadha lent munificent patronage to Buddha during his visit to Rājagṛha (present Rajgir), and subsequent to the parinirvāṇa of the Buddha, he sponsored the first Buddhist council at Rājagṛha. King Prasenajit of Kosala also sought to project and publicize his personal relationship with Śākyamuni Buddha, apparently to gain a political advantage over the rival monarchical states of the times. He is quoted as saying that the Lord Buddha was a Kosalan and so was he.

Buddhist Political Thought

Although B. G. Gokhale pointed out three stages over which the political ideology of Buddhism developed, two such strands are clearly noticeable. First was the theory of *mahāsammatta* (Great Elect), reflecting Buddha's nostalgia for tribal republicanism and second, the theory of an overarching principle of dhamma, that is, dhamma as undergirding the political philosophy of a cakravartin (wheel-turning universal ruler).

According to the theory of *mahasammatta* (Great Elect), in the times of the decline of public morality and the attendant need for the reorganization of society, an assembly of people was convened to select on the principle of unanimity the strongest and the finest person in the society as the leader. The chosen leader was entrusted with the task to perform judicial tasks of reward and punishment, and in return for his services, he received part of the produce at the time of harvest. He was called raja (king) because he brought happiness to the people and Kṣatriya (protector) because he protected their fields.

The age of the Buddha coincided with the age of transition from small tribal republics to aggressive monarchies. Apparently, the world of Buddhism was ambivalent and skeptical toward these new political patterns. The Buddha described kings as poisonous snakes, as robbers who violated people's property, and asked his followers to stay away from the domain of monarchical authority. Serving soldiers were not allowed to join the saṃgha, and monks were forbidden to watch military parades.

However, with the increasing growth of centralized monarchical power, Buddhism could no longer evade the inevitable – a grudging recognition of the "necessary evil" of monarchy. It revised its initial principle of "tribal republicanism" and formulated the Buddhist version of "cakravartin." Cakravartin symbolized normative kingship, an upholder of the dhamma (*dhammiko dhammarāja*). Evidently, Buddhism sought to inject into political institutions its sacred conceptions and world view encapsulated in the term dhamma.

The origin of the concept of the cakravartin can be traced to pre-Buddhist India. It was inspired, perhaps, by such Vedic rituals of royalty as *rajsuya* and *Asvamedha* (horse sacrifice) wherein a powerful ruler established his ceremonial sovereignty over the whole land by letting loose his horse. The horse was followed by the rolling chariot wheels of the army, and its unbridled advance signified the authentication of its owner's claim to sovereignty over the entire earth. The cakravartin in such ancient Indian texts (the *Purāṇas* and the *Upaniṣads*) is portrayed as a sage ruler possessing seven gems, including a wheel of divine attributes which rolls on unhindered and unchallenged over the earth. Its ever-onward movement symbolizes the ceremonial conquests of its possessor (the cakravartin) over all the lands where it goes. The seven treasures (Sanskrit: saptaratna) of a cakravartin in the pre-Buddhist texts include *cakra* (wheel), *ratha* (chariot), *maṇi* (gem), *bharya* (women), *nidhi* (wealth), *rāṣṭra* (people), and *gaja* (elephant). These seven treasures of a cakravartin represent seven constituents of the ancient Indian polity, and as the constituents and requirements of state power changed, the seven treasures too underwent modification. Kauṭilya, whose theories of statecraft are believed to have undergirded the administrative organization of the Mauryan Empire, conceived of the state as a body of seven organs (*saptāṅga*). They included the ruler (*svāmi*), councilors or ministers (*amātya*), the state (janapada), the fortified seat of the government (*durga*), machinery of control and coercion (danda), and ally/allies (mitra). The *Arthashastra* of Kautilya mentions the word *cakravartin ksetra* (the realm of a cakravartin), which denotes the entire Indian subcontinent stretching from the Himalayas to the Indian Ocean, that a king should bring under his sway.

This *dhammiko dhammarāja*, a cakravartin king, possesses seven gems, including a wheel of divine attributes, and the whole universe submits to his moral strength. The Buddhist "cakravartin" was a revised version of the concept of cakravartin that existed in the pre-Buddhist period.

Cakravartin is mentioned in a number of places in the *Dīgha Nikāya*, and a comparatively detailed discussion is provided in several subsequent texts. According to these texts, a cakravartin is generously endowed with physical strength and attributes and commands universal respect for his virtues. His kingdom enjoys peace and prosperity, and he possesses the seven treasures of wheel, horse, jewel, wife, gahapati, and parinayaka (general of the army). The texts describe in detail the function and significance of the seven treasures.

Seven is the number of totality. Cakra has been variously interpreted as a symbol of the cosmos, a solar disk, and the wheel of a war chariot. In many ancient societies, the cakra symbolized the cosmic sphere, and kings proclaimed their pivotal position in it by investing the architecture of their capital cities with cosmic significance.

It appears that Buddhism retained the original meaning of the Brāhmaṇical concept of cakravartin as cosmic sovereign but adapted it to its own values by imbuing it with a strong moral element. The cakravartin king of the Pali canons is paired with the Buddha as his secular counterpart and conqueror of the universe not by arms but by force of righteousness. He is generously endowed with the ten *rājadharmas* of liberality, good conduct, nonattachment, straightforwardness, mildness, austerity, non-anger, noninjury, patience, and forbearance. He protects his subjects and provides for those who are weak and destitute. His compassion is not confined to humankind but flows beyond for the well-being of even birds and beasts.

King Aśoka as a Cakravartin

The concept of cakravartin underwent several revisions in later centuries, beginning with Aśoka when he realized earlier imperial ideals and his conquest touched the limit of the land in the Indian subcontinent. The conversion of Aśoka to Buddhism was indeed one of the most important events in the history of the religion, for through his efforts, Buddhism spread beyond the borders of India. Aśoka seems to have been attracted toward Buddhism because, unlike Brahmanism, it was not enmeshed in elaborate and expensive rituals and possessed a broader social consciousness. The nightmare of the Kaliṅga war, in which myriads of human lives were lost, compelled Aśoka to redefine his political strategies. He declared that in the future, he would pursue the conquest through *Dhamma*. The event doubtless intensified his belief in Buddhist values, as is evidenced by his subsequent visits to important Buddhist sites such as Sarnath and Lumbini and by his reducing the tax burden at Lumbinī in deference to the sanctity of the place. Aśoka's political philosophy which he called *dhamma* is not identical with the Buddhist teachings, but it is doubtless influenced by Buddhism. *Dhamma*, Aśoka explained in his pillar Edict II, consists of causing no ill, doing good to all, sympathy, benevolence, truth, and purity. *Dhamma* meant observance of such principles as non-slaughter and noninjury of living beings, obedience to parents and elders, reverence for teachers, and kindness to slaves. One can hear the echo of the Buddhist text, *Dhammapada*, in these edicts.

In the Buddhist hagiography, Aśoka was hailed as a cakravartin, apparently because his initiatives led to the widespread popularity of Buddhism within India and beyond its borders and because his empire realized the political unification of India. The Buddhist world borrowed Aśoka's ideals and ideas to give the Vedic notion of cakravartin a systematic structure. The cakravartin ideal was redefined, apparently so as to accommodate, within the Buddhist hermeneutic, the military aspirations of monarchs. According to the new definition which can be found in Vasubandhu's *Abhidharmakoṣa*, there are four kinds of cakravartin – gold-wheel, silver-wheel, bronze-wheel, and iron-wheel, the last one also called *balacakravartin* (Armed Cakravartin) because of his inability to forsake brute force. A gold-wheel cakravartin brought all the four quarters of the universe under his suzerainty, but the jurisdiction of the other three types of cakravartin covered comparatively lesser areas in descending order.

Aśoka is credited in his Buddhist hagiographies with building 84,000 stūpas all over Jambudvīpa. Legends about Aśokan stupas became so popular that Tang China claimed 20 of them within its own borders. Indeed, several "Aśoka monasteries" were built by Chinese rulers in the early history of Buddhism but were retrospectively attributed to Aśoka. Eric Zurcher has correctly noted that the Buddhist ideal of cakravartin bore close resemblance with China's own tradition of sage-kings whose rule of "All Under Heaven" (*tianxia*) was legitimated by heavenly mandate. The fabricated "discovery" of the remains of Aśokan stupas in China was proclaimed as a portent of heaven's pleasure at the benevolent rule of the emperor.

According to the Korean historical text, the *Samguk yusa* one such stupa existed within the territory of the ancient Korean state of Koguryo. Japan too claimed one stone stupa in Sekitoji temple in Shiga prefecture as a genuine Aśoka stūpa. The myth was not confined to stupas, for though Buddha statues are post-Aśokan phenomena, many tales were manufactured in China about statues of the Buddha believed to have been cast by Aśoka or in some instances by his daughter, Saṃgharakṣita.

Development of Political Thought in the Mahāyānic Buddhist World

With the rise of powerful Kuṣāṇa states whose rulers styled themselves as "devaputra" (Son of Heaven) and the import of foreign ideas and institutions, the Buddhist recognition of the king's status as god-incarnate became less ambiguous. In the Mahāyānic text *Suvarṇa Prabhāsottam Sūtra*, the god Brahmā declares that king called the son of gods because a king enters his mother's womb by the authority of the great gods, and although he is born or he dies in the world of mortals, he rises from the gods.

When Buddhism reached China, the existing Mahāyāna scriptures written in India were not adequate to meet the challenges the religion faced both in the realms of metaphysical speculation and practical exigencies. As a result, several apocryphal texts appeared. The *Renwang jing* surpassed all other apocryphal texts in terms of political influence and appeal to the state in the Buddhist world of East Asia in the early medieval times, perhaps, because it addressed the central concern of rulers and attempted to establish a mutually empowering link between the sacred and profane domains. The sutra appears to have been inspired by the belief that monarchical support was crucial to the longevity of Buddhism, and this realization was made more acute during the millenarian nightmare of the late fifth century that manifested itself in the persecution of Buddhism in the Northern Wei in mid-fifth century. The sutra is underpinned with a strong political message that devout monarchs could be assured of heavenly protection for their kingdoms, while those who persecuted Buddhism and extended support to heterodox faiths (rivals of Buddhism) invited rebellion, crushing defeat in war, and natural calamities. It is apparent that a skeleton Sanskrit text was composed in central Asia or North China by an Indian monk who was conversant with the autocratic character of Chinese politics in the northern dynasties and also with the challenges which Buddhism faced there. It was subsequently given its current elaborate form when it was translated into Chinese.

Buddhism was lavishly patronized by states in central Asia and Northeast Asia because it introduced several new concepts, including the theories of karma and "Buddha nature" (tathāgatagarbha doctrine), which doubtless facilitated the preservation of the social and political order of the state. The theory of karma could be seen as justifying social hierarchy and the related practice of institutionalized discrimination by suggesting that low status in the hierarchical social structure came from demerits (bad karma) earned by individuals in their past lives. Early Buddhist texts explain karma as a natural law determining the consequence of human volition.

The doctrine of karma, therefore, became a persuasive explanation of failure and suffering, including human inequality, which was determined by birth and beyond human control. When He Shangzhi, an official of the Southern Song Dynasty, suggested to Emperor Wen (424–453) that propagation of Buddhism would facilitate the cultivation of good manners and customs in the people, he meant that faith in the Buddhist doctrine of karma would bring into focus the concept of individual responsibility. It would make people realize that their social status, however low, and their obligations to the state, however exorbitant, derived exclusively from their own sins, past and present.

The doctrine of karma also suggested to people the possibility of improving the nature and condition of their existence, present and future, by being "virtuous" and obeying the law of the land. It is remarkable that when the king of the ancient Korean kingdom of Paekche advised the court of Yamato Japan to embrace Buddhism, he emphasized the doctrine of karma as an outstanding feature of Buddhism, writing to him that the Buddhist doctrine was the most excellent, hard to explain, hard to comprehend, and its ability to "create religious merit and retribution without measure and without bounds."

Buddhism and royalty forged a mutually empowering relationship in the central Asian states on the Silk Road and beyond in East Asia. In the oasis states on the Silk Road, Buddha was given the epithet of "all knowing wise, the god of gods, Buddha king," and the rulers proclaimed themselves as "King of Kings" and "Sacred Lord" because "their respect and honor toward the Buddha was expressed in the same literary styles as respect and honor for the worldly power of the king." The "Household Bodhisattva" ideal was expressed in these oasis states in the form of frescoes which still exist.

Buddhism succeeded in expanding its appeal and influence in China because of the limitation of Confucianism. Confucianism had become so inextricably embedded in the political institutions of Han China that when the dynasty fell in 220 C. E., Confucianism, its underpinning ideology, also lost credence and credibility. After the disintegration of Han dynasty, China was divided into non-Han northern states and native southern China. During this "period of disunity," Buddhism became a force of cohesion. As a system of belief common to the ruling elites and the common masses and the so-called "barbarian" regimes north and the Han states of the south, it emerged as a significant force of unity and cultural integration in Chinese society.

Nonetheless, the emperors of the northern dynasties belonging to the Turkic race turned to Buddhism for legitimation with greater ingenuity and imaginative appeal than their Han counterparts in the south because the political philosophy of Buddhism conformed to their own tradition of "ordained by Heaven" (corresponding closely to the doctrine of cakravartin or the universal ruler, possessing distinctive physical marks of greatness and a divine wheel which appears mysteriously before him). The statement of a non-Han ruler of the Northern Wei that "since Buddha is a barbarian god and we are barbarians, the Buddha is naturally our god" needs to be placed within this political context. A significant adaptation of the Buddhist political philosophy also appeared in the north in the fifth century. An influential monk Faguo argued that the ruling emperor was the Tathāgata of today, and in worshipping the emperor, the laity and the monastic community worshipped the Buddha. Unlike South China where the monastic community maintained its autonomy vis-a-vis state and monks and nuns were exempted from bowing before the emperor, the Buddhist church in the north was subjugated to the interests of the rulers.

Political Uses of Maitreya Symbolism

The rulers of the central Asian states invoked the notion of cakravartin and lent immense authority to the Maitreya, the future Buddha. Vijayasambhava and Vijayavirya, two rulers of Khotan in the first century C.E., were considered to be incarnations of Maitreya. The popularity of the Maitreya cult is also evident in the cave paintings of Kizil in present-day Xinjiang. The Maitreya cult spread to the Dunhuang area and further to North China whose rulers invoked the ideal of the cakravartin and Maitreya in order to emphasize the divine element of royalty. Apparently, the symbolic significance of Maitreya added a Messianic dimension to the institution of kingship.

The interface between royalty and the Maitreya cult is more convincingly evidenced in the contemporary iconographical and epigraphical data. A votary inscription engraved on a Maitreya statue (dated 443) in North China reads that it was made with the prayer that the crown prince, his (benefactor's) parents, and all sentient beings may take part in the Three Assemblies of Maitreya when he descends to earth. The nuanced political symbolism of the Maitreya cult is identifiable even in the cave temples of Longmen and Yungang. It is believed that five cave temples at Yungang (numbered 16–20) were built in honor of five past and present Northern Wei emperors and the Maitreya statue, installed in cave 17, was dedicated to the reigning Emperor Wencheng. Furthermore, a cave temple of seven emperors built during the Northern Wei era contains statues of six past Buddhas and Shakyamuni Buddha of the present era, each representing past emperors of the dynasty. And, interestingly, in the center of the temple stands a huge Maitreya statue (also called *Manusi* Buddha or Human Buddha), which is a likely representation of Xiaowen, the reigning emperor. The significance of the cult of Maitreya was apparently manipulated by rulers along the Silk Road to bolster their claim of sacrality and emphasize their role as saviors.

The period witnessing the rise of the Maitreya cult in China was also the age when an eschatological belief in the "end of the dharma (Chinese: mofa)" embedded itself in the popular consciousness. Both the trends, perhaps, dialectically interpenetratied and influenced each other. In this period of social convulsion, the dividing line between Buddhism and Daoism became increasingly faint, and as has been suggested by Anna Seidal, the Daoist belief in the appearance of a "divine redeemer" and the Buddhist vision of a messiah converged. This process led to an alteration in the character of the future Buddha, Maitreya, who was originally to descend in the domain of a cakravartin marking "the peaceful golden age of the next kalpa's apogee." Maitreya was now recast as an "apocalyptic hero" and was now envisioned as a savior who would make his advent in the period of chaos and cataclysm. It was this Buddhist-Daoist synthesis and confluence of messianic expectations and apocalyptic fears that led the popular imagination to create a new Bodhisattva, Candraprabha kumara (Chinese: *Yueguang tongzi*).

In the sixth century when the cult of Yueguang was widespread in China, many popular disturbances and uprisings sought to manipulate its symbolic significance. Yueguang became synonymous with Maitreya, and the people now turned to this savior messiah with the hope that the climate of decline and despair would soon be replaced by justice and happiness. When Monk Fajing, calling himself Dacheng (Mahayana), raised a rebellion in Yizhou (together with Li Guibo and other commoners), he gave the slogan "The New Buddha will make an advent, Old Devils will be wiped out." In 524, a group of believers in Wucheng county holding white parasol and clad in white clothes raised similar attempt to express their grievances against moral decline and material discomfort and articulate their vision of a just and peaceful world. Xinfo (new Buddha) and Mongwang (shining king) which contemporary rebellions invoked as their source of inspiration have a clear resonance of Yueguang. The fact that Buddhism got increasingly enmeshed into millennial aspirations in the sixth century is evident in the decree of Emperor Wu of the Northern Zhou in the years 574–577 who declared that "Buddhism must be suppressed because it practiced unfilial conduct, wasted wealth and instigated rebellion." In the first state suppression of 446, Buddhism was not openly criticized for subversive acts against the state. The imperial edict had noted that Buddhism taught "the equality and unity of all classes, withdrawal from society, exemption from taxation, and celibacy." As noted earlier, Yueguang tongzi seems to have originated in the lower section of the Chinese society, but its growing popularity compelled the monastic elites to acknowledge its value. The fact that Narendrayasas, an Indian monk in Sui China, inserted a prophesy in one of his translations in 583 to the effect that Yueguang will be reincarnated as a powerful ruler of the Great Sui and patronize and propagate Buddhism with great devotion suggests the pervasive influence of the new bodhisattva on the Chinese mind.

When Buddhism spread to the ancient Korean state of Silla, the Silla royalty in the sixth century discerned immense political possibilities in the Maitreyan symbolism – king as cakravartin and Bodhisattva – in conformity with the tradition of the Chinese state of Northern Wei. King Chinhung of Silla (r. 534–576) promoted the Maitreya cult centered on Yueguang symbolism among the Silla youth by creating Hwarang, an order of the aristocratic youth of Silla, and in so doing, he was successful in blunting the millenarian edge of Maitreya cult. By projecting the scions of Silla nobility as the Maitreya-incarnate, King

Chinhung was also able to harness the significance of Maitreya as a force of national cohesion and a source of political dynamism in the times of political upheaval and uncertainty. The symbolism of Maitreya and the notion of bodhisattva kingship during the reign of King Chinhung served as an ideological underpinning of the consolidation of royal power and supported his ambitious campaigns of peninsular conquest.

Based on these traditional resources, Buddhism developed a more nuanced and sophisticated program of political action in the modern times. The two Nobel laureates of Asia, Dalai Lama and Aung San Suu Kyi, and interestingly, the responses to them by the political establishments have sought to appropriate the theoretical resources of Buddhism for legitimatory functions. Aung San Suu Kyi has declared herself to be an inheritor of the legacy of her father Aung San who was a devout Buddhist. Furthermore, in her first open letter addressed to Thura U Kyaw Htin, secretary of the Council of State in Burma, she made it clear that her campaign for democratization of Burma accorded with the advice of the Venerable Sayadaws (Buddhist Abbots) of the Sangha Maha Nayaka Committee. China has sought to legitimize its rule over Tibet in the Buddhist terms by sponsoring the enthronement of the 11th Panchen Lama amid colored banners inscribed with the slogan "*huguo anmin*" (protect the country and comfort the people). The Burmese government's importation of Buddha's relic from China and organization of festivity and jubilation may be cited as a counterresponse of Aung San Suu Kyi's political legitimacy from the Buddhist perspective. The followers of Ambedkar in India, attempting to integrate the dalit (down-trodden) section of Indian society within the orbit of Buddhism and various political parties owing their allegiance to Ambedkar's philosophy, the visibility of Soka Gakkai, primarily a Buddhist sect, on the political landscape of Japan and the formation of Jathika Hela Urumaya (National heritage party), a political party in Sri Lanka founded and run by Buddhist monks, may be cited to illustrate the ever-increasing linkage between Buddhism and politics in contemporary Asia.

Cross-References

▶ Ajātaśatru
▶ Ambedkar
▶ Aśoka
▶ Cakra
▶ Dhamma
▶ Dīgha Nikāya
▶ Karma
▶ Lumbinī
▶ Magadha
▶ Parinirvāṇa
▶ Vasubandhu

References

1. Basham AL (1954) The wonder that was India: a study of the culture of the Indian subcontinent before the coming of the Muslims. Sidgwick and Jackson, London
2. Chakravarti U (1987) The social dimensions of early Buddhism. Oxford University Press, Delhi/Oxford
3. Erdösy G (1995) City states of North India and Pakistan at the time of the Buddha. In: Allchin FR (ed) The archaeology of early historic South Asia: the emergence of cities and states. Cambridge University Press, Cambridge/New York
4. Gernet J (1995) Buddhism in Chinese Society: an economic history from the fifth to the tenth centuries (English trans: Franciscus Verellen). Columbia University Press, New York
5. Gokhale BG (1966–1967) Early Buddhist kingship. J Asian Stud 26(11)
6. Gokhale BG (1969) The early Buddhist view of the state. J Am Orient Soc 89(4)
7. Gonda J (1966) Ancient Indian kingship from the religious point of view. Brill, Leiden
8. Liu X (1988) Ancient India and ancient China: trade and religious exchanges A.D. 1–600. Oxford University Press, Oxford/New York
9. Matthews B (1993) Buddhism under a military regime: the Iron Heel in Burma. Asian Survey 3(4)
10. Mohan P (2001) Maitreya cult in early Shilla: focusing on Hwarang in Maitreya-Dynasty. Seoul J Korean Stud 14
11. Mohan P (2003) Buddhist kingship in sixth century Korea. J Orient Soc Aust 35
12. Nattier J (1991) Once upon a future time: studies in a Buddhist prophecy of decline. Asian Humanities Press, Berkeley
13. Orzech CD (1998) Politics and transcendent wisdom: the scripture for humane kings in the creation of Chinese Buddhism. The Pennsylvania State University, University Park

14. Reynolds F (1972) The two wheels of Dhamma: a study of early Buddhism. In: Obeyesekere G, Reynolds F, Smith B (eds) The two wheels of Dhamma: essays on the Theravada tradition in India and Ceylon. American Academy of Religion, Chambersburg
15. Seidel A (1990) Chronicles of Taoist studies in the West 1950–1990. Cahiers d'Extreme-Asie 5
16. Seneviratne A (ed) (1994) King Aśoka and Buddhism: historical and literary studies. Buddhist Publication Society, Kandy, Sri Lanka
17. Sponberg A, Hardcare H (eds) (1988) Maitreya, the future Buddha. Cambridge University Press, Cambridge/New York
18. Strong JS (1983) The legend of King Aśoka: a study and translation of the Aśokāvadana. Princeton University Press, Princeton
19. Tambiah SJ (1976) World conqueror and world renouncer: a study of Buddhism and polity in Thailand against a historical background. Cambridge University Press, Cambridge, UK
20. Thapar R (1973) Aśoka and the decline of the Mauryas, 2nd edn. Oxford University Press, Bombay
21. Trainor K (1997) Relics, ritual and representation in Buddhism: rematerializing the Sri Lankan Theravada tradition. Cambridge University Press, Cambridge
22. Warder AK (1970) Indian Buddhism. Motilal Banarsidass, Delhi
23. Wright A (1959) Buddhism in Chinese history. Stanford University Press, Stanford
24. Wright A (1990) Studies in Chinese Buddhism. Yale University Press, Yale
25. Zürcher E (1959) The Buddhist conquest of China. Brill, Leiden
26. Zurcher E (1982) Prince moonlight: Messianism and eschatology in early medieval Buddhism. T'oung-Pao 68

Polyandry

▶ Polygamy (Buddhism)

Polygamy (Buddhism)

Jagbir Singh
Department of Buddhist Studies, University of Delhi, Delhi, India

Synonyms

Bigamy; Concubinage; Group marriage; Polyandry; Polygyny

Definition

Polygamy can be most succinctly defined as any form of marriage in which a person has more than one spouse or having the grilling relationship with different females at one time. In social anthropology, sociobiology, and sociology, polygamy is referred as a practice of a person making himself/herself available for two or more spouses to mate with.

Connotations of the Term

Polygamy exists in three specific forms: polygyny, polyandry, and group marriage. Under polygyny, a man is either married to or involved in grilling relationship with a number of different females at one time. This is the most common form of polygamy. Polyandry is a breeding practice where a woman has more than one male grilling partner simultaneously. In the case of group marriage, the family unit consists of multiple husbands and multiple wives.

Historically, all these three practices have been found, but polygyny is by far the most common form referred. Confusion arises when the broad term "polygamy" is used instead of a specific form of polygamy which is being referred to. Here, the term polygamy is discussed with reference to Buddhism.

Polygamy and Buddhism

Buddhist texts are broadly silent on the subject of monogamy or polygamy; the Buddhist laity is, however, advised to confine themselves to one wife. The Buddha did not lay rules on married life but gave necessary advice on how to live a congenial married life. Such inferences can be gathered from His sermons that it is wise and advisable to remain faithful to one wife and not to be sensual enough to indulge in extramarital affairs. The Buddha realized that one of the main causes of man's downfall is his involvement with other women. *Gotama* himself, as a prince, was brought up surrounded by concubines and dancing girls. This indicates that it was not expected that young men would lead a life of much restraint. As a matter of fact, polygamy was common in the contemporary society. For instance, *Ambapāli*, the courtesan from whom the Buddha accepted gifts, was a person of the same consequence [1]. Therefore, after considering the frailties of human nature, the Buddha advised His followers to refrain from committing adultery or sexual misconduct in one of His precepts. Five precepts, the fundamental code of Buddhist ethics, contain an admonishment of sexual misconduct. Though what constitutes such misconduct from a Buddhist perspective varies widely depending on the local culture.

It is said in the *Parābhava Sutta* that "not to be contented with one's own wife and to be seen with harlots and the wives of others – this is a cause of one's downfall. Going to women who are dear unto others as their own lives – this is a cause of the decline just as the moon during the waning half. Being past one's youth, to take a young wife and to be unable to sleep for jealousy of her – this is a cause of one's downfall" [2]. In other words, if a married man goes to another woman out of wedlock, that could become the cause of his own downfall and he would have to face numerous other problems and disturbances [3]. Other fragments in the Buddhist scripture can be found that seem to treat polygamy unfavorably, leading some authors to conclude that Buddhism generally does not approve of it [4] or alternatively if it is tolerated, then in a subordinate marital model [5].

Sigālovāda Sutta of the *Dīgha Nikāya* describes the respect that one should give to one's spouse. In this Sutra Buddha advises *Sigāla*, a lay boy, that husband and wife should be faithful towards each other to lead a happy married life [6]. The Buddha's way of teaching is just to explain the situation and the consequences. People can think for themselves as to why certain things are good and certain things are bad. The Buddha did not lay down rules for the lay people about number of wife or wives a man should or should not have. However, if the laws of a country stipulate that marriages must be monogamous, then such laws must be complied with, because the Buddha was explicit about His followers respecting the laws of a country, if those laws were beneficial to all [3].

In Buddhist and pre-Buddhist India, monogamy was the established system of marriage. The western commentators on Buddhist scriptures have fallen into the common error about Buddhist marriage when they try to represent marriage in Buddhist India as polygamous. They have misunderstood the Pāli words for "girl," "maid," "woman," "housekeeper," and "queen" as meaning wife. The result is that they give in some instances 500 or 600, or even 16,000, wives to a king. In Pāli scriptures "*mehesika*" is the word used for the wife of a king, for she is the head of the household women, and "*bhojinī*" is a woman attendant or a lady of the court [7].

At the time of the Buddha, women were enjoying freedom; therefore, they could not have possibly given room for polygamy as the recognized form of marriage. The Buddhist scriptures abound in instances have shown the independent spirit of women. *Pabhāvati*, the queen of *Kusā*, went back with her retinue to her parents when she did not like to live with her ugly-faced husband (*Kusā Jātaka*). In another instance, the daughter of a rich noble man was prepared to go back to her parents when her father-in-law tried to impose his views of religion on her. Ultimately he gave in to his daughter-in-law (*Dhammapada Aṭṭhakathā-Visākhā*) [7].

Women could not marry more than one man at a time nor marry twice in her life as a general rule, though there were exceptions. For example, according to the story mentioned in *Nakkhatta Jātaka* (no. 49), the bride was given in marriage to another bridegroom on the failure of the selected bridegroom's coming to the bride's house on the appointed day. When the first bridegroom came, he was told that the girl could not be married twice over. It was not the custom for a wedded wife to take another mate even if she was not loved by her husband [8]. But there are instances in which married women who were either kidnapped or seduced were kept as wives. However, some examples of polyandry and polygyny are found in Buddhist literature. The case of polyandry occurs in *Kuṇāla Jātaka*

(*Jātaka* no. 536) in which Princess *Kaṇhā* was allowed to have at a time five husbands selected by her in a *Swayamvara* assembly. While a woman does not generally appear to have taken more than one husband, a man appears to have married more than one woman. In the *Vimānavatthu* commentary, *Bhaddā* being a barren woman told her husband to marry her sister *Subbhaddā*. The husband did so. In the *Babbu Jātaka* (no. 137), there is reference of a wife who delayed in coming back to her husband's house from her father's house and the husband took a second wife [9].

In Modern Perspective

For Buddhists, like the Hindus, there is a strong division between the religious and the legal foundations for polygamy on one side and its cultural foundations on the other. Legally, there is no ground for polygamy in most Buddhist countries, although it has been customary for rich men to have more than one wife or concubines. For example, in Malaysia about 30 % of the population is Chinese and primarily Buddhist. Buddhist Malaysians had a tradition to engage in polygamy. The government tried to control it by amending the marriage law and abolishing polygamy for non-Muslims. But the practice did not disappear but simply took another form. Today, a Chinese man can be married only to one wife legally in Malaysia but can then marry a second one by performing the traditional tea ceremony through which they were married according to the customary laws of the Chinese community [10]. As cultural practice overrules religions and legal codes, therefore a dual society with respect to polygamy is created, i.e., formal and informal.

Technically, since the Han Dynasty, Chinese men could have only one wife. However, in Chinese history, it was common for rich Chinese men to have a wife and various concubines. Polygyny is a by-product of the tradition of emphasis on procreation and the continuity of the father's family name. Before the establishment of the People's Republic of China, it was lawful to have a wife and multiple concubines within Chinese marriage. Emperors, government officials, and rich merchants had up to hundreds of concubines after marrying their first wives [11].

However, in some polygamous Buddhist populations, the practice is based on a cultural foundation. This has made Buddhist Tibet home to the largest and most flourishing polyandrous community in the world today. Tibetans typically practice fraternal polyandry where brothers become husbands to a common wife but also allow polyandry of father and sons who sometimes combine to have one wife in common. Among peasants, this helps prevent the division of precious family lands; among nomadic herdsmen, it meant that the wife was not left alone when one of the husbands was away. Another reason for polyandry is that the mountainous terrain makes some of the farmland difficult to cultivate, requiring more physical strength. Women take multiple husbands because they are strong and able to help to tend the land. In such marriage, the power and influence were considerable [10]. This is a unique phenomenon not found elsewhere in the world. Indeed every form of marriage appears to be permissible according to the cultural diversity of the area [12]. Presently, in rural Thailand, marriages are almost entirely monogamous. A few well-to-do farmers might have more than one wife, and this is more common in urban areas. If a second wife is taken, the first must give permission and is considered senior to the second. Both are usually provided with their own living quarters to manage independently [13]. In premodern Japan, polygamy was a recognized form of marriage, but the 1868 Meiji code recognized monogamy as a rule [14].

There is no doubt that polygamy was a part of different communities, but there is a need to understand the reasons behind the adaptation of polygamy. Anthropologists have suggested that polygamy was followed to:

1. Increase the probability of children, particularly when a wife is barren or gives birth to female children only
2. Increase the labor supply within a kinship network
3. Deal with the "problem" of surplus women

P

4. Expand the range of a man's alliances so he is able to maintain or acquire a position of leadership
5. Perhaps provide sexual satisfaction to men, particularly in societies with lengthy postpartum sexual taboos [15]

The Buddha did not discuss any particular form of marriage. However, among the Buddhists of a certain cultural and social milieu the practice of polygamy was followed. Cases of polygamy can also be traced in modern time in different Buddhist countries where people are more concerned with the tradition and customs, rather than religious and legal codes. Thus, polygamy can be referred in the context of Buddhism only in indirect ways.

Cross-References

▶ Jātaka

References

1. Walshe MOC (1986) Buddhism and sex. Buddhist Publication Society "Wheel" No. 225, Kandy
2. Thera N (tr) (1985) Everyman's ethics: four discourses by the Buddha. Buddhist Publication Society, Kandy
3. Sri Dhammananda K (1995) A happy married life: a Buddhist perspective. The Buddhist Missionary Society, Kuala Lumpur/Berkeley
4. Tachibana S (1992) The ethics of Buddhism. Routledge, New York/London
5. Harvey BP (2003) An introduction to Buddhist ethics: foundations, values, and issues. Cambridge University Press, Cambridge
6. Sinha SDJ (1987) Buddhist rules for the laity. Singapore Buddhist Meditation Centre, Singapore
7. De Zoysa AP (1955) Indian culture in the days of the Buddha. M.D. Gunasena, Colombo
8. Fausbōll (1880) Rhys Davids TW (tr) Kanhadīpāyana Jātaka, Jātaka, vol IV. Trtfbner, London
9. Law BC (1981) Women in Buddhist literature. Indological Book House, Sonarpur, Varanasi
10. Zeitzen MK (2008) Polygamy: a cross cultural analysis. Library of Congress Cataloging-in-Publication Data, New York
11. http://wimvincken.18.forumer.com. Accessed 15 Dec 2012
12. Bell C (1928) The people of Tibet. The Clarendon Press, Oxford
13. Hanks LM, Hanks JR (1963) Thailand: equality between the sexes. In: Ward BE (ed) Women in new Asia. UNESCO, Paris
14. MayKovich MK (1979) The Japanese family. In: Das MS, Bardis PD (eds) The family in Asia. Allen and Unwin, London
15. Macfarlane A (1986) Marriage and love in England, 1300–1840. Basil Blackwell, Oxford; Mair L (1971) Marriage. Penguin, Harmondsworth/Middlesex

Polygyny

▶ Polygamy (Buddhism)

Popular Buddhism

▶ Folklore (Buddhism)

Posaha

▶ Uposatha

Prajāpatī

▶ Pajāpati Gotamī

Prajāpatī Gautamī

▶ Pajāpati Gotamī

Prâjapati Gautami

▶ Pajāpati Gotamī

Prajñā

▶ Paññā

Prajñāpāramitā

James B. Apple
Department of Religious Studies,
University of Calgary, Calgary, AB, Canada

Synonyms

Mother of the Buddhas; Perfect wisdom; Perfection of insight; Perfection of understanding; Perfection of wisdom

Definition

The perfection of wisdom or insight in Mahāyāna forms of Buddhism that is worshipped as a feminine deity and embodied in a vast corpus of Buddhist scriptures.

The *Prajñāpāramitā* ("Perfection of Insight" or "Perfection of Discernment," commonly known as the "Perfection of Wisdom") is a vast and complex corpus of literature that initially developed in South Asian forms of Buddhism. As a genre of literature, the *Prajñapāramitā* is comprised of subtle teachings, techniques, and practices, which eventually come to be affiliated with invocation rituals and visualizations. In its earliest formulations, *Prajñāpāramitā* was concomitant with a boundless and luminous nonconceptual state of awareness. *Prajñāpāramitā* was also construed as a feminine force, the "mother of the Buddhas" (Sanskrit *sarvabuddhamātā*), and became a hypostatized deity. The communities that were devoted to *Prajñāpāramitā* were comprised of diverse interrelated groups within Indian Buddhist traditions that cultivated this literature for over the course of a thousand years in South Asia. These traditions later spread into Central, East, and Southeast Asia. Contemporary indigenous Buddhist traditions that preserve and cultivate the literature and practices related to *Prajñāpāramitā* are primarily found in Nepal, Tibet, and Japan.

The beginnings of *Prajñāpāramitā* discourses in South Asia emerge out of mainstream forms of early Buddhism. Within early discourses among the various Indian Buddhist ordination lineages (*nikāya*), the Indic term *prajñā* (Pali, *paññā*; Tibetan *shes rab*; Japanese *hannya*), signified a higher type of knowledge based on analysis. The word *prajñā* is made up of the nominalized verbal root "*jña*," which signifies "knowing, knowledge, perception," and the nominal prefix "*pra*," which signifies "superior" ([1], p. 209) Hence the word *prajñā* may literally be rendered as "insight" or "discernment." The concept of *prajñā*, and its related cognitive states, was central to all the various early Buddhist groups. Within such groups, *prajñā* was primarily understood as a complete comprehension (*abhisamaya*) of the nature and aspects of conditioned existence (*saṃsāra*), the forces that govern the conditioned (*karma*), the method of becoming liberated from the contaminated and conditioned (*mārga*), and the means form actualizing the reality of the unconditioned (*nirvāṇa*).

The Beginnings and Development of *Prajñāpāramitā*

At some time in early Buddhist history, possibly around the time of King Aśoka's reign (268–233 B.C.E), ordination lineages (*nikāya*) with a particular preoccupation with *prajñā* most likely composed mnemonic lists of categories (*mātṛkā*) for memorization and analysis of the Buddha's teachings (*dharma*) ([2], pp. 511–514). Discourses that focused on categorical lists of topics subject to analytical discernment (*prajñā*) developed into the Abhidharma literature as well as the *Prajñāpāramitā*. Early *Prajñāpāramitā* discourses asserted the excellence or perfection (*pāramitā*) of *prajñā* in relation to a luminous nonconceptual mind that attains an omniscient cognition synonymous with Buddhahood. The early discourses also assert that one courses in the *Prajñāpāramitā* while practicing a concentration (*samādhi*) that does not grasp at anything at all (*sarvadharmāparigṛhīta*) ([3], pp. 80, 81). This may signify that the discourses on *Prajñāpāramitā* may go back to practices among bhikṣus who dwell without strife (*araṇavihārin*) and who avoid conceptional determinations, as embodied in the figure of the Buddha's disciple Subhūti ([4], p. 72).

The exact geographical region for the beginnings of the *Prajñāpāramitā* literature and its practices in India is unknown. Edward Conze (1904–1979), the foremost modern scholar on *Prajñāpāramitā*, advocated for the origins of the *Prajñāpāramitā* among early monastic lineages of the Mahāsaṃghikas in Southern India, in the Andhra country on the Kṛṣṇā river ([5], pp. 10, 11). Étienne Lamotte (1903–1983), an eminent Belgian Indologist, argued for the origins of the *Prajñāpāramitā* in northwest South Asia and Central Asia ([6], p. 386). The idea of the *Prajñāpāramitā* having its beginnings in the south is indicated in several Mahāyāna Buddhist scriptures. The *Aṣṭasahāsrikā* (8,000 verse) *Prajñāpāramitā* (p. 225) states that "after the passing away of the *Tathāgata*" the perfection of wisdom will "proceed to the South." Also the *Mañjuśrīmūlatantra* specifies four regions for the recitation of various Mahāyāna Sūtras with the *Prajñāpāramitā* to be recited in the South ([5], p. 11]. This theory of the southern origin of the *Prajñāpāramitā* is complementary to the traditional Mahāyāna Buddhist historical accounts followed by indigenous Buddhist scholars. They trace the origins of the *Prajñāpāramitā* scriptures to the second major cycle of teachings taught by the Buddha himself in the fifth or sixth century B.C.E. These scriptures are said to have been lost in India until they were rediscovered by the legendary mystic sage Nāgārjuna in about the first century C.E. in southern India [7].

The *Prajñāpāramitā* Literature

Edward Conze distinguished four phases in the historical development of the *Prajñāpāramitā* literature, stretching over more than a thousand years ([5], pp. 1–25). The first phase lasted from about 100 B.C.E. to 100 C.E. with the elaboration of a basic root text. The earliest text of the *Prajñāpāramitā* has been theorized to be the *Aṣṭasāhasrikā* (8,000 verse) *Prajñāpāramitā* [8]. The earliest extant edition of the *Aṣṭasāhasrikā* is preserved in the Chinese translation of the Indo-scythian translator Lokakṣema, the *Daoxing Banruo Jing* 道行般若經 in 179 C.E. [9] A significant development in modern Buddhist Studies is a recently discovered Gāndhārī manuscript dating to the first century which appears to be a Gāndhārī *Prajñāpāramitā* (G. *prañaparamida*) that compares in form and content with Lokakṣema's translation [10, 11]. Fragments of the *Aṣṭasāhasrikā* have also been recovered from Bāmiyān which date back to the Kuṣāṇa period. An initial study of these manuscripts indicates that the *Aṣṭasāhasrikā* existed in multiple recensions at an early stage in its history [12]. During the following 200 years after the initial development of the *Prajñāpāramitā,* the basic text of the *Aṣṭasāhasrikā* was expanded in varying lengths comprising a textual family that scholars call the "Larger *Prajñāpāramitā*" consisting of redactions of size ranging from the *Aṣṭādaśasāhasrikā* (18,000 verse) and *Pañcaviṃśatisāhasrika* (25,000 verse) up to the *Śatasāhasrikā* (100,000 verse) *Prajñāpāramitā* [13].

The subsequent 200 years of *Prajñāpāramitā* development, lasting until about 500 C.E., consisted of a period of contraction in which the basic ideas of *Prajñāpāramitā* were distilled into shorter sūtras on the one hand, and versified summaries on the other. The best known among such smaller sūtras are the *Vajracchedikā* (commonly "Diamond sūtra") and the *Prajñāpāramitāhṛdaya* (commonly "Heart sūtra"). The *Vajracchedikā*, perhaps dating from the early third century, has been translated and studied in nine published editions. The earliest preserved Indic manuscripts date from the sixth and seventh centuries and come from Bāmiyān and Northern Pakistan. The *Vajracchedikā* was translated into Chinese, Khotanese, Sogdian, and Tibetan. Kumārajīva's *Jingang boruo bolumi jing* 金剛般若波羅蜜經 (translated 402 C.E.) is the earliest among the six extant Chinese translations [14]. The *Prajñāpāramitāhṛdaya* is one of the most cherished of Buddhist scriptures and is recited daily among Mahāyāna Buddhists in China, Tibet, and Japan. The "Heart sūtra" exists in a long and short version with Sanskrit manuscripts preserved from Japan, Tibet, and Nepal [15]. The text was also translated numerous times into Chinese, Khotanese, Sogdian, Uighur, and Tibetan. The smallest of contracted *Prajñāpāramitā* scriptures is the *Ekākṣarāmātānāma-sarvatathāgata* whose doctrinal content consists of just one letter "A." Technical digests (*śāstra*) on *Prajñāpāramitā* were also composed during this time period. Two of the more well known among such commentaries are the *Mahāprajñāpāramitāśāstra* and *Abhisamayālaṃkāra*. The *Mahāprajñāpāramitāśāstra*, attributed to Nāgārjuna and preserved in Kumārajīva's Chinese translation, the *Dazhidulun* 大智度論, is an enormous commentary on the "Larger Prajñāpāramitā" [16]. The most famous versified summary is the *Abhisamayālaṃkāra*, the "Ornament for Clear Realization," which is attributed to the bodhisattva Maitreya [17].

The final period of *Prajñāpāramitā* development, from 600 to 1200 C.E., coincided with the emergence of Tantric forms of Buddhism that emphasized the ritual use of *Prajñāpāramitā* texts and cultivated visualizations of *Prajñāpāramitā* as a hypostasized deity with attributes. In this period of literature, texts such as the *Prajñāpāramitānayasatapañcaśatikā* ("The 150 methods") begin to contain Tantric terms like *vajra*, *guhya*, and *siddhi*. The literature at this time also shows signs of hypostatizing the qualities of *Prajñāpāramitā* into a wisdom goddess (*prajñā*). This is evident in the *Prajñāpāramitānāmāṣṭaśataka* ("The 108 qualities") and the *Prajñāpāramitāstrotra* ("Hymn to the Goddess") [18]. Texts for constructing *maṇdalas*, like the *Prajñāpāramitāmaṇḍalavidhi*, are also prevalent. But in terms of the anthropomorphic characteristics of the goddess *Prajñāpāramitā*, the *sādhanas* preserved in the *Sādhanamālā* and the Tibetan Buddhist canon are most important. These are invocation texts which describe the proper methods for visualizing the goddess and experiencing direct communion with her. After this third period, around 1200 C.E., the presence of *Prajñāpāramitā* as scripture or religious praxis dissipates due to the institutional disappearance of Buddhism from the land of India. The huge corpus of literature on *Prajñāpāramitā*, ranging from dialectical discourses on nonconceptual discernment to the invocation of her in the form of a goddess, represents a complex religious and philosophic ideology that forms the basis of a great amount of Mahāyāna Buddhist literature.

Prajñāpāramitā **Doctrine**

Prajñāpāramitā was the insight or wisdom that constituted Omniscient cognition (*sarvajñatā*) and was identified with the end itself, perfect awakening (*saṃbodhi*). *Prajñāpāramitā* was considered to be non-dual (*advaya*) awareness that was beyond all thought constructions (*vikalpa*) permeated with insight that was absolutely pure (*atyantaviśuddhi*), neither born nor extinguished (*anutpādānirodha*), and imperishable (*akṣaya*). *Prajñāpāramitā* was *nirvāṇa*, *tathatā* ("suchness"), luminous *citta* ("mind"), and *buddhatā* ("buddhahood"). It was unattainable (*anupalabdha*), unthinkable (*acintya*), and beyond grasp (*aparāmṛiṣṭā*), yet it was seeing things just as they are, in their suchness (*yathābhūtatā*) ([19], pp. 159, 160). In this sense, *Prajñāpāramitā* was generally regarded as exclusively teaching the realization of emptiness (*śūnyatā*), the reality of the essencelessness of things (*dharmanairatyma*) and of people (*pudgalanairatyma*).

The teaching of the *Prajñāpāramitā* consisted in defining the essence of Bodhisattva-hood through the practices of the six virtues of perfection (*pāramitā*): (1) *dānapāramitā* (generosity), (2) *śīlapāramitā* (discipline), (3) *kṣāntipāramitā* (patience), (4) *vīryapāramitā* (effort), (5) *dhyānapāramitā* (concentration), and the most important, (6) *Prajñāpāramitā* (wisdom). The sūtras of the *Prajñāpāramitā* regarded *prajñā* as the directing principle of the other five virtues.

For without *prajñā*, the other five perfections are like a group of lost blind people. In this practice and philosophy, *Prajñā* was singled out and given the highest prominence. The denotation of the word *pāramitā* as applied to *Prajñā* is that "She is called *pāramitā*, because she arrives at the other shore (*pāra*) of the ocean of insight, because she arrives at the extremity (*anta*) of all the insights and attains the summit (*niṣṭhāgata*)" ([20], p. 1066). Alternatively, the Tibetan translation of *Prajñāpāramitā* is *shes-rab-kyi pha-rol-tu-phyin pa*. Scholars interpret it to mean wisdom (*prajñā*, *ses-rab*) which has gone (Sanskrit *ita*, Tibetan *phying pa*) to the other (Sanskrit *pāram*, Tibetan *pha-rol*) shore; that is, gone away from suffering and imperfection to the other shore of perfectly blissful and awakened liberation ([21], p. 166).

The late Indian Mahāyāna Buddhist scholastic tradition admitted only two kinds of fundamental interpretations of the *Prajñāpāramitā*, the Mādhyamika treatises of Nāgārjuna that elucidated the direct subject matter of the *Prajñāpāramitā Sūtras*, the teaching of the emptiness (*śūnyatā*) of all the elements of existence, and the interpretation of the *Abhisamayālaṃkāra* and its commentators, who found a hidden or implicit meaning (Tibetan *sbas-don*) in the *Prajñāpāramitā* indicating the cognitions and realizations (*abhisamaya*) of ultimate reality and the stages of the path (*mārga*) leading to the attainment of Buddhahood and final *Nirvāṇa* [22]. Along with these two main doctrinal interpretations, the Mahāyāna scholastic tradition used the term *prajñāpāramita* in reference to several different meanings. These different usages of *prajñāpāramitā* are stated in Dignāga's *Prajñāpāramitārthasaṃgraha*: (a) the highest wisdom personified as the Buddha in his *dharmakāya* aspect, and free from the differentiation of subject and object (*grāhya-grāhaka)*; (b) the Path leading to the attainment of this wisdom; and (c) the sūtras, or scriptures, containing the teaching which is conducive to the former two. Sometimes a fourth aspect is added, as essence (*svabhāva*, *rang bzhin*). In this case, the "essential" *Prajñāpāramitā* is emptiness, the essence, or final nature of all phenomena. Of the three, the first meaning of *Prajñāpāramitā* is the direct sense of the word, whereas the Path and the text are likewise designated by the name *Prajñāpāramitā*, as being the factors bringing about the attainment of the highest knowledge ([23], p. 7).

This attainment of the highest knowledge as *Prajñāpāramitā* was considered by the *Abhisamayālaṃkāra* and its commentators to consist of three kinds of omniscience. These three are the omniscient knowledge of all the objects of the empirical world (*sarvajñatā*), the omniscience in regard to knowing all the paths of salvation for the benefit of sentient beings (*mārgajñatā*), and the special omniscience of a Buddha, which is the knowledge of all the aspects of existence as being devoid of an independent separate reality (*sarvākārajñatā*) ([24], p. 58).

The *Prajñāpāramitā*, as manifesting itself in these three forms of omniscience, was glorified as the "mother" (*matṛ/yum*) of the *śrāvakas*, *Bodhisattvas*, and *Buddhas*. The name "mother" is given to the three kinds of wisdom, because each of them is like a mother that aids her child (the *ś rāvaka* or *Bodhisattva*) in the realization of the desired aim and a mother that fosters the virtuous elements in the spiritual streams of the practitioners. *Prajñāpāramitā* was also considered the mother of the different spiritual types of practitioners because she is their cause. Just as the mother is one of the two principal causes of a child, so too is wisdom (*prajñā*) one of the two chief causes of awakening. The other cause was skillful means (*upāya*). Just as a mother must bear the child in her womb for ten (lunar) months, the traditional gestation period, so too does wisdom nurture the adept along the way through the ten *bhūmis*, the stages of the bodhisattva path. Here, in this case, it was the gestation in the mother wisdom's womb that brings about the birth of awakened beings. Therefore, whether viewed as a scripture, spiritual state of mind, the goal of enlightenment, or emptiness, *Prajñāpāramitā* in the Mahāyāna Buddhist scholastic tradition was identified not only as a feminine force but as a mother, a source that produced Buddhahood ([25], p. 185).

Worship of *Prajñāpāramitā*

The expansion of the *Prajñāpāramitā* literature into texts containing thousands of verses was the result of the veneration of *Prajñāpāramitā* as a progenitor for the omniscience qualifying Buddhahood. The merits of worshipping *Prajñāpāramitā* were thought to exceed the veneration of a Buddha, Buddha relics, or a reliquary monument (*stūpa*), as she was the real source of a Buddha's omniscience. Quite early in the development of this set of discourses, *Prajñāpāramitā* was not only venerated as subtle Buddhist teachings, but the *Prajñāpāramitā* manuscripts themselves, in the form of books (*pustaka*), were to be worshipped as material objects that conferred sanctity [26]. The 8,000-verse *Prajñāpāramitā* in many places recommends the writing, reading, reciting, contemplating, copying, and distributing of the text as a powerful source of religious merit ([27], pp. 107, 108, 116, 117, 266, 267). Here, the "sons or daughters of good family" are enjoined to put up a copy of the *Prajñāpāramitā* on an altar, and to pay respect to it, to revere, worship and adore it, and pay regard and reverence to it with flowers, incense, powders, umbrellas, banners, bells, and rows of burning lamps ([27], p. 299). In this way, practitioners "study it prayerfully and venerate its visible symbol, the scriptural text, through traditional modes of worship, thereby absorbing its subtle energy more fully and directly, as nourishment is absorbed into the bloodstream" ([28], p. 22).

With the beginnings of the devotion to and worship of the *Prajñāpāramitā* texts themselves, the hypostasis of *Prajñāpāramitā* as a feminine deity with attributes developed as well. Her characterization as the "Mother of the Buddhas" in the scholastic sense of all-knowledge which produces Buddhahood carried meaning in the devotional aspect of her worship. The *Prajñāpāramitāstrotra* ("Hymn to the Goddess") described her as having a faultless body that is unclothed like space and that she was like meeting the light of the moon. In this praise, *Prajñāpāramitā* was called the sole mother, herself being the single path of liberation ([29], pp. 147–149). Personification, together with the worship of the texts themselves prepared the foundation for *Prajñāpāramitā* to become a female deity with attributes.

Tantric Developments

Although *Prajñāpāramitā* was personified as a mother, teacher, and guide for giving rise to Buddhahood, her iconographic forms did not develop, as based on written and archeological evidence, until the seventh century during the sociocultural era of the Pāla dynastic period. Previous doctrines and qualities of personification were incorporated into the ethos of the Buddhist Tantric developments. As previously mentioned, *Prajñāpāramitā* was a feminine power and archetype that arose in relation to the Buddha's doctrine of emptiness (*śūnyatā*) and dependent co-arising (*pratītyasamutpādā*) that presented a non-substantial (*niḥsvabhāvatā*) and non-dichotomous (*advaya*) view of reality. This view cognized reality as co-emergent and codependent with mind, allowing for no polarization of consciousness and nature or other dichotomies. Faith and insight in *Prajñāpāramitā* meant letting go of conceptual thinking and attachment and gaining meditative cognition of luminous space-like awareness, which was construed as possessing omniscient knowledge and was imperishable. These cultural understandings of *Prajñāpāramitā* were carried over into the sociocultural developments of Buddhist Tantra.

In Buddhist Tantrism, *Prajñāpāramitā* represented the prototype and essence of all the female figures in Tantric interplay [30]. In Tantric meditations *prajñā* was explicitly identified with *nirvāṇa* and *upāya* (means) with *saṃsāra*. Ultimate reality was described in the Tantras as the union (*yuganaddha*) of wisdom and means. The conjunction of means and wisdom was held to be indispensable for obtaining the state of Buddhahood. In ritual and meditational practices, *prajñā* was symbolized by a bell (*ghanta*), a lotus (*padma*), or a sun (*sūrya*), as well as by the vowels of the Sanskrit alphabet (*āli*). *Upāya* was symbolized by a *vajra*, moon (*candra*), or Sanskrit consonants (*kāli*). In yogic ritual practices involving a female partner, *prajñā* was identified with a *yoginī* (female yogin). In the union of *prajñā* and *upāya*, it was *prajñā* which played a dominant role, for even though the state of Buddhahood was unattainable without means, it was *prajñā* that embraced the highest reality of emptiness (*śūnyatā*) [31]. In the Tantric texts, a synonym of female *prajñā* was *Nairātmyā* ("selflessness"), and it was with a female *prajñā* that a Tantric practitioner, as *upāya*, united.

In Buddhist Tantric meditational practices, deities such as *Prajñāpāramitā* were evoked from seed-mantras (*bīja*) and were mentally cultivated in visible form. Incorporating the philosophy of *śūnyatā* from the *Prajñāpāramitā* literature, Tantrists held that one could dissolve one's individuality into essencelessness and reconstitute one's identity as a visualized Buddhist deity empowered with awakened qualities and characteristics. The idea was that if a practitioner could identify themselves with a Tantric deity, they could absorb the empowered forces and characteristics of the deity and come closer to awakening. The Tantric meditational liturgies used to perform these practices were known as *sādhanas* (Tibetan *sgrub thabs*, literally "means of achievement") [32]. The Tantric practitioner who performed these rites was called a *sādhaka* or *siddha*, "one who has power." *Sādhanas* guided a Tantric practitioner's efforts to imagine magnificent panoramas, to visualize superhuman beings, and to perform correct ritual utterances (*mantra*), gestures (*mudrā*), and other ritual activities with the aim of achieving Buddhahood. The complex mental, verbal, and physical practices prescribed constituted a practice known as "deity yoga" (*devatā yoga*). The deity yoga practices of *Prajñāpāramitā* are mainly preserved in the *Sādhanamālā*.

The *Sādhanamālā* (before 1100 C.E.) has preserved nine *sādhanas* for the invocation of the goddess *Prajñāpāramitā* and an additional one attributed to Kamalaśīla is contained in the Tibetan Buddhist canon. *Prajñāpāramitā* as envisioned in these instruction manuals was most often golden in color, although she appeared in white as well. She appeared with either two or four arms. She was imagined as having one face and all the ornamental characteristics of a goddess (Tibetan *lha mo'i mtsan nyid thams cad yongs su rdzogs pa*), including a jeweled diadem, bracelets, and earrings. *Prajñāpāramitā* was visualized seating in the diamond posture (*vajraparyaṅkasthāḥ*), a posture that represented a level of concentration (*samādhi*), which, like a diamond that cuts through all substances, cuts through all delusions of dualistic thinking. The symbolism employed in these sādhana visualizations involved ritual gestures (*mudrā*), attributes, and implements that correlated with awakened qualities. *Prajñāpāramitā* was often depicted in the ritual gesture of teaching (*dharmacakramudrā*, *vyākhyānamudrā*), which symbolized the "turning of the wheel of Dharma," and expressed the fact that *Prajñāpāramitā* had the central function of giving exposition to the Buddha's doctrine. The gesture of argument (*vitarkamudrā*), with the hand raised and the ring finger touching the tip of the thumb, was a symbol of the dialectic method of the *Prajñāpāramitā Sūtras* to shake the hearer of all logical preconceptions and dualistic thinking, allowing insight into nonconceptual (*nirvikalpa*) and non-dual awareness (*advayajñāna*). The gesture of fearlessness (*abhayamudrā*), with the arm raised and the palm turned outward, correlated to two aspects of *Prajñāpāramitā*. First, *Prajñāpāramitā* was known as the supreme source of protection and, second, the absence of all fear was thought be a sign that the teachings of *Prajñāpāramitā* had been understood and cognized. *Prajñāpāramitā* was visualized and depicted with numerous attributes and implements. Foremost was the pan-Buddhist symbol of the lotus, either in blue (*utpala* flower) or red (*padma*) color, that signified purity. Next, *Prajñāpāramitā* often appeared holding a book (*pustaka*) of the *Prajñāpāramitā* scripture itself. Usually held in the left hand (*vamahaste*), the book symbolized the teachings of the *Prajñāpāramitā sūtras* [33].

Besides cultivating the presence of *Prajñāpāramitā* by the means of *sādhanas*, the ethos of the Tantric literature represents *Prajñāpāramitā* with an uncompromising attitude of respect and veneration of the feminine in human form. In this practice, all women were considered embodiments of *Prajñāpāramitā*, being emanations of her divine qualities. This form of reverence is found in a statement by the Tantric siddha *Lakṣmīṅkarā* in her *Adhvayasiddhi* saying:

> One must not denigrate women,
> In whatever social class they are born,
> For they are Lady Perfection of Wisdom (*Prajñāpāramitā*),
> Embodied in the phenomenal realm. ([34], p. 39)

Prajñāpāramitā Outside of South Asia

Prajñāpāramitā was cultivated and worshipped in India until the close of Buddhism in the late twelfth century. By that time, the literature and practices associated with *Prajñāpāramitā* had spread into Nepal, Tibet, Central Asia, and East Asia. *Prajñāpāramitā* had a profound effect on the development of Buddhist thought in Chinese forms of Buddhism. Throughout premodern Japanese history, *Prajñāpāramitā* texts were ceremoniously recited under royal sponsorship to avert calamities. Ritual and meditation practices that focus on *Prajñāpāramitā* are current in both Tibetan and Nepalese forms of Buddhism. In Tibetan forms of Buddhism, *Prajñāpāramitā* is known as "wisdom mother" (*sher-phyin-ma*) or "the Great Mother" (*yum chen mo*) [26]. All Tibetan schools and orders study the *Prajñāpāramitā* and cultivate her visualization practices in some form. Machig Labdron (1055–1153 C.E.) was thought to be a living embodiment of *Prajñāpāramitā* and developed a distinctive lineage of practice "cutting off" (*gcod*) that cultivated a non-dual and selfless realization of *Prajñāpāramitā* utilizing rituals containing Tantric factors fused with exorcistic elements [35]. In Nepal, the veneration of *Prajñāpāramitā* takes place through the ritual recitation and worship of *Prajñāpāramitā* manuscripts in which the goddess is able to channel blessings that produce religious merit, cure illnesses, and gain success in worldly affairs [36]. In sum, *Prajñāpāramitā* was a distinctive feminine force throughout the history of Buddhism that produced an astonishing amount of literature, ritual practices, and distinct cultural religious formations.

Cross-References

▶ Abhidharma (Theravāda)
▶ Aṣṭasāhasrikāprajñāpāramitā
▶ Bodhisattva
▶ Mahāyāna
▶ Upāya
▶ Vajrachhedika
▶ Vajrayāna (Buddhism)

References

1. Waymen A (1984) Nescience and insight according to Asaṅga's Yogācārabhūmi. In: Elder G (ed) Buddhist insight, Motilal Banarsidass, New Delhi, pp 193–214
2. Migot A (1954) Un grand disciple du Buddha: Sâriputra. Son rôle dans l'histoire du bouddhisme et dans le développement de l'Abhidharma. In: Bulletin de l'Ecole française d'Extrême-Orient. Tome 46, pp 405–554
3. Verboom A (1998) A text-comparative research on "The Perfection of Discriminating Insight in Eight Thousand Lines, Chapter I." PhD dissertation, Leiden
4. Vetter T (2001) Once again on the origin of Mahāyāna Buddhism. Wiener Zeischrift fur die Kunde Südasiens 45:59–90
5. Conze E (1960) The Prajnāpāramitā literature. Mouton, 's-Gravenhage
6. Lamotte É (1954) Sur la formation du Mahāyāna. In: Asiatica: festchrift Friedrich Weller, zum 65. Otto Harrassowitz, Leipzig, pp 377–396
7. Venkata Ramanan K (1966) Nāgārjuna's Philosophy as presented in the Mahā-prajnāpāramitā-śāstra. Charles E. Tuttle, Tokyo
8. Lancaster L (1975) The oldest Mahayana sutra. East Buddh 8:30–41
9. Harrison PM (1993) The earliest Chinese translations of Mahayana Buddhist sutras: some notes on the works of Lokaksema. Buddh Stud Rev 10(2):135–177
10. Karashima (2010) A glossary of Lokaksema's translation of the Astasāhasrikā Prajnāpāramitā. International Research Institute for Advanced Buddhology, Soka University, Tokyo
11. Falk H (2011) The 'Split' collection of Kharoṣṭhī texts. Sōka daigaku kokusai bukkyōgaku kōtō kenkyūjo nenpō 創価大学国際仏教学高等研究所年報 14.13–23
12. Sander L (2000) Fragments of an Aṣṭasāhasrikā manuscript from the Kuṣāṇa period. In: Braarvig J (ed) Buddhist manuscripts (Oslo 2000), vol 1, Hermes Publishing, Oslo
13. Zacchetti S (2005) In praise of the light: a critical synoptic edition with an annotated translation of chapters 1–3 of Dharmarakṣa's Guang zan jing, being the earliest Chinese translation of the Larger

Prajñāpāramitā. The International Research Institute for Advanced Buddhology, Soka University, Tokyo
14. Harrison P (2006) Vajracchedikā Prajñāpāramitā: a new English translation of the Sanskrit text based on two manuscripts from greater Gandhāra. In: Braarvig J, Harrison P, Hartmann J-U, Matsuda K, Sander L (eds) Buddhist manuscripts in the Schøyen collection. Hermes, Oslo
15. Conze E (1948) Text, sources, and bibliography of the Prajnñāpāramitā-hṛdaya. J Roy Asiatic Soc (New Series) 80:33–51
16. Lamotte É (1944–1980) Le Traité de la Grande Vertu de Sagesse de Nāgārjuna, vols I–V. Institut Orientaliste, Louvain
17. Sparham G (2006–2009) Abhisamayālaṃkāra with Vṛtti and Ālokā, 3 vols. Jain, California
18. Conze E (2002) Perfection of wisdom: the short Prajñāpāramitā texts. Buddhist Publishing Group, Totnes
19. Frauwallner E, Sangpo L (2010) The philosophy of Buddhism = Die philosophie des Buddhismus. Motilal Banarsidass, New Delhi
20. Lamotte É (1949) Le Traité de la Grande Vertu de Sagesse de Nāgārjuna, vols II. Institut Orientaliste, Louvain
21. Dayal H (1970) The Bodhisattva doctrine in Buddhist Sanskrit literature. Motilal Banarsidass, Delhi
22. Apple JB (2008) Stairway to Nirvāṇa: a study of the twenty Saṃghas based on the works of Tsong Kha Pa. State University of New York Press, Albany
23. Obermiller E (1984) The doctrine of Prajñā-pāramitā as exposed in the Abhisamayālaṃkāra of Maitreya. Canon, Talent
24. Obermiller E, Sobatī HS (1988) Prajñāpāramitā in Tibetan Buddhism. Classics India, Delhi
25. Cabezón JI (1992) Buddhism, sexuality, and gender. State University of New York Press, Albany
26. Shaw ME (2006) Buddhist goddesses of India. Princeton University Press, Princeton
27. Conze E (1973) The perfection of wisdom in eight thousand lines & its verse summary. Four Seasons Foundation, Bolinas; distributed by Book People, Berkeley
28. Hixon L (1993) Mother of the Buddhas: meditation on the Prajnaparamita sutra. Quest Books, Wheaton
29. Conze E (1964) Buddhist texts through the ages. Harper and Row, New York
30. Snellgrove DL (1957) Buddhist Himalaya. Philosophical Library, New York
31. Wayman A (1962) Female energy and symbolism in the Buddhist Tantras. Hist Relig 2(1):73–111
32. Cozort D (1996) Sādhana (sgrub thabs): means of achievement for deity yoga. In: Tibetan literature, studies in genre, Snow Lion, Ithaca, pp 331–343
33. Conze E (1949) On the iconography of the Prajñāpāramitā. Orient Art 3:47–52; 3(1950–1951)
34. Shaw ME (1994) Passionate enlightenment: women in Tantric Buddhism. Princeton University Press, Princeton
35. Edou J (1996) Machig Labdrön and the Foundations of Chöd. Snow Lion, Ithaca
36. Gellner DN (1996) 'The Perfection of Wisdom' – a text and its uses in Kwā Bahā, Lalitpur. In: Lienhard S (ed) Change and continuity: studies in the Nepalese culture of the Kathmandu Valley. CESMEO, Turin, pp 223–240

Prajñāpāramitā-Hṛdaya Sūtra

► Heart Sūtra

Prajñapti-pada

► Puggalapaññatti

Prākrit

Sanjay Kr. Singh
Department of Buddhist Studies, University of Delhi, Delhi, India

Definition

The classical languages of Jaina texts and Sanskrit dramas.

Introduction

The term Prākrit (*prākṛta*) means "natural" and is used by grammarians as a general term to refer to all the languages of India, except Vedic and Sanskrit languages of the Old Indic. Western scholars have, however, narrowed the use of the term for only the Middle Indic or Middle Indo-Aryan languages. In this sense, Prākrit languages are those that came into existence and use after the Old Indic and prior to the modern vernaculars, which developed around 1000 C.E. Moreover, the Buddhist canonical language of Pāli is excluded from this definition, although it is a Middle Indic language.

Prākrit languages differ from Vedic and Sanskrit in several significant linguistic tendencies. Simplification of consonant clusters, use of simple vowels, general simplification of syllabic types, etc., can be seen in Prākrit languages. Morphologically, too, there have been simplifications which came gradually with time. It is believed that both the noun and the verb lost the dual number in the initial stages of development of Prākrit languages. Also, the system of noun was gradually simplified to two cases, an oblique and an absolute.

The verb morphology of the Vedic period was simplified in Sanskrit and was further cut down in Prākrit languages. There seems to be a great propensity to base the whole morphological system of any verb on the present tense. In contrast, in the Old Indic system, each tense and the passive participles showed separate types of formation.

During the periods between the Old Indic system and the onset of modern vernaculars, several Prākrit dialects developed. However, only a small number of them had a written form, and literatures were written in only a few of them.

The earliest records of Prākrit literatures are the inscriptions of the Mauryan emperor Aśoka written around third-century B.C.E. These inscriptions were written in three main varieties of dialect: northwestern, southwestern (Gujarat), and eastern. However, the later writings of the Hīnayāna or the southern school of Buddhists are chiefly in Pāli. But, the languages used by other Buddhist sects and local communities are in Prākrits. For instance, extensive fragments of an anthology of the type of the *Dhammapada* written in the northwestern type of Prākrit have been found in Ho-t'ien in China (ancient Khotan).

Buddhist Sanskrit (BS) is a language that came into being due to gradual Sanskritization of an original Prākrit language. Hence, this language has a similarity with Sanskrit and several important Buddhist texts, belonging to both the Hīnayāna and the Mahāyāna sects are in this language.

Ardhamāgadhī is another Prākrit language, which is a halfway speech between Śaurasenī, the upper Gaṅgā valley dialect, and the eastern Māgadhī. The canonical writings belonging to the Śvetāmbara sect of Jains are written in this language.

Jaina Mahārāṣṭrī is a Prākrit language in which later Jain works, epics, commentaries to the canon, etc., were written. This language owes its origin to the Mahārāṣṭrī language of the Marāthā country, which is considered as a southern Prākrit.

Jaina Śaurasenī is also a Prākrit language in which the Digambara sect of Jains wrote their scriptures. Actually, this language consists of various forms of Śaurasenī.

Apabhraṃśa is a later type of Prākrit language, and numerous Jain romances are written by various prolific writers over many genres.

Mahārāṣṭrī Prākrit was a language in which Brahmanical lyric love poetry developed. This poetry initially began as a popular form for poetry writing, but later on it was adopted and expanded by literary men. A good example of a poetry written in this language is the *Sattasai* (Seven Hundred Verses) of Hala (c. 200–450 C.E.). Besides poetry, verse epics were also written in this dialect. Pravarasena's *Setu-bandha* (Rama's Bridge; sixth-century C.E.) and Vakpati's *Gaudavaha* (The Slaying of the Gauda Prince; eighth-century C.E.) are two examples.

Paiśācī is another dialect of Prākrit languages in which a great novelistic tale *Bṛhatkathā* (Great Story; before 600 C.E.) was written by Guṇāḍhya. This work is, however, not available, and only three Sanskrit reworkings of it are found, two of them have been written as late as eleventh-century C.E.

All these Prākrit dialects have been used in the classical Indian drama. Scholars opine that originally all the dialects might have been not very far apart. In their attempt to be realistic, the dramatists of those periods would have made changes in the dialect with the passage of time, leading to a number of variations and dialects.

As soon as a dialect was begun to be used in literature, that particular dialect was cultivated for centuries as a literary language, generally on the basis of the descriptions laid down by grammarians. While the Middle Indic languages of the Jains and the Buddhists existed independently, the Prākrits of the Hindus were mere Prākrit versions of Sanskrit, translated as per the rules laid by grammarians.

In short, the Prākrit languages have been used by Brahmanical, Buddhist, and Jain writers. These languages are also found on numerous inscriptions and other nonliterary documents, especially those belonging to the period between third-century B.C.E. and fourth-century C.E.

Scholars of medieval India have used the word Prākrit in a restricted sense, and they include only the four most important literary Prākrits, while some scholars include the Dravidian languages in the Prākrit group of languages, which have many borrowed words of Indic languages. But, in general, the Indian scholars include only the Prākrits used by Hindu and Jain writers in their literature and exclude the languages used by Buddhist writers. They also sometimes exclude the Apabhraṃśa dialects.

The theory generally agreed about the birth of Prākrit languages is that the dialects different from Vedic and Sanskrit were existent, while those languages were still in use until roughly the fifth-century B.C.E. While the two literary languages became standardized and their usage remained unchanged in practice, the newly developing vernacular dialects continued to diverge. With the passage of time, spoken languages became different from the literary languages. These spoken languages were then progressively used by writers and thus began the literary cultivation of Prākrit languages.

The first literature to be written in Prākrit languages has not yet been ascertained, but the religious texts of the Jains and the Buddhists were among the earliest literature written in these languages. It is because the Buddha directed that his disciples teach in their own vernacular dialects. Thus, during the first few generations after the Buddha, many Middle Indic languages came to be used in Buddhist preaching. The availability of religious inscriptions belonging to Emperor Asoka in several Prākrit dialects is a testimony to this fact.

Over a period of time, the languages used for teaching also began to be used in literature owing to the gaining influence of Buddhist centers. Like Sanskrit, the teaching dialects also became standardized and started differing from the spoken vernaculars. Several of the Mahāyāna schools used a type of Prākrit for their voluminous literature.

This raised a difficulty in philosophical discourses with Brahmanism. As a result, Sanskrit came to be used by Buddhists leading to a partial Sanskritization of the verse texts and prose written in it. No pure examples of this form survive, and their geographical origin or chronology is also not known. But Sanskritized versions of these texts are found, and the language used in them is called Buddhist Sanskrit which seems to have originated in a more westerly Prākrit dialect, but it is still to be identified whether it was central or west central in the Gaṅgā valley. However, it is highly possible that there might have existed other Prākrits in the early centuries of Buddhism literatures than the known, Buddhist Sanskrit, Prākrit, and Pāli dialects.

Similarly, the Jain canonical texts can be found in various Prākrit languages. The literature of Digambara sect is found in Jain Śaurasenī, while that of Śvetāmbara sect is available in two dialects of Ardhamāgadhī. Then, there are the later texts like the commentaries on the canon and epics like Vimala Suri's *Paumacariya* that are found in Jain Mahārāṣṭrī.

In Brahmanical too, several Prākrit languages have been used, perhaps at the end of the pre-Christian era. Subsequently, Mahārāṣṭrī became quite popular and was particularly used in writing lyric poetry. This dialect is estimated to have begun to flourish during the third–fourth centuries C.E. *Sattasai*, the anthology by Hāla, is the most significant individual work of this kind.

The classical period of Sanskrit drama beginning with Kālidāsa used Mahārāṣṭrī in lyric verses. The epics of the *kāvya* were also composed in this dialect. Other important examples of literature in this dialect are the *Rāvaṇavaha* or *Setubandha*, the *Gauḍavaha*, and the last eight cantos of the poem *Dvyāśraya-mahākāvya*, the *Kumārapālacarita* written by Hemacandra in twelfth-century C.E. These cantos in Prākrit illustrate the Prākrit section of the grammar in Hemacandra's Sanskrit and Prākrit grammar, the *Siddha-hemaśabdānuśāsana*.

An important source for gaining information on Prākrit is the Sanskrit drama. Sanskrit, the literary language that is termed to be par excellence was spoken by educated men such as the kings, nobles, and the brahmans. They also sang in this language. All others spoke the vernacular languages, i.e., the Prākrit languages. Again, among the masses, the dialects differed from region to region and also on the basis of caste. As such, in Sanskrit dramas, one can come across people speaking different dialects, which would have been their own.

Slowly, however, the dialects in the dialogue began to be considered as appropriate, and they took rigid form as conventions started to harden. In Sanskrit dramas, one can find that most women, especially belonging to upper caste, speak Śaurasenī but sing in Mahārāṣṭrī. Śaurasenī is also spoken by some other characters in the drama like children and the brahman clown. Another vernacular, Māgadhī, is found to be spoken in the dramas by low-caste men, servants, and fishermen. There are other vernaculars that also appear in the Sanskrit drama. In fact, the appearance of these vernaculars in the Sanskrit drama gives credence to the theory that Prākrits were the spoken languages used by common men in their everyday activities. But, once the forms of dialects were prescribed according to characters by grammarians, it became a rule and the later dramas were composed adhering to the rule rather than using the living forms of speech.

There is also a mention of a Prākrit language called Paiśācī in works of some grammarians. It is believed that Guṇāḍhya's *Bṛhatkathā* was composed perhaps around the first or second-century C.E. in this dialect. This work is known through much later reworkings, especially Somadeva's *Kathāsaritsāgara* (eleventh-century C.E.), but unfortunately the Paiśācī text has not yet come to light.

Prākrit languages can also be found in nonliterary materials like early coin and stone inscriptions (third-century B.C.E. to fourth-century C.E.). The Aśokan inscriptions, of course, are the earliest nonliterary inscriptions of Prākrit languages. But, the materials obtained from Niya in Chinese Turkestan are the most interesting. Dating back to the third-century C.E., these are the official documents belonging to the Kroraina kingdom, and their Prākrit is similar to that found in *Dhammapada*. The original home of this Prākrit language was the region of Peshawar in northwest India, now in Pakistan. This unnamed Prākrit language was the literary and administrative language of the Kuṣāṇa Empire and its central Asiatic branches.

Scholars have been able to locate geographical area of some Prākrit languages with a certain degree of accuracy. Śaurasenī dialect was used in the region around the modern day Mathurā in Uttar Pradesh. This language was used in the Gangetic doab and extended eastward till the convergence of the rivers Yamunā and the Gaṅgā. Westward, it extended till Lahore in modern day Pakistan and also to Rajputana and Gujarat.

Māgadhī dialect was spoken in the area to the east of the place where the rivers Yamunā and the Gaṅgā converge, probably near Banaras or the modern day Varanasi in Uttar Pradesh. However, its eastern extent is yet to be ascertained by scholars.

Mahārāṣṭrī dialect was spoken in the Mahārāṣṭra (the great kingdom) region, south of the river Narmada. In modern times, Marathi is spoken in this geographical area.

Paiśācī dialect is estimated to have been spoken in the Vindhya region south of the Gaṅgā valley, but scholars have not located its geographical area as precisely as other dialects.

Out of the many Prākrit languages, Mahārāṣṭrī has been described at the greatest length by grammarians owing to its literary merit. This dialect has been described by Vararuci and Hemacandra, among others. Grammarians sketchily describe other Prākrits used in the dramas and also numerous other dialects which do not even appear in the literature. However, all these descriptions are generally made as deviations from Mahārāṣṭrī.

Over a period of time, the various Prākrits acquired standard literary form, but the vernaculars continued to change and thus slowly diverge from the standards. Again, the new vernaculars after sometime acquired literary forms. The best example of this type is the Apabhraṃśa, which means "downward departure (from speech)." The earliest reference to this language is found in the seventh-century C.E.

Western Apabhraṃśa belonged to the same region as the Śaurasenī. It is found in numerous texts such as Dhanavāla's *Bhavisattakaha* (tenth-century C.E.), Haribhadra's *Sanatkumāracaritam* (1159 C.E.), and Somaprabha's *Kumarapālapratibodha* (1195 C.E.). Majority of the writings in this language are by Jain authors.

Southern Apabhraṃśa belonged to the same region as the Mahārāṣṭrī. Similarly, eastern Apabhraṃśa belonged to the region where Māgadhī was used.

The Apabhraṃśa dialects are thus the immediate predecessors of the modern languages. These languages existed as late as the twelfth-century C.E. However, the relations between the modern languages and the Apabhraṃśa dialects are not very clearly available.

Characterization of the Languages

The Middle Indic languages depict a progressive change from the Old Indo-Aryan languages. (Sanskrit = Sanskrit; Śaurasenī = Śaurasenī; Mahārāṣṭrī = Mahārāṣṭrī).

Phonetic change is clearly noticeable as the complex consonant clusters of Sanskrit are simplified, most frequently by assimilations or losses and sometimes by insertions of vowels, e.g., *putra* "son" > *putta*, *ratna* "jewel" > Śaurasenī *radana*, Māgadhī *ladana*. Stop consonants between vowels were liable to many types of changes. Voiceless stops (*k*, *t*, *p*) remained in Pāli, became voiced (*g*, *d*, *v*) in some dialects, e.g., Śaurasenī and Apabhraṃśa, but were lost in Mahārāṣṭrī, e.g., Sanskrit *śata* "100" > Pāli *sata*, Śaurasenī *sada*, Mahārāṣṭrī *saa*. The cumulative effect of all changes was to produce words which are very far from their Sanskrit origins, e.g., Vāppairāa = Sanskrit *Vākpatirāja* "king Vākpati"; *prākṛta* "Prākrit" > Śaurasenī *pāuda*, Mahārāṣṭrī *pāua*.

Noun morphology becomes simplified with progress of time, e.g., by loss of the dual number. The eight-case system of Sanskrit got reduced by loss and amalgamation of cases. In some dialects, dative forms were completely lost, and syntactically the dative merges with the genitive. In feminine stems in ā, the instrumental, genitive, and locative singular have identical forms. In the Apabhraṃśa stage, case declension moved further toward the modern vernacular system of only two cases, absolute and oblique. The system of three genders remained intact in early Prākrits, but in Apabhraṃśa, masculine and neuter genders almost merged. The several declensional types of Sanskrit are somewhat decreased in number. In the consonantal stems, particularly tend to add vowels and merge with the vocalic declensions.

Verb conjugation in Prākrit languages shows even greater departures from the Sanskrit system. With some minor exceptions, the Sanskrit consonantal conjugation was replaced in Prākrit by the conjugation type in which a vowel appears between the final consonant of the root or stem and the inflectional suffix. In Middle Indic languages, the vowel is often *-a-* as in Sanskrit, but there has been a great extension of use also of *-e-*, which derives from *-aya-* of the Sanskrit causative and denominative conjugations.

The causative stem, on the other hand, often had a suffix *-ve-*, in which *v* represents Sanskrit *p*, which appears in only a few verbs in Sanskrit exceptional remnants of the Sanskrit consonantal conjugation including the highly irregular enclitic verb "to be," (e.g., *mhi* "I am" (< *asmi*), *si* you are (< *asi*)); the third person singular form *atthi* (< *asti*) is not enclitic.

In the Prākrit dialects, very little remains of the past tenses, except such forms as *āsī* "was, were" (< *āsīt*). The present tense has an imperative and an optative. The future tense remains usually formed with a suffix *-issa-* or *-ihi-* (< Sanskrit *–iṣya-*) added to the present stem. Passive stems either derive from Sanskrit passive stems, with Sanskrit *-y-* appearing in Mahārāṣṭrī as *-jj-* (e.g., *dijjai* "it is given" < Sanskrit *dīyate*), or add a suffix (Śaurasenī *-ia-*, Mahārāṣṭrī *-ijja-*) to the present stem.

In the Prākrit languages, gerunds, infinitives, gerundives, and three participles – all survive with many phonetic and other changes. Most important, however, is the past participle, which is active in intransitive verbs and passive in transitive verbs. Syntactically, it occurs most frequently with an instrumental case of a noun to replace the old past tense and its subject. In fact, this is the precursor of the peculiar past tense of modern languages.

Very frequently, the past participle shows a suffix Śaurasenī *-ida-*, Mahārāṣṭrī *-ia-* (< Sanskrit *-ita-*) added to the present stem. This part of the verb system shows more irregularities of form than any other, because of inheritance of old forms from Sanskrit, e.g., Śaurasenī *gada-*, Mahārāṣṭrī *gaa-* "gone" (< Sanskrit *gata-*) beside present stem *gacch-;* Śaurasenī *kida-*, Mahārāṣṭrī *kaa-* "made" (< Sanskrit *kṛta-*) beside present stem *kar-;* Śaurasenī *nāda-*, Mahārāṣṭrī *ṇāa-* "known" (< Sanskrit *jñāta-*) beside present stem *jān-*.

Thus, the vocabulary of Prākrit is in general derived from Old Indic languages of Vedic and Sanskrit, but there are also many words that are not so derivable. These words are called Deśī or "provincial" words, and the Indian grammarians have made a list of such words.

Cross-References

- ▶ Dhammapada
- ▶ Mathurā
- ▶ Pāli

References

1. Banerjee SR (1977) The Eastern School of Prakrit Grammarians: a linguistic study. Vidyasagar Pustak Mandir, Calcutta
2. Bhandarkar RG (1999) Sanskrit and the derived language. Motilal Banarsidass, Delhi
3. Chatterji SK (1953) Introduction to Indo-Aryan. Calcutta University, Calcutta
4. Pischel R, Grammar of the Prakrit languages (Eng. Trans. Jha Subhadra). Motilal Publishers, New York
5. Sen S (1960) A comparative grammar of middle Indo-Aryan. Deccan College, Poona
6. Winternitz M (1977) A history of Indian literature, reprint, vol II. Munshiram Manoharlal, New Delhi
7. Woolner AC (1996) Introduction to Prakrit, reprint. Motilal Banarsidass, Delhi

Pranidhāna

▶ Mantra

Prātimokṣa

▶ Pātimokkha

Pratītya Samutpāda

▶ Middle Way (Buddhism)

Pratyeka-Buddha

Shanker Thapa
Faculty of Buddhist Studies, Lumbini Buddhist University, Lumbini Rupandehi, Nepal

Synonyms

Pacceka-Buddha; Solitary Buddha

Definition

Pratyeka-buddha or solitary Buddha is one who has attained enlightenment without the benefit of a teacher, but he does not proclaim this truth to the world. Pratyeka-buddha is the Buddhist model of spiritual life. He wanders like rhinoceros.

The early Buddhist schools referred to three vehicles to attain enlightenment, Śrāvakayāna, the vehicle of the Arhat (Pali: Arahant) to be taken by the greatest number of disciples, and Pratyekabuddhayāna, the vehicle of the solitary practitioners who attain realization without the help of a spiritual teacher. They do not teach to others, and the Bodhisattvayāna, the vehicle of the aspirants to Buddhahood. Puggalapaññatti, an

Abhidhamma text in Pāli canon, mentions about the hierarchy of nine individuals with different kinds of attainments thereby providing definition of the Pratyeka-buddha. According to it, among the nine individuals, the first three are Samyaksambuddha, Pratyeka-buddha, and Srāvaka. Another classification occurring in the Pāli commentarial literature speaks of four kinds of Buddhas: the omniscient Buddha, the Pratyeka-buddha, the Four Noble Truths Buddha, and the learned Buddha. Pratyeka-buddha is one who, like the Buddha, attained enlightenment without the support of a spiritual teacher. In this way, he is someone who has thoroughly realized the truth concerning all dhammas which he had never known before. Pratyekabodhisattva lives the life of an ascetic and dedicates himself to meditation practices. The aspirant for Pratyekabodhi has to make every effort to reach the goal through the practice of meditation. But he lacks the capacity to teach others. Thus, he does not proclaim the Dharma to the world. A Pratyeka-buddha is described as a spiritual personality who is parsimonious of speech and cherishes solitude. *Puggalapaññatti* mentions, "What individual is the Pratyeka-buddha? To this world a certain individual awakes by himself to the truths that are not heard of before and then he does not attain omniscience or mastery of the powers; this individual is called a Pratyeka-buddha." A future Pratyeka-buddha is often mentioned as a disciple of a Buddha during one of his former lives. Not being able to become an Arhat at that time, he eventually attains Pratyekabodhi. The difference between Samyaksambuddha and Pratyeka-buddha is in the attainment of omniscience and the mastery over the fruits. The difference between the Buddhas and Pratyeka-buddhas is the following: Pratyeka-buddhas do not bring others to enlightenment, they do not understand the full range of the dhamma, and they are not able to formulate dhamma by way of concepts. Samyaksambuddhas possess supernatural powers, reach high levels of meditation, and can influence others indirectly to take up a religious life.

Pratyeka-buddha is the Buddhist model of spiritual life. He is similar in many respects to Arhats except that the latter attain enlightenment under the guidance of the Buddha. On the contrary, a Pratyeka-buddha gains enlightenment without outside guidance or support. He is one among three enlightened beings that Buddhism has recognized.

Pratyeka-buddha attains enlightenment with his own efforts. There is nobody to support him in his efforts of attaining enlightenment. Other discourses in the *Ekottarikāgama* confirm that Pratyeka-buddhas awaken on their own without a spiritual guide. He is described as the one who is enlightened through his own efforts. Thus, he attains the supreme and perfect insight but dies without proclaiming the truth to the world. A Pratyeka-buddha is a Buddha living in solitude and does not reveal his knowledge to the world. Pratyeka-buddha may be called a solitary Buddha. So the Pratyeka-buddhas die without proclaiming the truth they revealed. Because Pratyeka-buddha is a Buddha, he is also assigned with a higher place in terms of Buddhist practice and the notion of enlightenment. The life of a Pratyeka-buddha is solitary who live on alms and reside in mountains performing behavior (*caryā*). The historical Buddha himself has enumerated four categories of bodily relics of individuals who are worthy to be enshrined in the stūpa. One among them is the Pratyeka-buddha. Thus, Pratyeka-buddhas are worthy of veneration. In regard to enlightenment, there is no difference between the Arhats and the Tathāgatas. They are identical without any distinction.

He is devoid of the intention to pass on the dhamma and lacks the ability to teach although he is an enlightened being. They did not teach others to obtain the path to Nirvāṇa while they were alive. On the contrary, Buddha practices and teaches the dhamma that is good in the beginning, middle, and the end. All Buddhas, Pratyeka-buddhas, and Arhats had fulfilled all perfections and entered into Nirvāṇa. The Buddha, Pratyeka-buddha, Arhat, and the universal monarchs rank highest who are worthy of honor and respect. Pratyeka-buddha is described as parsimonious of speech and cherishes seclusion. Pratyeka-buddha appeared in this world at a time when there was no supreme Buddha. Only in times in which there are no Buddhas, it is possible to attain Pratyeka-buddhahood. Only in this situation, aspirants could attain enlightenment by becoming the Pratyeka-buddha or Arhat. During the course of becoming Pratyeka-buddha, one acquires the seeds of egolessness (*anattā bhāvanā*).

It is believed that adaptation of the Buddhist concept of the Pratyeka-buddha was probably inspired by the Indian tradition of asceticism. It was further upheld by the tradition of reverence and esteem for ascetics, wandering religious practitioners and sages. The tradition of renouncing worldly desires for religious pursuit has been one of the outstanding features of Indian religious behavior.

Pratyeka-buddha is one of the three fully enlightened beings. The other two are Arhat and the Buddha. However, Pratyeka-buddhas are mentioned rarely in Buddhist canons. The *Isigili Sutta* mentions that Isigili (Rishigiri) Mountain has served as the abode for several Pratyeka-buddhas. They preceded the Buddhas. It is said that, at one time, there were 500 Pratyeka-buddhas who dwelt on the Isigili Mountain, the abode of Seers.

Cross-References

- ► Abhidhamma Piṭaka
- ► Arhat (Sanskrit)
- ► Dhamma
- ► Enlightenment
- ► Nirvāṇa
- ► Omniscience
- ► Pāli
- ► Samyaka Sambodhi
- ► Śrāvaka
- ► Stūpa
- ► Tathāgata

References

1. Anālayo B (2010) Paccekabuddhas in the Isigili-sutta and its Ekottarika-āgama Parallel. Can J Buddh Stud 6:6–36
2. Dhammananda KS (2002) What Buddhists believe. Buddhist Missionary Society, Kuala Lumpur
3. Indaratana Mahathera, E (2002) Vandanā: the album of Pāḷi devotional chanting & hymns. Mahindarama Dhamma Publication, Penang
4. Isigili Sutta, Majjhima Nikaya – 116
5. Kloppenborg R (2006) The Paccekabuddha: a Buddhist ascetic a study of the concept of the Paccekabuddha in Pali canonical and commentarial literature. Buddhist Publication Society, Kandy
6. Norman KR (1996/2001) Solitary as a rhinoceros horn. In; Collected papers, vol 7. Pali Text Society, Oxford, pp 33–41
7. Piyadassi T (1999) The book of protection. Buddhist Publication Society, Kandy
8. Rahula W (1996) Gems of Buddhist wisdom. Buddhist Missionary Society, Kuala Lumpur
9. Ven Bhikkhu B (2010) Arahants, Bodhisattvas, and Buddhas. Access to Insight, 22 Aug 2010

Prausudha

► Uposatha

Problem of Evil

► Theodicy

Proponents of Non-nature

► Mādhyamika

Proponents of the Middle Way

► Mādhyamika

Pṛthivī

► Earth (Buddhism)

Psalms of the Brethren

▶ Thera- and Therīgāthā

Psalms of the Sisters

▶ Thera- and Therīgāthā

Psychology (Buddhism)

Madhumita Chattopadhyay
Department of Philosophy, Jadavpur University, Kolkata, West Bengal, India

Synonyms

Study of mind or consciousness

Definition

Science of the nature, functions, and phenomena of human mind.

Buddhist Psychology

In his earnest zeal to remove the sufferings of human beings, Lord Buddha gave much importance on the mental factors which have a decisive role to play in the determination of the worth of human actions. So, though Lord Buddha himself did not designate any specific part of his teaching as psychological, it is to be admitted that discussion on the mental occupies an important position in Buddhism. What sequences an individual faces in life, namely, enjoyment of happiness or suffering of pain, are all the results of his/her psychological states. This is vividly stated in the first two verses of the most important manual *Dhammapada*: All that a man is is the result of what he has thought – it is founded on his mind; it is made up of his thoughts. If a man speaks or acts with an evil thought, with a wicked mind, pain follows him just as the wheel follows the foot of the ox which drives the cart. On the other hand, happiness follows the man who speaks or acts with good thoughts, with a pure mind, and never leaves him like the shadow of the man himself. Through these two verses Lord Buddha wanted to emphasize that mind is the principal element both in the performance and the assessment of human deeds or actions. It is the mind that rules and shapes human actions, physical, mental, and verbal. The actions become good or bad in accordance with whether they are performed with pure or impure state of the mind. In short, ordinary human life is completely ruled by the mind. The mind to each individual can be his greatest enemy or best friend. Whatever harm an enemy can do to one, or a hater can do by hating, the harm caused by the misdirected mind is even greater. Neither mother nor father nor any relative can do as much good to an individual as the well-directed mind thus. In the *Dhammapada* it is said that the mind is very difficult to see, very delicate and subtle; it moves and lands whenever it pleases. The wise one should guard his mind, for the guarded mind alone can bring happiness. The mind occupies the central position in Buddhist thought – it is the focal point and at the same time it becomes the culminating point, the objective being to attain a pure and liberated mind. In short, the whole philosophical enterprise of Lord Buddha is closely connected with the psychological speculations and these speculations gave his philosophical opinion a new direction in the form of non-substantiality, anti-essentialism. Hence, Buddhist psychology occupies an important position in the whole philosophical scenario.

Buddhist psychology differs in certain fundamental respects from Western psychology which is a more recent development. Western psychology developed as a branch of medical science. For example, William James, one of the noted psychologists of modern period was a medical person and he had the opportunity to dissect and analyze the physical structure of human brain. On the basis of that analysis, and with the help of introspection and observation of the behavior of other human beings, William James tried to provide us with the analysis of consciousness. Buddha, on the other hand did not have any experience of the actual physical structure of the human brain. He confined himself to the methods of observation and introspection and provided an analysis of consciousness.

Another point of difference between Buddhist psychology and modern Western psychology lies in the fact that in the West, starting from the days of Freud till the present, emphasis has been given on the development of an individual since the childhood period. This is the period when the individual develops into a person. That is, in the West it is assumed that when a child is born he is a *tabula rasa*, a clean slate, and does not have any trace or impression in his mind. So everything that the child acquires during this development stage is carried on later in his life and forms his personality. In Buddhism, the story is a different one. A concept like a *tabula rasa* is completely unknown in their philosophical framework. As an ardent believer in the doctrine of causality, known technically as *pratītyasamutpāda* or *paṭiccasamuppāda*, they believe that every moment conditions the next one. So what is called the present is an effect of the past. Thus each child is born with an accumulation of the traces (*saṁskāras*) of their past lives which have a profound influence on their development as a person. Thus in Buddhism psychology has a close relationship with its religious beliefs, specially the belief in rebirth, in the doctrine of *karma*, etc., which are totally absent in Western psychology.

In Western psychology a dichotomy is drawn between mind and body, the former having consciousness as its essence while the latter possesses extension. Because of this dichotomy, the Western psychologists face a grave difficulty in providing the mind its locus. To avoid this sort of dualism, attempt has often been made to explain consciousness as an epiphenomenon or at best as an emergent property. But the case is different with the Buddhists. Within their philosophical framework of momentariness and the doctrine of dependent origination, they try to explain human being as a collection of processes. These processes might be physical or psychological, but they are not independent of each other. There is a close affinity and interdependence of *nāma* (psychological) and *rūpa* (physical or bodily processes). The conscious processes and corresponding material processes are only different aspects of the same reality. An individual is nothing but this *nāma-rūpa* complex. Thus in Buddhism it is possible to give a holistic interpretation of human being without getting involved in a dualistic framework.

As a strong adherent of the doctrine of momentariness, the Buddhists believe that there is no self or soul. But the difficulty arises in accounting for the personality of an individual which is believed to persist in him or her throughout life. The different states, physical as well as mental, may change; but is not there anything changeless amidst all the changing processes to whom the agency is ascribed and by which the question of responsibility can be determined? The Buddhists resolve this problem by their doctrine of causality. One moment conditions the next one. So there is continuity. Even it it is wrong to believe in any self, it cannot be denied that actions occur as events in this process. So there is agency, there is feeling and there is cognition occurring in the process. This process, thus, possesses all the three properties ascribed to the self. Hence, without admitting the existence of a permanent unchanging self, the Buddhists can explain the notion of a person who is eligible to bear the responsibilities and enjoy the privileges as a member of the society. Individual is a mind-body compound (*nāmarūpa*) and the personality or *attabhāva* is an aggregate of changing mental processes. The Buddhists provide a psycho-metaphysical analysis of the human being who according to them is constituted by fivefold aggregates or *pañcaskandha* consisting of the inner and the outer worlds in all acts of cognition. The *pañcaskandha* or the five aggregates are material form (*rūpa*), sensation (*vedanā*), perception (*saṁjñā*), disposition (*sankhāra*), and intellect or self-consciousness (*viññāna*). Of these, the first one, that is, the *rūpaskandha*, includes the body, the sense organs, the sensible objects, and sensations. The second aggregate comprises of feelings. There are three kinds of feeling: pleasure, pain, and neutral feeling. Feeling of pleasure arises from the enjoyment of the desired object, while the feeling of pain arises from the experience of an undesirable one. Neutral feeling arises from the experience of an object which is neither desired nor undesired. The *saṁjñāskandha* includes determinate perceptions of objects to which names are attached involving recognition. It does not consist of the mere sensation which is devoid of all sorts of determination. Such indeterminate sensation is included within the first variety of *rūpaskandha*. *Saṁjñā* includes cognitive assimilation of sense-impressions and cognitive assimilation of ideas by naming. There are in fact two stages in such *saṁjñā skandha* – one where the sense-impressions are contemplated and the other in which such sense-impressions are associated with designations. The fourth *skandha* includes composite mental states and synthetic mental activity. All mental dispositions – intellectual, volitional, or emotional – are *saṁskāras*. They are compound psychoses. Elementary psychoses are combined into dispositions which imply synthetic activity. The *vijñānaskandha* includes the intellectual process or self-consciousness. It includes object-consciousness and self-cognitions. Feeling, perception, and self-consciousness are inseparable from each other. *Vijñāna* is awareness of the mind.

The explanation of an individual in terms of the five aggregates (*pañcaskandha*) may be considered as similar to the analysis of human personality made in Western psychology. In Western psychology, the word "personality" refers to the unity of organized individual traits and processes which distinguish one person from another. When the Buddhists consider an individual as an aggregate of five *skandha*-s, they are actually referring to the process character and the function of the different factors, giving emphasis on the fact that there is no real unity behind such processes and parts. In one of the *Nikāya* texts, namely, the *Saṁyutta Nikāya*, this is explained with the analogy of a string musical instrument called *vīṇā*. Once a king listened to the music of a *vīṇā* for the first time and was very much delighted. He was shown the instrument but he wanted to find out the music in the *vīṇā*. He was told by the persons around him that the music is produced because the instrument is composed of different parts. He still went on insisting to show the part that is music. Then he broke the musical instrument into smaller parts, but nowhere did he find the music. In a similar man an inquisitive person may investigate the body, the sensation, the feeling, the perception, the dispositions, and the consciousness, but nowhere will he find anything that can be said as "I," "mine," or "I am." The *vīṇā* is a functional unit; without proper organization of its different parts, there can be no music. Human personality is like the music which also is very much dependent on the organization of the parts. The emphasis always is on the parts; there is no real permanent unity like a soul or a self to identify the individual with. In the *Questions of King Milinda* (*Milindapañhā*), Nāgasena, a Buddhist monk, compares a person with a chariot. Just as the term "chariot" is used to denote the whole where the parts like the spoke, axles, wheels, etc., are put together, it is a convention to denote the word "being" when the factors are taken together. The examples used by the Buddhist thinkers to show that there is nothing which can be regarded as a person reminds one of the modern Western view of the "Ghost in the Machine" put forwarded by Gilbert Ryle. A human being is nothing but a functional organized unit; it is only a mass of processes. There is no permanent identity.

According to the Buddhists, though an individual is composed of five factors, all the factors are not of equal importance. For example, the consciousness factor or *viññāna-skandha* is the most important one and the other factors are considered to be its seat or locus. The *viññāṇa*-processes are said to create the foundation of a new individual. The different passages in the *Saṁyutta Nikāya* speak of the special role played by *viññāna* in the process of rebirth. Depending on the desire for and attachment to the body, sensation, dispositions, etc., the *viññāna* processes are placed and difference is observed among different individuals. For example, one may long for a particular body in future or a particular sensation or a particular consciousness in future, that is, there may be a variety of wish and desire for the five personality factors. With reference to such wishes in the present life, changes can be realized in the afterlife. Passages in the *Majjhima Nikāya* (*Middle Length Discourses of Lord Buddha*) indicate that the collecting or building activity goes on during the present life. So ordinary persons who want to have a particular collection of body, sensation, disposition, consciousness, etc., will be conditioned by that collection and by that collection his growth will be determined. On the other hand, one who has taken the noble path, who wants to reduce and not to accumulate anything additional, who scatters and does not bind, will reduce his accumulations rather than heap up. He will reduce his body, sensations, etc., which will not be heaped up again. A monk or a *bhikkhu* who is possessed of a free mind, *vimuttacitta*, neither heaps up nor reduces. Having reduced he remains without abandoning and having abandoned he remains without gathering. Thus, the Buddhists recognize three possible phases of human personality – one of the ordinary men where there is expansion and growth and which continues as a preparation for the next life. The effects of the actions performed by him are accumulated and his personality is changed accordingly; he becomes more and more involved in this worldly existence. But with the beginning of the Buddhist training, the whole scenario starts changing. And when the aspirant attains the stage of an *Arhat*, the effects of his past actions are reduced to the minimum. He still possesses personality factors but those factors are in some way empty or unsubstantial and do not bind him to the worldly existences. In this way the Buddhist try to account for the differences in the personality of an ordinary individual, a disciple, and an *Arhat* in the framework of their *pañcaskandha* theory.

Denial of any permanent self or soul happens to create a problem in the explanation of rebirth and accounting for the punishment/reward of actions performed. The Buddhists also have solved this issue in their psychology. The state of existence connecting the previous birth with the subsequent birth is known as *antarābhāva* or intermediate state of existence in the *Abhidharmakośa*. Between death and rebirth, there is found this state of intermediary existence which is a "body" of the five elements (*pañcaskandha*) and that goes to the place of rebirth. Some Buddhists, like the Sthaviravādins, do not recognize this intermediary state of existence. According to them, death (*cyuti*) is immediately followed by *pratisandhiskandha* which is constituted by the five subtle elements. This *pratisaṁdhiskandha* remains inherent in the mind. Thus the mind or the *mana-indriya* constitutes the prime condition for the stream of becoming. The *maraṇabhavacitta* or *cyuticitta* or death consciousness is transplanted into *pratisaṁdhivijñāna* when all other conditions are matured. This *pratisaṁdhicitta* functions as a link between the *maraṇabhavacitta* (consciousness at the time of death) and *utpattibhavacitta* (consciousness at next birth). This stream of consciousness is recognized by some schools of Buddhism as *bhavāṇgacitta* in the prenatal and postnatal stages. This *bhavāṇgacitta* has been conceived as an unmodified, undetermined unit of flowing consciousness (*vijñānasantāna*). Though the term *bhavaṇgacitta* does not occur anywhere in the text *Abhidharmakośa*, it is assigned a very important position in other Buddhist texts like *Aṭṭhaśalinī* or *Abhidhammatthasaṁgaha* and others. It is sine qua non of the continuity of existence and has been compared to the current of a river. When a being is conceived, Buddhist belief gives him a congenital mind simultaneously with the inception of physical growth, as the result of the past generative act (*janaka kamma*). That mind at the moment of conception is but a bare state of subconsciousness, identical with the more adult *bhavāṇga* consciousness during dreamless sleep. Vasubandhu gives a nice exposition of the mental consciousness (*manovijñāna*) which exists at the moment of death and rebirth (*upapatti*). Such a consciousness at the time of death from one existence to rebirth in another existence is characterized by the following features – (1) rupture (*cheda*), that is, destruction of good states by wrong views; (2) resumption (*pratisaṃdhāra*), that is, resumption of good states by right views; (3) detachment (*vairāgya*), that is, detachment from the world and from other states (like first state of meditation, etc.) through concentration of mind; (4) loss of detachment on account of improper states (*vairāgyahāni*); and (5) death by the cessation of the functions of the five sense organs (*cyuti*) and rebirth (*upapatti*) of those with adverse thoughts. As the whole process is due to wrong views or adverse thoughts, those who have been able to overcome them, such as those who are in higher stages of trance like *asaṃjñisamāpatti* or *nirodhasamāpatti*, are not subject to the cycle of death and rebirth. For them death or *cyuti* takes place either in the heart or in the head.

The whole process of the functioning of the mind from the past birth to the formation of several consciousnesses in the present birth has been referred to as *cittavīthi* in the *Abhidhamma* literature. The Pāli word *vīthi* means road. The term *cittavīthi* figuratively indicates the road along which the mind travels. To illustrate this aspect of the functioning of mind Buddhaghoṣa offers the simile of a man sleeping under a mango tree. A man in deep sleep lies under a mango tree with his head covered. A wind blows, and stirs the branches and a fruit falls down near him by the stirring thereof. Consequently he awakes, removes his head-covering and sees the fruit. He picks it up, examines and comes to the conclusion about it. He eats it up, swallows the last remnants left in the mouth and again falls asleep. In the simile, the deep sleep is similar to the unperturbed current of the stream of being (*bhavāṇga*). The striking of the wind is like the past mental moment during which the object comes across the stream without perturbing it. The striking of the branches in the wind is like the past mental moment during which the object comes across the stream without perturbing it. The striking of the branches by the wind corresponds to the vibration of the stream of being. The falling of the mango represents the cutting off the stream. The waking of the man is comparable to the arresting of attention by the consciousness turning to impressions at the five sense-doors, the seeing of the fruit to the function of the visual consciousness, and the picking of it to the act of receiving by the recipient consciousness. The examination of the fruit corresponds to the momentary examination by the investigating consciousness and the coming to the conclusion about it to the function of determining by the consciousness turning toward impression at the mind-door. The eating of the fruit is like the active operation of apperceptive consciousness occupying seven mental moments. The swallowing of the last remnants left in the mouth represents the function of registering. The man's falling asleep again resembles the subsiding of the mind into the stream of being at the end.

Thus the Buddhists conceive of consciousness as a stream of flowing existences undergoing states like death, linking states of existence, prenatal and postnatal states of next birth, sleep, senselessness and the trance stages of meditation. When consciousness does not arise in a particular process of thought, there prevails the subconscious state of mind called the *bhavāṅgasota*, the stream of being. When the different sense organs like eye, ear, etc., come in contact with their respective objects like color, sound, etc., there arises a vibration in the stream of being. This is called the arising of mind or consciousness and may be compared to the occurrence of ripples in the water of a pond because of strong wind. In mentioning the mind, mention is to be made of the mental faculties also. The arising of consciousness is the assemblage of both. The mental faculties are nothing but the elements of the mind which go to form the consciousness. Just as the crops need a land to grow, the consciousness cannot occur without the objects such as color, sound, etc., on which the mind acts. At the same time for the occurrence of consciousness a base is needed which serves as its shelter. The sense organs like eye, ear, nose, tongue, body and mind serve as the bases of mind and the mental faculties which function in the occurrence of respective consciousness. On the basis of the contact of the sense-organs with their respective objects, there occur five different consciousnesses like visual consciousness, etc., each of which has a specific object of its own. The function of these consciousnesses is to be aware of the objects. In each of such consciousness, there are three phases in this process, origination (*uppāda*), development (*sthiti*) and dissolution (*bhaṇga*). Each of these is called an instant (*khaṅa*); three such instants make one mental moment (*cittakhaṅa*).

In Buddhist psychology, the mental faculties or the *caitasika*-s play important roles in determining the nature of consciousness. These mental faculties are roughly classified into four categories – universal (*sabba citta sādhāraṇa*), distinctive (*pakīṇṇaka*), immoral (*akuśala*), and moral (*śobhana*). As the name suggests, the first variety of mental faculties consists of those that are present in all consciousnesses. No consciousness, mundane or supra-mundane, can arise without them. Being necessary for the occurrence of any form of consciousness, these mental faculties are called universal. As distinguished from them, the second variety of mental faculties is regarded as distinctive or *pakīṇṇaka* in the sense that these mental faculties lie scattered in both moral and immoral consciousness. The moral and immoral mental faculties occur, respectively, in moral and immoral consciousness, but these distinctive mental faculties are manifested in both of them irrespective of their division. However, they are not present in all consciousnesses like the universal ones. That is why they are considered as a separate variety. The third variety of mental faculties consists of those that defile, debase, and degenerate the mind. They play dominant roles in the origination of immoral consciousness. Greed (*lobha*), hatred (*doṣa*), envy (*issā*), conceit (*māna*), dullness (*moha*), misconception (*diṭṭhi*) are some such immoral mental faculties which are either direct cause or indirect cause of immoral consciousness, since some of them create a hindrance before the mind, making it unable to realize the true nature of objects, or they poison the mind by creating attractions and attachments or by bringing in ill feelings toward others. As contrasted with such immoral mental faculties, there are moral or beautiful (*śobhana*) mental faculties which remove the ill thoughts of the mind and bring in such good thoughts that pave the way to the right path.

In addition to all these, in the Pāli Abhidhamma tradition, five function-events are mentioned. These are *vitarka*, *vicāra*, *prīti*, *sukha*, and *cittaikāgratā*. The first of these terms, *vitarka*, stands for the initial stage of concentration, a process of positing, implying examination leading to judgment and decision. It may be regarded as a process mediating between the already present and prepared content of the particular or general attitude of the individual and the new content. Insofar as *vitakka* precedes every act of the more subtle discursive reasoning, it is something robust like the beating of the bell; ensuing subtler activity is called the *vicāra* which denotes the steadily moving reflection, the quiet and serious consideration and study of that which has been brought into the circle of interest by the gross *vitarka*. It is by this activity that all details are taken in and all coexistent events and processes of the psyche are activated and involved. While *vitarka* and *vicāra* refer to the cognitive aspect in the process of concentration, the two events, *prīti* and *sukha*, point to the emotive aspect which is never absent in any of the mental processes though individuals are apt to overlook and underrate its importance because of the more intellectual orientation of the mental life. Of the two, *prīti* stresses the perceptible bodily processes and thus comes closer to sensation while *sukha* is differentiated from it as a feeling of pleasure which imparts itself to both the function patterns and to the whole attitude of the individual. It is out of the blending of the cognitive processes as expressed by *vitarka* and *vicāra* and of the emotive process as pointed out by *prīti* and *sukha* that concentration in the proper sense of the term is possible. Concentration combines both the cognitive and the emotive aspects of the mental processes and hence is called "one-objectedness" inasmuch as it does not allow of being distracted and torn away from its goal. Concentration or *cittasya ekāggatā* means that one's whole being and whole mental process is directed toward one object (*ekagga*), thus it is another term for absorption through concentration (*samādhi*). This concentration is the highest goal of human life for it is through this concentration that one can attain the state of *Nibbāṇa*.

There are two classes of consciousness arising with the concomitance of mental faculties, namely, mundane (*lokīya*) and supra-mundane (*lokuttara*). The consciousness that arises having *Nibbāṇa* as the object is called supra-mundane (*lokuttara*), and other varieties of consciousness are regarded as mundane or *lokīya*. This mundane consciousness is again classified into three types known as *kāmāvacāra* (concerned with sensual objects), *rūpāvacāra* (concerned with forms), and *arūpāvacāra* (concerned with the formless). Consciousness which arises in the realm of sensual desire grasping sight, sound, etc., as its object, is called *kāmāvacāra citta.* The *rūpāvacāra citta* and the *arūpāvacāra citta*, on the other hand, are attained through the practices of meditation and controlling the sensual desires. They are known as supra-normal consciousness or *mahaggata citta.*

In short, the *kāma* consciousness can be transformed into *rūpa* consciousness and the *rūpa* consciousness into the *arūpa* or formless one. This transformation is necessary for a distinct development of the mind required for spiritual upliftment of the individual. Whatever spiritual upgradation these *rūpa* consciousness and *arūpa* consciousness bring about in the mental life of an individual, they are not able to put an end to all the sufferings of the individual or reduce their span of life. The consciousness which does away with the worldly cycle of birth and death and leads the individual to the blissful state of *Nibbāṇa*, a state completely free from all types of suffering, is known as supra-mundane consciousness (*lokuttara citta*).The promotion of the mind from the mundane stage to the supra-mundane one is an ineffable one.

Just as the *kāma* consciousness is transformed to the *rūpa* consciousness and the *rūpa* consciousness to the *arūpa* one through the practices of meditation, similarly having *Nibbāṇa* as its object the *rūpa* consciousness or the mundane one develops into the supra-mundane one through a process of the mind known as *magga citta. Magga citta* is a *citta* or consciousness which is the path or means to *Nibbāṇa*. The Buddhists recognize four varieties of such *magga citta*: (1) *Sotāpatti magga citta* or consciousness relating to the path of attaining the stream. This is the attainment of the first stage when the mind is made free from all misconceptions. (2) *Sakadāgāmī magga citta* or consciousness relating to the path of once-returning. When one has attained the first stage of consciousness one's mind is bent toward enlightenment. One, then, is on the noble eightfold path standing for moral perfection, mental development, and insight. Such a person then reaches the second stage of the realization of *Nibbāṇa* in the depth of meditation. This is called *sakadāgāmī magga citta* that is the path of once-returning. That is, by attaining this stage one is reborn on this earth once only, no further rebirth will happen thereafter. The progressive cultivation of the noble eightfold path leads one to the third stage of the realization of *Nibbāṇa.* When this stage is attained, the sensual desire and the ill will are completely removed. This stage is described as the stage of (3) *anāgāmi magga citta* or consciousness relating to the path of never-returning. It is so designated because one who has attained it is not expected to return to the mundane world of sensual desires any more. At the first stage of meditation, misconceptions and evil thoughts are destroyed while in the third stage of meditation the fetters of sensual desire and ill will are shattered completely; other fetters like the ego-sense or ignorance are weakened but are not completely removed. That is why such a person after his death takes birth in the *Brahmaloka* in accordance with his stage of meditation. Just as with the arrival of dawn the dark sky shines with the rays of the morning sun, the mind promoted to the fourth stage of meditation after cultivating the eightfold noble paths to its optimum form finds itself in the full glory of light of the supreme *Nibbāṇa.* No darkness of any form remains anywhere in the person. He is free from fetters of all sorts. This unfettered free supra-mundane consciousness is regarded as (4) *Arahatta magga citta.* It is the stage of consciousness in which all the *ara* or the cycles of existence are destroyed. This is the acme of spiritual development and the highest attainment of life.

In short, the Buddhists recognize three degrees of consciousness – the subconscious, the conscious and, the super-conscious. Subconsciousness is concerned with desire (*kāma*), the material (*rūpa*), or the immaterial (*arūpa*). Normal consciousness (*kāmacitta*) is concerned with objects of desire. Super-normal consciousness is sublime. It is concerned with the material (*rūpaloka*), the immaterial (*arūpaloka*), or the supra-mundane (*lokuttara*).

Another important aspect of Buddhist psychology is their emphasis on the cultivation of certain good qualities of the mind which enable a man to rise above his selfish nature and develop a feeling for the world at large. In the Buddhist framework, these feelings are compassion (*karuṇā*), friendliness (*mettā*), appreciation (*muditā*), and equanimity (*upekkhā*), altogether these are known as *Brahmavihāra*. The cultivation of these qualities removes the immoral feelings like hatred, enmity, etc., which generally create a distance between one individual and another. Thus in their psychological discussion the Buddhists did not confine themselves to the mere analysis of the function of mind but also extended it to the moral sphere so that all people can lead a good moral life which will be beneficial to the society at large.

Cross-References

- ▶ Abhidharma (Theravāda)
- ▶ Antarābhava
- ▶ Āsavas (Āśravas)
- ▶ Avijjā
- ▶ Bhāvanā
- ▶ Brahmavihāra
- ▶ Dhammapada
- ▶ Dhyāna
- ▶ Enlightenment
- ▶ Kamma
- ▶ Karuṇā
- ▶ Kilesa (Kleśa)
- ▶ Knowledge (Buddhism)
- ▶ Majjhima Nikāya
- ▶ Metta
- ▶ Mind (Buddhism)
- ▶ Muditā
- ▶ Nāma-rūpa
- ▶ Paṭiccasamuppāda
- ▶ Philosophy (Buddhism)
- ▶ Rebirth (Buddhism)
- ▶ Sakadāgāmin
- ▶ Saṃsāra
- ▶ Senses (Buddhism)
- ▶ Sthaviravāda

References

1. Aung SZ (1910) Compendium of philosophy (revised and edited by Mrs Rhys Davids). Pali Text Society, Oxford
2. Brahmachari S (1990) An introduction to Abhidhamma. Barua, Calcutta
3. Chaudhuri S (1976) Analytical study of the Abhidharmakośa. Sanskrit College, Calcutta
4. Johansson REA (1979) The dynamic psychology of Buddhism. Curzon Press, Sri Lanka
5. Nāṇmoli B (1991) The path of purification: Viśuddhimagga. Buddhist Publication Society, Kandy
6. Pettifor E (1996) Buddhist psychology. In: Psybernetica. Winter
7. Poussin LV (1991) *Abhidharmakośabhāṣyam* (trans: Pruden LM). Asian Humanities Press, Berkeley
8. Radhakrishnan S (ed.) (1999) *The Dhammapada*, with introductory essays, Pāli texts, English translations and notes, 4th impression. Oxford University Press, New Delhi
9. Ryle G (1984) The concept of mind. Penguin Books Ltd, Middlesex, England, Reprint 1980
10. Sinha JN (1999) Indian philosophy. Matilal Banarsidass, Delhi
11. Nanamoli B, Bodhi B (1995) The Middle length discourses of the Buddha, Buddhist Publication society, Kandy, Sri Lanka
12. Rhys Davids CAF (1996) A Buddhist manual of psychological ethics. Munshiram Monoharlal Pub. Pvt Ltd, New Delhi, Indian edition
13. Gyatso GK (2002) Understanding the mind. Motilal Benarsidas Pub. Pvt Ltd, Indian Edition, Delhi
14. Nyanaponika Thera (1998) Abhidhamma studies: Buddhist explorations of consciousness and time. Buddhist Pub. society, Kandy, Sri Lanka

Psychophysical Aspects of Existence

▶ Khandha

Pu Xian and Bian ji

▶ Samantabhadra

P

Puḍgala (Puggala)

Ana Bajželj
Department of Philosophy, Faculty of Arts, University of Ljubljana, Ljubljana, Slovenia
Polonsky Academy, The Van Leer Jerusalem Institute, Jerusalem, Israel

Synonyms

Individual; Individuality; Person; Person (Buddhism); Personhood; Self

Definition

(1) A person, self, or an individual. (2) Personhood, the central concept of the doctrine of Puḍgalavāda, developed by various streams of early Buddhism in India, such as the Vātsīputrīyas, the Dharmottarīyas, the Bhadrāyanīyas, the Sāṃmitīyas, and the Ṣaṇṇāgārikas.

The notion of a person(hood) in Buddhism

One of the essential tenets of Buddhist philosophy is the notion of no-self (anātman), which proclaims concepts such as self, personality, and individuality as untrue and fabricated. This fundamental principle was challenged by certain groups of early Indian Buddhism, which are sometimes referred to as the Puḍgalavādins or the Personalists, meaning those who advocate the doctrine (vāda) of puḍgala. The earliest Puḍgalavādins were the Vātsīputrīyas that were followed by the Bhadrāyanīyas, the Dharmottarīyas, the Sāṃmitīyas, and the Ṣaṇṇāgārikas. Of these five, the Vātsīputrīyas and the Sāṃmitīyas were the most prominent. The Pāli canon, the Chinese *Saṃyuktāgama*, and the Mahāyāna *Mahāparinirvāṇasūtra* document that Vātsīputra or Vacchagotta was a wanderer, who spoke to the Buddha, converted, and attained nirvāṇa. The split between the Puḍgalavādins and the Sthaviravādins occurred in the third century B. C.E and the Puḍgalavādins flourished until the eleventh century C.E. During their time, they represented one of the leading traditions of Indian Buddhism and according to the Chinese Buddhist pilgrim Xuanzang the supporters of the Sāṃmitīya branch were the second largest group besides the adherents of Mahāyāna during the seventh century C.E., which means that at that time they constituted about a quarter of the whole Indian monastic community. However, nearly all of their texts have been lost with the decline of Buddhism in India and consequently the remaining evidence is very scarce. Due to the fragmentary and somewhat ambiguous nature of the textual sources, a great deal of the doctrine of puḍgala remains uncertain and difficult to reconstruct. Their teaching has been nevertheless partly retrieved from the preserved translations (mostly Chinese) and the accounts of their tradition in the literature of other branches of Buddhism. Still, for the time being every restoration of Puḍgalavāda and the contentious notion of puḍgala remains indefinite and to some extent speculative. Accordingly, scholarly reconstructions of the doctrine of puḍgala tend to differ quite substantially.

The adherents of the doctrine of puḍgala accepted the existence of impersonal psychophysical elements of existence or dharmas proposed by other Buddhist traditions but they additionally introduced a positive notion of personhood (puḍgala) that they claimed to be true and ultimate. The Puḍgalavādins maintained that their teaching was not merely consistent with the original teaching of the Buddha but that their interpretation was the most credible of all. They based their arguments on the references to the "personhood" in the Suttas. Other Buddhist traditions understood these occurrences of the word puḍgala as only conventional references to the five aggregates of form (skt. rūpa), feelings (skt. vedanā), cognition (skt. saṃjña), volitions (skt. saṃskāra), and consciousness (skt. vijñāna). Declaring that the expression "personhood" has no real referent, they discarded all affirmative conceptions of individuality as conflicting with the fundamental Buddhist principle of anātman. Conversely,

Puḍgalavādins declared personhood to be real, although they did not consider it to be absolutely unchanging like ātman of the Upaniṣads. As they admitted the reality of the aggregates in addition to puḍgala, this allowed them to develop a unique position on the concept of puḍgala that would distinguish their doctrine of personhood from the doctrine of a changeless self. Regarding the relationship between puḍgala and the five skandhas, they insisted that puḍgala is a substratum for the skandhas but does not contain the aggregates and similarly, they do not contain puḍgala. For that reason they concluded that it cannot be asserted that one is either the same or different person over time. Puḍgala is therefore neither identical with the conditioned aggregates (as it does not discontinue when they cease) nor entirely different from them, for it is not identical with the unconditioned ultimate reality (as it shares certain traits with the caused, for example, the enjoyment of happiness and unhappiness). It is these views of complete identity with or difference from the aggregates that, according to the Puḍgalavādins, represent two of the three wrong views, the third one being the view that there is no self. Certain textual sources illustrate that due to the ambiguous nature of puḍgala, the Puḍgalavādins claimed that it is impossible to attribute any predicates to it (e.g., whether it is eternal or non-eternal, conceptual or substantial, etc.). Hence, they concluded that the nature of puḍgala is inexplicable (avaktavya), which does not necessarily mean that it is not possible to conceive of what puḍgala is but rather that it is impossible for it to be explained as either identical or different in relation to the five aggregates. One is thought to be aware of one's own existence by means of perception that is inexplicable and that accompanies one's ordinary perception of an object. Its inexplicability means that this incidental perception is neither the same nor different from the perception of an object.

This implies that even though puḍgalas are considered to be conventional realities their inexplicability distinguishes them from the rest of the conventional realities ([4], p. 11). Accordingly, due to the fact that the notion of puḍgala cannot be reduced to any other constituents of existence, it may be ascribed ultimate existence as it does not exist merely as a mental construct. So, despite their contention that the notion of puḍgala is conventional and indeterminable, the Puḍgalavādins granted it truth and ultimacy. Puḍgalas are therefore conventional when considering their reliance upon the five skandhas and ultimate when regarding that they exist by themselves apart from being conceived on the basis of clusters of skandhas ([4], pp. 20, 21).

According to Puḍgalavāda persons therefore exist but they are not identical with their psychophysical structure. The Vasubandhu's *Abhidharmakośa* clarifies this uncertain nature of puḍgala and its ambiguous relationship with the aggregates to a certain degree by comparing the latter to the relationship between fire and fuel, a metaphor Puḍgalavādins used to represent their perplexing doctrine. Just as fire relies on the fuel but cannot be reduced to it, so also puḍgala continues to be supported by the skandhas although it does not contain them nor can it be classified as any single one of them or all of them combined. This analogy indicates the continuity of fire although it does seem to imply that the fire vanishes completely once there is no more fuel. However, concerning the status of the person in parinirvāṇa, Puḍgalavāda maintains that they can not be said to exist nor to not exist. Upon the cessation of the aggregates puḍgala therefore seems to vanish into nirvāṇa but does not become non-existent. Priestley illuminates this confusing statement by examining the relationship between the skandhas, puḍgala and nirvāṇa. He suggests that the Puḍgalavādins may have placed puḍgala into a separate category that is distinguished from both nirvāṇa as the sole uncreated dharma on the one hand and the created dharmas of past, present and future on the other. Neither of the three (aggregates, puḍgala and nirvāṇa) can be considered to be identical with one another ([7], p. 194). However, in *Kathāvatthu* the Puḍgalavādin holds that these three are not completely different either. In fact, it seems as if the notion of puḍgala takes part in all three categories of truths that Puḍgalavāda proposes, the practical truth (as a person functioning in the world), the characteristical truth (as a person being sustained by the five skandhas) and the ultimate truth (as a person who has attained parinirvāṇa) ([7], p. 212).

Resembling fuel supporting fire, the five aggregates therefore sustain puḍgala and allow it to be identifiable by reference to them. Here the impermanence of the skandhas allots puḍgala an impermanent status as well. However, once the five skandhas come to an end, puḍgala does not cease with them but continues its life in parinirvāṇa even though its existential status becomes ambiguous. According to Priestley, the fire metaphor calls for a careful reading and seems to imply a specific notion of fire as something that can be discerned from its particular manifestations and which persists despite the eventual extinction of its specific appearances ([7], pp. 191–198). Similarly, a particular manifestation of puḍgala relies on the fuel of the five skandhas and Priestley suggests that what is manifested, is nirvāṇa as a selfless reality, the worldly appearance of which is puḍgala ([7], p. 195). In the fire analogy, nirvāṇa would therefore not be represented by the burning fire but by the extinction of the fiery saṃsāric cycle and its returning to its infinite persisting non-burning essence ([7], p. 223). Priestley introduces a useful analogy of puḍgala being like the image of the sky as one may see it from the window, where nirvāṇa represents the sky and the aggregates symbolize the window ([7], p. 197). This comparison of the self as a finite representation of the selfless infinite elucidates how puḍgala may be considered as permanent in regard to what it is the manifestation of and impermanent in relation to its individual appearance that arises, is maintained by and ceases with the five aggregates. This would also imply that puḍgalas as a matter of fact are substantial (although not separate substances) but remain indeterminate in relation to the skandhas. Priestley does, however, acknowledge that extending the fire analogy to the topic of the relationship between pudgalas and nirvāṇa is somewhat speculative and Duerlinger suggests that Priestley's reconstruction of Puḍgalavāda comes to resemble the Vedic doctrine more than the Buddhist ([4], p. 64).

Thus, Puḍgalavāda concurs with the Buddhist teaching of no-self if self is understood as something either identical with the aggregates or entirely independent of them. This refutation of self evidently does not exclude the Puḍgalavāda concept of puḍgala and the intricate relationship between the five aggregates, puḍgala and nirvāṇa sheds light on the tradition's contention that due to its subtle nature puḍgala is indeterminate ([7], p. 195). Even though the notion of self is accepted, all dharmas (created and uncreated) are considered to be selfless and yet there is no self to be found apart from them as persons do not have separate identities. According to the Puḍgalavādins, the path to liberation from the endless cycles of rebirths is attained through the realization that there are no independently identifiable selves even though they ultimately exist ([4], p. 28).

The Puḍgalavāda doctrine of personhood seems to have advanced as a response to the fairly impersonal doctrines of dharmas that other early Buddhist school developed. The Puḍgalavādins maintained that merely dharmas could not sufficiently explain the working of the karmic law and the cycle of rebirths for it is persons and not fleeting dharmas that receive the karmic retribution and eventually attain liberation from saṃsāra. Similarly, compassion and kindness may only be attributed to actual individuals and not inanimate collections of dharmas without a foundation. Consequently, the Puḍgalavādins insisted that a certain notion of personhood is necessary for the Buddhist doctrine to be comprehensible ([7], p. 211).

Cross-References

- ▶ Abhidhamma Piṭaka
- ▶ Abhidharma (Theravāda)
- ▶ Anattā (Buddhism)
- ▶ Ātman
- ▶ Causality (Buddhism)
- ▶ Death (Buddhism)
- ▶ Enlightenment (Buddhism)
- ▶ Kathāvatthu

- ▶ Khandha
- ▶ Liberation (Buddhism)
- ▶ Mahāsāṅghika
- ▶ Nāma-Rūpa
- ▶ Parinirvāṇa
- ▶ Person (Buddhism)
- ▶ Psychology (Buddhism)
- ▶ Pudgalavādins
- ▶ Saṃkhāra
- ▶ Saṃskāra
- ▶ Sarvāstivāda
- ▶ Sarvāstivāda Abhidharma
- ▶ Sautrāntika
- ▶ Soul
- ▶ Sthaviravāda
- ▶ Theravāda
- ▶ Vaibhāṣika
- ▶ Vasubandhu
- ▶ Vijñāna
- ▶ Xuanzang (Hieun-Tsang)

References

1. Bareau A (1955) Les sectes bouddhiques du petit vehicule. École Française d'Extrême-Orient, Paris
2. Conze E (1959) Buddhist scriptures. Harmondsworth, Penguin (192–197: a variety of selections from the 9th ch. of Vasubandhu's Abhidharmakośabhāṣya translated from Tibetan into English)
3. Dube SN (1990) Genesis and development of *pudgalavāda*. J Dep Buddh Stud 14:93–97
4. Duerlinger J (2003) Indian Buddhist theories of persons: Vasubandhu's "Refutation of the Theory of a Self". RoutledgeCourzon, London/New York
5. Dutt N (1970) Buddhist sects in India. Firma K. L. Mukhopadhyay, Calcutta (207–213: section on puḍgala)
6. Dutt N (1971) The Sammitīyas and their *puggalavāda*. Mahābodhi, 79:129–136
7. Priestley LCDC (1999) Pudgalavāda Buddhism: the reality of the indeterminate self. Centre for South Asia Studies, University of Toronto, Toronto
8. Schayer S (1931–1932) Kamalaśīla's Kritik des Pudgalavāda. Rocznik Orientalistyczny 8.68–93
9. Stcherbatsky TH (1919) Soul theory of the Buddhists. Bulletin de l'Academie des Sciences de Russie 1919: 823–854, 937–958 (includes the 9th ch. of Vasubandhu's Abhidharmakośabhaṣya translated from Tibetan into English)
10. Thien Chau T (1999) The literature of the personalists of early Buddhism. Motilal Barnasidass, Delhi

Pudgalavādins

Leonard C. D. C. Priestley
Department of East Asian Studies and Centre for South Asian Studies, University of Toronto, Richmond Hill, ON, Canada

Synonyms

Personalists

Definition

Buddhists who affirmed the reality of the person or self.

The Pudgalavādins were early Buddhists (Śrāvakayāna) who maintained the reality of the self (ātman) or person (pudgala), which they held to be neither the same as the five skandhas or aggregates (body, feeling, ideation, volition, and consciousness) nor different from them. They were naturally regarded with suspicion by other Buddhists, since they seemed to deny one of the fundamental tenets of Buddhism, the doctrine of non-self (anātman). Yet their presence could not be ignored: two of the Pudgalavādin schools, the Vātsīputrīya and the Sāṃmitīya, were influential in India for at least half a millenium, and the Chinese pilgrim Xuánzàng, who traveled widely in India in the seventh century, reported that roughly a quarter of the monastic population at that time was Sāṃmitīya [1].

The Vātsīputrīya was among the earliest of the Śrāvakayāna schools to appear, separating from the Sthaviras about two centuries after the Buddha's Parinirvana. From the Vātsīputrīya sprang four other schools: the Dharmottarīya, the Bhadrayāṇīya, the Sāṃmitīya, and the Ṣaṇnagarika. The Sāṃmitīya later divided into the Avantaka and the Kaurukulaka. Of these schools, the Vātsīputrīya and the Sāṃmitīya seem to have been by far the most important.

But the Pudgalavādins were never numerous outside of India, and when Buddhism disappeared in its homeland, there was no longer a living tradition to preserve their literature. The Mahāyāna found it useful to translate many works of the Sarvāstivāda into Chinese, but only a few of the Pudgalavāda. The result is that the sources for the study of this important branch of Buddhism are extremely limited. Only three Pudgalavādin works have survived, and these only in Chinese translations: the Āśrayaprajñapti or Upādāyaprajñapti (Yīshuō lùn), translated as A Treatise of the Sāṃmitīya School (Sānmídǐbù lùn) and accordingly often referred to as the Sāṃmitīyanikāyaśāstra; the Tridharmakhaṇḍaka, in two translations, the Sānfǎdù lùn and the Sì ēhánmù chāojiě; and the Vinayadvāviṃśativyakti (Lǜ èrshíèr míngliǎo lùn). There is also material quoted from Sāṃmitīya sources in Daśabalaśrīmitra's Saṃskṛtāsaṃskṛtaviniścaya, which survives in a Tibetan translation. Only the first two of these works contain discussions of the self or person. What can be learned from these sources may be supplemented with information from several brief histories of the development of the schools, and from critiques of the Pudgalavāda such as Vasubandhu's in his Abhidharmakośabhāṣya; but the latter obviously have to be used with caution.

It has to be remembered that the Pudgalavādins did not regard themselves as heterodox. In holding that the self was real, they believed that they were not denying the doctrine of non-self, but interpreting it correctly: the aggregates are not the self, and there is no self apart from them. The self is thus neither the same as the aggregates nor entirely different from them. For schools like the Theravāda and the Sarvāstivāda, this indeterminacy of the self in relation to the aggregates was proof of its unreality; for the Pudgalavādins, it defined the nature of the real self.

They regarded themselves as orthodox because their position was founded upon the sutras. They pointed out that the Buddha often spoke in terms of a person or self; their opponents argued that in these cases the Buddha was only speaking conventionally, as a convenient and customary way of referring to the five aggregates. But there was one sutra at least which was not easy to explain in this way: "The Bearer of the Burden" (Bhārahārasutta). There, the Buddha says that the burden is the five aggregates of appropriation and the bearer of the burden is the person. If "person" is simply a conventional term for the five aggregates, in what sense are the aggregates supposed to be the bearer of themselves? In the Abhidharmakośabhāṣya, Vasubandhu explains that the burden and the bearer of it are not the same aggregates but earlier and later aggregates in the same series: "Those aggregates which are earlier lead to the injury of those aggregates which are later, and so they are called the burden and the bearer of the burden; for 'burden' is used in the sense of injury." In other words, what one has been (and done) causes injury to what one is; a sentient being bears the burden of its own karma. The explanation is reasonable (given Vasubandhu's convictions), but hardly obvious. The Pudgalavādins accept the sutra as simply saying what it seems to say.

But what sort of being was this indeterminate person or self supposed to be? According to the Upādāyaprajñapti and the Tridharmakhaṇḍaka in its two versions, they thought of it as existing in three modes: conceived (or designated) according to the basis, according to approach, and according to cessation. The first of these is the person conceived according to its present aggregates. The second, though explained somewhat differently in the three sources, seems in general to be the person conceived indirectly according to who the person was in the past or will be in the future, or according to the aggregates by which the person is identified in the present. The third is the person conceived as having attained Parinirvana. The first of these three is evidently primary.

In what sense did they understand the person so conceived to be real? The easiest and in some ways the most attractive interpretation is that they saw the self very much as their opponents did, as the five aggregates taken together as a whole, but differed from them in regarding this whole as not reducible to its constituents (neither the same as the aggregates nor different from them) and in that sense real.

But there are serious difficulties with this interpretation. In the first place, it is not supported by the analogy which the Pudgalavādins evidently preferred in explaining their doctrine. They say that the person is related to the aggregates as a fire is to its fuel. Their opponents regard the aggregates as the constituents of a conceptual entity known conventionally as a person or self. But the logs that a fire depends on are not the constituents of the fire. The fire is not simply the logs taken together as a whole; otherwise, a stack of wood could be called a fire.

A further problem is that the Pudgalavādins deny that the person is nonexistent even in Parinirvana. In the Kathāvatthu, the Pudgalavādin says initially that the person is existent in Parinirvana (literally, "in the Goal"), but then denies that the person is either eternal or annihilated, which seems to be equivalent to describing it as neither existent nor nonexistent. Now, if the person were unreal, this could mean simply that to describe it as either existent or nonexistent in Parinirvana is ultimately meaningless, just as it is even while the person is alive. But if a person consisting of the aggregates is supposed to be real, it can be meaningfully described as existent while alive, and then ought to be simply nonexistent in Parinirvana, when its constituent aggregates have passed away and no further aggregates arise. The Pudgalavādins understand the person to be something which in Parinirvana, when there is no longer anything for it to consist of, is still not actually nonexistent, and may even be described (perhaps loosely) as existent. The nature of such a person is certainly mysterious; but it is clearly not that of a whole consisting of the five aggregates.

How then is it to be understood? A passage in the Upādāyaprajñapti sheds a little light on the matter:

> When one gains Nirvana without residue (i.e. Parinirvana), then the unshakeable joy is attained. But if the person were eternal, it would have neither birth nor death, like Nirvana; its body, having neither birth nor death, would not change; its wisdom, whatever the realm in which it lived, also would not change.... It would also have neither bondage nor liberation.

The "unshakeable joy" must be joy for the person who attains Parinirvana (otherwise how is it relevant?), and that certainly seems to imply that the person is in some sense still existent. But the author denies that it follows that the person is eternal, for the person is certainly subject to change right up to the time of Parinirvana. According to Bhāvaviveka (Bhavya) in his Tarkajvālā, "The Vātsīputrīyas say that (Nirvana) has the nature of both existence and non-existence; for as there is no body, faculty or thought in Nirvana, it is non-existence; but as the supreme, everlasting joy is there, it is existence."

Now the unshakeable joy would seem to be an essential feature of Nirvana, and would thus have been attained by the Buddha, or perhaps more accurately, realized, even while he was alive, at the time of his enlightenment. And Nirvana is agreed by all the schools to be uncreated (asaṃskṛta), so it was not brought into existence when the Buddha attained it. The unshakeable joy cannot be something extraneous to his being; otherwise, he would attain it only to lose it again at death, when his aggregates all pass away. It must be something not identifiable with the aggregates which was mysteriously present in his being throughout his life and all previous lives. And this something, Nirvana present within the limits of the five aggregates as if reflected there, would be the pudgala, the person.

From the limited evidence available, it is impossible to be sure that this is how the Pudgalavādins thought about it, but it seems by far the most plausible interpretation of such evidence as there is. To confirm that such an interpretation is not unbuddhist, it is only necessary to look at a passage in the Mahāyāna Mahāparinirvāṇasūtra in which the Buddha explains to Pūrṇa (as he does in the Pali canon to Vacchagotta) that the Buddha after death is like a fire that has been extinguished; he is not to be found anywhere at all. But instead of saying simply that after death he is "deep, immeasurable, unfathomable as the great ocean," as in his explanation to Vacchagotta, he says,

> Son of good family, the Tathāgata has extinguished his impermanent physical form (and the other aggregates) up to impermanent consciousness, and so his body is eternal. If his body is eternal, it is impossible to say that there is any east, west, south or north for him.

This is not to say that the Pudgalavādins had a doctrine of an "eternal body," but only that such a doctrine is consistent with what seems to have been their understanding of the relationship between the Buddha (and other persons) and Nirvana. And it is by no means impossible, of course, that the development of the Mahāyāna doctrine of the eternal body or Dharmakāya of the Buddha owed something to the traditions of the Pudgalavādins.

Cross-References

- ▶ Abhidharma (Theravāda)
- ▶ Anātman
- ▶ Ātman
- ▶ Bhāvaviveka
- ▶ Decline of Indian Buddhism
- ▶ Kathāvatthu
- ▶ Mahāyāna
- ▶ Majjhima Nikāya
- ▶ Parinirvāṇa
- ▶ Puḍgala (Puggala)
- ▶ Sarvāstivāda
- ▶ Saṃyutta Nikāya
- ▶ Śrāvaka
- ▶ Sthaviravāda
- ▶ Theravāda
- ▶ Vasubandhu
- ▶ Xuanzang (Hieun-Tsang)

References

1. Lamotte É (1958) Histoire du Bouddhisme indien. Institut Orientaliste, Louvain
2. Priestley LCDC (1999) Pudgalavāda Buddhism: the reality of the indeterminate self. Centre for South Asian Studies, University of Toronto, Toronto

Puggalapaññatti

K. T. S. Sarao
Department of Buddhist Studies, University of Delhi, Delhi, India

Synonyms

A designation of human types; Concept of a person; Description of human individuals; Prajñapti-pada

Definition

The Puggalapaññatti is the fourth book of the Abhidhamma Piṭaka.

The Puggalapaññatti is the fourth of the seven books of the Abhidhamma Piṭaka. It is, however, generally considered to be the earliest of the Abhidhamma books (see [9], p. 188). The *mātikā* (table of contents) of the Puggalapaññatti specified six paññattis, i.e., group (*khandha*), locus (*ayatana*), element (*dhātu*), truth (*sacca*), faculty (*indriya*), and person (*puggala*). Of these six, the last one is the subject matter of the text wherein the different types of puggala are arranged in groups from one to ten. S. Z. Aung while discussing the word *paññatti* points out that this word might be used for both name-and-notion and term-and-concept and that it covers a great range of concepts or ideas ([1], p. 264). According to the Pañcappakaraṇa–aṭṭhakathā, the commentary of the Puggalapaññatti, the word *paññatti* means "explanation," "preaching," "pointing out," "establishing," "showing," and "exposition." The six *paññattis* amount to so many (a) designations, (b) indications, (c) expositions, (d) affirmations, and (e) depositions (paññāpanā, desanā, *pakāsanā*, *ṭhapanā*, and *nikkhipanā*) ([6], p. 329).

The compiler of the Puggalapaññatti follows the methodology of the Aṅguttara Nikāya in grouping human types first under one term, then under two, and so on up to ten. The book is most closely allied to the texts of the Sutta Piṭaka in terms of not only the treatment of the subject matter but also with regard to materials. Several of its sections can be seen almost entirely in the analogous sections of the Aṅguttara Nikāya as well as the *Saṅgīti Sutta* of the Dīgha Nikāya (see [3], p. 70; [6], p. 330; [8], p. 102; [10], p. 290; [11], p. 162). As pointed out by Winternitz, some of the chapters of the Puggalapaññatti "read exactly like Suttas in one of the Nikāyas and stand out favourably from their environment" ([11], p. 162). But Hinüber feels that the borrowing has not been done mechanically and that the "rembered orality" "prevalent in the Suttantas. . . has been given up in favour of the style adequate for a treatise on philosophy" ([3],

p. 70). In any case, there is general agreement that despite its presence in the Abhidhamma Piṭaka, the Puggalapaññatti owes much, in both form and content, to the Sutta Piṭaka ([8], p. 102). Moreover, its "non-metaphysical nature… is emphasised by the fact that in it *puggala* is not used in the sense of "underlying personality" (that is almost synonymous with *attā*), which is found in the Kathāvatthu and the Milindapañha, but simply in the sense of "person, individual"" ([8], p. 102).

It is difficult to date this text though it "can be said with certainty that it was written after the nikāyas" ([6], p. 328). "The redactor of Puggalapaññatti limited his efforts to a collection of material from other parts of the canon without developing any ideas of his own on the concept of person. Therefore, it is impossible to relate Puggalapaññatti to the history of philosophical ideas and to other Abhidhamma texts in order to arrive at a relative date. Moreover, there is no parallel text in any other Buddhist school. … Consequently, Puggalapaññatti seems to be a typical Theravāda creation not belonging to the common stock of Abhidhamma texts" ([3], p. 70). Commenting on the literary merits of this text, Winternitz has pointed out that in this book one only rarely comes across "passages of undeniable literary value. Generally speaking, even the parables are as barren and as tedious as the remaining parts of the book, the object of which is to classify individuals according to their ethical qualities" ([11], p. 163).

From a Buddhist perspective, the *puggala* does not have a real existence and is only conventionally true (*sammuti sacca*) as against being ultimately true (*paramattha sacca*). Thus, the *puggala* not ultimately real ([2], pp. 8–9) and it is incorrect to say that the *puggala* is conditioned ([2], p. 65). However, the Puggalavādins (Personalists) disputed such an understanding of the *puggala* and this must have led to disputes in the Buddhist saṃgha. K.R. Norman has suggested that the Puggalapaññatti "probably represents the results of the disputes which took place in early Buddhism about the nature of the "person", and which are referred to in the first section of the Kathāvatthu. The Theravādins came to the conclusion that the *puggala* had no reality, was not one of the *dhammas*, but was a mere concept (*paññatti*). It was therefore not correct for it to be included in the Vibhaṅga, which dealt with the real *dhammas* which existed, but it was made into a text by itself. The title "the concept of a person" shows that to the Theravādins the subject was unreal" ([8], p. 103).

Cross-References

- ▶ Abhidhamma Piṭaka
- ▶ Aṅguttara Nikāya
- ▶ Dhamma
- ▶ Dīgha Nikāya
- ▶ Kathāvatthu
- ▶ Puggalapaññatti
- ▶ Saṃgha
- ▶ Sutta Piṭaka
- ▶ Theravāda

References

1. Aung Shwe Zan, Rhys Davids CAF (trans) (1910) Compendium of philosophy. Pali Text Society, London
2. Aung Shwe Zan, Rhys Davids CAF (trans) (1915) Points of controversy or subjects of discourse, being a translation of the Kathāvatthu from the Abhidhammapiṭaka. Pali Text Society, London
3. von Hinüber O (1996) A handbook of Pāli literature. Walter de Gruyter, Berlin
4. Landsberg G, Rhys Davids CAF (eds) (1972) Puggala-paññatti-Aṭṭhakathā, combined reprint with corrections. Pali Text Society, London, pp 170–254
5. Law BC (trans) (1924) A designation of human types. Pali Text Society, London
6. Law BC (1983) A history of Pali literature, reprint, vol 1. Indological Book House, Delhi
7. Morris R (ed) (1972) Puggala-Paññatti, combined reprint with corrections. Pali Text Society, London, pp 1–94
8. Norman KR (1983) A history of Indian literature: Pāli literature, vol VII, Fasc. 2. Otto Harrassowitz, Wiesbaden
9. Rhys Davids TW (1903) Buddhist India. Unwin, London
10. Warder AK (2000) Indian Buddhism, 3rd rev edn. Motilal Banarsidass, Delhi
11. Winternitz M (1983) History of Indian literature (trans: Sarma VS), rev edn, vol 2. Motilal Banarsidass, Delhi

P

Punarāvṛtti

▶ Rebirth (Buddhism)

Punarbhava

▶ Rebirth (Buddhism)

Punarjanman

▶ Rebirth (Buddhism)

Punarjīvātu

▶ Rebirth (Buddhism)

Punarutpatti

▶ Rebirth (Buddhism)

Puñña

▶ Good (Buddhism)
▶ Responsibility (Buddhism)

Pupphavatī

▶ Vārāṇasī (Buddhism)

Pure Land

▶ Sukhāvatī

Purgatory

▶ Hell (Buddhism)

Pūrṇa Kāśyapa

Mangala Ramchandra Chinchore
Department of Philosophy, Centre for Studies in Classical Indian Buddhist Philosophy and Culture, University of Pune, Pune, Maharashtra, India

Definition

Ājīvaka, Akiriyāvādi, one of the six well-known *Śrāmaṇic* thinkers, learned, well-known ascetics, and acclaimed philosophers.

Akriyāvādi Buddha's Opponent

There is no detailed information available representing his thoughts and life. It is through scattered references available in different works, like *Sūtra-kṛtāṅga*, a Jaina work and Buddhist sources, viz. *Brahmajāla-sutta* (i.e., first part), *Sāmaññaphala-sutta* (i.e., second part) of the *Dīgha-Nikāya*, and *Visuddhi-magga* of Buddhaghoṣa that one comes to know about Pūraṇa Kassapa. He was *Ājīvaka* (died approximately in 530 B.C.), indifferent to moral-distinctions, believer in in-action, and indeterminism (Pali-*Akiriyāvādi*/Sk. *Akriyāvādin*), whose views were (indirectly) rejected by the Buddha.

At the time of the Buddha, many prominent intellectuals were not believing in the *Vedic* tradition, and following their own independent modes of thinking and living (like *Śrāmaṇic*) a wandering mode of life. Among the six [1] well-known *Śrāmaṇic* thinkers, viz. (Pali) Pūraṇa-kassapa/(Sk.) Pūrṇa-kāśyapa was the advocate of the doctrine of in-action (Sk. *Akriyāvāda*). The remaining five were physicalist/materialist (Sk. *Bhautikavādī*) and nihilist

(Sk. *Ucchedavādī*) Ajita-keśa-kaṁbalī, Pakudha-kaccāyana who was defender of the in-action/null-effect theory (Sk. *Akṛtatāvāda*), Makkhali-gosāla who was advocate of fatalism (Sk. *Daivavāda*), Sañjaya-belaṭṭhi-putta who was upholder of skepticism (Sk. *Vikṣapavāda*) and uncertainty (Sk. *Aniścitatāvāda*), and Nigaṇṭha-nāṭa-putta who was promoter of and believer in the four sacrifices for renunciation of the world and recluse of self (Sk. *Caturyāmasaṁvara*) and of pluralism (Sk. *Anekāntavāda*).

In the *Sāmaññaphala-sutta* of the *Dīgha-Nikāya*, [2] one comes across a reference that Kosala king Prasenajita once challenged the credentials of the Buddha, and informed him that in front of learned people, well-known ascetics, and acclaimed philosophers like Pūrṇa-kāśyapa, how can you, who is not yet ordained, beginner of spiritual carrier, young by age, and novice by practice be compared? On the basis of this, it is inferred that all of them (mentioned above) must be Buddha's senior contemporaries – both by age and knowledge. The Buddha rejected all these prevalent theories and asserted an independent novel alternative.

According to the *Brahmajāla-sutta* of the *Dīgha-Nikāya*, [3] Pūraṇa Kassapa advocated a view that all that one does are physical actions, which body performs and not self. Hence, they are not (voluntarily performed moral) actions at all. So, neither good/righteous action (Sk. *Satkṛtya*) brings in merits/reward (Sk. *Puṇya*), nor bad/ill-action/crime (Sk. *Duṣkṛtya*) derives sin (Sk. *Pāpa*). By killing/injury /murder or stealing/theft/robbery, violence, barbaric act like rape, or using other's property, women and wealth, unlawfully taking away things, etc., no sin (*Pāpa*) can be attached to self (Sk. *Ātman*). No one by performing scared fire (Sk. *Yajña*), sacrifice/ charity (Sk. *Dāna*), self-mortification, renouncing world (Sk. *Tapas*) by controlling instincts and passions or following rules strictly (Sk. *Saṁyama*) can amass piousness (Sk. *Puñya*). He denied determinate /essential relation between action and its fruits – a moral theory of causation (Sk. *Kriyā-phala*), and hence is known as *Akriyāvādin* (or an opponent of *Kriyāvāda* – in-action theory).

A dialogue between Magadha-Nareśa (king) Ajāta-śatru and the Buddha in the *Sāmaññaphala-sutta* [4] too throws light on the views of Pūraṇa Kassapa. All are equal to do what they want and free to find out their own happiness, without obeying eternal (*Vedic*) rules and regulations, which bring in hierarchy and discrimination. There is nothing like right and wrong, good and bad, moral and immoral, etc. which can be called as quality to be attached to self. When there is no possibility to establish essential co-relation between what you do and in return what you get in this world itself, then why to think of its correlation in the other world (Sk. *Paraloka*). It is non-sensical to hope for rewards and punishments (Sk. *Karma-phala*) in terms of happiness and pain (Sk. *Sukha-Duḥkha*) of good or bad actions (Sk. *Satkṛtya-Duṣkṛtya*) respectively in this world, or else trans-world (Sk. *Paraloka*) placement in terms of heaven (Sk. *Svagra*) and hell (Sk. *Naraka*) after death. His theory of action and retribution of their results is based on the doctrine of passivity of soul (Sk. *Niḥṣkriya*), which is said to be a unique contribution of Pūraṇa Kassapa.

According to Buddhaghoṣa, [5] Pūraṇa-kassapa was not a believer in the relation between action and its results and consequences. For, the traditional action theory is based on eternality of Self (*Ātman*) and its identity as a doer (*Kartā*) and enjoyer/sufferer (*Bhoktā*). However, according to Pūraṇa-kassapa, Self (*Ātman*) does not get affected by present actions. So, do things freely according to your will. If life and events in it are all predetermined, then present world and one's state of affair in it is only manifestation of the past deeds. Entire world and life at present is not possible to be changed, it is predestined. Obviously, one has to passively look at it. If at all one has any freedom, then it is restrictive only to shape the future, and not the present. But who is going to guarantee about future? Hence, present life is to be accepted as it is. The only alternative left before one is to passively submit oneself to whatever happens, or else enjoy the present without bothering about their implications. There simply is no point in being moral and social.

Why things happen at a particular time and place? There is no answer and proper reasoning for it. It is futile to find out co-relation between what happens and why it happens. Nothing in this world can be predicted and determined rationally. There is nothing like causality (Sk. *Kārya-kāraṇa-vāda*) or intentionality (hence *Ahetu-vāda*), either in human life or in the outside world. Events and happenings in the world can be explained only on the basis of un-intentionality/indeterminism (Sk. *Ahetu-vāda*). Things happen abruptly by chance, accident, and contingency, in an indeterminate manner. Hence, it is better not to do things, and expect that their results could be reaped and enjoyed.

Buddha understood the ebb and flow in such dogmatic understanding, and drew a lesson of futility of entertaining them. He was neither interested in metaphysical things and speculations, nor in blind rituals. But so too anarchy in thoughts can lead to chaos in facts of life in the society and morality – individual and social – gets dragged in it, which the Buddha wanted to avoid. He was not willing to accept dictates of the Supernatural powers (like God) over morality, by making man inactive. He was neither a promoter of licentiousness (like *Ājīvakas, Lokāyatas*, or *Cārvākas*), nor that of authoritarianism (of the *Vedic* traditions). He rejected all kinds of extremes and dogmas, like eternalism and nihilism, hedonism, and self-mortification. Rather, he insisted on the self-conscious righteous actions and insisted on the need of allocation of responsibility to organize society in a moral way. That is why he made a distinction between right-wrong/wholesome-unwholesome actions (Pali-*Kusala-Akusala-Kamma*), and emphasized on following the Eightfold-path (Pali-*Aṭṭaṅgika-Magga*) [both in terms of prescription of *sacca* (in Sanskrit *Satya* – correct/true) and prohibition of *micchā* (in Sanskrit *mithyā* – false/illicit)] by all – monks-nuns on the one hand, and laity (men and women) on the other. According to the Buddha, before doing action itself, one has to be cautious and careful about its results and consequences. Even with regard to nonvoluntary, nondeliberate, and unintended actions one is responsible, if it causes harm to others. Innocence does not allow one to be irresponsible or immoral. Thus, Buddha gave a new alternative theory of the Four Noble Truths (*Ārya-Satya*), by criticizing Pūraṇa-kassapa indirectly, and consequently emphasizing on the need of morality, accountability, and social responsibility.

Cross-References

- ▶ Buddhaghosa
- ▶ *Dīgha Nikāya*
- ▶ *Kuśala-akuśala*
- ▶ *Śramaṇa*
- ▶ *Uccheda-vāda*
- ▶ *Visuddhimagga*

References

1. Warder AK (2000) Indian Buddhism, 3rd edn. Motilal Banarsidass, Delhi, pp 38–41
2. Kasyapa BJ (ed) (1961) *Digh-Nikaya*. Pali Text Publication Board, Bihar Govt, Nalanda
3. Walsh M (1995) The long discourse of the Buddha: a translation of the *Dīgha-Nikāya* (1. *Brahmajāla-sutta*, pp 67–90 and 2. *Sāmaññaphala-sutta*, pp 91–109). Wisdom, Boston
4. Winternitz M (1993) *Sāmaññaphala-sutta* (i.e. the second sutta) of the *Dīgha-Nikāya*. History of Indian literature, vol II. Motilal Banarsidass, Delhi, pp 36, 191
5. Buddhaghosa, Revanta Dhamma (ed) (1969–1972) *Visuddhi-magga*, vols I, II, III. Varanaseya Sanskrit Vishwavidyalaya, Varanasi

Puṣpamitra

▶ Puṣyamitra Śuṅga

Puṣyamitra Śuṅga

K. T. S. Sarao
Department of Buddhist Studies, University of Delhi, Delhi, India

Synonyms

Gomimukhya; Gomiṣaṇḍa; Puṣpamitra

Definition

Founder of the Śuṅga dynasty (circa 184–178 B. C.E.) who is sometimes accused of having persecuted the Buddhists.

Introduction

Puṣyamitra Śuṅga (ruled circa 184–148 B.C.E.) who was the commander in chief of the last Mauryan king, Bṛhadratha, assassinated his master, captured power, and laid foundations of the Śuṅga dynasty ([26], pp. 30–31). He is generally regarded as the symbol and leader of the revival of Brāhmaṇical Hinduism that is said to have taken place after the dynasty of the Mauryas, the alleged supporters of non-Brāhmaṇical faiths, was brought to an end. His large empire with its capital at Pāṭaliputra included the cities of Ayodhyā, Vidiśā, and Vidarbha (Berar) and extended up to river Narmadā in the south. The accounts in the *Aś okāvadāna*, the *Divyāvadāna*, and *Tāranātha's History of Buddhism* also portray him as being the master of Jālaṃdhar and Śākala in the Punjab. Though Pāṇini connects the Śuṅgas with the well-known brāhmaṇa gotra Bhāradvāja, the *Purāṇas* mention Puṣyamitra as a brāhmaṇa of the Śuṅga clan ([10], p. 46). There is also a reference to his son Agnimitra as being from the Naimbika family of the Kāśyapa lineage in Kālidāsa's *Mālavikāgnimitra* ([11], Act I).

Puṣyamitra's Difficulties

It appears that the Śuṅgas were surrounded by many hostile powers and fought wars with the Andhras, Kaliṅgas, Yavanas/Yonas (Indo-Greeks), and probably the kingdoms of Pañcāla and Mathurā (which may not have been under Puṣyamitra's rule) ([20], pp. 47–48; [23], pp. 110, 267). Puṣyamitra himself fought at least three major wars. One of these wars was fought against Yajñasena, the king of Vidarbha, who had remained loyal to the Mauryan dynasty after the coup d'état. He fought the other two wars against the Yavanas, in all probability against King Menander (King Milinda of the *Milindapañha*). After the toppling of the Mauryan Empire by the Śuṅgas, the Greco-Bactrians expanded into India, where they founded the Indo-Greek kingdom. Even though the Śuṅgas were in control of some of the important centers of power, they do not appear to have had either the strength or the resources to recover the whole of the Mauryan empire, despite the fact that Puṣyamitra's two *aś vamedha yajñas* suggest that they tried it ([23], pp. 16, 110). Under such a state of political affairs, it was not surprising that the new power of the Greco-Bactrians should invade and occupy parts of the outlying provinces of the Mauryan Empire. Having consolidated their power, the Greco-Bactrians attacked the Punjab and, still later, appear to have made occasional incursions deeper into the Gaṅgā valley ([23], pp. 17, 110). Being surrounded by hostile powers such as the Greco-Bactrians, the Śuṅgas, particularly Puṣyamitra, must have felt very insecure.

Allegations of Persecution of the Buddhists

After seizing power, Puṣyamitra is alleged to have run the affairs of his kingdom with the help of his contemporary brāhmaṇa scholars such as Manu (the author of the *Manusmṛti*) and Patañjali (the author of the *Mahābhāṣya*) and reestablished the sacrificial ceremonies of Vedic Brāhmaṇism (see [8], p. 215). As animal sacrifices and old Vedic rituals were completely discouraged by the Mauryan rulers who were followers of *heterodox* faiths such as Buddhism and Jainism, his performance of two aśvamedha yajñas is viewed as an anti-Buddhist activity of a king who was a fundamentalist brāhmaṇa (see [13], p. 203). Haraprasad Sastri has suggested that Aśoka's actions such as discouraging animal sacrifices were a direct attack on brāhmaṇas who derived most of their power and prestige through the performance of sacrifices and by acting as intermediaries between the people and the gods ([28], pp. 259–262). Sastri further maintains that the *dhamma-mahāmattas* (superintendents of Dharma) employed by Aśoka for the propagation

P

of his policies, destroyed the reputation of the brāhmaṇas and such actions, coming from a śūdra king, were particularly resented by the brāhmaṇas ([28], pp. 259–262). It is further alleged that Aśoka had acted against Brāhmaṇism by "showing up the false gods" who had been till then worshipped in Jambudvīpa. Further, the propagation of Buddhism during the reign of the Mauryas is alleged to have disturbed the Brāhmaṇical social and religious order ([9], p. 258). Thus, the end of the dynasty of the Mauryas at the hands of Puṣyamitra Śuṅga is seen as a victory of anti-Buddhist Brāhmaṇical forces which had been silently at work. In other words, it is generally held that after the end of the Mauryan rule, Buddhism not only lost the royal favors that it had enjoyed under kings such as Aśoka, but, as a result of the persecution by Puṣyamitra Śuṅga, it is alleged, Buddhism also lost most of what it had gained earlier. Other than destroying Buddhist monastic institutions and personally ordering the killing of Buddhist monks, Puṣyamitra Śuṅga is also accused of having caused greater damage to Buddhism by letting loose unfavorable forces against it. In support of such a hypothesis, P.C. Bagchi has forcefully pointed out that Puṣyamitra's behavior was inimical toward the Buddhists and that their persecution took place at his hands ([2], pp. 405–406). It has been further suggested that even if the atrocities and massacres perpetrated by Puṣyamitra as mentioned in the *Divyāvadāna* and elsewhere are exaggerated, "the acute hostility and tensions between Pushyamitra and the monks cannot be denied" ([4], pp. 166–167).

These above-stated allegations against Puṣyamitra are based upon the testimony of the following texts and archaeological material.

The Divyāvadāna and the Aśokāvadāna

The most important and perhaps the earliest reference is from the *Divyāvadāna* (and its constituent the *Aśokāvadāna*). This Sarvāstivādin text of the second century C.E. says that after being advised by one of his brāhmaṇa priests, Puṣyamitra

> Set out for the Kukkuṭārāma [monastery at Pāṭaliputra]... [where he]... slaughtered the monks and destroyed the residence of the saṃgha. Applying such methods (on the way), he arrived in Śākala [Sialkot in the Pakistani Punjab]. (Here) he issued the edict: "Whoever brings me the head of a śramaṇa, I shall reward him with a dīnāra [a gold piece]." ... [Then in]... Koṣṭhaka.... Yakṣa Kṛmiśa, having seized an enormous mountain, crushed king Puṣyamitra along with his army... Thus, King Puṣyamitra got killed and the Maurya dynasty ended. ([22], pp. 133–135; [34], p. 282)

The Vibhāṣā

This Sarvāstivādin-Vaibhāṣika text dated in the second century C.E. points out that Puṣyamitra "a brāhmaṇa king... set fire to the Sūtras, destroyed Stūpas, razed Saṃghārāmas and massacred Bhikṣus.... Gradually destroying the Law of the Buddha, he reached the Bodhi tree. The deity of that tree, named *Ti yü* (Satyavāk) ... killed him and slew his army" (quoted from [16], p. 387).

The Śāriputraparipṛcchā

This Mahāsāṃghika text translated into Chinese between 317 and 420 C.E. mentions that in Pāṭaliputra

> By means of a decree, he summoned the seven assemblies; bhikṣus, bhikṣuṇīs, śrāmṇeras and śrāmṇerīs, śikṣamāṇas, śramaṇas and śramaṇīs assembled [and]... put them all to death, great and small indiscriminately. Blood flowed in streams. The king destroyed more than eight hundred saṃghārāmas and stūpas.... Five hundred Arhats went up to *Nan shan* (Dakṣiṇāgiri) where they took refuge, and since the mountains and valleys [in that place] were deserted and steep, the army could not reach them. That is why the king, fearing that they would not be annihilated, proposed rewards and appealed to all the kingdoms, saying: "If I obtain a head [of a religious), I will give three thousand pieces of gold as a reward." ... Puṣyamitra then went to the *Ya ch'ih t'a* "Stūpa of the Tooth" (Daṃṣṭrā-stūpa?). [Here]... Yakṣa Kṛmiśa ... grasping a huge mountain in his hand, crushed the king and his four army units with it, and they all died in an instant. (Reproduced from É. Lamotte, pp. 389–391)

The Āryamañjuśrīmūlakalpa

This early medieval text says that "In the Low Age (*yugādhame*) there will be a king, the chief Gomimukhya [Puṣyamitra Śuṅga], destroyer of my religion (*śāsanāntadhāpako mama*). ... he the fool, the wicked, will destroy vihāras and venerable relics (*dhātuvara*) and kill monks of good conduct. ... he will die, being killed along with his officers (*sarāṣtrā*) and his animal family by the fall of a mountain rock" ([14], pp. 530–541. English translation based on [16], p. 391).

Tāranātha

This well-known Tibetan Buddhist historian mentions that "the *brāhmaṇa* king Puṣyamitra, along with other *tīrthikas*-s, started war and thus burnt down numerous Buddhist monasteries from the *madhyadeśa* to Jalandhara. They also killed a number of vastly learned monks. As a result, within 5 years, the doctrine was extinct in the north" ([15], p. 121).

Archaeological Evidence

It has been suggested by some scholars that archaeological evidence available from different sites also suggests that Puṣyamitra targeted Buddhist places of worship. For instance, according to John Marshall, there is evidence of some damage done to the Buddhist establishments at Takṣaśilā at about the time when he was the ruler [17]. Marshall further points out that the Sāñcī stūpa was vandalized during the second century B.C.E. before it was rebuilt later on a larger scale, suggesting the possibility that the original brick stūpa built by Aśoka was destroyed by Puṣyamitra and then restored by his successor Agnimitra ([18], p. 38). Similarly, it has been pointed out that the gateway of Bhārhut was built not during the reign of Puṣyamitra but his successors who followed a more tolerant policy toward Buddhism as compared to Puṣyamitra who was a leader of Brāhmaṇic reaction ([8], pp. 215–217). The destruction and burning of the great monastery of Ghositārāma at Kauśāmbī in the second century B.C.E. is also attributed to the Śuṅgas ([11], Act I). G.R. Sharma who was responsible for most of the excavation work at Kauśāmbī was inclined to connect this phenomenon with the persecution of Buddhism by Puṣyamitra ([24], p. 294). Similarly, the Deorkothar stūpas, located between Sāñcī and Bhārhut, are also said to have suffered destruction under the Śuṅga rulers. It has been alleged that "[t]he exposed remains at Deorkothar bear evidence of deliberate destruction datable to his reign. The three-tiered railing is damaged; railing pillars lie broken to smithereens on stone flooring. Twenty pieces of pillar have been recovered, each fragment itself fractured. The site offers no indication of natural destruction" [19].

Skepticism About the Truthfulness of the Buddhist Legends

However, many leading scholars including H.C. Raychaudhury ([27], pp. 354–355), R.C. Mitra ([21], p. 125), É. Lamotte ([16], p. 392), K.P. Jayaswal ([12], pp. 257–265), R.S. Tripathi ([33], p. 187), Romila Thapar ([32], pp. 198–201), and D. Devahuti ([5], p. 48) have expressed serious doubts about the truthfulness of the Buddhist legends regarding the persecution of Buddhism by Puṣyamitra Śuṅga. Raychaudhury, for instance, points out that the ban on animal sacrifices did not necessarily entail antagonism toward the brāhmaṇas for the simple reason that the Brāhmaṇical literary texts, such as the *Chāndogya Upaniṣad* (iii.17.4), themselves advocate *ahiṃsā* and mention the futility of violent sacrifices. Aśoka did not ban only those animals which were sacrificed in *yajñas* but even others as clear from the list given in his Major Rock Edict no. 1. Thus, the ban was not exactly on those animals which were sacrificed (see [32], p. 250). It is reasonable to presume that though Puṣyamitra may have been staunch adherent of orthodox Brāhmaṇism, he was not as intolerant as portrayed in some of the Buddhist texts. Apropos the śūdra origin of the Mauryas, apart from the fact that the Mauryas are mentioned as kṣatriyas in the *Divyāvadāna*, Raychaudhury has pointed out that the *Purāṇa* statement that all kings

P

succeeding Mahāpadma Nanda will be of śūdra origin implies that Nanda kings after Mahāpadma were śūdras and not the Mauryas because if it referred to succeeding dynasties, then even the Śuṅgas and Kaṇvas would have to be listed as śūdras ([27], p. 354). In fact, not only that some of the *dhamma-mahāmattas* were concerned specifically with safeguarding the rights and welfare of the brāhmaṇas, but some of the Mauryan kings themselves were also followers of Brāhmaṇism. For instance, Jalauka was not only a zealous Śaiva and an open supporter of Brāhmaṇism, but he was also quite unfriendly toward Buddhism ([25], Vol. I, pp. 108–152; [27], p. 354). R.C. Mitra feels that, "The tales of persecution by Puṣyamitra as recorded in the *Divyāvadāna* and by Tāranātha bear marks of evident absurdity" ([21], p. 125). As pointed out by Lamotte, "The only point over which the sources concur is the destruction of the Kukkuṭārāma of Pāṭaliputra 'in the east.' If there was an encounter between Puṣyamitra and . . . Kṛmiśa, it is not known exactly where it took place: at Sthūlakoṣṭhaka in the Swāt valley, at the Dakṣiṇāvihāra on the heights above Rājagṛha or in Avanti at gates of Kaśmīr or in Jālandhar. As for the death of Puṣyamitra, it is in turn located under the Bodhi tree at Bodh-Gayā, on the shores of the Southern Ocean or somewhere 'in the north.' To judge from the documents, Puṣyamitra must be acquitted through lack of proof" ([16], p. 392). Agreeing with Lamotte, D. Devahuti also feels that the account of Puṣyamitra's sudden destruction with all his army, after his promulgation at Śākala of a law promising *dīnāras* for the heads of Buddhist monks slain by his subjects, "is manifestly false" ([5], p. 48). As suggested by Romila Thapar, Sastri's contention that Aśoka was powerful enough to keep the brāhmaṇas under control, but after him a conflict began between his successors and the brāhmaṇas which only ended when Puṣyamitra assumed power, and that Puṣyamitra's action was the manifestation of a great Brāhmaṇical revolution is also indefensible. After all, Aśoka's frequent exhortations in his edicts for showing due respect to brāhmaṇas and samaṇas hardly point to his being anti-Brāhmaṇical in outlook ([32], p. 200). "Since the Mauryan empire had shrunk considerably and the kings of the later period were hardly in a position to defend themselves, it did not need a revolution to depose Bṛhadratha" ([32], p. 201). The fact that he was assassinated while he was reviewing the army does not indicate a great revolution. On the contrary, it points rather strongly to a palace coup d'état which took place because by this time, the organization of the state had sunk so low that subordinate officials were happy to work under anyone who could give them assurance of a more competent administration ([32], p. 201). Moreover, had it been a great Brāhmaṇical revolution, Puṣyamitra would have received the assistance of other neighboring kings such as the descendants of Subhāgasena from the northwest ([32], p. 201).

It is also important to notice that the earliest of the texts that mention these legends are chronologically far removed from the Śuṅgas. The traditional narrative in the *Divyāvadāna*, for instance, can at the earliest be dated to two centuries after Puṣyamitra's death. It is more likely that the *Divyāvadāna* legend is a Buddhist version of Puṣyamitra's attack on the Mauryas and reflects the fact that, with the declining influence of Buddhism at the Śuṅga imperial court, Buddhist monuments and institutions would naturally receive less royal attention. Moreover, the source itself in this instance being Buddhist, it would naturally exaggerate the wickedness of anti-Buddhists ([32], p. 201). Further, *dīnāra* coins (Roman *denarius* gold coins) were not prevalent at the time of the Śuṅgas. The earliest period during which these coins came into circulation in India was the first century C.E. Most interestingly, this legend of persecution in which a *dīnāra* is offered as an award for the head of a monk is first related in the *Aśokāvadāna* in connection with the persecution of the Jainas and the Ājīvikas by Aśoka and most clearly appears to be a fabrication: "In the city of Puṇḍravardhana [north Bengal], a lay follower of Nirgrantha Jñātiputra [Mahāvīra Jaina] drew a picture showing Buddha prostrating himself at the feet of the Nirgrantha. . .. When Aśoka heard of this, he became merciless. He forced the man along with his whole family to enter their home and burnt it to the ground. He then issued a proclamation that whosoever brought him the head of a Nirgrantha would be rewarded with a dīnāra" ([22], pp. 67–68. English translation is based on [31], p. 232). To say that Aśoka, whose devotion to all religious sects is undeniable through his edicts, persecuted the Nirgranthas or the Ājīvikas is simply absurd and so is the story of Puṣyamitra Śuṅga. Thus, "the carbon-copy allegation against Puṣyamitra may very reasonably be dismissed as sectarian propaganda" [6]. Reliability of the *Divyāvadāna* is also grievously marred by the fact that Puṣyamitra Śuṅga is mentioned as a descendent of Aśoka whereas he did not belong to the Mauryan dynasty of non-Brāhmaṇical background. In fact, this very fact flies in the face of the hypothesis that Puṣyamitra persecuted the Buddhists because he was a brāhmaṇa and represented fundamentalist form of Brāhmaṇism.

There is, in fact, no concrete evidence to show that any of the Mauryan kings discriminated against Brāhmaṇism. Aśoka, the most popular Mauryan king, did not appear to have any vulgar ambition of exalting his own religion "by showing up the false gods" of Brāhmaṇism. Thus, the hypothesis of a Brāhmaṇical persecution under Puṣyamitra loses much of its *raison d'être* ([27], p. 126). The policy of Puṣyamitra Śuṅga appears to have been tolerant enough for the simple reason that if he were against the Buddhists, he would have dismissed his Buddhist ministers. There is overwhelming evidence to show that Buddhism actually prospered during the reign of the Śuṅga kings. And it has actually been argued that archaeological evidence casts doubt on the claims made by Buddhist texts that the Śuṅgas persecuted the Buddhists (see, for instance, [32], p. 200). An archaeological study of the celebrated stūpa at Sāñcī proves that it was enlarged and encased in its present covering during the Śuṅga period ([1], p. 160). The Aśokan pillar near it appears to have been wilfully destroyed, but this event may have occurred at a much later date ([18], p. 90). The Bhārhut Buddhist Pillar Inscription of the time of the Śuṅgas actually records some additions to the Buddhist monuments "during the supremacy of the Śuṅgas" (*Suganaṃ raje... dhanabhūtina karitaṅ toranāṃ silā-kaṅmaṅto ca upaṃṇa* ([30], p. 87. See also [18], p. 11)). The *Mahāvaṃsa* admits the existence of numerous monasteries in Bihar, Avadha, Malwa, and surrounding areas during the reign of Sri Lankan king Duṭṭhagāmaṇī (circa 101–177 B.C.E.) which is synchronous with the later Śuṅga period (see [7], XXIX).

Conclusion

It may not be possible to deny the fact that Puṣyamitra Śuṅga showed no favor to the Buddhists, but it is not certain that he persecuted them ([8], pp. 210–217). The only thing that can be said with certainty on the basis of the stories told in Buddhist texts about Puṣyamitra is that he might have withdrawn royal patronage from the Buddhist institutions. This change of circumstance under his reign might have led to discontent among the Buddhists. It seems that as a consequence of this shifting of patronage from Buddhism to Brāhmaṇism, the Buddhists became politically active against him and sided with his enemies, the Indo-Greeks. "The Greek struggle with Puṣyamitra gave the Buddhists the prospect of renewed influence... What may be sensed is that strategic reasons made some Greeks the promoters of Buddhism and some Buddhists supporters of the Greeks" ([29], p. 141). This might have incited him to put them down with a heavy hand ([3], p. 99). Thus, if in some parts of Puṣyamitra Śuṅga's kingdom, a few monasteries were at all pillaged, it must be seen as a political move rather than a religious one. Moreover, in such cases, the complicity of the local governors also cannot be ruled out. Jayaswal has referred to another interesting aspect of the declaration made by Puṣyamitra Śuṅga setting a price on the head of every Buddhist monk ([12], p. 263). It was made at Śākala, the capital city of Menander. The fact that such a fervid declaration was made not only at a place which was far removed from the center of the Śuṅga regime but also in the capital city of his archenemies points to reasons motivated by political considerations. After Aśoka's lavish sponsorship of Buddhism, it is quite possible that Buddhist institutions fell on somewhat harder times under the Śuṅgas, but persecution is quite another matter. "Far more than the so-called persecution by Puṣyamitra, the successes of the Viṣṇuite propaganda during the last two centuries of the ancient era led the Buddhists into danger, and this was all the more serious in that it was long time before its threat was assessed" ([16], pp. 392–393). Thus, it would be fair to say that where the Buddhists did not or could not ally themselves with the invading Indo-Greeks, Puṣyamitra left them alone.

Cross-References

- ▶ Aśoka
- ▶ Decline of Indian Buddhism
- ▶ Divyāvadāna
- ▶ Persecution (Buddhism)
- ▶ Xuanzang (Hieun-Tsang)

References

1. Archaeological Survey of India (1953) Ancient India: bulletin of the archaeological survey of India, vol IX. New Delhi
2. Bagchi PC (1921) Decline of Buddhism and its causes. In: Sir Ashutosh Mukherjee Silver Jubilee, vol III. Calcutta University, Calcutta, pp 405–406
3. Bhattacharyya H et al. (eds) (1953) Cultural heritage of India, 2nd enl. and rev edn, vol 2. Ramakrishna Mission Institute of Culture, Calcutta
4. Chakravartty G (1994) BJP-RSS and distortion of history. In: Lahiri P (ed) Selected writings on communalism. People's Publishing House, New Delhi, pp 161–172
5. Devahuti D (1998) Harsha: a political study, 3rd revised edn. Oxford University Press, New Delhi
6. Elst K (2007) Why Pushyamitra was more 'secular' than Ashoka? http://koenraadelst.bharatvani.org/print/articles/ayodhya/pushyamitra. Accessed 20 Apr 2007
7. Geiger W (ed) (1908) The Mahāvaṃsa. Pali Text Society, London
8. Ghosh NN (1945) Did Puṣyamitra Śuṅga persecute the Buddhists. In: Bhandarkar DR et al. (eds) B.C. Law, vol I. Bhandarkar Research Institute, Poona, pp 210–217
9. Ghoshal UN (1957) Studies in Indian history and culture. Orient Longmans, Bombay
10. Hazra KL (1995) The rise and decline of Buddhism in India. Munshiram Manoharlal, New Delhi
11. Iyer KAS (ed) (1978) Mālavikāgnimitra of Kālidāsa, critical edn. Sahitya Akademi, New Delhi
12. Jayaswal KP (1918) Revised notes on the Brahmin Empire. J Bihar Orissa Res Soc, Patna IV(Pt III):257–265. Patna
13. Jayaswal KP (1923) An inscription of the Śuṅga dynasty. J Bihar Orissa Res Soc, Patna X(1923):203
14. Jayaswal KP (ed and trans) (1934) The text of the Mañju-śrī-mūlakalpa: an imperial history of India. Motilal Banarsidass, Lahore
15. Lama C, Chattopadhyaya A (trans) (1970) Tāranātha's history of Buddhism in India. Indian Institute of Advanced Study, Simla
16. Lamotte É (1988) History of Indian Buddhism: from the origins to the Śaka Era (trans: Sara Webb-Boin). Insitut Orientaliste, Louvain-la-Neuve
17. Marshall JH (1951) Taxila, vol I. Cambridge University Press, Cambridge
18. Marshall JH (1955) A guide to Sanchi, 3rd edn. Manager of Publications, Delhi
19. Mishra PK (2001) Does newly excavated Buddhist temple provide a missing link? In: Archaeology. A Publication of the Archaeological Institute of America, April 2001. www.archaeology.org/online/news/deorkothar/. Accessed 15 Apr 2007
20. Mitchiner JE (ed and trans) (2002) The Yuga Purāṇa: critically edited, with an English translation and a detailed introduction, 2nd rev edn. Asiatic Society, Kolkata
21. Mitra RC (1954) The decline of Buddhism in India. Visva-Bharati, Santiniketan, Birbhum
22. Mukhopadhyaya S (ed) (1963) The Aśokāvadāna. Sahitya Akademi, New Delhi
23. Narain AK (2003) The Indo-Greeks: revisited and supplemented, 4th rep. with supplement. B.P. Publishing Corporation, Delhi
24. Negi JS (1958) Groundwork of ancient Indian history. Allahabad University Press, Allahabad
25. Pandit RS (ed) (2001) Kalhaṇa's Rājataraṅgiṇī: the saga of the kings of Kaśmīr. Sahitya Akademy, New Delhi, Third reprint
26. Pargiter FE (1962) Purāṇa texts of the dynasties of the Kali age, 2nd edn. Chowkhamba Sanskrit Series, Varanasi
27. Raychaudhury HC (1923) Political history of ancient India: from the accession of Parikshit to the extinction of the Gupta dynasty. University of Calcutta, Calcutta
28. Sastri H (1910) Notices. J Asiatic Soc Bengal, Calcutta LXXIV:259–262
29. Seldeslachts E (2007) Greece, the final frontier? The westward spread of Buddhism. In: Heirman A, Bumbacher SP (eds) The spread of Buddhism. E.J. Brill, Leiden
30. Sircar DC (ed) (1965) Select inscriptions bearing on Indian history and civilization, 2nd rev. and enl. edn, vol 1. University of Calcutta, Calcutta
31. Strong JS (1983) The legend of King Aśoka: a study and translation of the Aśokāvadāna. Princeton University Press, Princeton
32. Thapar R (1991) Aśoka and the decline of the Mauryas. Oxford University Press, New Delhi
33. Tripathi RS (1960) History of ancient India. Motilal Banarsidass, Delhi
34. Vaidya PL (ed) (1959) Divyāvadāna. Mithila Institute of Post-Graduate Studies and Research in Sanskrit Learning, Darbhanga

R

Rāga

► Kilesa (Kleśa)

Rāhula

K. T. S. Sarao
Department of Buddhist Studies, University of Delhi, Delhi, India

Synonyms

Rāhula Thera; Rāhulabhadda

Definition

The only son of Gautama Buddha.

Rāhula was the only son of Siddhārtha Gautama, the buddha-to-be, and his wife Yaśodharā (known as Bhaddakaccānā or simply Rāhulamātā in the Pāli Canon). Rāhula was born on the day on which his father left the household life ([1], Vol. i, p. 60; [17], Vol. i, p. 82). It is said that as soon as the news of Rāhula's birth was brought to Siddhārtha, he decided to renounce the world then and there as he saw in the birth of a son, a new bond tying him to the life of a householder ("*Rāhulajāto, bandhanaṃ jātaṃ*" the word *rāhula* meaning *bond*) ([1], Vol. i, p. 60; [9], Vol. i, p. 70). However, according to the *Apadānaaṭṭhakathā*, the name *Rāhula* literally means "little Rāhu," Rāhu being the demon who is believed to have caused eclipses by blocking the sun and the moon ([3], p. 37). Another account given in the *Mūlasarvāstivāda vinaya* mentions that Rāhula was given his name in accordance with an eclipse of the moon caused by Rahu ([4], p. 119).

Seven years after he had left home, the Buddha visited Kapilavastu after attaining Enlightenment on the invitation of his father. While the Buddha was having his meal, Rāhula's mother sent him to the Buddha to ask for his inheritance (*dāyajja*). The Buddha remained silent and after having finished his meal left the palace. Rāhula followed him and continued to repeating his request till finally the Buddha told Sāriputta to ordain him. Moggallāna was appointed his teacher who taught the *kammavācā* (rules and ritual regarding admission to the saṃgha) to him ([1], Vol. ii, p. 393; [14], Vol. i, p. 340). Later, the Buddha's father, Suddhodana, and Rāhulamātā complained that the boy had been taken away without their permission. Consequently, the Buddha declared that no one should be ordained without parental consent ([9], Vol. i, p. 98f; [10], Vol. i, p. 82f). The Buddha took keen interest in Rāhula's moral and spiritual education. He constantly (*abhinhovādavasena*) preached many *suttas* to Rāhula for his guidance ([17], Vol. i, p. 145). When Rāhula was 7 years old, the Buddha preached to him the *Ambalaṭṭhika Rāhulovāda Sutta* as a warning that he should

K.T.S. Sarao, J.D. Long (eds.), *Buddhism and Jainism*, Encyclopedia of Indian Religions,
DOI 10.1007/978-94-024-0852-2

never lie, even in fun. Rāhula used to accompany the Buddha on his begging rounds, and occasionally he would also accompany Sāriputta on his begging rounds. Rāhula was present when Sāriputta's mother roundly abused the latter for having left her ([9], Vol. iv, p. 164f). When Rāhula was 7 years old, the Buddha preached to him the *Ambalaṭṭhika Rāhulovāda Sutta* as a warning that he should never lie, even in fun. Rāhula often used to accompany the Buddha, and sometimes Sāriputta, on their begging rounds. Rāhula was present when Sāriputta's mother roundly abused the latter for having left her ([9], Vol. iv, p. 164f). Rāhula is said to have been himself eager to get instructed by his teachers as well as the Buddha. He used to get up early in the morning and, taking a handful of sand, used to express a wish: "May I have today as many words of counsel from my teachers as there are here grains of sand!" The monks often spoke of Rāhula's zealousness and obedience, and once the Buddha, aware of the subject of their talk, went among them and related the *Tipallatthamiga* and the *Tittira* Jātakas ([1], Vol. iii, p. 64ff; Vol. i, p. 160ff) to show them that in his previous births also Rāhula was equally obedient.

Three important suttas, namely, the *Mahā Rāhulovāda Sutta* ([16], Vol. i, pp. 420–426), *Cūla Rāhulovāda Sutta* ([15], Vol. iii, pp. 277–280; this *sutta* is also found in the *Saṃyutta Nikāya* ([2], Vol. iv, p. 105ff) where it is called the *Rāhula Sutta*), and the *Ambalaṭṭhika Rāhulovāda Sutta* ([15], Vol. i, pp. 414–420), were preached by the Buddha directly to Rāhula. In the *Mahā Rāhulovāda Sutta*, the Buddha tells Rāhula about *anattā* and the latter two *suttas* formed the topics for Rāhula's meditation (*vipassanā*). The *Cūla Rāhulovāda Sutta* was preached by the Buddha when he learnt that Rāhula's mind was ripe for final attainment, and after hearing this discourse, Rāhula became an arahant. The *Ambalaṭṭhika Rāhulovāda Sutta*, in which the Buddha warns against the use lies, was preached to Rāhula when he was only 7 years old ([17], Vol. ii, p. 636).

According to the *Paramatthajotikā*, Rāhula never lay on a bed for 12 years ([13], Vol. iii, p. 736). In the assembly of monks, he was declared by the Buddha as the foremost among those of his disciples who were eager for training (*sikkhākāmānaṃ*) ([8], Vol. i, p. 24). A story in the Vinaya refers to Rāhula's complete scrupulousness toward observing the rules. According to the story, one evening when he arrived at the gates of Badarikārāma at Kosambī, he was told that a new rule had been laid down according to which no novice was allowed to sleep under the same roof as a fully ordained monk. As he was unable to find any resting place which did not violate this rule, he spent the night in the Buddha's jakes. However, when the Buddha found him there the next morning, he modified the rule ([1], Vol. i, p. 161f; [10], Vol. iii, p. 16). On another occasion, Rāhula spent the night in the open, in front of the Buddha's cell as he found no place in which to sleep because monks who had arrived late had taken his sleeping place. Māra, seeing him there, tried unsuccessfully to frighten him by assuming the form of a huge elephant. This incident took place 8 years after Rāhula had attained arahantship ([9], Vol. iv, p. 69f).

In numerous Jātakas, Rāhula is mentioned as having been the bodhisatta's son. The *Apadāna* says that in many births Uppalavannā and Rāhula were born of the same parents (*ekasmiṃ sambhave*) and had similar inclinations (*samānacchandamānasā*) ([6], Vol. ii, p. 551). During the time of Padumuttara Buddha, Rāhula was born as a rich householder at Haṃsavatī, who, realizing the vanity of riches, gave all away to the poor and ascetics. As a result, he was born in the Nāga world as Pathavindhara. It was in this birth that he had expressed a wish that he might be born as the son of a future buddha. In the time of Kassapa Buddha also, Rāhula was born as Pathavindhara, the eldest son of King Kiki, later becoming his viceroy. During this birth, he built 500 residences for the monks ([14], Vol. i, p. 341; [17], Vol. i, p. 141ff; [18], Vol. ii, p. 722). According to the *Apadāna*, Rāhula gave Padumuttara Buddha a carpet (*santhara*), as a result of which, 21 *kalpas* (eons) ago, he was born as a khattiya named Vimala in Renuvatī ([6], Vol. i, p. 60f).

Four verses uttered by Rāhula are included in the *Theragāthā* ([11], pp. 295–298), and the

Milindapañha also contains several stanzas attributed to Rāhula ([15], p. 413). Rāhula was known to his friends as Rāhulabhadda (Rāhula, the Lucky) which he himself justified by saying that he deserved the title because he was twice blessed in being the son of the Buddha and an arahant ([9], Vol. i, p. 124; [11], p. 295f; [15], p. 410; [18], Vol. i, p. 537). Rāhula is said to have died before the Buddha, Moggallāna, and Sāriputta ([12], Vol. ii, p. 549; [18], Vol. iii, p. 172). Aśoka built a stūpa in his honor to be particularly worshipped by novices ([5], p. 281).

Cross-References

▶ Arahant
▶ Aśoka
▶ Buddha Śākyamuni
▶ Jātaka
▶ Moggallāna
▶ Śāriputra
▶ Thera- and Therīgāthā

References

1. Fausböll V (ed) (1977–1897) The Jātaka, 6 vols. Luzac, London
2. Feer ML (1884–1898) The Saṃyutta Nikāya, 5 vols. Pali Text Society, London
3. Godakumbura CE (ed) (1954) Visuddhajanavilāsinī nāma Apadānaṭṭhakathā. Pali Text Society, London
4. Gnoli R (ed) (1975) The Gilgit manuscript of the Saṃghabhedavastu. Instituto Italiano per il Medio ed Estremo Oriente, Roma
5. Li R (trans) (1996) The great Tang dynasty record of the western regions. Numata Center for Buddhist Translation and Research, Berkeley
6. Lilley ME (2000) The Apadāna, 2 vols. Pali Text Society, London
7. Malalasekera GP (1937–1938) Dictionary of Pāli proper names, 2 vols. Pali Text Society, London
8. Morris R, Hardy E (eds) (1885–1900) The Aṅguttara Nikāya (1885–1900), 5 vols. Pali Text Society, London
9. Norman HC (1906). The commentary of the Dhammapada, 4 vols. Pali Text Society, London
10. Olderberg H (ed) (1879–1883) The Vinaya Piṭakaṃ, 5 vols. Pali Text Society, London
11. Oldenberg H, Pischel R (eds) (1990) The Thera- and Therīgāthā (with Appendices by K.R. Norman & L. Alsdorf), 2nd edn. Pali Text Society, Oxford
12. Rhys Davids TW, Carpentier JE, Stede W (eds) (1886–1932) The Sumaṅgala-Vilāsinī: Buddhaghosa's commentary on the Dīgha Nikāya, 3 vols. Pali Text Society, London
13. Smith H (1916–1918) Sutta-Nipāta commentary being Paramatthajotikā II, 3 vols. Pali Text Society, London
14. Trenckner V (ed) (1880) The Milindapañho. Williams and Norgate, London
15. Trenckner V, Chalmers R (1888–1896) The Majjhima Nikāya, 3 vols. Pali Text Society, London
16. Walleser H, Kopp H (eds) (1924–1956) Manorathapūraṇī: Buddhaghosa's commentary on the Aṅguttara Nikāya, 5 vols. Pali Text Society, London
17. Woods JH, Kosambi D, Horner IB (eds) (1922–1938) Papañcasūdanī: Majjhimanikāyaṭṭhakathā of Buddhaghosācariya, 5 vols. Pali Text Society, London
18. Woodward FL (ed) (1929–1937) The Sāratthappakāsinī, Buddhaghosa's commentary on the Saṃyutta Nikāya, 3 vols. Pali Text Society, London

Rāhula Thera

▶ Rāhula

Rāhulabhadda

▶ Rāhula

Rājagaha (Pāli)

▶ *Rājagṛha*

Rājagṛha

Robert Harding
Faculty of Asian and Middle Eastern Studies, University of Cambridge, Cambridge, UK

Synonyms

Rājagaha (Pāli); Rāyagiha (Ardhamagadhi)

Definition

The city that was the earliest known capital of the kingdom of Magadha. Both Mahāvīra and the Buddha spent much time here, and it was an important early center for Buddhism.

Introduction

Rajgir lies at 25° 0'N: 85° 26'E to the southeast of Patna (ancient Pāṭaliputra). It is the oldest-known capital of Magadha, the kingdom that would evolve into the Mauryan Empire. In the absence of all but a few small-scale excavations, its origins as a town and as a capital are unclear, although it has legendary beginnings. Jain sources refer to predecessor capitals that are otherwise unknown. The *Mahābharāta* recounts the story of King Jarāsandha, who imprisoned many other kings in his capital (here called Girivrāja) until Kṛṣṇa, Arjuna, and Bhīma defeated him and set the kings free. The name (Giri = mountain) shows a strong association with the local topography. *Rājagṛha* (House of the King) accurately denotes its political functions.

Topography

The present town lies on the edge of a large earthen embankment, roughly pentagonal in shape and with a c. 5-km circuit. A rectangular stone wall with semicircular bastions lies in its southwest corner. To the west of the embankment, opposite the main gate, is the area's largest stupa, identified by the Chinese pilgrim Faxian (who visited in 405) with one of the 84,000 founded by Aśoka. Carbon 14 suggests dates for the embankment of the later first millennium BCE, although medieval bricks and a local folk tale suggest the stone wall was refortified under the Afghan king Sher Shah. The interior of this city is largely unknown although the pilgrim Xuanzang, who visited in the seventh century, suggested there were two monasteries there for Chinese pilgrims.

A short distance to the south, the Rajgir hills open to form a wide valley, with northern and southern entrances (Fig. 1). The town is identified with five hills that encircle this valley; unfortunately, different sources have different lists, and these are impossible to reconcile. The Pāli Canon list, found in the *Isigili Sutta* of the *Majjhima Nikāya*, is Vebhāra, Pāṇḍava, Vepulla, Gijjhakūta (Sanskrit Gṛdhakūta), and Isigili. The most important hill in Buddhist sacred geography is Gṛdhakūta (Vulture Peak); a number of Mahāyana texts, including the Lotus Sūtra, were reportedly delivered there, and Xuanzang saw a stūpa on the spot where it had been preached.

Today, the hills have what appear to be the Jain names of Vaibhāra and Vipula, flanking the north passage; Ratnagiri to the northeast; and Udaya and Soṇagiri flanking the southern exit. Gṛdhakūta has been identified with Chhaṭhāgiri, a small peak close to Ratna, on which are terraces of the Gupta period and some caves. Close by is the Japanese-built Shanti Stupa, opened in 1969.

Xuanzang identified this valley as Old Rajgir, abandoned for the new town to the north under King Bimbisāra. Faxian suggested Bimbisāra's son as the author of the move. Whoever is responsible, it should be noted that the present landscape suggests settlement outside the hills and religious structures within; and Francis Buchanan in 1811 was quick to point out how hot and flooded the plain would be ([2], p. 204).

Archaeology

However, the oldest settlement evidence, from the late second to the early first millennium BCE, comes from the Jāradevī Mound just inside the North Gate. In addition, the so-called Inner Fortification (Fig. 2), which encloses an area of the plain in the shape of a boot and which is associated with an outer ditch, would seem to constitute a defensive structure (though also a flood barrier) ([3], p. 263). Ceramics from the early to mid-first millennium BCE are embedded in it. Enclosing a much larger area is the Outer Fortification, a stone rubble wall that runs from Old Rajgir up

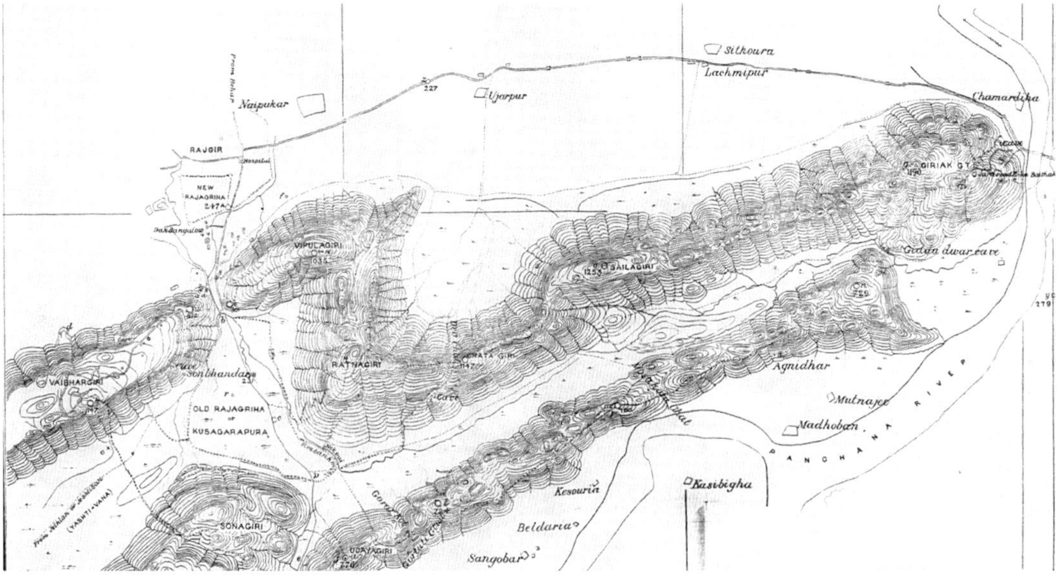

***Rājagṛha*, Fig. 1** Map from Marshall survey [7]

***Rājagṛha*, Fig. 2** The inner fortification with Ratnagiri in the background [photograph by author]

to Giriak at the eastern edge of the Rajgir hills (Fig. 1).

Giriak itself has a history going back to the Early Historic, as evidenced by ceramics including Northern Black Polished Ware and the terracotta ring wells typical of the period. They are to be found at the base of the Daktar English mound, which runs for 500 m next to the Panchana river, and the site was a large one at least into the early centuries CE. Both Rajgir and Giriak have connections south to the Chota Nagpur Plateau, with its rich resources of timber and minerals; and this is the probable explanation for the siting of the capital so far in the south of Magadha. It also underlines the fact that Giriak should be considered an integral part of the Rajgir complex. On Giriak hill itself is a monastery and stūpa complex, visible for miles around, described by Xuanzang as the Wild Goose Stūpa.

If it were complete, the stone wall would be about 35 km. long; however, it is quite incomplete on both the northern and southern sides. It is assumed to be a defensive structure ([4], pp. 464–466); however, only on either side of the passages (the North and South Gates) are there bastions that give it a military character (there are also some freestanding watchtowers). In a number of sections, the walls are quite indefensible; and in others, the path of the walls has no defensive meaning (for instance, the Zigzag Wall running from the base to the top of Ratnagiri). Whatever the age of the Outer Fortification, it has an association with the religious structures on the tops of the hills, now Jain, earlier Buddhist. Given that parts of this complex are identified as roads, it is likely that it was used primarily as a communication route, at least in the medieval period. In fact, they were used as pathways by Jains in the nineteenth century to access their temples, and local tribespeople referred to them as Jarāsandha's Staircase ([1], p. 240).

Buddhist Sites

Both Bimbisāra and his son were responsible for Magadha's expansion; and coincidentally, they were contemporaries of the Buddha, who visited Bimbisāra both before and after his Enlightenment – Bodh Gaya and Rajgir are separated by the Jethian valley and a short walking distance. It was Bimbisāra who donated the first monastery site to the Saṅgha – Veḷuvana (Sanskrit Veṇuvana) Garden. The royal physician Jīvaka also donated a site and by the time Buddha had finished his ministry the Saṅgha was in possession of numerous sites. Although Śrāvastī became more of a headquarters later, Rājagaha remained extremely significant. When Buddha set out for his journey to Kuśināgara, he recited what seems to be a set list (repeated twice in the *Vinaya*) of significant place names: Gijjhakūṭa, Corapapāta (Robber's Cliff), Sattapaṇṇi Cave, the Jīvakamrāvana (Jīvaka's Mango Grove), and so on (*Dīgha Nikāya* 16.3.41–43).

The city was soon after abandoned as a capital by Ajataśātru or his grandson for Paṭalipūtra; however, it is assumed one of the original relic stūpas is located somewhere in the town. It is now identified with a small earthen mound first excavated by Marshall ([7], p. 95), but there is no corroborating evidence. The First Buddhist Council, where 500 arhats recited for 6 months to establish the Sutta and Vinaya Piṭaka, was held at the Sattapaṇṇi Cave.

Sacred Geography and Archaeology

Modern Buddhist sacred geography, and the agenda of most archaeological work, was set by Faxian (337–422) and Xuanzang (596–664). They gave similar lists of places that were important for Buddha's biography, although details vary.

Both emphasized the Sattapaṇṇi Cave, first identified by James Beglar with a cave on the north slope of Vaibhāra. It has an artificial platform built up in front of it and as such is probably an example of an archaic type of ascetic residence. The Pippala Cave, mentioned in the Canon and by both monks, has been variously identified due to ambiguities in translations of the Chinese between "house" and "cave." Opinion (e.g., [1], pp. 89–90) has settled on a watchtower on the western side of the North Gate; but even if this was the structure identified as Pippala by the monks, there is nothing remotely religious about it.

The Elephant Stūpa marks the point where Buddha tamed the mad elephant Nālagiri, who attacked him at the instigation of Devadatta and Ajataśātru. This event was the one that gave Rajgir its place as one of the eight most sacred sites in Buddhist pilgrimage, a status established by the later first millennium CE. The most physically imposing stūpa is on the north slope of Vipula hill. A more likely location might be Bālarāma's Temple, which has evidence of being a decayed stūpa and is just inside Old Rajgir near the North Gate.

The Jīvakamrāvaṇa, identified by both monks as located near Ratnagiri, has been excavated and proved to be an archaic monastery, with apsidal halls, and dating to the third to second centuries BCE.

The archaeologist John Marshall, during his survey of 1905–1906, made a number of identifications, including the Kaḷanda Tank and the Veṇuvana Monastery (a Japanese Veṇuvana is now located there). These identifications are not necessarily firm, but they have become fixed in modern tourist and Buddhist ideas of the site ([5], pp. 213–217).

There are other features of the modern site not mentioned by the monks. The Son-Bhāndār Cave, on the west side of Old Rajgir, was once two caves with crude carvings of Jain *Tīrthāṇkaras* and a large Jain sculpture that has since been lost. An inscription claiming it as a Jain cave from the fourth to fifth centuries CE may be correct; however, one of the caves has a high polish inside that may indicate a Mauryan date.

A survey by V.H. Jackson in 1914–1915 found a number of stone structures on the valley floor, suggesting a history of occupation that is now largely lost. However, he identified a rectangular stone building with cells, towers at each corner, and a manacle or ring. Bimbisāra was imprisoned by his son and starved; however, he could view the Buddha on Gṛdhakūta from a window. Based on the manacle and the view of Chhaṭhagiri, Jackson called it Bimbisāra's jail ([6], p. 269); and though it is most likely a medieval Buddhist vihāra, the name has stuck.

In the center of Old Rajgir is Maṇiyār Māṭh, a temple located under a mound that had a Jain shrine on top. Archaeology has identified a circular building with associated platforms and a construction history going back to the second century BCE if not before. By the sixth century, a series of terracotta plaques around the outside of the circular structure portrayed nāgas and nāgīs, as well as Hindu deities; this, plus a many-headed jar similar to one used on serpent rites in Bengal, a second-century CE image of the nāga Maṇibhādhra, and the dedication of the Jain shrine to the same deity, suggests a serpent cult that at some point was brahmanized. Further south, a Gupta temple has recently been excavated by the Archaeological Survey of India; and a shell script, which is as yet undecipherable, has been found close to the South Gate. Nearby cart ruts, worn into the rock, are now "Bimbisāra's Chariot Tracks."

At the base of both Vaibhāra and Vipula, faults in the rock have created a series of hot and cold springs (kuṇḍs). These are the main focus of Hindu pilgrimage to the site, although Xuanzang connected them to the four past Buddhas. However, one is sacred to the Sikhs and another to Muslims. The most prominent modern buildings are Jain temples on the hills, the Jains having taken over many old Buddhist sites. Many Buddhist images are now in worship as Hindu deities; thus, a continuity of belief is established.

Cross-References

- ▶ Ajātaśatru
- ▶ Asoka
- ▶ Buddhist Councils
- ▶ Devadatta
- ▶ Faxian (337–422 C.E.)
- ▶ Jainism (Yakṣa)
- ▶ Magadha
- ▶ Monastery
- ▶ Xuanzang (Hieun-Tsang)

R

References

1. Broadley AM (1872) The Buddhistic remains of Bihar. J Asiatic Soc Bengal 41:209–312
2. Buchanan F (1936) An account of the districts of Bihar and Patna in 1811–1812. Bihar and Orissa Research Society, Patna
3. Chakrabarti DK (1976) Rajagriha: an early historic site in Eastern India. World Archaeology 7:261–268
4. Cunningham A (1924) Cunningham's ancient geography of India. Chuckervertty, Chatterjee & Co, Calcutta
5. Harding R (2010) Cunningham, Marshall and the Monks: an early historic city as a Buddhist landscape. In: Guha S (ed) The Marshall Albums: photography and archaeology. Mapin and Alkazi Collection, New Delhi, pp 202–227
6. Jackson VH (1917) Notes on old Rajagriha. Archaeological survey of India Annual report 1913–14:265–271
7. Marshall J et al (1909) Rājagṛha and its remains. Archaeological survey of India annual report 1905–06:86–106

Rājanīti

▶ Politics (Buddhism)

Rāma Paṇḍita

▶ Rāma, Indian Buddhism

Rāma, Indian Buddhism

K. T. S. Sarao
Department of Buddhist Studies, University of Delhi, Delhi, India

Synonyms

Rāma Paṇḍita

Definition

The Buddha in one of his previous births when he lived as Rāma, the son of King Dasaratha.

According to the Dasaratha Jātaka (no. 461) of the Jātaka-book ([2], pp. 1–12, 13–17; [3]: iv.123–130; [1]: iv.78–82), the Buddha was born as Rāma in one of his previous births, i.e., as a bodhisatta (Sk: bodhisattva). In the Dasaratha Jātaka, Rāma Paṇḍita (Rāma the Wise) is shown as a righteous king and also as a person who had conquered sorrow and was not affected by eight conditions of this world (gain and loss, fame and dishonor, praise and blame, bliss and woe) ([1]: iv.78 fn.2). Thus, when he received the news of the death of his father, he neither showed any emotions nor did he feel sorrowful.

According to the story told in the Dasaratha Jātaka, Dasaratha who ruled righteously at Bārāṇasī had 16,000 wives. His chief queen bore him two sons called Rāma Paṇḍita (Rāma the Wise) and Lakkhaṇa Kumāra and a daughter called Sītā Devī. After giving birth to these three children, the chief queen died and Dasaratha raised another queen to the status of chief queen. She bore him a son who was named Bharata Kumāra. The king was so pleased that he offered the queen a boon and asked her to choose. Though she accepted the offer, she put it off for the time being. When Bharat Kumar was seven, she reminded Dasaratha of his promise and asked him to give the kingdom to her son. The king would not give her this gift and she kept on nagging him about it day after day. The king thought to himself: "Women are ungrateful and treacherous. This woman might use a forged letter or a treacherous bribe to get my sons murdered" ([1]: iv.79). So he called astrologers and asked them to calculate the time of his death for him. They calculated it to 12 years thenceforth. In the light of this, he commanded Rāma Paṇḍita and Lakkhaṇa Kumāra to go to some neighboring country or the forest and return only after 12 years to avoid any mischief that might befall them. The two sons made a promise to follow their father's advice. Sītā Devī also insisted on accompanying her brothers. So the three took leave of their father and went away from Bārāṇasī. They found a suitable place in the Himālaya and built a hermitage there. Here Lakkhaṇa Kumāra and Sītā Devī took care of Rāma Paṇḍita as he was like father to them.

The grieving King Dasaratha died in the ninth year and the queen gave orders that Bharata Kumāra be crowned as the king. However, the courtiers and Bharata Kumāra refused to oblige her. Bharata Kumāra declared that he would go and fetch Rāma Paṇḍita from the forest and would crown him as the king. He pitched his camp not far away from the hermitage and approached Rāma Paṇḍita with a few courtiers, and at a time when Lakkhaṇa Kumāra and Sītā Devī were away in woods gathering fruit, Bharata Kumāra told him weepingly all that had occurred in the kingdom. Rāma Paṇḍita being immune to emotions gave a discourse to Bharata Kumar and the accompanying courtiers on the doctrine of impermanence and they lost all their grief. Now Bharata Kumāra begged Rāma Paṇḍita to accept the Kingdom of Bārāṇasī. But he refused saying that he could do so only at the end of 12 years as otherwise it would amount to disobedience to their father's command. However, when Bharata Kumar asked as to who would carry on the government all this while, he gave him his straw slippers and said: "Until I come, these slippers shall do it" ([1]: iv.81). Then Lakkhaṇa Kumāra, Sītā, and Bharata Kumāra returned to Bārāṇasī with the slippers. Henceforth, the kingdom was ruled by the straw slippers for 3 years. Whenever justice had to be delivered, the courtiers would place the slippers on the royal throne. If the slippers stayed quiet, the decision was deemed as correct. However, if the slippers beat upon each other, then the sign was viewed as an indication that the decision was wrong and the case was reexamined.

At the end of 3 years, Rāma Paṇḍita returned to Bārāṇasī and took his seat in the royal park. On hearing of the news of his arrival, Lakkhaṇa and Bharata Kumāra came to receive him at the park along with the courtiers. Sītā Devī was made the chief queen and then both Rāma Paṇḍita and Sītā were given the ceremonial sprinkling. Thereafter, riding a magnificent chariot and making a ceremonial right-wise circuit, Rāma Paṇḍita entered the city of Bārāṇasī. He reigned righteously for 16,000 years and Sītā's devotion to him became legendary ([2]: iv.559, 560; [4]: lxxiii.137). At the end of his reign, he went to heaven.

Rāma's battle with Rāvaṇa and many episodes narrated in Vālmīki's Rāmāyaṇa are mentioned in the later Pāli chronicles, such as the Cūḷavaṃsa ([4]: lxiv.42; lxviii.20; lxxv.59; lxxxiii.46, 69, 88). Interestingly, some of the ruling princes of Southeast Asia and Sri Lanka claimed descent from Rāma. King Jagatipāla (1047–51 C.E.) of Sri Lanka is one such example. He came from Ayojjhā (Sk: Ayodhyā) and declared Lord Rāma to be his ancestor. Having killed King Vikkamapaṇḍu, he ruled in Rohaṇa until his own death at the hands of the Coḷas ([4]: lvi.13f). King Jagatipāla's daughter called Līlāvatī later became the queen of King Vijayabāhu I ([4]: lix.23f).

Cross-References

▶ Bārāṇasī
▶ Bodhisattva
▶ Jātaka
▶ Rāmāyaṇa, Indian Buddhism

References

1. Cowell EW, Chalmers R, Francis HT, Neil RA, Rouse WHD (trans) (1895–1907) The Jātaka or the stories of the Buddha's former births. Cambridge University Press, Cambridge
2. Fausböll V (ed and trans) (1971) Dasaratha-Jātaka, being the Buddhist story of King Rāma, vol 6. Trübner, London
3. Fausböll V (ed) (1977–1897) The Jātaka, vol 6. Luzac, London
4. Geiger W, Rickmers CM (trans) (1929–1930) The Cūlavaṃsa: being the more recent part of the Mahāvaṃsa, vol 2. Pali Text Society, London

R

Rāmāyaṇa, Indian Buddhism

K. T. S. Sarao
Department of Buddhist Studies, University of Delhi, Delhi, India

Synonyms

Dasaratha Jātaka

Definition

The story of Rāma Paṇḍita.

The story of Rāma is known as the *Dasaratha Jātaka* in Indian Buddhism. It is *jātaka* no. 461 of the Jātaka book in the Khuddaka Nikāya of the Pāli Tipiṭaka ([2], pp. 1–12, 13–17; [3]: iv.123–130; [1]: iv.78–82). As per the Jātaka book, this story was told by Śākyamuni Buddha in the Jetavana at Śrāvastī. The backdrop to the story provided in the Jātaka book is that a landowner was overwhelmed with sorrow due to his father's death and consequently had neglected his duties. When the Buddha learned of this, he went to the landowner's house to allay his sorrow and consoled him saying that wise men in the past who were aware of the eight conditions of this world (gain and loss, fame and dishonor, praise and blame, bliss and woe) did not feel miserable at a father's death ([1]: iv.78 fn.2). Then on being requested by the landowner, the Buddha told him a story of the past.

The Buddha told him that once a great king called Dasaratha ruled righteously at Bārāṇasī. He had 16,000 wives. His chief queen (*jeṭṭhikā aggamahesī*) bore him two sons called Rāma Paṇḍita (Rāma the Wise) and Lakkhaṇa Kumāra and a daughter called Sītā Devī. After giving birth to these three children, the chief queen died and Dasaratha raised another queen to the status of chief queen. The king loved her dearly and in time she gave birth to a son who was named Bharata Kumāra. The king was so pleased that he offered the queen a boon (*vara*) and asked her to choose. Though she accepted the offer, she put it off for the time being.

When Bharat Kumar was seven, she reminded Dasaratha of his promise and asked him to give the kingdom to her son. The king would not give her this gift and she kept on nagging him about it day after day. The king thought to himself: "Women are ungrateful and treacherous. This woman might use a forged letter or a treacherous bribe to get my sons murdered" ([1]: iv.79). So he called astrologers and asked them to tell him the time of his death. They told him that he would live for another 12 years. So he told his sons, Rāma Paṇḍita and Lakkhaṇa Kumāra, to go to some neighboring country or the forest and return only after 12 years to avoid any mischief that might befall them. The two sons made a promise to follow their father's advice. Sītā Devī also insisted on accompanying her brothers. So the three took leave of their father and went away from Bārāṇasī weeping. They found a suitable place in the Himālaya which was well watered and where wild fruits were available in abundance. The three built a hermitage here and Lakkhaṇa Kumāra and Sītā Devī took care of Rāma Paṇḍita as he was like father to them.

King Dasaratha died in the 9th year. The queen gave orders that Bharata Kumāra be crowned as the king. However, the courtiers and Bharata Kumāra refused to oblige her. Bharata Kumāra declared that he would go and fetch Rāma Paṇḍita from the forest and would crown him as the king. He pitched his camp not far away from the hermitage and approached Rāma Paṇḍita with a few courtiers and at a time when Lakkhaṇa Kumāra and Sītā Devī were away in woods gathering fruit, Bharata Kumāra told him weepingly all that had occurred in the kingdom. Rāma Paṇḍita being immune to emotions gave a discourse to Bharata Kumar and the accompanying courtiers on the doctrine of impermanence and they lost all their grief. Now Bharata Kumāra begged Rāma Paṇḍita to accept the Kingdom of Bārāṇasī:

> Brother," said Rāma, "take Lakkhaṇa and Sītā with you, and administer the kingdom yourselves." "No, my lord, you take it." "Brother, my father commanded me to receive the kingdom at the end of twelve years. If I go now, I shall not carry out his bidding. After three more years I will come." "Who will carry on the government all that time?" "You do it." "I will not." "Then until I come, these slippers shall do it," said Rāma, and doffing his slippers of straw he gave them to his brother. So these three persons took the slippers, and bidding the wise man farewell, went to Benares with their great crowd of followers. ([1]: iv.81)

The kingdom was ruled by the straw slippers for 3 years. Whenever justice had to be delivered, the courtiers would place the slippers on the royal throne. If the slippers stayed quiet, the decision was deemed as correct. However, if the slippers beat upon each other, then the sign was viewed as an indication that the decision was wrong and the case was reexamined.

When 3 years were over, Rāma Paṇḍita came to Bārāṇasī and took his seat in a park. When the princes heard of this, they came to the park along with the courtiers. They made Sītā Devī the chief queen (*aggamahesī*) and then both were given the ceremonial sprinkling. Thereafter, riding a magnificent chariot and making a ceremonial right-wise circuit, Rāma Paṇḍita entered the city. Thereafter he reigned righteously for 16,000 years and at the end of his reign went to heaven.

At the end of the discourse, the Buddha identified the characters in the story as follows: King Suddhodana was King Dasaratha, Rāhulamātā was Sītā Devī, Ānanda was Bharata Kumāra, and the Buddha himself was Rāma Paṇḍita.

Though some scholars have suggested that the Dasaratha Jātaka is older than Vālmīki's Rāmāyaṇa (e.g., [6], p. 258), mostly it is agreed that the Dasaratha Jātaka is not the most ancient story but a later distortion (see [5], pp. 64–67; [4], pp. 433–434). In fact, Richard Gombrich goes so far as to call the Dasaratha Jātaka "a tissue of arbitrary events and even *non sequiturs*" ([4], p. 434) which is "not a genuine story" ([1], p. 436). According to him, the Dasaratha Jātaka "is a (perhaps intentionally) garbled story which cannot be taken seriously as an early version of the Rāma legend, let alone as proving that early Buddhists let brothers marry sisters" ([4], pp. 427–437). Interestingly, in the Southeast Asian countries such as Laos, Thailand, and Cambodia where Theravāda Buddhism is followed, none of the many versions of the Rāmāyaṇa including the *Khmer Reamker*, the *Lao Phra Lak Phra Lam*, and the *Thai Ramakien* is a variant of the Dasaratha Jātaka.

Cross-References

- ▶ Bārāṇasī
- ▶ Jātaka
- ▶ Ramma
- ▶ Śrāvastī

References

1. Cowell EW, Chalmers R, Francis HT, Neil RA, Rouse WHD (trans) (1895–1907) The Jātaka or the stories of the Buddha's former births. Cambridge University Press, Cambridge
2. Fausböll V (ed and trans) (1971) Dasaratha-Jātaka, being the Buddhist story of King Rāma, vol 6. Trübner, London
3. Fausböll V (ed) (1977–1897) The Jātaka, vol 6. Luzac, London
4. Gombrich R (1985) The Vessantara Jātaka, the Rāmāyaṇa and the Dasaratha Jātaka. J Am Orient Soc 105(3):427–443
5. Jacobi H (1960) The Rāmāyaṇa (trans: Ghosal SN). Oriental Institute, Baroda
6. Sadasivan SN (2000) A social history of India. A.P.H Publishing, New Delhi

Ramma

▶ Vārāṇasī (Buddhism)

Rammaka

▶ Vārāṇasī (Buddhism)

Rammanagara

▶ Vārāṇasī (Buddhism)

Rammavatī

▶ Vārāṇasī (Buddhism)

Ratnagiri

Claudine Bautze-Picron
Centre National de la Recherche Scientifique (CNRS), UMR 7528 'Mondes Iranien et Indien', Paris, France

Synonyms

Ratnāgiri

Definition

Monastic site

Ratnagiri is a site in Orissa (lat. 20°38' N.; long. 86°20' E.) situated very closely to two other contemporary sites, Udayagiri and Lalitagiri, all three constituting a major Buddhist nucleus from the eighth up to the late twelfth century or early thirteenth century. This region is associated with the Puṣpagiri monastery known from Buddhist historical sources, but no archaeological or epigraphic evidence would sustain the identification of this monastery with one of the three sites. Inscribed seals locally found reveal, however, that Ratnagiri was a "great monastery" or *mahāvihāra* ([5], p. 226). Although it is difficult to ascertain a date for the earliest phase of these sites – the Gupta period being a possibility ([1], p. 46; [5], p. 227) – it is evidently between the eighth and the twelfth centuries that these sites knew their peak of activity. Royal patronage during the rule of the Śailodbhavas in the seventh and of the early Bhaumakaras in the eighth century seems to have been active in the region, favoring the Buddhist community ([1], p. 44).

Architecture, Stūpas

The Archaeological Survey of India has led extensive excavations and restored the monuments of Ratnagiri. The main monument (monument 1) at Ratnagiri was a *stūpa* built in bricks on the top of the hillock before the ninth or tenth century on an earlier one perhaps originally erected during the Gupta period. The hemispheric dome, now destroyed, rested then on a square *medhi* or plinth measuring nearly 4.20 m in height and 14.50 in length; the platform is basically of the *triratha* type, i.e., the front surface of each side shows one projection in the center with two side surfaces setting thus back from it. Moreover, each one of these three surfaces or *rathas* has been divided in two, thus making a total of six *rathas* on each side. At a later period, the monument was restored and the square base with its projections disappeared within a structure, circular from the bottom ([6], Vol. 1, pp. 25–151) (Fig. 1).

Ratnagiri, Fig. 1 Main *stūpa* (Photo © Ken Ishikawa)

Ratnagiri, Fig. 2 Group of *stūpas*, those in the foreground with images of the Tārā, Hevajra and Ṣaḍakṣarī Lokeśvara (Photo © Ken Ishikawa)

A large number of smaller *stūpas* (or *caityas*) of different sizes were erected all around the central monument. Some were constructed and only their lower level survived while many others were carved out of a single piece of stone. The monolithic *stūpas* of Ratnagiri present the classical structure of the monument with a high pedestal supporting the hemispheric part which can be plain and only adorned with flat bands or contains one or four niches with images of various deities of the late Buddhist pantheon either carved out of the monoliths or fixed within their niches. The square pavilion or *harmikā* which surmounts the monument and protects the pole with umbrellas arising out of it is usually an added element which has been lost in the course of time. In the absence of inscriptions, it is rather difficult to propose a proper explanation justifying the presence of such a large number of small *caityas* in Ratnagiri; a similar situation is encountered at Bodhgaya, the site where Śākyamuni reached his spiritual enlightenment and became, thus, *Buddha*. True, such monuments are found in practically all Buddhist sites, but some sites, Ratnagiri or Bodhgaya for instance, evidently attracted more the attention of private donors, probably monks but perhaps also lay persons, who financed the carving of images and *stūpas* in honor of the Buddha, the site, the monument, or the institution. Structural *stūpas* could eventually fulfill their fundamental function which was to hide relics; seals inscribed with *dhāraṇīs*, "magic verses," were, for instance, found in the core of the *stūpa* 2, but also in monastery 1 ([1], pp. 46, 67).

Beside the fact that these small *caityas* were produced and offered as a gesture of devotion, those having images in their niches were probably also understood to be small shrines (Fig. 2).

The Monasteries

Two monasteries were constructed at Ratnagiri around the seventh and eighth centuries. Both, like another one erected at Udayagiri ([1], p. 75), have a square ground plan with an inner courtyard

Ratnagiri, Fig. 3 View of the façade of monastery 1 (Photo © Ken Ishikawa)

on which the monastic cells open. Both monasteries are open to the south whereas the one in Udayagiri is directed to the north. Monuments are built in bricks but stone has been massively used for covering the courtyard or for ornamental purposes – being used for door frames for instance. Images carved in stone could also be inserted in niches distributed in some walls.

Monastery 1 is the most important of them. It is the largest dwelling site built north of the great *stūpa*; it measures nearly 55 m long and has an impressive entrance made up of two porches, one to the outside and one in the direction of the courtyard. The inner courtyard, nearly 27 m in width, has a pillared veranda running in front of the cells which are distributed on two levels. A shrine has been inserted in the middle of the rear row of cells, reproducing, thus, a ground plan which probably traces its origin at Ajaṇṭā ([6], Vol. 1, pp. 152–245). The monastery underwent a thorough restoration named "Period II" by Debala Mitra who excavated the site; this period which has been variously dated between the tenth and the eleventh centuries saw, for instance, the façade of the shrine being completely renewed ([1], p. 49; [4], p. 371; [6], Vol. 1, p. 155) (Figs. 3 and 4).

The doorways to the monastery and the shrine were framed by a sculpted ornamentation of high quality showing groups of attendants at ground level, or characters such as Bodhisattvas or *nāgarājas*, "serpent-kings," and a similar structure is observed at the monastery of Udayagiri. Lakṣmī watered by two elephants is carved on the lintel, retaining thus a position which she has since the very beginning of Indian art, protecting the gate and symbolizing the welfare brought by the sacred place. As mentioned above, the façade of the shrine was completely renewed in Period II through a very ornamental screen which has been rebuilt by the excavators in the western part of the courtyard, thus not at its original position (Figs. 5 and 6).

Iconography, Images, or Richness

Sculptures were inserted in niches distributed around the main entrance to the courtyard, on the outer wall or on the side walls of the inner

Ratnagiri, Fig. 4 Entrance to monastery 1 (Photo © Ken Ishikawa)

Ratnagiri, Fig. 5 View of the façade of the shrine, monastery 1 (Photo © Ken Ishikawa)

Ratnagiri, Fig. 6 Screen initially built in front of the shrine, monastery 1 (Photo © Ken Ishikawa)

porch where Hārītī and Pāñcika face each other, an iconographic program which traces its origin in Maharashtra where it is observed at Ajaṇṭā, Aurangabad, or Ellora. Two further images of Jambhala, god of richness, are displayed on either side of the door frame; Jambhala is the Buddhist echo to the Hindu Kubera and evolved out of Pāñcika, showing also deep closeness to the two earlier "treasures of the lotus and the conch" (*padma* and *śaṅkhanidhis*) that were a common motif at Ajaṇṭā and other sites of Maharashtra. This iconography is here deeply rooted into the belief that richness and fertility were brought by the nature or by gods and goddesses, as seen in the exquisitely carved foliated volutes intermingled with dwarfs, the row of lotus petals and that of pearls which frame the entrance, or in the presence of Lakṣmī, the two portly male figures outside and Hārītī and Pāñcika inside. This iconography protects the threshold between the profane and sacred spaces, at the same time it clearly refers to the sacred space, here the monastery, as a place which is the source of (spiritual) richness.

The Buddha

The images installed in the shrine of Monastery 1 illustrate likewise an iconographic program which traces its source in Maharashtra, showing the Buddha displaying the gesture of enlightenment, i.e., touching the earth with the right hand (*bhūmisparśamudrā*) and being flanked by Avalokiteśvara and Vajrapāni. This is also the main image of the Buddha to be depicted and worshipped in Eastern India up to the end of the twelfth century, showing the importance which Bodhgaya, the site of enlightenment, had at that period, being a place where monks from all over South Asia and the Asian world were converging.

The image which used to stand in the shrine of Monastery 2 shows the Buddha standing and displaying the gesture of generosity, the right hand open toward the devotees who stand or kneel at his feet. This image stands in a tradition inaugurated in Orissa in the sixth century at Lalitagiri and which through its style and iconography relates to practically contemporary images at

Ratnagiri, Fig. 7 Shrine of monastery 1 (Photo © Ken Ishikawa)

Sarnath and Ajaṇṭā where they were all present on the façades of monuments 19 and 29. The same type of image can be seen at Udayagiri (Figs. 7, 8, and 9).

Maṇḍalas

The triad which stands in the shrine of Monastery 1 reflects esoteric tendencies which emerged in Maharashtra, in sites like Ellora and Nasik in the sixth and seventh centuries, the central Buddha, symbol of the *buddhakula* ("family of the *buddha*"), being surrounded by Vajrapāni at his proper left, symbol of the *vajrakula* ("family of the thunder or *vajra*"), and Avalokiteśvara at his proper right, image of the *padmakula* ("family of the lotus or *padma*").

Another esoteric aspect which arose within the context of Maharashtra before finding its way in Orissa is the *maṇḍala* where the Buddha is surrounded by eight Bodhisattvas. In Orissa, the Bodhisattvas can not only be depicted around the Buddha on a single image but also by the objects

Ratnagiri, Fig. 8 Shrine of monastery 2 (Photo © Ken Ishikawa)

Ratnagiri, Fig. 9 Rock-cut images at Udayagiri (Photo © Ken Ishikawa)

of eight stelas forming a group. Among them, four act as main Bodhisattvas, i.e., Avalokiteśvara, Vajrapāni, Maitreya and Mañjuśrī, and occupy positions which are close to the central Buddha whereas the four remaining ones have a rather "secondary" position, these are Samantabhadra, Kṣitigarbha, Ākāśagarbha, and Sarvanivaraṇaviṣkambhin. The group can also be seen distributed around Avalokiteśvara who is then depicted twice. Both topics, the triad or the group of eight Bodhisattvas form either the basic structure of a *maṇḍala* mentioned in the *Mahāvairocanasūtra* or a *maṇḍala* as such [2, 3] (Fig. 10).

Ratnagiri, Fig. 10 Avalokiteśvara being surrounded by eight Bodhisattvas, two of them being depicted in the pedestal, Udayagiri (Photo © Ken Ishikawa)

Bodhisattvas and Female Images

Beside belonging to the groups of eight Bodhisattvas, Avalokiteśvara is the most commonly met character who presents various aspects, he can be two-armed and standing under a tree in his Cintāmaṇi Lokeśvara form, be depicted meditating on the sufferings of the universe in his

Ratnagiri, Fig. 11 Four-armed Avalokiteśvara (Amoghapāśa Lokeśvara) accompanied by the Tārā, Bhṛkuṭī, and Hayagrīva, and two further female seated images in the upper part, near monastery 1, Ratnagiri (Photo © Ken Ishikawa)

Ratnagiri, Fig. 12 Aṣṭamahābhaya Tārā, Ratnagiri (Photo © Ken Ishikawa)

Cintāmaṇicakra Lokeśvara form, or be four-armed in his Ṣaḍakṣarī Lokeśvara aspect for instance. A common form encountered at Ratnagiri shows him four-armed, displaying the gesture of generosity with the right hand and holding a specific set of attributes, i.e., the *padma*, the water flask (*kamaṇḍalu*), the rosary (*akṣamālā*), and the noose (*pāśa*) to which this form owes its name: Amoghapāśa Lokeśvara. These forms are described in *sādhanas* or "propitiations," texts describing very precisely images to be mentally visualized with which the adept or *sādhaka* identifies himself. These texts, written at different periods, were compiled during the eleventh/twelfth century in the *Sādhanamālā* which constitutes a precious source for identifying contemporary images from all over Eastern India (Fig. 11).

Numerous images of Bodhisattvas show them standing and often accompanied by two female attendants. As a matter of fact, and also in the line of the development noted in Maharashtra from the sixth to the early eighth century, much attention is paid to the representation of the female in iconography. This increasing importance is also portrayed by the fact that the Tārā who is the image par excellence of compassion and generosity for all beings inherits Avalokiteśvara's function of protecting devotees from dangers encountered while traveling (lion, wild elephant, snake, fire, shipwreck, robbers, imprisonment, threaten of death) – this function being earlier illustrated by images of the Bodhisattva in the excavated sites of Maharashtra (Ajaṇṭā, Aurangabad, Kanheri). Acting as such, she is named Aṣṭamahābhaya Tārā. Besides, the Tārā is also, in company of Bhṛkuṭī, an attendant to Avalokiteśvara, as already observed at an earlier period in Ellora.

Another main female deity to be depicted is Mārīcī, the "Sun Goddess," who symbolizes the light which pervaded the universe when Śākyamuni reached enlightenment and who is

Ratnagiri, Fig. 13 Mārīcī, Ratnagiri (Photo © Ken Ishikawa)

depicted riding her chariot pulled by seven wild sows (Figs. 12 and 13).

Beside such large images of Bodhisattvas, a number of sculptures were recovered illustrating characters belonging to the late Buddhist pantheon of the "way of the Vajra" or Vajrayāna. Wrathful characters, known as *krodha*, are introduced, such as Hayagrīva who becomes a faithful attendant of Avalokiteśvara. Such images, mostly dating back to the eleventh century, were often integrated in the small *caityas* distributed in the site. In this context, Hevajra, a supreme aspect of the Buddha, is often depicted in his most traditional aspect. He is seen dancing on a corpse and holding the *vajra* in the upraised right hand and the skull (*kapāla*) in the left hand while retaining in his left arm his third attribute, i.e., the *khaṭvāṅga*. Details cannot always be clearly visible in the small images inserted in the *caityas*, but mention must be made that his hair stands on end, his facial features show wide open eyes and fangs in the open mouth whereas a long garland of heads hangs from his shoulders. Beside the philosophical background of such images like Mārīcī and

Ratnagiri, Fig. 14 *Caitya* with image of Hevajra in its niche (Photo © Ken Ishikawa)

Hevajra, one cannot fail to suggest them also to be images of violence illustrating the reaction of the Buddhist community confronted at that period by a tragic historical situation, progressively losing the royal patronage and being reduced to the sole walls of the monastery, whereas the Hindu temple was gaining in importance and power (Fig. 14).

Cross-References

- ▶ Ajaṇṭā
- ▶ Aurangabad
- ▶ Avalokiteśvara
- ▶ Ellora
- ▶ Stūpa

References

1. Bandyopadhaya B (2004) Buddhist centres of Orissa, Lalitagiri, Ratnagiri and Udayagiri. Sundeep Prakashan, New Delhi
2. Bautze-Picron C (1997) Le groupe des huit Grands Bodhisatva en Inde: genèse et développement. In: Eilenberg N, Subhadradis Diskul MC, Brown RL (eds) Living a life in accord with Dhamma: papers in honour of professor Jean Boisselier on his eightieth birthday. Silpakorn University, Bangkok, pp 1–55
3. Bautze-Picron C (2000) Nāsik: the late Mahāyāna caves 2, 15, 20 & 23–24. In: Taddei M, De Marco G (eds) South Asian archaeology 1997, Proceedings of the fourteenth international conference of the European association of South Asian Archaeologists, held in the Istituto Italiano per l'Africa el'Oriente, Palazzo Brancaccio, Rome, 7–14 July 1997. Istituto Italiano per l'Africa e l'Oriente, Rome III, pp 1201–1227
4. Donaldson T (2001) Iconography of the Buddhist sculpture of Orissa. Indira Gandhi National centre for the Arts/Abhinav Publications, New Delhi
5. Mitra D (1971) Buddhist monuments. Sahitya Samsad, Calcutta
6. Mitra D (1983) Ratnagiri (1958–61). Archaeological Survey of India, New Delhi

Ratnāgiri

▶ Ratnagiri

Rāyagiha (Ardhamagadhi)

▶ *Rājagṛha*

Ṛddhi

▶ *Iddhi*

Reality (Buddhism)

Ana Bajželj
Department of Philosophy, Faculty of Arts, University of Ljubljana, Ljubljana, Slovenia
Polonsky Academy, The Van Leer Jerusalem Institute, Jerusalem, Israel

Abbreviations

M	Majjhima-nikāya
S	Samyutta-nikāya
Sn	Sutta-nipāta

Synonyms

The state of the true existence of things; The way things really are; What there is

Definition

The Buddhist conception of reality is based on the way one experiences the world. Rather than developing abstract theories on the true nature of things, the Buddhist endeavor to explain reality is primarily aimed at transforming the lives of practicing individuals. The Buddhist articulation of reality therefore goes hand in hand with the practical path that leads one, who has realized the way things truly are, to enlightenment.

The Buddhist View of Reality

The notion of reality that Buddhism puts forward is primarily experiential reality, the analysis of which begins with the experience of human suffering. The Buddha is said to have renounced the world upon seeing a sick man, an old man, a dead man, and an ascetic. These encounters inspired him to start searching for a path that would lead to release from affliction. Upon the attainment of enlightenment, he realized the true nature of reality, the paradigmatic exposition of which is referred to as the four noble truths or catvāri ārya-satyāni, a term also variously translated as "the truths of the noble one(s)," "the truths for a noble one," or "the ennobling realities." These truths represent the core of the Buddhist doctrine, but ought not to be taken as dogmas. In fact, the Sanskrit word for truth is satya, which is derived from the verbal root √as-, meaning "to be." The term satya may then literally be translated as "that which stands in relation to being," "that which has being," "that which is real," "that which is actual," or "that which expresses the nature of things as they really are." The four noble truths are therefore not propositional truths. On the contrary, they are considered to be universal truths or realities that can be unconditionally asserted. Hence, all the other aspects of the Buddhist doctrine in one way or another build on the basic structure of the noble truths and articulate the implications that follow from them. Accordingly, these truths represent the foundation of all later Buddhist deliberations on the nature of reality. Here, the four noble truths will be outlined as the basic assertions about the nature of reality. Additionally, later developments of certain aspects of the doctrine of the four noble truths will be indicated. The Buddha explained the nature of reality through the lens of these four truths during his first sermon at Sārnāth that took place after his attainment of enlightenment. This teaching is described in the discourse titled The Setting in Motion of the Wheel of the Dharma or the Dharmacakra-pravartana-sūtra (Pāli Dhammacakkappavattana-sutta) (S V 420 ff.). The four noble truths are the following:

1. Life is marked with unsatisfactoriness (Skt. duḥkha).
2. There is a cause (Skt. samudaya) for unsatisfactoriness, namely, craving (Skt. tṛṣṇā).
3. There is an end (Skt. nirodha) to unsatisfactoriness and craving, namely, nirvāṇa.
4. There is a path (Skt. mārga) leading to the cessation of unsatisfactoriness, namely, the noble eighthfold path.

The four truths are frequently compared to a medical diagnosis: the recognition of a disease, the identification of its cause, the determination of its curability, and the description of the treatment leading to the cure. While the first two noble truths analyze the nature of reality as unsatisfactory, the third noble truth asserts the possibility of the end of unsatisfactoriness, and the fourth noble truth outlines the way to this goal. Even though the Buddha takes the role of a doctor in this analogy, the Buddhist doctrine maintains that everyone must tread the way to the cure on their own, since all beings are ultimately individually responsible for their unsatisfactoriness.

The first teaching of the Buddha pronounces that the first noble truth ought to be understood, the second abandoned, the third realized, and the fourth cultivated.

The *first noble truth* is the truth of unsatisfactoriness. It is articulated as follows:

(a) Birth, old age, sickness, and death are duḥkha.
(b) Sorrow, lamentation, pain, grief, and despair are duḥkha.
(c) Union with what is displeasing, separation from what is pleasing, and not to get what one wants are duḥkha.
(d) In short, the five aggregates subject to clinging are duḥkha.

As noted, the statement that life is unsatisfactory is not a value judgment but a truth statement. In other words, the recognition of reality as unsatisfactory is not aimed at proving that life is unpleasant, but at exposing the fundamental fact of empirical existence and most importantly explaining its nature. The term duḥkha is normally translated as suffering but in actual fact has numerous nuances and essentially refers to all kinds of unsatisfactoriness and unease. The first noble truth illustrates the character of duḥkha with several descriptions. Besides sorrow, lamentation, pain, grief, and despair, the four phenomena of birth, old age, sickness, and death are enumerated as examples of unsatisfactory experiences. It is self-evident why the events of old age, sickness, and death may lead to anguish and distress. Apart from being physically and mentally painful, they also reflect discomfort at losing something pleasant, e.g., youthfulness, health, and life. Furthermore, birth is considered to be unsatisfactory since it is at birth that one starts to grasp at things. The Buddha recognized that craving (Skt. tṛṣṇā) eventually leads to attachment (Skt. upādāna), this being the origin of unsatisfactoriness. When a relation of attachment is established, changes in the character of the relation often result in unrequited yearning that leads to mental unease, such as sorrow, lamentation, pain, grief, and despair. The discourses classify duḥkha into three types, namely, duḥkha as physical pain, duḥkha due to change, and duḥkha of conditioned phenomena (S IV 259). The first two have already been clarified. The third refers to states of happiness and contentment as imperfect states that are merely conditionally satisfactory.

Further, it is said that "union with what is displeasing," "separation from what is pleasing," and "not to get what one wants" are unsatisfactory. Unsatisfactoriness is therefore defined as a non-fulfilled want or a lack that one will sooner or later experience throughout one's life, even though one may normally be contented and happy. This corresponds to the abovementioned experience of unease when change occurs in the relation of attachment.

Lastly, the first noble truth explains the five aggregates subject to clinging (Skt. upādana-skandha) as unsatisfactory. The Buddhist doctrine refutes the notion of an abiding self that undergoes experience. By critically analyzing the human experience, the Buddha upheld that what is normally considered to be a self is merely a constant flux of the five aggregates (Skt. skandha). These are groups of phenomena that represent continuously changing fundamental psychophysical constituents or factors of existence. The five are form (Skt. rūpa), feelings (Skt. vedanā), cognition (Skt. saṃjñā), volitions (Skt. saṃskāra), and consciousness (Skt. vijñāna). They are considered to be causally conditioned and, as noted, independent of any kind of underlying permanent substance. However, even though they are impersonal, they are normally grasped at and are identified as "mine," "I," and "my self" (M I 138–139), and due to their impermanent nature, such clinging unavoidably generates unsatisfactory relations. The skandha analysis reveals the more subtle nuance of the term duḥkha. If the whole range of physical and mental factors of experience is considered to be duḥkha, this means that the most common translation of the term as suffering leaves out a large spectrum of its implications. It is not simply unpleasant experiences that are duḥkha, but all conditioned phenomena, including pleasant experiences. This feature of reality is bound to the impermanence of experiential events and their impossibility to ever be enduringly satisfactory. It corresponds to one of the three marks (Skt. trilakṣaṇa) of dependent existence. The three are impermanence (Skt. anityā), unsatisfactoriness (Skt. duḥkha), and non-self (Skt. anātman). The last is supposed to follow from the realization of the first two. From the realization that reality is essentially impermanent and therefore unsatisfactory follows an insight into the last mark of conditioned existence, namely, the selfless nature of the five aggregates. In other words, as all the five aggregates are realized to be impermanent and unsatisfactory continua, what is normally considered to be a person is comprehended to actually be empty (Skt. śūnya) of an independent and permanent self (S II 66–68). Besides the skandha scheme, there are two other common models to analyze human experience. One is the classification of the 12 spheres (Skt. āyatana), namely, the six senses (the sixth being the mind), and their respective sense objects, and the other the classification of the 18 elements (Skt. dhātu), which includes the six senses, their corresponding objects, and the six respective kinds of consciousness.

The apprehension of the universal nature of unsatisfactoriness, expounded with the first noble truth, is tightly linked to the *second noble truth* that recognizes the origin (Skt. samudaya) of unsatisfactoriness and thereby the foundation of the human predicament. This is formulated as follows:

(a) Craving (Skt. tṛṣṇā), accompanied by delight and attachment, leads to renewed existence.
(b) The objects of craving are sensual pleasures, existence, and nonexistence.

Tṛṣṇā literally means thirst and refers to cravings. Since no phenomenon lasts in the essentially impermanent reality, any wish to prolong a certain experience is bound to inevitably lead to unsatisfactoriness; craving can never be lastingly satisfied. The first part of the second noble truth states that craving leads to renewed existence. On a large scale, craving can be seen as the ultimate explanation of why beings are continually born and die and are reborn and redie. Renewed existence in the beginningless cycle of rebirths (Skt. saṃsāra) is stimulated by the principle of craving which creates karmic influences that guide the five aggregates throughout life and determine their postmortem fate. On a more subtle level, craving is the source that brings forth renewed existence all the time. Every thought, word, or deed caused by craving forms new conditions that perpetuate and affect the future existence.

Even though the Buddha refuted the notion of a persistent identity, he therefore did not reject the doctrine of saṃsāra and the empirical continuity within it. This approach is regarded to be the middle path (Skt. madhyamā pratipad) between eternalism (Skt. śāśvata-vāda), i.e., the idea that the self survives death, on the one hand, and annihilationism (Skt. uccheda-vāda), i.e., the idea that material death is the definite end of life, on the other. The former corresponds to the view of the Upaniṣads and the latter to the view of the Indian materialists. The two standpoints were rejected by the Buddha since they both remain rooted in the notion of the self.

The Buddhist doctrine maps out the continuity of existence within the framework of the cycle of rebirths with a 12-fold scheme of dependent origination (Skt. pratītya-samutpāda). The twelve links (Skt. nidāna) are (1) ignorance (Skt. avidyā), (2) volitions (Skt. saṃskāra), (3) consciousness (Skt. vijñāna), (4) name-and-form (Skt. nāma-rūpa), (5) six sense spheres (Skt. ṣad-āyatana), (6) contact (Skt. sparśa), (7) feelings (Skt. vedanā), (8) craving (Skt. tṛṣṇā), (9) grasping (Skt. upādāna), (10) becoming (Skt. bhava), (11) birth (Skt. jāti), and (12) old age and death (Skt. jarā-maraṇa). This scheme represents the basic law of conditionality, namely, that phenomena arise in dependence upon certain conditions – if A exists, B arises. From this follows that with the elimination of these same conditions, the conditioned phenomena also cease to exist – if A does not exist, B does not arise. Early Buddhism used this model of causal interdependence of various phenomena to explain the arising of duḥkha, the operation of personality, as well as the functioning of the karmic law and the doctrine of rebirth, without resting on the notion of a permanent self. Volitions as karmic forces are said to condition consciousness and thus present a key link in the operation of rebirth. If at the moment of death the karmic impetus of volitional activity is not discontinued, the flow of consciousness carries on into another life. This passage from one form of existence to the next is compared to the passing of a flame from one candle to the next. Accordingly, it is said that the person in the previous life and the person in the next life are neither completely alike nor entirely different. The two are conditionally interconnected through consciousness and karmic impulses. Thus, whereas the fivefold aggregate formula represents the static model of personality, the model of dependent origination represents a dynamic illustration of how the aggregates function and condition one another from one life to the next.

Further, the chain of dependent origination demonstrates that craving leads to attachment and this relation, as the second noble truth highlights, is regarded to be the locus of the inception of duḥkha. The Buddhist doctrine names four types of attachments, namely, attachment to the objects of sense desire, attachment to views, attachment to precepts and vows, and attachment to the doctrine of the self. It is important to note that it is not the objects of craving that are the source of suffering. The conditioned phenomena are characterized only with unsatisfactoriness and not suffering, the latter being the result of an unenlightened experience of them. What determines a relationship to a certain object to be a relationship of suffering is therefore one's mental attitude. In other words, although duḥkha is considered to be a universal fact, craving arising from it rests on personal reactions of ignorant worldlings to the intrinsically unsatisfactory nature of reality. The first factor on the 12-linked chain of dependent origination is, as noted, ignorance, which is evidently the fundamental underlying condition behind craving and thus the main factor perpetuating saṃsāra. The term ignorance refers to not knowing things as they really are, i.e., not knowing the true nature of reality.

The last part of the second noble truth enumerates three different objects of craving, namely, sensual pleasures, existence, and nonexistence. Craving for sensual pleasures may arise in relation to any of the six senses and their corresponding objects. Both craving for existence and craving for nonexistence derive from the attachment to the sense of self. Craving for existence refers to the urge for the protection of the ego and the prolongation of life of the self after death. Craving for nonexistence, on the other hand, finds gladness in the idea of death as the definite end of the self.

The *third noble truth* is stated as follows: The cessation of duḥkha lies in the cessation of craving.

The logic behind it is that if craving results in duḥkha, then it must also hold that when craving is completely rooted out, then there is no more duḥkha. This is possible by transforming the essential factor behind craving, namely, ignorance. Only by seeing things as they truly are and clearly comprehending how one is conditioned may craving and therefore duḥkha be completely eradicated. The complete ending of duḥkha is termed enlightenment or nirvāṇa, and a person who has attained it, a "worthy one" or an arhat. Nirvāṇa literally means the extinguishment of a lamp or a fire (the fire of duḥkha) and the conditions that bring it about (the fuel of duḥkha). The fire does not become extinct by blowing out but rather by the running out of fuel. Hence, nirvāṇa is defined as the overcoming of the three root poisons or fiery defilements (Skt. kleśa), namely, greed (Skt. rāga), hatred (Skt. dveṣa), and delusion (Skt. moha). Since it is reached by transcending all factors of existence that are conditioned and subject to birth and death, nirvāṇa is referred to as the "unconditioned," "unmade," "unconstructed," "unborn," "unbecome," and "deathless." Nirvāṇa is thus not a metaphysical concept but an event. This is indicated in references to persons who have attained it as those who have nirvāṇa-ed. The term is therefore used as a verb, meaning "to be extinguished." The attainment of nirvāṇa during one's life is named "nirvāṇa with a remainder" (Skt. sopadhiśeṣa-nirvāṇa) and nirvāṇa at death "nirvāṇa without a remainder" (Skt. nirupadhiśeṣa-nirvāṇa). A person who has attained the former remains in the framework of the five aggregates and continues to undergo pleasant and unpleasant experiences, whereas for the latter the aggregates discontinue and with them these experiences as well. Nevertheless, nirvāṇa is not regarded to be mere annihilation (S III 109–112). When asked the question of what happens to the Tathāgata (the name the Buddha used when referring to himself) after death (does he exist; does he not exist; does he, both, exist and not exist; or does he neither exist nor not exist), the Buddha did not answer (S IV 373–400). This is firstly because such questions are not deemed conducive to the advancement on the path toward enlightenment (M I 426–431). For this reason, the early Buddhist discourses shy away from philosophical speculation and instead focus on the explanation of the practical path toward enlightenment. Next, the notions of existence and nonexistence, as noted, are both considered to rely on the false doctrine of an enduring self. Additionally, once all the factors of existence have been transcended, one may not continue to be referred to in terms of conventional categories, just as if compared to a flame, once extinguished, an arhat can no longer be regarded in terms of a flame (Sn 1074, 1076). Hence, nirvāṇa is also known as the "unelaborated."

Unlike the Theravāda tradition, Mahāyāna Buddhism maintained that the flux of life processes need not be completely transcended in order for the attainment of the complete cessation of duḥkha to take place. This doctrine was supported by a particular notion of reality, developed within the tradition of Mahāyāna Buddhism, called Mādhyamika or the school of the "middle way." It was already the Abhidharma schools that insisted on the distinction between substantial existence (Skt. dravya-sat) and nominal existence (Skt. prajñapti-sat). This led them to distinguish between fundamental elements of existence (Skt. dharma) and secondarily fabricated conceptual wholes. They deemed the former, namely, the mental and material constituents of existence, to represent the ultimate level of reality, or in other words, that which really exists. The latter, i.e., the concepts of second-order entities (such as persons, trees, chairs), were claimed to represent merely the conventional categories that are projected onto the reality of dharmas as primary level psychophysical events. The adherents of Mādhyamika radicalized this reductionist technique of the Abhidharma and applied the notion of non-self to the whole of reality, including the dharmas. They achieved this by universalizing the doctrine of dependent origination into a general scheme of conditionality, termed emptiness (Skt. śūnyatā). This means that for Mādhyamika all of reality is empty of independent existence or own-being (Skt. svabhāva), since the arising of every constituent of reality depends on some conditioning factor other than itself. This branch of Buddhism also reformulated the doctrine of the two levels of reality that was implied in the Abhidharmic distinction between nominal and substantial existence. It articulated the notions of the conventional (Skt. saṃvṛti) level of reality on the one hand and the ultimate or absolute (Skt. paramārtha) level of reality on the other. The former is the everyday reality of subject-object dualisms and the latter the reality that highlights these dichotomies as superimposed upon the real picture of reality as mutual relativity of all there is. Mahāyāna Buddhism uses various terms to refer to the ultimate reality, a common one being tathatā, which literally means "suchness" or "thusness", i.e., the way things really are, in contrast with the fabricated notions of reality. It must be noted, however, that the Mādhyamika distinction between the two levels of reality is not ontological. Emptiness is not some substantive reality but merely a statement of the fact that everything is empty of independent existence. The fact of being empty therefore applies to the notion of emptiness as well, and this is put into a formulation "emptiness of emptiness." From this follows that in the light of emptiness, even saṃsāra and nirvāṇa cannot be differentiated. In fact, the very notion that there is a distinction between them is still a product of a dichotomizing mind that does not realize that the seemed difference is its own feature and not a feature of reality. In line with these conclusions came the Mahāyāna development of practical goals, considered to be more perfect than leaving the cycle of rebirths. The notion of the arhat as the highest ideal was replaced by the ideal of the bodhisattva (lit. buddha-to-be), a practitioner that renounces the release from saṃsāra in order to help other living beings.

The other main branch of Mahāyāna Buddhism, namely, Yogācāra or Vijñānavāda, maintained that nirvāṇa lays in the realization that the objects of experience can never be distinguished from the process of experience itself. In other words, the experiencing subject and the object of experience are inseparable. The erroneous notion of duality is thus considered to be superimposed upon the true nature of things, which is their interdependence (i.e., emptiness). The Yogācārins concluded that the fundamental and only reality must be consciousness (Skt. vijñāna), which is also the prime factor upon which all experience depends. They postulated eight levels of consciousness. Six of them are types of consciousness that arise with the contact between sense organs (i.e., the five sense organs and the mind) and their corresponding objects. The seventh type of consciousness is the coordinating faculty of the mind (Skt. manas), and the eighth is termed the store-consciousness (Skt. ālaya-vijñāna) in which karmic seeds of past actions are accumulated. The fruition of these seeds taints the true picture of reality and thus prevents one from seeing it as it really is, i.e., empty of independent existence. Yogācāra therefore adopted the Mādhyamika notion of emptiness and included it in an expanded model of three levels of reality or three realms of experience. These are as follows:

1. The "constructed aspect" (Skt. parikalpita-svabhāva), which refers to the incorrect reified understanding of the world as comprised of subjects and objects
2. The "dependent aspect" (Skt. paratantra-svabhāva), which refers to the Mādhyamika understanding of reality as empty of independent existence
3. The "perfected aspect" (Skt. parinişpanna-svabhāva), referring to the Yogācāra understanding of reality, according to which there is one inherently existing thing, namely, the continuously transforming consciousness, devoid of the secondary projections of the first aspect.

According to the Yogācāra, enlightenment is achieved by clearing the store-consciousness of all the seeds and thereby attaining an insight into the true nature of reality. Saṃsāra and nirvaṇa are therefore again considered to be merely two ways of being oriented toward the same reality, namely, the constant flow of consciousness events.

The *fourth noble truth* outlines the way leading to the "cure" in the form of the noble eightfold path (Skt. ārya-aṣṭaṅgika-mārga). This path is referred to as the middle way of the appropriate practical life, which avoids the extremes of indulging in sensual pleasures on the one hand and self-mortification on the other. Its eight-dimensional delineation entails the development of various factors (Skt. aṅga) that are defined as "right" or "perfect" (Skt. samyak). These are (1) right view (Skt. samyag-dṛṣṭi), (2) right intention (Skt. samyak-saṃkalpa), (3) right speech (Skt. samyag-vāc), (4) right action (Skt. samyak-karmānta), (5) right livelihood (Skt. samyag-ā jīva), (6) right effort (Skt. samyag-vyāyāma), (7) right mindfulness (Skt. samyak-smṛti), and (8) right concentration (Skt. samyak-samādhi). These are sectioned into three larger groups of wisdom (Skt. prajñā, 1–2), morality (Skt. śīla, 3–5), and meditative cultivation (Skt. samādhi, 6–8). The eight factors are not to be taken as consecutive steps on the path to enlightenment, but rather different aspects of development needed to reach this goal. Right view refers to the clear comprehension of reality as expounded in the four noble truths, where holding this view ought to be without attachment. In accordance with the insight into the nature of reality, the next factor of right intention implies a mind free from lust, ill-will, and cruelty. Right speech is speech without lies, gossip, slander, etc., and corresponds to the fourth of the five moral precepts (Skt. pañca-śīla) of Buddhism. Right action corresponds to the first three of the five precepts, namely, restraint from killing living beings, stealing, and misconduct in matters of sensual pleasures. Right livelihood refers to a way of living that avoids causing harm to living beings, be they human or animal. Right effort means an endeavor to foster wholesome states of mind. Right mindfulness refers to being always mindful of the nature of one's experience, namely, the arising and passing away of psychophysical phenomena. Right concentration refers to the training of the mind to focus attention on an object, necessary to achieve the four meditational trances (Skt. dhyāna). These are highly refined states of mental collectedness, tranquility, and calm during which attention is entirely absorbed in the object.

Cross-References

▶ Anattā (Buddhism)
▶ Anicca
▶ Dukkha
▶ Middle Way (Buddhism)
▶ Philosophy (Buddhism)
▶ Truth (Buddhism)

References

1. Anālayo B (2009) From craving to liberation – excursions into the thought-world of the Pali discourses (1). The Buddhist Association, New York

2. Anālayo B (2010) From grasping to emptiness – excursions into the thought-world of the Pali discourses (2). The Buddhist Association, New York
3. Bodhi B (2000) A comprehensive manual of Abhidhamma, the Abhidhammattha Saṅgaha of Ācariya Anuruddha. Buddhist Publication Society, Kandy
4. Collins S (1982) Selfless persons. Imagery and thought in Theravāda Buddhism. Cambridge University Press, Cambridge
5. Collins S (1982) Self and non-self in early Buddhism. Numen 29(2):250–257
6. Collins S (1994) What are Buddhists doing when they deny the self? In: Tracy D et al (eds) Religion and practical reason. State University New York Press, Albany, pp 59–86
7. Collins S (2006) Nirvana and other Buddhist felicities: utopias of the Pali imaginaire. Cambridge University Press, Cambridge
8. Conze E (1983) Buddhist thought in India. Three phases of Buddhist philosophy. Allen and Unwin, London
9. de Silva P (1991) An introduction to Buddhist psychology. Macmillan, London
10. Duckworth DS (2010) Two models of the two truths: ontological and phenomenological approaches. J Indian Philos 38:519–527
11. Eckel MD (1992) To see the Buddha: a philosopher's quest for the meaning of emptiness. Princeton University Press, Princeton
12. Garfield J (1995) The fundamental wisdom of the middle way: Nāgārjuna's Mūlamadhyamakākarikā. Oxford University Press, Oxford/New York
13. Gethin R (1986) The five Khandas: their treatment in the Nikāyas and early Abhidhamma. J Indian Philos 14:35–53
14. Govinda LA (1991) The psychological attitude of early Buddhist philosophy and its systematic representation according to Abhidhamma tradition. Motilal Banarsidass, Delhi
15. von Guenther H (1991) Philosophy and psychology in the Abhidharma. Motilal Banarsidass, Delhi
16. Hamilton S (1995) Anattā: a different approach. Middle Way 70(1):47–60
17. Hamilton S (1996) Identity and experience: the constitution of the human being according to early Buddhism. Luzac Oriental, London
18. Hamilton S (1997) The dependent nature of the phenomenal world. In: Dhammajoti KL et al (eds) Recent researches in Buddhist studies. Y Karunadasa Felicitation Committee/Chi Ying Foundation, Colombo/Hong Kong, pp 276–291
19. Harris IC (1991) The continuity of Madhyamaka and Yogācāra in Indian Mahāyāna Buddhism. Brill, Leiden/New York
20. Harvey P (2004) The selfless mind: personality, consciousness and Nirvāna in early Buddhism. RoutledgeCurzon, Oxon
21. Harvey P (2010) An introduction of Buddhism. Cambridge University Press, Cambridge
22. Hiriyanna M (1996) Essentials of Indian philosophy. Diamond Books, London
23. Huntington CW (2003) The emptiness of emptiness. An introduction to early Indian Mādhyamika. Motilal Banarsidass, Delhi
24. Jayasuriya WF (1963) The psychology and philosophy of Buddhism. YMBA Press, Colombo
25. Johansson REA (1985) The dynamic psychology of early Buddhism. Curzon, London
26. Kalupahana DJ (1976) Buddhist philosophy. A historical analysis. University of Hawaii Press, Honolulu
27. Kalupahana DJ (1986) The philosophy of the middle way. Mūlamadhyamakakārikā. State University of New York Press, Albany
28. Kalupahana DJ (1987) The principles of Buddhist Psychology. State University of New York Press, Albany
29. Kalupahana DJ (1992) A history of Buddhist philosophy. Continuities and discontinuities. University of Hawaii Press, Honolulu
30. King R (1994) Early Yogācāra and its relationship with the Madhyamaka School. Philos East West 44(4):659–686
31. King R (1999) Indian philosophy. An introduction to Hindu and Buddhist thought. Edinburgh University Press, Edinburgh
32. Laumakis S (2008) An introduction to Buddhist philosophy. Cambridge University Press, Cambridge
33. Malalasekera GP (1968) Aspects of reality as taught by Theravāda Buddhism. Buddhist Publication Society, Kandy
34. Matilal BK (2008) Logic, language and reality. An introduction to Indian philosophical studies. Motilal Banarsidass, Delhi
35. Murti TRV (2006) The central philosophy of Buddhism. A study of the Mādhyamika system. Munshiram Manoharlal, New Delhi
36. Perez-Remon J (1981) Self and non-self in early Buddhism. Mouton, The Hague/Paris/New York
37. Ramanan KV (2002) Nāgārjuna's philosophy as presented in the 'Mahā-prajñāpāramitā-śāstra'. Bharatiya Vidya Prakashan, Varanasi
38. Reat NR (1987) Some fundamental concepts of Buddhist psychology. Religion 17:15–28
39. Ronkin N (2010) Early Buddhist metaphysics. The making of a philosophical tradition. Routledge, London/New York
40. Schmithausen L (1987) Ālayavijñana: on the origin and the early development of a central concept of Yogācāra philosophy. International Institute for Buddhist Studies, Tokyo
41. Siderits M (1989) Thinking on empty: Madhyamaka anti-realism and canons of rationality. In: Biderman S et al (eds) Rationality in question. On eastern and western views of rationality. Brill, Leiden/New York, pp 231–249

42. Stcherbatsky T (1994) The central conception of Buddhism. Motilal Banarsidass, Delhi
43. Warder AK (1956) On the relationships between early Buddhism and other contemporary systems. Bull Sch Orient Afr Stud 18(1):43–63
44. Warder AK (1970) Indian Buddhism. Motilal Banarsidass, Delhi
45. Williams P (1981) On the Abhidharma ontology. J Indian Philos 9:227–257
46. Williams P (1991) On the interpretation of Madhyamaka thought. J Indian Philos 19:191–218
47. Williams P (2009) Mahāyāna Buddhism. The doctrinal foundations. Routledge, London/New York

Reality (Jainism)

Ana Bajželj
Department of Philosophy, Faculty of Arts, University of Ljubljana, Ljubljana, Slovenia
Polonsky Academy, The Van Leer Jerusalem Institute, Jerusalem, Israel

Abbreviations

Sas Sarvārtha-siddhi
Tas Tattvārtha-sūtra

Synonyms

The state of the true existence of things; The way things really are; What there is

Definition

Jain doctrine of reality is grounded in the exposition of the plurality of existing substances and the description of the dynamic relationship between the living and the material substances as the basis of both the entrapment in and release from the cycle of rebirths. As it is also the case with many other Indian religious traditions, Jainism considers knowledge of reality to be one of the essential factors in the attainment of liberation.

Jain Doctrine of Reality

Jain authors have answered the question of "what there is" with a doctrine of the nature of existence (Skt. sat) as well as the description of the basic mechanism of bondage (Skt. bandha) and liberation (Skt. mokṣa) of living beings. They describe existence as the character (Skt. lakṣaṇa) of substance and so understand substance as that which exists (Sas 5.29, cf. [2], p. 155). Substances (Skt. dravya) are said to be infinite (Skt. ananta) in number and they are described as sharing the same basic structure. They all possess the essential qualities (Skt. guṇa), which are permanent and coexist with the substances they qualify, and the accidental qualities or modes (Skt. paryāya), which are continually arising and passing away. While substances always possess their essential qualities, they are then also invariably changing; they are permanent, yet at the same time constantly in transformation (Skt. pariṇāma) (cf. [5], pp. 75–88). This dynamic makeup of substances agrees with the Jain definition of existence as constituted of origination (Skt. utpāda), cessation (Skt. vyaya), and persistence (Skt. dhrauvya), that is, as enduring through modification (Tas 5.29, cf. [5], p. 135). Existence is therefore multifaceted or non-one-sided (Skt. anekānta).

This specific kind of ontology, which is sometimes referred to as permanence in change, has allowed Jain authors to distinguish their doctrine from those that accepted permanence as the only real, from those that completely rejected the reality of permanence in favor of change, as well as from those which subordinated one to the other ([4], p. 123). Jains consider alternative views of reality to be only partial or one-sided (Skt. ekānta) truths about reality, which are a result of the karmic obscuration of the capacity of knowing that is inherent to all living beings. They claim that only an omniscient being (Skt. kevalin) possesses immediate, unobscured, and fully reliable knowledge of reality in all its complexity. The knowledge of the omniscient has thus served Jains as a source of and continuous support for all the various aspects of their descriptions of reality.

The Jain teaching on the nature of existence categorizes all substances into two basic types, that is, living (Skt. jīva) and nonliving (Skt.

ajīva). Jīvas, which are sometimes translated as selves or souls, possess many qualities, the main ones of which are consciousness (Skt. caitanya), bliss (Skt. sukha), and energy (Skt. vīrya). These distinguish them from the rest of the substantial world, and with regard to the particular modal modifications of their qualities, jīvas can also be distinguished from one another. Their modes may arise either in relation to external causes or independently of any exterior factors, but only the independently arisen modes are considered to be perfect. Jīvas have been infinite in number since beginningless times and their number remains constant; it neither grows nor diminishes with time. They are divided into those that are trapped in the cycle of recurring rebirths (Skt. saṃsāra) and those that have attained liberation (Skt. mokṣa) from it; the first occupy bodies and the second are disembodied. Jīvas are immaterial in nature, but are, nevertheless, regarded to be extensive substances (Skt. asti-kāya), which means that they are able to occupy numerous space points (Skt. pradeśa). They are said to adapt to the bodies they come to inhabit just as a lamp shines only inside the room in which it is located. This adaptation to diverse kinds of bodies in no way affects their essential nature; all jīvas are said to possess an innumerable (Skt. asaṃkhyeya) number of space points and this number stays the same, regardless of how large or small the body they occupy is. Due to such adaptability, they are compared to a piece of cloth, which may be folded in many different ways while still remaining the same piece of cloth ([3], p. 102). The existence of jīvas is restricted to cosmos (Skt. loka) and they cannot exist in acosmic space (Skt. aloka-ākāśa); the border of cosmos thus also determines the largest size any jīva may extend to. Whether inhabiting a body or being free of it, jīvas are then never all-pervasive. Even upon attaining liberation, they retain a certain size, which is sometimes said to be slightly smaller than the size of the last body they occupied. They also remain individual throughout both their embodied and liberated lives, and once liberated, they never enter the cycle of rebirths again. Jain authors have, furthermore, identified jīvas as having a specific function of offering service to one another.

Nonliving substances are classified into material and immaterial kinds. Matter (Skt. pudgala) is the only kind of substance that belongs to the first class and it is described as a nonliving substance with form (Skt. rūpi-ajīva). It exists in the form of innumerable indivisible particles (Skt. parama-aṇu), which are eternal, and their aggregates (Skt. skandha), which are impermanent. Material particles possess four basic qualities of color (Skt. varṇa), taste (Skt. rasa), smell (Skt. gandha), and palpability (Skt. sparśa). These continually undergo transformations, and just like modes of jīvas, modes of matter may also arise either in dependence to or independently of external conditions. Due to the varying degrees of palpability, material particles are attracted to one another and thus form aggregates; different combinations of material particles result in diverse aggregates of various sizes. In the form of aggregates, matter can occupy a numerable or an innumerable number of space points and is therefore also considered to be an extensive kind of substance. It pervades all of cosmic space, beyond which, like jīvas, it cannot exist. The function of matter is said to be providing the body, speech, mind, and breath, as well as bringing pleasure, pain, life, and death to jīvas.

The immaterial nonliving kinds of substances are referred to as nonliving substances without form (Skt. arūpi-ajīva). They are space (Skt. ākāśa), medium of motion (Skt. dharma), medium of rest (Skt. adharma), and time (Skt. kāla). Space, medium of motion, and medium of rest are single and unified substances. Space is the only substance of all that occupies an infinite number of space points and is thus infinitely extensive. Its function is said to be allowing the immersion (Skt. avagāha) of the other substances. Not all of it is, however, inhabited by them. Even though the substance of space is one, it is "divided" into two parts, that is, the cosmic portion, where all the other substances may be found, and the acosmic portion, where only empty space exists. Like all the other substances, space also undergoes transformations, but unlike modes of jīvas and matter, its modes always arise independently of any external factors.

Medium of motion (Skt. dharma) and medium of rest (Skt. adharma) are substances which are unique to the Jain tradition. They are both extensive in nature, but in contrast with the substance of space, which extends over an infinite number of space points, they extend over an innumerable number thereof. In fact, it is their border that delineates the boundary of cosmic space and no substance other than space may exist beyond them. This is so because of their specific functions. The medium of motion allows motion and the medium of rest enables rest; only where they are present is it possible to move and rest. However, they do not act as direct causes of motion and rest but perform merely as auxiliary or instrumental causes (Skt. nimitta-kāraṇa) of them. This function of theirs also bears no consequences on their own being; the medium of motion does not cause itself to move and the medium of rest itself to rest. These characteristics are often described with metaphors. The medium of motion is likened to a body of water, which allows fish to swim in it, while neither causing the fish nor itself to move. The medium of rest is, similarly, compared to earth or a shade of a tree, which enables rest, but neither causes themselves nor anything else to come to rest. Like modes of space, modes of medium of motion and medium of rest only arise independently of any exterior conditions.

Jain authors are divided regarding the inclusion of time in the list of substances. Digambaras unanimously consider it to be substantial in nature and deem its inclusion among substances necessary in order to account for the occurrence of change in the world, whereas Śvetāmbaras disagree over this issue and some of them do not distinguish time from the modes of other substances. Digambara authors propose the existence of an innumerable number of time particles (Skt. kāla-aṇu), which pervade the entire cosmos and each of which occupies precisely one space point. Their nature is such that they cannot form clusters and remain always separated in their space points, like a heap of unjoined jewels. Due to this, time is regarded as the only non-extensive substance. Rather than speaking of time particles, some Śvetāmbara authors propose a unitary theory of time. All theories, which accept time as a substance, understand it to be dynamic in nature like the rest of the substances, and they identify the continually changing modes of time as moments (Skt. samaya).

Jain authors developed their doctrine of existence in view of their soteriological goal of liberation; only by clearly understanding the nature of the saṃsāric entrapment was it deemed possible to achieve release from it. They recognized that the substances of space, medium of motion, medium of rest, and time are the background stage for the drama that occurs in the relationship between jīvas and matter. As noted, it is the substance of matter which provides the material dimension of non-liberated jīvas as well as participates in the arising of pleasure, pain, life, and death, and this is the basis of the distinct karmic theory proposed by the Jain tradition. This theory, which identifies karma as material, distinguishes two kinds of material aggregates, namely, those that may be karmically bound and those that may not be so. Under certain conditions, which arise when bodily, verbal, and mental activities of jīvas are informed by passions (Skt. kaṣāya), karmically bondable material aggregates flow to jīvas and adhere to them like dust sticks to moist ground. This is the basic mechanism of karmic bondage.

Jain doctrine speaks of eight principle kinds of karmic matter that bind jīvas, four are destructive (Skt. ghātiyā) and four nondestructive (Skt. aghātiyā). The destructive kinds of karmic matter obstruct, obscure, and defile the essential qualities of jīvas by disabling them from fully manifesting. As long as the arising modes of jīvas are externally affected by them, they are thus considered to be imperfect and impure. Since the cycle of rebirths is beginningless, jīvas have always been in an impure state and there is no living being, not even among those who have achieved liberation, who has not been subject to the destructive effects of karma. The nondestructive kinds of karmic matter do not pollute jīvas' qualities, but merely bring about the nature, conditions, and experience of particular embodiments of jīvas. In order to achieve liberation, the inflow of new karmic matter must be prevented and the old karmic matter must be removed, and Jain practice has been oriented towards the accomplishment of both. It is possible to perfect the modal manifestations of all qualities by the complete removal of destructive karmic matter while still being bound by nondestructive karma and thus remaining in an embodied state. In order to achieve actual liberation, nondestructive karmic matter must then also run its course. Upon its attainment, jīva detaches itself from the body and rises up to the very top edge of the cosmos where it forever remains in a perfected and motionless state.

These basic features of reality, which take account of existence as a plurality of eternal yet forever changing substances as well as the mechanisms of continuity and discontinuity of karmic bondage, have been gradually systematized and classified into fundamental principles of reality or reals. These are commonly termed tattvas (literally thusness) or padārthas (literally meaning/object of the word). A list of the basic principles, which captures all of the abovementioned aspects of the Jain theory of reality, is the following: (1) living substance (Skt. jīva), (2) nonliving substance (Skt. ajīva), (3) karmic influx (Skt. āsrava), (4) binding of karma (Skt. bandha), (5) stopping of karmic influx (Skt. saṃvara), (6) disjointing of bound karma (Skt. nirjarā), and liberation (Skt. mokṣa) ([1], p. 96). Some authors have added the principles of inauspicious (Skt. pāpa) and auspicious (Skt. puṇya) kinds of karma to the list. Knowledge of these basic principles is considered instrumental in the attainment of liberation. The path to achieving liberation is described with a three-fold formula, namely, proper faith/insight (Skt. samyag-darśana), proper knowledge (Skt. samyag-jñāna), and proper conduct (Skt. samyak-cāritra). Proper faith/insight, that is, the first step towards liberation, is described as faith in the doctrine of the tīrthaṅkaras and insight into the basic principles of reality.

Cross-References

- Dharma (Jainism)
- Dravya (Jainism)
- Jainism (Yakṣa)
- Jīva (Jainism)
- Karma (Jainism)
- Nayavāda
- Omniscience
- Philosophy
- Rebirth
- Relativity (Jainism)
- Saṃsāra
- Self (Jainism)
- Syādvāda (Jainism)
- Time (Jainism)
- Truth (Jainism)

References

1. Dundas P (2002) The Jains. Routledge, London/New York
2. Jain SA (tr) (1992) Reality: English translation of Shri Pujyapada's Sarvarthasiddhi. Jwalamalini Trust, Madras
3. Jaini PS (1998) The Jaina path of purification. Motilal Banarsidass, Delhi
4. Padmarajiah YJ (1963) A comparative study of the Jaina theories of reality and knowledge. Jain Sahitya Vikas Mandal, Bombay
5. Tatia N (tr) (2011) Tattvārtha sūtra: that which is. Yale University Press, New Haven/London

Rebirth

- Kamma

Rebirth (Buddhism)

Ana Bajželj
Department of Philosophy, Faculty of Arts, University of Ljubljana, Ljubljana, Slovenia
Polonsky Academy, The Van Leer Jerusalem Institute, Jerusalem, Israel

Synonyms

Bhavacakra; Punarāvṛtti; Punarbhava; Punarjanman; Punarjīvātu; Punarutpatti; Saṃsāra; Wheel of life

Definition

Rebirth is an eschatological notion that denotes a continuation of life after death. According to the Buddhist doctrine the cycle of rebirths has no beginning and is maintained by ignorance, craving, attachment, and the fruition of the karmic forces that determine the nature of future existences. One may attain release from the endless succession of births and deaths by extinguishing the factors that fuel its persistence.

The Continuation of Life After Death According to the Buddhist Doctrine

According to Buddhism death is not the annihilation of life as it is, but is merely a transitory state incessantly followed by rebirths in a beginningless succession. This pattern of progression is referred to as saṃsāra. The doctrine of the cyclical chain of rebirths that pertains to all forms of existence is one of the basic elements of the Indian religious paradigm. It is shared by most Indian religions and only repudiated by the materialists who, on the contrary, claim that death is the definitive end of life. The idea of rebirth is present in a number of diverse religious traditions around the world but it is the Indian tradition that ethicized the eschatology of rebirth by linking it to the theory of karma. In accordance with the karmic principle, one's actions have a significant bearing on one's future existence and likewise, one's present state is largely an outcome of one's past doings.

Despite striking similarities, there is an element in the Buddhist tradition that fundamentally differs from the other Indian traditions that also accept the theory of rebirth. The majority of them postulate that after death the living substance (ātman, jīva, etc.) reincarnates into a new physical body. However, for Buddhists, rebirth is not equivalent to reincarnation as they maintain that there is nothing that persists throughout the arising of new births. In other words, there is no such thing as a permanent soul or an individual entity that exists behind the modifications of different existences and that would re-*incarnate* after passing away. This feature of the Buddhist teaching is termed the doctrine of no-self (anātman). The Buddha holds that what is commonly considered to be a self is nothing more than a continually changing web of interactions between the five basic factors of existence, namely, aggregates (skandha). These are form (rūpa), feelings (vedanā), cognition (saṃjña), volitions (saṃskāra), and consciousness (vijñāṇa). Other common schemes of analyzing the basic constituents of beings are the twelve spheres (āyatana), namely, the six senses (including the mind) and their corresponding sense objects, as well as the eighteen elements (dhātu), namely, the six senses, their respective sense objects, and the six corresponding types of consciousness. According to the Buddhist doctrine, there is therefore no primary substance that remains the same throughout the changing of its secondary qualities. On the contrary, the only existing things are the qualities themselves, which are causally interlinked and ceaselessly changing. Whereas the five skandhas represent the "now" of experience, Buddhism explains the selfless temporal continuity of birth, existence, death, rebirth, and redeath with the doctrine of dependent origination (pratītya samutpāda). Its basic postulate is that phenomena arise when conditioned by particular factors, and hence if those factors are eliminated, the phenomena do not arise. Apart from explaining the empirical continuity and the functioning of personality over time, the scheme of dependent origination also explains the conditions that bring about the arising of unsatisfactoriness (duḥkha). Buddhism considers the latter to be one of the three marks of dependent existence, besides impermanence (anityā) and no-self. Since according to the Buddhist doctrine reality is considered to be essentially impermanent and selfless, craving and clinging to certain phenomena inevitably result in nonfulfillment and, consequently, unsatisfactoriness.

The pattern of dependent origination is normally depicted in a scheme, comprised of several links (nidānas) that successively condition one another. There are diverse formulations of it, however, the standard rendering has the following twelve links: (1) ignorance (avidyā), (2) volitions (saṃskāra), (3) consciousness (vijñāna), (4) name-form (nāma-rūpa), (5) six sense spheres (ṣadāyatana), (6) contact (sparśa), (7) feelings (vedanā), (8) craving (tṛṣṇā), (9) grasping (upādāna), (10) becoming (bhava), (11) birth (jāti), and (12) old age and death (jarāmaraṇa). The implications of individual links and relations between them have been variously understood. There is, however, a prevalent reading put forward by Buddhaghosa and Vasubandhu. Their interpretation maintains that the twelve links relate to three successive existences, where links 1 and 2 correspond to the past life, links 3–10 to the present life, and links 11 and 12 to the future life. The first link is ignorance, referring to the delusion regarding the true nature of reality. Due to the fact that one has not observed the Buddha's teaching in order to attain the insight into the way things really are, volitions as karmic forces continue to be effective. They in turn condition consciousness to arise in the mother's womb and thus present the main link by which consciousness passes onto another life. Functioning as a bridge between different modes of existence, the continuous stream of consciousness performs as means of transmitting karmic forces from one form of existence into the next. Despite facilitating basic continuity between successive existences, consciousness remains essentially transient and incessantly perishing. However, its instants are causally connected and this basic conditionality allows karmic seeds to pass from one life to the next without interruption. The next link in the change of dependent origination is name-form, which is an umbrella term for the five aggregates, that is, the modality of person's existence in the world. After that follow the links of the six sense spheres and contact, referring to the way one experiences the world, namely, contacting it through the six senses. Conditioned by the previous links is one's response to the sensory experience, that is, a feeling, which may be pleasant, unpleasant, or neutral. This fairly quickly leads to a habitual craving for more of an appealing kind of feeling, which sooner or later develops into a clinging to specific stimuli that bring about the experience one seeks. These habits shape one's way of being and come to represent how one exists in the world. This tenth link of "becoming" is the last link of the present life. The momentum of previous factors and craving for more of sought for experience leads to a new birth, old age, and death, which constitute links eleven and twelve.

The doctrine of dependent origination is considered to be the middle way between the eternalist idea that the self survives death, a view pertaining to the Upaniṣads, and the annihilationist idea that death is a complete cessation of life, held by the Indian materialists. The notion of a selfless empirical continuity, illustrated with the scheme of dependent origination, avoids both extreme viewpoints. Here, the continuity of one life passing into another is considered to be akin to the continuity during an individual lifetime. Accordingly, since there is no persisting agent behind this process, the reborn being is thought to be neither exactly the same as nor entirely different from the previous one, the relationship between them being like the one between a condition and its effect. In other words, two conditionally linked beings are like two moments of existence in the continuity of a single life span. They are not the same, since they are essentially changing and have changed from one instant to the next, nor are they different, since they belong to the same causal linkage of events. This process is compared to a flame passing from one candle to the next. The relationship between the two flames is equally neither one of complete identity nor one of complete difference.

Some schools of Buddhism proposed an intermediate period (antarābhava) between death and rebirth, in order to account for the continuance of existence amid two lives. This doctrine was supported by the Sarvāstivāda, Sautrāntika, Sāṃmitīya, Dārṣṭāntika, and Pūrvaśaila schools of early Buddhism, which, however, did not agree on the proper interpretation of this idea. Nevertheless, Vasubandhu's rendition in his Abhidharmakośabhāṣya from the fifth century C.E. came to be considered a standard understanding of the notion. He explains that the transitional period between two lives consists of seven short segments, which do not last longer than a week each, thereby making the duration of the intermediate period no longer than seven weeks. The being that exists during this interval is described as an entity that arises between death in the previous life and birth in the next form of existence. This entity survives on odors and is thus called a gandharva, literally meaning "that which eats scents." The form of the gandharva is similar to the shape of beings in the realm of its next existence. It has subtle but functional senses and may only be seen by beings of its kind and beings with divine eyes. It is composed of subtle forms of the five aggregates. Rebirth takes place when the gandharva sets eyes on its future parents during a sexual intercourse and the emotional aspect of its mind thrusts it into the next life. The gender it takes on is the gender of the parent it is repulsed by, or in other words, the opposite gender of the one it is attracted to. This intense experience of repulsion and attraction results in the coming together of the mind, the blood, and the semen, which combine in the mother's womb. Once conception occurs, the five aggregates become denser, thereby forming a new life. At the same time the gandharva passes away. Even though the idea of a transitional phase between lives received a noteworthy support among various Buddhist branches, it was opposed by many schools of early Buddhism, namely, the Theravāda, Vibhajyavāda, Mahāsāṅghika, and the Mahīśāsaka schools. Still, the notion was later adopted and further developed by the Mahāyāna tradition.

As noted, the Buddhist doctrine of rebirth is tightly related to the doctrine of karmic retribution, the idea that executed deeds have inevitable future echoes in the form of karmic fruit (phala), which correspond to the nature of the already performed actions. This means that the progression of rebirths is not arbitrary but follows an ordering principle, according to which the nature of the next rebirth is determined by the moral quality of one's past actions. The karmic law is not effective in the present or subsequent life only, but extends over several existences. This governing law is thought of as a natural law, since it does not have a purpose nor is it managed by anyone. Its operation follows a simple causal logic that wholesome actions condition pleasant and unwholesome unpleasant reverberations. Different types of rebirths are hence not understood as rewards or punishments for the past actions, but are rather deemed to be natural effects of particular types of actions. None of the different rebirths, no matter how pleasant or horrid, is, however, everlasting and eventually the potency of good or bad accrued karma is exhausted and beings are reborn again. Since the cycle of rebirths is regarded to be beginningless, everyone has supposedly had innumerable previous lives. This means that every human being has passed through all the possible realms of rebirth.

The term for a domain of rebirth is gati, which literally means "manner of going." Buddhism distinguishes between six different modes of saṃsāric existence or, in other words, six diverse domains into which a being can be reborn. These are realms of humans (manuṣya), animals (tiryañca), hungry ghosts (preta), gods (deva), semi-gods (asura), and hell beings (naraka). Ordinarily, people are able to perceive only the first two kinds of beings. Occasionally, hungry ghosts too may be perceived of as hovering between the shadows, since these beings are thought to inhabit the dim margins of the human realm. The last three forms of existence, however, are invisible to the human eye. There is an old tradition of representing the sixfold model in a form of the so-called "wheel of life" (bhavacakra), a round diagram, in which three of the six realms are allocated in the upper part of the circle and the other three in its lower part. The lower realms of animals, hungry ghosts, and hell beings are considered to be unfortunate realms of rebirth. In contrast, the upper realms are those of gods, semi-gods, and human beings, and are regarded to be fairly fortunate domains to be reborn into. The outer rim of the "wheel of life" diagram normally depicts the twelve links of the chain of dependent origination, thus indicating the conditioned continuity of the cycles of existences. The middle of the diagram additionally portrays a cockerel, a pig, and a snake, representing the fundamental causes of saṃsāric migration, namely, greed (rāga), delusion (moha), and hatred (dveṣa), respectively. Actions bound with greed are thought to result in a rebirth in the realm of the hungry ghosts, those with delusion in the animal realm, and those with hatred in hell. On the other hand, moral actions bound with generosity and kindness are thought to lead to a rebirth in the human or divine form.

Of the six domains of rebirth, animals are predominantly driven by impulses and lack reason by which they could be able to recognize their situation and learn the way out of it. They undergo suffering by being prey targets, either of humans or other animals. Plants do not belong to this category, even though they are considered to possess a basic form of consciousness, that is, being sensitive to touch.

Hungry ghosts are beings which are, due to their previous lives of greed and selfishness, condemned to a life of constant frustration. Although there are a variety of different kinds of hungry ghosts, they are frequently depicted as having bloated stomachs and very small mouths, as to where they can never satisfy their insatiable urges of hunger. As noted, they live on the margins of the human world due to their deep earthly attachments.

Hell beings exist in extremely hot or cold areas in which they endure painful experiences, such as being burnt, frozen, cut up, eaten, etc. This continues until the bad karma, which they had accumulated throughout their previous lives, is spent. Hells are manifold and each rebirth in hell is considered to reflect the nature of the bad deeds that have led to it. All lower forms of existence primarily only bear the outcomes of their previous actions and are mainly not able to affect the nature of their present actions. However, eventually the unwholesome karma is used up and the consequences of some previous wholesome actions lead them to a rebirth in more auspicious realms.

In opposition to the lower domains of existence, life is very pleasant in the heavenly realm. Its denizens are gods that were born there due to the good karma they had formerly accrued. They mainly enjoy the wholesome karmic consequences. Like the realm of hell, the heavenly realm is also multilayered. The top five heavenly tiers are called the pure abodes. These are the domain of the so-called nonreturners (anāgamin), namely, human beings who are on their way to attain nirvāṇa and will never be reborn in the human realm again. Around the fifth century C.E. the splitting up of the heavenly realm amounted to twenty-six divisions, hierarchically arranged from less to more sublime. Gods are thought to live for a very long time, their life span increasing with the levels. However, even gods are considered to be mortal and eventually must be reborn.

The next realm of rebirth is the sphere of the semi-gods. These are greedy warrior-like beings who are dominated by aggression, hatred, and craving for power. Early models of saṃsāric domains are only fivefold and are short of the semi-godly realm which was added later on, perhaps in order for the domains to add up to an even number, that could be depicted more easily.

Lastly, there is the human domain. This realm is considered to be the most auspicious destination to be reborn into, even more than the heavenly domain, since it is here that beings may gain a clear insight into suffering that is needed in order for the cycle of rebirths to discontinue. This is so because the ratio between pleasure and pain is suitable enough to inspire beings to step onto the path toward realization. Furthermore, humans possess reason needed to comprehend their predicament and understand the teaching of the Buddha, which teaches the way out of saṃsāra. To be born as a human being is thus regarded to be a rare opportunity which ought to be grasped.

Taking into account the splitting of the heavenly domain, there are all together thirty-one possible domains of rebirth. These different abodes of existence are frequently put forward in another model of three tiers. In this scheme, human beings populate the earthly realm, also known as the "realm of sense-desire" (kāmāvacara). This sphere of existence contains all the forms of existence that are below the seventh heavenly layer. Beings that exist in the "realm of the sense-desire" evaluate perceived objects according to whether they desire them or not. Gods that populate this realm are referred to as devas. From this coarse level of existence up, matter is considered to increasingly thin out until it ultimately diminishes.

The next sphere up from the "realm of sense-desire" is the domain spanning from the seventh heavenly layer up, containing eleven further godly domains. It is called the "realm of pure form" (rūpāvacara). Together with the levels increases the subtlety and calmness of their nature. Denizens of the domain of "pure form" are gods, commonly named brahmās, who telepathically interact. In contrast with the "realm of sense-desire," these beings, who lack senses of smell, taste, and touch, do not perceive objects according to their desirability but conceive them in their pure form. Nevertheless, they are still not free from other various kinds of clinging.

The uppermost sphere, which includes the four final heavenly layers, is the "realm of formlessness" or the "formless realm" (arūpāvacara). As the name suggest, beings in these highest domains possess no form, since they consist of pure mental energy. The gods inhabiting the last four layers are considered to perceive phenomena in four different ways, the subtlety of apprehension increasing with each domain. On the twenty-eighth level of the heavenly realm gods conceive everything as infinite space, on the twenty-ninth as infinite consciousness, and on the thirtieth as nothingness. The thirty-first level is a level where all the previous conceptions have been surpassed and is therefore referred to as the level of "neither perception nor non-perception."

Within these numerous realms of rebirth, the nature of one's character, outlook on the world, as well as events that occur in one's lives are greatly influenced by the accumulated karma. However, despite the fact that various forms of existence are significantly regulated by the karmic law, life is still not deemed to be deterministic in nature. A particular factor of individual existence, that according to the Buddhist teaching affects the nature of karmic seeds, is volitions that accompany the acts of body, speech, and mind. This significance of volitions is indicated in the fact that they represent the second link in the dependent origination scheme. It is thus not deeds themselves that produce karmic forces, but the wholesome and unwholesome intentions behind them. This means that actively contemplating an unwholesome act is sufficient to generate unwholesome karmic seeds. In contrast, letting go of such thoughts generates wholesome karmic forces. Hence, even though the accrued karma may affect the nature of one's attitude, it does not determine the present volitional tendency. In other words, the choice of intention at a particular moment is a free choice. This freedom of intention, which is necessary for the karmic forces to terminate, may be exercised with least difficulty in the human realm.

Once this possibility of choice is comprehended and the working of the mechanism of the succession of rebirths understood, it is logical for one to endeavor to be reborn in one of the upper realms of existence. However, to a Buddhist, it is ultimately undesirable to remain in the cyclical continuity of births and deaths as every subsequent existence merely prolongs the experience of unsatisfactoriness (duḥkha). For that reason, Buddhism outlines a path of salvation, suggesting soteriological techniques that help practitioners in the search for a way out of saṃsāra and assist others to equally do so. This is done by the attainment of enlightenment or nirvāṇa by which the fuel that maintains the fire of duḥkha is extinguished. Once an insight into the true nature of things as an antidote to ignorance is realized, all the links of the mechanism of dependent origination come to an end. A person who attains nirvāṇa is called a "worthy one" or an arhat.

Mahāyāna Buddhism, however, holds that a release from the continuous cycles of existence is neither necessary for the cessation of duḥkha nor is it the highest goal a practitioner may attain. This Buddhist tradition thus posits the ideal of the bodhisattva, namely, a being who attains nirvāṇa but postpones the final release from saṃsāra in order to help other living beings.

Some interpreters of Buddhism have attempted to dismiss the doctrine of rebirth, either regarding it to be a metaphor for the changing mental states or an unimportant and even inauthentic element of the Buddhist doctrine. However, the idea of a karmically conditioned continuity of existences is undoubtedly such an essential part of the Buddhist doctrine that its elimination would render much of the remaining doctrine incomplete.

Cross-References

- ▶ Anattā (Buddhism)
- ▶ Anicca
- ▶ Antarābhava
- ▶ Arahant
- ▶ Ātman
- ▶ Bodhisattva
- ▶ Brahmā
- ▶ Causality (Buddhism)
- ▶ Craving
- ▶ Death (Buddhism)
- ▶ Demon
- ▶ Dhyāna/Jhāna
- ▶ Dukkha
- ▶ Enlightenment (Buddhism)
- ▶ Eschatology (Buddhism)
- ▶ God (Buddhism)
- ▶ Heaven (Buddhism)
- ▶ Hell (Buddhism)
- ▶ Insight
- ▶ Jarā-Maraṇa
- ▶ Kamma
- ▶ Karma
- ▶ Khandha
- ▶ Liberation (Buddhism)
- ▶ Mahāsāṅghika
- ▶ Mahāyāna
- ▶ Māra
- ▶ Materialism (Buddhism)
- ▶ Middle Way (Buddhism)
- ▶ Nāma-Rūpa
- ▶ Parinirvāṇa
- ▶ Paṭicca Samuppāda
- ▶ Person (Buddhism)
- ▶ Psychology (Buddhism)
- ▶ Reality (Buddhism)
- ▶ Saṃkhāra
- ▶ Saṃskāra
- ▶ Sarvāstivāda
- ▶ Sautrāntika
- ▶ Sentient Beings
- ▶ Sin (Buddhism)
- ▶ Soul
- ▶ Theravāda
- ▶ Transcendental Virtues
- ▶ Vasubandhu
- ▶ Vijñāna

References

1. Anālayo B (2009) From craving to liberation – excursions into the thought-world of the Pāli discourses (1). The Buddhist Association, New York
2. Anālayo B (2010) From grasping to emptiness – excursions into the thought-world of the Pāli discourses (2). The Buddhist Association, New York
3. Banerjee B (1988) Karman–rebirth: Buddhism. In: Sengupta PK (ed) Freedom, transcendence and identity: essays in memory of Prof. Kalidas Bhattacharya. South Asia Books, Delhi, pp 116–123
4. Braarvig J (2009) The Buddhist hell: an early instance of the idea. Numen 61:254–281
5. Collins S (1982) Selfless persons. Imagery and thought in Theravāda Buddhism. Cambridge University Press, Cambridge
6. Collins S (1982) Self and non-self in early Buddhism. Numen 29(2):250–257
7. Collins S (1994) What are Buddhists doing when they deny the self? In: Tracy D et al (eds) Religion and practical reason. State University New York Press, Albany, pp 59–86
8. Collins S (2006) Nirvana and other Buddhist felicities: utopias of the Pali imaginaire. Cambridge University Press, Cambridge
9. Cuevas BJ (1996) Predecessors and prototypes: towards a conceptual history of the Buddhist *antarābhava*. Numen 63:263–302
10. Gethin R (1986) The five Khandhas: their treatment in the Nikāyas and early Abhidhamma. J Indian Philos 14:35–53
11. Gethin R (1996–1997) Cosmology and meditation: from the Aggaññasutta to the Mahāyāna. Hist Relig 36:183–217
12. Hamilton S (1995) Anattā: a different approach. Middle Way 70(1):47–60
13. Hamilton S (1996) Identity and experience; the constitution of the human being according to early Buddhism. Luzac Oriental, London
14. Hamilton S (1997) The dependent nature of the phenomenal world. In: Dhammajoti KL et al (eds) Recent researches in Buddhist studies. Y. Karunadasa Felicitation Committee/Chi Ying Foundation, Colombo/Hong Kong, pp 276–291
15. Harvey P (2004) The selfless mind: personality, consciousness and Nirvāṇa in early Buddhism. RoutledgeCurzon, Oxon
16. Jayasuriya WF (1963) The psychology and philosophy of Buddhism. YMBA Press, Colombo

17. Johansson REA (1985) The dynamic psychology of early Buddhism. Curzon, London
18. Marasinghe MMJ (1974) Gods in early Buddhism. University of Sri Lanka, Vidyalankara
19. Matthews B (1983) Craving and salvation. A study in Buddhist soteriology. Canadian Corporation for Studies in Religion, Waterloo
20. McDermott JP (1973) Nibbāna as a reward for Kamma. J Am Orient Soc 93:344–347
21. McDermott JP (1980) Karma and rebirth in early Buddhism. In: O'Flaherty WD (ed) Karma and rebirth in classical Indian traditions. University of California Press, Berkeley
22. McDermott JP (1984) Development in the early Buddhist concept of Kamma/Karma. Motilal Banarsidass, Delhi
23. Mittal KK (1990) Various perspectives on karma and rebirth. J Dep Buddh Stud 14:1–16
24. Obeyesekere G (1980) The rebirth eschatology and its transformations: a contribution to the sociology of early Buddhism. In: O'Flaherty WD (ed) Karma and rebirth in classical Indian traditions. University of California Press, Berkeley, pp 137–164
25. Perez-Remon J (1981) Self and non-self in early Buddhism. Mouton, Paris/New York
26. Saddhatissa H (1969) Concept of rebirth in Buddhism. Mahabodhi 77:135–138
27. Reat NR (1977) Karma and rebirth in the Upaniṣads and Buddhism. Numen 24:163–185, Fasc. 3
28. Reat NR (1987) Some fundamental concepts of Buddhist psychology. Religion 17:15–28
29. Wayman A (1974) The intermediate-state dispute in Buddhism. In: Cousins L et al (eds) Buddhist studies in honour of I. B. Horner. Reidel, Dordrecht, pp 227–237

Relativity

► *Anekāntavāda* (Jainism)

Relativity (Buddhism)

Ana Bajželj
Department of Philosophy, Faculty of Arts, University of Ljubljana, Ljubljana, Slovenia
Polonsky Academy, The Van Leer Jerusalem Institute, Jerusalem, Israel

Synonyms

Emptiness; Śūnyatā

Definition

The Buddha proposed a dynamic model of reality that avoids the extremes of eternalism and annihilationism. This middle approach is termed the doctrine of dependent origination, a scheme that describes the arising of phenomena of experience in relation to specific conditions. The Mādhyamika tradition applied this model of conditionality to all of reality, which resulted in the proposition of universal relativity of all things and the exposition of the theory of two truths, the distinction between which was considered to be relative to one's orientation.

The Buddhist Notion of Relativity

The Buddhist ontological theory draws a middle path (madhyamā pratipad) between eternalism (śāśvatavāda) and annihilationism (ucchedavāda), two views that were prominent during the time of the Buddha and which he considered to be extreme standpoints that ought to be evaded. Eternalism refers to the brahmanical approach to reality that proposed an eternal and permanent substance or self (ātman) which survives the death of a being. Conversely, annihilationism, a position held by the Indian materialists, disavowed the idea of a changeless essence and maintained that one's death is a definitive end of one's life. The Buddha, on the other hand, retained the notion of the continuity of rebirths (saṃsāra), but discarded the idea that there is an enduring independent entity that undergoes these changes. In order to explain the continuity of existence from one life to the next without accepting a changeless agent, he proposed a doctrine of dependent origination (pratītya samutpāda), a notion that experiential events arise in relation to specific conditioning factors. The standard rendition of the model consists of twelve links (nidāna). They are as follows. (1) ignorance (avidyā), (2) volitions (saṃskāra), (3) consciousness (vijñāna), (4) name-form (nāma-rūpa), (5) six sense spheres (ṣadāyatana), (6) contact (sparśa), (7) feelings (vedanā), (8) craving (tṛṣṇā), (9) grasping (upādāna), (10) becoming (bhava), (11) birth (jāti), and (12) old age and death (jarāmaraṇa). This scheme demonstrates how unsatisfactoriness (duḥkha) comes about, and further provides a temporal description of the dynamic functioning of the basic components (skandha) of personality and an explanation of the working of the karmic law and the cycle of rebirths.

One of the traditions of Mahāyāna Buddhism, namely, Mādhyamika or the school of "the middle way," expanded this scheme into a universal model of relativity, according to which everything arises and ceases in relation to certain conditions that are, in turn, again conditioned by other factors. The pioneer of Mādhyamika is regarded to be Nāgārjuna, a Buddhist monk who lived in the second century C.E. Nāgārjuna maintained that there is no persistent ontological support for the continuously changing world; on the contrary, all components of reality are connected and mutually interdependent. This means that subjects and the objective world around them do not exist independently, but conversely completely depend upon other factors for their existence. Phenomena are therefore neither intrinsically existent nor nonexistent; they rather exist interdependently, lacking intrinsic nature. This absence of independent existence (svabhāva) is referred to as emptiness (śūnyatā), meaning that things exist in complete relativity to other things, every event being conditioned by a preceding event. In this manner, Mādhyamika Buddhism uncompromisingly applied the basic Buddhist notion of no-self to the whole of reality and therefore radicalized the Abhidharma teaching on the emptiness of wholes. Various schools of Abhidharma suggested that in order to clearly comprehend reality, it is necessary to distinguish between nominal existence (prajñapti sat) and substantial existence (dravya sat). In line with this proposition, they argued that what is real is not the whole world of subjects and objects that are labeled and conceptualized, but rather only the momentary stream of ever-changing basic constituents of existence (dharma). These momentary events were considered to be substantial existents upon which the discourse of fabricated concepts is secondarily superimposed.

However, according to Nāgārjuna, it is not just the wholes, but also dharmas, that is, the fundamental components of existence, that are empty of intrinsic nature. In other words, there are no substantial existents at all. Furthermore, in order to universally apply the method of deconstruction, Nāgārjuna did not spare even emptiness itself. Emptiness is hence not considered to be some reified absolute principle, but is like everything else, also stated to be empty of intrinsic nature. This reasoning resulted in the notion of emptiness of emptiness. In fact, emptiness is regarded to be nothing more than a clear comprehension that nothing exists independently. In view of this, the only proper way to use the notion of emptiness is to employ it as an adjective (i.e., This room is empty.), rather than a substantive (i.e., There is emptiness independent of the room.). To sum up, Nāgārjuna maintained that there are no unconditioned phenomena and no absolute self-established existents. Consequently, for him, the only acceptable discourse on the nature of reality is one of nonaffirmative nature, since both the notion of existence (bhāva) as well as the notion of nonexistence (abhāva) depend on the idea of independent existence (svabhāva), and are hence considered to be erroneous. This position thus decried all ontological endeavors which purport to study what does or does not exist. The notion of emptiness was also adopted by the Yogācāra or Vijñānavāda branch of Mahāyāna Buddhism, which included it in its theory of reality as a continuously changing flow of consciousness (vijñāna), empty of dualisms.

The doctrine of emptiness also led to a reformulation of the theory of two truths, which was insinuated definitely as early as the Abhidharmic exposition of the difference between the nominal and the substantial existence. With the Mahāyāna radicalization of the Abhidharmic reductionist approach, there also followed a different articulation of the truth of reality. Two levels of reality or two truths were now proposed, this being conventional (saṃvṛti) on the one hand and ultimate (paramārtha) on the other. Entities, as one normally understands them, were asserted to be real at the conventional level. However, at the ultimate level they were declared to have no independent existence. In accordance with the doctrine of emptiness, these two levels were, however, not deemed to represent separate realities but rather to correspond to two different kinds of understanding reality, namely, that of unenlightened and enlightened beings. The distinction between them was thus not regarded to be ontological but cognitive, that is, not representing a particular feature of reality but rather revealing it as essentially relative to one's viewpoint.

Cross-References

- Abhidhamma Piṭaka
- Abhidharma (Theravāda)
- Anattā (Buddhism)
- Causality (Buddhism)
- Dukkha
- Enlightenment
- Idealism (Buddhism)
- Insight
- Kamma
- Karma
- Khandha
- Mādhyamika
- Mahāyāna
- Majjhimā Paṭipadā
- Materialism (Buddhism)
- Nāgārjuna
- Nāma-Rūpa
- Paṭicca Samuppāda
- Philosophy (Buddhism)
- Psychology (Buddhism)
- Reality (Buddhism)
- Rebirth (Buddhism)
- Saṃkhāra
- Saṃskāra
- Soul
- Śūnya
- Śūnyatā
- Vijñāna
- Vijñānavāda
- Yogācāra

References

1. Berger DL (2001) The special meaning of the middle way: the Mādhyamika critique of Indian ontologies of identity and difference. J Dharma 26:282–310
2. Burton D (1999) Emptiness appraised: a critical study of Nāgārjuna's philosophy. Curzon, Richmond
3. de La Vallée Poussin L (1928) Notes on (1) *śū nyatā* and (2) the middle path. Indian Hist Q 4:161–168
4. Garfield J (1995) The fundamental wisdom of the middle way: Nāgārjuna's Mūlamadhyamakākarikā. Oxford University Press, Oxford/New York
5. Gómez LO (1976) Proto-Mādhyamika in the Pāli canon. Philos East West 26(2):137–165
6. Harris IC (1991) The continuity of Madhyamaka and Yogācāra in Indian Mahāyāna Buddhism. E.J. Brill, Leiden/New York
7. Huntington CW (2003) The emptiness of emptiness. An introduction to early Indian Mādhyamika. Motilal Banarsidass, Delhi
8. Kalupahana D (1986) The philosophy of the middle way. Mūlamadhyamakakārikā. State University of New York Press, Albany
9. King R (1994) Early Yogācāra and its relationship with the Madhyamaka School. Philos East West 44(4):659–686
10. Mansfield V (1990) Relativity in Maādhyamika Buddhism and modern physics. Philos East West 40(1):59–72
11. Priest G (2009) The structure of emptiness. Philos East West 59:467–480
12. Robinson RH (1972) Did Nāgārjuna really refute all philosophical views? Philos East West 22(3): 325–330
13. Tatia N (1995) The non-absolutistic view and the middle way (*anekānta* and *madhyamā pratipad*). Indian Int J Buddh Stud 5(1):1–21
14. Westerhoff J (2007) The Madhyamaka concept of Svabhāva: ontological and cognitive aspects. Asian Philos 17(1):17–45
15. Williams DM (1974) The translation and interpretation of the twelve terms in the Paṭiccasamuppāda. Numen 21:35–63, Fasc. 1
16. Williams P (1991) On the interpretation of Madhyamaka thought. J Indian Philos 19:191–218

R

Relativity (Jainism)

Wm. Andrew Schwartz
Claremont Graduate University, Claremont, CA, USA

Synonyms

Anekāntavāda; *Nayavāda*; *Syādvāda*

Definition

The Jain doctrine of relativity consists of three different "relativity" doctrines – *anekāntavāda*, *nayavāda*, and *syādvāda*. In short, these three doctrines, when brought together, insist that reality can be approached from a variety of different but correct perspectives.

Anekāntavāda

Anekāntavāda is the Jain metaphysical doctrine of relativity and non-one-sidedness (see entry on "► *Anekāntavāda*"). According to this doctrine, reality is complex, multifaceted, and many-sided. Furthermore, entities are endowed with innumerable characteristics. As such, reality cannot be reduced to a single concept or characteristic [1]. The many-sided nature of reality is a metaphysical relativity. The world is made up of mutually dependent and interconnected parts. According to Jain scripture, "Existence is characterized by origination, disappearance (destruction) and permanence" (*Tattvārthasūtra* 5.30). Unlike other schools of Indian thought that affirm impermanence or permanence as the absolute nature of reality (Buddhism and Advaita, respectively), Jainism says yes to both – though this "yes" is conditional. It's both-and, not either-or. In Jainism, permanence and impermanence, being and non-being, are all characteristic of reality. These contradictory characteristics are synthesized in Jainism, when understood as being asserted in different senses and from different perspectives, which seek to capture the many-sided nature of reality. In this way, they are all true, but only partially so. Such relativity should not be confused with relativism, by which there is no absolute. On the contrary, Jainism does affirm an absolute perspective, attained and passed down by the omniscient *jiva* of Mahavira.

A common example used to explain this doctrine is the ancient Indic story of the blind men and the elephant (Fig. 1). As the stories goes: There were six blind men who were brought before the king and asked to describe an elephant. One man, holding onto a leg, describes the elephant as being like a tree trunk. A second man, holding onto an ear, disagrees and suggests that the elephant is like a fan. A third man trips and falls into the side of the elephant and argues that the elephant is like a wall. A fourth man, holding on to the tail, retorts that the elephant is like a rope. The fifth man, grabbing a tusk, describes the elephant as similar to a spear. Finally, the sixth man, holding onto the trunk, describes the elephant like a giant snake. They continue to argue about their differing perspectives, until the king (who was watching this spectacle) interjects. He explains that each of the men was holding onto a part of the enormous elephant and that, ultimately, each of them was partially right.

Relativity (Jainism), Fig. 1 The elephant and the blind men (From http://www.jainworld.com/literature/story25.htm)

The elephant, as a symbolic representation of the world, depicts the many-sided nature of reality. Most strictly, *anekāntavāda* is a doctrine about the elephant. *Nayavāda*, on the other hand, is a doctrine about the blind men.

Nayavāda

Nayavāda is the Jain epistemological doctrine of the relativity of standpoints (see entry on "► *Nayavāda*"). According to this doctrine, reality can be approached from a variety of perspectives (*nayas*). Since reality is many-sided, there are many ways to approach reality (via the many sides). From the metaphysical doctrine of a complex reality with innumerable attributes flows an epistemology which considers knowledge of an object incomplete insofar as it fails to account for the many-sided nature of that object. The term *naya* is used to refer to "standpoints." These standpoints (or perspectives) represent the many ways that one can approach reality.

Inferred from this epistemology is that the fullness of "truth" is the summation of all *nayas*. As H.R. Kapadia writes, "Every judgment that we pass in daily life is true only in reference to the standpoint occupied and that aspect of the object considered" [2]. In that sense, all claims, which are made from single standpoints, are at best partially true and never absolutely true. Therefore, Jain epistemology (of which *nayavāda* is only a piece) encourages the knower to explore alternative perspectives, in order to formulate a more complete understanding of reality.

Naya (knowledge attained from a limited standpoint) is contrasted by *pramana* (knowledge attained via the pure soul). Whereas knowledge from *naya* results in one-sided and partial knowing, knowledge from *pramana* is pure and absolute. This kind of knowledge comes when seeing reality from the summation of all standpoints [3]. Confusing *naya* for *pramana* results in *ekānta* (one-sidedness) and error. In other words, treating a relative perspective as the absolute perspective is to fall prey to the error of one-sidedness (*ekānta*).

Although there are innumerable *nayas* from which reality can be known, Jain epistemology formally includes seven basic viewpoints that can be taken with respect to a given object. These seven *nayas* are the following:

1. *Naigama*: the undifferentiated
2. *Samgraha*: the general
3. *Vyavahara*: the practical
4. *Rjusutra*: the clearly manifest
5. *Sabda*: the verbal
6. *Samabhirudha*: the subtle
7. *Evambhuta*: the "thus-happened"

"The first three. . .are standpoints from which to investigate the thing itself, whereas the remaining four are standpoints from which to investigate the modifications that things undergo" [4]. In other words, these *nayas* refer to the different kinds of standpoints from which reality can be known.

To be clear, this perspectivism is not to be confused with relativism. These different valid perspectives are not validated by virtue of their being a perspective. If so, it would become an "agree to disagree" sort of relativism, whereby each person is allowed to have their own opinion, and all opinions are valid because they are nothing more than opinion. Rather, *nayavāda* is a deep epistemology of perspectivism, for which knowledge (of this variety) is always bound by one's limited ways of knowing. In philosophical discourse, this view has been stated in many different ways: There is no objectivity, we have no God's-eye point of view, there is no neutral perspective, etc., all of which make one thing clear – there are limits to the way humans come to understand. To say that there are limits to human knowledge may be mistaken as placing limits on the capacity for knowledge (i.e., the human brain can only hold a finite amount of data). While this too is true, it is different than the current claim that there are limits to the way one comes to know – which is always from a particular perspective.

Just like the story of the blind men and the elephant, everyone has a particularized engagement with reality, and this particularity is a limitation. Therefore, one can only know reality from a limited perspective (one's own perspective). Insofar as someone is not omniscient, that someone can only encounter the elephant (the world, ideas, philosophical notions, etc.) from one side at a time. As such, a fuller understanding of this complex reality requires that one synthesizes this plurality of perspectives – bringing together the parts to make a whole. According to Jain relativity, each person has a piece of the puzzle, that is, reality. In order to see the big picture (or at least a bigger picture), the many perspectives must be brought together in a unified whole.

Syādvāda

To help articulate this relativity, Jainism developed the doctrine of *syādvāda* (the dialectical doctrine of qualified assertion) (see entry on "▸ *Syādvāda*"). According to the Jain doctrine of *syādvāda*, all assertions should be predicated with the particle *syāt*, in this context meaning "from a certain perspective." In doing so, assertions are qualified as conditioned by and relative to the perspective of the one doing the asserting.

Again, using the example of the blind men and the elephant, each of the blind men commits an error when they treat their perspective (e.g., "an elephant is like a rope," "an elephant is like a spear," etc.) as true to the exclusion of the others. The reason this happens is that the truths of the blind men, which are actually relative truths, are being asserted as absolute truths, which leaves no room for the relative truth of others. But, by following the Jain doctrine of *syādvāda*, the relative nature of the truths can be captured – resulting in the mutual inclusion of a plurality of truth claims.

By predicating the statement, "an elephant is like a wall" with the particle *syāt*, the absolute and exclusive statement becomes "from a certain perspective an elephant is like a wall." And for the blind man who falls into the side of the elephant, this is certainly true. But, since the statement is now qualified as being "from a certain perspective," it no longer excludes the perspectives of the others. This dialectic of relativity is a means of qualifying assertions as to capture the relative nature of the claim in question.

For some, this example of the elephant seems insufficient. While it may be true that there are many sides to elephants and that these blind men are groping at different parts of that large animal, is it the case that all assertions can be seen from many valid perspectives? Can, for example, something be said to both exist and not exist? Here, it is helpful to consider the sevenfold logic of *syādvāda* (*saptabhangī*).

According to the Jain doctrine of *syādvāda*, there are seven types of statements – or seven modes of predication (*saptabhangī*). Often used to describe these seven forms of assertion are examples of existence:

1. From a certain perspective (*syāt*) *p* certainly (*eva*) exists.
2. From a certain perspective (*syāt*) *p* certainly (*eva*) does not exist.
3. From a certain perspective (*syāt*) *p* certainly (*eva*) exists AND certainly (*eva*) does not exist successively.
4. From a certain perspective (*syāt*) *p* certainly (*eva*) exists AND certainly (*eva*) does not exist simultaneously.
5. From a certain perspective (*syāt*) *p* certainly (*eva*) exists AND p certainly (*eva*) exists and does not exist simultaneously.
6. From a certain perspective (*syāt*) *p* certainly (*eva*) does not exist AND p certainly (*eva*) exists and does not exist simultaneously.
7. From a certain perspective (*syāt*) *p* certainly (*eva*) exists and does not exist successively AND p certainly (*eva*) exists and does not exist simultaneously.

A more abstract formulation of these seven alternatives includes the following:

1. Affirmation
2. Negation
3. Both affirmation and negation successively
4. Inexpressible (both affirmation and negation simultaneously)
5. Affirmation and inexpressible

6. Negation and inexpressible
7. Affirmation and negation and inexpressible

According to the Jain doctrine of *anekāntavāda*, the multifaceted nature of a thing includes the qualities of both existence and non-existence [5]. Consider the following assertion: "The pen exists." The first step, in *syādvāda*, is to qualify this assertion. So, we add a *syāt* particle to the phrase and we get, "from a certain perspective the pen exists." This is not too problematic. What complicates things a bit more is when a contradictory assertion is made, "the pen does not exist." Again, we qualify the statement and are left with, "from a certain perspective the pen does not exist." Now, how can both perspectives be valid? One way to makes sense of this phenomenon is to distinguish between "exists" and "exists as." The pen can be said to exist (*qua* pen), insofar as it *exists as* a pen – meaning, it has the qualities essential for being a pen. Likewise, the pen can be said not to exist (*qua* pot), insofar as it does not *exist as* a pot – meaning, it does not have the essential qualities of a pot. In this way, two seemingly contradictory assertions regarding the existence and nonexistence of a pen can be mutually inclusive and reconciled as both being true (albeit partially so).

Critiques of Jain Relativity

Despite the above distinctions about assertions being from different perspectives or meant in different senses, there is one critique still facing the Jain doctrine of relativity today – the critique of self-refuting incoherency. In short, the problem can be framed in a single question – is the doctrine of relativity itself relative? If the Jain doctrines of *anekāntavāda*, *syādvāda*, and *nayavāda* are themselves treated as universals, then they appear to run contrary to their own claim that all doctrines should be treated as relative attempts at describing a many-sided absolute. If everything is relative, then relativity itself is an absolute. But if there is an absolute, then everything is not relative. But, the absolute which undermines relativity *is* relativity itself. What results is a paradox that critics argue results in incoherency.

These sorts of questions are part of a larger critique of the Jain position. Consider the example of the blind men and the elephant. There are three elements to the story (at least the version told above): (1) the elephant that represents reality, (2) the blind men who represent all men and women attempting to know reality, and (3) the king – the only sighted observer who sees the situation of the blind men and recognizes the many sides of reality. While the doctrine of *nayavāda* suggests that all non-omniscient beings can only know reality from within the confines of limited perspectives, represented by the blind men, the story seems to suggest that Jains are in a privileged position – the position of the king. This becomes apparent in the application of Jain relativity to the disagreement between Buddhism and Advaita Vedanta. Buddhists are considered advocates of the view that reality is ultimately impermanent, whereas Advaitins are considered advocates of the view that reality is ultimately permanent. But, according to Jainism, both are only relatively true since the Buddhists and the Advaitins are like the blind men – neither sees the big picture. As such, the Jain position (represented by the position of the sighted king) is deemed a superior position in that it recognizes the one-sided nature of the Buddhist and Advaitin claims, as well as the multi-sided nature of reality.

Graham Priest describes the problem like this: "A Jain is committed, presumably, to the view that Jainism is a more accurate perspective of how things are than are others. If not, why be a Jain rather than a Buddhist or a Hindu? On the other hand, Jains hold that reality is multi-faceted, and no one view completely captures how things are: each captures one of the facets. . .This puts Jains in a somewhat awkward position when they argue with a Buddhist, Hindu, etc. If they disagree with such an opponent, they must hold that they are right in a way that the opponent is not; but also that the opponent is just as right as they are" [6].

According to Priest, "such tension would seem to be resolvable in one of only two ways: either

R

with the insistence that all views are not, after all, equal, that the Jaina view is privileged in some way, or in a thoroughgoing relativism" [6]. Historically, the dominant Jain approach has been the former, one that embraces the superiority of the Jain perspective. This view was championed by Hemachandra (eleventh-century Jain thinker) [7], a view that is criticized on two counts. First, insofar as the absolute is the doctrine of relativity, it seems self-contradictory. And two, insofar as other philosophical and theological Jain doctrines (doctrines of karma, cosmology, *jivas*, etc.) are posited as definite truths – of an absolute and not relative nature – they contradict the Jain doctrine of relativity.

Regarding the absolutization of the principle of relativity, Jain scholar Jeffery D. Long calls this a logical necessity in order to avoid relativism. He writes, "The introduction of this absolute perspective [the perspective of the omniscient lords] is a logical necessity if the error of relativism, which negates itself by undermining its own validity, is to be avoided" [8]. What then of the other Jain doctrines? Are the doctrines of karma, the soul, etc., to be understood in a relative or absolute sense?

One solution has been presented by second-century Jain scholar Kundakunda. According to Kundakunda, Jain doctrine itself should *not* be treated as an absolute. Rather, its doctrines (whether doctrines of the soul, of karma, etc.) should be treated as relative truths that simply point to a larger truth beyond all words and conceptualization [9]. Although Kundakunda was an important and revered Jain thinker, this "two truths" doctrine, which treats Jain truth as among the relative truths of other perspectives, has been controversial in the history of Jain thought. Nevertheless, it does serve as a viable response, within the Jain tradition, to the critique of "absolute relativity."

In essence, Kundakunda identifies the absolute perspective as being beyond all words and conceptualization. Insofar as the Jain doctrines are purported by non-omniscient beings, it is necessary to do so via the medium of language and concepts which are relative attempts at naming an absolute truth. Therefore, Kundakunda's solution avoids relativism, insofar as it retains the existence of an absolute (albeit a transcendent one), and it avoids absolutism, insofar as it puts the Jain perspective on par with other relative perspectives. In other words, positing the existence of an absolute that is beyond the purview of non-omniscient beings is one solution, internal to the Jain tradition, that allows Jains to walk the line between absolutism and relativism – which is what the Jain doctrine of relativity attempts to do.

Cross-References

▶ *Anekāntavāda*
▶ Jainism (Yakṣa)
▶ *Syādvāda*

References

1. Long JD (2010) Jainism: an introduction. I.B. Tauris, New York, p 117
2. Kapadia HR (1947) Introduction to Haribhadra Suri's Anekantajayapataka with his own commentary and Municandra Suri's supercommentary. Oriental Institute, Baroda, p cxviii
3. Koller JM (2000) Syādvāda as the epistemological key to the Jaina middle way metaphysics of Anekāntavāda. Philos East West 50(3):403 (University of Hawai'i Press)
4. Koller JM (2000) Syādvāda as the epistemological key to the Jaina middle way metaphysics of Anekāntavāda. Philos East West 50(3):402 (University of Hawai'i Press)
5. Jain P (2000) Saptabhangi: the Jaina theory of seven fold predication: a logical analysis. Philos East West 50(3):395 (University of Hawai'i Press)
6. Priest G (2008) Jaina logic: a contemporary perspective. Hist Philos Logic 29:275
7. Long JD (2010) Jainism: an introduction. I.B. Tauris, New York, p 163; and Hemachandra, *Anyayogavyavacchedika* 30
8. Long JD (2000) Plurality and relativity: whitehead, Jainism, and the reconstruction of religious pluralism. Unpublished doctoral dissertation, University of Chicago, Chicago
9. Long JD (2010) Jainism: an introduction. I.B. Tauris, New York, p 62

Further Reading

Bhargava D (2000) A few modern interpretations of non-absolutism. In: Shah NJ (ed) Jaina theory of multiple facets of reality and truth (Anekantavada). Motilal Banarsidass, Delhi, pp 111–117

Bharucha F, Kamat RV (1984) *Syadvada* theory of Jainism in terms of deviant logic. Indian Philos V 9:181–187

Bhattacharya KC (2000) The Jaina theory of Anekanta. In: Shah NJ (ed) Jaina theory of multiple facets of reality and truth (Anekantavada). Motilal Banarsidass, Delhi, pp 17–31

Bhattacharya KC (1953) Anekantavada. Jaina Atmananda Sabha, Bhavnagar

Charitrapragya S (2004) Mahavira, Anekantavada and the world today. In: Sethia T (ed) Ahimsa, Anekanta and Jainism. Motilal Banarsidass, Delhi, pp 75–84

Cort JE (2000) 'Intellectual Ahimsa' revisited: Jain tolerance and intolerance of others. Philos East West 50(3):324–347 (Hawai'i: University of Hawai'i Press)

Dundas P (2004) Beyond Anekantavada: a Jain approach to religious tolerance. In: Sethia T (ed) Ahimsa, Anekanta and Jainism. Motilal Banarsidass, Delhi, pp 123–136

Ganeri J (2002) Jaina logic and the philosophical basis of pluralism. Hist Philos Logic 20:267–281 (Taylor & Francis)

Gopalan S (1991) Jainism as meta-philosophy. Sri Satguru Publications, Delhi

Haribhadrasuri (1949) Saddarsanasamuccaya. Caukhamba Sanskrit Series Office, Varanasi

Jain G (ed) (2009) Eternal, quotes from Lord Mahavira. Deepak Traders, Chennai

Jain P (2000) Saptabhangi: the Jaina theory of seven fold predication: a logical analysis. Philos East West 50(3):385–399 (University of Hawai'i Press)

Kapadia HR (1947) Introduction to Haribhadra Suri's Anekantajayapataka with his own commentary and Municandra Suri's supercommentary. Oriental Institute, Baroda

Koller JM (2000) Syādvāda as the epistemological key to the Jaina middle way metaphysics of Anekāntavāda. Philos East West 50(3):400–407 (University of Hawai'i Press)

Koller JM (2004) Why is Anekantavada important. In: Sethia T (ed) Ahimsa, Anekanta and Jainism. Motilal Banarsidass, Delhi, pp 85–98

Kulkarni VM (2000) Relativity and absolutism. In: Shah NJ (ed) Jaina theory of multiple facets of reality and truth (Anekantavada). Motilal Banarsidass, Delhi, pp 61–66

Kumar JA, Dak TM, Mishra AD (eds) (1996) Facets of Jain philosophy, religion and culture: Anekantavada and Syadvada. Jain Vishva Bharati Institute, Ladnun, Rajasthan

Long JD (2009) Jainism: an introduction. I.B. Tauris, New York

Mahaprajna A (1996) An introduction: the axioms of non-absolutism. In: Kumar JA, Dak TM, Mishra AD (eds) Facets of Jain philosophy, religion and culture: Anekantavada and Syadvada. Jain Vishva Bharati Institute, Ladnun, Rajasthan

Matilal BK (1981) The central philosophy of Jainism: Anekantavada. L.D. Institute of Indology, Ahmedabad

Matilal BK (2000) Anekanta: both yes and no. In: Shah NJ (ed) Jaina theory of multiple facets of reality and truth (Anekantavada). Motilal Banarsidass, Delhi

Mookerjee S (1978) The Jaina philosophy of non-absolutism: a critical study of Anekantavada. Motilal Banarsidass, Delhi

Padmarajiah YJ (1963) A comparative study of the Jaina theories of reality and knowledge. Jain Sahitya Vikas Mandal, Bombay

Priest G (2008) Jaina logic: a contemporary perspective. Hist Philos Logic 29(3):263–278 (Taylor & Francis)

Sethia T (ed) (2004) Ahimsa, Anekanta and Jainism. Motilal Banarsidass, Delhi

Shah N (2000) Jaina theory of multiple facets of reality and truth (Anekantavada). Motilal Banarsidass, Delhi

Shah N (ed) (1998) Jaina philosophy and religion. Motilal Banarsidass, Delhi

Shah SM (1987) The dialectic of knowledge and reality in Indian philosophy. Eastern Book Linkers, Delhi

Sharma A (2001) A Jaina perspective on the philosophy of religion. Motilal Banarsidass, Delhi

Sinari R (1996) A pragmatist critique of Jain relativism. Philos East West 19(1):59–64 (University of Hawai'i Press)

Tatia N (1951) Studies in Jaina philosophy. P.V. Research Institute, Varanasi

Vallely A (2004) Anekanta, Ahimsa and the question of pluralism. In: Sethia T (ed) Ahimsa, Anekanta and Jainism. Motilal Banarsidass, Delhi, pp 99–112

Religion

► Dharma (Jainism)

Religious Diversity

► Pluralism (Buddhism)

Renunciation

► Ordination

Renunciation (Buddhism)

Angraj Chaudhary
Vipassana Research Institute, Dhammagiri, Nashik, Maharashtra, India

Synonyms

Abhiniṣkramaṇa

Definition

Renunciation is leaving home for a homeless life. It precedes ordination.

Renunciation means leaving home for a homeless life. It means leaving the household life and retire. One who renounces home takes ordination and then becomes an ascetic, a sādhu, or a wanderer or a bhikkhu. Thus renunciation precedes ordination.

There are various causes for renouncing home. One may do so because he is jilted by his fiancée or his love is not reciprocated or he finds worldly life very troublesome or he finds it too much with him or finds it very difficult or he might have had some sad and shattering experience in his life in losing somebody who was his near and dear one or who might have had some harrowing experience because of the loss of wealth or loss of name and fame or because of poverty or some kind of court case or if he gets unexpected bad treatment from somebody in his life.

Buddha's Renunciation

But the kind of renunciation that is found in Buddhism is qualitatively different. It is not related to any of the causes enumerated above. It is a kind of spiritual dissatisfaction, which is called "ennui" in French. Siddhārtha left home not to lead a retired life as many ordinary mortals would do, but he did so to find out the cause of universal suffering and its remedy. The cause of his leaving home was very exalted as he wanted to find out the cause of universal suffering and also the path walking on which one can end one's suffering forever. And that meant the greatest good of the suffering people. And that also meant a lot of hard work and a very active life [1].

A Tide in Buddha's Life

Siddhārtha was very sensitive. Often, even amidst a lot of pleasures, he would retire to a lonely place and ponder. Even though he might have seen old men, diseased men, dead men, and ascetics earlier as pointed out by other critics, the avalanche came just before he left home. Why old age? Why disease? And why death? And what is the answer to these fundamental questions? This was actually the moment when the tide came in his thought, and he caught it at that moment. As Shakespeare has said, "There is a tide in the affairs of man, which taken at the flood, leads on to fortune, Omitted, all the voyage of their life is bound in shallows and miseries" [2].

Many people do not believe this story of seeing these four signs and making the Great Renunciation [3]. They argue that as Siddhārtha was quite grown up, he must have seen several old men (in fact, his parents were quite old), he must have seen diseased men, and he must have heard of death. Some people must have died in his own family. So the story of seeing the four signs and making the Great Renunciation does not seem to be true, as it is not logical. It does not appeal to them. But such things do happen in life. One event like this seen at a particular moment in life by a sensitive man can turn the course of his life. At a particular moment in his life, Siddhārtha felt very much disturbed and troubled when he saw that he was also subject to old age, disease, and death as others are. Therefore he naturally wanted to know if there was any way to get rid of these sufferings. He wanted to make a quest of the deathless and the peaceful. He also found household life "crowded and dusty" [4]. In these circumstances he decided to leave home to search for the deathless and the peaceful.

Other causes for his renunciation are gross in comparison to this great tide that came in his life.

D.D. Kosambi says that he left home because he saw people fighting for the water of the River Rohini. They were ready to shed precious blood for not so precious water. He also reflected that "the household life is close and dusty, the homeless life is free as air" [5]. So he decides to leave home. But if one thinks a little deeper, he will find it a half-truth. If an ascetic or a monk does not eradicate the root cause of suffering, he also has to suffer. So Siddhārtha did not leave home for a homeless life and adopt an ostrich policy but he left it to face the problems of life squarely and find out their causes to root them out. This cause to leave home is more meaningful, logical, and convincing than leaving home to keep himself away from taking part in the fight between the Śākyas and the Koliyas.

The cause for his renunciation is underlined by what he himself says in the Ariyapariyesanā Sutta [6]. He left home for making a noble search, not the ignoble one. He says there that if one who is himself subject to birth, aging, sickness, and death looks for something which is also subject to birth, aging, sickness, and death, this is an ignoble search. But if he himself subject to birth, aging, sickness, and death looks for something which is not subject to them, then that is a noble search. He saw everything in the world as impermanent. All objects of attachment are impermanent [7].

Siddhārtha abandoned his great property and left his great circle of relatives, left even the prosperity, majesty, and splendor of a wheel-turning king and renounced his home to live an ascetic life [8]. What does this mean? It means he abandoned greed and attachment and greed for wealth and attachment to his relatives.

Then he discovered the Noble Eightfold Path while learning in the school of experience. He walked on it very carefully and sincerely and discovered the root cause of the universal suffering. He also discovered the path walking on which one can end one's suffering and attain peace and tranquillity.

It is clear from what he says in the Ariyapariyesanā Sutta that he shaved off his hair and beard, donned the yellow robe, and went forth from the homelife into homelessness.

This is known as renunciation (abhinikkhamana), which in the Aṭṭhakathā came to be known as the Great Renunciation (Mahābhinikkhamana) [9].

Cross-References

▶ Renunciation

References

1. M 1. Ariyapariyesanā Sutta or Pāsarāsi Sutta (Unless otherwise mentioned all books referred to here are published by Vipassana Research Institute, Dhammagiri, in 1998)
2. Julius Caesar, pp iv, ii, 269–276
3. Kosambi DD, Buddha B (1996) Jīvana aur Darśana. Indian Press Pvt Ltd, Allahabad, pp 83–86, Koslyāyana A (trans) Baba Saheb Ambedkar, Bhagavāna Buddha aur Unakā Dhamma. Taiwan edn. pp 27–29
4. D.1.55 & Walsh M (trans) (1995) The Long Discourses of the Buddha. Wisdom Publications, Boston, p 99
5. ibid
6. M 1. Ariyapariyesanā Sutta or Pāsarāsi Sutta
7. Ñāṇamoli Bhikkhu, Bodhi Bhikkhu (trans) (1995) The Middle Length Discourses of the Buddha. Wisdom Publications, Boston, pp 254–256
8. Mūlapaṇṇāsa Ṭīkā, 2.120
9. DA 2.14

Resolution to Strive for Awakening

▶ Bodhicitta

R

Responsibility (Buddhism)

Asha Mukherjee
Department of Philosophy and Religion,
Visva-Bharati Central University, Santiniketan,
WB, India

Synonyms

Dhamma; Kusala; Puñña; Sīla; Vinaya

Definition

Any act or state or willing which removes suffering and leads to *nirvāṇa* is responsibility.

Introduction

In Buddhist system of thought, "responsibility" has an extremely important role to play. Everyone has a responsibility as either a layperson or monk toward oneself, responsibilities toward others including all sentient beings, and responsibilities toward the universe at large which is called *dhamma* (in Pali and *dharma* in Sanskrit), an all-inclusive concept. Responsibilities of everyone for the sake of understanding may be divided as moral, social, and metaphysical which emerge from the understanding of the cosmic order of the universe (including the monistic order). There are no deontological facets in Buddhism in the strong sense of the word like an impersonal categorical imperative as Richard E. Gombrich [6] while examining the duty in Buddhist Pali scriptures observed. The only central obligation or duty one could find is in relation to attainment of liberation from suffering but not in the sense of categorical imperative; rather, it is self-imposed duty. It is not a command but something emerges from the understanding of the nature of things as they are. Besides this there are contexts in which one finds rules, reciprocal duties, and obligations. The biggest responsibility of everyone toward oneself is to get liberation from suffering. The foundation of Buddha's teaching is the Four Noble Truths, the first being "there *is* suffering"; thus anything which has the possibility of leading to suffering cannot be good, and any state/action or nonaction which reduces suffering is good. The other three truths deal with the cause of suffering, the end of suffering, and the path that frees us from suffering. The main problem in Buddhism is how to get rid of suffering. In Buddhism, ceasing suffering is the only ideal of good life. But the question is, what is suffering? It is that craving that leads downward to rebirth, the craving for feeling, for rebirth. And "ceasing of suffering" means the utter passionless ceasing, the giving up, the abandonment of, the release from, and the freedom from attachment and craving. Suffering is the biggest evil due to the cycle of birth and death. "Countless are the births wherein I have circled and run seeking, but not finding, the builder of the house; ill is birth again and again" [13]. Breaking of the cycle of birth and to get rid of suffering, one can begin with simple practice of ordinary moralities of everyday life and continue without break to the transcendental state known as "Nirvāṇa" which can be attained in present life, and responsibility of each person is directed toward this highest goal. It can be achieved through the Noble Eightfold Path. The Eightfold Path consists of the following principles: right belief, to ponder on the reality of matter; right aims, knowing four truths (sorrows, development of sorrows, resistance of sorrows, and the way of eradication of sorrows); right speech, not to make false statements; right actions, to realize the right aims into actions; right means of livelihood with justification; right endeavors for right causes; right mindfulness for the renunciation from all indulgences; and right meditation to contemplate to achieve Nirvāṇa.

Social Responsibility

For all members of society, the prime responsibility is to maximize happiness and minimize suffering. Due to compassion, social institutions should aim at equity in distribution and opportunity and minimization of suffering for the least advantaged. The five ethical precepts (*pañca-sīla*) for laypersons refraining from killing, stealing, lying, sexual misconduct, and intoxication are part of the conception of good. Buddhist conception of social good can be seen as instrumental for ensuring the good of individuals. The important human virtues are generosity, patience, wisdom, moderation, and nonattachment, and these can be achieved by developing the traits of character to cultivate a sense of responsibility toward others not as imperatives but as natural and spontaneous. Almost similar to Aristotle [1], one needs to develop moral skill for the development of Buddhist virtues and attainment of good.

Responsibilities and duties are grounded in connectedness, in every relationship, like children and parents; husband and wife; teacher and pupil; servant and workpeople, with means of livelihood; and friends. Loyalty to one's friends brings service and support, freedom from enemies, a welcome at home, and success in one's activities. One should live up to one's promises and should regard with friendliness any person that has done one a service. A genuine friend is one who is a help and support always and especially in need, who is the same in happiness and sorrow, who advises for one's welfare, and who is sympathetic ([16], pp. 137–138). By associating with friends of high moral standard, one gains virtue of confidence, morality, charity, and wisdom displayed by the best of one's associates. One should lead a balanced life in the sense that neither one should be unduly elated in favorable time nor one should be depressed in difficult time. Achievement of wisdom lies in total destruction of suffering.

Bodhisattva takes the responsibility or burden of all suffering upon himself:

> At all costs I must bear the burdens of all beings, in that I do not follow my own inclinations. I have made the vow to save all beings. All beings I must set free. The whole world of living beings I must rescue, from the terrors of birth, of old age, of sickness, of death, and rebirth, of all kinds of moral offence, of all states of woe, of whole cycle of birth-and-death, of the jungle of false views, of the loss of whole-some dharma, of the concomitants of ignorance,-from all the terrors I must rescue all beings.... My endeavors do not merely aim at my own deliverance. For, with the help of the boat of the thought of all-knowledge, I must rescue all these beings from the stream of Samsara.... I am resolved to abide in each single state of woe for numberless aeons; and so I will help all beings to freedom, in all the states of woe that may be found in any world system whatever.

Bodhisattva with the help of skills achieved enters into the trances, and yet he is not reborn in the heaven, and he instigates others to do the same. It is the primary responsibility of Bodhisattva to show the path to others and the persons should follow the path to get rid of suffering.

The first five precepts (*pañca-sīla*) for the path to better rebirths or enlightenment for laity and monks are prohibit killing, stealing, lying, adultery, and the use of intoxicants (*satya, ahiṃsā, asteya, aparigrah).* Abstaining from drinks, dance, singing, instrumental music and visiting shows, abstaining from use of garland, scent, cosmetic ornamenting and decorating, abstaining from use of high and luxurious beds and seats, abstaining from the acceptance of gold and silver. These are the grounds to facilitate the development of morality and social harmony as well as providing germination ground for concentration and developing wisdom with pragmatic considerations. The duties and obligations emerge to bring the Buddhist community of monks, laymen, and families together. In early Buddhism, separation of monks, nuns, and laity is found. The monastic life is conceived as necessary for the attainment of *nirvāṇa*. Laity will have to reach to the stage of a monk and monk in his future state to attain *nirvāṇa*. In Buddhism, besides *pañca-sīla*, one also finds ten precepts (*daśa-sīla* or *dasakusala*); they may seem basically self-centered, but they are to be seen in the wider context of virtues and values such as giving (*dāna-sīla*) and the four unlimited virtues of benevolence (*maître*), compassion (*karuṇā*), sympathetic joy (*muditā*), and equanimity (*upekṣā*). But neither of them can exhaust the description of Buddhist path toward enlightenment. Five sins (*papa*) are also mentioned in Mahāyāna Buddhism, and they are killing of bodhisattva or a nun, sacrilege, slander, and wrong views about teaching, including the karmic or natural moral effects of good and bad deeds. Basically, the wrong viewing rather than bad will is the root of all evils.

Moral Responsibility

Whole domestic and social duty, with most comprehensive details, or Vinaya of the houseman is discussed in a canon called Siṅgālavadāsutta [14]. The entire Sutta is devoted to the outlook and relations of layman and his surroundings and the reciprocal duty resulting therefrom. Anukampanti is the word for the protecting tenderness of the stronger for the weaker and means vibrating along after. Thus the emotional force is even stronger than our compassion or sympathy. And because the emotion is other-regarding, a feeling-together whatever the loved one feels, it is justifiable by love from smaller to greater.

The difference between the duties of householder and the recluse (monk) lie not in the faculties employed but in the specific ends to which they were directed. Both have to acquire the habit of virtue and practice with a mind-set for higher life. A high standard of duty is expected regarding one's family, friends, and associates, and if one is a householder, he must fulfill those duties. Only a moral person should expect and achieve success in his pursuits. First, by his work, elegance, and clear mind, he could make himself happy and his parents, wife, children, servants, and workpeople. Then he could make happy his friends and companions, and then he would be able to keep his property; make suitable offerings to his kin, guests, deceased, kings, and monks; institute patience and gentleness; and engage in every activity that would perfect himself and others. Householders should not engage in any kind of trade in weapons, in human beings, in flesh, in intoxicants, and in poison ([9], vol. III, p. 208).

Duties of a wife, a husband, a child, parents, a student, a teacher, employer, employee, and householder all are discussed in utmost details. The notion of reciprocity is emphasized always, and one can find a fine blending of care and rights. Buddhism does not emphasize much on morality of rights but much more on morality of responsibility as found in most of the Asian traditions. It is often felt that morality of rights gives rise to antagonism between the powerless and the powerful; thus it is better to lay emphasis on reciprocity. The notion of reciprocity is not a relation of dominance or subordination but for mutual respect and dignity with respect to other fellow beings, human as well as other living beings. In Siṅgālavādasutta, Buddha outlines the spirit of caring and fellow feeling relationship in the family. But in the life of a monk, he should move away from the network of relationship. Buddha spent 45 years after attaining enlightenment just in guiding people how to live a good life. He used the analogy of mother's love for the child as a paradigm of universal compassion. During the discourses, he would select a person and give sermons which would be relevant for others as well; they were addressed to particular, but they are universal in character, agent-centered as well as a way to lead to liberation which is always the same for every person, beginning with personal and gradually becoming impersonal, and transcending the "I-ness" and "my-ness."

Buddha refers to the duties of the monks to spread the *dhamma/dharma* for the welfare of many and the duties of the king to govern according to the principles of *dhamma* as kinship was the only institution to govern the country. Buddha tried to humanize the kinship system and gave a moral flavor. The kings are also guided by the duties to rule with principles or righteousness, impartiality, and equity. The king should govern with the approval and consent of the people was the main axiom to be followed; the king was described as *mahāsammata* as he was selected by the people. He was expected to follow the path of *dhamma* – moral and cosmic order of the universe.

Buddhism originated in a caste society, and the Asian societies where Buddhism flourished have for the most part been hierarchically structured. In such a structured society, it is natural to have duty-based discourse rather than right based. Each member of the society has a duty toward the other – a reciprocal responsibility. Under *dharma*, husbands and wives, kings and people, and teachers and students all have reciprocal responsibilities/obligations which can be analyzed and understood in terms of rights and duties, but the fact remains that they are always expressed in the form of duties rather than rights. "A husband should support his wife" and not as "wives have a right to be maintained by their husbands." On the other hand, the hierarchical structure of the society is also rejected in Buddhism due to the doctrine of no self; all individuals are equal. If there is no self, then there are only individual bodies which are also momentary, changing every moment.

Metaphysical Responsibility

Buddha believed in the doctrine of correlated action, which goes to suggest as existence of law and order in the progress of cause and effect. In Buddhism, this doctrine is known as *paṭiccasamuppāda*, which is meant to illustrate the law of the dependent origination of things, in Majjhima Nikāya [8]: "If this is, that comes to be, from the arising of this that arises; if this is not that does not come to be, from the ceasing of this that ceases." In the context of Buddha's enlightenment, 12 direct and indirect *nidānas* are mentioned including conditioned by birth, old age and dying, grief, sorrow, suffering, dejection, despair, and all kinds of evil. To get rid of all these evils or ills, one has to get rid of ignorance (*avijjā*) to stop the habitual tendencies and stop the consciousness ([7], vol. IV, pp. 1–2). The root of all suffering is *avijjā* or ignorance from which others follow, and each one of these constitute a cause for the next following from forming a chain. Thus destruction of each cause has been said to annual its effect, leading to the cessation of suffering. The three qualities to be destroyed are known as the three evil roots (*hetus*) and with them the *āsavas* (sense desires, craving for the existence, lack of higher knowledge (*avijjā*), and attachment to wrong views) also to be destroyed to attain the goal. *Nirvāṇa* is the state which is not recorded by the five physical senses and is devoid of sensuous happiness; the happiness arising from the five senses is merely sensuous happiness.

There are two corollaries of *paṭiccasamuppāda*: "All is impermanent and all in the world are devoid of a self." The world is in a process of continuous change; nothing remains same for two moments. Everything is changing every moment including the individual (unselfness). An individual is not a unity but an aggregate of the five *khandhas* (*rūpa*, *vedanā*, *saññā*, *saṅkhāra*, and viññāṇa), each of which has no substance of itself. But then the problem arises; if the self or the doer of an act and the experiencer is not there, then who is responsible for any act? Buddhist does not find any inconsistency between impermanence and *anattā* or no self. Individual is a pure product of his deeds, and it is in his own hands to continue or to stop his miseries. "Karma is one's own." It is in his own hands to allow his miseries to continue or to stop them. The whole phenomenal world is not-self, devoid of permanence, and is in flux, a continual denial of sameness at two consecutive moments. But the principle of continuity says no two things are the same, but there is similarity. The individual of a particular moment cannot be independent of one immediately proceeding as long as one is caused and conditioned by the other. To explain the continuity, Buddha gives example of married women – the married woman is not the same as the one who was unmarried, but she is not different from the one who was unmarried.

In Mahāyāna, the Dharmakāya of Buddha is considered to be constituted by *Śūnyatā* (essence) and represented in monistic conception of reality. Mahāyāna lays equal emphasis on *Śūnyatā* (*Prajñā*) and *Karuṇā*; they are two legs on which Mahāyāna stands on the unity of the two. If one does not care much for *Karuṇā* and adheres to *Śūnyatā* alone, then he/she can never have access to the right path; nor if one concentrates on *Karuṇa* alone, he can attain salvation even in thousand births; but the one who is able to mingle *Śūnyatā* with *Karuṇā* remains neither in *bhava* (*samsara*) nor in *nirvāṇa*. Buddha laid much emphasis on experience and refuses to accept anything which is beyond experience. But he makes a distinction between that which can be objectively experienced and that which can only be transcendentally experienced. One is phenomenal and the other is absolute. Phenomenal reality can be objectively experienced and communicated, but ultimate reality cannot be communicated. Ultimate truth is a matter of realization and beyond of logic and good and evil. In this sense, Buddhists are both positivistic and mystical.

The title of the dialogue *Dhammapada* itself has been interpreted in different ways:

> Under one interpretation *'Dhamma'* means religion- the religion taught by Buddha, or the law which every Buddhist should accept and observe, under other interpretation '*dhamma'* is virtue, or the realization of the law. *'Pada'* also has many meanings as explained in Abhidhana-padipika, it means place, protection, *Nirvāṇa*, cause, word, thing portion, foot, footstep. Thus '*Dhammapada'* may mean 'footsteps of religion', 'The Paths of Religion', 'Footpath of Virtue' or 'Path of the Law' etc. ([10], pp. iii–iv).

In the first chapter of Dhammapada, each twin verses represent good and evil side of actions. Pain, hatred, hatred by hatred, uncontrolled life and looking for pleasure, having robe without cleaning oneself from sin, seeing truth in untruth and untruth in truth, passion, mourning for evil doing, and foolishness are evil, but happiness, love, controlled life, cleaning oneself from sin, seeing truth in truth and untruth in untruth, a well-reflecting mind, rejoicing the purity of mind, a virtuous life which makes one happy in this world and in the next, true knowledge, and priesthood are good ([10], pp. 3–8).

The requirement for monks and nuns are intended to promote austerity; they have to practice strict celibacy with few specified objects like begging bowl and robe. The laity has a special duty to support, welcome, and respect the *saṃgha*, and monks and nuns participate and anchorage all works related to *saṃgha* and temple which are not for worshiping God but for paying respect to the vanished teachers. The monks and nuns are supposed to control and meditate and to teach the doctrines (*dhamma*) to the laity and faithful and improve themselves through following the path. The special training consists of mindfulness where the aspirant attempts to control his/her own motives. The rules for monks are often context dependent; they are aimed to develop a fine moral culture. In a perfect *arahant* (monk), the ideal moral qualities become second nature, spontaneous, and natural.

It is not a question of faith but of actively taking responsibility for one's own spiritual victory. Men and women both are advised to fulfill their social roles and responsibility. Social responsibilities such as being respectful and kind to family members and generous to monks and nuns and avoiding jealousy, ill temper, vengefulness, lust, etc., were for both men and women, and they are part of their onward journey. There is a story about how the first *bhikṣuṇī* (nun) *saṃghas* was founded. Initially, it was not welcomed, and even when *bhikṣuṇī saṃgha* was allowed, a *bhikṣuṇī* had to accept much more strict eight rules: "(1) that every *bhikṣuṇī*, even if she has been ordained a hundred years, shall rise and salute every monk, even if he was just ordained that very day; (2) A *bhikṣuṇī* must spend the rainy season only in a place where there is a *bhikṣu*; (3) Every half month, the *bhikṣuṇī* must request the exhortation of dharma from the monks, and instructions as to when the fortnightly *Uposatha* ceremony is to be performed; (4) at the end of the rainy season, the *bhikṣuṇī* must report any misdeeds she might have committed, before the *bhikṣu Saṃghas* as well as before the *bhikṣuṇī Saṃghas*; (5) a *bhikṣuṇī* who has transgressed a Vinaya rule must submit to discipline by both the bhikṣu and *bhikṣuṇī* Saṃghas; (6) a *bhikṣuṇī* must be ordained by both the bhikṣu and *bhikṣuṇī Saṃghas*; (7) a *bhikṣuṇī* must never abuse or revile a monk; (8) a *bhikṣu* may formally admonish a *bhikṣuṇī*, but she may not admonish him" ([15], p. 43). But in spiritual matters women were equal to men although a strict hierarchy is clear in the above rules and male superiority is maintained. Women were not suited for taking positions of leadership and responsibility in secular affairs outside the home. *Bhikṣuṇī* accepted the rule gladly and disciplined them as Buddhism offered a way of life to women which were not available in Indian society at that time. From various sources, the names of *bhikṣuṇīs* can be found who attained high levels such as Dhammadinnā, Khemā, Paṭacārā, Buddhamitrā, and Mañjuśrī.

If one does not fulfill one's responsibility, or neglects it, it is considered as evil. After one has done some evil, he/she has to mourn: "The evildoer mourns in this world, and he mourns in both. He mourns and suffers when he sees the evil (result) of his own work" ([10], p. 15). *Visuddhimāgga* deals with how one can get rid of the effects of the evil doings; this method is called *visuddhi.* The evil path and good path are also technical expressions for descending and ascending scales of worlds through which all beings have to travel upward or downward, according to their deeds: "An evil deed, like newly-drawn milk, does not turn (suddenly); smoldering, like fire covered by ashes, it follows the fool" ([10], p. 71). "Good men indeed walk (warily) under all circumstances; good men speak not out of a desire for sensual gratification;

whether touched by happiness or sorrow wise people never appear elated or depressed" ([10], p. 83). "He who is calm, having left behind good and evil, free from defilement, having understood this and the other world, and conquered birth and death, such a one is called a *Samaṇa* by being so" [7].

One must note that in Buddhism there are several different lines along which both speculation and edifying teachings for conduct run. The first is one where conduct laid out for the ordinary Buddhist layman is found in various *Nikāyas*. In such context, Buddhism does not go away much from the current ethics of the day. The second is the rules as outward conduct of the members of the order laid down in various texts where we find simple incorporation of the Brahman and non-Brahman rules (with in Hinduism) with some minor changes and additions; the third is a system of self-training in higher things prescribed for members of the order, which also cannot be considered as exclusively Buddhist; and the last is the method of self-training laid down for those who have entered upon the Path of Arahatship, the Eightfold Path, where the exclusive Buddhist doctrines are to be found. But all the four kind of rules of conduct form a very well-welded consistent whole, and each part plays an important role in the whole.

In later Mahāyāna literature, there is a tendency to ascribe sacred properties to the text. The essence of the Buddha's teaching is considered as being "truth body." It is interesting to note that through the mystical experience and cooperative and altruistic considerations, a life of humanistic compassion follows interacting with a mystical worldview. Rabindranath Tagore's *Religion of Man* [20] comes very close to such kind of Buddhism – the relation between the individual and the universal; the individual finds meaning in identifying himself/herself with the universal, the transcendental.

Cross-References

▶ Dhamma
▶ Evil (Buddhism)
▶ Four Noble Truths
▶ Good (Buddhism)
▶ Karma

References

1. Aristotle, Nicomachean ethics in Works of Aristotle (1925) 9 vols (trans: Ross WD) Oxford Carendon Press
2. Bilimoria P, Mohanty JN (eds) (1997) Relativism, suffering and beyond, essays in memory of Bimal K. Matilal, Oxford University Press, Delhi
3. Conze E (1953) Buddhist texts through the ages. Oxford University Press, Oxford
4. Conze E (1964) Saṃyutta Nikāya in Buddhist texts through the ages. Harper Torchbooks, New York
5. Keown D (1992) The nature of Buddhist ethics. Macmillan, London
6. Gombrich RE (1978) The duty of a Buddhist according to Pali scripture. In: Doniger W et al (eds) The concept of duty in South Asia. Vikas, New Delhi
7. Horner IB (1958) Translation ofMahavagga. In: Book of the discipline of the Vinaya. Nalanda-Devnagari Pali Series, Pali Publication Board, Bihar Government
8. Bhikshu Jagdish K (ed) (1958) Majjhima-Nikāya, Nāl edn [As the middle length sayings], 3 vols (trans. Horner IB). PTS, London
9. Morris H, Hardy H (eds) (1959) Aṅguttara Nikāya, vols 1–5. Pali Text Society, London, 1885–1900, reprint
10. Max MF (1965) The Dhammapada – a collection of verses, translation from Pāli. Motilal Banarsidass, Delhi
11. Diana P (1979) Maharatnakūṭa. In: Women in Buddhism (trans). Asian Humanities Press, Berkeley
12. Rhys Davids TW (Mrs) (ed) (2005) Saṃyutta-Nikāya [The book of the kindred sayings], 5 vols (trans: Woodward FL). Motilal Banarsidass, Delhi
13. Rhys Davids TW (Mrs) (2007) Dīgha-Nikāya. In: Dialogues of the Buddha, vols 1–3. Motilal Banarsidass, Delhi
14. Rhys Davids TW (Mrs) (2007) Singalavadasutta. In: Dialogues of the Buddha, vol 3. Motilal Banarsidass, Delhi
15. Sharma A (2006) Women in Indian religions. Oxford University Press, Oxford
16. Saddhatissa H (1970) Buddhist ethics – essence of Buddhism. George Braziller, New York
17. Stcherbatsky Th (1961) The central conception of Buddhism and the meaning of the word 'Dharma', 3rd edn, Sushil Gupta, Calcutta
18. Suzuki DT (1963) Outlines of Mahāyāna Buddhism. Schocken Books, New York
19. Doniger W et al (eds) (1978) The concept of duty in South Asia. Vikas, New Delhi
20. Tagore R (1993) Religion of man. Indus, New Delhi

Revelation

▶ Mysticism (Buddhism)

Revelation of the Good Religion in Laṅkā

▶ Laṅkāvatāra Sūtra

Righteous War

▶ Warfare (Buddhism)

Rje-btsun Tārānātha

▶ Tāranātha

Root Language

▶ Divya-dhvani

Royal Consecration

Madhumita Chattopadhyay
Department of Philosophy, Jadavpur University, Kolkata, West Bengal, India

Synonyms

Royal patronage

Definition

Declaration of something as sacred by the king. Formal dedication by the king of some property or land to an institution for religious purposes.

Introduction

In the history of the world, it is observed that a religion can flourish well in a country or attain greatest popularity among the countrymen only when that religion receives its patronage from the ruler of the country, may be a king or an army officer or whatever status he may have. For example, Christianity would not have attained the form which it has now, unless it received the active support and patronage of emperors like Constantine. This happened not only with Christianity but with all great religions of the world. Buddhism is no exception in this regard.

Royal Connection

The founder of the religion of Buddhism, Siddhārtha Gautama, came from a royal family of Kapilavastu and as such was in an advantageous position to win over the royal favor and patronage. When Siddhārtha attained the stage of Bodhi and became known as Buddha and founded the religion of Buddhism, the popularity of his religion was not confined to his birthplace or to that royal family only but spread among different empires. This is evident from the fact that after his death, there was a craze among the different emperors to receive the relics after the cremation of his body and to erect *stūpas* for worshipping. In this regard mention may be made of Ajātasatru of Magadha, the Licchavis of Vesāli (Vaiśālī), the Śākyas of Kapilavastu, the Koliyas of Rāmagrāma, the Mallas of Pāvā, etc. History tells that Buddhism could spread so fast during this period under the royal consecration of many monarchs of this time, among whom mention must be made of Aśoka, Menander, and Kaniṣka whose only concern was to follow the religion of Buddha with great devotion.

Contribution of Aśoka

Aśoka Maurya was a religious person and rendered valuable service in the form of working for the spread of Buddhism to different parts of India and abroad and resolving the conflicts arising among the Buddhist saṃghas regarding the proper interpretation of Buddha's teachings [1]. From the minor pillar edicts of Aśoka found at Sārnāth, Kauśāmbi, and Sāñcī, it can be known that since the time of the second council, the atmosphere in the Buddhist saṃgha was not peaceful. There would occur disturbances and conflicts among the different groups of Buddhists. To resolve the conflicts and put an end to such disturbances, King Aśoka took precautionary measures against the unsettled conditions in the Buddhist saṃgha [2]. He, moreover, convened the Third Buddhist Council with Moggaliputta Tissa as the President and under his patronage the text *Kathāvatthu* was composed. For preaching Buddhism, Aśoka after this council sent nine missionaries to nine different countries. In his rock edicts II and XIII, mention is made of the names of the countries where the missionaries were sent for the purpose of *Dharmavijaya* or spread of Buddhism [3]. Aśoka tried to popularize the teachings of Lord Buddha in respect of providing medical services to both men and lower animals. His edicts point out the close connection between the court of Aśoka and several religious institutions. His love for Buddhism was so great that he wanted to regain its past glory. It was because of his earnest zeal that Buddhism as a religion took its firm roots in different parts of India and spread to foreign countries [4].

Contribution of Other Kings

After the fall of the Maurya Empire, the northern, western, and central parts of India went under the rules of foreign powers. Among the foreign rulers mention should be made of the Greek king Menander (probably of the first century) who being a lover of Buddhism adopted Buddhism as his personal faith and became a devout follower. He rendered valuable services for popularizing Buddhism during his reign. Because of his important contribution to the Buddhist world and his pious activities, he was known as *Dharmarāja*. The royal consecration of Buddhism during the reign of this Indo-Greek ruler has been mentioned in several inscriptions which also refer to the donations received from them.

During the reign of the Kuṣāṇa emperors, especially of Kaniṣka (78–101 A.D.), Buddhism received much patronage from the royal emperors. One important contribution of Kaniṣka is that it was during his reign that the Buddhist monks and nuns established the images of the Buddha and Bodhisattva and worked for the advancement of the welfare of Buddhism. On the model of Aśoka, Kaniṣka arranged for the Fourth Buddhist Council with the aim to reconcile the opinions of the various sects of Buddhism and explain the Vinaya, the Sūtra, and the Abhidharma texts properly [5]. This Fourth Buddhist Council may be looked upon as one of the most important events in the history of Buddhism as in this council, Sanskrit was first used as a medium of expressing the Buddhist doctrines. This council was organized at Kashmir and for this purpose a monastery was erected there by Kaniṣka to accommodate all the monks coming to attend the council. To make Buddhism popular among ordinary people, several statues of Buddha, stūpas, and religious buildings were erected in different parts of his kingdom. From the monasteries and statues of this period, it is generally believed that the Sarvāstivāda sect of Buddhism attained prominence at the time of Kaniṣka.

During the rule of the Sātavāhana kings, Buddhism reached the zenith of its popularity. From several inscriptions it is known that the Sātavāhana kings established rock-cut *caityas*, *stūpas* and hall of reception for the Buddhists. They also donated villages, lands and money to the monks for the construction of new buildings or renovation of already existing ones. This is an instance of the royal patronage of these kings.

In the Gupta period traces of patronage to Buddhism by the kings can be found from epigraphical sources. From the records of Hiuen Tsang, it is known that kings like Chandragupta I, Samudragupta, and Skandagupta of the Gupta empire revered the three gems – the Buddha, the *dhamma*, and the *saṃgha*. During the times of

Chandragupta II and Samudragupta, Bodhgayā and Sāñcī became famous places of Buddhism. Samudragupta also built a monastery at Nālandā, the great center of Buddhist learning. From the seals discovered at the site of Nālandā, it is inferred that other rulers of the Gupta dynasty were patrons of Buddhism and closely related with the Buddhist Nālandā University which was then growing very fast [6]. In the Gupta age Buddhist literary work and art started developing. There was a trend for Buddhist logic and critical school of philosophy with Dignāga as the pioneer. During the fourth, fifth, and sixth century A.D., artists used to create beautiful images of Buddha and Bodhisattva. Such literary and artistic excellences clearly indicate that Buddhism received great patronage from the royal families, from the noble families, and also from the rich people. All of them contributed much for patronizing Buddhism and donate for that sake land, money, and other assistances according to their own ability.

Cross-References

▶ Ajātaśatru
▶ Aśoka
▶ Bimbisāra
▶ Bodhgayā
▶ Dharmavijaya
▶ Gandhara
▶ Greeks
▶ Kaniṣka
▶ Kingship
▶ Kumārajīva
▶ Monastery
▶ Nālandā
▶ Sanchi
▶ Sārnāth
▶ Stūpa
▶ Vaiśālī

References

1. Akira H (1998) A history of Indian Buddhism: from Śākyamuni to early Mahāyāna. Motilal Banarsidass Publishers, Delhi
2. Hazra KL (2007) Aśoka as depicted in his Edicts. Munshiram Manoharlal, Delhi
3. Barua BM (1968) Aśoka and his inscriptions. New Age Publishers, Calcutta
4. Chattopadhyay DP (1997) Tārānātha's history of Buddhism in India. Motilal Banarsidass Publishers, Delhi
5. Bapat PV (1971) 2500 years of Buddhism. Publications Division, Ministry of Information and Broadcasting, Government of India, New Delhi
6. Hazra KL (1984) Royal patronage of Buddhism in ancient India. D.K. Publications, Delhi

Royal Patronage

▶ Royal Consecration

Rummendei

▶ Lumbinī

Rummindei

▶ Lumbinī

Rupadihi visayehi suttu aggo ti saggo

▶ Heaven (Buddhism)

Ryūmō (Japanese)

▶ Nāgārjuna

S

Sabar

▶ Tolerance (Jainism)

Śabda

Madhumita Chattopadhyay
Department of Philosophy, Jadavpur University, Kolkata, West Bengal, India

Synonyms

Testimony or verbal cognition

Definition

A variety of cognition which arises from the utterance of words or linguistic signs.

Buddhists on Sabda

The Nyāya as well as the Mīmāṃsā systems of Indian thought made very detailed analysis of the notion of *śabda pramāṇa* or testimony as a means of valid cognition in order to provide rational arguments for justifying the authenticity of the Vedas. The Buddhists, on the other hand, in their insistence on admitting only two *pramāṇa*s found no need to accept *śabda* as an independent source of cognition, but reduced it to inference. *Śabda* or testimony has been defined by the Nyāya thinkers as the instruction (*upadeśaḥ*) of a reliable person. This testimony is admitted as different from sense perception since the object apprehended by it is beyond the reach of the senses nor can it be regarded as a case of inference, since it does not fulfill the three conditions required for a valid inference. But the cognition that is generated by testimony with regard to such supernatural objects as *svarga, agnihotra*, etc., is free from all sorts of doubt, and hence has to be admitted as valid. The Buddhists, however, do not accept this view regarding testimony. Their observation is that there is no real connection between a word and its object; that is, no word can give us any information regarding the reality of an object. The Buddhist logician Dharmakīrti in his text *Pramāṇavārttikam* holds that since words do not have any inseparable relation (*nāntarīyakatva*) with the objects, the words cannot establish the existence of the objects. They are only expressive of the intention of the speaker. At the basis of this observation lies the main thesis of Buddhist epistemology, namely, that one can prove the existence of an object on the basis of something else only if there exists an inseparable relation between the two. In the case of *āgama*, any inseparable relation between the word and the object cannot be found. If there were such a relation, the nature of the object could have been ascertained from the utterance of the word. But that is not the case.

K.T.S. Sarao, J.D. Long (eds.), *Buddhism and Jainism*, Encyclopedia of Indian Religions,
DOI 10.1007/978-94-024-0852-2

From the mere utterance of the word "fire" no one is able to get fire. Hence, the existence of the object cannot be proved from words. In other words, testimony is not a *pramāṇa* with regard to the actual real object. From this, however, it would be wrong to conclude that *śabda* or testimony does not have any worth. The worth of it lies in expressing the intention of the speaker. These words are produced on the basis of the intention (*vivakṣā*) of the speaker. Since there is a causal relation between the words and the intention of the speaker, a necessary relation (*nāntarīyakatābhāva*) between them has to be admitted. Thus being inseparably connected, words can make the intention of the speaker known. So words, even though they form an *āgama* fundamentally cannot provide one with any information regarding the reality of the object.

Dignāga, the master logician of the Buddhist school, has regarded the knowledge based on the words of a reliable person to be an inference on the ground that both inference and testimony are *avisaṁvādaka*, that is, do not disagree with reality. He includes it within inference. By regarding *ś abda* to be an inference the Buddhist logician wants to recognize the fact that human behaviors are often dependent on the guidance of such *ś abda*. From the *āgama* a person comes to know about the great blessings and the great misfortunes which result or do not result when one performs or does not perform some act. So when an act, positive or negative, has to be performed, the ordinary individual feels it better to act in the manner as prescribed by the *āgama*. Taking such practical considerations into account Dignāga regarded *āgama* to be a *pramāṇa* that is an inference.

According to the Buddhists, an *āgama* or a reliable statement is one (1) whose words are coherent, (2) for which there are means that are appropriate for attaining the desired end, and (3) which expresses what is useful to a human being. The trustworthiness of such *āgama* statements about perceptible and imperceptible entities can be determined through the two *pramāṇa*s recognized by the Buddhists, namely, perception and inference. The basis of such determination is that the information contained in such sentences is not contradicted by either perception or by inference. The statement of a trustworthy person (like Buddha and others) can easily be regarded as reliable with reference to objects which are directly verifiable. Even when the statement refers to an object which is not directly verifiable, it can be considered equally as reliable, so long as no contrary results are perceived. Since the knowledge generated by the statements of a trustworthy person reveals the object in an indirect manner, Dignāga considers such knowledge to be of inferential nature. Dharmakīrti offers two arguments to justify the view of Dignāga. The first justification for considering the *āgama* as a sort of inference centers round the character of non-disagreement with reality (*avisaṁvādaka*) which is shared in common by the *āgama* and inference as *pramāṇa*. The knowledge of inaccessible objects, though is produced by the words of a reliable person, does not only inform of the intention of the speaker but informs about the nature of reality also. The second justification that is offered by Dharmakīrti is that through his own power of perception and inference a person can apprehend the correctness of the truth concerning the objects to be abandoned (namely, suffering) and of the truth of the object to be attained (namely, the avoidance of suffering) as also of the causes for such suffering and absence of suffering. All of these have been taught by a reliable person, namely, Lord Buddha. These statements are true since they do not disagree with reality. So it can be concluded that the cognition originating from *āgama* with regard to things beyond the grasp of a human being is an inference. However, there is a word of caution. Since words do not have any inseparable connection with reality, in the context of *āgama* as inference the possibility of error cannot be eliminated. So any inference based on words cannot be authentic. The authenticity of the *āgama* variety of inference depends on the authenticity of the speaker.

The question that arises immediately is concerning an authentic speaker: Is there really such a speaker whose words can enable one to have valid knowledge about such inaccessible objects? The Buddhists do not accept the notion of an *āptapuruṣa* as admitted by the Naiyāyikas nor can they deny the existence of such a person.

So they try to prove their existence through an argument of the following form:

1. Ordinary human beings are possessed of virtues and faults which determine the rightness and wrongness of their behavior.
2. All things which are sometimes inferior and sometimes superior must have an opposite.
3. The faults have the quality of becoming inferior and superior.
4. Therefore, there is an increase and decrease of the faults by the influence from the opposite thing.
5. The faults are produced from ideas (*vikalpa*).
6. Therefore, even if a person has the material cause of all faults, these faults are decreased by means of the repeated practice of a certain virtue of the mind.
7. When this virtue attains a maximum, the faults are bound to be completely destroyed.
8. Therefore, it is quite possible that a person free from faults exists.

The question that arises immediately is, even though a person is free from faults at present, how can it be ascertained that he will remain so afterward also. The answer that the Buddhists offer is that the person who has once made himself free from faults cannot fall prey to faults later. Their argument is as follows: First he has given up all the faults, secondly he is free from the suffering which is connected with the actual occurrence of anger, etc., or with future existence, and thirdly he does not shrink from the taste of felicity in the perfect calmness. Moreover, all kinds of faults originate from the notions of "I," "mine," etc., (*satkāyadṛṣṭi*) which arise because of nescience. So long as such nescience exists in human beings there is attachment to the self which is the root cause of all hatred, anger, and other faults. Hence for the person who has set himself free from the nescience through the repeated practice of no-self, there is no possibility that these defects will arise once again in him.

Dignāga in the introductory verse of his *Pramāṇasamuccaya* has regarded Buddha as *pramāṇabhūta*, a pramāṇa on religious matters. It seems that Dignāga is using the word *pramāṇa* in two different senses, the first one in a purely epistemological sense, meaning the source of valid cognition, and the second sense has a more general connotation where authority means right measure. According to Dignāga, Lord Buddha is a means of valid cognition regarding religious authority through his perfection in cause and effect, in order to produce reverence. The cause here refers to the Buddha's striving for the welfare of the world and his being the teacher while effect refers to Buddha's being the well-gone and his being the savior. Buddha has perfected and saved himself, but he has also saved others by teaching them the road to ultimate salvation, a road which he himself has traversed. This constitutes, according to Dignāga, the condition for Buddha's being a *pramāṇa*. In the second chapter of the text *Pramāṇavārttika* Dharmakīrti also offers arguments to prove that the doctrines of Lord Buddha are *pramāṇa*. For Dharmakīrti *ś abda* or testimony refers to words used in a coherent meaningful sentence which teaches suitable means and expresses what is useful to man. Coherently formulated sentences which refer to practicable methods to gain something and which disclose a desirable human goal, can communicate knowledge of objects really helpful to the hearer, even though such sentences do not reveal particular objects themselves as direct perception does. The teachings of Lord Buddha constitute trustworthy knowledge and reveal to the hearers objects that were not known before. Buddha has pointed out to others the facts of the useful things that are to be realized and informed them of the truths which were so far unknown to them. Further Buddha does not deceive others with regard to the ultimate goals of human aspiration. Since his words are nondeceptive in character and provide new information, he can be considered as a source of valid cognition. The trustworthiness of Buddha is proved to the extent to which a person really acquires for himself the objects taught by him. With regard to objects which are accessible to perception and inference, the teachings of Buddha are found to be trustworthy when the hearer finds the objects producing desired results. On the other hand, with regard to objects which are imperceptible, the trustworthiness of his teachings is inferred from his trustworthiness regarding perceptible matters. Thus Dharmakīrti limits the scope of scripturally based inferences to cases where the objects are radically inaccessible and hence beyond the range of ordinary ratiocination. By such limitation he is able to preserve inferences to be objectively grounded and at the samc time show his difference from the Mīmāṁsā and Sāṁkhya schools that cite scriptural passages as a means of proof even in the context of ordinary properties like the impermanence of sound. Hence, according to the Buddhists, testimony or *śabda* can be considered as an inference when it is applied to radically inaccessible objects. It is a special indirect case of inference because of the fact that it turns on inductive generalization presupposing the correctness of direct perception or ordinary inferences. In a nutshell, the Buddhist's view is that there is no need to postulate *śabda* as a separate means of knowledge; it is to be considered as a special variety of inference.

Cross-References

- ▶ Dharmakīrti (c. A.D. 600–660)
- ▶ Dignāga
- ▶ Knowledge (Buddhism)
- ▶ Logic (Buddhism)
- ▶ Mantra
- ▶ Omniscience
- ▶ Philosophy (Buddhism)

References

1. Chattopadhyay M (2007) Walking along the paths of Buddhist epistemology. D.K. Printworld, New Delhi
2. Dharmakīrti (1989) The Pramāṇavārttika of Acārya Dharmakīrti with the commentaries Svopajñavṛtti of the author and Pramāṇavārttikavṛtti of Manorathanandin, ed. Pandeya RC. Motilal Banarsidass, Delhi
3. Van Bijlert, Vittorio A (1989) Epistemology and spiritual authority: the development of epistemology and logic in the old Nyāya and the Buddhist school of epistemology with an annotated translation of Dharmakīrti's Pramāṇavārttika-II(Pramāṇasiddhi), vv 1–7, WSTB 20. Arbeitskreis fur Tibetische und Buddhistische Studien, Vienna
4. Yaita H (1987) Dharmakirti on the authority of Buddhist scriptures (Agama): an annotated translation of the *Pramāṇavārttikasvavṛtti*, adv 213–217. J Nanto Soc Buddh Stud 58:1–57
5. Yaita H (1988) Dharmakīrti on the person free from faults: an annotated translation of the *Pramāṇavārttikasvavṛtti*, adv 218–223. Nanto Bukkyo Kenkyukai II:433–445
6. Hayes RP (1988) Dinnaga on the Interpretation of Signs, Studies of classical India 8, Dordrecht: Kluwer Academic Press
7. Kajiyama Y (1966) An introduction to Buddhist Philosophy, Memoirs of the Faculty of Letters, Kyoto University, Kyoto
8. Hattori M (1968) Dinnaga on Perception, being the Pratyaksa paricchedah of Dinnaga's Pramanasamuccaya from the Sanskrit Fragnents and the Tibetan versions, Cambridge: Hervard University Press

Sacred Biography (Buddhism)

▶ Hagiography (Buddhism)

Saddharmapuṇḍrīka Sūtra

Mangala Ramchandra Chinchore
Department of Philosophy, Centre for Studies in Classical Indian Buddhist Philosophy and Culture, University of Pune, Pune, Maharashtra, India

Synonyms

The Lotus *Sūtra*

Definition

Mahāyāna-Buddhist text, one of the *Vaipulya-sūtras*, sacred *Nava-dharmas* (nine-texts) of the Nepālese Buddhism

Lotus of the Right Mode to Live Life

It is a *Mahāyāna*-Buddhist text [1] originated in India, having popularity and high respect all over the world among the practitioners of Buddhism, especially followers of Tendai sect in China and Nirchiren sect in Japan. It is translated into European languages like French, German, English, and is also available in Tibetan translated form by Surendrabodhi as well as Chinese along with six commentaries. It is one among the sacred *Navadharmas* (nine-texts) of the Nepalese Buddhism venerated with devotion and known as a part of the *Vaipulya-sūtras*. It consists of 27 chapters (*Parivratas*).

It is a mixed form of writing - combination of verse and prose. The First part is prose and it is then followed by verses. Verses present summary of the proceeding portion in details. "Lotus" is a symbol of purity and perfection, because it originates in mud but not defiled by mud, just like the Buddha, who was born as a human being in this world but he was above the worldly affairs. "Lotus" seeds/fruits are ripped is indicated when it is blossomed, same is the case with the Buddha, when he had realization of the *Bodhi* (ultimate truth/enlightenment), then only he started preaching the truth on request of the interested ones. It is "*Puṇḍarīka* (white-lotus)" clean and simple truth, taught by the Buddha having various petals of (chapters) of the doctrines exposing its natural beauty and glory. It is "lotus" of moral hues and colors attracting those bees to suck the honey readily available, like the Buddha's thoughts distributing sweet honey to all kinds of devotees without any discrimination.

Historically it is an important text [2] where paradigm shift from *Hīnayāna* to *Mahāyāna* is noticeable, or a mode of synthesizing the three *Yānas* into one, viz., *Śrāvaka-yāna*, *Pratyeka-buddha-yāna*, and *Bodhisattva-yāna* into *Buddha-yāna*. It is seen that there was a need to synchronize and systematize the differences of opinion and respectively various strands taken by the exponents of them from early Buddhist tradition, and by transcending the limitations or by bracketing the internal contradictions, an inclusive model of understanding teaching of the Buddha is insightfully articulated and put forth by the *Mahāyāna*. In such a context, perhaps, it was important to confront the problems originated that are faced by the then followers of Buddhism. Buddhism is not only meant for intellectuals, nor for strict practitioners, but it is a means to attain *Nirvāṇa* to all, without any kind of discrimination – rich and poor, men and women, children and age-old, belonging to any religion and region, etc. Naturally very few *Bhikkhus*, who were following *Vinaya* with extreme austerities alone are entitled to attain *Nirvāṇa*, a belief predominant among the followers of early Buddhism, was required to be altered by new version that all can attain *Nirvāṇa*, and to give hope and popularize the thoughts of the Buddha. Expansion cannot be made unless inclusive and accommodative framework is adopted, and that task was undertaken by some such works in the initial stages of *Mahāyāna* Buddhism and *Saddharma-puṇḍarīka-sūtra* was one among them.

A lay-person is not able to understand and digest highly philosophical thoughts; rather, she/he is most of the time governed by emotions, instincts, and passions. But if she/he is convinced by telling the stories and dialogues, by giving beautiful similes and parables, she/he can understand doctrines of Buddhism [3]. And, exactly this new mode of presentation is adopted by the *Saddharma-puṇḍarīka-sūtra*. At that time, people were interested in attaining the highest enlightenment by faith and trying to seek compassion (*Karuṇā*) of the Buddha and *Bodhisattvas*; hence, emphasis is on devotion to the Buddha. They were worshiping, by using whatever was available with them – externally or potentially – the relics, erecting *Stūpas*, scribbling pictures, constructing images and idols of the Buddha. By using devotion as a means one can attain the Buddha-hood: This was their belief. In this context, especially *Upāsakas*, *Upāsikas* and *Śrāvakas* believed in the compassion of the Buddha, that he is the only survivor and final solace to all kinds of problems they are facing and hence surrender to him unconditionally. Faith and reason can go together which is the backbone of *Mahāyāna* Buddhism: This is elaborated in this work. Even though one is living in a house, which is set on fire of craving and ignorance, one can survive and successfully lead a life, provided Buddha pours his grace. Thus, he is physician and protector, to provide medicine to our spiritual illness. So by using whatever is good, it is essential to obtain his grace [4].

Although one (any human being) is born as human a being and is distinctively different, if one uses the present life as a chance, one can morally and spiritually progress. All human beings have at least two assets and they are endowed with certain capacities as skillful means to develop – *Prajñā* (wisdom) and *Karuṇā* (compassion). If everybody uses these two assets skillfully, each one can become perfect and attain the *Nirvāṇa* (emancipation). It is this thought that is used and expanded in this book. That is why through this book, it is learnt that Buddhist arts and crafts were used as a means to attain perfection and tranquility. There is a glorification of the Buddha and his preachers in the form of *Bodhisattvas*, which appear to be endowed with strange and mystical powers. It also speaks of *Dhārinīs* (mystical-spells) to overcome difficulties faced, and when one is surrounded by annoying states of affairs. Some scholars [5] have attempted to find out similarities of the present text with Brahmanical texts like *Brāhmaṇa-granthas*, *Atharvaveda*, etc. on the one hand and Christian legends on the other.

When this work originated, perhaps, due to the passage of time, people were finding it difficult to correlate themselves with the Buddha. In order to establish the proximity and make Buddha's thoughts relevant even in changing circumstances and situations, it was, perhaps, felt essential to find out new ways and means. *Mahāyāna* Buddhism provides that skillful-bridge by creating a new idea of *Saṁbhoga-kāya* (emergence of the Buddha from time-to-time). In the early Buddhist texts, one never comes across the idea of *Tri-kāya*. However, in the *Saddharma-Puṇḍarīka-Sūtra*, for the first time, perhaps, it is articulated and expounded. The Buddha or reality is manifested in three different ways (*Kāyas* – bodies/forms/modes of existence): (I) *Nirmāṇa-kāya* (human form of embodiment) The Buddha actually lived as a human being in this world – i.e., his spatiotemporal emergence in this world, (II) *Dharma-kāya* (thoughts/doctrines as an embodiment of truth) – Thoughts of the Buddha emerged through his enlightenment and realization of truth and he taught it to others, and further it is preserved by his followers; and (III) *Saṁbhoga-kāya* (enjoyment through creative embodiment) – The images one imagines and creates through the inborn potentialities and gets manifested in archetype-forms are embodiments for joy and happiness for years together for all. In the early Buddhist literature, one can at the most trace the former two but the last one is a unique contribution of this text.

It is believed by the followers that even by reading or worshiping this text, one can get enlightenment (*Bodhi*) and attain *Nirvāṇa* (emancipation).

Cross-References

- *Bhikkhunī*
- *Bodhi*
- *Bodhisattva*
- *Dhāraṇī*
- *Dharma*
- *Hīnayāna*
- *Karuṇā*
- *Mahāyāna*
- *Mahāyāna Laṅkāvatāra Sūtra*
- *Nirvāṇa*
- *Prajñā*
- *Pratyeka-Buddha*
- *Śrāvaka*
- Stūpa
- *Tri-kāya*
- *Upāsaka*
- *Vinaya*

References

1. Vaidya PL (ed) (1960) Saddharma-Puṇḍarika-Sūtra. Mithila Institute, Darbhanga
2. Obermiller E (1999) Bu-Ston: the history of Buddhism in India and Tibet. Sri Sadguru Publications, Delhi
3. Warder AK (2000) Indian Buddhism, 3rd edn. Motilal Banarsidass, Delhi
4. Sangharakshita (1987) A survey of Buddhism: its doctrines and methods through ages. Tharpa Publications, London
5. Winternitz M (1993) History of Indian literature, vol II. Motilal Banarsidass, Delhi, pp 290–297, 367, 397

Sadharana

▶ Nigoda

Sadharmachakra Prāvartana Mahāvihāra

▶ Sārnāth

Sadhu

▶ Śramaṇa

Sagga

▶ Heaven (Buddhism)

Sahishnutaa

▶ Tolerance (Jainism)

Sakadāgāmin

Bhikkhu Anālayo
Center for Buddhist Studies, University of Hamburg, Balve, Germany

Synonyms

Once-returner; *Sakṛdāgāmin* (Sanskrit)

Definition

The *sakadāgāmin* is one who has reached the second of the four levels of awakening recognized in early Buddhism. A *sakadāgāmin* has thereby become a "once-returner," in the sense of being one who "returns," *āgāmin*, only "once," *sakid*, more to be reborn in the sensual world before reaching final liberation and thereby freedom from any rebirth.

The Once-returner

In early Buddhist thought, the scheme of the four levels of awakening reflects the gradual eradication of the fetters, *saṃyojana*, that are considered to be what binds an unawakened worldling to continued existence in the cycle of *saṃsāra*. A stream-enterer, who has gained the first level of awakening, has eradicated three of these fetters. These three are the fetter of personality view, *sakkāyadiṭṭhi*, in the sense of the notion of a permanent self, the fetter of doubt, *vicikicchā*, in particular doubt regarding the nature of what is wholesome and what is unwholesome, and the fetter of dogmatic clinging to rules and vows, *sīlabbataparāmāsa*, as in themselves sufficient for reaching liberation.

The next two fetters to be overcome are sensual lust, *kāmarāga*, and ill will, *vyāpāda*. In regard to their overcoming, a once-returner has already made substantial progress, since he or she has considerably weakened both. Their complete eradication, however, is only accomplished with the next and third level of awakening, the attainment of non-return, *anāgāmin*, whereby one will no longer return to be born in the sensual world.

The realization of once-return requires the development of insight, *vipassanā*, and tranquility, *samatha*, a meditative development of the mind that needs to be based on a firm foundation in moral conduct. To proceed from stream-entry to once-return and from there to the higher stages of awakening calls for contemplating the five aggregates affected by clinging as impermanent, unsatisfactory, and devoid of a self ([2], Vol. III, p. 168). These five aggregates are according to early Buddhism the chief constituents of an individual, comprising the aggregates of bodily form, feeling, perception, volitions, and consciousness. The above contemplation therefore implies that all aspects of subjective experience should be seen as constantly changing, as therefore unable to provide lasting satisfaction, and as therewith not fit to be considered as a permanent self. Indeed, if one takes anything to be permanent or satisfactory or a self, or else if one does not regard Nirvāṇa as happiness, then one is incapable of gaining once-return or any of the other levels of awakening ([3], Vol. III, p. 442).

The development of insight for the attainment of once-return comes into being through having had association with superior persons, having heard the Dharma, having attended wisely, and having practiced in accordance with the Dharma ([2], Vol. V, p. 410). The most basic requirement for the gaining of once-return, however, is the existence of a Buddha, since due to his teaching the path to once-return and to the other stages of awakening is revealed to humanity ([3], Vol. I, p. 23).

Although a once-returner has made substantial progress when compared to a stream-enterer or even an unawakened worldling, he or she has not yet fully realized the Buddha's teaching ([1], Vol. II, p. 252). This is only accomplished by those who have gained the highest level of awakening: the arahants. An arahant has also fully developed five mental faculties, *indriya*, that are of central importance for progress along the early Buddhist path to deliverance. These are confidence or faith, energy, mindfulness, concentration, and wisdom. A once-returner has developed these five mental faculties only to some degree ([2], Vol. V, p. 202).

Some discourses indicate that, unlike a non-returner, a once-returner has only completed the training in morality, but not necessarily in concentration ([3], Vol. I, p. 232 and [3], Vol. IV, p. 380). This suggests that, in order to become a once-returner, concentration does not need to be developed up to the level of absorption, *jhāna*. This much can also be deduced from a once-returner's level of rebirth. A once-returner is so called because he or she will be reborn once again in "this world," the *kāmaloka*, which according to early Buddhist cosmology comprises the human world and the lower celestial spheres. Someone who has developed concentration up to the ability to attain absorption, *jhāna*, however, is not going to return to "this world" in the next life ([3], Vol. II, p. 126). Such a one will be reborn in a higher heavenly sphere beyond the sensuous field, namely, in the fine-material or immaterial heavenly worlds, the *rūpaloka* and *arūpaloka*.

This certainly does not mean that all once-returners are bereft of deeper levels of concentration. But if all once-returners were at the same time also able to attain absorption, the concept of a "once-returner" would be superfluous, since not a single once-returner would ever return "to this world." Hence, the very expression "once-return" shows that the development of concentration up to the level of absorption attainment cannot be a requirement for gaining this level of awakening.

Some once-returners may, however, develop deep levels of concentration and even gain the immaterial attainments, *arūpa samāpatti*, where according to early Buddhist meditation theory the deeply concentrated mind perceives merely boundless space, or boundless consciousness, or nothingness, or else reaches such depth of concentration that perception as such appears almost absent. Such a once-returner could then be reckoned a "body witness," *kāyasakkhin*, in the sense of having directly witnessed these profound experiences ([3], Vol. I, p. 120). If, however, the faculty of confidence or faith should have been predominant during progress along the path, then the resulting once-returner is "freed by confidence" or "freed by faith," *saddhāvimutta*. In case wisdom was foremost, then such a type of once-returner belongs to those who have "attained to view," *diṭṭhipatta*.

A discourse reports how differences between once-returners, who emphasized different qualities during their progress on the path, caused some confusion in the mind of a lay disciple. The father of this lay disciple had lived a celibate life, while the uncle had not done so, yet the Buddha declared both to have passed away as once-returners ([3], Vol. III, p. 347). According to the explanation given in this discourse, both had been able to gain the same level of awakening because the uncle's stronger wisdom had compensated for his comparatively less developed moral conduct.

This passage also shows that the gain of once-return is not the sole domain of monastics. In fact, other discourses report that many lay followers had reached this level of awakening ([1], Vol. II, p. 93 and [1], Vol. II, p. 218). Gender also has no say in these matters, since women are most certainly capable of gaining once-return, just as they are able to attain any of the other stages of awakening ([3], Vol. IV, p. 276). A discourse records that even some women from the harem of a king had been able to become once-returners ([4], p. 79).

The gaining of once-return is reckoned in early Buddhism as one of the supreme fruits of living the celibate life ([2], Vol. V, p. 26). In fact, it is for the sake of this and the other stages of awakening that such a life should be lived under the Buddha ([1], Vol. I, p. 156). A monk who gains once-return will be able to reach the other shore just like a young ox will be able to cross the Ganges ([5], Vol. I, p. 226). Among unawakened mankind, whose predicament is comparable to being immersed in water, the once-returner is one who emerges from the water and is in the process of crossing over ([3], Vol. IV, p. 12).

Cross-References

▶ Anāgāmin
▶ Arahant
▶ Insight
▶ Liberation (Buddhism)
▶ Sotāpanna

References

1. Carpenter JE, Rhys Davids TW (eds) (1890–1911) The Dīgha Nikāya, 3 vols. Pali Text Society, London
2. Feer L (ed) (1888–1898) The Saṃyutta Nikāya, 5 vols. Pali Text Society, Oxford
3. Morris R, Hardy E (eds) (1885–1900) The Aṅguttara Nikāya, 5 vols. Pali Text Society, London
4. Steinthal P (ed) (1885) The Udāna. Pali Text Society, London
5. Trenckner V, Chalmers R (eds) (1888–1896) The Majjhima Nikāya, 3 vols. Pali Text Society, London

Sāketa

▶ Ayodhyā (Buddhism)

Sakṛdāgāmin

▶ *Sakadāgāmin*

Śāliputra

▶ Sāriputta

Sallekhanā (Jainism)

Whitny M. Braun
Center for Jain Studies, Claremont Lincoln University, Claremont, CA, USA

Synonyms

Anasana; *Samadhi-marana*; *Santhara*

Definition

The centuries-old ritual of fasting combined with meditation unique to Jain *dharma* in which the adherent gradually and systematically reduces their food consumption until death.

Introduction

Sallekhana is considered by Jains, both *Swetambara* and *Digambara*, to be the ideal method of meeting death [1]. In Jain *dharma*, Sallekhana embraces death voluntarily and is the ultimate act of *ahimsa* or nonviolence, which prevents the practitioner from accruing *karma* [2]. The origin and precise definition of the word

Sallekhana are unclear, but the most commonly accepted definition is "properly thinning out the passions of the body" [3, 4].

The Rationale of Sallekhana

The concept of *ahimsa* is at the core of the Jain faith. Each Jain throughout their life should ideally avoid thoughts that give rise to passions or violence. The existential goal is to avoid the accumulation of *karma* by practicing *ahimsa* throughout one's life. *Karma* prevents the soul or *jiva* from separating from the physical form and achieving ultimate liberation or *moksa* which is understood as the permanent release from the cycle of birth and death [2]. Accumulated *karma* will also influence the physical form and circumstances in which the soul may manifest in the next life [5]. Thus, when a Jain reaches the end of their life, they can opt to take the vow of *Sallekhana* and in doing so endeavor toward either achieving liberation or improving the physical form their *jiva* will next inhabit. A Jain can do this by striving to practice the ultimate form of *aparigraha* or nonpossession by (a) giving up all of their worldly possessions, including possession of their own body, and (b) gradually reducing their consumption of other *jivas* in the form of food and drink [5]. Ultimately, *Sallekhana* brings about the end of life through the rejection of life-sustaining elements such as food and water.

The Ritual

The decision to take the vow of Sallekhana is open to both lay Jains and ascetics who foresee that the end of their life is very near due to either old age, senility, mental illness, terminal illness, severe famine, attack from an enemy or a wild animal, or in some cases loss of chastity [6–8]. Any Jain who is faced with any of the aforementioned conditions can approach their *guru* or spiritual mentor and express their wish to take the vow of *Sallekhana*. They do so by saying the words:

> Please instruct me sir. I have come forward to seek. . .*Sallekhana*, (the vow of) which will remain in force as long as I live. I am free of all doubts and anxieties in this matter. I renounce, from now until the moment of my last breath, food and drink of all kinds. [3]

Assuming that permission is granted, the person either decides independently or consults with their physician as to the approximate amount of time he or she has left to live and then develops a program of fasting prescribing the gradual decrease in the amount of food and drink they consume to coincide with the level of rigor that has taken in their vow of *Sallekhana* [9].

According to Jain teaching, a member of the laity who accepts this vow should give up all personal relationships, friendships, and possessions as well as both physical and emotional attachments of any form to this life [10]. They forgive relatives, companions, friends, enemies, and servants or acquaintances and should ask for the pardon of all the sins and suffering he or she committed or caused in his or her lifetime. They then discuss honestly with their *guru* all the sins, including sinful acts that they asked others to commit, as well as the acts of sins they encouraged others around them to commit. During the period of this vow, the adherent should eliminate from their mind all the grief, fear, regret, affection, hatred, prejudice, and other passions to the fullest extent [11].

The vow can be taken in three different forms representing three different levels of rigor.

1. The longest vow of Sallekhana is 12 years in duration.
2. The medium vow is 1 year in duration.
3. The short vow is anything up to 6 months in duration [7].

The process of Sallekhana is meant to be a gradual one. Initially, the adherent should gradually reduce food consumption until they only survive on liquids and then downgrade slowly from drinking only milk to drinking only juice and finally water. Ultimately, they will give up water as well and experience a complete and total fast. During this process, the adherent should also give up all the passions they once had as they are considered mental weaknesses, and they should become engrossed in their meditation without paying attention to their physical body. There are five transgressions the adherent is advised to avoid, which are:

1. Wishing to postpone death
2. Wishing death would come sooner
3. Fearing death
4. Thinking of friends and relatives at the time of death
5. Hoping for some sort of reward after death [3, 7]

It is recommended that a person who has taken the vow of *Sallekhana* select a place to sit for the fast where legal authorities do not object to such a vow. Ideally, it should be a place where other people do not visit and are unlikely to interfere with the process. Traditionally, a person taking Sallekhana should find a quiet place in the forest, preferably under a tree, and then focus on nothing and nothingness and allow themselves to be overtaken by the natural forces around them, their body reclaimed, and their soul released for either reincarnation or released into the cosmos if it has attained liberation or *moksa* [12]. The translations of the original texts say that in order for *Sallekhana* to commence properly, the person must sit in silent meditation and bear all discomfort [12]. It says that if insects and vermin bite him, he must not defend himself or rub the wound because that would interfere with natural process [3].

Sallekhana in India Today

In India today, *Sallekhana* most commonly takes place in an *ashram* or holy place, however, because it is sanctioned as a religious death, and it is technically acceptable to perform *Sallekhana* in the home, in a monastery, or in the wilderness. In most current cases, the process of *Sallekhana* is a more public event than described in the *sutras*, with Jains from around the country traveling to pay their respects to the adherent. However, since 2006, the High Court of Rajasthan in Jaipur has been deliberating over a public interest litigation filed by human rights activists seeking to have *Sallekhana* classified as "suicide" and thus illegal under the Indian constitution. Further, the legal argument against Sallekhana posits that because women are statistically more likely to engage in the practice, it is inherently misogynistic and akin to the Hindu ritual of widow self-immolation known as *Sati* which has been illegal in India since 1829 [9], though there is no evidence in classical Jain teaching to suggest the presence of misogyny or gender bias.

Debate over the legality of Sallekhana stems from the argument over whether or not the ritual, which is in essence voluntary death, is by definition suicide. Jain teaching argues that Sallekhana is not suicide as suicide implies an act of instant violence directed toward oneself due to grief, depression, emotional imbalance, or perhaps the expectation of fame. However, Sallekhana is seen as the ultimate act of nonviolence because it is not instigated by any of the aforementioned motives nor does it result in the destruction of *jivas* [13].

According to the *sadhus* and *sadhvis*, who are male and female mendicants, as well as Jain scholars, *Sallekhana* is a pleasant death freely chosen by the adherent. The practitioner leaves the world without a care or concern, and a great euphoria is experienced followed by a peaceful death. Many eyewitness accounts tell of the *Sallekhana* adherent laughing and smiling during the final stages of their death. Opponents of Sallekhana counter that this perceived euphoria is simply a physiological response to the body being deprived of nutrition [9].

Directives Against Sallekhana

While *Sallekhana* is encouraged in Jain teaching and is put forth as the most noble method of reaching the end of one's life, there are clear and definite directives against the adoption of this vow.

If one is a productive member of society or a *sadhu* or *sadhvi* who is still fully capable of studying the Jain scriptures, then *Sallekhana* is not permitted [14]. A classic example of this is the story of the great Jain *sadhu* and scholar Acharya Samantabhadra. He suffered from a chronic and incurable disease which some say was leprosy. He wished to take the vow of *Sallekhana* due to the impossibility of living a life in accordance with the religious restrictions placed on a *sadhu*. He approached his guru for permission. His guru told him that because he was of such great intelligence and capable of significant scholarship, he must live on and contribute to Jain literature and deal with whatever hardships might confront him. Permission to die was denied, and Acharya Samantabhadra wrote several works before he ultimately died as a result of *Sallekhana* years later. Today, he is regarded as one of the greatest minds in the history of Jain philosophy [3, 15].

Alternatives to Sallekhana

For Jains who fear that they may die an accidental death or possibly pass away in their sleep before ever being able to take the vow of *Sallekhana*, there is a prayer ritual known as *Pratikramana*. This prayer ritual allows for the practitioner of the faith to express remorse for the acts of *himsa* committed while they were awake and the acts of *himsa* they may commit in their sleep. The evening ritual, known specifically as *Devasi Pratikramana*, may be performed before bedtime and ostensibly serves to allow the person to express their desire to strive toward *ahimsa*, divine consciousness, and liberation [3].

Demographics

Sallekhana has rarely been documented outside of India. However, an increasing number of aging members of Jain Diaspora communities are seeking to practice the ritual in their adopted homelands [9]. There have been documented cases in the United States [16]. However, accurate records are not publicly kept in India or within the Diaspora communities because of fear of possible legal interference [9].

Cross-References

▶ Ahiṃsā (Jainism)
▶ Dharma (Jainism)
▶ Karma (Jainism)

References

1. Jain J (1999) Religion and culture of the Jains, 4th edn. Bharatiya Jnanpith Publishing, Delhi
2. Glasenapp H (1991) Doctrine of Karman in Jain philosophy. P. V. Research Institute, Varanasi
3. Jaini P (1979) The Jaina path of purification. Motilal Banarsidass, Delhi
4. Varni J (1999) Saman suttam. Bhagwan Mahavir Memorial Samiti, New Delhi
5. Babb L (1994) The great choice: worldly values in a Jain ritual culture. Hist Relig 34:23
6. Sogani K (2005) Jainism: ethico-special perspective. Jaina Vidya Samsthana Publishing, Rajasthan
7. Tukol T (1976) Sallekhana is not suicide. Lalbhai Dalpatbhai Institute, Ahmedabad
8. Vallely A (2002) Guardians of the transcendent: an ethnography of a Jain ascetic community. University of Toronto Press, Toronto
9. Braun W (2008) Sallekhana: the ethicality and legality of religious suicide by starvation in the Jain religious community. Int J Med Law 27(4):913–924
10. Laidlaw J (1995) Riches and renunciation: religion, economy and society among the Jains. Clarendon, Oxford
11. Laidlaw J (2005) A life worth leaving: fasting to death as telos of a Jain religious life. Econ Soc 34:178–200
12. Choudhury P (1956) Jainism in Bihar. Indu Roy Choudhury, Patna
13. Chapple C (2002) Jainism and ecology: nonviolence in the web of life. Harvard University Press for the Center for the Study of World Religions, Cambridge, MA
14. Jain C (2004) Selections from the Jaina Law. Jaina Vidya Samsthana, Rajasthan
15. Roy A (1984) A history of the Jainas. Gitanjali Publishing House, New Delhi
16. Davis D (1990) Old and thin. Second Opin 15:6

Samadhi-Marana

▶ *Sallekhanā* (Jainism)

Samantabhadra

Ram Kumar Rana
Department of Buddhist Studies, Faculty of Arts, University of Delhi, Delhi, India

Synonyms

Fugen (Japanese); Kuntu Zangpo (Tibetan); Pu Xian and Bian ji (Chinese); Viśvabhadra

Definition

Samantabhadra, the patron of the *Lotus Sūtra*, is a celestial Bodhisattva of Eastern region in Mahāyāna Buddhism associated with Buddhist practices and meditation.

Preliminary

The word *Samanta* signifies Universally Extending or General whereas *Bhadra* means Great Virtue or Sage [5]. Samantabhadra, therefore means Universal Virtue or Universal Worthy, which is derived from these words. Samantabhadra also represents the principle of universal love or compassion. He is also known as the Bodhisattva of Great Activity. Samantabhadra is a Bodhisattva in Mahāyāna Buddhism associated with Buddhist practice and meditation. He is the patron of the *Lotus Sūtra* and, according to the *Avataṃsaka Sūtra*, made the ten great vows which are the basis of a Bodhisattva. In China, Samantabhadra is known as *Pu Xian* (Universal Worthy) and *Bian ji* (Universal Fortune), and is also associated with fundamental principle (Ch. *Li*), whereas the Bodhisattva Mañjuśri is associated with wisdom (Ch. *Zhi*) [5].

Samantabhadra in the *Avataṃsaka Sūtra*: One of the primary scriptural sources for Samantabhadra is the *Avataṃsaka Sūtra*, venerated as one of the most important scriptures of Mahāyāna Buddhism in China, where he is the principal Bodhisattva. In the *Avataṃsaka Sūtra*, "the Buddhas of ten directions describe the Bodhisattva Samantabhadra as present in all lands, sitting on a Jeweled Lotus Throne, beheld by all. He manifests all psychic powers, and is able to enter infinite meditations. The Samantabhadra always fill the universe, With various bodies flowing everywhere, With concentration, psychic power, skill and strength, In a universal voice teaching extensively without hindrance" [7].

Based on the above, Samantabhadra is not an ordinary Bodhisattva, but a being of cosmic proportions and implications. He symbolizes the practices and merits of all Bodhisattvas which must be fulfilled in order to attain Buddhahood. His vows and practices exemplify the ideal course of conduct for the Buddhists. This course of conduct is exemplified by the pilgrimage of youth Sudhana in the final chapters of *Avataṃsaka Sūtra* (*Bhadracarīpraṇidhāna*) [6]. The result is the knowledge of, and the merging into, the universe of identity and interdependence, which is the experience of the perfectly enlightened Buddhas. One must, in a sense, become Samantabhadra in order to truly take up the Bodhisattva way.

The *Gaṇḍavyūha Sūtra* prescribes the extensive worship and makes offerings to the innumerable Buddha's of the ten directions whom the devotees visualize face to face through the power of Samantabhadra's vows, with deep faith and understanding. Among all, the offerings of the Dharma are paramount, which include the offering of following all the Buddha's instructions, of benefiting all sentient beings, of embracing and sustaining all sentient beings, of taking upon oneself the sufferings of others, of vigorously fostering the root of merit, of swerving not from the Bodhisattva's duty, and of never departing from the thought of Enlightenment [1]. There upon, the Bodhisattva resolves: "I will never abandon, but continue to practice, this vast, great and supreme offering without cessation in bodily, vocal, and mental deeds without wariness" [1].

In the *Avataṃsaka Sūtra*, the Buddha states that Samantabhadra made ten great vows in his path to attain Buddhahood [6]:

1. To pay homage to all Buddhas
2. To praise all the Buddhas
3. To make abundant offerings (i.e., give generously)
4. To repent misdeeds and evil *Karmas*
5. To rejoice in others' merits and virtues
6. To request the Buddhas to continue teaching
7. To request the Buddhas to remain in the world
8. To follow the teachings of the Buddhas at all times
9. To accommodate and benefit all living beings
10. To transfer all merits and virtues to benefit all beings

The ten vows constitute the most important practices extolled in the popular *Mahāyāna Sūtras* and have become a common practice in East Asian Buddhism, particularly the tenth vow, with many Buddhists traditionally dedicating their merit and good works to all beings during Buddhist liturgies.

The Samantabhadra Bodhisattva Dhyāna Sūtra: The Samantabhadra Bodhisattva *Dhyāna Sūtra* introduces the true nature of Samantabhadra as boundless in the size of his body, boundless in the sound of his voice, and boundless in the form of his image. Desiring to come to this world, he makes use of his free transcendental powers and shrinks his stature to the small size (of a human being). Because the people in Jambudvipa have the three heavy hindrances, by his wisdom power he appears transformed as mounted on a white elephant [2].

A kind of visualization of Samantabhadra and countless Buddhas is also described in this *Sūtra* which prescribes practitioners to focus their minds uninterruptedly on the Great vehicle for a day or three times for 7 days. Then they will be able to visualize Samantabhadra taking time according to the magnitude of the impediment of their Karmic burdens ranging from 7 days, one birth, two births, to the three births [2]. The practitioner has to begin with a resolve to see Samantabhadra on the basis of his previous blessings than he should pray Samantabhadra to reveal himself. Having done this, the followers should pay homage to the Buddhas in all directions and the law of repentance which includes the purification of six sense organs. When the purity of his repentance is achieved, the Samantabhadra will appear before him and accompany him all the time, even in his dream continuously preaching in the Law [2].

The Samantabhadra, abiding before him, will also teach and explain to him all *karmas* and environments of his former lives, and will cause him to confess all the sins he committed in the course of his innumerable past lives. This would lead him to the contemplation of the revelation of the Buddha to the men. Then by the power of this contemplation and by the adornment of the preaching of the Samantabhadra, the follower will obtain the purity of the six organs, he will feel the joy of body and mind, and freedom from evil thoughts. Consequently, he will devote himself all the more to this Law. Such six laws are the aspiration to Buddhahood and are the ones that beget the Bodhisattvas before the Buddhas, if they confess their previous sins and repent six organs sincerely. The devotees are exhorted to observe the law of meditating on the Samantabhadra, and discriminate and explain it widely to all the gods and men of the universe. So that after the extinction of the Buddha, all his disciples obediently follow the Buddha's words and practice repentance; in such case all these practitioners are doing the work of Samantabhadra and those who practice in this manner see neither evil aspects nor the retribution of evil *karmas*. Having received the sixfold laws, next he must zealously practice the unhindered brahma-conduct; raise the mind of universally saving all living beings [2].

This *Sūtra* also illustrates that "The Samantabhadra was born in the eastern Pure Wonder Land" [2]. He is usually depicted on a six-tusked, seven-legged magical snowy white elephant holding a wish-fulfilling gem and a book of the Dharma (*Lotus Sūtra*). Here, the elephant symbolizes practice and awareness, while the six tusks represent overcoming attachment to the six senses. They also represent the Six Perfections in which the Bodhisattva pursues his spiritual cultivation to attain enlightenment also to save other sentient beings.

The Lotus Sūtra: Samantabhadra also plays an important role in the *Lotus Sūtra*, another important *Sūtra* in Mahāyāna Buddhism, in which his role as the Dharma Protector and Propagator of the *Lotus Sūtra* are discussed [7]. In this *Sūtra*, the chapter on Samantabhadra opens with arrival of Samantabhadra along with equally endowed countless Bodhisattvas, and other beings from the eastern direction arrive dramatically on the Vulture peak to pay homage to the Śākyamuni Buddha and to listen to the preaching of the *Lotus Sūtra* and accept it [8].

In the presence of the Buddha, Samantabhadra makes a vow to protect and guard all those who accept and uphold this *sūtra*. Not only this, he assured for them freedom from decline and any harm from all sorts of evil beings. Samantabhadra also promises to help the person(s) who accepts, upholds, reads, and recites the *Lotus Sūtra* properly so that they can gain insight and acquire *Samādhis* and *Dharanis* of repetition and the Dharma sounds expedient. Further, if the practitioner recites the sūtra for 21 days then Samantabhadra manifests himself riding on his six-tusked white elephant surrounded by innumerable Bodhisattvas before that person to preach and instruct him the Law for his benefit and joy. He also gives a *Dharani* capable of protecting him from all possible harms physical as well as spiritual. So, Samantabhadra bears responsibility to guard and protect *Lotus Sūtra* as well as the devotees who copy it, make others to copy, accept, uphold, read, recite, and memorize this sūtra correctly and practice as prescribed in the *Lotus Sūtra*. This resolution is further strengthened by the vow the Samantabhadra has taken to employ his transcendental powers to guard and protect *Lotus Sūtra*, and Śākyamuni Buddha promises to use his transcendental powers to guard and protect those who accept and uphold the name of Bodhisattva Samantabhadra [8]. For this reason, in Japan, Samantabhadra (Jap. Fugen) is worshipped as the patron and protector of their favorite text, the *Lotus Sūtra*, particularly by the Tendai, Shingon, and Nichiren sects.

In Mahāyāna Buddhism: Unlike his more popular counterpart Mañjuśri, Samantabhadra is only rarely depicted alone and is usually found in a trinity on the right side of Śākyamuni, riding on a white elephant. In those traditions that accept the *Avataṃsaka Sūtra* as their basic instruction, Samantabhadra and Mañjuśri flank Vairocana Buddha, the principle Buddha of this particular *Sūtra*. Samantabhadra has other identities in the Tang Dynasty Tantric School of Buddhism, which was popular and influential in few metropolitan centers of the eighth and ninth centuries, as Pu Xian Yan Ming (Samantabhadra Who Lengthens Life span). Samantabhadra is believed by many Chinese Buddhists to have resided at Mt. E Mei of Si Chuan Province [5].

In Esoteric Buddhism: In Esoteric Buddhism, Samantabhadra is also known as Vajradhara and Viśvabhadra [5], the different names represent different attributes and essence qualities, lineages of Sadhanā, and esoteric transmission. Samantabhadra appears in the Vajrayāna tantric text the Kunjed Gyalpo Tantra as the Primordial Ādi Buddha, the "embodiment" (Sanskrit: *kaya*) or "field" (Sanskrit: *Kṣetra*) of "timeless awareness, gnosis" (Sanskrit: *Jñāna*) awakened since from the time immemorial. Therefore, in Tibetan Buddhism the Nyingma, or "Old Translation" school, the Śākya, and the Bon schools view Samantabhadra as the Primordial Buddha. In the Nyingma school of Tibetan Buddhism, Vajrayāna, Samantabhadra is considered a Primordial Buddha, who is the embodiment of enlightenment or ultimate reality (*Dharmakāya*) in indivisible Yab-yum union with his consort Samantabhadri [4]. However, the Kagyu and Gelug schools use Vajradhara to represent the Primordial Buddha.

In short, Samantabhadra embodies all the virtues extolled in the Mahayana Tradition; physically he is beyond the limits of time and space, and he is described in an Esoteric tradition as the unity of awareness, appearances, and emptiness, the nature of mind, and natural clarity with unceasing compassion. This is how the Samantabhadra is known from the very beginning [3].

S

Cross-References

- ▶ Bodhisattva
- ▶ Mañjuśrī
- ▶ Vajrayāna (Buddhism)

References

1. Chang GCC (1972) The Buddhist teachings of totality: the philosophy of Hua Yen Buddhism. G. Allen, London
2. Kato B, Tamura Y, Miyasaka K (tr) (1975) There three fold lotus sutra. Weather Hill/Kosei, New York/Tokyo
3. Khyentse D (1990) Introduction: the significance of this biography. In: Palmo AJ (Eugenie de Jong; translator); Nyingpo Y et al (compiler) (2004) The great image: the life story of Vairochana the translator. Shambala, Boston
4. Rinpoche D, Dorje JY (1991) The Nyingma School of Tibetan Buddhism: its fundamentals and history, vol 2. Wisdom, Boston
5. Soothhill WE, Hodous L (2005) A dictionary of Chinese Buddhist terms. Munshiram Manoharlal, New Delhi
6. T10, No. 293
7. T9, No. 262
8. Watson B (tr) (1993) The lotus sutra. Sri Satguru, Delhi

Samatha

Bhikkhu Anālayo
Center for Buddhist Studies, University of Hamburg, Balve, Germany

Synonyms

Calm; *Śamatha* (Sanskrit); Tranquility

Definition

In conjunction with insight, *vipassanā*, *samatha* as mental calm or tranquility is a central aspect of the systematic cultivation of the mind in Buddhism.

Tranquility

In early Buddhist meditation theory, to develop *samatha* means to "settle" the mind, in the sense of making it steady, quiet, and concentrated. The development of *samatha* requires in particular the overcoming of certain mental states or conditions that are considered detrimental to deeper concentration. A standard listing of such conditions speaks of five "hindrances," *nīvaraṇa*, which are sensual desire, ill will, sloth-and-torpor, restlessness-and-worry, and doubt.

After their successful removal, the attainment of absorption, *jhāna*, becomes possible. Such attainment can take place based on mindfulness of breathing, or else by developing the mental attitudes of loving kindness, compassion, sympathetic joy, and equanimity, just to mention some out of the range of possible meditation practices that can lead to absorption attainment.

Systematic deepening of concentration in this way proceeds through a series of four absorptions, experiences of deep mental tranquility where the meditating subject and the object employed for meditation are experienced as merging with each other. The standard descriptions qualify the first absorption as aloof from any type of sensual distraction and being accompanied by spiritual forms of rapture, *pīti*, and happiness, *sukha*, that are the result of such aloofness. The first absorption is an experience of unification of the mind, which is maintained with the help of initial and sustained application of the mind, *vitakka* and *vicāra*. The degree of unification and inner pervasion with rapture and happiness experienced at this point is, according to the early Buddhist discourses, comparable to mixing bath powder with water for the purpose of taking a bath, where all the powder is thoroughly permeated and mixed with the water ([1], Vol. I, p. 74).

With further deepening of concentration, initial and sustained application of the mind fall away and the mind remains effortlessly stable and unified. At this point, the experience of rapture and happiness is not only based on aloofness from sensuality, but additionally born of the inner confidence and stability that result from the depth of concentration, once the second absorption has been reached. The aloofness and stability of such concentration accompanied by intense inner rapture and happiness finds an illustration in the image of a lake on top of a mountain which is fed by spring water welling up from within.

Eventually rapture, *pīti*, fades away and only happiness, *sukha*, remains. A sense of balance and inner clarity pervades this experience which by way of further deepening of concentration has become the attainment of the third absorption. The discourses compare the degree to which the whole experience at this stage is one of being immersed in happiness and profound concentration with the example of lotus flowers that are completely immersed in water.

Once even the subtle happiness of the third absorption is left behind, the fourth absorption can be attained, which transcends the dichotomy of pleasure and displeasure, being firmly and unshakably established in equanimity and deeply stable concentration. The inner purity of this experience and its total withdrawal from the outer world finds an illustration in the image of a person who is completely wrapped up in a white cloth, from head to toe.

Based on the attainment of the fourth absorption, according to early Buddhist meditation theory the mind has acquired such inner power and ability that the development of various supernatural abilities and powers becomes possible. These include telepathic knowledge of the minds of others and the recollection of one's own past lives, just to mention two examples.

Alternatively, based on the fourth absorption the immaterial attainments can be developed, profound experiences of mental tranquility that transcend any experience related to what is material. Experiencing these requires going beyond the object of meditation, which formed the basis for the progress through the four absorptions, and which now is replaced by a set of progressively subtler notions.

With the first of these immaterial attainments, the former meditation object, which due to the unification of the mind during absorption has become an all embracing experience, is refined by being replaced with the notion of "boundless space." In other words, the boundlessness of the former object remains, but the object itself is allowed to disappear, whereby the experience of matter is fully left behind.

The next step requires turning attention back to the mind that, by being absorbed in the notion of boundless space, has become boundless itself. In this way, the second immaterial attainment can be reached, which is based on the notion of "boundless consciousness." At this point, not only matter is left behind, but also space.

Attending to this refined experience of boundless consciousness as something that is insubstantial in every respect, the notion of "nothingness" can become the basis for attaining the third immaterial attainment. By now, not only matter and space, but even the notion of the experiencing mind is being transcended.

Still another step can be taken at this point. This requires letting go of any notion at all, whereby the fourth immaterial attainment of "neither-perception-nor-non-perception" can be reached. At this stage, the experience is so subtle that it is no longer possible to say whether there is perception or not.

Progress through the four immaterial attainments thus takes place by a sublimation of the object of meditation, based on the depth of concentration reached with the fourth absorption. In other words, the development of the four absorptions depicts a deepening of concentration with any meditation object, whereas the four immaterial attainments are based on a specific progressive refinement of the meditation object.

Within the context of the noble eightfold path, which succinctly describes what from an early Buddhist perspective is required for progress to liberation, the development of *samatha* by way of the four absorptions has its place under the heading of "right concentration." Such right concentration needs to be developed in cooperation with rightly directed view, intentions, speech, action, livelihood, effort, and mindfulness.

The development of *samatha* leads to a high degree of mastery over the mind and thereby forms a basis for the development of insight, *vipassanā*. When insight is developed by a calm and steady mind, such insight will be able to penetrate into the deeper regions of the mind and thereby bring about true inner change.

While *vipassanā* has the purpose of leading to the destruction of ignorance, the practice of tranquility is reckoned to be specifically aimed at the abandoning of passion ([2], Vol. I, p. 61). This, however, does not mean that these two aspects of meditation represent two different paths leading to two different goals. The above distinction only intends to draw attention to the specific task or quality of these two interdependent aspects of Buddhist meditation.

The experience of deep stages of concentration is one of intense pleasure and happiness, brought about by purely mental means, which eclipses any pleasure arising in dependence on material objects. In this way the development of *samatha* can become a powerful antidote to sensual desires, by divesting them of their former attraction.

Even though *samatha* on its own would not be able to lead to awakening, it thus does have an important function to perform for progress toward that aim. Hence, the path leading to the unconditioned requires both *samatha* and *vipassanā* ([3], Vol. IV, p. 359), both have to be developed as integral parts of the noble eightfold path. To borrow from a poetic image found in the discourses, mental tranquility and insight are a "swift pair of messengers," capable of carrying the message of Nirvāṇa along the road of the noble eightfold path ([3], Vol. IV, p. 195).

The basic difference between *samatha* and *vipassanā* can be illustrated with the help of mindfulness of breathing, since this meditation practice can be developed in both modes. The difference here depends on what angle is taken when observing the breath, since emphasis on various phenomena related to the process of breathing stays in the realm of variegated sensory experience and thus is more geared toward the development of insight, while emphasis on just mentally knowing the presence of the breath leads to a unitary type of experience and is thus capable of producing deepening levels of mental tranquility.

In the early Buddhist discourses, the terms *samatha* and *vipassanā* seldom occur alone and most often are found together. This conveys the impression that their relationship should be one of coexistence and cooperation. A calm mind supports the development of insight and the presence of insight in turn facilitates the development of deeper levels of tranquility. Therefore, tranquility and insight are at their best when developed in skilful cooperation.

Concerning the interrelation between tranquility and insight, the discourses indicate that there is no fixed pattern to be followed in this respect. One type of practitioner may have gained mental tranquility but is not yet endowed with the higher wisdom of insight, while another may be endowed with the higher wisdom of insight without having gained mental tranquility ([2], Vol. II, p. 92). In both cases, an effort should be made to develop what is still lacking. Some may practice insight first and then develop tranquility, others may build up mental tranquility right at the outset and only then turn to insight, and still others may develop both in conjunction ([2], Vol. II, p. 157). According to early Buddhist meditation theory, any of these approaches is capable of leading to liberation, if eventually insight and tranquility are both brought into being. Thus, there appears to be no fixed rule, according to which the development of one of these two meditative qualities inevitably has to precede the other. Much rather, the task appears to be one of developing both in harmonious cooperation. As a stanza proclaims:

> There is no meditative absorption for those without wisdom,
> There is no wisdom without meditation,
> Those who have meditative absorption and wisdom,
> Are close to Nirvāṇa ([4], 372).

Cross-References

- ▶ Ānāpānasati
- ▶ Bhāvanā
- ▶ Dhyāna/Jhāna
- ▶ Iddhi
- ▶ Insight
- ▶ Liberation (Buddhism)
- ▶ Meditation
- ▶ Metta
- ▶ Muditā

References

1. Carpenter JE, Rhys Davids TW (eds) (1890–1911) The Dīgha Nikāya, 3 vols. Pali Text Society, London
2. Morris R, Hardy E (eds) (1885–1900) The Aṅguttara Nikāya, 5 vols. Pali Text Society, London
3. Feer L (ed) (1888–1898) The Saṃyutta Nikāya, 5 vols. Pali Text Society, Oxford

4. von Hinüber O, Norman KR (eds) (1994) The Dhammapada. Pali Text Society, London (references are by stanza)
5. Bodhi (2002) The Jhānas and the lay disciple. In: Premasiri PD (ed) Buddhist studies, essays in honour of Professor Lily de Silva. University of Peradeniya, Sri Lanka, pp 36–64
6. Brahmāli (2007) Jhāna and Lokuttara-jjhāna. Buddh Stud Rev 24(1):75–90
7. Bucknell RS (1993) Reinterpreting the Jhānas. J Int Assoc Buddh Stud 16(2):375–409
8. Cousins LS (1973) Buddhist Jhāna, its nature and attainment according to the Pali sources. Religion 3:115–131
9. Cousins LS (1992) Vitakka/Vitarka and Vicāra, stages of Samādhi in Buddhism and yoga. Indo-Iranian J 35:137–157
10. Griffiths PJ (1983) Buddhist Jhāna, a form-critical study. Religion 13:55–68
11. Gunaratana H (1996) The path of serenity and insight, an explanation of the Buddhist Jhānas. Motilal, Delhi
12. Shankman R (2008) The experience of Samādhi, an in-depth exploration of Buddhist meditation. Shambala, Boston
13. Stuart-Fox M (1989) Jhāna and Buddhist scholasticism. J Int Assoc Buddh Stud 12(2):79–110

Śamatha

► *Samatha*

Samavasaraṇa (Jainism)

Brianne Donaldson
Claremont School of Theology, Claremont, CA, USA

Definition

Samavasaraṇa (also Samosaraṇa) refers to the "the coming together" of the great assembly of people, gods (devas), and animals of that occurs when a great Jain teacher, called a tīrthaṅkara, achieves kevala-jñāna. Kevala-jñāna is often translated as omniscience. However, it is more accurately described as the moment in which a jīva, meaning the immanent life force within every living entity experiences its true nature and also attains complete awareness of every other existent entity in the universe in all their qualities and continually changing modes. As the fourth of five auspicious events (kalyāṇaka) in the lives of a tīrthaṅkara, or Jina, the moment of omniscience is a central focus in Jain dharma. Thus, the samavasaraṇa is one of the most elaborate symbolic images of Jainism. It is frequently represented in art and architecture, but it also functions as an ethical ideal of planetary peace and coexistence among people, devas, and creatures, inspired by the Jina's teachings.

The *Ādipurāṇa* of Jinasena, among many other Jain āgamas and commentaries, contains a detailed description of the samavasaraṇa, both as a cosmological event and an architectural marvel. In this account, the samavasaraṇa arena is constructed by multiple devas, often atop a large mound, immediately after a tīrthaṅkara attains omniscience. The structure itself is an elaborate and highly precise architectural design meant to ensure the seamless arrival of innumerable and diverse guests, a receptive state of listening and collective harmony throughout the tīrthaṅkara's message, and the peaceful departure of all. It disappears after the speech concludes ([3], p. 117).

The samavasaraṇa consists of four circular (or rarely, square) layers. The base of the assembly is the widest, surrounded by a tall wall and covering an area of 12 km^2 that was prepared by the devas specifically for the occasion. Gates are embellished with Jain motifs such as umbrellas, crocodiles, and svastikas and strategically placed at the four cardinal points of the circular structure to ensure guest's unimpeded movement and visual access to the Jina located at the apex of the samavasaraṇa under a sacred Aśoka tree.

The tree provides refuge for the tīrthaṅkara in the tradition of a forest sanctuary. It also mimics the shelter designs of traditional Buddhist and Jain shrines (caitya-gṛha) that offer a covered space for pilgrims to visit a stūpa or reliquary. The Aśoka tree, native to India and renowned for its medicinal properties, is said to have sheltered Mahāvīra when he renounced the world. Some commentaries describe an inner chamber beneath the tree made of crystal and gems that reflect all the entities in the universe, akin to the Jina's omniscience. Below the branches, the tīrthaṅkara sits on a soft cushion. The body of the Jina is often depicted as four-sided, having been replicated three times, either by devas or by a self-replicating power, so that four images of the omniscient teacher face each of the cardinal directions. The terms pratimā-sarvatobhadrikā and caumukha designates an image that is auspicious on all four sides ([9], p. 20).

Surrounding the tīrthaṅkara on the second level are the gaṇadharas, or disciples, who are venerated leaders of ascetic communities, followed by omniscient ascetics who have not yet achieved karmic liberation. Other highly developed monastics join the audience, followed by female ascetics, male and female devas, and lay men and women. Each group enters serenely by paying homage to the enlightened teacher through salutation and circumambulation. Five-sensed animals such as fish, reptiles, birds, and mammals fill the third level, coexisting without any animosity between one another or with humans. The samavasaraṇa is considered to be an event of such rare inspiration that ascetics, laypeople, animals, and gods are encouraged to come in spite of great distance. Hence, the fourth and lowest level is reserved for the celestial vehicles and any mode of transport used to travel to the event. Crowds of people and animals also gather peacefully and orderly around the periphery of the structure, calmed and transfixed by the presence of the all-perceiving Jina.

The appearance of the tīrthaṅkara sitting in the samavasaraṇa is considered one of the most auspicious acts of beauty, humility, wisdom, and truth that any creature can witness. It is captured in the opening line of the Namaskāra-mantra that honors those Jinas, also called arhats, who have overcome anger, ego, deceit, and greed and who possessed certain karmic impressions that enabled their spiritual leadership. The tīrthaṅkara's sermon begins with an acknowledgment of the mokṣa-mārga, the central Jain affirmation that the "three-jewel" path of right knowledge, right perception, and right action leads to liberation.

The speech of the tīrthaṅkara is characterized by unique attributes. Not only is it amplified to reach the ears of all five-sensed creatures in the universe, but it also emanates as a monolingual, divine sound (divya-dhvani) that is transformed into the language or communicative mode of each listener. The message is believed to instruct (deśanā-labdhi) a listener on the soul's potential for right knowledge and inspire a renewed commitment to spiritual practices, full or partial renunciation, virtuous conduct, nonviolence, and a fresh reception of the sūtras, texts, and spiritual teachings of the ācāryas, even among animals.

The *Aupapātika Sūtra* within the Śvetāmbara canon, one of many explanatory āgamas elucidating the original 12 Jain aṅgas, includes narratives to the laity regarding devas and Mahāvīra's preaching that figure significantly in later ideas of the samavasaraṇa, becoming an important feature of Jain art and temple architecture.

Sculptors, painters, artisans, architects, and temple builders were given creative license to represent the samavasaraṇa as long as they maintained the central design elements, most specifically the Jina in the center, preferably in a seated position ([8], p. 231). As a flat painting, the samavasaraṇa might be confused with a maṇḍala, but the presence of a four-faced teacher in the center and three concentric rings of people, animals, and vehicles will always reveal the image to be of the Jain assembly. Metal, marble, or handmade replicas of the layered auditorium are also found in many Jain temples including a bronze recreation thought to be over 400 years old in the Neminātha temple in Ghogha, India. At Mount Śatruñjaya in Gujarat, a sacred Śvetāmbara pilgrimage site, visitors can gaze on large panels decorated with circular depictions of samavasaraṇa. At Pāvāpurī in Bihar, the location of Mahāvīra's death and liberation circa 527 B.C.E., visitors can find an older and newer samavasaraṇa shrine near the main mandir, or temple.

In some cases, temple architecture itself reflects the symbols, staircases, and hospitable levels of the assembly arena. One primary example of this is the māna-stambha columns that stand before Digambara temples. These "pillars of pride" are thought to destroy conceit in those who gaze on them. Each is topped with four faces of the Jina seated in samavasaraṇa.

Although the samavasaraṇa is said to be a refuge of equality and welcome for all, Vijayadharmasūri, a revered ācārya of the Śvetāmbara Tapā Gaccha subsect, composed a collection of responses in the seventeenth century addressing various aspects of the assembly hall. In his commentary, he points out that female ascetics and divine beings must stand while male human and divine beings sit as a sign of traditional (and persistent) gender hierarchy ([4], p. 123). Jain scholar Paul Dundas has further demonstrated that, according to Vijayadharmasūri's responses, some of the 363 types of heretics established by medieval Jainism may also be excluded from the assembly ([4], p. 124). This raises the question whether the samavasaraṇa truly represents an inclusive vision wide enough to accommodate diverse viewpoints and species or if it depicts an under-examined vision of philosophical, patriarchal, and humanist superiority latent within Jain dharma. Among devout Jains, however, the samavasaraṇa remains a preeminent motivating image of personal devotion, spiritual expansion, and nonviolent coexistence.

At this point in the current time cycle (kālacakra), there are no more samavasaraṇa gatherings expected, as Mahāvīra was the last tīrthaṅkara of this epoch. However, the holy assembly will convene again during the upswing (utsarpiṇī) of the next time cycle. Additionally, Jain cosmography posits the ongoing presence of 20 tīrthaṅkaras in mahāvideha-kṣetra, a geographical zone separated from our current universe that remains conducive to the perpetual teaching and gathering of the samavasaraṇa.

Cross-References

▶ Namaskāra Mantra
▶ Tīrthaṅkara (Jainism)

References

1. Balbir N (1994) An investigation of the textual sources on the samavasaraṇa. In: Bruhn K, Balbir N, Bautze J (eds) Festschrift Klaus Bruhn. Verlag für Orientalistische Fachpublikationen, Reinbek
2. Caillat C (1999) Traces of a "trifunctional" structure in the Jaina tradition? Approach Jaina Stud Philos Logic Ritual Symb 11:60
3. Cort J (2010) Framing the Jina: Narratives of Icons and Idols in Jain History. Oxford University Press, New York.
4. Dundas P (2004) Beyond anekāntavāda: a Jain approach to religious tolerance. In: Sethia T (ed) Ahimsā, Anekānta and Jainism. Motilal Banarsidass, Delhi
5. Harini MR (2005) Jaina paintings. Jaina archaeological heritage of Tamilnadu, (Lucknow: Bharatvarshiy Digambar Jain Mahasbha, 2005) p 68
6. Hegewald J (2007) Meru, Samavasarana and Siihhasana: the recurrence of three-tiered structures in Jaina cosmology, mythology and ritual. In: Bhattacharya G, Mitra GMM, Sinha S (eds) Kalhār (white water-lily): studies in art, iconography, architecture, and archaeology of India and Bangladesh. Kaveri Books, Delhi
7. Owen L (2012) Carving devotion in the Jain Caves at Ellora, vol 41. Brill, Boston
8. Titze K (2001) Jainism: a pictorial guide to the religion of non-violence. Motilal Banarsidass, Delhi
9. Tiwari MNP (1995) Jaina iconography: evolution and appraisal. Studies in Jaina art and iconography and allied subjects in honour of Dr. UP Shah, p 15

Samaya

▶ Time (Buddhism)

Sambodhī

▶ Bodhagayā

Same-Sex Desire

▶ Homosexuality (Buddhism)
▶ Homosexuality (Jainism)

Saṃgha

K. T. S. Sarao
Department of Buddhist Studies, University of Delhi, Delhi, India

Synonyms

Sangha; Saṅgha

Definition

The order of ordained Buddhist monks and nuns.

The word *Saṃgha*, derived from *saṃ* [adj. indeclinable prefix implying conjunction and completeness] + √*ghan/han* [to go (used rarely in classical literature, and when used it is regarded as a fault of composition)], is a word in Pāli and Sanskrit meaning *association*, *assembly*, or *community* and most commonly refers in Buddhism to the order of ordained Buddhist monks and nuns (see [4]). The Saṃgha is the third of the Tisaraṇa (Three Jewels) in Buddhism, the Buddha, the Dhamma, and the Saṃgha. The Saṃgha has a twofold meaning in Buddhism, i.e., it is not only an organization of monks and nuns but also a confederation that makes them one unified institution. In other words, the Saṃgha is far more than an organized proselytizing institution.

The foundations of the Saṃgha were laid in an environment of ancient India's homeless almsmen's community. It was in this type of environment that not only provided the basic guiding principles to the Buddhist Saṃgha but also molded its fundamental character in many ways. However, with the passage of time, the Saṃgha developed its own unique character. Members of the wandering community took up residence in well-endowed monasteries, and the unitary Saṃgha became plural. Some of these monasteries became metamorphosed into well-known centers of learning in the concluding phase and began drawing scholars from places located far and wide.

Originally, one could enter into the Saṃgha by just responding the Buddha's call to come forward. However, as time went by, admission to the Saṃgha was properly regulated through an intricate and well-defined procedure that consisted of two stages: *pabbajjā* ("the going forth") or the lower ordination and *upasampadā* (ordination) or the higher ordination. One must be at least 8 years old to be admitted to the *pabbajjā*. On being admitted one becomes a *sāmaṇera* (novice) and gets an *upajjhāya* (preceptor or spiritual teacher) and an *ācariya* (master). In order to become a *sāmaṇera*, the prospective candidate shaves one's beard and head, puts on the *kasāyavattha* (yellow/red/orange-colored robe), prostrates before the *upajjhāya*, and declares thrice his faith in the Tisaraṇa (Three Jewels) consisting of the Buddha, the Dhamma, and the Saṃgha. Thereafter, the *ācariya* teaches the ten rules (*dasasikhāpadāni*) to the *sāmaṇera*. As per these ten rules, he is expected to refrain from stealing, unchastity, lying, taking intoxicants, eating food at inappropriate times, entertaining programs consisting of singing, dancing, music, etc., wearing perfume and using decorative accessories, sitting on high chairs and sleeping on luxurious beds, and accepting gold and silver. The *sāmaṇera* becomes a regular member of the Saṃgha, i.e., a bhikkhu (fully ordained monk), only after the *upasampadā* for which one must be at least 20 years old. Initially, ordination into the Saṃgha took place through the Buddha alone. However, with the expansion of the work of ordination, the Buddha vested the power of ordination in other *bhikkhus* and *bhikkhunīs*.

The Buddhist Saṃgha is an order of persons who live by receiving alms. They must take a vow of poverty, renounce all material possessions, and must not practice any profession in order to make profit. They depend upon the munificence of the laity for the supply of essentials for sustenance: food, clothing, shelter, and medicines. Initially, the monks lived at roots of the tress, in grottoes and caves, on hills, in cemeteries, in forests, open spaces, or on straw heaps. A small percentage of monks still live like this and are generally known as the *araññakas* (forest dwellers). However, with the passage of time, as the Saṃgha grew in size as well as popularity, influential and rich patrons offered support for the construction of permanent residences. As a consequence, majority of the monks and nuns began to live in monasteries located in the vicinity of human settlements and became known as the *ārāmikas* (monastery dwellers). Originally, the monks were enjoined to live only on alms, but in courses of time, the rule was relaxed and they were allowed to accept invitations when extended to a particular Saṃgha as a body, or to a group of individual monks or nuns. Each Saṃgha was defined by a shared recitation of the Pātimokkha at the bimonthly *Uposatha* (confession ceremony) and an earmarked *sīma* (boundary) established for the purposes of the different ceremonies such as the *Vassāvāsa* (rainy retreat) and the *Uposatha*.

Initially, the general code of behavior followed by the Buddhists was not much different from the one followed by other ascetics. However, after the number of Buddhist monks and nuns grew substantially and it became imperative to have an appropriate code of conduct to control undisciplined members, the Buddha decided to formulate a disciplinary code of conduct (*Vinaya*) in tune with his own teaching (*buddhavacana*). Once this process of preparing the code of conduct began, revision, emendation, and expansion of these rules continued till final form in the shape of the *Vinaya Piṭaka* was achieved. All aspects of the lives of the *bhikkhus* and the *bhikkhunīs* have been dealt with in the *Vinaya Piṭaka*. The code of conduct consists of matters relating to the probationary period and initiation, training under the *ācariya* and *upajjhāya*, daily chores of life pertaining to food, dress, and other articles of use, lodgings and the manner of residing in them, different religious ceremonies such as the *Uposatha*, the *Vassāvāsa*, the *Pavāraṇā*, and the *Kaṭhina*, ecclesiastical procedure for the imposition of punishment, as well as release from guilt, schism in the Saṃgha, and the procedure for settling disputes among the members. The *bhikkhus* and the *bhikkhunīs* were provided with separate codes of conduct by the Buddha.

Cross-References

- ▶ Bhikkhunī
- ▶ Dhamma
- ▶ Pātimokkha

References

1. Horner IB (1938–1966) The book of the discipline (Vinaya Piṭaka), 6 vols. Pali Text Society, London
2. Prebish C (1975) Buddhist monastic discipline: the Sanskrit Prātimokṣa Sūtras of the Mahāsaṃghikas and Mūlasarvāstivādins. Pennsylvania State University Press, University Park
3. Sparham G (2004) Saṅgha. In: Buswell RE (editor-in-chief) Encyclopedia of Buddhism. Macmillan Reference USA, New York, pp 740–644
4. https://archive.org/details/EtymologyOfSangha. Accessed 24 Nov 2014

Samjhanaa

▶ Education (Jainism)

Saṃkhāra

Bhikkhu Anālayo
Center for Buddhist Studies, University of Hamburg, Balve, Germany

Synonyms

Formations; Saṃskāra (Buddhism); *Saṃskāra* (Sanskrit)

Definition

The term *saṅkhāra* combines *kāra*, "making," with the prefix *saṃ*, "together," and thus has the literal sense of a "making together." Such making together can convey an active as well as a passive sense, representing that which makes together and that which is made together.

In its early Buddhist usage, the term *saṅkhāra* thus has three main meanings:

- As the fourth of the five aggregates, *khandha*
- As the second link in the formula of dependent arising, *paṭicca samuppāda*
- As anything conditioned, this being the most general sense of the term

S

The Aggregate of *Saṅkhāras*

In early Buddhist thought, the individual is analyzed into five aggregates affected by clinging, which are bodily form, feeling, perception, *saṅkhāra*s, and consciousness. The *saṅkhāra*s as the fourth of these five aggregates represent the conative aspect of mental experience and thus stand predominantly for volition. In this role, the aggregate of *saṅkhāra*s comprises past, present, and future volitional formations, be they internal or external, gross or subtle, inferior or superior, (concerned with what is) far or near.

While the aggregates of feeling and consciousness relate to the sense doors, the aggregates of perception and *saṅkhāra*s relate to the sense objects, that is, to forms, sounds, smells, tastes, touches, and mental objects ([1], Vol. III, p. 60). This suggests that, whereas feeling and consciousness are to some degree more on the inner and receptive side of mental experience, perception and *saṅkhāra*s reach out to the object, so to say, recognizing it and reacting to it. In short, as an aggregate the *saṅkhāra*s represent that part of the mind which reacts to experience.

A discourse describes how someone with telepathic powers is able to recognize the operation of the *saṅkhāra*s in another's mind ([2], Vol. III, p. 104). According to this passage, once the volitional direction of such a *saṅkhāra* has been recognized through the exercise of telepathic powers, it will be possible to predict the type of thought that is about to arise in the other person's mind. This indicates that the *saṅkhāra*s as volitional formations represent the beginning stages of mental activity, the first inclination or tendency that precedes the arising of thought, whose nature is determined by the directional input provided by the *saṅkhāra*s.

During later developments of Buddhist philosophy, the connotations of the term *saṅkhāra* as an aggregate expanded until it came to cover a wide range of meaning, becoming an umbrella term for various mental factors. In this way, the *saṅkhāra*s came to stand for anything mental apart from the other three aggregates of feeling, perception, and consciousness.

This goes beyond the implications of the aggregate of *saṅkhāra*s in the early Buddhist discourses, which represents mainly the volitional aspect of mental experience. The fact that in descriptions of the aggregates the term *saṅkhāra* usually occurs in the plural form as well as the inherent nuance of the expression as a referent not only to what "makes together" but also to what "is made together" may have influenced the choice of the *saṅkhāra*s as a heading for other mental factors and qualities.

Saṅkhāras in Dependent Arising

Early Buddhism analyzes the arising of *dukkha* – a term whose meaning ranges from barely noticeable dissatisfaction to outright suffering as inherent features of human existence – with the help of a series of conditions. The standard way of representing these conditions is by way of 12 links, which begin with ignorance as the root cause and lead up to the arising of *dukkha*.

In the context of this scheme, the *saṅkhāra*s form the second link that leads from the first link of ignorance, *avijjā*, to the third link of consciousness, *viññāṇa*. According to the traditional interpretation, *saṅkhāra*s in this context represent the karmically active volitional formations responsible for rebirth and continued existence. That is, in the context of dependent arising the *saṅkhāra*s are the creative principle responsible for various forms of existence.

The function of the *saṅkhāra*s in the context of rebirth can be seen, for example, in a discourse which describes how someone endowed with confidence or faith, morality, learning, generosity, and wisdom may have the aspiration to be reborn in a favorable situation as a human or in a heavenly realm. If this mental aspiration is developed and repeatedly cultivated, the person in question will indeed be reborn in that situation or realm ([3], Vol. III, p. 99). That is, repeatedly developing these types of *saṅkhāra*s is what leads to the particular type of rebirth. Another discourse indicates that an aspiration for a favorable rebirth can also become effective if it is based on the meritorious deed of giving to recluses and Brahmins ([2], Vol. III, p. 258).

The importance of one's mental inclination is again highlighted in another discourse, which reports a discussion between the Buddha and two ascetics who had undertaken the practice of adopting the behavior of a dog and a cow, respectively ([3], Vol. I, p. 387). The discourse indicates that the mental inclination resulting from such a way of practice will simply lead to rebirth as a dog or a cow. The principle behind this is that *saṅkhāra*s of a particular type will lead to a corresponding type of rebirth. Hence, someone whose *saṅkhāra*s are similar to those of an animal will be reborn as an animal.

In more general terms, if *saṅkhāra*s are of a harmful nature, for example, they will lead to a rebirth where harmful types of experiences are predominant. The same principle holds for *saṅkhāra*s of a wholesome nature, which will lead to a positive type of rebirth. In this way, according to early Buddhism, each living being creates and forms its own character and existence, both in past lives and at every moment of present existence. This continuous process of creating and forming takes place through the medium of *saṅkhāra*s.

Saṅkhāras in General

The term *saṅkhāra* in its general sense can cover all five aggregates. Such a usage occurs in a verse by a monk, who told a gang of criminals intending to murder him that he was free from fear, since from his perspective there was no "I" to be killed, but only *saṅkhāra*s will pass away ([4], 715). A similar usage recurs in a verse by a nun ([1], Vol. I, p. 135), who in reply to a challenge points out that the challenger's notion of a (substantial) "being" was mistaken, since in reality there is just a heap of *saṅkhāra*s.

As mentioned above, the term *saṅkhāra* can assume an active as well as a passive sense. In the case of the more general usage of the term, the active mode underlies occurrences where the expression *saṅkhāra* represents the cause or condition for something, while in the passive mode the *saṅkhāra*s stand for whatever is a product of conditions.

An example of the active sense can be found in a passage which explains that unwholesome things arise due to a cause, *sasaṅkhārā*, not without a cause ([5], Vol. I, p. 82). The same general sense recurs in another passage according to which pain or pleasure arises due to a cause, *sasaṅkhārā* ([1], Vol. V, p. 213). In these instances, *saṅkhāra* refers to the presence of a "cause" or a "condition."

The passive mode of the term *saṅkhāra*s in its general usage stands for all conditioned phenomena. Examples of this usage can be found in two discourses ([2], Vol. II, p. 198 and [1], Vol. III, p. 146), which describe the splendor and immense wealth possessed by a former king, all of which has changed and passed away. The word used in this context to refer to the former splendor and wealth is *saṅkhāra*. A similar usage occurs in another discourse, which describes a worldwide drought that leads to the drying up of all water and the destruction of all life, illustrating the impermanent nature of all *saṅkhāras* ([5], Vol. IV, p. 100). Thus, all of existence can be covered by the term *saṅkhāra*, in the sense of things that are produced through conditions.

The same general usage underlies what according to tradition was the last instruction given by the Buddha before passing away, which highlights the impermanent nature of all conditioned phenomena, *vayadhammā saṅkhārā* ([2], Vol. II, p. 156). This theme recurs in a set of stanzas, according to which all *saṅkhāra*s are impermanent and unsatisfactory and all dharmas are not-self ([6], 277–279).

Of all *saṅkhāra*s (in the sense of conditioned phenomena), the noble eightfold path is the best ([5], Vol. II, p. 34). This noble eightfold path is a summary of what according to early Buddhism is required for progress to liberation, namely, rightly directed view, intentions, speech, action, livelihood, effort, mindfulness, and concentration. Although the noble eightfold path is conditioned and thus takes part in what is covered by the term *saṅkhāra* in its widest usage, the goal itself is beyond all *saṅkhāra*s ([6], 154). According to early Buddhism, Nirvāṇa is neither "formed" nor "made up" or "conditioned," but rather is "unconditioned," *asaṅkhata* ([7], p. 80).

Thus, only Nirvāṇa lies beyond the range of *saṅkhāras* even in their most general sense, being in fact the "stilling of all *saṅkhāras*." Such stilling of all *saṅkhāras*, a stanza exclaims, is happiness indeed ([6], 368, 381).

Cross-References

- ▶ Causality (Buddhism)
- ▶ Khandha
- ▶ Paṭicca Samuppāda

References

1. Feer L (ed) (1888–1898) The Saṃyutta Nikāya, 5 vols. Pali Text Society, Oxford
2. Carpenter JE, Rhys Davids TW (eds) (1890–1911) The Dīgha Nikāya, 3 vols. Pali Text Society, London
3. Trenckner V, Chalmers R (eds) (1888–1896) The Majjhima Nikāya, 3 vols. Pali Text Society, London
4. Alsdorf L, Norman KR (ed) (1966) Thera- and Therīgāthā. Pali Text Society, London (references are by stanza)
5. Morris R, Hardy E (eds) (1885–1900) The Aṅguttara Nikāya, 5 vols. Pali Text Society, London
6. von Hinüber O, Norman KR (eds) (1994) The Dhammapada. Pali Text Society, London (references are by stanza)
7. Steinthal P (ed) (1885) The Udāna. Pali Text Society, London
8. Hamilton S (1996) The saṃkhārakkhanda. In: id. Identity and experience, the constitution of the human being according to early Buddhism. Luzac Oriental, London, pp 66–81
9. Vetter T (2000) Saṅkhāra. In: id. The 'Khandha Passages' in the Vinayapiṭaka and the four main Nikāyas. Österreichische Akademie der Wissenschaften, Wien, pp 27–63

Sammādiṭṭhi

▶ Ethics (Buddhism)

Saṃsāra

▶ Rebirth (Buddhism)

Saṃsāra (Buddhism)

K. T. S. Sarao
Department of Buddhist Studies, University of Delhi, Delhi, India

Synonyms

Bhavacakka; Bhavacakra; Transmigration

Definition

Nonstop cycle of birth, decay-and-death, rebirth, redecay-and-redeath whose beginning is unknown and which is characterized by mental and physical suffering.

In Buddhism, the term *saṃsāra* (transmigration lit. faring on, journeying, circulating, continuously flowing [like a river]) refers to the nonstop cycle of birth (*jāti*), decay-and-death (*jarāmaraṇa*), rebirth (*abhijāti, āgati*), and redecay-and-redeath. This process is also known as *bhavacakka* (Sk, *bhavacakra*) ([9], pp. 529, 576) that arises out of *avijjā* (Sk, *avidyā*, ignorance) and is characterized by impermanence and psychophysical suffering (Pāli, *dukkha*; Sk, *duḥkha*) ([1], Vol. ii, p. 6). The commencement of this process cannot be known with certainty. In fact, it is viewed as beginningless. As described by the Buddha to monks in one of the suttas: "Incalculable is the beginning, brethren, of this faring on. The earliest point is not revealed of the running on, fairing on, of beings cloaked in ignorance, tied to craving" ([5], Vol. ii, p. 120). Every living being (*jīva*) in the universe participates in this process of one existence after another (*gati bhavābhava cuti upapatti.* [8], p. 664) running into myriads of existences. In the Buddhist view of *saṃsāra*, "beings generally rise and fall, and fall and rise through the various realms, now experiencing unhappiness, now experiencing happiness. This precisely is the nature of saṃsāra: wandering from life to life with no particular direction or purpose" ([2], p. 119). The only way to escape *saṃsāra* is through the attainment of *nibbāna* (Sk, nirvāṇa).

The driving force behind this stream-like continuous flow of existences is determined by the moral consequences of a being's kamma (Sk, karma, volitional act) of body, speech, and mind in the present existence and in the preceding existences. These moral consequences are called *kammavipāka* (fruition of the volitional acts) ([6], Vol. iii, pp. 150, 160) which can occur in the present existence or in a future existence. It is generally postulated that within *saṃsāra* the effects of good moral actions lead to wholesome rebirths, while the effects of bad moral actions lead inevitably to unwholesome rebirths. Thus, as pointed out by Damien Keown, "karma functions as the elevator that takes people from one floor of the building to another. Good deeds result in an upward movement and bad deeds in a downward one" ([4], p. 797).

> In general, though with some qualification, rebirth in the lower realms is considered to be the result of relatively unwholesome *(akuśala/akusala)*, or bad *(pāpa)* karma, while rebirth in the higher realms the result of relatively wholesome *(kuśala/kusala)*, or good *(puṇya/puñña)* karma. Correspondingly, the lower the realm, the more unpleasant and unhappy one's condition; the higher the realm the more pleasant, happy, and refined one's condition. One should note, however, that this hierarchy does not constitute a simple ladder which one, as it were, climbs, passing out at the top into nirvāṇa. ([2], p. 119)

Release from the cycle altogether, *nibbāna* (Sk, nirvāṇa) can be realized only by those beings who attain correct insight and realization of the truth of the Buddha's teachings.

Cosmologically, the saṃsāra consists of six distinct domains of existence within which living beings are reborn depending upon their kamma. These six domains of existence are the *devaloka* (the *deva* realm), *asuraloka* (the realm of the *asuras* or demigods), *manussaloka* (Sk, *manuṣyaloka*, human realm), *tiracchānaloka* (Sk, *tiryagyoniloka/tiraścayoniloka*, animal realm), *petaloka* (Sk, *pretaloka*, hungry ghost realm or realm of the spirits of the dead), and *niraya* (Sk, *naraka*, the hell realm). These six realms are typically divided into three higher realms and three lower realms: the three higher realms are the realms of the gods, demigods, and humans; the three lower realms are the realms of the animals, hungry ghosts, and hell beings. Life in none of these realms is eternal. Nor is it free from the prospect of suffering. In other words, irrespective of the real, higher or lower, a wandering being cannot escape the sufferings of birth, death, and rebirth.

The *devaloka* consists of different heaves where the *devas* lead extremely long lives full of pleasure and abundance. The devas are overwhelmed with the joys and pleasures so much that they constantly remain distracted and never think to practice the dharma. On exhausting their good karma, they are reborn in one of the other realms. The *asuras* have pleasure and abundance almost as much as the gods, but they suffer from jealousy and constant wars among themselves and with the *devas*. Animals suffer from being exploited by humans and attacked and eaten by other animals. They generally lead their lives under constant fear. Hungry ghosts suffer from extreme hunger and thirst. The lives of the hell beings are the worst of all. They have to undergo extreme forms of suffering for very long periods of time in different hells. The *manussaloka* is considered the best realm to attain liberation from the *saṃsāra*. This is so because it is considered as the most appropriate realm for practicing the dharma due to the fact that humans are not completely distracted by pleasures like the devas or *asuras* or by extreme suffering like the beings in the lower realms.

S

Cross-References

▶ Kamma

References

1. Feer ML (ed) (1889) The Saṃyutta Nikāya, reprint, vol 2. Pali Text Society, London
2. Gethin R (1998) Foundations of Buddhism. Oxford University Press, Oxford
3. Halder JR (1977) Early Buddhist mythology. Manohar, Delhi

4. Keown D (2000) Buddhism: a very short introduction. Oxford University Press, Oxford
5. Rhys Davids CAF, Woodward FH (eds) (1922) The book of the kindred sayings (Saṃyutta Nikāya), vol 2. Pali Text Society, London
6. Rhys Davids TW, Carpenter JE (eds) (1911) The Dīgha Nikāya, vol 3. Pali Text Society, London
7. Sadakata A (1997) Buddhist cosmology: philosophy and origins (trans: Gaynor Sekimori). Kōsei, Tokyo
8. Stede W (ed) (1918) Cullaniddesa. Pali Text Society, London
9. Tin, Pe Maung Tin (trans) (1971) The path of purity, being a translation of Buddhaghosa's Visuddhimagga, combined reprint. Pali Text Society, London
10. Williams P (2002) Buddhist thought. Taylor & Francis, London

Saṃskāra

► *Saṃkhāra*

Saṃskāra (Buddhism)

► *Saṃkhāra*

Samyaka Sambodhi

► *Bodhi Tree*

Saṃyutta Nikāya

K. T. S. Sarao
Department of Buddhist Studies, University of Delhi, Delhi, India

Synonyms

Book of the kindred sayings; Collection of connected discourses; Mixed Āgama; Saṃyuttāgama

Definition

The third of the five divisions of the Sutta Piṭaka.

The Saṃyutta Nikāya is a Buddhist scripture, the third of the five *nikāyas* (collections) in the Sutta Piṭaka, which in turn is one of the "three baskets" (Tipiṭaka). It is one of the basic works in which early Indian Buddhist teachings on topics such as suffering, impermanence, selflessness, four noble truths, and the eightfold path have been given in detail. It has received its title from the fact that its discourses (*suttas*) have been grouped together (*saṃyutta*) in accordance with their respective subject matters. According to the tradition, the total number of *suttas* in the Saṃyutta Nikāya should be 7,762 ([10], Vol. i, p. 17). However, the number as given in the edition of the Pali Text Society comes to only 2,889. The reason for this ambiguity is that the manuscripts often just have key words to be worked-out into full-fledged *suttas* in the absence of unambiguous guidelines as to how this is to be done. As a result, this kind of manuscript tradition differs entirely from the one that exists in either the Dīgha Nikāya or the Aṅguttara Nikāya, where the text is given in full and only occasionally passages repeated verbally have been left out. The Saṃyutta Nikāya, on the other hand, can be contracted into a basic minimum and can then again be expanded by using the key words. Buddhaghosa wrote a commentary (*aṭṭhakathā*) on it called the Sāratthappakāsinī in the fifth century.

The Saṃyutta Nikāya is divided into five main *vaggas* consisting of a total of 56 sections, called *saṃyuttas*. Each of these 56 *saṃyuttas* has been further subdivided into minor *vaggas* (chapters). The five main *vaggas* are as follows:

1. The Sagātha Vagga consisting of 11 *saṃyuttas* contains verses.
2. The Nidāna Vagga consisting of 10 *saṃyuttas* explains the chain of causation (*paṭiccasamuppāda*).
3. The Khandha Vagga consisting of 13 *saṃyuttas* explains the five *khandhas*.
4. The Saḷāyatana Vagga consisting of 10 *saṃyuttas* explains the six sense organs with their objects.
5. The Mahā Vagga consisting of 12 *saṃyuttas*.

The *suttas* in the different *saṃyuttas* have been put together on the basis of at least three different criteria. The *suttas* of a *saṃyutta* either (1) deal with any specific point or any specific area of the Buddhist doctrine or (2) they speak of some categories of gods, demons or human beings or (3) in them some admirable person appears as a hero or speaker ([12], p. 53). For instance, the Dhātu Saṃyutta (*saṃyutta* no. 14) contains *suttas* where the Buddha speaks on the *dhātus* (elements), while the Bala Saṃyutta (*saṃyutta* no. 50) is composed of *suttas* which deal with the five *balas* or powers, viz. *saddhā* (faith), *viriya* (energy), *sati* (mindfulness), *samādhi* (equanimity), and *paññā* (wisdom). However, this method is very repetitive. For instance, the 207 *suttas* of the Saḷāyatana Saṃyutta (*saṃyutta* no. 35) just relate to the six sense organs. It has been suggested that most probably this repetitiveness arose due to the fact that there existed a large number of *suttas* on the same subject, collected from different individuals and monasteries, etc., all being of equal religious merit and hence deserving to be included in the collection ([12], p. 57). At the same time, it must be recognized that this method of arrangement also means that the Saṃyutta Nikāya contains some of the most important tenets of Buddhism. A good example of this is the Sacca Saṃyutta (*saṃyutta* no. 56). It contains 131 *suttas* that relate to various aspects of the Four Noble Truths. Thus, the large number of the *suttas* is basically the outcome of a practice that involved a thorough treatment of the same topic from all angles in accordance with a fixed pattern to the complete exhaustion of both the topic and the reader. As suggested by K.R. Norman, this type of arrangement, however, represents an obvious editorial practice, and the existence of a number of the *suttas* elsewhere in the canon probably indicates a conscious selection of material to group together in this way ([7], p. 50). Further, as the *suttas* were classified in two different ways and as some of the *saṃyuttas* deal with numerical subjects, there is inevitably an overlap between the Saṃyutta Nikāya and the Aṅguttara Nikāya in the Pāli canon. Occasionally, different versions of the same *sutta* in the Saṃyutta Nikāya and within the *nikāyas* elsewhere show substantial differences among themselves. These differences indicate that changes were introduced into one another, or both, of the narratives at some time, but the tradition has not changed since then for the obvious reason that the texts were preserved by the Dīgha-*bhāṇakas* and the Saṃyutta-*bhāṇakas* independent of each other ([7], p. 50).

The *suttas* of the Saṃyutta Nikāya generally are much shorter than those of the Dīgha Nikāya or the Majjhima Nikāya. The Sagātha Vagga is totally different from the other *vaggas* and is rather similar in some respects to the Sutta-Nipāta. The most important part of this vagga are the verses which also occur occasionally elsewhere in the Tipiṭaka. It has been suggested that parts of the Sāgatha Vagga appear to be very old, actually well near to the Vedic texts [5].

The Saṃyutta Nikāya corresponds to the Saṃyukta Āgama found in the Sūtra Piṭakas of various Sanskritic early Buddhists schools, fragments of which survive in Sanskrit and in Tibetan translation. A complete Chinese translation from the Sarvāstivādin recension, known as the *Zá Ahánjīng* ("the Mixed Āgama"), appears in the Chinese Buddhist canon. It was translated into Chinese by Baoyun in the years 435–436 C.E. [1]. An examination of the *Zá Ahánjīng* shows that it includes a number of sūtras which appear in the Aṅguttara Nikāya of the Pāli Tipiṭaka ([8], p. 181). This would seem to indicate that at the time when the *āgamas* were collected, the distinction between the "connected" and the "numerical" classifications was not very clearly drawn ([7], p. 54). A comparison of the Sarvāstivādin, Kāśyapīya, and Theravādin texts reveals a substantial consistency of content, although each recension contains sūtras/suttas not found in the others [4]. On this basis, it has been argued that the remarkable congruence of the various recensions suggests that the Saṃyutta Nikāya/Saṃyukta Āgama was the only collection to be finalized in terms of both structure and content in the pre-sectarian period ([11], pp. 31, 37–52).

Cross-References

▶ Aṅguttara Nikāya
▶ Buddhaghosa

S

▶ Buddhist Councils
▶ Dīgha Nikāya
▶ Four Noble Truths
▶ Majjhima Nikāya
▶ Paṭiccasamuppāda
▶ Rājagaha (Pāli)
▶ Tipiṭaka

References

1. Anālayo B (2007) Mindfulness of breathing in the Saṃyukta-āgama. Buddh Stud Rev 24(2): 137–150
2. Feer ML (1884–1898) The Saṃyutta Nikāya, 5 vols. Pali Text Society, London
3. von Hinüber O (1996) A handbook of Pāli literature. Walter de Gruyter, Berlin
4. Keown D (2004) A dictionary of Buddhism. Oxford University Press, London
5. Lanman ChR (1893) Rigveda V.40 and its Buddhist parallel. In: Festgruss an Rudolf von Roth zum Doktor-Jubillaum, 24 August 1893. Stuttgart, pp 186–190
6. Law BC (1983) A history of Pāli Literature, reprint, vol 1. Indological Book House, Delhi
7. Norman KR (1983) A history of Indian literature: Pāli literature. Otto Harrassowitz, Wiesbaden
8. Pande GC (1957) Studies in the origins of Buddhism. University of Allahabad, Allahabad
9. Rhys Davids CAF, Thera SS, Woodward FL (trans) (1917–1930) The book of the kindred sayings. 5 vols. Pali Text Society, London
10. Rhys Davids TW, Carpentier JE, Stede W (eds) (1886–1932) The Sumaṅgala-Vilāsinī: Buddhaghosa's commentary on the Dīgha Nikāya, 3 vols, Pali Text Society, London
11. Sujato B (nd) A history of mindfulness: how insight worsted tranquility in the Sattipaṭṭhāna Sutta. https://sites.google.com/site/santipada/bhantesujato'swork. Accessed 15 Jan 2012
12. Winternitz M (1983) A history of Indian Literature, revised edn (trans) V, vol 2. Motilal Banarsidass, Srinivasa Sarma, Delhi
13. Woodward FL (ed) (1929–1937) The Sāratthappakāsinī, Buddhaghosas commentary on the Saṃyutta Nikāya, 3 vols. Pali Text Society, London

Saṃyuttāgama

▶ Saṃyutta Nikāya

Sanchi

▶ Sāñcī

Sāñcī

K. T. S. Sarao
Department of Buddhist Studies, University of Delhi, Delhi, India

Synonyms

Boṭaśrī-Parvata; Cetiyagiri; Kākanādaboṭa; Kākaṇāva; Kākaṇāya; Kanakheda; Sanchi; Vedisāgiri

Definition

A Buddhist monastic complex located in central India near Vidiśā.

The monastic complex of Sāñcī (modern spelling: Sanchi) (lat. 23°29′ N and long. 77°45′ E) occupies a hilltop at a distance of about 10 km from the prosperous central Indian town of Vidīṣā where major road and river routes crisscross. In the ancient sources, this site has been variously mentioned as Cetiyagiri, Kākanaya, Kākanādaboṭa, and Boṭa-Śrī-Parvat. Sāñcī is one of the oldest and most continuously occupied extant Buddhist sites in India. Sāñcī's over 50 monuments including stūpas, vihāras, assembly halls, temples, and freestanding pillars date from the reign of King Aśoka (third century B.C.E.) to around 1200 C.E. Sāñcī is particularly significant as it has almost all types of Buddhist architectural forms. Some of these structures were erected on the foundations of earlier ones. General Taylor, a British officer, was the first known Western historian to document in English the existence of Sāñcī in 1818. The site was looted and ravaged by treasure hunters and amateur archeologists till the initiation of proper restoration work in 1881. John Marshall was largely responsible for restoring

Sāñcī, Fig. 1 The Great Stūpa (Stūpa no. 1)

Sāñcī, Fig. 2 Stūpa no. 3

S

most of the structures to their present condition between 1912 and 1919.

Of the important monuments on the main terrace are Great Stūpa (also known as Stūpa 1) (Fig. 1), Stūpa 3 (Fig. 2), Pillar 10 (Aśoka Pillar), Temple 18 (Mauryan apsidal), and Temple 17 (fourth century). Temple 17 (Fig. 3), consisting of a flat-roofed square sanctum with a portico and four pillars, was built during the early Gupta period and is possibly the earliest extant stone temple in the Indian subcontinent. Its interior and three sides of the exterior are plain, but the front and the pillars are carved quite elegantly. Temple 45 (tenth century C.E.) is located in the eastern area, and Temple 40 is in the southern area. Begun during Aśoka's rule, Temple 40 was enlarged during the Śuṅga period (ca. second to first centuries B.C.E.) and again later. Monastery 51 (Fig. 4) and Stūpa 2 are located on the western slope. Cetiyagiri Vihāra, housing the remains of Sāriputta and Moggallāna, is a modern temple built in the 1960s to mark the celebrations of 2,500 years of Buddhism.

Sāñcī, Fig. 3 Temple 17

Originally commissioned by King Aśoka (third century B.C.E.), the Great Stūpa is the oldest stone structure in India. Aśoka installed by the side of this stūpa, a polished pillar of the Chunar sandstone with a capital similar to the one at Sārnāth. Built over the relics of the Buddha, the nucleus of this stūpa was a simple hemispherical brick structure. Its construction work was personally supervised by Aśoka's wife, Devī, who was the daughter of a merchant of Vidiśā. The stūpa was vandalized sometime in the second century B.C.E. It has been suggested by some scholars that Puṣyamitra Śuṅga who overtook the Mauryan kingdom in a coup d'état may have been behind this vandalism. However, during the reign of later Śuṅga kings, the stūpa was enlarged with stone slabs to nearly twice its original size. The dome was flattened near the top and crowned by three superimposed *chatras* (parasols) within a square railing. The dome was set on a high circular drum meant for circumambulation, which could be accessed via a double staircase. Copiously carved monumental gateways (*toraṇas*) (Fig. 5) facing the cardinal directions and a stone pathway enclosed by a balustrade encompassing the entire edifice were added in the first century B.C.E. With their *yakṣīs* (Figs. 6 and 7), the whole of the surface of the toraṇas is covered with bas-reliefs portraying incidents from the life of the Buddha (such as the Great Departure: see Figs. 8 and 9) and depictions of the various Jātaka tales such as *Vessantara* (Figs. 10 and 11), *Mahākapi, Chhaddanta, Sāma*, and

Sāñcī, Fig. 4 Monastery 51

Sāñcī, Fig. 5 Temple no. 18

Sāñcī, Fig. 6 Stūpa no. 2

Sāñcī, Fig. 7 Temple and Monastery no. 45

Alambusā Jātaka. Four-seated images of the Buddha, each under a *chatra* and facing the four *toraṇas* against the drum of the stūpa, were the last addition to the stūpa made during the Gupta period. Although made of stone, the gateways were carved and constructed in the manner of wood and were covered with narrative sculptures showing scenes from the life of thc Buddha. There was no direct royal patronage, and the Great Stūpa's 600 short inscriptions in Prakrit show that its patrons almost entirely consisted of monks, nuns, merchants, and commoners. It has been suggested that devotees, who donated money toward a sculpture, would often choose their favourite scene from the life of the Buddha and then have their names inscribed on it, thus, accounting for the random repetition of particular episodes on the stūpa. On these stone carvings the Buddha is not depicted as a human figure, but is represented by various attributes, such as his footprints, the horse on which he left home, or a canopy under the bodhi tree at the time of his enlightenment.

Sāñcī, Fig. 8 The Great Departure (north toraṇa)

Stūpas 2 and 3 were built during the second century B.C.E. Stūpa 2 (Fig. 12) yielded the body relics of ten Buddhist therās, including Kaśyapagotra and Majjhima who had been given the task of spreading Buddhism in the Himalayas. This stūpa is also noteworthy for its decorative bas-reliefs, mostly enclosed inside medallions. Stūpa 3, modeled after Stūpa 1 and located by its side, is of great sanctity as it contained the relics of Moggallāna and Sāriputta. The ground balustrade and a single *toraṇa* of this stūpa were constructed during the first century B.C.E. and first century C.E., respectively. Stūpa 5, built in the sixth century C.E., is known for an image of the Buddha built against its southern face. Stūpas 12, 13, 14, and 16, with square bases, belong to the sixth and seventh centuries C.E.

Apart from the Aśokan pillar (Fig. 13), there are other freestanding stone pillars of which Pillar 25 belongs to the Śuṅga period and Pillars 26 and 35 to the fifth century C.E. Pillar 35, now broken, had originally on its abacus a standing image of Vajrapāṇi, now exhibited in the local Museum. Temple 18 (Fig. 14), a seventh-century apsidal sanctuary with a stūpa (now extinct), was

Sāñcī, Fig. 9 The Great Departure (east toraṇa)

Sāñcī, Fig. 10 North gateway (toraṇa)

Sāñcī, Fig. 12 Aśokan pillar

Sāñcī, Fig. 11 A Yakṣī on the north toraṇa

Sāñcī, Fig. 13 A Yakṣī on the east toraṇa

constructed on top of the base of an earlier Śuṅga-period apsidal hall. Temple 31, which contains a large image of the Buddha, is an oblong-pillared shrine with a flat ceiling. None of the vihāras can be dated earlier than the sixth century C.E., though some of them were built over the ruins of earlier ones. The most imposing among these vihāras is Monastery 51, planned in the typical monastic style with an open brick-paved courtyard with an enclosing veranda and beyond it an assortment of

Sāñcī, Fig. 14 Vessantara Jātaka

Sāñcī, Fig. 15 Vessantara Jātaka

cells. Monasteries 36, 37, and 38, dateable to the seventh century C.E., are almost of the same design, except on a smaller scale. Monasteries 36 and 37 had central platforms. Monasteries 36 and 38 were originally two storied. The remains of Monastery 45 (Fig. 15) belong to two different periods, the seventh–eighth and tenth–eleventh centuries C.E. This monastery is noteworthy for its temple built over the ruins of an earlier temple which is still standing with the lower part of its spire. Monasteries 46 and 47, dated to the eleventh century C.E. and built on the ruins of earlier monasteries, belong to one complex. Monastery 46, reachable via Monastery 47, has a courtyard with cells on three sides. Monastery 47 is a court flanked by a pillared veranda with a small cell and a long room behind it on the south, a covered colonnade on the west, and a pillared veranda on the north leading to an antechamber and shrine at the western end and at the back to a corridor with five cells.

Sāñcī has been listed among the UNESCO World Heritage Sites since 1989.

Cross-References

- ▶ Aśoka
- ▶ Jātaka
- ▶ Puṣyamitra Śuṅga
- ▶ Stūpa
- ▶ Vihāra

References

1. Cunningham A (1854) The Bhilsa topes or Buddhist monuments of Central India. Smith, Elder, London
2. Dehejia V (ed) (1966) Unseen presence: the Buddha and Sanchi. Marg, Bombay
3. Dehejia V (1992) Collective and popular bases of early Buddhist patronage: sacred monuments, 100 BC-AD 250. In: Miller BS (ed) The powers of art. Oxford University Press, Delhi, pp 35–45
4. Dehejia V (1997) Indian art. Phaidon, London
5. Maisey FC (1892) Sanchi and its remains: a full description of the ancient buildings, sculptures, and inscriptions. Reprint, Indological Book House, Delhi, 1972
6. Marshall JH (1936) A guide to Sanchi, 2nd edn. Manager of Publications, Government of India, Delhi
7. Marshall JH (1940) The monuments of Sāñchī. Probsthain, London
8. Mitra D (1971) Buddhist monuments. Sahitya Samsad, Calcutta

Sandha(ka)

▶ Homosexuality (Jainism)

Sandhi/Saṃdhi-nirmocana-Sūtra

▶ *Sandhinirmocana Sūtra*

Sandhinirmocana Sūtra

Mangala Ramchandra Chinchore
Department of Philosophy, Centre for Studies in Classical Indian Buddhist Philosophy and Culture, University of Pune, Pune, Maharashtra, India

Synonyms

Sandhi/Saṃdhi-nirmocana-Sūtra; *Scripture unlocking the mysteries*; *The sutra of the explanation of the profound and secrets meaning*

Definition

Mahāyāna Buddhist text, text of the *Sūtra* literature-form, *Abhidharma*-text, *Yogacara*-text.

Sandhi/Saṃdhi-nirmocana-Sūtra, is a *Mahāyāna* Buddhist text, and is written in the *Sūtra* literature-form. It consists of mixed-style, having both verse and prose. It was originally written in Sanskrit, which unfortunately is lost. Like many early *Mahāyāna-Sūtras*, it is very difficult to get the exact date of origin and name of author of the *Sandhinirmocana-Sūtra*. It is a general consensus that *Mahāyāna-Sūtras* were composed, perhaps, in the beginning of the first century, when earlier Buddhism was felt to be restrictive and internal controversies were attempted to be transcended by articulating such a new more accommodative framework. This new form attempted to reconcile two kinds of controversies – one, 18 sects within early Buddhism, and another, to combat the charges from external non-Buddhist opponents. It was an attempt to settle the incompatibilities due to expansion and adoption of new framework, by way of providing clarification and establishment of a new transformational format in consonance with the teachings of the Buddha. Hence, *Sūtra* is a transit literature form, which is attempting to connect early Buddhism with later Buddhism, traditionally known as *Hīnayāna* with *Mahāyāna*. On the one hand orthodoxy of traditional practitioners and on the other hand the need to conceptually philosophize are the constraints under which *Mahāyāna-Sūtras* seem to be composed. It is in this context that the present text also seems to be written.

Originally, it might have been composed, in first or second century, because it attempts to provide definitive explanations and systematic clarifications for contradictory statements from the earlier *Sūtras*. It attempts to develop a kind of Buddhist hermeneutic [1], transcending the apparent paradoxes, which had emerged in the then intellectual climate. On the one hand, there was a need to understand Buddha's thoughts formulated in the form of doctrines for common masses, and on the other, some strict practitioners of Buddhism stressed on a view that conceptual understanding is imaginary fabrication (Sk. *Prapañca*), and hence is ultimately void/meaningless (Sk. *Śūnya*). It is a *Yogācāra* text attempting to highlight the importance of *Yoga* essential to be practiced by all without exception and discrimination for developing virtues through the Perfection of Wisdom (Sk. *Prajñā-pāramitā*) [2]. Further, since Asaṅga (fourth century) has written a commentary on it, it is generally held that it cannot be later than Asaṅga.

Both the *Sandhinirmocana-Sūtra* and its *Bhāṣya* (commentary) by Asaṅga exist in Tibetan [3] and Chinese [4]. The scholars hold a view that the present form of its composition in which it is available in Tibetan and Chinese, seems to have been not earlier than the third century C.E. It is reported by the historians that this *Sūtra* was translated from Sanskrit into Chinese four times at different periods, though currently complete and reliable versions of its translation in Chinese by Xuanzang and in Tibetan by Woncheuk exist. Further, it is claimed that Tibetan translation is, perhaps, influenced by Chinese version of it. The *Sandhinirmocana-Sūtra* available in Chinese is popularly known as "the *Sutra* of the Explanation of the Profound Secrets" and is translated from Tibetan into English as "*Scripture Unlocking the Mysteries*" [5].

Etymologically "*Sandhi*" means "connection, conjoining, combining, union, reconciliation, transition." "*Nirmocana*" means "*nir* + $\sqrt{}$*muc*

= to loose, to make free, to liberate from, to abandon." It means liberating from conjunction, freedom from union, loosing the bonds of attachments, abandoning the ties of alliance. Thus, "*Sandhinirmocana*" connotes "making free from the bondage of worldly affairs (Sk. *Saṃsāra)*, which conjoins man with the world." It is a text that enables to untie the knots of conceptual confusions, or provides insights into the modes of release from the bonds of mundane world (*Saṃsāra*) to attain emancipation (Sk. *Nirvāṇa*). Secondarily, it may mean abandoning the ties of restrictive or delimited understanding of the teachings of the Buddha, emanating from the earlier (*Tripiṭakas*-scriptures) and new *Sūtra's* (*Mādhyamika* tradition of Buddhism). It emphasizes on practicing *Yoga* instead of mere speculative philosophization and conceptual understanding.

It is an attempt to present *Abhidharma* (that which leads one toward the highest teaching) tradition of early Buddhism in a novel manner, while people were facing dilemmas of understanding true nature of the Ultimate reality (Sk. *Paramārtha-sat*). It is a text which for the first time clearly asserts positively that the Ultimate reality exists, and is of the nature of pure consciousness (Sk. *Citta*). It advocates triple-tiered nature of reality, based on the functions of consciousness.

The conventional world, which one normally experiences, is dependent upon and determined by subjective sensations (Sk. *Vijñapti*), that is, existence of things/beings in the external world depends on the other/knower (Sk. *Paratantra*). But the nature of consciousness (Sk. *Vijñāna*/ *Citta*) is dependent on cognition, which is a function of consciousness. Both, things cognized in the world and the cognition of it, could be explained by the relation of interdependence (Sk. *Paratantra*).

Cognition of existence is explained with the help of concepts and ideas, which is imaginary construction or articulation of expression of thoughts (Sk. *Parikalpita*). However, behind experiential world (Sk. *Paratantra*), ultimate reality (Sk. *Paramārtha-sat*/*Pariniṣpanna*) in the pure form of consciousness (Sk. *Vijñāna*/*Citta*) exists, which can be realized by the full perfection of awakening (Sk. *Pariniṣpanna*). It is absolute and ideal reality having its own nature (Sk. *Sa-svabhava*).

Ultimate reality or absolute consciousness itself is not null and void (Sk. *Śūnya)*, but any expression to communicate its nature is empty (Sk. *Śūnya*) and is impossible to communicate (Sk. *Nirabhilapya*). Ultimate reality is beyond thoughts and imagination (Sk. *Vijñapti*), though it involves consciousness (Sk. *Vijñāna*). And there is a difference between content of consciousness (Sk. *Vijñapti*) and consciousness (Sk. *Vijñāna*/ *Citta*), the former is causative and the latter is nominative. Realization of the ultimate reality is free from conceptual construction – characterization and differentiation based on it. It is because of attachments on the conventional plane that names and characteristics are attached to things, objects, and entities. Conventional reality/imaginary world (Sk. *Saṁvṛtti*/*Vyavahāra-sat*) is based on experiential reality (Sk. *Paratantra*), though ultimately nothing exists having characteristics/ nature (*Svabhāva*) of its own. It is due to series of consciousness (Sk. *Citta-Santati*) or the act of being conscious (Sk. *Vijñapti*), apparently in the conventional world (Sk. *Vyavahāra-sat*), traces of attachment (Sk. *Vāsanās*) take the form of characteristics (Sk. *Kalpanā*). Only on the level of thoughts (*Parikalpita*), there is repetition of existence (Sk. *Punarbhava*) of continuity/transmigration of consciousness (Sk. *Santāna*), but not on the facts as everything is susceptible to change and hence is impermanent (Sk. *Anitya*). Ultimately, everything is realized to be empty (Sk. *Śūnya*), having no substantial existence (Sk. *Anātma*), however it is real conventionally (Sk. *Paratantra*).

It is essential first to start philosophical inquiry with the present status of having wrong opinions/ illusory ideas (Sk. *Parikalpita*), in order to arrive at correct comprehension of the ultimate reality (Sk. *Pariniṣpanna*), and then acquire clarity in understanding current trends of ideas and increase profundity. By denying all principles, beliefs, and characteristics, it is possible to cognize true nature of the ultimate reality. If one starts philosophical inquiry with nothingness (Sk. *Pariniṣpanna*) of which the true nature of the ultimate reality is, then one cannot understand anything. Hence, one gets confused or baffled. The nature of Ultimate Reality (Sk. *Paramārtha-sat/Tathatā*) is inconceivable and beyond expression, nonetheless it is to be experienced and realized by developing insight/wisdom (Sk. *Prajñā*) by oneself.

In the *Sandhinirmocana-Sūtra*, great *Bodhisattvas* question the Buddha about the nature of consciousness, the character of the ultimate reality, the stages of the *Bodhisattva-yāna*, and the embodiment of the *Tathāgata*. The Buddha responds with the clear voice of perfect realization, illuminating the ten steps (Sk. *Daśa-bhumis*) in meditative practices (Sk. *Samādhi-Yoga*) and views that eliminate obstacles in enlightenment (Sk. *Bodhi*) [6]. *Śūnyatā* is a perspective/point of view to look at reality (Sk. *Dṛṣṭi*) and by adopting it insightfully everybody has to overcome ones own illicit understanding or misconceptions by himself. By clear and exact comprehension of meaning, one can understand the true nature of reality.

Sandhinirmocana-Sūtra is divided into eight parts/sections/chapters (Sk. *Parivratas*), presented in the form of series of dialogues between the Buddha and various *Bodhisattvas*. During these dialogues, the Buddha attempts to clarify disputed meanings present in the early *Mahāyāna* and the early Buddhist schools, and ultimately emphasizes on the need to practice *Yoga* in the form of *Prajñā-pāramitā*.

Cross-References

▸ *Abhidharma (Theravāda)*
▸ *Anātman*
▸ Asaṅga
▸ *Bodhisattva*
▸ *Citta*
▸ *Dāsa*
▸ *Hīnayāna*
▸ *Mādhyamika*
▸ *Mahāyāna*
▸ *Mahāyāna Laṅkāvatāra Sūtra*
▸ *Nirvāṇa*
▸ *Paramārtha*
▸ *Prajñāpāramitā*
▸ *Saṃsāra*
▸ *Śūnyatā*
▸ *Tathāgata*
▸ *Tripiṭaka*
▸ *Vijñāna*
▸ Xuanzang (Hieun-Tsang)
▸ *Yogācāra*

References

1. Keenan JP (2000) The scripture on the explication of underlying meaning [translated from Chinese of Hsiian-Tsang (Taisho Volume 16, Number 676) into English]. Numata Center for Buddhist Translation and Research
2. Powers J (1995) Wisdom of Buddha: the Saṃdhinirmocana-Sūtra [translated from Tibetan into English]. Dharma, Berkeley
3. Thomas C (1999) Buddhist yoga: a comprehensive course [translated from Tibetan into English]. Shambhala, South Asia Editions
4. Warder AK (2000) Indian Buddhism, 3rd revised edn. Motilal Banarsidass, Delhi, pp 407–411
5. Sutra of the explanation of the profound and secrets meaning, PDF of the Sandhinirmocana-sutra in Tibetan
6. Sangharakshita MS (1987) A survey of Buddhism: its doctrines and methods through ages. Tharpa, London

Sangha

▸ Saṃgha

Saṅgha

▸ Saṃgha

Saṅgīti

▸ Buddhist Councils

Saṅgītipariyāyapada

▸ Dhammasaṅgaṇī

Sañjaya Belaṭṭhiputta

Mangala Ramchandra Chinchore
Department of Philosophy, Centre for Studies in Classical Indian Buddhist Philosophy and Culture, University of Pune, Pune, Maharashtra, India

Definition

Ájīvaka, holder of *Amarāvikkhapavāda*, one of the six well-known *śrāmaṇic* thinkers, learned, well-known ascetics and acclaimed philosophers, and senior contemporary of the Buddha.

Amarāvikkhapavādi Buddhas' Opponent

At the time of the Buddha, thinkers were haunted and obsessed by mental unrest. It was a search for peace, joy, and happiness undertaken by all. They realised the futility of speculations and extreme austerity of asceticism, and hence society was denouncing worldly affairs. People were disillusioned by philosophy, and lost in the fog of mystical religious practices. Enthusiasm was replaced by vulgarised quibbling and wrangling, with indecisive thoughts. Glorification of Gods and annoyed by injuring multitude of supernatural powers led mankind to disappointment and suffering. This situation culminated into making man sceptic and lost in confusion.

Obviously, unending questions and, without behaving morally, rejecting the social sanctions and faith was the mode adopted by some people. Amongst them, Sañjaya-Belaṭṭhiputta (/Bolāṭṭhiputra) is prominently known for his doctrine of *Amarāvikkhapavāda* (in Sanskrit *Vikṣapavāda*) (skepticism). He was a senior contemporary of the Buddha. He was from Rajagrha, the capital of Magadha.

Sañjaya-Belaṭṭhiputta was not only an upholder of the *Vikṣapa-vāda* (scepticism, which diverts mind from metaphysical theories), but also an advocate of *Aniścitatā-vāda* (uncertainty) [1]. In the *Brahmajāla-sutta* of the *Dīgha-Nikāya*, Sañjaya perhaps has denied the fourfold categorisation of understanding the world, namely, is, is not, neither is-is not, nor is-is not. When one does not have any definite and firm answer to anything, one prefers to be silent over everything. It is a kind of indeterminism and Agnosticism, leading toward pluralism. In the entire world including human life, there is uncertainty and complete chaos. He was sceptical about trans-world identity, God, and morality.

Nothing is absolutely good or bad, what one calls good becomes bad also. It is not only due to variation in time, place, context, or individual, but even simultaneously nothing can be held as good or bad essentially. Everything is contextual and uncertain. One is often caught in a hopeless and helpless situation, which cannot be controlled. Rather, one is a passive recipient of what happens in the life and the world at large. One cannot create new, nor can apriorily anticipate destruction. There are neither laws of nature operating exceptionlessly nor is human purpose able to plan one's own destiny with certainty, or even God to determine without discrimination at his will. Hence, it is better to take things as they happen and live with them passively.

No one can ascertain firmly answers to issues like existence of the other world (Sk. *Paraloka*), existence of God as a creator, sustainer, or destroyer, relation between actions and reward/punishment, etc. Rather, by dealing with such eternal metaphysical questions, one's mind gets diverted from actual facts of life. Sañjaya [2] denied giving answer to: Is world eternal/non-eternal, infinite/finite? Whether a perfect man continues to exist after death Is there any reward/punishment – retribution for one's own right/wrong deed? He preferred silence [3]. Instead of responding to and entangling ourselves in such unending futile questions, it is better to enjoy the present state of life in which one is placed. By finding out conclusive and convincing answers to such questions, one is lost in the jungle of ideas and loses peace and happiness, as there is no end to such discussion and reflection. That is why it is known as eternal unending questions (Pali-*Amarāvikkhepikās*).

Can one be assured that by giving alms, performing rituals, sacrificing things, or by making penance one can get happiness in the present life or in future, or can one guarantee that those who do wrong deeds are punished and suffer for what they do? Hence, everything that happens is unknown and unknowable from the point of view of establishing conclusive proof.

Similar questions were also put forth to the Buddha, but he remained silent. This was because, contrarily, the Buddha believed that although chance and contingency play a vital role in the happenings in the world or human life, there is a need to be moral. Life is not hopeless and helpless, rather one can plan rightly and follow proper modes of action to build moral character (Sk. *śīla*) and emancipate oneself (Sk. *Nirvāṇa*). There is a possibility to develop and hope for betterment in each one's life. Like a rationalist or a positivist, he was not interested in destroying the common man's psychological support derived from the concept of God, but that does not mean he advocated and upheld the metaphysical entity of God, or possibility of existence of the other world. Interdependence (Sk. *Pratītya-samutpada*) on the one hand opens the possibility of explaining pain and suffering in human life, and on the other hand the Eightfold path (Sk. *Aṣṭāṅgika-mārga*) articulates the possibility of its control. The former is substituting causal determinism by sequential order of explication of facts, which is a blow given by the Buddha to the indeterminism advocated by Sañjaya. But even on the account of the latter, purposiveness and intentionality is involved, which too is opposition to uncertainty upheld by Sañjaya. Thus, there is neither complete chaos and disorder, nor absolute/strict determinism. There is a possibility to bring in order and hope for peace in human life. Rather, even a bad person, if follows the path laid down by the Buddha, can become good, like Aṅgulimāla, and emancipate in this world itself. And this great sense of hope is important in human life given by the Buddha.

On the background of the collapse of morality and disintegration of social order, which Sañjaya upheld and attempted to promote as the nature of reality, contrarily Buddha provided the foundations of morality, accountability, and responsibility by his new world order (Pali- *Dhamma*). It is because of this reason perhaps, Mahā-moggallana and Sāriputta, who were previously disciples of Sañjaya, became, later on, well-known disciples of the Buddha [4].

Cross-References

- ▶ *Aṣṭāṅgamārga*
- ▶ *Dhamma*
- ▶ *Dīgha Nikāya*
- ▶ God (Buddhism)
- ▶ *Śīla*
- ▶ *Śramaṇa*
- ▶ *Nirvāṇa*
- ▶ *Pratītya Samutpāda*

References

1. Kasyapa BJ (ed) (1961) Dīgha-Nikāya. Pali Text Publication Board, Bihar Govt, Nalanda
2. Walsh M (1995) The long discourse of the Buddha: a translation of the Dīgha-Nikāya (1. *Brahmajāla-sutta*-pp 67–90 and 2. *Sāmaññaphala-sutta* – pp 91–109). Wisdom, Boston
3. Warder AK (2000) Indian Buddhism, 3rd edn. Motilal Banarsidass, Delhi, pp 38–41
4. Winternitz M (1993) Sāmaññaphala-sutta (i.e. the second *sutta*) of the *Dīgha-Nikāya*. History of Indian literature, vol II. Motilal Banarsidass, Delhi, pp 36–191

Sankrityayan, Rahul

K. T. S. Sarao
Department of Buddhist Studies, University of Delhi, Delhi, India

S

Definition

Indian scholar, linguist, traveller, nationalist, and author of more than 150 books. He is particularly known for his contribution to Tibetan Studies and

Electronic supplementary material: The online version of this chapter (doi:10.1007/978-94-007-1988-0_1879) contains supplementary material, which is available to authorized users.

Buddhism, especially his feat in bringing a large collection of manuscripts from Tibet, now housed in the Patna Museum.

Rahul Sankrityayan, often called *mahāpaṇḍita* (great scholar), was one of the most widely travelled scholars of India, who spent 45 years of his life on travel and away from home. He became a Buddhist monk and eventually moved towards Marxist Socialism. He was arrested and jailed for nearly 3 years for his anti-British writings and speeches.

Rahul Sankrityayan was born Kedarnath Pandey on 9 April 1893 to an Orthodox Hindu Bhūmihār-Brāhmaṇa family in Pandha village of Azamgarh district in Uttar Pradesh. He was the eldest of five brothers and one sister. As his mother died early, he was brought up by his grandmother. Though he received formal education only up to grade eight in his village *pāṭhaśālā* through the medium of Urdu language, Sankrityayan later learned and mastered many languages (as many as 34 according to his biographer Machwe). However, he mostly wrote in Hindi. He picked up his wanderlust from his maternal grandfather, Ram Sharan Pathak, who was an ex-soldier and had impressed young Kedarnath with his tales of adventure. He points out in his autobiography that reading a couplet of Ismael Meruthiin grade three Urdu-book (*Śair kar duniyā kī ghāfil zindgānī fir kahāṅ, zindagī gar kuchh rahī to naujavānī phir kahāṅ*) added fuel to this fire to wander. At age 9, he ran away from home in order to see the world. After having gone to Calcutta via Varanasi, he later returned and completed his middle school.

He lived as a Vaiṣṇava sañnyāsī from 1914 till 1930 and was known as *Damodar Svāmī*. Later, he took up the name *Rahul* after converting to Buddhism in 1930. Between 1921 and 1927, he participated in the freedom movement. As a result, he was arrested and spent some time in the prisons at Buxar and HazariBagh. Between the years 1936 and 1944, he actively participated in peasant movement and spent 29 months in jail (1940–42) for being a member of the Communist Party of India. Besides extensive travels within the Himalayas especially Ladakh and northern Himachal, he went to Tibet at least four times disguised as a Buddhist monk. He also travelled extensively in Sri Lanka, Soviet Union, Far East, Iran, Afghanistan, and Western Europe. His travels earned him the sobriquet as the originator "science of travel." During one of his trips to Tibet, this polymath managed (in the guise of a Buddhist monk) to travel to Tibet thrice, bringing back with him 1619 valuable manuscripts and *thankha* paintings preserved there employing 16 mules to bring these to India and translating many of them en route. A special section of the Patna Museum houses these manuscripts and paintings and is named after Sankrityayan.

Sankrityayan was married when very young and never came to know anything of his child-wife (though she is said to have been in the crowd that came to see him when he visited his village after 34 years). Although he did not have any formal education, in view of his knowledge and command over the subject, University of Leningrad appointed him Professor of Indology in 1937–1938 and again in 1947–1948. Accepting an invitation for teaching Buddhism at Leningrad University during his stay in Soviet Russia a second time, he met and got married to Ellena Narvertovna Kozerovskaya and had a son (Igor) with her. Ellena and Igor were denied exit visa by the Communist authority to accompany Sankrityayan to India when the latter completed his assignment. Later in India, Sankrityayan got married to Dr Kamalā (1920–2009) of Indo-Nepalese origin and with her had a daughter (Jayā Pathak) and a son (Professor Jeta Sankrityayan of North Bengal University). In the 1950s, he accepted a teaching job at a Sri Lankan University and was made a *Tripiṭakācāriya.* While in Sri Lanka, he suffered seriously from diabetes, high blood pressure, and a mild stroke. After returning to Darjeeling, he was struck by a second stroke in 1961 and lost his memory as a result. His wife took him to Russia in 1962 for treatment, but there was no improvement. He was brought back to Darjeeling where he breathed his last on 14 April 1963.

Sankrityayan was an Indologist, a multilingual linguist, a Marxist theoretician, and a creative writer of varied interest. One of his most famous books is *Volgā se Gaṅgā* in which historical elements are remarkably interwoven with fiction whereby he provides an account of the migration of Āryans from the steppes of Eurasia to the regions around Volga River and thence across the Hindu Kush into the India subcontinent. *Merī jīvan-yātrā*, an autobiography in five lengthy volumes, offers a captivating account of his life. His other important books, running into a total of about 50,000 pages, include *Baudh Darś an, Darshan Digdarshan, Ghumakkar Shastra, Ghumakkar Swami, Kanaila ki Katha, Kinnar desh mein, Lhasa ki or, Madhya Asia kā Itihās, Mahamanav Buddha, Manava Samaj, Mansik Gulami, Rgvedic Arya, Sāmyavād hī kyoṅ, Sūdkhor kī Maut, Tibbat mein Baudh Dharm, Tumhārī Kṣāyā, and Vaigyānik Bhautikvād.*

Born a Brāhmaṇa, Kedarnath Pandey's peripatetic life took him from being an orthodox Hindu saññyāsī to an Ārya Samājist proselytizer, to becoming a Buddhist monk and then a dedicated Marxist. He was drawn to the rationality of Buddhism while studying it as an Ārya Samājist proselytizer primarily with the aim of discrediting it but becoming a Buddhist monk in Sri Lanka and acquiring the name by which he became known. His visits to the Soviet Union converted his Congress socialism into fully fledged communism. Sankrityayan felt that despite being a rational modern system of thought that offers a progressive agenda and freedom from moribund customs, Buddhism did not exactly meet his expectations as it remained status-quoist in nature and was a *religion*, due to "belief in rebirth, yogic mysticism and some other views."

He wrote in very simple Hindi so that common readers may be able to take advantage of his writings. He was also aware of the limitations of Hindi literature and took pains to make up for this shortcoming (Fig. 1). He was awarded the Sahitya Akademi Award in 1958 for his book *Madhya Asia kāItihās* and the Padma Bhushan by the Government of India in 1963. The Government of India has constituted two awards in his honor, viz., *Rahul Sankrityayan National Award* for contribution to Hindi travel literature and *Mahāpanḍit Rāhul Sānkrityāyan Paryaṭan Puraṣkār* for contribution in the field of travelogue, discovery, and research in Hindi. In 1993, the Government of India honored

Sankrityayan, Rahul, Fig. 1 Commemorative Stamp on Rāhul Sankrityayan

him by issuing a commemorative stamp on him (Fig. 1).

References

1. Ahir DC (1993) Himalayan Buddhism, past and present: Mahapandit Rahul Sankrityayan centenary volume. Sri Satguru Publications, New Delhi
2. Gaeffke P (1978) Hindi literature in the twentieth century. Otto Harrassowitz, Wiesbaden
3. Machwe P (1978) Rahul Sankrityayan. Sahitya Akademi, New Delhi
4. Sankritayan R (1951–1967) Merījīvan-yātrā, 5 vols. ĀdhunikPustak Bhavan, Kalkattā (vol 1)/KitābMahal, Ilāhābād (vols 2–5)
5. Sankrityayan R (1970) Buddhist dialectics. In: Sankrityayan R et al (eds) Buddhism: the Marxist approach. People's Publishing House, New Delhi, pp 1–8
6. Sharma RS (1993) Rahul Sankrityayan and social change. In: Indian history congress, 1993
7. Sharma RS (2009) Rethinking India's past. Oxford University Press, New Delhi

Sannyāsī

► Śramaṇa

Santati

► Time (Buddhism)

S

Santhara

► *Sallekhanā* (Jainism)

Śānti Varnam

► Śāntideva

Śāntideva

Mangala Ramchandra Chinchore
Department of Philosophy, Centre for Studies in Classical Indian Buddhist Philosophy and Culture, University of Pune, Pune, Maharashtra, India

Synonyms

Bhusukū; Śānti Varnam; Shyiwa Lha; Zhi ba lha

Definition

Śāntideva was a Tantric-Buddhist master and the author of *Śīkṣā-samuccaya* and *Bodhicaryāvatāra.*

Śāntideva was born to King Kalyāṇavarman in the southern country of Saurāṣṭra (modern Gujarat) [1]. His father was King Kalyāṇa Varnam, and his given name was Śānti Varnam. A mythical-story is in vogue about his life. He had a great faith in the *Mahāyāna* teachings, great respect for his teachers, and he was diligent in his studies. He was always helpful to the king's ministers and to all the subjects. He was very compassionate to the poor, the sick, and the downtrodden, and used to help them by giving aid and protection. He also became very learned and skillful in all the arts and sciences.

During his youth, he met a wandering *Yogī*, who gave him the teachings of the extreme austerities to get the (*Tīkṣṇa Mañjuśrī Sādhanā*), and through this practice, he established a strong connection with the *Bodhisattva Mañjuśrī* and attained a high level of realization.

When Śāntideva's father passed away, the ministers of the kingdom wanted to make Śāntideva the next king, and they prepared for his enthronement ceremony. But before the ceremony, Śāntideva had a dream indicating that there is no use to become a king. So he left everything behind.

He went to the monastic university of Nālandā, where he became a monk under *Paṇḍita* Jayadeva, who gave him the name Śāntideva. Although directions were given, he studied and practiced on his own focusing on teachings of the Buddha and putting it into practice. He secretly composed two treatises, viz., the *Śīkṣā-samuccaya* [*Compendium of Trainings*] and the *Sūtra-samuccaya* [*Compendium of Sutras*] that consolidated the meaning of the *Piṭakas*. Although Śāntideva had these great qualities of realization and renunciation, he remained composed and silent in Nālandā, without doing anything outwardly. To the other students, he seemed to be the laziest person, so they called him *bhusukū*, [one who just eats, sleeps, and goes out to the toilet (*Bhu* comes from *bhukta*, which means eating. *Su* comes from *susta*, which means sleeping. And *kū* comes from *kuchiwa*, which means just walking)]. The contemporary students thought that he was a disgrace and liability to them, because everybody else was studying and debating, and giving teachings – busy in doing something and in contrast Śāntideva was doing nothing. They wanted to expel him, but they could not find an excuse, because he had done nothing wrong. If you do not do anything, you cannot do anything wrong! So he did not break any rules or do anything that was against the law. Since they could not just ask him to go away, they tried to find a vicious/cunning way to expel. Somebody formulated a new rule and made it mandatory to all the students to give a teaching. So that when his turn will come he will be exposed and will run away. They took the permission and requested the teachers to execute it. They planned and plotted it in such a way that his teacher will have to order him to teach, and then he will fail to teach. They invited the whole community around the university to come and listen to Śāntideva. They really wanted to make him run away!

Finally, when the time came for him to give the teaching, Śāntideva just appeared on the throne. No one saw him arrive or climb onto the thorny-seat deliberately prepared to make fun of him, and they could not find out how he got there. Then Śāntideva said, "What kind of teaching should I give? Something that has been given before or something which has never been given before?" Of course, everybody shouted, "Something new!" Śāntideva replied, "I have three modes of teachings, but I will not prefer to present before you the *Śīkṣā-samuccaya* (*Compendium of Trainings*), which is too long and you will be tired to know the details. So too I will not give the teaching in brief form, viz, *Sūtra-samuccaya* (*Compendium of Sūtras*), because you will not be able to digest it. Rather taking into consideration the ability of mixed audience, I will give you the *Bodhicaryāvatāra*, which is of middle length discourse."

Śāntideva then recited the *Bodhicaryāvatāra* from memory, and it is said that many people saw *Mañjuśrī* in the sky above his head as he recited the text. It is a legend that when Śāntideva reached the thirty fourth verse of the ninth chapter, which is said to be the most difficult part of the work, he and *Mañjuśrī* were lifted off the ground, and rose up higher and higher into the air until they disappeared. Afterward, everyone was very impressed! A few *Paṇḍitas* with extraordinary memory had written down notes, but when they tried to compare their notes, there were different opinions on what was said. According to the *Paṇḍitas* from Kāshmīra, the text had nine chapters and seven hundred stanzas. But a group of *Paṇḍitas* from central India thought it had ten chapters and one thousand stanzas. In addition, they did not know what Śāntideva meant by these two books, i.e., *Śīkṣā samuccaya* [*Compendium of Trainings*] and *Sūtra-samuccaya* [*Compendium of Sūtras*], which were merely referred to in the teaching. So they searched for Śāntideva all over India, and after quite some time, they found him at the Stūpa of Sri Dakṣiṇa, in the South. The Nālandā scholars went there and invited Śāntideva to come back to Nālandā and teach. He refused their proposal, but settled their differences and doubts about the work, viz., *Bodhicaryāvatāra*, saying that it has 10 chapters and 1,000 stanzas. Then he told them the location of the two other books. Śāntideva had written the texts on palm leaves and hidden them under the thatched straw-roof in his room. He gave them the reading transmission and explanations of these texts also.

The *Bodhicaryāvatāra* was written for all beings generally, but especially for the then present 500 Paṇḍitas of Nālandā, to show them the genuine path of a *Bodhisattva*. It is said that there were 108 commentaries written on the *Bodhicaryāvatāra* in India.

Śāntideva [2], composed three works, viz., first he wrote *Śīkṣā-samuccaya* [3] [*Compendium of Trainings*], which is an explanation in detail and/or elaboration of teaching of the Buddha, then *Sūtra-samuccaya* [4] [*Compendium of Sūtras*] which is citation of extracts in the form of *Sūtras* in brief from various (approximately 110) works, and finally *Bodhicaryāvatāra* [5], which is a middle length mode of preaching the doctrines. The *Sūtra-samuccaya* does not seem to be a separate work, but appears to be a brief commentary on his *Śīkṣā-samuccaya* only.

Śāntideva was, perhaps, interested in highlighting the importance of practice, rather than philosophical aspect of Buddhism [6] that is reflected in his works, viz., *Śīkṣā-samuccaya* and *Bodhicaryāvatāra.* According to all the philosophical traditions in general and Buddhism in particular, human birth is a rare opportunity to purify the *Śīla* (moral-character) by practicing the *Bodhisattva-yāna*. To live life as a human being is a golden chance to rise oneself to the status of *Bodhisattva* in this very life, provided one follows the Six-*Pāramitās*, viz., *Dāna* (charity), *Śīla* (moral-character), *Kṣānti* (peace and tranquility), *Vīrya* (brevity), *Dhyāna* (meditation), and *Prajñā* (insightful wisdom) [7]. By constant recollection of the three jewels, viz., Buddha (the exemplar), *Dhamma* (the way to follow), and *Saṁgha* (a group of true followers/practitioners), one can understand teaching of the Buddha, but practicing it in individual life insightfully alone can bring in integrity and perfection. Morality is not a matter of theoretical discussion on universal abstract principles, but it has something to do with performing certain actual practices – the ethical codes of conduct – in individual life.

A lay person can start with reverence and faith to the Buddha and *Bodhisattvas*, and slowly can progress with perseverance and consistency to get *Bodhi* (enlightenment). Nonetheless, enlightenment is not individual selfish goal, rather it is to be used for the benefit of those who are suffering in the society. In the *Mahāyāna* Buddhism, it is living life for the sake of others that is emphasized and hence use/application of the realization of truth is essential. Thus, *Bodhi* (enlightenment) does not become the final goal of life but actually living life selflessly for removing pain and suffering (*Duḥkha*) of others – all kinds of living creatures – in society is the significant purpose of life. And while doing this humane-duty, one has to find out creative ways and means skillfully [8] – either hidden in oneself or others – to overcome the problems of life. Obviously, various aspects of personality need to be developed, taking into consideration different problems faced contextually. In doing service to humanity, one has to minimally use his own endowed potentialities, viz., *Karūṇā* (compassion) and *Prajñā* (wisdom). By using *Karuṇā* (compassion) and *Prajñā* (wisdom) insightfully, one can follow the path of ideal human being (*Bodhisattva*); and gradually become a perfect person or an exemplar.

As compared to *Śīkṣā-samuccaya*, it seems *Bodhicaryāvatāra* is much popular among the Western scholars, perhaps, due to its theological/religious character; and having some apparent similarity with Christen devotion and faith [9]. It is because of this reason perhaps *Bodhicaryāvatāra* is translated into modern European languages like French, German, English, Italian, etc. Both the above-mentioned works are available in Tibetan and Chinese [10]. Śāntideva is dated in between Dharmapāla and Sri Harsa, i.e., approximately middle of the seventh century C.E.

May be due to the mystical story about life and works, Śāntideva was known as a Tantric-Buddhist [11]. He was followed and referred to later on by Dipaṅkar Śrijñāna alias Ātiṣa, especially his *Śīkṣā-samuccaya*, and held to be a great *Siddha* among the 84 *Siddhas* of *Vajrayāna* Buddhism [12].

Cross-References

▶ *Bodhi*
▶ *Bodhisattva*
▶ *Dhamma*
▶ Dipaṅkara Śrijñāna
▶ *Dhammacakkappavattana-sutta*
▶ *Mahāyāna*
▶ *Mañjuśrī*
▶ Nālandā
▶ *Pāramitās*
▶ *Piṭakas*
▶ *Prajñā*
▶ *Śīla*
▶ *Tantric Buddhism*

References

1. Chattopadyaya D (ed) (1997) Taranatha's history of Buddhism. Motilal Banarsidass, Delhi
2. Chattopadyaya D (ed) (1997) Taranatha's history of Buddhism. Motilal Banarsidass, Delhi
3. Vaidya PL (ed) (1961) Śīkṣā-samuccaya. The Mithila Institute, Darbhanga
4. Winternitz M (1993) History of Indian literature, vol II. Motilal Banarsidass, Delhi
5. Vaidya PL (ed) (1960) Bodhicaryávatára. The Mithila Institute, Darbhanga'
6. Warder AK (2000) Indian Buddhism, 3rd edn. Motilal Banarsidass, Delhi
7. Obermiller E (1999) Bu-Ston: the history of Buddhism in India and Tibet. Sri Sadguru Publications, Delhi
8. Winternitz M (1993) History of Indian literature, vol II. Motilal Banarsidass, Delhi
9. Nariman JK (1972) Literary history of Sanskrit Buddhism, 2nd edn. Motilal Banarsidass, Delhi
10. Sangharakshita (1987) A survey of Buddhism: its doctrines and methods through ages. Tharpa Publications, London
11. Keith D (1998) Buddhist masters of enchantment: the lives and legends of the Mahasiddhas. Inner Traditions, Rochester
12. Sankrityayana RB (1937) 84 Siddhas of Buddhism. Indian Press (in Hindi), Chaukhambha, Varanasi

Saptabhangī

► Syādvāda (Jainism)

Śāradvatīputra

► Sāriputta

Sāraṅganāth

► Sārnāth

Śāriputra

► Sāriputta

Sāriputta

K. T. S. Sarao
Department of Buddhist Studies, University of Delhi, Delhi, India

Synonyms

Śāliputra; Śāradvatīputra; Śāriputra; Sāriputta Thera; Sārisambhava; Śārisutta; Upatissa

Definition

Chief disciple of the Buddha.

Sāriputta (Sk: Śāriputra) was the chief disciple (*aggasāvaka*) of Gautama Buddha. He was born to brāhmaṇa parents called Vaṅganta and Rūpasāri. It was because of his mother's name that he came to be known as Sāriputta (Son of Sāri). His personal name was Upatissa, which he perhaps took from the village where he was born. Besides him, at least seven members of the family, including three younger brothers (Cunda, Upasena, and Revata), three sisters (Cālā, Upacālā, and Sisupālā), and a nephew (Uparevata), are known to have joined the Buddhist saṃgha. He was older than the Buddha and was born on the same day as Moggallāna. Both Sāriputta and Moggallāna belonged to rich families and were childhood friends, their families having maintained an unbroken friendship for seven generations. Once after having watched a mime play, the two friends realized that the world is impermanent and hence decided to give up the lives of householders. Initially, they became the disciples of Sañjaya Belaṭṭhiputta, one of the six famous heretical teachers of the Buddha's time. However, having found no satisfaction under him or many other teachers, they wandered unsatisfied all over India. Later, promising that whoever first found what they were looking for would tell the other, they parted company.

While wandering about in Rājagaha, Sāriputta met the Buddhist monk Assaji who converted him to Buddhism. He became a *sotāpanna* (entered the stream to enlightenment) after hearing from Assaji a stanza on *Paṭiccasamuppāda* (Sk: *pratītyasamutpāda, Dependent Arising*). Thereafter, he found Moggallāna and repeated before him the stanza that he heard from Assaji. Moggallāna also became a *sotāpanna*. Then the two decided to pay a visit to the Buddha at Veḷuvana. They also requested Sañjaya, their former teacher, to accompany them. But he refused. However, 250 disciples of Sañjaya joined them and were ordained by the Buddha. Except Sāriputta and Moggallāna, they all attained arahantship. Moggallāna attained arahantship on the seventh day after his ordination, but it was not till a fortnight later that Sāriputta became an arahant after hearing the Buddha preach the *Vedānapariggaha Sutta* to Dīghanakha at Rājagaha.

On the day that Sāriputta and Moggallāna were ordained, the Buddha declared them to be his chief disciples. Some monks were upset at the newcomers being shown such an honor. But the Buddha pointed out that they deserved this due to their dedication and resolve in their previous lives. The Buddha also pointed out that the other monks should follow the examples of these two ideal disciples. In the *Saccavibhaṅga Sutta* of the *Majjhima Nikāya*, the Buddha thus distinguishes them from the others by saying that "Sāriputta trains in the fruits of conversion, Moggallāna trains in the highest good. Sāriputta can teach and clarify the Four Noble Truths; Moggallāna, on the other hand, teaches by his psychic marvel." In the *Anupada Sutta* of the *Majjhima Nikāya*, the Buddha acclaims Sāriputta as a quintessential example of a perfect disciple who had perfected himself in virtue, concentration, perception, patience, and deliverance. However, at the same time, the Buddha did not hesitate in censuring Sāriputta whenever needed. For instance, once when the Buddha sent away some novices for making noise, Sāriputta was censured for having misunderstood the purpose behind such a move. According to one of the Jātaka stories, Sāriputta had a weakness for meal cakes (*piṭṭhakhajjaka*); however, on realizing that they tended to make him greedy, he took a vow not to eat them ever.

Sāriputta was declared by the Buddha as foremost among those who possessed wisdom and as inferior only to himself in wisdom. The Buddha would often just suggest a topic, and Sāriputta would give a detailed discourse on it, and hence win approval of the Buddha. There are several instances in the Pāli Tipiṭaka of Sāriputta instructing and preaching to monks on different topics. From time to time, these discourses supplemented the Buddha's own discourses. Consequently, he became known as *Dhammasenāpati* (commander of the Dhamma). Sāriputta's special proficiency was in the Abhidhamma, and the textual order of the Abhidhamma is said to have originated with him. Perhaps the best known of Sāriputta's discourses are the *Dasuttara Sutta* and the *Sangīti Sutta*. Mention is also made of special discourses the *Mahā Rāhulovāda Sutta* and the *Anāthapiṇḍikovāda Sutta* which were preached by Sāriputta to Rāhula and Anāthapiṇḍika, respectively. At the end of the discourse, Anāthapiṇḍika is said to have remarked that he had never heard such a sermon before.

Being the chief disciple, Sāriputta was entrusted by the Buddha with the task of looking after matters relating to the welfare of monks. The Buddha placed great faith in him and Moggallāna for the purposes of keeping the Buddhist Order pure. When Devadatta created a schism in the Buddhist Order and went away with 500 of the monks to Gayāsīsa, the Buddha entrusted the task to Sāriputta and Moggallāna of winning those monks back. They did so successfully. It was quite usual for Sāriputta and Moggallāna to travel together at the head of the monks. When Rāhula, the Buddha's son, was ordained, Sāriputta was his preceptor and Moggallāna his teacher. Both Moggallāna and Sāriputta not only deeply cared about each other but also had great mutual admiration. Sāriputta's verses (nos. 1179–1181) in praise of Moggallāna and Moggallāna's in praise of Sāriputta (nos. 1176–1778) in the *Theragāthā* are a good example of their respect and admiration for each other. Their love for the Buddha was their strongest bond, and whenever they were away from him, they were able to converse with him through extrasensory means.

He was a scrupulous follower of the discipline rules laid down by the Buddha. Thus, a rule had been laid down that forbade the eating of garlic by monks, and when Sāriputta was afflicted by an illness and knew that by eating garlic he could be cured; even then he did not violate the rule till permission was given by the Buddha for him to do so. The *Dhammapada Commentary* describes how, at the monastery where Sāriputta lived, he often took round of the whole building, arranging things, cleaning and sweeping the un-swept areas, and filling up empty pots with water, etc. Despite this there were occasions when he was criticized by other monks. For instance, in a story related in the *Dhammapada Commentary*, Sāriputta was once charged with greed and the Buddha had to personally explain to the monks that Sāriputta was innocent. It was Sāriputta's habit to regularly visit sick monks. Moreover, Sāriputta was so enthusiastic in encouraging and recognizing merit in fellow monks that he once went around lavishing praise on Devadatta for his psychic (*iddhi*) powers, which made it hard for him when subsequently he had to declare, at the behest of the saṃgha, Devadatta's wickedness.

Sāriputtā's compassion for the poor and his eagerness to help them are the subject-matter of several incidents mentioned in the Pāli Tipiṭaka. Sāriputta was also known for the possession of boundless patience. This is testified by a story related in the *Dhammapada Commentary* in which a brāhmaṇa struck him on the head, to test his patience, as he entered a town for alms. Another quality for which Sāriputta was known was his ever willingness to learn from others, however lowly. Sāriputta is identified with various characters in as many as 73 Jātakas. While Śāriputta is depicted consistently positively in the Theravādin texts, his portrayal in some of the Mahāyāna texts is not so flattering. For instance, in the *Vimalakīrtinirdeśa Sūtra*, Śāriputra is portrayed as someone who was not able to comprehend the Mahāyāna doctrines easily delivered by Vimalakīrti and others, and is either reprimanded or overpowered in debate by a number of discussants.

According to the Dhammapada Commentary, when Sāriputta once went to his native village to visit his mother, she abused both him and his companions profusely. She was completely against the Buddha as all her children had joined the Order and left her desolate in spite of the vast wealth which lay her house. However, shortly before he died, Sāriputta preached to her, and she became a *sotāpanna*. Sāriputta's death took place a few months before the Buddha and 2 weeks before Moggallāna on the full moon day of the month of Kattikā. The *Saṃyutta Nikāya* records that he died at Nālagāmaka, his native village where his body was cremated. Cunda wrapped Sāriputta's relics in the latter's water-strainer and took them to Sāvatthī with his begging bowl and outer robe. Xuanzang saw the stūpa erected over the relics of Sāriputta in the town of Kālapināka.

Cross-References

- ▶ Abhidhamma Piṭaka
- ▶ Anāthapiṇḍika
- ▶ Devadatta
- ▶ Iddhi
- ▶ Jātaka
- ▶ Mahāyāna
- ▶ Rāhula
- ▶ Rājagaha (Pāli)
- ▶ Saṃyutta Nikāya
- ▶ Sāvatthī
- ▶ Sotāpanna
- ▶ Theravāda
- ▶ Tipiṭaka
- ▶ Vimalakīrti
- ▶ Vimalakīrti-Nirdeśa-Sūtra
- ▶ Xuanzang (Hieun-Tsang)

References

1. Fausböll V (ed) (1977–1897) The Jātaka, 6 vols. Luzac, London
2. Feer ML (ed) (1884–1889) The Saṃyutta Nikāya, 5 vols. Pali Text Society, London
3. Hecker H (1994) Maha-Moggallana. Buddhist Publication Society, Kandy
4. Li R (trans) (1996) The great Tang dynasty record of the western regions. Numata Center for Buddhist Translation and Research, Berkeley
5. Ñyānaponika T, Hecker H (2003) Great disciples of the Buddha: their lives, their works, their legacy. Wisdom, Boston
6. Ñyānaponika T (1966) Sāriputta: the marshall of the Dhamma. Buddhist Publications Society No. 90/92, Kandy
7. Norman HC (ed) (1906) The commentary on the Dhammapada, 4 vols. Pali Text Society, London
8. Olderberg H (ed) (1879–1883) The Vinaya Piṭakaṃ, 5 vols. Pali Text Society, London
9. Oldenberg H, Pischel R (eds) (1990) The Thera- and Theīgāthā (with appendices by K.R. Norman & L. Alsdorf), 2nd edn. Pali Text Society, Oxford
10. Thich H-V (1989) A critical study of the life and works of Sāriputta Thera. Linh Son Research Institute, Vietnam
11. Trenckner V, Chalmers R (eds) (1888–1896) The Majjhima Nikāya, 3 vols. Pali Text Society, London

Sāriputta Thera

▶ Sāriputta

Sārisambhava

▶ Sāriputta

Śārisutta

► Sāriputta

Sārnāth

Arvind Kumar Singh
Department of Buddhist Studies, Faculty of Arts, University of Delhi, Delhi, India
School of Buddhist Studies and Civilization, Gautam Buddha University, Greater Noida, UP, India

Synonyms

Dharmachakrajinavihāra; Isipatana; Khema-uyyāna; Migadāya; Sadharmachakra Prāvartana Mahāvihāra; Sāraṅganāth; Silun or Silulin

Definition

Sārnāth (Mrigadāva, Migadāya, Rishipattana, Isipatana) is the *Deer Park* where Siddhārtha Gautama delivered his first sermon called *The Turning of the Wheel of the Dhamma* (*Dhammacakkappavattana*) which resulted into the birth of Buddhism [1], and Buddhist *Saṃgha* was founded by the Buddha with *Pañcavaggiyas*, yassa, and others.

Introduction

In Sārnāth, being the spot of *Dharmachakra Prāvartana*, a number of temples and monasteries had been constructed since the age of the Buddha [2]. The name is applied to an extensive group of Buddhist ruins situated near Vārānasī (Banārasa) district of Uttara Pradesh in India. The name Sārnāth probably initially associated with Deer Park but later on associated with Śaiva temple called to the southeast of the *Dhammekha Stūpa*. The place seems to have been sacred and the resort of ascetics from very ancient times, even before the emergence of the Buddha. Sārnāth enjoys a high position in the Buddhist world and is one of the four great places named by Buddha at the time of his death in the *Mahaparinibbāna Sutta* ([3], Vol. ii, p. 141). The seed of the *Saṃgha* was also sown here with the conversion of Yasa and his 54 friends [4].

Origin of the Names

Sārnāth represents the site of the ancient Ṛṣipatana or Mrigadāva (variantly Mrigdāya). The first name owes its origin to the fall (*Patana*) of the bodies of 500 *Pratyeka-Buddhas* (*Ṛṣis*) at this place after their attainment of *Nibbāna* (*isayo ettha nipatanti uppatanti cāti-Isipatanaṃ*) [5], while the latter is derived from the legend that the king of Varanasi, moved by the spirit of self-sacrifice of *Bodhisattva*, born as a dear named *Nyāgrodha-miga* (Banyan Deer), granted security to the herds of deer to roam freely in the wood of Sārnāth ([6], Vol. i, p. 145f). Isipatana *Migadāya*, associated with Sārnāth, has been described as the scene of *Nandiyavatthu* [7]. *Mrigadāva* meaning "deer park" is the place where holy men (Pāli: *Isi*, Sanskrit: *Ṛṣi*) fell to earth. Now the question that calls for solution is about "*Migadāya*" and "*Mrigadāva*" where "*Dāya*" means gift and forest but in Childer's *Pāli Dictionary*, it was used in the sense of forest. No scholar has raised any objection. So, we inclined to accept that it was *Mrigadāva*. Buddhaghoṣa in his commentary on *Mahāpadāna Sutta* says that it was *Isipatana Migadāya* that came to be called *Dharmachakra Prāvartana* [7]. The French scholar Senart does not admit that the name Isipatana comes from Isipatana. He says that besides this name, two other names of the place are known, viz., *Ṛṣipatana* and *Ṛṣivadana*. According to the *Mahāvastu*, this place is also known as *Ṛṣivadana* and also occurs in the *Gāthās* of the *Lalitavistāra*. It-sing and other Chinese writers have used the word "*Silun*" or "*Silulin*" to translate the word "*Migadāya*" which means "the land given to the deer" [7].

No antiquarian, whether Foreign or Indian, has yet properly dealt with the age and origin of the modern name of Sārnāth. During the sixth century B.C.E., it was called *Mrigadāva*, and *Pāli Literature* bears the testimony to this fact. It had also been known by this name during the time of Aśoka and Kaṇiṣka as well as at the time of the pilgrimage of Faxiang and Xuanzang. When this place was devastated by the Mohammedans, the temple of the Sāraṅganāth was not in existence and most probably built here in consequence of the same movement which led to the establishment of a holy place at Bodhagayā. The meaning of Sāraṅganāth is "the lord of deer." Hence, it seems that the Hindus have been worshipping the Buddha as Mahādeva Sāraṅganāth [7]. Sārnāth, according to Alexander Cunningham, is a contraction of Sāraṅganāth [8]. Owing to the sanctity thus attached to it, the place continued to be a leading center of Buddhism till the last days of the faith in northern India, under such names as Dharmachakra Vihāra, Saddharmachakra Vihāra, and Saddharmachakra-pravartana Vihāra.

According to the *Pāli Aṭṭhakathās*, in the past, Isipatana was known by the same name at the time of Phussa Buddha, Dhammadassī, and Kassapa, who were born here. But more often, Isipatana was known by different names at the time of other different Buddhas like in Vipassī's time known as Khema-uyyāna. It is the custom for all Buddhas to go through the air to Isipatana to preach their first sermon [5].

Depiction in Buddhist Literature

The Buddha after attaining the Bodhi, he left Uruvelā and traveled to Isipatana to join and teach *Pañcavaggiya Bhikkhus*, who left him in the middle when he gave austere penances and came here. The Buddha was of the view that they were able to understand his *Dhamma* quickly. It was here that he preached his first sermon, the *Dhammacakkappavattana Sutta*, on the full moon day of *Āsālha* ([9], Vol. i, p. 10f). According to commentaries on Buddhist literature, it is believed that all the Buddhas preached their first sermon at the *Migadāya* in Isipatana; it is one of the four *avijahitatthānāni* (unchanging spots).

Several other incidents connected with the Buddha, besides the preaching of the first sermon, are mentioned as having taken place in Isipatana. The Buddhist *Saṃgha* was originated here after the conversion of Yassa and his followers into it ([9], Vol. i, p. 15f), the rule which prohibits the use of sandals made of talipot leaves ([9], Vol. i, p. 189), the rules forbidding the use of certain kinds of flesh, including human flesh ([9], Vol. i, p. 216ff), and twice Māra visited him ([10], Vol. i, p. 105f). Apart from *Dhammacakkappavattana Sutta*, several other *Suttas* were preached by the Buddha while staying at Isipatana which are the *Pañca Sutta* ([10], Vol. iii, p. 66f), the *Rathakāra* or *Pacetana Sutta* ([11], Vol. i, p. 110f), the two *Pāsa Suttas* ([10], Vol. i, p. 105f), the *Samaya Sutta* ([11], Vol. iii, p. 320ff), the *Katuviya Sutta* ([11], Vol. i, p. 279f.), a discourse on the *Metteyyapañha of the Parāyana* ([11], Vol. iii, p. 399f), and the *Dhammadinna Sutta* ([10], Vol. v, p. 406f). According to Pāli Literature, it is evident that some of the prominent *Bhikkhus* had conversations at Isipatana from time to time, viz., between Sāriputta and Mahākotthita ([10], Vol. ii, p. 112f, Vol. iii, p. 167f, Vol. iv, pp. 162f, 384ff) and one between Mahākotthita and Citta-Hatthisāriputta ([11], Vol. iii, p. 392f), and another discourse helps Channa in his difficulties ([10], Vol. iii, p. 132f).

According to the *Mahāvaṃsa*, there was a large community of monks at Isipatana in the second century B.C.E. which is corroborated by the description found in the *Mahāvaṃsa* that 12,000 monks under Dhammasena from Isipatana went to Sri Lanka at the foundation ceremony of the *Mahāthūpa* in Anurādhapura ([12], Vol. xxix, p. 31). Xuanzang [8] found, at Isipatana, 1,500 monks studying the Hīnayāna. The *Divyāvadāna* mentions Aśoka as intimating to Upagupta his desire to visit the places connected with the Buddha's activities and to erect *thūpas* there, and his visit is confirmed by Aśoka's Rock Edict (No. viii).

History of Sārnāth

According to V. A. Smith, "The history of Indian sculpture from Aśoka to the Mahommedan conquest might also illustrated with fair completeness from the finds of Sārnāth alone". The history of Sārnāth begins from the Pāli sources which are indicated by the ruins of monuments, and inscriptions found here attest the rule of Aśoka, the Suugas, the Guptas, and later kings [7]. King Aśoka visited Sārnāth in 249 B.C.E. and erected several monuments to mark his pilgrimage, notably, the *Dhamek Stūpa*, *Dharmarājika Stūpa*, and the Aśokan pillar surmounted by the famous Lion Capital, which is now the crest of India. Archeological excavations have brought to light about a dozen carved railing pillars ascribable to the Sunga period. An inscription of King Aśvaghosa, written on the pillar of Aśoka at Sārnāth, indicates that toward the beginning of first century C.E., he exercised control over Sārnāth [7]. During the reign of King Kaṇiṣka (78 C.E.), Sārnāth was a center of religious activity, and the famous colossal *Bodhisattva* image with a large parasol was installed by the Bhikkhu Bala. Though the Gupta kings did not do anything directly tending to the improvement of this place, yet there is no doubt that some of the architectural improvements were affected during their rule [7]. During the Gupta period (fourth to sixth century C.E.), the *Dhamek Stūpa* was encased with carved stones, the *Mūlagaṅdhakuṭi* main shrine was enlarged, and the famous Preaching Buddha image, a gift of King Kumāragupta, was added [13].

In 520 C.E., Sārnāth had its share of destruction during the invasion of the Huns under Mihirakula. But after the Huns were defeated, Sārnāth again flourished under the Buddhist king, Harṣavardhana (606–647 C.E.), and continued to be a living shrine under the Pāla kings (eighth to twelfth century C.E.). The reign of Harṣavardhana must have initiated fresh religious activity and restorations of the earlier building at Sārnāth. Xuanzang visited Sārnāth during the time and left a vivid description of it. The last known patron of Sārnāth was Queen Kumāradevi, wife of King Govindachandra Gahadwala (1114–1154 C.E.) who built *Dhammacakka Jina Vihāra* at Sārnāth, the ruins of which were exposed during excavations in the early twentieth century. For how long after Xuanzang's visit Sārnāth continued to flourish is not definitely known, but the evidence of monuments and inscriptions proves that it was still thriving at least in the twelfth century C.E. and probably owed its downfall to Qutbuddin Aibak, who devastated Benares in 1194 C.E. [14]. Things took a turn for the worse when Muslim hordes overran India and started their trail of destruction. After the diaspora of the *Saṃgha* in India, Sārnāth became deserted and was forgotten for about 600 years [13].

Discovery of Sārnāth

In 1794, Sārnāth came to the notice of the world under tragic circumstances. Jagat Singh, Dewan of Raja Chet Singh of Benares, dismantled the famous *Dhammarājika Stūpa* to collect bricks and stones for building a market [7]. A stone box containing green marble casket with human relics, probably of the Buddha, was found which was thrown into Gaṅgā River by Jagat Singh. So, they were lost forever. This act of vandalism would have gone unnoticed. But a report was published by Jonathan Duncan in *Asiatic Researches* about discovery of Sārnāth due to which in 1815, Mackenzie began explorations and discovered some more sculptures. In 1835–1836, Cunningham carried out excavations and recovered over 40 sculptures and carved stones. Another tragedy struck when they were carted away in his absence together with 60 cartloads of stones from the shrines as construction material for two bridges and some buildings in Benares [13]. Further excavations were continued on and off from 1851 to 1922, which exposed the *Dhamek Stūpa*, the *Dhammarājika Stūpa*, *Mūlagaṅdhakuṭi*, *Aśokan Pillar*, and the ruins of several monasteries [14].

Objects of Worship at Sārnāth

Chaukhandi: It is an ancient *stūpa* which commemorates the spot where the Buddha met the *Pancavaggiya Bhikkhus*, dating back to fifth century B.C.E., and later enhanced by the addition of an octagonal tower constructed to commemorate the visit of Mughal King Humāyun to Sārnāth in 1588.

Dhamek Stūpa: According to Cunningham, this is remains of an earlier *Mauryan Stūpa*, probably raised by Aśoka on his visit to Sārnāth. During the Gupta period, the lower portion was encased in stone, having beautiful carvings all round. No bodily relics were found inside this *stūpa*, but a slab with Buddha's creed, "ye dhamma hetuppabhava, etc." [4] was discovered. According to an inscription of the Pāla king Mahipāla I (1026 C.E.), its original name was *Dhammacakka Stūpa*, and on the basis of this, the Archeological Survey of India claims that this spot marks the site of the first sermon [13].

Dhammarājika Stūpa: The ruins of the *Dharmarājika Stūpa* are a short distance north of the *Dhamek Stūpa* and consist of a circular base of what remained after the wanton act of destruction by Jagat Singh. The original *stūpa* built by King Aśoka was enlarged twice during the Gupta period [8]. The *Dhammarājika Stūpa* was built by Aśoka to enshrine the bodily relics of the Buddha at the time of his redistributing the relics from the seven original *stūpa*s and enshrining them in a number of other *stūpas* at different places. However, some scholars are of the opinion that the *Dhammarājika Stūpa* marks the site of the first sermon [4].

Mūlagandhakuṭi: North of the *Dhammarājika Stūpa* are the ruins of it where the Buddha spent the first rains retreat. According to the Dhammapada Commentary, it was donated by the rich man Nandiya, and as soon as the Buddha accepted the gift, a celestial mansion arose in Tavatimsa heaven awaiting its owner, Nandiya – the area between the ruins of the main shrine and believed to be the site of the *Cankamana*, the promenade where the Buddha did his walking meditation which is supported by the discovery of the famous colossal *Bodhisattva* image installed at this site by Bhikkhu Bala [7]. Another modern *Mūlagandhakuṭi* was built by Mahābodhi Society where enshrined certain Buddhist relics discovered at Taxilā, Nāgārjunikoṇḍa, and Mirpur-khās in Sindh [1].

Aśokan Pillar: It is situated to the west of *Mūlagandhakuṭi* under a flat roof and enclosed by railings and surmounted by the famous Lion Capital kept at Sārnāth Museum. On the pillar is an inscription called Schism Edict, and it is believed that Aśoka issued this to promote harmony among the various Buddhist sects.

Pañcāyatana: To the east of the *Dhammarājika Stūpa* is a sunken shrine under a concrete platform made of terra-cotta bricks and modeled to resemble one of the four square temples of the Gupta period called "*Pañcāyatana*" believed to be the place *Dhammacakkappavattana*.

Lion Capital: It is the most magnificent sculpture of Mauryan art, which once crowned the Aśokan Pillar at Deer Park. The abacus has a *Dhammacakka* wheel and four animal, i.e., bull, elephant, horse, and lion, representing four auspicious signs of the Buddha. The four lions represent the roar of the Buddha in the four directions. The Lion Capital is the crest of India and the *Dhammacakka* wheel is the emblem of its national flag [2].

Colossal Bodhisatta Image: This colossal standing image is of red sandstone donated by the Bhikkhu Bala during the reign of King Kanishka and represents the best tradition of Mathurā art.

Preaching Buddha Image: The seated Buddha image, in *Dhammacakka Mudrā* or *Preaching Posture*, is one of the magnificent creations of Gupta art. This famous sculpture was a gift of King Kumāragupta.

Sārnāth School of Buddhist Art

With the advent of the Kushāna Dynasty in north India, Buddhism witnessed a new phase of religious and artistic activities. Though Mathurā was the center of this renaissance, Sārnāth also flourished. The colossal image of *Bodhisattva* was one of the master pieces of this period. The ancient relics discovered at Sārnāth serve as an ideal school and excellent examples of the various styles of art of ancient India [7]. Buddhist art reflects very faithfully all the important aspects of Buddhism. Sārnath became a prominent center of Buddhist Art during the Gupta period which marks the golden era of Indian Art. The main centers of Buddhist art during this period were Mathurā, Sārnāth, and Nālandā. The Buddhist images of Mathurā and Sārnāth are some of the best specimens of Indian art, never equaled by any art creations of later period. Sārnāth sculpture used cream-colored sandstone capable of high levels of detail and finish. Speaking of Sārnāth style, Sārnāth Buddha image is quite possibly the fifth century Chunār sandstone image of the seated Buddha in *Dharmachakra Mudrā*. Sārnāth style was active from about 300–700 C.E. It is believed that Xuanzang must have visited Sārnāth and seen the seated Buddha, the purest incarnation of the Gupta ideal in Art [1]. Overall, the Buddha image developed into a proportional, harmonious, and refined figure during the Gupta dynasty. This classical figure had such visual appeal that it influenced the art of many other countries.

Cross-References

▶ Aśoka
▶ Banaras (Buddhism)
▶ *Bodhi Tree*
▶ Buddhaghosa
▶ Buddhist Art
▶ Faxian (337–422 C.E.)
▶ *Jātaka*
▶ *Saṃgha*
▶ Xuanzang (Hieun-Tsang)

References

1. Bapat PV (1987) 2500 years of Buddhism, Reprint. Publication Division, Delhi, 1956
2. Ahir DC (1986) Buddhist shrines in India. B. R. Publishing Corporation, Delhi
3. Rhys Davids TW, Rhys Davids CAF (eds) (1899, 1910 & 1957) Dīgha Nikāya (the dialogues of the Buddha), vols 3. PTS, London
4. Mitra D (1971) Buddhist monuments. Sahitya Sansad, Calcutta
5. http://www.palikanon.com/english/pali_names/i_/isipatana.htm
6. Fausböll V (ed) (1877–1897) The Jātakas, vol I. Trubner, London
7. Bhattacharya BC (1924) The history of Sārnāth or the Cradle of Buddhism. Pilgrims Publishing, Varanasi
8. Beal S (2008) Buddhist records of the Western world, Reprint. Low Price Publication, Delhi
9. Oldenberg H (ed) (1879–1883) The Vinaya Piṭaka, 5 vols. Williams and Norgate (PTS), London
10. Freer ML (ed) (1884–1898) The Saṃyutta Nikāya, vols 3. PTS, London
11. Morris R, Hardy E (eds) (1885–1900) The Aṅguttara Nikāya, vol IV. PTS, London
12. Gieger W (tr) (1908 & 1912) The Mahāvaṃsa. PTS, London
13. Chan KS (2001) Buddhist pilgrimage. Buddha Dhamma Education Association, Malaysia
14. Annual reports on Sārnāth, 1906–1907, p 68; 1907–1908, p 43; 1914–1915, p 97; 1919–1920, p 26; 1921–1922, p 42 of Archaeological Survey of India, Government of India

Sarvabījaka

▶ Ālaya-vijñāna

Sarvajñatā, Sabbaññutā (Pali)

▶ Omniscience

Sarvāstivāda

Charles Willemen
International Buddhist College, Songkhla, Thailand

Definition

Sarvāstivāda is a Buddhist school, "claiming (°*vāda*) that everything (*sarvam*) exists (*asti*)." Its adherents split from the main Sthaviravāda trunk during Aśoka's council, ca. 244 B.C.

Because a very considerable part of the primary literature only exists in the Chinese language, and because the Sarvāstivādins of

Kaśmīra are traditionally seen as representative of all Sarvāstivādins, quite some confusion has existed about the question: Who are the Sarvāstivādins? Authors such as Paramārtha (499–569 A.D.), who probably is himself responsible for the text of the so-called *Samayabhedoparacanacakra*, Taishō ed.2033, attributing the text to Vasumitra of the Sarvāstivāda synod of ca. 170 A.D., lists Sarvāstivāda and Sautrāntika separately, giving the impression that these may be two different schools, *nikāyas*. Recently Sanskrit *vinaya* texts and other texts of Sarvāstivādins, based on Central Asian manuscripts from Turpan, have been published. In Gilgit, Sanskrit texts have been found. Mūlasarvāstivāda literature exists in Sanskrit (e.g., *Udānavarga*), in Tibetan (e.g., *Vinaya*), and in Chinese.

History

During the reign of Aśoka (ca. 264–227 B.C.) a Sthaviravāda synod was held in Pāṭaliputra, presided over by Maudgalyāyana. The Vātsīputrīya Pudgalavādins, Personalists, had already split from the main Sthaviravāda trunk, ca. 280 B.C. [2]. Aśoka's synod resulted in a split between Sarvāstivādins and Vibhajyavādins, who were declared "orthodox." Sarvāstivādins had new views. Sarvāstivādins then spread along the Ganges to the Gulf of Bengal, but mainly West to Mathurā and to the Gandharan cultural area. Upagupta, one of the patriarchs, is linked with Mathurā and with a long *vinaya*. Madhyāntika is said to have taken Buddhism to *Jibin* (northwestern Indian cultural area, i.e., mainly Gandhāra, but also Bactria, and from ca. 200 A.D. on also Kaśmīra) in the time of Aśoka. He is also linked with Mathurā. So, Sarvāstivādins with an ancient long *vinaya* were in the Gandharan cultural area (Uḍḍiyāna, Swat Valley; Gandhāra; Bactria, West of the Khyber Pass) before the arrival of the Kuṣāṇas. A Sarvāstivāda synod of traditionally 500 arhats was held in Kaśmīra ca. 170 A.D., a new cultural center. The Kuṣāṇa king Kaniṣka agreed. They revised existing Gandharan texts and sometimes added new compositions. They used Sanskrit and established a new "orthodoxy" in Kaśmīra. The *vinaya* was abbreviated to ten recitations, called *Daśabhāṇavāra*. Many stories (*avadāna, jātaka*) were left out, but the rules were not changed [8]. A basic Gandharan *abhidharma* text, the *Aṣṭagrantha*, was rewritten in Sanskrit and renamed *Jñānaprasthāna*. Six more texts were established, forming an *Abhidharmapiṭaka* of seven texts, said to be proclaimed by the Buddha himself, *Buddhabhāṣita* [6]. The traditional *Aṣṭagrantha* had its commentaries, *Vibhāṣās* [7]. So, the revised text needed a new commentary, the *Mahāvibhāṣā*, ca. 200 A.D. The new Sanskrit Kāśmīra "orthodoxy" was ever since that time also known as Vaibhāṣika. The traditional western Sarvāstivādins did not immediately adopt the new "orthodoxy." They kept believing that only the *sūtras* were Buddha's word. The term Sautrāntika just makes sense as opposed to a *Buddhabhāṣita Abhidharmapiṭaka*. Kumāralāta, author of the *Kalpanāmaṇḍitikā*, Taishō ed.201, is the reputed first *ācārya*, master of Sautrāntikas (second century A.D.) [14]. He is mentioned in Dharmatrāta's *Udāna* (Taishō ed.212), the sixth member (*aṅga*) of a *Kṣudrakapiṭaka*. He is known as a Dārṣṭāntika and lived ca. 150 A.D. The old long *vinaya* with its numerous stories (*avadāna, dṛṣṭānta*) lived on. Some now believe that the term Dārṣṭāntika applies to the western Sarvāstivādins who held on to the long *vinaya*. Some Sautrāntikas may have adopted the "modern" brief *vinaya* from Kaśmīra. The western Sarvāstivādins gradually adapted to the new "orthodoxy," as is seen in the commentaries on the *Aṣṭagrantha* and in the commentaries on the Bactrian *Abhidharmahṛdaya* [16]. This last text, a systematic explanation on how to become an arhat, was composed by Dharmaśreṣthin (often wrongly called Dharmaśrī), probably first century B.C [9]. It is the oldest systematic abhidharmic yoga manual. The *Abhidharmakośabhāṣya* [13] of Vasubandhu (ca. 350–430) is, via the *Miś rakābhidharmahṛdaya* (early fourth century), an enlarged *Abhidharmahṛdaya*. This work of the Gandharan Vasubandhu provoked the anger of Saṅghabhadra in Kaśmīra [5]. Śrīlāta, a teacher of Vasubandhu but not a direct disciple of Kumāralāta, was also criticized. But as the westerners became ever more like the "orthodoxy," between 650 and 700 A.D., that is, between the presence in India of Xuanzang and of Yijing, the term Mūla (basic, root, original) sarvāstivāda appears. Now all Sarvāstivādins were united again. Their language was Sanskrit. Their *vinaya* was the long one, but it probably had known a long evolution ever since the early period in Mathurā.

In Central Asia both Gandharan and Vaibhāṣika Sarvāstivādins were represented. In Kumārajīva's Kuqa (344–413) one encounters non-Vaibhāṣikas. In China *abhidharma* is of western origin, Sautrāntika. Sautrāntikas also had an *Abhidharmapiṭaka*. *Abhidharma* is all about the *dharma (sūtras)*, which is Buddha's word. This *abhidharma* was really introduced by Saṇghadeva (late fourth century), translator of the *Aṣṭagrantha* and of the *Hṛdaya*. After the translation of the *Miśraka°* in Nanjing in 435 A.D., an *Abhidharma* School appeared in southern China. It was replaced by a "*Kośa*" School when Paramārtha's translation of the *Abhidharmakośabhāṣya* came out in 568 A.D. This development shows that *abhidharma* in China is Sautrāntika Sarvāstivāda. Xuanzang introduced the Vaibhāṣika *abhidharma* in the seventh century, just before it disappeared in India itself. Nālandā was a center of non-Vaibhāṣikas. Tibet enters the Buddhist world in Mūlasarvāstivāda times.

Literature

Besides the already mentioned *abhidharma* literature [1, 10, 11, 15], it is now known that *yogācāra* (*bhūmi*), (stages) in the practice of yoga, is the subject of quite a few manuals which are of Sarvāstivāda affiliation, for example, Saṇgharakṣa's *Yogācārabhūmi* (Taishō 606), translated in Chinese in 284 A.D. The subdivision of all factors, *dharmas*, in five categories (matter, *rūpa*; thought, *citta*; factors associated with thought, *caitta*; factors not associated with thought, *cittaviprayukta*; unconditioned factors, *asaṃskṛta*) is a Sarvāstivāda view. Western Sarvāstivādins often adopted useful ideas of their opponents, the Mahāsāṅghikas, for example, Mindfulness of Buddha, *Buddhānusmṛti*, and Contemplation of emptiness. The *Yogācārabhūmi*, Taishō ed.1579, of Vasubandhu's elder brother, Asaṅga, incorporates Madhyamaka emptiness of Mahāsāṅghika origin in its yoga [12].

Some now think that Sukhāvatī is an excellent intermediate existence, that Pure Land (Sukhāvatī) Buddhism is of Bactrian Sarvāstivāda origin.

Much of *avadāna* literature (*Divyāvadāna*, etc.) may be said to be Sarvāstivāda.

Recent studies about *vinaya* offer the original Indian text of parts of the (Mūla) sarvāstivāda *vinaya* [4].

The Sarvāstivāda *Dharmapada* was used by the Dārṣṭāntika Dharmatrāta (second century) to establish an *Udāna*, the sixth of 12 parts, *aṅgas*, of Buddha's teaching. Later, a *Dharmapada* was collected again from this *Udāna*, forming a text known as *Udānavarga* of Mūlasarvāstivāda affiliation [3].

Famous non-Vaibhāṣikas from Central India, influenced by Mahāsāṅghika ideas, are Harivarman (ca. 300 A.D.) and Aśvaghoṣa (ca. 100 A.D.) [17].

It is important to put Sarvāstivādins in place (Central India, Gulf of Bengal, Northwestern India, Central Asia, China) and in time (before or after Kaniṣka's synod). Before ca. 170 one may see old Sautrāntika-Dārṣṭāntika Sarvāstivādins, and new ones after that time.

Cross-References

- ► Abhidharma (Theravāda)
- ► Antarābhava
- ► Aśvaghoṣa
- ► Buddhist Councils
- ► Gandhara
- ► Kaniṣka
- ► Paramārtha
- ► Sautrāntika
- ► Sthaviravāda
- ► Upagupta
- ► Vaibhāṣika
- ► Vasubandhu

▶ Xuanzang (Hieun-Tsang)
▶ Yijing
▶ Yogācāra

References

1. Banerjee AC (1957) Sarvāstivāda literature. K. L. Mukhopadhyay, Calcutta
2. Bareau A (1955) Les sectes bouddhiques du petit véhicule. École Française d'Extrême-Orient, Saigon
3. Bernhard FI (1965), II (1968) Udānavarga. III (1990) Byams pa thub bstan rdzoṅ rtse, with the cooperation of Dietz S, ed. Champa Thupten Zongtse. Vandenhoeck & Ruprecht, Gőttingen
4. Chang Jin-il, Vogel C, Wille K (eds) (2002) Sanskrittexte aus dem buddhistischen Kanon: Neuentdeckungen und Neueditionen IV. Vandenhoeck & Ruprecht, Gőttingen
5. Cox C (1995) Disputed dharmas: early Buddhist theories on existence. International Institute for Buddhist Studies, Tokyo
6. Dhammajoti Bhikkhu KL (2009) Sarvāstivāda abhidharma, 4th edn. Centre of Buddhist Studies, The University of Hong Kong, Hong Kong
7. Enomoto F (1996) A Sanskrit fragment from the Vibhāṣā discovered in Eastern Turkestan. In: Sanskrit-texte aus dem buddhistischen Kanon: Neuentdeckungen und Neueditionen III. Vandenhoeck & Ruprecht, Gőttingen
8. Finot L (1914) Le Prātimokṣa des Sarvāstivādins, Paris
9. Frauwallner E (1995) Studies in abhidharma literature and the origins of Buddhist philosophical systems (trans: Kidd S). SUNY Press, New York
10. Gómez L (2005) Sarvāstivāda. In: Jones L (ed) Encyclopedia of religion, 2nd edn. Macmillan Reference USA, Gale Virtual Reference Library, Detroit
11. Jaini P (1977) Abhidharmadīpa with Vibhāṣāprabhāvṛtti. Kashi Jayaswal Research Institute, Patna
12. La Vallée Poussin L de (1988) Abhidharmakośabhāsyam, 4 vols (trans: Pruden L). Asia Humanities Press, Berkeley
13. Lamotte É I (1966), II (1967), III (1970), IV (1976), V (1980) Le traité de la grande vertu de sagesse de Nāgārjuna. Mahāprajñāpāramitopadeśa. Université Catholique de Louvain, Institut Orientaliste, Louvain-La-Neuve
14. Lüders H (1979) Bruchstücke buddhistischer Dramen: Bruchstücke der Kalpanāmaṇḍitikā des Kumāralāta. Steiner, Wiesbaden
15. Willemen C (2006) The essence of scholasticism. Abhidharmahṛdaya. Motilal Banarsidass, Delhi
16. Willemen C (2008) Kumārajīva's explanatory discourse about abhidharmic literature. J Int Coll Postgrad Buddh Stud 12:27–83
17. Willemen C, Dessein B, Cox C (1998) Sarvāstivāda Buddhist scholasticism. Brill, Leiden

Sarvāstivāda Abhidharma

K. L. Dhammajoti
Centre of Buddhist Studies, The University of Hong Kong, Hong Kong, China

Definition

The Sarvāstivāda system developed for the proper understanding and true insight into the nature of existence.

Historical Origin

The Abhidharma is a system aiming at a systematic analysis and proper understanding of the Buddha's teachings. Its origin is to be traced to the *sūtras*. However, the term *Abhidharma*, although occurring therein, often alongside *abhivinaya*, does not refer to the *Abhidharma* texts constituting the third *piṭaka*; for in the *sūtra*s, the meaning of *Abhidharma* seems to be "about the *dhamma*," or "the profound doctrines." The following types of *sūtra* are particularly noteworthy as having features which contributed to the development of the *abhidhamma*/*Abhidharma* in the later specialized sense:

(a) Those featuring *Abhidharma-kathā* – a solemn dialogue between two monks concerning the spiritual path; others listening are not permitted to interrupt. An example is the *Mahāgosiṅga-sutta* (*Majjhima*, I, 212 ff).
(b) Those featuring *vedalla* (Skt. *vaidalya*): Derived from √*dal* meaning to "crack"/ "open," this feature signifies the extensive unraveling of the profound doctrinal meanings that have been hidden. In form, it consists of a question and answer session on doctrinal matters with a scope apparently broader than that in *abhidhamma-kathā* – either between the Buddha and the fourfold disciples (with others listening) or among the disciples themselves. *Vedalla-kathā* is also sometimes

juxtaposed to *abhidhamma-kathā*, as in *Aṅguttara*, ii, 107. Cf. *Mahā-vedalla-sutta* (*Majjhima*, i, 293 ff).

(c) Those featuring the *vibhaṅga* ("analysis/exposition") style – a brief, summarized teaching is elaborated upon by the Buddha or a competent disciple. The significance of *vibhaṅga* being the elaboration on brief teachings became distinctive at least by the time of formation of the *nikāya/āgama* collections. In the *Madhyamāgama*, there are some 35 *sūtras* grouped as "**vibhaṅga* recitations." Likewise, there are some 12 *suttas* grouped under the Pāli *Vibhaṅga-vagga*.

(d) Those featuring *mātṛkā/mātikā* – originally, meaning a matrix or list of headings purporting to systematically summarize the Buddha's teaching, e.g., the list of 37 doctrinal topics often known as *bodhipakṣya-dharmas*. The term *mātṛkā* came to be further developed to connote whatever textual basis that serves as a standard source. The Vaibhāṣikas mention *mātṛkā* unambiguously as being synonymous with *Abhidharma* and *upadeśa* (see below) and cite as *mātṛkā* the early Sarvāstivāda canonical texts: the *Saṅgītiparyāya*, the *Dharma-skandha*, and the *Prajñapti-śāstra*. Many scholars in fact believe that *Abhidharma* evolves from *mātṛkā*.

(e) Those featuring *upadeśa* – an expository or exegetical discourse. This refers to the last of the twelvefold classification of the Buddha's teachings. Saṃghabhadra explains this as follows, equating it with *mātṛkā* and *Abhidharma*:

> *Upadeśa* refers to the non-erroneous (*aparyasta*, *aviparīta*) revealing, answering of objections and ascertainment, of the preceding [eleven] members. (See § **3**) According to some, *upadeśa* also refers to analytical explanations, in accordance with reasoning, given by those who have seen the truth of the profound meanings of the *sūtras*, or by other wise ones. It is none other than what is called *mātṛkā*, for, when the meaning of other *sūtras* is to be explained, this serves as the *mātṛkā*. It is also called *abhidharma*, on account of its being face to face (*abhi*) with the characteristics of *dharmas*, and of its being a non-erroneous unraveling of the characteristics of *dharmas*. ([23], p. 595b).

The Major Abhidharma Texts

Like the Theravādins, the Sarvāstivādins too maintain that the *Abhidharma* was taught by the Buddha himself. But unlike the Theravādins who claim that the whole set of their canonical Abhidhamma texts was authored by the Buddha, the Sarvāstivādins ascribe their seven canonical texts to individual authors: (1) *Dharma-skandha* by Śāriputra, (2) *Saṅgīti-paryāya* by Mahākauṣṭhila, (3) *Prajñāpti-śāstra* by Mahāmaudgalyāyana, (4) *Vijñānakāya* by Devaśarman, (5) *Prakaraṇa-śāstra* by Vasumitra, (6) *Jñānaprasthāna* by Kātyāyanīputra, and (7) *Dhātukāya* by *Pūrṇa*. Of these, the first three belong to the earlier period, and the rest may be grouped under the later period. The *Jñānaprasthāna* was upheld as the supreme authority by the Vaibhāṣikas who called it the "body," in contrast to the other six which were called the "feet."

The Sarvāstivāda school may be said to have been effectively established by Kātyāyanīputra (ca. 150 B.C.) with his *Jñānaprasthāna*. Eventually the orthodox Sarvāstivādins based in Kaśmīra composed the *Abhidharma-mahāvibhāṣā*, a gigantic commentary (translated by Xuan Zang into 200 fascicles) on the *Jñānaprasthāna*, and came to be known as the Vaibhāṣikas on account of their upholding the sanctioned Sarvāstivāda views in it. But encyclopedic as this commentary is, its organization leaves much to be desired as a text for a systematic comprehension of the Sarvāstivāda doctrines. This partly results from its structure being dictated by that of the *Jñānaprasthāna* and partly owing to the compilers' style of branching off too frequently from one topic to another in discussing a given doctrinal position. This fact, coupled with a reaction on the part of some masters to its excessive adherence to the *Jñānaprasthāna* orthodoxy, led to the subsequent compilations of various manuals, culminating in Vasubandhu's famous *Abhidharmakośa-bhāṣya* which came to be commented upon by various masters of varying degrees of orthodoxy. Vasubandhu (ca. fourth century C.E.) states that he, in the main, follows the Kaśmīrian Vaibhāṣikas in expounding the Sarvāstivādin doctrines. However, in many places, he explicitly favors the doctrinal standpoints of the Sautrāntikas, a group of masters "who take the *sūtra*s but not the *śāstra*s as the authority" ([28], p. 11). Vasubandhu's brilliant critique of the Vaibhāṣika doctrines was answered by the equally brilliant Saṃghabhadra, his contemporary and a staunch Vaibhāṣika, in the **Nyāyānusāra*. Other more concise manuals followed, such as Skandhila's *Abhidharmāvatāra* which aims at expounding the totality of the Sarvāstivāda doctrines in a scheme of eight categories (*Padārtha*) – five aggregates (*skandha*) and the three unconditioned (*asaṃskṛta*) – while steering clear of sectarian disputations.

Definition, Nature, and Purpose

Although the term Ābhidharmika can refer generally to anyone who specializes in the study and transmission of the Abhidharma doctrines, it is often used specifically to refer to the mainstream Sarvāstivāda masters. Thus, when the *Mahāvibhāṣā* enumerates the various interpretation of "*Abhidharma*," the first is given as that of the Ābhidharmikas, followed by other interpretations ascribed to individual masters – such as Vasumitra and Dharmatrāta – and to other schools, such as the Dharmaguptaka. This Ābhidharmika interpretation is as follows:

> According to the Ābhidharmikas, it is so called because (i) it can properly and utterly determine (*vi-niś-√ci*) the characteristics of all *dharmas*; (ii) it can properly examine and penetrate the *dharma*s, (iii) it can directly realize (*abhi-sam-√i*) and realize (*sākṣāt-√kṛ*) with regard to all *dharma*s; (iv) it can get to the very bottom of the profound nature of *dharma*s; (v) through it, the wisdom-eye of the noble ones comes to be purified; (vi) it is only through it that the nature of the *dharma*s, subtle from beginningless time, comes to be revealed; (vii) what it expounds is not contradictory to the nature of the *dharma*s – one who is extremely well-versed with regard to the specific and common characteristics in the *abhidharma* cannot be faulted in any way and made to contradict the nature of the dharmas; (viii) it can refute and defeat all the heretical views. ([3], pp. 4a13–25)

More succinctly, Abhidharma is the proper examination and determination of the nature of all *dharma*s. This is called "*dharma-pravicaya*." This true determination is ultimately achieved when true spiritual insight – as opposed to mere intellectual understanding – into the true nature of things is generated in a process known as "direct realization" (*abhisamaya*).

A *dharma* is an ultimate constituent of reality – or an ultimate real – and is articulately defined as "that which sustains its intrinsic characteristic (*svalakṣaṇa-dhāraṇād dharmaḥ*) (see [2], p. 2). Thus, matter (*rūpa*) is a *dharma* because it always possesses a unique intrinsic characteristic of *rūpaṇa*/*rūpaṇā*: the nature of visibility and possessing resistance and susceptibility to gradual decay. Likewise, sensation (*vedanā*) is a *dharma*, being always a real force uniquely enabling the fact of sensation; likewise, understanding (*prajñā*) which uniquely enables the fact of understanding, etc. Abhidharma investigates into these intrinsic characteristics as well as the common characteristics (*sāmānya-lakṣaṇa*) obtaining among a given connected group of *dharmas*. On the basis of this, Abhidharma further examines the mutual inclusion/subsumption (*saṃgraha*) of *dharma*s in respect of intrinsic characteristics as well as the causal interaction.

"*Dharma-pravicaya*" is also the Ābhidharmika definition for *prajñā*. This *prajñā* is a faculty of understanding, i.e., a force which enables our experience of understanding. In the Sarvāstivāda system, therefore, *prajñā* must not be taken to mean exclusively "wisdom," less still, the wisdom of an *arhat* or the Buddha. It denotes the force of understanding that can assume various forms and admits various levels: an understanding that may be either correct or erroneous, pure or impure, with-outflow (*sāsrava*) or outflow-free (*anāsrava*), strong or weak, etc. In its outflow-free form, it is that which properly determines the nature of *dharmas*. And at its highest sublimated level, it is the perfect wisdom of the Buddha.

The above Ābhidharmika definition of "*Abhidharma*" clearly speaks of *Abhidharma* as true or pure wisdom. In keeping with this Ābhidharmika definition, Vasubandhu gives this as the definition of "*Abhidharma*" in the absolute sense, i.e., at the level of absolute truth. At the conventional truth, however, "*Abhidharma*" also

S

refers to the with-outflow *prajñā* – derived from listening, reflection, and cultivation (*śruta-cintā-bhāvanā-mayī prajñā*) or innately acquired (*upapattipratilambhikā*) – which helps to bring about the pure (i.e., outflow-free) *prajñā*. The *Abhidharma śāstra*s, too, inasmuch as they serve as a means or as requisites (*saṃbhāra*) for the acquisition of this pure *prajñā*, are also to be considered as *Abhidharma*.

The prefix "*abhi-*" in the above definition of *Abhidharma* signifies "facing" or "being face to face" (*abhimukha*) which underscores the signification of direct realization (*abhi* = *abhisamaya*) into the true nature of *dharma*s. The definition of Abhidharma as direct realization and pure *prajñā* too brings out its soteriological function: While it is true that in the course of development the Abhidharma methodology came to acquire a distinctive feature of what might be called "scholasticism," it preserves throughout the centuries its primacy of spiritual motivation and its commitment to systematically mapping out the Buddhist path of emancipation from the unsatisfactoriness (*duḥkha*) of sentient existence. This soteriological function from the perspective of Sarvāstivāda Abhidharma is presented; thus:

> Because apart from the examination of *dharmas* (= *prajñā* = *abhidharma*),
> there is no excellent means for the appeasement of the defilements.
> And it is on account of the defilements that beings wander in the existence-ocean.
> For this reason, therefore, it is said, the [*abhidharma*] is taught by the Master. ([2], p. 2)

For the Sarvāstivāda Ābhidharmikas, the Abhidharma is "the word of Buddha" (*Buddha-vacana*) as much as the sūtra and the Vinaya. Nay, it is *sūtra par excellence* and indeed the very authority/criterion for ascertaining the true *sūtra*s (*sūtra-pramāṇa*) – true teachings of the Buddha. Saṃghabhadra argues that in the twelvefold division of the *sūtra-piṭaka* (*sūtra*, *geya*, *vyākaraṇa*), *upadeśa* ("exposition," the 12th division) represents the *Abhidharma*; it serves as the criterion for non-erroneously unraveling and ascertaining the true meanings of all the other 11 divisions ([23], p. 595b). In brief, Abhidharma is the explicit (*nītārtha*) and definitive (*lākṣaṇika*) teachings of the Buddha, in contrast to the *sūtra*s which are generally implicit (*neyārtha*) and intentional (*ābhiprāyika*).

The 75 *Dharmas* Grouped Under Five Categories

In the process of *dharma-pravicaya*, by thoroughly subjecting the complexity of sentient experience to a process of analysis – whether based on direct empirical observation or on a deduction of the unique causal efficacy a particular entity (e.g., a mental force) – the Sarvāstivāda Abhidharmikas arrive at the following list of some 75 types of ultimate reals (*dharma*), divided into five fundamental categories:

I. ***Rūpa*** (matter, 11):

1. *Cakṣur-indriya* (visual faculty)	6. *Rūpa-artha* (visual object)
2. *Śrotra-indriya* (auditory fac)	7. *Śabda-artha* (auditory obj)
3. *Ghrāṇa-indriya* (olfactory fac)	8. *Gandha-artha* (olfactory obj)
4. *Jihvā-indriya* (gustatory fac)	9. *Rasa-artha* (gustatory obj)
5. *Kāya-indriya* (tangible fac)	10. *Spraṣṭavya-artha* (tangible obj)
11. *Avijñapti-rūpa* (noninformative matter)	

II. ***Citta*** (thought)

III. ***Caitasika dharmas*** (thought-concomitants, 46):

1) *Mahābhūmika dharma*s (universal *dharma*s, 10):

1. *Vedanā* (sensation)	6. *Prajñā* (understanding)
2. *Cetanā* (volition)	7. *Smṛti* (mindfulness)
3. *Saṃjñā* (ideation)	8. *Manaskāra* (mental application)

(*continued*)

4. *Chanda* (predilection)	9. *Adhimokṣa* (resolve/determination)
5. *Sparśa* (contact)	10. *Samādhi* (concentration)

2) *Kuśala-mahābhūmika dharmas* (skillful universal *dharmas*, 10):

1. *Śraddhā* (faith)	6. *Apatrāpya* (shame)
2. *Apramāda* (diligence)	7. *Alobha* (non-greed)
3. *Praśrabdhi* (calm)	8. *Adveṣa* (non-hatred)
4. *Upekṣā* (equanimity)	9. *Avihiṃsā* (harmlessness)
5. *Hrī* (modesty)	10. *Vīrya* (vigor)

3) *Kleśa-mahābhūmika dharmas* (universal *dharmas* of defilement, 6):

1. *Moha* (delusion)	4. *Āśraddhya* (lack of faith)
2. *Pramāda* (non-diligence)	5. *Styāna* (torpor)
3. *Kauśīdya* (slackness)	6. *Auddhatya* (restlessness)

4) *Akuśala-mahābhūmika dharmas* (unskillful universal *dharmas*, 2):

1. *Ahrīkya* (non-modesty)	2. *Anapatrāpya* (shamelessness)

5) *Parīttakleśa-bhūmika dharmas* (defilements of restricted scope 10):

1. *Krodha* (anger)	6. *Mrakṣa* (concealment)
2. *Upanāha* (enmity)	7. *Mātsarya* (avarice)
3. *Śāṭhya* (dissimulation)	8. *Māyā* (deceptiveness)
4. *Īrṣyā* (jealousy)	9. *Mada* (pride)
5. *Pradāśa* (depraved opinionatedness)	10. *Vihiṃsā* (harmfulness)

6) *Aniyata dharmas* (indeterminate *dharmas*, 8):

1. *Kaukṛtya* (remorse)	5. *Rāga* (greed)
2. *Middha* (sleep)	6. *Pratigha* (hostility)
3. *Vitarka* (reasoning)	7. *Māna* (conceit)
4. *Vicāra* (investigation)	8. *Vicikitsā* (doubt)

IV. ***Cittaviprayukta saṃskāra dharmas*** (conditionings disjoined from thought, 14):

1. *Prāpti* (acquisition)	8. *Jāti-lakṣaṇa* (production-characteristic)
2. *Aprāpti* (non-acquisition)	9. *Sthiti-lakṣaṇa* (duration-characteristic)
3. *Nikāyasabhāga* (group homogeneity)	10. *Jarā-lakṣaṇa* (deterioration-characteristic)
4. *Āsaṃjñika* (ideationlessness)	11. *Anityatā-lakṣaṇa* (impermanence-characteristic)
5. *Āsaṃjñi-samāpatti* (ideationless attainment)	12. *Nāma-kāya* (words)
6. *Nirodha-samāpatti* (cessation attainment)	13. *Pada-kāya* (phrases)
7. *Jīvitendriya* (vital faculty)	14. *Vyañjana-kāya* (syllables)

V. ***Asaṃskṛta dharmas*** (unconditioned *dharmas*, 3):

1. *Akāśa* (space)
2. *Pratisaṃkhyā-nirodha* (cessation through deliberation)
3. *Apratisaṃkhyā-nirodha* (cessation independent of deliberation)

I. The totality of *rūpa-dharmas* comprises (i) the primary matter comprising the four great elements (*mahābhūta*; "great reals") – earth (*pṛthivī*), water (*ap*), fire (*tejas*), and air (*vāyu*); (ii) 11 derived matter (*upādāya-rūpa*/*bhautika*) – five sense faculties (*indriya*), five corresponding objects (*artha/viṣaya*), and noninformation matter (*avijñapti-rūpa*). The four great elements are also subsumed under the objects of touch (*spraṣṭavya*) together with other derived tangibles because their functions can only be experienced through touch. They have the intrinsic nature of solidity (*khara*), humidity (*sneha*), heat (*uṣṇatā*), and mobility (*īraṇā*), respectively, and perform the functions of supporting (*dhṛti*), cohesion (*saṃgraha*), maturation (*pakti*), and extension (*vyūha*), respectively. The Sarvāstivāda acknowledges a total of 11 tangibles. The other seven are smoothness (*ślakṣṇatva*), coarseness (*karkaś atva*), heaviness (*gurutva*), lightness (*laghutva*), coldness (*śīta*), hunger (*jighatsā*), and thirst (*pipāsā*).

The four great elements exist inseparably from one another, being coexistent causes (*sahabhū-hetu*; see § **6**.(4)) one to another. Nevertheless, *rūpa-dharma*s are manifested and experienced in diverse forms on account of the difference in intensity or substance of one or more of the four elements.

Although the so-called derived *rūpa*s are already existing as ontological entities, their arising and functioning are dependent (*upādāya*) on the great elements. In this sense, the latter are said to be their cause. One set of the four great elements serves as the cause of an atom (*paramāṇu*) of the derived *rūpa* in a fivefold manner: (i) As generating cause (*janana-hetu*) – the derived *rūpa*s arise from them, like a child from the parents. (ii) As reliance cause (*niśraya-hetu*) – they are influenced by them, like a pupil under a teacher. (iii) As supportive cause (*pratiṣṭhā-hetu*) – they are supported by them. (iv) As maintaining cause (*upastambha-hetu*) – they are their cause of non-interruption. (v) As development cause (*upabṛmhaṇa-hetu*) – they are their cause of development ([2], p. 102 f; [3], p. 663a).

The non-informative (*avijñapti*) matter is a special type of *rūpa*, being invisible, nonresistant, and nonspatialized. Nevertheless, it is said to be of the nature of matter since its supporting basis (*āśraya*) – the four great elements – is resistant matter. In terms of the *āyatana* classification, it is subsumed under the *dharma-āyatana* rather than the *rūpa-āyatana* and is referred to as "matter subsumed under the *dharma-āyatana*" (*dharmāyatana-saṃgṛhīta-rūpa*). This is the medium of preservation of the karmic efficacy projected from a momentary bodily or vocal *karma*. It is "noninformative" because it is a karmic action that does not inform us of the mental state of its doer. Once projected, it continues to exist as a series until either the corresponding karmic effect is retributed or when a certain condition is met with – such as the person's death. Eventually, it came to be particularly emphasized as the karmic efficacy projected when one solemnly takes an ordination vow (*saṃvāra*, "restraint"), e.g., of abstaining from killing (2, 8, 205, 208, etc.).

II–III. No thought or thought-concomitant can arise singly; they necessarily arise in conjunction (*saṃprayoga*). For instance, any thought necessarily arises with the set of 10 universal thought-concomitants (sensation, etc.). When a skillful thought-concomitant arises, it necessarily does so together with the thought involved, the set of 10 universal *dharma*s, and the set of 10 skillful universal thought-concomitants (faith, etc.).

In a conjunction, the thought and thought-concomitants (i) arise at the same time, (ii) share the same basis (*āśraya*), (iii) take the same cognitive object (*ālambana*), (iv) have the same mode of activity/understanding (*ākāra*), and (v) each has a singularity of substance (*dravya* – e.g., a single thought conjoined with a single species of sensation, a single species of ideation).

IV. The category of "conditionings disjoined from thought" represents an Abhidharma development going beyond the matter–mind dualism of the Theravāda and other schools. These *dharma*s are forces that are neither physical nor mental, but whose efficacy can exercise in both domains.

Their nature and function are best illustrated with the example of "acquisition" (*prāpti*), a force which links a *dharma* – whether physical or mental, conditioned or unconditioned – to a sentient being. Thus, when, say, a sensual craving arises in the sentient being, he comes to "possess" this *dharma* called sensual craving, which has always been existing in the universe, thanks to this force, "acquisition," which as it were ties (like a rope) the craving to him. The acquisition of this craving, once projected, serially flows on in the person even when the craving does not arise manifestly – e.g., when the person's mental stream is of a skillful or neutral nature. For this reason, he is continuously possessed of this craving. When, as a result of spiritual praxis, the person comes to be freed from (to "abandon," *pra-*√*hā*) this craving, it is not that the *dharma* called craving as an ontological entity comes to be destroyed, but rather, that the serial continuity of its acquisition is cut off from him.

When one comes to attain *Nirvāṇa*, it cannot be that the unconditioned *dharma* arises as an effect of a path which is conditioned (see below). What is produced by the path is the acquisition (itself a conditioned *dharma*) of the *Nirvāṇa*, which links the latter to the practitioner.

V. In the Sarvāstivāda system, the domain of the unconditioned, just as the domain of the conditioned, is pluralistic. There are three types of conditioned *dharma*s:

1. "Cessation through deliberation (*pratisaṃkhyā-nirodha*)," namely, through an effort of understanding (*prajnā*; *pratisaṃkhyā* is explained as *prajñā-viśeṣa*) the true nature of *dharma*s. For each instance of abandoning a defilement, there arises a corresponding instance of its cessation (*nirodha*) which is a real entity – and not a mere absence of the defilement – contributing to the absolute prevention of the defilement's future arising. There are therefore as many instances of cessation through deliberation as they are instances of with-outflow entities to be disconnected from.
2. "Cessation independent of deliberation" (*apratisaṃkhyā-nirodha*). These are cessations acquired without specifically applying any effort of understanding but simply on account of deficiency in the required conditions for a *dharma*'s arising. For example, when the present eye and the mental faculty are focusing on a particular object giving rise to its visual consciousness, it is not possible for any of the five sensory consciousness to arise with regard to any of the other objects (visibles, sounds, etc.) existing in that same moment. There arise accordingly the cessations independent of deliberation of these latter instances of sensory consciousness by virtue of the deficiency in the conditions for their arising. However, these cessations are not mere absence of conditions; they are in each case a distinct, real entity efficacious in absolutely preventing the possible re-arising of the said consciousnesses. Besides such mundane occurrences in our daily experience of cognizing sensory objects, there are other spiritually significant instances, e.g., when through spiritual striving one attains stream-entry (*srota-āpatti*), one also thereby acquires the cessations independent of deliberation, of all forms of unfortunate rebirth (*durgati*) – one will no longer be reborn in any such unfortunate plane of existence.
3. Space (*ākāsa*). This is not to be confounded with conditioned space, called the space element (*akāśa-dhātu*), which is visible in the openings in windows, doors, cleavages, etc. Such spaces, though nonobstructive in nature, are nonetheless obstructed by material things. The unconditioned space, in contrast, is beyond space and time and is characterized by being neither obstructive to, nor obstructed by, any material thing. Its reality is to be comprehended from the fact that there exists the conditioned space which accommodates conditioned things and provides the venues for their activities. This does not mean that space can exercise any activity, but that it serves as a necessary contributing factor – a "dominant condition" (*adhipati-pratyaya*) – through a sequence of conditionality, making possible the fact of cognition of things in space–time:

> The unconditioned Space has no activity. Nevertheless, it can serve as the proximate *adhipati-pratyaya* for the various space elements. These various space-elements can serve as the proximate *adhipati-pratyaya* for the various Great Elements. These various Great Elements can serve as the proximate *adhipati-pratyaya* for the resistant derived matters. These resistant derived matters can serve as the proximate *adhipati-pratyaya* for the various mental *citta-caitta-dharma*s.
>
> If Space were non-existent, such a successive causal sequence cannot be established. Hence the intrinsic nature and characteristic of Space exist, lest there be such a fallacy; they must not be denied. ([3], p. 389a)

The conditioned *dharma*s, which arise into space–time and their operation therein, are described by two terms: (1) *saṃskṛta* ("compounded"), indicating their aspect of being causally produced, and (2) *saṃskāra* ("conditioning"), indicating their aspect of being conditioning forces that contribute to the arising and operation of other conditioned *dharma*s. The unconditioned *dharma*s are in complete contrast:

S

Being transcendent to space and time, they are neither causally produced nor do they operate as causes. However, they can serve as "condition qua object" (*ālambana-pratyaya*) inasmuch as they can be apprehended as cognitive objects. The Sarvāstivāda Ābhidharmikas would also concede that in some special sense and in conformity to worldly parlance, it is permissible to speak of the unconditioned *dharmas* as "efficient causes" (*kāraṇa-hetu*; see § **6**) inasmuch as they do not hinder the arising of other *dharmas*. Although not causally produced, the cessation through discernment may also be expediently spoken as a "disconnection-fruit" (*visaṃyoga-phala*) inasmuch as it is acquired (*pra-√āp*) through the efficacy of the noble path – even though it is not directly produced by it ([2], p. 91).

Sarvāstivāda vs. Vibhajyavāda

The Sarvāstivāda's fundamental standpoint is that all the above categories of *dharmas* – both the conditioned and the unconditioned – as unique, ultimate reals exist throughout time. This doctrine is expressed by the statement "all exists" (*sarvam asti*), hence the name of the school, Sarvāstivāda. This "all" therefore firstly indicates the reality of each and every ultimate factor that is truly a "*dharma*," i.e., that exists uniquely in its intrinsic nature (*svabhāva*) and that uniquely "maintains its intrinsic characteristic" (*svalakṣaṇa-dhāraṇa*; see § **3**). It further indicates that every conditioned *dharma* is existent throughout the three periods of time, future, present, and past, and this fact is expressed by stating that its intrinsic nature "always exists" (*sarvadā asti*). But this tritemporal existence must not be misunderstood as permanent existence – all conditioned *dharma* necessarily traverses time; the unconditioned *dharmas* alone, which transcend temporality, are permanent.

Although the intrinsic nature of a *dharma* exists always, its "activity" (*kāritra*) is momentary, being exercised only in the single present moment. This "activity" is defined as a *dharma*'s efficacy for inducing the next moment of its own existence in its serial continuity. It is its "efficacy for projecting its own fruit" (**svaphala-ākṣepa-sāmarthya*). Since this efficacy exists necessarily and uniquely in every present *dharma*, it comes to be officially adopted by the Sarvāstivādins as the criterion for temporal distinction of conditioned *dharmas*: When a *dharma* has not yet exercised this "activity," it is said to be future; when this activity is being exercised, it is said to be present; and when it has been exercised, it is said to be past. This theory is ascribed to Vasumitra who asserts that while a *dharma*'s intrinsic nature remains unchanged always, its temporal distinction is possible in terms of its three distinctive temporal "positions/stages" (*avasthā*) distinguished in respect of its activity. The Vaibhāṣikas – certainly Saṃghabhadra, for one – also advocate Dharmatrāta's theory that the same *dharma*, though always unchanged in respect of its intrinsic nature, exists in different "modes" (*bhāva*) in the three temporal periods ([23], pp. 632c, 633c).

In this tenet of "all exist," Saṃghabhadra articulates on the nature of the "existent" (*sat*). He defines an existent as "that which is capable of serving as the object-domain for generating a cognition (*buddhi*)" ([23], p. 621c). Accordingly, any act of cognition at all – be it a true cognition (as that through spiritual insight), or an imagination, or an illusion, or even a cognition of "absence," etc. – necessarily presupposes an existent object. These existent objects, of course, may be either relative existents such as a "person" (a notion derived from a composite comprising the five aggregates: matter, sensation, ideation, conditionings, and consciousness) or absolute existents such as matter, sensation, and other *dharmas*. This Sarvāstivāda doctrine that a notion or concept (*prajñapti*) is necessarily based ultimately on some absolute reals came to importantly influence the epistemological and ontological doctrines of the subsequent Buddhist schools, particularly the Yogācāra.

This standpoint of *Sarvāstivāda* (/*sarvāstitva*) is diametrically opposed by those known as the "distinctionists," Vibhajyavāda, who include the Sautrāntikas, the Mahāsāṃghikas, and others. They hold, in contrast, that only the present – or, for some, the present and those *karmas* that have not yet given fruits (*adattaphala*) – exists; the future and the past *dharma*s do not exist. The long-drawn-out controversy on *Sarvāstivāda* vs. *Vibhajyavāda* is an extremely important historical fact that must not be overlooked by any Buddhist historian for a proper perspective of the understanding of the development of Buddhist thought in which its reverberation is continuously seen in various forms throughout the centuries (both within and outside India).

Doctrine of Causality

Another important doctrinal contribution of the Sarvāstivāda is their theory of causality, innovated by Kātyāyanīputra in his *Jñānaprasthāna*. Prior to this, the Sarvāstivādins had been sharing with other Buddhists the doctrine of the four conditions: (1) condition qua cause (*hetu-pratyaya*), (2) equal-immediate condition (*samanantara-pratyaya*), (3) condition qua object (*ālambana-pratyaya*), and (4) condition of dominance (*adhipati-pratyaya*).

Kātyāyanīputra proposes for the first time, the doctrine of six causes:

1. Efficient cause (*kāraṇa-hetu*). This is the most generic cause, either in the sense of a general causal contribution or simply of being nonobstructive: "A conditioned *dharma* has all *dharma*s, excepting itself, as its efficient cause, for, as regards its arising, [these *dharma*s] abide in the state of non-obstructiveness" ([2], p. 82).
2. Homogeneous cause (*sabhāga-hetu*). This obtains in the case of a mental series, and among physical matter. "The similar *dharma*s are the homogeneous causes of *dharma*s similar [to them], for, e.g., the five *skandha*s which are skilful, are [the homogeneous causes] of the five skilful *skandha*s, among themselves. Likewise the defiled and the non-defined five *skandha*s, [in each case, among themselves]. . ." ([2], p. 85).
3. Universal cause (*sarvatraga-hetu*). "The universal *dharma*s arisen previously and belonging to a given stage (*bhūmi*) are the universal causes of later defiled *dharma*s belonging to their own stage. . .. On account of their being a cause applicable to all defiled *dharma*s, they are established [as a cause] separate from the homogeneous causes and [also] because they are the cause of [defiled *dharma*-s] belonging to other categories [of abandonability] (five categories: (i)–(iv) defilements are abandonable either through insight into the four Truths, or (v) through the path of cultivation) as well, for, through their power, defilements belonging to categories different from theirs are produced" ([2], p. 89). The Vaibhāṣikas hold that three defilements are universal: doubt (*vicikitsā*), view (*dṛṣṭi*), and ignorance (*avidyā*), which are abandonable by insight into unsatisfactoriness, the cause of unsatisfactoriness, together with their conjoined and coexistent *dharma*s" ([3], p. 90c; [23], p. 416c).
4. Coexistent cause (*sahabhū-hetu*). "The coexistent [causes] are those that are reciprocally effects. . .. For example: the four Great Elements are co-existent [causes] mutually among themselves; so also, thought and the *dharma*s that are thought-accompaniments (*cittānuvartin*). . . [The case of the co-existent cause] is like the staying in position of three sticks through their mutual strength/support – this establishes the causal relationship (*hetuphalabhāva*) of the co-existents" ([2], pp. 83–85). Co-nascence is a necessary, but not sufficient, condition for two or more *dharma*s to be coexistent causes. Saṃghabhadra articulates that in brief, this causal category obtains in only three cases: "[i] among those that share the same effect; or [ii] that are reciprocally effects; or [iii] where by the force of this, that *dharma* can arise. Such co-nascent [*dharma*s] have a cause–effect relationship, [i.e., are coexistent causes]" ([23], p. 419c).
5. Conjoined cause (*saṃprayuktaka-hetu*), a subset of the coexistent causes. As stated above, thought and concomitants necessarily arise in conjunction (§ **4**.II–III). Mental factors, in their role of contributing to their mutual arising and operational coordination, are called "conjoined causes." Moreover, being so

S

conjoined and coordinated, they accomplish the same activity in grasping the same object.

6. Retribution (/maturation) cause (*vipāka-hetu*). This is the karmic cause, leading to a corresponding karmic fruit – i.e., determining the specific type of rebirth that a sentient being will experience. The fruit is necessarily morally neutral (*avyākṛta*); if the retribution cause leads to a desirable (*iṣṭa*) fruit, it is "skillful" (*kuśala*); if it leads to an undesirable (*aniṣṭa*) fruit, it is "unskillful" (*akuśala*). Neutral and outflow-free *dharma*s do not yield any retribution fruit.

Since the time of the *Dharma-skandha*, the Sarvāstivādins have held that retribution causes and fruits comprise all five *skandha*s. That is, not only thought and the thought-concomitants but also the matter accompanying thought (*cittānuvṛttaka-rūpa*) and the conditionings disjoined from thought – the ideationless attainment (*asaṃjñī-samāpatti*), the cessation attainment (*nirodha-samāpatti*), all acquisitions which are unskillful, and skillful but with-outflow (*sāsrava*), and the accompanying characteristics of the conditioned (*saṃskṛta-lakṣaṇa*) – can constitute retribution causes (cf. [3], pp. 96a–c).

Of the six causes, the coexistent cause is the most important. For the Sarvāstivādins, the fact of direct perception (*pratyakṣa*) cannot be established without the type of simultaneous causality represented by the coexistent cause. This is because, given that a sensory faculty and its object last only one single moment (a doctrine commonly accepted by all Abhidharma schools with the exception of the Sāṃmitīya, etc.), if the corresponding consciousness (*qua* effect) were to arise in the second moment (as claimed by the Sautrāntikas and others), it would not have an existent object. If direct perception cannot be established, then inferential knowledge too would be impossible – and this would result in the absolute impossibility of any knowledge of the external world!

More importantly, the coexistent cause serves as the only valid paradigm of causation. In general, if *A* causes *B*, both *A* and *B* must be existent at the same time (an utter void or a nonexistent cannot be causally efficacious) – although they may belong to different time periods with respect to their own temporal frame of reference. That is, *A* may be past or present or future, and *B* may also be past or present or future – *but they must coexist, although not necessarily be co-nascent*. To borrow Dharmatrāta's terminology, they are both existent but not necessarily of the same "mode of existence" (*bhāva*). Where *A* and *B* are necessarily co-nascent, i.e., both existing at the same *present* moment, it reduces to the category known as the coexistent cause. In fact, in the Sarvāstivāda conception, all *dharma*s in their essential nature have always been existent; it is only a matter of inducing their arising through causes and conditions. This is the fundamental principle underlining the Sarvāstivāda doctrine of causality. Past and future *dharma*s are also endowed with efficacies including that of actually giving an effect, although it is only a present *dharma* that has "activity" – the efficacy of establishing the specific causal relationship with the *dharma* to be produced as its effect.

Cross-References

- ▶ Abhidhamma Piṭaka
- ▶ Abhidharma (Theravāda)
- ▶ Buddhist History
- ▶ Causality (Buddhism)
- ▶ Dharma
- ▶ Karma (Buddhism)
- ▶ Paññā
- ▶ Philosophy (Buddhism)
- ▶ Psychology (Buddhism)
- ▶ Sarvāstivāda
- ▶ Sautrāntika
- ▶ Sthaviravāda
- ▶ Theravāda
- ▶ Time (Buddhism)
- ▶ Tipiṭaka
- ▶ Vaibhāṣika
- ▶ Vasubandhu
- ▶ Vijñāna

References

1. Jaini PS (ed) (1959) Abhidharmadīpa with Vibhāṣāprabhāvṛtti. Patna
2. Pradhan P (ed) (1975) Abhidharmakośabhāṣyam of Vasubandhu. Patna
3. Abhidharma-mahāvibhāṣā. T29, no. 1545
4. Samtati NH (1971) Arthaviniścaya-sūtra-nibandhana. Patna
5. Bareau A (1952) Les sectes bouddhiques du Petit Véhicule et leurs Abhidharmapiṭaka. Bulletin de l'École Française d'Extrême-Orient XLIV:1–11. Paris
6. Cox C (1995) Disputed Dharmas: early Buddhist theories on existence. An Annotated Translation of the Section on Factors Dissociated from Thought from Saṃghabhadra's Nyāyānusāra. Tokyo
7. Demiéville P (1931–1932) L'origine des Sectes Bouddhiques d'après Paramārtha. Mélanges Chinois et Bouddhiques I:15–64. Bruxelles
8. Dietz S (1984) Fragmente des Dharmaskandha – Ein Abhidharma-text in Sanskrit aus Gilgit
9. Dhammajoti KL (1998) The defects in the Arhat's enlightenment: his *Akliṣṭa-ajñāna* and *Vāsanā*. Bukkyō Kenkyū XXVII:65–98. Hamamatsu
10. Dhammajoti KL (2005) Abhidharma and Upadeśa. J Centre Buddh Stud, Sri Lanka II. Colombo
11. Dhammajoti KL (2009) Abhidharma doctrines and controversies on perception, 3rd edn. Hong Kong
12. Dhammajoti KL (2008) Entrance into the supreme doctrine, 2nd edn. Hong Kong
13. Dhammajoti KL (2009) Sarvāstivāda Abhidharma, 4th edn. Hong Kong
14. Dhammajoti KL (2011) Śrīlāta's *Anudhātu* doctrine. Bukkyō Kenkyū XXXIX:19–75. Hamamatsu
15. Frauwallneer E (1995) Studies in Abhidharma literature and the origins of Buddhist philosophical systems. Eng. tr. by Sophie Francis Kidd under the supervision of Ernst Steinkellner, New York
16. Hirakawa A et. al. (1973) Index to the Abhidharmakośabhāśya – Part I: Sanskrit-Tibetan Chinese. Tokyo
17. Kajiyama Y (1985) An introduction to Buddhist philosophy – an annotated translation of the translation of the Tarkabhāṣā of Mokṣākaragupta. Tokyo
18. Karunadasa Y (1967) Buddhist analysis of matter. Colombo
19. Karunadasa Y (1983) Vibhajyavāda versus Sarvāstivāda: the Buddhist controversy on time. Kalyāni: J Human Soc Sci Univ Kelaniya (Sri Lanka) II:1–28. Colombo
20. Karunadasa Y (2010) The Theravāda Abhidhamma: its inquiry into the nature of conditioned reality. Hong Kong
21. La Vallée Poussin L de (1923–1931) L'Abhidharmakośa de Vasubandhu, vol I–VI. Paris
22. Masuda J (1925) Origin and doctrines of early Indian Buddhist Schools. Asia Major II:1–78
23. **Nyāyānusāra*. T29, no.1562
24. Prasad HS (1991) Essays on time in Buddhism. Delhi
25. Pruden L (1988) Eng. tr. of L'Abhidharmakośa de Vasubandhu (vols I–VI by La Vallée Poussin L de). Berkeley
26. Samtani NH (tr) (2002) Gathering the meanings: the Arthaviniścaya Sūtra and its commentary Nibandhana. Berkeley
27. Stcherbatsky Th (1970) The central conception of Buddhism and the meaning of the word 'Dharma'. Delhi
28. Wogihara U (ed) (1932–1936) Sphuṭārthā Abhidharmakośa-vyākhyā of Yaśomitra. Tokyo
29. Willemen C (2006) The essence of scholasticism. Abhidharmahṛdaya. T 1550. Revised edition with a completely new introduction. Delhi
30. Willemen C, Dessein B, Cox C (1998) Sarvāstivāda Buddhist scholasticism. Leiden

Satipaṭṭhāna

Bhikkhu Anālayo
Center for Buddhist Studies, University of Hamburg, Balve, Germany

Synonyms

Establishing of mindfulness; *Smṛtyupasthāna* (Sanskrit)

Definition

Satipaṭṭhāna stands for the systematic development of mindfulness as an essential aspect of the early Buddhist path to deliverance.

Establishing Mindfulness

Satipaṭṭhāna is a compound of *sati*, "mindfulness" or "awareness," and *upaṭṭhāna*, with the *u* of the latter term being dropped due to vowel elision. The Pāli term *upaṭṭhāna* literally means "placing near," and in the present context refers to a particular way of "being present" and "attending" to something with mindfulness. Thus *satipaṭṭhāna* is mental presence through established *sati*, in the sense of fully attending to the current situation. The word *satipaṭṭhāna* can then be translated as "establishing of mindfulness," in the sense of a "presence of mindfulness" by way of "attending with mindfulness" to whatever is happening.

Satipaṭṭhāna is the seventh of the factors of the noble eightfold path ([1], Vol. IV, p. 371), which combines the development of mindfulness with rightly directed view, intentions, speech, action, livelihood, effort, and concentration. According to the standard description of the noble eightfold path, *satipaṭṭhāna* consists in being mindful of the following four aspects of experience:

- Body
- Feelings
- Mental states
- Phenomena

A more detailed exposition of these four can be gathered from the *Satipaṭṭhāna-sutta* ([2], Vol. I, pp. 55–63, cf. also [3], Vol. II, pp. 290–315) of the Theravāda tradition. The Chinese *Āgamas* have preserved two parallels to the *Satipaṭṭhāna-sutta*. These occur in the *Madhyama-āgama*, probably stemming from a Sarvāstivāda transmission lineage (Taishō 1.582b), and in the *Ekottarika-āgama* (Taishō 2.568a), whose school affiliation is uncertain. Comparison of these three versions shows considerable variations, in particular in relation to the first and the fourth area for the development of mindfulness.

The three parallel versions do, however, agree on the basic scheme of four *satipaṭṭhānas*. This basic scheme occurs also in numerous discourses elsewhere, which usually mention only the bare outline of this scheme, without going into the details of their possible applications as found in the *Satipaṭṭhāna-sutta*.

In regard to the various meditations detailed in each area, one of the Chinese versions describes a total of 18 body contemplations, against only 6 types of body contemplations found in the Pāli version and only 4 exercises for contemplation of the body in the other Chinese version. Common ground among the parallel versions can be found in the following three practices:

- Contemplation of the anatomical constitution of the body
- Contemplation of the body as made up of material elements
- Contemplation of the decay of the body after death

This agreement among the parallel versions suggests that a central theme of contemplating the body as a *satipaṭṭhāna* is to gain insight into its true nature and constitution.

According to the fairly similar instructions given in the parallel versions, contemplation of the anatomical constitution of the body requires reviewing its various parts, such as its hair, nails, teeth, etc. Such reviewing could take place by way of an internal scanning of the body or else as a reflective recollection. This exercise can act as an antidote to conceit and sensual desire. The first five anatomical parts mentioned in this listing are usually taught to Buddhist monks and nuns on their day of ordination, no doubt as an encouragement to embark on this particular exercise as a protective and supportive practice for their celibate life.

Contemplation of the body in terms of the elements is in most versions based on the four elements of earth, water, fire, and wind, with one Chinese version additionally mentioning space and consciousness. According to the traditional explanation, the four elements stand representative for basic qualities of matter, such as hardness, cohesion, temperature, and motion. Thus, the point of such contemplation is to recognize the presence of these elements as qualities within the body. Undertaking this exercise can lead to insight into the not-self nature of the body, which is but a combination of material elements and thereby no different from any other manifestation of these elements found elsewhere in nature.

The third body contemplation found in all parallel versions directs mindfulness to different stages of a dead body in decay. Undertaking such contemplation can be based on having seen a rotting corpse, a vision that can later be recollected and applied to one's own body or that of others, understanding that they all share the same nature. Similar to the contemplation of the anatomical parts, this exercise can act as an antidote to conceit and sensual desire. It also quite vividly documents the impermanent nature of the body, whose final destination is none other than death.

According to the instructions found in all parallel versions, the second *satipaṭṭhāna* requires distinguishing feelings according to their affective quality into pleasant, unpleasant, and neutral types. Here, the task is to be aware of the affective input provided by feeling during the early stages of the process of perception, before the onset of reactions, projections, and mental elaborations in regard to what has been perceived.

These three types of feelings are moreover differentiated into worldly, *sāmisa*, or unworldly, *nirāmisa*, occurrences. This introduces an ethical distinction of feelings, aimed at the crucial difference between worldly feelings caused by "carnal" experiences and unworldly feelings related to renunciation and spiritual practice.

The third *satipaṭṭhāna* of contemplation of the mind covers the presence or absence of unwholesome states of mind, enjoining recognition whenever the mind is under the influence of lust, anger, delusion, or agitation. The main task here is to avoid being carried away by any particular train of thought and instead to clearly recognize the state of mind underlying this thought. In this way, the motivating forces at work in one's mind are uncovered and insight into the working mechanism of the mind becomes possible. Contemplation of the mind also involves recognizing the presence or absence of higher states of mind, thereby covering experiences that take place during more advanced stages of meditation practice.

Concerning the fourth *satipaṭṭhāna*, what remains as the unanimously accepted core of practice in the Pāli and Chinese versions are two exercises:

- Contemplation of the five hindrances (not fully spelled out in one Chinese version)
- Contemplation of the seven factors of awakening

The same two contemplations are also the only exercises listed under the fourth *satipaṭṭhāna* in the *Vibhaṅga*, the historically perhaps earliest text in the canonical Pāli Abhidharma collection ([4], p. 199). This agreement between the parallel versions and the *Vibhaṅga* throws into relief the importance of abandoning the hindrances and developing the factors of awakening for progress on the path to realization.

Regarding the first of these two exercises, the hindrances are those factors that particularly obstruct the proper functioning of the mind and therewith all attempts at meditation. The standard listing enumerates sensual desire, ill will, sloth-and-torpor, restlessness-and-worry, and doubt. In regard to these five hindrances, the task of *satipaṭṭhāna* is to recognize their presence or their absence and to gain insight into how they arise and how they can be overcome.

The awakening factors are those seven mental qualities that have to be brought into being in order to be able to gain awakening. Mindfulness constitutes the first and foundational factor in this set, followed by investigation of phenomena, energy, joy, tranquility, and concentration, with equanimity as the seventh awakening factor constituting the culmination point of practice. Contemplation of the awakening factors as a *satipaṭṭhāna* is to be aware of their presence or absence and to be aware of how they can be brought into being and further developed.

Traditional exegesis sets the four *satipaṭṭhānas* in opposition to the four distortions, *vipallāsa*, which are to mistake what is unattractive, unsatisfactory, impermanent, and not-self, for being attractive, satisfactory, permanent, and a self. From this perspective, contemplation of the body has the potential to reveal the absence of bodily beauty, observation of the true nature of feeling can counter one's incessant search for fleeting pleasures, awareness of the succession of states of mind can disclose the impermanent nature of all subjective experience, and contemplation of phenomena can reveal that the notion of a permanent self is nothing but an illusion.

This presentation points to the main theme that underlies each of the four *satipaṭṭhānas*. Although the corresponding insights are certainly not restricted to one *satipaṭṭhāna* alone, nevertheless this particular correlation indicates which *satipaṭṭhāna* is particularly suitable in order to correct a specific distortion. In the end, however, all four *satipaṭṭhānas* partake of the same essence and each of them is capable of leading to realization, like different gateways leading to the same city.

According to a set of verses in the *Satipaṭṭhāna-saṃyutta*, these four *satipaṭṭhānas* form the direct path, *ekāyano maggo*, for crossing the flood in past, present, and future times ([1], Vol. V, p. 168). The *Satipaṭṭhāna-sutta* uses the same expression in order to introduce *satipaṭṭhāna* as the direct path for the purification of beings and for the realization of Nirvāṇa ([2], Vol. I, p. 55). Another discourse indicates that, whosoever have escaped, are escaping, or will escape from this world, all of them do so by way of well developing the four *satipaṭṭhānas* ([5], Vol. V, p. 195).

Satipaṭṭhāna stands, however, in necessary interdependence with the other factors of the noble eightfold path, so that it would be a misunderstanding to believe that by practicing only mindfulness, awakening can be gained.

Another important requirement for successful undertaking of *satipaṭṭhāna* is that such practice should issue in insight into the arising and passing away of phenomena. This importance is highlighted in a discourse, according to which such insight marks the distinction between mere establishment of *satipaṭṭhāna* and its complete and full "development," *bhāvanā* ([1], Vol. V, p. 183). This passage indicates that mere awareness of the various objects listed under the four *satipaṭṭhānas* may not suffice for the task of developing penetrative insight. What is additionally required is to move on to a direct vision of their impermanence, to contemplating their arising and passing away, a requirement in fact explicitly mentioned in the *Satipaṭṭhāna-sutta* after each of the exercises. The same section of the *Satipaṭṭhāna-sutta* also highlights that contemplation should be undertaken internally and externally, presumably in the sense of covering one's own subjective experience as well as that of others.

In regard to the Buddha, the discourses present a set of three *satipaṭṭhāna*s specifically related to his role as a teacher ([2], Vol. III, p. 221). These are his balanced attitude toward three situations:

- His disciples do not listen to and do not follow his teachings.
- Some disciples listen and follow his teachings, others do not.
- His disciples do listen to and follow his teachings.

In each of these cases, the Buddha remains mindful and equanimous. This additional set of three *satipaṭṭhāna*s thus throws into relief a central aspect of mindfulness practice in early Buddhism, namely, clear awareness of what is taking place combined with a balanced and equanimous attitude.

Cross-References

▶ Ānāpānasati
▶ Bhāvanā
▶ Insight

References

1. Feer L (ed) (1888–1898) The Saṃyutta Nikāya, 5 vols. Pali Text Society, Oxford
2. Trenckner V, Chalmers R (eds) (1888–1896) The Majjhima Nikāya, 3 vols. Pali Text Society, London
3. Carpenter JE, Rhys Davids TW (eds) (1890–1911) The Dīgha Nikāya, 3 vols. Pali Text Society, London
4. Rhys Davids CAF (ed) (1904) The Vibhaṅga. Pali Text Society, London
5. Morris R, Hardy E (eds) (1885–1900) The Aṅguttara Nikāya, 5 vols. Pali Text Society, London
6. Anālayo (2003) Satipaṭṭhāna, the direct path to realization. Windhorse, Birmingham
7. Gethin R (1992) The Establishing of mindfulness. In: id. The Buddhist path to awakening: a study of the Bodhi-Pakkhiyā Dhammā. Brill, Leiden, pp 29–68
8. Kuan TF (2008) Mindfulness in early Buddhism. Routledge, London
9. Ñāṇaponika (1992) The heart of Buddhist meditation. BPS, Kandy
10. Ñāṇaponika (1986) The power of mindfulness. BPS, Kandy
11. Sīlananda U (1990) The four foundations of mindfulness. Wisdom, Boston
12. Soma (1981) The way of mindfulness. BPS, Kandy

Satya Vacana

▶ Mantra

Satyātman

▶ Tathāgatagarbha

Sautrāntika

Charles Willemen
International Buddhist College, Songkhla, Thailand

Definition

Sautrāntikas are non-Vaibhāṣika Sarvāstivādins (from the second century on), preceding Mūlasarvāstivādins (end of the seventh century).

The term means: "relying on the *sūtras*" as the word of the Buddha. Sautrāntikas are a group of Sarvāstivādins who do not believe that the *Abhidharmapiṭaka* was proclaimed by the Buddha himself, *buddhabhāṣita* [10]. The Chinese term is *Jingliang*, meaning *sūtrapramāṇika*, taking the *sūtras* as the measure of truth [8, 9]. In Chinese they are referred to as *bu, nikāya*. They are also known as Saṃkrāntivādins, saying that the five aggregates, *skandhas*, pass through existences [1, 5]. It is now known that the Dārṣṭāntikas (those who use similes, stories, *dṛṣṭānta*) are Sautrāntikas. It is likely that the two terms go together as *dharma* (Sautrāntika) and *vinaya* (Dārṣṭāntika) [11]. Dārṣṭāntikas use the traditional long *vinaya* from Mathurā, with its many stories (*avadāna, dṛṣṭānta*). The term Sautrāntika makes sense as opposed to the Kaśmīra Vaibhāṣikas, who appear at the end of the second century A.D., in the time of the Sarvāstivāda synod during the reign of king Kaniṣka. Vaibhāṣikas, thus called because of their *Mahāvibhāṣā*, *Great Commentary*, on the *Jñānaprasthāna*, insisted that their *abhidharma* was spoken by the Buddha himself. Sautrāntikas also had an *Abhidharmapiṭaka*, because their treatises, *śāstras*, taught "about the *dharma* (*abhidharma*)." The Sautrāntika *Udāna*, which exists only in Chinese translation, *Chuyao jing*, Taishō ed.212, of the Dārṣṭāntika Dharmatrāta (ca. 150 A.D.), also known as just *bhadanta*, even mentions the contents of a fourth *Piṭaka*, called *Kṣudrakapiṭaka*, the contents of which are the Buddha's teaching in 12 parts, *aṅga*. The sixth part is called *Udāna*. This text also mentions Kumāralāta, the reputed first master, *mūlācārya*, of the Sautrāntikas, who must have lived in the second century A.D. He was from Takṣaśilā in Gandhāra. He wrote the *Kalpanāmaṇḍitikā* [7]. Its Chinese version, Taishō ed.201, has for a long time been erroneously attributed to Aśvaghoṣa (ca. 100 A.D.), a Sautrāntika influenced by Mahāsāṅghika ideas. Much, if not most of the confusion about the identity of the Sautrāntikas, of Sarvāstivādins, etc., is the result of the Sarvāstivāda synod in Kaśmīra, held during Kaniṣka, ca. 170 A.D. At that occasion an "orthodoxy," using Sanskrit and new texts, was established. The *vinaya* was abbreviated to ten recitations, called *Daśabhāṇavāra*, leaving out many stories of the traditional long *vinaya*. An *Abhidharmapiṭaka* of seven texts, said to be proclaimed by Buddha himself, was established. Some reasons to hold this synod were as follows: diversity among Sarvāstivādins was too great; rivalry with the Mahāsāṅghikas; and establishing Kaśmīra as a new cultural center, to the East of the traditional Gandharan cultural area.

History

Sarvāstivādins, "claiming (°*vāda*) that everything (*sarvam*) exists (*asti*)," split from the main Sthaviravāda trunk during the reign of Aśoka (ca. 264–227 B.C.), in Pāṭaliputra, ca. 244 B.C. This happened during the so-called third council presided over by Maudgalyāyana, who is still being refuted in the Vaibhāṣika *abhidharma*

(Vijñānakāya). The "orthodox" Sthaviravāda group called itself Vibhajyavāda, "Analysts." Sarvāstivādins then spread East along the Ganges, but mainly West to Mathurā. Upagupta, one of the patriarchs, is linked with Mathurā and with the long *vinaya*. Madhyāntika, who also had a link with Mathurā, is said to have taken Buddhism to the northwestern area, to the Gandharan cultural area, called *Jibin* in Chinese. *Jibin* is Uḍḍiyāna and Gandhāra, and also Bactria to the West of the Khyber Pass. From ca. 200 A.D. Kaśmīra is part of *Jibin* too [11]. In the Gandharan cultural area in the first century B.C. the two main Sarvāstivāda texts were the Gandharan *Aṣṭagrantha* of Kātyāyanīputra and the Bactrian *Abhidharmahṛdaya* of Dharmaśreṣṭhin (often erroneously called *Abhidharmasāra* of Dharmaśrī) [4]. When the Vaibhāṣika Sarvāstivādins came into existence in the second century A.D. the traditional Sarvāstivādins were called Sautrāntikas. Those who did not adopt the new shorter *vinaya, Daś abhāṇavāra*, were called Dārṣṭāntikas. It is now possible to call Dharmaśreṣṭhin and Aśvaghoṣa Sautrāntikas, even though the term did not exist in their time.

The western Sarvāstivādins were very heterogeneous. All agreed on "everything exists," but they had different ideas about what "everything" or "exists" really meant. "Everything" may mean all *dharmas*, factors, but how many factors are there (100, 43, 75)? Or does "everything" mean the aggregates, *skandhas*? Does "exist" mean now, in the present only? This is what most seem to have believed, but there was no agreement among Sautrāntika Sarvāstivādins [11]. The split between the Vaibhāṣika and the non-Vaibhāṣika Sautrāntika Sarvāstivādins lasted until the end of the seventh century. Between the presence in India of Xuanzang, middle of the seventh century, and the presence in India of Yijing, ca. 700 A.D., the term Mūlasarvāstivāda appears. They used Sanskrit and followed the traditional long *vinaya* which by then had undergone quite a long development. Vaibhāṣikas disappeared. An important reason why the western Sarvāstivādins gained the upper hand may be the fact that the westerners were hardly different from the Vaibhāṣikas any longer. Ever since ca. 200 A.D. they had gradually adapted to the new "orthodoxy." This can be seen in the Gandharan *Vibhāṣā* commentaries on the *Aṣṭagrantha* and in the different *Abhidharmahṛdaya* texts. The *Miśrakābhidharmahṛdaya* of Dharmatrāta (early fourth century) is an enlarged °*Hṛdaya*, and Vasubandhu's (ca. 350–430 A.D.) *Abhidharmakośabhāṣya* is based on the *Miśraka*° [6]. The Gandharan Vasubandhu had to face the anger of the Vaibhāṣika Saṅghabhadra for his Sautrāntika views [3]. It is possible to distinguish between old and new Dārṣṭāntikas, namely, before and after the Kaśmīra synod. When the Mūlasarvāstivādins appear, the term Sautrāntika did not immediately disappear. When Tibet enters the Buddhist world, it is in a time of Sautrāntika Mūlasarvāstivādins. In Central Asia both Gandharan and Vaibhāṣika Sarvāstivādins were represented. In Kuqa one sees a Sautrāntika presence in, for example, the fifth century, in Kumārajīva's (344–413 A.D.) time.

In Jiankang (Nanjing) in southern China *abhidharma* was Sautrāntika. Saṅghadeva, probably of Bactrian origin, introduced the *Aṣṭagrantha* and the *Hṛdaya* at the end of the fourth century, but when the *Miśraka*° was translated by Saṅghavarman in 435 A.D., an *Abhidharma* School was formed. It was replaced by a "*Kośa*" School when Paramārtha's translation of the *Kośabhāṣya* came out in 568 A.D. In China *abhidharma* is definitely Sautrāntika. Xuanzang introduced the Vaibhāṣika *abhidharma* in the seventh century, just before it disappeared in India itself. Nālandā was a non-Vaibhāṣika center.

Literature

Abhidharma literature has already been mentioned. It is very important to know that Sautrāntika *abhidharma* is "practical," teaches how to become an arhat, how to obtain the superknowledges, *abhijñā*. For example, the *Hṛdaya* is a guide book, teaching how to eliminate ignorance, etc. Sautrāntika manuals develop knowledge, *jñāna*. Sautrāntikas have a multitude of yoga manuals, often with *yogācāra (bhūmi)* in the title. The inspiration often comes from Maitreya, for example, Saṅgharakṣa's *Yogācārabhūmi*, translated by Dharmarakṣa in 284 A.D., Taishō ed.606. The *Yogācārabhūmi*, Taishō ed.1579, of Vasubandhu's older brother Asaṅga, incorporates Madhyamaka emptiness of Mahāsāṅghika affiliation in its yoga. It is very characteristic of non-Vaibhāṣika Sarvāstivādins to use "useful" ideas of their Mahāsāṅghika rivals in their own meditative practice. So-called Yogacāra, Vijñānavāda, as known from Vasubandhu's and Asaṅga's work, is of Gandharan Sautrāntika affiliation. Asaṅga, a Mahīśāsaka monk, continued the Gandharan *yogācāra* tradition. It should be remembered that, as Paramārtha has shown, ever since the first centuries A.D. Mahīśāsakas were doctrinally hardly any different from Sautrāntika Sarvāstivādins. Vasubandhu just continued his Gandharan Sautrāntika tradition.

Recently the idea was put forward that *Sukhāvatī* is an excellent intermediate existence, *antarābhava*, that Pure Land Buddhism is of Bactrian Sautrāntika origin.

Much of *avadāna* literature (*Divyāvadāna*, etc.) may be said to be of Dārṣṭāntika, Sautrāntika affiliation.

In the second century A.D. the Dārṣṭāntika Dharmatrāta used the Sarvāstivāda *Dharmapada* to establish an *Udāna* as the sixth part of a *Kṣudrakapiṭaka*. Later, a *Dharmapada* was collected from this *Udāna* again, forming the Mūlasarvāstivāda *Udānavarga* [2, 12].

The *(Jñānakāya) Prodbhūtopadeśa*, often called *Tattvasiddhiśāstra*, Taishō ed.1646, of the converted brahmin from Central India, Harivarman (ca. 300 A.D.), a late disciple of Kumāralāta, is a Sautrāntika work, influenced by Mahāsāṅghika ideas. The other brahmin from the same area, Aśvaghoṣa (ca. 100 A.D.), author of the *Buddhacarita*, may also be called a Sautrāntika, influenced by Mahāsāṅghika ideas.

Buddhist logic, as seen in the work of Dignāga (ca. 480–540 A.D.), is of Sautrāntika (Yogācāra) affiliation.

Cross-References

- Abhidharma (Theravāda)
- Antarābhava
- Asaṅga
- Aśvaghoṣa
- Buddhist Councils
- Gandhara
- Kaniṣka
- Paramārtha
- Pudgalavādins
- Sarvāstivāda
- Sthaviravāda
- Upagupta
- Vaibhāṣika
- Vasubandhu
- Xuanzang (Hieun-Tsang)
- Yijing
- Yogācāra

References

1. Bareau A (1955) Les sectes bouddhiques du petit véhicule. École Française d'Extrême-Orient, Saigon
2. Bernhard F I (1965), II (1968) Udānavarga III (1990) Byams pa thub bstan rdzoṅ rtse, with the cooperation of Dietz S, ed. Champa Thupten Zongtse. Vandenhoeck & Ruprecht, Gőttingen
3. Dhammajoti Bhikkhu KL (2009) Sarvāstivāda abhidharma, 4th edn. Centre of Buddhist Studies, The University of Hong Kong, Hong Kong
4. Frauwallner E (1995) Studies in abhidharma literature and the origins of Buddhist philosophical systems (trans: Kidd S). SUNY Press, New York
5. Jaini P (1959) The Sautrāntika theory of *Bīja*. Bull Sch Orient Afr Stud 22:236–249
6. La Vallée Poussin L de (1988) Abhidharmakośabhāsyam (trans: Pruden L), 4 vols. Asia Humanities Press, Berkeley
7. Lüders H (1979) Bruchstücke buddhistischer Dramen: Bruchstücke der Kalpanāmaṇḍitikā des Kumāralāta. Steiner, Wiesbaden
8. Singh A (2007) Buddha's original logical: the Sautrāntika analytical philosophy. Eastern Book Corporation, Delhi
9. Skorupski T (2005) Sautrāntika. In: Jones L (ed) Encyclopedia of religion, vol 12, 2nd edn. Macmillan Reference USA, Gale Virtual Reference Library, Detroit, pp 8136–8139
10. Willemen C, Dessein B, Cox C (1998) Sarvāstivāda Buddhist scholasticism. Brill, Leiden

S

11. Willemen C (2008) Kumārajīva's explanatory discourse about abhidharmic literature. J Int Coll Postgrad Buddh Stud 12:27–83
12. Willemen C (1978) The Chinese Udānavarga. Mélanges Chinois et Bouddhiques 19. Institut Belge des Hautes Études Chinoises, Brussels

Sāvaka

► *Śrāvaka*

Sāvatthī

K. T. S. Sarao
Department of Buddhist Studies, University of Delhi, Delhi, India

Synonyms

Shravasti; Śrāvastī

Definition

Capital city of Kosala at the time of the Buddha.

Sāvatthī (Sk: Śrāvastī) was the capital city of Kosala at the time of the Buddha ([14], Vol. iii, p. 233). King Pasenadi had a palace here with some kind of enclosure around it ([19], Vol. i, p. 149). The Buddha passed most of his monastic life at Sāvatthī. The city was situated on the banks of river Aciravatī (modern Rāptī) on which there was a bridge of boats. The river carried a considerable volume of commercial traffic conducted by commercial carriers, and it was also a source of livelihood for numerous fishers ([14], Vol. i, pp. 191, 293; Sn.194). Though Sāvatthī once ran short of alms ([14], Vol. iii, p. 64), the *Jātakas* are full of the glory and richness of Sāvatthī, and the fact that it was the home of the greatest merchant banker, Anāthapiṇḍika, is an indication of the accumulation of mercantile capital in the city ([5], Vol. iv, pp. 144ff, 236ff; Vol. vi, p. 68). A certain guild of merchants (*pūga*) at this city once offered food to the Buddhist saṃgha ([14], Vol. iv, pp. 30, 83). Sāvatthī was an entrepot from where caravans started with as many as 500 cartloads of wares on the well-recognized routes that connected this city to various parts of the country and major commercial centers as far to the south as Patiṭṭhāna ([5], Vol. iv, p. 350). While a considerable volume of commodity production within the environs of the city may be assumed, the more important activity may have been in commodity exchange, as the city was very conveniently located for the distribution of goods along the sub-Himālayan highlands on the one hand, and the riverine territories to the south. It was perhaps the most important center of early Buddhism before the rise of imperial Magadha. A number of celebrated personalities, monks, nuns, laymen, and laywomen were either from the city or first converted to the faith here (See [16]: Appendices Va and Vb).

Sāvatthī was 30 *yojanas* from Saṃkassa ([5], Vol. iv, p. 265). The road from Rājagaha to Sāvatthī passed through Vesāli, Setavya, Kapilavatthu, Kusinārā, Pāvā, and Bhogagāmanagara ([14], Vol. ii, p. 159f). From Sāvatthī the road went southwards through Sāketa to Kosambī ([6], Vol. v, p. 302). Sāketa was six yojanas from Sāvatthī, a distance which was once covered by Pasenadi with seven relays of chariots ([14], Vol. i, p. 88; Vol. iii, p. 211; [19], Vol. i, p. 149). We are also told of a certain festival being celebrated here ([14], Vol. iv, p. 179). Monasteries such as Rājakārāma, Pubbārama, and Mahallaka Vihāra were situated near the city ([13], Vol. ii, p. 183; [14], Vol. iv, p. 44; [19], Vol. iii, p. 271). There was also a public rest house in the neighborhood of Sāvatthī ([14], Vol. iv, p. 69). Jetavana, a royal garden which included Anāthapiṇpiṇḍka's monastery and an assembly hall and became a favorite retreat of the Buddha, was situated at a distance of about one mile to the south of Sāvatthī ([15], Vol. i, p. 178; [19], Vol. iii, p. 88). Andhavana, the black forest, was located at a distance of one *gāvuta* (league) from the city ([14], Vol. iii, pp. 37, 64). Of the four *Nikāyas*, 871 *suttas* are said to have been preached at Sāvatthī, 844 of which were in the Jetavana, 23 in the Pubbārāma, and 4 in the suburbs ([20], Vol. v, p. xviii). According to C.A.F. Rhys Davids, this city was the earliest emporium for the collection and preservation of the discourses as the Buddha mainly lived at this place ([19], Vol. iv, p. vi). When Faxian (399–414 C.E.) visited here, he only saw few inhabitants in Śrāvastī ([3], p. 73). Xuanzang (629–644 C.E.) saw Śrāvastī in desolation with derelict vihāras including the ruined Jetavana ([12], pp. 165–166).

Saheṭh-Maheṭh, on the south bank of the Rāptī, on the borders of the Gonḍā and Bahraich districts of Uttar Pradesh, is the modern equivalent of the ancient site of Sāvatthī ([4], p. 330ff; [17], pp. 133–138). The archaeological records show that Sāvatthī's earliest phase, which is predefense, may be dated to c. 500 B.C.E. ([9], pp. 2, 47–50). Saheṭh-Maheṭh has two distinct sites, 300-m apart, the former representing the Jetavana and the latter the city proper ([1], Vol. i, pp. 317ff, 330ff; Vol. xi, p. 78fff; [10], p. 286). The site of the city is now represented by a rampart of crescent shape enclosing an area of about 395 acres. This rampart which may be dated between c. 275 200 B.C.E., circuiting about 5 km, later came to be topped by a burnt-brick wall [18]. It has been suggested that this brick wall was thrown up as a protection against an Indo-Greek invasion during the Śuṅga period ([7], p. 65). Apart from an inscribed Kuṣāṇa Bodhisattva sculpture which says that it was set up in the Jetavana of Sāvatthī, a large number of stūpas, temples, and monasteries have been laid bare here ([1], Vol. i, pp. 317ff, 330ff; Vol. xi, p. 78ff). On the basis of the Bhārhut relief, depicting the Jetavana scene, showing in it two buildings, the Gandhakuṭi and the Kosambakuṭi, were identified with the two brick structures in the monastic area ([17], pp. 133–138). Though the settlement continued in a weak state for quite some time, its decline began with the downfall of Kosala. As indicated by the ruins, the suburb outside the walls of the city must have been very limited. According to an inscription of 1130 C.E., Sāvatthī was granted six villages for the maintenance of the monks ([2]: 1907–1908, p. 39). The Buddhist inscription of 1219 C.E. found at Śrāvastī mentions the establishment of a convent by Vidyādhara, a councillor of the king of Gādhipura ([8], p. 61).

Cross-References

- Anāthapiṇḍika
- Faxian (337–422 C.E.)
- Kapilavatthu
- Kusinārā
- Pasenadi
- Rājagaha (Pāli)
- Sāketa
- Saṃgha
- Vesālī
- Xuanzang (Hieun-Tsang)

References

1. Archaeological Survey of India, Government of India, New Delhi
2. Archaeological Survey of India Reports, Government of India, New Delhi
3. Beal S (trans) (1869) Travels of Fa-Hien and Sung-Yun: Buddhist Pilgrims from China to India (400 A.D. and 518 A.D.). K. Paul, Trench & Trübner, London
4. Cunningham A (1871) Archaeological survey of India: four reports 1862-63-64-65, vol 1. Govt. Press, Simla
5. Fausböll V (ed) (1877–1897) The Jātakas. Trübner & Co, London
6. Feer ML (ed) (1884–1898) The Saṃyutta Nikāya, 5 vols. Text Society, London
7. Ghosh A (1973) The city in early historic India. Indian Institute of Advanced Study, Simla
8. Indian Antiquary, vol xvii, 1888, Calcutta
9. Indian Archaeol Rev, 1858–1859, New Delhi
10. J Asiatic Soc Bengal lxii, Calcutta
11. Journal of the Royal Asiatic Society, London
12. Li R (trans) (1996) The great Tang dynasty record of the western regions. Numata Center for Buddhist Translation and Research, Berkeley
13. Morris R, Hardy E (eds) (1885–1900) The Aṅguttara Nikāya, 5 vols. Pali Text Society, London
14. Oldenberg H (ed) (1879–1883) The Vinaya Piṭakaṃ, 5 vols. Pali Text Society, London
15. Rhys Davids TW, Carpenter JE (eds) (1890–1911) The Dīgha Nikāya, 3 vols. Pali Text Society, London
16. Sarao KTS (2009) Origin and nature of ancient Indian Buddhism. Munshiram Manoharlal, New Delhi
17. Sahni DR (1908–1909) A Buddhist image inscription from Śrāvastī. Annual report of the Archaeological Survey of India. Government of India, New Delhi, pp 133–138
18. Sinha KK (1967) Excavations of Sravasti: 1959. BHU, Varanasi
19. Trenckner V, Chalmers R (ed) (1888–1896) The Majjhima Nikāya, 3 vols. Pali Text Society, London
20. Woodward FL (ed) (1956) The book of kindred saying, vol V. Pali Text Society, London, reprint

Savvaṇṇutā (Ardhamāgadhī)

► Omniscience

Schools of Early Buddhism

► Theravāda

Science (Buddhism)

Angraj Chaudhary
Vipassana Research Institute, Dhammagiri, Igatpuri, Nashik, Maharashtra, India

Definition

Science has been defined as "knowledge about the structure and behaviour of the natural and physical world based on facts that you can prove, for example by experiments" [1]. Its knowledge is the physical, chemical, and biological laws, which operate, respectively, in the physical, chemical, and biological world. The veracity or otherwise of these laws discovered by external observation can be proved or disproved by experimenting in outside labs.

The laws propounded by the Buddha, on the other hand, are concerned with how one's mind works, what makes it work, and why it works the way it works. These laws are psycho-ethical. What is the nature of the mind and how it works are related to the psychology of the mind, and what are wholesome and unwholesome actions and what are their results are related to ethics.

Nature of Buddha's Science

The science found in Buddha's teachings is not what one generally understands by it. It is a science in the sense that the laws propounded here can also be experimented and proved right or wrong. Like the physical, chemical, and biological laws, it also deals with cause and effect. Here also there is no effect without a cause. And with the disappearance of the cause, the effect disappears.

But it is a science with a difference. It is a science, which cannot be observed, experimented and understood by a man who does not live an ethical life. Devoid of ethics, in other words, without living a virtuous life and without attaining purity of mind, nobody can fully understand the laws of nature discovered by the Buddha.

One may call them spiritual laws or psycho-ethical laws and know them at the intellectual level, but one cannot understand them in depth. The Buddha himself could discover these laws by living a pure and ethical life, by making his mind "concentrated, purified, bright, unblemished, rid of imperfection, malleable, wieldy, steady and imperturbable" [2]. Because these laws are related to how mind and matter work together, they cannot be understood outside of one nor can they be experimented in any lab outside of one's fathom-long body, where the veracity of these laws can be proved if the mind of the man making experiment is purified. For precisely understanding these laws, one has to concentrate one's mind. And how can one's mind with various defilements be concentrated unless he observes ethical precepts to free his mind from them.

As far as the physical, chemical, and other laws are concerned, they have been discovered by persons who were not necessarily absorbed in meditation. They kept on observing what happened in nature and why and propounded these laws. Of course, some amount of concentration on their part must have been there, but leading an ethical life to achieve concentration of pure mind was not a necessary condition and was not an absolute condition for them.

Besides, the laws discovered by them can be experimented by others in any suitable lab. Neither the discoverers of the laws nor those who make experiments to prove their veracity are required to lead a life of virtue, concentration, and wisdom.

On the other hand, as the Buddha discovered the laws like the Law of Dependent Origination, or *Vedanā paccayā taṇhā* (sensation gives rise to desire) or *Pubbe hanati attānaṃ, pacchā hanati so pare* (he first hurts his own self before he hurts others), so a man walking on the path shown by him can verify these laws. These laws will remain a sealed book to those who do not walk on the path shown by him – the path consisting of *sīla*, *samādhi*, and *paññā*. Only those who achieve purity of mind are capable of verifying and understanding these laws.

Buddha's Scientific Discoveries Based on Observation by a Mind Purified and Sharpened by Leading an Ethical Life

Buddha's scientific discoveries are, therefore, based on observation by a mind purified and sharpened by leading an ethical life. All the laws that he discovered relate to how one's mind works, how cravings are caused, where precisely they arise, and why they cause suffering. If one knows all these, one can eliminate the causes and get rid of suffering.

One of the constituents of the discovery of these laws is observation. But this is not an ordinary observation. It is an observation made by a man who leads a pure ethical life as said above and who has made his mind so sharp, pointed, and pure that he can observe all the minutest things that happen within him. He can also understand how he hurts himself first when he is angry with somebody before he hurts him if he enables himself to see what happens inside him when he is angry with somebody.

No great scientist, not even a Nobel laureate, can understand the laws propounded by the Buddha unless he walks on the path shown by him and unless he achieves concentration of his mind by purifying it. And for this he has to observe precepts.

Buddha's Philosophy of Suffering Is Not Speculative but Born Out of His Own Experience

The philosophy of suffering propounded by the Buddha is not speculative, but it is born out of his own experience. It was the direct experience not of a common man but of a very sensitive and pure man, who was free from defilements such as greed, aversion, jealousy, anger, etc., which he had annihilated by practicing Vipassana.

His philosophy, therefore, is not based on abstractions. It does not speculate on "empty first principles" [3] in the words of Robert N. Beck – a pragmatic thinker. Buddha's attitude to speculative philosophy becomes clear from what he says to Poṭṭhapāda and Mālunkyaputta [4]. When Poṭṭhapāda put ten questions relating to the world and the soul like "Is the world eternal or not eternal, Is the world finite or not finite, Does the Tathāgata live after death or not and so on, the Buddha did not answer these questions. Why? Because he called them indeterminate questions. Answering such questions, according to him, is not 'conducive to the purpose, not conducive to Dhamma, not the way to embark on the holy life, it does not lead to disenchantment, to dispassion, to cessation, to calm, to higher knowledge, to enlightenment, to Nibbāna" [5]. Instead he explained the Four Noble Truths because their enunciation "is conducive to the purpose, conducive to Dhamma, the way to embark on the holy life; it leads to disenchantment, to dispassion, to cessation, to calm, to higher knowledge, to enlightenment, to Nibbāna" [6].

From this it is clear that the philosophy propounded by the Buddha is not speculative but pragmatic. This is also clear from what he says to Cūlamālunkyaputta who also like Poṭṭhapāda wanted to know from him the answer to such speculative questions. The Buddha said to Mālunkyaputta that to insist on knowing the answer to such questions before one agrees to lead the holy life is as foolish and fruitless as a man pierced with a poisoned arrow not agreeing to have the arrow taken out by a surgeon until he knows all about the arrow and the person who shot it. What would be the result? The result would be that he would suffer great pain and die, but the questions would remain unanswered [7].

The Buddha was a different kind of philosopher. The philosophies propounded by other philosophers are based on logic and reasoning and abstract thinking. They, therefore, may be

S

controversial and may not be logical. And certainly they are not useful at all for solving the existential problems of human life.

He was not like Leibnitz nor like Heraclitus. Leibnitz talks about monad – the indivisible simple entity. But how can this concept of monad enable one to end one's suffering, which is the greatest truth and an incontrovertible fact of life? Heraclitus said that one cannot step twice into the same river, and he definitely understood that all things are in a constant state of flux [8]. But this he realized at the intellectual level. Had he, like the Buddha, realized it at the experiential level, he would also have become the Buddha by developing nonattachment to worldly things, which attract one and cause desire in him. One's desires are not always fulfilled because the things, which one longs for, are not permanent. Therefore, when they change they cause suffering in him. Had Heraclitus realized the impermanent nature of things at the experiential level and trained his mind not to long for those impermanent things, he would have definitely gone the Buddha way.

The Buddha wanted to grapple with the problem of suffering which is ubiquitous and universal. Suffering is an existential problem not only of mankind but also of all living beings. No being is free from it. All are subject to different kinds of suffering, physical and mental. One who is born is subject to old age, disease, and death. He is also separated from the one he likes. This is suffering. He also has to live with somebody he does not like. This is also suffering. He does not get what he wants. This is also suffering. All these are sufferings from which nobody is free. The Buddha saw it very sensitively and wanted to find a way out to end it [9].

This is from where he started. He started with the real problem that faced mankind, with nothing abstract and speculative. He saw the problem facing him starkly. He saw the disease. His effort was to know the cause of the disease and find out its medicine as also how and when to take the medicine to be completely free from the disease.

In his spiritual journey he learned from his own experience. While practicing meditation he went deep into it and realized that one's suffering is caused by one's desires for the things one likes. One's desires are never fulfilled because the things one desires are not permanent. They are in a constant state of flux. This realization came to him after practicing meditation. This was a sort of "eureka" for him.

For practicing meditation concentration of mind is a *sine qua non*. The Buddha realized this while practicing meditation that so long as the mind is not free from defilements like greed, aversion, jealousy, hatred, etc., it cannot be concentrated. This was another big discovery. He thus concluded that in order to drive out defilements from mind observation of precepts (*sīla*) is necessary. Gradually he learned that observation of *sīla* helps one to achieve concentration of mind, and with the help of this concentration, one realizes the true nature of the objects of the world.

When one comes to know the true nature of things, ignorance goes away and one begins to see their true nature. In other words, true knowledge dawns upon him. He sees the objects of one's attachment impermanent, becomes disillusioned, and concludes that if the objects he longs for are transient and impermanent, how can they make him happy? This again was a great realization born out of his direct experience.

Thus the Buddha concluded that one's suffering is caused by one's desires and one has desires for things the real nature of which one does not know. There is a built-in dynamo inside everybody. So long as one is ignorant of the real nature of the objects of the world, the dynamo within one fueled by desires keeps on generating desires. And multiplication of desires causes endless suffering. But once one comes to know the real nature of the objects one hankers after, one begins to develop nonattachment for them. Practice of Vipassana meditation helps him a lot. Whenever one practices Vipassana one experiences that what arises passes away. Nothing is permanent. So one experiences impermanence (*aniccatā*). And whatever is impermanent is *dukkha* [10]. Thus one either reduces one's desires and reduces one's suffering proportionately or completely annihilates one's desires and completely eradicates one's suffering.

Practice of Vipassana helps one understand this law as it had helped the Buddha.

The Buddha thus realized the cause of suffering. It was then just the second step for him to know that suffering can be eliminated by removing its cause which is desire.

Thus he propounded the philosophy of suffering from his own experience. He had realized the great importance of observing moral precepts in concentrating his mind. He had also experienced the great role of a concentrated mind in seeing things sharply and clearly as they are, and by practicing Vipassana, he had seen how cravings are caused and how they can be eliminated. By practicing Vipassana, it became clear to him that "wherever in the world there is anything agreeable and pleasurable, there this craving arises and establishes itself" [11].

It did not take the Buddha long to conclude that cravings can be eliminated by eliminating the cause of cravings. And what is the cause of cravings? The agreeable and pleasurable in the world are the causes of cravings. By practicing Vipassana he knew that even the most beautiful objects of the world are impermanent. They do not last forever. The natural question was then why crave for them? Thus he trained his mind to see the transitory nature of objects and give up his craving for them. In this way by practicing Vipassana he ended his suffering. It means that anybody can end his suffering by practicing Vipassana.

Because he had realized how suffering is caused and also because he had realized the role of morality (*sīla*) in eliminating it, so, while propounding the philosophy of suffering, he ethicized it [12]. He was also a great psychologist. He saw the role of our mind in causing craving; he also saw how to tame this monkey mind, which now craves for this object and now for that.

The Buddha thus propounded his philosophy of suffering with his *bhāvanāmayā paññā*, (experiential wisdom) which is *yathābhūtañāṇadassana* (wisdom arising from seeing the truth as it is). *Bhāvanāmayā paññā* means insight wisdom developed at the experiential level. There is no question of it being false or speculative or abstract. It is experiential knowledge (*paññā*) with which he saw the cause of suffering. The philosophy of suffering propounded by the Buddha, therefore, is based on his direct experience. Anybody who practices Vipassana can see for himself why craving is caused, where suffering arises, and how craving and suffering can be ended.

The Buddha realized all this at the experiential level by practicing Vipassana and developing his *paññā* (insight wisdom or understanding based on his direct experience).

He propounded the Four Noble Truths of suffering, viz., suffering, its cause, its cessation, and the way leading to its cessation, and preached them to the first five disciples. He explained three aspects of each truth. One should know the first noble truth. This is the first aspect of the first noble truth. The first noble truth of suffering should be comprehended (*pariññeyaṃ*). This is called *kicca ñāṇa*, i. e., knowledge gained while doing. This is its second aspect. When it is thoroughly comprehended (*pariññātaṃ*), it is called *kata ñāṇa*, i.e., knowledge gained when done. This is its third aspect. Similarly the rest of the truths should also be known comprehensively. The second noble truth of suffering should be abandoned (*pahātabbaṃ*). This is *kicca ñāṇa*, and when it is completely abandoned (*pahīnaṃ*), it is called *kata ñāṇa*. The third noble truth should be realized (*sacchikātabbaṃ*). This aspect of this truth is *kicca ñāṇa*, and when it is realized (*sacchikataṃ*), it is called *kata ñāṇa*. The fourth noble truth should be developed (*bhāvetabbaṃ*). This is called *kicca ñāṇa*, and when it is developed (*bhāvita*), it is called *kata ñāṇa* [13].

The Buddha propounded the philosophy of suffering by developing his *bhāvanāmayā paññā*. Therefore his philosophy of suffering can be understood by developing *bhāvanāmayā paññā* for which practice of Vipassana meditation is inevitable.

Requisites Necessary for Practicing Vipassana

For practicing Vipassana, the nature of the mind has got to be understood. The mind is very fickle and unsteady [14]. This is psychology. And for concentrating mind observation of *sīla* is inevitable. *Sīla* comes under ethics. When one understands the true nature of the objects of the world for which one craves, this is metaphysics, Buddhist metaphysics if one may call it so. Apart from these, Vipassana also means training one's mind to give up the old habit pattern of reacting to sensations that arise on one's body. Thus Vipassana is a very comprehensive practice to know the nature of the mind and nature of reality. Besides, it is also an effective tool to train one's mind to learn to behave in a particular way.

Practicing Vipassana the Buddha propounded the Law of Dependent Origination, which explains how one creates *saṅkhāras* in ignorance, how *saṅkhāras* give rise to consciousness, consciousness to *nāma-rūpa*, etc., and how *bhava* gives rise to *jāti* and *jāti* gives rise to old age, disease, death, and all sorts of sorrows and suffering. The Buddha also concluded that as effect has a cause and as it can be eliminated by eliminating its cause, so suffering can be extirpated by eliminating cravings [15].

All the links of *paṭiccasamuppāda*, each of which is a law, can be understood by practicing Vipassana.

One's Fathom-Long Body Is the Only Laboratory Where the Laws Propounded by the Buddha Can Be Experimented

But there is a basic difference between the physical laws and the laws connected with the Four Noble Truths. In no other laboratory outside this fathom-long body can it be proved that sensations cause desire. This will be possible only when one, who wants to prove it, lives a pure life, practices Vipassana, and observes one's sensations, pleasant or unpleasant. He will see that he wants to have more of pleasant sensations and none of the unpleasant ones. The former is craving and the latter is aversion. Both are the causes of suffering.

Physical laws can be experimented and proved in outside laboratories by anybody. He may be of greedy temperament. He may have several defilements. It does not matter. But the laws relating to the Four Noble Truths propounded by the Buddha can be experienced and proved by those who live a virtuous life, i.e., who observe *sīla*, practice *samādhi*, and are on the way to develop *paññā* [16].

References

1. Hornby AS (2000) Oxford Advanced Learner's Dictionary. OUP
2. Ñāṇamoli B, Bodhi B (trans) (1995) The Middle Length Discourses of the Buddha. Wisdom Publications, Boston, p 341
3. Beck RN (1979) Handbook in Social Philosophy. Macmillan, New York, p 123
4. See the Poṭṭhapāda Sutta in the Dīgha Nikāya and the Cūlamālunkya Sutta in the Majjhima Nikāya (Unless otherwise mentioned all books referred to here are published by Vipassana Research Institute, Dhammagiri in 1998)
5. See the Cūlamālunkya Sutta in the Majjhima Nikāya
6. Walsh M (trans) (1995) The Long Discourses of the Buddha. Wisdom Publications, Boston, pp 164–165
7. See the Cūlamālunkya Sutta in the Majjhima Nikāya
8. You cannot step twice into the same river, for fresh waters are ever flowing in upon you –quoted from the foot note no 1 on p. no 26 of What the Buddha Taught by Walpole Rahula
9. D.2.228
10. S.2.21 Yad aniccaṃ taṃ dukkhaṃ, yaṃ dukkhaṃ tadanattā
11. Walsh M (1995) The Long Discourses of the Buddha. Wisdom Publications, Boston, p 346
12. Chaudhary A (2013) Ehicisation makes Buddhism a World Religion. In: Essays on Buddhism and Pali literature, 2nd edn. Eastern Book Linkers, Delhi, pp 90–96
13. S.3.484
14. Dh. verse 33
15. Yaṃ kiñci samudayadhammaṃ sabbaṃ taṃ nirodhadhammaṃ
16. M1. pp 1–8

Scripture of the Descent into Laṅkā

▶ Laṅkāvatāra Sūtra

Scripture Unlocking the Mysteries

▶ *Sandhinirmocana Sūtra*

Secret

► Mysticism (Buddhism)

Self

► Jīva (Jainism)
► Puḍgala (Puggala)

Self (Jainism)

Sean Butler
Claremont Graduate University, Claremont, CA, USA

Synonyms

Ātman; *Jīva*

Definition

An unperceivable, eternal entity whose primary characteristic is sentiency and whose essential element is knowledge; contrasted with a*jīva* or non-sentient substance.

The Ambiguity of the Self in Jainism

The first thing that one should note when investigating the Jain notion of the self is that the notion is ambiguous. "Self" might appear in Jain literature as *ātman*, *jīva*, *sattva*, or *jeta*, to name only a few possible translations. In turn, each of the above terms has various meanings that a Western audience might understand as only loosely correlated to a distinct concept of self (e.g., *ātman* might mean "breath"). Further, whereas the self is often conceptually distinguished from its attributes and manifestations, there is no such clear distinction in the Jain religion. Further still, different texts categorize the modes and attributes of the self differently. The self, then, is a concept that is integrated into a greater philosophical system and cosmology, a concept understood only in relation to its place in the greater system. As a full exploration of Jain philosophy and cosmology is not possible here, the following exposition will focus on the self as it relates to the three primary subsystems of which it is a part: *saṃsāra* (the cycle of rebirth and re-death), *mokṣa* (liberation), and the *karma* (moral law of cause and effect) path that links them.

The Self in Saṃsāra

The non-liberated self is known as the mundane self, the self that is embodied and is in *saṃsāra*. The mundane self is said to be identical with the body and thus distinct from the "real" self in that *jīva* identifies both living substances in the world of *saṃsāra* and the self/soul that transcends this existence and is capable of liberation. There are five types of embodiment of the self: the physical body, the divine or infernal body, the astral body, the consummative body, and the *karma* body. The mundane self is endowed with the qualities of remembrance, desire for knowledge, desire for activity, desire for movements, and doubt [1]. It is one of an infinite number of selves, it exists independently as a substance, and, according to Kundakunda, the most famous of Jain philosophers, it consists of knowledge, action, and fruit [2–6]. The mundane self has four possible modes of existence in *saṃsāra*: hellish existence, subhuman or animal existence, human existence, and divine existence. The mundane self is thus anchored in *saṃsāra* by its *karmas*, imperceptible matter that attach themselves to the self literally weighing down the self and counteracting the self's natural tendency to float up to heaven. The mundane self, which is bound by *karma*, is defiled by its *karma* which perverts its relation to knowledge, perception, feeling, belief, age, physicality, status, and power [1, 4, 7, 8]. It is the goal of the mundane self to transcend itself through the elimination of *karma* and achieve liberation.

The Liberated Self

The liberated self or the real self is the self that is free of all *karmas*. This self is understood as the real or true self because it is purified from the defiling influence of *karma* and thus is the distinct self, unbound to existences other than its own. The liberated self is said to be pure and perfect existence with infinite consciousness and omniscience [1, 4, 5, 8, 9]. Though there is some debate among Jain philosophers today about the omniscience of the liberated self, it is generally agreed that the liberated self is omniscient due to the inward direction of its consciousness [5, 8]. The liberated self is two-thirds the size of its last bodily incarnation and resides in *siddha-loka*, the crescent-shaped abode of the enlightened beings located at the top of the Jain universe. The essential attributes of the liberated self are knowledge, faith, energy, and bliss. The liberated self is immaterial but still substantial and eternal [3–5, 10]. One should note, however, that the boundary between the mundane and liberated self is not pristinely clear. Many maintain that *arhats* (sages), *Tīrthaṅkaras* (fordmakers), *Jinas* (conquerors), and *siddhas* (fully liberated beings) are each properly liberated, though not all free of *karma* (though all free of bad *karma*) [1, 11]. This distinction is important because it allows for omniscient beings to have been embodied in the world and deliver what the Jain religion considers to be the truth(s) about the world and the path to liberation.

The Path to Liberation

Much of the ambiguity or seeming inconsistency in the Jain notion of self becomes more comprehensible when viewed from the perspective of its goal of liberation. On its path to liberation, the self is often divided into three types: the external self, the internal self, and the highest self. The external self takes itself to be the body, the internal self understands that it is distinct from the body, and the highest self is the liberated, luminous self [11]. These three types of self may be understood in terms of a process from outward to inward perception. The least advanced selves on their path to liberation focus their consciousness outward and thus understand the world in terms of bodies and materiality. The self that has progressed in its path to liberation to some extent focuses its consciousness outward but also inward, recognizing that the soul is distinct from its material incarnation. The liberated self exists outside of *saṃsāra*, is free from *karmas*, and focuses only reflexively on its infinite luminosity. One thus understands the ambiguity of the self as a relation between the real (liberated) self, *karma*, and the relative state of the self in its journey to liberation. Because the nature of the liberated self is immaterial and free from *karmas*, the self that is in *saṃsāra* must be differentiated from the liberated self, and this differentiation directly relates to the presence of *karmas*. *Karmas*, thus, make the self dependent on the world around it, perverting the self's faith and knowledge which is pure in the liberated, *karma*-free, state. Thus, the essential attributes of the liberated self are overpowered or bound by *karma* [1]. The goal of every self is to break free from *karma*, purifying itself from the defiling influences of *karma*. It does this through the cessation of outward action and the inward orientation of faith and perception. Through this process, the self transforms through purification to total self-realization [8, 11]. Beginning in a state so bound up with materiality that it is undifferentiable from its material existence, moving through a process of right action, faith, and perception, to unadulterated, pure, existence. Each of these stages and their subprocesses identify the dynamism of the Jain notion of self as a process reality aiming at liberation.

Cross-References

- ▶ Dharma (Jainism)
- ▶ Jīva (Jainism)

▶ Karma (Jainism)
▶ Omniscience

References

1. Muniji S (2007) The doctrine of karma and transmigration in Jainism. Sanskar Jain Patrika, Chennai
2. Cort JE (1995) Genres of Jain history. J Indian Philos 23(4):469–506
3. Jain JP (2006) Religion and culture of the Jains. Bharatiya Jnanpith, New Delhi
4. Jaini PS (2001) The Jaina path of purification. Motilal Banarsidass, Delhi
5. Jain SC (2006) Structure and functions of soul in Jainism. Bharatiya Jnanpith, New Delhi
6. Muniji S (2007) The doctrine of the self in Jainism. Sanskar Jain Patrika, Chennai
7. Glasenapp HV (1942) Doctrine of karman in Jain philosophy. PV Research Institute, Varanasi
8. Muniji S (2006) Return to self. Sanskar Jain Patrika, Chennai
9. Sikdar JC (1991) Jaina theory of reality. PV Research Institute, Varanasi
10. Umaswami A (2010) Key to reality in Jainism. Digambar Jain Trilok Shodh Sansthan, Hastinapur
11. Muniji S (2007) The Jaina pathway to liberation. Sanskar Jain Patrika, Chennai

Seniya Bimbisāra

▶ Bimbisāra

Sensation

▶ Senses (Buddhism)

Senses (Buddhism)

Madhumita Chattopadhyay
Department of Philosophy, Jadavpur University, Kolkata, West Bengal, India

Synonyms

Faculty; Feeling; Sensation

Definition

Special bodily faculties by which sensation is aroused; bodily organ conveying external stimuli to the inner state of the mind.

Buddhist Notion of Sense-organs

In their search for finding out the way for removing suffering, the Buddhist philosophers put emphasis on the importance of knowledge regarding the real objects of the world. Though understanding or *paññā* is required for such an aim, they believed that it itself is not sufficient. It has to take help of others, for example, the faculties or the *indriya*s together with aggregates, bases, elements, etc. It is out of such belief that the discussion of *indriya* is made in Buddhist literature.

The term "*indriya*," the Sanskrit term for sense organs, is derived from the root "*idi*" signifying supreme authority (*paramaiśwarya*). Whatever exercises supreme power or authority is called an *indriya*. Thus, in general, *indriya*s signify *adhipati* or ruler – they are controlling faculties in the sense of bringing about action and are controlling faculties in the sense of sovereignty which is called the dominant influence. There are 22 such controlling faculties which include not only the cognitive faculties but something more which plays dominant influence on other aspects of the individual. 22 such controlling faculties are eye, ear, nose, tongue, body, mind, femininity, muscularity, vital principle, pleasure-physical, pain-physical, mental-pleasure, mental-pain, equanimity, faith, energy, mindfulness, concentration, understanding, I-shall-come-to-know-the-unknown faculty, final knowledge faculty, and final knower faculty.

In support of the view that the sense organs are of supreme power, the Buddhists point out that the six sense organs, namely, the visual one or the auditory one, are the supports of consciousness (*cittāśraya*). They are the principal organs of a being (*maulam sattvadravyam*) who is again identified as masculine or as feminine on the basis of *puruṣendriya* and *strīndriya*. The duration of

S

a being is maintained by the *jīvitendriya* or the vital principle. The individual being becomes contaminated (*samkleśa*) by the faculties of sensation *sukha*, etc. Its purification is prepared (*sambhāra*) by the five moral qualities, for example, *śraddhā*, and is completed by the last three *indriyas*. In other words, for the Buddhists, mere predominance is not the mark of an *indriya*, but predominance with regard to the constitution, the subdivision, etc., of a living being and with regard to the basis of his volition and cessation is considered to be the predominating feature of *indriya*.

Another account of the senses or the *indriyas* is found in Buddhist literature. In this account, interpretation of the elements of existence was made with a view to distinguish between the cognitive faculties and their corresponding objects. The cognitive faculties are believed to be six and their corresponding objects are also believed to be six in number. These cognitive faculties as well as the six categories of objects constitute the *āyatana*s. The term *āyatana* means entrance. It is an entrance for consciousness and mental phenomena. Consciousness never arises alone, since it is pure sensation without any content. It is always introduced by two elements: a cognitive element and a corresponding objective element. Thus, there are doors (*dvāra*) through which consciousness appears, and these doors are the senses. For example, through the door of vision (*caksur-indriyam-āyatanam*) arises the visual consciousness of color and shape. This classification in terms of *āyatana* is peculiarly a Buddhist one which covers all objects of cognition into sense objects and nonsensuous ones.

An alternative account of *indriya* has been proposed in the Buddhist text *Vibhāṣā*. There, 14 *indriyas* as support of transmigration, origin, duration, enjoyment of this support are admitted. The other *indriyas* have the same function with regard to *Nirvāṇa*. According to this view, the six organs (*ṣaḍāyatanas*), starting with the visual sense organ to the sense organ of mind, are the supports of this repeated existence in this world since they are the principal organs of a being. It is through the two sexual organs of masculinity and femininity that the two organs of touch and mind directly arise, and the other four organs, namely, eye, ear, nose, and tongue, gradually come into existence. These sense organs, however, last on the basis of the vital organ (i.e., the *ṣaḍāyatana*s last so long as the vital organ is there). It is through the five sensations that the *ṣaḍāyatana*s enjoy. On the other hand, the five faculties, namely, faith, force, memory, absorption, and discernment, are the support of cessation since they are considered to be the very basis of that ultimate stage. *Nirvāṇa* is generated for the first time through the organ *ājñāsyāmīndriya*, for it is the first pure faculty. *Nirvāṇa* is developed through the second pure organ and is *experienced* by the third pure organ *ājñātāvīndriya*, for it is through this faculty that one experiences the satisfaction and well-being of deliverance.

The Buddhists refute the views of the Sāmkhya philosophers who maintain that voice (*vāk*), hands (*pāṇi*), feet (*pāda*), the anus (*pāyu*), and the sexual organs (*upastha*) are also *indriyas* since they also have predominance over their respective functions like speaking, taking, walking, excretion, enjoyment of pleasure and pain, etc. According to the Buddhists, voice cannot be regarded as *indriya*, since it is not the sole predominating factor with regard to words; some sort of training regarding the operation of the tongue is essential, which is not the case with other sense organs like eye, etc. A newborn baby without any instruction can see the form but cannot speak without any training. So the character of *indriya* is not satisfied in the case of voice and, hence, cannot be considered an *indriya*. In fact, the Sāṁkhya philosophers regard the organs of action (*karmendriya*) to be suprasensible like the organs of consciousness, while the Buddhists believe that words are action of the tongue which is the locus of the organs of taste. Similarly, hands and feet cannot be regarded as *indriya*, for they are not predominant with regard to grasping and walking. Grasping and walking are simply arousing the hands and feet in a second moment in another place and with a new figure. Moreover, it is a fact that hands and feet are not indispensable for grasping or walking since lizards and the like can perform similar functions of grasping and walking even in the absence of hands and feet. Further, if the hands and the feet were considered as *indriyas*, the throat, the teeth, the eyelids, and the joints also would have to be accepted as *indriyas*, since they function respectively with regard to swallowing, chewing, opening and closing, and folding up, and anything that exercises its action with regard to its effect. Hence, the term "*indriya*" is reserved for that which possesses predominance.

The important feature of the Buddhist discussion of *indriya* is the emphasis on the notion of the "supreme development of the faculties". In the other schools of Indian philosophy, it is generally believed that in the ultimate stage of liberation, the sense organs do not perform their normal function. That is, one does not see forms with the eyes, nor does one hear words with the ear, etc. Under this interpretation the liberated person will have to be regarded as blind or as deaf, etc., which no one will accept. So the view of Lord Buddha is that in the stage of liberation a *bhiksu* also sees a form with the eyes or hears a word with the ear, and there also arises in him the idea of what is agreeable or what is disagreeable or what is both agreeable and disagreeable, but he does not allow his mind to be overcome by them. Hence, the teaching of Lord Buddha toward his disciples is not to shut the sense organs but to suppress the defilements of the mind like greed, lust, etc., and try to establish equanimity of insight.

Cross-References

- ▶ Abhidharma (Theravāda)
- ▶ Knowledge (Buddhism)
- ▶ Mind (Buddhism)
- ▶ Psychology (Buddhism)

References

1. Choudhury S (1996) Analytical study of the Abhidharmakośa. Sanskrit College, Calcutta
2. Guenther HV (1999) Philosophy and psychology in the Abhidharma. Motilal Banarsidass, Delhi
3. Haldar A (2001) Some psychological aspects of early Buddhist philosophy based on Abhidharmakosah of Vasubandhu. Asiatic Society, Kolkata
4. Poussin L (1990) Abhidharmakośabhāṣyam (trans: Pruden LM), vol 1. Asian Humanities Press, Berkeley
5. Rhys Davids CAF (1976) The compendium of philosophy (tr. of the *Abhidhammaṭṭhasangaha*). Pali Text Society, London
6. Sāmkṛtyāyana R (ed) (1988) Abhidharmakośah: Ācārya Vasubandhupraṇītaḥ. Kāśī Vidyāpīth, Varanasi
7. Sastri SD (ed) (1998) The Abhidharmakosa and Bhasya of Acarya Vasubandhu with Sphutartha commentary of Acarya Yasomitra. Bauddha Bharati, Varanasi
8. Chattopadhyay M (2004) Analysis of Indriya: a Buddhist reflection. In: Narasimha Murthy ML, Sadasiva Murty R (eds) Work culture and efficiency with special reference to indriyas. Rashtriya Sanskrit Vidyapeetha, Deemed University, Tirupati

Sentient Beings

Sarah Whylly
Religion Department, Florida State University, Tallahassee, FL, USA

Definition

Beings with consciousness or sentience; capable of subjective experience. In Buddhist thought and literature it is a being of the five *skandhas* or aggregates that is not enlightened.

Characterizations of Sentient Beings in Buddhist Thought

A sentient being is one that possesses Buddha-nature within them. This Buddha-nature is a potential which may lead the being to attain enlightenment and reach Buddhahood. However, sentient beings as such are not yet enlightened. These beings are ones in whom the five aggregates are thought to be present. These five aggregates are form, sensation, perception, categorical or volitional judgments, and consciousness. It is these five aggregates that lead to grasping and attachment. Beings of the five aggregates are still subject to the cycle of samsara and experience suffering.

What Kinds of Beings Are Sentient Beings?

Ideas regarding which beings are sentient and which are not are varied. Considerations for sentience have been made with regard to animals and plants in addition to humans and other sorts of beings such as hungry ghosts, demons, or gods. Although all sentient beings are caught up in samsara, human sentience is viewed as being special since in humans it is characterized by a greater degree of freedom and a greater ability to comprehend. Thus, humans are morally and spiritually more capable than other sorts of beings. This is not to say that other types of beings are not capable of morality and do not have freedom – it is a matter of degree. There are varying views upon whether or not plants can be considered sentient beings. There has been some suggestion from scholars that Pāli Buddhism, particularly early Pāli Buddhism, was at least ambiguous on this question while others claim that Tibetan and Japanese forms of Buddhism include plants in sentient beings. That which is non-sentient is part of the background environment, the only possible exception being plant life, as mentioned earlier.

The Role of Compassion Among Sentient Beings

The position of humans as unique sorts of sentient beings does not mean that humans should exploit other sentient beings or dominate them. In fact, humans, along with all other sentient beings, are expected to have compassion toward their fellow beings. The idea of *ahiṃsa* is particularly relevant in the conversation on sentient beings. *Ahiṃsa* is noninjury or nonviolence. The first precept of the five Buddhist Precepts is to keep from or avoid intentional violence toward or the intentional killing of living beings. Emphasis upon the intentionality of an act implies that one might be held less morally blameworthy or perhaps not blameworthy at all in instances where harm is caused but not intentionally. Not only does one bring harm to another being but, because of the effects of karma, they bring harm to themselves. Toward this end, some Buddhist practitioners are careful even when they drink water to try to avoid harming beings which might live in it, while others confine such observances to the dietary practice of vegetarianism or veganism [1]. It is sometimes unclear in Buddhist literature to whom certain injunctions regarding the treatment of other sentient beings are directed. Some rules are meant exclusively for *sangha* members, others for laity.

It should be noted, however, that compassion toward living beings is frequently characterized in Indian Buddhist literature as being the lowest form of compassion of the three types of compassion that exist. This classification involves levels of awareness of the nature of all things. The first level is compassion toward living beings. The second is compassion on the impersonal events of the world after someone realizes that living beings do not exist. The third level is compassion which acts within the universe of emptiness. Thus, the first level or compassion toward living beings is a kind of emotion that brings about the motivation to help others. This level should also contain the caveat that this sort of emotion is dependent upon a view of others as distinction beings. The second level acknowledges that the lives of people are not separate or distinct identity units. The third level eradicates a view of life as a thing at all and acknowledges the emptiness of everything [2].

The Bodhisattva Vow and Sentient Beings

A *bodhisattva* is any person who, in response to compassion for all sentient beings, aspires to Buddhahood so as to benefit all such beings. This person possesses *bodhicitta* or a wish for enlightenment which will be of benefit to all sentient beings still in *samsāra*. The *bodhisattva* is one whose sole motivation for all activity is the goal of benefiting all sentient beings in *samsāra*.

The *bodhisattva* takes a vow toward this motivation often called the *Bodhisattva Vow* or *Precept*. This vow involves committing oneself to working for the liberation of all sentient beings from *samsāra* and to leading them to enlightenment for the entirety of *samsāra*.

The Concept of Sentient Beings and Buddhist History

Buddhists have less strict views than other traditions such as Jainism with regard to sentient beings, although the rules governing this treatment vary depending upon the kind of Buddhists involved and the time and place under consideration. Although there is a tradition of vegetarianism in Buddhism, some Buddhists were allowed to eat meat if it was not killed for them in particular. There have also been injunctions for Buddhists to avoid destroying foliage, as sentient beings rely upon them for food and shelter.

This does not mean that Buddhists have necessarily been pacifists. Although nonviolence is a tenet particularly in the Pali Canon, this has not been evidenced in the historical record. Frequently, war and conflict are viewed as unavoidable aspects of human life and defensive action was sometimes viewed as required. However, this does not mean that war should be waged arbitrarily. Attempts at peaceful resolutions are encouraged and the demand for right attitudes requires that persons cultivate mental tranquility in order to avoid engaging in violent behaviors.

In the twentieth century, concern arose over animal research testing that has inspired continued debate among some Buddhists. Some Buddhists take the view that even vaccinations developed from animals are to be shunned while others believe that animal testing allows humans a gain that is worth the price paid by the suffering of animals. This view is further qualified by requiring that the benefit to humans needs to be profoundly measurable and that new alternatives for testing be explored constantly. In earlier times, objections to the use of animals in ritual sacrifice or killing animals as part of the halal practice of the purification of meat were made by Buddhists. This has translated into laws at certain times against certain practices considered exploitative of animals as in the cases of King Aśoka or King Alaungpaya who attempted to legislate killing according to the Buddhist injunctions.

Cross-References

- ▶ Ahimsa
- ▶ Asoka
- ▶ Ethics (Buddhism)
- ▶ Vegetarianism (Buddhism)
- ▶ Warfare

References

1. Findly EB (2002) Borderline beings: plant possibilities in early Buddhism. J Am Orient Soc 122(2):252–263
2. Goodman C (2009) Consequences of compassion. Oxford University Press, New York
3. Harvey P (2000) An introduction to Buddhist ethics. Cambridge University Press, Cambridge
4. Lecso PA (1988) To do no harm: a Buddhist view on animal use in research. J Relig Health 27(4):307–312
5. Saddhatissa H (1970) Buddhist ethics: essence of Buddhism. George Braziller, New York
6. Spencer RF (1966) Ethical expression in a Burmese Jātaka. J Am Folklore 79(311):278–301
7. Swearer DK (1998) Buddhist virtue, voluntary poverty, and extensive benevolence. J Relig Ethics 26(1):71–103

Sentient Substance

▶ Jīva (Jainism)

Sepulchral Monument

▶ Cetiya

Servants

▶ Slaves (Buddhism)

S

Sgrolma'imgonpo

► Tāranātha

Shengtian (Chinese)

► Āryadeva

Shin Upago

► Upagupta

Shingon

► Vajrayāna (Buddhism)

Short Overview of Buddhism

► Philosophy (Buddhism)

Shoten (Japanese)

► Āryadeva

Shravasti

► Sāvatthī

Shuen Shang

► Xuanzang (Hieun-Tsang)

Shyiwa Lha

► Śāntideva

Siddha-loka

► Heaven (Jainism)

Sīla

► Good (Buddhism)
► Responsibility (Buddhism)

Śīla

Mangala Ramchandra Chinchore
Department of Philosophy, Centre for Studies in Classical Indian Buddhist Philosophy and Culture, University of Pune, Pune, Maharashtra, India

Synonyms

Sk. *Śīla-śikṣā/Adhi-śīla*,

Śīla consists of the three factors, namely, right speech (Sk. *Samyak-vāk*), right action (Sk. *Samyak-Karmānta*), and right livelihood (Sk. *Samyak-Ājīvikā*).

Definition

Śīla (Sk.: *Śīla-śikṣā/Adhi-śīla*) (translated into English as moral conduct/character) is a part of the Noble Eightfold Path (Sk. *Aṣṭāṅgika-mārga*), which is a way to destroy/control suffering (Sk. *Duḥkha-nirodha-gāmini-pratipad*), the fourth Noble Truth (Sk. *Ārya-satya*). *Śīla* is translated into English as moral conduct/character, personality development facilitative factors, and/ or virtues convenient in practical life.

The Buddhist way of life forms three modes of educating/training/culturing (Sk. *Tri-Śikṣā*), namely, training/developing moral character (Sk. *Śīla-śikṣā*/*Adhi-śīla*), training mind/developing concentration of consciousness (Sk. *Samādhi-ś ikṣā/Citta-śikṣā*), and developing wisdom and insight (Sk. *Prajñā/ Adhi-prajñā*), [1] where training moral character is given first priority.

Buddhist Character-Building Norms

Śīla is the characteristic mark and fundamental basis of Buddhist ethics. It is not merely ethical theory but physical, mental, and verbal modes of performing actions and practicing them consistently and conducting conscientiously throughout life. Whosoever is a follower of Buddhism should observe with his own will certain codes of conduct and adopt certain modes of life which are conducive to building excellence of character and/or develop perfection in personality on the one hand [2] and correspondingly enable to form a social order and peace on the other. These codes are neither authoritative eternal rules nor commandments nor mere theoretical principles. They are formulated by enlightened human beings after experiencing and/ or contemplating on life and then, onward, they are meant to be used with one's own conviction for the benefit of all human beings. These vows are commonly observable (Sk. *Saṁdṛṣṭika*), timeless (Sk. *Akālika*), verifiable (Sk. *Aihipaśyika*), fruitful (Sk. *Anupānāyika*), sensed/discovered (Sk. *Vedayiyavya*), and individually experienced (Sk. *Pratyātman*) by discerning personal insights (Sk. *Vijñu*) [3].

In Buddhism, one can be considered honorable, gentleman, and excellent (Sk. *Ārya*) provided one has good habits, exercises good intensions, and uses ethically altruistic means to get freedom from pain and suffering (Sk. *Duḥkha*), which is the goal of all human beings. To realize the true nature of human beings in particular and all sentient beings in general (i.e., *Duḥkha*) is, in a sense, enlightenment (Sk. *Bodhi*). But Buddhism does not end by merely presenting fact-finding analysis, it also inquires into the possibility of overcoming it by stipulating concretely certain ways and means to regulate life. For that, it stresses on conduct, which has to be controlled and channelized by some codes of moral conduct (Sk. *Śīla*).

Development of moral conduct/character has two aspects [4]. One, prohibitive/negative: refraining from certain things already prevalent as habits or, at present, likely to overpower and hence need regulating modes and, in future, abstaining from attractions, lures, and temptations of any kind. Second, constructive/positive: they are helpful to develop personality in mundane life and/or insight in spiritual life. Moral character (Sk. *Śīla*) is a stepping-stone toward enlightenment. For enlightenment, first one should have faith in teachings of the Buddha and Buddhist way of life, first-hand experience of pain and suffering as the nature of human life and of the reality correspondingly; and then onwards apply one's own in-depth observations by understanding things properly. What is right and what is wrong cannot be decided once and for all eternally, uniformly, and abstractly in the form of theoretical principles. These codes of conduct prohibit, refrain, and abstain from doing wrong/ evil acts and inhumane practices on the one hand and enable to regulate and channelize conduct and develop ideal personality and virtues and are conducive to the well-being of humanity at large on the other.

Generally, in Buddhism, it is held that by nature one is neither totally good nor completely bad, though in the circumstances and situations prevailed and predominated, one behaves wrongly. But if one is trained, cultured, and nurtured in an appropriate way, one can confront situations courageously, respond to things in the right way, and regulate behavior in proper direction. Buddhism holds that even though the circumstances in which one lives are adverse, one should not be hopeless to bring in change using moral modes of action. It depends by and large upon how one is trained and develops psychological attitude of taking things. Generally, they emphasize on proper/right training of mind, which takes care of the other two aspects of behavior, namely, bodily and verbal modes of actions. In other words, Buddhism advocates that both bodily and verbal actions are regulated by psychological states of mind. Although conventionally it is held that in totality, mind, body, and speech understood in depth builds character, according to Buddhism, it mainly depends upon the development of psychological states of mind. The more one dives deep into the inner world, the height of spiritual growth and/or insightful understanding towards perfection springs up and blossoms. Thus, proper spiritual training (Sk. *Adhi-Śikṣā*) is important.

There are certain codes of conduct or modes of training discovered by the Gautama Buddha and taught to his then prevalent disciples that are later on used generally for the positive development of character. They are facilitative to practice Buddhist way of life taking into consideration two forms of life, stipulated in the form of two sets: one for ordained monastic followers (Sk. *Bhikṣu-saṁgha*), namely, monks and nuns (Sk. *Bhikṣu-Bhikṣuṇī*), and another for lay disciples (Sk. *Puthujana*) consisting of householders – men and women (Sk. *Upāsakas-Upāsikās*). One begins with faith and initiates with reciting three refuges (Sk. *Tri-śaraṇas*), namely, the Buddha, teachings of Buddhism (Pāli-*Dhamma*), and the community of followers (Sk. *Saṁgha*), as a devotional religious regular practice. Accompanied with it then is taking the five precepts/vows/voluntary promises (Sk. *Pañca-Śīla*), which are common to all, since Buddhism believes that anyone can get perfection or develop excellence of character. Those who are practitioners, they recite them daily to remind promises given by oneself in the morning and evening. Any lay person can undertake them voluntarily to facilitate practicing Buddhism. These promises are:

1. To refrain from destroying life of any sentient being, i.e., killing excessively living creatures (Sk. *Pāṇātipāta*)
2. To refrain from taking that which is not given, i.e., stealing (Sk. *Adinnādanā*)
3. To refrain from sexual misconduct, i.e., illicit sex (Sk. *Kāmesu-micchācāra*)
4. To refrain from wrong speech, i.e., lying, abusing, harsh words, etc. (Sk. *Musāvāda*)
5. To refrain from intoxicating drinks and drugs that lead to carelessness (Sk. *Surāmerayamajjā-pamādatthāna*)

Over and above these five precepts/vows/voluntary promises (Sk. *Pañca-Śīlas*), if one wishes to practice a bit more strictly than the usual one, leading more toward ascetic life, one undertakes the eight precepts (Sk. *Aṣṭa-Śīla*), i.e., three more percepts in addition to the above-mentioned five precepts. One observes a 1-day or a week fast (Sk. *Uposatha*) on the new moon, first quarter moon, full moon, and last quarter moon days living in the monastery and practicing the eight precepts, namely:

6. To refrain from eating untimely before sunrise and after sunset (Sk. *Aparānha-bhojana*)
7. To refrain from dancing (Sk. *Nṛtya*), music/singing (Sk. *Saṅgīta*), playing instrumental music (Sk. *Vādya*), and attending entertainment performances (Sk. *Samārādhana*)
8. To refrain from wearing perfume/scents and using cosmetics (Sk. *Gaṅdha-vilepana*) and garlands/decorative accessories (Sk. *Mālā-dhāraṇa*)

Further, additionally, two more precepts are there, thus making it, in total, ten precepts (Sk. *Daśa-Śīla*) that are mandatory for all ordained monks and nuns (Sk. *Bhikṣu-Bhikṣuṇī*). They are:

9. To refrain from sitting on luxurious high chair or sleeping on luxurious and soft bed, which may cause overindulging in sleep (Sk. *Uccāsana-mṛduśayyā-śayana*)
10. To refrain from accepting gold (Sk. *Suvarṇa*), silver (Sk. *Rajata*), and/or money (Sk. *Mudrā*)

Over and above these ten precepts/moral codes, there are 227 rules for ordained monks (Pāli-*Bhikkhus*) and 311 for nuns (Pāli-*Bhikkhuṇī*), known as codes of disciplining for release (Pāli- *Pātimokkha*) and [5] discussed in detail in the *Vinaya-Piṭaka*. It is with reference to practicing these codes strictly or flexibly that there were disputes between *Sthaviravādins* and *Mahāsāṁghikas* of Buddhism.

In practicing these codes, one concentrates on refraining or abstaining from evil tendencies prevalent within each one by nature, which are likely to predominate, and because of which one experiences pain and suffering further. Moreover, by observing these promises as daily practices, one attempts to reduce predominance of instincts and regulates passions to develop moral virtues, which lead to perfection or excellence. Here, it is important to note that Buddhist regulations emphasize on individual conduct and concentrate on personal/individual aspect of life to be morally governed first and, through collection of such individuals who are observing ethical codes, hope to build a society. These codes are facilitative and conducive to practice Buddhist way of life for any lay person who desires to follow it by conviction. In the context of Eightfold Path (Sk. *Aṣṭāṅgika-mārga*) in general and right action (Sk. *Samyak-Karmānta*) in particular, Gautama the Buddha has explained five precepts (Sk. *Panca-Śīla*) and ten precepts (Sk. *Daśa-Śīla*), respectively. Eightfold Path (Sk. *Aṣṭāṅgika-mārga*) is nothing else but a way to control/destroy pain and suffering (Sk. *Duḥkha-nirodha-gāminī-pratipad*) innovatively discovered by the Buddha and taught to all his disciples – known and unknown, universally.

In Buddhism, ideal personality could be built from the three avenues provided by the Buddha and training of spiritual life is insisted, which consists of the three modes of training (Sk. *Adhi/Tri-Śikṣā*), namely, character/morality (Sk. *Śīla*), wisdom/insight (Sk. *Prajñā*), and meditation/concentration (Sk. *Samādhi*). Ideal/perfect moral conduct (Sk. *Śīla*) is essential for opening the possibility of getting insight/developing wisdom (Sk. *Prajñā*) and then only further can one have meditation/concentration (Sk. *Samādhi*). Thus, there is a sequential order of its enumeration (Sk. *Anuloma*) for the beginners, but for those who have already developed control over one's own conduct, it is indicated and can be verified in their practice in converse order (Sk. *Pratiloma*), excellence in meditation/concentration (Sk. *Samādhi*) is reflected in the insightful understanding (Sk. *Prajñā*), and further, wisdom is seen in practicing moral character (Sk. *Śīla*). Right comprehension and insightful understanding are the indicators of wisdom in behavior [6]. The three modes of training (Sk. *Tri-Śikṣā*), namely, wisdom/insight (Sk. *Prajñā*), character/morality (Sk. *Śīla*), and meditation/concentration (Sk. *Samādhi*) are also known as precious touchstones of perfection/jewels of ideal personality (Sk. *Tri-ratnas*). It is, perhaps, because before getting introduced or knowing the Buddhist way of life, they are the modes of training (Sk. *Adhi/Tri-Śikṣā*), but after learning/getting command over them, they turn out to be the indicators of what one has been learnt through practicing moral conduct/actual behavior and form virtuous characteristics of an individual having precious jewels of ideal perfection (Sk. *Tri-ratnas*). Buddhist ethics is based on these *Tri-ratnas*, which enables one to learn the importance of responsibility, accountability, and independence. They are the three aspects of personality that are interlinked or interdependent. They are not mutually exclusive, but they conjointly form the core of teaching of the Buddha and operate as indicators of the development of personality. They are the avenues of becoming free from pain and suffering (Sk. *Duḥkha*) and mundane life/world (Sk. *Saṁsāra*). They are relevant universally with regard to all and give hope to all by reminding the potentiality to attain the state of emancipation (Sk. *Nirvāṇa*).

Śīla consists of positively adopting and observing in practice wholesome actions (Sk. *Kuśala-Karma*) that are associated with motives and intensions. They have creative psychological and ethical basis. And, negatively, they make one cautious and refrain anybody from doing unwholesome actions (Sk. *Akuśala-Karma*), respectively. For the *Hīnayāna* tradition of Buddhism, good actions (Sk. *Kuśala-Karmas*) are those which are free from the three defilements, namely, greed (Sk. *Lobha*), hate (Sk. *Dveṣa*), and delusion (Sk. *Moha*). However, in the *Mahāyāna* tradition of Buddhism, it has to be inspired positively by compassion (Sk. *Karuṇā*) and benevolent love (Sk. *Maitrī*) as well [7]. In the *Mahāyāna* tradition, positive development of virtues and ideal personality development are stressed more by practicing virtues par excellence (Sk. *Pāramitās*). Freedom to grow and develop is ethically based on true independence and equality without any kind of discrimination, but it is embedded by responsibility and accountability because, freedom is not to be confused with licentiousness. On the contrary, in the *Hīnayāna* tradition, emphasis seems to be on wholesome/unwholesome actions (Sk. *Kuśala/Akuśala-Karmas*) and the five/ten precepts (Sk. *Śīlas – Pañca* or *Daśa*), respectively. *Mahāyānists* prefer to consider virtues par excellence (Sk. *Pāramitās*) more and perhaps because of this, in the list of virtues (Sk. *Pāramitās*), character/morality (*Śīla*) gets second enumerative important status.

Cross-References

- ▶ *Aṣṭāṅgamārga*
- ▶ *Ārya Satyāni*
- ▶ *Bodhi*
- ▶ *Dharma*
- ▶ *Duḥkha*
- ▶ *Karma*
- ▶ *Karuṇā*
- ▶ *Mahāsāṅghika*
- ▶ *Nirvāṇa*
- ▶ *Pañca-Śīla*
- ▶ *Pāṭimokkha*
- ▶ *Pāramitās*
- ▶ *Prajñā*
- ▶ *Saṃsāra*
- ▶ *Samadhi-Marana*
- ▶ *Upāsaka*
- ▶ *Uposatha*

References

1. (1995) Majjhima-Nikāya, Tipiṭaka, Chaṭṭha Saṇgāyana edn (CD-ROM Version-3). Vipassana Research Institute, Igatpuri
2. Deo AN (1901) Bauddha-Dharma-Darsana (in Hindi), 2nd edn. Bihar Rashtrabhasa Parisad, Patna
3. (1995) Khuddakapāṭha, Aṅguttara-Nikāya, Tipiṭaka, Chaṭṭha Saṇgāyana edn (CD-ROM Version-3). Vipassana Research Institute, Igatpuri
4. (1995) Sāmaññaphala-Sutta (Dīgha-Nikāya-II), Tipiṭaka, Chaṭṭha Saṇgāyana edn (CD-ROM Version-3). Vipassana Research Institute, Igatpuri
5. (1995) Pātimokkha, Vinaya-Piṭaka, Tipiṭaka, Chaṭṭha Saṇgāyana edn (CD-ROM Version-3). Vipassana Research Institute, Igatpuri
6. Kasyapa BJ (ed) (1961) Dīgha-Nikāya. Pali Text Publication Board, Bihar Govt, Nalanda
7. Vaidya PL (ed) (1961) Śāntīdeva's Bodhicaryāvatāra (with Pañjikā of Prajñakaramati). Mithila Institute, Darbhanga

Śīla-śikṣā

▶ *Śīla*

Silulin

▶ Sārnāth

Silun

▶ Sārnāth

Sin (Buddhism)

Madhumita Chattopadhyay
Department of Philosophy, Jadavpur University, Kolkata, West Bengal, India

Synonyms

Pāpa, evil action

Definition

Sin stands for the evil elements that defile the mind and have a bad effect on the psyche making it difficult to attain the stage of enlightenment.

Nature of Sin

The term "sin" does not have any special connotation in Buddhism, as it has in major theistic religions like Christianity, Judaism, or Islam. In all these religions, the general belief is that sins are individual actions which are contrary to the will of God or to the will of the Supreme Being. As Buddhism does not believe in any personal God or any Supreme Being, the word "*pāpa, apuñña*" or sin stands for the evil elements that defile the mind and have a deadening effect on the psyche making it difficult for its upliftment. In the Theravāda tradition, the mind (*manas* or *citta*) is considered to be the most important factor in the determination of the moral quality of an action. If an individual performs or acts with an evil or wicked mind, suffering follows as the consequence [1]. Accordingly in the different Buddhist texts, advice has been given to get rid of all kinds of evils or sins. It has been said that greed (*lobha*), attraction (*rāga*), hatred (*dosa*), and delusion (*moha*) are the sources of all kinds of evil acts [2]. There are ten kinds of evil acts (*pāpa*): three related to the body, namely, killing, stealing, and sexual misconduct; four related to speech (*vāk*), namely, lying, slandering, and use of harsh words and frivolous words; and three related to mind (*manas*), namely, covetousness, ill will, and false views. These ten types of acts done with the body or the speech or thought are evil or *pāpa* in the sense that they bring about undesired result. The Buddhists believe that a single act of evil has the ability to remove all the merits acquired through the performance of good acts. So it is absolutely essential to free one's mind from all sorts of evils (*pāpā cittam nivāraye*). To show the importance of avoidance of evils, the analogy of a merchant carrying lots of wealth but small escorts is given. Just as a merchant with great wealth but small escorts avoids the perilous route or just as a man willing to live avoids poison, similarly, it is the duty of all to shun evil things [1].

The Upanisadic seers speak of the acts of stealing (especially gold), drinking liquor, dishonoring one's teacher, and murdering a Brāhmana as the most heinous acts. These are considered to be the great sins (*mahāpāpa*). The Buddhist texts also consider some acts as root sins. For example, in the *Akāsa- garbha sūtra*, five root sins have been elaborately discussed. The first one is stealing the goods from a *stūpa*, the second one is showing disrespect or hatred to the *dharma* or creating any hindrance to the moral order, the third one is disobeying a monk in the form of taking away his saffron robes or sending him to prison or to kill him, the fourth one is taking the life of a relative or a monk or an Arhat, and the fifth one is either himself following the paths of unrighteousness or to indulge others to do so.

Apart from these root sins, other types of sins are also mentioned in the same *sūtra*, like creating divisions in villages, districts, town, or kingdom. The text *Śikṣāsamuccaya* [3] speaks of eight root sins which cause the young men and women, the Bodhisattvas, to stumble and which destroy the merits they have earned in their past lives. These are disrespect shown to Buddhas, laws, ascetics, Pratyekabuddhas, Bodhisattvas, and to those who uttered the Good Law. It also includes disrespect shown to one's parents and also to other virtuous persons. The *Śikṣāsamuccaya* refers to the *Suvarṇaprabhāsottama Sūtra* where it has been shown that sins may occur in other ways also. For example, sins done in one birth might be accumulated in the series of subsequent births with various embodiments. Sins may occur also by association with a bad friend or out of fear and passion, by fault or delusion. However, sin occurring in connection with hatred has been regarded as the great root sin. This is because sin connected with hatred makes for the abandonment of people. The *Upāli–paripṛcchā-sūtra* considers sin connected with delusion (*moha*) to be similar to sin connected with hatred since both of them are very heinous in nature. In the *Sutta-Nipāta* [4], it has been pointed out that the ignorant persons out of delusion get involved in sins or evil actions and also induce others to such sinful acts. Thus, the main cause of sin can be found in ignorance. Hence, to avoid sins, ignorance is to be removed. The *Dhammasangāni* [5] regard five acts – matricide, parricide, slaying an Arhat, slaying a Buddha, and causing division among priesthood to be five unpardonable sins.

However, the Buddhists admit cases where committing an act which is generally considered to be sinful has not been looked upon as sins. For example, the *Śikṣāsamuccaya* refers to the text *Ratnamegha* where it has been specifically said that the slaying of a man who was intending to commit a deadly sin is permissible. The same idea has been upheld in the *Śrāvaka-vinaya* where it has been said that there is no sin in the releasing of animals for the sake of pity. In short, the Buddhists think that such slaying though apparently seems to be sinful is not really sinful for it actually puts an end to further deadly sins. It would be wrong to think that to avoid sin, the general recommendation of the Buddhists would be to get involved in some other similar action. Rather, their attitude in this regard would be frank confession of the sin committed. Depending on the nature of the sin, prescription has been made as regards the audience or persons before whom the confession has to be made. For example, in the *Upāli–paripṛcchā-sūtra*, it has been pointed out that confession for the sin of evil thought is to be made before one or two persons while committing the five unpardonable sins require confession in the presence of the 35 blessed Buddhas or by calling upon their names day and night and by engaging in the recitation of the *dharma* and entering into meditation. It may, however, not be possible for all beings, even the multitude of the ascetics and the Pratyekabuddhas, to recite the names of so-many blessed Buddhas day and night or get involved in meditation to purify themselves from all the sins committed. Here also, the recommendation of the Buddhists is to get acquainted with the sacred books. Moreover, if through practice, one is able to have an idea of what is sin and what is not and also of what is discipline and what is not and of what is impurity and what is purification, then through that knowledge, one will be able to get rid of the effects of past evil actions. In short, the Buddhists do not simply stop by pointing to the sins committed by a person, but at the same time, they have suggested ways for the removal of such sins.

Cross-References

▸ Dhammapada
▸ Evil (Buddhism)
▸ Good (Buddhism)
▸ *Kilesa (Kleśa)*

References

1. Narada Thera (1978) The Dhammapada: a translation. B.M.S Publication, Colombo
2. Santideva (1995) Santideva: the Bodhicaryavatara (trans: Crosby K, Skilton A). Oxford University Press, Oxford
3. Santideva (1999) Śikṣāsamuccaya: a compendium of Buddhist doctrine compiled by Santideva (trans: Bendall C, Rouse WHD). Motilal Banarsidass, Delhi
4. Max Muller F, Fausboll (tr) (1881) Sacred books of the east: the Dhammapada & Sutta Nipata, vol 10. The Clarendon Press, Oxford
5. Rhys Davids CAF (2003) Buddhist manual of psychological ethics. Kessinger, Montana

Sineru

▸ Meru (Buddhism)

Six Perfections

▸ Pāramitā

Skanda

▸ Khandha

Skandha

▸ Khandha

Skepticism

Madhumita Chattopadhyay
Department of Philosophy, Jadavpur University, Kolkata, West Bengal, India

Synonyms

Doubtfulness; Dubiety; Hesitancy; Incredibility

Definition

The view that is unconvinced of the truth of a particular fact or denies the possibility of knowledge; doctrine of persons who take cynical views regarding knowledge.

Buddhist View on Skepticism

Skepticism is a critical philosophical attitude questioning the reliability of the knowledge claims made by philosophers and others. Skepticism unlike dogmatism questions the possibility of knowledge either in its general form or in any one or other of its accepted varieties. To the skeptic, the ordinarily accepted methods of knowing like perception, inferences, etc., appear to be highly questionable. They hold that it is a mistake for the dogmatist to claim to have true knowledge about any entity without examining ways through which an object is claimed to be known.

In the West, skepticism, starting from the days of the Greek period to the modern ages, has been prescribed in different forms. There are some skeptics who do not raise doubt on all the ways of knowing, but only on one or more of them. This type of skepticism is regarded as moderate skepticism. As contrasted with them, there are others who do not admit authenticity of any cognitive method and even challenge the validity of sense-perception. Accordingly, their view is known as "absolute skepticism." Thus, among the philosophers known to us, the Cārvākas can be regarded as moderate skeptics, since they challenge the other sources of knowledge, after accepting the validity of sense-perception. On the other hand, extreme form of skepticism is found in the philosophy of the Mādhyamika thinker Nāgārjuna, who has challenged the validity of every mode of knowing.

To illustrate how the skeptics work in refuting the views of others, the arguments offered by Nāgārjuna to refute the possibility of knowledge may be considered in brief. In his *Vigrahavyāvartanī*, the view of absolute skepticism or extreme skepticism is established with the help of arguments. From verses 30–51, he tries to show with different arguments that anything called *pramāṇa* does not exist, and hence one cannot speak of the existence of objects apprehended through such *pramāṇa*s. In almost all the schools of Indian philosophy, the authority of the *pramāṇa*s is accepted unquestioningly (though there might be controversy regarding the nature and number of such *pramāṇa*s) and it is on the basis of the *pramāna* that objects in the reality are admitted. The Mādhyamika philosophers throw a challenge to this basic assumption, by questioning the authenticity of the *pramāṇa*s themselves: How are the *pramāṇa*s themselves established? There can be two answers to this question – first, the *pramāṇa*s are established without the help of any other *pramāṇa* or they are established with the help of other *pramāṇa*s. In either of the case, one is faced with grave consequences. First, if it is said that the *pramāṇa*s are established without the help of *pramāṇa*s, then the proposition that all objects are established through *pramāṇa*s cannot be maintained, since the *pramāṇa*s or the means of cognition themselves are objects (*artha*). To avoid this consequence, if the second alternative is accepted, that is, if it is said that the *pramāṇa*s themselves are established with the help of other *pramāṇa*s, one gets involved in infinite regress. In that case, there would not be any beginning of the process. Since the *pramāṇa*s are established through other *pramāṇa*s, and those others again through others, there cannot be any beginning. And when there is no beginning, there cannot be any middle, nor can there be an end. Consequently, the statement that

S

the *pramāṇas* are established through other *pramāṇas* does not stand. To avoid the fallacy of infinite regress, if it is said that the *pramāṇas* are themselves established without any *pramāṇa*, then that cannot be accepted also. For in the first place, the position that everything is established through *pramāṇa* will not hold. Secondly, there will bc discordance, since it is to be said that some objects are established through *pramāṇas* while some objects are not, and the special reason has to be provided as to why some objects can be established through *pramāṇa* and some cannot. But no philosopher has presented such special reasons. So this alternative is not acceptable.

To save the situation, one may give the analogy of fire and say that just as fire does not require any other object to illuminate itself while illuminating others, *pramāṇas* do not need the help of any other *pramāṇa* to establish themselves. Nāgārjuna's observation here is that such an argument also cannot be accepted, since it rests on a false proposition. Fire is not illuminated by itself in the way an object pot is illuminated. Before being illuminated by fire, the object pot is first not perceived in darkness. Then being illuminated by fire, it is perceived. Hence, it is said that the pot is illuminated by fire. In the same manner, if it is to be said that fire is illuminated by fire, then it has to be the case that before being illuminated by fire, fire existed in darkness and was not perceived, and then it were illuminated. But such a thing never happens. Therefore, this assumption that fire illuminates itself does not stand. There is another problem also in this assumption. If it is said that fire illuminates itself just as it illuminates others, it has to be said that fire can burn itself just as it can burn other objects, which is also impossible. Accordingly, the statement that fire illuminates itself as it illuminates others cannot be admitted. Since the basic statement is false, comparison of *pramāṇa* with fire does not stand. Those who are in favor of the *pramāṇa* theories may argue that without taking the help of any analogy, it can simply be said that the *pramāṇas* are self-established. That is, the means of valid cognition are established independently of the objects of true cognition. But this view also is not justified. For, in that case there will be nothing with reference to which one can speak of the *pramāṇas* as *pramāṇas*. Nor can the *pramāṇas* be established in terms of the *prameyas*. So all these arguments show that the *pramāṇas* are not established by themselves, nor by anything else, nor by other *pramāṇas*, nor even by the *prameyas*. In short, one cannot speak of *pramāṇas* at all. And this holds for all the *pramāṇas* or sources of knowledge, irrespective of whether the *pramāṇa* is perception, inference, comparison, testimony, or anything else. So, the position holds that knowledge is not possible at all.

Cross-References

▸ Ajita Keśakambali
▸ Knowledge (Buddhism)
▸ Logic (Buddhism)
▸ Mādhyamika
▸ Nāgārjuna

References

1. Bhattacharyya (Chakrabarti) B (1987) Absolute skepticism: eastern and western. Prajñā, Calcutta
2. Bhattacharyya K (1978) The dialectical method of Nāgārjuna. Motilal Banarsidass, Delhi
3. Vaidya PL (1960) Mulamadhyamakasastra of Nagarjuna, The Mithila Institute of Post-graduate Studies and Research in Sanskrit Learning, Darbhanga

Śīla-samādhi-prajñā

▸ Ethics (Buddhism)

Slaves (Buddhism)

Madhumita Chattopadhyay
Department of Philosophy, Jadavpur University, Kolkata, West Bengal, India

Synonyms

Dāsa; Servants

Definition

Slaves are persons born of a low class and purchased through wealth (*dhana*) for the purpose of getting service in household activities and other activities where physical labor is required.

Slaves

In the early days of Buddhism, society was divided among four classes of people – the *khattiya* (*kṣatriya*) or the warrior class, the *brāhmaṇa* or the priests, the *vessa* (*vaiśya*) or the ordinary citizens, and the *sudda*s (*śūdra*) or the people who were engaged in lower profession or to some acts which were considered to be low vocation (*hīnasippāni*) [1]. All these people were free citizens, that is, they could do their works according to their own will. They could exert their own wish or choices for choosing a particular profession or doing a particular act. In addition to these people, there were some who were not allowed any freedom; this group of people was known as the *dāsa* or the slaves. Buddhaghosa in his commentary *Sumangala-vilāsini* defines a slave as *antojāta*, one who is born to a low class. In another context of the same commentary, a more detailed account of a slave or a *dāsa* can be found from which it is clear that *dāsa* or slaves are persons purchased by money or wealth. The definition is *antojāta-dhanakkīta-karamarānīta-samaṃ dāsabyaṇ upagatānaṇ aññataro* [2] – that is, slaves are those born of a low class and are purchased through wealth (*dhana*) for the purpose of getting service and in this respect are different from other classes of people. From this definition of Buddhaghosa, it can be said that slaves were persons purchased for some money. This account of slaves is also found in the Jataka stories where it is mentioned that a *dāsa* was purchased for 700 *kahāpaṇa*s (currency of those days). But this is not the only way of obtaining a *dāsa* or the only reason for someone's being regarded as a *dāsa*; there were other reasons as well. One possible way was through war or battle between two countries or two kingdoms. At the end of such a war or battle, the citizens of the defeated kingdom were captured and reduced to slavery by the conquerors [3]. Another possible reason for slavery was judicial punishment – that is, someone might have been deprived of freedom as a kind of judicial punishment [4]; another reason was hereditary, that is, the children of the slaves were considered as slaves. Apart from all these reasons, there was another possibility – someone could opt for slavery out of his own choices.

The most explicit treatment on slavery is found in the Vinaya text [5] in connection with the discussion on the restrictions of ordination. There it has been stated categorically that a slave cannot be ordained as a *bhikkhu* (*dāso na pabbājetabbo*). However, in the Vinaya text, no explicit reason has been offered for such restriction. The probable reason that can be suggested is that the *bhikkhus* were not allowed to be the owner of anything. Slaves were considered to be objects owned. Naturally the *bhikkhus* who were prohibited from having anything of their own could not have slaves. And since the slaves did not have any freedom of their own, they were debarred from ordination, because only persons with free choice could opt for becoming a *bhikkhu*. In short, in the Buddhist literature, slave ownership was not considered to be anything different from ownership of other properties. In fact, in the Buddhist society, stock description of wealth included ownership of slaves as also of other properties. And there were also instances where the gifts offered to Lord Buddha included slaves, both male and female, along with other gift items.

In spite of the presence of slave systems in Buddhist society, it would be wrong to say that slaves were ill-treated as is heard of in other Western countries, for example, in the Christian society, the life of slave was one of misery and oppression. But in the Buddhist society, slaves were household servants and not badly treated. The only case of slave oppression recorded in Buddhist literature is found in the Jātaka stories where a slave girl was let out to work for wages but had to return home without receiving any money [6]. In most cases, the slaves were looked upon as members appointed for doing household works or as laborers who can offer physical labor for daily works. As such in different texts like the *Dīgha Nikāya* or the Vinaya texts, the slaves have been referred to as *kammakaro* (*dāso kammakaro* or *dāsa ca kammakarā*). It has been repeatedly advised to the common people to behave well with the servants. The *Sigālovāda Sutta* of the *Dīgha Nikāya* recommended that a person must look after his servants in a humanitarian way "by arranging their work according to their strength, by supplying them with food and wages, by looking after them when they are ill, by sharing delicacies with them, and by letting them off work at right time." The *dāsa*s were also advised to be diligent and honest in return and try to uphold the employer's reputation [7]. Similar advice is found in the rock edifices of King Aśoka. In short, the position of the slaves was not considered to be derogatory in the Buddhist society. This gets confirmed by the fact that people of the higher classes or castes did not feel themselves dishonored or degraded to call themselves *dāsa* or servant of Lord Buddha.

Cross-References

▶ Engaged Buddhism
▶ Justice

References

1. Kalupahana D (2008) Ethics in early Buddhism. Motilal Banarsidass, Delhi
2. Rhys Davids TW, Stede W (1975) Pāli-English dictionary. Oriental Books Reprint Corporation, Delhi
3. Rhys Davids TW (1911) Buddhist India. T. Fischer Unwin, London
4. Rhys Davids TW (2001) Dialogues of the Buddha. Low Price Publications, Delhi
5. Rhys Davids TW, Oldenberg H (tr) (1996) Vinaya Texts (in 3 vols) published in the series Sacred books of the east, vols 13, 17, 20 (ed. MaxMuller). Motilal Banarsidass, Delhi
6. Mookerji RK (1958) Local Government in ancient India. Motilal Banarsidass, Delhi
7. Harvey P (2000) An introduction to Buddhist ethics. Cambridge University Press, Cambridge

Smṛtyupasthāna

▶ *Satipaṭṭhāna*

Socially Engaged Buddhism

▶ Engaged Buddhism

Sociology (Buddhism)

Renuka Singh
Department of Sociology, Centre for the Study of Social Systems, School of Social Sciences, Jawaharlal Nehru University, New Delhi, India

Definition

Sociology of religion is primarily the study of the practices, social structures, historical backgrounds, development, universal themes, and roles of religion in society; in this context, Buddhism is held as a religion that deals with salvation.

Sociology can be traced back to enlightenment thought, shortly after the French Revolution, as a positivist science of society. Its genesis is owed to various key movements in the philosophies of science and knowledge [7]. Social analysis in a broader sense, however, has origins within the generic gamut of philosophy and necessarily predates the field. The emergence of modern academic sociology has been catalyzed by factors such as modernity, capitalism, urbanization, rationalization, and secularization, and bears a particularly strong interest in the emergence of the modern nation state – its constituent institutions, its units of socialization, and its means of surveillance. A manifest preference of modernity over enlightenment then is one of the chief distinguishing features of sociology.

Sociology acquired a keen diversified and expansionist tendency, in terms of topic as well as of methodology. Such a tendency is attributed to a protracted opposition to empiricism [7]. History is wrought with thriving debates marking the distinction between structure and agency and the relative supremacy of one over the other. Contemporary social theorists have tended toward the attempt to reconcile such quagmires. While postmodernist trends in recent years have seen a rise in highly abstracted theory, new quantitative data collection methods have also emerged, mostly for dealing with various ethnocentric issues. Despite being a derivative of sociology, the method of social research has quickly cut itself a niche in the very heart of social sciences as it has gained the repute of becoming a uniform analytical tool across myriad fields of social sciences. This, in turn, has bestowed on social science the status of an umbrella discipline, with a broad gamut, including diverse sciences dealing with every human phenomenon.

Scholars have argued that religion, as an aspect of human society, has been supported by both historians and anthropologists as being universal. Both primitive and civilized humans have sought to come to terms with unexplainable situations and experiences in everyday life [26]. Thus, religion has been associated with the human attempt to find purpose and meaning in life – both of self and the universe. In the past, religion had occupied a central place in human society and human thought. In the age of enlightenment and scientific rationalism, it was relegated to a secondary position, so much so that the secularization theorists had even predicted the demise of religion. However, in recent times, we see religion returning to the forefront of human concern. Religion, as a component of human behavior, is of utmost importance to the understanding of the evolution of society, and the various approaches involved to comprehend the entirety of the intellectual scope that study of religion prerequisites have made it difficult to describe or define sociology of religion in any unilateral sense of the term.

Sociology of Religion

The study of religion in its social aspects and consequences emerged as part of the nineteenth-century nomothetic ambition. Sociologists of religion have in general been committed to a would-be scientific analysis of the role played by religion in the emergence, persistence, and evolution of social and cultural systems [13]. The sociology of religion is primarily the study of the practices, social structures, historical backgrounds, development, universal themes, and roles of religion in society [9]. Sociologists of religion attempt to explain the effects of society on religion and the effects of religion on society, in other words, their dialectical relationship [2]. The historical background and, therefore, the respective philosophy and theology of the era, and consecutively, the intellectual, scientific, and eventually the rationalist arguments help to understand the contemporary religious fields [4]. The trajectory through the functional and positivist approach of thinkers like Durkheim in classical sociology, to the more anthropological outlooks of Frazer and Tylor, to the rationalist arguments of Weber, finally arrives at the postmodern phenomena of secularism and globalization [9]. Peter Berger argued that the world was becoming increasingly secular, but has since recanted. He wrote that pluralism and globalization have changed the experience of faith for individuals around the world as dogmatic religion is now less important than is a personal quest for spirituality. Thomas Luckmann provides another fruitful analysis of the discipline, although he maintains that there is today an absence of developing theory in the sociology of religion. This absence of theory is both a conceptual and methodological problem [13].

Modern academic sociology began with the analysis of religion in Émile Durkheim's 1897 study of suicide rates among Catholic and Protestant populations, a foundational work of social research which served to distinguish sociology from other disciplines, such as psychology [26]. Religion, he argued, was an expression of social cohesion, and not *imaginary*, although he does deprive it of what many believers find essential [6]. Religion is very real; it is an expression of society itself, and indeed, there is no society that does not have religion. Individuals perceive a force greater than themselves, which is their social life, and give that perception a supernatural face. They then express themselves religiously in groups, which for Durkheim makes the symbolic power greater. Religion is an expression of their collective consciousness, which is the fusion of all of their individual consciousnesses, creating a reality of its own [6].

In the works of Karl Marx, religion is held as a significant hindrance to reason, inherently masking the truth and misguiding followers. He views social alienation as the heart of social inequality. The antithesis to this alienation is freedom. Thus, to propagate freedom means to present individuals with the truth and give them a choice to accept or deny it. Central to Marx's theories is the oppressive economic situation in which he dwelt. Not only are workers exploited, but in the process they are being further detached from the products they helped create. By simply selling their work for wages, "workers simultaneously lose connection with the object of labor and become objects themselves. Workers are devalued to the level of a commodity – a thing…" [14]. From this objectification comes alienation. The common worker is told he or she is a replaceable tool, alienated to the point of extreme discontent. Here, in Marx's eyes, religion enters. Capitalism utilizes our tendency toward religion as a tool or ideological state apparatus to justify this alienation.

Max Weber emphasizes the relationship between religion and the economic or social structure of society. For Weber, religion is best understood as it responds to the human need for theodicy and soteriology [3]. Human beings are troubled, he says, with the question of theodicy – the question of how the extraordinary power of a divine god may be reconciled with the imperfection of the world that he has created and rules over [5]. People need to know, for example, why there is undeserved good fortune and suffering in the world. Religion offers people soteriological answers, or answers that provide opportunities for salvation, for example, relief from suffering, and reassuring meaning [28]. The pursuit of salvation, like the pursuit of wealth, becomes a part of human motivation.

A religion of salvation may very well have its origin within socially privileged groups [3]. The charisma of the prophet is normally associated with a certain minimum of intellectual cultivation. But as a rule, salvation religion changes its character as soon as it has reached lay circles who are not particularly or professionally concerned with intellectualism, and more changes its character after it has reached into the lowest social strata to whom intellectualism is both economically and socially inaccessible. One characteristic element of this transformation, a product of the inevitable accommodation to the needs of the masses, may be formulated generally as the emergence of a personal, divine, or human-divine savior as the bearer of salvation, with the additional consequence that the religious relationship to this personality becomes the precondition of salvation [5]. One instance of this is the substitution for the Buddha ideal, namely, the exemplary intellectualist salvation into enlightenment (*nirvana*), by the ideal of a *Bodhisattva*, namely, a savior who has descended upon earth and has sacrificed his own entrance into *Nirvana* for the sake of saving his fellow humans [1]. In the Buddhist doctrine, any proletarian denunciation of wealth would have been equally alien to the Buddha, for whom the unconditional withdrawal from the world was absolute presupposition for salvation. Buddhism constitutes the most radical antithesis to every type of resentment religiosity [23].

Buddhism

The origin of Buddhism can be archeologically traced back to approximately 2,500 years, in the *ś rāmānic* traditions of the *Sākyā* tribe in the foothills of Himalayas in present-day Nepal [8]. The values and teachings of Buddhism then were those that stood in opposition to the *Hindu* variety of differentiation and intolerance. Buddhism sought to assimilate all humans from diverse strata of the Indian culture of the *Vedic-Brahmanic* order [8]. The Buddhist ideologies were teachings of the "awakened one" or the *Buddha*, who imparted his knowledge and experience or *Dharma* into the community or *Samgha* of his followers [10].

These elements were characteristic of an inner awakening or liberation taught as lessons, which transcended material bondage to stratification, and thus provided a linear spiritual direction for those who subscribed to the teachings, removed from the dogmatized and heavily segregated history of *Hindu* traditions [1].

Buddhism passed through the political associations of its time with dynasties such as the *Sākyā*, *Māuryā*, and *Śūnga*, and reached its pinnacle through their support [8]. In this period between its genesis and the impending foreign invasions, of about 300 years, Buddhism became a systematized doctrinal practice. The decline and fall of the *Māuryā* dynasty brought an end to the assured association for Buddhist monastic institutions [3]. It was then that the scriptural traditions within the Buddhist framework started to acquire internal shapes, and the canons indoctrinated scholastic variations divided on linguistic lines. "Apart from the Theravāda recension of the Pāli canon and some fragments of the Sarvāstivādin Sanskrit canon nothing survives of what must have been a diverse body of literature. For most of the collections we only have the memory preserved in inscriptions referring to pitakas and nikāyas and an occasional reference in the extant literature" [8]. These facts led to the disintegration of Buddhism based on scriptural lineage, and the *Mahāyāna* and *Hināyāna* sects arose from it, and spread in every direction culminating in the fact that eventually certain areas became dominantly *Mahāyāna* or *Hināyāna*, of which the *Mahāyāna* tradition bore more ground-level acceptance. The Buddhist tradition has always encompassed a spiritual deconstruction of the self-conception to incorporate the idea of the *bodhisattva* path as the first aspiration to awakening, and the *bodhisattva* ideal also implied new ethical notions as themes in its own ethical speculation [8].

Buddhism clearly arose as the salvation teaching of an intellectual stratum, originally recruited almost entirely from the privileged castes, especially the warrior caste, which proudly and aristocratically rejected the illusions of life, both here and hereafter [3]. The Buddhist monk (*bhikshu*) does not desire the world at all, not even a rebirth into paradise, nor to teach the person who does not desire salvation (*nirvana*). Precisely, this example of Buddhism demonstrates that the need for salvation and ethical religion has yet another source besides the social condition of the disprivileged and the rationalism of the citizens, who were conditioned by their practical situation of life [20]. This additional factor is intellectualism as such, more particularly the philosophical needs of the human mind as it is driven to reflect on ethical and religious questions, driven not by material need but by an inner need to understand the world as a *meaningful* cosmos and to take up a position toward it [1].

At the opposite extreme from economic ethics of this worldly religion stands the ultimate ethic of world-rejection, the mystical illuminative concentration of original ancient Buddhism [18]. Even this most world-rejecting ethic is *rational*, in the sense that it produces a constant self-control of all natural instinctive drives, though for purposes entirely different from those of inner-worldly asceticism. Salvation is sought, not from sin and suffering alone, but also from transitoriness as such; escape from the *wheel* of *karma*-causality into eternal rest is the goal pursued. This search is, and can only be, the highly individualized achievement of a particular person [17]. There is no predestination, no divine grace, no prayer, and no religious service. The *karma*-causality of the cosmic mechanism of compensation automatically rewards or punishes all single good or evil deeds. This retribution is always proportional, and hence always limited in time. So long as the individual is driven to action by the thirst for life, one must experience in full measure the fruits of one's behavior in ever-new human existences. Whether their momentary situation is animal, heavenly, or hellish, one necessarily creates new chances in the future [20].

The achievement of salvation is possible for only a few, even for those who have resolved to live in propertyless, celibacy, and unemployment (for labor is end-oriented action), and hence in begging. These chosen few are required to wander ceaselessly – except at the time of heavy rains – freed from all personal ties to family and world, pursuing the goal of mystical illumination by fulfilling the commandments of the correct path (*dharma*). When such salvation is gained, the deep joy and tender, undifferentiated love characterizing such illumination provide the highest blessing possible in this existence, short of absorption into the eternal dreamless sleep (*nirvana*), the only state in which there is no suffering [18].

The decline of Buddhist traditions in India was marked by the Turkish conqueror *Muhammad Ghūrī* and the consequent destruction of the universities of *Nālandā* in 1197 and *Vikramaśīla* in 1203. After this, Buddhism became a walled-in philosophy that only survived in isolated pockets [20]. As the Turkish occupation spread in India, the Buddhist scholars escaped from Kashmir and Bihar into Nepal and Tibet [27]. Himalayan Buddhism of direct Indian ancestry remains only in Nepal, partly fused with the local Hindu traditions. Buddhism of Tibetan origin survives in the subcontinent mostly in Ladakh, Bhutan, and Sikkim [20].

The Buddhist revivalism only started as recent as the late nineteenth century through the *Mahābodhi Society* and *Theosophical Society* popularized in Sri Lanka by Henri S. Olcott. The most significant revivalist attempt at Buddhism in the new age was through the emancipatory ideals of equality and justice of Buddhism; B. R. Ambedkar took up the cause of the marginally excluded and exploited castes within Hinduism and provided them with a chance to liberate their social position through the indiscriminate spirituality of Buddhism [10]. The most detailed and persistent effort at rediscovering Buddhism has come primarily from the Western scholars, who have repeatedly attempted at reviving the Buddhist scriptures, including a modern critical edition of the complete *Pāli* canon and the recovery of original texts of the *Sarvāstivāda* canon. Japanese scholarship has also revived the Chinese canons between 1880 and 1929, and their productive critical research has placed Japan ahead of many more such attempts at the head of modern research into Indian Buddhism. The neo-Buddhists, as sects or groups who adopt the Buddhist teachings and philosophies, in Europe and America have also contributed to the global revivalism of Buddhism, through their critical and modernist stands [23].

In the West, however, postmodern paradigms of Buddhism have undergone some important changes in the last few decades; in other words, Buddhism has cross-pollinated with modernity with inspiration from the processes of detraditionalization, demythologization, and psychologization [19]. It also provides insight into the three overlapping constitutive discourses of modernity: western theism, scientific rationalism, and romanticism including its successors [15]. However, despite being theologically disconnected with Buddhism, these discourses offer to illustrate the historicity and hybridity of the doctrine, as well as provide paradigmatic explanations for the spread of its spiritual message all over the world through the past few decades.

Buddhism and Modernity

The hybridity of Buddhist modernism, its protean nature, its discarding of much that is traditional, and its often radical reworking of doctrine and practice naturally invite questions of authenticity, legitimacy, and definition [15]. What seems to be the order here is that Buddhism being a relatively liberal and egalitarian conception instills a sense of inner peace through its spiritual teachings, whereas modernity encourages isolated individuality and increased competition between the isolated individuals, thus creating a spiritual vacuum within the system. Buddhism, if considered for the sake of the argument, as a sermon provides an escape from the never-ending rat race of the postmodern world, where no one ever rests, sleeps, or stops, and offers a peaceful meditative alternative realization that transcends the material matters of this world [22]. This particular alternative of Buddhist teaching is what gave the Western world – where inner-spirituality was already on the decline and individuality based compensation on its pinnacle – the creation of the *Zen* or, in other words, the Western implementation of Buddhist teachings, wherein some elements of Buddhism were adapted with the modern realities to merge and create a suitable alternative that fitted the psyche of those who subscribed to it [15]. Thus, globalization and decentering of legitimacy contextual to the time-space recurrence of Buddhism as a philosophy will pertain to the debate that Buddhism as a spiritual guide shall face revivalism whenever there would arise a need for global folk religion that surpasses the politicization that the other major religious systems of the world face [25].

Buddhism is the most consistent doctrine of salvation produced by the intellectualism of noble lay educated Indian strata [11]. Its cool and proud emancipation of the individual from life as such, which in effect stood the individual on one's own feet, could never become a mass religion of salvation. Buddhism's influence beyond the circle of the educated was due to the tremendous prestige traditionally enjoyed by the *śrāmānic* members, who possessed magical and idolatrous charisma. As soon as Buddhism became a missionizing *folk religion*, it accordingly transformed into a savior religion based on karma compensation, with hopes for the world beyond guaranteed by devotional techniques, cultic and sacramental grace, and deeds of mercy [15]. Naturally, Buddhism also tended to accept purely magical notions.

In India, Buddhism took its place among the upper strata, by a renewed philosophy of salvation based on the Vedas [12], and it met competition from *Hinduistic* salvation religions, especially the various forms of *Vishnuism*, from *Tantristic* magic, and from orgiastic mystery religions, notably the *bhakti* piety (love of god). In Tibet, Buddhism became the purely monastic religion of a theocracy which controlled the laity by churchly powers of a thoroughly magical character. In East Asia, original Buddhism underwent striking transformation as it competed and entered into diverse combinations with Chinese Taoism, thus, which was specifically concerned with this world and the ancestral cult and which become a typical mass religion of grace and salvation [11].

Although Buddhism has been called a museum piece primarily preserved at Nalanda, Kushinagar, Ajanta, Ellora, Sarnath, Sanchi, and Bodhgaya, one cannot overlook the fact that Buddhism's middle path and culture of wisdom have been reflected in the lives of ordinary Indians and that Buddhism is coming alive again in India, as mentioned earlier [12]. Even though worldwide there has been a rapid growth of interest in Buddhism in the last quarter of the twentieth century, His Holiness the Dalai Lama does not see any special significance in this phenomenon, especially the tendency toward sectarianism among new practitioners in the West. His Holiness sees this as a disturbing development. Religion, he asserts, should never become a source of conflict [24].

Today, Buddhism has spread in a rather thin manner and for it to have any future, one requires a solid foundation of the Buddhist realizations. As Ven. Lama Zopa Rinpoche says:

> When one talks about the propagation of Buddhism, one has to remember that there are two types of teaching – the words and the realizations. Of these, it is the latter that makes the difference. It is easy for the words to continue for centuries – all one needs is a few good libraries. But without the living experience of the meanings of the words that comes through purification, creation of merit and effective meditation, the words are dry and tasteless and cannot be a vehicle for Buddhism to continue into the distant future. For this to happen, one needs serious meditators spending years, if not their lives, in retreat under the supervision of experienced masters. Is this happening today? [24].

Cross-References

- ▶ Bodhisattva
- ▶ Dharma
- ▶ Karma
- ▶ Nālandā
- ▶ Nirvana

References

1. Bailey G, Mabbett IW (2003) The sociology of early Buddhism. Cambridge University Press
2. Berger PL (1999) The desecularization of the world: resurgent religion and world politics. Wm. B. Eerdmans
3. Buss AE (1985) Max Weber in Asian studies. Brill Archive
4. D'Souza L (2005) The sociology of religion: a historical review. Rawat

S

5. Davidson RM (2004) Indian esoteric Buddhism: a social history of the tantric movement. Motilal Banarasidass
6. Durkheim E (2003) Elementary forms of religious life (reprint) (trans: Cosman C). Oxford University Press
7. Giddens A (1986) Sociology (reprint). Macmillan
8. Gomez LO (2002) Buddhism in India. In: Kitagawa JM (ed) The religious traditions of Asia: religion, history and culture. Routledge Curzon, London/New York
9. Hamilton MB (2001) Sociology of religion: theoretical and comparative perspectives, 2nd edn. Routledge
10. Jones KH, Ken J (2003) The new social face of Buddhism: a call to action. Wisdom
11. Law BC (1922) Historical gleanings. Calcutta
12. Ling TO (1980) Buddhist revival in India: aspects of the sociology of Buddhism. Macmillan
13. Luckmann T, Bryan W (1995) Religion isn't what it used to be. In: Greely AM (ed) Sociology and religion: a collection of readings. Harper Collins
14. Marx K, Friedrich E (2008) On religion (reprint). Dover
15. Mcmahan DL (2008) The making of Buddhist modernism. Oxford University Press
16. Mitra RC (1954) The decline of Buddhism in India. Calcutta
17. Nakamura H (1980) Indian Buddhism: a survey with bibliographical notes (Narain AK ed). Delhi
18. Omvedt G (2003) Buddhism in India: challenging Brahmanism and caste. SAGE
19. Paine J (2004) Re-enchantment: Tibetan Buddhism comes to the west. W. W. Norton
20. Robinson RH, Johnson WL (1982) The Buddhist religion: a historical introduction. Belmont
21. Ruegg DS (1967) The study of Indian and Tibetan thought. Leiden
22. Sangharakshita (Bhikshu) (1992) Buddhism and the west: the integration of Buddhism into western society. Windhorse
23. Sarkar BK (1985) The dynamics of Buddhist thought. In: The positive background of Hindu sociology: introduction to Hindu positivism. Motilal Banarasidass
24. Singh R (ed) (2004) The path of the Buddha: writings on contemporary Buddhism. Penguin Books
25. Thomas EJ (2003) The history of Buddhist thought. Asian Educational Services, New Delhi (AES reprint)
26. Turner BS (ed) (2010) The new Blackwell companion to the sociology of religion. Wiley-Blackwell
27. Ven Pategama G (1998) Aspects of early Buddhist sociological thought. Buddha Dharma Education Association
28. Weber M (1993) Sociology of religion (reprint). Beacon Press. Translated by Ephraim Fischoff, with a new Foreword by Ann Swidler
29. Weber M (2000) Religion of India: the sociology of Hinduism and Buddhism (reprint) with Hans Heinrich Gerth and Don Martindale. Munshiram Manoharilal

Solitary Buddha

▶ Pratyeka-Buddha

Sotāpanna

Bhikkhu Anālayo
Center for Buddhist Studies, University of Hamburg, Balve, Germany

Synonyms

Srotāpanna (Sanskrit); Stream-enterer

Definition

The term *sotāpanna* refers to one who has reached the first of the four levels of awakening recognized in early Buddhism. A *sotāpanna* has thereby become a "stream-enterer," in the sense of being one who has irreversibly entered the "stream" that will ultimately lead him or her to full liberation.

Stream-enterer

The stream which the *sotāpanna* has entered is the noble eightfold path ([3], Vol. V, p. 347), a succinct description of the Buddhist conception of what is required to progress to liberation, namely, rightly directed view, intentions, speech, action, livelihood, effort, mindfulness, and concentration. This noble eightfold noble path constitutes a stream in the sense that it leads toward Nirvāṇa just as the Ganges leads toward the sea ([3], Vol. V, p. 38).

The time required for this stream to lead to the highest is at most seven lives, none of which will take place in a lower sphere of rebirth. Not every *sotāpanna* requires seven lives to reach the final goal, hence stream-entrants can be distinguished into three main types ([4], Vol. IV,

p. 381): those who need up to seven more lives in human or heavenly realms to reach liberation, *sattakkhattuparama*, those who are reborn twice or thrice among humans before reaching full liberation, *kolankola*, and those who are reborn only once more as a human being before attaining the final goal, *ekabījī*. Such differences reflect the circumstance that a stream-enterer might neglect to retire regularly into seclusion for the purpose of meditative practice and, due to neglecting the practice, gains neither concentration nor deeper insight ([3], Vol. V, p. 398).

Some discourses report staggering numbers of disciples of the Buddha who had been able to gain stream-entry ([2], Vol. II, p. 218). The attainment of stream-entry is not restricted to a particular caste or gender, as women are as capable as men to progress toward this or any of the other three levels of awakening ([4], Vol. IV, p. 276). Not only humans can attain stream-entry, but also gods ([4], Vol. III, p. 333). A case in point is Sakka, the king of gods, who visited the Buddha in order to pose a set of questions and on hearing the Buddha's replies attained stream-entry ([2], Vol. II, p. 284).

In the numerous instances of stream-entry reported in the discourses, the actual attainment similarly takes place during a visit paid to the Buddha. This begins with the Buddha delivering a gradual discourse on the importance of morality and generosity and on the need to renounce sensuality. When in the course of listening to this gradual instruction the listener's mind reaches a state free from the hindrances, the Buddha expounds the four noble truths, a teaching that begins by identifying the scope of *dukkha* (first truth), a term whose meaning ranges from barely noticeable dissatisfaction to outright suffering as inherent features of human existence. The same teaching then proceeds by delineating the arising of *dukkha* (second truth), its cessation (third truth), and the path that leads to its cessation (fourth truth). Upon receiving this teaching of the four noble truths, the "eye of the Dharma," *dhammacakkhu*, arises in the listener's mind, with the insight that whatever is of a nature to arise is also of a nature to cease.

With the arising of this "eye of the Dharma," which would correspond to the first direct experience of Nirvāṇa, the noble disciple has seen, reached, understood, and penetrated the Dharma. In this way having gone beyond doubt, the stream-enterer has attained such a degree of personal independence in regard to the teaching that he or she no longer needs to depend on anyone else. The attainment of stream-entry is in fact clearly recognizable as an event that occurs at a particular moment of time, comparable to one's going forth ([4], Vol. I, p. 107).

The discourses report several rather striking cases of the arising of the "eye of the Dharma," such as the case of a leper who had apparently mistaken a crowd listening to the Buddha for a group assembled at a charitable food distribution and approached them only in the hope of receiving a meal ([6], p. 49). Instead of getting food, he was able to hear a gradual instruction by the Buddha, resulting in his attainment of stream-entry.

Another discourse reports a layman who was slightly inebriated, but then sobered up through the impact of meeting the Buddha for the first time and realized stream-entry during a gradual discourse given at that same first meeting ([4], Vol. IV, p. 213). Another layman is on record for having passed away as a stream-enterer even though earlier he had been unable to abstain completely from intoxicating drinks ([3], Vol. V, p. 375).

Possibly even more surprising is the case of several hired killers, one of whom even had the mission of killing the Buddha. Instead of completing their mission, they all are reported to have become stream-enterers, after having received a gradual discourse by the Buddha ([5], Vol. II, p. 192).

On considering the frequent occurrence of stream-entry during a discourse by the Buddha, it needs to be taken into account that if someone had realized stream-entry while meditating alone and in seclusion, this did not occasion a discourse and therefore was not recorded later. But when someone realized stream-entry while listening to the Buddha's instruction, this became part of the later reported discourse. Thus, it is to be expected that mainly the latter type of stream-entry realizations are recorded in the discourses. These instances thus reflect the Buddha's outstanding capability as a teacher, who apparently was able to deliver a talk in such a way that it would lead to stream-entry of even those who otherwise would probably not so easily have reached such a lofty attainment.

Listening to the Dharma and associating with worthy men, together with rightly directed attention and practice in accordance with the Dharma, are in fact the factors that are required for the attainment of stream-entry ([3], Vol. V, p. 411).

At the moment of attaining stream-entry, three of the fetters that according to early Buddhism bind the unawakened worldling to continued existence in the cycle of *saṃsāra* are eradicated ([1], 231). These three are the fetter of personality view, *sakkāyadiṭṭhi*, in the sense of the notion of a permanent self, the fetter of doubt, *vicikicchā*, in particular doubt regarding the nature of what is wholesome and what is unwholesome, and the fetter of dogmatic clinging to rules and vows, *sīlabbataparāmāsa*, as in themselves sufficient for reaching liberation.

The meditative development of insight culminating in the attainment of stream-entry could be based on contemplating the impermanent, unsatisfactory, and therefore selfless nature of the five aggregates affected by clinging ([3], Vol. III, p. 160). These five aggregates are according to the early Buddhist analysis the chief constituents of an individual, covering the aggregates of bodily form, feeling, perception, volitions, and consciousness. Alternatively, subjective experience can be analyzed from the perspective of the six senses and their objects ([3], Vol. III, p. 225), a mode of analysis that reckons the mind as a sixth sense alongside the five physical senses of the eye, ear, nose, tongue, and body.

In any case, insight into the conditioned nature of all phenomena needs to be part of the development of insight that leads to stream-entry, since an understanding of conditionality forms one of the qualities of a stream-enterer ([4], Vol. III, p. 441). In sum, what needs to be realized by direct personal experience in order to attain stream-entry is what early Buddhism reckons the true nature of reality, namely, its being conditioned and marked by impermanence, unsatisfactoriness, and the absence of a self.

One who has become a stream-enterer is endowed with the four limbs of stream-entry: unwavering confidence or faith in the Buddha, the Dharma, and the community of noble ones, together with a firm commitment to moral conduct ([3], Vol. V, p. 357). Though minor breaches of morality may still occur, a stream-enterer will be unable to commit a serious crime ([1], 231). Even in the case of a smaller breach of moral conduct, a stream-enterer will immediately confess the breach ([1], 232).

Other qualities of a stream-enterer are no longer being obsessed by mental defilements, possessing a certain degree of inner tranquility, being firmly convinced of the uniqueness of the insight gained, being willing to admit any committed offence, being fully dedicated to the development of morality, meditation, and wisdom, and having a keen interest in the Dharma ([7], Vol. I, p. 324). Even on the worldly level, the attainment of stream-entry apparently has its repercussions, since according to one discourse a stream-enterer is endowed with long life and beauty, happiness, and a good reputation ([3], Vol. V, p. 390). In sum, from an early Buddhist perspective, neither lordship over the whole earth, nor rebirth in an exalted heavenly realm, nor dominion over the entire universe can compare to the attainment of stream-entry ([8], 178).

Cross-References

▶ Anāgāmin
▶ Arahant
▶ Insight
▶ Liberation (Buddhism)
▶ Sakadāgāmin

References

1. Andersen D, Smith H (eds) (1913) The Sutta-nipāta. Pali Text Society, London (references are by stanza)
2. Carpenter JE, Rhys Davids TW (eds) (1890–1911) The Dīgha Nikāya, 3 vols. Pali Text Society, London

3. Feer L (ed) (1888–1898) The Saṃyutta Nikāya, 5 vols. Pali Text Society, Oxford
4. Morris R, Hardy E (eds) (1885–1900) The Aṅguttara Nikāya, 5 vols. Pali Text Society, London
5. Oldenberg H (ed) (1879–1882) Vinayapiṭakaṃ, 5 vols. Pali Text Society, Oxford
6. Steinthal P (ed) (1885) The Udāna. Pali Text Society, London
7. Trenckner V, Chalmers R (eds) (1888–1896) The Majjhima Nikāya, 3 vols. Pali Text Society, London
8. von Hinüber O, Norman KR (eds) (1994) The Dhammapada. Pali Text Society, London (references are by stanza)

Soul

► Jīva (Jainism)

Southern Tradition of Buddhism

► Theravāda

Spiritualism

► Mysticism (Buddhism)

Śramaṇa

Angraj Chaudhary
Vipassana Research Institute, Dhammagiri, Igatpuri, Nashik, Maharashtra, India

Synonyms

Ascetic; Parivrājaka; Sadhu; Sannyāsī; Yati

Definition

One who is completely free from all evil actions is a *śramaṇa*.

'*Śramaṇa*' in Sanskrit is "*samaṇa*" in Pali.

The word "*śramaṇa*" in Sanskrit is derived from the root "*śram*," which means 'to strive' or 'to labor hard'. A *śramaṇa* has to work hard to drive out different defilements like craving and aversion from his mind. If he works to achieve this end, he is called a *śramaṇa*.

The word "*samaṇa*" in Pali is derived from the root "*sama*" which means 'to become quiet', to attain peace and tranquillity. It also means to be free from burning. Its other meaning is equanimity, which means to remain unmoved in all circumstances of life [1].

Because a *samaṇa* works hard to get rid of defilements, to attain peace, and to develop equanimity, the derivation of the word *samaṇa* from both the roots is justified.

One who has ceased to do evil actions and one who commits no evil actions (*pāpakā akusalā dhammā*) is called a *samaṇa* [2].

What are evil or unwholesome actions? They are unwholesome physical and vocal actions like killing, stealing, committing sexual misconduct, telling lies, slandering people, making harsh speech, talking uselessly, and taking intoxicants.

One who has destroyed all his cankers or taints is also called a *samaṇa* [3].

From all these definitions it is clear that one who is on the path of refraining from unwholesome actions is a *samaṇa* and one who is completely free from them is also a *samaṇa*.

Categories of Samaṇa

There are, therefore, several categories of *samaṇa*. The first category is *sotāpanna*, who has entered into the stream that will ultimately take him to nibbāna

As soon as he becomes a *sotāpanna*, three of the fetters such as doubt, belief in a soul, and clinging to rites and rituals are abandoned. A *sotāpanna* is not subject to birth in lower worlds; he is firmly established in *dhamma*, and he is sure to attain nibbāna. He has to be born for not more than seven times to be free from all taints and become an arhat. Besides he develops other qualities such as he cannot conceal any of his wrong actions and he cannot commit any of the six heinous crimes such as killing his mother, killing his father, killing an arahant, causing schism in the saṅgha, wounding a Buddha, and upholding wrong views [4].

The second category is *sakadāgāmī*, i.e., once returner. It means that he will be born only once in this world and attain nibbāna. He dilutes and makes feeble the two other fetters, viz., sensuality (*kāma rāga*) and ill will (*vyāpāda*).

The third category is *anāgāmī*, i.e., he will not be born in this world and attain nibbāna in some other deva world. The most important characteristic of an *anāgāmī* is that he is completely free from the 5 lower fetters.

The fourth category is *arahant*, who has destroyed all his taints and attained nibbāna. He will never be born in any *loka*, and he is free from the cycle of birth and death. He becomes free from the 5 higher fetters such as craving for fine material existence (*rūpa rāga*), craving for immaterial existence (*arūpa rāga*), conceit (*māna*), restlessness (*uddhacca*), and ignorance (*avijjā*). He attains both the kinds of deliverance, deliverance of mind (*ceto vimutti*) and deliverance through wisdom (*paññā vimutti*). Deliverance of mind means to be free from *rāga* (craving) and *dosa* (aversion) and deliverance through *paññā* (wisdom) means deliverance from *avijjā* (ignorance) [5].

Buddha: A Mahāsamaṇa

The Buddha is called a *mahāsamaṇa* as is clear from what Assaji says to Sāriputta.

> Ye dhammā hetuppabhavā, tesaṃ hetu Tathāgato āha/
> Tesaṃ ca yo nirodho, evaṃvādī mahāsamaṇoti// [6]

The Great Samaṇa, the Tathāgata, explains the causes of those dhammas, which have causes to arise. He also explains how those causes can cease to be.

Many brāhmanas and others call the Buddha a *samaṇa* [7].

One can be a *samaṇa* if he walks on the Eightfold Path. If there is no Noble Eightfold Path in any Dhamma and Discipline, there is no *samaṇa* there [8].

The Buddha also says in the *Cūḷasīhanāda Sutta* that as there is the Noble Eightfold Path here, four kinds of *samaṇas* are found in his order, in his teaching. They cannot be found anywhere else. Why? Because others' orders and teachings do not make a good field where seeds can grow. Just as mustard seeds cannot stay on the tip of an awl, nor can fire burn by the side of water, nor can seeds grow on a flat stone, in the same way all the four kinds of *samaṇas* can be found in the order of the Buddha, in the teachings of the Buddha, not in the teachings of other sectarian teachers because the Noble Eightfold Path is not there [9].

It has also been said here that just as a lion does not live in a cemetery, nor on the rubbish heap, but in the jeweled cave of the Himalayas, a six-tusked elephant is born in his own family and not in the nine ordinary elephant families, just as the dark horse king is not born in the family of ass or in the family of ordinary horse, but in a Saindhava family on the bank of the river Sindhu, just as an all pleasure fulfilling jewel is not found on the heap of rubbish or on the heap of dust but in the inside of mountain Vaipulla. . .so not even a single *samaṇa* is found in other sects but found only in the order of the Buddha where monks walk on the Eightfold Path [10].

A true *samaṇa* is endowed with eight kinds of pleasure. He has no desire for collecting riches; he earns his livelihood by pure means; what he eats, he eats without craving; he does not have to give trouble to anybody for his alms like a king; he has no attachment to the objects of the world; he does not fear thieves; he does not have the desire to meet the king and his ministers; and he is free to go in any direction [11].

References

1. Dh, verse 388 (Unless otherwise mentioned all books referred to here are published by Vipassana Research Institute, Dhammagiri in 1998)
2. M 1.351; Sīlakkhadhavagga Ṭīkā 1.238 Sīlakkhadhavagga Abhinava Ṭīkā 1.28, Dh. verse 265
3. Sīlakkhadhavagga Ṭīkā,1.28.

4. Sn p. 118, Ratana Sutta
5. A.1.273
6. Mv p. 46; A3 160
7. M1.268, D.197,125
8. A 1.273
9. MA 1.317
10. MA 1.313
11. JA 1.10

Śrāvaka

Mangala Ramchandra Chinchore
Department of Philosophy, Centre for Studies in Classical Indian Buddhist Philosophy and Culture, University of Pune, Pune, Maharashtra, India

Synonyms

Sāvaka (Pāli)

Definition

Sāvaka (Pāli)/*Śrāvaka* (Sanskrit) etymologically means 'hearer' or 'listener,' which is generally translated as 'disciple' or 'follower' of the traditional Buddhist way of life. Since at the time of the Buddha, it was oral tradition, *Śrāvaka* connotes those who listen (direct voice) to teachings of the Buddha [or indirectly through the elders (Sk. *Sthavira*)] [1]. It also connotes one who is ready to follow the teachings/advices/instructions (Pāli-*Sikkhā*/Sk.-*Śīkṣā*) given by the Buddha, (strictly by letters) with conviction and commitment [2]. *Śrāvaka* is a term used by both Jainism and Buddhism to denote followers of the *Śrāmaṇic* tradition.

Disciple' or 'Follower' of the Traditional Buddhist Way of Life

In this context, it is worth to note that all sayings of the Buddha in the *Nikāya* literature begin with the phrase 'thus I have heard or this is what I have been given to understand' (Sk. '*etaṁ mayāś rutam*'), indicating that Buddhist tradition was in the original form oral and later on came down in the written form.

At that time, 'listening' (Sk. *Śravaṇa*), 'thinking/contemplating' (Sk. *Manana*), and rethinking/memorizing daily (Sk. *Nididhyāsana*) was the *Vedic* method of comprehension and understanding (Sk. *Abhyāsa*) used to preserve tradition by the *Brāhmaṇas*. *Śrāmaṇic* traditions, both Jainism and Buddhism, at the initial stages adopted similar modes/practices. That is why one often comes across the term *Śramaṇa-Brāhmaṇa* in the Pāli *Tripiṭaka* literature to indicate similarity of following and preserving the tradition faithfully. It helped both Jainism and Buddhism to preserve the tradition authentically by the *Śrāvakas*, who were strict adherents.

Sāvaka/Śrāvaka is a term used by both the *Śrāmaṇic* traditions – Buddhism and Jainism. '*Sāvaka/Śrāvaka*' primarily means lay-male disciple; however, for women, lay-disciple correlate separate term is available that is *Sāvikā/Śrāvikā*. Similarly, it connotes two different meanings in the *Śrāmaṇic* traditions. In Jainism, a *Śrāvaka* is any 'lay-follower.' Contrastively in Buddhism, the term is restrictively used for 'distinguished or ordained disciples only' of the Buddha [Sk. *Sādhujana* – monks (Pāli-*Bhikkhu/ṣ*) and/or nuns (Pāli-*Bhikkhuṇīs*)]. *Śrāvaka* is one who has believed and entered the stream of adopting practice of teachings of the Buddha, preserved and prescribed by the tradition. For lay-disciple, separately they prefer to use another term '*Puthujana,*' which connotes laymen/laywomen (Sk. *Upāsakas* and/or *Upāsikās*). However, such subtle discrimination and distinction was later on noted and removed appropriately in the *Mahāyāna* Buddhism, and the term *Bodhisattvas* was used commonly to connote *Arhat*, in contrast to *Śrāvaka*. Roughly speaking, *Śrāvaka* seems to connote a lower sense (Pāli-*Hīna)*, referring to the earlier/orthodox followers of the Buddha, but in the *Mahāyāna* Buddhism, there was a possibility to become *Bodhisattva* (ideal human being) open to all without discrimination of gender or marital status.

S

Any lay-disciple men/women (Sk. *Śrāvaka/ Śrāvikā)* should follow moral codes of discipline prescribed in the Eightfold Path (Sk. *Aṣṭāṅgika-mārga*) in general and the five precepts (Sk. *Pañca-Śīla*) in particular. He/she should respect but should not have attachment toward the six kinds of relationships, namely, parents, teachers, wife and children, friends, and servants. He/she should regard the six directions, namely, East–West, South-North, up-down, showing gratefulness toward earth and one's placement on it [3]. He/she should abide by the three refuges (Sk. *Tri-Śaraṇas*) – Buddha, his teachings (Pāli-*Dhamma*) and the group of people following it (Pāli-*Saṁgha*). He/she should give up the four kinds of defilements/impurities (Sk. *Kleśas/ Doṣas*) in action, which bring in infringement in the moral/social principles, namely, taking away life or doing violence to (Sk. *Hiṁsā*), craving and clinging to what is not given/stealing (Sk. *Parigraha*), misconduct in joy of sensual pleasure/indulgence in sex (Sk. *A-brahmacarya*), and speaking lies (Sk. *A-satya*) since they are enemies of humanity, namely, greed (Sk. *Rāga/Lobha*), envy, jealousy and hatred (Sk. *Dveṣa*), delusion (Sk. *Moha*), etc. He/she should not practice bad actions related to the four circumstances (Sk. *Sthānas*), namely, will, wish, inclinations, desire, etc. (Sk. *Chandas*), hatred/anger (Sk. *Dveṣa*), lures/temptations/delusions (Sk. *Moha*), and fear (Sk. *Bhaya*). He/she should not indulge in the six kinds of openings to loss of property due to habit/ practice (Sk. *Anuyoga*) or negligence due to intoxication (Sk. *Pramāda*), etc. Thus, he/she should avoid the 14 kinds of evils and behave appropriately in an ethical and religious way [4].

Within the fold of Buddhism, roughly speaking, there are two sects – *Hīnayāna* and *Mahāyāna*, and there are three paths/vehicles/modes of emancipation (*Yānas*) [5], corresponding to the three goals of life, namely, wisdom/insight (Pāli-*Paññā*/Sk. *Prajñā*), character/morality (Sk. *Śīla*), and meditation/concentration (Sk. *Samādhi*). *Hīnayāna* tradition advocates the two modes of emancipation – *Śrāvaka-yāna*, one who has heard the teachings of the Buddha and has strictly abided oneself by the practices prescribed by the traditional ways and by adhering to the instructions laid down by the Buddha by letters to become *Arhat*. Here, it is important to note that the word generally used is *Śrāvaka-yāna* and not *Śrāvikā-yāna*, though the instructions given are meant for both *Śrāvaka* and *Śrāvikā*, without bringing in any kind of discrimination, because the emphasis is not on the gender or marital status of the person concerned but on emancipation (Sk. *Nirvāṇa*) and one's eligibility or entitlement (Sk. *Arhatatā*). In the *Śrāvaka-yāna*, the ideal for a *Śrāvaka* is to become eligible/entitled to (*Arhat*) emancipation (Pāli-*Nibbāna*/Sk. *Nirvāṇa*). It is a path preserving the authenticity and reliability of the tradition without changes and hence is orthodox mode of life. They are also called as *Samyak-sambuddhas* (Pāli-*Sammā-sambuddhas*) in contrast to another form of emancipation, namely, *Pratyeka-Buddha* (Pāli-*Pacceka-buddha*).

Pratyeka-Buddhayāna implies that one who has attained enlightenment (*Bodhi*) by self-effort, following his/her own conscience, as per the advices of the Buddha, is becoming guide of oneself (Pāli-*Attāno padīpo bhava*). One follows middle way (Sk. *Madhyamā-pratipad*) but has the capacity to interpret the appropriate meaning and makes changes according to contexts and situations in which one lives. One takes the full moral responsibility of any action performed by oneself. Each one has a potentiality to become Buddha, provided one strives very hard to actualize it.

In contrast to these two, in the *Mahāyāna* tradition, there is only one mode, namely, *Bodhisattva-yāna* (one who is living selflessly for the sake of emancipation of all sentient beings and sacrificing one's own personal goals of life). *Bodhisattva* primarily practices wisdom (Pāli-*Paññā*/Sk. *Prajñā*) and compassion (Sk. *Karūṇā*) and has transcended the limitations of self-interests. It is claimed by the *Mahāyānists* that their consideration of goals of life is more profound and altruistic, as compared to the earlier *Hīnayāna* conception of *Śrāvaka-yāna* and/or *Pratyeka-Buddha-yāna*. However, unless one becomes a *Śrāvaka* and becomes eligible or entitles oneself as *Arhat*/*Pratyeka-Buddha*, one cannot help others and become *Bodhisattva*. Thus, in the *Bodhisattva-yāna*, the person concerned has not completely disregarded the importance of the teachings of the Buddha or the methods and modes of practicing Buddhist way of life but is expanding the vistas of making sense of the teachings of the Buddha in an altruistic sense truly (Sk. *Nairātmya-Darśana*). In other words, becoming *Śrāvaka* appears to be a precondition for becoming *Bodhisattva* too.

In the *Tripiṭakas*, one comes across three more terms indicative of the hierarchical order of monks, namely, chief disciple (Pāli-*Agga-Sāvaka*/Sk.-*Agra-Śrāvaka*) like Śāriputra, Mahāmaudgalāyana, Kṣemā, Utpalavarṇā, etc. Another term is great disciples (Pāli-*Mahā-Sāvaka*/Sk.-*Mahā-Śrāvaka*) like Mahākāśyapa, Ānanda, and Mahākātyāna. The third one is ordinary disciples (Sk. *Prakṛti-Śrāvaka*/*Ārya-Śrāvaka*), who have not yet irreversibly entered the path of emancipation (*Anāgāmin*) and is still subject to infinite rebirths. Buddhist *Saṁgha* was basically consisting of all such *Śrāvakas*/*Śrāvikās*.

For *Śrāvaka*/*Śrāvikā*, the final stage of life and ideal is to become eligible/entitled (Sk. *Arhat*), who gets emancipation (Pāli-*Nibbāna*/Sk. *Nirvāṇa*) in this life and the world. The path for getting emancipation (Pāli-*Nibbāna*/*Nirvāṇa*) followed by any *Śrāvaka*/*Śrāvikā* is known as *Śrāvaka-yāna*. There are three stages/preconditions in a sequential forward order (Sk. *Auloma*) to obtain the fourth stage, namely, entitlement (*Arhat*). They are as follows: (a) stream enterer (Pāli-*Sotāpanna*/Sk. *Srotāpanna*) – one starts realizing the importance of living Buddhist way of life and following teachings of the Buddha, and because of practicing the Eightfold Path (Sk. *Aṣṭāṅgika-mārga*), one gets freedom from ignorance (Sk. *Avidyā*) and realizes futility of craving (Pāli-*Taṇhā*/Sk. *Tṛṣṇā*). It is an attempt to eradicate basically three things, which are impediments in the spiritual growth, namely, illusion of the eternality of self (Pāli-*Sakkāya-diṭṭhi*/Sk. *Satkāya-dṛṣṭi*), vacuousness of doubt, and hair-splitting analysis (Pāli-*Vicīkiccā*/Sk. *Vicīkitsa*) and undertakes critical examination of indulgence into wrong/illicit rites and ceremonies (Pāli-*Silabbata-parāmassa*/Sk. *Śīlavrata-parāmarśa*). (b) Prima-facie enterer (Pāli-*Sakadāgāmi*/Sk. *Sakṛdāgāmin*) – one who has started purification of mind and body by following the seven steps of meditation (*Sati-paṭṭhāna*) and achieved control over craving and desires (Sk. *Kāma*/*Rāga*) and ill will toward others (Sk. *Pratigha*). (c) Non-returnee (Sk. *Anāgāmin*) – one who has destroyed all kinds of bindings and become free from the cycle of birth and death. There is no possibility of relapsing to get entangled in the world of attachment again (Sk. *Saṁsāra*). It is his/her last birth in human world. After following all the three stages, one becomes entitled (*Arhat*) to get freedom from all kinds of sufferings (Sk. *Duḥkha-nirodha*) – the final goal of human life to realize emancipation (Pāli-*Nibbāna*/Sk. *Nirvāṇa*).

Cross-References

- *Anāgāmin*
- *Arhat (Sanskrit)*
- *Aṣṭāṅgamārga*
- *Bodhisattva*
- *Karuṇā*
- *Madhyamā Pratipad*
- *Nirvāṇa*
- *Pañca-Śīla*
- *Prajñā*
- *Pratyeka-Buddha*
- *Sakadāgāmin*
- *Samyaka Sambodhi*
- *Satipaṭṭhāna*
- *Sthaviravāda*
- *Upāsaka*

References

1. Warder AK (2000) Indian Buddhism, 3rd edn. Motilal Banarsidass, Delhi, pp 175–194
2. Obermiller E (1999) Bu-Ston: the history of Buddhism in India and Tibet. Sri Sadguru Publications, Delhi
3. Kasyapa BJ (ed) (1961) Dīgha-Nikāya. Pali Text Publication Board, Bihar Govt, Nalanda
4. (1995) Dīgha-Nikāya, Tipiṭaka, Chaṭṭha Saṇgāyana edn (CD-ROM Version-3). Vipassana Research Institute, Igatpuri
5. Sangharakshita (1987) A survey of Buddhism: its doctrines and methods through ages. Tharpa Publications, London, pp 106, 239, 395

S

Śrāvastī

► Sāvatthī

Sri Gaudapada Acarya

► Gaudapada

Sri Mahābodhi

► *Bodhi Tree*

Srigcodrdorje

► Tāranātha

Śrīparvata

► Nāgārjunakoṇḍa

Srotāpanna

► *Sotāpanna*

Sthaviravāda

Charles Willemen
International Buddhist College, Songkhla, Thailand

Synonyms

In Pāli called Theravāda

Definition

Those who proclaim the principles of the Elders (Sthaviras), as opposed to the majority, Mahāsāṅghikas. This fundamental split in the Buddhist order occurred in Pāṭaliputra, shortly before Aśoka (ca. 264–227 B.C.).

Origin

There is more than one tradition concerning the origin of Sthaviravāda. The southern Theravāda tradition mentions a council in Vaiśālī. It concerned the allegation that some *bhikṣus*, monks, permitted ten unlawful practices, infringements on the *vinaya*. For example, eating after midday and handling money. The elder Sarvagāmin condemned these ten points. There was, however, no schism. A second meeting, not mentioned in the Theravāda tradition, took place some years later in Pāṭaliputra. The king of Magadha, Mahāpadma Nanda (ca. 362–334 B.C.), decided in favor of the majority, *Mahāsaṅgha*, Great Community. The other party was referred to as the S*thaviras*, Elders. These claimed that the majority was distorting the original teaching and was too lax. But the Mahāsāṅghika *Śāriputraparipṛcchā*, *Questions of Śāriputra*, which exists only in a Chinese translation of the Eastern Jin (317–420 A.D.), Taishō ed.1465, makes it clear that the oldest *vinaya* is the one of the Mahāsāṅghikas. The majority refused to accept the addition of minor rules to the *vinaya*, as the *Sthaviras* wanted. This text does not mention Mahādeva's five theses concerning the *arhat*, which are doctrinal matters. Mahādeva appears in a later split within the Mahāsāṅghikas in Southern India. So, Sthaviravāda begins in Patna, ca. 340 B.C., as the result of disagreement about the *vinaya* [7].

Sectarian Development

Both Sthaviravādins and Mahāsāṅghikas spread out from Patna [2, 3]. The first to split from the main Sthaviravāda trunk, ca. 280 B.C., were the

Vātsīputrīyas. They held that a *pudgala*, personality, really exists. They are known as Pudgalavādins. It is quite possible that the large number of converted brahmins, who used to believe in an *ātman, ego*, is at the basis of this split. But this school, *nikāya*, was still Sthaviravāda. It had its *abhidharma* in nine parts from Rāhula, who had received it from Śāriputra. Śāriputra is the ultimate authority of all Sthaviravāda *abhidharma* [9]. The Pudgalavāda *abhidharma* consisted of three factors, *dharmas* (*guṇa*, quality; *doṣa*, fault;*āśraya* basis), which were each subdivided in three sections, *khaṇḍa (ka)*. The text exists in Chinese translation, called *Sanfa du lun*, *Tridharmakhaṇḍa(ka)śāstra* (?), Taishō ed.1506. It is the work of (the Bactrian?) Saṅghadeva in 391 A.D., and it inspired Huiyuan (334–416 A.D.) on Mount Lu to write his *San bao lun, Treatise about the Three Kinds of Retribution*, Taishō ed.2102, 34 bc. The Vātsīputrīyas subsequently split in four groups: Dharmottarīya, Bhadrayānīya, Ṣaṇnagarika, and Sāṃmitīya. The Sāṃmitīyas were most numerous. They became very influential in Bactria and in Central Asia, but also in the area of the Gulf of Bengal and in the area of Mumbai.

At the so-called third council in Pāṭaliputra during Aśoka's reign (ca. 264–227 B.C.), ca. 244 B.C., a Sthaviravāda meeting was held. It is known in the Theravāda tradition. It was presided over by Maudgalyāyana, Moggalliputtatissa, and resulted in a split between the Sarvāstivādins and the Vibhajyavādins, "Analysts," who were declared "orthodox." Sarvāstivādins had new views, their name meaning "Claiming (°*vāda*) that everything (*sarvam*) exists (*asti*)." They subsequently spread to the Gulf of Bengal, but mainly to Mathurā and to the Gandharan cultural area [4]. The "orthodox" Sthaviras called themselves Vibhajyavādins in Patna. Vibhajyavādins, that is, non-Vātsīputrīya Sthaviras who opposed Sarvāstivāda ideas, are known to consist of four groups: Mahīśāsaka, Dharmaguptaka, Kāśyapīya, and Tāmraparṇīya or Tāmraśātīya, that is, Vibhajyavādins in Śrī Laṅkā. After the "third" council Vibhajyavādins spread out from Patna. The Theravāda tradition claims that they themselves are the original Vibhajyavādins, brought to Śrī Laṅkā by Mahendra, Mahinda, and that Pāli is the language of Magadha. It has been suggested that the Vibhajyavādins who went South to Andhra are the Mahīśāsakas, and that those who continued on to Śrī Laṅkā are the Theravādins [1]. But there is the very distinct possibility that the Vibhajyavādins on the one hand went South to Andhra and on to Śrī Laṅkā, and on the other hand also went to the Gandharan cultural area. They then became known as Mahīśāsakas, "converting the earth," the earth being India. In Śrī Laṅkā a conservative movement, returning to the Vibhajyavāda of Aśoka's council, developed, establishing an *Abhidhammapiṭaka* in Śrī Laṅkā, said to be expounded by the Buddha himself. The final inclusion in this *Piṭaka* is the *Kathāvatthu, Points of Controversy*, maybe finalized at the end of the second century B.C., and attributed to Moggalliputta himself [5]. The seven texts of this *Piṭaka* constitute the *Abhidhammapiṭaka* of the Theravādins. Mahīśāsaka Vibhajyavādins were all over India, including Śrī Laṅkā, where during the years 410–412 A.D. Faxian received their *vinaya* in five parts. This *vinaya* was translated in 422–423 A.D., after Faxian had passed away. It is the work of Buddhajīva, a Mahīśāsaka monk from the Gandharan cultural area, *Jibin*. This is the *Wu fen lü, Vinaya in Five Parts*, Taishō ed.1421.

In the Gandharan cultural area the Dharmaguptakas split from the Mahīśāsakas. There was disagreement about the question who to give *dāna*, gifts, to: to the Buddha, the *saṅgha*, or to the *stūpa*. This split may have occurred shortly before 200 B.C. Dharmaguptakas seem to have had five *Piṭakas*. Their *abhidharma* is the *Śāriputrābhidharma, Shelifu epitan lun*, Taishō ed.1548, the work of Dharmayaśas in 414–415 A.D. Their *vinaya* is the *vinaya* in four parts, *Si fen lü*, Taishō ed.1428, the work of Buddhayaśas and Zhu Fonian in Chang'an, 410–412 A.D. They also may have had a now lost *Bodhisattvapiṭaka* and a *Dhāraṇīpiṭaka*, according to Paramārtha. A *bodhisattva* is an excellent preacher, *dharmabhāṇaka*, who used the mnemotechnic means of *dhāraṇī* to preach. The Dharmaguptakas seem to have disappeared in

India in the sixth century, but their *vinaya* became the main *vinaya* in East Asia.

In the Gandharan cultural area the Mahīśāsakas lost to the Sautrāntika Sarvāstivādins. In Kuṣāṇa times, first centuries A.D., they are known as "later" Mahīśāsakas [8], seemingly a subgroup of Gandharan Sarvāstivādins. Spread thinly throughout India, they always lost to the local majority.

Kāśyapīyas seem to have split from the main Vibhajyavādins ca. 240–230 B.C., in the Gandharan cultural area. They disappeared before 600 A.D. They hold an intermediate doctrinal position between Sarvāstivādins and "orthodox" Vibhajyavādins. It has been thought that Kāśyapīyas, whose *abhidharma* was very similar to the Dharmaguptaka *abhidharma*, are the same as Haimavatas [1]. So, Vibhajyavāda Sthaviravāda developments occurred both in the Gandharan cultural area and in Śrī Laṅkā. In the Gandharan cultural area, especially in the Bactrian part, Sarvāstivāda Sthaviras eventually became preponderant. There they determined Sthaviravāda history. In Śrī Laṅkā the conservative Sthaviras became preponderant, known as Theravādins.

Pāli, a mixed Prākrit, basically a language of the Avanti area, dating from the early post-Aśokan period, is a term for the sacred texts and for the language of these texts in Śrī Laṅkā [6]. The Vibhajyavādins in the Gandharan cultural area used Gāndhārī(s). The Mahīśāsakas in Andhra seem to have used a Prākrit which is very similar to Pāli.

Theravāda in Śrī Laṅkā continued to develop. Abhayagiri monks split there from the old and mainstream Mahāvihāra monks in the first century B.C., a period when the *Tripiṭaka* was first written down in the South. In the fourth century A.D. Jetavanīya split off. In the twelfth century Mahāvihāra Theravādins finally won.

Cross-References

- ▶ Abhidharma (Theravāda)
- ▶ Buddhist Councils
- ▶ Faxian (337–422 C.E.)
- ▶ Gandhara
- ▶ Kaniṣka
- ▶ Kathāvatthu
- ▶ Mahāsāṅghika
- ▶ Pāli
- ▶ Paramārtha
- ▶ Prākrit
- ▶ Pudgalavādins
- ▶ Śāriputra
- ▶ Sarvāstivāda
- ▶ Sautrāntika
- ▶ Theravāda
- ▶ Vaibhāṣika

References

1. Bareau A (1955) Les sectes bouddhiques du petit véhicule. École Française d'Extrême-Orient, Saigon
2. Cox C (2004) Mainstream Buddhist schools. In: Buswell R (ed) Encyclopedia of Buddhism, vol II. Macmillan Reference USA, New York, pp 501–507
3. Dutt N (2007, reprint of 2nd ed of 1978) Buddhist sects in India. Motilal Banarsidass, Delhi
4. Gómez L (2005) Sarvāstivāda. In: Jones L (ed) Encyclopedia of religion, 2nd edn. Macmillan Reference USA, Gale Virtual Reference Library, Detroit
5. Hirakawa A (1st ed 1990 Hawaii; Indian ed 1993) A history of Indian Buddhism (trans: Groner P). Motilal Banarsidass, Delhi
6. Lamotte É (1988) History of Indian Buddhism: from the origins to the Śaka Era (trans: Sara Webb-Boin). Université Catholique de Louvain, Institut Orientaliste, Louvain-La-Neuve
7. Skilton A (2001, reprint of 2nd edn of 1997) A concise history of Buddhism. Windhorse, Birmingham
8. Tsukamoto K (2004) The cycle of the formation of the schismatic doctrines. BDK English Tripiṭaka. Numata Center for Buddhist Translation and Research, Berkeley
9. Willemen C (2008) Kumārajīva's explanatory discourse about abhidharmic literature. J Int Coll Postgrad Buddh Stud 12:27–83

Sthiti

▶ Time (Buddhism)

Storehouse Consciousness

▶ Ālaya-vijñāna

Stories of Celestial Mentions

► Vimānavatthu

Stream-Enterer

► *Sotāpanna*

Study of Mind or Consciousness

► Psychology (Buddhism)

Stūpa

Kanoko Tanaka
Komazawa University, Tokyo, Japan

Synonyms

Caitya

Definition

"*Stūpa*" in Sanskrit, and "*thūpa*" in Pāli, literally meaning "knot of hair," "top of a house," "summit," "heap of clay and soil or firewoods for cremation" from Vedic periods up to the time of the Buddha Śākyamuṇi.

The mound-like structure of a *stūpa* in Buddhist context was originally containing the relics (śarīra) of Śākyamuṇi (= Buddha śarīra), built by Buddhists under the patronage of the ruler who paid homage to *tri-ratna* (= the three jewels): the Buddha, his teachings (= Buddha-dharma), and the community of his disciples (= Saṃgha). "*Caitya*" (in Sanskrit. "*ceitya*" in Pāli) also literally means "heap" which may suggest the place of the Buddha's cremation where the firewoods should be piled up, and it was also the general term for the sacred tree (e.g., bodhi tree) under which Śākyamuṇi attained the Awakenings (= bodhi), where Buddhists naturally feel as if they were listening to his sermon. *Caitya* caves at Ajantā and Bājā were always built near *vihāra* caves (= monastery of Buddhist monks). A caitya (= stūpa-shaped rock hollowed out of a cave) did not generally contain the Buddha *śarīra*. In the same way, all of the *stūpas* were not always the container of the physical remains of the Buddha, but would rather contain the scrolls of *sūtras* and precious jewels as the symbol of Buddhist spirits to concentrate on what the Buddha himself taught in his lifetime. Even today, it does not matter to Buddhists whether the Buddha *śarīra* may be authentic or not. Probably because the *stūpa* has been built and worshipped not as a tomb of the deceased One in the narrowest sense, but as a complex of ancient Indian symbolism in the broadest sense, which will be discussed later in this entry.

For the purpose of defining the significance of *stūpa*, it is helpful to see Fig. 1 (the Great Stūpa at Sāñcī, India, whose original component was built by King Aśoka in the third century, B.C.). This Stūpa No. 1 dedicated to the Buddha Śākyamuṇi is known as an ideal archeological evidence to tell about early Buddhist architecture and decorative art (approximately from the first century, B.C. up to the second century, A.D.).

First of all, you can see the tripled umbrellas (*cattra*) supported by one pole (*yūpa yaṣṭi*) surrounded by a railing (*harmikā*) on the top of the *stūpa*. From ancient times, a *cattra* was usually raised for a noble or a sacred man to protect him against the sultry sunlight. The triple ones suggest that the Buddha was regarded as much more precious and sacred than any other saints of the ancient times. The term *yūpa yaṣṭi* in Vedic context means "the pole to which a sacrifice animal should be chained," but in Buddhist theory, it is nothing but a pole of supporting the place where the Śākyamuṇi attained the Awakenings (= *bodhi*) and preached the importance of non-killing (= *ahiṃsā)* as well as Mahāvīra, one of the Jinas in the history of Jainism stressed that *ahiṃsā* had to become the supreme dharma to reach the final goal of a life. The *harmikā*,

Stūpa, Fig. 1 Great Stūpa (Stūpa No. 1) on the hill of Sāñcī, India. A view from the east. This stūpa was gradually built and expanded during the Mauryan, Śuṅgan, and Āndhran dynasties (Photographed by Kanoko Tanaka)

therefore, seems to describe "the palace of the Buddha as the King of Dharma" (= *Dharma-rāja*). Buddhist laymen came together looking up at the *cattra* and the *harmikā*, offer flowers, water, foods, incense, songs, and dances (= the acts of *pūjā*, in contrast to *yajña*, animal sacrifice) as if they were invited by *Dharma-rāja* at his own palace. Moreover, it is worthy to mention that the shape of *cattra* and *yūpa yaṣṭi* looks like the *Tree of Life* to fulfill one's wish without fail.

Secondly, the semicircular mound of a *stūpa* is called "*aṇḍa*"(= egg) which reminded ancient Indian people of "a golden egg" in the beginning of the world. Moreover, the Buddha *śarīra* was also taken as "*bījā*" (= seed). This obviously suggests that a *stūpa* was regarded as "*garbha*" (= womb or treasury) from which life energy should be arisen again and again. In fact, the jar full of water (= *pūrṇa-ghata*) as a symbol of auspiciousness and eternal life became a model for a *stūpa* under construction and was often chosen as a motif of bas-relief carved on *toraṇa* (= gateway) and *vedikā* (= railing; originally pointed to *vedi*: an alter for fire rituals or animal sacrifice) surrounding a *stūpa.* Regarding the image on "water," a stūpa-motif was also connected with *nāga* worship. "Nāga" is a sacred serpent with five heads that rains and guards a saint like the Buddha under the sunlight. The bas-reliefs depicting "a *stūpa* protected by a king of *nāga*" were found at Amarāvatī in south India. As far as the yearning for life energy is concerned, the shape of a *stūpa* came to be identified with that of a *liṇga* (= phallus) with the rise of Tantric Buddhism, a metamorphosis from Śākyamuṇi's teachings.

The basement on which the *aṇḍa* should be placed is called "*medhī*" (originally used for animal sacrifice to gods, for example, on the occasion of *aśva medha* held by a powerful king; also meaning "wisdom" and "the power of understanding"). The term *medhī* for Buddhists is also a symbol of their protest against the animal sacrifice. On the other hand, the *medhī* meaning "wisdom" is able to emphasize "*prajñā*"(= wisdom of seeing this phenomenal world *as it is*, without distorting *it* from selfish and biased viewpoints) as the basic philosophy of Buddhism.

Thirdly, you will see a twofold *vedikā* around a *stūpa*, which is found on the inner and outer side of the *pradakṣinapatha* (= the *path* for pilgrims who should go around a *stūpa right-handedly*). Pilgrims usually go around a *stūpa* three times right-handedly, just as the Buddha's disciples used to do the same whenever visiting their great Master to ask for his guidance. A *stūpa*, in this sense, takes a role of the Buddha who should give his sermon to all the visitors. Such visitors came to the *stūpa* from all directions of India. Four gateways (= *toraṇa*) at the south, the north, the east, and the west may signify that everybody, no matter whether the visitor is a Buddhist or not, is most welcome to make a pilgrimage to a *stūpa*, purify his mind, and continue to live a good life. Such pilgrims as this can be seen even in the modern times at the precinct of Sāñcī Stūpas, including the Stūpa No. 2 (enshrining the relics of Sāriputta and Mahā-Moggallāna, the greatest disciples of Śākyamuṇi Buddha) and the Stūpa No. 3 (enshrining the relics of Moggaliputta Tissa who is said to have been King Aśoka's teacher). The *stūpa* was painted white, and the *toraṇas* were colored in red.

Then, how could the visitors to Sāñcī listen to the sermon from a *stūpa*? Probably some monks and laymen took the role of interpreter who guided them to look around the bas-reliefs on the four gateways describing the scenes of *jātaka* (= stories of the Buddha's previous lives), the last and greatest life of the Buddha, and any other subjects to enhance faith in Buddhism.

It is noteworthy that the *sukhāvatī* (= the land of happiness where Buddhists can fulfill their dream of seeing and listening to the Buddha's sermon in order to attain the Buddhahood) was the idealized image of a huge *stūpa* with a sevenfold *vedikā*, according to the *Smaller Sukhāvatīvyūha*. Indeed, it must be a long-cherished desire for those who had never seen the Buddha in person. Such a desire as this is not regarded as a delusion. It is an interesting logic of religious faith.

Stūpa, Fig. 2 Bas-relief on Bhārhut Vedikā, Bhārhut, India, second century, B.C. So many floral garlands decorating over the stūpa may signify how devotees were attached to the object of worship (A. K. Coomaraswamy, *La Sculputre de Bhārhut*, Paris, 1956)

Since Sāñcī, as well as Bhārhut, was dominated by Theravāda Buddhism, a *stūpa* did not remind visitors of *sukhāvatī* in Mahāyāna context. Bhārhut was also in the same situation, but the bas-reliefs of Bhārhut Stūpa show us so many happy elements to urge everybody to yearn for the ideal world to fulfill any wish. Please see Fig. 2 (a bas-relief on the Bhārhut vedikā, the second century, B.C.). This is one of the best examples of depicting the reality of stūpa-worship. Two noble men or gods in human form with decorative turbans are doing *pradakṣina* (= right-handed circumambulation) around the *stūpa*. One is coming back closer and the other is turning to the rear of the *stūpa*, showing his back. Here everybody on the ground is joining their hands in prayer (= *anjali*). For what are they praying? For example, a lady sitting on her heels seems to wish if she could be blessed with a *male* child who will have the responsibility of holding a memorial service for ancestors. Nine hand-prints seen at the base of a *stūpa* are auspicious marks to protect people against evil powers, which can be seen also in the prehistorical painting on the cave. From the heavens, two

S

Stūpa, Fig. 3 The slab of Stūpa, Nāgārjuṇakoṇḍa, India, third century, A.D. "Use unknown" regarding the five angular-pillars (called Āyaka Kambha), although it is said that they put offerings on the top. Is "he" a Buddha image or the Buddha himself? That is a question (British Museum, photographed by Kanoko Tanaka)

angels are flying to offer garlands. Even today, Indian people like very much to make garlands for offering them to an image of god in the shrine and the temple, made of Marigold and other colorful flowers.

Now, please see Fig. 3 showing a bas-relief of "*stūpa*," carved at Nāgārjunakoṇḍa in the third century, A.D. If you do not have any background information about this work of art, but if you are versed in the topic of Mahāyāna Buddhism and its relationship to the stūpa-worship, this "*stūpa*" may remind you of the climax scene of the *Stūpadarśana-parivarta* (in the *Saddharma-puṇḍarika-sūtra*), where the whole body of the Buddha Prabhūtaratna, the symbol of timeless truth of the Dharma, appears from the inside of the *stūpa*, as if he has just resurrected from bones and ashes (= Buddha *śarīra*) left after the cremation. At the "*stūpa*" of Fig. 3, two devotees are looking up at the standing Buddha. Is *he* just a Buddha image enshrined in the "*stūpa*" or a *real* Buddha who raised from the historical *parinirvāṇa*? When thinking of the advanced idea of visual art, *this* Buddha might be regarded as the One with flesh and blood. However, it is proved that the samgha at Nāgārjunakoṇḍa belonged to the Aparaśaila, one of the Nikāya Buddhist sects. There was no relationship with Mahāyāna Buddhism at all, but monks of this sect could not ignore the importance of stūpa-worship as well as their own daily practice of meditation and study of the sutras. Or rather, they positively came to yearn for the Buddha through the medium of a *stūpa* in hope of attaining the Buddhahood sometime in the future.

It was believed that karmic merits coming from stūpa-worship should be equally given to all the Buddhists, no matter whether the person may observe the full set of precepts required of a monk or can only perform *pūjā* around a *stūpa* in prayer. When visiting the *vihāra* caves of Ajantā (around the first century, B.C.), we can see how monks thought much of living near the *caitya* caves where they could fully meditate on the Buddha and his teachings by doing *pradakṣina*.

It is probable that Mahāyānistic movement in later periods arise from such a universal popularity of *Stūpas* built over India, especially after the Buddha image was created for the first time at Mathurā and Gandhāra approximately from the late first up to second century, A.D. Stūpa-worship does not directly connect with the rise of Mahāyāna Buddhism, but it is very interesting to research more.

According to the *Mahāparinibbāna-suttanta* of the *Dīghanikāya*, the Buddha in his last days advised Ānanda and other monks *not* to be concerned with the worship of the Tathāgata's śarīra, and laymen should hold the ritual for stūpa-worship. This must be a paradoxical evidence to confess how monks, as well as laymen, were concerned with the construction and worship of a *stūpa* after the moment of *parinirvāṇa*. Actually the *Mahaparinibbāna-suttanta* itself is telling that the Buddha's corporal remains would not burn at all until Mahākaśyapa, who became the successor to his Master, arrived at Kuśinagara after a long journey from faraway places and finally ignited firewoods for the cremation. This fact may suggest that monks, from the beginning, took charge of supervision over various issues related to a *stūpa*. Inscriptions of donors who contributed to build Sāñcī and Bhārhut Stupas prove that not a few nuns and monks positively took part in the construction work.

Looking back on how the matters on "*stūpa*" have been important to the history of Indian Buddhism, they found one question: Why did only the Buddha's relics came to be enshrined by Indian people, in spite of the traditional fact that a dead body even of a king is always cremated at the riverbank even today? A possible answer is: "Because *parinirvāṇa* of the Buddha was too rare to forget, and at the same time, the Buddha, who was originally the Crown Prince from Śākya clan, was blessed with powerful patrons of kśatriya caste who would like to enshrine the Buddha's bones and ashes in a *stūpa*"? Or, is there any more better answers? This is a good subject to tackle with, and it may be better to keep this in suspense for the present.

Just as the *parinirvāṇa* was not a mere death of the Buddha, the *stūpa* was not a mere tomb containing his relics. From the beginning of constructing the Buddha Stūpa for the first time, they intentionally regarded it as the complex of rich symbolism, because the shape of semicircle is universally able to give a sense of psychological stability to those who need to relieve from sufferings of this world. It is just according with an aim in a Buddhist life (= *nirvāṇa*).

Cross-References

▶ Caitya, Parinirvāṇa

References

1. Coomaraswamy AK (1956) La Sculputre de Bhārhut, Vanoes. Editions d'Art et d'Histoire, Paris
2. Government of India, Ministry of Information and Broadcasting (1956) The Way of Buddha. (published on the occasion of the 2500th anniversary of the Mahāparinirvāṇa of Buddha), Delhi
3. Hirakawa A (1963) The rise of Mahāyāna Buddhism and its relationship to the worship of Stūpa. Memoirs of the Research Department of the Toyo Bunko (The Oriental Library) No.22. The Toyo Bunko, Tokyo
4. Lüders H (1963) Bharhut inscriptions (corpus inscriptionum indicarum). Government of Epigraphist for India, Ootacamund
5. Marshall SJ (1955) A guide to Sāñchī. The Government of India, Calcutta
6. Marshall SJ, Foucher A (1982) The monuments of Sāñchī. Swati Publications, Delhi
7. Sugimoto T (1984) Studies in Buddhist Stūpa-Cult in India. Heirakuji Shoten, Kyoto (Japanese edition)
8. Sugimoto T (2007) The story of Stūpa. Daihourinkaku, Tokyo (Japanese edition)
9. Tanaka K (1998) Absence of the Buddha image in early Buddhist art – toward its significance in comparative religion. D.K. Printworld, New Delhi

Subjective Idealism

▶ Idealism (Buddhism)

Subjects of Discourse

▶ Kathāvatthu

Substance

▶ Dravya (Jainism)

Substratum Consciousness

▶ Ālaya-vijñāna

Sudatta

▶ Anāthapiṇḍika

Sugatagarbha

► Tathāgatagarbha

Suicide (Buddhism)

K. T. S. Sarao
Department of Buddhist Studies, University of Delhi, Delhi, India

Synonyms

Ātmaghāta; Ātmavadha; Attaghañña; Attaghāta; Attavadha

Definition

The act of purposely causing one's own death.

Making death one's aim, wishing death, or setting out on any course that leads to death, is considered immoral in Buddhism ([9], Vol. ii, p. 464). By virtue of its belief in rebirth and retributive kamma (Sk: karma), Buddhism teaches that suicide does not offer a permanent solution to problems encountered by a human being. As Buddhism views the whole *saṃsāric* existence itself as suffering, suicide merely leads to the postponement of the problems to be faced in the next birth and with the added retribution of the evil kamma produced by such an act. Irrespective of the motive, suicide being an act of violence, is contrary to the principle of *ahiṃsā* which says that the taking of any life (including one's own) goes against the first precept. Thus, from Buddhist perspective, any attempt to put a complete end to suffering through suicide is a completely futile exercise as ultimately it would not achieve the intended purpose. Buddhism values life as against death, thus, suicide is seen as morally wrong.

There are many other reasons offered in the Buddhist texts on the basis of which suicide is viewed as an irrational act and contrary to basic Buddhist values. For instance, Buddhism believes that birth as a human being is very rare in the *saṃsāra* and cutting it short amounts to losing an invaluable chance for spiritual growth. Suicide by virtuous human beings is seen with particular disfavor as suicide by such people deprives others of the benefits they might bring to them ([8], Vol. ii, p. 330f; [11], pp. 44, 195f). Moreover, suicide brings life to a premature end which goes against the Buddhist view of life being allowed to follow its natural course. Suicide is also contrary to the third *pārājika* ([11], p. 195). Apart from this, self-destruction was associated by the Buddha with ascetical practices which were rejected since "Buddhism had better methods of crushing lust and destroying sin" (see [13], p. 26). Buddhism teaches that by understanding that life is impermanent and subject to suffering of various kinds, one can develop an attitude of enlightened detachment enabling one to remain untroubled by any kind of suffering. Buddhism attempts to instill this kind of realistic understanding of life and mindfulness in a follower so that such a person is not driven to a state of desperation to the extent that he/she may commit suicide.

Interestingly, there are at least three well-documented cases in the Pāli Tipiṭaka which seem to indicate that suicide may be condoned under certain circumstances. These are the cases of Channa ([2], Vol. iv, p. 55; [12], Vol. iii, p. 263), Vakkali ([2], Vol. iii, p. 119), and Godhika ([2], Vol. i, p. 120f). Scholars such as Lamotte, Woodward, Harran, and Wiltshire ([1], p. 137; [3], p. 129; [5], pp. 106–110; [14], pp. 126–140; [15], p. 8) have attempted to explain away these cases by pointing out that though suicide is prohibited for an unenlightened person (*puthujjana*), it is permitted under two conditions for a person who is not unenlightened. One, this person is an arahant (Sk: arhat), i.e., a fully enlightened person at the time of the act of suicide taking place and thus is free of anger, hate, or fear. It has been indicated that such a person's act of suicide does not produce further fruit, and hence the person escapes from the world of rebirths. Two, this person is suffering from a terminal disease and does not want to become an unnecessary source of burden to those who are taking care of him. Thus, it has been pointed out that it is necessary to appreciate that such an "act is not gratuitously performed, but constrained by force of circumstances" ([14], p. 132). "An Arahant neither wishes for death nor wishes not to die: it will come when it comes" ([6], pp. 1002–1003). According to Buddhaghosa, it is legitimate in the case of one, suffering from a painful and terminal illness, to withdraw from food in the knowledge that he is on the brink of a spiritual breakthrough and exerts himself in his meditation subject or if he sees that the caretakers are worn out and his life cannot be prolonged even with intensive care (see [9], Vol. ii, p. 467). It is indicated through this example that Buddhism does not consider it morally obligatory to preserve life at all costs.

Damien Keown has suggested that this popular but doctrinally dubious notion has gained currency by being linked to the idea that the arahants go beyond conventional moral norms, a view that no longer commands wide respect (see [4]). To quote him, "To say that suicide is wrong because motivated by desire, moreover, is really only to say that *desire* is wrong. It would follow from this that someone who murders without desire does nothing wrong. The absurdity of this conclusion illustrates why a subjectivist approach to the morality of suicide is inadequate. Subjectivism leads to the conclusion that suicide (or murder) can be right for one person but wrong for another, or even right and wrong for the same person at different times, as his state of mind changes, and desire comes and goes" ([4], p. 9).

Cross-References

- ▶ Ahimsa
- ▶ Arahant
- ▶ Buddhaghosa
- ▶ Kamma
- ▶ Rebirth
- ▶ Saṃsāra

References

1. Becker CB (1993) Breaking the circle: death and the afterlife in Buddhism. Southern Illinois University Press, Carbondale
2. Feer ML (ed) (1884–1898) The Saṃyutta Nikāya, 5 vols. Pali Text Society, London
3. Harran MJ (1993) Suicide (Buddhism and Confucianism). In: The encyclopedia of religion, vol 14. Macmillan, New York, p 129
4. Keown D (1996) Buddhism and suicide: the case of Channa. J Buddh Ethics 3:8–31
5. Lamotte E (1987) Religious suicide in early Buddhism. Buddh Stud Rev 4:105–126
6. Oldenberg H, Pischel R (eds) (1990) Theragāthā, 2nd edn (with appendices by K.R. Norman & L. Alsdorf). Pali Text Society, Oxford
7. Rāhula W (1978) Self cremation in Mahāyāna Buddhism. In: Rāhula W (ed) Zen and the taming of the Bull. Gordon Fraser, London, pp 55–67
8. Rhys Davids TW, Carpenter JE (eds) (1890–1911) The Dīgha Nikāya, 3 vols. Pali Text Society, London
9. Takakusu J, Nagai M (eds) (1947–1975) Samantapāsādikā: Buddhaghosa's commentary on the Vinaya Piṭaka (including index by H. Kopp), 8 vols. Pali Text Society, London
10. Thakur U (1963) The history of suicide in India. Munshiram Manoharlal, New Delhi
11. Trenckner V (ed) (1880) Milindapañha. Williams and Norgate, London
12. Trenckner V, Chalmers R (eds) (1888–1896) The Majjhima Nikāya, 3 vols. Pali Text Society, London
13. Vallée Poussin L de la (1922) Suicide (Buddhist). In The encyclopaedia of religion and ethics, vol XII, pp 24–26
14. Wiltshire MG (1983) The 'Suicide' problem in the Pāli Canon. J Int Assoc Buddh Stud 6:124–140
15. Woodward FL (1922) The ethics of suicide in Greek, Latin and Buddhist literature. Buddh Ann Ceylon 4–9

Sukha

▶ Good (Buddhism)

Sukhāvatī

Charles Willemen
International Buddhist College, Songkhla, Thailand

Synonyms

Also known as *Jingtu* (Chinese); *Jōdo* (Japanese); Pure Land

Definition

Sukhāvatī is usually translated as Land of Bliss. Bliss renders *sukha*. The Western Paradise, ruled over by Amitābha.

In Gandharan (Lokottaravāda Mahāsāṅghika) circles developed a belief in countless Buddha-fields in the ten, that is in all directions. Some became well known. For example, The Paradise of the Buddha Akṣobhya in the East, known as Abhirati. But more than one *nikāya*, school, then developed this belief. Most popular is Amitābha's Paradise, Land of Bliss, in the West. This Paradise may be seen as an ideal intermediate existence, *antarābhava*, of Sautrāntika affiliation [8]. It is described in the *Sukhāvatīvyūhasūtras, Sutras About the Display of the Land of Bliss.* They describe a Paradise inhabited by Buddhas and bodhisattvas. There also is an impure realm, inhabited by transmigrating beings. The Buddha Amitābha, who rules over Sukhāvatī, has promised to save these beings, so that they may be reborn in his Paradise after death [4, 3]. Amitābha's eighteenth vow, as found in Chinese literature, is a commitment to save all. It just asks that one sincerely calls Amitābha's name to mind a minimum of ten moments, after which one may be reborn in the Land of Bliss.

Sukhāvatī is rendered in Chinese as *Jingtu* Pure Land. *Jing* actually translates *śubha* pleasant, in ancient Chinese translations based on Gāndhārī(s) and on Kharoṣṭhī script. In the *Aṣṭasāhasrikāprajñāpāramitā* one reads the expression *buddhakṣetrapariśuddhi*, purification of the Buddha-field. Amitābha's Buddha-field is purified *(śuddha)*, made beautiful by the presence of a Buddha or bodhisattva(s). Chinese *jing*, Japanese *jō*, literally means "pure, purified," but used in the translation of Sukhāvatī, Chinese *Jingtu*, Japanese *Jōdo*, it also means *śubha*, pleasant.

The sutras which describe the Pure Land of Amitābha number mainly two: (1) Kumārajīva's *Amituo jing* (*Sutra About Amitābha*), Taishō ed.366, of 402 A.D. in Chang'an, that is, the *Smaller Sukhāvatīvyūha*; (2) Baoyun's *Wuliangshou jing (Sutra About Amitāyus)*, Taishō ed.360, of 421 A.D. in Jiankang (Nanjing), that is, the *Larger Sukhāvatīvyūha* [6]. This last text is often erroneously said to be the work of Kang Sengkai (Saṅghavarman) in 252 A.D. Fei Zhangfang's catalogue of 597 A.D., *Lidai sanbao ji*, is responsible for the mistake. There further are two ancient versions of the *Larger Sukhāvatīvyūha*. P. Harrison has established that Taishō ed.361 is the work of Zhi Qian (third century) and that Taishō ed.362 is a revision of a text linked with Loujia Chen, commonly called Lokakṣema (end of second century A.D.). Xuanzang brought out a new version of the *Smaller Sukhāvatīvyūha* in 650 A.D., that is, Taishō ed.367. There also is a Tang version by Bodhiruci of the *Larger* text in Chang'an, Taishō ed.310 [5], and also two Song versions, Taishō ed.363 by Dharmabhadra in 991 A.D. and Taishō ed.364 by Wang Rixiu in 1162 A.D.

The Pure Land School in East Asia uses Kumārajīva's text and Baoyun's text as canonical [1, 2, 7].

Cross-References

- ▶ Amitābha
- ▶ Avalokiteśvara
- ▶ Kharoṣṭhī Script
- ▶ Sautrāntika

References

1. Blum M (2002) The origins and development of pure land Buddhism: a study and translation of Gyonen's Jodo Homon Genrusho. Oxford University Press, Oxford
2. Foard J, Solomon M, Payne R (eds) (1996) The pure land tradition: history and development. Regents of the University of California, Berkeley
3. Fujita K (2005) Pure and impure lands. In: Jones L (ed) Encyclopedia of religion, 2nd edn. Macmillan Reference USA, Gale Virtual Reference Library, Detroit
4. Gómez L (1996, 3rd printing 2000) The land of bliss: the paradise of the Buddha of measureless light. University of Hawaii Press, Honolulu
5. Inagaki H (2003) The three pure land sutras. Numata Center for Buddhist Translation and Research, Berkeley
6. Kao Kuan-ju (1964) Amitābha-Vyūha. In: Malalasekera G (ed) Encyclopaedia of Buddhism, vol I. Government of Colombo, Colombo, pp 464–468

7. Payne R, Tanaka K (eds) (2004) Approaching the land of bliss: religious praxis in the cult of Amitābha. Kuroda Institute in East Asian Buddhism. University of Hawaii Press, Honolulu
8. Willemen C (2013) Early Yogācāra and visualization (Bhāvanā). In: Volume in memory of L. Kawamura. Contemporary Issues in Buddhist Studies Series. Institute of Buddhist Studies, University of Hawaii Press, Berkeley

Sumeru

▶ Kailash
▶ Meru (Buddhism)

Śūnya

Madhumita Chattopadhyay
Department of Philosophy, Jadavpur University, Kolkata, West Bengal, India

Synonyms

Empty; Nothing; Unreal; Void

Definition

The concept that things do not have any essence of their own and in that sense they are unreal.

Buddhist Notion of Sunya

The term *śūnya* (Pāli *suñña*) in ordinary language is understood to stand for a place or a locus which is vacant, which is not occupied by anybody. In the grammatical tradition, the term is analyzed as *ś une kukkurāya hitam*. The term *hita* generally means "good" (*mangala*), but in this context it means "offered." So the whole expression means "that which is offered to the dog." In the Indian tradition, the dog is considered to be something not good or sacred but as something bad. So if anything is dedicated to the dog, it is meant that the object is completely worthless, it is no longer of any use, it is as if nothing. In accordance with such grammatical analysis, the term *śūnya* comes to mean "empty, vacant, nothing."

In the Buddhist literature, for example, in the *Dhammapada, Saṃyutta Nikāya*, or in the *Jātaka* stories, there are such expressions as *suññāgāra* (an empty room), *suññavana* (an empty forest), *śūnyaṃ vāsagṛham* (a house which is bereft of people), etc. In all such expressions, the term *śūnya* indicates the absence of entities like animals, persons, etc. This sense of the term is not anything special to Buddhism; rather it is very common. The Buddhist philosophers, however, give this term a new dimension for which their philosophy begets a new orientation. All the objects in the world are said to be characterized by four features: *anitya* (impermanence), *duḥkha* (suffering), *śūnya*, and *anātman* (selfless). Of these, the term *śūnya* was interpreted as selfless or devoid of self in the early literature. For example, Aśvaghoṣa explains that the elements are *śū nya* or void because there is neither producer nor enjoyer in them ([1], p. 17.20). This explanation indicates that for Aśvaghoṣa, *śūnya* is to be taken as selfless or soulless or *anātman*. Buddhaghoṣa, also, interprets *śūnya* as soulless. He elucidates the point with the illustration of a wooden machine. Just as a wooden machine is *śūnya*, being devoid of a soul and will, and yet can walk or sit because of the fitting of wood and rope and behaves as if it were willing and living, similarly the man, namely, the *nāmarūpa*, is devoid of soul and will, yet it walks and sits because of the conglomeration of different *dharmas* and appears as if it were willing and living. This understanding of *śūnya* as *anattā* has been presented by Buddhaghoṣa from different perspectives. According to one perspective, things are *śūnya* means that they are devoid of (1) soul/substance, (2) anything pertaining to the soul, (3) permanence, (4) eternality, (5) impermanence, and (6) everlastingness. According to another perspective, *śūnya* is (1) non-perception of soul in oneself, (2) non-perception of one's self elsewhere, (3) non-perception of any other soul anywhere, and (4) non-perception of anyone else's soul in oneself. In short, for Buddhaghoṣa, the notion of *śūnya* comes to mean *anattā*.

The difficulty with such an interpretation of the early Buddhist thinkers is that according to it, a problem occurs. If *śūnya* means selfless, then the fourth feature, namely, *anātman*, would become redundant. To avoid this problem, Aśvaghoṣa points out the difference in significance between the two terms *śūnya* and *anātman*, thereby justifying his sense of the term. According to him, *śūnya* means no-soul and no-soul merely and nothing more, while the term *anātman* signifies that entities are devoid of desire/will (*nirīha*), are not independent (*asvatantra*), and they are dependently originated. Yaśomitra points out the difference in another way. He equates *anātman* with the negation of *ātmadṛṣṭi* or the view of the soul, while *śūnya* is the negation of *ātmīyadṛṣṭi*, view of things concerning the soul. Some other philosophers hold that *śūnya* means merely being empty. For example, when one says that the pot is empty or *śūnya*, what one means is that there is no water in it. So when it is said that everything is *śūnya*, what is meant is that there is no soul in the body. On the other hand, *nairātmya* or *anātman* means *naiḥsvābhāvya* or essencelessness or negation of everything whatsoever.

In the Buddhist literature, the term *śūnya* is also used in the sense of being non-substantial. Nāgasena in his *Milindapañhā* equates *śūnya* with essencelessness (*nihsvabhāvatā*) when he speaks of bringing to light the self-character of things as the supremely *suñña*, free from willing and living, absolutely *suñña* ([5], p. 76). The Sarvāstivādin thinkers hold that all entities of the world are characterized by the four characteristics of *anitya, duhkha, śūnya*, and *anātman*. The text *Theragāthā* adds to this list two other features, namely, *agham* (sinful) and *vadham* (destructive). The Thera or the elderly person or the monk addresses his mind to be watchful of things in their true characteristics in order that it may remain aloof from them. The watchfulness of the mind over the separate personality elements is considered to be one of the four ways of being mindful (*satipaṭṭhana*). In the *Nikāya*s, it is explained as keeping watch over the fact that the different factors of *Bodhi*, four noble truths, etc., are truly realized. But Vasubandhu holds that to be mindful is to penetrate into the elements in their four aspects, namely, *anitya* (impermanence), *duhkha* (suffering), *śūnya* (void), and *anātman* (selfless). Modern scholars believe that this interpretation is not to be viewed as originally one of Vasubandhu, but it is based on the teachings of the thinkers of the early Sarvāstivāda school. The Sarvāstivādins insist that the comprehension of the four noble truths (*Āryasatya*) is possible under each of these four aspects. For instance, the first noble truth, known as *duhkha-satya*, is characterized as *anitya, duhkha, śūnya*, and *anātman*. Since this first noble truth holds for the entire universe, the different Buddhist philosophers selected one of these topics and founded their ontological outlook on it. Nāgārjuna and his followers picked up the aspect of *śūnya* of the elements and constructed the superstructure of their philosophy on it. The term *śūnya* according to this Buddhist logician stands for the lack of independent existence, inherent existence, or essence of things. A thing can be said to have an essence or *svabhāva* of its own if it does not depend on anything else for its existence. On the contrary, if anything is dependent on anything else for its existence, it cannot be regarded to have any own essence. The fact is that all the entities of the world depend for their origination on certain causes (*hetu*) and conditions (*pratyaya*), and hence they cannot be said to have any essence. And that which is devoid of an intrinsic essence of its own is regarded as *śūnya*. So everything is regarded as *śūnya*. While showing that everything is *śūnya*, Nāgārjuna is relying on the principle that dependent origination, lack of intrinsic nature, and being *śūnya* mean the same thing. Nāgārjuna in the text *Mūlamadhyamakaśāstra* relentlessly analyzes the phenomena or processes that appear to exist independently and shows that they cannot so exist. Naively from the common sense standpoint, it is believed by all that all entities exist and they all have their own inherent essence, independent of others. Nāgārjuna's argument strikes at the basis of this common sense belief and shows that such naïve belief is the root of all delusions that lead to human suffering. So, for the extirpation of the very root of human suffering, it is to be admitted that these phenomena are not real in the true sense of the term – they are only conventionally real. Whatever may be the empirical value of the categories like substance, change, permanence, etc., for interpreting the phenomena, they are not assignable determinations of the Absolute. They belong to the region of the empirical truth or *samvṛti satya*. From the ultimate standpoint, they are all *śūnya*. The Mādhyamikas believe that there is no term, category, or concept, however general it may be, that is applicable to both the Absolute and the phenomena in the same sense. The Absolute and the phenomena do not stand on the same plane; they cannot be related, compared, and contrasted. Words cannot describe or denote the Absolute in any recognizable sense. The Absolute is incommensurable and inexpressible and is completely transcendent to thought. As such, the Absolute is regarded as *śūnya*.

Some Absolutist thinkers, however, believe that there is a double process – the transformation of the Absolute into phenomena and the reconversion of the phenomena to its pristine state of the Absolute through knowledge. The Vijñānavādins, for example, speak of the consciousness as underlying defilements and then overcoming them through purification (*vyāvadāna*). Even in the early stages of Vedānta, there is the notion of retransformation of the world into the Brahman, which implies that these Vedāntins believed in the degradation of the Brahman originally. However, such Absolutist thinking is rejected by the Mādhyamikas. They point out that there is no initial fall and, hence, there is no need for retransformation. So the Mādhyamikas hold that through wisdom the real things are not made unreal; things are themselves unreal (*śūnya*) in nature. So the doctrine of *śūnyatā* does not bring about a change in the nature of things but a change in the outlook of people. This view of the Mādhyamikas that everything is *śūnya* is not shared by all the Buddhist thinkers. In the *Tathāgatagarbha Sūtra*, only impermanent, changeful things and states which constitute the world of *samsāra* are regarded as empty or *śūnya* in a negative sense, but not the Buddha or the Nirvāṇa which are stated to be real, eternal, and filled with inconceivable enduring virtues. The Lotus Sūtra also holds that seeing all phenomena as empty cannot be the highest final attainment; the objective is to attain that ultimate wisdom of *Bodhi* which supersedes the knowledge of emptiness.

In short, for the Buddhists, the doctrine of *śūnya* is not an arbitrary prescription to view things as unreal; it is the revelation of the intrinsic nature of objects, and this revelation helps to free the human mind from all sorts of false views and misconceptions and can lead one to the path of realizing the highest truth.

Cross-References

- Aśvaghoṣa
- Idealism (Buddhism)
- Mādhyamika
- Middle Way (Buddhism)
- Nāgārjuna
- Philosophy (Buddhism)
- Reality (Buddhism)
- Śūnyatā
- The Lotus Sūtra

References

1. Aśvaghoṣa (2001) Saundarananda. Motilal Banarsidass, Delhi
2. Harivarman (1975) Satyasiddhiśāstra: restored from the Chinese (Shastri NA ed). Gaekwad Oriental Series, Baroda
3. Murti TRV (2006) The central philosophy of Buddhism: a study of Mādhyamika system. Munshiram Manoharlal, Delhi
4. Nagao G (1990) The foundational standpoint of Mādhyamika philosophy, first Indian edn. Sri Satguru, Delhi
5. Rhys Davids TW (1997) The questions of king Milinda. Motilal Banarsidass, Delhi, Indian Reprint
6. Vaidya PL (ed) (1960) Mulamadhyamakasastra of Nagarjuna. The Mithila Institute of Post-Graduate Studies and Research in Sanskrit Learning, Darbhanga
7. Nanamoli B, Bodhi B (ed) (1995) The middle length discourses of the Buddha. Buddhist Publication Society, Kandy, Sri Lanka
8. Nanamoli B (1991) The path of purification: Visuddhimagga. Buddhist Publication Society, Kandy, SriLanka
9. Maitreyanatha (1971) Madhyantavibhagasastrakarika (Pandeya RC ed). Motilal Banarsidass, Delhi

S

10. Asanga (1964) Mahayanasutralankara (Bagchi S ed). The Mithila Institute of Post-Graduate Studies and Research in Sanskrit Learning, Darbhanga
11. Suzuki DT (1999) Studies in the Lankavatarasutra. Motilal Banarsidass, Delhi, Indian edition

Śūnyatā

Madhumita Chattopadhyay
Department of Philosophy, Jadavpur University, Kolkata, West Bengal, India

Synonyms

Emptiness; Nothingness; Voidness

Definition

Doctrine about the nonexistence of a perceiving subject and the perceived objects.*Abassara Brahma* Loka

Buddhist Account of Śūnyatā

The term *śūnyatā* often translated as "emptiness" in English is generally associated with the Mādhyamika school of Buddhism, and is the main reason for the appellation "*śūnyavādin*" of this school. However, a thorough study of the history of Buddhism reveals that the term *śūnya* or the concept *śūnyatā* was not the innovation of this particular school; rather the concept has its origin in the teachings of Lord Buddha himself. This concept of *śūnyatā* has been discussed by other Buddhist schools also. Early reference to this term is found in the *Majjhima Nikāya* in the context of elucidation of *śūnyatāvihāra* ([1], pp. 965–978). There, a monastery is described as *śūnya* in the sense that it is devoid of elephants, cows, horses, etc., but not devoid of monks. A person residing in a forest may be devoid of villagers, but not devoid of the forest trees. In a similar manner, it is said that when a person meditates on the earth as a single object, without making any distinction of the rivers, mountains, oceans, etc., the earth remains, for him, devoid of men, rivers, mountains, etc., but not of the earth-oneness. When the aspirant attains a higher stage in the process of his meditation, like the fifth stage of meditation where his mind concentrates on infinite space, other things become *śūnya* for him and only the infinite space remains as a real object, *aśūnya*. As he proceeds to higher and higher states of meditation, like infinite consciousness, the state of nothingness, and the state of neither consciousness nor no-consciousness, his meditation becomes free or bereft of all other objects, but not of the objects meditated. These objects of meditation are considered as real, *aśūnya*. At the last stage of meditation, which is on the absence of any object, the meditator finds that even this concept is not everlasting or permanent, and thereby he gets himself free from the impurities related to thirst, rebirth, and ignorance. But still he retains the sense of his body as constituted of the sense-organs which remain till his death. That is, in this last stage of meditation, all other things become *śūnya* for him, but his body constituted of the different sense-organs still is not *śūnya*. This indicates that in this early treatise, a distinction between external voidness and internal voidness was made. The former is the absence of some object in a particular place, whereas the latter is the deliverance of one's mind from all sorts of impurities. Such distinction between these two types of *śūnyata* has been referred to as *śūnyata* and *patiśūnyattva*, emptiness and internal purification, in the text *Saṃyutta Nikāya*, Book II. Understanding *śūnyatā* in terms of internal purification is a very common phenomenon in early Buddhist literature. In the *Dhammapada*, it is said that when one's mind is completely free from the three impurities, it is regarded as the stage of *śūnyatā-vimokṣa*. In the *Kathāvatthu*, it is said that the Buddha while speaking of the five *dharmas* compared them with different unreal objects. Thus, the five senses were regarded to be like dots of foam, feeling (*vedanā*) like bubbles, perception (*saññā*) like mirages, impression (*saṃskāras*) like the banana tree, and awareness like illusion (*māyā*). The objects with which the comparison is made are all accepted as unreal; hence, it implies that all the five elements are to be regarded as unreal also. The unreality of all objects is more specifically spelled out in the *Dhātuvibhangasutta* of the *Majjhima Nikāya*, where it is said that depending upon the oil and wick does a lamp burn, but the lamp is neither in the one nor in the other, nor is it anything in itself. Phenomena are like such lamps – they have nothing in themselves. Therefore, all phenomenal objects are unreal; they are deceptions. The only real thing is the *Nirvāṇa* ([2], pp. 74–75). In the Pāli canonical texts like the *Cūla-Suññatā-Sutta* of the *Majjhima Nikāya*, the doctrine of *suññatā* has been praised as veridical (*yathābhucca*), changeless (*avipallattha*), pure (*parisuddha*), and supremely unsurpassable (*paramānuttara*). The *Anguttara Nikāya* and the *Saṃyutta Nikāya* declare that all of the discourses of Lord Buddha are concerned with *suññatā*. In the text *Visuddhimagga*, Buddhaghoṣa regards the insight into *suññatā* of all things as the insight into the soullessness of the elements and it is regarded as one of the gateways to liberation ([3], p. Book XXI.67). It is the non-perception of soul in oneself, non-perception of one's own soul elsewhere, non-perception of any other soul anywhere, and non-perception of anyone else's soul in oneself. Aśvaghoṣa in the text *Mahāyānaś raddhotpādaśāstra* interprets *śūnyatā* as being devoid of phenomena and explains it with the simile of space. Space is nothing; it has no existence and is not a reality; but in ordinary life people speak of this place or that place and that is done in order to distinguish things. This means that what is found in ordinary usages does not always reveal the reality. Similarly, though the phenomenal world appears to be real, it does not have any really outward form; all phenomena are only in the Mind. Hence, it is a mistake to think that there is something outside. All phenomena arise from the false notion of the mind. So when the mind is made free from all false ideas and misconceptions, all phenomena will disappear.

In the Abhidhamma literature, the term *śū nyata* is often understood in the sense of no-soul. Vasubandhu in his *Abhidharmakośabhāṣya* points out that this is a collection of different *saṃskāras*, because there is no *sattva* or sentient being. In the *Milindapañha*, Nāgasena tells us that the nature of all the manifest elements is supreme voidness or *parama-śūnyatvam* because of the absence of any living being. Certain Mahāyāna texts point to the fact that the concept of *śūnyatā* counteracts the *satkāyadṛṣṭi* or belief in the soul. Another sense of the concept of *śūnyatā* is found in the *Samādhirājasūtra*, where it is said that *śūnyata* does not arise nor does it die, because all things are devoid of their own essences (*svabhāva*). In short, in the early Buddhist thought, *śūnyatā* conveyed three different senses: (1) the sense of inner purification, (2) the sense of no-soul, and (3) the sense of being devoid of one's own essence. In some later Buddhist texts like *Pañcaviṃś atisahasrikā*, *Abhisamayālaṃkārāloka*, and *Madhyantavibhāgaṭīkā*, various modes of *śū nyata* have been discussed. Haribhadra, for example, in his *Abhisamayālaṃkāra* treats these different modes of *śūnyatā* either as identical with the ten planes of concentration (*daśabhūmi*) or as preparatory to or as posterior to these stages. The number of modes of *śūnyatā* stated in these texts is not always the same. For instance, in the *Madhyantavibhāgaṭīkā*, the number is stated to be 16, whereas in the *Pancaviṁśatisahasrikā*, the number is 20. These 20 modes are enumerated as follows: (1) the unreality of internal elements of existence (*adhyātmaśūnyatā*), (2) the unreality of external objects (*bahirdhaśūnyatā*), (3) the unreality of both as in the sense-organs or the body (*adhyātmabahirdhasunyatā*), (4) the unreality of unreality (*sunyatā sunyatā*), (5) the unreality of the infinite space (*Mahāsunyatā*), (6) the unreality of the ultimate reality (*paramārthasunyatā*), (7) the unreality of the conditioned (*samskrta sunyāt*), (8) the unreality of the unconditioned (*asamskrta sunyāt*), (9) the unreality of the limitless (*atyantasunyatā*), (10) the unreality of that which is beginningless and endless (*anavaragarasunyatā*), (11) the unreality of the undeniable (*anavakārasunyatā*), (12) the unreality of the ultimate essences (*prakrtisunyatā*), (13) the unreality of all elements of existence (*sarvadharmasunyatā*), (14) the unreality of all determination (*laksanasunyatā*), (15) the unreality of the past, present, and future (*anupalambhasunyatā*), (16) the unreality of

S

relation conceived as absence (*abhāvasvabhāvasunyatā*), (17) the unreality of the positive constituents of empirical existence (*bhāvasunyatā*), (18) the unreality of absence (*abhāvasunyatā*), (19) the unreality of self-being (*svabhāvasunyatā*), and (20) the unreality of independent being (*parabhāvasunyatā*) ([4], pp. 350–356).

In spite of all these explanations or elucidations of the notion of *śūnyatā* by different Buddhist logicians, the notion has come to be closely associated with the name of the Mādhyamika philosopher Nāgārjuna. In his *Mūlamadhyamakakārikā*, he makes different statements on different occasions to remove the various misconceptions regarding *śūnyatā* and bring out its proper significance. With the application of the *prasaṇga* form of argument (a sort of method analogous to the *reductio ad absurdum* argument of the West), Nāgārjuna discusses the different alternative views regarding the notions of motion, senses, agent and action, fire and fuel, essence, suffering, bondage, etc., and shows that none of these views stand the test of scrutiny or all of them lead to some kind of absurd consequences. Hence, ultimately everything is to be considered as *śūnya*. Thus, Nāgārjuna widened the application of *śū nyatā* to the entire field of philosophical speculations. Some Buddhist thinkers objected to such a wide application of the term on the ground that the Buddha used this concept as a means to gain insight into the no-soul notion (*anattā*); hence, application of the notion of *śūnyatā* to other cases cannot be justified. Such an objection was countered by Nāgārjuna with the argument that the doctrine of *śūnyatā* was preached by Lord Buddha to remove all kinds of misconception. So there is nothing wrong to apply this concept of *śūnyatā* to all cases. Nāgārjuna explicitly argues that *śūnyatā* means the lack of essence (*nihsvabhāvatā*) and so *śūnyatā* cannot itself be considered as an essence that things can have; rather it is the total lack of essence or inherent existence. The doctrine of *śūnyatā* is very subtle and hence can be easily misinterpreted. Proper understanding of the notion of *śūnyatā* makes one understand the true nature of everything, whereas lack of clarity in the understanding of this notion makes other notions unclear ([5], p. XXIV.14). So proper understanding of the notion of *śūnyatā* is the primary requirement. In the context of explaining the notion of *śūnyatā*, Nāgārjuna makes a critical three-way relation between *śūnyatā*, dependent origination, and verbal convention and asserts that this relation itself is the middle way. His argument is that dependent origination, technically known as *pratītyasamutpāda*, means the origination of an object as dependent on causes and conditions. Just as in the physical plane the germination of a seed takes place by depending on its cause and other conditions, in the psychical plane, consciousness (*vijñāna*) occurs by depending on its respective cause and condition. That is, everything in the world can occur only by its dependence on other causes and conditions. That which depends for its occurrence on other causes and conditions cannot be said to have an essence of its own. So, all the objects in the world being dependent on causes and conditions for their occurrences are said to be devoid of any essence of their own. And that which is devoid of an intrinsic essence of its own is regarded as *śūnyatā*. Thus, according to Nāgārjuna, dependent origination, lack of intrinsic nature, and *śūnyatā* mean the same thing. In verse 18 of Chapter 24 of the text *Mūlamadhyamakaśāstra* [5], Nāgārjuna holds that whatever is dependently co-arisen, that is explained to be emptiness. That being a dependent origination is itself the middle way. Here, Nāgārjuna is asserting the identity of (1) emptiness (*śūnyatā*), (2) the dependently originated entities, that is, all phenomena, and (3) verbal convention. Basic to this assertion of the emptiness of all phenomena stand two fundamental theses of Nāgārjuna's philosophy: (a) doctrine of dependent origination, namely, that everything is dependent on their respective cause (*hetu*) and condition (*pratyaya*), and (b) whatever is so dependent has to be regarded as devoid of any essence. In his elucidation of the notion of causality, Nāgārjuna makes a distinction between a cause (*hetu*) and a condition (*pratyaya*). What he means by cause or *hetu* is an event or state or process that can be appealed to in explaining another event, state, or process without any metaphysical commitment to any occult connection between the *explanandum* and the *explanans* [6]. Taking cause and condition in this way, Nāgārjuna points out that if one views phenomena as having and as emerging from causal powers, one views them as having essences and as being connected to the essences of other phenomena. But, this is ultimately incoherent since it forces one to admit the inherent existence of things in virtue of their essential identity and at the same time it asserts their dependent and productive character in virtue of their causal history. But such dependence and relational character are incompatible with their inherent existence. So that which has dependent origination is to be regarded as devoid of inherent existence and, hence, is empty (*śūnya*). Therefore, it is established that to say of something that it is dependently originated is to say that it is empty and to say of something that it is empty is another way of saying that it arises dependently.

For Nāgārjuna, *śūnyatā*, therefore, stands for a denial of all metaphysical constructions and it itself cannot be regarded as a metaphysical doctrine of nihilism or absolutism or anything of that sort. Unfortunately, the notion of *śūnyatā* has often been criticized to be so by the opponents. Nāgārjuna refutes their views by referring to the words of Lord Buddha. The Buddha in his instruction to Kāśyapa holds that he considers the man to be incurable who considers *śūnyatā* itself to be a theory. If a drug administered to a patient is able to remove all his discomforts, but at the same time were to affect the stomach by remaining in it, the patient cannot be said to be cured. In the same manner, *śūnyatā* is an antidote to all dogmatic views, but if anyone regards it to be a theory or a view in itself, then he fails to realize the true spirit of *śūnyatā* (*Kāśyapa-parivarta-Sūtra* quoted in [4] and [7]). The significance of this way of presentation of *śūnyatā* is that it clearly points out that it is wrong to interpret *śūnyatā* as a doctrine of voidness or doctrine of nihilism. *Śūnyatā* of *dṛṣṭi* (views) is not one more *dṛṣṭi*, but is *prajñā* or their reflective awareness. This *śūnyatā* or the reflective awareness of reason belongs to a higher level of consciousness. From that level alone, it can be regarded as a review of views. In the *Aṣṭasahasrikāprajñāpāramitā* and other *Prajñā Pāramitā* texts, it has been said that *rūpa* is *śūnya* and *śūnyatā* is *rūpa*, and similar is the case with other aggregates (*skandhas*) like *vedanā, samjñā, samskāra, and vijñāna*. If *śūnyatā* were different from them, things will not be devoid of essential reality. Mādhyamika philosophers have repeatedly warned people not to consider *śūnyatā* as nonexistence or *abhāva*. To deny the accessibility of thought to real is not to deny the real but to point out the limitations of thought. Thought always looks at the real through conceptual patterns, through differentia, and distinction. It sunders and distorts the real. *Buddhi* or thought is characterized as the conventional or *saṃvṛti*, a cover that veils the real. The essence of thought consists in the different modes or attributes as for instance "is" or "is not" or a combination of both "is and is not". So to have proper knowledge of the real, it is essential to get rid of all the functions of thought, that is, to remove the different modes of thought. The total negation of thought modes is *prajñā* or intuition. *Prajñā* is Absolute, the real. As such, the Mādhyamikas consider this *prajñā* as the *śūnyatā* of *dṛṣṭi*, the negation of concepts. This *śūnyatā* as the dissolution of the conceptual function of the mind is freedom. Viewed from the standpoint of *prajñā, samsāra* and *nirvāṇa* are identical; there is no difference between them. *Nirvāṇa* is the reality of *saṃsāra*, while *saṃsāra* is the falsity of *Nirvāṇa*. *Nirvāṇa* is actually the *saṃsāra* without the birth and the decay. The difference consists in one's way of looking at them. It is epistemological and not metaphysical. This *śūnyatā* is truly universal, it constitutes the whole reality. Accordingly, the Mādhyamikas contend that the final release is possible only through the understanding of such *śūnyatā*. The paths shown by other philosophical systems can lead to partial release or to a preliminary stage. All of them speak of the attainment of liberation through the knowledge of the true nature of reality either as substance or as Prakṛti or as Brahman, etc. Consideration of the real in any such particular modes, for instance, as substance or as being, necessarily creates an other and distinguishes the real from that other. So while upholding that reality is such and such, these systems are being attached to one particular view and rejecting other views. Such restriction or determination is the root of *saṃsāra*. Nāgārjuna holds that when the self is posited, an other confronts it; with the division of things into self and nonself, attachment and aversion result. Depending on these all vices spring up. Attachment brings in the thirst for pleasure, and thirst hides all flaws of the objects. Blinded by attachment and thirst, man imagines qualities in things and looks for upon the means to achieve pleasure. *Saṃsāra* is thus present as long as there is the attachment to the "I" ([4], p. 270).

The root cause of all our sufferings, according to the Mādhyamikas, lies in indulgence in the wrong views (*dṛṣṭi*) or *kalpanā*. *Kalpanā* is *avidyā* par excellence. The real is the indeterminate; associating it with a character, determining it as "this" or "not this" is to apprehend the real as one-sided, partial, and unreal. This is unconsciously negation of the real, for all determination is negation. So what is required is the denial of all the standpoints which are the initial negation of the real that is essentially indeterminate, and this is *śūnyatā*. So *śūnyatā* properly understood will lead one to correct this initial unconscious falsification of the real and, hence, can lead one to the stage of *Nirvāṇa*.

The Yogācāra school of Buddhism has also spoken of the notion of *śūnyatā*, but their interpretation is somewhat different from that of the Mādhyamikas. Like the Mādhyamikas, the Yogācāra philosophers believe that the objective world which is experienced by human beings is a false reflection of the human mind. It is one phase of the store consciousness (*ālayavijñāna*) which is an accumulation of the past impressions (*vāsanā*) from time immemorial. This store consciousness has to be checked and substituted by a pure supramundane cognition. To do away with it is considered as the summum bonum (*mukti*). The Yogācāra philosopher Maitreyanātha regards this as *śūnyatā* because it is the cleansing of all the defiling factors which generate the illusive appearance of the external objects and human attachment toward them. This *śūnyatā* is not an absolute nonentity but something more [8]. His argument is that liberation is acquired as a result of purifying one's own mind from all sorts of misconceptions. Since consciousness presents an illusive appearance before human beings, the existence of such consciousness cannot be denied altogether. So what is denied is the illusive character of such consciousness which occurs in the form of the apprehender (*grāhaka*) and the apprehended (*grāhya*). But the self-substance of the consciousness itself is beyond the reach of the ordinary mind; still it can hardly be denied. Thus, the Yogācāra notion of *śūnyatā* differs from the Mādhyamika notion. For the Mādhyamikas, *śūnyatā* conveys the idea of non-substantiality (*niḥsvabhāva*) and serves as an antidote to all misconceptions and false ideas, but this *śūnyatā* itself is not regarded to possess any essence of its own, while for the Yogācāras, *śūnyatā* has an essence which cannot be denied, though that essence cannot be realized by ordinary human intellect. The Vijñānavādins sometimes also talk in the language of the Mādhyamikas. For example, Sthiramati equates *śūnyatā* with the exclusion of all views (*sarva-dṛṣṭi-niḥśaraṇa*). Asaṃga also seems to follow the Mādhyamika dialect of the four-cornered negation: negation of being, negation of nonbeing, negation of being and nonbeing, and negation of neither.

Often a distinction is made between emptiness of one thing by another (*itaretaraśūnyatā*) and emptiness concerning characters (*lakṣaṇaśū nyatā*). The former type of emptiness is that of one thing by another. This is exemplified in the case when one perceptually apprehends a certain place as being free of another object. This emptiness of one thing by another is not regarded as ultimate, but depends on the conventional truth. That is, although all entities are not different from each other on account of their being of the same nature in being ultimately destructible, momentary, they appear to be mutually different to the ordinary person. Hence, for the ordinary beings, this emptiness of one thing by another is a commonly accepted fact, since they grasp one entity as being free of another, but it is not ultimately established. In actual fact, dreamt and illusory entities do not admit among themselves any distinct nature. Therefore, Lord Buddha regarded this kind of emptiness as the worst of all, not being founded on ultimate reality, and asked people to abandon this view. As such, when the Mādhyamikas speak of *śūnyatā*, they mean by it *lakṣaṇaśūnyatā*, that is, emptiness concerning characters. All *dharmas* are regarded to be ultimately devoid of intrinsic nature because their particular and universal characters (*svasāmānyalakṣaṇa*), as they are established, are void. This voidness is apprehended through the occurrence of the wisdom in which no *dharma* appears. If the character, both particular and universal, truly existed, it would have been apprehended by the seers through their yogic apprehension. But the yogins never apprehend any such ultimate aspects of objects. Hence, all the dharmas would have to be regarded as *śūnya*. As such, it is stated in the *Madhyamakāloka* that the Mādhyamikas accept the absence of the real, intrinsic nature of all dharmas due to the emptiness concerning characters and not due to the emptiness of one thing by another ([9], pp. 110–112).

Because of this understanding of *śūnyatā* as the absence of the intrinsic nature of things, the Mādhyamika philosophers hold that everything is consistent for him for whom essencelessness is proper, while everything becomes inconsistent for one for whom essencelessness is not proper. Therefore, in the text *Vigrahavyāvartanī*, Nāgārjuna points out in clear terms that all activities and all values and interests will remain in a secure position for one who believes in the ultimate truth of *śūnyatā*. On the other hand, for one who does not subscribe to *śūnyatā*, nothing becomes secure. To the enlightened person who understands *śūnyatā* properly, the triple jewel (*triratna*), namely, the Buddha, the Dharma or the Law, and the monastic order, will become a matter of conviction. So *śūnyatā* helps one not simply in the matter of spiritual practices, but the mundane laws of individual conduct, social behavior, etc., also derive their significance from the concept of *śūnyatā*. As such, in the Mahāyāna tradition it is believed that understanding of *śūnyatā* leads one to the path of liberation. Liberation is achieved through the realization of the doctrine of emptiness. In the text *Bodhicaryāvatāra*, *śūnyatā* is regarded as the path of Bodhi (*Bodhimārga*), as the cause of *Nirvāṇa* (*nirvāṇakāraṇam*). Through the rejection of all the empirical modes of the transcendent, the mind becomes free not only from all the alternatives, but from all the *kleśa*s, namely, passions, attachment, and aversion, since they all have their root in false construction. This is the state of *Nirvāṇa*. Thus, *śūnyatā* leading to *prajñā* leads one to the ultimate state of *Nirvāṇa*. In the text *Laṇkāvatārasūtra*, the concept of *śunyata* is frequently used with the concepts of no-birth (*anutpāda*), no self-substance (*asvabhāva*), and non-duality (*advaya*) to mean the same entity or express different aspects of the same fact. When it is said that everything is empty, what is meant is that all the particular objects of the world do not have any ultimate reality. Nothing exists in the world which can be said to be absolutely real in the sense of possessing self-substance. Because of emptiness there is no birth, and as there is no birth there is no world of particulars in which the notion of self-substance (*svabhāva*) or the notion of duality can occur. So when one realizes the notion of emptiness properly, one is said to have compliance with reality not born (*anutpattikādharmakṣānti*) and is able to attain the realization of the highest knowledge (*anuttara-samyak-sambodhi*) [10].

The *Laṇkāvatārasūtra* speaks of seven types of emptiness: (1) emptiness of appearance (*lakṣaṇa*), (2) emptiness of self-substance (*svabhāva*), (3) emptiness of nonaction (*apracarita*), (4) emptiness of action (*pracarita*), (5) emptiness by which is meant the unnameability of existence (*sarva-dharma-nirabhilāpya*), (6) emptiness of the highest degree, that is, the ultimate reality (*paramārtha*), and (7) emptiness of reciprocity (*itaretara*). By the emptiness of appearance is meant that appearance is not a final fact. Emptiness of self-substance indicates that talk of individual nature of objects is a construction of our own mind. It is an illusion to think that individual objects exist in reality. Since the individual objects do not have any self-substance or essence of their own, they are regarded as empty. By the emptiness of the nonaction is meant that what is described as the activities of the different elements or *skandhas* is not real, the *skandhas* in their nature are nonacting, and in that sense they are described as emptiness. The question obviously arises that if there is in reality no activity of the elements, how is it that their activities are perceived. In reply, it is explained that these elements or *skandhas* are not by themselves independent creating agencies; there is nothing in them that can be regarded to be their self. The activities or *karmas* which are perceived are due to different causes and conditions. In that sense, the emptiness of action is stated. As existence of everything is dependent on the imaginative power of human mind, their existence is a constructed one or *parikalpita*. They do not have any self-substance of their own by which they can be named and described by the terminology of relative knowledge; and this incapability of being named by designation is regarded as the emptiness of the unnameability. But the great emptiness or emptiness of the highest degree is the supreme wisdom (*Āryajñāna*). When this supreme wisdom is realized by inner consciousness, all the theories, wrong ideas, and traces of beginningless memory altogether disappear. This is another form of emptiness. As compared to others, the emptiness of reciprocity is considered to be of the lowest kind and is to be avoided by all. This emptiness occurs when the quality possessed by one entity is lacking in another. For example, a monastery where there are no horses and elephants is regarded as empty, but that does not mean that there are no monks there. A monastery is a monastery and a monk is a monk, each retaining its own characteristic. Elephants and horses may be found in places where they belong; only they are absent in places which is occupied by another. Such sort of absence is regarded as the emptiness of reciprocity ([10], pp. 287–291).

Regarding the notion of emptiness or *śūnyatā*, one faces a problem: If everything in the world is considered as empty, what will be the status of emptiness itself? Is it to be regarded as empty also? In reply, it can be said that Nāgārjuna does not consider emptiness as an additional entity. As such, when he rejects all other concepts, he rejects the notion of emptiness also. His point is that if there were something nonempty, there could be something empty (*śūnya*), but since there is nothing nonempty, there cannot be anything called emptiness. What is left after negating everything conceivable can be characterized neither as nonbeing, nor as *śūnya* for the simple reason that there is nothing in opposition to which these concepts could be logically framed. Candrakīrti, the chief commentator of Nāgārjuna, explains this point clearly. According to him, if there were something like *śūnyatā* over and above the objects, the essence of objects would depend upon it. But this is not the case. Here, *śūnyatā* is propounded as the generic characteristic feature of all reals. There is no non-*śūnya* real, and hence non-*śūnyatā* itself does not exist. That is to say, all reals being *śūnya*, there is no non-*śūnya* real, and hence *śūnyatā*, in default of its opposite, simply does not exist. So the point that Nāgārjuna and other Buddhist thinkers want to emphasize is that the main objective of the doctrine of *śūnyatā* was to point out the defective character of all ontological thesis. But it would be wrong to regard the *śūnyatā* itself as a thesis in its turn. If it were itself regarded as a view and a negative view, it would be as absurd as other theories. Hence, *śūnyatā* itself cannot be regarded as a real entity while rejecting the reality of other entities. This is what is meant by the emptiness of emptiness itself. The abandonment of even the notion of *śūnyatā* is referred to as *Mahāśūnyatā* or great emptiness in the Mahāyāna tradition.

Cross-References

▶ Anattā (Buddhism)
▶ Bodhidharma
▶ Idealism (Buddhism)
▶ Mādhyamika
▶ Majjhimā Paṭipadā
▶ Middle Way (Buddhism)
▶ Nāgārjuna

▶ Paṭiccasamuppāda
▶ Philosophy (Buddhism)
▶ Prajñāpāramitā
▶ Yogācāra

References

1. Ñāṇamoli B, Bodhi B (eds) (1995) The middle length discourses of the Buddha: a new translation of the Maqjjhima Nikāya. Buddhist Publication Society, Kandy, pp 965–978
2. Narain H (1997) The Mādhyamika mind. Motilal Banarsidass, Delhi
3. Ñāṇamoli B (tr) (1991) The path of purification. Buddhist Publication Society, Kandy, Book XXI.67
4. Murti TRV (2006) The central philosophy of Buddhism: a study of Madhyamika system. Munshiram Manoharlal, Delhi
5. Vaidya PL (1960) Madhyamakaśāstra of Nāgārjuna with the commentary Prasannapadā by Candrakīrti. Mithila Institute of Post-Graduate Studies and Research in Sanskrit Learning, Darbhanga
6. Garfield JL (2002) Empty words: Buddhist philosophy and cross-cultural interpretation. Oxford University Press, New York
7. Nayak GC (2001) Mādhyamika Sunyatā: a reappraisal. Indian Council of Philosophical Research, New Delhi
8. Shastri NA (1975) Śūnyatā and its significance in Buddhism. In: Bulletin of tibetology. Namgyal Institute of Tibetology, Gangtok, pp 5–18
9. Keira R (2004) Mādhyamika and epistemology: a study of Kamalaśīla's method for proving the voidness of all Dharmas. Arbeitskreis für Tibetische und Buddhistische Studien, Universität Wien, Wien
10. Suzuki DT (1999) Studies in the Laṇkāvatāra Sūtra. Motilal Banarsidass, Delhi, Indian edition

Śūnyatā

▶ Middle Way (Buddhism)
▶ Relativity (Buddhism)

Supernatural Power

▶ *Iddhi*

Supremacy

▶ Pāramitā

Surāmerayamadya

▶ Alcoholic Drinks and Drinking (Buddhism)

Surāmerayamajja

▶ Alcoholic Drinks and Drinking (Buddhism)

Śūraśena

▶ Mathurā

Surundha

▶ Vārāṇasī (Buddhism)

Surundhana

▶ Vārāṇasī (Buddhism)

Suryapura

▶ Mathurā

Sūtra Piṭaka

▶ Sutta Piṭaka

Sutta Piṭaka

K. T. S. Sarao
Department of Buddhist Studies, University of Delhi, Delhi, India

Synonyms

Sūtra Piṭaka; Suttanta Piṭaka

Definition

The second of the three divisions of the *Tipiṭaka*.

Introduction

The Sutta Piṭaka which is one of the three *piṭakas* (collections) of the Tipiṭaka contains more than 10,000 *suttas* (Sk: *sūtras*, discourses) attributed to the Buddha or his close associates. It consists of five *nikāyas* (divisions): Dīgha, Majjhima, Saṃyutta, Aṅguttara, and Khuddaka. Whereas the first four *nikāyas* are homogeneous and cognate in nature, the fifth one is quite heterogeneous. Some *suttas* appear in two or more of the *nikāyas*. Though tradition claims that the Sutta Piṭaka was composed in the First Buddhist Council that took place shortly after the demise of the Buddha, it is generally agreed that it would have been impossible that such a huge collection was finally composed and settled within a short period of 3 months. Most probably, only short speeches, sayings, and verses conveying important doctrines of Buddhism were collected in the First Buddhist Council, and these were was expanded into full-length suttas over the next 100 years or so.

The Dīgha Nikāya

The Dīgha Nikāya is known as the "Collection of Long Discourses" in English. A complete version of the Dīrgha Āgama of the Dharmaguptaka School survives in Chinese translation under the title of *Cháng Ahánjīng*. There are 30 *sūtras* (discourses) in it as compared to 34 *suttantas* (discourses) of the Theravādin Dīgha Nikāya. Fragments of the Sarvāstivādin School's Dīrgha Āgama are also extant in their Sanskrit as well as Tibetan translations [9].

The Theravādin Dīgha Nikāya appears to be composed of earlier and later portions and is not the earliest work of the Pāli Tipiṭaka ([30], p. 44). In it, though there are some long *suttas*, majority of the *suttas* are short. The second *vagga* consists of the longest *suttas*, some of which have grown into their present bulky size as a result of interpolations ([30], p. 35). Each of the *suttas* of the Dīgha Nikāya treats intensively some particular point or points of doctrine and may be as well considered an independent work ([30], p. 35). Its 34 *suttas* have been put together into three *vaggas* (groups), and this threefold division is a purely formal division with no direct link to the subject matter or content (see [7], p. 26).

More than half of the *suttas* of the Dīgha Nikāya are debates with either Brāhmaṇas or members of other sects that were contemporaries of early Buddhism and hence contain much information on sects, some of which is the only available information on these sects ([12], p. 75; [7], p. 28). It has been suggested that these debates in the Dīgha Nikāya were probably used to win followers, and in all probability, once Buddhism established itself, the content of the Dīgha Nikāya may have become outdated ([12], pp. 71, 78).

Majjhima Nikāya

The Majjhima Nikāya is known as the "Collection of Middle Length Discourse/Sayings" or "Middle Collection" in English. It consists of 152 *suttas* grouped into three books (*paṇṇāsas*) called *Mahāpaṇṇāsa* (first 50 *suttas*), *Majjhimapaṇṇāsa* (*sutta* nos. 51–100), and *Uparipaṇṇāsa* (*sutta* nos. 101–152). Each of these three books is subdivided into groups of ten *suttas*. Occasionally, these *suttas* are also clustered into pairs called *Cūḷa* (Small) and *Mahā* (Great) *suttas*. At the First Buddhist Council that took place at Rājagaha three months after the death of the Buddha, the job of memorizing the Majjhima Nikāya and of transmitting it further intact was assigned to the "school" of Sāriputta ([19]: i.15). The Majjhima Nikāya corresponds to the Madhyama Āgama found in the Sūtra Piṭakas of various Sanskrit-based early Buddhist schools, fragments of which are extant in Sanskrit. Portions of the Sarvāstivāda Madhyama Āgama also survive in Tibetan translation. A complete translation of the Madhyama Āgama of the Sarvāstivāda School, known as the *Zhōng Ahánjīng* (Taishō 26) containing 222 *sūtras*, was done by Saṃghadeva in the Eastern Jin Dynasty in 397–398 C.E. [9].

Almost all the important tenets of Buddhism have been dealt with in the Majjhima Nikāya, and light has been thrown not only on the life of the Buddhist monks and nuns but also on subjects such as Brāhmaṇical *yajñas* (sacrifices), different forms of asceticism, the relation of the Buddha to the Nigaṇṭhas (Jainas), the four noble truths, the doctrine of kamma, refutation of the self, different modes of meditation, and the social and political conditions prevalent at that time that have all been discussed in this *nikāya* ([11], p. 116). In some of the *suttas* of the Majjhima Nikāya, it has been stated that the particular dialogue took place after the Mahāparinibbāna indicating that these *suttas* are younger than those in the Dīgha Nikāya ([7], p. 34).

The Saṃyutta Nikāya

The Saṃyutta Nikāya is known as "Book of the Kindred Sayings" or "Collection of Connected Discourses" in English. It is one of the basic works in which early Indian teachings on topics such as suffering, impermanence, selflessness, four noble truths, and the eightfold path have been given in detail. The Saṃyutta Nikāya is divided into five main *vaggas* consisting of a total of 56 sections, called *saṃyuttas*. Each of these 56 *saṃyuttas* has been further subdivided into minor *vaggas* (chapters). The five main *vaggas* are as follows:

1. The Sagātha Vagga consisting of 11 *saṃyuttas* contains verses.
2. The Nidāna Vagga consisting of ten *saṃyuttas* explains the chain of causation (*paṭiccasamuppāda*).
3. The Khandha Vagga consisting of 13 *saṃyuttas* explains the 5 *khandhas*.
4. The Saḷāyatana Vagga consisting of ten *saṃyuttas* explains the six sense organs with their objects.
5. The Mahā Vagga consisting of 12 *saṃyuttas*.

The *suttas* in the different *saṃyuttas* recur repetitively. It has been suggested that most probably this repetitiveness arose due to the fact that there existed a large number of *suttas* on the same subject, collected from different individuals and monasteries, etc., all being of equal religious merit and hence deserving to be included in the collection ([30], p. 57). Thus, the large number of the *suttas* is basically the outcome of a practice that involved a thorough treatment of the same topic from all angles in accordance with a fixed pattern to the complete exhaustion of both the topic and the reader. As suggested by K.R. Norman, this type of arrangement, however, represents an obvious editorial practice, and the existence of a number of the *suttas* elsewhere in the canon probably indicates a conscious selection of material to group together in this way ([15], p. 50). Further, as the *suttas* were classified in two different ways and as some of the *saṃyuttas* deal with numerical subjects, there is inevitably an overlap between the Saṃyutta Nikāya and the Aṅguttara Nikāya in the Pāli canon. Occasionally, different versions of the same *sutta* in the Saṃyutta Nikāya and within the *nikāyas* elsewhere show substantial differences among themselves. These differences indicate that changes were introduced into one another, or both, of the narratives at some time, but the tradition has not changed since then for the obvious reason that the texts were preserved by the Dīgha-*bhāṇakas* and the Saṃyutta-*bhāṇakas* independent of each other ([15], p. 50).

The Saṃyutta Nikāya corresponds to the Saṃyukta Āgama found in the Sūtra Piṭakas of various Sanskritic early Buddhists schools, fragments of which survive in Sanskrit and in Tibetan translation. A complete Chinese translation from the Sarvāstivādin recension, known as the *ZáAhánjīng*, appears in the Chinese Buddhist canon, and it includes a number of *sūtras* which appear in the Aṅguttara Nikāya of the Pāli Tipiṭaka ([17], p. 181). This would seem to indicate that at the time when the *āgamas* were collected, the distinction between the "connected" and the "numerical" classifications was not very clearly drawn ([15], p. 54).

The Aṅguttara Nikāya

The Aṅguttara Nikāya is known as "Book of Gradual Sayings" or "Numerical Discourses" in English. It has *suttas* (Sk: *sūtras*, discourses) grouped in "higher" (*uttara*) "parts" (*aṅgas*), i.e., in groups of numerical ascendency with an arithmetical progression from 1 to 11 on the basis of the number of *dhamma* (Sk: dharma) items referenced in them. Thus, the *Eka-nipāta* (the *Book of Ones*) deals with a great variety of subjects but always from one single aspect at a time; the *Book of Twos* comprises of *suttas* concerning pairs of things (e.g., a *sutta* on two kinds of fools, another about two kinds of happiness); and the *Book of Threes* contains *suttas* concerning three things (e.g., a *sutta* on three governing principles that keep one's Dhamma practice on track, a *sutta* about the three levels on which becoming (*bhava*) operates in relation to consciousness). Each of the eleven books (*nipātas*) of the Aṅguttara Nikāya is divided in turn into groups of *suttas*, called *vagga* or chapter, according to some similarity of subject or of treatment. Though the exact count of *suttas* in the Aṅguttara Nikāya depends on the particular edition (Sri Lankan, Thai, or Burmese) as well as the way in which these *suttas* are counted, the number of *suttas* distinctive in character is generally calculated between 1,000 and 2500 ([8], p. 12; [7], p. xv; [28], p. 26). Majority of these *suttas* are short, some being very short, though there are some *suttas* of sizeable length. The Sanskrit parallel of the Pāli Aṅguttara Nikāya is the Ekottarāgama of which only fragments have been found among the remains of manuscripts discovered in Xinjiang. However, a complete version of the *Ekottarāgama* survives in Chinese by the name of *ZēngyīAhánjīng* (*TaishōTripiṭaka* 125).

The Aṅguttara Nikāya contains the greatest number of quotations from the other three *nikāyas* (the Dīgha, the Majjhima, and the Saṃyutta), though these *nikāyas* are never cited as such. However, as there is no substantial difference among the first four *nikāyas* in terms of either their style or language, there could not have been much chronological gap between the composition of the Aṅguttara Nikāya and the other three *nikāyas*. Thus, as regards the earliest accessible sources of the *Buddhavacana* (teachings of the Buddha), there is no particular *nikāya* which could rightly lay any claim thereto, as all of them contain very ancient as well as comparatively late components. According to *Manorathapūraṇī*, the commentary of the Aṅguttara Nikāya, when the Buddha's dharma comes to an end, the first portion of the Sutta Piṭaka to vanish will be the Aṅguttara Nikāya, starting with the *Book of Elevens* and ending with the *Book of Ones* ([29], p. 881).

The Khuddaka Nikāya

The Khuddaka Nikāya (Minor Collection) consists of 15 texts, viz., Khuddakapāṭha, Dhammapada, Udāna, Itivuttaka, Sutta-Nipāta, Vimānavatthu, Petavatthu, Theragāthā, Therīgāthā, Jātaka, Niddesa, Paṭisambhidāmagga, Apadāna, Buddhavaṃsa, and Cariyāpiṭaka. Four more texts, viz., Suttasaṃgaha, Nettippakaraṇa, Petakopadesa, and Milindapañha, were added to this *nikāya* in Myanmar. The full list of these 18 books is included in the inscriptions as approved by the Fifth Council of Myanmar and in the printed edition of the text recited at the Sixth Council.

According to the Paramatthajotikā, the Khuddakapāṭha commentary, the Khuddaka Nikāya is a collection of numerous units of the Dhamma which are small and variegated and hence the name of the collection Khuddaka Nikāya ([24], p. 12). This *nikāya* contains, besides complete *suttas* and verses, small portions of the teachings of the Dhamma on different subjects credited to the Buddha and his chief disciples. Major portion of this *nikāya* is in verse and contains nearly all the important works of Buddhist poetry. The texts of the Khuddaka Nikāya are very heterogeneous works of widely varying length. The shortest of its texts is the Khuddakapāṭha which consists of less than ten printed pages, whereas the Jātaka is over a 100 times as bigger. Only three of its texts contain suttas similar to those in the first four nikāyas: nine are collections of verses, one is a commentary, one is a philosophical text, and one (the Khuddakapāṭha) has been assembled from short pieces found elsewhere in the canon ([7], pp. 41–42). It has been suggested that the Khuddaka Nikāya was the repository for materials that were left out of the four *nikāyas* (the Dīgha Nikāya, Majjhima Nikāya, Saṃyutta Nikāya, and Aṅguttara Nikāya) and thus included both early and late texts ([2], p. 128). Though Buddhist schools such as the Mahisāsaka, Dharmaguptaka, and Mahāsaṃghika included a Khuddaka Piṭaka in their canons, the Khuddaka Nikāya of the Theravāda school is the only extant example of such a Khuddaka Piṭaka ([2], p. 128).

There does not seem to be any recognizable system in the arrangement of the texts in the Khuddaka Nikāya, and this uncertainty prevails in Theravāda, the only school to possess a complete Khuddaka Nikāya. The long history of the uncertainty about the contents of the Khuddaka Nikāya has been described by Lamotte [10]. The earliest lists of the texts contained in this *nikāyas* are found in the description of the canon at the beginning of the commentaries on the various texts of the Pāli *Tipiṭaka*. For instance, Samantapāsādikā, the commentary of the Vinaya, refers to the existence of 15 texts. However, Atthasālinī, the Abhidhamma commentary, refers to only 14 of them, probably leaving out the Khuddakapāṭha ([7], p. 42). According to Sumaṅgalavilāsinī, the commentary on the Dīgha *Nikāya*, whereas the *Dīghabhāṇakas* (the reciters of the Dīgha Nikāya) rehearsed 11 of the 15 texts (except Khuddakapāṭha, Apadāna, Buddhavaṃsa, and Cariyāpiṭaka), called them collectively the *Khuddakagantha*, and included them in the Abhidhamma Piṭaka, the *Majjhimabhāṇakas*, on the other hand, mention 14 of these texts (leaving out the Khuddakapāṭha) and included these texts in the Sutta Piṭaka ([19]: i.15). According to another classification, the whole of the Vinaya Piṭaka and the Abhidhamma Piṭaka and the teachings of the Buddha not included in the other four *nikāyas* are considered as constituting the Khuddaka Nikāya ([19]: i.23; [9]: i.27).

It has been suggested that the texts Suttanipāta, Itivuttaka, Dhammapada, Therīgāthā, Theragāthā, Udāna, and Jātaka belong to the early stratum and the texts Khuddakapāṭha, Vimānavatthu, Petavatthu, Niddesa, Paṭisambhidāmagga, Apadāna, Buddhavaṃsa, and Cariyāpiṭaka can be categorized in the later stratum ([1], p. 113). Although the Theravādin tradition accepts that the five *nikāyas* of the Sutta Piṭaka were rehearsed at the First Council and that the Khuddaka Nikāya includes all other sayings of the Buddha that are not included in the first four Nikāyas, the Khuddaka Nikāya is generally believed to have been developed and completed during a long period of time, beginning from the Buddha's time up to about the time of the Third Council. On the basis of the use of the word *pañcanekāyika* (knower of the five *nikāyas*) in a third century B.C.E. inscription, Rhys Davids has suggested the existence of Khuddaka Nikāya by the third century B.C.E. ([20], p. 168).

The Khuddaka Nikāya as a whole is considered traditionally as less important compared with the first four *nikāyas* as it is believed that the first four *nikāyas* contain discourses preached by the Buddha, whereas the texts of the Khuddaka Nikāya are compositions of the disciples ([1], p. 16). It has also been suggested that outside the first four *nikāyas*, there were a number of texts regarded as of inferior importance, either because they were compositions of the followers of the Buddha or because their genuineness was uncertain ([27], pp. 202–203). However, the Theravādin tradition considers the Khuddaka Nikāya as an integral part of its canon.

Cross-References

- ▶ Aṅguttara Nikāya
- ▶ Apadāna
- ▶ Buddhavaṃsa
- ▶ Cariyāpiṭaka
- ▶ Dhammapada
- ▶ Dīgha Nikāya
- ▶ Itivuttaka
- ▶ Jātaka

▶ Khuddaka Nikāya
▶ Majjhima Nikāya
▶ Paṭisambhidāmagga
▶ Petavatthu
▶ Saṃyutta Nikāya
▶ Sutta-Nipāta
▶ Thera- and Therīgāthā
▶ Tipiṭaka
▶ Udāna
▶ Vimānavatthu

References

1. Abeynayaka O (1984) A textual and historical analysis of the Khuddaka Nikāya. Tisara Press, Colombo
2. Akira H (1993) A history of Indian Buddhism (trans & ed: Groner P). Motilal Banarsidass Publishers, Delhi
3. Bodhi B (trans) (2000) The connected discourses of the Buddha: a new Translation of the Saṃyutta Nikāya. Wisdom Publications, Boston
4. Bodhi B (trans) (2012) Numerical discourses of the Buddha: a complete translation of the Aṅguttara Nikāya. Wisdom Publications, Boston
5. Feer ML (ed) (1884–1898) The Saṃyutta Nikāya, 5 vols. Pali Text Society, London
6. Horner IB (trans) (1954–1959) The collection of the middle length sayings, 3 vols. Pali Text Society, London
7. von Hinüber O (1996) A handbook of Pāli literature. Walter de Gruyter, Berlin
8. Jayawardhana S (1993) Handbook of Pāli literature. Karunaratne, Colombo
9. Keown D (2004) A dictionary of Buddhism. Oxford University Press, London
10. Lamotte É (1988) History of Indian Buddhism. Peters Press, Louvain, Paris
11. Law BC (1983) A history of Pāli literature, reprint, vol 1. Indological Book House, Delhi
12. Manné J (1990) Categories of Sutta in the Pāli Nikāyas and their implications for our appreciation of the Buddhist teaching and literature. J Pali Text Soc 15:29–87
13. Morris R, Hardy E (eds) (1885–1900) The Aṅguttara Nikāya (1885–1900), 5 vols. Pali Text Society, London
14. Ñāṇamoli B, Bhikkhu B (trans) (1995) The middle length discourses of the Buddha: a new translation of the Majjhima Nikāya. Wisdom Publications, Boston
15. Norman KR (1983) A history of Indian literature: Pāli literature. Otto Harrassowitz, Wiesbaden
16. Nyanaponika T, Bodhi B (eds) (1999) Numerical discourses of the Buddha. AltaMira Press, Lanham
17. Pande GC (1957) Studies in the origins of Buddhism. University of Allahabad, Allahabad
18. Rhys Davids CAF, Thera SS, Woodward FL (trans) (1917–1930) The book of the kindred sayings, 5 vols. Pali Text Society, London
19. Rhys Davids TW, Carpentier JE, Stede W (eds) (1886–1932) The Sumaṅgala-Vilāsinī: Buddhaghosa's commentary on the Dīgha Nikāya, 3 vols. PTS, London
20. Rhys Davids TW (1903) Buddhist India. G.P. Putnam's Sons, London
21. Rhys Davids TW, Carpentier JE (eds) (1890–1911) The Dīgha Nikāya, 3 vols. Pali Text Society, London
22. Rhys Davids CAF, Thera SS, Woodward FL (trans) (1917–1930) The book of the kindred sayings, 5 vols. Pali Text Society, London
23. Rhys Davids TW, Rhys Davids CAF (trans) (2000) Dialogues of the Buddha, reprint, 3 vols. Motilal Banarsidass, Delhi
24. Smith H (ed) (1915) The Khuddaka-Pāṭha together with its commentary Paramatthajotikā I. Pali Text Society, London
25. Trenckner V, Chalmers R (eds) (1888–1896) The Majjhima Nikāya, 3 vols. Pali Text Society, London
26. Walshe M (trans) (1995) The long discourses of the Buddha: a translation of the Dīgha Nikāya. Wisdom Publications, Boston
27. Warder AK (1970) Indian Buddhism. Motilal Banarsidass, Delhi
28. Webb R (1975) An analysis of the Pāli Canon. Buddhist Publication Society, Kandy
29. Walleser H, Kopp H (eds) (1924–1956) Manorathapūraṇī: Buddhaghosa's commentary on the Aṅguttara Nikāya, 5 vols. Pali Text Society, London
30. Winternitz M (1983) A history of Indian literature (trans: SrinivasaSarma V), rev edn, vol II. Motilal Banarsidass, Delhi
31. Woods JH, Kosambi D, Horner IB (eds) (1922–1938) Papañcasūdanī: Majjhimanikāyaṭṭhakathā of Buddhaghosācariya, 5 vols. Pali Text Society, London
32. Woodward FL, Hare EM (trans) (1932–1936) The book of the gradual sayings, 5 vols. Pali Text Society, London

Sutta-Nipāta

K. T. S. Sarao
Department of Buddhist Studies, University of Delhi, Delhi, India

Definition

The fifth book of the Khuddaka Nikāya.

The Sutta-Nipāta ("The Sutta Collection") is the fifth book of the Khuddaka Nikāya which in turn is part of the Pāli Tipiṭaka of Theravāda Buddhism. This remarkable text is not only one of the oldest collections of Buddhist discourses in the Pāli Tipiṭaka but is also one of the most popular texts of Theravāda Buddhism. It consists of 1,123 verses, interspersed with some prose passages, put together into five *vaggas* (chapters), namely, (a) Uragavagga (The Snake Chapter), (b) Cūḷavagga (The Lesser Chapter), (c) Mahāvagga (The Great Chapter), (d) Aṭṭhakavagga (The Octet Chapter), and (e) Pārāyaṇavagga (The Chapter on the Way to the Far Shore). The first three *vaggas* consist of 12, 14, and 12 suttas, respectively, and the fourth and fifth vaggas contain 16 suttas each.

The Sutta-Nipāta contains some of the most lyrical and evocative poetry in the Pāli texts which makes very liberal use of natural environmental imagery. For example, a teacher is compared to "a skilled boatman who knows firsthand how to cross to the opposite shore" or a monk is exhorted to "wander alone like a rhinoceros" and to "give up the here and the beyond just as a serpent sheds its worn-out skin." The Sutta-Nipāta is an important reference point for texts offering guidance to lay Buddhists. The first three suttas, namely, the Ratana Sutta, the Mahāmaṅgala Sutta, and the Mettā Sutta, are among the most popular suttas in Theravāda Buddhism. They are virtually the key to understanding, practice, and attitude in the cotemporary Theravādin Buddhist society. Thus, these three suttas are often taught to lay men and women so that they may absorb the Buddhist values and ideals in their lives. They also serve as *paritta suttas* (protective discourses) which are recited to offer blessings and protection in situations of trouble and danger. The first sermon on the Ratana also provides very useful introduction to the Sutta-Nipāta in general as well as its place and history in the Sutta Piṭaka.

The Sutta-Nipāta offers valuable information on the nature of the earliest form of Buddhism. In it, for instance, can be seen not only the saṃgha in its youngest days but also the lives of monks and nuns in their pristine phase. The Sutta-Nipāta mainly focuses on the nature and qualities of a saint. The Sutta-Nipāta shows through the description of the spiritual qualities as to how by practicing them one may be able to develop oneself into a saint. Instead of the realization of some abstract metaphysical truth, the Sutta-Nipāta primarily focuses on the cultivation of different virtues and comparatively less attention is paid to the cognitive aspects of wisdom. Though terminology relating to "wisdom" and "insight" does exist in the Sutta-Nipāta, much reticence is shown in the presentation of metaphysical ideas. In fact, it advises restraint and caution in the adoption of any views at all, and makes it clear that the saint eventually exists beyond all views. The goal is defined mainly in terms of psychology and ethics rather than intellect. Enlightenment is not normally described as an epistemological transformation as if one were earlier struggling under a cognitive mistake that has now been fixed. On the contrary, the goal is seen in terms of a thorough modification of one's mental states and behavior in sharp contrast to the ones administered by unenlightened motivations. The language of renunciation and purification is extensively employed throughout the Sutta-Nipāta. It provides a vision of Enlightenment as a state of being rather than a state of knowing, though ultimately these two cannot be separated. The enlightened being is shown as the one who has developed particular kind of qualities to an exceptional and irreversible degree and who lives in a particular type of way. One may move closer to enlightenment by attaining a deeper sense of its sublime nature through the cultivation of the necessary virtues applied to a saint.

On the basis of its language and contents, it has been suggested that some parts of the Mahāvagga and nearly the whole of the Aṭṭhakavagga of the Sutta-Nipāta are perhaps the oldest in the whole of Buddhist literature. Hence some of the discourses of the Sutta-Nipāta are placed among the oldest discourses in the Pāli Tipiṭaka. In this text can be found the fuller Vedic forms of nouns and verbs in the plural, the shorter Vedic plurals and instrumental singular nouns, and Vedic infinitives, apart from many unusual forms and words. There are also some difficult and irregular constructions, and very condensed expressions. V. Fausböll has suggested that the portions of the Sutta-Nipāta where these are found are much older than the suttas in which the language is not only fluent but of which some verses are even singularly melodious.

Of the 38 poems in the first three *vaggas* of the Sutta-Nipāta, 6 can also be found in other texts of the Pāli Tipiṭaka. On this basis, B.C. law has suggested that these had perhaps existed separately, as popular poems, before being amalgamated into the Sutta-Nipāta. There are references in the Saṃyutta Nikāya, the Vinaya Piṭaka, and the Udāna to the independent and separate existence of the Aṭṭhakavagga. T.W. Rhys Davids has suggested that initially the Aṭṭhakavagga was quite probably closely associated with the Pārāyaṇavagga philosophically as these two *vaggas* are the subject of a curious old commentary, the only work of this type, incorporated in the *nikāyas*. The fact that this commentary, the Niddesa, does not refer to any of the remaining *vaggas*, it seems to hint that when the Sutta-Nipāta was composed, all its five *vaggas* had not been put together in the form of a single text. Though the Sutta-Nipāta as a collection exists only in the Theravādin tradition, some of its individual *suttas* can be found in other Buddhist traditions as well. For instance, the Aṭṭhakavagga exists in the Chinese Tripiṭaka. The Sutta-Nipāta was included by the *Dīghabhāṇakas* in the Abhidhamma Piṭaka. A commentary on the Sutta-Nipāta, written by Buddhaghosa, is known as the *Paramatthajotikā*.

Cross-References

- ► Abhidhamma Piṭaka
- ► Buddhaghosa
- ► Khuddaka Nikāya
- ► Saṃyutta Nikāya
- ► Udāna

References

1. Andersen D, Smith H (eds) (1913) The Sutta-Nipāta. Pali Text Society, London
2. Geiger W (2004) Pāli literature and language (trans: Ghosh BK, reprint). Munshiram Manoharlal, New Delhi
3. Hinüber O (1996) A handbook of Pāli literature. Walter de Gruyter, Berlin
4. Law BC (1983) A history of Pāli literature, vol I, reprint. Indological Book House, Delhi
5. Norman KR (trans) (1992) The group of discourses (Sutta-Nipāta), 2nd edn, translated with Introduction and Notes. Pali Text Society, Oxford

Suttanta Piṭaka

► Sutta Piṭaka

Sutthu – Aggatta Sagga

► Heaven (Buddhism)

Swaartha

► Education (Jainism)

Syādvāda

► *Anekāntavāda* (Jainism)
► Relativity (Jainism)

Syādvāda (Jainism)

Wm. Andrew Schwartz
Claremont Graduate University, Claremont, CA, USA

Synonyms

Anekāntavāda; *Saptabhangī*

Definition

Syādvāda is the Jain doctrine of conditional predication. According to this doctrine, all philosophical statements should be predicated with the particle *syāt* (from a certain perspective), to capture the relative nature of the truth claim. In this way, seemingly contradictory assertions can be reconciled as being from different perspectives and in different senses.

Introduction

Syādvāda is the Jain doctrine of conditional predication (i.e., qualified assertion). The doctrine of *syādvāda* is so named for its notion of predicating statements with the particle *syāt*. In ordinary Sanskrit usage, *syāt* is translated as "maybe" or "perhaps." It is one of the three words used to answer a direct question. When asked, "is such and such the case," one could answer "yes," "no," or "*syāt* (maybe)" [1]. Translated this way, *syāt* suggests a degree of uncertainty. For example, if asked, "is it raining outside?" to respond by "maybe" or "perhaps" is similar to responding with "I don't know." In this way, the ordinary usage of *syāt* evokes a sense of skepticism. In Jain technical usage, however, *syāt* is not used this way. Rather than evoking uncertainty, in Jainism, *syāt* acts as a conditional "yes."

To understand this doctrine of predication more fully, one must first understand the Jain vision of reality, to which *syāt* statements refer. The Jain metaphysical doctrine of *anekāntavāda* postulates that reality is multifaceted (*anekānta* or non-one-sided) (see entry on "▸ *Anekāntavāda* (Jainism)"). And, since reality is many-sided, all statements should be qualified as being made with respect to only one of those many facets (from a particular perspective). In Jainism, the particle *syāt* does just that.

Since *syāt* (in its ordinary Sanskrit usage) is typically translated as "maybe" or "perhaps," the Jain doctrine of *syādvāda* has often been confusingly described as the "maybe doctrine." Preferred translations, however, include "in some respect," "from a certain perspective," and "under a certain condition." Nevertheless, as a one-to-one translation between Sanskrit and English does not exist, most Jain scholars prefer to use the original term *syāt*.

In Jainism, the particle *syāt* is used to turn categorical statements [*A* is *B*] into conditional statements [if *p* (*syāt*), then *A* is *B*]. For example, the statement "the pot exists" becomes "from a certain perspective (*syāt*), the pot exists." This qualification is necessary to accurately express a statement which is, according to Jainism, always asserted from and conditioned by a particular perspective (*naya*) (see entry on "▸ *Nayavāda*"). In this way, exclusive claims become inclusive claims – absolute claims become relative claims. For this reason, in contemporary Jain scholarship, the doctrine of *syādvāda* (along with the doctrine of *anekāntavāda* and *nayavāda*) has been used as the philosophical foundation of an inclusive or even pluralistic response to philosophical and religious diversity.

In an additional attempt to overcome the confusion between ordinary usage and Jain usage of the term *syāt*, Jains often use *syāt* in conjunction with the term *eva* (certainly) [2, 3]. This is done to avoid the skeptical and uncertain tone of *syāt* statements in favor of a qualified "yes." It is important for Jain's that *syādvāda* not be seen as a doctrine of skepticism. Rather, the predicative purpose of *syāt* is to qualify a proposition (a truth claim) as to take into account the plurality of *nayas* (perspectives) and the non-one-sided nature of reality. This has been the dominant interpretation since the second century when it was put forth by Jain philosopher Samantabhadra [4].

Sevenfold Logic of Predication (*Saptabhangī*)

According to the Jain doctrine of *syādvāda*, there are seven types of statements – or seven modes of predication (*saptabhangī*). Often used to describe these seven forms of assertion are examples of existence:

1. From a certain perspective (*syāt*), *p* certainly (*eva*) exists.
2. From a certain perspective (*syāt*), *p* certainly (*eva*) does not exist.
3. From a certain perspective (*syāt*), *p* certainly (*eva*) exists AND certainly (*eva*) does not exist successively.

4. From a certain perspective (*syāt*), *p* certainly (*eva*) exists AND certainly (*eva*) does not exist simultaneously.
5. From a certain perspective (*syāt*), *p* certainly (*eva*) exists, AND p certainly (*eva*) exists and does not exist simultaneously.
6. From a certain perspective (*syāt*), *p* certainly (*eva*) does not exist, AND p certainly (*eva*) exists and does not exist simultaneously.
7. From a certain perspective (*syāt*), *p* certainly (*eva*) exists and does not exist successively, AND p certainly (*eva*) exists and does not exist simultaneously.

A more abstract formulation of these seven alternatives include:

1. Affirmation
2. Negation
3. Both affirmation and negation successively
4. Inexpressible (both affirmation and negation simultaneously)
5. Affirmation and inexpressible
6. Negation and inexpressible
7. Affirmation and negation and inexpressible

Let us begin with statements of the form (1) and (2). According to *anekāntavāda*, reality is non-one-sided. Furthermore, the multifaceted nature of a thing includes the qualities of both existence and nonexistence [5]. Therefore, one way to makes sense of this phenomenon is to distinguish between "exists" and "exists as." Common examples of pots not having the qualities of pens, or cows not having the qualities of dogs, are littered throughout Jain literature as ways to explain this distinction. For example, a cow exists (*qua* cow) insofar as it has "cowness" (qualities essential for being a cow). Therefore, (1) from the perspective of cow attributes, **a cow exists** (*qua* cow). But, from the perspective of dog attributes (qualities essential for being a dog), a cow does not exist (*qua* dog). Therefore, (2) from another perspective, **a cow does not exist** (*qua* dog). This is the meaning of statements of the form (1) affirmation and (2) negation. When it comes to distinguishing between "exists" and "exists as," such examples seem to imply that the apparent contradiction lies in one's failure to keep claims of existence as relative claims. In philosophy, examples of existence are often used because they appear absolute – either the pen exists or the pen does not exist. However, if one keeps in mind the *anekānta* (non-one-sided) nature of reality, even claims of existence must be taken as relative claims. So, *syāt p* exists and *syāt p* docs not exist.

What then of the third mode of predication – both affirmation and negation successively? Imagine that the object being discussed is water inside a particular bottle. It may be appropriate at one moment to say (1) from a certain perspective the water exists. At another moment (perhaps after someone drinks all the water), it may be appropriate to say (2) from a certain perspective the water does not exist. And together, these give us predication three (3) that from yet another perspective the water both exists and does not exist successively (i.e., at one time it exists, at another time it does not exist). This mode of predication is essential for describing the Jain notion of reality which consists of "origination, destruction, and persistence" [6].

Predications 5, 6, and 7 are also not altogether complicated, in that they are simply combinations of the first three with the fourth: 5 (1 and 4), 6 (2 and 4), and 7 (3 and 4). As such, how one understands modes 5–7 is directly dependent upon one's interpretation of mode 4 (*inexpressible* – both affirmation and negation simultaneously).

Inexpressibility

Of the seven modes of predication, none has received more attention (and criticism) than the fourth mode. As such, there is not clear consensus on what is meant in the fourth mode by "inexpressibility" (*avaktavya*). Nevertheless, the above interpretation (simultaneous affirmation and negation) has been the dominant view since the time of Samantabhadra [7].

That existence and nonexistence can be simultaneously ascribed to a single object in the same sense, or that a single assertion can be both true and false at the same time in the same sense, will certainly warrant looks of confusion from many philosophers (Eastern and Western) [8]. After all, what could it possible mean to say that something is both true and false?

It is sometimes suggested by Jain scholars that language is incapable of expressing simultaneous existence and nonexistence. Therefore, the fourth mode of predication is considered "inexpressible." Not only so, but even if it was possible to express simultaneous existence and nonexistence [e.g., by using logically notion such as (p and $\sim p$) or even using the term *avaktavya* (inexpressible)], it is expected that the distinct notions of existence and nonexistence would always be presented to one's cognition successively [9]. In this way, the fourth predication (4), "from a certain perspective inexpressible," paradoxically takes an assertion to be both true and false simultaneously in the same sense. What this means with respect to truth values is highly debated in Jain philosophy. For some, this denotes an indeterminate truth-value [10]. For others, it denotes a neutralized truth-value by which the components of affirmation (+) and negation (−) are taken together to form a new determinate truth-value (0) [11]. And still others hold that inexpressibility is a product of unknowability and mystery [12]. Despite these disputes regarding inexpressibility, the majority of Jain thinkers agree that a proper understanding of *syādvāda* should be grounded in the metaphysical doctrine of *anekāntavāda*.

Syādvāda and *Anekāntavāda*

To be sure, the Jain doctrine of conditional predication (*syādvāda*) is intimately related and sometimes conflated with the metaphysical and epistemological doctrines of a*nekāntavāda* and *nayavāda*, respectively. As such, in coming to a clear understanding of the doctrine of *syādvāda*, it is important to consider the doctrines of a*nekāntavāda* and *nayavāda* as well.

According to the Jain doctrine of *anekāntavāda*, the non-one-sided nature of reality, objects are endowed with innumerably many attributes [13]. Ultimately, this means that objects are endowed with contradictory characteristics. Each of the seven *syāt* statements (not to be confused or conflated with the seven *nayas* shown below) is an example of assertion from seven different perspectives. In this way, there is a perspective where "the pot exists" and another perspective where "the pot does not exist." When it comes to predication 4, there is a perspective that is "inexpressible" where "the pot both exists and does not exist simultaneously." This means that statement 4 allows that contradictory attributes can be affirmed from a single perspective. Although, for whatever reason (whether linguistic, epistemic, etc.), this perspective is inexpressible.

To this end, Mahavira is quoted as saying, "Where there is truth, from there language returns, neither intellect, nor thoughts nor even the mind goes there" (Ayaro Sutra 5/123–125) [14]. Mahavira acknowledges that truth transcends linguistic and cognitive capacities – though such transcendence does not preclude immanence. Therefore, "As an omniscient being, with infinite knowledge at his disposal, Mahavira recognized that truth or reality can be experienced but cannot be expressed in its entirety through the medium of language" [15].

Syādvāda and *Nayavāda*

With respect to *nayavāda* (the Jain epistemological doctrine of standpoints), there are seven standpoints from which something can be known. These seven *nayas* are:

1. *Naigama*: the undifferentiated
2. *Samgraha*: the general
3. *Vyavahara*: the practical
4. *Rjusutra*: the clearly manifest
5. *Sabda*: the verbal
6. *Samabhirudha*: the subtle
7. *Evambhuta*: the "thus-happened"

"The first three. . .are standpoints from which to investigate the thing itself, whereas the remaining four are standpoints from which to investigate the modifications that things undergo" [16]. And, from each of these standpoints, there are seven ways (or modes) of assertion. What is important to realize about the relation between *nayavāda* and *syādvāda* is that according to the doctrine of standpoints, there are many ways of knowing. Therefore, given the multifaceted nature of reality (depicted by a*nekāntavāda*) and the plurality of ways of knowing that many-sided reality (depicted by *nayavāda*), all statements should be qualified and conditioned by these factors, being asserted from "a certain perspective" (as depicted by *syādvāda*).

Syādvāda and Truth

It is often suggested in Jainism that by adding a *syāt* particle to a statement, one has captured the truth [17]. However, the "truth" captured in this way is necessarily a relative truth, which is indicated by qualifying one's proposition with the particle *syāt* (see entry on "▸ Truth (Jainism)"). Therefore, the practice of qualifying an assertion with the *syāt* particle allows one to affirm the truth and validity of one's own perspective, without being obligated to reject the different or even contradictory views of others. For, seemingly contradictory statements are compatible, in so far as they are asserted from different perspectives and in different senses. As Siddhasena Divākara (fifth century) writes, "all the standpoints (*nayas*) are right in their own respective spheres. But, if they are taken to be refutations, each of the other, then they are wrong. A man who knows the 'non-one-sided' nature of reality never says that a particular view is absolutely wrong" [18].

The implication of *syādvāda* for expressing truth, then, is that "No judgment is true in itself and by itself without reference to the conditions under which it is made" [19]. As such, the Jain practice of qualified assertion can be used as a method of reconciliation – that is, it can take divisive and exclusive statements and bring them into an inclusive synthesis.

Jainism points to the long-standing disagreement between Advaitin permanence and Buddhist impermanence as an example of this. According to the Advaitin perspective, reality is ultimately characterized by permanence (Brahman). Contrarily, from the Buddhist perspective, reality is ultimately characterized by impermanence (sunyata). Jainism, however, brings these two positions into a synthesis, whereby both are true (though only partially so). The problem, as Jain philosophers have described it, is that both Advaitin and Buddhist thinkers perpetuate their doctrines to the exclusion of the other. In doing so, they commit the error of *ekānta* (one-sidedness). In other words, the failure of both the Advaitins and the Buddhists is to neglect the many-sided nature of reality – a failure which results in treating one's own limited perspective as the exclusively absolute perspective. Therefore, according to Jainism, both the Buddhist and Advaitin are only partially correct. This does not mean some sort of hopeless skepticism or vicious relativism. The Jain epistemological stance is a positive one, albeit qualified. By using the doctrine of *syādvāda*, these exclusive and absolutists statements are made relative and compatible. From a certain perspective (*syāt*), reality is permanent. From a certain perspective (*syāt*), reality is impermanent. And when these propositions are conditionally asserted, they are no longer found to be refutations of each other and can be seen as mutually inclusive. Specifically, from the perspective of substance, reality is permanent, while, from the perspective of mode, reality is impermanent. But, as Jainism asserts, reality consists of both substance and modes, both continuity and change, and both permanence and impermanence. This is how the Jain doctrine of *syādvāda* is used to reconcile that which was previously irreconcilable. It qualifies claims so they are no longer exclusive, which allows for seemingly contradictory notions to both be true.

Cross-References

▸ *Anekāntavāda* (Jainism)
▸ *Nayavāda*
▸ Relativity
▸ Truth (Jainism)

References

1. Matilal BK (1981) The central philosophy of Jainism (Anekānta-vāda). L.D. Institute of Indology, Ahmedabad, p 52
2. Jeffery D (2010) Long, Jainism: an introduction. I.B. Tauris, New York, p 147
3. Mahaprajna A (1996) An introduction: the axioms of non-absolutism. In: Kumar RA, Dak TM, Mishra AD (eds) Facets of Jain philosophy, religion and culture: Anekantavada and Syadvada. Jain Vishva Bharati Institute, Ladnun, Rajasthan
4. Samantabhadra (2002) Apta-mimamsa. Bharatiya Jnanpith, Delhi
5. Jain P (2000) Saptabhangi: the Jaina theory of seven fold predication: a logical analysis. Philos East West 50(3):395, University of Hawai'i Press
6. Tattvarthasutra v. 30
7. Dixit KK (1971) Jaina ontology. L.D. Institute Indology, Ahmedabad; or Long JD (2009) Jainism: an introduction. I.B. Tauris, New York
8. Priest G (2002) Beyond the limits of thought, 2nd edn. Clarendon, Oxford, p 4
9. Shah NJ (trans) (1998) Jaina philosophy and religion. Motilal Banarsidass, Delhi, p 351
10. Bharucha F, Kamat RV (1984) Syādvāda theory of Jainism in terms of deviant logic. Indian Philos Q 9:183
11. Matilal BK (1981) The central philosophy of Jainism (Anekānta-vāda). L.D. Institute of Indology, Ahmedabad, p 54
12. Matilal BK (2000) Anekānta: both yes and no. In: Shah NJ (ed) Jaina theory of multiple facets of reality and truth (Anekāntavāda). Motilal Banarsidass, Delhi, p 15
13. Kulkarni VM (2000) Relativity and absolutism. In: Shah NJ (ed) Jaina theory of multiple facets of reality and truth (Anekantavada). Motilal Banarsidass, Delhi, p 66
14. Jain G (trans) (2009) Eternal quotes from Lord Mahavira. Raj Rajendra Prakashan Trust, p 78
15. Charitrapragya S (2004) Mahavira, Anekantavada and the world today. In: Sethia T (ed) Ahimsa, Anekanta and Jainism. Motilal Banarsidass, Delhi, p 77
16. Koller JM (2000) Syādvāda as the epistemological key to the Jaina middle way metaphysics of Anekāntavāda. Philos East West 50(3):402 (University of Hawai'i Press)
17. Matilal BK (1981) The central philosophy of Jainism: Anekāntavāda. L.D. Institute of Indology, Ahmedabad, p 61
18. Siddhasena (1981) Sanmati-tarka, Chapter 1, Verse 28 (adapted from Matilal), p 31
19. Shah N (2000) Jaina theory of multiple facets of reality and truth (Anekantavada). Motilal Banarsidass, Delhi

Further Reading

Bharucha F, Kamat RV (1984) Syadvada theory of Jainism in terms of deviant logic. Indian Philos Q 9:181–187

Bhattacharya KC (1953) Anekantavada. Jaina Atmananda Sabha

Ganeri J (2002) Jaina logic and the philosophical basis of pluralism. Hist Philos Logic 20(4):267–281, Taylor & Francis

Gokhale PP (1991) The Logical Structure of Syadvada. J Indian Council Philos Res 8(3):73–81

Jain P (2000) Saptabhangi: the Jaina theory of seven fold predication: a logical analysis. Philos East West 50(3):385–399, University of Hawai'i Press

Koller JM (2000) Syādvāda as the epistemological key to the Jaina middle way metaphysics of Anekāntavāda. Philos East West 50(3):400–407, University of Hawai'i Press

Kumar JA, Dak TM, Mishra AD (eds) (1996) Facets of Jain philosophy, religion and culture: Anekantavada and Syadvada. Jain Vishva Bharati Institute, Ladnun, Rajasthan

Long JD (2009) Jainism: an introduction. I.B. Tauris, New York

Matilal BK (1981) The central philosophy of Jainism: Anekantavada. L.D. Institute of Indology, Ahmedabad

Matilal BK (2000) Anekanta: both yes and no. In: Shah NJ (ed) Jaina theory of multiple facets of reality and truth (Anekantavada). Motilal Banarsidass, Delhi

Mookerjee S (1978) The Jaina philosophy of non-absolutism: a critical study of Anekantavada. Motilal Banarsidass, Delhi

Padmarajiah YJ (1963) A comparative study of the Jaina theories of reality and knowledge. Jain Sahitya Vikas Mandal, Bombay

Priest G (2008) Jaina logic: a contemporary perspective. Hist Philos Logic 29(3):263–278, Taylor & Francis

Sarkar T (1992) Some reflections on Jaina Anekantavada and Syadvada. Jadavpur J Philos IV(2):13–35

Sethia T (ed) (2004) Ahimsa, Anekanta and Jainism. Motilal Banarsidass, Delhi

Shah N (2000) Jaina Theory of Multiple Facets of Reality and Truth (Anekantavada). Motilal Banarsidass, Delhi

Shah N (ed) (1998) Jaina philosophy and religion. Motilal Banarsidass, Delhi, 1998

Shah SM (1987) The dialectic of knowledge and reality in Indian philosophy. Eastern Book Linkers, Delhi

Tatia N (1951) Studies in Jaina philosophy. P.V. Research Institute, Varanasi

Sympathetic Joy

▶ Muditā

Syncretism (Buddhism)

Shanker Thapa
Faculty of Buddhist Studies, Lumbini Buddhist University, Lumbini Rupandehi, Nepal

Definition

Syncretism is an attempted union or reconciliation of diverse and opposite tenets or practices, especially in philosophy and religion. It is also the process of amalgamation, something existential meeting of two religions.

Syncretism is a conceptual model that denotes to alliance, amalgamation, or combination of features and tenets of different and opposing religious, philosophical, and cultural systems. The terminology was first used in 1625 to describe misguided attempt to reunite Catholic and Protestant churches as syncretism. Syncretism is a process by which the other gains acceptance in the broader context. Syncretism is the result of a process by which elements of distinct religions are merged into a unitary world view. The plural societies in Asia encouraged followers of various religions borrow tenets from each other's traditions.

An "attempted union or reconciliation of diverse and opposite tenets or practices, especially in philosophy and religion" is also defined as syncretism. J. H. Kamstra elaborates syncretism as amalgamation, something existential meeting of two religions. He has explained syncretism as the result of alienation in an existing religion. The criterion for syncretism is therefore alienation, which either comes in as alien from without or which is alienated from within. Similarly, Michael Pye defines syncretism as "the temporary ambiguous coexistence of elements from diverse religious and other contexts within a coherent religious pattern." It indicates syncretism as a result not as a process, and also as something man-made and not natural. Further, Judith Berling has a narrow definition, according to which syncretism is the borrowing, affirmation, or integration of concepts, symbols, and practices of one religion into another by a process of selection and reconciliation. This definition emphasizes on reconciliation and argues that tenets of distinct world views combine syncretically. In the process of syncretism, there is always reconciliation whether in the formulation of doctrine or in the construction of rites, or in the subjective or other perceptions of the follower.

Religious syncretism is the mixture of tenets with one of the religions. Syncretism as such is also an important component in the course of development of a religion. Broadly speaking, the terminology has been identified as "any mixture of two or more religions." It includes "cases when elements from one religion are accepted into another without changing the fundamental character of the other religion." The natural dissension between different systems of religious ideas, thoughts, gestures, views, or practices disappears through syncretism.

Christianity and Islam, which have cleaved historically to the notion of religion as revelation, conceptually resisted reconciliation with other traditions. This is true at the conceptual level. However, religious plurality in Asian countries possesses amazing features and the power of integration and amalgamation. Asian religious traditions particularly Hinduism, Buddhism, Taoism, Confucianism, or other minor religions are syncretic by nature. They are categorically integrative and responsive of tenets of other religions. Indian and Chinese religions encourage their adherents to borrow from each other's traditions and to look benevolently on pluralism, combination, and mutual influence. This world view has encouraged amalgamation of ideas and tenets of a religion to the other. This borrowing positively developed into religious syncretism in India as well. All major religions in India are syncretic by nature. Thus, in the Indian context of religious behavior, even Hindu and Muslims have shared common practices or ideas at least in certain practices. Applicability of the concept of syncretism is a prime concern in Indian religions since this has been a major feature of Hinduism, Buddhism, Jainism, Sikhism, and other minor religious traditions. When two religions or cultures meet, they exchange religious tenets and ideas with the dominant culture prevailing in the exchange. Syncretism has recently reemerged as a valuable tool for understanding the complex dynamics of ethnicity, interconnectedness, and postmodernism in the Indian context.

In the context of Indian religions, syncretism has been one of the important features both at the theoretical and the practical levels that has created harmony of nations and generation and development of hybrid cultures with very interesting features. Syncretism is the synthesis of religions and cultures. It has been a general feature of popular religions in India. Regarding syncretism in the context of Indian religions, it can be said that there is firm balance between cultural diversity and syncretism pervading the foundation of Indian civilization. It has reemerged as an effective tool to understand complex sociocultural and religious dynamics in the Indian context. The confluence of the two religions gradually produced a cultural syncretism as early as twelfth century in India. It has helped to create a composite culture not only in India but elsewhere. Religious synthesis or syncretism always has positive implication as a foundation and form of resistance to cultural dominance. Consequently, religious ideas, rituals, and cultural traits mediate between diverse ethnic and religious communities, sects, and cultural domains to give rise to a complex unity. The process of syncretism is considered basic not only to religions and rituals but to the predicament of cultures as well. The Hindu-Muslims syncretism is one of the characteristic features of religious behavior in India. In fact, syncretism of Hinduism and Islam and their cultures have deep cultural roots which has survived various sociocultural upheavals in history. There are many syncretic shrines across India which continued to attract people of Hindu and Muslim faiths. Hindu-Muslim syncretism has been spectacular and significant in the context of structure of history religion and culture of Indian subcontinent. The cult of saints has been one of the religious steps which has promoted Hindu-Muslim syncretism in India. During the course of history, religious syncretism turned out to be a synthetic product in India. Regarding syncretism in Indian religions, very spectacular process can be observed in Hindu-Buddhist relationship and coexistence in Nepal. Both the religions in Nepal borrowed tenets, concepts, ideas, practices, and rituals from each other. They share the same shrines with different identity. There are common rituals and celebrations among these religions. The borrowing and amalgamation of religious tenets from each other's religion, the Hindus and the Buddhists presents most outstanding example of religious syncretism.

Cross-References

▸ Religion
▸ Syncretism (Buddhism)

References

1. Berling J (1980) The syncretic religion of Lin Chao-en. Columbia University Press, New York
2. Birnbaum M (1966) Aldous Huxley's quest for values: a study in religious syncretism. Comp Lit Studies 3(2):169–182
3. Brook T (1993) Rethinking syncretism: the unity of the three teachings and their joint worship in late-imperial China. J Chin Relig 21:13–44
4. Clifford J (1988) The predicament of culture: twentieth century ethnography, literature and art. Harvard University Press, Cambridge
5. Das NK (2003) Introduction: an outline of syncretism. In: Culture, religion and philosophy: critical studies in syncretism and inter-faith harmony. Rawat Publications, Jaipur
6. Grierson GA (1911) A case of Hindu syncretism. J Roy Asiatic Soc Great Britain Ireland :195
7. Kamstra JH (1993) Encounter or syncretism: the initial growth of Japanese Buddhism. Leiden, 1967
8. Pye M (1993) Syncretism versus synthesis. Ramsden, Cardiff
9. Ringgren H (1969) The problems of syncretism. In: Hartmen S (ed) Syncretism. Almqvist and Wiksell, Stockholm
10. Roy A (1983) The Islamic syncretic tradition in Bengal. Princeton University, Princeton
11. Van der Veer P (1994) Syncretism, multiculturalism, and the discourse of tolerance. In: Stewart C, Shaw R (eds) Syncretism – anti-syncretism: the politics of religious synthesis. Routledge, London

S

T

Takkasilā

Robert Harding
Faculty of Asian and Middle Eastern Studies,
University of Cambridge, Cambridge, UK

Synonyms

Takṣaśilā; Taksaïla (Gandhāri); Taxila (Greek and Latin)

Definition

City that is mentioned in early Buddhist literature and which became famous in the classical Mediterranean because of its links with Alexander. The fertility of its hinterland and its location at the confluence of trade routes assured its prosperity and it became the location for many Buddhist monastic sites.

Location

The importance of Taxila (located at 33°46′N, 72°50′E) is owed to two happy circumstances. First, its hinterland was the fertile Potwar Plateau. Second, it was in a position that allowed to draw together a number of key trade routes – the road via Puṣkalāvati, the Khyber Pass, and Bactria to West and Central Asia; the route north through the Hunza Valley and the Karakoram Mountains into Kashmir and China; and the Uttarāpatha network that connected the cities of North India. There was also an overland route connecting Taxila to the ports along the western Indian coast, including Broach and Barbaricon. The wider region in which it was located was known in ancient times as Gandhāra (Fig. 1 Marshall's map of Taxila)

The immediate surroundings can be understood in terms of a valley divided in two by the east–west Hathial Ridge. To the south of the ridge, in a less fertile zone, can be found the majority of Buddhist sites. To the west of the ridge runs the Tamrā rivulet, far smaller than its ancient capacity. Hathial itself was the site of early settlement, and archaeology has yielded a sequence of three further "Taxilas"; the Bhīr Mound, on the west side of the Tamra; Sirkap to the northeast; and further north again, Sirsukh.

Early Sources

Legendary accounts are associated with etiologies of its name. The *Ramāyaṇa* ascribes its origin to Takṣa, son of Bhārata, who ruled here. In the *Mahābharāta* 1.3, the city was founded by the nāga king Takṣaka, who was overthrown by King Jānemajāya of Hāstinapura. The epic was recited publicly for the first time at the subsequent great nāga sacrifice. The more prosaic explanation of "city of cut stone" is a more likely one ([4], pp. 2–4; [10]).

K.T.S. Sarao, J.D. Long (eds.), *Buddhism and Jainism*, Encyclopedia of Indian Religions,
DOI 10.1007/978-94-024-0852-2

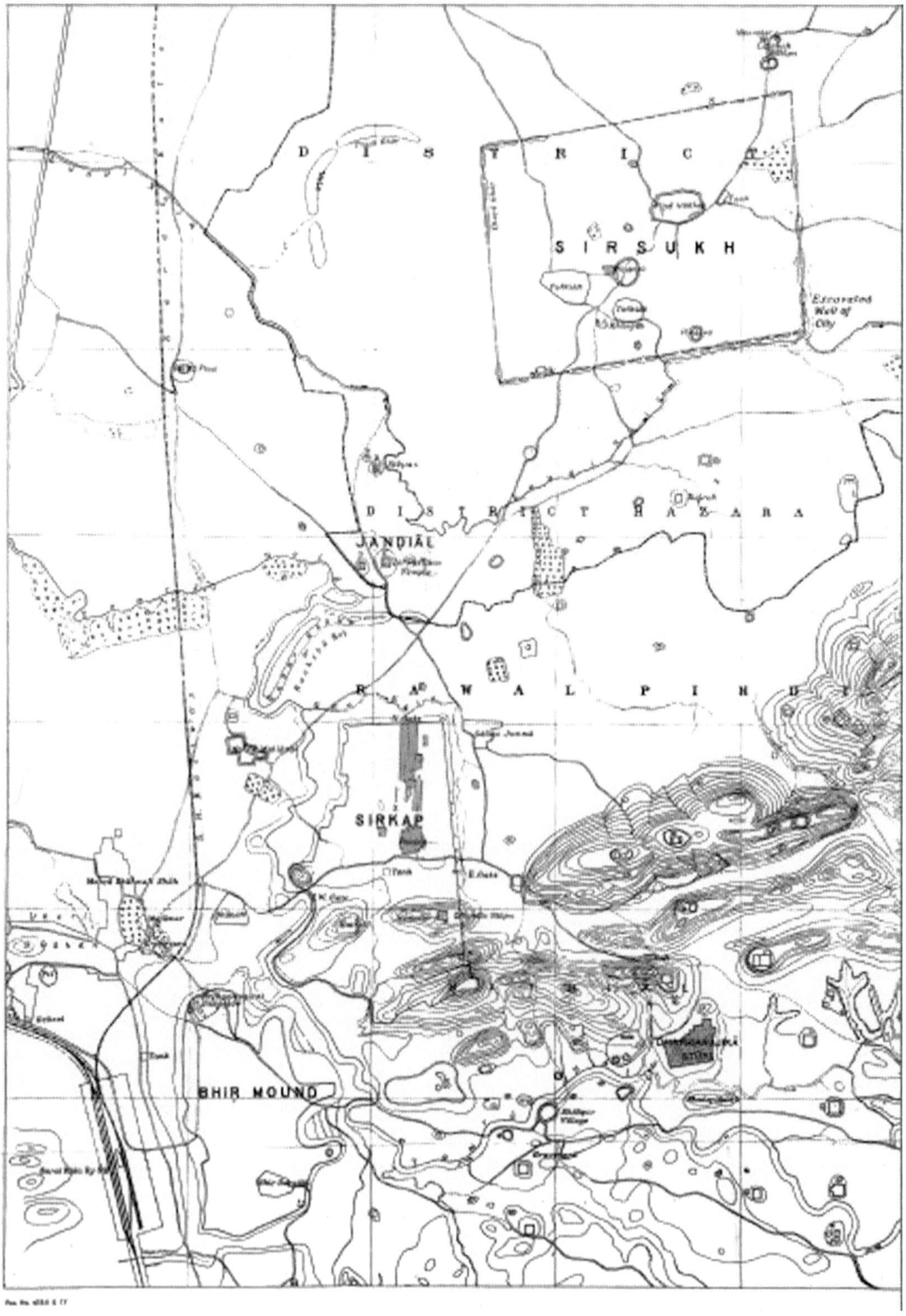

Takkasilā, Fig. 1 Marshall's map of Taxila (From Marshall, Guide to Taxila, Calcutta, Superintendent Government Printing, India, 1928)

Buddhist etiology connecting the name to head cutting is explained by Xuanzang's identification of an Aśokan stūpa marking where the Buddha, in his former life as Candraprabha, cut his head off as an act of alms giving ([12], pp. 95). Further away from the city, other significant sites mentioned by him were the lotus pond of the nāga king Elāpattra, associated with Kaśyapa Buddha and prayed to for rain or good weather; an Aśokan stūpa marking the spot where four great treasures would appear when Maitreya descended from heaven; and, on the other side of the Indus, a stūpa marking the spot where the Buddha as Prince Mahāsattva allowed himself to be eaten by a hungry tigress ([12], pp. 94–97).

The Pāli Canon connects Takkhaśila with a university, foremost in its time, that taught the Vedas, Vedaṅgas, and practical arts such as archery and military science. It was open to students from the three upper varṇas and consisted of a group of teachers who would take on students individually and on payment of a fee. Important donors such as Jīvaka, the royal physician of Magadha, and kings such as Prāsenājit were former pupils. It is notable that this university does not feature in the *Suttapiṭaka*, but in later texts such as the *Jātakas* and in Pāli commentarial literature including the *Dhammapadatthakathā* ([7], pp. 982–983).

Later History

Presumably, Taxila became part of the Persian Empire within the Gandhāran satrapy. It seems to have done so under Cyrus the Great in 518 BC and may even have been the satrapal capital. The archaeological evidence does not extend much beyond a few coins, but an Aśokan edict found in the city that was translated into Aramaic, and the presence of a regional script, Kharoṣṭhī, which is based on Aramaic, does suggest strong Persian influence. By the time Alexander the Great moved into South Asia in 327 B.C.E., local kings were again in control; and Ambhi, also called Taxiles, quickly submitted and became an ally. Macedonian occupation did not last very long. Soon afterwards, the region was occupied by the Mauryan Empire.

Literature offers up a close connection between Mauryans and Taxila, though the picture is confused. The *Divyavadāna* states Aśoka himself was ordered by his father to quell a rebellion. Another version found in the second century C.E. *Aśokāvadāna* has the rebellion occurring in his own reign, with the dispatch of his son Kuṇāla to deal with it. Kuṇāla's evil stepmother took the opportunity to engineer an order forcing him to take out his eyes. Xuanzang locates the blinding at a spot to the southeast of the city, where an Aśokan stūpa commemorating it rose to over 100 ft high ([12], 95–98). From the length of description Xuanzang devotes to the story, this it seems for him was the most important monument of the area. Whatever the truth of these stories, the evidence is consistent that Taxila was a capital of one of the major provinces of the empire.

With the end of the Mauryans, the region may have come under local control again. At some point in the early second century B.C.E., possibly as late as Menander (from c. 155 B.C.E.), the city came under Indo-Greek rule. The Heliodoros Pillar in Besnagar makes reference to Antialcidas the king of Taxila and Antialcidas is believed to have reigned from c. 130 to 120 B.C.E. From the mid-first century B.C.E., it came under a sequence of foreign dynasties – Śāka, Indo-Parthian and Kuṣāna – with the Central Asian Empire of the Kushans in particular doing nothing to damage Taxila's role as a trade center.

Archaeology

Unfortunately, little of the known history can be squared with the archaeology. The city was identified first by Alexander Cunningham, who conducted several surveys, cleared a number of the monuments, and tried to identify some of the sites mentioned by Xuanzang ([3], pp. 121–138). The major excavations were conducted by John Marshall [8], which were successful in exposing large areas, but which have raised many questions of chronology. Since then, a number of smaller projects have added extra pieces without resolving the major issues.

Settlement began with Saraikhola, about 2.5-km away, when a small agricultural community was first established. In the third millennium

B.C.E., a community allied to the Kot Dijian culture replaced it, and Kot Diji ceramics are also found on the Hathial Ridge. In the later second millennium B.C.E., Kot Diji was replaced in turn by a culture with strong affinities to the Swāt Valley to the northwest. Hathial was the main center of occupation up until the mid-first millennium B.C.E., though as far as can be ascertained, it was a town more than a city. The establishment of the Bhīr site gave Taxila a proper urban character. Though not as regular as its successor, it was still well organized into blocks with a court or market in the center of each. Problems with the archaeology mean the type of defensive wall, if any, is not known or to what extent the city was built of mud brick. The most striking building was a "palace" with a pillared hall, which Marshall took to be an early Hindu temple ([9], p. 47); though apart from some terracotta figurines, there was little to give it a non-secular character. The material culture is strongly Gangetic and so from this period, Taxila was clearly developing strong relations with North India. There is some dispute over the dating of Bhīr, with Marshall placing it at sixth/fifth century to at least second century B.C.E. ([9], p. 47) and Wheeler to fourth century B.C.E. onwards (and thus outside the Achaemenid period) ([4], pp. 44–45).

In the fourth to second century B.C.E., Hathial was subjected to massive reinforcement with layers of earth and slate with a stone facing. It seems the ridge was transformed into a citadel, perhaps under the Persians or the Greeks.

Numismatics and the central Asian character of the buildings (courtyards with many rooms to the side) would suggest that Sirkap was constructed in the mid-first century B.C.E. It had a three-meter-thick stone wall surrounding it and also part of Hathial which via a wall dividing it from the rest of the town became an acropolis. The wall was up to 30 ft high and incorporated bastions at irregular intervals. There was also a chessboard-style street plan. The types of residence suggest it was an elite district only and that the majority continued to live elsewhere, perhaps in Bhīr, but perhaps also in the unexcavated area to the south of Sirkap. In addition, the northern wall of Sirkap runs against a large earthen wall, possibly on a brick foundation (Kachhā Koṭ). This may be a (very grand) wall for a suburb or caravanserai area, or it may belong, along with the Hathial citadel, to the Indo-Greek period. Marshall was keen to ascribe Sirkap itself to the Greeks and pointed to Greek features, including the choice of location on a flat plain and the grid pattern of its streets ([8], p. 61). The palace, with later accretions taken away, also seems close to Indo-Greek palace forms such as at Ai Khanum in Bactria [2].

Sirkap continued to be occupied through the Kushan era until perhaps the time of Kaniṣka I or even Huviṣka. At that point, a large new city, Sirsukh, with massive walls and an area double that of the old town, was built. Its rectangular shape, circular towers, and loopholes for archers mark it as Central Asian in character; but the lack of excavation within the walls means little more can be said about it.

Other Secular Structures

In a glen at the far west of Hathial is a large building known locally as the Mahal, of the same size as the Sirkap palace and of roughly the same date (first century C.E.). It consisted of at least five courts and covered an area of c. 94×73 m ([7], pp. 214–216; [8], pp. 82–84). Dani's suggestion that it was actually a monastery ([4], pp. 40–42) is unlikely given that it doesn't look like a monastic complex.

The fort of Giri is located near the Margala Pass in the center of the Potwar Plateau. Marshall dated it to the fifth century C.E., and because of its association with a small Buddhist monastery, it was decided to be used by monks, especially during the destruction wrought by the Huṇas ([8], pp. 342–347). However, recent redating to at least the third century B.C.E. is more in line with its true role, as protection for an important east-running road that connected it to the main trade routes ([5], pp. 113–114).

Religious Structures

These are of two types: within the city sites and outside, including the nearby hills. The

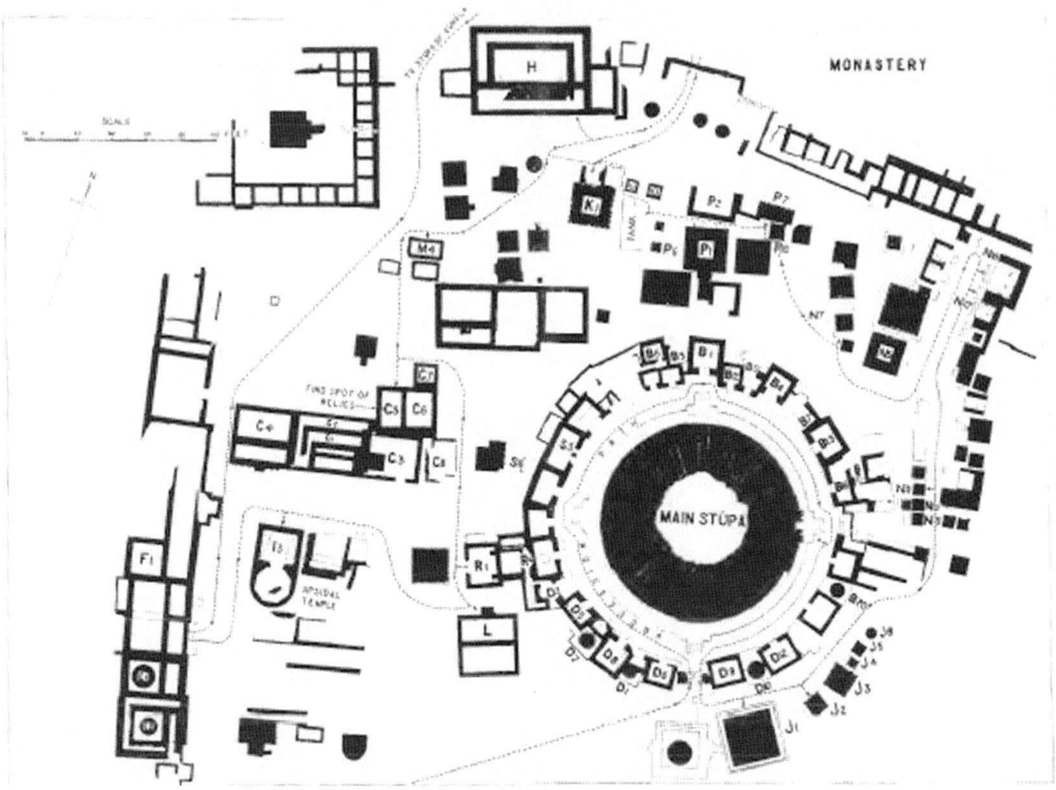

Takkasilā, Fig. 2 The Dharmarajika complex (From Marshall, Guide to Taxila, Calcutta, Superintendent Government Printing, India, 1918)

monasteries are the oldest in Gandhāra, beginning in the last centuries B.C.E., and consist at first of cells grouped around a main stupa. By the second century C.E., they had developed into quadrangular courts, with an increasing emphasis on images and image shrines. The oldest and the most important stūpa complex, with a number of associated vihāras, was Dharmarājika. Located just a few kilometers from the city, its name indicates the stūpa held relics of the Buddha; Marshall's assumption that it was originally Aśokan ([8], p. 102) cannot yet be backed by structural evidence, with Behrendt dating it to the second century B.C.E. ([1], pp. 39–40). The early emphasis terms of subsidiary building were on stupa shrines. From the second century, shrine for images (mainly stucco) became more prominent, especially around the northern avenue, through which the monks from nearby vihāras would process. Eventually, these spread throughout the site, and by the fifth century, shrines for monolithic statues appeared [1] (Fig. 2 The Dharmarājika Complex).

Jaṇḍiāl C

Jaṇḍiāl C and D were temples on either side of the main road from Sirkap to Puṣkalāvati and Kapiśa. C was 48 × 26 m in size and has many similarities to a Greek temple, with peristyle with Ionic columns, pronaos (front porch), and sanctuary. There are other features that are not as Greek, including a probable second story, an outer wall with windows (rather than a colonnade), and a walkway around the building. A rubble mass may indicate it had a tower. Comparison with Ai Khanum and the construction date of third century B.C. may indicate an Indo-Greek context; whether it was a Zoroastrian, Buddhist, or other temple type is still debated ([1], pp. 61–77). D was of similar

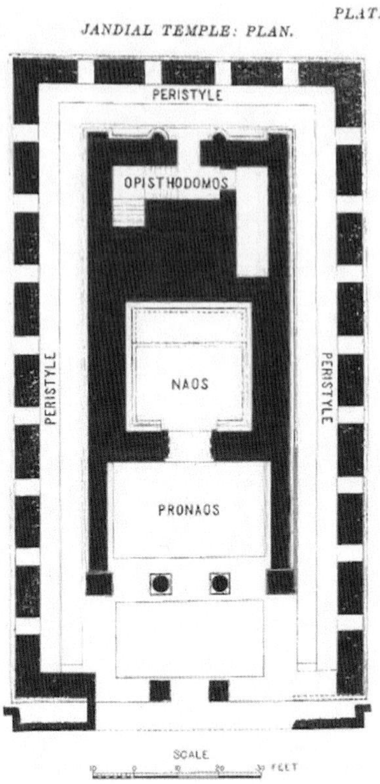

Takkasilā, Fig. 3 Marshall's plan of Jaṇḍiāl (From Marshall, Guide to Taxila, Calcutta, Superintendent Government Printing, India, 1918)

construction, though slightly smaller (Fig. 3 Marshall's plan of Jaṇḍiāl).

The post-Kushan period is an unclear one for Taxila. From the eighth century, Taxilan Buddhism, as elsewhere in Gandhāra, was losing patronage and in decline. Marshall argued the Huṇa invasion of the later fifth century visited destruction on the city and its Buddhist monasteries, with the area never recovering ([9], pp. 38–39). Xuanzang portrays the city as a victim of local quarrelling and Kashmiri domination ([12], pp. 93–94). But the region never went completely out of favor and the city is close to the more recent foundations of Rawalpindi and Islamabad.

Cross-References

▶ Asoka
▶ Faxian (337–422 C.E.)
▶ Gandhara
▶ Greeks
▶ Kharoṣṭhī Script
▶ Monastery
▶ Xuanzang (Hieun-Tsang)

References

1. Behrendt K (2003) The Buddhist architecture of Gandhāra. In: Handbook of oriental studies, section 2: India 17. Brill, Leiden
2. Coningham R, Edwards BR (1997/1998) Space and society at Sirkap, Taxila: a re-examination of urban form and meaning. Pak Archaeol 12:47–75
3. Cunningham A (2002) The ancient geography of India. Munshiram, Delhi [1924]
4. Dani AH (1986) The historic city of Taxila. UNESCO/ Centre for East Asian Cultural Studies, Paris/Tokyo
5. Dar SR (1993) Dating the monasteries of Taxila. In: Doris S (ed) Urban form and meaning in south Asia: the shaping of cities from prehistoric to post-colonial times. Yale University Press, New Haven, pp 103–122
6. Harding R (2010) Cunningham, Marshall and the Monks: an early historic city as a Buddhist landscape. In: Guha S (ed) The Marshall albums: photography and archaeology. Mapin and Alkazi Collection, New Delhi, pp 202–227
7. Malalasekara GP (1937) Dictionary of Pali proper names. Pali Text Society, London
8. Marshall J (1951) Taxila. Cambridge University Press, Cambridge
9. Sir Marshall J (1960) A guide to Taxila, 4th edn. Cambridge University Press, Cambridge
10. Salomon R (2005) The name of Taxila: Greek Τάξιλα, Gāndhārī Taksaïla, Sanskrit Takṣaśīla, PaliTakkasilā". East West 55:265–277
11. Srinivasan D (ed) (1993) Urban form and meaning in south Asia: the shaping of cities from prehistoric to post-colonial times. Yale University Press, New Haven
12. Xuanzang (1996) The Great Tang Dynasty record of the western regions. Numata Center for Buddhist Translation and Research, Berkeley

Taksaïla (Gandhāri)

▶ Takkasilā

Takṣaśilā

▶ Takkasilā

Ta-mo-po-lo

▶ Dhammapāla

Taṇhā

▶ Craving

Tantra

▶ Vajrayāna (Buddhism)

Tantrayāna

▶ Vajrayāna (Buddhism)

Tantric Buddhism

▶ Vajrayāna (Buddhism)

Tapas

▶ Asceticism (Buddhism)

Tārā (Buddhism)

K. T. S. Sarao
Department of Buddhist Studies, University of Delhi, Delhi, India

Synonyms

Ārya Tārā; Dara Eke; Dölma; Drölma; Jetsun Tārā; Tārā Bosatsu; Tārinī

Definition

The most important Buddhist savior-goddess in Northern Buddhism.

Tārā is the most important Buddhist savior-goddess in Tibet, Nepal, and Mongolia. Its Sanskrit name *Tārā* is derived from the root *tar* (to cross) and hence is taken to mean as *the one who helps to cross (to the other shore of the ocean of ignorance)*. To the Tibetans she is known as *sgrol-ma* (or *Dölma*), which means *saviouress* or *deliveress*, hence her name in Tibetan means *the one who saves/delivers* (see [3], p. 120). She is the feminine counterpart as well as consort of Avalokiteśvara and like him is a compassionate, succoring deity. She is the protectress of not only navigation and earthly travel but also of spiritual journey on the way to *bodhi*. She embodies purity and is usually shown standing on the right side of her consort, Avalokiteśvara, or seated with legs crossed, holding a lotus in full-bloom. She is mostly depicted as having a third eye and occasionally the soles of her feet and palms of hand are also depicted as having eyes. Quite often, the figure of the *self-born* Buddha, Amitābha, is shown in her headdress, as like Avalokiteśvara, she is also viewed as an emanation of Amitābha.

There are a large number of legends related to the origin of Tārā. One such legend is that she was born from a blue ray emerging from the eye of Amitābha. The widely popular legend, however, is that she was born from a tear shed by Avalokiteśvara, which formed a lake when it fell on the ground. Out of the waters of this lake emerged a lotus and the goddess emerged out of this lotus on its opening (see [3], p. 120).

Tārā symbolizes the very notion of female divinity and her name can therefore be included in the list of other goddesses who frequently appear as Tārā's specialized forms. Majority of the Tibetan temple banners display 21 different Tārās, colored white (10), red (5), and yellow (5), with a Green Tārā in the center. Tārā is also viewed as the female Buddha of enlightened activity of which there are four types each represented by a different color:

1. **White**: pacifying enlightened activity overcoming sickness, obstacles, etc.
2. **Yellow**: enlightened activity of increasing the positive qualities conducive to a long life, peace, and happiness.
3. **Red**: enlightened activity of overpowering external forces that cannot be tamed through the first two activities.
4. **Black/Blue**: wrathful enlightened activity involving use of forceful methods for accomplishing activities that cannot be accomplished through other means.

In the beginning Tārā had only two distinct forms (Green Tārā and White Tārā). However with the passage of time, her forms multiplied, forming a group of 21 Tārās. A practice text, *Praises to the Twenty-One Tārās*, is recited in the morning by Tibetan Buddhists of all the major traditions. The Tārās are invariably seated, except when accompanied by Avalokiteśvara or another prominent bodhisattva, when they generally adopt a standing posture. Tārā is also occasionally encircled by her own manifestations as well as other gods (see [3], p. 121).

The most widely known forms of Tārā are:

Śyāma Tārā (Green Tārā): She is viewed by some as the original Tārā and is known for supreme wisdom and active compassion. She was believed to be incarnated as the Nepali princess. She is mostly depicted as seated on a lotus throne with her right leg hanging down, wearing a bodhisattva's jewelry, and holding in her hand a closed blue lotus (*utpala*).

Sita Tārā (White Tārā): She is known for compassion, long life, healing, and serenity. The White and Green Tārās, with their contrasting symbols of the fully-blooming and closed lotus, are said to symbolize between them the never-ending compassion of the deity laboring day and night to relieve beings of their suffering.

Jāṅgulī Tārā (Dispeller of Poison): She protects against snake bite.

Bhṛkuṭī Tārā (the Frowning Tārā): She is associated with wealth and prosperity.

Ekajaṭā/Ekajaṭī (Tārā with one chignon)/Ugra Tārā (the Ferocious Tārā): She destroys all impediments, confers good luck, and deep religious gratification.

Khadiravaṇi Tārā: She is the Tārā of the Acacia Forest who offers protection against the eight great fears. She is sometimes referred to as the *Twenty-second Tārā.*

Kurukullā: She is the Red Tārā of fierce character linked to wealth.

Sarasvatī: She is the Tārā of music, poetry, and learning.

Uṣṇīṣavijayā: She is the Victorious Tārā with chignon who offers long life.

It is not clear whether Tārā came into origin as a Buddhist goddess independently or had a Brāhmaṇical-Hindu origin. In fact, there is no literary or archaeological evidence of the existence of Tārā as an independent Buddhist deity prior to the Gupta period in India. It has been suggested by M. Ghosh that Tārā originated as a form of the goddess Durgā in the Purāṇas of Brāhmaṇical-Hinduism ([4], p. 17). The earliest literary reference to her is in the *Āryamañjuśrīmūlakalpa*, a text that has been dated in c. sixth to eighth centuries C.E. ([7], p. 40). Her earliest images are dateable towards the end of the fifth or beginning of the sixth century C.E. ([4], pp. 10–14, 16, 31; also see [6], p. 317). It appears that the image of Tārā as she is known now evolved fully around Nālandā only by the sixth century and from there it appears to have spread towards the Deccan caves, particularly Ajaṇṭā and Ellorā ([4], pp. 10–14, 31). Xuanzang saw many images of Tārā in northern India in the first half of the seventh century. From the eighth century onwards she occupied a place among the most important deities of the Mahāyāna pantheon (see [3], pp. 119–120).

Cross-References

▸ Ajaṇṭā
▸ Avalokiteśvara
▸ Bodhi
▸ Bodhisattva
▸ Nālandā

References

1. Beyer S (1973) The cult of Tārā: magic and ritual in Tibet (Hermeneutics: studies in the history of religions). University of California, Berkeley
2. Bhattacharyya B (1987) The Indian Buddhist iconography. Firma KLM, Calcutta
3. Getty A (1978) The gods of northern Buddhism, 1st Indian edn. Munshiram Manoharlal, New Delhi
4. Ghosh M (1980) Development of Buddhist iconography in Eastern India: a study of Tārā, Prajñās of five Tathāgatas and Bhṛkuṭī. Munshiram Manoharlal, New Delhi
5. Sherab KP, Dongyal KT (2007) Tārā's enlightened activity: commentary on the praises to the twenty-one Tārās. Snow Lion Publications, Boston
6. Snellgrove D (1987) Indo-Tibetan Buddhism. Shambhala, Boston
7. Willson M (1992) In praise of Tārā: songs to the savioueress. Wisdom Publications, Boston

Tārā Bosatsu

▶ Tārā (Buddhism)

Tāranātha

Arvind Kumar Singh
Department of Buddhist Studies, Faculty of Arts, University of Delhi, Delhi, India
School of Buddhist Studies and Civilization, Gautam Buddha University, Greater Noida, Uttar Pradesh, India

Synonyms

Ānandagarbha [1]; Drolwai Gonpo [4]; "Groba"imgonpo; Jetsun Tārānātha; Jo-naṅrje-btsun Tārānātha; Kun dga' snying po; Kunga Nyingpo; Rje-btsun Tārānātha; Sgrolma'imgonpo; Srigcodrdorje

Definition

Tāranātha (1575–1634), a great accomplished master of the Jo-naṅ-pa sect of Tibetan Buddhism, was famous in Tibet as the author of many treatises on Tantra and philosophy but especially known for his masterly work *History of Buddhism in India (rGya-gar-chos-'byuṅ).*

Life of Tāranātha

Tāranātha, a Tibetan scholar, is known for his historical works on Buddhism and was a foremost expert on the *tantras* of the Sarma or new translation period. He was born at Karag (*kha rag*) [5] in the Tsang (*gtsang*) province of Western Tibet [8] in the hereditary line of the great Tibetan translator Ra Lotsawa Dorje Drak in 1575 C.E., on the same birthday as Padmasambhava, who was the founder of Buddhism in Tibet. His Tibetan name was *Kun dga' Snying po* (Ānandagarbha), but he is generally known as Tāranātha, which he received in a vision from a great Indian Jvālānātha [1]. Accounts of his life, corroborated by his autobiography, assert that he was recognized by Khenchen Lungrik Gyatso in his first year of childhood [5] as an incarnation of Kṛṣṇācārya and of the Jonaṅ master Kunga Drolchok. Later on, he was taken to a local monastery for a secret training [8]. But this was kept secret for several years [5].

At the age of about 4 years, he was brought to Kunga Drolchok's monastery of Cholung Changtse and formally recognized as his incarnation. He then began years of intense study and practice under the guidance of a series of great masters, many of whom had been major disciples of Kunga Drolchok. Guided by Kunga Drolchok's disciple, Jampa Lhundrup, Tāranātha first studied and mastered various subjects of *sūtra* and *tantra* [8]. Then he received a vast number of *tāntric* teachings and initiations, primarily of the Śākya tradition of Lamdre from Doring Kunga Gyaltsen. Kunga Drolchok's disciple Dragtopa Lhawang Dragpa taught Tāranātha many esoteric instructions, especially the six *Yogas* and *Mahāmūdrās*, which resulted into a sublime primordial awareness to arise in the young prodigy's mind. Jedrung Kunga Palsang, who was Kunga Drolchok's nephew and successor on the monastic seat of Jo-naṅ, transmitted to Tāranātha the teachings of *Kālacakra* and the dharma protector *Mahākāla*. From Kunga Drolchok's disciple Lungrik Gyatso, Tāranātha received many transmissions, especially the *Kālacakra* initiation, the explanation of the *Kālacakra Tantra*, the esoteric instructions of the sixfold yoga according to the Jo-naṅ tradition, and the collected writings of dharma lord Dolpopa Sherab Gyaltsen [7]. He gained a special experiential realization when he practiced the sixfold yoga [5]. Buddhagupta-nātha became one of Tāranātha's (14 years old) most important teachers, who taught him *tantras* and instructions of *Tārāyoginī*, the *Gūhyasamāja Tantra* according to the tradition of *Jñana-pada*, the *Dohas* of Jalandhara, *Varahī* according to the tradition of Jalandhara, the oral instructions of *Kusali* and its six branches on the perfection process for *Hevajra*, and several *Mahāmudrā* lessons [5]. Several other Indian *yogins* and scholars, both Buddhist and non-Buddhist, came to Tibet during Tāranātha's lifetime, such as Bālabhadra, Nirvānaśri, Puraṇanda, Purṇavajra, and Kṛṣṇa Bhadra. Some of them taught him profound instructions and scholarly topics and joined him in translating Sanskrit manuscripts into Tibetan. Several of Tāranātha's translations are now included in the Tibetan canonical collections of the *Kangyur* and *Tengyur* [1].

In his autobiography called *The Secret Biography*, Lama Tāranātha records that without any formal instructions from any teacher, he effortlessly acquired proficiency in various Indian languages. When he was just 4 years old, he overheard the conversation of Venerable Tenzin Ngawang with an Indian *Zoki* (*Yogi*) and he could understand the substance of it. He further says that because of his many previous births in India, he had vivid recollection of geography and topography of the country and knowledge of various Indian languages since his childhood. At 16, he was prophesied by his personal deity (*Iṣṭadeva*) that if he chose to go to Zanskar in Ladakh and Garsha (presently in Himachal Pradesh) before he was 20 years old, he would accumulate merit to do immense service to the sentient beings. But since the prophecy remained unimplemented, he thought his lifework could not be so prolific. Further, he tells that while in his twenties, he once fell sick with constant bleeding through his nostrils for about 3 months. At that time in a dream, he saw two Indian *Yogis*, one of them named Jvālanātha [1]. In 1588 C.E., Jedrung Kunga Palzang enthroned Tāranātha at Jo-naṅ, who took upon himself the responsibility of causing the dharma lord Dolpopa's insights to once again reach a wide audience. He was determined to revive what he saw as a priceless transmission lineage in danger of being lost. During the 1590s, Tāranātha's teacher Jampa Lhundrup advised him to restore the Great Stūpa of Jo-naṅ that Dolpopa had built about 260 years before at Jo-naṅ. Tāranātha put all his energy into the project [7].

In 1604 C.E., after a decade of efforts to revive the original Jo-naṅ teachings, all of Tāranātha's work was threatened by serious political conflict between the regions of Jang (*byang*) and Tsang. Jo-naṅ itself was in immediate danger of being attacked by hostile armies. He became despondent and wished only to go into retreat. But Dolpopa then appeared to him in a vision, encouraged him to continue as before, and assured him that his efforts would not be in vain. As a result of these events, Tāranātha said he gained realization, and all his uncertainties and doubts were completely removed. As an expression of his realization, he composed a versified text entitled, *Ornament of the Zhentong Madhyamaka*, which is one of his most important works solely devoted to the explication of the Zhentong view. Tāranātha said that he received several prophecies from Dolpopa and thereafter met him many times, in both reality and dreams [5].

In 1614 C.E., Tāranātha established Puntsokling Monastery three miles down the side valley, near the south bank of the Tsangpo. The main buildings of the monastery were built on a high knob overlooking the river and offering spectacular views up and down the valley. The Puntsokling Monastery eventually became famous for its printing workshop which among many other items published the 16-volume collected works of Tāranātha himself. According to some accounts, Tāranātha went to Mongolia not long after founding Puntsokling and established several monasteries there. Almost nothing is known about his years in Mongolia, and it is unclear what monasteries he may have founded in those pre-Zanabazar days. In any case, he died in Mongolia in 1634 C.E., and his body was returned to Tibet [6]. In 1615, the powerful Tsang ruler Desi Phuntsok Namgyal provided a special piece of land and the necessary supplies and workers to begin construction of a monastery to serve as a center for the teachings of the definitive meaning of the Buddha's doctrine. This monastery, which was finally completed in 1628 C.E., became Tāranātha's main residence and was known as Takten Damcho Ling [5]. Shortly before his death, Tāranātha appointed his disciple Sangye Gyatso as his successor on the monastic seat of Takten Damcho Ling and made many prophetic statements about the Jo-naṅ tradition and the great political troubles that would soon sweep through Tibet. Unfortunately, Sangye Gyatso passed away not long after Tāranātha himself. Thus, another of the great master's disciples, Kunga Rinchen Gyatso, was appointed to the monastic seat and led the Jo-naṅ tradition for the next 15 years [5].

Jo-naṅ-pa Sect

In the thirteenth century, Kunpang Tukje Tsötru (1243–1313 C.E.) founded the original Jo-naṅ monastery about three miles up a small side valley of the Tsangpo. Reportedly this monastery was modeled on the traditional layout of the kingdom of Shambhala as shown on Shambhala *thangkas*. In 1327 C.E., Dolpopa Sherab Gyeltsen built nearby an enormous seven-story stūpa, the Jo-naṅ Kumbum, similar in appearance but older than the much more famous kumbum in the city of Gyantse [5]. The sect of Tibetan Buddhism which had Jo-naṅ as its stronghold came to be known as Jo-naṅ-pa sect, which was founded by Phyogs-las-rnam-rgyal (Digvijaya) [1]. *Kālacakra Tantra* constituted an important feature of this sect. In Tibetan writings, Tāranātha is usually mentioned as "Jo-naṅ Tāranātha" or rje-btsun (*Bhaṭṭāraka*) Tāranātha of the Jo-naṅ-pa sect where Jo-naṅ is the name of the place with a *chaitya* and a convent to the northwest of the Tashilhunpo [1]. Tāranātha himself, a later leader of the Jo-naṅ-pa sect, was famous as an author of several works and "guidebooks" (*Khrid-yig*) on the *Kālacakra* doctrine [1]. The basic teachings of the school had appeared early as the eleventh century, but it is Dolpopa Sherab Gyeltsen (1292–1361 C.E.) who is credited with fully developing the Jo-naṅ-pa belief system [7]. The sect is best known for its philosophical doctrine of ultimate truth called *shen-tong*, or "other emptiness." This is different from the rang-tang doctrine of *self-emptiness* expounded by Nāgārjuna, Caṅdrakīrti, and other Indian teachers. *Shen-tong* asserts that "emptiness, in dispelling the illusive relative truths of the world", reveals an ineffable transcendental reality with positive attributes. The *rang-tang* view claimed that emptiness is merely the elimination of falsely imagined projections upon the relative truths of the world and does not imply anything else. As Tibetologist Stephen Batchelor [6] points out, "While such distinctions may strike us today as theological hair splitting, in Tibet they became (and still are) crucial articles of faith." In addition to the shen-teng doctrine, the Jo-naṅ-pa had a special interest in the *Kālacakra*. Numerous Jo-naṅ-pa monks besides Tāranātha wrote on the *Kālacakra*, and a unique line of *Kālacakra* teachings has been passed down to this day by the Karma Kagyu school [6]. The first Jebtsundamba, also known as Zanabazar (1635–1723 C.E.), was identified as the reincarnation of Tāranātha of the Jo-naṅ-pa school of Tibetan Buddhism. He also is believed to be the incarnation of Tāranātha and Khyungpo Naljor, founders of the Jo-naṅ-pa and Shangpa lineages. Prior to his incarnation as Tāranātha, he was known as Jamyang Choje, who established Drepung Monastery outside Lhasa [3].

Works of Tāranātha

Tāranātha spent much of his life traveling throughout Central Tibet (a penchant reflected in the nickname he gave himself *Gyalkampa*, "the wanderer"), studying under a number of eminent lamas, teaching extensively, rebuilding temples and monasteries, and composing an outstanding number of texts on various aspects of Buddhist doctrines, practice, and history [8]. He was a great Tibetan scholar, teacher, and founder of monasteries in Tibet and Mongolia, where he taught for 20 years; his collected writings fill 23 volumes. He was the most suitable person of his age to write an account of the development of Buddhist teachings in India because of his interest in writing accounts of the past and the lives of personages of lineages, mastery over Sanskrit and other Indian dialects, and access to the authentic works of Pandits, viz., Kṣemendrabhadra, Indradatta, and Bhataghati [1]. Tāranātha wrote a life story of Padmasambhava based exclusively on Indian sources. His best known work is the 143-folio *dpalduskyi 'khorlo'ichosbskorgyibyungkhungsnyermkho* of 1608 C.E. [2], which is usually referred to as *rGya-gar-chos-'byuṅ*, which means *History of Buddhism in India*, but brief title Tāranātha himself chose for it was *dGos-'dod-kun-'byuṅ*, literally "that which fulfils all desires" [1]. Though it is full of superstitious beliefs, fanciful traditions, and wild stories, Tāranātha's "history" preserves an indispensable account of the spread of Buddhism in India and particularly of the lives of distinguished âcāryas of India who composed learned philosophical works as also of the missionaries engaged in the spread of Buddhism in India [2].

His other works are *the Seven Instruction Lineages* and the *Origin of the Tārā Tantra*, as well as his *Kālacakra* and Vajrabhairava histories, which give us a fairly good account of the development of many Siddha lineages in India and their continuation onto Tibetan soil. The source for many of these accounts was a result of his interactions with an Indian master whom Tāranātha met around the year 1594 C.E. near Narthang in Central Tibet, while he himself stayed in a hermitage called "Mahābodhi." That master was none other than the Mahāsiddha Buddhagupta-nātha, who was a disciple of the very famous Mahāsiddha Shanti-Gupta. Shanti-Gupta's biography is added as an appendix to Tāranātha's *Seven Instruction Lineages*, whereas his biography of Buddhagupta-nātha appears as a separate text [1]. Among the works of Tāranātha, we have no text translated by him, but he mentions in his autobiography that he did translations of minor texts also. He states to have studied several Sanskrit manuscripts belonging to Atisa which he found preserved in the Rading Monastery. "His scholarship of Sanskrit is evidenced from many of his extensive works on the *Kālacakra Tantra* and other philosophical texts" [1]. Tāranātha in his autobiography lays emphasis on his utter honesty, straightforwardness, and impartiality in his writings and also pays deep respect to all the lineages of various Buddhist scholars which are substantiated by his extensive works ranging from psalms and verses (*dohas* and *gathas*) to the most sophisticated philosophical and Tantrika treatises, including commentaries of *sutras* and *tantras* besides his original compositions [1].

Later Life of Tārānātha

Probably not long after 1614 C.E., Tāranātha went to Mongolia, where he reportedly founded several monasteries. According to some accounts, Tāranātha went to Mongolia not long after founding Puntsokling and established several monasteries [3] and spent 20 years propagating Buddhism among the Khalkha Mongols. He died probably in Urga, Mongolia. According to Italian Tibetologist Giuseppe Tucci, Tāranātha was buried at Dzingi, five miles northeast of Oka, "A large silver chorten is said to hold the mortal remains of Tāranātha, a well-known Tibetan polymath . . . As tradition has it, Tāranātha's relics were thrown into the river and carried by the stream to Katrag, midway between Zangrikangmar and Oka, where they were collected and transported into the Dzingji temple" [6]. He was canonized under the title of "The Reverend Holiness," Jetsun Dampa. And his "reincarnate" successors are now installed with great magnificence as Grand Lāmas at Urga in the Khalkha province of Mongolia, to the east of Lop Nor [9]. His rebirth became known as Zanabazar, the First Bogd Gegen, or Jetsun Dampa of Mongolia. His current reincarnation is known as Khalkha Jetsun Dampa.

Tārānātha and His Indian Connection

According to David Templeman, Tārānātha's fascination with India and his literary recreation of himself as a "Virtual Indian" have been based upon evidence which shows that, especially in his earlier years, Tārānātha envisaged himself as an Indian, somehow "accidentally" born in Tibet which was reinforced in his last writings too. As a means of legitimating his sense of being Indian, like many other Tibetan prelates, Tārānātha deliberately locates himself at certain epochal moments in Indian Buddhist history which are as follows: "as a close confidante of the Buddha Vipaśyi, present as an auditor when the Buddha preached the Great Drum Sūtra (Mahābheri Sūtra), being the King Arvanti of Li yul (Khotan), actually being the Mahāsiddha Kṛṣṇācārya one of the 84 Mahāsiddhas, as priest to the founder of Nālandā Mahāvihāra, as a friend of Abhayākaragupta, being a student of Jo boAtīśa, etc." [4]. One can find throughout in his Secret Autobiographies written at different stages of his life that he was indeed Indian in spirit, if not in body. A series of life incidents which he records are as follows [4]: "his life was saved by Indian yogis and their blessing made his life firm, belonged to Indian yogic groups before, demonstrated through his strong desire to emulate their lives in his youth, his true 'home' was in the very heart of Buddhist India, Bodhgāya to where he is transported in visions upon the sight of Indian yogis, his ability to converse easily with Indian yogis as a natural speaker of various Indian vernaculars, he reaffirms that the languages of India were his natural preserve, and in his childhood visions he discovers that his innermost nature is identical and inseparable from that of Cakrasavara, generally regarded as the consummate Anuttārayoga deity in Indian tantric practice." This is not merely some sort of relationship but an affection and relationship with India where he has never visited. Instead he built up a personal, idealized, and idiosyncratic vision of India which was both flawed and yet touchingly human.

Cross-References

- ▶ Bodhagayā
- ▶ Jaananaa
- ▶ Tantra
- ▶ Vajrayāna (Buddhism)

References

1. Chimpa L, Chattopadhyaya A (tr) Tāranātha's history of Buddhism in India (Chattopadhyaya DP, ed). Motilal Banarsidass, New Delhi, Reprint: 1990
2. Dutt N (1969) Synopsis of Tāranātha's history. In: Namgyal GH, Sherab Gyaltshen T, Sinha NC (eds) Bulletin of tibetology. Namgyal Institute of Tibetology, Gangtok, Sikkim
3. http://keywen.com/en/TĀRĀNĀTHA#MONASTERY. Accessed 31 Mar 2012
4. http://ltwa.tibetanbridges.com/tibet_journal/Special_issue-2009-2010/09%20Templeman.pdf. Accessed 1 Apr 2012
5. http://www.Jo-naṅfoundation.org/Tārānātha. Accessed 24 Mar 2012
6. http://www.zanabazar.mn/Life/zanabazar.12.html. Accessed 31 Mar 2012
7. Stearns C (1999) The Buddha from Dolpo: a study of the life and thought of the Tibetan master Dolpopa Sherab Gyaltsen. State University of New York Press, Albany
8. Tārānātha (2005) The essence of ambrosia: a guide to Buddhist contemplations (trans: Baker W). Library of Tibetan Works and Archives, Dharmashala
9. Waddell A (1972) Tibetan Buddhism: with its mystic cults, symbolism and mythology, and in its relation to Indian Buddhism. Dover Publications, New York, Reprint

Tārinī

▶ Tārā (Buddhism)

Tarka-śāstra

▶ Logic (Buddhism)

Tarka-vidyā

► Logic (Buddhism)

Tathāgata

Bhikkhu Anālayo
Center for Buddhist Studies, University of Hamburg, Balve, Germany

Synonyms

Thus-gone One

Definition

Tathāgata is the epithet that according to the early Buddhist sources the Buddha regularly used to refer to himself and hence can be taken to represent what was considered the most fitting expression of the Buddha's nature and realization.

The Tathāgata

The word *tathāgata* can be derived from the adverb *tathā*, "thus," and the past participle *gata*, "gone." On this derivation, *tathāgata* can be translated as "thus gone." This way of understanding the term *tathāgata* would be similar to another epithet of the Buddha, *sugata*, "well gone."

Alternatively, the second part of the compound could be the past participle *āgata*, "come" or "arrived," on which derivation the term *tathāgata* can be translated as "thus come," *tathā* + *āgata*. The Chinese translators of Buddhist texts opted for the rendering "thus come," *ru lai*, in order to translate *tathāgata*. The other nuance of having "thus gone," however, is still present in the Tibetan rendering of the same term as *de bzhin gshegs pa*, which similar to the Pāli and Sanskrit expressions combines the two meanings "thus come" and "thus gone."

The term *tathāgata* seems to have been in common use in ancient India and the form *tahāgaya* occurs also in Jain scriptures. A non-Buddhist usage of the term *tathāgata* is reflected in Buddhist texts, which present a set of four ways of predicating the destiny of a *tathāgata* after death. This fourfold predication, or tetralemma, regarding the destiny of a *tathāgata* after death appears to have been a current topic of debate among ancient Indian recluses and wanderers. The problem it takes up is whether a *tathāgata*:

- Exists after death
- Does not exist after death
- Both exists and does not exist after death
- Neither exists nor does not exist after death

Tradition unanimously reports that the Buddha consistently refused to take up any of these four propositions. The reason for this refusal has a close bearing on the Buddhist understanding of the term *tathāgata* and therefore deserves closer inspection.

The discourses report one occasion when a monk, on being questioned by outside wanderers regarding the tetralemma on the *tathāgata* after death, proposed that there was yet another way of making a statement on this matter ([1], Vol. III, p. 116). The outside wanderers took him for a fool, since the tetralemma exhausts the possible ways of predication according to ancient Indian logic, so that a fifth proposition is simply impossible.

The monk then reported what had happened to the Buddha, who with a question and answer catechism led this monk to the realization that even here and now a *tathāgata* cannot be identified with any of the five aggregates affected by clinging. These five aggregates are what early Buddhism considers to be the constituents of an individual, comprising bodily form, feeling, perception, volitional formations, and consciousness.

A *tathāgata* can also not be identified as being in these five aggregates or apart from them. Since here and now a *tathāgata* cannot be found in truth and fact, how could any predication about his future destiny be made? This line of reasoning clarifies why the Buddha would without fail be unwilling to grant any of the four positions proposed by the tetralemma.

Another discourse points out that only those who consider any of the physical senses or the mind as being "mine," "I," or "my self" will uphold one or the other of these four propositions on the future destiny of a *tathāgata* ([1], Vol. IV, p. 393). The tetralemma on the *tathāgata* is thus, from a Buddhist perspective, an expression of the belief in the existence of a permanent self. Hence, for one who has realized that a permanent self does not exist, any such view or proposal becomes just meaningless.

In the early Buddhist discourses, the term *tathāgata* stands at times for arahants in general (e.g., [2], Vol. I, p. 140). The most frequent use of the term *tathāgata*, however, refers specifically to the Buddha, who is the one to discover and teach the path to liberation. Such path-finding *tathāgatas* arise rarely in the world ([3], Vol. II, p. 149).

The role of a *tathāgata* in the spiritual realm is parallel to the role of a wheel-turning king, *cakkavatti rāja*, who is the worldly counterpart to a *tathāgata*. Both are supreme in their respective sphere. A characteristic of a wheel-turning king is that he possesses seven treasures: a wheel, an elephant, a horse, a jewel, a woman, a steward, and a counselor, each endowed with magical qualities. The counterparts to these seven treasures are the seven factors of awakening, *bojjhaṅga*, whose disclosure forms a characteristic of a *tathāgata* ([1], Vol. V, p. 99). These seven mental qualities, required for reaching awakening, are mindfulness, investigation of phenomena, energy, joy, tranquility, concentration, and equanimity.

The Buddha in his role of being a *tathāgata* possesses ten powers, *bala*. These "ten powers of a *tathāgata*" are ([2], Vol. I, p. 69):

- Knowledge of what is possible and what is impossible
- Knowledge of karma and its result
- Knowledge of the ways to all (rebirth) destinations
- Knowledge of the various elements that make up the world
- Knowledge of the different inclinations of living beings
- Knowledge of the faculties of beings
- Knowledge of the attainment of concentration and realization in all its aspects
- Knowledge of his past lives
- Knowledge of the arising and passing away of beings in accordance with their deeds
- Destruction of the influxes, *āsava*

In addition to these ten powers, a *tathāgata* is also in possession of four intrepidities, *vesārajja*. These four intrepidities are ([2], Vol. I, p. 71):

- He has fully awakened
- He has successfully eradicated all influxes
- He knows what are obstructions to the development of the path
- He is able to lead others to freedom from *dukkha*

Endowed with these ten powers and four intrepidities, a *tathāgata* can claim the role of a leader and roar his lion's roar in assemblies. Another set of qualifications explains that the Buddha deserves to be called a *tathāgata* because ([4], Vol. II, p. 23):

- He has fully comprehended the world, its arising and cessation, and is free from it
- He has penetrative insight into whatever is seen, heard, experienced, cognized, etc.
- From the time of his awakening to his final Nirvāṇa, he speaks only what is true
- He acts in accordance with what he says and speaks in accordance with his action
- He is supreme in the world

Due to having developed the four roads to power, *iddhipāda*, a *tathāgata* is able to live for a long time ([3], Vol. II, p. 103). Yet, rebirth is extinct for a *tathāgata*; hence gods and men will not be able to see him after death ([3], Vol. I, p. 46). With later traditions, however, the *tathāgata* becomes increasingly invested with transcendent qualities, and buddhological speculation arrives at identifying the *tathāgata* with ineffable, omnipotent, and unchanging suchness.

Cross-References

- Arahant
- Buddha (Concept)

References

1. Feer L (ed) (1888–1898) The Saṃyutta Nikāya, 5 vols. Pali Text Society, Oxford
2. Trenckner V, Chalmers R (eds) (1888–1896) The Majjhima Nikāya, 3 vols. Pali Text Society, London
3. Carpenter JE, Rhys Davids TW (eds) (1890–1911) The Dīgha Nikāya, 3 vols. Pali Text Society, London
4. Morris R, Hardy E (eds) (1885–1900) The Aṅguttara Nikāya, 5 vols. Pali Text Society, London
5. Anesaki MN (1921) Tathāgata. In: Hastings J (ed) Encyclopaedia of religion and ethics, vol 12, T. & T. Clark, Edinburgh, pp 202–204
6. Chalmers R (1898) Tathāgata. J Roy Asiatic Soc 103–115
7. Endo T (2002) Buddha in Theravāda Buddhism. BCC, Dehiwala
8. Harvey P (1983) The nature of the Tathāgata. In: Denwood P (ed) Buddhist studies: ancient and modern. Curzon, London, pp 35–52
9. Hopkins EW (1911) Buddha as Tathāgata. Am J Philol 32:205–209
10. Norman KR (1990) Seven Pāli etymologies – Tathāgata. J Pali Text Soc 15:154
11. Thomas EJ (1936) Tathāgata and Tahāgaya. Bull Sch Orient Stud 8:781–788

Tathāgatagarbha

A. W. Barber
Department of Communication and Culture, University of Calgary, Calgary, AB, Canada

Synonyms

Buddhadhātu; *Satyātman*; *Sugatagarbha*

Definition

Tathāgatagarbha: "*tathāgata*-womb, *tathāgata*-seed, *tathāgata*-matrix"; indicating the "Buddha within" understood as originally or inherently awakened or as one's potential for awakening.

The Buddha Within

Tathāgatagarbha, buddhadhātu, and similar terms are used to indicate the Mahāyāna idea of a "buddha within." The "buddha within" idea is found in a number of *sūtras* that research indicates originated around the Krishna River basin with the Mahāsaṃghikas [2, 4, 14, 15]. Probably the earliest *sūtras* are the *Tathāgatagarbha sūtra* [3, 9, 13, 17, 18] and the *Śrīmālādevī-siṁhanāda-nāma mahāyānasūtra* [3, 7, 13, 16] "published" in approximately the third century C.E. Shortly after the "publication" of these first *sūtras*, works such as the *Mahāparinirvāṇa sūtra,* the *Laṅkāvatāra sūtra* [3, 13], and others all of which have *tathāgatagarbha* teachings as an important theme were also "published." The meaning of the term "*tathāgatagarbha*" has received considerable scholarly debate with *tathāgata*-womb, *tathāgata*-seed, *tathāgata*-matrix, and other possibilities being presented as translations. Most of these renderings of the Sanskrit into modern languages have been assisted by the Chinese translation which can be read as either "are" or "having" a *tathāgatagarbha* and the Tibetan translation as "having" a *tathāgatagarbha*. The first *sūtra's* introduction of the term can be understood as sentient beings are the womb/container of the *tathāgata* [12].

In part, the *tathāgatagarbha* theory can be associated with notions put forward to deal with the major problems that arise from the *anātman* theory. The first is how to explain the experience of luminosity (i.e., pristine awareness) as testified to in the **Aṅguttara Nikāya's** *Pabhassara sutta* [5] and elsewhere if there is no self. Second is how to account for teachings such as in the **Samyutta Nikāya's** *Bearer Sutra* (*Bhāra-sutta*) [10] which holds out the idea of a bearer of the five aggregates (*skandhas*). Also how to account for transmigration, who experiences liberation, memory, and who experiences karma become problematic with a radical no-self doctrine. All of these were issues of concern for the Buddhists in the Andhra region. Various *śrāvaka* schools put forward different theories. The Mahāsaṃghika schools in general did not hold to as thoroughgoing *anātman* theory as the Theravada school and, thus, posited a root consciousness (*mūlavijñāna*) to address these problems. Another example of addressing these concerns is from the Yogācāra school which held out a storehouse consciousness (*ālayavijñāna)* [6, 11]. Therefore, *tathāgatagarbha* theory should be viewed in this light.

The *Tathāgatagarbha sūtra* [1], after listing the audience present, states that the Buddha Śākyamuni caused those attending to have a vision of countless brilliant Buddhas sitting on thousand-petaled lotuses floating in the sky. Suddenly, the flowers became putrid but the Buddhas were untouched. He explains that when he views sentient beings covered with *kleśas* (greed, confusion, anger, and delusion) within, he sees a perfectly formed Buddha including his wisdom, vision, and body. The teaching here is that the *kleśas* are not intrinsic but adventitious and universally beings are already awakened. This *sūtra* speaks in metaphors, and some scholars have argued that at least some of the metaphors can be understood as only implying a "potential" to buddhahood.

The *Śrīmālādevīsiṃhanāda sūtra* considerably advances the development of this basic idea. Herein, the *tathāgatagarbha* is understood as the one vehicle (*ekayāna*), the *Dharmakāya* within defilements, ultimately free of defilements, not void of Buddha qualities (*Buddha-dharmas*), the *śūnyatā* knowledge of the Tathāgata. It is permanent (*nitya*), unchangeable (*dhruva*), calm (*śiva*), and eternal (*śāsvata*). The *tathāgatagarbha* is the source for both awakening and *saṃsāra* in that it is the origin (*niśraya*), support (*ādhāra*), and base (*pratiṣṭhā*) of the constructed (*saṃskṛta*) and for one's aspiration to follow the spiritual life. The *sūtra* is careful to distinguish between the *ātman* and the *tathāgatagarbha.* However, there is a tension between understanding *tathāgatagarbha* as innate Buddhahood or one's potential for awakening. Other *sūtras* also have this tension.

The *Laṅkāvatāra sūtra* presents both innate Buddhahood and potential for awakening without resolving the issues. It also claims that *tathāgatagarbha* is distinct from the *ātman,* and is emptiness (*śūnyatā*), reality limit (*bhūtakoṭi*), *nirvāṇa,* the unborn (*ajāti*) [8], deathless (*aniruddha*), and non-fixed (*apraṇihita*). In addition to the above, this *sūtra* also says that the Buddha sometimes teaches *tathāgatagarbha* as a skillful means (*upāya*) to attract non-Buddhists.

The Mahāyāna *Mahāparinirvāṇa sūtra* breaks new ground in many ways. First, it is critical of the more thoroughgoing interpretation of *anātman* familiar to us from Theravada doctrine. It introduces the idea of Great Nirvāṇa (*mahā-nirvāṇa*). It also states that there is a true self (*ātman*) which is discussed in many of the same terms as the *tathāgatagarbha* (i.e., *nitya, dhruva, śiva*) and which is the Buddha's *Dharmakāya.* This true self is the Buddha element (*buddhadhātu*) and all beings have it, but it is covered by the *kleśas.* This true self is also the *tathāgatagarbha*, and *tathāgatagarbha* is wisdom. Using *buddhadhātu* and *tathāgatagarbha* interchangeably, the *sūtra* presents this information in a chapter entitled "The Tathāgatagarbha." In the Tibetan version, it declares that the *buddhadhātu* is the inherent nature of beings.

The only recognized Indic commentary presenting *tathāgatagarbha* material is the *Ratnagotravibhāga Mahāyānottaratantraśāstra* [13]. The Chinese and Tibetan traditions differ on the author(s) of this work which with its *Vyākhyā* is multilayered. Part of the verse portion often refers to the *Tathāgatagarbha sūtra*, and the *Ārya-Śrīmālādevīsiṁhanāda* is often quoted. Speaking of tainted and untainted thusnesses *(tathatā*), it equates the tainted thusness with *tathāgatagarbha.* This work shows considerable Yogācāric influences when taken as a whole.

Unlike the consolidation of the *śūnyatā* theory in Mādhyamaka or the consciousnesses (*vijñāna)* theory in the Vijñānavāda, *tathāgatagarbha* theory never develops into a school of philosophy/praxis in India, although it had a major impact on the Vajrayāna, particularly in the Mahāsandhi and Mahāmudrā traditions. Some Mādhyamakins take *tathāgatagarbha* to be a synonym of emptiness (*śūnyatā*), and the Yogācāra school understands it in connection with *ālayavijñāna.* Proponents from the Mādhyamaka and Yogācāra schools understand *tathāgatagarbha* as only a potential. Some of the *sūtras* teaching *tathāgatagarbha* become highly significant in East Asia, and

Tibetan philosophical inquiries into the *tathāgatagarbha* are primarily based on the *Ratnagotravibhāga*. Outside of India, tathāgatagarbha theory becomes one of the most significant doctrines in Buddhism, touching every major school and acting as the foundation for Chan/Zen.

Cross-References

▶ *Ālaya-vijñāna*
▶ Buddha (Concept)
▶ *Dhamma*
▶ Mādhyamika
▶ *Saṃsāra*
▶ *Śrāvaka*
▶ *Śūnyatā*
▶ *Upāya*
▶ Yogācāra

References

1. Barber AW (1999) The Anti-Sukhāvatīvyūha stance of the Tathāgatagarbha Sūtra. Pure Land 16:190–202
2. Barber AW (1999) The practice lineage of Tathāgatagarbha. Stud Zen Buddh 77:29–45
3. Barber AW (ed) (1991) The Tibetan Tripitaka: Taipei edition. SMC, Taipei: Nos. 92 (Śrīmālādevīsiṁhanāda); 107 (Laṅkāvatāra); 120, 121 (Mahāparinirvāṇa); 258 (Tathāgatagarbha); 5525 (Ratnagotravibhāga Mahāyānottaratantraśāstra)
4. Barber AW (2008) Two Mahāyāna developments along the Krishna River. In: Padma S, Barber AW (eds) Buddhism in the Krishna River Valley of Andhra. State University of New York Press, Albany
5. Bhikkhu T. Pabhassara Sutta. Captured 10/10/2011. http://www.accesstoinsight.org/tipitaka/an/an01/an01.049.than.html
6. Brown BE (1991) The Buddha nature a study of the Tathāgatagarbha and Ālayavijñāna. Motilal Banarsidass, Delhi
7. Chang GCC (1983) A treasury of Mahāyāna Sūtras (19). The Pennsylvania State University Press, University Park
8. Grosnick WH (1981) Nonorigination and Nirvāṇa in the early *Tathāgatagarbha* literature. J Int Assoc Buddh Stud 4/2:33–43
9. Grosnick WH (1995) The Tathāgatagarbha Sūtra. In: Lopez DS Jr (ed) Buddhism in practice. Princeton University Press, Princeton
10. Kashyap BJ (1959) The Samyutta Nikāya, vol II, No. 22:22 (Bhāra Sutta). Pāli Publication Board, Varanasi
11. Nagao GM (1991) What remains in *Śūnyatā*. In: Nagao GM (ed) Mādhyamika and Yogācāra. State University of New York Press, Albany
12. Rawlinson A (1983) The ambiguity of the Buddha-nature concept in India and China. In: Lai W, Lancaster LR (eds) Early Ch'an in China and Tibet. Berkeley Buddhist Studies Series, Berkeley
13. Takasaki J (1966) A study on the Ratnagotravibhāga (Uttaratantra) being a treatise on the Tathāgatagarbha theory of Mahāyāna Buddhism. Instituto Italiano Per Il Medio Ed Estremo Oriente, Roma
14. Takakusu J (ed) (1922–1933) Taishō shinshū daizōkyō. Daizō shuppan kai, Tokyo: Nos. 310(48), 353 (Śrīmālādevīsiṁhanāda); 374, 375, 390, (Mahāparinirvāṇa); 666 (Tathāgatagarbha); 670, 671, 672 (Laṅkāvatāra); 1611 (Ratnagotravibhāga Mahāyānottaratantraśāstra)
15. Wayman A (1978) The Mahāsāṃghika and the Tathāgatagarbha (Buddhist Doctrinal History, Study 1). J Int Assoc Buddh Stud 1/1:35–50
16. Wayman A, Hideko W (1974) The Lion's Roar of Queen Śrīmālā a Buddhist scripture on the Tathāgatagarbha theory. Columbia University Press, New York
17. Williams P (1991) The Tathāgatagarbha. In: Williams P (ed) Mahāyāna Buddhism the Doctrinal Foundations. Routledge, London
18. Zimmermann M (2003) A Buddha within: the Tathāgatagarbhasūtra the earliest exposition of the Buddha-nature teaching in India. The International Research Institute of Advanced Buddhology Soka University, Tokyo

Tattvārthādhigama-Sūtra

▶ Tattvārtha-Sūtra

Tattvārtha-Sūtra

Ana Bajželj
Department of Philosophy, Faculty of Arts, University of Ljubljana, Ljubljana, Slovenia
Polonsky Academy, The Van Leer Jerusalem Institute, Jerusalem, Israel

Synonyms

Tattvārthādhigama-sūtra

Definition

Tattvārtha-sūtra is a text written by a Jain mendicant, Umāsvāti/Umāsvāmin, sometime between the second and fifth centuries C.E. With its sūtra style, it follows the sūtras of other traditions that were composed around that time, and it is the first Jain text of this kind. Its aim was to systematize the previously unorganized teachings on the Jain doctrine, including soteriology, ontology, cosmology, epistemology, ethics, and practice. It is recognized as an authentic and authoritative text by all traditions of Jainism.

What is Tattvārtha-sūtra?

Tattvārtha-sūtra is a very significant text for both Śvetāmbaras and Digambaras. The date of its composition is uncertain and has stirred up many discussions, but it is estimated that it must have been written between the second and fifth centuries C.E. by a Jain mendicant named Umāsvāti (for Śvetāmbaras) or Umāsvāmin (for Digambaras). It is the first Jain text that was written in the form of short Sanskrit aphorisms or sūtras modeled after the central texts of non-Jain traditions of the time such as the Yoga-sūtra of Patañjali, the Vaiśeṣika-sūtra of Kaṇāda, etc. These were compilations of terse mnemonic rules that encapsulated the essence of their respective doctrines. The intention behind Tattvārtha-sūtra was similar; it was an attempt to organize and systematize the contents of Jain teachings that were prior to that more or less scattered throughout various texts. Although not agreed by everyone, it is often suggested that it particularly drew from the content of the Śvetāmbara canon, which was written in Prākrit. The fact that the text was not written in Prākrit but Sanskrit indicates a willingness and endeavor to step into debates with other, rival traditions of the time ([1], p. 87; [2], p. 81).

The name *Tattvārtha-sūtra* has been variously translated as "Mnemonic Rules on the Meaning of the Reals," "Aphorisms on the Understanding of Principles," "Aphorisms for the Comprehension of the Jaina Fundamentals," etc. It consists of three Sanskrit words, that is, "tattva," "artha," and "sūtra." "Tattva" literally means "that-ness" and is often translated as "real," "verity," "truth," or "true principle," referring to that which exists. "Artha" translates as "meaning," and "sūtra," as already noted, "mnemonic rule" or "aphorism." The name of the text, then, indicates its form and content; it is an explication of the meaning of the basic principles of reality, that is, of the reals, in the sūtra form.

Structure and Content

The number of sūtras in the Tattvārtha-sūtra varies from 344 to 357 due to discrepancies between Śvetāmbaras and Digambaras ([3], p. v); some sūtras may be recognized as authentic by one group but not by the other, and occasionally certain sūtras are merged into one or divided into two parts. The complete collection of sūtras consists of 10 chapters without chapter titles. These address a great variety of topics (soteriological, ontological, cosmological, ethical, epistemological, and practical), which are interwoven with the basic explanation of the seven tattvas. The tattvas are (1) living substance, (2) nonliving substance, (3) influx of auspicious and inauspicious karmic matter, (4) karmic bondage, (5) stoppage of karmic influx, (6) dissociation of karmic matter, and (7) liberation.

The first chapter famously defines the path to liberation (Skt. mokṣa-mārga) from the cycle of rebirths (Skt. saṃsāra) as the proper view of reality (Skt. samyag-darśana), proper knowledge (Skt. samyag-jñāna), and proper conduct (Skt. samyak-cāritra). It is because of its orientation toward the attainment of liberation that the Tattvārtha-sūtra is also referred to as the Mokṣa-sūtra or Mokṣa-śāstra. The second sūtra describes belief in tattvas as constituting the proper view of reality and the fourth sūtra lists them. The first chapter then continues by expanding on the varieties of cognition ([4], pp. 1–27).

The second chapter discusses the living substance, or jīva. It starts by listing the five states (Skt. bhāva) of jīvas, four of which arise in relation to karmic matter and one of which does not. It continues by defining the application of consciousness (Skt. upayoga) as the basic characteristic of jīvas and divides the latter into two main groups, namely, worldly (Skt. saṃsārin) and liberated (Skt. mukta). After that, it enumerates different classes within the group of worldly jīvas ([4], pp. 29–63).

The third chapter introduces the lower and middle cosmic abodes; it describes their geography, the types of living beings that inhabit them, the sorts of lives they live, and how long they live and lists the temporal and geographical conditions for the attainment of liberation ([4], pp. 65–88). The fourth chapter does similarly for the heavenly abode and also makes mention of the animal and plant category (Skt. tiryañc) of living beings ([4], pp. 91–117).

The fifth chapter moves on to describe the nonliving (Skt. ajīva) kinds of substances. These are medium of motion (Skt. dharma), medium of rest (Skt. adharma), space (Skt. ākāśa), matter (Skt. pudgala), and, according to some, time (Skt. kāla). It explains how many of which there are and their other characteristics such as extendedness, mobility, number of space units they contain, the space they occupy, and their functions. It also once again brings in the jīvas and specifies their characteristics. After this, the chapter goes on to define existence (Skt. sat) as the character of substance (Skt. dravya) and explains existence as constituted by origination, cessation, and persistence ([4], pp. 119–145).

The sixth chapter is the explanation of karmic influx (Skt. āsrava). It lists its causes as the bodily, verbal, and mental actions (Skt. yoga) and differentiates between the good (Skt. śubha) and the bad (Skt. aśubha) kinds of action, which respectively cause the influx of auspicious (Skt. puṇya) and inauspicious (Skt. pāpa) karmic matter. It also points out that activities informed by passions (Skt. kaṣāya) cause long-term influx, whereas those devoid of passions cause instantaneous influx of karma. It then moves on to describe what the activities that attract each of the eight basic kinds of karmic matter are ([4], pp. 147–163).

The seventh chapter lays the foundation for Jain ethics and practice of both mendicants and laity. It begins by listing the five vows (Skt. vrata): abstention from violence (Skt. hiṃsā), falsehood (Skt. anṛta), stealing (Skt. steya), carnality (Skt. abrahma), and possessiveness (Skt. parigraha). It then distinguishes between complete abstention as a great vow (Skt. mahā-vrata) and partial abstention as a small vow (Skt. aṇu-vrata). After describing the types of behavior that support these vows, the chapter goes on to define each one of the vows and expands on who observes which vows, how they may be supplemented, and what kinds of activities transgress them ([4], pp. 165–183).

The eighth chapter explains the causes of karmic bondage (Skt. bandha) and lists the types of bondage with their particular characteristics such as duration, intensity of fruition, and mass ([4], pp. 185–206). The ninth chapter describes the different ways and stages of inhibiting (Skt. saṃvara) the karmic influx and wearing off (Skt. nirjarā) of karmic matter ([4], pp. 209–247). The tenth chapter defines liberation (Skt. mokṣa) as the elimination (Skt. kṣaya) of all types of karma and describes the upward travel of liberated jīvas toward the edge of the cosmos as well as the circumstances under which jīvas may be liberated ([4], pp. 249–264).

Authority and Commentaries

The Tattvārtha-sūtra is one of the small number of texts that is considered as authoritative by all Jain traditions; both Śvetāmbaras and Digambaras claim it for their own and consider it as the heart of their teachings. The differences in their versions of it reflect the differences between their doctrines and practices and concern topics such as the necessity for mendicant nudity, the intake of food by omniscient beings, the acceptance of time as a substance, etc. (cf. [2], p. 82). It is not clear which tradition Umāsvāti/Umāsvāmin himself was affiliated with, but it may be presumed that he lived and wrote before the split of the Jain community had fully taken shape ([1], pp. 86–87).

Many authors from Śvetāmbara and Digambara traditions alike wrote commentaries to the contents of the Tattvārtha-sūtra. According to the Śvetāmbaras, Umāsvāti/Umāsvāmin wrote an autocommentary to the Tattvārtha-sūtra. It is called the Svopajña-bhāṣya and is not recognized as authentic by the Digambaras. The Śvetāmbara author Siddhasena Gaṇi (Gandhahastin) wrote a subcommentary to this autocommentary in the eighth century C.E. The most significant Digambara commentaries include Pūjyapāda's (Devanandi's) Sarvārthasiddhi (sixth century C.E.), Akalaṅka's Rājavārtika (eighth century C.E.), and Vidyānanda's Ślokavārttika (ninth century C.E.) ([1], p. 87; [2], pp. 82–83).

Cross-References

- Dravya (Jainism)
- Environmental Ethics and Jainism
- Jainism (Yakṣa)
- Jīva (Jainism)
- Karma (Jainism)
- Philosophy
- Reality (Jainism)
- Self (Jainism)

References

1. Dundas P (2002) The Jains. Routledge, London/New York
2. Jaini PS (1998) The Jaina path of purification. Motilal Banarsidass, Delhi
3. Ohira S (1982) A study of the Tattvārthasūtra with Bhāṣya. L. D. series no. 86. L. D. Institute of Indology, Ahmedabad
4. Tatia N (2011) That which is. Yale University Press, New Haven/London

Tattvasaṁgraha

Madhumita Chattopadhyay
Department of Philosophy, Jadavpur University, Kolkata, West Bengal, India

Definition

The text written by the Buddhist philosopher Sāntarakṣita.

Of the different texts which try to establish the essential doctrines of Buddhist philosophy in a critical manner by refuting the views of the opponents, *Tattvasaṁgraha* is an important one. This text is composed in verses. In Tibetan language this book is known as *De kho na ñid bsdus pahi tsig lehur byas pa,* a work containing the memorial verses on a summary of the *tattvas.* The author of this text is Śāntarakṣita, who is credited in the Tibetan tradition as one of the three persons who helped to establish Buddhism in the Land of Snows. He along with Khri Sang Lde Brtsan and Padmasambhava established the first monastery in Tibet named Samyen. The chief commentator of this text is Kamalaśīla whose commentary is known as *Tattvasaṁgrahapañjikā.*

From the very title of the text "*Tattvasaṁgraha*," it is indicated that this book is a compendium, a *saṁgraha* of the *tattva*-s, the true doctrine. The true doctrine here stands for the doctrine of dependent origination, and to establish that this is *the* true doctrine, doctrines of other schools, like those advocated by the Sāṁkhya, the Vaiśeṣikas, the Jainas, the Mīmāṁsakas, the Naiyāyikas, the Vedāntins, the Grammarians are refuted. The term *saṁgraha* indicates that in this book the author's task is to compile, to bring together to the mind the true doctrines scattered here and there in the Buddhist literature. The advantage of this act of compilation of true doctrines in one place is that it will be easier for the generation of the learners to apprehend those doctrines which would be very difficult for them to comprehend when they are scattered in different places. But mere comprehension of the true doctrines cannot be the sole aim for the composition of such a treatise since that task has already been done by older teachers. Hence, in this text, the motive is something more. Even though the true doctrines have been duly set forth by elder teachers, yet it is not easy for students of less intelligence to apprehend them since they are scattered. So, the target group of this book is such dull-witted students; for their easy comprehension of all the doctrines, they all are compiled under two covers. It is for this reason that the title is "Compendium of the true doctrines" and not the "Determination of true doctrines." Another important motive for this compilation has been indicated by the author himself in the introductory chapter of the text. That motive is described to be the desire to bring about the welfare of the world. Apparently, there is no connection between "the desire to bring about the welfare of the world" and "the compilation of the true doctrines." But the connection becomes clear when what the Buddhists mean by the welfare of the world is realized. The welfare consists in the attainment of prosperity and the Highest Good. And for this what is required is the removal of the misconceptions or the false notions, since all troubles are rooted in ignorance. The wrong notions can be removed only when there is true knowledge of the real connection between an action and its result, the doctrine of *pudgala*, *dharma*, and of no-soul. Right cognition of all this can be obtained from the present text through the elucidation of the doctrine of dependent origination; by listening to the elucidation, pondering over that elucidation, and contemplating it will generate proper knowledge of it. As such, it is claimed that the welfare of the world results from the act of compiling the true doctrines. In short, the aim of this treatise is twofold – the first one is compilation of the Buddhist doctrines scattered here and there within two covers so that any person, even the dull ones can have knowledge of them from a single treatise and the second one is the removal of false notions.

The text *Tattvasaṁgraha* consists of several chapters. Since the main aim of this book is to present the true doctrines of Buddhism and one such fundamental doctrine is the doctrine of dependent origination, the book starts with the examination of the doctrine concerning the origination of the world as advocated by different schools of Indian philosophy. So, first there is the discussion of the Sāṁkhya doctrine of primordial matter (*Prakṛti*) as the origin of the world. Then it proceeds to discuss the doctrine of God, the doctrine of both God and primordial matter, doctrine of "thing-by-itself," of word-sound (*Śabdabrahma*) as origin of the world. The second topic of discussion is the doctrine of soul or *ātman* as has been advocated by the Nyāya-Vaiśeṣikas, the Mīmāṁsakas, the Sāṁkhya, the Digambara Jainas, the Advaita Vedāntins, and the Vātsīputrīyas. The essential teaching of Lord Buddha consists in the doctrine of perpetual flux implying the doctrine of impermanence. From the point of view of this perpetual flux, all the various entities admitted by other schools like the *Prakṛti* or the primordial matter, God, the Soul, or *ātmā* can be easily discarded. As such, the author proceeds to establish with special care the doctrine of perpetual flux for the purpose of refuting all the entities discussed so far starting with primordial matter of the Sāṁkhya and ending with the *pudgala* admitted by the Vātsīputrīyas; and also those entities like the universal, substance, quality, etc. A problem arises at this point. If things are held to be impermanent or in perpetual flux, how could there be any such relation as the one subsisting between action and its results. It would also be difficult to explain different philosophical issues relating to (1) the apprehension of the causal relationship, (2) recognition following apprehension, remembrance (4) decisions taken after the cessation of doubt, (5) bondage and liberation. As such, after establishing the doctrine of perpetual flux, the author takes up for discussion in several chapters one after another the examination of action and reaction; examination of inherence; examination of different means of cognition like perception, inference, testimony, analogical cognition, presumption, negation, ratio-cination (*yukti*), non-apprehension (*anupalabdhi*), probability, tradition (*aitihya*), and *pratibhā*; examination of the doctrine of *traikālya* or things continuing to exist during three points of time; doctrine of self-sufficient validity; and examination of the person with super-normal vision. The text concludes with the hope that after going through all the discussions made here the whole mankind may attain the character of a lotus blooming under the rays of the sun of the Great Teachings.

Cross-References

▶ Insight
▶ Knowledge (Buddhism)

- Paṭiccasamuppāda
- Philosophy (Buddhism)
- Reality (Buddhism)
- Śabda
- Time (Buddhism)
- Universal

References

1. Jha GN (1986) The Tattvasaṃgraha of Shāntarakshita with the commentary of Kamalashīla. Motilal Banarsidass, Delhi, Reprint
2. Mookerjee S (1975) The Buddhist philosophy of universal flux. Motilal Banarsidass, Delhi, Reprint
3. Sāntarakṣita (1968) Tattvasaṃgraha with Tattvasaṃgrahapañjikā (Dvārikadas Sāstri, ed). Bauddha Bharati, Varanasi
4. Vidyabhushan SC (1977) A history of the mediaeval school of Indian logic. Oriental Books Reprint Corporation, New Delhi

Taxila (Greek and Latin)

- Takkasilā

Teaching

- Dharma (Jainism)

Testimony or Verbal Cognition

- Śabda

Thabs

- Upāya

The Bhaiṣajya Buddha

- Bhaiṣajyaguru

The Book of Analysis

- Vibhaṅga

The Book of Double Questions

- Yamaka

The Book of the Gradual Sayings

- Aṅguttara Nikāya

The Book of the Middle Length Sayings

- Majjhima Nikāya

The Buddha of Healing

- Bhaiṣajyaguru

The Diamond Cutter

- Vajrachhedika

The Diamond Sutra

- Vajrachhedika

The Healing Buddha

▶ Bhaiṣajyaguru

The Jewel of Transcendental Wisdom

▶ Vajrachhedika

The Lotus *Sūtra*

▶ Saddharmapuṇḍrīka Sūtra

The Medicine Buddha

▶ Bhaiṣajyaguru

The Pairs-Book

▶ Yamaka

The Path of Purification

▶ Visuddhimagga

The Path of Purity

▶ Visuddhimagga

The Perfection of Wisdom in Eight Thousand Lines

▶ *Aṣṭasāhasrikāprajñāpāramitā*

The Prakaraṇapada

▶ Yamaka

The State of the True Existence of Things

▶ Reality (Buddhism)
▶ Reality (Jainism)

The Sutra of the Explanation of the Profound and Secrets Meaning

▶ *Sandhinirmocana Sūtra*

The Tathagata

▶ Vajrachhedika

The Third Text of the Theravāda Abhidhamma Piṭaka

▶ Dhātukathā

The Vajrachchedika Prajñāpāramitā Sutra

▶ Vajrachhedika

The Way Things Really Are

▶ Reality (Buddhism)
▶ Reality (Jainism)

Theodicy

Walter Menezes
Department of Humanities and Social Sciences, Indian Institute of Technology Bombay, Mumbai, Maharashtra, India

Synonyms

Problem of evil

Definition

Theodicy can be defined as the "effort to defend God's justice and power" in a world marred by suffering.

Introduction

Theodicy is the defense of divine omnipotence and perfect goodness in the light of the problem of evil and suffering in the world. In the words of Milton's famous preface to *Paradise Lost*, theodicy means, to "justify the ways of God to men" (John Milton, *Paradise Lost* 1:25–26). It is an effort to justify the illness, suffering, and death of the children and the innocent persons at the hands of the wicked, and the unjust prosperity of the wicked at the expense of the just persons. Theodicy may thus be construed of as the effort to defend God's justice and power in the face of suffering in a world believed to be ruled by a morally good God [1].

The term theodicy was apparently coined by the philosopher Gottfried Leibniz (1646–1716) and is a compound of the Greek words *theos* (god) and *dike* (justice). Through the work of Leibniz and Christian Wolff the term came to encompass the general philosophical treatment of questions concerning God's existence and attributes. The term attempts to show why, given the world's evil, God may still be seen as good. Theodicy then, proceeds on the presumption that God is a responsible being, who bears responsibility for the world; and further, that His rulership ought to make some significant difference to the worldly condition [1, 2].

The Evil

The problem of theodicy is the result of the tension, found mainly in monotheistic religions, between the belief that the world is created by a God who is omnipotent, omniscient, and wholly good, and the observation that there exists immense evil and suffering in the world. Skeptics contend that the existence of evil is logically inconsistent with the fundamental religious beliefs – God's omnipotence, benevolence, and omniscience, etc. (see ► Omniscience). If evil exists, it seems either that God is unable to obliterate evil, whereby his omnipotence is denied, or that God does not want to obliterate evil, in which case his goodness is denied [2, 3]. Many religious systems have grappled with the problem of the existence of evil in a world, thought to have been created by a God that is infinitely good. In monotheistic religions, evil does not originate within the divinity nor, in general, within a divine world as it does, for instance, in Gnosticism; it arises instead from the improper use of freedom by created beings. In monistic religions, which are based on the opposition between the One and the many, there is a notion of evil as being that which is caused by decay or fragmentation of the One [1].

Theodicy Is in Various Religions

In accordance with their doctrines, each religion is challenged with the problem of evil in different ways. What is interesting to note is that only those religions which believe in absolute power of God are faced with the problem of evil, while atheistic religions are able to produce convincing defense for the problem of evil.

Theodicy in Judaism

The problem of evil has mainly challenged Christianity, Judaism, and Islam. In Judaism, the incomprehensibleness of God and of God's justice is emphasized. The rabbinical discussion contains several approaches to the problem of theodicy. The Hebrew Scriptures provided the basis for both Jewish and Christian theodicies [4, 5]. It emphasizes more prominently the freewill theodicy or retributive theodicy. This can be seen in Genesis, where in the beginning man had the freedom to choose good or bad. Later his suffering is seen as the consequence of human disobedience to God. In wisdom literature, especially the book of Job, the older theodicy is rejected. Job is an innocent man, blameless and righteous in every way; yet he suffers (Job. 1–2). The most decisive response to the problem of theodicy is found dissolved when God asked Job, "Where were you when I laid the foundations of the earth?" (38:4). Job repents his presumption: "I have uttered what I did not understand, things too wonderful for me, which I did not know" (42:3). Jewish teaching also stresses the educational and disciplinary value of suffering [6].

Theodicy in Christianity

New Testament assumes the theodicy of biblical and rabbinic thought. The crucifixion of Jesus clearly forms the focal point of New Testament for all Christian thinking about suffering. But the interpretation of this special event varies widely in accordance to the theodicies it brings forth [1, 5]. It is true that the crucifixion provides for Christians decisive evidence that not all who suffer are guilty. Nevertheless, the death of Jesus is also the result of almost every form of human weakness. Factionalism, nationalism, militarism, religious hypocrisy, greed, personal disloyalty, and pride all conspire here to effect the death of an innocent man. The fact that Christ is blameless provokes further questions of why he should be allowed to suffer at all. On one level, in many New Testament texts a qualified dualism makes its appearance, Evil and suffering are traced to the agency of demonic forces or to Satan (e.g., Mk. 5:1–13; Mt. 9:32–34; 12:22–24). On the another level, eschatological theodicy is vigorously reasserted, with Christ's resurrection furnishing proof that the righteous are able to vanquish all the forces of wickedness and to surmount suffering and death. The apostle Paul typically insists that the Resurrection is a source of personal hope and confidence for all who follow Christ (1 Cor. 5:15–19; 2 Cor. 4:14). Side by side with this and found everywhere from the Gospels to revelation is a vivid apocalyptic expectation. Christ is the "son of man" whose life (and death) will usher in the kingdom of God. In this kingdom, worldly hierarchies of reward will be overturned: "Many that are first will be last and the last will be first" (Mk. 10:31; Mt. 5:19), [6, 7].

St. Paul in Rom. 5:4–5 gives the educative theodicy, which calls upon Christians to rejoice in suffering because it produces endurance, character, and hope. Suffering also presents the opportunity to imitate Christ (1Cor. 11:1), who has shown that power is made perfect not in strength but in weakness (2 Cor. 12:9). Since all are sinners, what is extraordinary is not that some suffer in a world ruled by God, but that anyone is spared the divine wrath (Rom. 9:22–24). The fact that not all are punished is explained in terms of God's grace being manifest in Christ's vicarious suffering and in God's willingness to suspend the punishment for sin (Rom. 3:24), [6]. Thus, in the later part of the New Testament the retributive theodicy is strongly reinterpreted in strong eschatological and apocalyptic atmosphere of the time.

Theodicy in Calvinism

John Calvin went beyond Luther's idea of gratuitous salvation to that of the complete sovereignty of God. God is all in the order of ends as well as of means; everything tends toward His glory. "His essence is incomprehensible; hence his divineness far escapes all human perception" (*Institutes* 1.5.1). Thus Calvin conceives of God in terms of His supreme will that is absolute law, ". . .the truly just cause of all things" (*Institutes* 1.17.1). From it comes every decree by which all is ordered: God has "decreed what he was going to do, and now, by his might, carries out what he has decreed" (*Institutes* 1.16.8). Calvin's doctrine of double predestination to election or reprobation is on his conviction on the absolute sovereignty of God and on man's complete inability to contribute to his salvation. All are created by "God's eternal decree, by which he determined with himself what he willed to become of each man. For all are not created in equal condition; rather, eternal life is foreordained for some, eternal damnation for others" (*Institutes* 3.21.5). Calvin declares: "God's will is so much the highest rule of righteousness that whatever he wills, by the very fact that He wills it, must be considered righteous. When, therefore, one asks why has God so done, we must reply: because he has willed it" (*Institutes* 3.23.2). Thus every suffering is already predetermined by God [8, 26].

Theodicy in Arminianism

A system of belief that takes its name from Arminius (Jacobus Hermandszoon) expressed dissatisfaction with rigid Calvinist principles, especially the teaching that God had predestined some to be saved and others to be lost even before the Fall. These held the milder doctrine that while God foresaw the Fall, the formal decree was not made until after Adam's transgression. The major points of departure from stricter Calvinism contained there are: atonement was intended for all men and that man needs grace, yet is able to resist it and can even lose it. They denied the Calvinistic principle of absolute predestination and admitted the concurrence of free will and grace [9, 26].

Theodicy in Zoroastrianism

Zoroastrianism, ancient and current religion of Persia (modern Iran), named after its prophet Zarathustra, has often been said to have much in common with biblical teaching. Many scholars hold that Jewish beliefs on Satan and spirits good and evil, and especially eschatological beliefs such as judgment, resurrection, heaven, and a fiery burning hell, came into Judaism from Zoroastrianism during the exilic period through Israelite contact and association with the Persians. The eschatology of Zoroastrianism seems to point to the same restoration of idyllic perfection as does the book of Revelation, when good conquers evil. In Zoroastrianism, Angra Mainyu, the destroying spirit, is equated with the devil in Bible, is a primordial being equal in power to Ahuramazda [10, 11, 26]. Highlighting their complementarities this dual power, Prophet Zarathustra declared that "when these two spirits first came together, they created life and death" [12].

Theodicy in Islam

In Islamic tradition there is a strong emphasis on the omnipotence of God. This applies not only to the strong tradition of divine predestination, but also to the belief that human beings must obey and surrender to the will of God and that God is not accountable to human moral judgment. In his book *The House of Islam* (1975), Kenneth Cragg observes that because of its emphasis on God's transcendence, Islam "...does not find a theodicy necessary either for its theology or its worship" (p. 16). With one or two important qualifications, this is a reasonably accurate assessment of the state of theodicy in a tradition that insists on surrender to the divine will (one meaning of Islam) and finds it blasphemous to hold that God is accountable to human moral judgments. Nevertheless, while theodicy has not been a major preoccupation of Muslims, there are, especially in the earliest texts, implicit efforts to understand the sources of suffering and why God might allow it to exist. In the Quran the most persistent explanations and justifications of human suffering rests on the abuse of freedom by the creatures [11, 13].

Theodicy in Hinduism and Buddhism

The actuality of evil is a concern in many religions. India has found altogether a different answer to the problem of theodicy. In Buddhism and Hinduism since their principal goal is to be released from the suffering in the world, the question of divine justice and its possible conflict with suffering has not been a main concern. In Buddhism and Hinduism, the suffering is the fruit of the actions of the individual, which is known as the law of karma (see ▶ Karma); suffering cannot be blamed on the gods, for even the gods are submitted to karma [1, 14].

Pain or is a prominent feature of Hinduism, manifesting itself in an abundance of vicarious sacrifices. And the pervasiveness of the sacrifice principle shows up in the Aupaniṣadic statement that "All living bodies subsist on food grains, food grains are produced from rains, rains come from performance of sacrifice, and sacrifice is born of prescribed duties" ([15]; Ch. 3:14, p. 50). The whole purpose of different types of sacrifice is to arrive gradually at the status of complete

T

knowledge, then to gain release from material miseries, and ultimately, to engage in loving transcendental service to the Supreme Personality of Godhead (Kṛṣṇa). More fundamentally, all this sacrifice is based on Vedic understandings of origin of the cosmos. Human sacrifices are metaphorically linked with the original sacrifice by which the universe was created, namely, the dismemberment of the *Puruṣa*, the primal Being, by the Gods [15, 16].

In Hinduism karma or reincarnation is progressive. Over countless lifetimes an individual ātman (see ▶ Ātman) moves from mineral forms to plant, to animal, and to human. In incarnations as a Brahman, one comes closest to transcending māyā, and these are the only incarnations in which yogic and other spiritual practices are relevant. Each ātman eventually achieves conscious awareness of its true nature and escapes from the cycle of birth and death, a transformation commonly referred to as mokṣa, or liberation. The further implication of this teaching is that the gods may be neither blamed nor appealed to when suffering occurs. In Buddhism, belief in karma helps explain the subordinate place of God or the gods in the schema of salvation. Even gods are subject to law of karma, that they can plunge down from their lofty state should they err in their divine state. Thus, gods cannot be accountable for the human sufferings [17, 18].

Buddhism explicitly denies the gods any role in creation. The universe is conceived of as an ongoing, eternal, and cyclical process of becoming, and only an error on the part of the first born Tathāgata (see ▶ Tathāgata) allows him to think himself as the creator. Hinduism gives a more active role to the gods in this cyclic process of evolution and devolution. In Hinduism the creation is a process whereby every potentiality within the great God is allowed to manifest itself in the world of differentiation. This means that everything in creation, blessings and suffering, the gods and the demons, all good and all evil represent the working out of the divine plenitude. If creation is conceived in anthropomorphic terms at all, it is not a morally intentioned act for which God is accountable but an expression of the deity's spontaneous creativity or play [14, 18].

The answer to the question of how one may escape samsāra (see ▶ Saṃsāra) constitutes the core of teachings of Hindu and Buddhist traditions. The answers range from Hinduism's stress on the profound recognition that one's soul (ātman) is identical with being-itself (Brahman), and hence basically unaffected by the flux of becoming, to Buddhism's opposing insistence that there is no eternal soul capable of being affected by samsāra (the doctrine of anātman). Despite the enormous differences between these teachings, due to their independent tradition, in the issue of theodicy both traditions share a common perspective on suffering. Suffering or Dukkha (see ▶ Dukkha) is viewed as endemic to the world process, and the goal is extrication from this process. Suffering is not a reason for praising or blaming God. The legacy of the law of karma thus colors Indian thought from beginning to end, from its conception of the problem of suffering to that problem's resolution. The law of karma holds that suffering is the result of the operation of automatic law of moral retribution. In his sociology of religion (Boston, 1963), Max Weber characterized karma as "the most radical solution of the problem of theodicy" (p. 47). Because karma traces suffering to one's own thoughts and deeds, and because it denies the Gods any involvement in or control over the process of suffering, it is not a theodicy in our sense at all. But it is a fundamental dissolution of the theodicy problem as we encounter it in ethical monotheism [14, 19].

Within this intellectual context, theodicy in its classic sense finds little room for development. There is, therefore, in neither of these traditions any question of morally justifying the gods, and there is no real theodicy. Instead, the paramount religious questions become how (in popular Hinduism especially) one can procure some favor from the gods, how one can produce good karma, and how, finally, one can altogether escape samsāra, the world of karmic determined becoming. This question becomes more important when we realize that suffering is the part and parcel of this world.

Theodicy in Jainism

Jainism is a religious tradition that stretches back into the mists of Indian prehistory. It is originated by the practices and doctrines of wandering forest ascetics, known as *munis* or *shramanas*, who predated the arrival of the Vedas with the Aryan invasions. Historically documented Jainism is based upon the system of ideas and practices developed by Vardhamana Mahavira (c. 540–468 B.C.E.) in the sixth century B.C.E. The teachings of Mahavira have considerable overlap with those of the Buddha and of the late Upanishads, which developed around the same time. All three traditions integrate emphases of the ancient Shramana tradition, including reincarnation, karma, and liberation from *māyā,* or illusion, by ascetic and meditative practices. Jainism and Buddhism differ from the yoga and ascetic practices discussed in the Upaniṣads, however, in being atheistic and in regarding liberation as an individual matter rather than involving union with a transcendent God [16].

The principle of nonviolence or Ahimsā (see ▸ Ahimsa) dominates Jaina Philosophy. Their behavior inspires gentleness toward the rest of the beings. They subject themselves to the extreme act of self-denial, including notable indifference to pain. The Jainas do not believe in God. Their way to spiritual liberation lies in non attachment and patient, indifferent forbearance of all difficulties [16].

From the Jain perspective, the universe consists of two sorts of entities, *jivas,* or individual souls, and *ajīva,* or nonliving matter. Jīvas are in their essence free and omniscient, but their knowledge and freedom are obscured by a subtle form of matter, called karma. To the Jains, karma, the law of action and reaction, is a form of materialistic determinism, which keeps the soul bound to the world of illusion through many lifetimes [16].

Survey of Various Theodicies

Judeo-Christian Theodicies

Process Theology

Process philosophy is a movement by William James and Charles Hartshorne primarily by virtue of seeking to show how religion and science can be fused into one rational scheme of thought. It is a philosophy or a natural theology, because it bases its truth-claims not on the authority of any putative revelation but solely on the general philosophical criteria of adequacy and self-consistency. They maintain that the alleged contradiction between monotheism and suffering does not exist. The key to these positions is an understanding of what it means to say that God is omnipotent. Typically, it is argued that while God can do anything he wills himself to do and anything that is capable of being done, he cannot do what is logically impossible. This is not because his power is limited, but the very idea cannot be conceived, or renders nonsense. The best example could be "square circle." According to Process theology, the Christian understanding of God as almighty is not identical to the philosophical idea of a capacity to predetermine everything that happens, which is known as supernaturalism. It implies that God simply cannot occasionally interrupt the basic causal principles by which the world usually operates. God is all powerful in the sense of having all the power that one being could possibly have, but not in the sense of essentially having literally all the power, because that is impossible. To ask why god does not prevent various evils implies, therefore, a false metaphysics [9, 20–22].

God Wills Greatest Goodness

It is also not true that the all-powerful God necessarily wants to eliminate all the sufferings in the world. It could be conceived that the perfect being wants to bring about the greatest goodness in the world, and creating such a state may involve the creation of some specific goods whose existence logically entails the possibility of certain evils, and these evils may be the source of the suffering we see around us. The enterprise of theodicy, therefore, essentially involves the identification of those eminently valuable goods whose existence may entail certain states of suffering or evil. The proponents of theodicies claim that the world would be lesser good without the existence of such goods, whose existence brings about some evil [3].

The Freewill Theodicy

One of the most powerful and most frequently adduced explanations of suffering is the freewill theodicy. This position maintains that a world containing creatures who freely perform good actions and who freely respond to their creator's goodness is far better than a world of automatons, who are free determined to do right. To create a creature freely capable of doing what is morally right, therefore, God must create a creature that is also capable of doing what is morally wrong. Therefore, suffering is caused by the free exercise of the freedom applied wrongly, while some sufferings are the result of the punishment by God for the misconduct. The defenders of the freewill theodicy have sometimes traced natural evil to the agency of demonic beings, (fallen angels or Satan) whose own malevolence results from a perverse exercise of free will. They have also sometimes argued that natural evils are ongoing punishments for wrongful acts by humankind's first parents, so that suffering is a result of original sin [1].

Educative Theodicy

Another form of theodicy is the claim that suffering is an unavoidable means to a greater end. God's main goal is not to create a paradise on earth, but rather this world is a kind of school to prepare for heaven. Christian teaching often goes beyond the harmonious vision of Leibniz. Not only is suffering seen as an integral part of life, but God is also described as engaging in human misery by taking suffering upon himself through Jesus Christ. Within Christianity, there are divergent interpretations of why Christ assumes this vicarious suffering and what function it has. This theodicy of suffering educates to mold us into better beings, so that we can march toward the ultimate goal, which is liberation or mokṣa [1].

Eschatological Theodicy

Since human life is very short, justice should be calculated in terms of life after death. Millennialism is the belief expressed in the biblical Book of "Revelation to John" that Christ will establish a 1,000 year reign of the saints on earth before the Last Judgment. Millennialism offers a concrete vision of the fundamental eschatological belief that at the "end time" God will judge the living and the (resurrected) dead. This belief in an ultimate divine justice has provided a solution to the problem of Theodicy in the face of suffering and oppression for countless generations of believers – Jews, Christians, Muslims, and Buddhists. It has, therefore, had immense appeal in every age. All these efforts to defend the goodness of God in the face of the evil continue to be widely debated, but many give only partial explanations of evil. However, a theodicy must not only provide an intellectually satisfying explanation for evil, the explanation must be morally convincing [1].

Denial of Theodicy

The "problem of Theodicy" arises when the experienced reality of suffering is juxtaposed with two sets of beliefs traditionally associated with ethical monotheism. One is the belief that God is absolutely good and compassionate, and the other is that the all-powerful (omnipotent) and all-knowing (omniscient) God controls all events in the history. This belief entails a belief that the good and powerful being prevents sufferings of the humanity. Theodicy may be thought of as the effort to resist the conclusion that logical inconsistency exists when there is suffering in the world. It aims to show that traditional claims about God's power and goodness are compatible with the fact of suffering. According to J. L. Mackie "The problem of evil…, is a problem only for someone who believes that there is a God who is both omnipotent and wholly good" [23].

Denial of Justice

Some religious positions avoid theodicy by denying that God is morally good. Wendy Dongier O'Flaherty in her book *The Origins of Evil in Hindu Mythology* (Berkeley, 1976) has argued that at least one important motif in Hindu mythology traces suffering to the God's pettiness and fear of human power. It is a claim that God's justice is somehow quantitatively different from our ordinary human ideas or right or wrong. Sometimes what would be regarded as wickedness on the part of a human being, for example, the slaughter of children, may not be unjust where God is concerned. This view is dominant even in Islam and in Calvinist Christianity [17].

Denial of God's Omnipotence

Some religious thinkers avoided theodicy by qualifying divine power. This view is especially characteristic of religious dualism, which speaks of good and bad as two basic forces in the universe. In Zoroastrianism, for example, imperfections and suffering in this world are traced to an ongoing cosmic struggle between the good deity, Ahura Mazdā (Ohrmazd), and his evil antagonist, Angra Mainyu (Ahriman) [10]. Similarly, the Gnostic religion explains suffering in terms of a struggle between a "spiritual" God of goodness and light and an evil "creator" demon associated with darkness and matter [24]. Apart from religious dualism there are other ways by which religions can deny God's omnipotence. One of the most important of these is found in Buddhism, where suffering is traced to the automatic operation of the moral law of retribution known as law of karma. The law of karma eliminates the need to justify god in a world of suffering because it places that suffering almost wholly beyond divine control.

Denial of Suffering

We can avoid the problem of theodicy by denying the existence of the suffering in the world. Though it may seem to be impossible, in various ways, religious thinkers and religious traditions have sometimes denied the ultimate reality or the significance of suffering. Spinoza affirmed that the world is filled with evil only because we see it from erroneous human point of view. From the perspective of the divine, the world is a necessary perfect whole. Some Hindu thinkers also denied the reality of suffering by advocating adoption of the divine point of view. According to the vedāntic tradition, what we call evil or suffering is really an aspect of māyā, the cosmic principle of dynamism and individuation. This principle is not ultimate, and the seeker who attains the divine perspective sees māyā as an illusory process that does not really affect the eternal soul [7, 25].

Theodicy in Indian Religions

Comparison between the godlessness of Jainism or Buddhism, on the one hand, and the "god fullness" of Hinduism, on the other, exemplify clearly enough the insignificance of the god-notion in terms of human experience of pain and suffering. Jainism, much like its fellow non-Vedic Indian religion of Buddhism, advocates obliviousness to suffering. Jain positions exclude possibility of any meaningful discussion on other standard terms of theodicy such as "justice" or "fairness." In relation to demonstrating God's justice, Jainism and Buddhism might be called anti-theodicies, except that none of the two religions involves personal deities either culpable or justifiable. At the same time, it becomes evident that Hinduism's ubiquitous sacrifice makes no attempt to absolve its deities from accusations of injustice. Sacrifice in Hinduism teaches how the universe began; worship of the goddess Kali may even involve human sacrifice. Thus, contrary to the popular expectations, godliness and godlessness do not necessarily present with the appropriate alternatives for relating to the misery of pain and suffering.

This limited survey of theodicy in various religions clarify how some human beings have related to the presence of pain and suffering with carefully developed philosophical systematizations on suffering as a part of their religious experience. Across the range of integrative attempts there appears to be some general distinction between those whose response is "God-bound," and others whose view is atheistic. Therefore, the statement of Mackie can be slightly modified, as "that the problem of evil is only a problem for someone who believes that God is sovereign, and in control over the creation. For it would be no more or less a problem if God, however conceived, were incapable of control, than if he is simply denied existence." In accordance with this, above theories can be summarized in as many as six positions (see Table 1), beginning, not with atheistic irreligion, but with godless religions such as Jainism and Buddhism which, self-evidently, do not involve systematizations on the relation of God to suffering. In relation to demonstrating God's justice, these religions produce what may be called anti-theodicies. The second position would be occupied by the godless nonreligion where, despite

Theodicy, Table 1 Religions continuum on "Religious Faiths and the Problem of Evil"

Position 1	**Position 2**	**Position 3**	**Position 4**	**Position 5**	**Position 6**
Godless Religions -Jainism, Buddhism etc	Godless non-Religions -Atheism, Agnosticism	Polytheism -Hinduism, Animism	Dualism -Zorastrianism	Christian Theodicy–A -Double Predestinariam Calvinism	Christian Theodicy-B -Arminianism

the denial of God, humans agonize over life's unfairness and injustice. The third position would be occupied by the polytheistic uncertainty of Hinduism, animism, and indigenous religions where there is a noticeable degree of relation between God and suffering of humankind, in which the law of karma is the measuring scale. A fourth position would be occupied by the dualism of Zoroastrianism, in which polarity of the position would noticeably entail pain and suffering and thereby, to a larger extent, the application of the notion of theodicy, while the final two positions would both be held by Calvinism and Arminianism, which attempt to show that salvation by grace integrates fully with the presence of the physical pain in the world. While Calvinism does not fully accommodate human freedom, Ariminianism believes in a God of unmodified omniscience, power, and love, whose grace is concurrent with the free will of beings.

Conclusion

Along with the corrosive effect of modern scientific knowledge, the problem of innocent suffering poses one of the greatest challenges to ethical monotheism in our day. In the wake of the present-day mass sufferings, we may be impelled to conclude the nonexistence of God. Some others have been drawn to various dissolutions of the theodicy problem, ranging from the eastern stress on karma to an extreme fideism that abandons the insistence of God's justice. Before rejecting ethical monotheism or the theodicies it has stimulated, however, it is worth keeping in mind that both spring from a profound moral intentionality. Ethical monotheism expresses the conviction that a supreme power guides reality and that this power is characterized by righteousness and love. Theodicy is the effort to sustain this conviction in the face of innocent suffering. Theodicy need not be defense or a justification for supreme power, for it sounds absolutely absurd to justify that which is not accessible to human reason. It becomes more sensible to understand and assume the fundamental designs of the world in relation to the authorship of a Supreme Power. Very many religions justify the notion of world-order, fancied by the erroneous human rationality. But the problem of theodicy refuses to be contained by the human reason, and occasionally gives the glimpse of the authorship of a higher being, which is capable of designing the world independent of human involvement. Theodicy, therefore, is often less an effort to provide an account of the hope and confidence that despite various resistances, goodness, and righteousness will triumph. Theodicy may not violate the requirements of logic, nor may it ignore the experienced reality of suffering. Theodicy's deepest impulse, however, is not to report the bitter facts of life but to overcome and transform them.

Cross-References

▶ Ahimsa
▶ Ātman
▶ Dukkha
▶ Karma
▶ Omniscience
▶ Saṃsāra
▶ Tathāgata

References

1. Latto A, De Moor JC (eds) (2003) Theodicy in the world of the Bible. Brill, Boston
2. Pinnock SK (2002) Beyond theodicy. State University of New York Press, Albany
3. Wainwright WJ (1982) The Oxford hand book of philosophy. Wisconsin, Milwaukee
4. D'souza PJ (2010) Stronger than death; intimations of afterlife in the book of psalms. Dhyanavana, Bangalore
5. Crenshaw JL (2005) Defending god; biblical responses to the problem of evil. Oxford University Press, New York
6. Wansbrough H (ed) (2007) The New Jerusalem Bible. The Bombay Saint Paul Society, Bandra, Bombay
7. Stoeber M (2005) Reclaiming theodicy; reflections on suffering, compassion and spiritual transformation. Palgrave Macmillan, New York
8. McNeill JT (ed) (1960) Institutes of the Christian religion, 2 vols. Westminster Press, Philadelphia
9. Thomas LE (ed) (2001) Issues in contemporary philosophy of religion, vol 23. Kluwer, London
10. Yamauchi EM (1990) Persia and the Bible. Baker, Grand Rapids
11. Hick J (1977) Evil and the god of love, 2nd edn. Macmillan, London
12. Stanley I (Tr) (1977) Yasna 30: in the Gathas of Zarathustra. Prentice Hall, Upper Saddle River
13. Nasr SH (2003) Islam; religion, history and civilization. HarperCollins, New York
14. Herman AL (1976) The problem of evil and Indian thought. Motilal Banarsidass, Delhi
15. Prabhupada AC, Swami B (1972) Bhagavad-Gita as it is, abridged. The Bhaktivedanta Book Trust, Los Angeles/New York
16. Fisher MP (1997) Living religions, 3rd edn. Prentice Hall, New Jersey
17. O'Flahery WD (1976) The origin of evil in Hindu mythology. Motilal Banarsidass, Delhi
18. Obeyeskere G (1968) Theodicy, sin, and salvation in a sociology of Buddhism. In: Leach ER (ed) Dialectic in practical religion. Cambridge University Press, Cambridge
19. Weber M (1963) Sociology of religion. Beacon, Boston
20. Frankenberry N (1981) Some problems in process theodicy. Relig Stud 17:181–184
21. Peterson ML (1988) God and evil: an introduction to the issues. Westview Press, Oxford
22. Griffin DR (1976) God, power, and evil: a process theodicy. Westminster Press, Philadephia
23. Mackie JL (1990) Evil and omnipotence. In: Adams MM, Adams RM (eds) The problem of evil. Oxford Readings in Philosophy. Oxford University Press, USA
24. Pagels E (1989) The Gnostic gospels. Vintage Books, New York
25. Bowker J (1970) Problem of suffering in the religions of the world. Cambridge University Press, Cambridge
26. Obeyeskere G (1963) Theodicy, salvation, and Rebirth. In: Weber's sociology of religion (trans: Fischoff E). Beacon Press, Boston

Thera- and Therīgāthā

K. T. S. Sarao
Department of Buddhist Studies, University of Delhi, Delhi, India

Synonyms

Elders' verses; Poems of early Buddhist monks; Poems of early Buddhist nuns; Psalms of the brethren; Psalms of the sisters; Verses of the elder monks; Verses of the elder nuns

Definition

Theragāthā and Therīgāthā are respectively the eighth and ninth books of the *Khuddaka Nikāya*

T

which in turn is the fifth of the five divisions of the Pāli *Sutta Piṭaka.*

The *Theragāthā* and the *Therīgāthā* are the eighth and the ninth books respectively of the *Khuddaka Nikāya. Theragāthā*, often translated as *Verses of the Elder Monks* (Pāli: *thera* = elder (masculine noun) + *gāthā* = verse), is a collection of 107 poems with 1,279 *gāthās* (verses), arranged into 21 chapters (*nipāta*s). These short poems were apparently narrated by early members of the Buddhist saṃgha. Whereas some of these poems contain biographies of the *theras*, there are some others which are paeans to the newly discovered freedom, joyfulness, and solitude by these *theras*. A large number of the *gāthās* of the *Theragāthā* relate to efforts by monks to overcome the snares of Māra (the Evil One). The procedure followed in the arrangement of these *gāthās* is what is generally followed in the Buddhist literature, namely, the single verses are place in the beginning, followed by the dyads, triads, etc. The number of *theras* who are supposed to have uttered these *gāthās* is 264. Notable poems from the *Theragāthā* include the third poem of Chap. 17, in which Ānanda mourns the passing away of the Buddha, his esteemed cousin and master and the eighth poem of Chap. 16, which consists of *gāthās* uttered by Aṅgulimāla, the reformed killer. A commentary on the *Theragāthā*, as part of the *Paramatthadīpanī*, was written by Thera Dhammapāla, probably in the sixth century C.E.

The *Therīgāthā*, the ninth book of the *Khuddaka Nikāya*, is the natural companion to the *Theragāthā.* It is often translated as *Verses of the Elder Nuns* (Pāli: *therī* = elder (feminine noun) + *gāthā* = verse). It consists of 73 short poems apparently uttered by early members of the saṃgha. These poems, consisting of 494 *gāthās*, are organized into 16 chapters. The actual number of nuns who spoke these verses is 73 ([2], p. 81). The importance of the *Therīgāthā* lies in the fact that this is the first surviving poetry supposed to have been composed by women in India. Thus, despite its small size, this text is an extremely important document not only in the study of early Indian Buddhism but also in gender studies. Some of the *gāthās* of the *Therīgāthā* strongly support the view that women are equal to men in terms of spiritual accomplishment. It is worthy of notice that the poetically excellent quality of these verses is not matched by Indian poetesses of later periods ([7], p. 54). Some of the important *gāthās* in the *Therīgāthā* are of a former courtesan who became a nun ([5], Vol. v, p. 2), a mother who was traumatized by the death of her child ([5], Vol. vi, pp. 1, 2), an affluent woman who gave up her life of luxuries and abundance ([5], Vol. vi, p. 5), and above all, of Gotamī Pajāpatī, the Buddha's stepmother and officially the first nun of Buddhism ([5], Vol. vi, p. 6). Some of the nuns whose *gāthās* exist in the *Therīgāthā* also have their *gāthās* is the *Apadāna*, another book of the *Khuddaka Nikāya.* As for the *Theragāthā*, Dhammapāla also wrote a commentary on the *Therīgāthā*, as part of the *Paramatthadīpanī.*

As the *gāthās* of the *Theragāthā* and the *Therīgāthā* are utterances of monks and nuns, these two texts cannot be thought of as *buddhavacana.* Moreover, although they are largely parallel in terms of their structure and contents, there are some differences of minor nature between the two of them. While all the *gāthās* of *Theragāthā* are unambiguously ascribed to a monk, some of the *gāthās* of the *Therīgāthā* are anonymous ([7], p. 52). Another peculiarity of the *Therīgāthā* is the vocatives in the verses: the nun is either addressed by someone or she addresses herself; which is the case cannot be decided ([7], p. 52). Probably both *Theragāthā* and *Therīgāthā* grew over a long period of time, slowly absorbing verses commemorating monks and nuns living at quite different periods of time ([7], p. 53). In fact, some of the *gāthās* appear to be as late as the Third Council which took place during the reign of King Aśoka ([3], p. 73). The importance of the *Theragāthā* and the *Therīgāthā* lies in the fact that their *gāthās* provide an exclusive glimpse into very early Indian poetry which is otherwise entirely lost. Thus, poetical figures (*alaṃkāra*) known from much later poetry can be found here for the first time and they are an example "of the highly valuable and beautiful poetry once existing in ancient India" ([7], p. 53). No doubt, it has been suggested by an eminent scholar that the *Theragāthā* and the *Therīgāthā* "can stand with dignity by virtue of their power and beauty by the side of the best products of Indian lyric – right from the hymns of the Ṛgveda up to the lyrical poems of Kālidāsa and Amarsu" ([8], p. 98).

Cross-References

▶ Apadāna
▶ Aśoka
▶ Dhammapāla
▶ Khuddaka Nikāya
▶ Nuns (Buddhism)
▶ Saṃyutta Nikāya
▶ Thera- and Therīgāthā

References

1. Lienhard S (1984) A history of classical poetry in Sanskrit, Pāli, Prakrit. Otto Harrassowitz, Biesbaden
2. Mizuno K (1993) A comparative study of the Theragāthā and the Therīgāthā. Buddh Stud (Bukkyō Kenkyū) 22:3–83 (in Japanese)
3. Norman KR (1983) Pāli literature including the canonical literature in Prakrit and Sanskrit of all Hīnayāna Schools of Buddhism. Otto Harrassowitz, Wieswaden
4. Oldenberg H, Pischel R (eds) (1990) Theragāthā (with Appendices by K.R. Norman & L. Alsdorf), 2nd edn. Pali Text Society, Oxford
5. Oldenberg H, Pischel R (eds) (1990) Therīgāthā (with Appendices by K.R. Norman & L. Alsdorf), 2nd edn. Pali Text Society, Oxford
6. Pruitt W (ed) (1997) Therīgāthā commentary (Paramatthadīpanī VI): commentary on the Therīgāthā by Dhammapāla. Pali Text Society, Oxford
7. von Hinüber O (2008) A handbook of Pāli literature, 3rd Indian edn. Munshiram Manoharlal, New Delhi
8. Winternitz M (1983) History of Indian literature (Eng. trans: Sarma VS), rev. edn, vol II. Motilal Banarsidass, Delhi
9. Woodward FL (ed) (1940–1959) Paramatthadīpanī: Theragāthā-Aṭṭhakathā. The commentary of Dhammapālācariya, 3 vols. Pali Text Society, London

Theravāda

Ana Bajželj
Department of Philosophy, Faculty of Arts, University of Ljubljana, Ljubljana, Slovenia
Polonsky Academy, The Van Leer Jerusalem Institute, Jerusalem, Israel

Abbreviations

S	Samyutta Nikāya
Vin	Vinaya

Synonyms

Doctrine of the elders; Early Buddhism; Hīnayāna; Mainstream Buddhism; Nikāya Buddhism; Orthodox Buddhism; Schools of early Buddhism; Southern tradition of Buddhism

Definition

Theravāda literally means the doctrine (vāda) of the elders (thera). The term is used to refer to the only school of the pre-Mahāyāna Indian Buddhism that has survived up to the present day. Today, this tradition continues to be present mainly in Śri Laṅka, Cambodia, Laos, Thailand, and Burma, with approximately 100 million followers.

Name

Theravāda Buddhism is frequently referred to as Hīnayāna Buddhism. This name is problematic in several ways. The term Hīnayāna has a pejorative connotation as it literally denotes the lesser or the inferior (hīna) vehicle (yāna). As such, it was used by the later Mahāyāna (lit. great vehicle) Buddhism, in order to emphasize the difference between the two and the constrictive nature of the former. Due to such a polemical nature of the term Hīnayāna, several alternative names have been suggested to indicate the period of Indian

T

Buddhism that preceded Mahāyāna, namely, early Buddhism, mainstream Buddhism, Nikāya Buddhism, orthodox Buddhism, etc. Furthermore, it is problematic to equate Hīnayāna with Theravāda since the former term is much broader than the latter. Following the Buddha's death, the early period of Indian Buddhism saw a gradual split of the Buddhist community into several branches or ordination lineages (nikāya). As a result, already in the first century B.C.E. there were supposed to exist at least 18 schools of Buddhism and the texts make reference to even more than that. Out of them, only one has survived up to the present times, namely, Theravāda Buddhism. Today, this branch of Buddhism continues to exist in Śri Laṅka, Cambodia, Laos, Thailand, and Burma. Because of its prevalence in the countries of South Asia, Theravāda Buddhism is also referred to as southern Buddhism. What is important to point out is that Theravāda school represents only one of the many early schools of Buddhism, and consequently may not simply be equated with terms used to denote early Buddhism in general, such as Hīnayāna. However, as the only survivor of the early Buddhist tradition, it is often referred to in this way. Additionally, there are other grounds on which Theravāda may be directly associated with Hīnayāna. The Mahāyāna notion that all fundamental components of existence are empty of an independent self, as proposed in the Prajñāpāramitā-sūtras, is contested in the text called Kathāvatthu (Points of Discussion) of the Theravāda Abhidhamma-piṭaka. Furthermore, this same text refutes the Mahāyāna proposition that numerous Buddhas may simultaneously exist in different worlds. Additionally, the two traditions of Theravāda and Mahāyāna are typically set apart with regard to the ideal of a bodhisattva that is considered to have been accepted merely by the Mahāyāna tradition in contrast with the arahant (Skt. arhat) ideal of the Theravāda. This distinction is then taken to rationalize the linking of the Theravāda with the lesser vehicle. However, this last point is a mistaken assumption since the Theravāda tradition also accepted the bodhisattva ideal even though its role may not have been as prominent as in the Mahāyāna tradition.

The origin of the name Theravāda goes back to the initial split of the original body of the followers of the Buddha into the Mahāsāṃghika and Sthavira schools. The latter is considered to be the more orthodox of the two and the name "sthavira" is a Sanskrit equivalent of the Pāli term "thera." The term literally means the doctrine (vāda) of the elders (sthavira/thera), indicating that this school is the oldest (and thus the most authentic) of all. The Theravāda tradition considers itself to be the direct descendent of this early orthodox tradition.

Origins

As noted, the Theravāda school of Indian Buddhism originated from the Sthaviravāda branch that arose as a result of the first split of the original Buddhist community (saṅgha). During the life of the Buddha, the Buddhist community was one of the samaṇa (Skt. śramaṇa) groups in India, that is, one of the several groups of wandering ascetics. During the rainy season, the saṅgha stopped for a more concerted religious practice. Additionally, the Buddhist monastics would use this time to reach the laity. The monks or bhikkhus (Skt. bhikṣu) and nuns or bhikkhunīs (Skt. bhikṣuṇī) would regularly spend their rainy periods at same places and soon these turned into permanent settlements for monastic communities. The Buddha conveyed the rules of monastic discipline and encouraged the saṅghas to hold recurrent assemblies to establish agreements over the nature of the monastic conduct. At the time of the Buddha's death, the number of monks and nuns that followed him is considered to be around 1,250. Soon (probably a couple of weeks) after their teacher's death about 500 arahants gathered in Rājagaha (Skt. Rājagṛha) for a communal recitation in order to compare the memorized doctrines. By doing so, they were set to authenticate the discourses as the words of the Buddha (buddha-vacana) and accordingly establish the true content of the Buddha's teaching. The aim was also to form a corpus that would be possible to commit to memory and hence would be suitable for oral transmission. This outlining of the common ground of the Buddhist community intended to restrict its disintegration into various segments. At the first council, the instructions of the Buddha were recited by Ānanda, a monk, a loyal disciple, and a close relative of the Buddha. He was chosen to be the final evaluator in verifying the authenticity of the content of the Buddha's teaching that was being recollected. The parts of the content that Ānanda authorized were then assembled into various collections. These were memorized by several monks who were set with a task to pass them on to others, and these accounts of the Buddha's original teaching were orally transmitted to the next generations. This part of the Buddhist teaching or dhamma (Skt. dharma) is known as the suttas (Skt. sūtra). Another part of the buddhadhamma is the monastic discipline or vinaya, which was recited at the first council by a monk named Upāli. Vinaya is composed of rules of monastic conduct or pāṭimokkha (Skt. prātimokṣa) and imparts the historical account of their establishment as well as further development. Around 70 years after the first council, the Buddhist monastic community gathered again at Vesālī (Skt. Vaiśālī) in order to reprimand monastics who were negligent in observing certain vows, that is, receiving money, etc. About 16 years later the third council took place at Pāṭaliputta (Skt. Pāṭaliputra) and this is where the first split (saṅgha-bheda) of the Buddhist community, that was previously unified, is thought to have occurred. According to the textual sources, after that yet another council at Pāṭaliputta, convened by king Asoka (Skt. Aśoka), took place. During the reign of the King Asoka, Buddhism was adopted as the state religion and was spread around the whole of India. There is a speculation that during the second council in Pāṭaliputta the principal method employed was analysis or vibhajja (Skt. vibhajya), otherwise used by the Vibhajjavādins, the monastic precursors to Theravāda Buddhism. This council is deemed to have been managed by a Buddhist monk by the name of Moggaliputta Tissa (Skt. Maudgaliputra Tiṣya) and was primarily aimed at resolving the disagreements over the Buddhist monastic practice, and at refuting the heterodox views. As a consequence, 60,000 monks are thought to have been banished from the community. Around a 1,000 from those that remained were chosen to verify which contents of the canon were the genuine instructions of the Buddha. The record of this doing is preserved in the abovementioned Moggaliputta Tissa's Kathāvatthu (Points of Discussion), a text that outlines the deviating views, recording around 200 points of disagreement, and puts forward their repudiations. Moreover, King Asoka declared an edict critical of the splitting up of the Buddhist community. The fifth council took place in the first century C.E. in the northwestern part of India. It was organized by another early school of Buddhism, called Sarvāstivāda.

The first split, that perhaps occurred as a reaction to an attempt of somewhat expanding the list of monastic rules or rather as a refusal to accept new monastic practices that had emerged, resulted in the arising of two separate branches, namely, the reformist Sthaviravāda (lit. the doctrine of the elders) and the prevailing Mahāsāṃghika (lit. the great monastic community). It is probable that the followers of the former which were in minority, tried to integrate a few novel regulations that were more restricting and could not reach a consensus about the reform with the majority of the followers of the latter, which resulted in a split. Even though the initial division of the Buddhist community is generally linked to the third council, it should be noted that the Chinese pilgrims and translators as well as later chronicles in the Pāli language associate the first fragmentation of the original body of Buddhists with either the first or the second council mentioned. Whichever the case, the cause of the division was most likely some sort of a disagreement over different ordination lineages and the correct monastic discipline, which were possibly the main reasons for further divisions within the Buddhist community as well. This supposition is supported by the Mahāsāṃghika and Theravāda sources. Six different codes of discipline have been preserved to this day, namely, the Sarvāstivāda, Mahāsāṃghika, Mahīśāsaka, Dharmaguptaka, Theravāda, and Mūlasarvāstivāda. These six thus represent separate monastic communities with

T

independent lineages. Despite the differences in codes of discipline the relationship between these groups is supposed to have been respectful rather than adverse. The Sthaviravāda sources, on the other hand, claim the doctrinal differences to be the root of the communal fragmentation. However, it is generally accepted that different interpretations of the doctrine were most likely not the foremost cause for actual sectarian divisions, unless they affected the rules of monastic conduct. In fact according to the Pāli Vinaya, the only view that a monastic could be denounced for was an unrelenting contention that sensual pleasure is acceptable. This fairly noninterventionist atmosphere implies that monastics with a specific doctrinal conviction probably lived in a variety of monastic communities. Various names, given to different doctrinal interpretations, thus primarily had a methodological purpose for teaching and scholastic discussions rather than a noteworthy implication for the way of the monastic living. The doctrinal differences thus initially led merely to the delineation of different schools of interpretation (vāda) and these, only by around the second century B.C.E., started to also entail the differences between monastic communities. By the first century C.E., the doctrinal dissimilarities had the potential to result in sectarian divisions and accordingly the distinction between what was considered to be a "monastic community" and a "school" diminished as well. However, it must be emphasized that even after the splitting up, the schools would frequently continue to share the same monasteries. It was therefore the monastic discipline, the initial important function of which was to distinguish Buddhist monastics from their contemporaries that belonged to other religious traditions, which was most likely also the cause of the fragmentation within the Buddhist monastic community itself.

It is traditionally put forward that from the initial split of the community to the first century B.C.E. 18 different schools of Buddhism had developed. However, it seems that the number 18 is merely symbolic and that the schools were even more numerous. Since Theravāda Buddhism emerged from the Sthaviravāda branch of early Buddhism, this line of schools will be considered in more detail than the Mahāsṃghika tradition. At least six different schools (Ekavyāvahārika, Lokkottaravāda, Gokulika, Bahuśrutīya, Prajñaptivāda, and Caitika) of thought emerged from the Mahāsāṃghika branch. The Mahāsāṃghikas introduced the doctrine called lokottara-vāda, which declares the Buddha to be supramundane (lokottara), transcending the limitations of the human world. For them, the Buddha was thus never actually in the world but merely appeared to be so out of compassion. By the third century B.C.E., three schools developed from the Sthaviravāda branch of early Buddhism, namely, Puggalavāda (Skt. Pudgalavāda), Sabbatthivāda (Skt. Sarvāstivāda), and Vibhajjavāda (Skt. Vibhajyavāda).

At their time Puggalavāda represented one of the most dominant traditions of Buddhism and it is recorded that in the seventh century C.E. the only larger group were the adherents of Mahāyāna Buddhism. Their textual sources are, however, scarce and consequently the information on this school of early Indian Buddhism remains indefinite to a large extent. The point of differentiation with the other early Buddhist traditions was their acceptance of the reality of the concept of personhood or puggala (Skt. pudgala). The other schools marked the notion of personhood as untrue and understood it as a mere conventional denotation for a constantly changing stream of the five factors of existence or khandhas (Skt. skandha), namely, form or rūpa, feelings or vedanā, cognition or saññā (Skt. saṃjñā), volitions or saṅkhāra (Skt. saṃskāra), and consciousness or viññāṇa (Skt. vijñāna). Accordingly, they recognized the Puggalavāda's insistence on the reality of puggala as contradicting the basic Buddhist doctrine of no-self or anattā (Skt. anātman). However, the Puggalavādins claimed puggala, which they accepted as real, to be different from the changeless self of the Vedic streams of thought. Furthermore, they maintained that the relationship between the puggala and the five khandhas may not be described either as a relationship of identity or difference. They consequently declared the nature of puggala to be inexplicable. The adherents of Puggalavāda got sectioned into several schools, amongst which were the Vātsīputrīyas, the Dharmottarīyas, the Bhadrayānīyas, the Sāṃmitīyas, and the Ṣaṇṇāgārikas.

The Sabbatthivāda school of early Buddhism reified the notion of dhamma (Skt. dharma) and defined it as an undividable element of reality that has a unique own-nature or sabhāva (Skt. svabhāva) that is inherent to it. The name of this school of thought derives from its distinctive doctrine that not only the present dhammas but also the past and the future dhammas exist. Therefore, the name "sabba atthi" or "everything exists." Later the school was also named Vaibhāṣika, referring to the tradition that follows the commentary of the Sabbatthivāda-abhidhamma, titled Mahāvibhāṣā. An important offshoot of the Sabbatthivāda tradition was the school of Sautrāntika which rejected many of the dhammas introduced by the Sabbatthivāda as well as its notion that "everything exists," and maintained the existence of dhammas to be momentary.

The third school was known as the Vibhajjavāda or the school of analysis and got its name after the analytical method of the suttas, called a vibhajja (Skt. vibhajya). The Vibhajja school of thought for the most part rejected the reification of the basic constituents of reality and followed the more traditional interpretation of their nature as experiential. Its adherents claimed dhammas to be conditioned, the only unconditioned one amongst them being nibbāna. Their interpretation of sabhāva or own-nature differed from the Sabbatthivāda understanding of this term. For Vibhajjavādins own-nature implied merely dhamma's distinctiveness due to its conditioned nature. Additionally, this school of thought contested the Sabbatthivāda and Puggalavāda stance on the nature of an arahant. Whereas the latter two maintained that it is possible for an arahant to regress from this level of attainment, the Vibhajjavādins claimed the one who could regress from arahantship not to be a true arahant. The Theravāda tradition followed this branch of the Sthaviravāda school, which considered itself to be the most orthodox interpreter of the old tradition. Other offshoots of the Vibhajja branch were the Mahīśāsaka and the Kāśyapīya as well as the Dharmaguptakas that developed from the former of the two.

Texts

The canon of the Theravāda school is called the Tipiṭaka (Skt. Tripiṭaka) or the Pāli canon and is regarded by the Theravādins to be the true word of the Buddha, either directly or indirectly through his approval. The Pāli canon is the only canon of the early Buddhist schools that has been maintained in its entirety to this day. This collection of texts is also the only early Buddhist canon that has been completely preserved in the original Indian language, namely, Pāli. The word Pāli probably originates with the commentarial tradition which referred to the language of the canonical texts as Pāli or Pāḷi, a word literally meaning "a line" or "a text." Pāli was one of the vernacular languages of India, called Prākrits, and is closely related to Sanskrit. The name Tipiṭaka (lit. three baskets) refers to the structure of the canon that consists of three major units or piṭakas (lit. baskets) of texts, these being the Vinaya-piṭaka, the Sutta-piṭaka (Skt. Sūtra-piṭaka), and the Abhidhamma-piṭaka (Skt. Abhidharma-piṭaka). The Vinaya basket contains texts that mostly deal with the monastic order and discipline. The second basket of Suttas is largely comprised of the Buddha's discourses and is divided into four parts, which are termed Nikāyas (lit. collection or group) or Āgamas (lit. canonical text, tradition, or authority). They are subdivided into Dīgha-nikāya (Skt. Dīgha-nikāya), Majjhima-nikāya (Skt. Madhyama-nikāya), Samyutta-nikāya (Skt. Samyutta-nikāya), and Aṅguttara-nikāya (Skt. Ekottara-nikāya). The Dīgha-nikāya or The Collection of Long Discourses contains the most extensive discourses, the Majjhima-nikāya or the Collection of Middle Discourses contains the medium-length discourses, the Samyutta-nikāya or Connected Discourses comprises short discourses that are thematically linked, and the Aṅguttara-nikāya or Discourses Increasing by One contains discourses organized in an ascending arrangement according to the number of terms they attend to. It is of particular importance here to mention the fifth Nikāya that has not been included in the list above. This Nikāya is titled Khuddaka-nikāya (Skt. Kṣudraka-nikāya) and is sometimes considered to represent the oldest

T

strata of the canon. However, certain early Buddhist schools rejected it as inauthentic. The third basket, namely, the Abhidhamma, represents the foundation of the doctrinal developments of the Theravāda tradition. It contains systemized scholastic study and philosophical interpretation of the topics dealt with in the Buddha's instructions. It is traditionally explained that the Abhidhamma articulates the Buddhist dhamma in general philosophical terms in contrast with the Suttas in which these abstract notions are applied to specific situations. The term abhidhamma is very complex in meaning, and according to the traditional sources, it may be translated either as a "higher" or a "further" (abhi) exploration of "the Buddhist teaching" (dhamma) or "with regard to" (abhi) "the instructions of the Buddha" (dhamma). It is speculated that abhidhamma originates in the standardization of the Buddhadhamma, which includes the making of systematic lists of basic teachings, called mātikā (Skt. mātṛkā). Some accounts in the traditional sources suggest that the first time these lists were compiled was during the first council, along with the sutta and vinaya recitations. The abhidhamma elaborated on these key instructions and explained the implicit aspects of the Buddhist doctrine, that is, those that may have been left out in the suttas. Thus, it attempted to outline an intellectual framework for soteriological purposes. Whereas the vinaya and sutta texts of different early Buddhist canons mostly overlap, their abhidhammas differ greatly. Despite the fact that the teaching of abhidhamma evolved with a practical intention to further explain the received instruction of the Buddha by applying new techniques, it soon resulted in novel doctrinal developments and the production of accompanying texts. In fact, various abhidhammas developed concurrently with the fragmentation of the Buddhist community into different schools of thought. They represented the basis and the means for the formation of schools, and furthermore, interscholastic debates. The abhidhammas thus became the focal point of the scholarly Buddhist monastics. In this manner they had an enourmous influence on the Mahāyāna philosophies as well. The Theravāda Abhidhamma-piṭaka is divided into seven books:

1. Dhammasaṅgaṇī (Enumeration of factors) specifies and elaborates on various aspects of experience that are ultimately real.
2. Vibhaṅga (Analysis) categorizes these ultimate factors of experience. It also puts forward the differences in the sutta and abhidhamma accounts of the dhammas.
3. Dhātukathā (Discussion of elements) presents the contents of the first two books in the form of questions and answers.
4. Puggalapaññatti (Designation of persons) describes various kinds of human beings, with a particular focus on those who are progressing on the path to liberation.
5. The Kathāvatthu (Points of discussion) records various points of controversy between different schools of thought.
6. Yamaka (Pairs) deals with different topics such as the five aggregates; the four noble truths; the categorization of mental states into wholesome, unwholesome, and neutral, etc.
7. Paṭṭhāna (Foundational conditions) explains the doctrine of dependent origination.

If the recitation of the taxonomic lists of basic teachings, which the abhidhamma is supposed to rest upon, may really be traced back to the first council, this would imply a direct link between the abhidhamma and the Buddha. Several schools of early Buddhism have granted it authority on this basis. However, the topic of authorship and genuineness of the abhidhamma has been a contested issue and there were schools that rejected the authenticity of the abhidhamma as the words of the Buddha.

As noted, the Pāli canon was orally transmitted for at least one century (if not two or three) after the Buddha's death and while it was being passed on in this manner, some changes were inevitably introduced. In fact, the preserved collections reveal that a structure that preceded the three baskets and arranged the texts into various numbers of sections (3, 4, 9, and 12) must have existed. The tradition of Theravāda Buddhism traces the preserved canon back to the times of King Asoka. He is thought to have ordained his son (or, alternatively, his younger brother) Mahinda (Skt. Mahindra), who is then supposed to have brought the Theravāda tradition of Buddhism to Śri Laṅka in the third century B.C.E. This transmission was still oral and the texts are supposed to have been finally written down in the first century B.C.E. in Śri Laṅka. The early periods of the arrangement and transmission of the Pāli canon were followed by a scholastic commentarial tradition, the most authoritative contributor of which is generally considered to be Buddhaghosa, an Indian monk who lived in the fifth century C.E. He is supposed to have traveled from northern India to Anurādhapura in Śri Laṅka and stopped to reside in Mahāvihāra. Using early commentaries that were available there, Buddhaghosa composed a digested account of the Theravāda tradition of Buddhism, called Visuddhimagga or Path of Purification. Along with that he produced commentaries to the Pāli texts in which he regards Theravāda Buddhism to be the orthodox branch of Buddhism.

Canons of other schools of early Buddhism have similar structures to the Pāli canon but are by no means identical to each other. They vary in the number and types of suttas that particular sections contain and, as has been pointed out, particularly in their abhidhammas. However, the preserved texts reveal that the various canons share the same origin and the differences seem to be merely a result of the unavoidable modification introduced by passing on of the teaching in separate environments as well as translational and redactional additions and reductions. The other versions of the canon in original Indian languages remain very fragmentary. More extensive portions of the canons have been preserved in translations. A particularly important collection is the Chinese Tripiṭaka, the Nikāyas of which are usually referred to as Āgamas. These are Dīrgha-āgama, Madhyama-āgama, Saṃyukta-āgama, and Ekkottar(ik)a-āgama.

The Buddha

The central figure in the exposition of the Theravāda doctrine is the historical Buddha, namely, Siddhattha Gotama (Skt. Siddhārtha Gautama). It must be pointed out that many of the traditional descriptions of the story of the Buddha generally do not rest on the accounts in the Pāli canon. Nevertheless, certain elements of his life ought to be pointed out. According to the Theravāda tradition Siddhattha Gotama was a real person who was born and lived in the middle Gangetic plain, an area that is now divided between India and Nepal. He grew up in the community called the Sākya, Sakka, or Sākiyā (Skt. Śākya) and later spent most of the time in the towns of Rājagaha, Vesālī, and the Sāvatthī (Skt. Śrāvastī). The tradition depicts Siddhattha Gotama as a son, born in an affluent family, who decided to "go forth" (i.e., renounce the life of worldly pleasures) after seeing a sick man, an old man, a dead man, and an ascetic. His path of a wandering mendicant thus began with an insight into the nature of life as suffering. According to the Pāli canon, he was 29 years old at the time. Thereupon, he began to search for a release from afflictions. He first became a student of two spiritual teachers, who instructed him in techniques of meditation. Even though Siddhattha Gotama was an exquisite student, these methods did not satisfy him in what he was looking for. Afterward he joined a group of five ascetics and led a severely austere life for several years, but eventually let go of these methods, which he realized to be ineffective. After 6 years of searching in this manner, he is considered to have one day sat under a tree where he remained in tranquility for 49 days. This resulted in his attainment of enlightenment or nibbāna (Skt. nirvāṇa) at the age of 35. Due to this insight into the nature of reality, Siddhattha Gotama is referred to as the Buddha, a descriptive title literally meaning "the enlightened one" or "the awakened one." Otherwise, the Pāli canon most commonly refers to the Buddha as bhagavā (the nominative form) or bhagavat (the stem form), which may be translated as "the blessed one," "the exalted one," "the fortunate one," "the lord," etc. When the Buddha referred to himself, he used the term "tathāgata," literally meaning "thus-gone" or "thus-come."

The contemporary Theravāda Buddhists claim the date of the Buddha's enlightenment to be 544/3 B.C.E. Nevertheless, the majority of the Buddhist scholars today are of an opinion that this date is set too far in the past. The canon records that the Buddha was 80 years old when he died and entered final nibbāna or parinibbāna (Skt parinirvāṇa). However, the date of his death is, together with the other dates of his life, a contested topic. A general agreement has been reached that he probably died around the year 400 B.C.E. The main reference for calculating the dates of the Buddha is the inauguration of King Asoka. However, since different chronological records report different relationships between the inauguration and the death of the Buddha, this inevitably leads to disagreements over the correct one.

According to Buddhaghosa, the Theravādins hold that the Buddha's physical body or rūpa-kāya remains in the form of relics, whereas his spiritual body or dhammakāya (Skt dharma-kāya) continues with the textual tradition, final stages of the path to liberation and nibbāna. Both of these became the focal elements of the Theravāda Buddhist communities. On the one hand, rūpa-kāya resulted in the thūpa (Skt stūpa) and image worship. Thūpas or cetiyas (Skt caitya) are mound-like structures that are considered to contain the relics of the Buddha. Three kinds of objects are recognized by the Theravādins to qualify as rūpa-kāya, namely, bodily relics, objects the Buddha used, and his reminders like footprints and alike. On the other hand, dhamma-kāya set the foundation for further Buddhist scholarly developments.

Doctrine and Practice

The Theravāda tradition holds that after having attained nibbāna, the Buddha did not intend to preach what he had realized. However, the highest god, Brahmā, was sent to convince him to communicate the content of his enlightenment to other beings. The Buddha agreed to his request and delivered his first lecture in the deer park in Sārnāth, where he instructed his former five ascetic fellows on the nature of human condition as well as the practical method leading to liberation. The details of this first teaching are documented in the discourse titled The Setting in Motion of the Wheel of the Dhamma or the Dhammacakkappavattana-sutta (Skt. Dharmacakrapravartana-sūtra) (S V 421–423). Here, the term dhamma refers to the teaching of the Buddha. The Buddha opened his first instruction with the declaration of Buddhism as the middle way or majjhimā paṭipadā (Skt madhyamā pratipad) between the indulgence in sensual pleasures, which is low and vulgar, on the one hand and strict austerities, which are painful, on the other. These were the two extremes that the Buddha himself experienced as unsatisfactory. After this opening statement, the Buddha put forward the principles of reality in the framework of the so-called four noble truths or cattāri ariyasaccāni (Skt. catvāri ārya-satyāni), sometimes also translated as "the truths of the noble one(s)," "the truths for a noble one," or "the ennobling realities." These truths offer an insight into the true nature of things as they really are, and are not to be taken dogmatically. The four truths are:

1. Life is characterized with unsatisfactoriness or dukkha (Skt duḥkha).
2. There exists a cause or samudaya for unsatisfactoriness, which is described as thirst or taṇhā (Skt tṛṣṇā), referring to craving.
3. There exists an end or nirodha to unsatisfactoriness and craving, namely, nibbāna.
4. There is a path or magga (Skt mārga) leading to the cessation of unsatisfactoriness, namely, the eighthfold noble path or ariya aṭṭhaṅgika-magga (Skt. ārya-aṣṭāṅgika-mārga).

The Pāli canon often points to an analogy between the Buddha explaining these four truths and a doctor giving a medical diagnosis. First, the disease is identified, second, the cause is revealed, third, the possibility of restoration back to health is affirmed, and fourth, the method of a healing therapy is outlined. This path of rehabilitation is open to everyone. However, the patient ought not to passively wait for a cure but actively follow the Buddha's steps to liberation. This ought to be done by clearly comprehending the first noble truth, disposing of the second, realizing the third, and developing the forth.

The first noble truth identifies life as marked with unsatisfactoriness or dukkha, which is understood to be a universal truth, that is, an actuality of empirical existence. The term dukkha is frequently translated as suffering but in fact embraces a wider range of meaning. In essence, it stands for the whole spectrum of uneasy and unsatisfactory experiences. The first noble truth explains birth, old age, sickness, and death as dukkha. Furthermore sorrow, lamentation, pain, grief, and despair are pointed out as dukkha. Then union with what is displeasing, separation from what is pleasing, and not to get what one wants is described as dukkha. Finally, the five aggregates subject to clinging are recognized as dukkha. This exposition is fundamentally linked to the second noble truth, namely, the recognition of craving as the cause leading to attachment or upādāna, and thence, due to the nature of reality as essentially impermanent, to dukkha. Not obtaining an object of desire, be it life, health, or any other target of longing, leads to the experience of dukkha. In other words, any unresolved relationship of craving results in unsatisfactoriness. This is an inevitable consequence deriving from the basic nature of reality which is according to Buddhism, as has been pointed out, continually changing. The Buddha rejected the Upaniṣadic notion of an immutable self or attā (Skt ātman) and instead taught that there is no such thing as a permanent and changeless underlying reality of experience. This came to be known as the doctrine of no-self or anattā (Skt anātman) and was introduced by the Buddha in his second instruction (Vin I 13). In contrast to the idea of a persistent self, the Buddha dissected human experience into various fundamental factors, which were then shown to be in a perpetual flux and not resting on any kind of substratum. Three of the most prominent schemes that derive from such an analysis are the five aggregates, the 12 sense spheres, and the 18 elements. The five aggregates, already mentioned above, are form or rūpa, feelings or vedanā, cognition or saññā (Skt. saṃjñā), volitions or saṅkhāra (Skt saṃskāra), and consciousness or viññāṇa (Skt vijñāna). The classification of the 12 spheres or āyatanas divides human experience into six senses (the sixth being the mind), and their corresponding sense objects. Lastly, the scheme of 18 elements or dhātus comprises of the six senses, their corresponding objects, and the six respective kinds of consciousness. All of the above factors of experience are ordinarily grasped at and considered to be one's belonging. It was therefore taught by the Buddha that the impersonal nature of these experiential aspects of existence ought to be comprehended.

The abhidhamma expanded the notion of no-self and introduced a differentiation between substantial and nominal existence, namely, basic elements of existence or dhammas and secondarily fabricated conceptual wholes respectively. According to the abhidhamma, the former category consisted of mental and material constituents of existence. These were considered to correspond to the ultimate, truly existing level of reality. The latter category, however, was deemed to comprise of mere conventional labels that were projected onto the fundamental level of continually fluctuating events.

Apart from identifying craving as leading to the arising of dukkha in the second noble truth, the Buddha also taught that it is precisely craving that generates forces that maintain the continuity of rebirths. Here, it may be noted that the Buddha accepted the paradigm of his time which considered a single life to be merely one link in the beginningless chain of rebirths or saṃsāra and the law determining the nature of the next existence was referred to as the karmic law. According to the karmic principle, every thought, word, and action leads to a reaction and thus upholds the continuation of existences. According to the Buddha, craving is the vital link that produces karmic formations. The aim of a Buddhist practitioner, who aspires to be released from the saṃsāric cycle, is consequently aimed at diminishing the karmic influences by eradicating the craving. In place of the idea of a permanent and changeless attā, the Buddha therefore proposed a selfless empirical continuity in saṃsāra. The Pāli canon asserts this view to be the middle way between the position claiming an eternal persistency of a soul and the position that life ends with the death of the body. The former view is referred to as eternalism or sassata-vāda (Skt. śāśvata-vāda) and corresponds to the position of the Vedic streams of thought. The latter view of annihilationism (Skt. uccheda-vāda) corresponds to the position of the Indian materialists. The Buddha refuted both of these traditions since he understood them as still resting on the notion of a self. In order to explain the continuity of existence without an underlying self, the Buddha proposed a model of temporal conditionality. This element of the Buddha-dhamma is termed paṭicca-samuppāda (Skt. pratītya-samutpāda) or dependent origination. It maintains that all phenomena arise in dependence upon certain conditions and similarly, with the eradication of those very conditions, the conditioned phenomena likewise cease to arise. Theravāda Buddhism employs this scheme of interconditionality to elucidate the mechanism behind the occurrence of dukkha as well as the working of the karmic principle within saṃsāra. Ordinarily, the model is subdivided into 12 links or nidānas. These are: (1) ignorance or avijjā (Skt avidyā), (2) volitions or saṅkhāra (Skt saṃskāra), (3) consciousness or viññāṇa (Skt vijñāna), (4) name-form or nāma-rūpa, (5) six sense spheres or saḷāyatana (Skt ṣaḍāyatana), (6) contact or phassa (Skt sparśa), (7) feelings or vedanā, (8) craving or taṇhā (Skt tṛṣṇā), (9) clinging or upādāna, (10) becoming or bhava, (11) birth or jāti, and (12) old age and death or jarā-maraṇa. The individual links and relations between them have been interpreted in several different ways. Buddhaghosa suggested that the chain of dependent origination embraces three consecutive existences. According to his explanation, the first and the second links relate to the past existence. Ignorance of the true nature of reality results in the arising of karmic formations or volitions, which in turn condition the arising of consciousness and thereby maintain the mechanism of rebirth by impelling consciousness to continue in the next life. Despite being constantly changing, consciousness operates as a transmitter of karmic formations. Links 3–10 correspond to the present existence. Name-form refers to the mode of human existence and the six sense spheres and contact present the manner in which one experiences the world, that is, by contacting it through the six senses. Any such experience leads to the arising of a certain feeling, be it pleasant, unpleasant, or neutral, and before long more of a specific type of a feeling is desired. This then leads to the arising of clinging or attachment to the phenomena which are experienced to produce the longed for effects. The present life linkage that has been described so far is what one is considered to "become," that is, they compose the way of one's worldly existence, which constitutes the tenth link of dependent origination. The impetus of all of the described factors results in the links 11 and 12 which are birth, old age, and death, representing the third or future existence.

According to the nature of accumulated karma one may have a fortunate or an unfortunate rebirth. According to the Kathāvatthu, Theravāda Buddhism proposed there to be five possible domains of rebirth or gatis (lit. manner of going). These are the realms of humans, animals, hungry ghosts, gods, and hell-beings. Out of these, rebirth in hell is considered to be the most painful whereas rebirth in heavens is deemed to be the most delightful. However, none of the enumerated modes of existence is considered to be permanent. Theravāda Buddhism regards the transmission from one existence to the other to be like the passing of a flame from one candle to the next. In his third instruction, the Buddha described all of perceptual objects as being ablaze (Vin I 34). He claimed them to be on fire due to the three "roots of evil," which may also be termed defilements, or kilesas (Skt kleśa), namely, greed or rāga, hatred or dosa (Skt dveṣa), and delusion or moha.

The first two noble truths rest on the realization of the three marks or tilakkhaṇa (Skt trilakṣaṇa) of dependent existence. These are first, impermanence or aniccā (Skt. anitya), second, unsatisfactoriness or dukkha (Skt duḥkha), and third, no-self or anattā (anātman). Since reality is impermanent and selfless, any relation of craving is bound to give rise to dukkha. The third noble truth turns this formula of craving resulting in dukkha around, and asserts that consequently the cessation of craving must bring about the cessation of dukkha. This may be attained by eradicating ignorance or in other words, gaining an insight into the true nature of reality. The stopping of dukkha is named nibbāna, which is, in accordance with the analogy of the candle flame, explained as the extinguishment of the three fires or "roots of evil" and thereby the cessation of the passing on of the flame. It ought to be stressed that nibbāna is not some sort of a metaphysical concept but is rather an event, a verb rather than a noun, and it is said that the one who has attained it has nibbāna-ed. The occurrence of the attainment of nibbāna during one's lifetime is termed "nibbāna with a remainder" or saupādisesa-nibbāna (Skt. sopadhiśeṣa-nirvāṇa), since one continues to operate within the framework of the factors of existence. Nibbāna at death is termed "nirvāṇa without a remainder" or anupādisesa-nibbāna (Skt. nirupadhiśeṣa-nirvāṇa), as it is here that the factors of existence also discontinue. The Buddha, however, did not answer the question of what happens to the Tathāgata after death, (S IV 373–400) since he considered these types of questions to be detrimental to progression on the path to liberation, which revolves around human experience rather than philosophical speculation. Furthermore, he considered this very question to still rest on the notion of attā. Additionally, nibbāna may not be explicated in everyday terminology. Thus, for the Buddha, trying to answer the posed question would be similar to attempting to describe the extinguished fire in the language of the flame.

Since the aim of Theravāda Buddhist practitioners is the attainment of liberation, the teaching of the Buddha is not meant to be passed on simply as theoretical information, but rather as instructions for individual development of the skills for achieving this goal. The early texts therefore frequently refer to the Buddhist doctrine as a system of training or sikkhā (Skt śikṣā) and accordingly his students engaged in this training are spoken of as sekha (Skt śaikṣa). The Buddha described the path to the healing from unsatisfactoriness and to the release from the cycle of existences in the exposition of the fourth noble truth, which is also the practical method of the middle way. This path is subdivided into eight limbs, namely, (1) right view or sammā-diṭṭhi (Skt. samyag-dṛṣṭi), (2) right intention sammā-saṅkappa (Skt. samyak-saṃkalpa), (3) right speech or sammā-vācā (Skt. samyag-vācā), (4) right action or sammā-kammanta (Skt. samyak-karmanta), (5) right livelihood or sammā-ājīva (Skt. samyag-ājīva), (6) right effort or sammā-vāyāma (Skt. samyag-vyāyāma), (7) right mindfulness or sammā-sati (Skt. samyak-smṛti), (8) right concentration or sammā-samādhi (Skt. samyak-samādhi). Buddhaghosa grouped these eight into three larger units of wisdom or paññā (Skt prajñā; 1–2), morality or sīla (Skt śīla; 3–5) and meditative cultivation or samādhi (6–8). Despite the systematic consecutive presentation of the practical way to nibbāna, these eight dimensions ought not to be taken as a ladder of successive attainments but rather as various facets of the practical life that leads one to liberation. Right view refers to the clear apprehending of things as they really are. This factor goes hand in hand with the right intention which refers to thinking in accordance with the right view. This means a nonattached experience of the world and the abolishing of all wrong intentions. Right speech is speech that is not harsh and does not contain lies, gossip, slander, and the like. Right action means restraining from harming living beings, taking what is not given, and misconduct in matters of sensual pleasures. Right livelihood refers to avoiding activities that would result in harming others, that is, trading weapons, engaging in slavery business, selling poisons and intoxicants, etc. Right effort means a conscious prevention of the arising of negative and harmful mental states, like hatred, sluggishness, sensual desire, worry, fear, and doubt. Instead, beneficial states of mind, like the seven factors of enlightenment (mindfulness, investigation of phenomena, energy, rapture, tranquility, concentration, and equanimity) should purposely be cultivated. Right mindfulness means always being mindful of the arising and ceasing of all the experiential phenomena. By employing this practice, one endeavors to see reality as it really is, that is, impermanent, selfless, and unsatisfactory. Right concentration is aimed at achieving one-pointedness of the mind, which may lead to the four meditational trances or jhānas. These are refined states of mental collectedness and tranquility, in which a complete absorption in the object is achieved.

The path to the realization of nibbāna is considered to be open for everyone and is divided into stages or paths of four noble persons or ariyapuggala (Skt. ārya-pudgala) that ought to be completed over the course of numerous lifetimes. The first one is the path of a stream-enterer or sotāpatti-magga (Skt. srotāpatti-mārga) the path of a once-returner or sakadāgāmi-magga (Skt. sakṛdāgāmi-mārga) the path of a no-returner or anāgāmi-magga (Skt. anāgāmi-mārga) and lastly, the path of an arahant. An arahant is an individual who has attained the complete cessation of afflictions and fetters that bind one to the cycle of rebirths. Buddhaghosa, the Theravāda commentator, has thus described the arahant as the one who has completed the path to nibbāna. In this way, an arahant is regarded to be the same as the Buddha, the only difference between the two being that the Buddha was not taught the dhamma by someone else like the arahant. Unlike some other schools of early Buddhism, the Theravāda tradition maintains that arahantship is a permanent attainment and that it is therefore not possible for one to regress once this stage is reached.

Community

As noted above, the Buddha delivered his first lecture to his former ascetic fellows in Sārnāth. The five of them received an introductory ordination into monasticism or pabbajjā (Skt pravrajyā), which literally meant "going forth" from the household life into homelessness, and full ordination or upasaṃpadā. The ordination was carried out by the Buddha's call "come, O monk" or "ehi bhikkhu" (Skt ehi bhikṣu). This is considered to be the origin of the Buddhist monastic community, also referred to as saṅgha. Various mendicants or bhikkhus continued to gather around the Buddha and once their number reached 60, the Buddha requested that they themselves go and spread the doctrine further. During the initial growth of the saṅgha, the Buddha himself ordained the new monastics. However, since the community was expanding so rapidly, the monastics themselves were granted a permission to confer ordinations as well and this led to the formalization of the procedure. Additionally, the introductory and full ordinations were set apart into two different ceremonies. The pabbajjā was understood to ordain one into a novice or sāmaṇera (Skt śrāmaṇera) and according to the Vinaya-piṭaka one is old enough to undergo this initial ceremony when he is able to scare away crows. Every newcomer had to shave their head, put on a robe, and recite the taking of refuge in the three jewels or tiratana (Skt triratna), namely, the Buddha, the dhamma, and the saṅgha, which are hence called the three refuges or tisaraṇa (Skt triśaraṇa). Furthermore, he had to concur with the system of training by accepting the ten precepts or sikkhāpada (Skt śikṣāpada). These were refraining from (1) harming living beings, (2) taking what is not given, (3) misconduct in matters of sensual pleasure, (4) false speech, (5) intoxication, (6) eating after midday, (7) entertainment, (8) wearing jewelry and perfumes, (9) sleeping on luxurious beds, and (10) handling silver and gold. Additionally, a teacher of at least 10 years' standing was appointed to every new member of the saṅgha and in this manner the students could efficiently learn the texts as well as rules of monastic conduct. This provided for a well-organized system of oral transmission. At 20 years of age one was allowed to undergo the upasaṃpadā ceremony, which made one a bhikkhu proper. In order for the ceremony to be valid, the presence of five fully ordained monks of at least 10 years' standing was required. The full ordination concludes with the statement that the four requisites or nissaya (Skt niśraya) of food, clothing, lodging, and medicine ought to be alms, robes made of old rags, the foot of a tree, and the fermented urine correspondingly. As noted, the original community of monks and nuns were wandering mendicants who were allowed to settle only during the rainy season. This style of living obliged them to keep their possession at minimum and according to one of the lists of requisites they were allowed to carry three robes, a belt, a needle, a razor, an alms bowl, and a water strainer. Following the full ordination into a bhikkhu or a bhikkhunī, one's life is thus regulated by the monastic rules of which according to the Theravāda tradition, there are

227. These are a further elaboration of the monastic lifestyle based on the ten abovementioned fundamental precepts. This traditional model of ordination persisted in the Theravāda tradition until today.

Buddha was initially reluctant toward the ordination of women as he deemed that the order of nuns would accelerate the deterioration of the dhamma. However, he considered them to be able to attain arahantship. The monastic rules of bhikkhunīs were generally very similar to those of bhikkhus. It is important to note, however, that probably around the eleventh century C.E. the Theravāda order of nuns was discontinued. This means that the nuns may nowadays be ordained as novices but cannot be fully ordained since there are no fully ordained nuns who ought to participate in the full ordination ceremony in order for it to be legitimate. Nevertheless, there has emerged an endeavor to restore the Theravāda bhikkhunī lineage of ordination.

Furthermore, it must be noted that the lay community has always played a significant role in the history of Theravāda Buddhism, since the monastic community depended on its generosity or dāna. Lay followers of the Buddha are divided into male disciples or upāsaka and female disciples or upāsikā, the Pāli words literally denoting the "sitting by the teacher's feet (and listening to his instructions)." According to the Theravāda doctrine, a lay follower is defined as a person who has taken the refuge in the Buddha, the dhamma, and the saṅgha. The Pāli canon records the teachings of the Buddha to the laity to be predominantly concerned with morality. Instructions for the practical life of laity are laid out in the form of the five precepts or pañcasīlāni (Skt pañcaśīlāni), namely, the first five of the ten monastic precepts. Sometimes (typically on special occasions) lay followers can abide by the eight precepts, where in addition to the basic five (in which refraining form sexual misconduct is replaced with absolute sexual abstinence) refraining form eating after midday, refraining from entertainment, and wearing jewelry and perfumes, etc., as well as refraining from sleeping in luxurious beds are adhered to. This conduct basically corresponds to the ten monastic precepts.

The Diffusion of Theravāda Buddhism from India

As noted above, Theravāda Buddhism was most likely brought to Śri Laṅka in the third century B.C.E. and during the following 1,000 years Śri Laṅka was a notable center of Buddhist studies. In many ways, the later spreading of the Theravāda tradition was affected by the deterioration of Indian Buddhism, which started with the weakening of the Buddhist Pāla rule in the eleventh century C.E. With the later Islamic invasions to India, Buddhism there gradually saw its decline. Consequently, the Buddhist community fled from Northern India to the south (which still resisted the Muslim rule), and further into Asia. The Theravāda tradition remained in South India until at least seventeenth century C.E. Already in the eleventh century C.E. it also reached Burma and in the following couple of centuries it spread to Thailand, Laos, and Cambodia. Its establishment in these countries of South and Southeast Asia thus greatly contributed to its survival during the downfall of Buddhism in India. In fact, in the sixteenth century the Theravāda tradition started again being introduced from Burma to parts of Northeast India.

Today Theravāda Buddhism is a religion of the majority in Śri Laṅka, Burma, and Thailand. On the other hand, the communist regimes of Laos and Cambodia were profoundly detrimental to its development there, although it is nowadays slowly recovering. It must be highlighted that the Theravāda tradition in all these countries is nowadays not entirely uniform. However, it still belongs to a single monastic lineage and accepts the authority of the Pāli canon as well as its commentaries.

T

Cross-References

- ▶ Buddhist Councils
- ▶ Mahāsāṅghika
- ▶ Sarvāstivāda
- ▶ Sautrāntika
- ▶ Sthaviravāda
- ▶ Tipiṭaka

References

1. Anālayo B (2008) Satipaṭṭhāna. The direct path to realization. Windhorse, Cambridge
2. Anālayo B (2009) From craving to liberation. The Buddhist Association, New York
3. Aronson HB (1979) The relationship of the karmic to the Nirvanic in Theravāda Buddhism. J Relig Ethics 7(1):28–36
4. Bareau A (1955) Les sectes bouddhiques du petit véhicule. École Française d'Extrême-Orient, Saigon, Vietnam
5. Bodhi B (1976) Aggregates and the clinging aggregates. Pāli Buddh Rev 1(1):91–102
6. Bodhi B (2000) A comprehensive manual of Abhidhamma, the Abhidhammattha Saṅgaha of Ācariya Anuruddha. BPS Pariyatti Edition, Kandy
7. Boisvert M (1997) The five aggregates: understanding Theravāda psychology and soteriology. Si Satguru, Delhi
8. Bond GD (1984) The development and elaboration of the arahant ideal in the Theravada Buddhist tradition. J Am Acad Relig 52(2):227–242
9. Burford GG (1994) Theravāda Buddhist soteriology and the paradox of desire. In: Buswell RE et al (eds) Paths to liberation. Motilal Banarsidass, Delhi, pp 37–62
10. Burns DM (1994) Buddhist meditation and depth psychology. BPS, Kandy
11. Carter JR (1977) A history of "Early Buddhism". Relig Stud 13(3):263–287
12. Cohen RS (1995) Discontented categories: Hīnayāna and Mahāyāna in Indian Buddhist history. J Am Acad Relig 63(1):1–25
13. Collins S (1982) Selfless persons: imagery and thought in Theravāda Buddhism. Cambridge University Press, Cambridge
14. Collins S (1982) Self and non-self in early Buddhism. Numen 29(2):250–257
15. Collins S (1990) On the very idea of the Pāli canon. J Pali Text Soc 15:89–126
16. Collins S (1992) Notes on some oral aspects of Pali literature. Indo-Iran J 35:121–135
17. Collins S (1994) What are Buddhists doing when they deny the self? In: Tracy D et al (eds) Religion and practical reason. State University New York Press, Albany, pp 59–86
18. Conze E (1962) Buddhist thought in India: three phases of Buddhist philosophy. University of Michigan Press, Ann Arbor
19. Cousins LS (1973) Buddhist *Jhāna*: its nature and attainment according to the Pāli sources. Religion 3:115–131
20. Cousins LS (1981) Paṭṭhāna and the development of the Theravādin Abhidhamma. J Pali Text Soc 9:22–46
21. Cousins LS (1984) Nibbāna and Abhidhamma. Buddh Stud Rev I:95–109
22. Crosby K (2006) A Theravāda code of conduct for good Buddhists: the "Upāsakamanussavinaya". J Am Orient Soc 126(2):177–187
23. Cruise H (1983) Early Buddhism: some recent misconceptions. Philos East West 33(2):149–166
24. de A Wijesekera OH (1964) The concept of Vinnāṇa in Theravāda Buddhism. J Am Orient Soc 84(3):254–259
25. de Silva L (1987) Sense experience of the liberated being as reflected in early Buddhism. In: Kalupahana DJ et al (eds) Buddhist philosophy and culture. N.A. Jayawickrema Felicitation Volume Committee, Colombo, pp 13–22
26. de Silva P (1991) An introduction to Buddhist psychology. Macmillan, London
27. Endo T (2002) Buddha in Theravada Buddhism. A study of the concept of Buddha in the Pali commentaries. Buddhist Cultural Centre, Colombo
28. Frauwallner E (1956) The earliest Vinaya and the beginnings of Buddhist literature, Serie Orientale Roma VIII. Is. M.E.O, Rome
29. Fuller P (2005) The notion of Diṭṭhi in Theravāda Buddhism. RoutledgeCurzon, London/New York
30. Gethin R (1986) The five Khandhas: their treatment in the Nikāyas and early Abhidhamma. J Indian Philos 14:35–53
31. Gethin R (1994) *Bhavaṅga* and rebirth according to the Abhidhamma. Buddh Forum 3:11–35
32. Gombrich R (1980) The significance of former Buddhas in Theravadin tradition. In: Balasooriya S et al (eds) Buddhist studies in honour of Walpola Rahula. Gordon Fraser, London, pp 62–72
33. Gombrich R (1992) Dating the Buddha: a red herring revealed. In: Bechert H (ed) The dating of the historical Buddha part 2. Vandenhoeck & Ruprecht, Göttingen, pp 237–259
34. Gombrich R (2005) How Buddhism began. The conditioned genesis of the early teaching. Routledge, London/New York
35. Gombrich R (2006) Theravāda Buddhism. A social history from ancient Benares to modern Colombo. Routledge, London/New York
36. Gómez LO (1976) Proto-Mādhyamika in the Pāli canon. Philos East West 26(2):137–165
37. Govinda LA (1991) The psychological attitude of early Buddhist philosophy and its systematic representation according to Abhidhamma tradition. Motilal Banarsidass, Delhi
38. Hallisey C (1991) Councils as ideas and events in the Theravāda. Buddh Forum 3:133–148
39. Hamilton S (1995) Anattā: a different approach. Middle Way 70(1):47–60
40. Hamilton S (1995) From the Buddha to Buddhaghosa: changing attitudes towards the human body in Theravāda Buddhism. In: Law JM (ed) Religious reflection on the human body. Indiana University Press, Bloomington, pp 46–63
41. Hamilton S (1996) Identity and experience: the constitution of the human being according to early Buddhism. Luzac Oriental, London
42. Harris EJ (2006) Theravāda Buddhism and the British encounter. Religious, missionary and colonial

experience in nineteenth century Sri Lanka. Routledge, London/New York
43. Harvey P (2004) The selfless mind: personality, consciousness and Nirvāna in early Buddhism. RoutledgeCurzon, Oxon
44. Hirakawa A (2007) A history of Indian Buddhism: from Śākyamuni to early Mahāyāna. Motilal Banarsidass, Delhi
45. Holt JC (1995) Discipline: the canonical Buddhism of the Vinayapiṭaka. Motilal Banarsidass, Delhi
46. Holt JC et al (2003) Constituting communities. Theravāda Buddhism and the religious cultures of south and Southeast Asia. SUNY Press, New York
47. Johansson REA (1985) The dynamic psychology of early Buddhism. Curzon, London
48. Jones RH (1979) Theravāda Buddhism and morality. J Am Acad Relig 47(3):371–387
49. Kalupahana DJ (1982) Buddhist philosophy: a historical analysis. University Press of Hawaii, Honolulu
50. Kalupahana DJ (1994) Buddhist philosophy: continuities and discontinuities. Motilal Banarsidass, Delhi
51. Karunadasa Y (1987) Anattā as via media. Sri Lanka J Buddh Stud 1:1–9
52. Karunadasa Y (1999) The Buddhist critique of Sassatavāda and Ucchedavāda: the key to a proper understanding of the origin and doctrines of early Buddhism. Middle Way 74(2):69–79
53. Kimura R (2007) Mahayana and Hinayana Buddhism: a historical study of the terms Mahayana and Hinayana and the origin of Mahayana Buddhism. Pilgrims, Varanasi
54. Lamotte É (1988) History of Indian Buddhism: from the origins to the Saka Era (trans: Webb-Boin S). Université catholique de Louvain, Institut Orientaliste, Louvain-la-Neuve
55. Love TT (1965) Theravāda Buddhism: ethical theory and practice. J Bible Relig 33(4):303–313
56. Malalasekera GP (1964) The status of the individual in Theravāda Buddhism. Philos East West 14(2):145–156
57. Malalasekera GP (1968) Aspects of reality as taught by Theravada Buddhism. BPS, Kandy
58. Marasinghe MMJ (1974) Gods in early Buddhism: a study in their social and mythological milieu as depicted in the Nikāyas of the Pāli canon. University of Sri Lanka, Vidyalankara
59. McDermott JP (1973) Nibbāna as a reward for Kamma. J Am Orient Soc 93(3):344–347
60. McDermott JP (1976) Is there group karma in Theravāda Buddhism? Numen 23:67–80, Fasc. 1
61. Misra GSP (1968) Logical and scientific method in early Buddhist texts. J Roy Asiat Soc 1(2):54–64
62. Nattier JJ et al (1977) Mahāsāṅghika origins: the beginnings of Buddhist sectarianism. Hist Relig 16:237–272
63. Perez-Remon J (1981) Self and non-self in early Buddhism. Mouton, Paris/New York
64. Premasiri PD (1987) Early Buddhist analysis of varieties of cognition. Sri Lanka J Buddh Stud 1:51–69
65. Ronkin N (2005) Early Buddhist metaphysics. The making of a philosophical tradition. RoutledgeCurzon, London/New York
66. Seneviratna A (1994) King Aśoka and Buddhism: historical and literary studies. BPS, Kandy
67. Vélez de Cea A (2005) Emptiness in the Pāli suttas and the question of Nāgārjuna's orthodoxy. Philos East West 55(4):507–528
68. von Guenther H (1991) Philosophy and psychology in the Abhidharma. Motilal Banarsidass, Delhi
69. von Hinüber O (1996) A handbook of Pāli literature. de Gruyter, Berlin/New York
70. Warder AK (1956) On the relationships between early Buddhism and other contemporary systems. Bull School Orient Afr Stud 18(1):43–63
71. Warder AK (2004) Indian Buddhism. Motilal Banarsidass, Delhi
72. Whiteman JHM (1957) The early Buddhist teaching concerning "Birth". J Relig 37(3):189–200
73. Williams DM (1974) The translation and interpretation of the twelve terms in the Paṭiccasamuppāda. Numen 21:35–63, Fasc. 1

Thought of Enlightenment

▶ Bodhicitta

Three Bodies of the Buddha

▶ *Tri-kāya*

Thullanandā

Angraj Chaudhary
Vipassana Research Institute, Dhammagiri, Igatpuri, Nashik, Maharashtra, India

Definition

Thullananda is the example of a woman who becomes a nun to live a lax and lewd life.

Notorious Thullanandā Creates Troubles in the Order

Thullanandā is the example of a nun who became ordained just to live a lax and lewd life. She took so much pleasure in breaking the rules that in fact she became notorious for creating trouble in the Order. For her actions the Buddha declared her committing pārājika (a grave transgression of the rules for bhikkhus and bhikhunis meriting expulsion from the Order), pācittiya (offense requiring expiation), etc.

She regarded great monks like Sāriputta, Moggallāna, Mahākaccāna, etc., as slaves (ceṭaka), but she regarded Devadatta, Kokālika, and Samuddadatta as great monks (mahānāga) [1].

She liked living with Ariṭṭha who was previously a vulture trainer and who had been expelled by the whole Bhikkhu Saṅgha [2].

It is said that a man is known by the company he keeps. What sort of a nun Thullanandā was is clear from the company she kept and took delight in.

The goal of a monk or a nun who leaves home for a homeless life is to be free from mental defilements like greed, aversion, sexual desire, anger, jealousy, etc., and attain nibbāna – the summum bonum of an ascetic life. But Thullanandā could not give up greed – the basic defilement according to the Buddha from which proceed all other defilements [3].

Greedy Thullanandā

She was very greedy for possessions. She had the habit of misappropriating the gifts meant for other nuns.

She would barter what was meant for others for her own use. She would distribute cīvaras (robes) among her own disciples and would not give to other nuns.

Once she ordained a woman. The woman was of bad character and was not loyal to her husband. He threatened to kill her. Out of fear she wanted to take ordination. Other ascetics refused to ordain her, but Thullanandā ordained her because she offered her a lot of belongings she had stolen from her husband's house [4].

She was in the habit of asking for cīvara for ordaining one who wanted to be trained. Before ordaining one, she also took promise from her to serve her (Thullanandā) for at least 2 years [5].

Once she took more garlic from the farmer's field than he wanted her to take [6].

She had the habit of going to her donor's house when it was regarded not proper to go, and even if she was not offered a seat, she would sit down there in the hope to get something [7].

Once she promised to stitch a cīvara of a nun which was not nicely stitched. The nun unstitched it and gave it to her for stitching it nicely but she did not do it [8].

Jealous Thullanandā

She wanted everything to be given to her. She was jealous of others. Once when a donor expressed his wish to give cīvara to all nuns, she prevented him from doing so. Thus all nuns were prevented from having cīvara, and, as a result, the upāsaka could not earn merit [9].

If something was given to her which she had asked for she would say she wanted something else. This annoyed the shopkeeper and the donor or the person who went to buy things [10].

Thullanandā did not attend to sick bhikkhuṇīs living with her nor did she ask others to attend to her [11].

An Eloquent Preacher

She had one quality. She could preach so eloquently that people were highly impressed by her eloquence. She was well versed in the doctrine [12], but she never lived her life according to the teachings of the Buddha. Even then she could impress not only the common people but also the elite like King Prasendi who allowed her to persuade him to part with his costly upper garment [13]. This also speaks of her greedy and discontented nature

But in spite of her being a good preacher, she lacked the character and conduct that can lead people to achieve the highest goal of life for which one becomes a monk or a nun.

A Woman of Strong Likes and Dislikes

She was a woman of strong likes and dislikes. She liked Ānanda but disliked Mahākassapa whom she called an aññatitthiya (one who belongs to a different sect). Once Mahākassapa asked Ānanda not to wander about with young bhikkhus who were unguarded in their sense faculties and immoderate in eating and be like them. This offended Thullanandā very much. She had great regards for Ānanda [14].

As she herself was of a doubtful character, she encouraged the nuns who followed her and who were many to indulge in all kinds of malpractices.

She liked the company of men. She had intrigues with them. In order to have their company, she frequented streets and crossroads unattended so that nobody could see and hinder her in her intrigues with them [15].

She knew what temptation is and therefore she had great sympathy with those women who fell a prey to it. In fact she shielded them on many occasions. When her sister Sundarīnandā became pregnant, she did not disclose it to good bhikkhuṇīs and bhikkhus. She said that her unwholesome deeds are theirs so why should she disclose all bad things about them [16].

She was very fond of listening to her praise. For this she bribed dancers and singers to sing her praise. She gave them cīvaras and food [17].

She was very jealous of others' achievement. Bhaddā Kāpilānī was also a great preacher. The Buddha had declared her first among those nuns who could remember their past lives [18]. So Thullanandā could not tolerate her. When she saw Bhaddā being worshipped first, she could not tolerate it. She caused so many discomforts to her [19].

Once Bhaddā Kapilani was living in Sāketa, she wanted to come to Sāvatthi. She sent a messenger to Thullanandā and asked her to arrange for her abode. Thullanandā agreed to do so. In fact she gave her shelter. But when she saw that Bhaddā Kāpilānī was worshipped first, she became jealous and asked her to leave [20].

She was herself quarrelsome [21], and when there was any quarrel between bhikkhunīs and she was requested to pacify, she did not do that nor did she ask anybody else to do that [22].

Thullanandā is the example of a nun who was very very greedy. She had so many bad qualities but at the same time she was a very good preacher of Dhamma.

References

1. Pācittiya p 93 (Unless otherwise mentioned all books referred to here are published by Vipassana Research Institute, Dhammagiri in 1998)
2. Pācittiya. 293
3. D.3 Aggañña Sutta
4. Pācittiya, 301
5. ibid., pp 458, 460
6. ibid., p 351
7. ibid., p 373
8. ibid., p 382
9. ibid., p 386
10. ibid., p 337
11. Ibid., p 397
12. ibid., p 346
13. ibid., 348
14. S.1.196
15. ibid., p 369
16. Pācittiya.291
17. Ibid., p 387
18. A.1.35
19. ibid., p 395
20. ibid., p 398
21. ibid., p 298
22. ibid., p 410

T

Thunderbolt

► Vajra

Thus-Gone One

► *Tathāgata*

Tibet

Radha Madhav Bharadwaj
Department of History, Deen Dayal Upadhyaya College, University of Delhi, Karampura, New Delhi, India

Synonyms

Bhoṭa deśa

Definition

A snowy mountainous country between India and China, Tibet came to limelight during the reign of its first great emperor Srong-brtsan-sgam-po (627–649/650) who not only introduced literacy but also welded it into a great political power and paved the way for the cultivation of knowledge, culture, and the religion of the Buddha in Tibet for another two centuries. The later kings of western Tibet (Purang, Guge, and Ladakh) continued the process and made it a land of Buddhist religion, philosophy, and spirituality which have survived till today through the office of the great Dalai Lama.

Tibet has the distinction of giving so much to the world in the field of religion, philosophy, literature, and art over the last 13 centuries but it is no longer an independent country now as it lost its sovereignty to China. In this short write-up, an attempt will be made to unravel the political and cultural achievements of this once great sovereign nation over the last 1,300 years in brief.

The present-day interest of the world in Tibet and its culture goes back to the year 1959, when the 14th Dalai Lama Tenzin Gyatso, the monk-ruler, left his Potala palace at capital Lhasa, along with his around 80,000 followers, to lead a life of exile in India. He established his Tibetan Government-in-exile and made Dharmaśālā its headquarter. He crossed over to India fearing for the life of his followers and the danger to the decimation of Tibetan culture and that is why he and his followers also brought along many important manuscripts and pieces of art. He has since established a Tibetan Higher Studies Centre there to save Tibetan religious culture by devising a curriculum of Tibetan studies for the new generation of Tibetans living in India and abroad. He has traveled widely and has attracted a large band of followers across many communities and has contributed to world peace.

The vast mountainous tract of country between 73° and 98° East Longitude from London, and 27° and 38° north latitude may be called by the general name of "Tibet." The whole of Tibet occupies high ground and lies among snowy mountains. The sources of the rivers Indus, Satluj, and the Brahmaputra are in *Nāri* (mount *Kailāś* in Sanskrit), the highest ground in Tibet. It lies south of the countries of the Turks and the Mongols, west of China (*Gyanak*), north of India (*Gyagar*), and east of India, Afghanistan, and Turkistan ([3], pp. 121, 122).

Origin of the Tibetans

Tibetans are ignorant of their origin. Some derive their origin from India, some from China, others from the Mongols. Csoma de Köros holds the view that it is very probable that the royal family which reigned from central Tibet with its capital at Lhasa, from 250 B.C. to the tenth century A.D., was derived from the race of the *Licchavis* (the royal lineage which ruled the republican state of *Vaiśālī* in northeast Bihar during the sixth and fifth centuries B.C.) and it is certain that their religion and literature is of Indian origin ([3], p. 127).

But, before launching on the achievements of Tibet, a brief historiography of the origin of Tibetology will help understand it better. The explorations made during the last two centuries in the land of snow-Tibet, Nepal, Central Asia, Mongolia, Turfan, Khotan, and some other South Asian countries by the western and Indian scholars like Brian H. Hodgson, Alexander Csoma de Koros, Giuseppe Tucci, H.P. Shastri, Sarat Chandra Das, Rajendra Lal Mitra, Rāhula Sānkṛtyāyana, Raghuvīra, and many others have provided new vistas to the study of Buddhology in general, and Tibetology in particular, in modern times. This has been, to quote Anant Lal Thakur, “the biggest achievement of the 20th century scholarship” which has made accessible some of the very important texts that were assumed to have been lost ([15], p. 75).

It would be quite interesting to look at the history of the early attempts at deciphering a leaf of the Tibetan canon. H.H. Wilson, the secretary of the Journal of the Asiatic Society of Bengal, in 1832, remarks that in the end of the seventeenth and the beginning of the eighteenth century, the Russians, during their incursions into Siberia, came upon various deserted temples and monasteries where considerable collections of manuscripts were deposited. Although, in general, these were destroyed and mutilated by the ignorant soldiers, fragments of them were preserved and found their way as curiosities to Europe. Amongst these, some loose leaves, supposed to have been obtained at the ruins of *Ablaikit*, a monastery near the source of the river Irtish, were presented to the emperor, czar Peter the great. Literature being, then, at a low ebb in Russia, no one attempted to decipher them and were sent by the czar to the French Academy, the most learned body in Europe at that time. In 1723, the Academy communicated to the czar that the fragments were portions of a work in the Tibetan language, and sent him a translation of one page made by Abbe Fourmont. The letter was translated in the transactions of the Academy of St. Petersburgh, and the text and translation reprinted by Bayer in his *Museum Sinicum*. Muller in his *commentatio de Scriptis Tanguticis* in Siberia *repertisi-Petropoli*, 1747, criticized Fourmont’s translation, and gave a new one of the first lines, prepared with the double aid of a *Tangutan* priest who rendered it into Mongolian, and a Mongol student of the Imperial College, who interpreted that version to Muller. Georgi, in his *Alphabetum Tibetanum*, reprinted it with corrections and a new translation. But his attempts were most ludicrously erroneous. Then, Csoma de Koros prepared a correct translation in 1831 and said that the fragments belong to the ninth volume of the *Gyut* class of *Kahgyur* and that a great part of the extract consists of *mantras* or mystical formulas, or invocations, and these are not in Tibetan but Sanskrit language. Now, neither of the former translators had any knowledge of Sanskrit nor were they aware that these passages were in Sanskrit. Fourmont considered them to be in Tibetan, as well as the rest, and translated the Sanskrit words with the help of his Tibetan dictionary. The failure of the early attempts at reading the fragment of the Tibetan text may be condoned as it were these scholars whose curiosity to know kept the flame of knowledge burning and which led to the reaching of the real meaning of the text and ultimately to the source of the vast knowledge contained in the Tibetan canon ([18], pp. 269–272).

The scholarly investigation of the textual source material began to gain momentum. Some names command respect for doing pioneering work in the field of Tibetology during the nineteenth century. Hodgson, as a British resident at Kathmandu, utilized his time discovering the enormous accumulation of Indian and Nepalese Buddhist palm-leaf manuscripts, many of them dating back to the period of the *Pāla* dynasty which ruled Bihar and Bengal from the eighth to twelfth centuries A.D. He obtained hundreds of works and deposited them to the academic community at Calcutta, London, Oxford, and Paris. He also produced a number of articles on Buddhism on the basis of Nepalese sources which he called Nepalese or Tibetan as Nepal served as a conduit of transmission of Buddhism from India to Tibet.

Another great name during the first half of the nineteenth century is that of a Hungarian scholar, Alexander Csoma de Koros. From 1823 onward, he led an ascetic life in the Indian Tibetan-speaking borderland of *Zangskar* to have a firsthand knowledge of the Tibetan People and their culture. He made an inventory of the contents of the Tibetan canon and also compiled a Tibetan grammar and dictionary. He conclusively showed that the Tibetan canonical works were almost entirely translations from Buddhist Sanskrit which opened up another great chapter in the history of Buddhism in India. He may rightly be regarded as the founder of Tibetan studies in the world.

The Italian scholar Giuseppe Tucci’s expedition in western and central Tibet during the 1930s and 1940s brought hitherto unknown treasures of

Tibetan religion, history, and art. He produced works on all aspects of Indo-Tibetan civilization. A great name in this field is that of reverend Rāhula Sānkṛtyāyana who made four hazardous journeys to Tibet in search of Sanskrit manuscripts between 1929 and 1938. In his fourth visit in 1938, he brought about 1,400 photographs of Sanskrit manuscripts and important objects of art ([14], pp. 137–163). Writing about him, K.P. Jayaswal said that although he brought 22 muleloads of Sanskrit manuscripts and 200 paintings from Tibet, his greatest achievement was to bring back to India the *Pramāṇavārttika*, supposedly the greatest work on Indian logic on which rested the reputation of Dharmakirti, and the commentaries on it in Sanskrit. The whole Tibetan library is now available at the *Bihar Research Society*, Patna, which is the biggest library on Tibetan studies outside Tibet ([8], pp. 159–164).There are many other great explorers and exponents in this field but their achievements cannot be discussed here for want of space.

Tibet's recorded history begins in the first half of seventh century A.D. during which period it emerged as a unified kingdom, with Yarlung valley as its center, some 55 miles southeast of Lhasa, which later became its capital. Tibet's history begins to be written down from the reign of Srong-brtsan-sgam-po (627–649/650 A.D.; the meaning of srong being straight and brtsan mighty) considered to be the greatest Tibetan and the father of Tibetan culture. Within the period of a few years, he built up a vast empire extending from the deserts of Gobi to the foot of the Himalayas, and from Central China to the Pamirs, by leading and disciplining his undaunted and intrepid countrymen into a great power, and by presenting them with the newly imported script ([13], p. 84). The glory of the valor of Sgam-po became so widespread and the Tibetan military pressure on China was so intense that the Chinese emperor Tai-tsung gave his daughter princess Wen-cheng in marriage to him in 641 A.D. Around the same time, a Nepalese princess also came to Lhasa as his wife. Marriage of the Tibetan emperor Sgam-po with the Chinese princess no doubt formed part of a determined Tibetan interest in learning all that could be won by closer contact with China. *Tang* Annals record that the young Tibetans of good families were sent to study statecraft, and not religion, at the Imperial College at the Chinese capital. The diplomatic relationship that was established with China in 641 A.D. proved fruitful to the Tibetans who evinced considerable respect for Chinese institutions, and when they later occupied an appreciable part of northwest China in relative peace for 60 years and more (c. 787–848 A.D.) with Chinese scholars at their beck and call, they took full advantage of the situation ([16], pp. 386 and 415).

According to traditional Tibetan accounts, the Holy doctrine of Buddhism was first introduced in Tibet during the reign of emperor Srong-brtsan-sgam-po but no one could read, write, or explain them at that time. Introduction of literacy became a necessity. Sgam-po then thought of reducing the spoken Tibetan to a system of alphabetic writing to facilitate the coming of Knowledge, and especially Buddhism, from India. The emperor took direct initiative and selected a brilliant Tibetan of his court, Thon-mī Sambhoṭa, to go to the famous seats of learning in India to study epigraphy, phonetics, and grammar. Sixteen other aspirants were also selected to accompany him in this mission. Thon-mī studied in Magadha the arts of both the *Brāhmaṇas* and the Buddhists under Devabit Siṃha and others. After a long period of study, he came back to his country in about 647 A.D. He devised an alphabetic script for the Tibetan language and established its grammatical rules ([4], p. 37). He wrote eight independent treatises on Tibetan writing and grammar. He also prepared the first Tibetan translations of certain Sanskrit Buddhist works, so that he came to be recognized as the father of Tibetan literature. His works provided a great impetus to the beginning of an era of great literary activity, which, to begin with, mainly consisted in the translation of Indian works. It is interesting to note Jaschke's remarks about the significance of Thon-mi's contribution: "Thon-mi's invention of the Tibetan alphabet made it possible that for several centuries the wisdom of India and the ingenuity of Tibet laboured in unison, and with greatest industry and enthusiasm, at the work of translation. It is most remarkable, how they managed to produce translations at once scientific, liberal and faithful to the spirit of the original" ([7], p. iv).

During his lifetime, Sgam-po promulgated laws to harmonize with the "Ten Virtues" prescribed by Buddhism. Both his wives had brought images and the philosophy of the Buddha which paved the ground for the cultivation of Buddhist thought and virtues. He built the famous temples of *Ramoche* and *Jokhang* at Lhasa and the grand architecture of the 11-storied Palace, called the *Potala*. The credit of ushering in a new era in the history of Tibet thus goes to the first great monarch of Tibet, Sgam-po, a contemporary of emperor Harsha of India, *Hazrat* Muhammad of Mecca, and Hieun Tsang, the famous Chinese traveler to India ([5], p. 66).

King Khri lDe-gtsug-brtsan's (Mes-ag-tshom; the meaning of Khri being throne, gtsug being crest, lDe being god, and brtsan being mighty) reign (c. 704–754 A.D.) is marked by the arrival of a second Chinese princess in Tibet and the good treatment given to the foreign Buddhist monks who settled at Lhasa from places such as Gilgit, Yarkand, Khotan, and Kashgar. The king also erected seven temples for them. But he had to expel them after the outbreak of an epidemic of smallpox, which was seen as a bad omen, and the revolt of his ministers. It shows how foreign a thing Buddhism was still felt to be in Tibet in the first half of the eighth century A.D.

The reign of his son Khri Srong-lde-brtsan's reign (c. 754–797 A.D.) is fruitful for political and cultural achievements. Politically, he was engaged in constant warfare in central Asia from the far northwest of the Indian subcontinent (especially Gilgit and Baltistan) to the distant confines of northwestern China. At times fighting and at times on truce with the Arabs and the Turks, his forces pressed their advantages against the Chinese, finally capturing temporarily the Chinese capital of Ch'angan in 763 A.D. and installing a puppet emperor there ([16], p. 421). Speaking at the Afro-Asian committee on Tibet in 1959, it was perhaps to this king that Jayaprakash Narayana, a veteran socialist leader in India, referred to, during whose reign in the eighth century A.D. Peking paid a yearly tribute of 50,000 (fifty thousand) yards of brocade to Tibet ([9], p. 417).

Khri Srong-lde-brtsan was perhaps the first really committed king of Tibet as his Buddhist interests are well attested – both by his words, as preserved in inscriptions and edicts, and by his actions, especially by the founding of *bSam-yas* monastery – the first officially recognized community of Tibetan monks. Despite his powerful *Phon* officials' opposition, he invited Śāntarakṣita, a professor at the Nālandā University, to Tibet to spread the genuine teachings of Indic Buddhism instead of that from China. Due to certain calamities, however, the latter was advised to leave by the king. He recommended the name of Padmasambhava of Swāt Valley who was well versed in the esoteric methods and beliefs of *Tantrism*. It was only he who could impress the people, steeped as they seemed to be in primitive sorcery and charlatanism. Padmasambhava became a great success there. Khri's personal views in matters of doctrine are expressed in the earliest stone inscription which still stands at *bSam yas* ("*Sam-ya*"), which reads as follows:

> The Buddha images set up in the temples of *Ra-sa* (Lha-sa) and elsewhere, as well as the practice of the Buddhist religion, are never to be abandoned. From now on in every generation, the king and his heir shall take a vow to this effect and that this vow may never be transgressed.

It is of interest to know that this inscription was copied in later Tibetan history, which quotes the relevant ordinance that there should never be an abandonment of the "Three Jewels" which are permanently good as the one island of refuge. From now on, the practice of the religion of the Buddha and the "Supports" of the "Three Jewels" shall never be destroyed in Tibet ([17], pp. 43–44 and 95–96).

In about c. 767 A.D., Khri Srong-lde-brtsan, with the help of Śāntarakṣita, who had returned to Tibet by that time, laid the foundation of the first monastery in Tibet – the *bSam-yas* – on the model of the monastic educational center of *Odantapurī* in Bihar and commissioned seven novice Tibetan scholars to become well versed in Buddhism. Śāntarakṣita also helped lay the foundation of the translation activities on sound lines. The establishment of school for translation (*Sgra bsgyur grva*) inside the *bSam-yas* monastery in the eighth century A.D. was a unique academic mission. A translation methodology was evolved, besides the precise Tibetan equivalent of each Buddhist term. Manuals were prepared for maintaining uniformity of renderings. Bilingual glossaries were prepared by the Indian *Paṇḍitas* (scholars) and the Tibetan interpreters (*lo-tsa-ba*). Thc first catalog of the translated Buddhist works was prepared.

Nālandā shaped the mind of the Tibetans ever since Śāntarakṣita accepted to be their guide. A monastery named *Na len dra* was built in the vicinity of Lha-sa. Śāntarakṣita framed a master plan to introduce the academic tradition of Nālandā in Tibet. As per the available materials, Nālandā had a syllabus of five subjects and several subsidiary subjects like lyrics, drama, rhetorics, prosody, Lexicon, polity, didactics, mathematics, astronomy, and astrology ([10], pp. 51–52). The translated versions of all these subjects form part of the *Kanjur* and *Tanjur* collections.

After Śāntarakṣita, who always emphasized the constructive aspect of Buddhism, the nihilistic tradition of Buddhist Philosophy propagated by some Chinese monks gained an upper hand there. The king invited his able disciple Kamalaśīla from Nālandā to meet their challenge. A debate was held between the two parties in the presence of the king, and Kamalaśīla was declared the winner but he was killed by the defeated party. His body was embalmed and preserved in a monastery to the west of Lhasa. King Khri Srong-lde died broken hearted soon afterward ([5], pp. 67–68).

His idealistic son Mu-ne-brtsan-po began ruling from c. 797 A.D. but was poisoned to death in 804 A.D. Then came Khri lDe Srong-brtsan alias Sad-ne-legs, father of Ral-pa-can, who ruled from 804 to 815 A.D. During his time, the Tibetan empire reached its greatest extent. In the east, it included the confines of China, including Tun-huang which the Tibetans held since 787 A.D., in the south it claimed suzerainty over the kingdom of Nepal, in the west it reached Baltistan and Gilgit, and in the north it dominated the whole of Takla Makan with several flourishing city-states. The lower section of Sad-ne-leg's tomb inscription talks of these conquests in grandiose imperialistic terms. It also reads that "the mighty one, the divine son established forever the dominion of his sons and grandsons, made ordinance relating to advice about keeping his people happy and to the methods of defence, better than anything known before, so the enemy might be kept in subjection." But, apart from political achievements, his reign also saw development in matters of religion and culture. His tomb inscription also reads that "the divine king established good religious customs. In accordance with this great law of eternity, he was the ruler of men" ([16], pp. 384, 385). He is also known to have given fresh impetus to translating Indian works into Tibetan by patronizing the composition and publication of the first Sanskrit-Tibetan dictionary called the *Mahavyutpatti* in 814 A.D ([5], p. 68).

Sad-ne-legs named his younger son Khri Gtsug-lde-brtsan (815–838 A.D.) better known by the name of Ral-pa-can, as his successor, in preference to his elder son Glang-dar-ma. Ral-pa-can is remembered by his countrymen as the third great royal protector of religion in the golden age of Tibetan Buddhism. He gave privileges and administrative authority to the priesthood. Richardson has averred that during his time a monk became his chief minister ([11], pp. 136, 137). Politically, he not only maintained the empire but also extended its boundaries and the first history of Tibet came to be written under his patronage. But it was in the field of religion and culture where his genius is discerned. Although the translation work that began in the seventh century A.D. continued till the end of the seventeenth century, it was actually in the reign of emperor Ral-pa-can that it reached its climax.

The translation of Sanskrit works was undertaken on a large scale. According to one estimate, more than half the books comprising the present Tibetan *Tripiṭaka* were translated about this time. The king issued an order to the effect that uniformity, both in the use of technical terms and modes of expression, was to be maintained; in no case were the rules of translation to be violated; and the titles were to be registered and written down to form an index. The codification of each draft of translation was followed rigorously. After the said procedure was over, the manuscript of each text was entered in the catalog (*dkar chag*) with the following details: (1) category, (2) title, (3) author, (4) number of chapters, (5) number of volumes, (6) number of pages, (7) whether translated work is complete or not, and (8) name of the team members who revised the text. The translated works were preserved either in important temples or in a royal palace ([10], p. 50). Each translation was generally a joint work of at least two scholars, one Indian, called *Paṇḍita*, and the other a Tibetan, called *lo-tsa-ba* (translator/interpreter). In some cases, there was a third scholar described as the "corrector." The translated drafts were placed before the revisers. This kind of two-tier or three-tier system of scholars for the best possible rendering reminds the people of the Vedic sacrificial chantings where the three priests – the *Hotṛ*, the *Adhwaryu*, and the *Udgātri* used to chant hymns from the *Ṛgveda*, and the *Atharvaveda*, in front of the fire. To ensure that they chanted grammatically and phonetically correct, there used to be an ultimate priest called the *Brahman*, who was supposed to know all the three *Vedas*, to supervise and set correct their chantings in case they misspelt them ([1], p. 91). The most important point about the nature of these translations is that they are not mere translations, but a word for word representation of a Sanskrit text into Tibetan. Moreover, apart from definite rules for translations, there were fixed Tibetan terms for technical words so that uniformity could be maintained. Thus, with a little bit of ingenuity and careful consideration of the Tibetan version, it becomes possible to reconstruct almost verbatim the Sanskrit one.

> According to a supplement attached to the *Derge* edition of the Kanjur and Tanjur, the number of Indian scholars engaged in the translation work was 107 and that from Tibet, 222. These translations are preserved even today in two grand collections called the *Kanjur* and the *Tanjur* which contain about 4,566 works, the former 1,108 and the latter 3,458. These collections are preserved in xylographs, printed from wooden blocks on handmade paper in red or black ink. These were prepared and preserved in different places in Tibet and that is why there are different versions or editions, generally known by the name of the place of its origin, for example, the *Derge* edition, the *Narthang* edition, etc. Michael Hahn says that the Tibetan canonical literature called the *Kanjur* and the *Tanjur* contains altogether 4,500 titles and texts and if printed in modern book form, these would be at least 400,000 (four hundred thousand) pages – more than the Chinese Buddhist canon, which would amount to about 300,000 (three hundred thousand) pages ([6], p. 3). Although the preferred aim of this literary activity was the propagation of the Buddha's teachings, the selection of a vast range of secular texts other than religion amply testifies to Tibetan hunger for all kinds of knowledge, for example, works of Buddhist logic and Philosophy by Dinnaga and Dharmakirti and commentaries thereon, Kālidāsa's *Meghadūta* and Māgha's *Śiśupālavadhaṃ*, *Chandoratnākara* by Ratnākara Śānti, *Bhāṣāvṛtti* by Purusottamadeva, Dandin, *Kāvyādarsa* Kokā's *Ratirahasya* Bhīmarjuna's *Subhāṣitaratnakoṣa*, and other texts by others like *Aśvāyurvedasaṃhitā*, *Citralakṣaṇa Vyākaraṇa* and *Amarkoṣaṭīkā* ([12], pp. 23–42). Among the several works on grammar that were translated into Tibetan, there is also a translation of Patañjali's *Mahābhāṣya* ([2], p. 112) which is regarded as the philosophy of Sanskrit grammar by many. These were some of the large number of works that were translated/transliterated from Sanskrit to Tibetan.

Khri-lde-sron-brtsan's naming his younger son Ral-pa-can as his successor angered his elder son Khri U'idum-brtsan, better known as Glang-darma, who killed him in 838 A.D. and usurped the throne as an enemy of Buddhism. Although he could rule only for a few years and was himself assassinated in 842 A.D., it was a dark period for Buddhism as Buddha's images were buried, monasteries closed, religious ceremonies banned, and monks forced to return to the life of laymen. His ruthless rule sounded the death knell of monarchical rule in Tibet and his weak successors lost their hold on their dependencies and disintegration set in. The son of the last king of Lhasa, Dpal-hKhor-brtsan (906–923 A.D.), bade farewell to the capital and migrated to western Tibet now known as *Nga-rī* (royal domain). The first representative of the line of Yarlung kings to be declared king of *Nga-rī* is named Nyi-ma-mgon. After his death, his kingdom got divided into three states between three sons – Ladakh was one, Zangskar and Spiti the second, and Guge and Purang formed the third unit. Guge and Purang got united during the tenth century A.D. when it was jointly ruled by king Srong-nge (grandson of its founder Nyi-ma-mgon) and his son lHa-lde. *Srong-nge* adopted the religious life and became known by the religious name of *Lha-lama* (royal lama) and Yeshes-Od (wisdom's light-*Jñānaprabha*). He died sometime toward the end of the tenth century and lHa-lde's son 'Od-lde ruled as coruler with his father. His two brothers, known by the religious names of Byang-chub-Od and Zhi-ba-Od, devoted themselves to Buddhist works, the younger of the two becoming a renowned translator. This is a noticeable fact that in tenth and eleventh centuries A.D. in western Tibet, monarchy appears in the dual role of head of state and of religion. This arrangement became a distinctive feature of later Tibetan governments. The royal family controlled religion insofar as they provided the cost of inviting foreign scholars, of financing expeditions to India in quest of even more books, in building monasteries and temples, and in establishing translation workshops. The royal *lama* Ye-shes-Od invited Dharmapāla, who was the greatest scholar in eastern India at that time. His son lHa-lde invited the great scholar from Kashmir, Subhūtiśrī Śānti, who translated many *Sūtras* and wrote *Abhisamayālaṃkārāloka* and *Abhisamāyālaṃkāraṭīkā* (a commentary on the perfection of wisdom in 8,000 verses). Dgeba'iblo-Gros, a pupil of the great translator Rinchen bzang-po, translated many texts such as the famous *Pramāṇavārttika* by Dharmakīrti and its matching commentary, thus setting a course for the study of logic and philosophy in Tibetan monasteries for the monk-pupils. In the time of 'Odlde, the princely lord (*Jo-bo-rje* or *Atiśa*) was invited to set correct the right doctrine ([8], pp. 471–476). The coming of *Atiśa* (982–1054 A.D.) to Tibet in 1042 A.D. may be said to have brought the last great spiritual impetus from India, with the result that Buddhism struck deep roots in Tibet and thenceforward flourished as an indigenous mode of religion and philosophy. At the request of his patron, the royal *lama* Byang-chub-Od, he composed a little compendium of religious principles called the *Bodhipatha-pradīpa* (guide to enlightenment path) and the 25 key texts. *Atisa's* teachings took a synthetic view of the teachings of both the *Hīnayāna* and *Mahāyāna*, enforced celibacy upon the monks, and discouraged magical practices. It taught moral virtues of monastic life and that one's primary concern should be for all other living beings. In 1056, his disciple Brom-ston founded the first distinctive religious order in Tibet called *bkahgdams-pa*, pronounced *ka-dam-pa* meaning "bound to the Buddha's words," to preserve and spread his master's teachings.

Atisa's coming to Tibet led some monks to reorganize the earlier heterogeneous and unreformed type of Buddhism to be called *rNying-ma-pa* or the "old school" and worshipped Padmasambhava as their founder and *guru* (also called monks with red caps). Two other schools, closely allied with the *bkah-gdams-pa*, came to be founded in the later half of the eleventh century A.D., namely, *bkah-rgyud-pa* and *Sa-skya-pa*. The *bkah-rgyud-pa* (oral traditionalists) was founded by the Tibetan *lama* Mar-pa. It later divided into many sects like *Karm-pa* (Sikkim) and *Hbrug-pa* (Bhutan). The second school *Sa-skya-pa* derived its name "Grey Earth" from the color of soil where its first monastery was founded in 1071 A.D. This sect was closely related to the *rNying-ma-pa* and its monks were not celibate either, and it was also based on Nagarjuna's *mādhyamika* philosophy.

A *Sa-skya* high priest called Hphags-pa became the spiritual teacher of the first Mongol emperor of China Khubilai Khan, who conferred the sovereignty of central Tibet on him in 1270 A.D. This was the beginning of the theocratic state in central Tibet. The famous Tibetan historian Bu-ston (1290–1364 A.D.) belonged to this sect who collected and arranged all the Tibetan translations into two comprehensive categories – *Bkah-hgyur* (*Kanjur*) the word of the Buddha in 100 volumes and the *Bstan-hgyur* (*Tanjur* – the treatises) in 225 volumes. These have come down to be known as the Tibetan Buddhist canon ([5], pp. 70–71).

The great Tibetan reformer Tson-kha-pa, a native of Amdo, founded the *dGelugs-pa* sect ("school of the virtuous," popularly called the Yellow hats) in 1408 which purified the *bkahgdams-pa* of much of its elaborate ritualism and today dominates Tibetan Buddhism both temporally and spiritually, through the religious succession of the Dalai Lamas, of whom the 14th is now the head of this theocracy. His followers founded many monasteries and propagated the doctrine in

Mongolia and Siberia so ably that when the power of the *Saskya-pas* disintegrated, the *dGelugs-pas* came to be favored by the powerful Mongol chiefs as spiritual and temporal heads. The Mongol chief Altan Khan came to regard their third high priest (1546–1587 A.D.), a Dalai (ocean of knowledge), and from that time on this title has been used by all the spiritual and temporal heads of Tibet. The most distinguished amongst the Dalai Lamas was the fifth one (1615–1680) upon whom the sovereignty of the whole country was conferred by the Mongol chief Gusri Khan. But before the Dalai Lama could establish himself, he had to vanquish the king of Tsang, with the Mongol clan as ally and patron. But this system of seeking patronage from an emperor ruling from China had its serious side effects, as from the next century, when the Manchus became the emperors of China, they acted as patron and suzerain which, in the long run, became a tool of justification for asserting its claim over Tibetan territory as one of her dependent states. The seventh Dalai Lama (1708–1758) was a man of deep learning and toleration during whose reign the Jesuits visited Lhasa. Religion and culture seem to have fallen into oblivion because of various factors. After the fall of the Manchu dynasty in 1911, Tibet regained independence, but from 1950 onward China began asserting its claim over Tibet and began sending ethnic Han Chinese to settle down in various parts of Tibet. It forcefully imposed land reforms which were vehemently opposed by the Tibetans, and from 1956 to 1959 the feudal lords and the monasteries rose in revolt at various places like Amdo and Lhasa which were brutally suppressed by the Peoples Liberation Army of China and Tibet was grabbed and made a part of it. The 14th and the last Dalai Lama had to flee Tibet and seek asylum in India. The freedom and civilization of a land which contributed so much in the field of spirituality, art, and culture during the last 12–13 centuries came to an ignominious end.

Cross-References

▶ *Bhoṭa deśa*
▶ *jo-bo-rje*
▶ Nālandā
▶ Padmasambhava

References

1. Bharadwaj RM (2010) The methods and stages of the preservation of scriptures in ancient India: oral tradition. In: Tripathi DS (ed) Tattvabodha, vol III. National Mission for Manuscripts, New Delhi
2. Chattopadhyaya DP (ed) (1970) Taranath's history of Buddhism in India. Indian Institute of Advanced Studies, Simla
3. Csoma de Koros A (1832) Geographical notice of Tibet. J Roy Asiat Soc Bengal (4)
4. Gangopadhyaya MK (2007) Tibetan tradition as complementary to Indian tradition. In: Basu R (ed) Buddhist literary heritage in India: texts and contexts, vol I, Samīkṣikā series. National Mission for Manuscripts, New Delhi
5. Gokhale VV (1987) 'The expansion of Buddhism in Tibet (central) and Ladakh. In: Bapat PV (ed) 2500 years of Buddhism. Publications Division, Government of India, New Delhi
6. Hahn M (2007) Buddhist literary texts. In: Basu R (ed) Buddhist literary heritage: texts and contexts, vol I, Samīkṣikā series. National Mission for Manuscripts, New Delhi
7. Jaschke HA (1958, reprint) A Tibetan-English dictionary. Routledge and Kegan Paul, London
8. Jayaswal KP (1937) Lost Sanskrit works recovered from Tibet. Modern Rev LXI(2)
9. Narayan J (2010) The tragedy of Tibet. In: Guha R (ed) The makers of modern India. Penguin/Viking, New Delhi
10. Pathak SK (2007) Buddhism and Indo-Tibetan literature in xylographs. In: Basu R (ed) Buddhist literary heritage in India: texts and contexts, vol I, Samīkṣikā series. National Mission for Manuscripts, New Delhi
11. Richardson HE (1952) Tibetan inscriptions at Zhvai-lha-Khang. J Roy Asiat Soc, London
12. Sāṇkṛtyāyana R (1935) Sanskrit palm leaf manuscripts in Tibet. J Bihar Orissa Res Soc xxiv (Part I), Patna
13. Sāṇkṛtyāyana R (1937) My impressions of Tibet. Modern Rev LXI(61) No. I, Calcutta
14. Sāṇkṛtyāyana R (1938) Search for Sanskrit manuscripts in Tibet. J Bihar Orissa Res Soc xxiv(Part iv), Patna
15. Shukla K (2007) Aspects of Buddhist tantric texts: the Sādhana literature in India. In: Basu R (ed) Buddhist literary heritage in India: texts and contexts, vol I, Samīkṣikā series. National Mission for Manuscripts, New Delhi
16. Snellgrove DL (1987) Indo-Tibetan Buddhism – Indian Buddhists and their Tibetan successors. Serindia, London

T

17. Tucci G (1950) Tombs of the Tibetan Kings. Instituto Italiano Per IL Medio Ed Estremo oriente (ISMEO), Rome
18. Wilson HH (1832) Translation of a Tibetan fragment by Mr. Csoma de Koros, with remarks by H. H. Wilson. J Asiat Soc Bengal (7)

Time (Buddhism)

Hari Shankar Prasad
Department of Philosophy, University of Delhi, New Delhi, Delhi, India

Synonyms and Related Terms

Adhva (temporality: past/*atīta*, present/*pratyutpanna*, and future/*anāgata*); *Kāla* (time); *Khaṇḍakāla* (empirical time); *Kṣaṇa* (moment, temporal unit); *Mahākāla/dravyakāla* (substantial, eternal, absolute time); *Samaya* (special moment); *Santati* (temporal continuity); *Sthiti* (duration)

Definition

The Sanskrit word for time is *kāla*, derived from the root *kal*, which means to devour, cook, count, measure, cause maturity from birth to death, etc. Time is the very mode of existence. Some Indian philosophical systems define it as an eternal absolute substance whose temporal qualities are past, present, future, before, after, simultaneous, oldness, youngness, etc. Time is also defined through metaphorical images, such as river, wheel, consumer of beings, God of death, and God of gods ([1], pp. 537–542).

Brief History and Meaning of Time

In the *Atharvaveda* ([2], Vol. XIX, pp. 53.1–8; [3], p. 537), which has the earliest reference to time, time is projected as the Supreme God, even God of gods, cosmic power, principle of causality, and an inexorable force which without discrimination matures all kinds of sentient beings from birth to death; metaphorically, it is said to cook and devour them. Time is their destiny. In other words, there is nothing which can escape the clutches of time. Even the Supreme God Prajāpati who is the Cosmic Creator is subjected to time; also even the cosmic principle as eternal duration is understood only with reference to time. Such myths and images of time are created to make human being to realize their ineluctable temporality – birth, duration, and death. Those who subscribe to this theory are called *kālacintaka*, *kālavādin*, or *kālakāraṇavādin* ([3], pp. 537–538). In the subsequent literature, the image and function of all powerful cruel time are transformed. Either time is subsumed under cosmic metaphysical reality (Brahman) and is declared as just a temporal aspect of beings as in the Upaniṣads or identified with the graceful and powerful Supreme Deity like Kṛṣṇa as in the *Bhagavadgītā* ([4], Vol. X, pp. 30, 33; Vol. XI, p. 32). In either case, the soul as life principle of a person is ultimately permanent in the cycle of birth-death-birth or merged into the cosmic reality. So there is no fear of ultimate termination of life which is now indestructible (*anaśvara*, *akṣara*).

Secondly, in the orthodox philosophical schools, time is taken in various ways. In the realist school like Nyāya-Vaiśeṣika, time is classified into two types: substantial time or great time (*mahākāla*) and the empirical time or temporality (*khaṇḍakāla*) [5]. The former is considered to be one of the nine substances. As substantial time, it is unique, inactive, all-pervasive, eternal, and ground of various linguistic usage (past, present, future), temporal priority (i.e., oldness), temporal posteriority (i.e., youngness), simultaneity, nonsimultaneity, *kṣaṇa*, before, after, and so on. In another orthodox school, such as Sāṃkhya, time loses its substantial status and is said to be a derived concept from change [5]. These descriptions of time are significant to understand the Buddhist discussions of time. The Buddhist responses to the above approaches are varied: (1) It nowhere takes time as an external cosmic power as the *Atharvaveda* accepts. (2) It outrightly denies Upaniṣadic and realist conceptions of time but follows Sāṃkhya. (3) The Mādhyamika *śūnyavādin* rejects all kinds of philosophical speculations whether Buddhist or non-Buddhist.

Background Framework of Buddhism

Against the Upaniṣadic doctrines of one, cosmic, eternal, absolute, conscious reality called self (*ātman*, *Brahman*) which is devoid of change, causality, plurality, and spatiotemporal structure, the Buddha's awakening emphasizes two basic truths: the law of dependent/interdependent/mutual arising (*pratītyasamutpāda*) covering both mental and material phenomena and middle path (*madhyamāpaṭipadā*). The latter is known for avoiding the two extremes of eternalism (*śāśvatavāda*) and accidentalism (*ucchedavāda*). The universal causal law of dependent arising defines the nature of coordinated functioning of plurality, change, temporality, and continuity. It makes a thing dynamic in nature. This law is the core of Buddhism. That is why it is identified with the Buddha's dhamma. It is famously said: "One who sees the principle of dependent arising sees the dhamma and one who sees the dhamma sees the dependent arising" ([6], pp. 190–191; [7], p. 384). An insight into the functioning of this law overcomes various false metaphysical beliefs, which are the root causes of suffering. This law is natural and ubiquitous. Together with the law of moral action, it is a replacement of any external creator agency like God. As a religion, Buddhism does talk of overcoming suffering and attainment of nirvana, which involve a methodological path leading to epistemological and moral transformation and development. Further, in Buddhism, whereas life is processional, temporal, and endowed with suffering, nirvana is a state of atemporality, peace, and happiness. A clear understanding of these and many more issues in Buddhism is possible only when one has a clear understanding of the debates on time and temporality among various schools of Buddhism.

It is without any doubt that Buddhism is a process philosophy. It treats every existence or thing having its own history in terms of change and temporality, which are to be ultimately conquered. As a consequence of the dynamic nature of existence in general, Buddhism highlights the three characteristics of a thing: (1) Everything is impermanent (*sarvam anityam*), (2) everything is non-substantial or without permanent essence (*sarvam anātman*), and (3) everything is dissatisfactory (*sarvaṃ duḥkham*) as a consequence of the first two. The impermanence theory later logically culminated into momentariness (*kṣaṇabhaṅgavāda*), which identifies an existence with a temporal unit called *kṣaṇa*. The Theravādins, Sarvāstivādins, and the Sautrāntikas have long debates on the issue of nature of a moment which is required to involve causality, change, and also continuity for both mental and material phenomena. An existence comes into existence because of a complex dynamic causes and conditions. Now the question is whether a dynamic existence has any duration before it comes to its destruction. The Theravādins and the Sarvāstivādins, although differently, do accommodate duration in order to complete causal process, and the Sautrāntikas reject any such proposal as it will go against the logic of change. They maintain that a thing is destroyed as soon as it comes into existence. Secondly, they take both kinds of phenomena, mental as well as material, subject to the same law of change. According to momentariness doctrine, an empirical thing like table or human being as a continuant is a temporal series of events. But how do events constitute a continuant and whether there is an underlying substantial base for these events are further questions of debate which one will see when four kinds of Sarvāstivādins present their different points of view and criticized by other Buddhists like the Sautrāntikas and the Mādhyamikas.

Buddhism is not a single coherent system of thought; it is rather a cluster of various conflicting schools of thought, which means there is not one common notion of time in it. At the same time, time is a very complex and intriguing concept, so no consensus among these schools can be expected. The strategy adopted here will be to analyze various Buddhist positions available in divergent forms of literature in a historical manner. Toward the end, one may thus arrive at some clear idea of the status of time in Buddhism.

Time in Pali Literature

Time as a Special Moment (Samaya)

In the canonical Pali literature, one can begin with the concept of dependent arising (*paṭiccasamuppāda*) which defines a thing's empirical identity as a dynamic whole built of complex factors, whose combination changes every moment. This is the process of ever-becoming nature of the thing. The continuity of this process, because of one's ignorance about the true nature of reality, is conceived epistemologically as a continuant and linguistically or conventionally identified as "table," for example. Thus, "a series of becoming" is actually called a spatiotemporal "being." The Buddha's awakening is about the realization of the true nature of being. This is an extraordinary experience which marks a special moment of occurrence. This is the temporality of that event. This is one of the meanings of the concept of *samaya* ([8], pp. 124–128). Further, temporally it is a transforming event, the experience of one's temporal life process itself and an awakening from the ignorance. *Samaya* indicates the experience of flow of becoming of one's own existence as *lived time*.

Buddhaghosa in his *Aṭṭhasālinī* ([9], pp. 48–51) uses the term *samaya* which denotes time (*kāla*), of course not the substantial time, as well as many other related concepts. He quotes a verse in which time (*samaya*) and consciousness are said to be determined mutually, but first it is time which determines consciousness, and the vice versa. Since temporality is the very nature of consciousness, it is given the primary focus. In the *Dhammasaṅgiṇi* ([10], p. 48), one often finds an indefinite locative "When" (*yasmin samaye...*) which is indicative of an appropriate time or occasion. The *Sumaṅgalavilāsinī* ([11], p. 31), the commentary of the *Dīghanikāya*, gives nine meanings of the word "*samaya*," all of which have somehow temporal sense: occurrence (*samavāya*), moment (*khaṇa*), time (*kāla*), group (*samūha*), condition (*hetu*), view (*diṭṭhi*), acquisition (*paṭilābha*), abandonment (*pahāṇa*), and penetration (*paṭivedha*). Since all these are happenings, they have one common characteristic of temporality. But here moment (*khaṇa*) has a special significance. It indicates the ninth, the culminating, moment of successional states of trance, which denotes the lived experience of holy life. This is also an experience of lived time.

Time as an Abstract Idea

In Buddhism, whereas temporality is considered as an essential aspect of process philosophy, the substantial time (*kāla*) is taken as an abstract idea derived from change which is temporal in nature. This is how Buddhaghosa defines time ([9], p. 49). In the same vein, the *Abhidhānappadīpikāsūcī* defines time in terms of three aspects: (1) Time is a concept by which the terms of life, etc., are counted or reckoned; (2) time is that "passing by" reckoned as "'so much has passed," etc.; and (3) time is eventuation or happening, there being no such thing as time except events ([8], p. 126).

In the *Milindapañha* too ([12], p. 39ff), time is denied unified substantial status, although it discusses the three time epochs (*addhā*) ([8], p. 128ff). When the King Milinda asks the Monk Nāgasena what time is, the Monk Nāgasena replies that it is nothing more than past, present, and future. This reply is based on the discussion of the concept of three time epochs (*addhā*) in the Nikāyas ([13], Vol. I, p. 197; [8], p. 129, n. 160; [14], Vol. I, p. 140). The next question is about the existence of past, etc. Nāgasena's reply is a bit puzzling but interesting and deep in meaning. He says that there is some time which exists and there is some which does not. This reply has its reference to the 12-link temporal formulation of the human personality (*dvādasanidāna*), which is a form of *paṭiccasamuppāda*. This position has been pronounced with reference to the kammic formations (*saṅkhāra*), the second term in the 12-membered *paṭiccasuppāda* of human life across the three times. But, he avers, there is no time for those kammic formations, which are past (*atīta*), gone (*vigata*), ceased (*niruddha*), and changed (*vipariṇata*). Again, there is no time for those dhammas which are ripened (*dhammavipāka*) or those *vipāka-dhammas* which still possess the potentialities of producing results (*vipākadhammadhamma*) or those which help rise reunion (i.e., rebirth, *paṭisandhi*). Also, time exists for those beings (*satta*) who will be reborn after death (*kalaṅkata*), but those beings who will not be reborn when dead and those who have attained *parinibbāna*, to them time does not exist ([8], pp. 128–130). This interesting way of dealing with the issues of time and temporality is not found anywhere else in the world literature of philosophy and religion.

Paṭiccasamuppāda: The Temporality of Human Existence

Paṭiccasamuppāda in early Buddhism represents the three temporal states of a becoming: past, present, and future. The temporal divisions of the 12-link formulation are as follows. A careful study of these links shows that they are stretching over all the three time epochs – past, present, and future ([8], pp. 132–134).

Past Phase as Cause
1. Ignorance (*avijjā*)
2. Kammic formations (*saṅkhāra*)

Present Phase I as Effect of Past
3. Consciousness (*viññāṇa*)
4. Name and form (*nama-rūpa*)
5. Six sense organs (*saḷāyatana*)
6. Contact (*phassa*)
7. Feeling (*vedanā*)

Present Phase II as Cause of Future
8. Craving (*taṇhā*)
9. Clinging (*upādāna*)
10. Becoming (*bhava*)

Future Effect
11. Rebirth (*jāti*)
12. Old age and death (*jarā-maraṇa*)

Causality, Change, Continuity, and Time

Buddhism from the very beginning talks of two forms of reality: events and continuants, actual and conventional, given and constructed, and empirical and transcendental. If change is the most fundamental universal fact of existence, then needless to say, it happens in succession, that is, temporally one after another in the sequence of before and after. In other words, an empirical thing is not only, according to the law of dependently arising, a functional cluster of multiple factors, a whole in parts, but it also acquires its empirical identity like tree or cow under the ignorance or epistemic failure to know the real nature of the processional reality whose constituting factors keep changing instantly. In this manner of existence, a thing is never the same in any two consecutive moments of its *being*, which is as a matter of fact a series of *becomings*. This is metaphysically the inherent nature of an existence. But when one analyzes intellectually and logically the process of change underlying a thing, one conventionally uses linguistic terms like past, present, and future explaining *metaphorically* its different states. This is one's tensed manner of speaking loaded with metaphysical connotations which one has learned since childhood. This habit guides one's entire thinking till one challenges one's own presuppositions, which the Buddhist process philosophy is doing. Technically past, present, and future are called temporal notions unlike spatial ones. Whereas the former is derived from the succession, which is in nature *linear*, *irreversible*, and *asymmetric*, the spatial ones are derived from the simultaneity of all things in the world.

Buddhism maintains the conceptual and also the empirical possibility of togetherness of both temporal and spatial characteristics without assigning space and time a metaphysical substantial status as substrata (*dravya*). The realists like Nyāya [5] will look for a substratum of the properties like pastness, presentness, futureness, now, earlier, and simultaneity in the case of time (the same is the case with space which is not being discussed further). Since these properties, through the process of elimination, do not find their loci in any one of the remaining substances, there must be a substance like time to be their substratum. They also find their support in the linguistic/conventional usages of these terms which in one's life are very effective in successful communication in and understanding of the common world. But Buddhism in its entire history nowhere propounds a theory of substantial time. Yes, it does talk of the reality of past, present, and future (*adhva*, *traikālyavāda*), especially in Sarvāstivāda ([15], Vol. V, pp. 23–25), but it should be understood in a *metaphorical sense* since they are the very modes of the existence of a dynamic reality. At other places, it also talks of time as an abstract notion or as derived from change denying substantial status to it.

Now, the most fundamental difficulty is as to how to explain the mutually related concepts of change and continuity in the process philosophy of Buddhism. The realist has a very easy way of solving this problem. They say, because of its dynamic nature, a thing changes its modes, but its essence or substance remains unchanged throughout the process. But since Buddhism in general maintains the non-substantiality of a thing, it has an arduous task to defend its basic tenets as well as to explain satisfactorily the issues of change and continuity. Other non-Buddhist schools like Advaitins of Śaṃkara type have an easy answer. They simply explain away change as false or mere appearance, which requires just epistemic correction leading to the realization of the cosmic absolute truth, that is, Brahman. Being anti-absolutism and antirealism, the Buddhists are the target of severe criticism, even face contempt and total rejection, by the realists and the Vedāntins. On the other hand, within Buddhism itself, one finds sharp differences among its schools on most of the philosophical issues including those of time and temporality, especially the Sarvāstivādins and their commentators Vaibhāṣikas are innovative and radical in their explanation as they talk of altogether change, unchanging substantial essence, reality of three time epochs, etc. As a result, there are fierce debates between them and other schools like Sautrāntikas, Mādhyamikas, and Yogācāra-Vijñānavādins.

The Sarvāstivāda-Sautrāntika Debate on Time

The debate between the Sarvāstivādins and the Sautrāntikas on various issues including the issue of temporality is presented by Sautrāntika Vasubandhu in his *Abhidharmakośabhāṣya*. Vasubandhu's distinction between primary existence (*dravyasat*) and secondary (*vijñaptisat*), or basic truth and conventional truth, is very interesting here. Through this difference, he tries to solve the problems arising from the togetherness of change and continuity. Now, one can elaborate this idea. A thing, say, a table, is dependently arisen entity which undergoes perpetual change. In other words, its constitutive dynamic factors keep changing in their combination, that is, some new factors join and some old ones get out under the influence of internal and external causal factors. In natural manner, these factors maintain coordinated functioning under parts-whole relationship. But because of the ignorance of this fact, one cognizes the whole as a spatiotemporally given fact which is one's empirical table. In Vasubandhu's analysis, the constitutive factors are primary existence or basic truth (*dravyasat*), while the table which is one's epistemic creation with ontological status is the secondary existence or conventional truth (*prajñaptisat*). Thus, the empirical object which one conventionally calls table, chair, tree, human body, or any other thing is the result of two processes: (1) complex functional combination of irreducible factors which lack spatiotemporal structure and mental interference and (2) cognitive failure to cognize the basic factors as they are and the imposition of mental structure on their complex combination. Whereas the former is inherently dynamic and so ever changing, the latter appears as a structurally given continuant. Again, the basic factors have their own essence (*svalakṣaṇa*), but an empirical reality is subject to the general law of impermanence or change, that is, they come into existence and ultimately disintegrate (*anityatā* = *sāmānyalakṣaṇa*). This whole process involves causality in temporal order. Now, one can discuss the viewpoints of the four Sarvāstivādins and their criticism by Vasubandhu.

Four Sarvāstivāda Views on Temporality

The Sarvāstivādins and their commentators, Vaibhāṣikas, are the champions of maintaining the reality of three time epochs – past, present, future – as against the Theravādins who accept the reality of present only. If one takes the Sarvāstivāda theory at its face value, that is, in literal sense, they are blamed to be playing in the hands of realists and thus going against the basic doctrines of Buddhism. Logically, also they seem to be nonsensical as assigning independent ontological status to past, present, and future will be preposterous. It is therefore advisable that one takes this thesis in a *metaphorical sense*. If one takes temporality – the past, present, and future – as the essential characteristic of an event which flows in linear manner from future to present to past, one can accept engagement in dialogue with the Sarvāstivādins. But logic demands that events, which are in flux and which are happenings, are grounded in some substantial reality. But the kind of language and arguments, as presented by Vasubandhu, the four Sarvāstivādins use for explaining the issues of temporality create problems and confusions and thus invite sharp criticisms by their opponents.

The Sarvāstivāda maintains that a factor or thing has three phases of its existence – past (*atīta*), present (*pratyutpanna*), and future (*anāgata*) ([15], Vol. V, pp. 23–25). This thesis faces lots of criticism because it assigns existence to all three phases of time. There is no problem if present is assigned existence, but how can past which has ceased to exist and future which is yet to come into existence by definition be considered at par or simultaneous with present if the sense of the term "existence" in each case is not different. Different attempts have been made to explain this problem by the four Sarvāstivādins, namely, Dharmatrāta, Ghoṣaka, Vasumitra, and Buddhadeva. Their problem is how to explain conceptually the fact of continuity amidst change. Note that change here is *not in time*, that is, change happening within the time as a vessel; rather it is indicative of *change of time* immanent in the very essence of a thing.

The Sarvāstivāda arguments are based on certain passages of the Sutta literature ([16], pp. 19–20; [3]) attributed to the Buddha in some cases and the demand of logic:

1. The Buddha is quoted as telling his disciples that a wise person does not take past and future into consideration. This statement presupposes the existence of past and future in the same sense as in the case of present.
2. In another *Sutta*, the Buddha is quoted as explaining the epistemological process of visual cognition involving contact of eyes and the material form. Mental awareness naturally follows visual cognition. In the sequence, the former is "earlier" and the latter "after." In this case, the earlier is now past and the after is now present. In this sequential continuity, the next stage, which is yet to happen, can be anticipated to happen. Thus, if there is no future, then there is no present, and if there is no present, then there is no past. This avoids not only accidentalism (*ucchedavāda*) and eternalism (*śāśvatavāda*) forms of causality but also all other forms of causality. It offers dependent arising (*pratītyasamutpāda*) form of causality which universally applies to both mental and material phenomena.

The Sarvāstivāda-Vaibhāṣika text *Saṃyuktābhidharmahṛdayaśāstra* summarizes its argument in support of the reality of the three times – past, present, and future – as follows:

> If there were no past and future, then there would be no present period of time; if there were no present period of time, there would also be no conditioned factors (*samskrta dharma*). That is why there are the three periods of time (*trikāla*). Do not state that there is a mistake. When stating that [the fact that] what is remote is past and that what will exist is future does not exist and that there only is the present, this is not right. Why? Because there is retribution (*vipāka*) of action. The world-honored One has been saying: "There is action and there is retribution." It is not the case that this action and retribution are both present. When action is present, it should be known that retribution is future; when retribution is present, it should be known that action is already past [. . .]. As has been said: "If there are no such five faculties as faith (*śraddhendriya*), I say this is the generation of worldling (*pṛthagjana*)." When the seeker (*śaiksa*) is the one who is bound by envelopers (*paryavasthāna*), such five faculties as faith are not present, because the path is not together with defilement (*kleśa*). That is why it should be known that there are past and future. If it were different, noble persons (*āryapudgala*) would have to worldling. ([16], p. 21)

In the Sarvāstivāda arguments, both kinds of series of time, to use McTaggart's terminology, A-series (past, present, and future) and

T

B-series (earlier than, simultaneous with, and later than), are interwoven:

3. If the existence of the three times is not existent, then the very possibility of the process of karma and its retribution will be impossible.

Now, one can see a strong point in the Sarvāstivāda thesis. They are clearly not maintaining the substantial absolute time. Even if they subscribe to the three-times theory (*traikālyavāda*), they do not recognize their independent existence from the processional reality. In the same vein, one can discuss the different interpretations of the four Sarvāstivādins ([15], Vol. V, pp. 23–25), which are elaborated below:

1. **Dharmatrāta's Theory of Modes (*bhāvānyathātva*)**: Dharmatrāta professes the theory of change as transformation of modes (*bhāva*). *Bhāva* is defined by Kamalaśīla [17] as a special quality (*guṇaviśeṣa*) on the basis of which the application of knowledge (*jñānapravṛtti*) of the three times – past, present, and future – is made possible. When a dharma, he continues, passes through the three phases of time, only its modes change, not its substance, just as gold is changed into different kinds of ornaments. In all these states, only the modes of gold change, not its substance and color (*varṇa*).
2. ***Ghoṣaka's Theory of the Change of Characteristics* (*lakṣaṇānyathātva*)**: Ghoṣaka maintains that there is change only in the characteristics (*lakṣaṇa*) of a dharma when it passes through different time. Thus, when a dharma attains its past characteristic, it does not lose its present and future characteristics. The same is the case with the present and the future characteristics of a dharma. For example, when a man is in love with a woman, at the same time, he does not abandon his passion for other women.
3. **Vasumitra's Theory of the Change of States (*avasthānyathātva*)**: Vasumitra propounds in disagreement with Dharmatrāta and Ghoṣaka that a dharma exists at all the three times and does not change in its substance, modes, or characteristics. When a dharma appears at different times, its conditions change, not its essence, and it receives different designations in reference to its state which it receives without any alteration in its substance. For example, when a small ball (*gulikā*) is thrown in the place of units, it means one; when thrown in place of 100, it means 100 and so on. In this theory, the state is determined by the causal efficiency (*kāritra*) of the dharma. Thus, when a dharma is in the state in which it has not yet attained its causal efficiency, it is called future; when it continues to be causally efficient, it is present; and when it has ceased to be causally efficient, it is past. But in all these states, the essence of the dharma remains intact.
4. **Buddhadeva's Theory of Change of Temporal Relativity (*anyathānyathātva*)**: Buddhadeva propounds a theory of change of relations (*anyathā*). According to him, a dharma passing through different phases of time is designated differently as past, present, and future in relation to its antecedent and subsequent moments without altering its essence. For example, a woman is called mother in relation to her children and daughter in relation to her mother at the same time. In this way, a dharma is future in relation to its antecedent moments past and present; likewise, it is present, when it has both its antecedent and subsequent moments, that is, past and future, respectively, and that which has only its subsequent moments, that is, present and future, is past.

Vasubandhu as a Sautrāntika evaluates and rejects these four theories but transforms and develops Vasumitra's theory, which like that of the Sautrāntikas talks of the concept of causal efficiency (*kāritra*). It is not to elaborate here this aspect of Vasubandhu for want of space. Instead, it is better to discuss below the Mādhyamika and Yogācāra views in brief.

The Mādhyamika Criticism of Time

Nāgārjuna is the champion of Mādhyamika philosophy. He is the propounder of no-view theory.

He examines all other views and shows their emptiness (*sarvadṛṣṭiśūnyatā*) because these views are product of conceptual networking, a mental form of dependent arising (*pratītyasamutpāda*) which is empty in ontological content and external reference. He and his followers like Candrakīrti and Śāntideva are called *prāsaṅgika* as they apply the destructive method of *reductio ad absurdum argument* to a philosophic view, and thus it examines and demonstrates emptiness of its ontological claims. Among other things, he is known for his ruthlessness against realism which subscribes to the view that a thing has its inherent nature (*svabhāva*), its own permanent essence independent of any change. This is a substantialist view, which is under examination by Nāgārjuna. His central point of view can be summarized in the following equation:

Dependent arising (existential, mereological, or conceptual-cum-linguistic) = emptiness of essence (śūnyatā, niḥsvabhāvatā) = emptiness of concepts and language = emptiness of all speculative views.

As discussed earlier, causation in the form of dependent/interdependent arising is the beginning and core of subsequent philosophical discussions in Buddhism. It is a universal law and one experiences it in all kinds of phenomena. The principle of causation gives rise to motion and change which are in temporal order. They are inherently bound up with temporality. In Nāgārjuna, anything which is supposed to exist comes into being and considered dependently arisen. Outside this law, everything is inexistent. Substantial time is one of them. Secondly, in the conceptual dependent arising, mind has multiple functions. It functions out of ignorance and shapes arguments on the basis of presuppositions in order to create a structured view which is superimposed on the dependently arisen empirical object. When analyzed in the Mādhyamika manner, the whole structure and its ontological claim are found to be empty in substantial essence. The epistemological, logical, and semantic enterprises also meet the same fate. Different conceptual frameworks with their implicit presuppositions and the subsequent ontological claims make the philosophical discourse impossible. Thus, world becomes the field of conflicts. The grand program of compassion miserably fails. Nāgārjuna is aware of this.

In the present context, Nāgārjuna in his *Madhyamakakārikā* in its two chapters ([7]. Vols. II and XIX) shows emptiness of ontology of both time and temporality. In Chapter II, he analyzes the concept of motion, which presupposes mover, motion, and the space in which the movement takes place. The whole process is seen in temporal order and relation, which are examined. He shows not only the interdependence of concepts involved in it but also the impossibility of motion and temporality. In Chapter XIX, he rejects the claims of the time theorists (*kālavādin*), substantialists-realist Nyāya, and temporalist-realist Sarvāstivāda. He finally concludes that the past, present, and future are not only derived concepts from temporally ordered change but also relative to each other. Their essencelessness is now proved beyond doubt.

In Yogācāra tradition, the significance of time is recognized, but not as a substantial reality. Since the cause-effect continuum is a fact and it is temporally ordered, that is, it has the moments in the temporal sequence of before and after, time is required to account for change and continuum. In other words, one can say that in the process of cause-effect series, it is the time which as a principle of relation binds the two consecutive events, cause and effect. This is the intrinsic mechanism of the flow of consciousness. To account for this phenomenon, one in natural manner invokes time, which is not an external reality. This is how one can interpret Asaṅga's definition of time (*kāla*) in his *Abhidharmasamuccaya* ([18], p. 11) as follows: "Time is a designation indicating the continuous succession of causes and effects" (*hetuphalaprabandhapravṛttau kāla iti prajñapti*).

To sum up, it can safely be said that nowhere in Buddhism any established school of thought has taken time as a substantial reality. Its entire discussion in various interpretations is focused on the issue of temporality – past, present, future, before, after and simultaneous with – and its other related concepts like causation, change, motion, and linguistic convention or our manner of speaking, which involve temporal concepts, ordering, and relations.

References

1. Prasad HS (2007) The centrality of ethics in Buddhism: exploratory essays. Motilal Banarsidass, Delhi
2. Sharama SR (ed & tr) (2000) Atharvaveda, 2 vols. Haridwar
3. Prasad HS (1982) The concept of time in Buddhism. Unpublished PhD thesis, Australian National University, Canberra
4. Bhagvadgītā. Gita Press Edition, Gorakhpur, year of publication not mentioned
5. Prasad HS (1984) Time as a substantive reality in Nyāya-Vaiśeṣika. East West 34:233–266, Rome
6. (1960–1964) Majjhimanikāya, 4 vols. Pali Texts Society, London
7. Vaidya PL (1060) Madhyamakakārikā of Nāgārjuna, with Candrakīrti's Vrtti. Darbhanga
8. Prasad HS (1988) The concept of time in Pali Buddhism. East West 38:107–136, Rome
9. Bapat PV, Vadekar RD (eds) (1942) Aṭṭhasālinī of Buddhaghosa. Poona
10. Bapat PV, Vadekar RD (eds) (1940) Dhammasaṅgiṇī. Poona
11. (1968) Sumaṅgalavilāsinī of Buddhaghosa. Pali Texts Society, Part I
12. Shastri DD (ed) (1979) Milindapañha. Bauddha Bharati, Varanasi
13. Warder AK (ed) (1961) Anguttaranikāya, 2nd edn. Pali Texts Society, London
14. Feer L (ed) (1973) Saṃyuttanikāya. Pali Texts Society, London
15. Shastri DD (ed) (1970–1973) *Abhidharmakośabhāṣya* of Vasubandhu, 4 vols. Bauddha Bharati, Varanasi
16. Cox C (1998) Sarvāstivāda Buddhist Scholasticism. Brill, Leiden
17. Kamalaśīla, see *Tatvasaṃgraha*
18. Pradhana P (ed) (1950) Abhidharmasamuccaya of Asaṅga. Visva-BHarati, Santiniketan
19. Bareau A (1957) The notion of time in early Buddhism. East West 7:353–364, Rome
20. Prasad HS (1984) Time in Sāṃkhya-Yoga. J Indian Philos 12:35–49
21. Prasad HS (ed) (1992) Essays on time in Buddhism. Satguru Publication, Delhi
22. Prasad HS (ed) (1992) Time in Indian philosophy: a collection of essays. Satguru Publication, Delhi
23. Shastri DD (1968) Tattvasaṃgraha of Śāntarakṣita with Kamalaśīla's Pañjikā, 2 vols. Bauddha Bharati, Varanasi

Time (Jainism)

Ana Bajželj
Department of Philosophy, Faculty of Arts, University of Ljubljana, Ljubljana, Slovenia
Polonsky Academy, The Van Leer Jerusalem Institute, Jerusalem, Israel

Abbreviations

Ds	Dravya-saṃgraha
Ns	Niyama-sāra
Paks	Pañcāstikāya-sāra
Ps	Pravacana-sāra
Sas	Sarvārtha-siddhi
Tas	Tattvārtha-sūtra

Synonyms

Kāla

Definition

According to the Digambara tradition of Jainism, time is one of the six basic types of substances. It exists in the form of innumerable time particles, which are present in the entire cosmos. Modal aspects of these particles are ever-changing and are called moments. Certain authors of the Śvetāmbara tradition agree with the substantial theory of time, whereas others do not accept time as an independent substance and do not distinguish it from the modes of other substances. Despite these differences, all traditions of Jainism understand existence as having neither a beginning nor an end in time. However, within the course of eternity, they speak of the recurrence of ascending and descending temporal cycles in certain geographical areas. These cycles relate to the quality of the living conditions and the possibility for the attainment of liberation.

Jain Theories of Time

There are two basic theories of time (Skt. kāla) in Jainism, one which accepts time as an independent substance (Skt. dravya) and the other which disputes the independence of time from the other substances. The opinion of the Śvetāmbara community is divided with regard to the two theories, whereas Digambaras only support the first one. Those Śvetāmbara authors who reject the idea of time as an independent substance claim that time is not different from the modes of other substances and that there is no need to introduce a separate substance of time in order to account for the temporality in the world. In fact, the theory of time as a substance is not developed in the early canonical doctrine of the Śvetāmbaras and even the word "kāla" appears less frequently than the word "addha-samaya" as "a stretch of time" ([3], pp. 78–80).

According to the other Śvetāmbara authors, time is, however, substantial and they agree with the Digambaras that it represents one of the six basic kinds of substances that make up reality (Sas 5.39, cf. [4], pp. 163–164). Time belongs to the category of nonliving substances (Skt. ajīva), the other substances in this category being matter (Skt. pudgala), space (Skt. ākāśa), medium of motion (Skt. dharma), and medium of rest (Skt. adharma). All of these are distinguished from the category of living substances (Skt. jīva). There is only a single substance of space. It is an extensive substance (Skt. asti-kāya), which means that it occupies many space-points (Skt. pradeśa). The extension of space is infinite, and it is said that it contains an infinite number of space-points. Medium of motion and medium of rest are likewise single and extensive substances, but albeit vast, their extension is limited. They delineate the limits of cosmos and beyond them no other substance but space may exist. Due to this limit, matter may only exist within the cosmic border, and it does so in the form of innumerable minute particles (Skt. parama-aṇu) and aggregates (Skt. skandha) thereof. Jīvas are infinite in number and although extensive, they are also confined to the cosmic part of space.

Digambara authors describe time as existing in the form of time particles (Skt. kāla-aṇu). Each particle of time occupies one space-point and does not combine with other time particles into aggregates like particles of matter but remains forever discrete. Due to this characteristic, time particles are considered to be non-extensive (Ns 34, cf. [6], p. 41) and are compared to a heap of unjoined jewels (Ds 22, cf. [1], p. 12). Just as it is the case with all the other substances apart from space, the existence of time particles is restricted to the cosmic realm. Since cosmos, and with it the number of space-points within it, is limited, the number of time particles occupying cosmic space-points is said to be innumerable, that is, great in number but still finite. Among those authors of the Śvetāmbara tradition who accept the existence of time as an independent substance, some, such as Hemacandra, agree with the Digambara theory of time as consisting of time particles. Others understand time to be a single substance, pervading the whole of cosmic space ([7], pp. 1292–1293; cf. [3], p. 76).

According to the Jain ontological theory, all substances have the same basic structure, that is, they all possess permanent essential qualities (Skt. guṇa) and momentarily changing accidental qualities or modes (Skt. paryāya). This also holds true for the substance of time; it has essential qualities and continually changing modes. The modes of time are called moments (Skt. samaya) and they are infinite in number (Tas 5.39, cf. [8], p. 144), their series having neither a beginning nor an end. A moment is defined as the time that it takes for one material particle to cross a single space-point (Ps II.46–47, cf. [9], p. 397). This duration cannot be measured in the ordinary sense; the smallest measurable time unit is called āvalikā and it consists of innumerable moments. The largest measurable time unit is said to be śīrṣaprahelikā, and time units beyond it are so immense that they are described only with the help of similes (cf. [8], pp. 273–274). Time is said to be measured with relation to the movement of the vehicles of the luminous gods, which are the sun, moon, stars, and planets (Tas 4.13–4.15, cf. [8], pp. 102–104).

These are stationary outside the human region, but are always moving inside it.

On the basis of the difference between the immeasurability of moments and the measurability of other time units, which are determined with regard to the movements of heavenly vehicles, Jain authors distinguished two levels of time. These are the ascertained (Skt. niścaya) level of time on the one hand, which refers to the substance of time with immeasurable moments as their modes, and the conventional (Skt. vyavahāra) or secondary level of time on the other, which is measurable and the measuring of which is performed with reference to the celestial movements. Apart from the practical measurements of time, some Jain authors have proposed that even theoretical measurement by movement of material particles belongs to the conventional level of time ([3], p. 75).

Movement as such, however, is said to be conditioned by the substance of time, which is itself motionless. Jain authors have correlated every substance with a specific function and they described the function of the substance of time as assisting becoming (Skt. vartanā), change (Skt. pariṇāma), motion (Skt. kriyā), and the sequence of before and after (Skt. paratva-aparatva) (Tas 5.22, cf. [8], pp. 131–132). All activity is then dependent on time, which is said to be the auxiliary or instrumental cause, enabling change in other substances (Paks 23, cf. [2], pp. 16–17). In order for the continuous succession of modes in other substances to take place, time must exist, and since substances are present everywhere, the substance of time must exist in the whole of cosmic space.

Cycles of Time

In accordance with Jain thought, certain geographical areas of cosmos (i.e., the continents of Bharata-kṣetra and Airāvata-kṣetra) go through cyclical periods of time (Skt. kalpa), each of which consists of an ascending (Skt. utsarpiṇī) and a descending half-cycle (Skt. avasarpiṇī) (Sas 3.27, cf. [4], pp. 97–98). Once one cycle of time is complete, another one follows immediately; there is then a continuous shifting between ascending and descending half-cycles, both of which last for a very long time. The ascending half-cycle is characterized by an improvement in the conditions of living: people live longer, they are taller, and there is more knowledge, happiness, morality, spirituality, and general prosperity. The descending half-cycle sees a decline in all of these.

Both of the half-cycles are further divided into six time phases (Skt. kāla), which is often diagrammatically represented as a wheel of time (Skt. kāla-cakra), consisting of twelve spokes. The descending half-cycle contains the following phases: (1) very happy (Skt. suṣamā-suṣamā), (2) happy (Skt. suṣamā), (3) more happy than unhappy (Skt. suṣamā-duṣamā), (4) more unhappy than happy (Skt. duṣamā-suṣamā), (5) unhappy (Skt. duṣamā), and (6) very unhappy (Skt. duṣamā-duṣamā). The ascending half-cycle begins with the "very unhappy" phase and then gradually moves through all the other phases up to the "very happy" one. The happy phases generally last longer than the unhappy ones. Furthermore, it is said that after an innumerable number of full time cycles, an irregular descending cycle occurs, when unusual events happen.

It is significant to note that liberation (Skt. mokṣa) is said to be attainable only during the third and fourth phases of either of the half-cycles, since that is when tīrthaṅkaras teach their doctrine and happiness is in the right proportion with unhappiness. During the third and fourth phases of each half-cycle, 24 tīrthaṅkaras are believed to be born; the first tīrthaṅkara of our half-cycle was Ṛṣabha and the last Mahāvīra. As noted, not all geographical areas undergo these cyclical changes and there are certain parts of the cosmos where tīrthaṅkaras always teach and where liberation is therefore constantly achievable. We live on the Bharata-kṣetra continent, which suffers the changing temporal phases, and are currently said to be in the fifth (i.e., unhappy) phase of the descending half-cycle. This means that liberation in our part of the world is at present not possible for anybody ([5], pp. 30–32).

Cross-References

▶ Dharma (Jainism)
▶ Dravya (Jainism)
▶ Jainism (Yakṣa)
▶ Jīva (Jainism)
▶ Philosophy
▶ Reality (Jainism)

References

1. Balbir N (tr) (2010) Dravyasaṃgraha. Hindi Granth Karyalay, Mumbai
2. Chakravarti Nayanar A (tr) (2002) Ācārya Kundakunda's Pañcāstikāya-sāra (The building of the cosmos). Bharatiya Jnanpith, New Delhi
3. Emmrich C (2003) How many times? Monism and pluralism in early Jaina temporal description. In: Balcerowicz P (ed) Essays in Jaina philosophy and religion. Motilal Banarsidass, Delhi, pp 69–88
4. Jain SA (tr) (1992) Reality: English translation of Shri Pujyapada's Sarvarthasiddhi. Jwalamalini Trust, Madras
5. Jaini PS (1998) The Jaina path of purification. Motilal Banarsidass, New Delhi
6. Sain U (tr) (2006) Acharya Kundakunda's Niyamasāra. Bharatiya Jnanpith, New Delhi
7. Shah NJ (2001) Conception of space and time. In: Singh NK (ed) Encyclopedia of Jainism, vol 5. Anmol Publications, New Delhi, pp 1283–1298
8. Tatia N (tr) (2011) Tattvārtha sūtra: that which is. Yale University Press, New Haven/London
9. Upadhye AN (tr) (1984) Pravacanasāra. Agas, The Parama-Śruta-Prabhāvaka Mandal, Shrimad Rajachandra Ashrama

Tipiṭaka

K. T. S. Sarao
Department of Buddhist Studies, University of Delhi, Delhi, India

Synonyms

Buddhist canon; Piṭakas; Tripiṭaka

Definition

A traditional term used by different Buddhist sects to describe their canons of scriptures.

The *Tipiṭaka* (Sk: *tripiṭaka*) (*tī/tri* = three + *piṭaka* = baskets), as the name suggests, traditionally consists of three "baskets" of teachings: a *Vinaya Piṭaka*, a *Sutta Piṭaka* (Sk: *Sūtra Piṭaka*), and an *Abhidhamma Piṭaka* (Sk: *Abhidharma Piṭaka*). Most likely, each of the early Buddhist schools had their own recensions of the *Tipiṭaka*. However, apart from Theravāda, Sarvāstivāda is the only early school which has a nearly complete *Sūtra Piṭaka*, *Vinaya Piṭaka*, and *Abhidharma Piṭaka*. Portions of the *Mūlasarvāstivādin Tripiṭaka* also survive in their Tibetan translation as well as in Nepalese manuscripts. *Dīrgha Āgama*, *Ekottara Āgama*, and *Vinaya* of the Dharmaguptaka School are extant in Chinese translations. *The Dharmaguptaka Tripiṭaka* is said to have contained a total of five *piṭakas*. These included a *Bodhisattva Piṭaka* and a *Mantra/Dhāraṇī Piṭaka*. Traditionally, the term *Tipiṭaka* has generally been used as an epithet for the Chinese and Tibetan collections of the Buddhist scriptures, although strictly speaking, the general divisions of the Chinese and Tibetan collections cannot be put together into three *piṭakas* in the way as has been done in Theravāda. In fact, in the Chinese tradition, the Buddhist texts have been categorized in such a manner that most of them have been put together in four or even more *piṭakas*. The Chinese form of *Tripiṭaka* (*sānzàng*) was also occasionally employed as a titular designation for such Buddhist monks who had mastered the teachings given in the *Tripiṭaka*.

The *Vinaya Piṭaka* consists of texts that deal with the rules of conduct governing the daily affairs within the saṃgha – the Buddhist Order consisting of ordained monks (*bhikkhus*) and nuns (*bhikkhunīs*). Apart from providing a list of the rules, the *Vinaya Piṭaka* also includes the stories behind the origin of each of these rules, offering in detail an account of the Buddha's prescription on issues relating to the maintenance of communal harmony within a large and diverse community of monks and nuns. Different portions of the *Vinaya Piṭaka* are the *Suttavibhaṅga*, the *Khandhaka*, the *Parivāra*, and the *Pātimokkha*. The *Suttavibhaṅga* is a wide-ranging methodical commentary on all the rules of the *Vinaya*. Each of the rules has been given along with an explanatory story in which the background to the origin of a particular rule has been narrated. This itself is followed by the promulgated rule along with additional conditions and the word by word explanation of the entire rule. The *Khandhaka* consists of the *Mahāvagga* and the *Cullavagga*. The *Mahāvagga* consists of ten chapters in which an uninterrupted account is given of the period following the Buddha's enlightenment, his first sermon at Sārnath, and stories of how some of his disciples joined the saṃgha and themselves attained enlightenment. In the *Mahāvagga* are also included the rules relating to ordination, recitation of the Pātimokkha, and the different procedures that monks and nuns are expected to observe during formal assemblies of the saṃgha. The *Cullavagga*, as the name suggests, is the minor of the two divisions and consists of 12 chapters. The first nine chapters relate to disciplinary procedures, different transgressions, prescribed punishments, and expiation, etc. In the tenth chapter, duties of the nuns are dealt with. The last two chapters relate to the first two Buddhist Councils that took place after the death of the Buddha. The *Parivāra* is a manual of instructions. It is a generally accepted view that the *Parivāra* is a later addition to the *Vinaya Piṭaka*. *Pātimokkha* contains in summary all the monastic rules, and it is intimately linked to the observance of *uposatha* at which the recitation of the *Pātimokkha* takes place.

With the passage of time, as Buddhism spread into different regions and cultures and as different schools of Buddhism came into origin, different Vinayas also came into existence. Three of these Vinayas are still in use. They are largely the same in substance and have only minor differences. The Vinaya of the Theravādin Buddhists in Sri Lanka, Myanmar, Thailand, Cambodia, and Laos consists of 227 rules for the monks and 311 for the now non-existent nuns. The *Dharmaguptaka Vinaya* followed by the Buddhists in China, Taiwan, South Korea, and Vietnam has 250 rules for the monks and 348 rules for the nuns. The *Mūlasarvāstivāda Vinaya* Buddhists followed by the Buddhists in Tibet and Mongolia consist of 253 rules for the monks and 364 rules for nuns, though in theory, as the nuns' order was never introduced in Tibet.

The *Sutta Piṭaka* (Sk: *Sūtra Piṭaka*) contains more than 10,000 *suttas* attributed to Śākyamuni Buddha or his close companions. It has five *nikāyas* (subdivisions or collections) – *Dīgha Nikāya*, *Majjhima Nikāya*, *Saṃyutta Nikāya*, *Aṅguttara Nikāya*, and *Khuddaka Nikāya*. The *Dīgha Nikāya* consists of 34 long discourses. The *Majjhima Nikāya* has 152 medium-length discourses. There are 2,889 (but according to the commentary 7,762) shorter *suttas* in the *Saṃyutta Nikāya* arranged in 50-odd groups by subject, person, etc. The *Aṅguttara Nikāya*, according to the commentary, consists of 9,565 short discourses arranged numerically from ones to elevens. The *Khuddaka Nikāya*, a miscellaneous collection of works in prose or verse, consists of *Khuddakapāṭha*, *Dhammapada*, *Udāna*, *Itivuttaka*, *Sutta-Nipāta*, *Vimānavatthu*, *Petavatthu*, *Theragāthā*, *Therīgāthā*, *Jātaka*, *Niddesa*, *Paṭisambhidāmagga*, *Apadāna*, *Buddhavaṃsa*, and *Cariyapiṭaka*. Apart from these, *Nettippakaraṇa*, *Petakopadesa*, and *Milindapañha* are also included in the Burmese edition of the *Tipiṭaka*.

The *Abhidhamma Piṭaka* (literally "higher dhamma") is a collection of texts in which the fundamental doctrinal principles specified in the *Sutta Piṭaka* are systematically restructured and organized. The *Abhidhamma Piṭaka* consists of seven books: *Dhammasaṅgaṇī*, *Vibhaṅga*, *Dhātukathā*, *Puggalapaññatti*, *Kathāvatthu*, *Yamaka*, and *Paṭṭhāna*. In the *Dhammasaṅgaṇī*, dhammas are enumerated, defined, and classified. The *Vibhaṅga* consists of the analysis of 18 topics by various methods. The *Dhātukathā* deals with interrelations between ideas mostly from the *Vibhaṅga*. The *Puggalapaññatti* consists of explanations of types of person, arranged numerically in lists from ones to tens. The *Kathāvatthu* comprises of over 200 debates on points of doctrine. The *Yamaka* consists of ten chapters, each chapter dealing with a different topic. The *Paṭṭhāna* deals with an analysis of 24 types of conditions.

Cross-References

- Abhidhamma Piṭaka
- Aṅguttara Nikāya
- Dhammapada
- Dīgha Nikāya
- Faxian (337–422 C.E.)
- Itivuttaka
- Jātaka
- Khuddaka Nikāya
- Majjhima Nikāya
- Saṃyutta Nikāya
- Sarvāstivāda
- Sutta-Nipāta
- Thera- and Therīgāthā
- Theravāda
- Udāna
- Xuanzang (Hieun-Tsang)

References

1. Chau TM (1991) The Chinese Madhyama Āgama and the Pāli Majjhima Nikāya: a comparative study. Motilal Banarsidass, Delhi
2. Chizen A (1991) Comparative catalogue of Chinese Āgamas and Pali Nikāyas. Reprint. Satguru Publications, Delhi
3. Jayawardhana S (1993) Handbook of Pāli literature. Karunaratne, Colombo
4. Keown D (2004) A dictionary of Buddhism. Oxford University Press, London
5. Lamotte É (1988) History of Indian Buddhism. Peters Press, Louvain, Paris
6. Law BC (1930) Chronology of the Pāli Canon. Ann Bhandarkar Orient Res Inst, Poona 12(Pt 2):171–201
7. Mizuno, K (1972) Essentials of Buddhism: basic terminology and concepts of Buddhist philosophy and practice, 1st eng. edn. Kosei, Tokyo
8. Nanjio (1883) Catalogue of the Chinese translations of the Buddhist Tripiṭaka. Clarendon, Oxford
9. Walser J (2005) Nāgārjuna in context: Mahāyāna Buddhism and early Indian culture. Columbia University Press, New York
10. Warder AK (1970) Indian Buddhism. Motilal Banarsidass, Delhi
11. Webb R (1975) An analysis of the Pāli Canon. Buddhist Publication Society, Kandy

Tipo

► Āryadeva

Tīrthaṅkara (Jainism)

Gregory M. Clines
Committee on the Study of Religion, Harvard University, Cambridge, MA, USA

Synonyms

Jina

Definition

The term *Tīrthaṅkara* refers to 1 of the 24 enlightened teachers of Jain dharma who are born in the descending arc (*avasarpiṇī*) of each cyclical world age. Synonymous with the title *Jina* (conqueror), the honorific title is formed by adding a verbal derivative of the Sanskrit root *kṛ*, meaning "to do" or "to make," to the word *tīrtha*, literally meaning "ford." In this sense the *Tīrthaṅkara* is a "ford maker," one who through his teachings erects a ford for crossing over the troubled waters of *saṁsāra*, the world of perpetual rebirth and suffering. The word *tīrtha* also refers to the fourfold community of Jain monks (*sadhu*), nuns (*sādhvī*), laymen (*śrāvaka*), and laywomen (*śrāvika*), and so the *Tīrthaṅkara* is also understood to be the teacher who establishes this fourfold community.

The Teachings of a *Tīrthaṅkara*

At the heart of the *Tīrthaṅkara's* teachings are the Three Jewels: right faith (*samyag-darśan*), right knowledge (*samyag-jñān*), and right conduct (*samyag-cāritra*). These teachings are considered to be universal and eternal; thus, *Tīrthaṅkaras* are thought to reintroduce or reactivate the dharma in the world at periods when it has been forgotten. Once the *Tīrthaṅkara* attains enlightenment, achieved through the burning away of all *karma* through rigorous asceticism and meditation, he gives his first sermon in a large and grandly decorated assembly hall built by the gods (*samavasarana*). Gods, men, and animals gather to listen to the *Tīrthaṅkara's* sermon, all of them understanding the *Tīrthaṅkara's* address in his or her own language. The body of the *Tīrthaṅkara* is markedly different from that of a normal human being and the *Tīrthaṅkara's* physical presence affects the environment in wondrous ways. His breath has the fragrance of lotus flowers, and while preaching he is shaded by an *ashoka* tree and fanned by divine yak-tail fans. He rests on a lion throne and his presence is accompanied by the sound of divine drums. In his presence war, drought, famine, and political turmoil are nonexistent ([3], pp. 21–23). Many of these distinguishing features draw from ancient Indian royal iconography, highlighting the deep-seated connection between the Jain *Tīrthaṅkara* and the heroic warrior king. Indeed, a common trope in Jain literature is to depict the *Tīrthaṅkara* as the fearless ascetic-warrior battling *karma* on the battlefield of *saṁsāra* ([1], p. 5).

The Historicity of *Tīrthaṅkaras*

The first *Tīrthaṅkara* of this world age was Ādinātha (also called Ṛṣabhadeva), who, as a great king before his renunciation, is believed to have introduced to the world such necessary skills as agriculture, the kindling of fire, and civilized society. The final *Tīrthaṅkara* of this world age was Lord Mahāvīra. The earliest reference to the 20 intermediary *Tīrthaṅkaras* between Ādinātha and Neminātha, the 22nd, is found in the *Kalpasūtra*, and scholars believe the list of exactly 24leaders to have been introduced sometime in the second or first century B.C.E. The list may have been at least partially inspired by similar lists in the Vedic *Upaniṣads* of Vedic seers ([4], p. 40). While Jains consider their dharma to be without beginning and eternal, only the final two *Tīrthaṅkaras*, i.e., Pārśvanātha and Mahāvīra, are believed by scholars to have been historical individuals. Mahāvīra is usually dated to sometime in either the sixth or fifth century B.C.E., with Pārśvanātha being dated to approximately 250 years prior. Scholars continue to debate the exact dates of Mahāvīra, however, and much of the evidence for his dates stem from Buddhist historical sources, as Mahāvīra is believed to have been the older contemporary of Gautama Buddha ([2], pp. 24–25).

Sectarian Controversy over Mallinātha

There is disagreement between the Śvetāmbara and Digambara sects concerning the gender of the 19th *Tīrthaṅkara*, Mallinātha. Digambaras claim that, like the other 23 leaders, Mallinātha was male, while the Śvetāmbaras, who usually refer to this *Tīrthaṅkara* simply as Mallī, assert that she was female; indeed the only female *Tīrthaṅkara* of this world age. According to Śvetāmbara versions of her biography, Mallinātha was previously born as a deceitful king named Mahābala. The king renounced the world along with seven friends, and the eight of them made an agreement to perform the same number of fasts during their time as ascetics. The deceitful Mahābala, though, persisted in finding reasons to cheat on his fasts, using excuses like poor health as reasons to end them early. Because of this, he accrued bad karma. The rest of his ascetic practice, though, was perfect, and so he was able to accrue karma that would mean his being born as a *Tīrthaṅkara* in a future birth. Therefore, the bad karma that stemmed from Mahābala's trickery manifested itself in Mallinātha's female body. The seven friends with whom Mahābala renounced the world were reborn as mighty kings who all sought Mallinātha's hand in marriage. Disgusted with being seen as a sexual object, Mallinātha renounced the world and attained omniscience. Even still, most Śvetāmbara iconic representations of Mallī are in no way noticeably female, and both Śvetāmbaras and Digambaras share the view that committing sins such as trickery or deceit will eventually lead to rebirth as a woman ([5], pp. 14–15).

The Five Auspicious Events in a *Tīrthaṅkara's* Life

In the life of each *Tīrthaṅkara*, there are five events that are considered especially auspicious (*pañc kalyāṇak*). These are, in order, the descent of the future *Tīrthaṅkara* from his existence as a god into the womb of his mother (*cyavan kalyāṇak*), his birth (*janam kalyāṇak*), his renunciation and acceptance of asceticism (*dīkṣa kalyāṇak*), his attainment of enlightenment (*kevaljñān kalyāṇak*), and his attainment of final liberation at death (*nirvāŋ kalyāṇak*) ([2], pp. 27–36).

The *Tīrthaṅkaras* in Biographical Literature

The biographies of most of the *Tīrthaṅkaras* are relatively standardized; Ādinātha and Mahāvīra have the most extensive and unique biographical literature, though Mallinātha and Pārśvanātha also have distinctive stories. Neminātha, too, because he is considered to be the nephew of Kṛṣṇa, the popular avatar of the Hindu god Viṣṇu, and is thus connected with Jain versions of the *Mahābhārata* story, has also been the object of extensive literary attention. In the Śvetāmbara literary tradition, the most famous biographical account of the lives of the 24 *Tīrthaṅkaras* is the twelfth-century monk Hemacandra's *Triṣaṣṭiśalākāpuruṣcaritra* (*The Lives of Sixty-Three Illustrious Persons)*, while in the Digambara tradition it is the *Mahāpurāṇa* (*Universal History*) of Jinasena and his pupil Guṇabhadra.

Tīrthaṅkara Iconography

Iconography of the *Jinas* has been standardized and consistent since soon after images first began to appear in approximately 100 B.C.E. The *Tīrthaṅkaras* are presented in one of two positions. The first is the Lotus Position (*padmāsana*), a cross-legged position in which the feet are placed atop the opposing thighs with the soles of the feet facing upward and hands folded in the lap. The second is the Abandonment-of-the-Body Position (*kāyotsarga*). This is a standing meditative posture in which the arms hang straight down with palms turned inward toward the body. Each individual *Tīrthaṅkara* is depicted as identical to every other *Tīrthaṅkara*; in many cases, the only way to differentiate among *Jina* icons is through the individualized symbol carved into the base of the image. Even this, though, is a later technology of identification; these individualized emblems did not begin to appear until the fourth century of the Common Era. Examining the individualized protector deities (*yakṣa* and *yakṣī*) of each *Jina*, one of which is usually carved on each side of the image, can also help in identifying *Tīrthaṅkara* icons. The only two exceptions to this rule of uniformity are Ādinātha, who in some early icons is represented with long, shoulder-length hair, and Pārśvanātha, who is always depicted with a cobra-hood parasol. This iconographic anomaly stems from an episode of Pārśvanātha's life story in which he was shielded from the torments of a menacing god by the hoods of two snake gods whom Pārśvanātha had attempted to save from death in their previous lives as earthly snakes. All *Tīrthaṅkara* icons, though, express a balanced symmetry and firm, tranquil stability that help to present the *Tīrthaṅkara* as having overcome the bonds of *karma*. Among modern Jain communities, five *Tīrthaṅkara* have emerged as the most popular objects of worship: Ādinātha (1st), Śāntinātha (16th), Neminātha (22nd), Pārśvanātha (23rd), and, of course, Mahāvīra (24th) ([3], pp 19–24). The *Tīrthaṅkara*, though, is not believed to be an active, present participant in ritual worship. Having overcome the bonds of *karma*, free from all desires and worldly attachments (*vītarāga*), including attachments to any followers, the *Tīrthaṅkara* resides in pure bliss at the top of the cosmos and is unable to interact with worshippers. Ritual worship is considered to be a reflexive activity, during which the worshipper attempts to emulate, to a lesser degree of course, the asceticism of the *Tīrthaṅkara* that is necessary for achieving final liberation ([1]).

Tīrthaṅkaras in Time and Space

In the extensive Jain cosmography, *Tīrthaṅkaras* live and preach in numerous areas of the universe. Thus, a *Tīrthaṅkara* named Simandhar Swami is currently preaching in a region called *Mahāvidehakśetra*. While *Mahāvidehakśetra* is inaccessible to most Jain followers, a few accomplished ascetics have claimed to have magically traveled to the region to hear Simandhar Swami preach and bring his teachings back to *Bharatakś etra*, the region inhabited by Mahāvira and the other 23 *Tīrthaṅkaras* of the current *avasarpiṇī*. Jains have also mapped out the 24 future *Tīrthaṅkaras* who will preach in *Bharatakśetra* in the next world age. The first will be Mahāpadma, also called Padmanabha, who in a previous life was the famed King Śrenik. While his soul currently resides in one of the many Jain hells, where it is burning off karma acquired because King Śrenik ended his life through suicide, Mahāpadma (also sometimes Padmanābha) will eventually be reborn as the *Tīrthaṅkara* contemporary of the future Buddha, Maitreya ([2], p. 41; [5], p. 26).

List of 24 *Tīrthaṅkaras* of the Current World Age Along with Symbol and Complexion

Ṛṣabhadeva/ Ādinātha	Bull	Golden
Ajitanātha	Elephant	Golden
Sambavanātha	Horse	Golden
Abhinandananātha	Monkey	Golden
Sumatinātha	Crow/heron	Golden
Padmaprabha	Lotus	Red
Suparśvanātha	Swastika	Golden
Candraprabha	Moon	White
Suvidhinātha	Makara/crocodile/ dolphin	White
Śītalanātha	Wish-fulfilling tree/ Śrīvatsa symbol	Golden
Śreyānsanātha	Rhinoceros	Golden
Vāsupūjya	Female buffalo	Red
Vimalanātha	Boar	Golden
Anantanātha	Hawk (Digambara), ram/ boar (Śvetāmbara)	Golden
Dharmanātha	Vajra/thunderbolt	Golden
Śāntinātha	Deer/antelope	Golden
Kunthunātha	Goat	Golden
Arahanātha	Fish/nandyavarta symbol	Golden
Mallinātha	Kalasa/water jug	Blue
Munisuvratanatha	Tortoise	Black
Naminātha	Blue lotus	Golden
Neminātha	Conch shell	Black
Pārśvanātha	Snake	Blue black or blue green
Mahāvīra	Lion	Golden

Cross-References

▶ Jina

References

1. Babb LA (1996) Absent lord: ascetics and kings in a Jain ritual culture. University of California Press, Berkeley/Los Angeles
2. Carrithers M, Humphrey C (1991) The assembly of listeners: Jains in society. Cambridge University Press, New York
3. Cort JE (2010) Framing the Jina: narratives of icons and idols in Jain history. Oxford University Press, New York
4. Dundas P (2002) The Jains, 2nd edn. Routledge, London/New York
5. Jaina PS (1991) Gender and salvation: Jaina debates about the spiritual liberation of women. University of California Press, Berkeley/Los Angeles

Further Reading

Cort JE (2010) Framing the jina: narratives of icons and idols in Jain history. Oxfrod University Press, New York

Cort JE (2001) Jains in the world: religious values and ideology in India. Oxford University Press, New York

Jaini PS (1979) The Jaina path of purification. University of California Press, Berkeley/Los Angeles

Kelting W (2001) Singing to the Jinas: Jain laywomen, maṇḍal singing, and the negotiations of Jain devotion. Oxford University Press, New York
Long JD (2009) Jainism: an introduction. IB Tauris, NewYork
Pal P et al (1994) The peaceful liberators: Jain art from India. Thames and Hudson, New York
Pereíra J (1977) Monolithic Jinas: the iconography of the Jain temples of Ellora. Motilal Banarsidass, Delhi
Titze K (1998) Jainism: a pictorial guide to the religion of non-violence. Motilal Banarsidass, Delhi
van Alphen J (2000) Steps to liberation: 2,500 years of Jain art and religion. Etnografisch Museum, Antwerp
von Glasenapp H (1999) Jainism: an Indian religion of salvation (trans: Shrotri SB). Motilal Banarsidass, Delhi

Tīrthayātrā

▶ Pilgrimage (Buddhism)

Titthayātā

▶ Pilgrimage (Buddhism)

Tolerance (Jainism)

Stephanie Varnon-Hughes
Claremont Lincoln University, Claremont, CA, USA

Synonyms

Sabar; Sahishnutaa

Definition

Tolerance is a concept that stems from the fundamental Jain understanding that one living being is not more valuable than another.

"Live and Let Live"

Tolerance refers to an underlying concept – nearly a practice – within Jainism. First, the Jain precept "live and let live" underscores the idea that all living things are on similar paths to enlightenment. One human's life is not more valuable than another. That is, inside, each person – and living being – is the same; one's worth does not come from external assets or circumstances such as wealth, beauty, skills, or acclaim. Jains understand these material or worldly values to be not only unrelated to the ascension of the soul but in fact a detriment to spiritual development.

Anekānta-vāda

Jains teach about the inherent nature of all living beings through self-meditation and through practicing *ahimsa*, *aparigraha*, and *anekānta-vāda* (nonviolence, nonpossession, and multiplicity of viewpoints). Mahavir emphasized that all living beings, irrespective of their size, form, or spiritual development, are equal and deserve love and respect. *Anekānta-vāda* is related to tolerance because the practice of non-absolutism allows us to think critically, entertain a variety of perspectives, and engage respectfully with others. These abilities are the foundation of tolerance.

In Jain theory, "tolerance" does not necessarily mean forbearance of the negative, out of compulsion or helplessness. Instead, the doctrine of *Anekānta-vāda* (particularly as it applies to tolerance) is a philosophy related to the reconciliation of (seemingly) opposite attributes [1]. Simply put, one cannot be the only right one; living in this world by practicing tolerance allows one to both practice flexibility of thought and experience and develop spiritually through right conduct.

T

Reality

According to Jains, commitment to only one way, or one opinion, is severely limited because it can only be a *partial* view of reality. The realities of the world are innumerable. When we are intolerant, we are denying ourselves access to understanding reality. Additionally, intolerance is a negative and harmful attribute – it is related to pride in one's own existence and supremacy and undercuts humility and a sense of respect to other living creatures.

Peaceful Coexistence

Jains believe that true tolerance has the capacity to both heal human conflict and resolve metaphysical issues. The idea of tolerance is essential to the former [2]. Accepting others, and their own way of life, is seen as essential to living in peace.

Tolerance is also related with ideas of *ahimsa* and karma; as such, it is one of the underpinnings of many aspects of Jain philosophy. When one remembers that all living beings are equal and should have neither friend nor foe (following the teachings of Mahavira), it becomes clear that intolerance becomes a kind of mental violence that often leads to material and physical violence. Jains also understand tolerance to be related to karma because it helps us understand the suffering of others and prevent harm we may otherwise cause.

Another reason to be tolerant is so that one might be humble. It is not possible, in this life, for one to access complete truth; humans are not omniscient. Accordingly, one should not insist that one's viewpoint is the only and correct one to follow. Being tolerant is a way to practice relativity and flexibility of thought. Humility is one of the ten observances of *daslakshan dharma*. Keeping one's heart tolerant is supreme humility.

Showing tolerance is also a way to foster reconciliation with those of differing viewpoints. In this way, tolerance is fertile ground for nonviolence, another foundational precept for Jainism. Indeed, tolerance, nonviolence, and compassion are related and intersect frequently in Jain philosophy and teachings. Tolerance cannot be understood or attempted without also practicing compassion. The humility that undergirds tolerance can feed compassion, for example. Intolerance can be thought of as "mineness," with the idea that "mine" is the most correct or only correct viewpoint. And so, when "mineness" dissolves, its parallel "otherness" also disappears, leading to equanimity. First, we must learn and understand that we are mistaken when we understand objects and ideas to belong to us. With guidance, and tolerance, we can begin to understand the fleeting falseness of "otherness."

To continue understanding the relationship between tolerance and nonviolence, it is worth noting that at the moment one recognizes one could be wrong, one's conduct can then never be dogmatic or fundamentalist. Once one begins to be tolerant, one's behavior is bound to be more amicable.

Right Belief

Finally, practicing tolerance can help one achieve right belief. Two characteristics of right belief, *prasama* or *sama* and *anukampa*, are related to tolerance. *Prasama* can be understood as calmness, or tranquility. When one lets go of the false belief that his or her belief is the only correct one, he or she can become more tranquil and perhaps achieve equanimity [3]. Without this, he or she will remain in spiritual bondage. *Anukampa* is compassion; compassion for others grows when one begins to understand the validity of all viewpoints. A right believer is not bigoted, but has respect for all. The more one clings to one's viewpoint, the more he or she remains intolerant; in this way, access to understanding reality and growing spiritually is thwarted.

And so, tolerance can be understood to be important socially and spiritually. Socially, tolerance can heal rifts in communities and provide leaders with ways to connect with those who have differing viewpoints and priorities. Spiritually, practicing tolerance can help cultivate compassion and achieve equanimity. Additionally, once one becomes softened to understanding another's perspective, he or she finds it easier to wish that person peace. It is no wonder that *anekānta-vāda*, the Jain doctrine of which tolerance is part, is a key part of Jainism. Without tolerance, one's sense of self becomes unclear and inflated and veers away from accessing the truth of reality – possible understandings are infinite.

Cross-References

- *Anekāntavāda*
- *Nayavāda*
- *Syādvāda*

References

1. Paul D (2004) Beyond Anekantavada: a Jain approach to religious tolerance. In: Sethia T (ed) Ahimsa, Anekanta and Jainism. Motilal Banarsidass, New Delhi, pp 123–136
2. Sagar Mal J (1997) The philosophical foundation of religious tolerance in Jainism. In: Studies in Jainism: reader 2. Jain Study Circle, New York, pp 157–164
3. Sangave VA (2006) Aspects of Jaina religion. Bharatiya Jnanpith, New Delhi

Trance

- Dhyāna/Jhāna

Tranquility

- *Samatha*

Transcendental Virtues

- Pāramitā

Transmigration

- Karma (Jainism)
- Saṃsāra (Buddhism)

Travel (Buddhism)

Pankaj Mohan
Faculty of International Korean Studies, The Academy of Korean Studies, Gyeonggi-do, South Korea

Synonyms

Yātrā

Definition

The movement of Buddhist monks and laity from one place to another.

Travel As a Means of Buddhist Evangelism

The spread and triumph of Buddhism beyond the borders of India can be attributed to the indefatigable zeal with which Buddhist monks traveled. In his sermon at Sarnath at the end of the rain retreat, the Buddha exhorted monks to wander forth for the benefit of the many: "in compassion for the world" and "for the welfare of gods and men." After attaining enlightenment, Buddha traveled to many places in the present-day Bihar and UP provinces, namely, Rājgīr, Pāṭaliputra (Patna), Vaiśālī, Sāranāth, and Śrāvastī. It is also interesting that the Third Buddhist Council, convened in Pāṭaliputra, decided to send missionaries to Sri Lanka, Gandhāra, Himalayan regions, and even Greece. In the subsequent centuries, Buddhist monks bridged the cultural gulf between India and other countries where Buddhism spread, through their translation works. Kumārajīva was such a pioneer translator of Buddhist texts in Chinese.

Kumārajīva (died 413) earned such renown as a scholar of Buddhism that he was captured by Lu Guang (382) on one of his military expeditions in

T

Central Asia and brought to Changan in 401. With the help of his assistants, he translated 98 of the Buddhist texts, 52 of which are still extant. Kumārajīva's translations of Buddhist scriptures in sophisticated Classical Chinese played a crucial role in the spread of Buddhism in East Asia.

While Kumārajīva was engaged in spreading the words of Buddha among the Chinese people, a Chinese monk Faxian (337 to c. 422 C.E.) undertook a death-defying journey to India to acquire original Buddhist scriptures in Sanskrit on Vinaya (monastic discipline). He left China in 399, and crossing the Gobi desert and passing through Lobnor, Kucha, Khotan, and Gandhāra, he reached the city of Pāṭaliputra in North India in 399 and stayed in this city for 3 years, studying Vinaya texts and copying Buddhist scriptures. He traveled to various parts of India and returned to China by sea route via Sri Lanka and Java. His travelogue *Faguoji* (*Records of the Buddhist Kingdoms*) offers a fascinating account of the history and geography of many countries on the Silk Road and an insight into the formative phase of Buddhism in Central Asia.

Numerous Buddhist monks from China followed the footsteps of Faxian and traveled to India in the fifth and sixth centuries, but the monk who left the most distinguished mark as a traveler on the history of Buddhism is Xuanzang. Xuanzang left China in 629, and crossing the Gobi desert and from there following the Tianshan, westward, he entered into the territory ruled by Tujue (The Western Turks). Subsequently, he passed through Samarqand, Sogdiana, Kapisa, and Gandhāra and reached the famous Nālandā monastery, the preeminent seat of Buddhist learning in the contemporary world. He studied Yogācāra (consciousness-only) texts at Nalanda for 5 years under the guidance of Monk Śīlabhadra. After he returned to China in 644, Emperor Taizong created an Office of Translation to facilitate his work of translation of Buddhist texts that he had brought from India. Xuanzang wrote *Xiyuji* (*Journey to the Western Region*) which is an invaluable source to study the history of early medieval India.

Another important Chinese pilgrim to India was Yijing (634–713) who took maritime route from Guangzhou to Tāmralipti (present-day Tamluk of West Bengal) by the way of Sri Vijaya in Sumatra. Besides an account of his travel to the countries he visited, he wrote a book *Datangxiyuqiufagaosengzhuan (Biographies of Eminent Monks who Traveled to India in Search of Law)*, containing short biographies of eminent Chinese and Korean monks in India. It is remarkable that out of 61 monks whose biographies Yijing wrote in his book, 7 are from the ancient Korean state of Silla and 1 is from another Korean kindom, Koguryo. Āryavarman, Hyeop, Hyontai, Hyongak, Hyeryun, and Hyunyu are some of these Silla monks noted by Yijing.

The unification of the Korean peninsula by the joint Silla (Korea)–Tang forces in 668 paved path for close political collaboration between Tang China and Silla which in turn facilitated an active cultural and religious interaction between the two states. In the mid-seventh century, the world of Korean Buddhism got further stimulus due to the introduction of Buddhist canons, translated by the famous Tang monk Xuanzang after his return from India in 645. Commencing from the mid-seventh century, monks from Silla and Japan traveled to China in large numbers.

In the early eighth century, a Korean monk Hyech'o set off for India. He studied esoteric Buddhism in Tang China in the early eighth century under a tantric master Vajrabodhi who praised him as "one of the six living persons who were well trained in the five sections of the Buddhist canons." It was apparently at his advice that he set out for India. His travelogue *Wangoch'onch'ukkuk chon* (Record of Travel to Five Indian States) lay hidden in oblivion until 1904 when a French scholar Paul Pelliot became aware of its significance. Later in 1908 when Pelliot discovered the text, although in a truncated and abridged version, in a Dunhuang grotto, many scholars from China, Japan, and Korea wrote about this important source on the history and culture of India in the eighth century.

Chikong is the last recorded Indian monk to visit China and Korea. He reached the kingdom of Koryo in 1326 and sought to inject fresh strength into decaying Korean Buddhism. As he came via Yuan China, records about him are available in China.

Travel played an important part in building a bridge of cultural understanding and linking India with Tibet and countries in Southeast Asia. Indian monk Padmasambhava who traveled to Tibet in the eighth century is regarded by followers of the Nyingma School as the second Buddha. Another Indian monk of seminal significance, *Atiśa*, visited Tibet in 1038 and initiated a major reform movement in that country.

Cross-References

- ▶ Buddhist Councils
- ▶ Faxian (337–422 C.E.)
- ▶ Gandhara
- ▶ Kumārajīva
- ▶ Sārnāth
- ▶ Śrāvastī
- ▶ Vaiśālī
- ▶ Xuanzang (Hieun-Tsang)
- ▶ Yijing

References

1. Xian Fa (1886) A Record of Buddhistic Kingdoms; Being an Account by the Chinese monk Fa-hien of his Travels in India and Ceylon, A.D. in search of the Buddhist Books of Discipline (trans: James Legge). Clarendon Press, Oxford
2. Hien Fa (1877) Record of the Buddhistic kingdoms by Fa-hien (414 AD). Tr. from the Chinese by Herbert A Giles. Trubner, London
3. Beal S (trans) (1911) The life of Hiuen-Tsiang. Trans. from the Chinese of Shaman Hwui li, 2nd edn. London. Munishiram Manoharlal, Delhi, 1973
4. Yung-hsi L (trans) (1959) The life of Hsuan-Tsang by Huili. Chinese Buddhist Association, Peking
5. Wriggins SH (1996) Xuanzang: a Buddhist Pilgrim on the Silk Road. Westview Press/Harper Collins, Boulder
6. I-Tsing (2005) A Record of the Buddhist Religion: as Practised in India and the Malay Archipelago (A.D. 671–695). Translated by J. Takakusu (1896). Reprint. AES, New Delhi
7. I-Tsing (1986) Chinese Monks in India, Biography of Eminent Monks who went to the western world in Search of the Law during the Great Tang Dynasty, Translated by Latika Lahiri. Motilal Banarsidass, Delhi
8. Jan Yun-hua et al (trans) (1984) The Hye Ch'o Diary: memoir of the Pilgrimage to the Five Regions of India (Religions of Asia Series) Asian Humanities Press, Berkeley, California and Seoul
9. Sankrityayana R (1984) Selected Essays. People's Publishing House, Delhi
10. Sen T (2003) Buddhism, Diplomacy, and Trade: the Realignment of Sino-Indian Relations, 600–1400. University of Hawaii Press, Honolulu

Tri-kāya

Mangala Ramchandra Chinchore
Department of Philosophy, Centre for Studies in Classical Indian Buddhist Philosophy and Culture, University of Pune, Pune, Maharashtra, India

Synonyms

Three bodies of thc Buddha

Definition

Three important aspects of nature of the Buddha and correspondingly that of the reality.

"*Tri-kāya*" literally means "Three Bodies" and connotes "three bodies of the Buddha." It concentrates on the three important aspects of nature of the Buddha and correspondingly that of the reality. *Tri-kāya* doctrine is a unique contribution of *Mahāyāna* tradition of Buddhism in general and of *Yogācāra* sect in particular, articulated and expounded perhaps for the first time in the *Saddharma-Puṇḍarīka-Sūtra* (The Lotus-*Sūtra*) [1], composed in the first century B.C.E. approximately, and then later on in the *Saddharma-Laṅkāvatāra-Sūtra* [2].

The Buddha or Reality is manifested in three different ways (*Kāyas* – bodies/forms/modes of physical existence): (1) *Nirmāṇa-kāya* (created-body) is origination or spatiotemporal emergence in this world, (2) *Dharma-kāya* (truth-body) is truth realized by the Buddha, and he taught it to others, and further it is preserved by his followers, and (3) *Saṁbhoga-kāya* (enjoyment-body) is manifestation in archetype form. It is historically interesting and philosophically important to know this doctrine in details.

Nirmāṇa-kāya (Created-Body)

Nirmāṇa-kāya of *Mahāyāna* Buddhism and/or *Rūpa-kāya* (physical form of bodily existence) of *Theravāda* Buddhism is a view that the Buddha was actually born as a human being with extraordinary qualities, at particular space and time, and lived till his natural death. Buddha is not a concept articulated or imaginarily fabricated by human intellect, but he actually lived in this world. In a nutshell, human birth and life of the Buddha is not a gospel.

After the passage of about four centuries between the demise (*Parinirvāṇa*) of the Buddha and his followers, the question was raised whether the Buddha really existed in space and time historically, or is it a mythical creation through human imagination. At that time it was essential to emphasize that the Buddha really existed in this world. It is not just a matter of belief and legend, but of truism, although at present one is neither clear about the exact date and year of his birth, nor that of his demise, and hence there are disputes (among scholars) about them. However, one is certain that he was born around 563 B.C.E. approximately at Lumbinī near Kapilavastu in the Śākya-clan, as a son of Śuddodana and Mahāmāyā. Mahāmāyā died just after 7 days of his birth, and her younger sister, Prajāpati Gautamī, brought him up. He lived his married life with Yaśodharā and had a son Rāhula. At the age of 29, he renounced his family life and adopted the ascetic mode of life. He passed through various stages of spiritual practices, realized the truth, and was enlightened at the age of 35. Till his death at the age of 80 approximately in 483 B.C.E., he delivered his thoughts and enlightened others [3]. His life as a human being is portrayed mystically and gloriously due to various legends connected with it, providing grounds for doubt/suspicion about his origination, passage of life, and acquisition of enlightenment through progressive stages of his spiritual career and finally making a landmark as the profounder of Buddhism.

The *Nirmāṇa-kāya* doctrine advocated by *Mahāyāna* Buddhism is a response to such doubts, like whether the Buddha was born as a superhuman being and descended down on the earth, or like a normal human being he too passed through the various problems and faced the facts of life. This doctrine enables one to connect with the Buddha and stresses on the point that anybody can become a Buddha, ascend one's own spiritual status by self-effort, and establish himself in this world as an exemplary ideal human being. It is possible to corelate oneself with the Buddha, irrespective of passage of time and place, to anybody without discrimination of age, gender, place/region, religion, etc., universally. Nobody is bestowed any status by grace, but one has to acquire perfection by self-help/self-efforts. Even though conditions are adverse, one has to fight by oneself against all kinds of odds. The Buddha was not enlightened by birth, and did not descend down on earth, but made strenuous efforts both psychophysically as well as spiritually to realize the ultimate truth. Buddha by birth was Siddhārtha Gautama, and later on he became the *Tathāgata* Buddha. In the Buddhist Canonical literature, physical existence of the Buddha was known as the *Rūpa-kāya*, which later on *Mahāyānists* presented in the universalized form of *Nirmāṇa-kāya.*

Dharma-kāya (Truth-Body)

When Buddha was alive, his life itself was an illustrious example giving direction to others and the truth was depicted in his thoughts. However, Buddha was clear about the difference between life and thoughts – death is the end of life, but thoughts can survive and continue endlessly, transcending the boundaries of space and time universally. That is why, Buddha says to Vasettha, "after my death my thoughts will survive and provide you guidance". Human existence is impermanent/non-eternal, constituted of *Putikāya* – (decomposing body) according to *Saṁyutta-Nikāya* ([4], 122.87) – but thoughts of the enlightened one (Buddha) can be eternal and universal. After enlightenment, the Buddha became

Dharma-bhūta (truth-incarnated or becoming truth) and *Tathāgata* (thus coming) (*Dīgha-Nikāya*). The term *Dharma-kāya* was in vogue even before *Parinirvāṇa* of the Buddha.

Dharma-kāya literally means "Embodiment of Truth" by the enlightened Buddha. Buddha recognizes the unchanging nature of the truth (*Dharma*), which is the universal principle and an unconditioned timeless phenomenon. This eternal aspect of Buddha's teaching is *Dharma-kāya*. It is also known as *Svabhāva-kāya* (self-existent body of truth). *Dharma* (truth or reality) exists by its own nature. Teaching of the Buddha is everything – manifested or unmanifested (free from characteristics and distinctions) – preserved orthodoxically by letters or by interpretation of thoughts too. *Dharma* does not restrictively mean teachings of the Buddha by letters only, but it also consists of interpretations of his teachings made by his enlightened and committed followers from time to time, making Buddhism relevant in the changing circumstances and situations. This provided scope to contribute to preserve tradition and become a part of the *Dhamma*, transcending the limitations of time. *Dharma-kāya* (truth-body) is the embodiment of the very principle of enlightenment in the inclusive sense, without any kind of limitation or restriction.

In Buddhism, "enlightenment" can "become truth" (*Dharma-bhūta*) ([5], pp. 27–29) or can be lived in this world and life. Truth can be realized by two ways, and hence correspondingly there are two types of Buddhas: *Samyak-saṁbuddha* (*Sammā-saṁbuddha*) and *Pratyeka Buddha* (*Pacceka-buddha*). In both the cases, there is a possibility to become Buddha respectively, and such a potentiality to realize *Nirvāṇa* lies in each one, but the ways and means differ, and hence correspondingly there is a differentiation between *Samyak-saṁbuddha* and *Pratyeka Buddha*.

(a) *Samyak-saṁbuddhas* are those who attain Buddhahood and decide to teach others the truth they discovered by themselves. They awaken others by teaching the *Dharma* – in the prevalent spatiotemporal context, where it has not been taught before, taught but misunderstood, or has been taught yet forgotten after a passage of time. They use their own discretionary powers to discover the truth, interpret the thoughts of the Buddha relevant to the prevalent circumstances, and live it through efforts courageously. They are enlightened noble ones, who discover the *Dhamma* without teacher or tradition by themselves. Historically, Siddhārtha Gautama Buddha is considered as *Samyak-saṁbuddha*. In short, *Samyak-saṁbuddha* is one who has become enlightened through self-reliance, self-effort and helps others to be enlightened.

(b) *Pratyeka-Buddhas* are similar to *Samyak-saṁbuddhas*. They too attain *Bodhi* (enlightenment) and *Nirvāṇa* (emancipation), acquire the similar powers as a *Sammā-saṁbuddha*, but they choose not to teach what they have discovered to others; that is why, they are known as "Silent Buddhas." They only concentrate on personal spiritual development, and stick to the path not discovered by themselves but abiding by tradition follow the directives given by the Buddha strictly. They are known as *Anu-buddhas/Śrāvaka-buddhas* (hearers or followers), who become Buddhas after getting instruction only.

Thus, in the *Hīnayāna* tradition itself one notices two forms of truth – one advocated by *Mahāsāṁghikas* primarily by developing one's own discretionary powers and realized by oneself, and further used for the benefit of the others, whereas the other advocated by *Sthaviravādins*, strictly following teachings of the Buddha by letters and adopting the ways laid down by the Buddha personally, but not willing to extend to teach the truth to others.

However, in both the forms, namely, *Samyak-saṁbuddha* and *Pratyeka Buddha*, one begins by practicing the Buddhist way of life and abiding by the Buddha's teaching (*Dharma-kāya*), which is regarded mandatory respectfully – if not primarily and strictly, at least secondarily and flexibly. Thoughts of the Buddha are known as *Arūpa-kāya* (not having any specific form), because they are substanceless/empty (*Śūnya*).

The Buddha could foresee that veneration is sometimes superficial and misguided. He warned people against turning him into an object of worship. He categorically instructed that there will be no heir to preserve my lineage authoritatively. He forbade carvings and sculptures representing him in physical form, and he told his follow-beings that "whoever sees the *Dhamma* sees me, whoever sees me sees the *Dhamma*" ([6], 22.87). *Dhamma* is above life, because life is lived in contingently emerged exigencies, and under circumstantial compulsions to survive. Nevertheless, after the demise of the Buddha, human psychology predominated. His bodily remains were preserved in *Stūpas* and religiously worshiped with great veneration. Preservation of his remains was done in physical form of pieces of his corpse, in verbal form giving rise to mythology, and in visual form of images, paintings, sculptures praising his mysterious powers and extraordinary accomplishments as divinized ideal perfections. He, as a person, became an illustrious example to be emulated and a universal role model to guide many. Taking into consideration likings and availability of the medium, people portrayed the Buddha in various ways, and that is symbolically represented in the Vairocana (etymologically Vai=various + ruci=likings) forms of the Buddha. Although these are creations, they are real in the mundane world and have creative value.

In the mythical process of development, concurrent ideas of perfection concerning the physical characteristics of divinized human beings were incorporated and absorbed. The creation of images of the Universal Buddha was necessary for the devotion of lay followers. It is a new mode of connecting followers, if not with the historical Buddha directly at least with his image getting proximity to protect, and symbolic representations were helpful to respect for many, especially in the process of popularizing of Buddhism [7]. This entire process of divinization of the Buddha is traceable in the *Hīnayāna* literature, but conversely the process of personification of enlightenment started from the emergence of *Mahāyāna* Buddhism. In the Pāli scriptures, it is claimed that all the Buddhas have 32 major marks and 80 minor marks of a superior being. These marks are not necessarily physical, though are symbolized as bodily features. They have something to do with ideal virtues, leading toward perfection and divinity depicted in the form of human reason and emotion both together synthesized in creations.

Another thing is that although Buddhism held the doctrine of *Anātmatā* (non-eternality of self), it has always recognized the existence of more than one Buddha. In the early Buddhist Pāli literature, previous to Siddhārtha Gautama Buddha, 28 Buddhas are mentioned, who lived in this world and guided humanity. Over and above that in the *Jātaka* stories various births of the Buddha were depicted.

Both the things produced impression on the later followers that there are contradictions within the teachings of the Buddha. Due to the passage of time, there was no authentic source to settle doubts and provide reliable clues to the then currently circulated thoughts. In order to reconcile apparently conflicting thoughts about the teachings of the Buddha, attempts were made by *Mahāyāna* Buddhists to connect various kinds of followers, various ways of presenting the thoughts and life of the Buddha together not merely by synthesizing them but by putting them forth in a neutral way, equidistancing from both tradition and contextual needs. Starting from the *Sūtra* period, various *Mahāyāna-Sūtras* attempted in a novel way to articulate a framework, which enabled them to present thoughts of the Buddha making it relevant, and *Tri-kāya* doctrine is one such attempt. It provided scope for innovative thinking and making Buddhism relevant. In this context particularly *Saṁbhoga-kāya* is a novel creation, which is supportive of the *Boddhisattva-yāna* advocated by *Mahāyāna.* Such an attempt was undertaken by both the *Saddharma-Puṇḍarika-Sūtra* and the *Saddharma-Laṅkāvatāra-Sūtra.*

Saṁbhoga-kāya (Body of Enjoyment)

Buddha was not only born as a human being, but he ascended himself to the level of the superhuman being, who could enjoy bliss and peaceful existence even with a physical body. Physical body is not an impediment or hurdle in the process of enlightenment; rather it can be used as an instrument to serve the needs of others with complete joy, peace, and contentment. Sacrificing one-self verbally, mentally, and spiritually is possible only when one lives physically by taking the birth of human being, and not in any other form of life. It is possible neither for God nor for other species to sacrifice oneself for the benefit of others, like the *Bodhisattva*. Human existence is not only filthy, due to which one has to experience *Duḥkha* (pain and suffering), but it is good as well, and essential to realize the ultimate truth. Human body turns out to be an instrument to reveal unlimited bliss and joy in the world, a need to manifest the principle of enlightenment. Without a physical body, there cannot be a possibility to comprehend the ultimate truth and get *Bodhi* (enlightenment) or experience *Nirvāṇa* (emancipation). Rather one is supposed to uplift oneself from the impure body, like a lotus, and remain unadulterated, by using *Prajñā* (wisdom) and *Karūṇā* (compassion), like a *Bodhisattva*.

Saṁbhoga-kāya is an ideal image of the Buddha created by others, portrayed in carvings and sculptures differently according to their likings and metaphorically represented in the form of Amitābha, Bhaiṣajyaguru, Vajrasattva, Tārā, and Mañjuśrī *Bodhisattvas* [8]. Buddha is one, but manifests in the conventional relative world in different ways, and appears in the form of *Bodhisattvas* to work for the liberation of all sentient beings. After the demise of the Buddha, there were only his thoughts to correlate with and highlight the transcendental aspect of the *Dharma*. Reality is transcendental but assumes various functional forms in the mundane world. Here, Buddha does not remain merely as a human being but becomes an aggregate of qualities by the acquisition of which one attains enlightenment (*Bodhi*) or Buddhahood. And for attaining that state, one has to use virtues like *Prajñā* (wisdom) and *Karūṇā* (compassion), which potentially exist within each one. This was possible only because of the *Tri-kāya* doctrine, especially by highlighting *Saṁbhoga-kāya*.

Saṁbhoga-kāya is best understood as the symbolic or archetype Buddha. In the *Mahāyāna* tradition, there is freedom to interpret thoughts of the Buddha according to the changing situations and context in which one lives, and thereby it is the non-substantiality or emptiness (*Śūnyatā*) of the core that is emphasized. At the same time, followers of the *Yogācāra* tradition attempted to highlight the cognitive aspect of it and the potentiality to become a Buddha. They hold that by nature one has certain abilities like the Buddha, and hence they stressed on the *Tathāgata-garbha* nature existing within oneself [9]. The mundane momentary existence of man, however, can continue in two forms: one, as a stream of consciousness in a linear way (*Eka-santāna-vāda*) such that there is no difference between inner/outer modes of comprehending life, which was emphasized by some, whereas others upheld the second possibility of differential ways of understanding the same reality (*Santānāntara-vāda*) in multidimensional ways of interpretation and alternative modes of existence. It is an attempt of transcending the limitations of space and time, melting the difference between inner and outer perspectives, and providing avenues of accounting for a variety of comprehensions of thoughts of the Buddha simultaneously and/or serially in the mundane world. It was possible due to at least two kinds of flexibilities: one, flexibilities existing within the thoughts of the Buddha, and second, through joyful creations making use of that flexibility in differential ways through expression and communication by his followers, by bracketing time and space. Both of them mutually provided grounds for making thoughts of the Buddha universal. Entertaining the thoughts of the Buddha was an enlightening and enjoyable play, and hence is known as *Saṁbhoga-kāya*. This metaphorical or psychic phenomenon was, it seems, first expounded in the *Saddharma-Puṇḍarika-Sūtra*, giving scope primarily for laypersons to use their own discretionary powers to comprehend the thoughts of the Buddha, not only verbally but imaginatively using various modes of expression artistically and creatively. Although it is a human creation, it is real. It is a glorious and spiritual manifestation of the fruits of discipline of the creator. It is the splendor and power of the Buddha nature. Although, *Rūpa-kāya/Nirmāṇa-kāya* and *Dharma-kāya/Arūpa-kāya* were present in one form or the other in the *Hīnayāna* tradition, after advent of the *Mahāyāna* tradition *Saṁbhoga-kāya* is not merely a simple addition to the prevalent two, rather it is a kind of three-dimensional understanding reality. Such a creative and enlightening *Tri-kāya* doctrine obviously brought in transformation to the foreground within Buddhism. It is the bliss of enlightenment and the reward of spiritual practice. The *Tri-kāya* doctrine became an important part of the *Mahāyāna* and particularly that of the *Yogācāra*, which was systematically crystallized later on by Asaṅga. It is a new mode of teaching, as a method/mechanism to reconcile the various and potentially conflicting interpretations and representations of the teachings of the Buddha found in the Buddhist texts. Similar to the earlier Buddhist thoughts, here too it is held that all the three forms of the Buddha teach the same *Dharma*. However, going a step ahead, it is held that truth can be expressed in different ways taking into consideration contextual needs and its significance. Introduction of the *Saṁbhoga-kāya* conceptually fits in between the *Nirmāṇa-kāya* and the *Dharma-kāya*.

The *Saṁbhoga-kāya* is that aspect of the Buddha or the *Dharma* which is a visionary unification of life and thoughts of the Buddha, in a state of deep meditation. Such a kind of enlightenment is not reserved restrictively for the ordained monastic followers, but is made available to laity primarily for the first time within Buddhism. It is an interesting historic fact that the number three has positive symbolic resonance across different cultures and religions. In the Buddhist iconography, how much one can be faithful (*Ekaniṣṭha*) to the thoughts and ideas depicts the extra-cosmic realm of meditational height of the practitioner on the one hand, and clarity and transparency of his vision (*Śuddhāvāsa*) on the other. It is a personification of super-mundane (*Lokottara*) qualities imagined and existing of enlightenment in the Buddha. It is creation of depth inside and experiencing the sublime. Enlightenment (*Bodhi*) is truest reality in the Universe and comprehension of the transcendental aspect of the *Dharma*. Here, the Buddha no longer remains essentially as a human being, but turns out to be the ultimate embodiment of the transcendental truth. The difference between mundane and super-mundane vanishes at the state of enlightenment, a unique experience of the ultimate reality. The Buddha becomes *Dhamma* and vice versa. The Buddha exists as a mode of *Dharma-kāya*, having universal non-substantial infinite life. And failure to recognize the Buddha's nature becomes a major obstacle in one's attaining the state of complete awakening (*Bodhi*). Hence, once the crux of the *Saṁbhoga-kāya* is realized, it becomes easier to awaken the inner reality and true nature, that is, Buddhahood.

Cross-References

- Amitābha
- *Anātman*
- Bhaiṣajyaguru
- *Bodhi*
- *Bodhisattva*
- *Dharma*
- *Dīgha Nikāya*
- *Duḥkha*
- *Hīnayāna*
- *Jātaka*
- *Karuṇā*
- *Mahāsāṅghika*
- *Mahāyāna*
- *Mahāyāna Laṅkāvatāra Sūtra*
- Mañjuśrī
- *Nirvāṇa*
- *Parinirvāṇa*
- *Prajñā*
- *Pratyeka-Buddha*
- *Saddharmapuṇḍrīka Sūtra*
- *Samyaka Sambodhi*
- *Saṃyutta Nikāya*
- *Sthaviravāda*
- *Śūnya*
- *Śūnyatā*
- Tārā (Buddhism)
- Vairocana
- *Yogācāra*

References

1. Vaidya PL (ed) (1960) Saddharma-Puṇḍarika-Sūtra. Mithila Institute, Darbhanga
2. Vaidya PL (ed) (1963) Saddharma-Laṅkāvatāra-Sūtra. Mithila Institute, Darbhanga
3. Warder AK (2000) Indian Buddhism, 3 revisedth edn. Motilal Banarsidass, Delhi, pp 407–411
4. (1995) Saṁyutta-Nikāya: 22.87, Dhamma-cakka-pabattana-sutta, Tipiṭaka, Chaṭṭha Saṇgāyana Edition (CD-ROM Version-3). Vipassana Research Institute, Igatpuri
5. Kasyapa BJ (ed) (1961) Dīgha-Nikāya. Pali Text Publication Board, Bihar Govt, Nalanda
6. (1995) Dīgha-Nikāya-I, Tipiṭaka, Chaṭṭha Saṇgāyana Edition (CD-ROM Version-3). Vipassana Research Institute, Igatpuri
7. Sangharakshita MS (1987) A survey of Buddhism: its doctrines and methods through ages. Tharpa, London
8. Nakamura H (1987) Indian Buddhism: a survey with bibliographical notes. Motilal Banarsidass, Delhi
9. Winternitz M (1993) History of Indian literature, vol II. Motilal Banarsidass, Delhi

Tripiṭaka

▶ Tipiṭaka

Tṛṣṇā

▶ Craving

Truth (Buddhism)

▶ Buddha (Concept)

Truth (Jainism)

Wm. Andrew Schwartz
Claremont Graduate University, Claremont, CA, USA

Definition

The notion of "truth" in Jainism has emerged in two distinct ways: (1) relative and (2) absolute. As relative, truth is a subjective status given to a proposition. As absolute, truth indicates a relation between a statement and "the way things are."

Relative Truth

In the spirit of the Jain doctrine of *anekāntavāda* (non-one-sidedness) (see entry on "▶ Anekāntavāda"), if a statement is made from a limited perspective (*naya*), it can only be relatively true. This is the kind of truth dealt with most of the time. Inevitably, to assert something is to do so from within a particular framework (time, place, etc.) as a particular person. Therefore, when I say, "it is raining," my statement may be true or false depending on my context. It may in fact be raining in Longview, WA, and not in Claremont, CA. Therefore, the statement, "it is raining," is only true or false in a relative sense. To treat relative truths as absolute truths is to commit the egregious error of *ekānta* (one-sidedness). Claims made from a certain perspective (*syāt*) are always relative claims. As such, they can only be true or false in a relative sense.

When it comes to the Jain theory of error, the primary way of committing falsehood is *ekānta*, to treat one-sided relative truths as absolute and universal truths, to the exclusion of all contraries. In short, one commits this error by making an unconditional dogmatic assertion. The way to avoid such error is to follow the path of *syādvāda*, the Jain doctrine of conditional assertion/predication (see entry on "▶ Syādvāda"). Accordingly, all claims should by predicated by the particle *syāt* (from a certain perspective), so that dogmatic assertions become conditional, and the relative truth of an assertion can be captured. In this way, the seemingly contradictory claims of others are seen as complimentary insofar as they are asserted in different senses and from different perspectives.

Truth, understood in this way, is a function of perspective, since the truth of an assertion is directly dependent on the perspective from which it is asserted. But if this were all that determined truth, then Jainism would devolve into a form of relativism, by which truth is simply a matter of perspective. Therefore, what is true for you in your perspective would be true because it is your perspective. And what is true for me in my perspective would be true because it is my perspective. This would mean that truth is a matter of perspective, with no objective criterion. Yet, Jains have gone to great lengths to defend against the charge of relativism.

For Jainism, unlike relativism, it is not the case that just any assertion can be true in just any sense. What saves the Jain position from relativism is the identification of two limiting factors, which act as fixed points by which the truth of an assertion can be measured. These limitations are (1) reality itself and (2) the normative claims of the Jain tradition [1]. Reality, as a limiting notion, is the result of Jain metaphysical realism. A true statement, even when expressed conditionally from a particular perspective, must be an accurate description of objective reality (if even partially so). Here, it is truth as correspondence that is an important notion of truth in the Jain tradition, whereby something is truth if it properly *corresponds* to reality. For Jains, there really is a "real world" to which each relative perspective is related. In this way, Jainism is a form of relativity, but not relativism. While it is possible to have a misguided perspective (i.e., improperly describe the objective reality), most of the time, reality – in its manifoldness and innumerable attributes – can be properly described from a plurality of seemingly contradictory perspectives. For this reason, Jainism suggests one begin by giving others the benefit of the doubt and assume they have a piece of the truth that one does not. In this way, it is possible to avoid the error of unnecessary exclusion and one-sidedness.

Absolute Truth

Whereas everyday truth is relative truth, Jainism has not given up on absolute truth. Whereas relative truth is one-sided truth, absolute truth is non-one-sided. Such truth can only be known by an omniscient *jiva* (soul) that has shed all knowledge obscuring karmas and subsequently transcends one-sidedness. This is the second limiting factor – the normative claims of Jainism itself, passed down from the absolute perspective of the enlightened omniscient Jinas (e.g., Mahavira). This limitation is the result of the Jain affirmation of a coherent worldview. Since the perspective of omniscience is an absolute and pure perspective, all truth (even partial truth) must properly cohere to this absolute perspective. Here, it is truth as coherence that is an important notion of truth in the Jain tradition, whereby something is truth if it properly *coheres* to the logic of a given system.

Absolute truth can only be grasped from an absolute viewpoint. Apart from omniscience, all viewpoints are non-absolute (or relative) and therefore can only grasp relative truth. As Siddhasena (fifth-century Jain philosopher) writes, "Since a thing has manifold character, it is comprehended (only) by the omniscient. But a thing becomes the subject matter of a *naya*, when it is conceived from one particular standpoint" [2]. To grasp absolute truth is to grasp the many-sided nature of reality. But from the standpoint of non-omniscience, and in order to avoid the error of *ekānta*, one should preface every claim with the participle *syāt* (from a certain perspective) to ensure that the claim is treated relatively.

Absolute truth is transcendent truth. Such truth is ultimately unknowable (for non-omniscient beings) and inexpressible (even for omniscient beings). To this end, Mahavira is quoted as saying, "Where there is truth, from there language returns, neither intellect, nor thoughts nor even the mind goes there" (Ayaro Sutra 5/123–125) [3]. Mahavira acknowledges that truth transcends linguistic and cognitive capacities – though such transcendence does not preclude immanence. Therefore, "As an omniscient being, with infinite knowledge at his disposal, Mahavira recognized that truth or reality can be experienced but cannot be expressed in its entirety through the medium of language" [4]. This is a crucial stance on the notion of truth in Jainism and undergirds the rationale for why Mahavira encourages his followers to "Find the truth yourself" (Uttaradhyayana Sutra

6/2) [5]. Truth – in its full complexity – can never be expressed and subsequently can never be taught. It can only be experienced. Now, one might wonder, if this is so, why does Mahavira continue to teach – why propose metaphysical doctrines, doctrines of the soul, of karma, principles like *ahimsa*, etc.? If ultimate truth cannot be expressed, why make all these attempts to express it? Not only so, but is not the claim that "absolute truth cannot be expressed" an expression of an absolute truth? If so, does it refute itself? Keeping in mind the Jain perspective on the transcendent nature of absolute truth, perhaps the best way to understand Jain metaphysical and other doctrines is not as attempts at defining the "truth" in its full complexity (in the absolute sense), but as symbolically pointing toward the absolute. In this way, Jain philosophical doctrines are not attempts at describing the indescribable, but a pragmatic means of using language as symbols that points one toward the goal – liberation. To truly understand absolute truth and the many-sided nature of reality, one must ultimately transcend Jain "doctrine" and experience the truth of eternal bliss. Therefore, another important notion of truth in Jainism is a "pragmatic" notion, for which truth is a means rather than an end.

Respect for the Truth of Others

Among the various aspects of the Jain conception of truth, the bottom line – the heart of the matter – is that conceptions of "truth" in Jainism facilitate respect and intellectual humility while simultaneously resisting skepticism and absolutism.

The recognition (through *anekāntavāda*) of the plurality of valid perspectives which yield a myriad of relative truths, and the transcendental nature of absolute truth which can only be experienced, demands humility with respect to truth claims. With relative truth, such humility is found in the admission that one's own claims to truth (like all others) are necessarily relative and should not be treated as exclusive and absolute. With absolute truth, such humility comes with the admission that as non-omniscient beings, one only has access to relative truths. All the while, such humility does not become a form of skepticism, nor does it default to an exclusive absolutism. Since the ultimate truth is beyond words or concepts, all truth claims should be asserted with an attitude of humility and dialectic of conditionality.

Cross-References

- *Anekāntavāda*
- Jainism (Yakṣa)
- *Nayavāda*
- Reality (Jainism)
- Relativity
- *Syādvāda*

References

1. Long JD (2010) Jainism: an introduction. I.B. Tauris, New York, p 150
2. Siddhasena, Nyayavatara (verse. 29)
3. Gyan Jain (trans) Eternal. Quotes from Lord Mahavira, 78
4. Charitrapragya S (2004) Mahavira, Anekantavada and the world today. In: Sethia T (ed) Ahimsa, Anekanta and Jainism. Motilal Banarsidass, Delhi, p 77
5. Gyan Jain (trans) Eternal. Quotes From Lord Mahavira, 12

Further Reading

Long JD (2009) Jainism: an introduction. I.B. Tauris, New York

Matilal BK (1981) The central philosophy of Jainism: Anekantavada. L.D. Institute of Indology, Ahmedabad

Mookerjee S (1978) The Jaina philosophy of non-absolutism: a critical study of Anekantavada. Motilal Banarsidass, Delhi

Padmarajiah YJ (1963) A comparative study of the Jaina theories of reality and knowledge. Jain Sahitya Vikas Mandal, Bombay

Sethia T (ed) (2004) Ahimsa, Anekanta and Jainism. Motilal Banarsidass, Delhi

Shah N (2000) Jaina theory of multiple facets of reality and truth (Anekantavada). Motilal Banarsidass, Delhi

Shah N (ed) (1998) Jaina philosophy and religion. Motilal Banarsidass, Delhi

Uma Swami A (2011) Jainism, key to reality (Tattvarthasutra) (trans Jain SC). Digambar Jain Trilok Shodh Sansthan, Hastinapur

T

Tso Rimpoche

► Mānasarovara (Buddhism)

Tumulus

► Cetiya

Tyaga

► Dāna (Buddhism)

Tyāga

► Cāga

U

Uccheda-vāda

▶ Materialism (Buddhism)

Udāna

K. T. S. Sarao
Department of Buddhist Studies, University of Delhi, Delhi, India

Synonyms

Inspired utterances; Udānavarga; Verses of uplift

Definition

The Udāna is one of the texts in the Khuddaka Nikāya of the Sutta Piṭaka.

The Udāna, one of the texts of the Khuddaka Nikāya of the Sutta Piṭaka, is a short collection of 80 stories. The stories have been put together in eight *vaggas* (chapters) of ten stories each, and each *vagga* has been named after one of the stories it contains. Each of the stories is a prose account of some special occasion which is concluded by an *udāna* (inspired utterance) of the Buddha. The *udānas* are composed for the most part in ordinary meters (*Śloka*, *Trisṭubh*, or *Jagatī*) and rarely in prose ([8], p. viii). Thus, each story contains a prose portion followed by a verse. At the end of each prose section, as run-up to the verse, the following formulaic text is included: "Then, on realizing the significance of that, the Blessed One on that occasion exclaimed: (*Atha kho bhagavā etam atthaṃ viditvā tāyaṃ velāyaṃ imaṃ udānaṃ udānesi*)." It is these "exclamations" (*udānas*) that have given the collection its name as pointed out in its commentary ([10], p. 2):

> "as the water which a reservoir cannot hold runs out, and that is called 'flood-water,' even so that accumulated thrill-wave of strong emotion, of thought directed and diffused (*vitakka-vipphāra*), which the heart cannot contain, when it grows to excess cannot stay within, but bursts forth by way of the door of speech, regardless of who receives it– in fact an extraordinary expiration (*udāhāra-viseso*)– that is called *Udāna*" ([11], p. vi). It has been suggested that most probably there was once an Udāna having only verses such as those in the Udānavarga ([2], p. 46).

The Udāna is closely connected to the Itivuttaka ([2], p. 46). Several prose texts of the Udāna appear to have been borrowed from the Vinaya Piṭaka and the *Mahāparinibbāna Suttanta* of the Dīgha Nikāya ([11], pp. vi–vii; [4], p. 226). However, Winternitz feels that they were probably not borrowed from these collections, but were based on earlier traditions on which the various collections have drawn ([9], p. 82). In his opinion "most of these short and beautiful utterances certainly bear the stamp of antiquity and... many of them are possibly the actual words of the Buddha himself or of his most prominent disciples" ([9],

K.T.S. Sarao, J.D. Long (eds.), *Buddhism and Jainism*, Encyclopedia of Indian Religions,
DOI 10.1007/978-94-024-0852-2

p. 82). Thus, there is general agreement that not only that some of the concepts developed in the Udāna are quite old, but they also have parallels in Jainism as well as the Upaniṣads (see [2], p. 46; [1]). The Udāna, as the prose-verse type of discourse (although not necessarily the existing collection itself), has also been identified as being part of the pre-canonical ninefold (*navaṅga*) categorization (*sutta, geyya, veyyākaraṇa, gāthā, udāna, itivuttaka, jātaka, abbhutadhamma*, and *vedalla*) of the *buddhavacana* (teachings of the Buddha) according to its form and style (see [2], pp. 7, 46). As pointed out by Winternitz,

> "the utterances themselves, are as a rule older, than the narratives into which they are inserted. Though a few of them may have come down from the very beginning in association with an introductory story, yet in the majority of cases it was the compiler who appended such a story to an old *udāna*. This is why many of the stories only contain very simple, in fact sometimes silly stories, inappropriate to the pathos of the utterances themselves" ([9], p. 82).

However, "only the Udāna verses belong to the genuine poetry of ancient Buddhism, while the prose-stories have been partly invented by one or more commentators and partly taken over from other texts" ([9], p. 86). The Dhammapada-aṭṭhakathā appears to have got not only its inspiration from the prose and verse stories of the Udāna but has also borrowed from it at least a dozen of its stories ([5]: I.*s.v.* Udāna). Following this line of argument, Winternitz has suggested that some of these stories were included in the Buddhist canon "may be due to the reason that they were perhaps older than the stories of the Dhammapada commentary; but the reason may perhaps also lie in this that these short pronouncements appeared to need elaboration through introductory stories" ([9], p. 86). Woodward was of the view that as the scene of the majority of these little stories was laid at Sāvatthī, the Udāna "is an independent collection of the reciters of the school of monks there" ([11], p. vii).

Some of the important points of Buddhism discussed in the Udāna include arhatship, paṭiccasamuppāda, monkhood versus worldly life, *taṇhā* and dukkha, life after death, kamma, anattā and puggala, four unthinkables, nibbāna, evolution, cosmos, heaven, and hell. The celebrated story of the blind men and an elephant also appears in the Udāna ([11]: VI.iv; [6]: VI.4).

Cross-References

- ▶ Anattā (Buddhism)
- ▶ Dīgha Nikāya
- ▶ Dukkha
- ▶ Itivuttaka
- ▶ Kamma
- ▶ Khuddaka Nikāya
- ▶ Paṭiccasamuppāda
- ▶ Sutta Piṭaka

References

1. Enomoto F (1989) On the annihilation of *karman* in Early Buddhism. In: Transactions of the international conference of orientalists in Japan, vol 34. Institute of Eastern Culture, Tōhō Gakkai, pp 43–55
2. von Hinüber O (1996) A handbook of Pāli literature. Walter de Gruyter, Berlin
3. Ireland JD (trans) (1990) The Udāna: inspired utterances of the Buddha. Buddhist Publication Society, Kandy
4. Law BC (1983) A history of Pali literature, reprint, vol 1. Indological Book House, Delhi
5. Malalasekera GP (2007) Dictionary of Pāli proper names. First Indian edn. Motilal Banarsidass, Delhi.
6. Masefield P (trans) (1994) The Udāna. Pali Text Society, Oxford
7. Masefield P (ed) (1994–95) The Udāna commentary, vol 2. Pali Text Society, Oxford
8. Steinthal P (ed) (1885) Udāna. Pali Text Society, London
9. Winternitz M (1983) History of Indian literature (trans: Sarma VS), rev edn, vol 2. Motilal Banarsidass, Delhi
10. Woodward FL (ed) (1926) Paramattha-Dīpanī: Udānaṭṭhakathā (Udāna Commentary) of Dhammapālācariya. Pali Text Society, London
11. Woodward FL (trans) (1935) The minor anthologies of the Pāli Canon, Part II, Udāna: verses of uplift and Itivuttaka: as it was said. Oxford University Press, London

Udānavarga

▶ Udāna

Understanding

► Paññā
► Wisdom (Buddhism)

Universal

Madhumita Chattopadhyay
Department of Philosophy, Jadavpur University, Kolkata, West Bengal, India

Synonyms

All-embracing; All-inclusive; Common property; General

Definition

A character or property belonging to all persons, individuals of a class. A common property applicable to all cases.

On Universals

The common man believes that every existing thing possesses some character which is unique to the object and at the same time it possesses some character which it shares with others. In Indian philosophy, especially in the Realist system, the former is regarded as particular or *viśeṣa* and the latter as universal or *sāmānya*. In perceiving a thing, one perceives it at the first moment vaguely without differentiating the individuality and the generality, but later on apprehends the object determinately by combining the individuality and the generality. For them, both the particulars as well as the universals are real. However, the Buddhists do not support this view. They admit the reality of particulars only which in their terminology is *svalakṣaṇa*; whereas universals are conceptually constructed by the mind through generalization from many individuals without any regard for their individuality. Since they are conceptually constructed they are devoid of reality. The Buddhists hold that universals are nonexistent, or even if existent, at least unknowable. Accordingly, they criticize and refute the notion of universal as has been admitted by the realist school like the Vaiśeṣikas. The realists regard the universal to be an entity which is itself one and indivisible but which resides in a plurality of individuals by inherence relation. First of all, the Buddhists do not admit such inherence relation. Moreover, they hold that the universal as an entity is logically impossible, since its two properties, namely "being indivisible" and "residing in a plurality of instances" are incompatible. To explain, if the universal is to reside in an individual, it can do it either completely or partially. That is, either the entire universal resides in an individual or only part of it does. If a universal U resides in its entirety in a given individual i_1, then it does not reside at all in other individuals i_2, i_3,. . . at the same time. So it cannot be regarded to reside in a plurality of instances at the same time. If, on the other hand, the universal is conceived as residing only partially in each of its individual instances, then it loses its indivisibility character, for then it will be said to have as many internal divisions as there are individuals in which it is supposed to reside.

In addition to the above argument against the possibility of universals as indivisible entities residing in a number of instances, there is another argument to the conclusion that universals are unknowable. The concept of universal appears to be that of an organizing principle by virtue of which a plurality of individuals is collected together in a class. Even if there is such a principle, knowing that is impossible without knowing each individual in the class determined by that principle. For, until one knows each individual in a class one cannot know what they have in common that qualifies them all for membership in that class. But to know each past, present, and future individual in a class is physically impossible for any finite individual. Thus, it would be impossible to know that "x is the locus of universal P," for it would require knowledge of both x and the universal P.

U

The question that arises next is whether there is any interpretation of the expression "x is the locus of the property P" by which it can express something knowable? The Buddhists think that there is an affirmative answer to this question. In order to understand their view, it is helpful to realize that the organizing principle by virtue of which a plurality of individuals is collected together may not be known. Thus, one may begin with the knowledge that there is a set or collection P made up of a number of individuals p_1, p_2, p_3,.... To make sense of the expression "the property P" or "the universal P," one must link it up somehow with "the collection P." The expression "the collection P" can in turn be seen as another way of saying "all p-s." It is obviously not the case that "the universal P" is simply an alternative way of saying "all p-s." For, then "x is a locus of the universal P" would simply be an alternative way of saying "x is a locus of all p-s," which is not what is intended. What actually is intended is to say "x is a locus of some p." This expression is easily arrived at by denying the expression "x is a locus of no p." So, whenever there is an expression of the form "x is a locus of the universal P" it has to be interpreted as saying "x is a locus of the deniability of the absence of every particular p" or "x is qualified by the exclusion of the absence of every p."

The advantage of this way of interpretation is that whereas the truth of "x is qualified by the universal P" cannot be known because of the unknowability of the universal P construed as an organizing principle, "x is qualified by the exclusion of the absence of every p" can be known by knowing only one particular. For, knowing that one particular p is present at x, is sufficient to falsify the proposition that "every particular p is absent from x."

The Buddhists do not stop simply by declaring that the various particular objects of a class, which have nothing common in them, do give rise to a notion of commonness by their very nature. They also try to provide a deeper analysis of this notion of commonness. According to them, this notion is caused not by any positive commonness residing in all the individual objects of a class but by a negative commonness which belongs to all the individual objects. For instance, all the cows of the world are different from each other and have nothing in common except the performance of a particular function and the fact of their birth from similar causes. Yet, all of them have a negative commonness in that they are all different from the non-cows, for example, the horses, the dogs, etc. The universal cow-ness according to the Buddhists is not an external reality but only a negation in the form of exclusion of non-cows. It is called *atadvyāvṛtti* or exclusion of what a thing is not. The technical term used for it is *apoha*, which is the Buddhist counterpart of the universal of the realist school.

Cross-References

▶ Knowledge (Buddhism)
▶ Logic (Buddhism)
▶ Philosophy (Buddhism)
▶ Śabda

References

1. Dravid RR (1972) The problem of universals in Indian philosophy. Motilal Banarsidass, Delhi
2. Katsura S (1991) Dignāga and Dhrmakīrti on apoha. In: Steinkellner E (ed) Studies in the Buddhist epistemological tradition. Osterreiche Akademie der Wissenschaft, Vienna
3. Matilal BK, Evans D (1986) Buddhist logic and epistemology: studies in the Buddhist analysis of inference and language. D. Reidel, Dordrecht
4. Mookerjee S (1975) The Buddhist philosophy of universal flux. Motilal Banarsidass, Delhi, Reprint
5. Sāntarakṣita (1968) Tattvasaṃgraha with Tattvasaṃgrahapañjikā (Dvārikadas Sāstri, ed). Bauddha Bharati, Varanasi
6. Sastri DN (1964) The philosophy of Nyāya-Vaiśeṣika realism and its conflict with the Buddhist Dignāga School. Bharatiya Vidya Prakashan, Delhi
7. Sharma DN (1969) The differentiation theory of meaning in Indian logic. Mouten, Paris
8. Shastri DD (ed) (1992) Apohavāda: a basic principle of Buddhist philosophy. Bauddha Bharati, Varanasi

Unreal

▶ Śūnya

Untouchable

► Caṇḍāla (Buddhism)

Upādāna

► Āsavas (Āśravas)

Upagupta

K. T. S. Sarao
Department of Buddhist Studies, University of Delhi, Delhi, India

Synonyms

Kisanāga Upagutta; Phra Uppakhuta; Shin Upago; Upagutta

Definition

A Buddhist saint who preached and taught meditative practices in ancient northern India and is now venerated in Myanmar, Thailand, and Laos as a protective deity.

Upagupta was a Buddhist saint and dharma master who preached and taught meditative practices in the region of Mathurā in northern India, sometime between the reign of King Aśoka (third century B.C.E.) and the first century of the Common Era ([8], p. 3). In the Sarvāstivādin tradition, he is the fifth patriarch in the succession beginning with Mahākāśyapa and including Ānanda; Madhyāntika; Upagupta's guru, Śāṇakavāsin; and Upagupta ([3], p. 150). Although Upagupta is not mentioned in the Pāli canon, via the influence of Sanskrit Buddhism in Southeast Asia, he emerged in the twelfth century as a prominent saint in legend and cult in Myanmar, Thailand, and Laos where he "is invoked primarily as a protective figure, a guardian against disorder. He is also thought to have great magical powers and to be able to intercede in favor of his devotees" ([8], p. 4).

A complete description of the biography of Upagupta is available in the *Divyāvadāna* (Chaps. 21 and 27). As a monkey in his previous life, Upagupta worked for the welfare of many, so it was prophesied by the Buddha that he would show compassion for the multitude ([8], pp. 44–45). According to the *Divyāvadāna* ([11], pp. 216–222), Upagupta was the son of a certain Gupta of Mathurā who was a perfume seller. He entered the Buddhist saṃgha at the age of seventeen under Śāṇakavāsin. He took up residence near Mathurā at the monastery founded by Naṭabhaṭika on the top of Mt. Urumuṇḍa ([11], p. 222). Three years later, he attained arahantship and became "Buddha without marks" (*alakṣaṇako buddho*). Thereafter, he began to work as a Buddha (*buddhakāryaṃ*) and converted many to Buddhism. His taming of Māra while here was perhaps his greatest achievement. According to Strong, perhaps by inclination, he was a follower of Sarvāstivāda and a forest monk, drawing to himself a number of disciples interested in meditation but at the same time staying in touch with laypersons ([8], p. 3). According to Xuanzang, there was a large cave into which Upagupta was in the habit of throwing a chip of wood to register the number of individuals who had become *arahants* (Sk: *arhats*) through him, until the cave ultimately became filled with the chips ([4], p. 123).

After having attained prominence at Mathurā, he is said to have gone to Pāṭaliputra at the invitation of King Aśoka. Subsequently, he became the spiritual adviser of King Aśoka (third century B.C.E.) and instructed him in the erection of monasteries and stūpas all over India. He also conducted Aśoka to important sites sanctified by the Buddha and his principal disciples. At Pāṭaliputra, his hermitage was, as in Mathurā, on a hill which is described by Xuanzang as "a rocky hill around which there are several tens of caves excavated on the steeps by divine labor under the command of King Aśoka for Upagupta and other Arhats" ([4], pp. 228–229). The only written work attributed to him, the *Netrīpada Śāstra*, would appear to have been a treatise presenting Sarvāstivādin viewpoints ([8], p. 6). Some Chinese sources credit him with the compilation of the *Sarvāstivādin Vinaya* ([8], p. 6). Some accounts mention his death having taken place at Mathurā, and his mountain monastery near here became a center of pilgrimage. According to Xuanzang, "At all the places where he sojourned, monasteries, stūpas, or both were erected as monuments to mark the sites" ([4], p. 346). Paying him ultimate homage, the Tibetan historian, Tāranātha, says that "since the death of the Guide (Buddha) no man has been born who has done so much good to living beings as this man" ([7], p. 164).

Though Upagupta himself is now thought of as being a monk, the cult of Upagupta is almost the exclusive preserve of Buddhist laypersons ([8], p. 4). In Southeast Asia, Upagupta is invariably associated with water and *nāgas* and believed not to have died but to live on in swamps, river bottoms, or in the ocean, in a meditative trance ([8], p. 4). Occasionally, it is believed that he may appear in person as a rough-looking monk. At such times, it is particularly beneficial to give him alms. Worship of him is thought to bring to the devotee good luck, protection, and prosperity in this life ([8], p. 14). According to a monograph prepared by Strong [8], the faithfuls often invite Upagupta from his watery abode to come and protect their festivals and rituals from interferences and disturbances caused by Māra and to give people an opportunity to make merit. After receiving his services, the devotees return Upagupta to his watery residence by floating his image downstream on a raft. In Myanmar, where statues of Upagupta are quit common, he is often depicted as having one of his hands in a begging bowl on his lap and his head tilted upward toward the sky. Two explanations are generally offered for this strange posture. One, Upagupta is a very strict monk and does not want to break the monastic rule by eating after noon (*vikālabhojana*); hence, he is looking skyward to check if the sun has passed the zenith. Two, it is maintained by others that the sun has already passed the zenith and that Upagupta is looking upward as he is putting his magical powers to use to stop the sun in its tracks so that he may continue to eat ([8], p. 14).

Cross-References

- ▶ Arahant
- ▶ Aśoka
- ▶ Buddhist Councils
- ▶ Divyāvadāna
- ▶ Māra
- ▶ Mathurā
- ▶ Sarvāstivāda
- ▶ Xuanzang (Hieun-Tsang)

References

1. Guruge AWP (2005) Who were Upagupta and his Aśoka? Indologica Taurinensia XXX1: 135–158
2. Lama C, Chattopadhyaya A (trans) (1970) Tāranātha's history of Buddhism in India. Indian Institute of Advanced Study, Simla
3. Lamotte É (1988) History of Indian Buddhism: from the origins to the Śaka Era (trans: Webb-Boin S). Insitut Orientaliste, Louvain-la-Neuve
4. Li R (trans) (1996) The Great Tang Dynasty record of the western regions. Numata Center for Buddhist Translation and Research, Berkeley
5. Kin M (1903) The legend of Upagutta. Buddhism (Rangoon) 1:219–242
6. Ray RA (1994) Buddhist Saints in India: a study in Buddhist values and Orientations. Oxford University Press, New York
7. Rockhill WW (1884) The life of the Buddha and the early history of his order. Trübner, London
8. Strong JS (1992) The legend and cult of Upagupta. Princeton University Press, Princeton
9. Vaidya PL (ed) (1958) Avadānaśataka, Buddhist sanskrit texts no. 19. The Mithila Institute of Post-Graduate Studies and Research in Sanskrit Learning, Darbhanga
10. Vaidya PL (ed) (1959) Divyāvadāna, Buddhist sanskrit texts no. 20. The Mithila Institute of Post-Graduate Studies and Research in Sanskrit Learning, Darbhanga
11. Waddell LA (1899) Upagupta, the fourth Buddhist Patriarch, and high priest of Açoka. J Asiatic Soc Bengal 1151(1):76–84

Upagutta

▶ Upagupta

Upāli

K. T. S. Sarao
Department of Buddhist Studies, University of Delhi, Delhi, India

Synonyms

Upāli Thera

Definition

One of the most eminent disciples of the Buddha and an expert on the Vinaya regulations.

Upāli, one of the most eminent disciples of the Buddha, was born in a śūdra family of barbers in Kapilavatthu (Sk: Kapilavastu). As a young person, he took service as a barber with the Sākiyan princes, including Siddhattha ([3], Vol. iii, p. 179). When the Śākyan prince Anuruddha and his cousins approached the Buddha seeking ordination, Upāli went along with them. The princes offered to give their valuable ornaments to Upāli which the latter refused and referred to join the saṃgha instead. It has been pointed out in the texts that Upāli refused to accept the ornaments for fear of reprisals from the hot-headed Śākyans who might suspect him of having plotted to grab their precious possessions. In order to humble the Śākyan princes, the Buddha ordained the low-caste Upāli before them ([7], Vol. i, p. 116f; [10], Vol. ii, p. 182). Kappitaka Thera, formerly a Jaṭila, was appointed Upāli's preceptor (*upajjhāya*) ([10], Vol. iv, p. 308; [14], Vol. iv, p. 937).

After having been initiated, Upāli expressed a desire to dwell in the solitude of the forest. However, the Buddha advised him against it as by living in the forest, he could learn only meditation, but by living among people, he could acquire knowledge of both meditation and the Dhamma. Upāli accepted the advice of the Buddha, and instead of becoming a forest-dweller (*araññika*), became a monastery dweller (*ārāmika*). After having practiced *vipassanā* (insight), he became an *arahant* in due course of time. He learnt the *Vinaya* from the Buddha who declared him in an assembly of the saṃgha to be the best among those who knew the Vinaya ([6], Vol. i, p. 24; [16], Vol. i, p. 172; [17], Vol. i, pp. 360f, 370). Many instances are given in the *Vinaya Piṭaka* where Upāli's arbitrations on the Vinaya rules earned him special praise of the Buddha ([1], Vol. i, p. 148; [4], Vol. iv, pp. 3, 5; [7], Vol. iii, p. 145; [10], Vol. iii, pp. 39, 66f, Vol. iv, p. 142). A complete list of questions asked by Upāli and answers given by the Buddha on matters pertaining to the Vinaya rules is given in the *Upāli-Pañcaka* chapter of the *Parivāra* portion in the *Vinaya Piṭaka* ([10], Vol. v, pp. 180–206). Even in the lifetime of the Buddha, monks are said to have considered it a great honor to learn the Vinaya from Upāli ([10], Vol. iv, p. 142; [14], Vol. iv, p. 876). He is known as having reached the pinnacle of the *Vinaya* (*Vinaye agganikkhitto*) ([4], Vol. iv, pp. 3, 5), and it was in this capacity that Kassapa entrusted him with compiling the *Vinaya Piṭaka* at the First Buddhist council at Rājagṛha ([2], Vol. iii, p. 30; [10], Vol. ii, p. 286f; [12], Vol. i, p. 11f).

Other than questions relating to the Vinaya that he asked the Buddha, there are only two references in the entire *Tipiṭaka* in the *Aṅguttara Nikāya* where Upāli is mentioned in connection with a discourse ([6], Vol. v, p. 201ff, Vol. iv, p. 143f). However, there are three verses in the *Theragāthā* that are attributed to Upāli ([9], pp. 249–251). There is also one verse in the *Milindapañha* in which he admonishes the monks to look for associates of tenacious character, to learn the Vinaya rules, and to practice solitude ([15], p. 108). The monks considered Upāli as their special friend to whom they could go for help in times of difficulty. Thus, for instance, when thieves dispossessed certain monks of their robes, it was Upāli whose help they sought ([10], Vol. iii, p. 212).

In one of his previous births at the time of Padumuttara, Upāli was a very rich brāhmaṇa named Sujāta. During this birth, he expressed a wish to see Gautama Buddha in the future and become the *Vinayadhara* (Knower of the Vinaya). With this purpose, he did many good deeds, including the construction of a monastery. As a result, he was born in heaven for 30,000 *kappas* (Sk: *kalpas*; aeons) and became a king of the *devas* 1,000 times. For another 1,000 times, he became a *Cakkavatti* (Sk: *chakravarti*) king. According to the *Apadāna*, as he had insulted the Pacceka Buddha Devala in one of his previous births, he was born as a barber in his last birth ([5], Vol. i, p. 37ff). The tradition of the Dotted Record of Guangzhou is said to have been initiated by Upāli and handed down in succession by the *Vinaya* teachers ([11], p. 346). After having been the Vinayapāmokkha for 30 years, Upāli died at the age of 74 in the sixth year of king Udāyibhadda's reign ([4], Vol. v, pp. 7, 103).

Cross-References

▶ Anuruddha
▶ Arahant
▶ Buddhaghosa
▶ Dhamma
▶ Kapilavatthu
▶ Pacceka-Buddha
▶ Saṃgha
▶ Thera- and Therīgāthā

References

1. Fausböll V (ed) (1977–1897) The Jātaka, 6 vols. Luzac, London
2. Geiger W (1908) The Mahāvaṃsa. Pali Text Society, London
3. Jones JJ (trans) (1949–1956) The Mahāvastu, Sacred books of the east, 3 vols (16, 18, 19). Luzac, London
4. Law BC (ed and trans) (1958) The chronicle of the Island of Ceylon or the Dīpavaṃsa. Ceylon Hist J, Colombo 7:1–266
5. Lilley ME (2000) The Apadāna, 2 vols. Pali Text Society, London
6. Morris R, Hardy E (eds) (1895–1900) The Aṅguttara Nikāya, 5 vols. Pali Text Society, London
7. Norman HC (ed) (1906) The commentary of the Dhammapada, 4 vols. Pali Text Society, London
8. Ñyānaponika T, Hecker H (2003) Great disciples of the Buddha: their lives, their works, their legacy. Wisdom, Boston
9. Oldenberg H, Pischel R (eds) (1990) The Thera- and Therīgāthā (with appendices by K. R. Norman & L. Alsdorf), 2nd edn. Pali Text Society, Oxford
10. Olderberg H (ed) (1879–1883) The Vinaya Piṭakaṃ, 5 vols. Pali Text Society, London
11. Pachow W (1965) A study of the dotted record. J Am Orient Soc 83(3):342–345
12. Rhys Davids TW, Carpentier JE, Stede W (eds) (1886–1932) The Sumaṅgala-Vilāsinī: Buddhaghosa's commentary on the Dīgha Nikāya, 3 vols. Pali Text Society, London
13. Rockhill WW (1884) The life of the Buddha and the early history of his order. Trübner, London
14. Takakusu J, Nagai M (eds) (1947–1975) Samantapāsādikā: Buddhaghosa's commentary on the Vinaya Piṭaka (including index by H. Kopp), 8 vols. Pali Text Society, London
15. Trenckner V (ed) (1880) The Milindapañho. Williams and Norgate, London
16. Walleser H, Kopp H (eds) (1924–1956) Manorathapūraṇī: Buddhaghosa's commentary on the Aṅguttara Nikāya, 5 vols. Pali Text Society, London
17. Woodward FL (ed) (1940–1949) Paramattha-Dīpanī: Theragāthā-Aṭṭhakathā, the commentary of Dhammapālācariya, 3 vols. Pali Text Society, London

Upāli Thera

▶ Upāli

Upāsaka

Angraj Chaudhary
Vipassana Research Institute, Dhammagiri, Igatpuri, Nashik, Maharashtra, India

Synonyms

Gahaṭṭha

Definition

A layman who goes to the three refuges, observes precepts, and earns his livelihood by honest means is an upāsaka.

Who is a layman or a lay devotee? How does he become one? Which are the precepts he observes? How does he earn his livelihood?

What are his misfortunes, and what are his fortunes [1]?

The Buddha explained to Mahānāna that one who goes to the refuge of the three gems, viz., the Buddha, the Dhamma, and the Saṅgha, is a layman or a lay devotee [1].

How does he become a lay devotee? He becomes one by worshipping the three gems. Anybody who worships the Buddha, the Dhamma, and the Saṅgha is a lay devotee. He will truly worship them if he remembers their qualities and tries to develop their qualities in him even though in a small measure.

Upāsaka Observes Five Precepts

He observes five precepts. He refrains from killing, stealing, committing adultery or sexual misconduct, telling lies, slandering people, making harsh speech, talking uselessly, and taking intoxicants.

Honest Means of Earning Livelihood

How does he earn his livelihood? A layman who has gone to the three refuges keeps himself from earning his livelihood by wrong means and earns it by right means. What are the right means of earning one's livelihood? If he does not sell weapons, does not sell human beings, does not sell meat, does not sell wine, and does not sell poison, he earns his livelihood by right means. Besides, if he is a shopkeeper and does not take more from a person who sells his good and gives less to a customer who buys from him and weighs and measures things dishonestly, he does not earn his livelihood by honest and pure means. If he sells weapons, he encourages killings; if he sells meat, he encourages killing; if he makes human beings slaves, he is devoid of compassion; if he sells wine, he is responsible for ruining many poor persons' family life and causing many kinds of trouble to them. If he sells poison he encourages people to poison others and sometimes poison themselves.

Upasaka's Misfortunes

What are his misfortunes? His misfortunes are not observing precepts of morality. If he does not observe them, he becomes an outcaste, a cāṇḍāla. Metaphorically he is called the dirt of layman (mala), and he is scorned and defamed (patikuṭṭhaṃ). If a person is without faith and without morality and if he is a diviner by curious ceremonies, he believes in luck and not in deeds, and he seeks a gift-worthy person from outside the order and offers first service there, he is a cāṇḍāla.

What Kind of Upāsaka Is the Jewel of Laymen?

But if he observes precepts, has faith, and believes in deeds, not in luck, he "is the jewel of laymen, the lily of laymen and the lotus of laymen" [2].

Tapassu and Bhallika were the first to become dvevācika upāsakas [3] by going to the refuge of the Buddha and the Dhamma. Others become upāsakas by pronouncing the whole saraṇa formula and are called tevācika upāsakas [4].

Laymen can be sotāpanna (stream enterer), sakadāgāmī (once returner), and anāgāmī (nonreturner). They can also become arahants, but as soon as they become arahants, they either become bhikkhus or die.

References

1. Sīlakkhandhavagga Aṭṭhakathā, 1.190 (Unless otherwise mentioned all books referred to here are published by Vipassana Research Institute, Dhammagiri in 1998)
2. ibid. 1.190
3. Sīlakkhandhavagga Aṭṭhakathā (1973) The Book of the Gradual Sayings (trans: Hare EM), vol III. PTS, London, p 152, Sīlakkhandhavagga Aṭṭhakathā, 1. 190
4. Sīakkhandhavagga Abhinava Ṭikā, Mahāvagga (Vinaya Piaka), p 5, 2.162

Upatissa

► Sāriputta

Upāya

Ram Kumar Rana
Department of Buddhist Studies, Faculty of Arts, University of Delhi, Delhi, India

Synonyms

Fangbian (Ch.); Hōben (Jp); Thabs (Tib.); Upāya-kauśalya (Skt)

Definition

Upāya is a Sanskrit word for *means* or *method* applied by the Buddhas and Bodhisattvas to enhance the spiritual potentialities of different people by words and actions, adjusted and adapted to their level of comprehension.

The term *Upāya* is often used as part of the compound *Upāya-kauśalya*. It generally connotes *skill in means, skillful means*, or *expedient* [4]. *Upāya-kauśalya* is a concept which emphasizes that practitioner may use his own most effective and appropriate specific methods toward actualizing the Buddha's teaching and maturing others for attaining liberation and enlightenment. Though, the implication of such a technique, view, etc., is not true in the highest sense, it may still be an expedient practice to follow or view to hold as it has the potential to lead the practitioner closer to true realization. In Chinese, the term *Upāya* is rendered as Fangbian (Jap. Hoben). Here, *Fang* means *Fangfa*, a method, mode, or plan. And *bian* is *bianyong*, i.e., convenient for use or expedient method [9]. It is also interpreted as partial, temporary, or relative (teaching of) knowledge of reality in contrast with *Prajñā* "the Absolute Truth or Reality." The exercise of skill to which it refers is the ability to adapt one's message to the audience by any suitable method or expedient beneficial to the recipient(s) [9]. This concept gained prominence in early Mahāyāna and expounded in texts such as the *Upāya Kauślya Sūtra, the Lotus Sūtra, the Vimalakīrtinirdeśa Sūtra*, and *the Prajñāpāramitā Sūtras*. In the Mahāyāna tradition, *Upāya* is a central concept which plays important role in Buddhist hermeneutics, soteriology, polemics, and ethics.

In Early Buddhism

The term *skill in means Upāya-kosalla* is relatively rare in Pāli canon and used only in the later texts. These texts portray the Buddha as "skilled in means" (*Upāya-kusala*) in a verse of the *Theragāthā* (158). A teacher of doctrine, like a good boatman, is a "skillful knower of means" or *Upāyaññu-kusalo* in a stanza of the *Nāvasutta* of *Sutta Nipāta* (321). In the *Sangāmāvacāra Jātaka* (No. 182), "skill in means" is applied when the Buddha converts Nanda from passion to religion; at other places, it is paired with *Paññā*, wisdom in general [6]. *Upāya* in the Pāli canon has its ordinary sense of the Buddha's skill in expounding the Dhamma.

Some widely known passages in Pāli canon quite clearly refer to the concept of *Upāya*. Among the famous simile of particular interest is that of the raft which represents the clearest and simplest statement of *skill in means* in the Theravāda canon (*Alagaddūpama Sutta in Majjhima Nikāya*). The story is about a man who crosses a great body of water by means of a raft prepared by using wooden sticks and straws. When he crosses over to the other shore, he ponders what to do with it. Should he carry it with him or just leave behind. The Buddha makes the point with this simile that Dhamma is just for crossing over, not for retaining. This point toward the provisional nature of the Buddhist teaching and their efficacy lay in crossing over from the suffering of *saṃsāra* to the bliss of *nirvāṇa*.

In the Lotus Sūtra

One more incident recorded in the Pali Canon is the legend of the Buddha's initial hesitation to teach Dhamma (Skt. dharma) immediately after his enlightenment. Then, it was only after the entreaty to preach by the god Brahma, He decides to preach. (The story is given in the section entitled *Mahāvagga* of the *Vinaya Piṭaka* and also in the *Āriyapariya senasutta* of the *Majjhima Nikāya*). This legend, inherited by all Buddhist, indicates the problem of communicating the Dhamma to people.

Upāya in the Lotus Sūtra

The *Lotus Sūtra* specifically focuses on the implications of this tradition when it emphasizes the Buddha's initial refusal to teach at all, and then only through *skillful means*, it became possible and worthwhile. Eventually, he decided to turn the wheel of the law following the way of all other Buddhas by employing the power of *skillful means* [11]. Accordingly, the Buddha then goes to Varanasi and teaches his five former companions. The *nirvāṇic* character of all dharmas cannot be stated in words, and hence, the necessity to employ provisional terms, concepts, and goal as an expedient to prepare them for supreme truth [11]. The concepts such as Buddha, dharma, *Saṃgha*, and the four noble truths, etc., are provisional in the sense that they are only useful as a means and not to be perceived as absolute reality but positively however these concepts are required, because it is only through the discriminated knowledge "the supreme principle" can be conveyed [6]. It refers to both the path which the Buddha provides for the salvation of beings and also to the system of methods used by these beings in their attainment of liberation. Thus, *Upāya* certainly is not simply a device or measure. On the contrary, the term can more or less be equated with the term Mahāyāna [6].

The Tathāgata has the capability to make various kinds of distinctions in order to expound the teaching skillfully. The true nature and characteristics of all phenomena can only be understood and shared among the Buddhas. The Buddhas preach the law in accordance with what is appropriate but the meaning and their intentions are difficult to understand. Since the Buddhas appear in evil worlds of five impurities viz. impurity of the age, desire, living beings, view, and life span. In such an impure age and chaotic times, the defilements of living beings are grave; they are greedy and jealous and possess evil roots [11]. Taking cognizance of this basic nature of theirs, the Buddhas utilizing the power of expedient means apply distinctions to the one Buddha vehicle and preach as though it were three, knowing fully well that living beings have various desires and attachments that are deeply rooted in their minds [11].

The primary objective of the Buddhas is to simply teach and convert the Bodhisattvas. They wish to use the Buddha wisdom to enlighten living beings and cause them to enter the path of Buddha wisdom. From the very beginning the Buddha vowed to make all persons equal to him, without any distinction. That is why he has converted all livings beings and caused them to enter the Buddha way [11]. But, the persons of dull capacities delight in a little law and lack confidence to attain Buddhahood. Those who greedily cling to birth and death fail to practice the profound and wonderful way; for them, the Buddha has resorted to the expedient means, preaching the way that ends all sufferings and showing them *nirvāṇa*. Yet this *nirvāṇa* preached by Him is not the true extinction. The Buddhas appear in the world to preach the law, in which all things are equal. The original vow of the Buddhas is to preach the way, which they themselves practice and should be shared universally among living beings so that they too may attain this Buddha way. In this endeavor though, they point out different paths; in truth, they do so for the sake of the Buddha vehicle [11].

Keeping in view, the actions of living beings, the deep rooted thoughts of their minds, the deeds they have performed in the past, their desires, their nature, the power of their exertions, and whether their capacities are acute or dull, the Buddhas employ various causes and conditions, similes, parables, and other words and phrases, adapting what expedient means are suitable to their preaching so that all of them may attain the one Buddha vehicle and wisdom of all modes [11]. It is for their sake the Buddha made distinctions and preach the three vehicles. Even though He preaches the three vehicles, but that are merely means to teach the Bodhisattvas. From infinite eons the Buddha had extolled and taught the law of nirvana ending the long sufferings of birth and death but the Bodhisattvas as and when they hear this law, will be freed from all entanglements of doubt [11].

Almost anything in the whole range of Buddhist teaching, ritual and practice can be described as skillful means. This applies not only to draw a Buddha image but also to such a central teaching as that of *nirvāṇa*. In the intentions and actions of a Buddha, skillful means signifies that provisional teachings are established only to be replaced by "the most wonderful supreme Dharma." Upāya is just about the nature, purpose, and style of Buddhist teaching and practice which characterizing the operation of the Buddhist religion. Apart from the skillful means of the Buddha, there is no other vehicle [6].

In the *Lotus Sūtra*, skill in means is used primarily as tool of hermeneutics. In its one Vehicle theory, it is proposed that voice hearers are given teachings that are not definitive but *skillful means*, as they are unable to cope with Bodhisattva teachings. In this sense, "skill in means" is derivative of "one vehicle" theory [10]. Skillful means and the doctrine of the one vehicle also form the subject of the main parables for which the *Lotus Sūtra* is well known. In the parable of the burning house, three sons of a rich man are trapped in a burning house, absorbed in playing their games without noticing the fire. The father, using a skillful device, persuades his children to come out by offering them goat, deer, and ox carriage as they like playing with carriages drawn by animals. The children immediately rush out of the burning house. The father then gives them the very best and wonderful carriage, drawn by a white ox (Chap. 3). In this parable the father is the Buddha; the burning house is *saṃsāra*, within which sentient beings absorbed in their playthings are trapped. The Buddha offers various vehicles (*yānas*) to entice, according to the tastes of sentient beings, but when they are saved from *saṃsāra* he gives them the very best, the only, vehicle of Buddhahood. Here, the question arises whether the father, or the Buddha, lied to his children? He is exonerated from such blame since truth usually depends upon motive and context. The Buddha as the father of beings simply uses skillful means out of compassion to save his children [11]. The use of skill in means to explain discrepancies among Buddhist doctrines was developed later as a Mahāyāna response to the apprehensions regarding the authenticity of the early *Mahāyāna Sūtras* [10].

Traditionally, the Buddha in certain respects is regarded superior to *arhats* and *pratyekabuddhas*, but in early Buddhism, *arhats*, *pratyekabuddhas*, and Buddhas are all placed at the level of enlightened ones [13]. In the Lotus Sūtra, the Buddha is portrayed as preaching that the goal of *arhat*ship and *pratyekabuddhahood* are no real goals, they are merely provisional devices, and that *arhatship* and *pratyekabuddhahood* is far from the true goal of full and complete Buddhahood [11]. The nature of *arhatship* and *pratyekabuddhahood* as goals is further illustrated by the parable of the Place of Jewels (Chap. 7). The Buddha is compared with a guide, leading men to the Place of Jewels, a fabulous utopia indeed. Midway, his followers become tired and want to give up. The guide, however, skilled in means and also a magician, creates a magical city in which they can rest before proceeding on to their true destination. Likewise, the Buddha creates the magical city of *arhatship* and *pratyekabuddhahood* [11].

In the *Lotus Sūtra*, and some texts belonging to certain non-Mahāyāna traditions, a gradual devaluation of *arhats* and *pratyekabuddhas*, and an elevation of the Buddha and his attainments are clearly evident. The *Lotus Sūtra* marks the culmination of this process [13]. There is in reality only one vehicle, not three. This one vehicle is the supreme Buddha vehicle. Just as the Buddha is infinitely superior to the *arhat* and the *pratyekabuddha*, so the only final vehicle is the one vehicle to perfect Buddhahood. All will eventually become Buddhas; the doctrines of the three vehicles were in reality nothing more than the Buddha's skillful means [11]. These were taught simply to encourage people. All will eventually take the path of the *Bodhisattva* and progress to perfect Buddhahood, including those who consider themselves to have attained already the goals of *arhatship* and *pratyekabuddhahood*. In the *Lotus Sūtra*, the Buddha predicts how *arhats* in his entourage, like Sāriputra, and others will eventually become full Buddha [11]. All the provisional teachings lead to the Buddha vehicle, or in other words, they dismantle in favor of the one Buddha vehicle which is the sole and consistent intention from the very beginning.

The *Lotus Sūtra* describes even the Buddha's own entry into *nirvāna* as skillful means. In reality, the Buddha has not really passed away. He is like a great physician whose sons have been poisoned. He quickly prepares the antidote, but the minds of some of the sons are so deranged that they ignore the medicine. The father fakes his own death and retires elsewhere. Brought to their senses by shock, the sons take the antidote. The father then reappears. His death was a skillful device (Chap. 16). This indicates; the so-called nirvana of the Buddha is not the true extinction but an expedient to help his disciples.

Upāya in the Upayakauśalya Sūtra

In Mahāyāna, *skillful means* generally refers to any compassionately motivated activity that helps others in spiritual progress. This "contextual" ethic makes moral decision making more flexible and defines virtue in terms of motive rather than conduct. The *Upāya-kauśalya Sūtra* refers to some cases of Bodhisattva monks who are suspected of breaking celibacy; the accused, however, is ultimately proved to be technically innocent. The complaints only highlight the irritability of the accusers; the Bodhisattva himself does not hesitate to commit an infringement, but he does so only when it is unavoidable to ensure the welfare of someone else. In such cases, the Bodhisattva is even prepared to sacrifice his own spiritual career and delay his obtainment of *nirvāṇa*. Those who maintain celibacy in the *Upāya-kauśalya Sūtra* are able to prove it by displays of levitation [10]. The Bodhisattva who is entitled to violate such serious precepts to commit murder or to break celibacy is called a *Mahāsattva*, "great hero." Bodhisattva-Mahāsattva may indulge himself in all manner of sensual pleasures and games in order to bring sentient beings to maturity without generating any craving for permanence in them. Even though he indulges himself in all means of pleasure games but does not possess himself of defilements that lead to great distress, nor does he lose the qualities of a Buddha. Bodhisattva skilled in means will focus his thought on omniscience cultivating emptiness, signlessness, and wishlessness (selflessness). He enters the swamp of sense desire but guarding well the thought of omniscience. Without omniscience there would be no possibility of universal compassion. Being fully aware that the offense would cause him to suffer in hell for 100,000 eons, the Bodhisattva, however, will incur transgression and sufferings of the hell enthusiastically rather than to relinquish the store of merit of a single sentient being. Bodhisattva who is skilled in means knows how to bring sentient beings to maturity and to introduce them to the three jewels and to supreme, right and full awakening [10]. Bodhisattvas dwell in inconceivable skill in means course in form, sound, smell, taste, and touch – all of which are occasions for attachment – yet they remain unattached to them with skillful means. In the process, he adapts himself to sentient beings; after they develop store of merit he proceeds to ignore and leave them without thought [10].

Ethics for the Bodhisattva too is based upon the *Vinaya* rules as for other monastics; yet he is not circumscribed by it. In practicing skill in means, he may supersede the monastic rule and act in a manner contrary to the "narrower" moral or monastic code of others. The *Upāya-kauśalya Sūtra* describes how the Buddha in a previous life as a celibate religious had sexual intercourse in order to save a poor girl who threatened to die for love of him [10]. A story well known among Mahāyāna followers tells similarly how in a previous life, the Buddha killed a man. This was the only way to prevent him from killing 500 other persons and consequently falling to the lowest hell for a very long time. The Bodhisattva's act was driven by pure compassion. Knowing fully well that he was violating the moral code, he was ready to suffer in hell himself out of his compassionate concern for others. Later, the *Sūtra* tells us, not only did the Bodhisattva progress spiritually and avoid hell, but the potential murderer was also reborn in a heavenly realm [13].

In employing skillful means, it becomes theoretically possible that many of the proscribed practices, such as violence, theft, and sexuality, could be seen as use of skillful means. The use of harsh words and violence to one's disciples has occasionally been used by the Chan masters as a way of opening their eyes to the nature of self and suffering and thus causing a deep insight in the disciple. There are a number of other stories of Buddhist masters taking part in quite eccentric and unusual behaviors in the practice of skillful means.

Prajñā-Upāya and the Bodhisattva Practice

In Mahāyāna soteriology, *Upāya* is paired with wisdom, one of the two aspects of the path perfected by Bodhisattvas toward Buddhahood. Here, *Upāya* refers to nearly any religious method not related directly to wisdom, and so includes the perfections of generosity, morality, patience, and effort and the practice of various ritual and meditative techniques, the development of the compassionately motivated aspiration to achieve enlightenment for the sake of all beings (*Bodhicitta*). His thought of enlightenment consists in the fact that he does not want to leave all beings behind.

Dāna, Pāramitā, etc., accompanied by *Prajñā* alone and in no other manner attain an identity a designation. *Skill in means* is also linked to dedication of merit. In the *Upāya Kauśalya Sūtra*, the Bodhisattva performs every good deed with an aspiration for Buddhahood and dedication of the merit created by the deed to the achievement of Buddhahood by all sentient beings. For instance, the Bodhisattva who practices charity renounces its short-term benefit and makes a wish instead that the merit counts toward Buddhahood; this surpasses the benefits of ordinary giving [10]. In addition, the act of dedication itself creates even greater merit. This requires both the recognition of a pattern of merit and freedom from seeing it in terms of characteristics. It requires in fact the combination known as "*Prajñāpārmitā* – skilful means" [6].

Upāya is bondage when unassociated with *Prajñā* and even *Prajñā* is also bondage when unassociated with *Upāya*; both of them can achieve liberation when the one is associated with the other. *Prajñā* as the passive principle is the *dharmakāya* the thatness (*Tathatā*) with perfect purity and perfect knowledge in her [5]. Except the perfection of wisdom (other perfections) all other virtuous accumulations are explained by the conquerors to be the means. Vigorous practice of the means and proper meditation on wisdom lead to enlightenment swiftly, while merely meditating on selflessness does not [1].

Prajñā and *Upāya* are compared with the two wings of a bird. *Upāya* is the knowledge of acquisition and *Prajña* is the knowledge of discrimination. Skill in *Upāya* is the acquisition of all dharmas and *Prajña* is the skill of analyzing all dharmas. *Prajñā* and *Upāya* are meant for the accumulation of all the perfections by Bodhisattva. Equipped with the twin path of *Prajñā* and *Upāya*, the Mahāsattva Bodhisattva will soon be linked with supreme perfect enlightenment [7].

The *Prajñā* of omniscience (*Sarvajñāta*) has compassion as its root, it is the essence of *Bodhicitta* and is the end of *Upāya*. Therefore, the Bodhisattvas must always practice both of them. *Prajñā* prevents the consequences of superimposition and *Upāya* prevents the consequences of contradiction [7]. A skillful means is to see there are ultimately no dharmas and sentient beings while saving living beings. Even though a Bodhisattva knows that all dharmas are void because of the power of skillful means, he does not abandon sentient beings. Even though he does not abandon living beings, he knows all dharmas are in reality void. A Bodhisattva should not get entangled in a particular attention to insight or emptiness as if it were something different from everything else. His power of skillful means enables him to recognize the equality of emptiness, the existence, and the needs of the living beings. In this manner, a Bodhisattva by his power of skillful means is able to avoid practicing in characteristics or marks [7].

If a Bodhisattva in his mind forms the aspiration not to abandon all beings but to set them free, and if in addition he aspires for the concentration on the emptiness, the signless, and the wishless; the three doors of deliverance, then the Bodhisattva should be known as one who is endowed with skillful means and he will not realize reality limit (nirvāṇa) midway without completing the Buddha dharmas. Without skillful means, had they realized the reality limit, then they come on the level of *pratyekabuddhas*, not that of a Buddha [3]. If a Bodhisattva endowed with *bodhicitta* does not midway realize reality limit, he does not lose his concentration on the four *brahmvihāras*. Upheld by skillful means, he increases his pure dharmas, more and more his faith becomes keener and keener, and he acquires powers, limbs of enlightenment, and the path [3].

In Buddhist literature, *Prajñā and Upāya* are practiced together. "*Prajñā*" is the wisdom of *Śunyatā*. Bodhisattva should practice emptiness through wisdom coupled with upāya in order to counter the wind of contradiction (*viparyāsa*) [7]. *Upāya* is the activity of *Prajñā*, which manifests as compassion (*karuṇā*). The paired dharmas are voidness and compassion; skillful means is the key to their correlation without being attached to the either. Skillful means refers to the ability of adeptness in practicing contradictorily on the basis of unique intention. So, wisdom is the sixth perfection, while skill in means embraces the first five. From skill in means arises a corresponding set of terms for the functions (the "bodies") of a Buddha, for "pure lands," and for the Bodhisattva stages [6].

In Tibetan Buddhist practice, clear-eyed awareness and a fundamental sense of kindness and acceptance applied to oneself and the world with equal generosity that benefits oneself and others. This is accomplished through the wisdom and skillful means (Tib: *Sherab and Thab*). Wisdom and means relate to the polarity of ultimate and relative reality, that strange paradox wherein the diverse forms and phenomena of the material world coexists alongside the ultimate, open, and luminous matrix from which they arise! [8]. In Vajrayāna practice, they are the stages of development and completion. Skillful means will permeate one's position by embracing the root of virtue. Growing wisdom will inform one's actions. Thus the skillful means is a path of action, whereas wisdom and compassion are matters of practical application, not mere concepts [8].

In China too, the relation between illusion and reality is reconfigured as the relation between provisional and ultimate truth in the Buddha's teaching. Zhiyi characterizes the *Lotus* teachings as the "opening of the provisional to reveal the real" (*kaiquan xianshi*), allowing one to see the provisional truths as both a means to and an expression of the ultimate truth. Provisional and ultimate truths are nondual, even when maintaining their contradiction [2]. On the basis of this doctrine, Zhiyi (538–597) established the most influential harmenuetical scheme in a comprehensive system of "classification of teachings (*Panjiao*)" in five progressively higher stages of the Buddha's teachings culminating in the *Lotus Sūtra*. Here, all Buddhist teachings are explained as the expressions of ultimate truth suitable for specific circumstance and listeners [2]. In this fashion, a hierarchical progression of teachings could be constructed, starting with the most elementary and leading to the most profound. This system was particularly used by the Tiantai and the Huayan schools of Chinese Buddhism.

Upāya in Vimalkīrti Nirdeśa Sūtra

In the *Vimalkīrti Nirdeśa Sūtra*, Vimalakīrti is portrayed as a wealthy layman who lives in Veśāli with family, wearing decorative ornaments and enjoying lavish food and drinks. But in living the household life, he is not attached to the world and takes delight in practicing the true Dharma [12]. The skillful means and the career of Bodhisattvas is superbly represented by Vimalakīrti who in his past births had attended to the countless Buddhas, deeply planted the wholesome roots, grasped the truth of birthlessness, successfully removed all impediments and penetrated deeply into the doctrine of the law, became proficient in the *Pāramitā* of wisdom, and a master in employing expedient means. He had successfully fulfilled his great vow and could clearly discern the minds of others and distinguish whether their capacities were sharp or dull. His mind was purified through the long practice of the Buddha Way and understanding the Great Vehicle. In dignity and authority, he equals a Buddha, and his mind was vast as the sea. He was admired by all thc Buddhas and commanded the respect of the Four Heavenly Kings. His faultless observation of the precepts served as a reproach to those who would violate prohibitions [12].

In fact, Vimalakīrti's living in Veśāli is his *skill in means* to fulfill his vow to save people. He frequently visited the gambling dens to enlighten all those there, listened to the doctrines of other religions, and he did not allow them to impinge on the true faith. He frequented the busy crossroads in order to benefit others, entered the government offices and courts of law to help all those he could. He visited the places of debate in order to guide others in the Great Vehicle, visited the schools and study halls to further the instruction of the pupils, also frequented brothels to teach the vanity of fleshly desire, entered wine shops to encourage those who wish to quit drinking [12].

In the teachings of Vimalakīrti, the model Bodhisattva aims at, as part of his skillful means, all the main forms of secular life and had a distinct social involvement. The rich honored him as foremost among them because he preached the superior law for them, the lay believers honored him as foremost because he freed them from greed and attachment, the Kshatriyas honored him because he taught them forbearance, and the Brahmans honored him because he rid them of their self-conceit. The great ministers honored him as foremost because he taught the correct law. The princes honored him as foremost because he showed them how to be loyal and filial. Within the women's quarters, he was most honored because he converted and brought refinement to them [12]. In this manner, in each case, he is able to give what is needed by those who are entangled in the various walks of life.

Using the expedient means, he feigned illness. Then he used his bodily illness to expound the law to numerous people belonging to all strata of the society who visited him to inquire about his illness. To the visitors, Vimalakīrti expounded the favorite subject of the Buddhist, the shortcomings of the physical body, and advised them to rather seek the Buddha body which is also called body of the Dharma, born of immeasurable numbers of pure and taintless things. If people wish to gain the Buddha body and do away with the ills that afflict all living beings, then they must set their minds on attaining supreme perfect enlightenment. Consequently, innumerable persons set their minds on attainment of *anuttara-samyak-sambodhi* [12]. The sickness of Vimalakīrti had two facets. On the one hand, it bears the marks of the sufferings of the world, but on the other hand, it has no marks. As a skillful means, Vimalakīrti's illness both follows the lines of the suffering of the world and bears within it the latent resolution of this suffering [6].

In some of the *Mahāyāna texts*, such as the *Lotus Sūtra*, *Upāya* is used as a polemic device against prior Buddhist traditions; it is said that the Buddha gave them various *Upāya*s rather than revealing the ultimate truth, for which they were not ready. The teaching of Vimalakīrti is more concerned with the polemics between the Bodhisattva Vimalakīrti himself and narrower interpreters of Buddhism [6].

The *Lotus Sūtra* suggests that all beings are Bodhisattvas, and all Bodhisattvas are Buddhas. The only difference between them is that of the capacity and ignorance which maintains their identities intact. The *Upāya*s work as long as they are not known to be *Upāya*. This means that intersubjective liberative relationship between Buddhas and sentient beings is primary and always operative, whichever role one may seem to be playing at any time. Being is the intersubjective, i.e., each being is always both liberating and being liberated by all others, even while also creating *Karma* (action) and *Dukkha* (suffering). Ontology is here made soteriological: All existence is instructive and revelatory, and can be understood as a salvational scheme devised by a Buddha to liberate sentient beings [2]. Thus, in terms of *skillful means*, a Bodhisattva's true practice and the deliverance of others belong together. The Mahāyānists saw the whole Buddhist religion as a vehicle for "crossing over" and for "bringing over," which are inseparable. In short, Buddhism is *skillful means* [6].

Cross-References

- Arhat (Sanskrit)
- Bodhisattva
- Karuṇā
- Mahāyāna
- Nirvāṇa
- Prajñā
- Pratyeka-Buddha
- The Lotus Sūtra
- Vimalakirti

References

1. Angrup L (tr), Tripathi RS (ed) (1990) Bodhipathapradīp of Acarya Dipankar Srijñāna. Central Institute of Buddhist Studies, Leh
2. Buswell RE (2004) Encyclopedia of Buddhism, vol II. MacMillan Reference USA, Thomson Gale
3. Conze E (tr) (1970) Aæṭasāhasrika Prjñāpāramitā, Bibliotheca Indica, a collection of oriental works. Asiatic Society, Calcutta
4. Edgerton F (1953) Buddhist hybrid Sanskrit dictionary and grammar. Yale University Press, New Heavens
5. Ghosh B (1992) Concept of Prajñā and Upāya. In: Bulletin of tibetology, vol 3. Sikkim Research Institute of Tibetology, Gangtok, Sikkim
6. Pye M (1978) Skilful means: a concept in Mahayana Buddhism. Gerald Duckworth, London
7. Sharma P (tr) (2004) Bhāvanākrama of Acarya Kamalśila, 2nd edn. Aditya Prakashan, New Delhi
8. Soeng M (2000) Diamond Sūtra: transforming the way we perceive the world. Wisdom, Somerville
9. Soothill WE, Hodus L (2005) A dictionary of Chinese Buddhist terms. Munshiram Manoharlal, New Delhi
10. Tatz M (tr) (2001) The skill in means (Upāya-Kauśalya Sūtra). Moti Lal Banarasi Dass, Delhi, Reprint
11. Watson B (1999) The Lotus Sūtra. Sri Satguru, Delhi
12. Watson B (1999) The Vimalakirti Sūtra, Buddhist tradition series. Motilal Banarasidass, Delhi
13. Williams P (1999) Mahayana Buddhism: the doctrinal foundations. Routledge, London, Reprint

Upāyakauśalya

► Ethics (Buddhism)

Upāya-kauśalya

► Upāya

Uposatha

Rajesh Ranjan
Department of Pali, Nava Nalanda Mahaviihara (Deemed to be University), Nalanda, Bihar, India

Synonyms

Jainism – Posadha (Skt.); Pausadha (Skt.); Prausudha (Skt.); Parva (Skt.); Posaha (Ardhamagadhi); Vedic religion – Upavasatha (Skt.)

Definition

The *Uposatha* (Sanskrit, *Upavasatha*) is a day of observance in Buddhist tradition. Initially, the monks used to hold *uposatha* on the 8th, 14th, and 15th days of each half month, but later on only 2 days, that is, 14th and 15th days of each half month, were designated as the *uposatha* days. The recital of the *pātimokkha* (disciplinary code) before the *bhikkhu saṅgha* was to be done once in a fortnight, that is, either on the 14th or the 15th day, which in due course of time fixed for the 15th day only. Lay people observe the eight precepts do meditation and confess commitment to the *Dhamma* on *uposatha* days. In pre-Buddhist times, the *upavasatha* was the fasting day preceding the Vedic sacrifice. In some ways, the *uposatha* is similar to the Jewish and Christian *Sabbath*, except that it is not obligatory to observe it.

Despite India being a country of multiracial and multiethnic society, there were some customs and observances pursued by all people alike irrespective of their faiths, that is, Brāhmanism, Jainism, Buddhism, and the like. Among such practices which were uniformly availed by people pursuing mendicant life since time immemorial was the practice of fasting in one form or the other, on certain days of a month. It was a characteristic feature of almost all ancient Indian religions referred to above. The followers of the Brāhmanical fold observed *upavāsa* on *amāvasyā* (the first day of the dark-fortnight – *kṛṣṇapakṣa*) and *purṇamāsī* (the full moon day of the bright-fortnight – *śuklapakṣa*) of the month and called them *darśa* and *pauraṇamāsa*, respectively. Thus *darśa* and *pauraṇamāsa* taken together were known as *upavasatha* days.

The observance of the *upavasatha* was an ancient Indo-Aryan ritual observed by the Brāhmanical laities since long time. As such, the earliest reference to the *upavasatha* is made in the *Śatapatha Brāhamaṇa* [4], which enjoins to perform the sacrificial rites on the eve of the *darśa* and *pauraṇamāsa*.

The Sanskṛit term *upavasatha* stood for the fast day, especially the day preceding the *Soma* sacrifice and the period of the sacrifice itself. According to *Kātyāyana Śrautasūtra* [2], the term *upavasatha* meant to live close to the deities, which was feasible only by performing certain sacrifices twice in a month, that is, on the last days of the dark-half (*amāvasyā*) and the bright-half (*pauraṇamāsa*) of every month. The fasting was observed by the sacrificers tending the fire on the lines prescribed by their priests. *Āruṇeyya Upaniṣada* [5] admonishes the sacrificers to complete the penances like fast, etc., and the Brāhmin priest to chant Upaniṣadas or Araṇyakas. It was, therefore, obviously a ritual to be performed by householders. According to *Hirṇyakesin* [1], the ritual of *upavasatha* was of utmost importance because it aimed at discarding the company of the impious and seeking the company of the pious. Thus, the sum total of the Brāhmanical *upavasatha* was to inculcate virtue and to eradicate vice.

The Ardhamagadhi/Prakrit equivalent to the Sanskrit term *upavasatha* is *posaha*. In Jaina Sanskrit literature, it is mentioned as *pauṣadha* or *poṣadha*. Like the Brāhmanical *upavasatha*, the *posaha* was observed exclusively by the Jaina laities. *Parva* is the word used as a synonym for *pauṣadha* by Umāswāti in his undisputed composition, the *Tattāvrthasūtra*. He mentions *Aṣṭamī*, *caturdaśī*, and *pañcadasī* or any other day (*tithi*) of the month suitable for observing the *pauṣadha*. The Jaina scriptures refer to *posahasālā*, a room or hall set apart for the purpose, where a Jaina *sāvaga* (lay follower) was enjoined to fast and behave strictly like a Jaina monk abstaining from bodily decoration like bathing, use of perfumes and powder, putting on jewelry and ornaments, etc. Besides, the *vrati* (the person who observes the *posaha*) was advised to sleep on mats of *kuśa* grass or wooden planks. Normally the *posaha* was observed for 1 day, but if continued for more than 1 day, the *vrati* was expected to desist from sleep so far as possible and practice various meditational postures and meditate on religious tenets and nature of self.

The *Bhagavatisūtra*, a Jaina Āgama, refers to a type of *posaha* known as *pakkhiya-posaha*, in which the *vrati* with a view to celebrate this type of *posaha* went out of his residence, prepared food and drink, and passed the day there in merriments. Very likely this *posaha*, which did not appear to be the least religious, was given the status of the *posaha* proper because of its being associated with the *parva* days, that is, *aṣṭamī* and *caturdasī*. It, therefore, may be inferred that ceremonies, religious or social, associated with *posaha*/*parva* days were indiscriminately given the importance of *posaha*, which accounts for the *Aṅguttaranikāya* reference to *gopālaka-uposatha*.

The Pali expression of the Sanskrit term *upavasatha* is *uposatha*. The Buddha introduced this Indo-Aryan ritual to his order of monks on the suggestion of the king Seniya Bimbisāra of Magadha who himself, according to the tradition, had been observing it being performed by the followers of the heretical religions (*titthiya*s) [3]. The idea behind such observances on appointed days, that is, 8th, 14th, and 15th days of each half month by the *titthiya*s, was to gain adherents by promoting faith in them through religious discourses. So the Buddha admonished the monks to assemble and hold *uposatha*. Though the monks began to assemble on 8th, 14th, and 15th days of each half month, they sat tight-lipped. Irritated by this sort of assembling of monks, people started passing scandalous remarks, which led the Buddha to enjoin upon them to recite the *Dhammā* on the *uposatha* days. In due course of time, the recitation of the *Dhamma* was replaced by the recitation of the *pātimokkha*, which was known as *uposatha-kamma*. On the *uposatha* day, a competent monk had to recite the *pātimokkha* and those who had committed any offense would have to confess it. As the monks were hesitant to confess their omissions and commissions in the presence of the lay devotees, consequently their participation in *uposatha* ceremony was banned.

Initially, the monks used to hold *uposatha* on the 8th, 14th, and 15th days of each half month, but later on only 2 days, that is, 14th and 15th days of each half month, were designated as the *uposatha* days. Likewise, the recital of the *pātimokkha* was to be done once in a fortnight, that is, either on the 14th or the 15th day, which in due course of time fixed for the 15th day only (*ajjuposatho paṇṇaraso*) [1].

Before referring to the places fit for solemnizing *uposatha*, it would not be out of place to throw some light on the terms *sīmā* and *āvāsa* first. Like the Christian diocese or parish, *sīmā* was the circuit of the jurisdiction of an *āvāsa*. It was obligatory for all monks living within the *sīmā* of an *āvāsa* to be present personally or send their consent (*chanda*) in absentia [3].

Normally, a *vihāra*, an *aḍḍhyoga* (pinnacled house), a *pāsāda* (storied building), a *hammiya* (attic), and a *guhā* (cave) were regarded as ideal venues for holding *uposatha*. The place for holding the *uposatha* was usually decided by the *saṅgha*. It was strictly forbidden to hold *uposatha* in one's own room or to fix two *uposathāgāra* (hall for holding the *uposatha*) within one *āvāsa*. In case of several *āvāsa*s within the same boundary, the *uposatha* was to be held in the *āvāsa* fixed by the *saṅgha* or in the *āvāsa* of the senior monks. Under constrained circumstances, it was also to be held in the personal room/cell of a monk [3].

The jurisdiction (*sīmā*) of an *āvāsa* which was decided usually by the *kammavācā* process was demarcated by some conspicuous marks like a mountain, a rock, a wood, a tree, a path, an anthill, a river, and a tank. In case of unsettled boundary (*sīmā*) of an *āvāsa* situated in a village, the starting point of the jurisdiction of the adjacent village was regarded as its *sīmā*. The *sīmā* of an *āvāsa* situated in a forest extended up to seven *abbhantara*s (a linear measure equal to 28 hands) all around. Normally, the *sīmā* in case of a river, sea, or a tank extended as far as an average man can throw water, but if there existed any regular communication, the *sīmā* ran up to the opposite side of the river. So also the boundary (*sīmā*) of more than three *yojana*s and overlapping or encompassing another *sīmā* could not be fixed [3].

Before the assembling of monks in the *uposathāgāra* to hold *uposatha*, it must be well furnished with the necessary articles. Duties like sweeping the hall, providing seats for the participating monks, arranging drinking water and food for the assembly, and putting a lighted lamp were assigned to junior monks. It was obligatory for the senior monks to assemble first [3].

After all the monks of an *āvāsa* had assembled in the *uposathāgāra*, the *ňatti* (declaration of resolution or motion) was proclaimed by a competent monk directing the assembly to confess one's offense during the recital of the concerned section of the *pātimokkha* and non-offenders to remain silent. Confession of offenses by monks led to the recommencement of the penalty (*mulāyapaṭikassanā*) or sentence of *mānatta* (a kind of ecclesiastical punishment which debars a monk from enjoying the usual privileges as a monk for a period of six nights) discipline, keeping in view seniority of the offending monks. So also rebuking anybody for his offense without the prior consent of the person concerned was forbidden. Nobody could either preach the *Dhamma* or put questions about the Vinaya or answer them without the permission of the assembly [3].

Normally, during the *uposatha* ceremony, the complete *pātimokkha* was to be recited. But in extraordinary circumstances, the abridged recital was also allowed. In case no senior monk was capable to recite the *pātimokkha*, a junior monk could be assigned the job. The recital of the *pātimokkha* was not allowed in an assembly where there was a nun (*bhikkhuni*), a nun under training (*sikkhamānā*), a novice (*sāmaṇera*), a female novice (*sāmaṇeri*), a renegade (*sikkhāpaccakkhātaka*), an enunch (*paṇdaka*), or the like or in an assembly otherwise impure [3].

So far as the *uposatha* ceremony observed by the *bhikkhuni saṅgha* was concerned, the *pātimokkha* was recited by monks on their behalf in the beginning. Such type of practice led the people to pass scandalous remarks. Ultimately, the nuns were trained to recite the *pātimokkha* themselves during their *uposatha* ceremony. However, they had to take permission from the *bhikkhu saṅgha* 2 or 3 days before fixing the date for holding the *uposatha* [3].

Among the various types of the *uposatha*, the first to be mentioned is the *saṅgha-uposatha*, that is, the *uposatha* performed by four or more than four monks or nuns, as the minimum quorum of the *saṅgha* competent to perform an ecclesiastical act is four. The second is named *sāmaggi-uposatha*, which is performed on any day by a competent *saṅgha* for the formal reconciliation of a dispute persisting from before but non-resolved. The third is the *uposatha* held by a group (*gaṇa*) of two or three monks or nuns, that is, less than the minimum quorum required for a *saṅgha* competent to perform an ecclesiastical act. In it, monks or nuns proclaim their *pārisuddhi* without the recital of the *pātimokkha*. Accordingly it is called *gaṇa-uposatha* or *pārisuddhi-uposatha*. The last to be mentioned is the *puggala-uposatha*, an *uposatha* performed by a lonely monk or nun. It is also called *adhiṭṭhāna-uposatha* because the monk or nun concerned resolves to perform *uposatha* only [3].

It is explicit from the foregoing perusal that the sole feature of the fortnightly meeting was the recital of the *pātimokkha*, though it had begun at its very outset, with the recital of the *Dhamma*. Along with the recital of the section of the *pātimokkha*, the concerned monks participating in the meeting had to declare, in order of seniority, their complete purification, *pārisuddhi*, and also to seek absolution from the offense, if incurred any. Thus, it is crystal clear that the nature of the Buddhist *uposatha*, at the time of its introduction, was out-and-out monastic. On the contrary, the *upavasatha* was being observed as a socioreligious ritual by the people since long before the advent of the Buddha. It is therefore feared that the abrupt change in the character of the ritual would not have proved pleasing to the newly converted populace. However, the Buddhist *saṅgha*, apprehending the displeasure of its laities, made an attempt to introduce the *uposatha* for them too. This view is substantiated by the information regarding *uposatha* recorded in the *sutta*s like *Lakkhaṇasutta* and *Uposathasutta*. The *Aṅguttaranikāya* contains one more *Uposathasutta*, but is related to the *uposatha* held by the order of monks [1].

Cross-References

- ▶ Dharma
- ▶ Pañcaśīla
- ▶ Pātimokkha
- ▶ Śīla
- ▶ Sin (Buddhism)
- ▶ Vinaya

References

1. Morris R, Hardy E (eds) (1885–1900) The Aṅguttaranikāya, 5 vols. PTS, London; Woodward FL (tr) (1955–1970) The book of the gradual sayings, vols I, II & V; Hare EM, vols III & IV, PTS, London
2. Oldenberg H (ed) (1879–1883) The Vinaya Pitaka, 5 vols. PTS, London; Horner IB (tr) (1938–1966) The book of the discipline, 6 vols. PTS, London; Rhys Davids TW, Oldenberg H (tr) Vinay texts, vols. 13, 17, 20. Reprint, (1982–1985) Sacred books of the east. Motilal Banarasidass, Delhi
3. Oldenberg H, Max Muller F (1892) Sacred books of the east, vol 30 (XXX): the Grihya-Sūtra: rules of Vedic domestic ceremonies, part II, Gobhila, Hirṇyakesin, Āpastamba, Yajña-Paribhāsā-Sūtras
4. Ranade RH (tr) (1978) Kātyāyana Śrautasūtra: rules for the Vedic sacrifices. Ranade Publication Series

5. Samasrami S (ed) (1900–1910) Śatapatha-Brāhmaṇa, Calcutta; Eggling (tr) (1882–1900) Oxford
6. Seshachari VG (tr) (1898–1899) Āruṇeyopaniṣada, Madras

Uppalavaṇṇā

Angraj Chaudhary
Vipassana Research Institute, Dhammagiri, Igatpuri, Nashik, Maharashtra, India

Definition

Uppalavaṇṇā was one of the two chief women disciples of the Buddha.

Uppalavaṇṇā and Khemā were Two Chief Women Disciples of the Buddha

Uppalavaṇṇā was one of the two chief women disciples. The other was Khemā. They were just like Sāriputta and Moggallāna to the Buddha.

She was born in Sāvatthi as the daughter of a very rich merchant. She was very beautiful to look at. Her skin was like the color of the heart of the blue lotus. So she was called Uppalavaṇṇā [1].

When she came of age and attained marriage-able age, the news of her incomparable beauty spread far and wide. Many kings and rich merchants of Jambudvīpa were eager to marry her. Who would not like to have such an extraordinary beautiful woman as a wife? They sent messages to her father asking for her hand in marriage. Her father did not know what to do. He did not want to offend and disappoint anybody [2]. But he could give his daughter to only one in marriage.

How Did She Solve Her Father's Problem

He thought out a way. If his daughter became a nun the problem would be solved. So he, unlike most of the fathers, who want their daughters to marry and live a happy conjugal life, advised Uppalavaṇṇā to renounce the world and become a nun. Uppalavaṇṇā was not an ordinary girl. She had the *upanissaya* (qualifications) for becoming an arahant. The desire to leave home and become a nun was there in her mind in the seed form. So when the proposal to renounce the world and become a nun came from her father himself, she gladly accepted it and willingly agreed to seek ordination. The words of the father were very soothing to her [3].

Tejo Kasiṇa as the Object of Meditation

When as a nun her turn came to sweep the hall where the Pātimokkha (a collection of various Vinaya rules framed by the Buddha) is recited, she did it. After that she lighted the lamp. She took the flame of the lamp as her visible object to meditate, and she developed *tejo kasiṇa* (external device of fire to develop concentration), attained to *jhāna*, and became an arahant. She also attained the magical or psychic power which is one of the six higher spiritual powers (*abhiññā*) [4].

As she was ravishingly beautiful, one of her own cousins was enamored of her. Once she was living in Andhavana. One day while she was out for begging alms, he came to her hut and hid himself. When she came back, he caught hold of her and raped her. She spoke about it to the bhikkhunīs. They spoke to the bhikkhus about it, and the bhikkhus spoke about it to the Buddha. The Buddha did not pronounce it as an offense called *pārājika* because whatever her cousin did he did forcibly, without her wanting it [5].

Once when the Buddha came to perform the twin miracle at the Gaṇḍamba tree, Uppalavaṇṇā offered to perform a few miracles. The Buddha did not permit her. But she was so expert in performing miracles that the Buddha declared her to be the chief of the women disciples who possessed the psychic (*iddhi*) power [6].

Her Dialogue with Māra and Her Ability to Perform Miracles

What she could do with her *iddhi* power is clear from what she said to Māra who came to seduce her. When Māra asked her whether she was not afraid of seducers in the forest with trees full of fragrant flowers (the spring season is the best season for lovemaking), she said she recognized him as Māra, and even if 100,000 seducers like him were to try to seduce her, they could not produce fear in her and could not curl the hairs of her body. She had become fearless by becoming an arahant [7].

She also spoke to Māra of her *iddhi* power. She said that she had gone completely beyond his powers. She could vanish at will, enter into his body, and stand between his eyebrows [8].

She further said to Māra that she knew very well what sensual pleasures are like. They are like spears and javelins which pierce and rend the mortal frame. She further said to him, "What you speak of as joys are not joys. They are so impermanent. What you think of as joys are not worth anything for me" [9].

She became ordained after realizing the dangers of sensual pleasures [10].

Uppalavaṇṇā: The Measure of Women Disciples

The Buddha also declared that Khemā and Uppalavaṇṇā are the measures of his women disciples. Any woman who would aspire after attaining the highest in the spiritual field should try to be like them [11].

References

1. AA.1.258; Para A 1.218 (Unless otherwise mentioned all books referred to here are published by Vipassana Research Institute, Dhammagiri in 1998)
2. AA.1.265
3. AA.1.265
4. Therīg A.p. 211
5. Pārā p 40
6. A 1.36
7. Thi G Verses 231, 232
8. ibid.
9. ibid 234
10. ibid. 225
11. S.1.213

Ūrdhva-loka

▶ Heaven (Jainism)

Uruvelā

▶ Bodhagayā

Uttara Madhurā

▶ Mathurā

V

Vacchagotta

Angraj Chaudhary
Vipassana Research Institute, Dhammagiri, Igatpuri, Nashik, Maharashtra, India

Definition

Vacchagotta's becoming a *tevijja* from the Brahminical learning point of view could not liberate him.

Vacchagotta Finds His Vedic Learning Useless

Vacchagotta was born as the son of a very rich brahmin at Rajgir. Because of his *gotta* (clan), which was Vaccha, he was called Vacchagotta. When he came of age, he studied Brahminical learning and became an expert. But his expertise in the Brahminical learning was of no avail to him as it did not help him to attain what he really sought. He wanted to become liberated but his learning of the Vedas could not help him. Finding his learning useless he became a wanderer. He wandered from place to place and then came in contact with the Buddha [1].

It is said that he asked some questions to the Buddha. The questions were whether the world is eternal or not eternal, finite or infinite, the soul and the body are the same, or the soul is one thing and the body another. The four other questions were related to whether the Tathāgata exists or does not exist after death or both exist and not exist after death or both exist and do not exist after death. The Buddha answered him that these questions cannot be answered, so he called them indeterminate [2]. He also said further that these questions are irrelevant as far as they are not helpful in living a holy life. The Buddha further explained to him that he did not explain them as he called them indeterminate because "it is unbeneficial, it does not belong to the fundamentals of the holy life, it does not lead to disenchantment, to dispassion, to cessation, to peace, to direct knowledge, to enlightenment, to nibbāna" [3].

Once he asked the same questions to Moggallāna, and when he gave the same answer as the Buddha, he expressed his admiration for the fact that the disciple knew what the teacher knew and their meaning and phrasing were exactly the same. There was no difference between them [4]. This impressed Vacchagotta very much.

What Does "Tevijja" Mean

There are three *suttas* related to Vacchagotta in the *Majjhima Nikāya*. From the *Tevijjavacchagotta sutta*, it becomes clear that Vacchagotta came to know the three higher knowledges of the Buddha on account of which he was a *tevijja* that he knew his past lives and could remember them and he could see beings passing away and reappearing in

K.T.S. Sarao, J.D. Long (eds.), *Buddhism and Jainism*, Encyclopedia of Indian Religions,
DOI 10.1007/978-94-024-0852-2

either fortunate or unfortunate state. He also knew why one appeared in a particular state. He also knew that he destroyed all taints and attained deliverance of mind and deliverance by wisdom [5]. From the brahminical learning point of view, Vacchagotta was a *tevijja*, but the Buddha was a real *tevijja* who went beyond suffering and attained nibbāna.

Speculative View "Is a Thicket of Views, a Wilderness of Views"

From the *Aggivacchagotta sutta*, it becomes clear that Vacchagotta learned from the Buddha why he does not take interest in answering speculative questions such as "is the world eternal or not eternal and so on." The Buddha said to him that the speculative view "is a thicket of views, a wilderness of views, a contortion of views, a vacillation of views, a fetter of views. It is beset by sufferings, by vexation, by despair, and by fever, and it does not lead to disenchantment, to dispassion, to cessation, to peace, to direct knowledge, to enlightenment, and to nibbana" [6].

From this *sutta* it becomes very clear how Vacchagotta went deep into the teaching of the Buddha and how greatly he appreciated it. He said to the Buddha that he found his teaching just like the heartwood of a tree completely pure without branches and foliage, without bark and sapwood [7].

From the *Mahāvacchagotta Sutta* it is clear that Vaccha learns from the Buddha what is wholesome and what is unwholesome and how one can become an arahant by destroying taints. After that he went to the refuge of the Buddha, the Dhamma and the Saṅgha. When he sought full admission, the Buddha asked him to live on probation for 4 months as it was a rule made compulsory by the Buddha for persons belonging to another sect. Vacchagotta was so much impressed by his teaching that he lived on probation for 4 months. Half a month after his full admission, he went to the Buddha and requested him to teach him the further Dhamma. The Buddha asked him to develop 'samatha' or 'serenity' and vipassana (insight) so that he would be able to penetrate many elements. In other words, he would be able to attain six *abhiññās* (higher knowledge or supernormal power) [8].

He Became a True *Tevijja*

Vacchagotta developed all six *abhiññās*, destroyed all his taints, and became an arahant. He attained the threefold true knowledge and had great supernormal power and might [9].

As is said in the *Apadāna*, he attained *abhiññāṣ*, became a true *tevijja*, and became a great meditator [10].

References

1. Therag A 1.241
2. S.2.361 (Unless otherwise mentioned all books referred to here are published by Vipassana Research Institute, Dhammagiri in 1998)
3. Ñaṇmoli B, Bodhi B (1995) The Middle Length Discourses of the Buddha. Wisdom Publications, Boston, p 536
4. S.2.360
5. M.2.157
6. Ñaṇmoli B, Bodhi B (1995) The Middle Length Discourses of the Buddha. Wisdom Publications, Boston, pp 591–592; M.2.162
7. M.2.165
8. M.2.171
9. M.2.174
10. Ap. Thera, 1.16 15–20; M.2. 171

Vādavidhi

► Logic (Buddhism)

Vādirājā

► Mañjuśrī

Vādisiṃha

▶ Mañjuśrī

Vāgīśvara

▶ Mañjuśrī

Vaibhāṣika

Charles Willemen
International Buddhist College, Songkhla, Thailand

Definition

Vaibhāṣika is a term used to designate the "orthodox" Kāśmīra Sarvāstivādins, who received this name because they are known for their "*Great Commentary*," *Mahāvibhāṣā*.

Before Kaśmīra completely entered the Buddhist world ca. 200 A.D., the Sarvāstivādins of the Gandharan cultural area had two basic texts, composed in Gāndhārī: The *Abhidharmahṛdaya*, erroneously called *Abhidharmasāra*, of Dharmaśreṣṭhin, erroneously called Dharmaśrī, in Bactria (Taishō ed.1550), and Kātyāyanīputra's *Aṣṭagrantha*, erroneously called *Aṣṭaskandha* in Gandhāra (Taishō ed.1543), both composed probably in the first century B.C [7]. Many commentaries, *vibhāṣās*, were composed on the latter text. Some are preserved in Chinese translation: *Vibhāṣāśāstra* (Taishō ed.1547), attributed to Sitapāṇi or Śītapāṇi (?), translated in 383 A.D. by Saṅghabhadra, sometimes erroneously called Saṅghabhūti, and further *Abhidharmavibhāṣāśāstra* (Taishō ed.1546), translated by Buddhavarman between 437 and 439 A.D. A Sarvāstivāda synod of 500 arhats was held ca. 170 A.D. in Kaśmīra, a new cultural center of the Kuṣāṇas. King Kaniṣka agreed. They revised existing Gandharan texts and sometimes added new parts. They used Sanskrit and established a new "orthodoxy." They are also known as Yuktavādins, proclaiming the right principles. They abbreviated the long *vinaya* from Mathurā to a "modern" version of ten recitations, called *Daśabhāṇavāra* (Taishō ed.1435, translated 404–409 A.D.), sometimes erroneously called *Daśādhyāya*. Many stories (*avadāna, dṛṣṭānta*) were left out, but the rules were not changed [6]. The basic Gandharan *Aṣṭagrantha* was rewritten in Sanskrit and renamed *Jñānaprasthāna* (Taishō ed.1544, translated by Xuanzang 657–669 A.D.). So, a new commentary was required, that is, the *Mahāvibhāṣā* (Taishō ed.1545, translated by Xuanzang's team 656–659 A.D.) [11]. Because of this text, probably completed shortly after 200 A.D., these "orthodox" Sarvāstivādins were also known as Vaibhāṣikas.

History

Sarvāstivādins, claiming (°*vāda)* that everything (*sarvam*) exists (*asti*), split from the main Sthaviravāda trunk during the reign of Aśoka (ca. 264–227 B.C.) in Pāṭaliputra, ca. 244 B.C. This happened during the so-called third council presided over by Maudgalyāyana [8]. They then spread mainly West to Mathurā, and to the Gandharan cultural area, known in Chinese as *Jibin*. From ca. 200 A.D. Kaśmīra was part of *Jibin* too [11]. During the reign of Kaniṣka, ca. 170 A.D., a Sarvāstivāda synod was held in his new cultural center, Kaśmīra. A new "orthodoxy" was established. Its "modern" *vinaya* was much shorter, consisting of ten recitations. A new central text, the *Jñānaprasthāna*, was written, said to be the "body," *śarīra*, of the *abhidharma*. Six more texts were established, forming a new *Abhidharmapiṭaka*, said to be proclaimed by the Buddha himself, *Buddhabhāṣita*. From that time on the traditional Sarvāstivādins, who were very

V

heterogeneous, became known as Sautrāntikas. The six new texts formed a collection (*kāya*) of Sanskrit texts. They were known as six *pādas*, six parts. Because *pāda* is translated as "foot" by Xuanzang, they are also known as "six feet." The new "orthodoxy" was established for more than one reason. It was supposed to bring unity for the very heterogeneous Sarvāstivādins and to oppose the rival Mahāsāṅghikas [10] in the area. Even Mahīśāsakas were doctrinally seen as a (Sautrāntika) Sarvāstivāda subgroup in the early centuries A.D. in the Gandharan cultural area. Western Sarvāstivādins gradually adopted more and more Vaibhāṣika views, as can be seen in the commentaries on the *Abhidharmahṛdaya*, especially the *Miśrakābhidharmahṛdaya*, erroneously called *Saṃyuktābhidharmahṛdaya*, early fourth century (Taishō ed.1552), and in the *Vibhāṣās* on the *Aṣṭagrantha*. The Gandharan Vasubandhu (ca. 350–430 A.D.) composed the *Abhidharmakośabhāṣya*, provoking the anger of Saṅghabhadra in Kaśmīra [5]. Now the "orthodoxy" had to defend itself. After Saṅghabhadra an *Abhidharmadīpa* and its *Vibhāṣāprabhāvṛtti* were composed, sixth century, refuting Vasubandhu's *Bhāṣya* and trying to uphold Vaibhāṣika "orthodoxy" [9]. But between the presence in India of Xuanzang and of Yijing, end seventh century, Vaibhāṣikas disappeared. Differences with other Sarvāstivādins, also called Sautrāntikas, had become minor. Sarvāstivādins were united again, now known as Mūlasarvāstivādins. Before this happened, Xuanzang translated the "orthodox" Sarvāstivāda texts in Chinese, all except the *Prajñaptiśāstra*. So, Vaibhāṣikas were in Kaśmīra between ca. 200 A.D. and the end of the seventh century, but because they are thought to be the "orthodoxy," Sarvāstivādins are often automatically seen as Vaibhāṣikas. Even though Vaibhāṣika *abhidharma* was in China with Xuanzang, *abhidharma* in China remained Sautrāntika. Xuanzang's translation of the *Koś abhāṣya* (Taishō ed.1558, 651–654 A.D.) was far more influential in East Asia. The impact of the Vaibhāṣikas in Central Asia was limited. Kumārajīva's Kuqa, ca. 400 A.D., rather was Sautrāntika. Tibet enters the Buddhist world in Mūlasarvāstivāda times.

Literature

The main text, *śarīra*, body, is the *Jñānaprasthāna* (Taishō ed.1544, translated by Xuanzang). Six more texts, parts of an *Abhidharmapiṭaka*, were established [1, 2, 4, 8]. They basically were rewritten Gandharan texts, namely, *Saṅgītiparyāya* (Taishō ed.1536, translated by Xuanzang, 660–663 A.D.), *Dharmaskandha* (Taishō ed.1537, translated by Xuanzang, 659 A.D.), and *Prajñaptiśāstra* (Taishō ed.1538) in eight parts. Part of the second part of a version of this latter text, known as *Kāraṇa* (reasons) *prajñapti*, was translated in China by Dharmapāla and Weijing, early eleventh century, but this Chinese text is Sautrāntika, not Vaibhāṣika. The Tibetan Mūlasarvāstivāda version (eighth to ninth century) contains three parts. There is no Vaibhāṣika version. The mentioned three texts belong to a first, old group. Later texts are *Dhātukāya* (Taishō ed.1540, translated by Xuanzang, 663 A.D.) and *Vijñānakāya* (Taishō ed.1539, translated by Xuanzang, 649 A.D.). This text is very significant in the development of many key Sarvāstivāda doctrines. It refutes Maudgalyāyana, the Vibhajyavādin, and also the *pudgala* (person) theory. So, it still reacts to the split during Aśoka's council. The text also formulates the causes (*hetu*) and conditions (*pratyaya*), for which Sarvāstivādins are famous. Western Sarvāstivādins, as seen in the *Abhidharmahṛdaya*, already had this elaborate theory about causes and conditions. That is why they are sometimes called Hetuvādins. The sixth text, the *Prakaraṇapāda*, is the most recent and the most significant among the six parts. Its eight parts were translated by Xuanzang in 660 A.D. (Taishō ed.1542). A non-Vaibhāṣika, Gandharan version exists in Chinese translation by Guṇabhadra and Bodhiyaśas (Taishō ed.1541, 435–443 A.D.). The Vaibhāṣika *Mahāvibhāṣā* (Taishō ed.1545), commentary on the *Jñānaprasthāna*, was translated by Xuanzang's team in 656–659 A.D. Saṅghabhadra's refutations of Vasubandhu's *Kośabhāṣya* also belong to Vaibhāṣika literature: *Nyāyānusāra* (Taishō ed.1562, translated by Xuanzang in 654 A.D.) and *Samayapradīpikā* (Taishō ed.1563, translated by Xuanzang in 652 A.D.) [3]. For the

Abhidharmadīpa and the *Vibhāṣāprabhāvṛtti*, probably sixth century, there is only a Sanskrit text.

The Sarvāstivāda synod in Kaśmīra also established a shorter "modern" version of the *vinaya*, that is, the *Daśabhāṇavāra* (Taishō ed.1435).

Cross-References

- Abhidharma (Theravāda)
- Buddhist Councils
- Kaniṣka
- Puḍgala (Puggala)
- Sarvāstivāda
- Sautrāntika
- Vasubandhu
- Vinaya
- Xuanzang (Hieun-Tsang)
- Yijing

References

1. Banerjee AC (1957) Sarvāstivāda literature. K. L. Mukhopadhyay, Calcutta
2. Bareau A (1955) Les sectes bouddhiques du petit véhicule. École Française d'Extrême-Orient, Saigon
3. Cox C (1995) Disputed dharmas: early Buddhist theories on existence. International Institute for Buddhist Studies, Tokyo
4. Cox C (1998) Kaśmīra: Vaibhāṣika orthodoxy. In: Willemen C, Dessein B, Cox C (eds) Sarvāstivāda Buddhist scholasticism. Brill, Leiden
5. Dhammajoti Bhikkhu KL (2009) Sarvāstivāda abhidharma, 4th edn. Centre of Buddhist Studies, The University of Hong Kong, Hong Kong
6. Finot L (1914) Le Prātimokṣa des Sarvāstivādins, Paris
7. Frauwallner E (1955) Studies in abhidharma literature and the origins of Buddhist philosophical systems (trans: Kidd S). SUNY Press, New York
8. Gómez L (2005) Sarvāstivāda. In: Jones L (ed) Encyclopedia of religion, 2nd edn. Macmillan Reference USA, Gale Virtual Reference Library, Detroit
9. Jaini P (1977) Abhidharmadīpa with Vibhāṣāprabhāvṛtti. Kashi Jayaswal Research Institute, Patna
10. Lamotte É I (1966), II (1967), III (1970), IV (1976), V (1980) Le traité de la grande vertu de sagesse de Nāgārjuna. Mahāprajñāpāramitopadeśa. Université Catholique de Louvain, Institut Orientaliste, Louvain-La-Neuve
11. Willemen C (2008) Kumārajīva's explanatory discourse about abhidharmic literature. J Int Coll Postgrad Buddh Stud 12:27–83

Vairocana

Anand Singh
School of Buddhist Studies and Civilization, Gautam Buddha University, Greater Noida, UP, India
Institute of Management Sciences, University of Lucknow, Lucknow, UP, India

Synonyms

Birojanabul; *Birushanabutsu*; *Daeil Yeorae*; *Dainichi Nyorai*; *Dārī Rūlāi*; Dhyanī Buddha; Mahāvairocana; *Pīlūzhénāfo*; Vairochana

Definition

Vairocana is one of the Dhyānī Buddhas interpreted as *dhammakāyā* of the Buddha. In Sino-Japanese Buddhism, Vairocana is represented as the embodiment of *Śunyata*. In Vajrayāna tradition, he is the first among the five Dhyānī Buddhas, and his consort is white Tārā. The doctrine of Vairocana is based on the teachings of *Mahāvairocana Abhisambodhi Tantra* and *Sarvatathāgatatattvasamgraha Tantra*. The worshipping of Vairocana is prevalent in Tibet, Nepal, China, Japan, Korea, and Mongolia and the Indian subcontinent [4]. In China, Vairocana is known as *Dārī Rūlāi* and *Pīlūzhénāfo*, and in Japan, it is represented as *Dainichi Nyorai* and *Birushanabutsu* [8].

Introduction

Vairocana is represented with other Dhyānī Buddhas in *Guhyasamāja*. He is white in color, and his mount is a dragon [1]. He is regarded as the oldest and the first Dhyānī Buddha. He is placed in the sanctum of the stūpa to be the master of the whole structure. In Nepal, he has been occasionally placed between Akṣobhya in the east and Ratnasambhava in the south [4].

Characteristics of Names

Vairocana originates from the white syllable "Om" placed on the eastern petal of the lotus and is white in color which is recognized with a white discus. He exhibits the *Bodhyāngī mūdrā* and is without any bad companions. He belongs to *Tathāgata* family, so known as *tathāgatkulika* and has been depicted as an embodiment of ideal knowledge. He represents the spring season, the sweet taste, and the morning and evening of the day [9]. His two hands are held against the chest with the tips of the thumb and forefinger of each hand united, and he is mounted on a pair of dragons or gryphon and is recognized with a *cakka* or the discus with two or more arms. When Vairocana is four faced and eight armed, he is called Vajradhātu, and in this form, he is seated in *Vajraparyanka mūdrā* and is white in color. His four faces reflect white, yellow, red, and green colors. His eight arms with two principal hands holding the *vajra* exhibit the *Bodhiyāngī* or *Dhammcakka mūdrā* and the second pair of hands holding the rosary and the arrow, and with two remaining left, he carries the discus and the bow [2]. He is widely represented in Tibet and China.

Depiction in Buddhist Literature

The pantheon of the northern Buddhist revolves around the theory of five Dhyānī Buddhas. Buddhism accepts that the world is composed of five cosmic elements or *Skandhas*. The five *Skandhas* are *Rūpa* (form), *Vedana* (sensation), *Samjna* (name), *Samskāra* (conformation), and *Vijnana* (consciousness). These elements are eternal cosmic forces and are without a beginning or an end, and these cosmic forces are worshipped in Vajrayāna as the five Dhyānī Buddhas [4]. In Vajrayāna, Ādibuddha is regarded as the highest deity of the Buddhist pantheon and the originator of the five Dhyānī Buddhas. The *Sadhanāmālā* says that the Dhyānī Buddhas are Vairocana, Ratnasambhava, Amitābha, Amoghsiddhi, and Akṣobhya. Their colors are white, yellow, red, green, and blue, and they represent the *Bodhyāngī* (teaching), *Varada* (boon), *Dhyāna* (meditation), *Abhaya* (protection), and *Bhumisparśa* (earth touching) *mūdrās* of hand, respectively [3].

In *Guhyasamāja*, Vairocana is given a *mantra*, a color, a direction, and a guardian of the gate who is not required to pass through the stage of Bodhisattva. He is always engaged in peaceful meditation and is represented as seated on a full-blown lotus in a meditative pose with leg crossed, the right foot crossing over the left, with the soles of both feet turned upward [1]. Vairocana is deity of the inner shrine and therefore is generally unrepresented. He is occasionally assigned a place between Ratnasambhava in the south and Akṣobhya in the east.

Emanations of Vairocana

The *Sadhanāmālā* says that all the deities that emanate from Vairocana have a white color. Some of the goddesses have the images of Vairocana on their crown, and several of them are expressed as *Vairocanakulodbhava* which means born in the family of Vairocana. The deities emanating from Vairocana reside in the sanctum of the stūpa as he is the lord of interior of the stūpa. The important emanations of Vairocana are as follows:

1. Nāmasangati
   He is one faced, white in color, represented in a meditative posture with a smiling face, and is decked with six precious ornaments and has 12 arms. He exhibited in the first pair of right and left hands the two *Abhaya mūdrās* against the chest and in the second pair, the *Anjali mūdrā* over the crown. The third right hand carries the

sword on the double *Vajra*, the fourth pair shows the *Tarpana mūdrā*, and the fifth pair is depicting the *mūdrā* of sprinkling nectar from the vessel. The sixth pair shows the *Samadhi mūdrā* with the vessel of nectar and the third left hand carries the *Khatvanga* with *Vajra* and he sits in the meditative pose on the lotus [1].

2. Mārici
   Mārici is invoked by the Lāmās of Tibet about the time of sunrise, and her chariot is drawn by seven pigs. Mārici appears singularly, and her consort is Vairocana himself. The *Sadhanāmālā* mentions six distinct forms of Mārici in which she may have one, three, five, or six faces and 2, 8, 10, or 12 arms. She is generally accompanied by her four attendants, Varttalī, Vadalī, Varalī, and Varāhamukhī. She is recognized by the sow face and the seven pigs that run her chariot. The needle and the string are characteristic symbols, to sew up the mouths and the eyes of the wicked [4]. Aśokakānta, Arya-Mārici, Māricipipicuva, Ubhayavarahanana, Dasbhujasta-Mārici, and Vajradhatvisvari-Mārici are important forms of Mārici [6].
3. Uṣnisavijaya
   Mārici Uṣnisavijaya also bears the image of Vairocana on his crown and resides within the womb of the *cetiya* who is one of the most popular deities of the pantheon and is very popular in Nepal [4]. She is white in complexion, three faced, three eyed, youthful, and decked with many ornaments. Her right and left faces are respectively of yellow and blue colors. Her four right hands display the Visvavajra, Buddha on lotus, the arrow, and the Varada pose, and her four left hands show the bow, the noose with *Tarjanī*, the *Abhaya* pose, and the well-filled water vessel [3].
4. Sitatapatra Aparajita
   She is also member of family of Vairocana who is three faced, six armed, and has three eyes in each of her faces. She is white in color, and her right and left faces are blue and red colored, respectively. She has angry looks and capable of destroying all sorts of evil spirits [7]. She is popular in Tibet and China [5].
5. Mahāsahasrapramardanī
   She is associated with Vairocana and is white in complexion. She is one faced and six armed. She carries in her three right hands the sword, the arrow, and the *Varada mūdrā*, and in three left hands, the bow, the noose, and the *Paraśu* are adopted. She is young and beautiful and bears the figure of Vairocana on her crown. She sits on the moon over lotus and is radiant like the moon [3].
6. Vajravārahī
   Vajravārahi is also known as Dākinī and associated with Vairocana. She is known as Vajravārahi because she has an excrescence near her right ear which resembles the face of a sow and has two forms known as Vajravairocani and Buddha Dākinī. She has either two arms or four arms. She is popular in Nepal, Tibet, and China [5].
7. Cunda
   Cunda is spiritual daughter of Vairocana. She is also known as Cundavajri. She has four arms, one face, and is of white complexion. She shows the *Varada mūdrā* with the right hand and holds the book on a lotus in the left. The two other hands hold the bowl. She is decked with beautiful ornaments [2].
8. Grahamatraka
   She is a family member of Vairocana and has three faces of white, yellow, and red colors. She displays *Dhammacakka mūdrā* carrying the *Vajra* and the arrow in her two right hands and in the two left, the lotus and the bow. She sits in the *Vajrasana* on a lotus of a thousand petals [3].

Vairocana and other four Dhyānī Buddhas are the cornerstone of Buddhist iconography on which the whole edifice of the Buddhist pantheon is erected. The five Dhyānī Buddhas are the progenitors of the five *kulas*. The community which worships them is identified as *Kaulas*, and the process of worship is called *Kaulkāra*.

Cross-References

▶ Buddha (Concept)
▶ Gandhara
▶ Vajrayāna (Buddhism)

References

1. Bhattacharya B (ed) (1931) Guhyasamāja Tantra. Gaikwad Oriental Series, Baroda
2. Bhattacharya B (ed) (1949) Niśpannayogavalī of Abhayakara Gupta. GOS, No. 109. Gaikwad Oriental Series, Baroda
3. Bhattacharya B (ed) (1925–1928) Sādhanamālā, 2 vols. GOS, No.26 &241. Oriental Institute, Baroda
4. Bhattacharya B (1968) The Indian Buddhist iconography. K.L. Mukhoupadhyaya Publication, Calcutta
5. Clark, WE (1937) Two Lamaistc pantheons, 2 vols. Harvard Yenching Institute, Cambridge, MA
6. Getty A (1914, 1978 reprint, Delhi) The Gods of Northern Buddhism. Oxford Clarendon Press, Oxford
7. Gordon AK (1939) The iconography of Tibetan Lamaism. Columbia University Press, New York
8. http://en.wikipedia.org/wiki/Vairocana
9. Sastri H (ed) (1927) Advayavajrasangraha. GOS, No. XL. Gaikwad Oriental Series, Baroda

Vairochana

▶ Vairocana

Vaiśālī

▶ Vesālī

Vaishali

▶ Vesālī

Vaivarṇika

▶ Caṇḍāla (Buddhism)

Vajra

Kai Ana Makanoe Kaikaulaokaweilaha Kaululaau
Department of Philosophy, University of Bristol, Bristol, UK
Department of Philosophy, California State University, Los Angeles, CA, USA

Synonyms

Chin-kang; Dorje, Jingang; Kongou; Thunderbolt

Definition

Vajra is a word of Sanskrit origin that means "diamond-like" or "thunderbolt." Vajra embodies the "indestructible nature" of the diamond that cannot be manipulated or broken. Yet, it is able to pierce or "cut through" any illusion, obstruction, affliction, or attachment ([1], p. 1; [4], p. 1; [5], p. 1; [6], p. 1; [7], p. 1).

The Vajra is an abrupt change in human consciousness, or the "thunderbolt of enlightenment," that acts as a pivotal experience in the lives of "great beings." In Tibetan Buddhism, Vajra is a transformative enlightenment for those who experience the "releasing of self," or "Great Death." In Vajrayana Buddhism, the Vajra is a symbol of the indestructible state of enlightenment or Buddhahood. Conjunctively, the term Vajrayana itself is translated as "Thunderbolt Way" or "Diamond Way" to describe the "thunderbolt experience" of Buddhist enlightenment. When worn as a pendant, the Vajra also symbolizes the supreme indestructibility of knowledge and the true "nature of reality" ([1], p. 1; [2], p. 1; [5], p. 1; [6], p. 1; [7], p. 1).

Vajra Legend

In ancient India, the Vajra became a primary armament to the Vedic sky god Indra; it was a weapon that controlled the forces of thunder and lightning as well as monsoon storm clouds ([1], p. 1). According to legend, Indra's thunderbolt weapon was created from the bones of Rishi Dadhichi, who was decapitated by Indra in sacrifice; consequently, Dadhichi's "indestructible" skull gave Indra the power to eliminate many of his enemy demons. In its mythological descriptions, Indra's Vajra is shaped either in the likeness of a discus with a hole at its center or in the form of a cross with circuitous bladed bars. According to a Buddhist legend, Shakyamuni took the Vajra weapon from Indra and forced its wrathful open points together, thus forming a peaceful scepter with closed prongs ([1], p. 1).

The Vajra as a Scepter

The Vajra is also a ritual scepter symbolically used in Buddhism, Jainism, and Hinduism that consists of (1) a center sphere and (2) three, five, or nine spokes that unfold at either end of the wand – depending on the sadhana ([1], p. 1; [7], p. 1; [7], p. 1).

The most commonly used Vajra is the five-pronged scepter. The center of the scepter is a spherical midway section between two symmetrical sets of five prongs. The two symmetrical sets of five prongs camber out from two eight-petaled lotus blooms, then come to an equal point from the center, thus giving the appearance of a "diamond scepter." The center spherical section represents Sunyata – the primordial nature of the universe or the underlying unity of all things. Emerging from the center sphere are two eight-petaled lotus flowers: One lotus flower represents the phenomenal world or Samsara; the other lotus flower represents the nominal world or Nirvana ([1], p. 1; [7], p. 1; [7], p. 1).

The five prongs are a correspondent between both the five poisons and the five wisdoms. The five poisons are described as (1) desire, (2) anger or hatred, (3) delusion, (4) greed or pride, and (5) envy. The five wisdoms are described as (1) discriminating wisdom, (2) mirror-like wisdom, (3) reality wisdom, (4) wisdom of calmness, and (5) all-accomplishing wisdom. In Tibetan Buddhism, the Vajra scepter (Dorje) embodies the brilliance of refracted illumination – a point of power called the axis mundi or hub of the world ([6], p. 1; [7], p. 1).

The Vajra as a Cross

The Vajra Cross (also called double Dorje) is an instrument that represents both the "intransience of the physical world" and "the universe as we experience its reality"; it is also the emblem of Buddhist deities whose influence encourages immoveable determination. In Tibetan Buddhism, the Vajra Cross represents the stability or foundation of the physical world. Additionally, the mark is often used as a seal or stamp that may be found impressed or incised on the plate base of a statue in order to protect and keep prayers or relics inside ([1], p. 1).

The Vajra as a Crown

The Vajra Crown or "Black Crown" is a crown in the Kagyu school of Tibetan Buddhism that signifies the capacity to help all sentient beings attain liberation through "true seeing." In representation, the top adornment of the Vajra Crown symbolizes "the pinnacle of wisdom" or Buddha wisdom. Its cloud ornaments on the left and right side of the crown have a twofold representation which is (1) the immeasurable and unbiased rain of wisdom and compassion and (2) the activities of tenth level Buddhas that benefit all sentient beings. Additionally, the four prongs of the crown represent the four enlightened activities – (1) pacifying, (2) enriching, (3) emanating, and (4) destroying; the four-cornered base of the crown represents the four immeasurables – (1) loving-kindness, (2) compassion, (3) joy, and (4) equanimity toward all sentient beings ([2], p. 1).

The Vajra and Buddhist Iconography

Akshobhya is the Vajra family Buddha associated with "consciousness," "space," or "ether." Akshobhya is the Vajradhara or "thunderbolt bearer" who is pictorially depicted with one face and two arms; he sits solidly fixed in a vajraparyanka pose with his left hand resting on his lap face up; his right forearm extends over the right knee while the tip of his middle finger touches the earth in the bhusparsha (earth-touching) pose ([1], p. 1; [8], p. 1).

Amoghasiddhi ("unfailing accomplishment") is the Karma family Buddha associated with the

Vajra Cross. Essentially, his endeavor is to subtly diminish klesha (the stain, or imperfection of jealousy) as well as its attachment. Pictorially, his left hand rests in his lap in the mudra (posture) of equanimity and his right at chest level palm outward that grants both guard and protection ([1], p. 1; [8], p. 1).

The Vajra is also symbolically portrayed with other Buddhist deities such as:

1. The Padmasambhava ("the lotus born") who holds the Vajra scepter in his right hand above his right knee ([1], p. 1; [8], p. 1)
2. The Vajrasattva ("Vajra-being" or "white bodhisattva of purification") who holds the Vajra scepter in his right hand, raised to his heart ([1], p. 1; [8], p. 1)
3. The Vajrapani ("Vajra in the hand" or "wielder of the Dorje") who raises and balances the Vajra scepter in his right hand, above his head. ([1], p. 1; [8], p. 1)
4. Vajrayogini ("the sky dancer") who holds a flaying knife with a vajra handle known as a "Vajra chopper" (used to cut off attachments) in her right hand ([4], p. 1)

The Three Vajras

In Tibetan Buddhism, the three Vajras (also known as the three jewels or three roots) are a representation that describe "body," "speech," and "mind" devoid of all "marks, senses, conditions, or qualities" ([8], p. 1; [9], p. 1).

The three Vajras are described as (1) the enlightened body – or the subtle intermediaries that illuminate Vajra extension which is the "truth body" or "reality body"; (2) the enlightened speech – words that expound "Vajra speech," in order to bring out the "Buddha nature" in all beings; and (3) the enlightened mind – also known as the "Buddha mind" which is attained by not just one, but countless Buddhas from the Buddhas of past, present, and future ([8], p. 1).

Respectively, the three jewels or three roots are described as (1) the Buddha (the realized one); (2) the Dharma (teachings); and (3) the Sangha (community); the three roots are described as (1) Lama which is the "root of blessing" or "root of grace"; (2) Yidham which is the "root of methods" or "root of accomplishment"; and (3) Khandroma or Chokyong which is the "root of protection" or "root of activity" ([9], p. 1).

Cross-References

▶ The Diamond Sutra
▶ The Tathagata
▶ Vajrachhedika
▶ Vajrayāna (Buddhism)

References

1. http://www.khandro.net/ritual_vajra.htm
2. http://buddhism.about.com/od/buddhismglossaryv/g/vajradef.htm
3. http://www.kagyuoffice.org/kagyulineage.blackcrown.html
4. http://www.britannica.com/EBchecked/topic/621707/vajra
5. http://www.visiblemantra.org/vajrayogini.html
6. http://buddhism.about.com/od/buddhismglossaryv/g/vajradef.htm
7. http://www.exoticindiaart.com/article/ritual/
8. http://www.en.wikipedia.org/wiki/Vajra
9. http://en.wikipedia.org/wiki/Three_Vajras
10. http://en.wikipedia.org/wiki/Three_Roots

Vajrachhedika

Kai Ana Makanoe Kaikaulaokaweilaha Kaululaau
Department of Philosophy, University of Bristol, Bristol, UK
Department of Philosophy, California State University, Los Angeles, CA, USA

Synonyms

The diamond cutter; *The diamond sutra*; *The jewel of transcendental wisdom*; *The Tathagata*; *The Vajrachchedika Prajñāpāramitā Sutra* ([1], 1)

Definition

The Vajrachchedika is a sutra that has no form as its source and no abiding as its substance; the Vajrachchedika is a sutra that examines the both the nature, and no-nature of wisdom with "subtle being" as its function ([2], 85).

Origin of the Text

The Vajrachchedika is a 300 line script within the Maha-Prajnaparamita or "Perfection of Transcendental Wisdom" that is a Sanskrit text composed in India between 100 B.C and 600 C.E. Although the date of initial composition is unknown, the Vajrachchedika was translated from Sanskrit to Chinese by Kumarajiva in 401 C.E. The Vajrachchedika was also translated from Sanskrit to Chinese by Bodhiruci in 509 C.E, Paramartha in 558 C.E, Xuanzang in 648 C.E, Yijing in 703 C.E., and Wang Chieh in 868 C.E ([3], 13; [4], 1; [1], 1; [5], 15)

The Wang Chieh translation was discovered in the early 1900s by Wang Yunalu in the Mogao Caves, also known as the "Caves of a Thousand Buddhas" near Dunhuang in North-West China. Initially, Yunalu offered the text to local Chinese officials in an attempt to gain funding for its conservation – however, the script was sold in 1907 to British archeologist Sir Marc Aurel Stein ([6], 1; [5], 1; [7], 1). The Wang Chieh translation consists as seven strips of yellow-stained paper imprinted from carved wooden blocks; the seven imprinted strips were pasted together to form a scroll which measures approximately 16 ft in length. The printed scroll was 1 of 40,000 other books, commentaries, apocryphal works, paintings, and Buddhist statues that were collected and hidden in the cave. The secret library is believed to have been sealed up around 1000 C.E, a time when province was under threat by the Hsi-Hsia kingdom to the north ([8], 8; [9], 3; [3], 14; [10], 1; [11], 1; [12], 1).

The Buddha and Subhuti

In the beginning of the Sutra, the Buddha completes his walk and gathering of alms in the city of Sravasti (also known as "The City of Wonders") in the Jeta Grove – within the garden of Anathapindika. After washing both his feet and hands, he begins to concentrate his attention on "the breath which is in front of him," then enters into a trance ([13], 1; [8], 1; [9], 1). In pictorial depiction of the script, the Buddha is seated cross-legged on a lotus throne with a swastika displayed to indicate that he is not a historical Buddha – but rather, a glorified body that expounds more spiritually profound, and esoteric truths to those ready to receive them ([8], 1; [9], 1).

Subhuti, who is one of the Ten Great Śrāvakas of Śākyamuni Buddha and foremost in the understanding of emptiness, ([14], 1) approaches the Buddha in a position of prostration – a position showing reverence to the Buddha, the Dharma, and the Sangha ([15], 1). After this, a dialogue concerning the "path of bodhisattva" such as: how the Bodhisattva should stand – meaning, how to abide; how the Bodhisattva should progress – meaning, how to nurture a steady growth in "the awakened mind"; how a Bodhisattva should "control thought" – meaning, how to deflect confusion or distraction from the inward mind ([2], 90; [9], 3).

The Buddha explains to Subhuti that the "path of the Bodhisattva" begins by the "vow of commitment" or "producing thought," toward enlightenment. The Buddha explicates that the "vow of commitment" or "producing thought" is vast because it refers to all beings; it is the calm and wise acceptance that "no being exists"; it is a path unmarred by false views of self and being. Thus, the "vow of commitment" or "producing thought" is the gentle and subtly rising ability to teach and liberate with kindness, compassion, joyfulness, and equanimity ([2], 90).

Regardless of however many species of living beings (whether they are born from eggs; from the womb, moisture, or spontaneously; whether they have form or do not have form; whether they have perceptions or do not have perceptions.) – The "vow of the bodhisattva" is to lead all beings toward "enlightenment." Yet, when immeasurable and infinite numbers of beings are liberated – there is no preponderance that any single being has been liberated ([2], 92).

Gift and Merit

The Buddha continues to explain that when a Bodhisattva acts in accordance to the source, they do not dwell in appearances. Accordingly, when a Bodhisattva practices charity – charity is not practiced by dwelling on "forms" or "non-forms"; charity is not supported by "material" or "sight-objects," nor is it led by the senses such as sounds, smells, tastes, touchables, or mind-objects ([2], 95). As such, a Bodhi-Being gives "gift" or "merit" in such a way that they are not supported by the notion of a sign; they are not influenced by the construction of representation. A Bodhi-Being is committed to giving "gift" or "merit" not for themselves but for the benefit of others ([2], 96; [9], 4).

In turn, when the Bodhi-Being is able to release such attachments to appearances, he has understood "the Perfection of Giving" such as: (1) Dana – the practice of cultivating unattached and unconditional generosity; it is the cultivation of "giving and letting go," thus purifying and transforming the mind of the giver. (2) Isla – the action of intentional effort and "good conduct"; it is the purity of thought, word, and deed, thus cultivating moral discipline or precept. (3) Kshanti – patience, forbearance, and forgiveness; Kshanti is the practice of mindfully and actively giving patience as a gift, rather than giving patience out of fixed necessity, shrewdness, or obligation. (4) Virya – refers to "strength of being," or "perseverance"; Virya signifies strength of character and persistent effort for the well-being of others. (5) Dhyana – refers to meditation or meditative states; Dhyana is described as profound stillness and concentration through mindfulness of being. (6) Prajna – refers to wisdom, understanding, or discernment; Prajna is the wisdom that extinguishes afflictions in order to bring about enlightenment ([16], 1).

The Roots of Goodness

Upon understanding that all appearances are illusionary, the Bodhi-Being is able to firmly plant the "roots of goodness" for countless Buddhas throughout the eons – such is true faith; ([2], 99; [5], 100) in turn, the Bodhi-Being who holds true faith continuously engrains and fosters "the roots of goodness." The Buddha explains to Subhuti that those who plant and foster the roots of goodness do so by committing themselves to the Buddhas and their teachings; they are respectful and mindful to all beings; they develop an attitude of mercy and compassion to those who suffer ([2], 99).

Those firmly planted in the root of goodness are gentle and tolerant toward all beings; they do not kill, harm, or cheat; they do not despise or disgrace beings nor do they partake in eating their flesh; they hold with true faith that "buddha-nature" is inherit in all beings ([2], 99). Through the root of goodness, bodhisattvas internalize and understand that both dharma and "no-dharma" are provisional. They have realized the emptiness of all beings, the emptiness of all dharmas as well as Emptiness itself.

To elucidate, the Buddha explains to Subhuti that Dharmas are like that of a raft: When the raft (cultivation) is used to traverse and end the sea of suffering (such as birth and death or the birth and death of a cycle) – it must be set aside and abandoned; further use of the "raft" would only serve to recreate illness, affliction, or attachment ([5], 101). Thus, the Tathagata cannot fully be known: Its "true nature" is "no-nature," and its "no-nature" is its "true nature"; its awareness and view do not abide nor do they fixedly remain. As such, the Tathagata's truth is non-dwelling, formless, and without origin; it has no destruction, pinpointed mark, or condition; yet, its unformulated wellspring is the foundation of the infinite systems for all the sages ([9], 90).

States of Realization

The Buddha explains to Subhuti that although states of realization exist, their forms are originally non-dual; such states are described as: (1) Stream-Entering – Stream-enterers go against the stream of birth and death; through understanding "formless truth" – they are unaffected by objects of the senses (nor do they desire the attainment of stream-entering itself). (2) Once-Returning – Once-returners have cast off the bonds of the world; they are once-returners because their ties to the world are over; for once their "eyes" have beheld the "true reality" of objects and/or substances (which are formless), there is no second arousal of returning or dormancy. (3) Non-Returning – a non-returner is one who abandons all conditions or marks of desire(s), contamination (s), and affliction(s) forever; it is pure conduct or the "emergence of pure mind" ([2], 105).

Pure Land

Once the emergence of pure mind manifests, the presence and transformation of "Pure Land" begins. The Buddha explains to Subhuti that Pure Land is a place where Bodhisattvas understand dharma and no-dharma regardless of whether it is one stanza of four lines or the entire sutra itself; Pure Land is a shrine – a place where one understands, spreads, and demonstrates the perfection of wisdom; it is a shelter for kings; a shelter of rest and final relief ([2], 107).

Although the adornments of Pure Land are essentially non-adornment, the Buddha explains to Subhuti that Pure Land is bejeweled by means of building sanctuaries, copying sutras, practicing charity, and giving alms; its beautification "by sight" is to act with respect toward all beings in view. The enhancement of Pure Land "by means of learning" is to apply Buddha-cognition and Buddha-mind in every moment ([2], 109). Therefore, any area of land on which true teaching is proclaimed can be a Pure Land – a land where gods, men, and asuras travel to make offerings; such a land is sacred, rare, and profound ([2], 108).

True Teaching

"The Diamond that Cuts Through Illusion" has the capacity to cut through all delusions, deceptions, and afflictions. As such, those who understand, internalize, and carry out the Tathagata acquire wisdom beyond; it is a perfection of wisdom that is not taught by one or two primary Buddhas – but countless Buddhas; it is taught as the highest perfection because it is the most innumerable ([2], 111). The Buddha explains to Subhuti that while the Tathagata is identified as the "highest transcendence of understanding," it is in fact it is not the highest transcendence of understanding – yet simultaneously, this is why the Tathagata is truly the highest transcendent understanding ([2], 111).

Yet, if one beholds the sutra for a single moment – both self and person immediately dissipate. The impure deeds they have carried out in their past or former lives are removed; their karma becomes exhausted; they no longer have images of self, person, being, or liver of life. They begin to internalize the dharma with Buddha-cognition; they begin to perceive the dharma with Buddha-Eye (or "Eye of Teaching"). As such, their illumination is a realization of enlightenment – a wisdom that is beyond, yet within their spectrum. Therefore, just as the dharma has given a doctrine that is essentially unknown or "unthinkable", so the bodhisattva's karma or karmic fate is essentially unknown or "unthinkable" ([2], 113; [5], 145; [17], 16).

Accepting and Holding True Teaching

Accepting and holding true teaching is boundless and immeasurable because it is a great vehicle of vast knowledge and wisdom; it does not establish "defiled things" as "things to reject" nor does it determine "pure things" as "things to seek." The Buddha explains to Subhuti that accepting and holding true teaching does not induce the Bodhi-Being to view "all living beings" as "beings to liberate" because the realm of nirvana leaves nothing behind ([2], 120).

Hence, if the Bodhisattva acquires the impression that "all living beings" are "beings to be liberated" – he possesses an image of "self"; if the Bodhisattva becomes imprinted with the sense that "they can liberate all living beings" – he carries an image of "person"; if the Bodhisattva contends that "nirvana can be sought" – there is an image of a "being"; if the Bodhisattva asserts the notion that "existence of nirvana can be realized" – he holds the image of a "liver of life"; therefore, those who have these four images (self, person, being, and liver of life) are not Bodhisattvas ([2], 126; [5], 198; [17], 25).

The Five Eyes

The Buddha explains to Subhuti that regardless of the many beings throughout various lands – the Tathagata understands them all. Similarly, in the view of "Oneness" just as one world contains many worlds – so one eye contains "five eyes"

([2], 130; [17], 26). The Buddha explains that by continuing to cultivate, nourish, and sustain "good roots," the five eyes begin to manifest themselves. The five eyes are: (1) The flesh-eye is the physical-eye that can see tangible objects as well as objects devoid of form or marks such as ghosts and spirits. While the range of the flesh-eye is much greater than the "ordinary eye," the flesh-eye can also examine things in the minutest detail, taking note of any distinguishing marks such as moles or birthmarks. (2) The heavenly-eye is the divine eye that can see clear into heaven but does not perceive material objects; through the heavenly-eye one is able to distinctly perceive all celestial and heavenly bodies. (3) The wisdom-eye is the eye that perceives the illusionary nature of all reality, thus seeing the emptiness of all dharmas; it is the eye that enables one to know clearly and instantaneously if something is right or wrong, true or false without any confusion (to explicate, only a fool would mistake falsity for truth, or truth as falsity.). (4) The Dharma-eye is the eye that differentiates the infinite dharmas; it is the eye that is able to see Buddha-dharma throughout all empty space and dharma realms. Consequently, the Dharma-eye also sees the suffering experienced by beings through illusion, cause and effect, as well as the penetration of past lives. (5) The Buddha-eye is the eye of omniscience; it is the eye that enables one to understand the true meaning of all Buddha-dharma; although the Buddha-eye can see all things (form and no-form) – it is essentially indescribable and incomprehensible in "ordinary terms"; it is the eye that can only be experienced ([5], 206–210).

Form and No-Form

The Buddha conveys to Subhuti that as the five eyes perceive the form and no-form of all dharma-bodies – all beings and teachings are therefore essentially empty. As such, the Tathagata cannot be perceived as "perfect form" or "perfect body," nor can it be perceived by any phenomenal characteristic; ([17], 28) Correspondingly, the reality of enlightenment is essentially formless and without high or low emotions or passions; it is a state of reality without obsession or fixation, a reality that is not ambitious or greedy for enlightenment ([2], 135). Parenthetically, the Buddha explains that whether it is through four lines in one stanza – if one can put the stanza into practice, they can attain Buddhahood ([2], 136). But importantly, the Buddha instructs Subhuti not to say that one can attain enlightenment "without cultivating the thirty-two practices" – to say this and do so would be to annihilate the lineage of countless Buddhas ([2], 138). As such, when one hears the sutra and realizes its way, then awakened insight constantly shines toward enlightenment throughout in both thought and action – this is true teaching and application ([2], 141).

The Great Mind

The Buddha explains to Subhuti that the Great Mind is patient and naturally free from greed; it "comes from nowhere and goes nowhere"; the Great Mind gives rise to virtue but is not caught in the idea of virtue and happiness ([2], 139). As such, the great mind understands and internalizes that all beings embody Buddha-nature; they understand and internalize that all beings have an intrinsic nature without afflictions; they understand, internalize, and cultivate formless truth – without sense of subject and object ([2], 143). Consequently, once other minds are inspired, emanations begin to foster and influence others in joy, wisdom, and compassion – thus, such acts are immeasurable blessings. Therefore, the great mind explains truth skillfully and expediently; they take others into account; they adapt to other beings within their capacities; they perfect a silent mind in accordance to thusness without any sense of gaining or losing, hope or expectation, excitement or oblivion – such is the reality, apart from forms, labels, and appearances ([2], 143–144; [5], 40; [17], 252).

Cross-References

- ▶ The Diamond Sutra
- ▶ Vajra
- ▶ Vajrayāna (Buddhism)

References

1. http://www.en.wikipedia.org/wiki/Diamond_Sutra
2. Cleary T (1998) The sutra of Hui-Neng – Grand Master of Zen. Shambhala Publications, Boston/London
3. Price AF (trans) (1947) The jewel of transcendental wisdom (Chin Kang Ching). Buddhist Society Publications, London
4. http://www.sinc.sunysb.edu/clubs/buddhism/sutras/diamond1.html
5. http://www.buddhanet.net/pdf_file/prajparagen2.pdf
6. http://www.en.wikipedia.org/wiki/Wang_Yuanlu
7. http://www.silk-road.com/artl/diamondsutra.shtml
8. Evans-Wentz WY, Humphreys C, Price AF (1974) (trans) The diamond sutra and the sutra of Hui-Neng. Shambhala Publications, Boston/London
9. Mou-Lam W, Price AF (trans) (1969) The diamond sutra and the sutra of Hui Neng. Clear Light series. Shambhala Publications, Boston
10. http://www.en.wikipedia.org/wiki/Mogao_Caves
11. http://www.idp.bl.uk/
12. http://www.bl.uk/onlinegallery/sacredtexts/diamondsutra.html
13. Conze E (trans) (1958) The diamond sutra. Ruskin House/George Allen & Unwin, London
14. http://www.en.wikipedia.org/wiki/Subhuti
15. http://www.en.wikipedia.org/wiki/Prostration_(Buddhism)
16. http://www.en.wikipedia.org/wiki/P%C4%81ramit%C4%81
17. http://www.hermetics.org/pdf/The_Diamond_Sutra.pdf

Vajrapani

Jens-Uwe Hartmann
Institut für Indologie und Tibetologie,
University of Munich, Munich, Germany

Synonyms

Guhyakādhipati

Definition

A nonhuman attendant of the Buddha, first a Yakṣa, later a Bodhisattva.

Vajrapani is a very remarkable figure whose origin and early relation with the Buddha are a matter of ongoing debate. The name means "Holding a/the Vajra in his Hand," and this connects him with Indra, one of the most powerful of ancient Vedic Gods. Indra is characterized by a specific weapon called a vajra, but the information preserved in the Vedic hymns on the form and use of this vajra remains vague. The vajra is commonly understood and translated as "thunderbolt" which fits Indra as a God connected also with rain, but does not agree with the Vedic descriptions of the use of the weapon. While the myth survived, knowledge of the concrete shape of the weapon was apparently lost and probably had to be reinvented when Vajrapāṇi emerged as a Buddhist figure and was pictorially represented in art.

The canonical texts of early Buddhism do not expressly link Vajrapāṇi with Indra, but at least the famous Pali commentator Buddhaghosa (fifth century) does so. He equates Vajrapāṇi (Vajirapāni in Pali) with Śakra (Pali Sakka), another name of Indra, who survives in Buddhist mythology under this name as the King of the Gods and the inhabitant of a specific heaven; he appears in many episodes in the life of the Buddha and often renders him some sort of help. In the canon, Vajrapāṇi is classified as a yakṣa; generally this is a term for a class of powerful and potentially dangerous nonhuman and pan-Indian beings often connected with trees. However, in Buddhism the term is sometimes also used as a name for the gods, among them Indra, and this facilitates the equation of Vajrapāṇi with Indra.

There are very few occasions in the canonical scriptures of early Buddhism where Vajrapāṇi appears. In the Sūtrapiṭaka, there are only two passages and both are identical, as follows. The Buddha is conversing with an opponent in front of a large audience. The Buddha asks him a question, and the opponent would be able to answer it, but refuses to do so, because in front of the audience the answer would be embarrassing for him and would refute his previous arguments. So he prefers to remain silent, but the Buddha urges him to answer and warns him that a refusal would be dangerous. Then the text goes on (example taken from the Pali Ambaṭṭhasutta): "And at that moment Vajirapāni the yakkha, holding a huge iron club, flaming, ablaze and glowing, up in the sky just above Ambaṭṭha, was thinking: 'If this young man Ambaṭṭha does not answer a proper question put to him by the Blessed Lord by the third time of asking, I'll split his head into seven pieces!' The Lord saw Vajirapāni, and so did Ambaṭṭha" [5]. At this frightening sight, the opponent is prudent enough to answer the question. That is all the text has to say about Vajrapāṇi, and exactly the same information is also found in the Sanskrit version of this discourse, the Ambāṣṭhasūtra, which has recently come to light in a manuscript from Pakistan. It should be noted that the Pali word *kūṭa,* translated above as "club," and by others as "hammer," means neither of these, and rather shows the problem that translators face in coming to terms with this strange implement. The Sanskrit version prefers *vajra* in this place.

In some Vinaya versions it is Vajrapāṇi who protects the Buddha when his cousin Devadatta tries to kill him with a rock; and in some versions of the story of the snake demon (nāga) Apalāla, it is Vajrapāṇi who accompanies the Buddha and helps him taming the ferocious opponent. Thus, early written sources on Vajrapāṇi are rare and offer very limited information. In a remarkable contradistinction to this paucity in the written material, he is very often found in Buddhist art as an attendant of the Buddha. At the beginning of the first millennium C.E. and after centuries of aniconic representation, the artists created an anthropomorphic image for Buddha. Whether this image was first created in Mathura or in Gandhara is a matter of dispute, but in both schools of art the Buddha is accompanied by a figure holding an implement apparently representing a *vajra*. In Gandhara, images of the gods and heroes of the Graeco-Roman world were available to the artists, and they chose the figure of Heracles as a model for Vajrapāṇi and equipped the latter with the former's lion skin, but substituted for Heracles' club a fairly large item resembling the form of an hourglass or a double pestle and grasped by the middle. Most likely the choice was inspired by representations of the thunderbolt carried by Zeus. The lion skin, sometimes knotted around the belly and sometimes worn with the lion's head covering the head of Vajrapāṇi, is still found on some paintings and busts of Vajrapāṇi along the Silk Road in Central Asia and equally in Mathura ([2] against [3]). The lion skin disappeared in later Indian art, while the hourglass-like vajra became the distinctive mark wherever the figure traveled. Its size varies greatly; in a wall painting in the famous caves of Ajanta (India), for example, the vajra is tiny, while the huge wooden figure of Vajrapāṇi at the entrance gate of the Todaiji temple in Nara (Japan) holds a very long weapon. The basic shape, however, remains the same.

In Gandhara, Vajrapāṇi is nearly omnipresent in reliefs depicting the life of the Buddha, from the great escape to the Parinirvana. This has been explained as resulting from the specific popularity of this figure in the northwestern part of the Indian Buddhist world. He usually stands somewhere in the vicinity of the Buddha, always easily recognizable from the *vajra* he carries in one of his hands. This frequency of representation in art, contrasted with his absence in written sources which could offer hints for explaining the popularity, and the choice of Heracles as a model, has initiated manifold deliberations about his function [1, 2, 4, 6]. None of the representations appears to convey a threatening attitude, and he often rather looks like a casual bystander, but the underlying relation between him and the Buddha is not made explicit in the reliefs. One theory that has been advanced, among others, is that he serves as a kind of protector spirit of the Buddha. The Buddha, however, is not likely to be in need of such protection. More convincing, perhaps, is the role of a powerful attendant who is employed whenever some additional force is needed for a specific conversion, as exemplified in the subjugation of the Nāga Apalāla, a story which is even set in the region.

When Vajrapāṇi appears in the Mahāyānasūtras, he has a remarkable career behind him. He is no longer classified as a *yakṣa* and thus a member of the spirit world, but has been advanced to the status of a Bodhisattva who counts among the interlocutors of the Buddha as do Avalokiteśvara, Mañjuśrī, and the other major Bodhisattvas. He is now a part of the salvific forces that help the suffering beings on the way to liberation, and some sources even credit to him a role similar to that of Ānanda as the person to whom the Buddha entrusts the transmission and protection of the Mahāyānasūtras.

He retained and even enforced this salvific status when he finally became incorporated into the pantheon of Vajrayāna Buddhism. Here he serves as a meditation deity and becomes the object of specific visualization practices where he represents the wholesome activity of the Buddha, in the same way as Avalokiteśvara stands for the Buddha's great compassion. Among the various meanings of vajra, that meaning "very hard stone = diamond" now comes to the fore. There is a close, but rather complicated relation with Vajradhara ("Holder of the Vajra") and Vajrasattva ("Vajra-Being"), both of eminent importance in Tantric Buddhism and both distinguished by holding a vajra, and they overlap to a certain degree. Finally, Vajrapāṇi's potentially fierce and threatening nature comes again to the fore: he is usually depicted as a wrathful deity, even when combined with the peaceful Bodhisattvas Avalokiteśvara and Mañjuśrī. This triad gained a specific popularity in Tibetan Buddhism, where the three are seen as important agents for the spread and preservation of Buddhism in Tibet; the three early Kings most important for the introduction of Buddhism into the country are each considered an emanation of one of these Bodhisattvas, with the last of the three kings, Khri Gtsug-lde-brtsan (Ral-pa-can), usually regarded as the emanation of Vajrapāṇi

Cross-References

- ▶ Avalokiteśvara
- ▶ Buddhaghosa
- ▶ Gandhara
- ▶ Mañjuśrī
- ▶ Mathurā
- ▶ Vajra
- ▶ Yakṣa

References

1. Bhattacharya G (1995/1996) The Buddhist deity Vajrapāṇi. Silk Road Art Archaeol 4:323–353
2. Flood FB (1985) Herakles and the perpetual 'Acolyte' of the Buddha: some observations on the iconography of Vajrapani in Gandharan art. South Asian Stud 1:17–27
3. Lamotte E (2003) Vajrapāṇi in India. Buddh Stud Rev 20.1:1–30, 20.2:119–144
4. Tanabe K (2005) Why is the Buddha Śākyamuni accompanied by Hercules/Vajrapāṇi? Farewell to Yakṣa-theory. East West 55:363–381
5. Walshe M (1987) Thus have I heard. The long discourses of the Buddha. Wisdom, London
6. Zin M (2009) Vajrapāṇi in the narrative reliefs. In: Fröhlich C (ed) Migration, trade and peoples, vol 2. The British Academy, London, pp 73–88

Vajrāsana

▶ Bodhagayā

Vajrayāna (Buddhism)

Joseph P. Elacqua
Center for Language and Learning Development, Mohawk Valley Community College, Utica, NY, USA

Synonyms

Esoteric Buddhism; Kongōjō; Mantranaya; Mantrayāna; Mikkyō; Shingon; Tantra; Tantrayāna; Tantric Buddhism; Yoga; Zhenyan

Definition

Vajrayāna refers to a highly ritualized and Esoteric form of Buddhism that seems to have emerged in India around the eighth century C.E. Two major types of Vajrayāna Buddhism survive today: one practiced in Japan and the other practiced by Tibetan exiles in India.

Introduction

Despite its still widespread use among scholars based in Asia, the term "Vajrayāna" is frequently avoided in Western scholarship. A number of Western scholars have rightly criticized the

V

terminology used to describe systematized Esoteric forms of Buddhism, especially within the last decade. ([13], pp. 5–8, 155–175) While the term "Vajrayāna" is attested in extant Sanskrit manuscripts as well as in Chinese and Tibetan translation, it seems that Western scholars avoid it largely due to a lack of clarity regarding what exactly Vajrayāna signifies within the larger tradition of Esoteric Buddhism. As a critical academic definition of this term has not yet been reached, this article will attempt to summarize the majority of the Esoteric Buddhist tradition, beginning in India and later expanding to China, Japan, and Tibet.

Generally speaking, Esoteric Buddhism originates in the sixth century, a number of texts were compiled that describe a heavily ritualized and Esoteric form of Buddhism. This new and systematized Esoteric Buddhism differs from Mahāyāna Buddhism primarily in its adaptation of Brahmanical practices such as *homa*, mantra recitation, coronation (Skt. *abhiṣeka*), the consecration of images, and the use of *mūdras*. For example, the initiation of a Buddhist candidate into the tradition of an Esoteric *maṇḍala* itself involves a number of mantras, mūdras, and also homa ceremonies ([3], p. 820). It also diverges from Mahāyāna Buddhism in that one may obtain buddhahood within this lifetime rather than after countless reincarnations. Esoteric Buddhism is also strongly associated with kingship; one of its strongest metaphors is that of the Buddhist practitioner as a supreme overlord (Skt. *rājādhirāja*) or a universal ruler (Skt. *cakravartin*) ([6], p. 114, [16], p. 30–31, and [14], p. 204). Other rites were appropriated from or otherwise influenced by Śaiva, Saurya, Gāruḍa, Pañcarātra, Jain, and folk sources, among others ([12], p. 21, [7], pp. 10–18, [18], 397–402).

Teachers (Skt. *guru*, *ācārya*) and the master-disciple relationship are also extremely important within Esoteric Buddhism. Masters are expected to maintain knowledge of all Esoteric doctrines and ritual practices, and it is likewise deemed impossible to learn such materials without the proper guidance of a teacher ([2], p. 220). Finally – as an Esoteric religious tradition – the rites, ceremonies, and other elements of this movement of Buddhism are kept secret.

Numerous buddhas and bodhisattvas are revered within Esoteric Buddhism. The most popular of these is [Mahā] Vairocana, the chief Esoteric Buddha. Other popular figures include Akṣobhya, Amitābha, Ratnasambhava, Amoghasiddhi, Mañjuśrī, Maitreya, Avalokiteśvara, Vajrasattva, and a host of others ([2], p. 211). Each divinity is equated with his own mantra and mūdra that are utilized throughout Esoteric Buddhist rituals.

The Indian Roots of Esoteric Buddhism

While its roots may trace back to India, Esoteric Buddhism is no longer practiced there. Consequently, the reconstruction of its history in India depends on textual analysis of related surviving Sanskrit scriptures as well as those in Chinese and Tibetan translation.

The first inklings of tantric phenomena within Indian Buddhism seem to have appeared around the third century C.E. with the emergence of a genre of Mahāyāna *dhāraṇī* literature. This textual genre is characterized by a number of dhāraṇī (mystical Sanskrit incantations) that were believed to invoke certain effects within the natural world such as the healing of illness. Dhāraṇī literature seems to have become incredibly popular, paving the way for a new Buddhist system altogether [17]. The earliest known tantric system to emerge within Buddhism involved texts relating to the Universal Emperor from the Buddha's Uṣṇīṣa (Skt. *Ekākṣara-uṣṇīṣa-cakravartin*). While describing themselves as dhāraṇī texts, they are the first to include practices that were chiefly foreign to Buddhism.

By the mid-sixth century, the Gupta empire collapsed in India, altering the way Buddhist monasteries were patronized. Some of the more prominent ones grew even larger, eventually evolving into monastic centers of education and instruction. The Indian monastery at Nālandā was a particularly prominent establishment, eventually becoming a great center for Esoteric Buddhist learning.

The earliest text presently known to include the core elements of mature Esoteric Buddhism is the *Dhāraṇī-saṅgraha-sūtra*, compiled around 654. While it contains the coronation of a candidate using *homa*, mantras, and mūdras, it also includes rituals derived from non-Buddhist practices and cults to deities of non-Buddhist origin ([12], p. 23). It also coordinated the use of mantras, mūdras, and maṇḍalas within rituals.

Since the popularization of dhāraṇī literature, Mahāyāna Buddhist texts seem to have also gradually acquired additional esoteric elements. For example, they began to include buddhas and bodhisattvas that later rose to great prominence within Esoteric Buddhist texts. Thus, it can be concluded that earlier esoteric texts were added to the Mahāyāna Buddhist corpus from roughly the third through the ninth centuries C.E. ([10], pp. 6–7). As time progressed, the range of practices deemed sacred was significantly widened as a result of the increase in Esoteric Buddhist influence. The five substances (Skt. *pañcamākara*) of wine, meat, fish, parched grain, and sexual intercourse came to be regarded not only as sacred but also as essential for attaining liberation. In later texts, even the enlightened mind (Skt. *bodhicitta*) is created through sexual union.

Scholarship on Esoteric Buddhism commonly notes that the aforementioned early developments could not have constituted an organized school of Esoteric belief. Chinese pilgrims to India from the fifth through seventh centuries – such as Faxian, Huishen, and Xuanzang – do not mention any sort of Esoteric belief system in their writings; such a system is not mentioned until the mid-seventh century. However, this conclusion neglects the Indian monk Puṇyodaya, who attempted to introduce Esoteric texts to China in 655. It was Xuanzang that prevented him from doing so, as he stated a lack of interest in such texts ([5], pp. 244–245). Thus, properly Esoteric texts (outside of simple dhāraṇī literature) must date to the mid-sixth century at the latest. Such literature may well have originated earlier while only remaining available through secret transmissions.

The Establishment of Mature Esoteric Buddhism

Despite their deep roots, these various Esoteric elements were not systematized until the mid-seventh century. According to extant records, Xuanzang dismissed ignorant users of spells in 646, the *Dhāraṇī-saṅgraha-sūtra* was compiled and translated into Chinese by 654, and Puṇyodaya failed to introduce Esoteric texts to China in 655 ([11], p. 89). Around 680, another Chinese monk, Wuxing, commented on the popularity of Esoteric practice in India and had purportedly obtained a copy of the first major Esoteric Buddhist scripture. Yet another Chinese monk, Daolin, is purported to have been greatly interested in Esoteric Buddhism during his time in India.

In the following decades, core Esoteric Buddhist texts were composed. Important Esoteric texts include the *Mahāvairocanābhisambodhi*, the *Susiddhikara*, the *Sarva-tathāgata-tattva-saṅgraha*, the *Guhyasamāja*, and the *Sarva-buddha-samāyoga*, among a number of others. The *Sarvatathāgata-tattvasaṅgraha* and the *Guhyasamāja* are among the earliest Indian texts to utilize the term Vajrayāna in describing the form of Buddhism they profess. Many of these Esoteric texts were quickly brought to China and began to be translated into Chinese. Tradition also ascribes the transmission of Esoteric Buddhism to Tibet during the latter half of the eighth century. However, within India, Esoteric Buddhism only had a few remaining centuries to prosper.

During the mid-eighth century, the Bengal-based Pāla Empire arose and quickly attained control over much of the Indian subcontinent. The Pāla Empire championed Buddhism, and it was under their protection that Indian Esoteric Buddhism (by this point, certainly known as Vajrayāna) reached its apex. A great number of texts – such as the *Cakrasaṃvara* and

Hevajra – were composed, large monastic institutions such as Vikramaśīla were founded, and extensive commentaries were written by eminent Indian monks such as Buddhaguhya and Śākyamitra.

Although the Pāla Empire ruled over much of India, it was threatened during the eighth century when the Rajputs took control in the northeast. The problem was exacerbated when the Chola dynasty rose to power in the south. Both of these groups championed the Hindu religion; thus, Buddhism was unable to flourish in lands under their control ([19], p. 13). As time progressed, more and more of India began to face the threat of possible Muslim occupation.

Eventually, Esoteric Buddhist teachings were only prosperous in eastern India, which remained under the control of the Pālas. In places such as Orissa, Esoteric Buddhism was able to thrive for several centuries. It was especially prosperous within Buddhist institutions such as Vikramaśīla and Nālandā, which continued to produce Esoteric masters such as Nāropā.

In time, India gave birth to a new genre of Esoteric scriptures known as the Highest yoga (Skt. yoganiruttara) Tantras. These scriptures – representing the apex of Vajrayāna thought – closely resembled non-Buddhist tantric scriptures, emphasizing the sexual union of Buddhist practitioners with female consorts, the latter of whom are identified with Buddhist deities. While some of these texts were eventually translated into Chinese, they never reached a notable level of popularity in East Asia. Quite oppositely, these texts received great attention in India and Tibet.

Esoteric Buddhism continued to blossom in eastern India until the Pāla Empire began to weaken. As time progressed, the Pālas faced pressure from the Sena dynasty in Bengal. Their kingdom was ultimately destroyed in 1174, when Muslim armies invaded India. Buddhists and Hindus were slaughtered, temples and monastic centers were destroyed, and sacred scriptures were burned as the last wave of Vajrayāna texts – such as the *Kālacakra* – were being compiled. Indian Vajrayāna effectively came to an end around 1203 when Muslim conquerors arrived in eastern India ([19], p. 13). Buddhists that survived the slaughter fled to Tibet, Nepal, southern India, and Java. All forms of Indian Buddhism, including Vajrayāna, were effectively silenced.

Esoteric Buddhism in China

Officially, Vajrayāna Buddhism was not introduced into China until the eighth century. However, dhāraṇī literature appeared in Chinese translation prior to the middle of the third century ([5], p. 242). A number of monks translated various dhāraṇī texts (some with and others without accompanying rituals) until Yijing returned from India at the end of the seventh century.

In 716, the Indian monk Śubhākarasiṃha (Ch. Shan Wuwei) arrived in China to spread tantric knowledge. However, extant Chinese records clearly exaggerate parts of his biography, and his existence is not recorded in any Indian documents. Śubhākarasiṃha's greatest credit is the translation of the *Mahāvairocanābhisambodhi* ([9], p. xiv). He is recorded to have translated a handful of other texts, some with the help of the Chinese monk Yixing, but at least 30 works bear his name in modern editions of the Chinese Buddhist canon. According to Chinese records, Śubhākarasiṃha died in 735. Some scholars have attempted to equate Śubhākarasiṃha with various Indian historical figures, but currently, there is no universally accepted theory.

While Śubhākarasiṃha was still alive, another Indian monk brought Esoteric scriptures to China in 720. This monk, Vajrabodhi (Ch. Jin'gangzhi), was famous for translating (or perhaps composing from memory) a summary of the doctrines of the *Sarva-tathāgata-tattva-saṅgraha* ([8], p. 7). Unlike Śubhākarasiṃha, Vajrabodhi brought a disciple with him named Amoghavajra (Ch. Bukong). Like their predecessor, there are no Indian records that refer to either Vajrabodhi or Amoghavajra, and Chinese records clearly embellish their biographies [5]. Vajrabodhi translated a number of scriptures before his death in 741. While only a few texts are known with certainty to have been translated by Vajrabodhi, the modern canon attributes more than 20 texts to him.

Around the time of Vajrabodhi's death, Amoghavajra was forced to leave China, conforming to an edict that expelled foreign monks. However, he returned in 746 with a veritable library of Vajrayāna (and other Esoteric) texts to translate. He is most famous for translating the first section of the Sarvatathāgata-tattvasaṅgraha into Chinese. Amoghavajra won the support of the emperor and became an extremely popular historical figure. He took a number of disciples himself before he died in 774. According to Amoghavajra's own record, he translated at least 77 texts, although more than double that number are attributed to him in the modern canon ([12], p. 357).

Śubhākarasiṃha, Vajrabodhi, and Amoghavajra are popularly considered to be the three great preceptors (Skt. *ācārya*) of Esoteric Buddhism in China. However, scholars have since determined that the teachings brought to China by these three monks did not constitute a group of organized teachings that could be considered a systematized denomination or "school" of Buddhism. Rather, these teachings seem to have been practiced by monks of various disciplines. Their teachings are generally referred to by the more ambiguous term Esoteric Buddhism (Ch. *mijiao*).

Regardless of how systematized their teachings were, the three preceptors certainly transmitted a number of definitive tantric scriptures to China, many of which then circulated throughout East Asia. The contributions of these monks cannot be overestimated as a number of the esoteric texts they were said to have translated (most notably the *Mahāvairocanābhisambodhi*) no longer survive in Sanskrit.

Even while the three monks were still alive, Esoteric Buddhism began to take on Chinese characteristics. Some Buddhist deities were confused with Chinese ones, unable to be extricated even by modern scholars. Esoteric scriptures were composed in China that utilized Chinese philosophical and folk terms, deities, and even Daoist vocabulary. While modern scholars are separating more of these apocrypha from the authentic Vajrayāna texts, it is still a difficult and time-consuming process.

Another major element of Chinese Esoteric Buddhism relates to two tantric maṇḍalas. No longer extant in China, the earliest copies of these maṇḍalas exist in Japan. The first is known as the Womb Realm maṇḍala (Jp. *Taizōkai mandara*), and it depicts more than 400 buddhas, bodhisattvas, and other deities. Stylistically and ritually speaking, it is intimately connected to the *Mahāvairocanābhisambodhi*, although scholars have demonstrated that the present version of the maṇḍala differs substantially from the maṇḍalas provided in the *Mahāvairocanābhisambodhi*. The second is called the Vajra Realm maṇḍala (Jp. *Kongōkai mandara*), and it generally depicts fewer than 40 deities. Like the Womb Realm maṇḍala, the Vajra Realm maṇḍala differs substantially from the maṇḍalas described in its companion scripture: the *Sarva-tathāgata-tattva-saṅgraha* [15].

The two scriptures notwithstanding, Indian precedents for these maṇḍalas have not been identified, so it is impossible to determine their country of origin. However, the monk Śubhākarasiṃha is said to have first brought iconographic images of the maṇḍalas' various deities to China in two works referred to today as the *Taizō zuzō* and the *Gobu shinkan*. Another work called the *Taizo kyūzuyō* is said to represent the divinities of the Womb Realm based on the tradition of Vajrabodhi and Amoghavajra. Only copies of these works survive, and the maṇḍalas they prescribe also differ from the maṇḍalas surviving today. Thus, if precedents for either maṇḍala did exist in India, it is clear that they differed considerably from the maṇḍalas used today.

Despite the appearance of two major maṇḍalas presented in two major esoteric scriptures, the Womb Realm and Vajra Realm maṇḍalas were not originally part of a unified system. Today, they are rarely separated and are often referred to as the Maṇḍala of the Dual Realms (Jp. *Ryōbu mandara*). Modern scholars attribute the joining of these two maṇḍalas to the Chinese monk Huiguo, Amoghavajra's most well-known disciple.

The popularity of Esoteric Buddhism continued during China's Tang (618–907) and Song (960–1279) dynasties, during which scriptures were both copied and created, catalogues and editions of the Buddhist canon were compiled, Esoteric art was produced, and Esoteric Buddhism continued to be subject to various Chinese influences. It became the official religion of China under Mongol rulers during the Yuan dynasty (1271–1368) ([12], p. 540). However, Esoteric Buddhism was deemed heterodox during the Ming dynasty (1368–1644) and was thenceforth abolished. However, Esoteric practices and the translation of scriptures continued beyond the Ming, despite this ruling.

Esoteric Buddhism in Japan

The history of Esoteric Buddhism (Jp. *Mikkyō*) is somewhat clearer in Japan. According to historical records, dhāraṇī literature appeared in Japan as from very early on. A dhāraṇī text dated to 686 C.E. is one of the oldest extant hand-copied sūtras in Japan. From as late as 660 through the eighth century, a host of dhāraṇī scriptures were brought to Japan. While most were received by Japanese pilgrims that traveled to China, some were brought over by Korean and Chinese pilgrims to Japan as well ([12], pp. 661–662).

The first crucial moment in the establishment of Japanese Esoteric Buddhism came in 736 when the Chinese monk Daoxuan came to Japan bearing a number of esoteric scriptures. Among the scriptures he brought with him were the *Mahāvairocanābhisambodhi*, the *Sarva-tathāgata-tattva-saṅgraha*, and the *Susiddhikara*, fewer than 15 years after they were originally translated into Chinese. These three scriptures also represented the core teachings of Chinese Esoteric Buddhism.

Despite the presence of Esoteric Buddhist scriptures in Japan, it is difficult to determine precisely how they were understood and what rituals were performed in relation to them. However, these scriptures were certainly circulated widely, and the dhāraṇī they contained were frequently recited. In fact, the vast majority of the Esoteric texts known to China by the year 730 had been transmitted to Japan within the following two decades ([1], pp. 153–156).

By the close of the eighth century, six separate "schools" of Buddhism were practiced in the Japanese islands. The first five were ultimately derived from Indian Buddhism: Vinaya (Jp. *Ritsu*), Satyasiddhi (Jp. *Jōjitsu*), Abhidharma (Jp. *Kusha*), Madhyamaka (Jp. *Sanron*), and yogācāra (Jp. *Hossō*). The last, Huayan (Jp. *Kegon*, Skt. *Avataṃsaka*), originated in China. While members of these schools came to frequently utilize Esoteric scriptures, dhāraṇī, and other rituals, it is notable that none of these schools were centered upon any level of esotericism, much less the level championed by masters such as Śubhākarasiṃha, Vajrabodhi, and Amoghavajra. Thus, despite the frequent use of various Esoteric scriptures, it is highly doubtful that the Japanese viewed these texts and their contents as having contained a wholly new set of beliefs and practices ([12], p. 692).

However, Japanese Buddhism was to be completely restructured in 806 when a monk named Kūkai returned from a 30-month stay in China with a collection of scriptures, commentaries, paintings, ritual implements, and a variety of other items. While in China, Kūkai had studied with Huiguo, one of Amoghavajra's disciples in China. Kūkai was fully ordained into Chinese Esoteric Buddhism within shortly after meeting Huiguo. He received initiation into both the Womb Realm maṇḍala and the Vajra Realm maṇḍala. Kūkai was designated an official Dharmic successor and could thus trace his transmission back through Huiguo and Amoghavajra at least as far as Vajrabodhi himself ([12], p. 697). Later, four other esoteric patriarchs were eventually added to extend Kūkai's transmission lineage as far back as the cosmic buddha, Mahāvairocana – the chief divinity of both the *Mahāvairocanābhisambodhi* and the *Sarva-tathāgata-tattva-saṅgraha*.

Upon his return to Japan in 806, Kūkai founded what would be known as Shingon (Skt. Mantra) Buddhism, centered at Mt. Kōya in Wakayama Prefecture. However, the Shingon denomination was not officially recognized by the government until 835, shortly before Kūkai's death. While Shingon is the closest approximation to a Japanese Vajrayāna denomination, it also centers on texts such as the *Vairocanābhisambodhi*, which are properly designated as Mahāyāna. It is thus, perhaps best understood as a hybrid Mahāyana/Vajrayāna denomination, especially when considering that a number of essential Indian Vajrayāna texts never took hold in East Asia. Based on extant records, Kūkai maintained a visible interest in differentiating between the Esoteric doctrines he transmitted to Japan and the remainder of "exoteric" Buddhism that had already been transmitted there. His new Buddhism provided theoretical explanations for the Esoteric texts and dhāraṇī already present in Japan and thus maintained a relationship with the previous six schools. Kūkai himself also wrote a number of works that served to legitimize this new denomination for the Japanese.

Kūkai, however, was not alone. Traveling on the same voyage to China was a monk named Saichō. However, Saichō's time in China seems to have been largely spent in absence of Esoteric teachings. He did receive an esoteric initiation from a monk named Shunxiao, but it seems that Saichō otherwise had little interest in Esoteric Buddhism. However, Saichō eventually understood the importance of Esotericism, as he frequently requested texts and other materials from Kūkai. Saichō established the Tendai (Ch. Tiantai) denomination of Buddhism at Mt. Hiei near Kyōto. Tendai was technically a Mahāyāna school, but Esoteric elements were eventually added to allow it to compete with Shingon Buddhism. Saichō himself even attested that there was no actual difference between Shingon and Tendai Buddhism. In modern times, at least three scriptures composed to legitimize Saichō's connection to esotericism were exposed as forgeries [4].

Japanese Esoteric Buddhism – exemplified by the Shingon denomination of Buddhism – continued to remain strong, even after Kūkai's death. Throughout its history, Shingon produced a great number of masters, commentators, and monks. During the twelfth century, a monk named Kakuban attempted to reform Shingon Buddhism ([19], p. 41). He incorporated some Tendai esoteric practices as well as Pure Land Buddhist teachings into Shingon. However, hostilities began to arise between those that championed Kakuban's reformed Shingon and those who preferred the original methods.

Around 1140, hostilities on Mt. Kōya forced Kakuban and his followers to flee and take refuge at a branch temple in Negoro, also located in Wakayama prefecture. This schism was the greatest to take place within Shingon, and even today, Kakuban's reformed denomination is known as Shingi Shingon (New Rite Shingon). Oppositely, the Shingon practiced at Mt. Kōya is referred to as Kogi Shingon (Old Rite Shingon). Today, Kogi Shingon and Shingi Shingon are each comprised of a number of branches practiced throughout the country.

Although somewhat obscure, one other branch of Shingon deserves mention. No longer extant, there was once a Shingon branch called the Tachikawa Ryū, established not long before Kakuban and his supporters left Mt. Kōya. Most Tachikawa Ryū scriptures have not survived. Existing polemics decry the branch, stating that it relied on a number of perverse and heterodox sexual practices. Despite this stigma, modern scholars have since demonstrated that these purported practices were commonly performed by Japanese Buddhists of numerous denominations and cannot be restricted simply to the Tachikawa Ryū itself ([12], pp. 805–814).

One of the most important elements in Japanese Vajrayāna is the Chinese Buddhist canon, on which it is heavily reliant. The Japanese *Taishō shinshū daizōkyō*, the most recently compiled and most prominent edition of the canon, was produced in Japan from 1924 through 1934. Its section on Esoteric Buddhism contains 573 individual works in four volumes (v. 18–21). However, this estimate does not include some texts from earlier editions of the Chinese canon or a large number of others appearing within the compilation's 12 volumes of iconographic texts. A vast number of texts are preserved here in Chinese as their Sanskrit originals have been lost.

Esoteric Buddhism in Tibet

According to tradition, Esoteric Buddhism was first brought to Tibet by Padmasambhava, when he was summoned there. He ordained monks and during that time, Esoteric scriptures began to be translated into Tibetan. Padmasambhava is also credited with the establishment of the Nyingma denomination, one of the four major branches of Tibetan Buddhism. Early Tibetan Esoteric Buddhism was fashioned to serve the Tibetan court and incorporated various elements of the indigenous Bön tradition, which was extremely influential at that time.

However, during the mid-ninth century, all Buddhist teachings were suppressed in Tibet, forcing the ordained monks to flee to the northeast. At the end of this period, transmissions from India continued. Texts such as the *Guhyasamāja*, the *Sarva-buddha-samāyoga*, the *Cakrasaṃvara*, and the *Hevajra* – which championed violent practices as well as sexual rites – were transmitted to Tibet. A number of these monks led by Rinchen Zangpo were sent to India to establish that these texts were truly orthodox. In India, Zangpo had studied in Kashmir as well as under the Indian master Atiśa at Vikramaśīla. Atiśa was invited to come to Tibet in 1040, advocating monastic celibacy despite practicing tantra. Buddhists in these areas decreed that these texts were indeed orthodox: this discovery ignited a rapid transmission of scriptures, rituals, and other practices to Tibet from the eleventh century forward ([12], p. 452).

Sexuality was not restricted to Vajrayāna texts that were largely transmitted to Tibet. Buddhist practices such as coronation came to involved sexual practices with a consort. Various maṇḍalas also betrayed this aspect, depicting male deities in sexual union (Tib. Yab-yum) with their consorts. This symbolism, frequently associated with Highest yoga tantras, is largely characteristic of Tibetan Buddhism because such texts were only rarely transmitted to China and then to Japan. As a result, East Asian Esoteric Buddhism is not nearly as sexualized.

It should be noted that Esoteric texts were transmitted to China while Indian Vajrayāna Buddhism was still comparatively young. Conversely, Tibetans did not receive the bulk of their Esoteric texts until the eleventh through thirteenth centuries, when the evolution of Vajrayāna in India was reaching its apex. This cultural phenomenon enforced a number of major differences between the types of Esoteric Buddhism practiced in each of the two countries. These differences are still observable in modern Japanese Shingon and Tibetan Vajrayāna.

During the eleventh century alone, a number of Tibetan Buddhist denominations were founded. Dromtön Gyelwé Jungné, a disciple of Atiśa's, is credited with founding the monastic Kadam denomination, which quickly led to the founding of others. Another translator, Marpa Chögi Lodrö, founded the Kagyü denomination shortly thereafter. Disciples of the yogī Milarépa continued to establish additional Kagyü lineages. The Sakya denomination was also founded by Khön Könchok Gyelpo during this period ([12], pp. 453–454). Together, the Kagyü and Sakya denominations would eventually become two of the four major branches of Tibetan Buddhism. Kagyü Buddhism emphasized intensive meditation, advanced yogic practices, and also utilized Mahāmudrā (Tib. Chagchen) techniques. Sakya Buddhism was a scholarly tradition heavily centered on the *Hevajra*.

As new denominations of Tibetan Buddhism arose during this period, the older denominations began to revise themselves. The more ancient Nyingma denomination was revised, and the indigenous Bön tradition evolved as well. These evolutions involved the appearance of new texts as well as ritual practices attributed to ancient masters such as Padmasambhava. Dzogchen (Skt. Atiyoga), viewed by the Nyingma denomination as the most definitive path toward enlightenment, also emerged during this period.

During the thirteenth century, the Sakya master Buston of Shalu monastery was instrumental in cataloguing the entire Tibetan Buddhist canon. Tibetan texts were categorized into two main divisions: the *Kagyur*, which held translations of texts attributed to the Buddha, and the *Tengyur*, which contains commentaries and other secondary materials. Today, the Tibetan canon holds more than 4,556 texts, almost 500 of which are tantric scriptures. These texts are generally divided into four main categories: Action (Skt. Kriyā) tantras, Performance (Skt. Caryā) tantras, Yoga tantras, and Highest yoga tantras ([3], p. 821). It should be noted that with respect to Indian Vajrayāna, these categories derive from a comparatively late period and thus tend not to represent how the tantras were organized or categorized in other countries ([12], pp. 435–436). In addition to its Esoteric scriptures, more than 2,000 texts in the Tibetan canon are commentaries. Like the Chinese Buddhist canon, many of these texts have no extant Sanskrit originals and survive only in Tibetan translation. It should be noted that Tibetans do not often differentiate between Mahāyāna and Vajrayāna Buddhism; in Tibet, the Mahāyāna path is equated with Esoteric Buddhism because both represent the bodhisattva path ([2], p. 208).

The next major developments came to Tibet in the fourteenth century. This period brought Tibet the so-called *Tibetan Book of the Dead* (Tib. *Bardo Thodol*), attributed to Padmasambhava, and one final major branch: the Geluk, founded by Tsongkhapa. Originally established as a reform order that emphasized the tantric system brought to Tibet by Atiśa, the Geluk denomination is perhaps the most well-known Tibetan denomination today. It is from this branch of Tibetan Buddhism that the figure of the Dalai Lama emerged.

Like Japanese Shingon, Tibetan Vajrayāna passed through periods of downfall as well as prosperity, seeing new masters, new texts, and new ritual techniques as time progressed. Between the four main branches of Nyingma, Kagyü, Sakya, and Geluk, Tibetan Buddhism ultimately thrived.

However, in 1949, newly Communist China sought to take over the Tibetan plateau. Shortly thereafter, His Holiness Tenzin Gyatso assumed his role as the fourteenth and current Dalai Lama. In 1951, the Tibetans were forced to sign their country over to China. In the following years, animosity and violence between the Chinese and Tibetans resulted in the Dalai Lama's escape from Tibet in 1959. He arrived in India, where he was welcomed and given political refuge ([3], p. 195). Tens of thousands of Tibetan refugees fled to India, where many of them currently reside. The Dalai Lama set up a government while in exile in Dharamśālā, India, where he still presently resides.

With the escape of the Dalai Lama and more than 10,000 Tibetan refugees, Esoteric Buddhism has come full circle, once again blossoming in its home country of India.

Cross-References

- ▶ Mantra
- ▶ Padmasambhava
- ▶ Tantra
- ▶ Vairocana
- ▶ Xuanzang (Hieun-Tsang)
- ▶ Yoga

References

1. Abe R (1999) The weaving of mantra: Kukai and the construction of Esoteric Buddhist discourse. Columbia University Press, New York
2. Bhattacharyya NN (2005) History of the tantric religion, 2nd rev edn. Manohar, New Delhi
3. Buswell RE (2004) Encyclopedia of Buddhism, 2 vols. Macmillan Reference USA, New York
4. Chen J (2009) Legend and legitimation: the formation of Tendai Esoteric Buddhism in Japan. Institut Belge des Hautes Études Chinoises, Brussels
5. Chou Y (1945) Tantrism in China. Harvard J Asiatic Stud 8(3):241–332
6. Davidson RM (2002) Indian esoteric Buddhism: a social history of the tantric movement. Columbia University Press, New York
7. Davidson RM (2005) Tibetan renaissance: tantric Buddhism in the rebirth of Tibetan culture. Columbia University Press, New York
8. Giebel RW (2001) Two esoteric sutras: the Adamantine pinnacle sutra, the Susiddhikara sutra. Numata Center for Buddhist Translation and Research, Berkeley
9. Giebel RW (2005) The Vairocanābhisaṃbodhi sutra. Numata Center for Buddhist Translation and Research, Berkeley
10. Hodge S (2003) The Mahā-Vairocana-Abhisaṃbodhi tantra with Buddhaguhya's commentary. RoutledgeCurzon, London
11. Huntington JC (1987) Note on a Chinese text demonstrating the earliness of tantra. JIABS 10(2):88–98
12. Orzech CD, Sørensen HH, Payne RK (2011) Esoteric Buddhism and the tantras in East Asia. Brill, Leiden
13. Payne RK (2006) Tantric Buddhism in East Asia. Wisdom, Somerville
14. Snellgrove DL (1959) The notion of divine kingship in tantric Buddhism. In: The sacral kingship: contributions to the central theme of the VIIIth International Congress for the history of religions, Rome, pp 204–218

15. Snodgrass A (1988) the matrix and diamond world mandalas in Shingon Buddhism, 2 vols. Rakesh Goel, New Delhi
16. Sullivan BM (2006) Tantroid phenomena in early Indic literature: an essay in honor of Jim Sanford. Pacific World 3rd Ser 8:9–20
17. Wayman A, Tajima R (1992) The enlightenment of Vairocana. Motilal Banarsidass, New Delhi
18. Williams P (2005) Buddhism: critical concepts in religious studies, vol 6, Tantric Buddhism (including China and Japan); Buddhism in Nepal and Tibet. Routledge, London
19. Yamasaki T (1988) Shingon: Japanese Esoteric Buddhism. Shambhala, Boston

Vaṇṇa

► Caste (Buddhism)

Vārāṇasī (Buddhism)

K. T. S. Sarao
Department of Buddhist Studies, University of Delhi, Delhi, India

Synonyms

Banārasa; Banaras (Buddhism); Bārāṇasī; Bārāṇāsī (Buddhism); Benares; Benaras (Buddhism); Brahmavaḍḍhana; Kashi; Kashi (Buddhism); Kāsi; Kāśī; Kāśī (Buddhism); Kāśinagara; Kāśipura; Ketumatī; Molinī; Pupphavatī; Ramma; Rammaka; Rammanagara; Rammavatī; Surundha; Surundhana

Definition

Capital city of the state of Kāśī in ancient India and an important place of pilgrimage.

Early Buddhist texts mention Vārāṇasī as the capital city (*rājadhānīya nagara*) of Kāsi (Sk: Kāśī) *janapada* (state) and a harbor (*pattana*), which was one of the six metropolitan cities (*mahānagaras*) at the time of the Buddha, the other five being Campā, Rājagaha, Sāvatthī, Sāketa, and Kosambi ([12], Vol. ii, p. 146). The Buddha is said to have visited Vārāṇasī several times and delivered many sermons here ([2], Vol. i, p. 105, Vol. v, p. 406; [6], Vol. i, pp. 110f, 279f; Vol. iii, pp. 392ff, 399ff; [9], Vol. i, pp. 189, 216f, 289). Apart from being an important place of pilgrimage, Vārāṇasī is mentioned in early Buddhist texts as a wealthy and prosperous place which was the center of trade and industry ([6], Vol. i, p. 213; [12], Vol. ii, p. 75). Vārāṇasī was particularly known for its manufacture of ships ([1], Vol. iv, p. 2), sandalwood, and cloths ([6], Vol. i, pp. 145, 245, Vol. iv, p. 281; Vol. v, p. 61f; [12], Vol. iii, p. 110) where various kinds of businessmen *(seṭṭhānuseṭṭhi)* lived ([9], Vol. i, p. 18). Hundreds of merchants are said to have frequented Vārāṇasī harbor to buy cargo ([1], Vol. iv, p. 121) and from where rich merchants are said to have sailed to Suvaṇṇabhūmi (Sk: Suvarṇabhūmi, Southeast Asia) ([1], Vol. iv, p. 15). Existence of locations, such as ivory-workers' street (*Dantakāravīthi*) within the city of Vārāṇasī ([1], Vol. iv, p. 320), and villages, such as a carpenters' village (*Vaḍḍhakigāma*) near its four gates ([1], Vol. i, pp. 121, 125, 231, 11.18, Vol. iii, p. 414, Vol. iv, p. 344, Vol. v, p. 288, Vol. vi, p. 170; [9], Vol. i, p. 15), indicates toward the existence of commercial importance of this city. Various festivals, especially the night festival of Kattīkā (Sk: Kārtikā), were celebrated here with pomp and show, and on such occasions, Vārāṇasī was decorated like a *devanagara* (city of the gods), and everybody kept a holiday ([1], Vol. i, p. 499, Vol. ii, p. 13). Isipatana with its famous Deer Park (*Migadāya*), where the Buddha had delivered his first sermon, was near here ([6], Vol. iii, p. 320; [16], Vol. i, p. 170f, Vol. ii, p. 157).

The extent of Vārāṇasī is often quoted as 12 leagues (*yojanas*) in the Jātakas ([1], Vol i, p. 314, Vol. ii, pp. 253, 402, Vol. iii, p. 410, Vol. iv, p. 377, Vol. v, p. 127, Vol. vi, pp. 160, 195). One Jātaka mentions that while the walls of Vārāṇasī (i.e., its fortifications) were 12 leagues in length, the city and its suburbs put together were 300 leagues as a whole ([1], Vol. i, p. 125). According to Xuanzang (seventh century C.E.), Vārāṇasī was about 18 or 19 *lī* (about 3–4 miles) in length and about 5 or 6 *lī* (about 1 mile) in breadth ([5], p. 195). The *Jātakas* speak of a seven-storied palace with fine terraces at Vārāṇasī ([1], Vol. iv, p. 104). It is said that Yasa, the son of a merchant, had three mansions (*pāsādā*) over here ([9], Vol. i, p. 15). According to one of the Jātakas, Vārāṇasī was properly defended with rampart wall, gates, towers, moats, and battlement ([1], Vol. ii, p. 94). Another Jātaka mentions that

> To this fortified city, dug with moats, approach is hard,While its trenches and its towers hand and sword unite to guard,
> Not the young and not the mighty entrance here can lightly gain. ([13], Vol. iv, p. 68)

The Pāli texts refer to Vārāṇasī by various names such as Brahmavaddhana ([1], Vol. v, p. 312), Kāsinagara ([1], Vol. v, p. 54), Kāsipura ([1], Vol. vi, p. 165; [8], p. 1.87), Ketumatī ([12], Vol. iii, p. 75), Molinī ([1], Vol. iv, p. 15), Pupphavatī ([1], Vol. vi, p. 131), Ramma ([1], Vol. iv, p. 119), Surundhana ([1], Vol. iv.104), and Sudassana ([1], Vol. v, p. 177). The *Jātakas* mention the names of numerous kings such as Aṅga, Uggasena, Udaya, Kikī, Dhanañjaya, Mahāsīlava, Vissasena, and Saṃyama who ruled from Vārāṇasī. The commonest king (perhaps only a title for the kings ruling from here), Brahmadatta, lived in a palace which had at least two stories ([9], Vol. i, p. 345). He was rich, wealthy, opulent, of great strength, with many vehicles, large territories, full storehouses, and granaries ([9], Vol. i, p. 342ff). According to the *Mahāgovinda Sutta* of the *Dīgha Nikāya* ([12], Vol. ii, p. 220f), when Mahāgovinda, the brāhmaṇa chaplain of king Reṇu, divided his empire, the administration of the kingdom of Kāsi with Vārāṇasī as its capital fell into the hands of Dhataraṭṭha (Sk: Dhaṛtarāṣtra) who is represented as a king of the line of Bharata. B.C. Law is of the opinion that the Bharata line of the Kāsi kings appears to have been supplanted by a new line of kings called the Brahmadattas who were probably of Videhan origin ([4], p. 128ff). Most of the Jātaka stories have been named with reference to the reign of this line of Brahmadattas. The commentary of the *Sutta-Nipāta* mentions several kings of Vārāṇasī by name who renounced the world and became *paccekabuddhas* ([15], Vol. i, p. 46ff). Many Jātakas, such as *Bhaddasāla Jātaka* (no. 465) and *Dhonasākha Jātaka* (no. 353), refer to the unsurpassed glory of Vārāṇasī and to the ambition of its rulers for paramount sovereignty over the whole of Jambudīpa (Sk: Jambudvīpa, South Asia). The *Vinaya* also bears testimony to the former greatness and prosperity of the city ([9], Vol. i, p. 342f). There was a time when king Manoja of Vārāṇasī was able to subdue the kings of Assaka, Kosala, Aṅga, and Magadha ([1], Vol. ii, p. 155, Vol. v, p. 312). During the pre-Buddhist period, kings of Kāsi and Kosala are mentioned as repeatedly struggling for supremacy, and the Kosalan king, Kaṃsa, appears to have eventually succeeded in annexing Kāsi to his kingdom ([1], Vol. ii, p. 403f). Later, Mahākosala, father of Pasenadi, appears to have been in control of Kāsī as he gave it in dowry to Bimbisāra, the king of Magadha ([2], Vol. i, pp. 82–85).

Though many princes and brāhmaṇas from Vārāṇasī used to go to Takkasilā to receive education ([1], Vol. ii, p. 47), there were some educational institutions at Vārāṇasī which were even older than those at Takkasilā ([8], Vol. iii, p. 445f). Kassapa Buddha is said to have been born at Vārāṇasī ([3], Vol. xxv, p. 33). It has been mentioned in the *Dīgha Nikāya* that at the time of the future Metteyya (Sk: Maitreya) Buddha, Vārāṇasī, known as Ketumatī, shall be the capital of Jambudīpa at the head of 84,000 towns, and Saṃkha would be the *cakkavatti* (SK: *cakravarti*) ruler there, but he will renounce the world and will become an arahant under Metteyya ([12], Vol. iii, p. 75f). The Jātakas point out that the kings of Vārāṇasī ruled with justice and equity, and hence, the country enjoyed good government. They are said to have been always on the alert to know their own faults and, with this purpose in view, often went about in the city in disguise ([1], Vol. ii, pp. 1 5).

Rajghat situated on the eastern bank of the Gaṅgā and to the northeast of present Vārāṇasī represents the ancient site of Vārāṇasī. Due to the limitations of the excavations conducted here, it is not possible to identify the various localities mentioned in the Pāli literature, lying either within or outside the settlement. However, a good number of small ancient settlements like Chiurāpura, Umdī, Sirsī, Matigāoṅ, Murdāhan, Machiyān, etc., have been located roughly within a radius of 12–22 kms from the Rājaghat mound [10, 14]. Archaeological information available so far indicates that this settlement sprang up around 800 B.C.E., and in the pre-Northern Black Polished Ware phase (till c. 615 B.C.E.), there is no evidence of any housing activity as no plan of any house could be recovered from the excavations. Perhaps the limited excavations are responsible for this. It also might have been possible that the early settlers here were poorly equipped and did not build houses of durable material. However, one can have some idea about the nature of house constructions from the available fragmentary evidence. The occurrence of postholes as well as some fragments of mud plaster with reed impressions suggests that wooden or bamboo screens plastered with mud were used at Vārāṇasī in making houses ([7], pp. 23 and 74). Floors were made of burnt clay and vertical pits of different types, and *kaccā* drains were used for sanitation. The pits had their beginnings from the early phase of this period, while the drains were noticed to occur from the late phase. It is difficult to compute the exact extent of the settlement during this phase, but it may be said, on the basis of the limited information available from the trenches dug, that the first settlers occupied much smaller area than those of subsequent periods. Between the sixth century B.C.E. and the second century C.E., there was an extension of the area of the settlement and hence the population. The settlement actually appears to have grown rapidly. Rajghat supported the extensive monastic community of Sarnath, although as far as published evidence goes, the monastic remains of Sarnath do not antedate the third century BCE. The original monastic settlement undoubtedly must have come into existence at the Buddha's time. The ramparts, which are datable to the fifth century B.C.E., enclosed an area of about 99 acres and the size of mounds outside the defenses though is not entirely known, but they covered at least 346 acres at the beginning of the Common Era. The ramparts, resting on a wooden platform, measure about 20 m at the base and are preserved to a height of 6 m. On the three sides, they are surrounded by river, and on the fourth side, a moat had to be dug for additional protection. As is the case with some other cities, the magnificence of Rajghat's defenses is not matched by the finds within the enclosed area. Only from the fourth-third century B.C.E. is extensive construction activity evident in the shape of baked brick structures, drains, wells, and tanks. Due to limited excavations, little light can be thrown on the city's functions beyond the usual range of manufacturing and trading activities, as shown by presence of seals, coins, ornaments of semiprecious stones, and a rich variety of terra-cotta figurines. Along the Gaṅgā, an embankment of wooden planks, later remade with clay, possibly served as a platform to facilitate loading and unloading of goods from ships in the harbor. Attention also may be paid to the evidence obtained from a study of the sculptural details on the Amarāvatī *stūpa* which show the city of ancient Vārāṇasī. Inside the city wall, the king's palace is depicted and the people are seen coming in and going out from its main gate ([11], p. 364). From about the beginning of the Common Era till c. 300 C.E., the structures became impressive with elaborate foundations, regular planning, use of tiles for roofing, brick-lined drains, large storage pits for sanitation, a well-paved brick platform, and a well. It seems this was the most prosperous period of Vārāṇasī, though some areas were abandoned. The intensive structural activity of this period continued in the next one (c. 300–700 C.E.) in which Gupta terracottas, boat-shaped bead of a carnelian, and inscribed terra-cotta sealings were discovered, and a decline in structural activity starts after this phase.

Cross-References

- Amaravati
- Dīgha Nikāya
- Jātaka
- Magadha

- ▶ Pasenadi
- ▶ Rājagaha (Pāli)
- ▶ Sāketa
- ▶ Sārnāth
- ▶ Sāvatthī
- ▶ Takkasilā

References

1. Fausböll V (ed) (1977–1897) The Jātaka, 6 vols. Luzac, London
2. Feer ML (ed) (1884–1898) The Saṃyutta Nikāya, 5 vols. Pali Text Society, London
3. Jayawickrama NA (ed) (1974) Buddhavaṃsa and Cariyāpiṭaka, Newth edn. Pali Text Society, London
4. Law BC (1941) India as described in early texts of Buddhism and Jainism. Luzac, London
5. Li R (trans) (1996) The great Tang Dynasty record of the western regions. Numata Center for Buddhist Translation and Research, Berkeley
6. Morris R, Hardy E (eds) (1995–1900) Aṅguttara Nikāya, 5 vols. Pali Text Society, London
7. Narain AK, Roy TN (1976–1978) Excavations at Rajghat: 1957–58, 1960–65, 4 Vols. Banaras Hindu University, Varanasi
8. Norman HC (ed) (1906) The commentary on the Dhammapada, 4 vols. Pali Text Society, London
9. Olderberg H (ed) (1879–1883) The Vinaya Piṭakaṃ, 5 vols. Pali Text Society, London
10. Radhakrishnan S (1964) A report on archaeological explorations in the Varanasi District. Unpublished MA thesis, Banaras Hindu University, Varanasi
11. Rai UN (1965) Prācīna Bhārata Mein Nagara Tathā Nagara Jīvana (in Hindi). Allahabad University Press, Allahabad
12. Rhys Davids TW, Carpenter JE (1890–1911) The Dīgha Nikāya, 3 vols. Pali Text Society, London
13. Rouse WHD (trans) (1902) The Jātaka or the stories of the Buddha's former births, vol 4. Cambridge University Press, Cambridge
14. Shukla MS (1963) Archaeological explorations in the Varanasi district. Unpublished M.A. thesis, Banaras Hindu University, Varanasi
15. Smith H (1916–1918) Sutta-Nipāta commentary being Paramatthajotikā II, 3 vols. Pali Text Society, London
16. Trenckner V, Chalmers R (eds) (1888–1896) The Majjhima Nikāya, 3 vols. Pali Text Society, London

Varṇa

- ▶ Caste (Buddhism)

Vasubandhu

K. T. S. Sarao
Department of Buddhist Studies, University of Delhi, Delhi, India

Definition

One of the most influential Buddhist monks of India who lived during the fourth–fifth centuries C.E. and cofounded the Yogācāra school along with his half brother Asaṅga.

Introduction

Vasubandhu was one of the most important figures in the development of Mahāyāna Buddhism in India. Though he is particularly admired by later Buddhists as cofounder of the Yogācāra school along with his half brother Asaṅga, his pre-Yogācāra works, such as the *Abhidharmakośa* and his auto-commentary (*Abhidharmakoś abhāṣya*) on it, are considered masterpieces. He wrote commentaries on many *sūtras*, works on logic, devotional poetry, works on Abhidharma classifications, as well as original and innovative philosophical treatises. Some of his writings have survived in their original Sanskrit form, but many others, particularly his commentaries, are extant only in their Chinese or Tibetan translations. Vasubandhu was a many-sided thinker, and his personality as it emerges from his works and his biographies shows him as a man who was not only a great genius and a philosopher but also a human being who was filled with great compassion.

Sources on the Biography of Vasubandhu

The most important and the only complete account of the life of Vasubandhu entitled *Posou pandoufa shijuan* (*Biography of Master Vasubandhu*) was compiled into Chinese by

Paramārtha (499–569 C.E.), one of the chief exponents of Yogācāra doctrine in China. It is preserved in the Chinese *Tripiṭaka* and its English translation was published by J. Takakusu in 1904. Apart from this account, *Xiyuji* of Xuanzang (600–664 C.E.) also provides important information about the life of Vasubandhu. Though Paramārtha and Xuanzang are the two most credible authorities for Vasubandhu's life, yet serious discrepancies exist between their accounts. Paramārtha's account not only contains legendary or even mythical elements, but the time sequence of events is also ambiguous and differs greatly in places from the account of Xuanzang's *Xiyuji*. Tibetan historians, Tāranātha and Bu-ston, also give some important information on Vasubandhu's life, but their account further disagrees with Paramārtha and Xuanzang in terms of certain names and events associated with the life of Vasubandhu.

Early Life of Vasubandhu

He was born at Puruṣapura (identified with modern Peshawar, capital of Khyber Pakhtunkhwa in Pakistan) in the state of Gandhāra. Gandhāra is best known today as one of the earliest regions to develop a distinctive form of Buddhist art noted for its Hellenistic influence. According to Tāranātha, Vasubandhu was born one year after his older brother Asaṅga became a Buddhist monk. His father was a brāhmaṇa of the Kauśika *gotra*. According to *Posou pandou fashi zhuan*, his mother's name was Viriñcī. But Bu-ston and Tāranātha mention the name of the mother of Asaṅga and Vasubandhu as Prasannaśīlā. According to these two Tibetan historians, Asaṅga and Vasubandhu were half-brothers, Asaṅga's father being a kṣatriya and Vasubandhu's a brāhmaṇa. Vasubandhu also had a younger brother called Viriñcīvatsa. Vasubandhu's father was a court priest and, according to Tāranātha, was an authority on the *Vedas*. In all probability, he officiated at the court of the Śaka princes of the Śīlada clan, who at that time ruled from Puruṣapura. During the formative years of his life, Vasubandhu may have been introduced by his father not only to the Brāhmaṇical tradition but also to the postulates of classical Nyāya and Vaiśeṣika, both of which had influence on his logical thought.

As a young student, he amazed his teachers with his brilliance and ready wit. According to Paramārtha, Vasubandhu's teacher was called Buddhamitra. The *Hsi-yü-chi*, however, never mentions Buddhamitra and names Manoratha as the teacher of Vasubandhu. At Vasubandhu's time, the dominant Buddhist school in Gāndhāra was the Vaibhāṣika (also called Sarvāstivāda). Vasubandhu entered the Sarvāstivāda order and studied primarily the scholastic system of the Vaibhāṣikas. Initially, he was quite impressed with the *Mahāvibhāṣā*. In time, however, Vasubandhu began to have grave doubts about the validity and relevance of Vaibhāṣika metaphysics. At this time, perhaps through the brilliant teacher Manoratha, he came into contact with the theories of the Sautrāntikas, that group of Buddhists who wished to reject everything that was not the express word of the Buddha and who held the elaborate constructions of the *Vibhāṣā* up to ridicule. That there was a strong Sautrāntika tradition in Puruṣapura is likely in view of the fact that it was the birthplace of that maverick philosopher of the second century, Dharmatrāta. In fact, the most orthodox Vaibhāṣika seat of learning was not in Gandhāra, but in Kashmir, whose masters looked down upon the Gāndhārans as quasi-heretics. Therefore, according to Xuanzang's pupil Pu Kuang, Vasubandhu decided to go to Kashmir disguised as a lunatic to investigate the Vaibhāṣika teachings more deeply. Vasubandhu studied in Kashmir with different teachers for 4 years and then came back to Puruṣapura.

After having returned to his native place, Vasubandhu began to prepare for an enormous project that had been in his mind for some time. At this time, he was unattached to any particular order and lived in a small private house in the center of Puruṣapura. Vasubandhu supported himself by lecturing on Buddhism before the general public, which presumably remunerated him with gifts. According to tradition, during the day, he would lecture on Vaibhāṣika doctrine and in the evening distill the day's lectures into a verse.

When collected together, the 600 plus verses (*kārikās*) gave a thorough summary of the entire system. He entitled this work the *Abhidharmakośa* (Treasury of Abhidharma). According to Paramārtha, Vasubandhu composed the *Abhidharmakośa* at Ayodhyā, but according to Xuanzang, it was composed in the suburbs of Puruṣapura. In the *Abhidharmakośa*, Vasubandhu analyzed and cataloged 75 *dharmas*, the basic factors of experience, for the purposes of attaining Bodhi. He divided them into various categories consisting of 11 types of *rūpāṇi*, i.e., "material forms" (the five sense organs, their corresponding objects, and *avijñapti-rūpa*, i.e., "gesture unrevealing of intent"); *citta* (mind); ten types of *mahābhūmikā*, i.e., "major groundings" (volition, desire, mindfulness, attention, etc.); ten types of *kuśala-mahābhūmikā*, i.e., "advantageous major groundings" (faith, vigor, equanimity, ahiṃsā, serenity, etc.); six types of *kleśa-mahābhūmikā*, i.e., "mental disturbance major groundings" (confusion, carelessness, restlessness, etc.); two types of *akuśala mahābhūmikā*, i.e., "nonadvantageous major groundings" (shamelessness and non-embarrassment); ten types of *paritta-kleśa-mahābhūmikā*, i.e., "secondary mental disturbance major groundings" (anger, enmity, envy, conceit, etc.); eight types of *aniyata-mahābhūmikā*, i.e., "indeterminate major groundings" (remorse, arrogance, aversion, doubt, torpor, etc.); 14 types of *citta-viprayukta-saṃskāra-dharmāḥ*, i.e., "embodied conditioning disassociated from mind" (life force, birth, decay, impermanence, etc.); and three types of *asaṃskṛta-dharmāḥ*, i.e., "unconditioned *dharmas*" (spatiality, cessation through understanding, and cessation without understanding). Not only were the definitions and interrelations of these 75 dharmas analyzed in the *Abhidharmakośa* but their karmic qualities also examined. Besides, Vasubandhu also elaborated upon causal theories, cosmology, practices of meditation, theories of perception, karma, rebirth, and the characteristics of an Enlightened Being in this text.

As the *Abhidharmakośa* was an eloquent summary of the purport of the *Mahāvibhāṣā*, the Kashmiri Sarvāstivādins are reported to have rejoiced to see in it all their doctrines so well propounded. Accordingly, they requested Vasubandhu to write a prose commentary (*bhāṣya*) on it. However, it seems that after having written the *Abhidharmakośa*, Vasubandhu began to have second thoughts about the Vaibhāṣika teachings. As a consequence, it is said, Vasubandhu prepared the *Abhidharmakośabhāṣya*. But as it contained a thoroughgoing critique of Vaibhāṣika dogmatics from a Sautrāntika viewpoint, the Kashmiri Sarvāstivādins soon realized, to their great disappointment, that the *Abhidharmakośabhāṣya* in fact refuted many Sarvāstivāda theories and upheld the doctrines of the Sautrāntika school. One major point that created bad blood between the Vaibhāṣikas and the Sautrāntikas was concerning the status and nature of the dharmas. The Vaibhāṣikas held that the dharmas exist in the past and future as well as the present. On the other hand, the Sautrāntikas held the view that they are discrete, particular moments only existing at the present moment in which they discharge causal efficacy. The Vaibhāṣikas wrote several treatises attempting to refute Vasubandhu's critiques.

Conversion to Mahāyāna

In the years directly following the composition of the *Abhidharmakośabhāṣya*, Vasubandhu seems to have spent much time in traveling from place to place. Finally, after having spent some time at Śākala/Śāgala (modern Sialkot in Pakistan), he shifted along with his teachers Buddhamitra and Manoratha to Ayodhyā (now located in Uttar Pradesh, northern India), a city far removed from Kashmir. According to *Posou pandou fashi zhuan*, Vasubandhu, now proud of the fame he had acquired, clung faithfully to the Hīnayāna doctrine in which he was well versed and, having no faith in the Mahāyāna, denied that it was the teaching of the Buddha. Vasubandhu had up to this time but little regard for the Yogācāra treatises of his elder brother. He had perhaps seen the voluminous *Yogācārabhūmi* compiled by Asaṅga, which may have simply repelled him by its bulk. According to Bu-ston, he is reported to have said, "Alas, Asaṅga, residing in the forest, has practiced meditation for 12 years. Without having attained anything by this meditation, he has founded a system, so difficult and burdensome, that it can be carried only by an elephant." Asaṅga heard about this attitude of his brother and feared that Vasubandhu would use his great intellectual gifts to undermine the Mahāyāna. By feigning illness, he was able to summon his younger brother to Puruṣapura, where he lived. However, Xuanzang differs with some of these details and the place provided by Paramārtha regarding Vasubandhu's conversion. According to the *Xiyuji*, the conversion of Vasubandhu took place at Ayodhyā. At the rendezvous, Vasubandhu asked Asaṅga to explain the Mahāyāna teaching to him, whereupon he immediately realized the supremacy of Mahāyāna thought. After further study, he is said to have equaled his brother in the depth of realization. Deeply ashamed of his former abuse of the Mahāyāna, Vasubandhu wanted to cut out his tongue, but refrained from doing so when Asaṅga told him to use it for the cause of Mahāyāna. Vasubandhu regarded the study of the enormous *Śatasāhasrikāprajñā-pāramitā-sūtra* as of utmost importance. In view of the fact that they were the texts that converted him to Mahāyāna, Vasubandhu's commentaries on the *Akṣayamatinirdeśa-sūtra* and the *Daśabhūmika* may have been his earliest Mahāyāna works. These were followed by a series of commentaries on other Mahāyāna *sūtras* and treatises, including the *Avataṃsakasūtra*, *Nirvāṇasūtra*, *Vimalakīrtinirdeśasūtra*, and *Śrīmālādevīsūtra*. He himself composed a treatise on *vijñaptimātra* (cognition only) theory and commented on the *Mahāyānasaṃgraha*, *Triratna-gotra*, *Amṛtamukha*, and other Mahāyāna treatises. According to the Tibetan biographers, his favorite *sūtra* was either the *Śatasāhasrikāprajñā-pāramitā-sūtra* or the *Aṣṭasāhasrikā*. Considering that these texts reveal the most profound insights into Mahāyāna thinking, it is not surprising that Vasubandhu liked them. Since the output of Vasubandhu's Mahāyāna works is huge, he was in all probability writing new treatises every year. According to *Posou pandou fashi zhuan*, Vasubandhu engaged in his literary activity on behalf of the Mahāyāna after Asaṅga's death. Xuanzang, however, tells a strange story that suggests that Vasubandhu died before Asaṅga.

Intellectual Debates

With the composition of the *Abhidharmakośa*, Vasubandhu came to enjoy the patronage and favor of two Gupta rulers, Vikramāditya and his heir Bālāditya. Vikrmāditya is identified either with Purugupta or Skandagupta (ruled circa 455–467 C.E.) and Bālāditya with Narasiṃhagupta (ruled circa 467–473 C.E.). The first important intellectual debate which Vasubandhu had was with Vasurāta. Vasurāta was a grammarian and the husband of the younger sister of Bālāditya. It was Bālāditya who had challenged Vasubandhu to a debate. Vasubandhu was able to defeat him successfully. Another well-known intellectual encounter which Vasubandhu had was with Sāṃkhyas. While Vasubandhu was away, his old master Buddhamitra was defeated in a debate at Ayodhyā by Vindhyavāsin. When Vasubandhu came to know of it, he was enraged and subsequently trounced the Sāṃkhyas both in debate and in a treatise the *Paramārthasaptatikā*. Candragupta II rewarded him with 300,000 gold coins for his victory over the Sāṃkhyas. Vasubandhu made use of this money to build three monasteries, one for the Mahāyānists, another one for his old colleagues the Sarvāstivādins, and a third for the nuns. Refutation of Vaiśeṣika and Sāṃkhya theories had been presented by Vasubandhu already in the *Abhidharmakośa*, but it was perhaps from this point onward that Vasubandhu was regarded as a philosopher whose views could not be lightly challenged. Saṃghabhadra, a Sarvāstivada scholar from Kashmir, also once challenged Vasubandhu regarding the *Abhidharmakośa*. He composed two treatises, one consisting of 10,000 verses and another of 120,000 verses. According to Xuanzang, it took 12 years for Saṃghabhadra to finish the two works. He challenged Vasubandhu to a debate, but Vasubandhu refused, saying, "I am already old, so I will let you say what you wish. Long ago, this work of mine destroyed the Vaibhāṣika (i.e., the Sarvāstivāda) doctrines. There is no need now of confronting you… Wise men will know which of us is right and which one is wrong."

Date of Vasubandhu

The date of Vasubandhu has posed a problem for historians. According to Paramārtha, Vasubandhu lived 900 years after the Mahāparinirvāṇa of the Buddha. At another place, Paramārtha also mentions the figure of 1,100. Xuanzang and his disciples, respectively, mention that Vasubandhu lived 1,000 and 900 years after the Mahāparinirvāṇa of the Buddha. Now, though it is generally believed that the Mahāparinirvāṇa of the Buddha took place within few years of 400 B.C.E., some scholars are still hesitant to accept this date. This has led to different scholars proposing different dates for Vasubandhu. Noel Péri and Shīo Benkyō give as Vasubandhu's dates the years 270–350 C.E. Steven Anacker proposes his date as 316–396 C.E.; Ui Hakuju places him in the fourth century (320–400 C.E.). Takakusu Junjirō and Kimura Taiken gave 420–500, Wogihara Unrai gives 390–470 C.E., and Hikata Ryūshō gives 400–480 C.E. Erich Frauwallner suggests that there were two Vasubandhus and hence two different dates. According to him, Vasubandhu the elder lived between about 320 and 380 C.E. and Vasubandhu the younger between around 400 and 480 C.E. However, this hypothesis of two Vasubandhus is no longer tenable in current scholarship as many of the early Chinese documents used by Frauwallner are of spurious nature, and thus, their testimony cannot be accepted.

Writings of Vasubandhu

Vasubandhu is said to have been the author of 1,000 works, 500 in the Hīnayāna tradition and 500 Mahāyāna treatises. But only 47 works of Vasubandhu are extant, 9 of which survive in the Sanskrit original, 27 in Chinese translation, and 33 in Tibetan translation. The *Abhidharmakośa* is the most voluminous among Vasubandhu's independent expositions. It attained the status of a primary textbook to be studied by all students of the tradition in the Northern Buddhist countries, including Tibet. As pointed out above, the *Abhidharmakośa* pictures the Buddhist Path to Enlightenment through the categorization and analysis of the 75 dharmas.

Vasubandhu's *Karmasiddhi* (Establishing Karma) is a short, quasi-Hīnayāna treatise colored, as is the *Abhidharmakośa*, by Sautrāntika leanings. His *Pañcaskandhaprakaraṇa* (Exposition on the Five Aggregates) discusses most of the subjects taken up in the *Abhidharmakośa*. In cataloging and categorization of dharmas in the *Pañcaskandhaprakaraṇa*, the dharmas are a bit different than the *Abhidharmakośa*. Moreover, whereas the *Abhidharmakośa* talks about 75 dharmas, not only have several dharmas been added, but many of the original 75 have been dropped in the *Pañcaskandhaprakaraṇa*.

In his *Karmasiddhiprakaraṇa* (Exposition on Establishing Karma), Vasubandhu challenged the views of those who held that dharmas are anything other than being momentary. The doctrine of momentariness (*kṣanikavāda*) perceived consciousness as a causal sequence of moments in which each moment is caused by its immediate predecessor. However, he felt that this theory could not explain certain categories of continuity. For instance, *kṣanikavāda* did not offer any satisfactory explanation for the reemergence of a consciousness stream after having been interrupted in deep sleep. Similarly, continuity from one life to the next could not be explained satisfactorily by this theory. To solve such inconsistencies, Vasubandhu introduced the Yogācāra notion of the *ālaya vijñāna* (storehouse consciousness). Through this concept, he explained that the seed (*bīja*) of a previous experience is stored subliminally and released into a new experience. In this way, Vasubandhu not only explained continuity between two separate moments of consciousness, but he also provided a quasi-causal explanation for the functioning of karmic retribution. In other words, Vasubandhu's *ālaya vijñāna* provided an explanation as to how an action performed at one time could produce its result at another time. This concept also did away with the necessity of a permanent ātman as the doer and recipient of karma since, like a stream, it is continuously changing with new conditions from moment to moment.

From the Yogācāra point of view, the most important of Vasubandhu's works are the *Viṃśatikā* (20 Verses), *Triṃśikā* (30 Verses), and *Trisvabhāvanirdeśa* (Exposition on the Three Natures). According to tradition, the *Trisvabhāvanirdeśa* was reputedly his last treatise, and his *Viṃśatikā* and *Triṃśikā* were written near the end of his life, though there is no actual evidence to support this order. Despite the fact that all these three texts are very concise and the *Trisvabhāvanirdeśa* was not even known in China (and is never read in Tibet despite being part of Tibetan canon), they form a kind of troika and represent Vasubandhu's final accomplishment as a Yogācāra-Vijñānavāda teacher.

The *Viṃśatikā* is perhaps the most original and philosophically interesting treatise of Vasubandhu. Vasubandhu devotes a major portion of this text in dealing with the Realist objections against Yogācāra. To the Realist position that external things must exist because they are consistently located in space as well as time, Vasubandhu responds by saying that objects also appear to have spatial and temporal qualities in dreams, whereas nothing "external" is present in the dreams. This means that the appearance of cognitive objects does not require an actual object external to the consciousness cognizing it. Vasubandhu, however, points out that without the consciousness nothing whatsoever can be apprehended. Therefore, it is consciousness that is the necessary condition and not an external object. Vasubandhu does not deny that cognitive objects exist. However, what he denies is that such cognitive objects have external reference points. From the Yogācāra point of view, what one believes to be external objects are actually nothing more than mental projections. Thus, whatever one thinks about, knows, experiences, or conceptualizes occurs to one only in one's consciousness and nowhere else. In other words, according to Vasubandhu, cognition takes place only in consciousness and nowhere else. Thus, everything that one knows is acquired through sensory experience. One is fooled by consciousness into believing that those things which one perceives and appropriates within consciousness are actually outside one's cognitive sphere. To the Realist objection that subjective wishes do not determine objective realities, Vasubandhu replies that due to collective karma, groups give rise to common misperceptions. He pointed out that it is the result of a person's own karma that determines the type of situation in which that person would be born. Thus, Vasubandhu points out that how people see things is shaped by previous experience, and since experience is inter-subjective, people gather in groups that see things the way they do. To another Realist objection that the objective world functions by determinate causal principles, Vasubandhu points out that the appearance of causal efficacy also occurs in dreams. Thus, people's conscious "dreams" can have causal efficacy.

The *Triṃśikā*, which became the basic text of the Faxiang (Japanese Hossoo) school, is one of Vasubandhu's most mature works. Through concise verses, he sums up his doctrine of *vijñapti-mātra* (cognition only) by explaining Yogācāra theories of eight consciousnesses, three natures, and the five-step path to Enlightenment. The eight types of consciousness are the five sense consciousnesses, the empirical consciousness (*mano-vijñāna*), a self-aggrandizing mentality (*manas*), and the *ālaya-vijñāna.* Vasubandhu describes and explains how each of these can be extinguished through *āśraya-paravṛtti*, i.e., through the overturning of the very basis of these eight types of consciousness. This overturning, i.e., achievement of the Bodhi, gradually takes place through the five-step path such that consciousness *(vijñāna)* is transformed into unmediated cognition *(jñāna)*. According to the theory of three natures, there are three cognitive realms at play: the delusional cognitively constructed realm, which is intrinsically unreal; the realm of causal dependency; and the perfectional realm which is intrinsically "empty." To Vasubandhu, Buddhism is a method of cleansing the stream of consciousness from "contaminations" and "defilements."

The *Foxinglun* (Treatise on Buddha Nature) exerted great influence on Sino-Japanese Buddhism by propounding the concept of tathāgatagarbha (Buddha Nature). The *Vādavidhi* (A Method for Argumentation) is another important text attributed to Vasubandhu. Though this text is not strictly speaking a "logic" text and does not make any distinction between techniques of debate and logic as such, still its importance in the field of logic cannot be overlooked. It not only provides information on the state of Buddhist logic prior to Dignāga but also paves the way for the revolutionary contribution of Dignāga and Dharmakīrti in the field of logic. Though not many details on the meditative career of Vasubandhu are available, his *Madhyāntavibhāgabhāṣya* (Commentary on the Separation of the Middle from Extremes) points to his keen interest in the techniques of meditation.

Vasubandhu's commentaries on *sūtras* and *śā stras* are by no means less important than the above-mentioned independent treatises. He wrote commentaries on three treatises: the *Madhyāntavibhāga* (Discrimination between the Middle and the Extremes), *Mahāyānasūtrālaṃkāra* (Ornament of the Mahāyāna Sūtras), and *Dharmadharmatāvibhāga/Dharmadharmtāvibhaṅga* (Discrimination between Existence and Essence). All these three treatises are important texts of the Yogācāra school and are ascribed to Asaṅga's teacher Maitreya. Vasubandhu also composed a commentary on Asaṅga's *Mahāyānasaṃgraha* (Compendium of Mahāyāna). It is the first methodical presentation of the doctrines of Yogācāra-Vijñānavāda. Vasubandhu's *Sukhāvativyūhasūtranirdeśa* (Commentary on the Sukhāvativyūha Sūtra) is another important text. This text became a fundamental treatise of the Pure Land faith in China and Japan. The Indian Yogācāra-Vijñānavāda is represented in China by three schools, and the development of all these schools is credited to the works of Vasubandhu. The first of these schools, called the Dilun school (which was established in the first half of the sixth century C.E.), took his *Daś abhūmikasūtranirdeśa* (Commentary on the Daśabhūmika Sūtra) as its basic text. The second, the Shelun School which originated in the second half of the sixth century C.E., developed around a translation of the *Mahāyānasaṃgraha* done by Paramārtha. The third school, known as the Faxiang school (founded by Xuanzang and his disciple Kuiji in the seventh century), adopted the *Triṃśikā* as its basic text.

Later in life, Vasubandhu went so far ahead with his contemplative exercises that he even refused to engage in a debate with his worthy opponent Saṃghabhadra. He died at the age of 80. Paramārtha says that he died at Ayodhyā, whereas Bu-ston says that his death took place in the northern frontier countries, which he calls "Nepal." In recognition of his contribution and achievements as a Mahāyāna teacher, he came to be reverently called a bodhisattva in various traditions from India to China. In fact, some go to the extent of even calling him the "second Buddha." As rightly pointed out in Bu-ston, he "was possessed of the wealth (*vasu*) of the Highest wisdom and, having propagated the Doctrine out of mercy, had become the friend (*bandhu*) of the living beings."

Cross-References

- Abhidharma (Theravāda)
- Ālaya-vijñāna
- Asaṅga
- Ātman
- Gandhara
- Mahāyāna
- Sautrāntika
- Vaibhāṣika
- Xuanzang (Hieun-Tsang)
- Yogācāra

References

1. Anacker S (1984) Seven works of Vasubandhu. Motilal Banarsidass, Delhi
2. de la Vallée Poussin L (trans) (1971) L'Abhidharmakośa de Vasubandhu, 6 vols, reprint, Bruxelles. Its English translation entitled Abhidharma Kośa Bhāṣyam by Leo Pruden, 4 vols. Asian Humanities Press, Berkeley, 1988–1990

3. Duerlinger J (2003) Indian Buddhist theories of Person: Vasubandhu's refutation of the theory of a self. Routledge Curzon, London
4. Frauwallner E (1951) On the date of the Buddhist master of the law, Vasubandhu. IsMeo, Rome
5. Hall BC (1986) The meaning of Vijñapti in Vasubandhu's concept of mind. J Intl Assoc Buddh Stud 9:7–23
6. Ryūshō H (1956) A reconsideration on the date of Vasubandhu. Bull Fac Kyushu Univ 4:53–74
7. Jaini PS (1958) On the theory of two Vasubandhus. Bull Sch Orient Afr Stud 21:48–53
8. Kaplan S (1990) A Holographic Alternative to a Traditional Yogācāra Simile: An Analysis of Vasubandhu's Trisvabhāva Doctrine. Eastern Buddhist 23:56–78
9. Kochumuttom T (1982) A Buddhist doctrine of experience: a new translation and interpretation of the works of Vasubandhu the Yogācārin. Motilal Banarsidass, Delhi
10. Kritzer R (1993) Vasubandhu on samapratyaya vijñānamam. J Intl Assoc Buddh Stud 16/1:24–55
11. Chimpa L, Chattopadhyaya A (trans) (1970) Tāranātha's history of Buddhism in India. Indian Institute of Advanced Study, Simla
12. Lévi S (1932) Un système de philosophie bouddhique: Matériaux pour l'étude du système Vijñaptimātra, Paris: Bibliothèque de l'École des Hautes Études, fasc. 260
13. Lusthaus D (2000) Buddhist phenomenology: a philosophical investigation of Yogācāra Buddhism and the Ch'eng wei shih lun. Curzon, London
14. Obermiller E (trans) (1986) The history of Buddhism in India and Tibet by Bu-Ston, 2nd rev. edn. Sri Satguru Publications, Delhi (First edition, Heidelberg: Harrassowitz, 1931–1932)
15. Péri N (1911) Á Propos de la Date de Vasubandhu. Bulletin de l'Ecole Francaise d'Extrême-Orient XI:339–390
16. Takakusu J (1905) A study of Paramārtha's life of Vasubandhu and the date of Vasubandhu. J Roy Asiat Soc 37:33–53
17. Thát LM (2006) The philosophy of Vasubandhu. Vietnam Buddhist University, Ho Chi Minh City
18. Tola F, Dragonetti C (eds) (1983) The Trisvabhāvakārikā of Vasubandhu. J Indian Philos 11:225–266
19. Waldron WS (2003) The Buddhist unconsciousness: the Ālaya-Vijñāna in the context of Indian Buddhist thought. Routledge Curzon, London
20. Yamada I (1977) Vijñaptimātratā of Vasubandhu. J Roy Asiat Soc 109:158–176

Vedic Religion – Upavasatha

► Uposatha

Vedisāgiri

► Sāñcī

Vegetarianism (Buddhism)

K. T. S. Sarao
Department of Buddhist Studies, University of Delhi, Delhi, India

Definition

The practice of subsisting primarily on plant-based diets.

Views on vegetarianism vary from sect to sect in Buddhism. The first precept in Buddhism is normally translated as "I undertake the precept to refrain from taking life." Some sects view this as implying that they should not eat meat whereas others feel that this is not so. Thus, in Theravāda, monks are allowed to eat meat, Mahāyāna generally recommends a vegetarian diet, and in Vajrayāna, meat eating is not always prohibited. In most Buddhist sects, one may adopt vegetarianism if one so desires, but it is not regarded a skillful practice to speak negatively of another person for eating meat.

According to the Theravādin scriptures, the Buddha taught "never to destroy the life of any living creature, however tiny it might be" ([7], Vol. xvii, p. 30, Vol. xx, p. 128) even "for the sake of sustaining life" ([15], Vol. iv, p. 129). A monk is allowed to gratefully accept "what has been put in his alms bowl" ([7], Vol. iii, p. 155), and hence Theravāda allows a monk to accept meat except that when he has (a) seen, (b) heard, or (c) suspected that the meat is especially acquired for him by killing an animal ([4], Vol. i, p. 298; [5], Vol. ii, p. 33). This rule is called the *Rule of Tikoṭiparisuddha* (*Pure in Three Ways*). Theravāda does not allow the use of raw meat ([9], Vol. ii, p. 5), except in case of sickness when "raw flesh and blood could be used" ([7], Vol. xvii, p. 49). The cooking and eating of the remains of the kills of lions, tigers, hyenas, and wolves are also allowed in Theravāda to be eaten by the monks ([4], Vol. i, p. 98). Indeed, fish and meat are mentioned among the delicate foods (*pāṇitabhojanīya*) which a monk who is ill is allowed to eat (Pātimokkha, Pacittiya Dhamma No.33). However, the meat of man, elephant, horse, dog, snake, lion, tiger, leopard, bear, and hyena is forbidden to be eaten by the monks due to a variety of reasons involved in their eating ([7], Vol. xvii, p. 85). In the Pāli Tipiṭaka, Buddha explicitly declared meat eating to be karma neutral and once explicitly refused suggestion by Devadatta to institute vegetarianism in the monks' Vinaya ([4], Vol. i, p. 297ff; [7], Vol. xi, p. 196ff). Thus, he pointed out that purity did not depend upon food ([14], p. 1.80), but on restraint over such bodily, mental, and moral conduct as could defile a man ([8], Vol. i, p. 221). The Buddha's advice on meat eating was directed specifically to monks and nuns, and the Tipiṭaka does not contain the Buddha's comments or advice to lay followers regarding meat eating. The distinction is rather crucial as monks and nuns beg for alms, eating leftover food of a householder. They are expected to eat whatever is given to them, including meat. However, in Theravāda Buddhism, avoiding meat eating for the purpose of cultivation of *mettā* (loving kindness) is also seen to be in accord with the teachings of the Buddha.

In relation to the issue of vegetarianism in Buddhism, also arises the question as to whether the Buddha died as a result of eating pork (which was putrid and, thus, poisoned the Buddha) at the home of one of his followers called Cunda ([9], Vol. ii, pp. 127–127), as claimed by some scholars, or from a poisonous mushroom, as asserted by others. This controversy has arisen from the different interpretations of the term *sūkaramaddava* which formed part of the Buddha's last meal. If some translate it as "pork," there are others who feel it simply means some sort of vegetable, mushroom, or truffles (See [11], p. 147). Interestingly, the word for pork in Pāli Tipiṭaka is mentioned as *sūkaramaṃsa* ([8], Vol. iii, p. 49).

The view of meat eating is sharply criticized and contradicted by some of the Mahāyāna Sūtras, also purporting to be the spoken words of the Buddha. They categorically assert that meat eating is contrary to the spirit and intent of the first precept since it makes one an accessory to the slaying of animals and therefore contravenes the compassionate concern for all life that lies at the core of Buddhism. The Mahāyāna Sūtras that consider meat eating as undesirable and karmically unwholesome include the *Nirvāṇa Sūtra*, the *Śūraṅgama Sūtra*, the *Brahmajāla Sūtra*, *Mahāparinirvāṇa Sūtra*, the *Aṅgulimāliya Sūtra*, the *Mahāmegha Sūtra*, the *Laṅkāvatāra Sūtra*, and the *Karma Sūtra*. Thus, according to the *Laṅkāvatāra Sūtra*, meat eating "in any form, in any manner, and in any place, is unconditionally and once, for all, prohibited for all" ([13], p. 156). Similarly, *Śūraṅgama Sūtra* asks, "how can those who eat the flesh of beings be called the disciples of Shakya?" ([12], Vol. vi, pp. 20–21). The *Śikṣā-Samuccaya* goes even further and points out that "Flesh free from the three objections, not prepared, unasked, unsolicited, there is none: therefore one should not eat flesh" ([1], p. 131).

The Vajrayāna position is that it is not necessary to be vegetarian, and vegetarianism among the Himalayan Buddhists is rare.

Cross-References

- ▶ Mahāyāna
- ▶ Metta
- ▶ The Healing Buddha
- ▶ Theravāda
- ▶ Tipiṭaka
- ▶ Vajrayāna (Buddhism)

References

1. Bendall C, Rouse WHD (trans) (1922) Śikshā-Samuccaya: a compendium of Buddhist doctrine compiled by Śāntideva. John Murray, London
2. Bodhipaksa (2004) Vegetarianism. Windhorse Publications, Cambridge
3. Chapple CK (1993) Nonviolence to animals, earth and self in Asian traditions. SUNY Press, Albany
4. Horner IB (trans) (1938–1966) The book of the discipline, reprints. Pali Text Society, London

5. Horner IB (trans) (1954–1959) The book of middle length sayings, 3 vols. Pali Text Society, London
6. Kapleau P (1986) To cherish all life. Zen Center, Rochester
7. Max Muller F (ed) (1973) The sacred books of the east, 50 vols, reprint. Motilal Banarasidass, Delhi
8. Morris R, Hardy E (eds) (1885–1900) The Aṅguttara Nikāya, 5 vols. Pali Text Society, London
9. Rhys Davids TW, Carpenter JE (eds) (1890–1911) The Dīgha Nikāya. Pali Text Society, London
10. Rhys Davids TW, Rhys Davids CAF (trans) (1899–1957) Dialogues of the Buddha, reprints, 3 vols. Sacred Books of the Buddhists, London
11. Sarao KTS (2010) Origin and nature of ancient Indian Buddhism, 3rd rev. edn. Munshiram Manoharlal, New Delhi
12. (2009) The Śūraṅgama Sūtra: a new translation with excerpts from the commentary by the venerable master Hsüan Hua. Buddhist Text Translation Society, Talmage
13. Suzuki DT (trans) (1932) The Laṅkāvatāra Sūtra. George Routledge & Son, London
14. Trenckner V, Chalmers R (eds) (1888–1896) The Majjhima Nikāya, 3 vols. Pali Text Society, London
15. Woodward FL, Hare EM (trans) (1955–1970) The book of gradual saying, reprints. Pali Text Society, London

Vehicles in Buddhism

Anand Singh
School of Buddhist Studies and Civilization, Gautam Buddha University, Greater Noida, UP, India
Institute of Management Sciences, University of Lucknow, Lucknow, UP, India

Synonyms

Yānas

Definition

Buddhism can be divided into three *Yānas* (vehicles) – Theravāda or Hīnayāna, Mahāyāna, and Vajrayāna. Theravāda is generally considered to be the earliest vehicle of Buddhism. Mahāyāna was a later development, though its traces have been found in the teachings of the Buddha. The third vehicle is Vajrayāna which is also known as Mantrayāna and Sahajayāna. This school is also influenced by *tantric* tradition [8].

Theravāda

Hīnayāna or Theravāda or Sthaviravādins are the oldest and the most orthodox vehicle of Buddhism. It adopted Pāli as its sacred language. This vehicle admits human character of the Buddha, though possesses certain superhuman qualities. The Buddha as a human being can attain *Nibbāna*, and he was subject to human frailties through his *yogic* power that can prevent everyday rigidities [1]. Theravādins were divided into eleven sects – Theravāda or Arya-sthavira-nikaya, Mahiśāsaka, Dharmagupta, Sarvāstivāda, Kasyapiya, Sankantika (Sautantrika), Vātsiputriya, Saṃmittiya, Dharmottriya, Bhadrayaniya, and Shan-nagrika [10].

Theravādins believe that all worldly phenomena are subject to three attributes – *anitya* (impermanent and transient), *dukkha* (suffering), and *anattā* (nonself). All compounded things have been made of *nāma* (nonmaterial) and *rūpa* (material). These are consistent of nothing but of five constituents (*skandhas*) as *rūpa*, the material quality, and other four nonmaterial qualities: *vedanā* (sensation), *saṃjnā* (perception), *saṃkhāras* (mental formatives), and *vijñāna* (consciousness). These elements have also been classified into 12 organs and object of senses (*ayatanā*) and 18 *dhātus* [3].

The Vaibhasikas and the Sautantrikas are two important schools of Philosophy of Hīnayāna. The Vaibhasikas are believed in *vibhasas* or commentaries and accept existence of phenomenal object on direct perception (*pratakshya*). Asvaghosa, Dharmottara, Dharmatrata, Vasumitra, Gunaprabha, and Buddhadeva were prominent teachers of this school. Vasubandhu was the most influential teacher of this school who composed *Abhidharma-kośa* and its commentaries. Vaibhasikas accept that external objects can be perceived. If external objects have not been perceived, they could not be inferred [3]. The Sautāntrika school was founded by Kumārlabhadda which emphasizes upon sūtras rather than commentaries or *vibhāṣas*. It accepts phenomenal objects as only appearances (*prajñapti*), the existence of which could be inferred only by inference. It also accepts transference of the *skandhamatras* from one existence to another but asserts that it will be ceased in *Nibbāna*. They believe in reality not only of the mind but also of the external objects. Without supposition of external objects, it is not possible to explain even the illusory appearance of external objects [3].

The earliest Pāli literature was *Buddhavacana*, the discourses delivered by the Buddha. Most of early literature was composed in Pāli language, the language through which the Buddha delivered his discourses and doctrines. The Pāli literature has been first time written in the form of *piṭakas* – *Vinaya*, *Sutta*, and *Abhidhamma* – in Sri Lanka in the first century B.C.E. during the reign of Vaṭṭagāmiṇi. Later on various *aṭṭhakathās* were written on these literatures in Pali, Sinhalese, and Sanskrit language. The scholars like Buddhaghosa, Buddhadatta, and Dhammapāla did their commendable work to write their commentaries [7].

The *Vinaya Piṭaka* deals with rules and regulations related to saṃgha and for the daily lives of monks and nuns. It consists of (1) *Sutta Vibhanga*, (2) *Khandhakas*, (3) *Parivara*, and (4) *Patimokkha*. The *Sutta Vibhanga* is further divided into *Parajika* and *Pacitiya*. Further *Khandhakas* have been divided into Mahāvagga and Cullavagga [7]. The *Sutta Pitaka* consists of discourses as a main source for the doctrine of the Buddha as expounded in arguments and dialogues. The *Sutta Pitaka* is divided into five *Nikāyas*: (1) *Digha Nikāya*, (2) *Majjhima Nikāya*, (3) *Samyutta Nikāya*, (4) *Aṅguttara Nikāya*, and (5) *Khuddaka Nikāya* [7]. The third *pitaka* is *Abhidhamma Pitaka* which deals with philosophy and metaphysics. It is dominantly composed in the form of questions and answers. It contains seven parts: (1) *Dhammasangini*, (2) *Vibhanga*, (3) *Kathavatthu*, (4) *Puggalapannatti*, (5) *Dhatukatha*, (6) *Yamaka*, and (7) *Patthana* [7].

Mahāyāna

Mahāyāna is the second important vehicle of Buddhism and can seek its origin from Mahāsanghikas who seceded from Theravādins in the Second Buddhist Council [1]. The Mahāsanghikas were divided into Mahāsanghika, Gokulika, Pannattivāda, Bahusrutiya, Chetiyavada, Ekvyaharika, and Lokottaravada. Siddhatthika, Rajagirika, Aparśaila, Purvaśaila, etc., are also important sects of Mahāyāna [4]. The real development of Mahāyāna took place in the Andhra region in Amaravati and Nagarjunakonda. The origin of Mahāyāna is also associated with Nāgārjuna who belonged to Andhra region [6]. Mahāyāna is embedded with *śunyata* (universal emptiness); the plurality of the Buddha and bodhisattvas and their *pāramitās* (virtues); and the worship of the Buddhas, bodhisattvas, and other gods, goddesses, and *dharinis*. Sanskrit was their main language. Mahāyāna develops the *trikāya* doctrine.

Mahāyāna developed the *trikāya* doctrine in which the Buddha has been represented into three forms. According to the *trikāya* doctrine, the rūpa or *nirmānakāyā* (human body) of the Buddha has been different from his *sambhogakāyā* (body with *mahāpurushalakkhana*) and *dharmakāyā* (cosmic body) [4]. The bodhisattva in Mahāyāna was further the development of the bodhisattva concept of Theravāda which believes that only Gautama Buddha was born as the bodhisattva in his previous existences. Mahāyāna says that the worldly beings by adhering to *bodhichitta* and *pāramitas* can become the Buddha. One should not desire to his own emancipation unless all others have achieved it. It says that it is not possible to attain all virtue perfections (*pāramitas*) in one life, but in several existences, a bodhisattva can perfect himself in six *pāramitas*: *dāna* (charity), *śila* (observance of precepts), *kshanti* (forbearance), *virya* (energy), *dhyāna* (meditation), and *prajna* (knowledge). By this method he crosses all ten *bhumis* (*dusbhumi*) to attain *bodhi* [4].

Mahāyāna philosophy was divided into Madhyamika and Yogacāra. Nāgārjuna was the founder of Madhyamika doctrine of *śunyata*. Nāgārjuna in his *Madhyamika Sastra* does not deny reality as interpreted by some scholars, but it is only the apparent phenomenal world. Behind this phenomenal world, there is reality which is not describable by any character, mental or nonmental, that we perceive. Being devoid of phenomenal character, it is called *śunya*. Yogacāra is the second school of philosophy, and Maitreyanātha was its founder. It admits all attributes of Madhyamikas except unreality of *citta* (mind). If the mind is unreal, then all reasoning and thinking will be false, and Madhyamikas could not establish their own arguments. The mind, consisting of a stream of different kinds of ideas, is the only reality. Things that appear to be outside the mind, body, as well as other objects are merely ideas of the mind. Yogacāra has also been known as Vijnanavada because it admits that there is only one kind of reality which is of the nature of consciousness, and objects which appear to be material or external to consciousness are really ideas or states of consciousness. It is also known as subjective idealism because existence of an object perceived is not different from the subject or the perceived mind [3].

Mahāyāna believed in dharma-*śunyata* or *tathata* and also speculated about the physical appearance of the Buddha. He could be identical with *dharma-śunyata* and a *tathagata* whose body could be *dharmakāyā*. Mahāyāna also believed that the Buddha appeared as *nirmānakāyā* for spiritually guiding the mortal beings. The metaphysical conception of the Buddha's body as *dharmakāyā* is a further step in the beginning of image worship in Buddhism. In Hinayāna, the bodhisattva means all the previous existence of the Buddha. Here as the Buddha, he lived life of an average being acquiring merits and avoiding demerits as far as possible. But Mahāyāna upheld the view that individuals can cherish the intention of becoming the bodhisattva. They also believe that the development of the bodhisattva should include the condition that one should dedicate his life in several existences to the service of others and should not care to attain his bodhisattvahood.

Mahāyāna accepts all Hinayāna literature, and besides it they have produced voluminous literature. The *Prajnaparamita Sutra* is supposed to be the most important literature of Mahāyāna, written in several versions: large, medium, and small. The *Sukhavati-vyuha*, *Saddharmapundarika Sūtra*, and *Dasabhumi Sūtra* are other important literatures of Mahāyāna. The *Prajnaparamitas*, *Saddharmapundarika*, *Lankavatara*, and *Gandavyuha* are supposed to be products of the first two centuries of the Christian Era [4]. These *sūtras* came early in the history of Mahāyāna and were followed by the *śāstras* of *ācaryas*. The exegesis of *sūtras* by the *ācaryas* was not a development of a particular concept but a compendium of inter-relating and systematizing *sūtras*. The best example of it is *Surangama Sūtra*, though it is termed a sūtra but in reality a *śāstra*. The tradition is that it was composed by Dharmapāla in Nālandā and was translated in Chinese in 705 C.E. [5]. The dialectics developed by *ācaryas* hold balance to two viewpoints, opposed diametrically to one another as thesis and antithesis. Its most pronounced form appears in Madhyamika of Nāgārjuna. The dialectic is considered to be the soul of Madhyamika philosophy and also gets prominence in the Yogacāra. From dialectics evolved logic. The Yogacāra was a nursery of logic. It became a potent intellectual instrument in public debate and disputations [5].

Mahāyāna also started image worshipping in Buddhism. On the basis of the bodhisattva doctrine, they developed a large pantheon of gods and goddesses and other subordinate deities. The image carved out may be that of the bodhisattva, and later on the Buddha images were also carved out in different postures. It is still a matter of debate which school made the first Buddha statue. Earlier it was Gandhāra but now it is acknowledged to be Mathura School [9]. The image worshipping with huge Mahāyāna deities and their consorts and supporters popularized Mahāyāna and contributed immensely to the field of art and architecture.

Vajrayāna

This vehicle of Buddhism is influenced by *Tantricism*. It is also known as Mantrayāna and

Sahajayāna. Vajrayāna vehicle includes *mantras* (syllabus), *yantras* (magical diagrams), *mandalas* (ritualistic circle), and *mudras* (physical gestures), with multiple pantheons of gods and goddesses and rituals [5]. The *mantra*/hymn sacred to a deity is an important characteristic of Vajrayāna. It has a vast pantheon of gods and goddesses related to Dhyāni Buddhas and *Śaktis* associated with them. The human Buddha, a bodhisattva, a family, a color, a vehicle, and a particular direction and location in human body have been also specified. The *bodhicitta* conception in Vajrayāna is at par with the Yogacāra school of Mahāyāna. It is like a continuous stream of consciousness of the previous movements giving rise or causing the consciousness of the succeeding movement. This chain of momentary consciousness, without a beginning or an end, operating in unison with the all-powerful act force, leads it to either degradation or emancipation. According to good or bad action. Vajrayāna says that *bodhicitta* is the stage where *śunya* and *karunā* work in unison. They also believe that external objects are not real but are just mirage or shadow and their reality cannot be proved by reason [2].

The *mantras* constitute the backbone of Vajrayāna, and it is believed that these mystic syllables are endowed with great powers which can confer Buddhahood. The repletion of the mantras is to be done with the greatest care. The mind at the time of repetition should be completely concentrated on exact pronouncement, and the person should be free from all evil thoughts. The dynamic power of the *mantras* lies in the arrangement of the syllables, the accuracy of which is to be guarded with the greatest care. When the mantras became powerful, the vibration let loose by the worshipper reacts to the universal *śunya*. The *śunya* expresses in consequence of the divine form of divinity which appears in his mind.

The *Prajnaparamita*, *Manjusrimulakalpa*, *Guhyasamaja*, and *Sādhanamala* are important literatures of Vajrayāna. In the later literature, list of gurus (*Siddhācaryas*) and their succession line has also been mentioned: Padmavajra, Anaṅgavajra, Indrabhūti, Bhagvatī Lakshmī, Līlāvajra, Dārikapā, Sahajayogini Cintā, and Dombī Heruka. Taranatha informs that Saraha (Rahulabhadra) introduced *Būddhakapālatantra*, Luipa the *Yoginisancarya*, Kambala and Padmavajra the *Hevajratantra*, Krishnācārya the *Samputatilaka*, Lalitavajra the *Krsnayamāritantra*, Gambhiravajra the *Vajamrtatantra*, and Kukkurīpā the *Mahamayatantra* [2].

Vajrayāna has given varied, extensive, and diversified pantheon to Buddhism. The *Manjusrimulkalpa* describes a number of gods and goddesses, and *Prajnaparamita Sūtra* informs the description of elaborate worshipping of the Buddha, but it was in *Guhyasamaja* where the idea of the Buddhist pantheon was properly and systematically crystallized. It gives description of the five Dhyāni Buddhas, their mantras and *mandalas*, and their *Śaktis*, *kulas*, and *kulesas*. The five *kulas* are *dvesa*, *moha*, *rāgas*, *cintammani*, and *samaya* which conduce to the attainment of all desires as well as emancipation. The *Advayavajra* says that deities are nothing but a manifestation of *śunya*. He has given four stages of evolution of a deity – the right perception of *śunyatā*, the connection with germ syllable the *bīja*, the conception of an icon, and finally the external representation of the deities. Sometimes deities have been represented in the form of Dhyāni Buddhas who are an embodiment of five *skandhas*, over each of which one Dhyāni Buddha presides. For example, Akshobhya presides over vijñāna, Vairocana for *rūpa*, Ratnasambhava for *vedanā*, Amitabha for *saṃjnā*, and Amoghasiddhi for *saṃskāra*. When one element among the five predominates, the deity is accepted as the emanation of that Dhyāni Buddha who presides over the element in question. When he is depicted in art, he bears on his head the same Dhyāni Buddha and is considered his offspring. The other Dhyāni Buddhas are generally depicted on the aureole over the head of the principal deity. In Vajrayāna specific color has been applied to all deities. The deity cannot have same color in all rituals because each rite has its own significance and specification. Sometimes deities have fierce appearance and have been invoked in terrible rites. These deities may be terrific externally but are extremely compassionate internally. They are always benevolent to their worshipper [2].

Cross-References

► Mahāyāna
► Nāgārjuna

References

1. Bapat PV (1956) 2500 years of Buddhism. Publication Division, Delhi
2. Bhattacharya B (2009) An introduction to Buddhist esoterism. Motilal Banarasidas, Delhi
3. Chatterji SC, Datta DM (1984) An introduction to Indian philosophy. University of Calcutta, Calcutta
4. Dutt N (1976) Mahāyāna Buddhism. Firma KLM, Calcutta
5. Dutt S (2000) Buddhist monks and monasteries of India: their history and their contribution to Indian culture. Motilal Banarasidas, Delhi
6. Joshi LM (1977) Studies in Buddhist culture of India (during 7th & 8th centuries A.D.). Motilal Banarasidas, Delhi
7. Law BC (1933) A history of Pali literature. Kegan Paul, Trench Trubener, London
8. Pande GC (1957) Studies in origin of Buddhism. Allahabad University, Allahabad
9. Singh A (2014) Buddhism at Sārnāth. Primus Press, Delhi
10. Warder AK (2008) Indian Buddhism. Motilal Banarasidas, Delhi

Verses of the Elder Monks

► Thera- and Therīgāthā

Verses of the Elder Nuns

► Thera- and Therīgāthā

Verses of Uplift

► Udāna

Vesālī

K. T. S. Sarao
Department of Buddhist Studies, University of Delhi, Delhi, India

Synonyms

Vaiśālī; Vaishali

Definition

An important capital at the time of the Buddha.

Vesālī was the capital city of the Licchavis at the time of the Buddha, and the Buddhist texts mention it as an opulent (*iddhā*), prosperous (*phitā*), populous (*bahujanā, ākiṇṇamanussā*), and well-fed (*subhikkhā*) river port ([1], Vol. i, p. 268) with many highways, byways, and crossroads ([1], Vol. iv, p. 187). It was encompassed by three walls at a distance of one *gāvuta* (league) from one another, and the walls had three gates with watchtowers ([2], Vol. i, p. 504). According to the *Samantapāsādikā*, Vesālī got its name from the fact that of being *viśāla* (extensive) ([3], Vol. ii, p. 393). It was connected to Rājagaha by a high road ([1], Vol. i, p. 287f). There were many pre-Buddhist *cetiyas* (Sk, *caityas*) at Vesālī, such as Bahuputta, Sārādada, Gotamaka, Udena, Bahupatta, Sattamba, and Cāpāla ([4], Vol. ii, pp. 102–103, 118; [5], Vol. i, p. 276; Vol. iv, pp. 18, 309; [6], Vol. v, pp. 159, 258–259. See also [7], p. 104). Near this settlement was a cemetery where the Chabbaggivya nuns had erected a *stūpa* over the ashes of one of their leaders ([1], Vol. iv, p. 308). According to the *Vinaya Piṭaka*, various temples, shrines, and monasteries were constructed here for the monks, who themselves superintended their construction ([8], Vol. xx, p. 189f). Ambapālī as a courtesan is credited for bringing prosperity to this city ([9], Vol. i, p. 268).

The *Jātakas* point out that there were 7,707 *rājās* and an equal number of viceroys, generals, and treasurers in Vesālī ([2], Vol. iii, p. 1). There was a Conference Hall (*Santhāgāra*) at Vesālī where the Licchavis assembled to discuss various matters ([1], Vol. i, p. 233; [9], Vol. i, p. 228). The auspicious *Pokkharaṇī* was the tank wherein the representatives of the khattiya families of Vesālī were anointed ([2], Vol. iv, p. 148). The Buddha stayed here either in the Ambapālīvana ([5], Vol. iv, p. 99) or Mahāvana's Gabled House (*Kūṭāgārasālā*) near Vesālī ([1], Vol. ii, p. 225, Vol. iv, p. 24; [5], Vol. i, pp. 220, 230; [9], Vol. i, p. 227). Important *suttas* preached at Vesālī are the *Mahāli, Mahāsīhanāda, Cūḷa Saccaka, Mahā Saccaka, Tevijja, Vacchagotta, Sunakkhatta*, and *Ratana*. Quite a few Vinaya rules are mentioned as having been laid down at Vesālī (see, e.g., [1], Vol. i, pp. 238, 287f; Vol. ii, pp. 118, 119, 127, 159f, etc.). It was during his stay in Vesālī that Mahāpajāpati Gotamī followed the Buddha with 500 other Sākyan women and, with the help of Ānanda, obtained permission for women's entry into the saṃgha ([1], Vol. ii, p. 253ff). After the Buddha's death, a portion of his relics was enshrined in this city ([4], Vol. ii, p. 167; [10], Vol. xxviii, p. 2). Later, the Second Buddhist Council was held here ([1], Vol. ii, p. 299f).

Faxian mentions derelict monasteries, missing monks, and innumerable number of heretics with their deva-temples at Vaiśālī ([11], p. 96). In the seventh century, Xuanzang found all the several hundred vihāras in ruins in the country of Vaiśālī except three to five which housed few monks ([12], p. 209). According to him, the wall of the city of Vaiśālī had badly collapsed while the palace city had few inhabitants inside ([12], p. 210). A 100 years later, Hye Ch'o saw "the monastery by deserted and ruined with no monks" ([13], p. 42). A few decades later, Oukong could find nothing at Vaiśālī other than the ruins of the vihāra of Vimalakīrti ([14], p. 355).

The mound locally known as *Rājā-Bisāl-kā-Garh* at Basārh was identified by Alexander Cunningham and others with the ancient city of Vesālī ([15], 1835, p. 129; [16], p. 55; [17], 1902, pp. 267–288). The total area covered by various mounds in and around Basārh is spread over 3.5 × 2.5 miles ([16], p. 56), and the habitations covered at least 617.8 acres in c. 100 C.E. The existence of a tank, now called Kharauṇāpokhrā, measuring 425 × 200 m^2 and located about half a mile to the northwest of the mound, was confirmed by the excavations carried out by A.S. Altekar ([18], 1957–1958, pp. 10–11; 1958–1959, p. 12; 1959–1960, pp. 14–16; 1960–1961, p. 6; 1961–1962, pp. 5, 7). Altekar reports that initially it was a small tank which was "enlarged and surrounded by a wall, represented by its present remains, in about the second century BCE, when the Licchavis might have once more become powerful after the decline of the Mauryan Empire ([18], 1957–1958, pp. 10–11; 1958–1959, p. 12). Next to Kharauṇāpokhrā, now stands the Japanese temple and the World Peace Pagoda built by the Japanese.

Excavations of an unpretentious low *stūpa*, about 800 m to the northwest of the fort, yielded interesting results. Originally, a mud structure with thin layers of cloddy clay, the *stūpa*, underwent four enlargements, in all of which burnt bricks were used. In the center of the original *stūpa*, seemingly lying in the midst of soil anciently disturbed by a trench, was besides other things a relic casket of soapstone containing a small quantity of ashy earth. The original *stūpa* appears to have been quite old, perhaps pre-Mauryan. From its primitive features and from the fact that a trench had been driven into its core in old times, it has been held that the *stūpa* is no other than the one erected by the Lichhavis over their share of the mortal remains of the Buddha, the trench being the one that was dug by Aśoka to reach the relics, some of which, according to Xuanzang, were left in their original position by Aśoka. If this identification is correct, the *stūpa* would be the earliest as yet discovered, but it must be added that the identification cannot be regarded as firmly established ([19], p. 75).

Studying the reports on archaeological activities, one gets the clear impression that so far as its antiquity goes, the date of the earliest habitation may be fixed around 600 B.C.E. While the main mounds were enclosed within a large rectangular mud-built enclosure, another rampart outside has been traced over a long stretch. There are remains of several *stūpas* inside and outside the fortification. The archaeological records indicate that the site was occupied till about 500 C.E. Two mud *stūpas* found in the excavations near Vesālī were constructed around 150 B.C.E. During the Kuṣāṇa days, the rampart was heightened with earth and encircled by a moat. Excavation records show that during the Gupta period the rampart was further improved with bricks and barracks and other structures were added to it.

Cross-References

- ▶ Cetiya
- ▶ Faxian (337–422 C.E.)
- ▶ Pajāpati Gotamī
- ▶ Saṃgha
- ▶ Stūpa
- ▶ Vimalakīrti
- ▶ Xuanzang (Hieun-Tsang)

References

1. Oldenberg H (ed) (1879–1883) The Vinaya Piṭakaṃ, 5 vols. Pali Text Society, London
2. Fausböll V (ed) (1877–1897) The Jātakas, 7 vols. Trübner, London
3. Takakusu J, Nagai M (eds) (1947–1975) Samantapāsādikā: Buddhaghosa's commentary on the Vinaya Piṭaka, 8 vols (including index by H. Kopp). Pali Text Society, London
4. Rhys Davids TW, Carpenter JE (eds) (1890–1911) The Dīgha Nikāya, 3 vols. Pali Text Society, London
5. Morris R, Hardy E (eds) (1885–1900) The Aṅguttara Nikāya, 5 vols. Pali Text Society, London
6. Feer ML (ed) (1884–1898) The Saṃyutta Nikāya, 5 vols. Pali Text Society, London
7. Rhys Davids TW, Stede W (1921–1925) Pāli-English dictionary. Pali Text Society, London
8. Max Muller F (ed) Sacred books of the east, 50 vols, reprint. Motilal Banarasidass, Delhi
9. Trenckner V, Chelmers R (eds) (1888–1896) The Majjhima Nikāya, 3 vols. Pali Text Society, London
10. Jayawickrama NA (ed) (1974) The Buddhavaṃsa. Pali Text Society, London
11. Beal S (trans) (1869) Travels of Fa-Hien and Sung-Yun: Buddhist pilgrims from China to India (400 A.D. and 518 A.D.). K. Paul, Trench & Trübner, London
12. Li R (trans) (1996) The Great Tang Dynasty record of the western regions. Numata Center for Buddhist Translation and Research, Berkeley
13. Yang Han-sung, Jan, Yün-hua et al (trans) (1984) The Hye Ch'o diary: memoir of the pilgrimage to the five regions of India. Asian Humanities Press, Berkeley
14. Lévi S, Chavannes E (1895) "L'Itinèraire d'Ou K'ong (751–790)" J Asiatique, NeuviçmeSèrie, Tome VI, 1895
15. J Asiat Soc Bengal, Calcutta
16. Cunningham A (1871) ASI: four reports 1862-63-64-65, vol I. Govt Press, Simla
17. J Roy Asiat Soc, London
18. Indian Archaeology: a review, New Delhi
19. Mitra D (1971) Buddhist monuments. Sahitya Samsad, Calcutta
20. Woodward FL, Hare EM (trans) (1955–1970) The book of gradual sayings, 5 vols, reprints. Pali Text Society, London

Vevaṇṇiya

▶ Caṇḍāla (Buddhism)

Vibhaṅga

K. T. S. Sarao
Department of Buddhist Studies, University of Delhi, Delhi, India

Synonyms

The book of analysis

Definition

It is the second book of the Abhidhamma Piṭaka.

The *Vibhaṅga* is the second of the seven books of the *Abhidhamma Piṭaka*. It consists of eighteen *vibhaṅgas* (chapters). Each of these *vibhaṅgas* deals with a separate topic. The following headings of the different *vibhaṅgas* provided in the edition of the Pali Text Society edited by C.A.F. Rhys Davids [6] are based on the subject matter of each of the *vibhaṅga: Khandhavibhaṅga* (chapter on the aggregates), *Āyatanavibhaṅga* (chapter on the sense bases), *Dhātuvibhaṅga* (chapter on the elements), *Saccavibhaṅga* (chapter on the truths), *Indriyavibhaṅga* (chapter on the faculties), *Paccayākāravibhaṅga* (chapter on the dependent arising), *Satipaṭṭhānavibhaṅga* (chapter on the recollections), *Sammappadhānavibhaṅga* (chapter on the right exertion), *Iddhipādavibhaṅga* (chapter on the base of power), *Bhojjaṅga-vibhaṅga* (chapter on the elements of knowledge), *Maggavibhaṅga* (chapter on the Path), *Jhānavibhaṅga* (chapter on the stages of meditation), *Appammaññāvibhaṅga* (chapter on the immeasurables), *Sikkhāpadavibhaṅga* (chapter on the training rules), *Paṭisambhidāvibhaṅga* (chapter on the analysis), *Ñāṇavibhaṅga* (chapter on the knowledge), *Khuddakavatthuvibhaṅga* (chapter on the small objects), and *Dhammahadayavibhaṅga* (chapter on the heart of the Dhamma).

Most of its chapters (except chapters no. V, VI, XIV, XVI, XVII, and XVIII) have three sections, viz., Sutta Method (*Suttantabhājaniya*), Abhidhamma Method (*Abhidhammabhājaniya*), and Question Method (*Pañhāpuchhaka*). The *Suttantabhājaniya* portion of each of the chapters that have it, the method of analysis, and the definitions used by the Buddha in general discourses have been mentioned. For instance, in the *Suttantabhājaniya* of the *Khandhavibhaṅga*, the constituent parts of *khandhas*, i.e., *rūpa*, *vedanā*, *saññā*, *saṃkhāra*, and *viññāna*, have been analyzed and examined individually with reference to time, space, and matter. Some of the analyses provided in the *Suttantabhājanīya* portions of the different chapters can also be seen in other parts of the *Tipiṭaka*. In the *Abhidhammabhājaniya* portion of each of the chapters, technical analysis and definitions of the same subject have been provided from a philosophical perspective. Thus, for example, in the *Abhidhammabhājaniya* of the *Khandhavibhaṅga*, in the case of *vedanā* (sensation), it has been shown that there are ten ways for the rise of *vedanā* and that it can also be categorized into various clusters such as*kusala* (good), *akusala* (bad), and *avyākata* (neither good nor bad). In the chapters which have a *Pañhāpuchhaka* section has been comprehensively explained as to how each of the particular terms is to be defined under the rubrics of triplets and couplets listed in the *Dhammasaṅgaṇi* ([4], pp. 313–314; [5], p. 100).

The *Vibhaṅga* was most probably conceived as a manual for students just like the *Dhammasaṅgaṇi* ([6], p. xx). It generally deals with the various categories and formulae dealt with in the *Dhammasaṅgaṇi*. The subject matter of many of the chapters of the *Dhammasaṅgaṇi* is repeated in the Vibhaṅga, but the methodology employed and the matter are largely different. For instance, the Vibhaṅga contains some terms and definitions that are not found in the *Dhammasaṅgaṇi* ([4], p. 313). According to C.A.F. Rhys Davids, there is no intention in this text on the part of the compilers of setting forth their ethical philosophy or psychological ethics in any complete and systematic order. Acquaintance with the Dhamma is taken for granted. The object is not so much as to extend knowledge as to ensure mutual consistency in the intension of ethical notions and to systematize and formulate the theories and practical mechanism of intellectual and moral progress scattered throughout the *Sutta Piṭaka* ([6], p. xx).

The *Vibhaṅga* systematizes old material and is considered to be the oldest among all the texts of the *Abhidhamma Piṭaka* ([2], p. 69). Bronkhorst has suggested that an early form of this text was compiled during the first century after the Mahāparinibbāna ([1], p. 309). However, Hinüber considers this too early a date ([2], p. 69). The last three chapters of *Vibhaṅga* were originally independent small books on Abhidhamma separate from the beginning of the text ([2], p. 69).

Cross-References

- Abhidhamma Piṭaka
- Dhamma
- Dhammasaṅgaṇī
- Sutta Piṭaka
- Tipiṭaka

V

References

1. Bronkhorst J (1985) Dharma and Abhidharma. Bull School Orient Afr Stud 48:305–320
2. von Hinüber O (1996) A handbook of Pāli literature. Walter de Gruyter, Berlin
3. Iggleden REW (1969) Introduction. In: Thiṭṭila U (trans) The Book of Analysis (Vibhaṅga). Pali Text Society, London

4. Law BC (1983) A history of Pali literature, reprint, vol 1. Indological Book House, Delhi
5. Norman KR (1983) A history of Indian literature: Pāli literature, vol VII, Fasc 2. Otto Harrassowitz, Wiesbaden
6. Rhys Davids CAF (ed) (1904) The Vibhaṅgha. Pali Text Society, London
7. Thiṭṭila U (ed) (1969) The book of analysis (Vibhaṅga). Pali Text Society, London
8. Winternitz M (1983) History of Indian literature (trans: Sarma VS), rev edn., vol 2. Motilal Banarsidass, Delhi

Vidya

▶ Mantra

Vihāra

K. T. S. Sarao
Department of Buddhist Studies, University of Delhi, Delhi, India

Synonyms

Monastery

Definition

A Buddhist monastic establishment.

Vihāra is a Pāli and Sanskrit term used for a Buddhist monastery. The *vihāras* passed through four main phases of growth and development in India. Originally, they simply referred to temporary shelters used by wandering monastics particularly during the *vassāvāsa* (rainy retreat). These shelters were simple thatched bamboo huts or wooden structures. People considered it a religiously meritorious act to offer food and shelter to mendicants. Consequently, when Buddhist saṃgha became an established institution, rich lay devotees began to make substantial donations for the construction of opulent *vihāra* s ([11], p. 51). Thus, during the second phase, a typical *vihāra* became an organized large permanent monastic establishment which besides working as a residence for the monks and nuns, it also worked as a place where various activities including meetings, recreation, religious work, meditation, and learning took place ([13], Vol. 1, p. 58, Vol. ii, p. 207, Vol. ii, p. 47; [15], Vol. i, p. 133). Typical *vihāras* during the second phase were located on the outskirts of human habitations, close enough for begging but far enough to offer seclusion for undisturbed meditation.

By about the second century BCE, a standard plan for the construction of a vihāra came into existence. Now a typical *vihāra* was either structural or rock-cut. It consisted of a walled quadrangular court which was surrounded by small cells fitted with rock-cut platforms for beds and pillows. A door was hewn out in the front wall. During the later periods, the back side usually had a shrine for the image of the Buddha ([11], p. 56). These *vihāra* s, usually built of stone or brick, mostly consisted of a square block formed by four rows of cells along the four sides of an inner courtyard. As the saṃgha grew, they became elaborate brick structures consisting of several stories containing stūpas and statues of the Buddha as well as various bodhisattvas.

During the third stage, the *vihāras* broke free of their usual supporters and began to mushroom on the trade routes. Trade routes became ideal locations for *vihāras.* Donations from wealthy merchants led to an increased economic clout of these vihāras. They also received a fillip due to the increasing demands for teaching in Mahāyāna Buddhism [1]. With the growth of mercantile and royal endowments, intricate facades were added to the exteriors of these *vihāras* and their interiors begun to be decorated with beautiful paintings and elaborate carvings involving highly skilled artisans and craftsmen. The Buddhist *vihāra* s also became mercantile in nature and began to provide capital loans and facilities for mercantile communities involved in interregional commerce in the Indian subcontinent ([9], pp. 100–114). In spite of the physical isolation of majority of the Buddhist monastic establishments and lack of artifactual or structural evidence pointing to military, storage, or industrial functions within monasteries ([5], p. 132), it has been suggested that by the early centuries of the Common Era, the saṃgha had certainly become a major holder of land and property ([14], p. 150). There is overwhelming evidence indicating that Buddhist vihāras actively participated in commercial activities such as banking and financing. *Vinaya* rules setting conditions for traveling with and seeking donations from merchant caravans and narratives about monks who participated in trade missions and traders who visited *vihāra* s along their routes reflect deep connections between mobile monastic and merchant communities. At sites such as Bhārhut and Sāñcī, the largest single group of donors were monks and nuns, who evidently owned personal property despite Vinaya rules to the contrary. As the prosperity of the urbanite merchants, traders, bankers, financiers, and artisans increased, they vied with each other in constructing stūpas and providing material support to Buddhist *vihāra* s. However, the dependence of the saṃgha solely upon urban mercantile communities was a serious drawback as "nothing could be more ruinous for an ideology than to have drawn its sanction only from such patronage" ([2], p. xiv). Urban orientation of the Buddhist *vihāra* s and their dependence upon urbanites alienated the rural communities from Buddhism. As time went by, isolation from and aversion to serve the rural communities and lack of interest in winning supporters among them, Buddhist *vihāra* s turned into some sort of islands with uncertain future. With the onset of urban crisis, the situation developed completely to the disadvantage of Buddhism. During this fourth phase, the Buddhist *vihāra* s were no longer attracting generous donations and political patronage on the same scale as before and the Brāhmaṇical-Hindu sects were certainly on the ascendant ([14], p. 150). Between 300 and 600 C.E., Brāhmaṇical-Hindu temples emerged as the focus of social and economic activity, and the first land grants were made to them ([12], pp. 316–317). They began to attract more and more land grants and played an important role in the consolidation and expansion of agrarian settlements. The dispersal of merchants, traders, bankers, financiers, and artisans sapped the socially and economically vital foundations of the saṃgha. The loss of traditional lay supporters as well as material support led to the dwindling in numbers of those who aspired to adopt renunciation in the Buddhist saṃgha. In such a newly emerged situation, the existence of the saṃgha became very precarious indeed. One direct consequence was that majority of the small *vihāra* s, which formally existed in the vicinity of urban settlements, became mostly derelict ([10], p. 414). Thereafter, the saṃgha became concentrated in fewer and fewer *vihāra* s. As time went by and as more and more urban settlements decayed, the number of Buddhist *vihāra* s became reduced significantly. Interestingly, in the Gupta and post-Gupta periods, when most of the urban settlements either declined or were deserted, some new settlements with urban features also emerged. However, these newly emerged urban settlements were different in nature from their predecessors. Whereas the early historical urban settlements were directly linked up with centers of authority with supra-regional loci, the early medieval urban settlements were more rooted in their regional contexts acting as nodal points in local exchange networks, corresponding to different ties of regional power. Though some support may still have accrued here and there from the few surviving or newly emerged urban settlements to an insignificant number of Buddhist *vihāra* s, the number of traditional supporters of Buddhism became grievously small.

The phase from the sixth to seventh centuries till the twelfth to thirteenth centuries CE was distinctive in the history of Indian Buddhism. During this phase, in order to survive in a situation of dwindling traditional support and the rising tide of rejuvenated Brāhmaṇical-Hinduism, the few surviving Buddhist *vihāra* s began to tune themselves to the emerging feudal situation by adopting new roles for themselves through the practice of self-supporting economies based on land grants ([16], p. 165). Further, the saṃgha liberalized learning and opened the doors of its *vihāra* s to secular education so as to make it more effective in debates and disputations ([3], p. 29). Thus, from the sixth century onwards, a number of *vihāra* s began to grow out of their conventional character into centers of laicized academic learning and scholarship. Here, the learning was not confined to saṃgha members alone, but was made available to all seekers after knowledge, Buddhists as well as non-Buddhists. As a consequence of such an unrestrained development, the Buddhist saṃgha began to tune itself to the moorings of the Brāhmaṇical-Hindu society. Like their Brāhmaṇical-Hindu counterparts, the Buddhist *vihāra* s also began to accept donations of arable land for religious purposes from the kings and the chiefs. Consequently, some of them at places such as Nālandā, Pahārpur, and Vallabhī became metamorphosed into reputed centers of Buddhist learning and developed into fully grown universities (*mahāvihāras*). In the new scenario, they had to manage not only large landed estates but also a whole lot of other things associated with such estates. Monastic landlordism naturally led to revolutionary changes in the very character of these newly sprung *mahāvihāras*. This phenomenon helped these few *mahāvihāras* to survive and even prosper for a while, independently of their traditional supporters.

Interestingly, from the Gupta period onwards, building *vihāras* and providing for their upkeep began to be regarded more as a service rendered to the cause of learning and culture than to the cause of Buddhism ([3], p. 331). A major share of the land grants to Buddhist institutions came from their Brāhmaṇical-Hindu patrons. Besides, these *mahāvihāras* turned out to be poor competitors to their Brāhmaṇical-Hindu counterparts as the latter had a clear advantage over *mahāvihāras* in the management of landed estates. A Brāhmaṇical-Hindu temple invariably ministered to the religious needs of a large village or a populous quarter of a town. In sharp contrast to this, a Buddhist *vihāra* had almost nothing to do with the familial rituals of a householder and only served as a center of intellectual and spiritual inspiration for anyone who wanted it. "Ritual remained a monopoly of the Brahman. Moreover, the Brahman at that time was a pioneer who could stimulate production, for he had a good working calendar for predicting the times of ploughing, sowing, and harvesting. He knew something of new crops and trade possibilities. He was not a drain upon production as had been his sacrificing ancestors, or the large Buddhist monasteries" ([8], p. 66). Thus, the Brāhmaṇical-Hindu temples, due to their better knowledge of agriculture (especially rice cultivation) and seasons ([4], pp. 3–21.), and their ingenuity in constructing origin myths and enormous capacity for legitimation, and thus wider sociopolitical functions [7], obtained an advantage over Buddhist *mahāvihāras*. This advantage was manifested in the shift of royal patronage from Buddhism to Brāhmaṇical-Hindu sects, which became more visible by the end of the eleventh century and is quite evident in the artistic record of the period ([6], pp. 179–201).

Cross-References

▶ Nālandā
▶ Stūpa
▶ Xuanzang (Hieun-Tsang)

References

1. Chakrabarti DK (1995) Buddhist sites across South Asia as influenced by political and economic forces. World Archaeol 27(2):185–202
2. Chattopadhyaya DP (1970) Preface. In: Chimpa L, Chattopadhyaya A (eds) (trans) Tāranātha's history of Buddhism in India. Indian Institute of Advanced Study, Simla
3. Dutt S (1962) Buddhist monks and monasteries of India: their history and contribution to Indian culture. George Allen and Unwin, London
4. Eaton RM (1993) The rise of Islam and the Bengal frontier, 1204–1706. University of California Press, Berkeley
5. Heitzmann J (1984) Early Buddhism, trade and empire. In: Kennedy KAR, Possehl DL (eds) Studies in the archaeology and palaeoanthropology of South Asia. Oxford University Press, New Delhi
6. Huntington SL (1984) The Pala-Sena schools of sculpture. Studies in South Asian Culture, Leiden
7. Jha A (2003) Patronage and authority: Buddhist monasteries in early medieval India. Teach South Asia, Internet J Pedagog II(1). www.mssc.edu/projectsouthasia/TSA/VIIN1/Jha.html
8. Kosambi DD (1957) Exasperating essays: exercises in the dialectical methods. People's Book House, Poona

9. Kosambi DD (1962) Myth and reality. Popular Prakashan, Bombay
10. Lamotte É (1988) History of Indian Buddhism: from the origins to the faka era (trans: Sara Webb-Boin). Insitut Orientaliste, Louvain-la-Neuve
11. Mitra D (1971) Buddhist monuments. Sahitya Samsad, Calcutta
12. Neelis J (2011) Early Buddhist transmission and trade networks: mobility and exchange within and beyond the Northwestern Borderlands of South Asia. K. Brill, Leiden
13. Olderberg H (ed) (1879–1883) The Vinaya Piṭakaṃ, 5 vols. Pali Text Society, London
14. Ray HP (1994) The winds of change: Buddhism and the Maritime links of early South Asia. Oxford University Press, Delhi
15. Rhys Davids TW, Carpentier JE, Stede W (eds) (1886–1932) The Sumaṅgala-Vilāsinī: Buddhaghosa's commentary on the Dīgha Nikāya, 3 vols. Pali Text Society, London
16. Sharma RS (1987) Urban decay in India (c.300–c.1000). Munshiram Manoharlal, Delhi

Vijānavāda

► Yogācāra

Vijayapuri

► Nāgārjunakoṇḍa

Vijñāna

► *Viññāṇa*

Vijñāna (Sanskrit)

► *Viññāṇa*

Vijñāṇapada

► Kathāvatthu

Vijñānavāda

C. D. Sebastian
Department of Humanities and Social Sciences, Indian Institute of Technology Bombay, Mumbai, India

Synonyms

Cittamātra; Consciousness-only; Mind-only; Vijñaptimātra(tā); Yogācāra; Yogācāra-Vijñānavāda

Definition

Vijñānavāda literally means the "doctrine of consciousness." The Vijñānavāda, sometimes called as the "Yogācāra-Vijñānavāda," is one of the most significant schools of Mahāyāna Buddhism. According to this school, the only existent is consciousness (*vijñānamātra, citta-mātra*, or *vijñapti-mātra*).

Introduction

Vijñānavāda literally means the "doctrine of consciousness" (*vijñāna* + *vāda*). The other name of this school is the Yogācāra (see ► Yogācāra). It is also, at times, called the Yogācāra-Vijñānavāda. It is one of the two major schools of Mahāyāna Buddhism. This school of Buddhist thought flourished in India from the third/fourth century A.D. to twelfth century. According to this school, the only existent is consciousness (*vijñāna-mātra, cittamātra*, or *vijñapti-mātra*). In Buddhism, *vijñāna* corresponds to the resulting activity when the mental and physical organs come into contact with external objects and the input derived from such contact is associated, recognized, and subsequently acted upon. Thus, the term "*vijñāna*," as it is understood in the entire Buddhist corpus, means "consciousness," and the doctrine (*vāda*) that upholds the theory of consciousness (*vjñāna*) is *vijñānavāda*. The adherents of this school are known as the Vijñānavādins or even as the Yogācārins.

Development

The Yogācāra school founded by Maitreya(nātha) and Asaṅga (see ▶ Asaṅga) and philosophically developed by Vasubandhu (see ▶ Vasubandhu) in the fourth century A.D. underwent certain changes and came to be known as the *Vijñānavāda* or even as the *Vijñaptimātratā-vāda*. According to Tibetan tradition, there are three basic *sūtras* where full-fledged *Vijñānavāda* could be seen: the *Saṁdhinirmocana*, the *Lankāvatāra*, and the *Ghanavyūha*. These texts must have been composed sometime in a period between the first century B.C. and the third century A.D. The fourth and fifth century A.D. is the classical period of Yogācāra where Maitreya(nātha), Asaṅga, and Vasubandhu are the greatest *ācāryas*.

After the halcyon days of the Yogācāra with Asaṅga, Vasubandhu, and Sthiramati (pupil and great commentator of Vasubandhu in the fifth century A.D.), its idealistic phase came to an end. There was a shift in the interest of the interpreters and *ācāryas* of this school to logic and epistemology. The Sautrāntika (see ▶ Sautrāntika) theory of *svalakṣṇa* (unique particular, or a conception of thing-in-itself) got restored, which effected in the development of the hybrid school of Sautrāntika-Yogācāra [1], "for which the name Vijñānavāda can be reserved" [2]. This does not mean that they rejected the Yogācāra tenets in toto and went in a Sautrāntika way. At the core, their approach lays a concern with cognition and conditions of knowing, aimed at correcting cognitive errors. Though their approach was epistemological, the goal was the same as that of the Yogācārins [3].

The school of Dignāga (see ▶ Dignāga) and Dharmakīrti, the Buddhist logicians *par excellence*, essentially accepted the doctrine of *vijñaptimātratā*, and the unreality of the object, but when they come into logical discussions, they endorse the Sautrāntika standpoint of something being given in knowledge. Their fundamental teaching was that of the Yogācāra, which could be traced from Dignāga's *Ālambanaparīkṣā* and Dharmakīrti's *Pramāṇavārtika* (particularly the section on *Vijñaptimātratācintā*), but their focal interest was logical elaboration. With these scholars, the trend in Buddhist philosophy tended to pertain predominantly to logical reasoning rather than scriptures. And thus, "these new philosophers now came to be called *Nyāyānusārī* rather than *Āgamānusārī*" [4]. With Dignāga and Dharmakīrti, new positional possibilities opened up by their logical and epistemological approach (which was due to the cutting critique leveled at the Yogācāra by other Buddhist schools – especially by Candrakīrti et al.), and the scheme of philosophizing turned into an epistemo-psychology. With Dharmakīrti, the critical epistemology of Buddhism with its logical sharpness eventually became the Buddhist thought of the time.

The logical school of Vijñānavāda never had an impact in China. Due to the influence of the Buddhist logicians, Buddhist logical school remained the fundamental Buddhist philosophy in India. "Chinese Buddhism" never could make a "shift from psychology to logico-epistemology. Instead it further developed the psychology into meta-psychology, an elaborate descriptive and prescriptive examination of the mind" [5]. The logical-epistemological shift of the Vijñānavāda never occurred in China, as this shift, on the whole, was unfamiliar to Chinese interests and the contemporaneous Chinese thought. Hsüan-tsang had introduced Indian logic in China by translating Indian logic texts for the first time, but it did not have any major impact in China. The great Buddhist logician Dharamkīrti and others like Śāntarakṣita and Ratnakīrti remained almost unknown in East Asian Buddhism.

The Buddhist logical acumen was unique in Nāgārjuna, and even earlier. But it was precisely with the Yogācāra-Vijñānavāda that logic, precisely syllogistic logic, received its foundation in Buddhism. Again, epistemological expertise could be seen even before, but it was with the Vijñānavāda that logic per se got prominence in Buddhist thought.

Major Thinkers

The Vijñānavāda school is synonymous with Yogācāra, and it is also known as the Yogācāra-Vijñānavāda. The Yogācāra doctrines were the foundation of the Vijñānavāda. After Vasubandhu, the Yogācāra bifurcated into two divergent directions: a logico-epistemic tradition led by Dignāga, Dharmakīrti, Śāntarakṣita, and Ratnakīrti; and an Ābhidharmika psychology represented by such thinkers as Sthiramati, Dharmapāla, and Vinītadeva [6]. The most celebrated *ācāryas* of the Vijñānavāda logical school were Dignāga and Dharmakīrti. According to them, the only existent or reality (*paramārthasatya*) was *vijñaptimātratā*, but for logical and epistemological reasons they took recourse to the *svalakṣaṇa* as empirically real (*paramārthasat*). Thus, their school could be termed as an idealism-cum-critical realism [7].

Maitreyanātha: (see Maitreya)

Asaṅga: (see ► Asaṅga)

Vasubandhu: (see ► Vasubandhu)

Dignāga: Dignāga is the founder of Buddhist logic, and perhaps, the most independent thinker among the successors of Vasubandhu. His main works are the *Pramāṇasamuccaya, Trikāla Parīkṣā, Hetucakranirṇaya*, and *Nyāyamukha*. Dignāga emphasized two *pramāṇas* (valid means of knowledge), namely, perception and inference, and each of which was a dissimilar type of knowledge and had a different sphere of objects to know. Perception is immediate knowledge and has as *content* undifferentiated exposed phenomena of objects, whereas inference is judgmental and constructs objects out of the reflexes. Thus, these two *pramāṇas* dichotomize knowledge as well as the knowable into intuitions and construct their *content*. Before the time of Dignāga, the Buddhist thinkers generally divided the "experience" into two parts: *nimittabhāga* (the objective presentation or *phenomena*. It is like *noema* in phenomenology) and *darśanabhāga* (the *cognition* of the objective presentation. It is like *noesis* in phenomenology). Dignāga added to it a third one: *samvittibhāga* (auto-referring consciousness which escorts all experience), which was also called *svasaṁvedana*. The conceptions of *ālayavijñāna* (see ► Ālayavijñāna) and the *kliṣṭamanas*, which was hitherto central to the Yogācāra system got discarded in the new frame of logical analysis. Thus, instead of eight *vijñānas*, only six were found sufficient and the sixth one, *manas* was labeled as *manovijñāna* and it got the functions of the other two *vijñānas* [8].

Dharmakīrti: Dharmakīrti's main treatises are the *Pramāṇavārttika*, the *Nyāyabindu*, and the *Hetubindu*. Dharmakīrti (Dharmakīrt's teacher was Īśvarasena, the pupil of Dignāga) revised Dignāga's definition of perception in his *Nyāyabindu*, adding an adjective *abhrāntam* (non-erroneous), with a purport that perception is non-erroneous. Dignāga had defined valid perception (*pratyakṣa*) as devoid of conceptual construction (*kalpanāpoḍha*) or without constructive imagination (*avikalpa*). Dharmakīrti revised it with an adjectival addition that it must also be non-erroneous or free of error (*abhrānta*). To be non-erroneous, it is implied being definite and without any ambiguity [9].

In his *Pramāṇavārtika*, Dharmakīrti formulated new arguments, and the most important is the *sahopalambha-niyama* or the "law of being apprehended together." It implies that the knowledge and its object are always found together. There is a nondifference between knowledge and its object, that is, object is not conceivable except as object of knowledge. The distinction unpretentiously made between the precept and its content is illusory. This is explained in this way: the blue and the consciousness of the blue are identical (*sahopalambhaniyamād abhedo nīla-taddhiyoḥ*). It does not mean that cognition and its object as empirical entities are observed to be identical, but what is argued is that *cognition* and the *content* are conceptually inseparable. The "blue" is inconceivable apart from the content of visual cognition, and the cognition is incomprehensible except as the exposé of a content like "blue." Connecting the cognition and the object there is an indispensable coordination which cancels out their independent existence.

Śāntarakṣita and Others: In Śāntarakṣita and Kamalaśīla could be found another interesting development of the Vijñānavāda thought.

Śāntarakṣita's major philosophical work is the *Tattvasaṁgraha* in which he refuted all the philosophical systems of his day, both Buddhist and non-Buddhist. Śāntarakṣita made an attempt to synthesize the Mādhyamika and the Yogācāra schools. He rejected the empirical reality of the external world and accepted an introspective perception. By differencing from the Yogācāra, he did not accept consciousness as *ultimate reality* either. In India, the period between the seventh to ninth centuries was a time of the Mādhyamika writers, and a slow decline of Yogācāra. Śāntarakṣita, Kamalaśīla, and Haribhadra criticized the Yogācāra by accepting the key conceptions of Yogācāra as a useful intermediary understanding for gradual realization of the ultimate truth. For this reason, these scholars are classified by Tibetan scholars as the Yogācāra-Mādhyamika. These Mādhyamika scholars appropriated Yogācāra standpoint of the conceptual construction of duality, the bodhisattva path, stages of meditation, and *trikāya* doctrine. Śāntarakṣita adopted the Yogācāra analysis of cognitive subject-object duality which is, according to the Yogācāra, is a mere conceptual construct. In his system, the Yogācāra theory of non-duality formed a valuable step to the realization of the *paramārtha satya* (ultimate truth) [10]. The other *ācāryas* who are in agreement with the position of Śāntarakṣita are Kamalaśīla, Vimuktasena, Haribhadra, Buddhajñānapāda, and Abhayākaragupta. Their system is known as the Yogācāra-Mādhyamika school or Svātantrika Mādhyamika school.

Cittamātra and Vijñaptimātra(tā)

The often quoted line of the *Daśabhūmikasūtra: cittamātram idaṁ yad idaṁ traidhātukaṁ* (*Daś abhūmik sūtra* 6: 16) looms large in entire *Vijñānavāda* tradition. It implies that *citta* (mind or consciousness) is the only existent. Modern scholars opine that the statement that the whole world is only mind (*cittamātra*) must be interpreted as directed *not* against the existence of real objects (phenomena), but against the existence of a substantial *ātman*. The use of *cittamātra* in this sense could be traceable to other texts like the *Abhidharmasamuccaya, Sūtrālaṁkāra-vṛttibhāṣya* of Sthiramati, and the *Lankāvatārasūtra* as well. This expression with the same connotation appears in Vasubandhu's commentary on the *Daś abhūmikasūtra* [11]. In contrast to the *Daś abḥumikasūtra*, the *Bhadrapālasūtra* presents the conception of *cittamātra* in the context of a perfect idealistic standpoint. Perhaps, the *Bhadrapālasūtra* is the first text to enunciate the thesis of universal idealism and express this by the term *cittamātra* [11]. The *Bhadrapālasūtra* highlights the universal illusion, the unreality of phenomena, thereby pointing toward an idealism.

Cittamātra is one of the complex and difficult terms, as it occurs in Mahāyāna texts with varying meanings. In the *Daśabhūmikasūtra*, the term *cittamātra* was first used within the context of the meditative practice. *Cittamātra* as a doctrine was the product of reflection upon meditational experience where the realization was arrived at that the totality of one's experience dependent upon one's mind. In Asaṅga and Vasubandhu, *cittamātra* had different meanings where an epistemological intent was implied. In ordinary cognition what is cognized is not an exact representation of an object existing outside the mind but an object-like mental image, or a conceptualized object, which is a creation of constructive imagination [12]. In the *Saṁdhinirmocana sūtra* and other texts, the term *vijñaptimātratā* was often used as a synonym for *cittamātra*, especially within meditative context. But with Vasubandu the term *vijñaptimātratā* gets a philosophical nuance. In Vasubandhu's *Vijñaptimātratāsiddhi* (the *Viṁśatikā* and the *Triṁśikā)*, the shift of emphasis from a discourse centering on *cittamātra* (in a meditative context) to that centering on *vijñaptimātratā* in a philosophical perspective, is clearly seen.

Here the notion of *vijñaptimātratā* would mean "consciousness alone exists," as it has been interpreted by the idealistic interpreters of Buddhism. But for those who oppose the idealistic (or even absolutistic) interpretation of the Vijñānavāda (or Yogācāra-Vijñānavāda), *vijñaptimātratā* does not have any ontological bearing at all. According to these latter interpreters, it implies that whatever is experienced is a projection of consciousness. It is an epistemic vigilance and not an ontological assertion. *Vijñaptimātra*(*tā*) also implies that within one's own experience of the phenomena, and the conceptual *cum* linguistic constructs one uses to make sense out of such experiences, one realizes what is the case in reality (*yathābhūtam*). In other words, Cittamātra or Vijñaptimātra(tā) system would signify that actions are intentions to act by means of body, speech, or mind. Since intention (*cetanā*) is a cognitive phenomenon, all phenomena, all that exists, can be said be under the control of mind [13].

Nimitta and Vijñaptimātra(tā)

The entire corpus of the Yogācāra-Vijñānavāda system upholds that meditation (*samādhi*) and wisdom (*prajñā*) are not widely divergent. One realizes *cittamātra* or *vijñaptimātra*(*tā*) in *samādhi*. In the meditative process, *ālambana* refers to the mental support of cognition, or object cognized; and *pratibimba* refers to "reflected image." In meditative contexts, *ālambana* is equivalent to *nimitta*, literally "sign" or "mark" which is applied both to the object and the subjective ideal of meditation.

In the early Buddhist theory, there are three levels of *nimitta*, and the Vijñānavāda is primarily concerned with the third level. First level is the preliminary sign in ordinary practice (*parikamma nimitta*) which refers a concrete object of an ordinary experience. The second level is the representation of the exact copy of the object internalized and given to the mind (*uggaha nimitta*). And the third and the last level is an after-image, which is a concentration divested of any sort of image, but only an ideation (or the transformation into an idea) without any trace of the object in it (*paṭibhāga nimitta*). At this stage, the senses do not have any role to play, no cognitive faculty is required, nor does the concrete object have any significance at all [14]. It is this last and the highest level of meditative ideation which the Vijñānavādins call *cittamātra* or *vijñaptimātra*. This could be seen in the *Yogācārabhūmi* (particularly the chapters *Bodhisattvabhūmi* and *Bodhisattvabhūmiviniścaya*), where it is stated that the external objects are mere denominations (*prajñaptimātra*). Thus, it is a theory that considers phenomena (*nimitta*) to be a product of false conception [11].

Conception of Liberation in Vijñānavāda

Taking the objective world as real is bondage. The liberation is the realization of the selflessness of phenomena. Getting rid of this ignorance, which is the root cause of continued rebirth, is only possible by wisdom. To believe that there is self and really existing external things that are meaningful to the self is delusion and it will cause suffering. To realize that self and the apparently real objects (phenomena) are just mental images and ideas is the focal point of the Vijñānavāda doctrine. Liberation is *āśrayaparāvṛtti* (see the title "Ālayavijñāna and Āśraya" under "Ālayavijñāna") (see ▸ Ālaya-vijñāna). It is the disappearance of the unreal object and the realization of Tathatā (*yathābhūtam*). It is not the acquisition of anything new, but only seeing things as they really are. It is said that realizing everything is imaginary, the Bodhisattva ceases to imagine anything at all, and this is *bodhi*, the enlightenment (*Mahāyānasūtrāṁkāra* 9: 81). It is seeing consciousness in consciousness (*cittasya citte sthānāt: Mahāyānasūtralamkāra* 18: 66)

Vijñānavāda Is Not Solipsism

The Vijñanavāda with its doctrine of *cittamātra* or *vijñāptimātra*(*tā*) does not advocate solipsism. It never argued that world is in God's mind either. Consciousness is intersubjective. Karma is personal as well as communitarian. Therefore, the existence of other minds is affirmed. There are many consciousnesses. In Vasubandhu's *Vimś atikā* (verse 18) with its auto-commentary, one gets a reference of other minds. Vasubandu's treatment of *vijñapti* in the above-mentioned text explains that a "concept" is not mere linguistic representation. A concept is also a convention based upon experience and dispositions (*vāsanā*). In the waking state, the thought process can be dominated by the concepts of others as well. Understanding "Vasubandhu's notion of vijñapti," as presented in his text, "one avoids attributing any solipsism to him" [15]. Dharmakīrt also gives this argument for the existence of other minds: One consciousness views another by inference based on observation of what the other is bodily or physically doing [16].

Vijñānavāda and Idealism

Vasunbadhu's *Vimśatikā* constitutes the first of his longer treatise on *vijñapti-mātratā* (consciousness only). In the verses one and two of this text, he gives the idealist position of *vijñaptimātratā*. Further, the first 14 verses of *Vimśatikā* are set in such way to establish idealism by refuting the reality of matter. Many scholars consider this school as idealism [17–19]. See also the title "Yogācāra Idealism and Ontology" under Yogācāra (see ▶ Yogācāra)

Sākāra and Nirākāra Vijñānavāda

The system of Yogācāra-Vijñānavāda was one of the prominent systems of philosophy in India. According to Advayavajra (978–1053 A.D.), there are two kinds of Vijñānavāda: *Sākāra* and *Nirākāra*. The *Sākāra Vijñānavāda* held that there is no subject-object duality. What appears is the form of mind. Here the mind itself is perceived in the perception form. Knowledge is endowed with form. In other words, the *Sākāra Vijñānavāda* school held that enlightened consciousness retains mental representations. According to the *Nirākāra Vijñānavāda* knowledge has no form. It is felt within. The mind which is formless can be experienced only within, and it is totally amorphous [20].

Vijñānavāda and Phenomenology

The Vijñānavāda has much in common with phenomenology. Phenomenology and the Vijñānavāda take *human experience* as their beginning and ending points. Both focuses on similar epistemological issues like perception, sensation, and cognition. The Vijñānavāda does not give importance to the existence of external objects and world, but focuses on the process how they are known in awareness. Western phenomenology with Husserl and others do not provide with an exact correlation to the Vijñānavāda. The Vijñānavāda vocabulary with *darśana* and *nimitta, grāhaka* and *grāhya, ālambaka* and *ālambana*, etc., in fact, is far richer and more intricate than the Husserlian version with *noesis* and *noema*. Buddhist phenomenology reached its zenith in the Yogācāra-Vijñānavāda school. The Vijñānavādins examined the constitution, formation, and function of cognition from epistemological, logical, psychological, ethical, and soteriological standpoints. They found that it was specifically in the dominion of cognition that the major problematic was situated, which they tried to analyze and resolve [6].

The conceptions of *nimiitabhāga* and *darś anabhāga* go in line with the phenomenological analysis of noema and noesis, respectively. *Nimittabhāga* is the cognitively produced part (the noema) and *darśanabhāga* is the seeing part (the noesis). In the Buddhist texts, *nimitta* means the sensorial marks by which a sense object is cognized and determined as what it is with a characterization with color, shape, texture, etc. For the Vijñānavāda, it implies the cognitive sensory marks by which a projection of consciousness gets an objective quality. *Darśanabhāga* is an active subjective constituent of perception and cognition. But this cannot be just reduced to simple subjective, nor objective components. The grasped (*grāhya*) and the grasper (*grāhaka*) do not have independent existence apart from consciousness. The main contention of the Vijñānavada has remained the same, in spite of the appearance of varied trends and texts in the long career of this school from the third/fourth century A.D. Despite the proliferation of Yogācāra-Vijñānavāda identities, it "does display a certain methodological consistency" and this methodology could be characterized as "phenomenology" [21].

Cross-References

- Ālaya-vijñāna
- Asaṅga
- Dignāga
- Sautrāntika
- Vasubandhu
- Vijñāna
- Yogācāra

References

1. Stcherbatsky T (1996) The conception of Buddhist nirvana, 2nd revised edn. Motilal Banarsidass, Delhi
2. Chatterjee AK (1999) The Yogācāra idealism, new edn. Motilal Banarsidass, New Delhi, pp 40, 41
3. Lusthaus D (2002) Buddhist phenomenology: a philosophical investigation of Yogācāra Buddhism and the Ch'eng Wei-shih lun. RoutledgeCurzon, London, p 63
4. Pande GC (1993) Studies in Mahāyāna. Central Institute of Higher Tibetan Studies, Sarnath, Varanasi, p 126
5. Lusthaus D (2002) Buddhist phenomenology: a philosophical investigation of Yogācāra Buddhism and the Ch'eng Wei-shih lun. RoutledgeCurzon, London, p 363
6. Lusthaus D (2002) Buddhist phenomenology: a philosophical investigation of Yogācāra Buddhism and the Ch'eng Wei-shih lun. RoutledgeCurzon, London
7. Chatterjee AK (1999) The Yogācāra Idealism, new edn. Motilal Banarsidass, New Delhi, pp 40–44
8. Pande GC (1993) Studies in Mahāyāna. Central Institute of Higher Tibetan Studies, Sarnath, Varanasi
9. Franco E (1986) Once again on Dharmakīrti's Deviation from Dignāga on Pratyakṣābhāsa. J Indian Philos 14:79–97
10. Makransky JJ (1997) Buddhahood embodied: sources of controversy in India and Tibet. State University of New York Press, Albany, pp 211–218
11. Schmithausen L (2005) On the problem of the relation of spiritual practice and philosophical theory in Buddhism. In: Williams P (ed) Buddhism: critical concepts in religious studies, vol 2. Routledge, London/New York, pp 242–254
12. Willis JD (1979) Two threads of the Yogācāra and some later confusions. In: Willis JD (tr) (ed) On knowing reality: the Tattvārtha chapter of Asaṅga's Bodhisattvabhūmi. Columbia University Press, New York, pp 20–36
13. Wilson JB Jr (1986) The meaning of mind in the Mahāyāna philosophy of mind-only (cittamātra): a study of a presentation by the Tibetan scholar Gung-tang Jam-bay-yang of Asaṅga's theory of mind-basis-of-all (ālayaviñāna) and related topics in Buddhist theories of personal continuity, epistemology and hermeneutics. PhD dissertation, University Microfilms International, Ann Arbor
14. Mahathera PV (1987) Buddhist meditation in theory and practice: a general exposition according to Pāli canon of the Theravāda school, 3rd edn. Buddhist Missionary Society, Kuala Lumpur
15. Kalupahana DJ (1992) The principles of Buddhist psychology. Sri Satuguru, Delhi, p 188
16. Dharmakīrti (1975) Santānāntara-siddhi, with Vinītadeva's Santānāntara-siddhi-ṭīkā. In: Gupta HC (ed) Papers of Th. Stcherbatsky. Reprint, Indian Studies Past & Present, Calcutta, pp 55–91
17. Chatterjee AK (1999) The Yogācāra idealism. Motilal Banarsidass, Delhi
18. Takakusu J (1975) The essentials of Buddhist philosophy. Motilal Banasrsidass, Delhi, p 81
19. Herman AL (1983) An introduction to Buddhist thought: a philosophic history of Indian Buddhism. University Press of America, Lanham/London, p 331
20. Advayavajra, Shastri H (ed) (1927) Advayavajrasaṁgraha. Gaekwad Oriental Institute, Baroda
21. Lusthaus D (2002) Buddhist phenomenology: a philosophical investigation of Yogācāra Buddhism and the Ch'eng Wei-shih lun. RoutledgeCurzon, London, p 9

Vijñaptimātra(tā)

- Vijñānavāda
- Yogācāra

Vikramaśilā

K. T. S. Sarao
Department of Buddhist Studies, University of Delhi, Delhi, India

Synonyms

Vikramaśīlā

Definition

A famous seat of Buddhist learning in India during the early medieval period

The Vikramaśilā Mahāvihāra was one of the two most important centers of Buddhist learning in India during the Pāla dynasty, along with Nālandā Mahāvihāra. Vikramaśilā is said to have been built in the second half of the eighth century by King Dharmapāla (r. 783–820 C.E.) supposedly because the quality of scholarship at Nālandā had declined. It continued to be the only center that imparted higher Buddhist studies and during the period it flourished Vikramaśilā was in regular intercourse with different Tibetan and Nepalese Buddhist monasteries. Most of the literary information on Vikramaśilā is primarily available in the Tibetan sources, particularly Tāranātha's work, the *History of Buddhism in India* [2]. Vikramaśilā has been identified with archeological remains in the neighborhood of Antichak village, close to Pātharghātā and located at a distance of about 50 km to the east of Bhagalpur in Bihar at 25°16′23″ N and 87°14′26″ E (see [4]).

It has been mentioned in the Tibetan sources that five important monastic institutions that grew up in early medieval eastern India during the Pāla period were Vikramaśilā, Nālandā, Somapura, Odantapura, and Jaggadāla. According to these sources, Nālandā, though still renowned, had gone past its prime, and Vikramaśilā had become the foremost center of learning. Together these five monastic institutions formed "a system of co-ordination among them... it seems from the evidence that the different seats of Buddhist learning that functioned in eastern India under the Pālas were regarded together as forming a network, an interlinked group of institutions," and it was quite common for eminent scholars to move from one position to another among the institutions (see [4], pp. 352–353). Vikramaśilā resembled Nālandā in many ways. Its main orientation was Mahāyānist, with an even stronger emphasis on Tantric beliefs and practices; the curriculum, though, may have been less extensive ([7], p. 156). Apart from Tantrism, which was the major branch of learning, subjects such as metaphysics, astrology, astronomy, philosophy, grammar, logic, and medicine were taught here. The *Guhyasamāja Tantra* was taught in as many as 53 vihāras of the Vikramaśilā Mahāvihāra. Vikramaśilā is credited with having produced eminent scholars who often traveled to foreign lands to spread the dharma. Some of the great scholars closely associated with Vikramaśilā Mahāvihāra were Ātiśa, Naropa, Santipa, Jetari, Ratnavajra, Buddhajñānapāda, Vairocanarakṣita, Prajñākaramati, Vāgīsvarakīrti, Jñānaśrīmitra, Ratnākaraśānti, Vīryasiṃha, Abhayākaragupta, and Tathāgatarakṣita ([4], p. 362).

The mahāvihāra consisted of six colleges, and each of these colleges had its own gate under the charge of a *dvāra-paṇḍita* (gate scholar). The *dvāra-paṇḍita* appears to have been in charge of admissions. The mahāvihāra was headed by an *adhyakṣa* (abbot), generally appointed by the king, of whom the most famous was Ātiśa Dīpaṃkara Śrījñāna (982–1054 C.E.) (see [2], pp. 313, 329). Like Nālandā, Vikramaśilā had strong ties with Tibet and Nepal from where students in large numbers came for higher studies in Buddhism (see [7], p. 156). According to Tibetan sources, Vikramaśilā eventually eclipsed Nālandā in royal patronage ([2], p. 319). According to a Tibetan report, it was a common practice at Vikramaśilā that before conferred to a position, a new scholar had to prove himself in a public debate presided over by the king (see [5], p. 20f). "One hundred and sixty *paṇḍita*-s and about a thousand monks permanently resided in Vikramaśilā... (and) five thousand ordained monks assembled there for occasional offerings" ([2], p. 313). However, the number of monks dwindled to about a hundred when Turuṣka raids began ([4], p. 359).

According to Tāranātha, at the height of its glory during the reign of King Canaka (955–83 C.E.), the *dvāra-paṇḍitas* (gate scholars) were as follows: Ratnākaraśānti (eastern gate), Vāgīsvarakīrti (western gate), Ratnavajra (first central gate), Jñānaśrīmitra (second central gate), Naropa (northern gate), and Prajñākaramati (southern gate) ([4], pp. 360–361). According to S. Dutt, Vikramaśilā appears to have had a more clearly defined hierarchy than the other *mahāvihāras*, as follows ([4], pp. 360–361):

1. Abbot (*adhyakṣa*), the head of the Mahāvihāra
2. Six gate protectors or gate scholars (*dvāra-paṇḍita*), one each for the six gates
3. Senior professors (*paṇḍita*), roughly 108 in number
4. Professors (*upādhyāya* or *ācārya*), about 160 in number
5. Resident monks (*bhikṣu*), about 1,000 in number

The remains of the ancient mahāvihāra, spread over an area of about 50 hectares, have been partially excavated. These excavations (see [8]) have exposed a gigantic square monastery with a two-terraced cruciform stūpa, a library building, and an assortment of votive stūpas. Each of the four sides of the gigantic square monastery consists of 52 residential cells making 208 cells in all. All the cells open into a common verandah and face the cruciform stūpa which is located in the center of the gigantic monastery. The stūpa, which is a brick structure, can only be accessed from the northern side. On each side of the stūpa, there is a chamber with an antechamber and a *maṇḍapa* (porch). Each of the four chambers had a large stucco image of the seated Buddha. Three of these images were found in situ, but the fourth one in the northern chamber was most probably replaced by a stone image after the stucco image either suffered some damage or was removed due to some other reason. About 100 ft to the south of the monastery and attached to it through a narrow corridor is a rectangular structure that has been identified as a library building [8].

Vikramaśilā flourished for about four centuries till it was destroyed by Bakhtiyār Khalji sometime between 1198 and 1206 C.E. who, "having razed it to the ground, had thrown the foundation stones into the Gaṅgā" ([6], p. 64). A few of the monks who survived the massacre fled to Tibet. The report suggests that even at the time of Śākya Śrībhadra's visit to Magadha (1206 C.E.), the mahāvihāra had not been entirely wrecked, but it was entirely obliterated by 1235. Vikramaśilā appears to have been subjected to repeated raids by the Turuṣkas, as the huge masses of brick and stone structures that Vikramaśilā presented to the raiders were difficult to demolish wholesale by a single assault (see [4], p. 359).

Cross-References

▶ Nālandā
▶ Stūpa

References

1. Bose PN (1923) Indian teachers of Buddhist universities. Theosophical Publication House, Madras
2. Chimpa L, Chattopadhyaya A (trans) (1970) Tāranātha's history of Buddhism in India. Indian Institute of Advanced Study, Simla
3. Dey N (1909) The Vikramasila monastery. Journal and Proceedings of the Asiatic Society of Bengal, new series, vol V. Asiatic Society, Calcutta, pp 1–18
4. Dutt S (1962) Buddhist monks and monasteries of India: their history and contribution to Indian culture. George Allen and Unwin, London
5. Guenther H (1963) The life and teaching of Nāropa. Oxford University Press, London
6. Roerich G (ed) (1959) Biography of Dharmasvāmin (Chag lo tsa-ba Chos rje-dpal): A Tibetan monk pilgrim (with a historical and critical intro. by Altekar AS). K.P. Jayaswal Research Institute, Patna
7. Sharfe H (2012) Handbook of oriental studies. Brill, Leiden
8. Vikramasila: excavation report. http://bhpromo.org.in. Accessed 22 Dec 2014

Vikramaśīlā

▶ Vikramaśilā

Vimalakirti

▶ Vimalakīrti

Vimalakīrti

James B. Apple
Department of Religious Studies, University of Calgary, Calgary, AB, Canada

Synonyms

Holy Teaching of Vimalakirti; Vimalakirti; Vimalakīrti Nirdeśa Sūtra; Vimalakīrti Sūtra

Definition

Legendary bodhisattva figure in the *Vimalakīrtinirdeśa.*

Vimalakīrti is a celebrated legendary bodhisattva most famously known for his teachings and miraculous activities in the Mahāyāna scripture called the *Vimalakīrtinirdeśa* ("The Teaching of Vimalakīrti"). The scripture has enjoyed for centuries great popularity among Mahāyāna Buddhists in India, Central Asia, China, Tibet, and Japan. The *Vimalakīrtinirdeśa* is one of the oldest and more famous texts of Mahāyāna Buddhist literature. Although the central figure of Vimalakīrti is presented as the ideal Mahāyāna lay practitioner and a contemporary of Gautama Buddha (sixth to fifth centuries B.C.E.), the *Vimalakīrtinirdeśa* was likely composed in India in approximately 100 C.E. ([1], p. xcviii). Indirect evidence for the presence of Vimalakīrti in ancient northwest Gandhāra has been found in a recently identified fragmentary Gāndhārī scroll which describes an encounter between the Buddha and the young son of Vimalakīrti, the *licchavikumāra* Sucitti ([2], p. 11). As far as currently known, no mention of Vimalakīrti appears in any text earlier than the sūtra.

The *Vimalakīrtinirdeśa* is known as the "jewel of the Mahāyāna sūtras" and exhibits a dramatic narrative, filled with dialogue and miraculous events that ostensively teach the wisdom of emptiness (*śūnyatā*) fused with skill in liberative technique (*upāya*) to indicate the inconceivable profundity of ultimate reality (*acintyavimokṣa*) ([3], p. 7). However, the *Vimalakīrtinirdeśa* is also a great example of the rhetoric of Mahāyāna discourse which recreates and relocates authority, legitimacy, and sanctity to overcome traditional forms of Buddhism in order to advocate textualized Mahāyāna forms of Buddhism in the reading or listening experiences of its audience [4].

Although the actual popularity in ancient India of the *Vimalakīrtinirdeśa* is not clearly known, the scripture was cited in the scholarly works of Indian Buddhist authors ([1], pp. cxi–cxv). The popularity of this scripture outside of India is attested by the number of translations preserved in Central and East Asia including eight Chinese translations, two or three Tibetan translations, as well as translations preserved in Sogdian and Khotanese. Chinese translations of the *Vimalakīrtinirdeśa* were made several times over the centuries, including those by Lokakṣema (188 C.E.), Dharmarakṣa (308 C.E.), Upaśūnya (545 C.E.), and Jñānagupta (591 C.E.). There are three classical Chinese translations extant: the 佛說維摩詰經 *Foshuo weimojie jing* (in two juans translated by Zhi Qian 支謙, ca. 222–252), the 維摩詰所說經 *Weimojie suoshuo jing* (in three juans translated by Kumārajīva 鳩摩羅什, fifth century), and the 說無垢稱經 *Shuo wugoucheng jing* (in juans translated by Xuanzang 玄奘, seventh century) [5]. The oldest translation preserved, and most likely representing the oldest available recension of the text ([1], p. xxviii), is that of Zhi Qian 支謙, carried out between 222 and 229 C.E. Two especially influential translations are the Kumārajīva version (406 C.E.), which is the most widely used, and the Xuanzang version (650 C.E.). Kumārajīva's Chinese translation consists of 14 chapters. Most Japanese versions are based on the Chinese Kumārajīva version. The Tibetan translation, *'Phags pa dri ma med par grags pas bstan pa zhes bya ba theg pa chen po'i mdo*, was translated by Dharmatāśīla (*Chos nyid tshul khrims*) at the end of the eighth century. In 1999, Prof. Hisao Takahashi of Taishō University discovered a complete Sanskrit manuscript of the *Vimalakīrtinirdeśa* among the Chinese Government's Potala collection in Tibet [6]. The manuscript was written in a Bengali-related script and dates to between the eleventh and thirteenth centuries. A facsimile edition of the manuscript [7] and a diplomatic edition of the Sanskrit [8] have been recently published. The Sanskrit version as well as the Tibetan version of the *Vimalakīrtinirdeśa* consist of 12 chapters (*parivarta*). The contents of the 12 chapters are outlined as follows.

1. Purification of the Buddha-Field (*Buddhakṣetrapariśuddhinidāna*)
   The opening vignette is set in the Āmrapālīvana in Vaiśālī where Śākyamuni Buddha gives a teaching to a large assembly of śrāvakas, bodhisattvas, and gods. A wealthy young Licchavi noble from Vaiśālī, the bodhisattva Ratnākara, leads a delegation of 500 Licchavi youths, each carrying a jeweled parasol, to meet and praise the Buddha. Upon the Licchavis arrival, the Buddha miraculously transforms all the parasols into a giant canopy that covers the universe. The Buddha then explains the purity of the Buddha-field (*buddhakṣetra*) and the purification of a bodhisattva's mind based on a Buddha-field's purity. The Buddha then quells the doubt of Śāriputra by teaching why a Buddha-field appears as impure to beings and then transforms the universe into a mass appearance of jeweled splendor by touching his big toe on the ground.
2. Inconceivable Skill in Liberative Technique (*Acintyopāyakauśalyaparivarta*)
   The scene shifts location to the house of Vimalakīrti. Out of compassion for the suffering of all beings and as a strategy liberative technique (*upāya*), Vimalakīrti feigns a serious illness and people from the town come to his house to inquire about his health. Vimalakīrti then gives a discourse to the townspeople on the impermanence of the human body and the qualities of the Tathāgata-body (*tathāgatakāya*).
3. The Disciples' and Bodhisattvas' Reluctance to Visit Vimalakīrti (*Śrāvakabodhisatvavisarjanapraśna*)
   Vimalakīrti then makes a "psychic" communication to the Buddha by thinking about why the Buddha has failed to show concern for him. The scene shifts back to the Āmrapālīvana in Vaiśālī where the Buddha proceeds to request ten of his great śrāvaka disciples, such as Śāriputra, Subhūti, and Ānanda, as well as bodhisattvas, such as Maitreya, Prābhāvyūha, and Jagtiṃdhara, to go visit Vimalakīrti and inquire about his health. All of them are reluctant to visit Vimalakīrti and decline the Buddha's request because of Vimalakīrti's eloquence in rendering them speechless during past encounters.
4. The Consolation of the Invalid (*Glānapratisaṃmodanāparivarta*)
   Mañjuśrī, the crown prince bodhisattva of wisdom, accepts the Buddha's request to visit Vimalakīrti. The scene then changes to the house of Vimalakīrti, where a vast number of visitors, including gods, goddesses, śrāvakas, and bodhisattvas, are miraculously accommodated to listen to the dialogue between Mañjuśrī and Vimalakīrti. The dialogue between Mañjuśrī and Vimalakīrti then proceeds to discuss emptiness (*śūnyatā*), the nature of sickness, and the range (*gocara*) of the bodhisattva.
5. The Vision of the Inconceivable Liberation (*Acintyavimokṣasaṃdarśanaparivarta*)
   The great śrāvaka Śāriputra then mentally inquires about seating arrangements. Thereupon Vimalakīrti teaches on the inquiry of dharma and then performs a miraculous feat that brings gigantic thrones sent by the Tathāgata Merupradīparāja from the Merudhvajā universe. Once all the beings in attendance are seated, Vimalakīrti explains the inconceivable liberation (*acintyavimokạ*) of Tathāgatas and bodhisattvas.
6. The Goddess (*Devatāparivartaḥ*)
   The discussion between Vimalakīrti and Mañjuśrī resumes where they discuss a number of topics including essencelessness (*dharmanairātmya*), compassion, joy, and equanimity, as well as baselessness (*apratiṣṭhāna*). A goddess (*devatā*) then appears whereby miraculous flowers fall from the sky and stick only to the śrāvakas. The goddess engages in a paradoxical dialogue with Śāriputra where she advocates

the superiority of the Mahāyāna and explains eight great wonders (*āścaryābhutadharma*) of Vimalakīrti's house. The goddess then employs her magical power to exchange appearances with the elder Śāriputra to demonstrate the equivalence of the sexes. Vimalakīrti then reveals that the goddess is actually an irreversible bodhisattva who has served innumerable previous Buddha's.

7. The Family of the Tathagatas (*Tathāgatagotraparivarta*)
   The dialogue between Vimalakīrti and Mañjuśrī continues on with Vimalakīrti teaching on the roundabout ways of a bodhisattva and Mañjuśrī giving a discourse on the family (*gotra*) of the Tathāgata. The elder Mahākāśyapa confirms Mañjuśrī's teaching. The chapter concludes with Vimalakīrti teaching in verse to the bodhisattva Sarvarūpasaṃdarśana.
8. Entering the Dharma-Gate of Non-duality (*Advayadharmamukhapraveśaparivarta*)
   Vimalakīrti inquires to the bodhisattva about how to enter the dharma-gate of non-duality (*advaya*). Thirty-one bodhisattvas reply each with their own ideas of what constitutes the dharma-gate of non-duality. Mañjuśrī, as the 32nd bodhisattva to reply, provides an explanation, and then asks Vimalakīrti for his response. Vimalakīrti gives a performative "great lion's roar of profound silence" ([3], p. 9) to convey the bodhisattva's dharma-gate of non-duality.
9. The Feast Brought by the Emanated Incarnation (*Nirmitabhojanānayanaparivarta*)
   The great elder Śāriputra, out of concern with Vinaya protocol, agonizes about the providing of food before noontime. Vimalakīrti, telepathically reading Śāriputra's mind, then miraculously reveals a meal scene from the Sarvagandhasugandhā universe where the Tathāgata Gandhottamakūṭa is together with a retinue of bodhisattvas. Vimalakīrti then creates an imaginary bodhisattva who goes to the Sarvagandhasugandhā universe to retrieve food. The imaginary bodhisattva receives meals remains from the Tathāgata Gandhottamakūṭa and instantly returns to the house of Vimalakīrti. The assembly at the house of Vimalakīrti shares the special food and then receives instructions regarding the Sarvagandhasugandhā universe, the Sahā universe of Śākyamuni, and the conditions for entering a pure Buddha-field.
10. Lesson of the Destructible and the Indestructible (*Kṣayākṣayo*)
    The scene translocates back to the Āmrapālīvana in Vaiśālī with Vimalakīrti magically transporting all the assemblies in his house directly into the presence of Śākyamuni. Ānanda then tells Śākyamuni of the meal shared at Vimalakīrti's house whereby Śākyamuni explains the duration and effects of the food. The Buddha then goes on to explain the variety and similarity of Buddha-fields, the sameness and inconceivability of the Buddhas, and the superiority of bodhisattvas over śrāvakas. Bodhisattvas from the Sarvagandhasugandhā universe then request a teaching from Śākyamuni to which he gives an exposition on the exhaustible and inexhaustible (kṣayo 'kṣayo). The Sarvagandhasugandhā bodhisattvas, having rejoiced and praised the exposition, then reenter the Sarvagandhasugandhā universe.
11. Vision of the Universe Abhirati and the Tathagata Aksobhya (*Abhiratilokadhātvāna yanākṣobhyatathāgatadarśanaparivarta*)
    Vimalakīrti, instigated by the Buddha, explains how to view the body of the Tathāgata. Śāriputra then inquires where Vimalakīrti is from. The Buddha then reveals that Vimalakīrti is an emanation form the Abhirati universe of the Tathāgata Akṣobhya. On request from Śākyamuni, Vimalakīrti miraculously brings the Abhirati universe into view which allows the assemblies in the Sahā universe to gain a vision of the splendors of the Abhirati universe. After Śākyamuni predicts the future rebirth of the assemblies into the Abhirati universe, Vimalakīrti puts the universe back in place.
12. Antecedents and Transmission of the Holy Dharma (*Nigamanaparīndanāparivarta*)
    Śakra, prince of gods, declares that he will protect and help those who uphold this

exposition of dharma (*dharmaparyāya*). Śākyamuni gives consent for Śakra to protect those who uphold the dharma discourse and then gives a Jātaka story of Ratnachattra regarding proper dharma-worship (*dharmapūjā*). Śākyamuni then entrusts the future Buddha and great bodhisattva Maitreya with his supreme awakening and ensures the transmission of the teaching. Śākyamuni then teaches Maitreya on the categories of beginner and veteran bodhisattvas. Maitreya, along with bodhisattvas and dharma protectors, pledges to protect dharma preachers (*dharmabhāṇaka*) of this dharma exposition. The transmission of the dharma exposition is given to Ānanda, and the various titles of the exposition are bestowed.

The *Vimalakīrtinirdeśa* enjoyed immense popularity in China during the Six Dynasties period (222–589 C.E.). The figure of an accomplished layperson like Vimalakīrti offered an influential model for Buddhists in East Asia, where Indian Buddhist monasticism conflicted with Chinese social values. The teachings of the *Vimalakīrtinirdeśa* (*Foshuo weimojie jing*) were well received in the second half of the fourth century among the gentry of the Eastern Jin in southeastern China after being translated by Zhi Qian (active 220–252 C.E.) [9]. Many famous artistic depictions of Vimalakīrti were made throughout Chinese history including stone stele depictions, paintings, sculptures, and frescoes. Multiple images of Vimalakīrti are found on the walls of the Buddhist cave complex of Dunhaung dating between 581 and 1036 C.E. [10]. Vimalakīrti had great purport in Japan as well, as a commentary to the *Vimalakīrtinirdeśa* is attributed to Prince Shotoku (574–622 C.E.), and an early enshrined statue of Vimalakīrti debating with Mañjuśrī is found in the first level of the five-story pagoda built at the Horyuji temple complex. Likewise, the *Yuima-e* ("Service of lecturing on the Vimalakīrtinirdeśa sūtra"), initiated by Fujiwara no Kamatari in the mid-seventh century, is an annual religious service held at the Kōfuku-ji temple in the ancient capital of Nara [11]. The *Vimalakīrtinirdeśa* is popular among contemporary modern Western Buddhist audiences and has been translated into English, French, and German several times.

Cross-References

▶ Bodhisattva
▶ Mādhyamika
▶ Mahāyāna
▶ Mañjuśrī

References

1. Lamotte É (1994) The teaching of Vimalakīrti (Vimalakīrtinirdeśa). Pali Text Society, London
2. Mark A, Salomon R (2010) New evidence for Mahayana in early Gandhāra. East Buddh 41(1):1–22
3. Thurman RAF (1976) The holy teaching of Vimalakīrti: a Mahāyāna scripture. The Pennsylvania State University Press, University Park
4. Cole A (2005) Text as father: paternal seductions in early Mahāyāna Buddhist literature. University of California Press, Berkeley
5. Harrison P 2008 (2010) Experimental core samples of Chinese translations of two Buddhist Sūtras analysed in the light of recent Sanskrit manuscript discoveries. J Int Assoc Buddh Stud 31(1–2):205–249
6. Yonezawa Y (2007) The Vimalakīrtinirdeśa and the (Sarvabuddhaviṣayāvatāra-) Jñānalokālaṃkāra. J Indian Buddh Stud (Indogaku Bukkyōgaku Kenkyū) 55(3):1085–1091
7. Takahashi H et al (ed) (2004) Vimalakīrtinirdeśa and Jñānālokālaṃkāra 2, Vimalakīrtinirdeśa: Transliterated Sanskrit text collated with Tibetan and Chinese translations. Taisho University Press, Tokyo
8. Takahashi H (2006) Vimalakīrtinirdeśa: a Sanskrit edition based upon the manuscript newly found at the Potala palace. Taisho University Press, Tokyo
9. Demiéville P (2004) Vimalakīrti in China (Translated in to English by Sara Boin Webb). Buddh Stud Rev 21:179–196
10. Bunker EC (1968) Early Chinese representations of Vimalakīrti. Artibus Asiae 30(1):28–52
11. Tamenori M (1988) Translated by Edward Kamens. The three jewels: a study and translation of Minamoto Tamenori's Sanboe (Michigan monograph series in Japanese studies)

Vimalakīrti Nirdeśa Sūtra

▶ Vimalakīrti

Vimalakīrti Sūtra

▶ Vimalakīrti

Vimalakīrtinirdeśa

Jens-Uwe Hartmann
Institut für Indologie und Tibetologie, University of Munich, Munich, Germany

Synonyms

Acintya-dharma-vimokṣa; Vimalakīrti-nirdeśa-sūtra

Definition

A discourse of Mahāyāna Buddhism.

The Vimalakīrtinirdeśa, the "Instruction by Vimalakīrti," counts among the best-known discourses (*sūtra*) of Mahāyāna Buddhism. It became especially popular in East Asia, where its popularity was derived from the main character of the story, Vimalakīrti, a follower of the Buddha. He is not a celibate monk or a secluded ascetic, but on the contrary a very wealthy householder living in the town of Vaiśālī. Although a member of the upper class, he is described as a highly accomplished Buddhist practitioner, a bodhisattva, whose mental brilliance and thorough understanding of the real nature of the world and its phenomena set him far apart from all the other well-known followers of the Buddha. One day Vimalakīrti feigns illness, and when all the people come to inquire after his health, he uses this opportunity to instruct them in the basic impermanence of all phenomena, by making reference to his own physical state. This leads up to the longest and probably most famous chapter of the text: At this time, the Buddha is also staying in the city of Vaiśālī together with a large community of monks and an even larger congregation of bodhisattvas. When he moves to send one of his followers to the home of Vimalakīrti in order to inquire after his health, it turns out that first all the famous monks, but then also the bodhisattvas refuse to go. One after the other they report an earlier encounter with Vimalakīrti in which they had been outwitted by him. In each case Vimalakīrti reveals a much deeper understanding of reality than the monk or the bodhisattva he is conversing with. It is easy here to see Vimalakīrti as a possible role model for an affluent and educated lay Buddhist who does not feel in a position to leave the worldly life and to seek salvation in solitude or at least to enter the "homeless" state of a celibate monk. There is a basic tension between the Buddhist ideal of a celibate world-renouncer and Confucian notions of the appropriate behavior of a male member of the society. As a lay person, Vimalakīrti is much closer to such Confucian notions, and this may explain the special popularity of the text in East Asian Buddhism.

Very little is known about the history of the sūtra in India. As in the case of all the other Mahāyāna sutras, the place and date of its origin lie in the dark. By the third century C.E., an Indian version existed, since it was translated into Chinese for the first time then. Recent sensational findings of Indic Buddhist manuscripts in Pakistan and Afghanistan also contain some Mahāyāna texts in Gāndhārī, a northwestern Middle Indian dialect. They push the evidence for the existence of such texts back to the first century C.E., but so far no trace of the Vimalakīrtinirdeśa has been found. There is, however, a sūtra that contains a story about the son of Vimalakīrti [1]. Although this son is unknown to the Vimalakīrtinirdeśa, the story suggests that the figure of Vimalakīrti was already established. Until recently, the text of the sūtra was known only from translations. Altogether three Chinese translations are preserved, the first by Zhi Qian between 222 and 229, the second by Kumārajīva in 406, and the third by Xuanzang in 650. There is a complete translation into Tibetan dated to the beginning of the ninth century, and there are fragments of translations into the Central Asian languages Sogdian, Khotanese, and Uighur, all produced in the latter half of the first millennium.

While the Sogdian and Uighur versions are based on Kumārajīva's Chinese translation, the Khotanese text is derived from a Sanskrit original. A number of quotations from the sūtra in Indian Buddhist commentaries attest to its spread in India, but the original text seemed lost until in 1999 a complete Sanskrit manuscript was found in the Potala palace in Tibet and published by a group of Japanese scholars [5].

The text is divided into 12 chapters of unequal length. The first chapter describes the wondrous setting of the sūtra: The Buddha stays in the town of Vaiśālī together with an enormous crowd of monks, bodhisattvas, and nonhuman beings. When several young men present parasols to him, the Buddha transforms them into one and expands its size so that it covers the whole world-system. The crowd marvels at this magical feat, and at the request of the young man the Buddha teaches about the purity of the Buddha fields and demonstrates that purity and impurity are nothing real and that their perception depends on the mental development of the spectator. In the second chapter, the scene switches to the house of Vimalakīrti who is described as the paradigmatic lay follower, excelling both in his command of skilful means (*upāya*) and in his understanding (*prajñā*) of emptiness or reality. These skilful means lead him to feign a sickness, and when all the townspeople come to inquire after his health, he instructs them extensively in the transitory and unreal nature of the body. The third chapter describes the futile attempts of the Buddha to send prominent members of his crowd of monks, bodhisattvas, and lay followers to Vimalakīrti. They all refuse and report how they have been humbled in a previous conversation by his eloquence and his deep understanding. Then, in the fourth chapter, the Buddha finally calls on the Bodhisattva Mañjuśrī, paragon of wisdom, to go, and the latter consents. The whole crowd accompanies him to the house of Vimalakīrti and listens to a dialogue between the two on illness, emptiness, wrong and correct views, skilful means, understanding, and the domain of the bodhisattva. When the monk Śāriputra wonders about seats for the whole assembly (Chap. 5), Vimalakīrti instructs him in non-grasping and, then, by his supernatural faculties, has a large number of thrones brought from a distant Buddha land, which all fit into his house. Śāriputra marvels at this sight, and Vimalakīrti advises him on the magical feats of bodhisattvas who possess the inconceivable liberation. In Chap. 6, Vimalakīrti and Mañjuśrī continue their discourse on the nonexistence of living beings, on benevolence, and on baselessness. Then the goddess of the house displays a miracle of flowers and engages the astonished Śāriputra in a conversation about how the correct understanding of reality is prevented by conceptual and dualistic thinking. Finally, she performs another miracle by transforming Śāriputra into a woman and herself into a man in order to demonstrate the baselessness of such dualistic categories. Again Mañjuśrī and Vimalakīrti resume their discourse (Chap. 7), this time on seeming contradictions in the behavior of a bodhisattva which again reveal the emptiness of such categories, and then they expand this reflection on the family of the Tathāgata. When a member of the assembly asks Vimalakīrti about his absent relatives, servants, and employees, he answers with a long series of metaphorical stanzas. In Chap. 8, Vimalakīrti asks the bodhisattvas about the entrance into the teaching of nonduality. In turn, 30 bodhisattvas offer statements on this topic, and then Mañjuśrī declares that not saying anything is the entrance into nonduality. Finally, Vimalakīrti is asked for a statement and simply remains silent. When Śāriputra, obliged as a monk to take his daily meal before noon, becomes concerned about eating (Chap. 9), Vimalakīrti, again by his supernatural powers, reveals another universe with another Buddha to the assembly and creates a phantom bodhisattva to be sent there in order to request the remains of the delicious food in the begging bowl of the distant Buddha. The request is fulfilled, and a large crowd of bodhisattvas from the other universe accompany the phantom on his way back in order to meet Vimalakīrti. He creates the necessary number of additional thrones in his house and receives the newcomers, and the seemingly little food brought from the other universe turns out to be inexhaustible. Asked by the foreign bodhisattvas about the teaching of Śākyamuni,

Vimalakīrti gives a short summary of the Buddhist doctrine and explains the specific requirements for the difficult conversion of beings in this world. In Chap. 10, Vimalakīrti performs another miracle by transposing the whole assembly from his house to the place where the Buddha stays. The Buddha explains to Ānanda the wondrous effects of the food brought from the other universe and then goes on to talk about the Buddha fields, the sameness of all the Buddhas, and how a bodhisattva neither abides in the unconditioned nor exhausts the conditioned. Delighted, the foreign bodhisattvas return to their universe. The Buddha goes on with a teaching on the nonexistence of all Buddhas (Chap. 11). Then Śāriputra asks about Vimalakīrti's former birth and learns that he came from the well-known Buddha field named Abhirati where the Buddha Akṣobhya resides. When the assembly wants to see this Buddha field, Vimalakīrti miraculously brings that universe in his right hand to this world, shows it to the assembly, and returns it without any damage. Once again, Śāriputra marvels at the sight. The final Chap. 12 describes the transmission of the sūtra and the merit acquired by those who spread and preserve it. The Buddha illustrates the need to preserve the dharma and the means of appropriately honoring it with a story about a previous birth. Finally, he entrusts the teaching first to the next Buddha Maitreya and then to Ānanda, who generally is the person responsible for transmitting the discourses of the Buddha.

The whole work is aimed at the elimination of dualistic thought seen as the root of ignorance and delusion. All mind objects arise from false imagination, and in reality they are baseless; understanding this leads to the acceptance of the sameness of all phenomena and to nonduality. Affirmation or negation of any proposition about a phenomenon is likewise false, and therefore the only possible position is the absence of any position. In the endeavor to illustrate this, the text deconstructs everything by means of miracles or dialogues: time, space, sex, morality, and even the Buddha himself. Thus, the whole text is a perfect expression of the middle way as understood by the Mahāyāna. The ideas put forward in the sūtra are highly sophisticated and often meant to irritate in their seeming contradictions, especially when viewed from the perspective of canonical Buddhism, but several times they are expressed with a touch of humor, and this makes the reading instructive, inspiring, and even entertaining to a degree not often met with in Mahāyāna sūtras.

There are many translations into Western languages [2, 3, 4, 6], the first already dating from the end of the nineteenth century. Most of them are based on the Chinese translation of Kumārajīva and, inspired to a certain extent by its popularity in East Asian Buddhism, are addressed to the nonacademic reader. This has made the text one of the best-known Mahāyāna sūtras in the West. The best philological study continues to be the work of Lamotte [2], who made use of the Tibetan and Chinese versions and added copious notes to his own translation (originally into French in 1962).

Cross-References

- ▶ Kumārajīva
- ▶ Mahāyāna
- ▶ Mañjuśrī
- ▶ Upāya

References

1. Allon M, Salomon R (2010) New evidence for Mahāyāna in early Gandhāra. East Buddh 41:1–22
2. Lamotte É (1994) The teaching of Vimalakīrti (Vimalakīrtinirdeśa). The Pali Text Society, Oxford
3. McRae J (2004) The Vimalakīrti Sūtra. Translated from the Chinese (Taishō Vol 14, Number 475), BDK English Tripiṭaka 20-I, 26-I, Berkeley, pp 63–201
4. Nattier J (2000) The teaching of Vimalakīrti (Vimalakīrtinirdeśa): a review of four English translations. Buddh Lit 2:234–258
5. Study Group on Buddhist Sanskrit Literature (2006) Vimalakīrtinirdeśa. A Sanskrit edition based upon the manuscript newly found at the Potala palace. Taisho University Press, Tokyo
6. Thurman RAF (1976) The holy teaching of Vimalakīrti. A Mahāyāna scripture. The Pennsylvania State University, London
7. Whitehead JD (1978) The Sinicization of the Vimalakirtinirdesa Sutra. Bull Soc Stud Chinese Relig 5:3–51

Vimalakīrti-Nirdeśa-Sūtra

► Vimalakīrtinirdeśa

Vimāna Stories

► Vimānavatthu

Vimānavatthu

K. T. S. Sarao
Department of Buddhist Studies, University of Delhi, Delhi, India

Synonyms

Stories of celestial mentions; Vimāna stories

Definition

The Vimānavatthu is the sixth book in the Khuddaka Nikāya of the Sutta Piṭaka of Pāli Tipiṭaka.

The Vimānavatthu which is the sixth book in the Khuddaka Nikāya of the Sutta Piṭaka of Pāli Tipiṭaka is an anthology of 85 short stories consisting of 1,282 verses. Each of the stories talks about a *deva* (divine being) who has attained residence in a *vimāna* (heavenly abode, celestial mansion) as a reward for a meritorious deed that this *deva* performed in his or her previous birth as a human being. The text of the Vimānavatthu consists of 7 *vaggas* containing 17, 11, 10, 12, 14, 10, and 11 stories, respectively. All the stories follow a similar pattern. Each story begins with an introductory verse (or verses) in which the *deva* is asked about the cause for his or her rebirth within that particular *vimāna*. The *deva* thereupon relates his or her previous good deed and the reward that it brought in accordance of the level of the merit. It has been mentioned that these stories were told by the *devas* themselves to Moggallāna, Vaṅgīsa, and others when they were on their visits to the *devalokas* (*deva* worlds), and they in turn reported these stories to Śākyamuni Buddha on returning. According to the Sri Lankan chronicle Mahāvaṃsa, the Vimānavatthu and the Petavatthu were taught by Mahinda to King Devānampiyatissa's queen Anulā and her 500 companions on the day of his arrival in Anurādhapura ([1]: xiv.58).

Its commentary (*Vimānavatthu-aṭṭhakathā*) written by Dhammapāla, sometimes called *Vimalatthavilāsinī*, forms part of the Paramatthadīpanī. According to this commentary, "*Vimānas* are the abodes of pleasure of the gods, and are so called as they have sprung up in accordance with the merits resulting from the amount of good deeds performed by them. They are of one and two *yojanas* in extent, are brilliant with gems, and being of variegated colours and forms are really worth seeing" (see [2], p. x). It has been further explained that these column-supported palaces could be moved at will by the resident *devas*. For instance, a *deva* could pay a visit to the Earth in a *vimāna*, and occasionally some of these *devas* are mentioned as descending to Earth in their *vimānas* when bade by the Buddha. The lives of the *devas* in these *vimānas* are shown as extremely delightful, and the *vimānas* themselves are depicted as centers of supreme joy and happiness.

In the stories told in the Vimānavatthu undoubtedly "with much forethought... peculiar stress is laid" ([2], p. v) on the description of these *vimānas*, in order to "induce listeners to lead a pure life and to do meritorious deeds in order to obtain bliss after death" ([7], p. 260). The Vimānavatthu, like the Petavatthu, is clearly addressed to the laity and is an important source for popular religion as it deals with stories of persons who after death are reborn as devas and enjoy the fruit of their good deeds.

Being a small treatise of questions and answers, the Vimānavatthu is written in easy and intelligible language ([2], p. xv). But it is generally considered a work of mediocre literary quality which is composed according to set pattern and is devoid of style (see [4], p. 50). Winternitz found it as "highly displeasing" and "fortunately not so voluminous" work ([10], p. 96). According to him, the doctrine of karma is explained through examples "most inartistically" in the "stereotyped" small stories of the Vimānavatthu in which "what is poetical is only the metrical form" ([10], p. 96). However, along with Petavatthu, the Vimānavatthu is quite popular among the laity wherever Theravāda Buddhism is followed. References have also been made frequently to the stories from the Vimānavatthu in later doctrinal Buddhist texts whenever a career of virtue is exemplified. For instance, Maṭṭakuṇḍalī and Sirimā Vimāna are referred to in the Commentary of the Dhammapada (Dhammapada-aṭṭhakathā) (see [2], p. v). Talking about the legacy and impact of the stories of the Vimānavatthu and the Petavatthu, T.W. Rhys Davids has pointed out that "The whole set of beliefs exemplified in these books. . . is historically interesting as being in all probability the source of a good deal of medieval Christian belief in heaven and hell"([9], p. 77).

The Vimānavatthu is one of the youngest texts of the Pāli Tipiṭaka. E. Hardy was of the opinion that the Petavatthu could have borrowed material useful for its purposes from other works of the Khuddaka Nikāya such as the Jātakas ([4], pp. 25–50). Its different portions appear to belong to different periods and it does not seem to be a uniform text ([4], p. 51). As it has strong associations with Moggallāna, a contemporary of King Aśoka, the text itself appears to have been composed in the post-Aśokan period, if not post-Mauryan.

Cross-References

- ▶ Aśoka
- ▶ Buddha Śākyamuni
- ▶ Dhammapada
- ▶ Dhammapāla
- ▶ Karma
- ▶ Khuddaka Nikāya
- ▶ Petavatthu
- ▶ Theravāda
- ▶ Tipiṭaka

References

1. Geiger W, Bode MH (trans) (1912) The Mahāvaṃsa or the great chronicle of Ceylon. Pali Text Society, London
2. Gooneratne ER (ed) (1886) Vimānavatthu commentary (Paramatthadīpanī III). Pali Text Society, London
3. Hardy E (1899) Eine Buddhistische Bearbeitunge der Kṛṣṇa-Sage. Z Deutsch Morgenl Ges 53:25–50
4. von Hinüber O (1996) A handbook of Pāli literature. Walter de Gruyter, Berlin
5. Horner IB (trans) (1974) Vimānavatthu: stories of the mansions, the minor anthologies of the Pāli Canon (assisted: Jayawickrama NA), Part IV, new edn. Pali Text Society, London
6. Jayawickrama NA (ed) (1977) The Vimānavatthu and the Petavatthu, new edn. Pali Text Society, London
7. Law BC (1983) A history of Pali literature, reprint, vol 1. Indological Book House, Delhi
8. Masefield P, Jayawickrama NA (trans) (1989) Elucidation of the meaning: so named the commentary on the Vimāna stories (Paramattha-dīpanī nāma Vimānavatthu-aṭṭhakathā). Pali Text Society, Oxford
9. Rhys Davids TW (1896) Buddhism, its history and literature (American lectures). G.P. Putnam's Sons, London
10. Winternitz M (1983) History of Indian literature (trans: Sarma VS), rev edn, vol 2. Motilal Banarsidass, Delhi

Vimokkha

▶ Liberation (Buddhism)

Vimokṣa

▶ Liberation (Buddhism)

Vimukti

▶ Liberation (Buddhism)

Vimutti

▶ Liberation (Buddhism)

Vinaya

► Responsibility (Buddhism)

Viññāṇa

Bhikkhu Anālayo
Center for Buddhist Studies, University of Hamburg, Balve, Germany

Synonyms

Consciousness; Vijñāna; *Vijñāna* (Sanskrit)

Definition

Viññāṇa in early Buddhist thought stands for "consciousness" by way of the senses and for the underlying stream of consciousness that sustains personal continuity during life and through subsequent rebirths.

Consciousness

Viññāṇa is the fifth of the five aggregates, *khandha*, that in early Buddhist thought are the chief constituents of an individual. These are, besides consciousness, bodily form, feeling, perception, and volitional formations. As long as attachment is present, the other four aggregates can be said to provide a "home" for consciousness ([1], Vol. III, p. 9).They are the fertile ground in which consciousness, comparable to a seed, will come to growth on being "watered" by lust and delight ([1], Vol. III, p. 55).

The "seed" of *viññāṇa* could alternatively be seen as being planted in the field of karma, with craving providing the moisture required for growth ([2], Vol. I, p. 223). Consciousness could also be compared to a tree, whose growth is nourished when whatever leads to bondage is mistakenly regarded as gratifying ([1], Vol. II, p. 91).

As an aggregate, *viññāṇa* comprises past, present, and future instances of consciousness, be these internal or external, gross or subtle, inferior or superior, (related to what is) far or near ([3], Vol. III, p. 17).

In the context of a series of similes that illustrate the nature of each aggregate, consciousness is compared to a magic show ([1], Vol. III, p. 142). Just as one who thoroughly scrutinizes the tricks and performances of a magician would find no essence in them, similarly, on closer investigation *viññāṇa* turns out to be devoid of any enduring substance.

Besides its role in the context of the scheme of the five aggregates, *viññāṇa* stands in the third position within the 12-fold standard representation of the dependent arising, *paṭicca samuppāda*, of *dukkha* – a term whose meaning ranges from barely noticeable dissatisfaction to outright suffering as inherent features of human existence. In this series of 12 links that culminate in the arising of *dukkha*, consciousness is conditioned by volitional formations, *saṅkhārā*, and in turn conditions name-and-form, *nāma-rūpa*. The conditional dependence of *viññāṇa* on the preceding link of volitional formations is such that what one plans and what one has a tendency toward becomes a basis for the maintenance of consciousness ([1], Vol. II, p. 65).

The positioning of consciousness at this junction between volitional formations and name-and-form is significant in view of the traditional three-life interpretation of the 12 links of dependent arising. From this perspective, *viññāṇa* represents what is reborn. A discourse in fact explicitly speaks of *viññāṇa* descending into the mother's womb ([4], Vol. II, p. 63), and another discourse refers to the evolving consciousness, *saṃvattanika viññāṇa*, that is reborn ([3], Vol. II, p. 262). Conversely, death occurs when *viññāṇa* as well as heat and the life faculty leave the body ([3], Vol. I, p. 296).

In such passages, *viññāṇa* clearly stands for the entire mental aspect of a being, thereby going beyond its meaning in the context of the aggregate analysis. The same can also be seen in a recurrent reference that speaks of being without conceit "in regard to this body with consciousness," *saviññāṇake kāye* (e.g., [1], Vol. III, p. 80). Another example would be the description of an insight into the nature of the body and its relation to consciousness as being supported by and bound to the body, a situation comparable to a gem strung on a string ([3], Vol. II, p. 17). In each of these passages, *viññāṇa* represents the whole of the mind.

To appreciate properly the nature of *viññāṇa* in relation to rebirth, it needs to be kept in mind that, from an early Buddhist perspective, it is not the same *viññāṇa* that is reborn ([3], Vol. I, p. 256). Instead, rebirth takes place by way of the flux of consciousness, *viññāṇasota* ([4], Vol. III, p. 105), a changing process devoid of any abiding permanent entity.

Iconographic presentations of consciousness in the context of the 12 links of dependent arising tend to employ the image of a monkey. This could be in reminiscence of a simile found in a discourse which illustrates the impermanent nature of consciousness with the example of a monkey, who while faring through a forest will take hold of one branch only to let go of it again and grasp another ([1], Vol. II, p. 95).

The inclusion of *viññāṇa* in the series of dependent arising, *paṭicca samuppāda*, implies that consciousness is a dependently arisen phenomenon and therefore lacks the property of intrinsic independence that apparently was part of the ancient Indian conception of a self. *Viññāṇa* is thus impermanent, unsatisfactory, and not-self, and needs to be contemplated as such in order to wean oneself from the tendency of appropriating consciousness as "mine" or even identifying with it as "I" or "my self."

In the context of dependent arising, *viññāṇa* is defined as consciousness by way of the six senses ([3], Vol. I, p. 53), namely, by way of the eye, ear, nose, tongue, body, and mind, *mano*. In regard to each of the six senses, *viññāṇa* can become aware of further details related to sensory experience, such as in the case of taste, for example, becoming conscious of sour, bitter, pungent, sweet, sharp, mild, salty, and bland ([1], Vol. III, p. 87).

The circumstance that the definition of *viññāṇa* mentions the senses points to a small but significant difference between consciousness and perception, *saññā*, whose definition instead speaks of the objects of the sense, that is, sight, sound, smell, taste, tangibles, and mental objects. In other words, perception reaches out to the objects by recognizing and conceptualizing them, whereas consciousness stands for the subjective experiencing of the same.

In this role, consciousness provides a reflective platform for the other mental aggregates. Thus, for example, feeling, *vedanā*, feels pleasure, displeasure, and neutrality ([3], Vol. I, p. 293). Consciousness, then, is aware of this experience as "pleasure," "displeasure," and "neutrality" ([3], Vol. I, p. 292). In other words, *vedanā* just feels, whereas *viññāṇa* is conscious of the experience of feeling.

In a simile that describes a border town with six gates, representing the six senses, *viññāṇa* is given the role of the lord of the town ([1], Vol. IV, p. 195). The point of this simile appears to be that consciousness is experienced as the functional center of personal experience. This role, however, may give the mistaken impression that consciousness is an independent observer. Yet, according to early Buddhism, closer inspection will bring to light that consciousness is a dependently arisen phenomenon, depending on the sense, based on which it arose, comparable to fire that depends on the fuel, based on which it burns ([3], Vol. I, p. 259). Although arising in dependence on the senses, consciousness is not the automatic product of the existence of a sense and its correspondent object. For the manifestation of the corresponding consciousness, there additionally needs to be the factor of engagement, *samannāhāra*, with the object ([3], Vol. I, p. 190).

Viññāṇa makes its appearance in several other schemes, in addition to the five aggregates and the 12 links of dependent arising. One of these schemes presents a listing of six elements, which besides consciousness comprises the elements earth, water, fire, wind, and space ([3], Vol. III, p. 31). This listing combines a detailed analysis of different aspects of matter with consciousness as representative of mind as a whole.

Another set lists four types of nutriment, *āhāra*, which besides material food, contact, and mental volition comprises *viññāṇa* as its fourth

([1], Vol. II, p. 11). These four types of nutriment single out what serves as a basis for the continuous existence of living beings in their present life as well as in future existences. The afflictive aspect of having to depend on the nutriment of consciousness is comparable to the predicament of a criminal who is being punished by having a 100 spears thrown at him in the morning, at noon, and in the evening ([1], Vol. II, p. 100).

Viññāṇa can also become an object of meditation in the context of the four immaterial attainments that can be developed after the concentrative depth of the fourth absorption, *jhāna*, has been reached. Once the mind has experienced the first of the four immaterial attainments, the sphere of boundless space, meditative experience can be further refined by turning attention to the fact that the mind, having taken boundless space as its object, has become boundless itself. This then leads to the attainment of the "sphere of boundless consciousness," *viññāṇañcāyatana*.

Yet another set is concerned with seven stations of consciousness, *viññāṇaṭṭhiti* ([4], Vol. II, p. 68). These cover different types of living beings who could be:

- Different in body and perception
- Different in body but alike in perception
- Alike in body but different in perception
- Alike in body and perception
- Perceptive of boundless space
- Perceptive of boundless consciousness
- Perceptive of nothingness

The central task of the early Buddhist scheme of deliverance is to go beyond rebirth in any of these seven stations, as well as beyond the nutriments, the elements, the conditioned series of links of dependent arising that lead up to the dependent arising of *dukkha*, and beyond clinging to any of the five aggregates. With the attainment of awakening, *viññāṇa* becomes signless, *anidassana* ([4], Vol. I, p. 223), and unestablished, *apatiṭṭha* ([1], Vol. III, p. 53). The experience of Nirvāṇa brings about an appeasement of consciousness, *viññāṇūpasama* ([5], 735), and the *viññāṇa* of one who has become fully awakened has become independent of any support, *nissita* ([3], Vol. I, p. 140).

Among subsequent developments of Buddhist thought, the conception of an eighth type of consciousness arose, in addition to the six types recognized in early Buddhism and a seventh type reckoned as representing the defiled mind, *kliṣṭamanas*. This eighth type of consciousness is the "storehouse consciousness," *ālayavijñāna*, which functions as a repository for the seeds of former deeds through the process of rebirth in *saṃsāra*. Eventually, the *ālayavijñāna* was considered by some to be the very source of the world, which in turn was seen as a projection of consciousness.

The position taken in early Buddhism, however, is that consciousness merely is that on which an actually existing world is projected by way of name-and-form, *nāma-rūpa*, which in a reciprocally conditioning relationship with *viññāṇa* forms the basic matrix of experience, any aspect of which is conditioned, impermanent, and without any abiding substance.

Cross-References

▶ Ālaya-vijñāna
▶ Mind (Buddhism)
▶ Nāma-rūpa
▶ Vijñāna

References

1. Feer L (ed) (1888–1898) The Saṃyutta Nikāya, 5 vols. Pali Text Society, Oxford
2. Morris R, Hardy E (eds) (1885–1900) The Aṅguttara Nikāya, 5 vols. Pali Text Society, London
3. Trenckner V, Chalmers R (eds) (1888–1896) The Majjhima Nikāya, 3 vols. Pali Text Society, London
4. Carpenter JE, Rhys Davids TW (eds) (1890–1911) The Dīgha Nikāya, 3 vols. Pali Text Society, London
5. Andersen D, Smith H (ed) (1913) The Sutta-nipāta. Pali Text Society, London (references are by stanza)
6. Hamilton S (1996) The Viññāṇakkhandha. In: id. Identity and experience, the constitution of the human being according to early Buddhism. Luzac Oriental, London, pp 82–120
7. de A Wijesekera OH (1964) The concept of Viññāṇa in Theravāda Buddhism. J Am Orient Soc 84(3):254–259

Violence

▶ Warfare (Buddhism)

Vipassanā

▶ Insight

Vipaśyanā

▶ Insight

Virtues

▶ Pāramitā

Virtuous Behavior

▶ Dharma (Jainism)

Visuddhimagga

Madhumita Chattopadhyay
Department of Philosophy, Jadavpur University, Kolkata, West Bengal, India

Synonyms

The path of purification; The path of purity

Definition

A well-known treatise written by Buddhaghoṣa on the exposition of the paths leading to the attainment of *Nibbāna* following the Tripiṭakas and different commentarial literature.

Visuddhimagga

The text *Visuddhimagga* is one of the most well-known treatises of Theravāda Buddhism. It may be viewed as an encyclopedia of Buddhist doctrines and meditation. It systematically summarizes and interprets the essential teachings of Lord Buddha as contained in the *Tripiṭaka*s. The author of this text is Acārya Buddhaghosha who is revered as the greatest commentator and exegetist in the history of Pāli Buddhist literature [1].

The title *Visuddhimagga* consists of two terms *visuddhi* or purification and *magga* or path. So the whole term "*Visuddhimagga*" means path of purification. Here, the term "purification" stands for "*nibbāna*" or liberation, and path stands for the means of approach to this stage of *nibbāna*. This path has been described to be different by different systems. Sometimes this path is said to consist of insight (*paññā*) alone; in some cases, it is said to be meditation (*jhāna*) and understanding. In the *Majjhima Nikāya*, deeds or *kamma* is said to be one path for the attainment of *nibbāna*; in other instances, virtue and mindfulness are also regarded as the path for the realization of *nibbāna*.

After referring to passages of different Buddhist texts regarding the path for the realization of the Ultimate Goal, the *Visuddhimagga* comes to the opinion that the Blessed One has recommended through his doctrine of eightfold means (*aṣ ṭāngika mārga*) three things, namely, virtue, concentration, and understanding as the path of purification. By virtue is meant the training of higher virtue, by concentration training of higher consciousness, and by understanding the training of higher understanding. Accordingly, the text *Visuddhimagga* [2] is divided into three parts, and each of them is devoted respectively to elaborate discussion on the nature of each of these three, virtue, concentration, and understanding. Each of these parts consists of several chapters dealing with specific issues related to the main one. For instance in Part I, the part dealing with virtue, there are two chapters dealing with description of virtue and the ascetic practices. Virtue or *śīla* is presented as the prevention of all defilements in one's conduct, and the reason for its being so called is that it is either a coordinating principle (*samādhāna*) in the sense of being a non-inconsistency of bodily action due to virtuousness or is the upholding (*upadhāraṇa*) in the sense of being a foundation (*ādhāra*) for profitable states. In the pursuit of virtue, the individual has to take note of the ascetic practices which have been advised by the Blessed One. Accordingly, after discussion of the nature of virtue or *śīla*, the author goes on to discuss the ascetic practices in the second chapter entitled *Dhutaṇga-niddesa*, for the purpose of gladdening good people.

The second part of the *Visuddhimagga* is dedicated to the discussion on concentration or *samādhi*. This part consists of ten chapters of which the first one entitled "*Kammaṭṭhāna-gahana-niddesa*" (Taking a Meditation Subject) deals elaborately on the nature of concentration. Since concentration can be of many types and can have various aspects, in the beginning Buddhaghosa finds it proper to specify the sense in which the term "concentration" is to be understood. The term "concentration" or *samādhi* is connected with the sense of concentrating (*samādhāna*) which means centring (*ādhāna*) of consciousness and consciousness-concomitants evenly (*samaṃ*) and rightly (*sammā*) on a single object, undistracted and unscattered. While in Buddhism there is no exclusive claim to teach *jhāna* concentration (*samatha* = *samādhi*), there is a claim that the development of insight (*vipassanā*) arises through penetration into the Four Noble Truths, as such the two, namely concentration and insight are to be combined together. In the next few chapters, there is a discussion on 18 faults (*kasina-doṣa*) which render a conduct as unfit and also on the exposition of the different types of evil acts. Gradually, there is the discussion on the divine abiding (*brahmavihāra*), immaterial states, and this part is concluded with a discussion on the benefits of developing concentration. The benefit of developing concentration has been different for an Arhat and for the lay person. For the Arhats, the benefit is one of blissful abiding, and for the ordinary persons, concentration provides the benefit of insight so that they can understand things in a correct way.

Part three of the text deals with purification of views which arises through different stages; first, there is purification through overcoming doubt; then, there is purification by knowledge and vision of what is and what is not the path. This knowledge arises through the recognition of the different imperfections, dissolutions, and dangers that exist in the path and also through the understanding of the ways to remove them. The text concludes with a discussion on the benefits of developing understanding. The benefits have been described to be (1) removal of the various defilements beginning with the fetters, (2) experience of the taste of the noble fruit, (3) ability to attain the stage of cessation of suffering, and (4) achievement of worthiness to receive gifts and so on.

In short, the text *Visuddhimagga* through a detailed and elaborate analysis of virtue, concentration, and understanding points out that when a wise man is established well in virtue and develops consciousness and understanding, he can succeed in disentangling this tangle. So through this text, the author provides one a summary of the three paths of *śīla*, *samādhi*, and *paññā*, as presented in the *Tripiṭakas* and different commentarial literature for the purpose of gladdening good people. Discussion on concentration is supplemented with discussion on other important topics like the Four Noble Truths and the doctrine of dependent origination. Elaborate analysis of such topics mainly occurs in the sixteenth and seventeenth chapters and provide "theoretic" discussion of what is to be learnt, whereas Chaps. 18–21 may be regarded as "practical" in the sense of giving instruction regarding the application of that theoretic knowledge to the individual's own experience and in pointing out what may be expected to happen in the course of development. Thus, this text serves as a good guide to the world of Buddhist philosophy indicating the steps to attain the ultimate goal of *Nibbāna*.

Cross-References

- ▶ Aryasacca
- ▶ Brahmavihāra
- ▶ Buddhaghosa
- ▶ Ethics (Buddhism)

References

1. Law BC (1997) The life and works of Buddhaghosa. Asian Educational Services, New Delhi
2. Nāṇamoli B (1991) The path of purification by Bhadantācariya Buddhaghosa. Buddhist Publication Society, Kandy, Sri Lanka

Viśvabhadra

▶ Samantabhadra

Void

▶ Śūnya

Voidness

▶ Śūnyatā

Vraja Veranjā

▶ Mathurā

W

War

▶ Warfare (Buddhism)

War(s)

▶ Warfare (Buddhism)

Warfare

▶ Warfare (Buddhism)

Warfare (Buddhism)

Mahinda Deegalle
Department of Humanities, Colgate University, New York, USA
Bath Spa University, UK

Synonyms

Ahimsa; Army; Battles; Dharmavijaya; Dharmayuddha; Holy war; Justice; Kamma; Kingship; Military; Pañcasila; Righteous war; Violence; War; War(s); Warfare

Definition

Engagement in battle

Introduction

Buddhism has become one of the most admired Indian religions for its espousal of a message of compassion, loving-kindness, sympathy, and nonviolence. As a doctrinal system, it was well grounded in the conviction that nonviolent actions are ultimately efficacious over violent reactions [3]. This is identified as an undisputed principle by presenting it as an eternal law. Throughout history, Buddhist institutions and Buddhists attempted to implement nonviolent convictions whenever and wherever they could. Physical violence found in traditional Buddhist societies in Asia can be seen as cases of abrogation of the first precept – abstention from taking the life of another living being – a voluntary commitment that Buddhists take to fulfill. Taking doctrinal and historical realities in living Buddhist traditions into account, this entry will examine Buddhist attitudes to violence and warfare.

At the very beginning, this entry makes an assertion. Though there are many accounts of the life and death of soldiers and episodes of wars and battlefields in Buddhist texts of both Mahayana and Theravada traditions, there is hardly any evidence of scholastic attempts within Buddhist traditions to

K.T.S. Sarao, J.D. Long (eds.), *Buddhism and Jainism*, Encyclopedia of Indian Religions,
DOI 10.1007/978-94-024-0852-2

develop systematically a theory of "righteous war" (Skt. *dharmayuddha*) even when Buddhists were/are fighting wars of all sorts in the name of nation, religion, or self-defense [6]. Unlike the monastic scholarship of the Christian tradition found in Catholic thinkers such as Augustine (354–430) under the Roman Empire and Aquinas (1225–1274) during the last decades of crusades, there is hardly any serious and systematic internal scholastic debates to develop a theory of just war within Buddhist societies. Why is it? Why are Buddhist thinkers relatively silent on the issue of practicalities of warfare? Is it because they did not foresee any meaningful result from waging war or even instrumentality of it for creating peace? Or did they reject warfare completely conceiving it as a contradiction in terms and hopeless to go to debate to justify the process?

The Historical Buddha's Teachings in Understanding Warfare

The *Dhammapada* (Verses of *Dhamma*), one of the prominent early Buddhist texts, which still remains to be the most popular Buddhist scripture in South and Southeast Asia, has many relevant insights on ethical aspects of warfare. It puts forward an eternal conviction with regard to the nature of violence, its repetitive and reactive aspects. This message has a profound impact on the thought patterns of Buddhists of many centuries.

Buddhism believes in the power of negative actions to reproduce even more devastating, counterproductive results. Constant battle between positive emotional qualities and negative feelings is quite strong and taken into serious consideration in Buddhist psychological analysis. This profound understanding of the nature of emotional factors results in a fundamental conviction, which Buddhism identifies as an eternal law (*dhammo sanantano*) candidly worded as "Enmity Never Quelled by Enmity." This conviction undergirds key Buddhist beliefs, teachings, and practices.

This conviction of an eternal law of the nature of emotional factors such as hatred is often illustrated figuratively through narratives of *kamma* ("intentional action," Skt. *karma*) and rebirth as seen in the story of the Demoness Kāli recorded in the Sinhala language in the thirteenth century *Saddharmaratnāvaliya* (The Garland of Jewels of the Good Doctrine, c. 1220–1293 C.E.) of Dharmasena Thera [9]. Dharmasena Thera provided a rich context for the original Pāli narrative in elaborating how the law of *kamma* works within the context of rebirth and how one's intention to revenge takes precedence over human lives in producing rather complex and vicious circle of misfortunes:

> As a bush fire burning off out of control stops only when it reaches a vast body of water, so the rage of one who vows vengeance cannot be quelled except by the waters of compassion that fill the ocean of Omniscience [9].

This narrative illustrates how a fervent rebirth wish leads to many lives of suffering and revenge:

> With that Fervent Rebirth-Wish, the hen died and was reborn as a tigress. The cat died and was reborn as a doe. Three times the tigress ate the young of the doe. Finally when she was about to eat the doe, the dying doe made a Fervent Rebirth-Wish. Three times this tigress has eaten the young I bore. Now she eats me, too. May I die and be born a demoness so that I can eat her and her children [9].

In the lifetime of the Buddha, the doe was reborn as a demoness:

> [T]he Buddha. . .was seated preaching . . . . The terrified woman cut through the crowds, went right up to the Buddha and. . .laid the tiny infant by the Buddha. . . . Though I may never hope to be a Buddha, this child I give to you. I see him in great danger. . . . I beg you, protect this child from the demoness that seeks to hurt him [9].

The Buddha knowing their *karm*ic and violent circumstances in the past and their present propensities for spiritual development, the Buddha comforted her with an advice:

> [W]hen your body is filthy with spit, phlegm, and snot, you cannot clean it with that same spit. . .in fact it will only get more filthy. So when you abuse those who abuse and revile you, or kill or beat up those murderers who beat you, or indulge in criminal acts against those who do criminal acts against you, it is like adding fuel to fire; enmity on both sides never ceases. Just as iron sharpened on steel cuts ever more keenly, so your rage increases. How then can that enmity be made to cease like a fire that is dampened?

> As spit, snot, and such like are washed off with clean water, and that water, because it is pure, can cleanse a filthy body, so hatred that burns on the fuel of justifications must be quenched with the water of compassion, not fed with the firewood of reasons and causes [9].

This narrative recommends compassion as antidote to hatred. From a Buddhist point of view, the cultivation of positive mental qualities such as loving-kindness and non-hatred feelings helps overcome negative emotions.

From a doctrinal point of view, aversion to war and violence is a prominent theme in Buddhist texts. This central feature of early Buddhist teachings can be seen clearly in Buddhist narrative literature such as the *Mūgapakkha Jātaka* (No. 538) [13]. According to it, the *bodhisattva* (who aspired awakening) was born as Prince Mūgapakkha, the son of King of Kāsi. On the day of his birth, there were rains throughout the kingdom; because the prince was born wet, he was called Temiya (J.VI.3) and the narrative itself sometimes identified as *Temiya Jātaka*. This *Jātaka* presents a context, which led *bodhisattva* Temiya to renounce any activities that contribute to harm and violence. According to it, his father, King of Kāsi, held the baby Prince Temiya on his lap when he issued an order to execute a convict. For the little prince, the very thought of probability of going to hell for issuing an order to kill a criminal was a scary feeling. As a result, the prince decided to feign deaf and dumb. He avoided becoming himself king in the future since he knew as a king he had to deal with issues of crime, punishment, violence, and war. This may be just a narrative, but it brings out certain fundamental convictions that Buddhists share in terms of avoiding violence and negative aspects that are inherent in kingship by raising questionable violent status of kingship.

The *Dharmayuddha* Concept in Theravada

In the English translation of the *Ummagga Jātaka* (The Story of the Tunnel), the term *dharmayuddha* (righteous war) has been translated as "The Battle of Justice" (Chap. 26) [10]. The battle between King Brahmadatta and Vedeha is the context for a discussion of *dharmayuddha* there. The narrative presents that in a previous life the historical Buddha was born as a wise man named Mahausada (great medicine). The key point in this discussion of *dharmayuddha* is to explain the use of nonviolent strategies in winning wars. Kevatta, the counselor of King Brahmadatta, advises him: "Your Majesty, it is better that the two forces do not fight. When the two wise men of the two kings get together and the one who prostrates before the other is the looser. The party that is respected will be victorious" [10].

In the last century, the Sanskrit term *dharmayuddha* (righteous war) gained currency in academic writings. Nowadays, in popular Sri Lankan writings, though one finds the term, this Sanskrit term and its related derivations do not have much history within Sri Lanka. It begins to appear in two senses in the late nineteenth century in the British colonial context. At that time, Sri Lankan Buddhists felt the necessity to defend Buddhist ideas, values, and practices in the context of widespread Protestant Christian missions and cultural intrusions.

In Sinhala publications, the term *dharmayuddha* has been used in two senses: first, its spiritual sense, which is prominent. It denotes the victory that the Buddha achieved by conquering defilements in confronting the challenges of Mara (the personification of death).

The spiritual meaning embedded in the term *dharmayuddha* has been used with military metaphors. In using the term *dharmayuddha*, some modern writers speak of the war figuratively:

> We, too, have a war to fight; but we do not need weapons such as guns. Our war is a "*dharma yuddhaya*." It is an opportunity to fight the demon of *mityadrsti* (false belief). Although we have been fighting this war for a while, victory is not yet ours because our weapons are old. We should get new weapons [1].

The second meaning of the term *dharmayuddha* is the struggle. In this case, it is used to explain the struggle that one faces in attempting to protect Buddhism in an unsuitable political and religious environment. Even then until the mid-twentieth century, the term *dharmayuddha* remained a nonviolent term limited in meaning to a reference to social struggle.

In 1951, writing to a Sinhala publication, *Buddha Lokaya* (Buddhist World), the late Pāli scholar, G.P. Malalasekera (1899–1973) used military metaphors to encourage people to get involved in social welfare activities:

> We should gather the weapons of *maitri* [loving-kindness], *karuna* [compassion] and *santi* [peace] and prepare for a *dharma yuddhaya* [righteous war]. We have to prepare for a religious fight, a long fight. This is not a revolution but an attempt to protect our ancestral religion – Buddhism. Thus, this is a *dharma yuddhaya*. This is not a war fought with the aid of weapons. We are fighting for the truth and the *dharma*. We have to start with loving-kindness and compassion. We have to fight to the end [1].

In this case, the term *dharmayuddha* is used in the sense of spiritual renewal rather than a war against another group or religion.

In the *English-Sinhalese Dictionary*, which Malalasekera compiled and published in 1948, a dictionary widely used today by students of English in Sri Lanka, the English term "holy war" is translated specifically with a religious meaning as *āgama udesā karana yuddhaya* (a war fought for the defense of religion) rather than a struggle for spiritual renewal [11]. In his explanation, Malalasekera did not use the term "*dharma yuddha*" as a definition. This dictionary also does not contain any entry either on "just" (Sin. *dharmistha*) or "righteous" (Sin. *dharmistha*) war.

For Malalasekera, as a Buddhist, spiritual renewal through the development of sublime qualities was essential to raise the profile of Buddhists at the time. Though he used military metaphors for that purpose, nonviolent engagement with Buddhism was essential for the Buddhist renewal in a colonial context.

In the political writings of Buddhist monks produced after the independence of Sri Lanka in 1948, one can detect quite frequent use of the term "*dharmayuddha*." One can detect some attribution of violent dimensions to its usage as opposed to the spiritual and moral meanings that it contained earlier.

In 1950s, one notices a monastic articulation of righteous war. Venerable Baddegama Wimalawansa (1912–1992), the Principal of Sri Lanka Vidyālāya, a monastic school located in Colombo, belonged to the monastic fraternity of Rāmaññanikāya. He was a monk of both nationalist and leftist political leanings. In the early 1950s, he published a series of pamphlets under the title *Dharma Yuddhaya* which exposed the anti-Buddhist and anti-Sinhala activities of the Sri Lankan government and the Christian missionaries. An examination of some of these pamphlets demonstrates the use of *dharmayuddha* as a reference to a social struggle in Sri Lanka. First of the series of the *Dharma Yuddhaya* pamphlet focused on the "Future of the Buddhist Monk." It argued that Christian missionaries had undermined the social significance of the Buddhist monk in Sri Lankan society. The second pamphlet was on the "Government and the Power of the Missionaries." The third one focused on "Buddhism Today." The seventh of the *Dharma Yuddhaya* series focused on the "Activities of the Christian Clergy" who had immense power and influence over education and health services [8].

Fighting for Rights: Battles in Politics

Postindependent Sri Lanka marks the rise of political activism and aggressive tone ushered in political platforms in defending the rights of Buddhists on an argument of the lost privileges of Buddhism during the colonial period. Sri Lanka's independence anniversary day on 4 February 1956 was an important day in terms of Buddhist assertions of their rights. An important report – The Report of the Buddhist Affairs Investigation (Bauddha Toraturu Parīksaka Sabhāve Vartāva), reprinted in 2006 – was presented to the Buddhist clergy and public at Ananda College, Colombo. This report included data gathered from 26 June 1954 to 22 May 1955 in 37 places around the country. The investigation team included leading monks and scholars of the time such as G.P.

Malalasekera. The report contained ten topics. The subject of chapter eight was on the topic of patience of Buddhists (*bauddhayāge ivasīma*, pp. 317–321). It is a brief chapter, but it includes details of Buddhist grievances under the colonial period and Buddhist assertion that Buddhists must stand up for their rights and fight for them. The tone here seems to have changed and taken an aggressive form. Rather than emphasizing duties as traditionally done, in this document, standing up and defending rights of Buddhists are highlighted. It asserts that Buddhists "must fight for rights" (p. 320). This defensive mode is further asserted by highlighting it as a defensive struggle: "a fight fought for self-defence when patience became ineffective" (p. 321). It further asserts the tragedy of the collective group: "We would like to inform kindly even though one can die as an individual, as a collective group we cannot die" (p. 321). It suggests "Buddhists do not want to have any need to be patient until this land of *dhamma* makes a fortress of Roman Catholicism in Asia" (p. 319).

Year 1956 was recognized as the Buddha Jayanthi (the 2500th anniversary of Buddhism). On the eve of the Buddha Jayanthi, *Bauddha Peramuna* (Buddhist Front) published an article in Sinhala entitled "Dharma Yuddhaya" with frequent use of the term. It argued "[s]ince he [Prime Minister] has not obeyed the 'monks' pleas [not to hold elections in the Buddha Jayanthi Year], they [monks] are launching a *dharma yuddhaya*" and "To save this *dharmistha* [righteous] land we have to launch a *dharma yuddhaya*. Its leaders are Buddhists monks."

A notion of a defensive war gradually emerged in their writings. On 27 April 1957, a Buddhist monk wrote: "Buddhism has always been a tolerant religion. . .Although tolerance is advocated, at this time of emergency when it is attacked in various ways, Buddhists cannot be tolerant; . . .Buddhists have to fight to save their lives" [1].

By 1961, the use of force in the defense of the *dharma* has been justified. An article published in *Bauddha Peramuna* on 11 March 1961 claimed: "According to Buddhist principles, believers should always practice *maitri* [loving-kindness]; however, in order to protect the religion we have to peacefully fight our enemies. When Buddhism is threatened, we cannot merely practice *maitri*" [1].

Modern Buddhist Articulations of Warfare

Twentieth and twenty-first century mark an important phase in relation to Buddhist involvements in war. Several countries, which had a Buddhist majority population such as Japan, Korea, Sri Lanka, and Vietnam, faced civil, national, and international wars. With the Japanese occupation of Korea, a devastating war began that later involved the USA in it. Japan also entered into a conflict with China, which led to serious destruction. Since 1959, with the exile of Dalai Lama to India and the Chinese occupation of Tibet, Tibetans are also facing increasing violence. In the late 1960s, Vietnam was heavily involved in war with France and the USA. Cambodia was completely devastated by war and internal annihilation created by the Khmer Rouge (1975–1979). Sri Lanka, primarily as a Theravada Buddhist nation, was involved heavily in managing a civil war that led to fierce battled between the Sri Lankan armed forces and the Liberation Tigers of Tamil Eelam since July 1983. This 26-year-old guerrilla warfare finally ended with the eradication of the LTTE in May 2009. With the increasing insurgency in southern Thailand in recent years, Buddhists in Thailand are also facing acute threats of terrorists. In these contexts, there are some Buddhist articulations of war.

Buddhism and Nationalism in Warfare

During the civil war period (1983–2009), there was the rise of nationalist and militant groups within the Sri Lankan society. One such nationalist group, which had a base in Buddhist institutions, was the Patriotic Young Bhikkhu Front (Dēsaprēmi Taruna Bhikshu Peramuna) headed by Ven. Bengamuvē Nālaka. Its undated joint publication with the Sri Lanka National Front named *Mavubima Urumaya* (Heritage of the

Motherland) [12] published between 1977 and 1990, having its immediate political context the Timpul Peace Talks, is dedicated to soldiers and contains comments on the importance of armed forces. It recommends the resettlement of armed forces in the dry zone by establishing soldier villages in problem areas and using them for economic victory of the country. It also advocates providing military training to civilians. It urges the need of creating an environment in which the armed forces can act with self-confidence and increasing the number of soldiers in the armed forces to 100,000 and the police force to 50,000.

Another nationalist, political group of the early 2000s, *Sihala Urumaya* (Sinhala Heritage), also gave much prominence of the armed forces. Its manifesto states:

> Nation's esteem and protection is the armed forces. We will establish the Army, Navy and Air Force with new modern equipment and national esteem. Military training will become mandatory to all citizens… It will be compulsory for all soldiers the study of the history of Sinhala, the study of *dharma yuddha* concept and spiritual training [2].

It is striking the Sihala Urumaya's insistence on the importance of soldiers studying the righteous war concept [7].

During the civil war period, some Buddhist monks assumed certain nonconventional and nonreligious roles. Venerable Elle Gunawansa, a radical monk in many ways, took a leading role in composing war songs for soldiers in the battlefield. His songs, very nationalist in tone as well as in their content, have drawn considerable attention of recent critical scholarship.

> My brave, brilliant soldier son
> Leaving [home] to defend the motherland
> That act of merit is enough
> To reach Nirvana in a future birth.
>
> When you march to battle…
> May the gods of the four directions protect you….
>
> Know that the mother and motherland
> Are nobler than kingly pleasure…
>
> Not an inch of another's land on this big earth we want
> Not an inch of this mother earth we'll give, but die…
> We'll shed the last drop of blood
> To defend the land which gave us birth…
>
> Where is a country without a nation
> A nation without a country, where?…
>
> The sword is pulled from the scaffold, it is
> Not put back unless smeared with blood,
> This is the way of the Sinhala of old…
>
> The Saṅgha is ever ready
> At the front
> If the race is threatened…
>
> If you die in the battlefield my lord
> I will come too, bearing arms, I am not lonely
>
> You my lord, do not come [home] without victory
> Searching for me here again.
>
> I will come to the battlefield
> Searching for you [16].

The late 1990s and early 2000s witnessed the emergence of several *bhikkhus* (monks) dominated political and religious associations. The Jātika Saṅgha Sabhāva (National Saṅgha Council), established in 1997, with the aim of unifying monks against the national crisis, published an undated booklet entitled *Nivanata manga pādana jīvana kramayak udesā* (For a Lifestyle that Opens Doors to Nirvana), dedicated to the pioneering politically activist monk, Ven. Dr. Walpola Rāhula (1907–1997), the author of the *Heritage of the Bhikkhu*. One section of the book, *Saturu balavegayanta erehiva dharma sangrāmaya* (holy war against enemy forces), asserts that "Perfect non-violence is a great thing," in the face of "injustice," however, rather than subordinating oneself, "one must fight" with good intention (*yahapat cētanaven satan kala yutu ya*). It maintains that "only by that path" (*e mangin ma pamani*), one can survive in the conventional society [14].

The notion of defensive war gradually emerged in the writings of Buddhists as demonstrated in the following statement made by a Buddhist monk writer on 27 April 1957:

> Buddhism has always been a tolerant religion…Although tolerance is advocated, at this time of emergency when it is attacked in various ways, Buddhists cannot be tolerant; …Buddhists have to fight to save their lives.

Toward the middle of the 1980s, the notion of justified war emerged in the context of terrorism and the protracted civil war in Sri Lanka.

The War for Creating Peace

The People's Alliance Government, a coalition led by the Sri Lanka Freedom Party (f. 1951) and headed by the former President Chandrika Bandaranaike Kumaratunga (b. 1945–), won the general elections of August 1994 and 2000. Initially as Prime Minister in 1994, Mrs. Kumaratunga proposed peace talks with the LTTE (f. 1975, Liberation Tigers of Tamil Eelam), which had waged guerilla war against the Sri Lankan state since mid-1970s for establishing a separate state for Tamils in the north and east of Sri Lanka. In the presidential election held in November 1994, Mrs. Kumaratunga was elected and became the first female Executive President of Sri Lanka. Because the People's Alliance sought power in 1994 promising to seek a long lasting solution to the continuing ethnic conflict, the government was obligated to initiate peace talks with the LTTE but was forced to abandon peace talks in April 1995.

President Kumaratunga projected an image that she believed in a political settlement for the Sri Lankan conflict. Her government put forward a package of constitutional reforms (which came to be known as "package") so that the Sri Lankan government can address Tamil grievances by devolving power to the provinces to meet Tamil demands for autonomy. The constitutional package, however, failed because the government was unable to get the two-thirds majority vote for constitutional amendments at the Parliament.

After 2 years of governing, the People's Alliance Government sought ways to resolve the ethnic conflict. In presenting its policies on resolving the conflict, President Kumaratunga claimed on 22 May 1996:

> [I]f peace cannot be established through peaceful means our government will act to establish peace by using any other means. Our battle (*satana*) is for creating peace. I stress that our battle is not at all against the Tamil public. Today we are in battle against those who oppose to political solutions that are anticipated from the bottom of heart by the entire Sri Lankan public including Sinhalas, Tamils and Muslims and those who oppose peace.

In the search for a political solution to the ethnic problem, the People's Alliance Government published a small pamphlet in 1996 entitled *Sāma Sangrāmaya: Yuddhaya edā saha ada* (The War for Peace: War in the Past and Today). It urges:

> Forget for a moment that you are a Sinhala, a Tamil and a Muslim.. . .considers and compares the war in the past and today's war as a [Sri] Lankan. . . .There are two sections who challenge real peace. With false reasons and unfair demands, the LTTE has again resumed the war and forced our government. . . . Whether we like it or not, to create peace in this country, we are forced to wage war again. To save Tamil, Sinhala and Muslim public who live in North and East from war, today we are forced to wage a war for peace. . .Is not this unfortunate war must be stopped by any means?. . .It may become essential stopping war. How can peace be created? Peace can be generated only through a political solution. You may definitely question: what kind of peace when members of the tigers have entered into war with arms? There is the truth in it. When one party has entered war, the other party cannot shrink its wings. Therefore, at this moment, war is a necessary factor. . .The tiger movement, which afflicts the Tamil and Sinhala public, must be definitely defeated. But we must not forget the war is against the tiger movement and not against the Tamil public. . .Tiger movement must not be given any opportunity to hide its Tamil racism. . . . No opportunity must be given to Sinhala racism [15].

This government publication elucidates its strong conviction that peace cannot be generated without resorting to war when the adversary has taken arms and resorted to brutal forms of violence and tactics of terror.

The notion of defensive war gradually emerged in the writings of Buddhists as demonstrated in the following statement made by a Buddhist monk writer on 27 April 1957:

> Buddhism has always been a tolerant religion. . .Although tolerance is advocated, at this time of emergency when it is attacked in various ways, Buddhists cannot be tolerant; . . .Buddhists have to fight to save their lives.

Toward the middle of the 1980s, the notion of justified war emerged in the context of terrorism and the protracted civil war in Sri Lanka.

A Sermon for Soldiers in the Battlefield

The late Venerable Gangodawila Soma (1948–2003) was a renowned popular preacher;

W

later in his life, he became increasingly controversial politically and held serious ambitions to get into politics as a Buddhist monk. His religious and ethnic roots are in suburban Colombo. He was a resident monk of the famous Siri Vajiragñāna Dhamāyatanaya located 12 miles south of Colombo. His teacher was a famous monk of Sri Lankan religious and ethno-politics scene, the late Venerable Madihe Paññāsīha (1913–2003). Venerable Soma was frequently invited by Colombo-based TV stations and had regular appearances both in television and local newspapers written in Sinhala. Beginning from 1997, after his return from Australia, he gradually emerged in the religious scene as a controversial and critical monk of the political affairs of the country and the ethnic minorities [5].

Two texts produced below – *A Sermon for Soldiers in the Battlefield* and *The War Is Not Against Tamils* – were originally published in Sinhala and now for the first time translated into English. They deal specifically with war situations and issues related to the life of soldiers in the battlefield. As a preacher, due to his popularity and availability for public speaking, he was invited often by people related to military, and he himself assumed the role of counselor to bereaved families of soldiers. These texts show that on occasions, he was very pragmatic and adapted Buddhist teachings in responding to war and the life of soldiers in the immediate war environment [17]:

> In Sri Lanka, is there a family that is not subjected to the curse of war? ... Is *karma* the reason for this curse of war?... It cannot be said that all of us are subjected to war due to our previous *karma*....It is just not enough becoming sad of the victims of war. Living cursing the war is equally meaningless.... We must not forget that Sri Lanka is consisted of Sinhala Buddhist heritage; we must also accept that Sri Lanka is the motherland of Sinhala, Tamil and Muslim ethnic groups. An introduction of an administration based on ethnic difference will spread seeds for a future war.
>
> Today in Sri Lanka the Sinhalese and Muslims have no rights. It is not only that both Sinhala and Muslim communities have become a target of terrorist hatred. But also how many Sinhalese, Tamils and Muslims have lost their villages and lands due to the war? What kind of sorrow do they have in their hearts? Therefore today we need a society where all ethnic communities live together harmoniously.
>
> How should we act with regard to relatives who die in the battlefield?...We must not forget them even for a moment since our heroic sons have selected the battlefield with the intention of protecting the country and nation...Heroic youth have gone to the battlefield with their feelings towards the country and nation. Parents must be proud of their brave children. Sorrow that arises due to the deaths of sons in the battlefield can be overcome by reflecting upon bravery of your children
>
> Previous *karma* is not the reason for going to the battlefield. The war is a result of cause and effect that emerge at the time. It is a natural thing. But the thoughts that arise in the battlefield shape the *karma* of the soldier. It cannot be stated certainly that the one who dies in the battlefield goes to hell. In the battlefield, there are acts of bravery, the use of strategic mind and the final victory over enemies.
>
> But if the soldier's external lifestyle is soft, generous and just, his *karma* will gradually become *kusala* (wholesome). When a soldier's mind is not overwhelmed with hatred and he or she leads a life endowed with good conduct, there is no obstacle for the soldier to obtain a better rebirth.
>
> The battlefield is a place where one is forced to destroy life. In war, one has to destroy the enemy who comes against oneself. But if one leads one's life with good conduct and engages in good activities, he or she can limit the impact of engaging in war to the battlefield.
>
> The primary concern here is the intention of the soldier who attacks the enemy for one's self-defence without a cruelty and hatred towards the enemy. When one attacks the enemy, the intention that arises in one's mind forms the *karma vipāka* (the result of the *karma*). The *karma vipāka* must be determined on the basis of thoughts that arise in the mind. A soldier does not always live with thoughts of war.
>
> ...At one time, the Buddha mentioned that as long as the world lasts, the war would last. Until one achieves victory over the mind overwhelmed by *trṣṇā* (craving), it is not possible to win the war. The birth at a time of war occurs due to our journey in the cycle of birth and death in the *samsāra*....
>
> The engagement in war is not a *kusala karma*. But when *kusala karma* arises powerfully in one's mind, the *karma vipāka* of engaging in war gets gradually erased.
>
> Therefore, it is needed to do *pinkam* on behalf of those who go to the battlefield and cultivate *kusala*. In the defeat or death in the battlefield, if that person reflects upon *budu guṇa* and Buddha's teachings, he or she will obtain a better rebirth due to that *kusala* action. On the other hand, if one can remove the sorrow by thinking of the reasons for going to war

> and the intention of war, if one can recollect the *kusala* actions performed, in such a occasion, beneficial *karma vipāka* become essential. Therefore the Buddha said: Monks I tell you the intention is karma [17].

In these sermons, Ven. Soma emphasized that the war was not against Tamils but a way of creating a peaceful society free from terrorism.

Conclusions

With a focus on Theravada Buddhism in South and Southeast Asia, this entry has examined in some detail ideas of warfare, the lack of systematic theorizations of "just war," and issues surrounding warfare at present and the past. It has examined a range of historical and contemporary perspectives on the nature of war, circumstances where war is sometimes justified in the Buddhist traditions, and the changing meaning in the concept of *dharmayuddha* throughout history of Buddhism in Sri Lanka. It had made clear the historical Buddha's injunctions against monks' involvement in war-related events. It has demonstrated the gradual adoption of the notion of *dharmayuddha* toward military ends. It has also demonstrated that extremist groups had an opportunity to modify and adapt Buddhist notions on war in order to respond to controversial political, ethnic, and religious issues. It has also explored various phases of development of a notion of righteous war, mostly, in rhetorical terms as expounded and employed by Buddhist thinkers. It has identified a gradual growth of a discourse on defending rights of Buddhists and implementing reactionary strategies, which might have led in time to occasional support and justifications of warfare in contemporary Sri Lanka in the mid-2000s. Sri Lankan political situation has been taken into account in examining both the discourse on rights and attitudes to war.

Cross-References

▶ Ahimsa
▶ Army
▶ Battles
▶ Dharmavijaya
▶ Dharmayuddha
▶ Holy War
▶ Justice
▶ Kamma
▶ Kingship
▶ Military
▶ Pañcasila
▶ Righteous War
▶ Violence
▶ War

References

1. Bartholomeusz TJ (2002) In defense of Dharma: just-war ideology in Buddhist Sri Lanka. RoutledgeCurzon, London, p 70
2. Daya Nanvana Sihala Manga: Sihala Urumaya Pratipatti Prakasanaya (Sinhala path to develop the country: Sinhala heritage manifesto of principles) (n. d.) Sihala Urumaya, Colombo, pp 6–7. Translated by Mahinda Deegalle
3. Deegalle M (2002) Is violence justified in Theravada Buddhism? Curr Dialogue 39:8–17
4. Deegalle M (2009) Norms of war in Theravada Buddhism. In: Popovski V, Reichberg GM, Turner N (eds) World religions and norms of war. United Nations University Press, Tokyo/New York/Paris, pp 60–86
5. Deegalle M (2009) Religious concerns in the ethno-politics of Sri Lanka. Mahachulalongkorn J Buddh Stud 2:79–109
6. Deegalle M (2012) Warfare in the Buddhist traditions of south and Southeast Asia. In: Reichberg GM, Syse H (eds) Cambridge sourcebook on religion, ethics and war. Cambridge University Press, Cambridge
7. Deegalle M (2012) Sinhala ethno-nationalisms and militarization in Sri Lanka. In: Tikhonov V, Brekke T (eds) Violent Buddhisms: Militarism and Buddhism in Asia. Routledge, New York
8. Dharmadasa KNO (1997) Buddhism and politics in modern Sri Lanka. In: Sobhita M et al (eds) Bhiksuva saha Lanka samajaya (Buddhist monk and Sri Lankan Society). Paravahara Sri Pannananda Nahimi Upahara Kamituva, Colombo, pp 259–260
9. Dharmasena T (1991) Jewels of the doctrine: stories of the Saddharma Ratnāvaliya (trans: Ranjini Obeyesekere). State University of New York Press, Albany/New York, pp 98–110
10. Karunaratne D (trans) (1962) Ummagga Jataka. M.D. Gunasena, Colombo. Sections translated by Mahinda Deegalle
11. Malalasekera GP (1978) English Sinhalese dictionary. M.D. Gunasena, Colombo, p 437

12. Mavubima Urumaya (Heritage of the Motherland) (n.d.) Desapremi Taruna Bhikshu Peramuna and Sri Lanka Jatika Peramuna, Kelaniya, pp viii+38
13. Mūga-Pakkha Jātaka (1995) The Jātaka or stories of the Buddha's former births, vol VI (trans: Cowell EB, Rouse WHD). The Pali Text Society, Oxford, pp 26–28
14. National Saṅgha Council (n.d.) Nivanata manga padana jivana kramayak udesa (for a lifestyle that opens doors to Nirvana). Systematic Printers, Dehiwala, pp 5–6
15. Sāma Sangrāmaya: Yuddhaya edā saha ada (the war for peace: war in the past and today) (n.d.), pp 3–49, translated by Mahinda Deegalle
16. Seneviratne HL (1999) The work of kings: the new Buddhism in Sri Lanka. The University of Chicago Press, Chicago/London, pp 272–276
17. Soma Himi G, Sumanasekra G (2001) Yuda bimaka miyayana soldaduvatat sugatigami upatak (A good rebirth for the solidier, who dies in the battlefield, in Sitata sahana dena budu bana (Buddha's sermons that comforts the heart). Dayavansa Jayakodi, Colombo, pp 135–140, translated by Mahinda Deegalle

Way of Comprehension

► Paṭisambhidāmagga

Wedding

► Marriage (Buddhism)

Westernization (Buddhism)

Jackie Ho
Department of Interdisciplinary Studies, University of Calgary Room 3168, Professional Faculties Building, Calgary, AB, Canada

Synonyms

American Buddhism; Buddhism in North America; Buddhism in the West

Definition

The development and characteristics of Buddhism in North America.

Historical Development

Introduction

Buddhism was first introduced to the West Coast of California in the 1840s by Chinese immigrant laborers that were drawn to the gold rush ([17], p. 3). In 1853, the first Buddhist temple was built by the Sze Yap Company followed by the establishment of a second temple in 1854 by the Ning Yeong Company, both of which were in San Francisco ([4], p. 73). They represented Chinese popular religion, a syncretic blend of Buddhism, Daoism, and Confucianism. Through the mining expeditions, Buddhism spread along the West Coast reaching British Columbia, Canada in the 1880s ([5], p. 5). At that time, Chinese laborers were commissioned for the construction of the Canadian Pacific Railway ([5], p. 5). At the end of the nineteenth century, there were an estimated 400 temples, predominantly Chinese, along the West Coast in places such as San Diego, Vancouver, and the Sierra Nevada ([4], p. 73). It is important to note that Jodo Shinshu Buddhism was also introduced, by chance, in Hawaii as early as 1839 when Japanese ships became lost around Hawaiian shores ([18], p. 4). However, Hawaii was not considered to be part of America until 1898 ([16], p. 5). Buddhism's arrival on North American soil was, thus, introduced by lay people.

Perhaps one of the most significant events that recognized the official presence of diverse Buddhist groups in America and which contributed to the early development of Buddhism was the meeting of the World's Parliament of Religions in Chicago in 1893 ([18], p. 6). The Buddhist tradition was represented mainly by Japanese Buddhists that included the Jodo Shinshu, Nichiren, Tendai, Shingon, and Zen schools ([18], p. 6). Most notably, it was Shaku Soen's involvement with the meeting, a monk from the Rinzai Zen order, that subsequently led Rinzai Zen to speak for Buddhism in the West up until the 1970s ([7],

p. 378). Immediately following the parliament, Soen's disciple, D. T. Suzuki (Daisetz Teitaro), a Zen lay practitioner, was commissioned to edit a series of Buddhist books ([18], p. 6). This thus began his assiduous career in writing and lecturing at American Universities, including Columbia University, until his death in 1966 ([8], p. 68). His influential contributions include translations of the *Lankavatara Sutra*, his *Essays in Zen Buddhism* (three volumes, 1927–1934), and his *Zen and Japanese Culture* (1959), though the accuracy of his works have been questioned by later scholars ([8], p. 68).

In Canada, Jodo Shinshu followers of the Nishi Honganji Temple, a school founded by Shinran Shonin (1173–1263), established a network of temples across Canada as early as 1905, beginning with the Japanese Buddhist Temple in Vancouver ([25], p. 39). This network expanded eastward to Southern Alberta through the purchase of old churches in Raymond and Lethbridge, and eventually reached Moose Jaw, Thunder Bay, Montreal, and Toronto [25]. During World War II (1939–1945), Japanese Canadians were placed in internment camps as a result of the War Measures Act (1941) ([25], p. 108). In order to avoid arousal of suspicion, the Jodo Shinshu members removed any Japanese orientation from their religious services and adopted the language and form of Christian fellowships ([25], p. 140). These changes represent an early attempt to apply a Western orientation to Buddhism, although these measures were not intended to convert non-Japanese. These Jodo Shinshu organizations are currently known as Jodo Shinshu Buddhist Temples of Canada and Buddhist Churches of America.

The conversion of non-Asian Canadians and Americans was slow during the first half of the twentieth century. Among the earliest converts were members of the Theosophical Society, founded by Helena Blavatski and Henry Olcott, who sponsored Buddhist publications and created Buddhist schools of learning ([18], p. 5). By 1920, Buddhist centers that were founded by Euro-American converts had sprouted on the American landscape ([3], p. 216). It was not, however, until the 1950s to the 1970s that Buddhism became popular. During that time, North America was swept by the Beat Generation, who were influenced by the writings of Allen Ginsberg, William S. Burroughs, and Jack Kerouac ([20], p. 1). Skerl writes:

> The Beats were a loosely affiliated arts community – one that encompassed two or three generations of writers, artists, activists, and nonconformists who sought to create a new alternative culture that served as a bohemian retreat from the dominant culture, as a critique of mainstream values and social structures, as a force for social change, and as a crucible for art ([20], p. 2).

Jack Kerouac explored the basic principle of *duhkha* or suffering, and Mahayana ideas such as the notion of *sunyata* or emptiness, in his novel *Dharma Bums* (1958) [9]. However, the Beat's portrayal of Buddhist ideas have been criticized by scholars as misrepresentations of Buddhist teachings.

Converts were especially attracted to the iconoclasm and meditative practices of the Zen tradition ([3], p. 216). The nontheistic spirit of Buddhist philosophy offered an appealing alternative to the "dogmatic monotheism" of the dominant Judeo-Christian society ([3], p. 215). In addition, meditation had an exotic appeal that encouraged spiritual experimentation, as opposed to requiring blind faith ([3], p. 215).

From the late 1970s to the late 1990s, there was a surge in Asian immigration to North America due to relaxations in immigration laws and an economic boom in Asia ([12], p. xviii and [3], p. 229). These migrations contributed to the diverse growth of Asian Buddhist groups, including the Taiwanese, Cambodian, Thai, Laotian, and Vietnamese, which resulted in the growth of a wider spectrum of Buddhist branches in North America. While many temples were independent of a particular lineage, others were satellite branches of new Buddhist organizations established in Asia that were seeking global expansion. In many cases, the founders of these new organizations began lecturing to Asian and Euro-American audiences in North America, which later led to the establishments of new temples. For instance, Master Hsuan Hua (1908–1995) of the Dharma Realm Association arrived in America in 1962 and built the City of Ten Thousand Buddhas, which now comprises over 488 acres and more than 60 buildings. Master Sheng Yen (1930–2009) of Dharma Drum Mountain began a series of lectures on Chan Buddhism in New York and hosted 49-day meditation retreats, and Master Sheng-Yen Lu (1945–) of True Buddha School delivered weekly dharma talks on Chinese Vajrayana in Redmond, Washington, for more than 30 years. Perhaps the most prominent writer and proponent of Tibetan Buddhism in the West is Tenzin Gyatso, the 14th Dalai Lama, whose writings have not only attracted convert Buddhists but have also appealed to Western intellectuals and general non-Buddhists. His works include the best-selling *The Art of Happiness* (1998), and recent releases *My Spiritual Journey* (2010) and *Emotional Awareness* (2009, with Paul Ekman). Though his earlier works promoted the teachings of Tibetan Buddhism, his later books emphasized religious tolerance and ecumenism, interfaith dialogue, and nonviolence, which gained widespread appeal.

From the 1990s and onward, the spread of Buddhist ideas continued to trickle into mass popular culture. Buddhist terminology such as "Zen," "karma," and "nirvana" became commonplace words and were adopted into marketing and advertising campaigns of national brands. The Buddhist presence in North America was also highlighted in music, film, and television, featuring major Hollywood celebrities like Brad Pitt in *Seven Years in Tibet* (1997) and Keanu Reeves in the film *The Little Buddha* (1994). Famous convert figures and celebrities were prominent such as Steven Seagal (Nyingma), Tina Turner (Soka Gakkai), and the fictional character Lisa Simpson from the hit cartoon series *The Simpsons*.

At the turn of the millennium and onward, access to Buddhist sutras, teachings, and online communities have increasingly become available through cyberspace. Websites such as www.buddhanet.net and www.sumeru-books.com connect a vast network of sanghas across the globe and offer instant access to Buddhist e-books, radio broadcasts, and digital libraries. Social networking sites such as Facebook, MySpace, and Twitter allow individuals to share up-to-the minute information about Buddhist activities and events. Local bookstores have also expanded their shelves to include dedicated sections on Buddhism, and a new genre of literature called Buddhist fiction has became popular, featuring chart toppers such as Kate Wheeler's *Nixon Under the Bodhi Tree* (2004), Keith Kachtick's *Hungry Ghost* (2004), and Todd Walton's *Buddha in a Teacup* (2008). The authors of such novels highlight the sentimental and emotional struggles of fictitious lay cultivators seeking to accept and apply Buddhist principles such as rebirth and *metta* or loving kindness in their lives. These novels suggest a growing desire for the experiences of convert Buddhists to be heard through the medium of fiction.

The recent decade has also resulted in a surge in the popularity of meditation retreats, attesting to the continuing appeal of meditative practice in the West. Although such retreats have been offered since the 1970s, the variety of retreats available by different Buddhist sects and branches has expanded. For instance, the Shambhala Mountain Center in Northern Colorado and the Hermitage, a Kagyu meditation center, in Denman Island, British Columbia, offer extensive meditation programs on basic *samatha* or tranquility meditation up to the advanced kundalini and Mahamudra meditations of Vajrayana Buddhism.

It is important to also note the contributions of scholars to the study of Buddhism in North America, whose extensive survey and research of Buddhist groups have helped to create networks between academics in all regions and have promoted a close working connection between scholars and local communities. In turn, information about the Buddhist communities has been added a nationwide database. Notable scholars in the field include Charles Prebish, Rick Fields, Paul Numrich, Kenneth Tanaka, Janet McLellan, and Donald S. Lopez, among others.

According to government census reports, there were a reported 300,000 Buddhists in Canada in 2001, and close to 1.2 million in America in 2008 [23, 24]. Today, every sect and branch of Buddhism is represented in North America.

A principal challenge in regard to the study of the Westernization of Buddhism lies in the ambiguity of who to regard as a Buddhist. Many claim to be influenced and inspired by the teachings of Buddhism while refusing to label themselves as Buddhists, despite the fact that they may practice daily meditation, read Buddhist books, and actively participate in Buddhist groups for many years. Part of this denial may be attributed to the perceived stigma of involvement in institutionalized religion. In regard to exclusive membership, many Asian Buddhists belong to more than one religious group since they also consider themselves to be Daoists and Confucians. Subsequently, one approach to the challenge has been to set aside the issue of identity and evaluate "who is involved in Buddhism and to what degree?" ([2], p. 187). In order to navigate through the ambiguity, some scholars have proposed a concentric model with outer layers surrounding an inner core to delineate the degree to which Buddhism plays a part in an individual's life. James Coleman writes, "On the outer edge are those with only a casual interest in Buddhism, and at the core are the most dedicated practitioners" ([2], p. 187). He explains, "Countless people have been indirectly influenced by Buddhist ideas that have filtered out into our popular culture, and they stand on the outer fringe of our concentric circles" ([2], p. 187). The so-called bookstore Buddhists may also be included on the outer fringe ([2], p. 187).

Other scholars have proposed different typologies in regard to the study of Buddhist groups. In the late 1970s, descriptions of Buddhists in North America were divided into two typologies: ethnic-Asian Buddhists and Euro-American converts [16]. These typologies were later rejected because they did not reflect the complexity of Buddhist groups and the diverse landscape of Buddhism in North America. In addition, the typologies suggested that both groups were static and practiced in isolation to each other. Assumptions and generalizations about both groups were challenged by new research, and subsequently, five new typologies were proposed to form a picture of Buddhism in the West, which include ethnicity, practice, democratization, engagement, and adaptation ([18], p. 53). Donald Mitchell writes:

> It should now be clear that in the United States, Buddhism is taking shape not as a single religious entity, but as a plurality of temples, practice centers, monasteries, fellowships, activist groups, and study facilities. ([14], p. 379)

Despite criticisms of the "Two Buddhisms" approach, a discussion of ethnic-Asian Buddhists and Euro-American converts, with respect to recent findings in scholarship, can serve as a starting point toward a nuanced view regarding the Westernization of Buddhism. Thus, it should be noted that these two typologies are only used as loose categorizations with no strict divides in this discussion. Another challenge with regard to the topic about the Westernization of Buddhism lies in the question of whether there is a new form of Buddhism that can be called American Buddhism or whether North America is simply another region in which Buddhism has been established. While scholars such as Coleman have suggested that there is indeed a new Buddhism, it can be argued that almost all Buddhist groups in North America, including ethnic-Asian communities, have made adjustments to adapt to their local landscape.

Ethnic-Asian Communities

According to Prebish, "It is clear that Asian Americans make up the vast majority of Buddhists in the United States" ([18], p. 57). The term ethnic-Asian Buddhists primarily applies to first-generation immigrants and their offspring. Labels such as "Baggage Buddhism" and "Ethnic Buddhism" have also been ascribed to this group, denoting that the tradition followed immigrants from their home country ([10], p. 190). While this arrangement might have been true for some groups, the description "Baggage Buddhism" does not reflect the situation that many immigrants did not convert to Buddhism until after their arrival in the new homeland. For many of these converts, the temple represented the preservation of their home culture, an activity center for social gatherings, and a central place for those who spoke the same native language. Thus, the term convert Buddhist equally applies to Asian Buddhists. Furthermore, among those who were Buddhists before their arrival, some converted to different sects of Buddhism due to the fact that their branch of Buddhism was not available. Thus, there was an initial homogenization of Asian Buddhists with various denominations practicing under one roof in the early establishment of Asian Buddhist groups. Furthermore, the status of Asian Buddhists has become more ambiguous because ethnic Buddhists have now become American Buddhists.

It should be clarified that the experiences of different Asian groups are not all the same. For example, the Chinese benefited from the economic prosperity in Asia during the 1990s and immigrated to North America to seek out new economic opportunities. The general Vietnamese population, however, came to North America as refugees. In fact, Southeast Asians account for half of all ethnic Buddhists in Canada, a large portion of which are Vietnamese ([1], p. 115). In the case of the Vietnamese, many of them suffered extreme oppression and brutality in their home land that forced them to escape by boat. Thus, they often arrived with no possessions or preparations for reestablishment. Factors such as these contribute to the unique identities of each sangha group.

Ethnic-Asian Buddhist communities have long been regarded as culturally exclusivist and insular ([12], p. xix). In other words, temple membership is often comprised of homogenized ethnic groups due to the "comfort of belonging to a particular community" ([12], p. xix). Furthermore, different ethnic groups are viewed as being separate from one another with little or no contact. The divisions, however, are not based on mandated discriminate bias toward other groups. Throughout the history of the tradition, Buddhist rulers have sought to convert others not by force but through Dharma conquest. Aside from obvious language barriers, many Euro-American converts, however, regard the devotional form of Buddhism practiced by many Asian Buddhists as being "too hierarchical, culturally enclosed, ritualistic and superstitious" ([12], p. xx). For the converts, ethnic-Asian Buddhism contains too much cultural baggage and thus, Buddhism needs to be purified of popular cultural practices such as the cult of ancestor worship, for example, to reveal Buddhism in its original form. Perspectives such as these highlight "issues of hegemony and racism that are implicit in the identity practices of American Buddhism" ([21], p. 43). Despite the outward forms of deity worship that are associated with Asian Buddhism, such practices embody deep layers of meaning and sophisticated presuppositions concerning detachment from the ego, inner transformation of *klesa* or defilements, and purification of the body, speech, and mind. At the same time, Coleman argues that Dharma must be "psychologically available to the potential participant" ([2], p. 203). Proximity to local Buddhist groups alone does not represent a real opportunity for taking refuge ([2], p. 203). There must be a shared "set of objective conditions and a symbolic understanding of those conditions" in order to attract newcomers ([2], p. 203). As a result, many ethnic-Asian groups, despite being established in the community for decades, are unknown to the general population due to wide differences in cultural concerns and backgrounds. It should be noted, however, that a number of Euro-Americans do join ethnic-Asian communities and are fully integrated and heavily involved in them, indicating that cultural barriers do not act as permanent boundaries.

In regard to whether ethnic-Asian groups have contributed to a new form of Buddhism in North America, the general literature appears to indicate that only Western converts have contributed to a new identity. However, ethnic Buddhists have made alterations to their practice outside of their home country. For example, local laws have democratized the administrative authority within temples such that they are operated by a board of directors that make collaborative decisions. In the True Buddha School, for example, there has been a shared effort in carrying out administrative and spiritual duties between the monastic sangha and the lay members, thus increasing the involvement of laypeople [6]. It should also be noted that it is common within the immigrant experience to actively seek integration with the wider community, as a part of upholding the values of responsible citizenship in the new nation.

Within the literature, four major characteristics of ethnic-Asian Buddhists are highlighted. It should be cautioned, however, that such generalizations do not apply to all groups due to their sheer range and diversity. First, there is an important emphasis on the continuity of monasticism. Monastics maintain the primary authority of disseminating the Dharma. They are also seen as ritual experts in regard to the conducting of ceremonies and rites such as funerals. Due to Western influences, monastics have increasingly had to adopt functions similar to Christian pastors, acting as personal counselors to the lay community and presiding over Buddhist weddings, which is a recent phenomenon in the twentieth century. Second, the temple or monastery remains centrally important as a field of merit. Providing dana for the temple through large sponsorships and monetary and food donations continue to be an important practice for laypeople to gain merit or *punya*. The names of donors are often prominently displayed in temples, and many temples serve as open houses where lay members may freely enter to perform *puja* or acts of bowing and making offerings. In addition, the temple serves to reinforce close relationships and mutual support between lay members and monastics. Third, while meditation is an integral component of practice, there is an equally important emphasis on sutra chanting. Popular sutras such as the Heart Sutra (*Prajnaparamita*), Amitabha Sutra (Shorter *Sukhavativyuha*), and Lotus Sutra (*Saddharma Pundarika*) are collectively chanted by the congregation, and dharma lectures often center on the expounding of sutras. Fourth, Asian groups are often characterized as being devotion based. For example, adherents rely on celestial Buddhas and bodhisattvas to transfer merit to devotees and offer them protection and blessings. Within the Mahayana and Vajrayana traditions, devotees often pray to figures such as Kuan Yin Bodhisattva (*Avalokitesvara*), Pu Xian Bodhisattva (*Samantabhadra*), Manjushri Bodhisattva, Medicine Buddha, and Vairocana Buddha. For instance, during the celebration of Vesak, the historical Buddha's birthday and liberation day, communities carry out the act of bathing statues of Sakyamuni while also presenting offerings of flowers, fruit, and incense as symbolic acts of reverence. The devotional orientation does not, however, apply to humanitarian-based groups such as Tzu Chi Buddhist Compassion Relief, founded by the nun Cheng Yen, and Dharma Drum Mountain.

Though many ethnic-Asian Buddhist groups have only been established in North America since the 1970s, the challenges faced by groups that arrived in the early twentieth century such as the Jodo Shinshu members, offer a glimpse of potential future challenges. As the first-generation members of a congregation age, it is of great significance to retain the second- and third-generation offspring in order to sustain membership [15]. These generations are charged with the critical role of anticipating the needs of their congregation and acting as a bridge of communication to the greater community. However, only a limited portion of offspring may return during adulthood due to the fact that some convert to other faiths or become disinterested in their parents' faith. As a result, membership numbers decline. The survival and continuity of the organization, thus, relies on the ability of the existing congregation to exert skillful means (*upaya*) and interpret Dharma in a way that is meaningful and relevant to new generations and audiences. Some organizations, however, have been successful at the outset in attracting a large audience of Euro-American converts, and these communities have been described as hybrid, blended, parallel, mixed ethnic, or inter-Buddhist communities in which both Asian and non-Asian groups practice together ([11], p. 61). Notable hybrid communities include the Order of Interbeing established by the well-known Vietnamese monk, Thich Nhat Hanh, and Soka Gakkai, founded by Tsunesaburo Makiguchi (1871–1944). Thich Nhat Hanh's Engaged Buddhism attracted large audiences due to its emphasis on human rights issues, social welfare, and environmental conservation. The Soka Gakkai, which literally means "Society for the Creation of Values," have attracted two to three million members outside of Japan, and its teachings center upon the Japanese monk Nichiren and the importance of reciting the name of the Lotus Sutra, which embraces the entirety of the Buddha's teachings ([13], pp. 1–2).

Euro-American Communities

Many charismatic leaders and their disciples have contributed to the global expansion of Buddhism. Regardless of whether the leaders are Asian or Euro-American, their success has relied on the ability to make the Buddha Dharma relatable to the daily concerns of a modern audience. Within Vajrayana Buddhism, "the vast majority of the tulkus teaching in the West are Tibetans" ([2], p. 135). This is attributed to the fact that in Asia, the role of scholar-monastics plays a more centralized role in the sangha [2]. Nonetheless, there are convert monastics that have gained followings in North America. For example, Pema Chodron, a Tibetan Buddhist nun and American convert, has been lecturing to audiences across the continent. She is a prolific writer of books such as *When Things Fall Apart* (2000) and *Smile at Fear* (2010), and she is also the principal teacher at Gampo Abbey in Cape Breton, Nova Scotia. Within the last 5 years, video sharing websites such as Youtube have helped to promote and popularize lectures by Western teachers such as Pema Chodron. Though Western Buddhism has mainly been regarded as a lay phenomenon, there is a thriving convert monastic community based in the Forest Tradition, a Thai Theravadin branch. Major monasteries include Sitavana in Birken, British Columbia; Tisarana in Perth, Ontario; and Bhavana Society in West Virginia.

Unlike Asia, where most people encounter Buddhism through temples, convert Buddhists typically learn about Buddhism through books. Regarding the demographics of such readers, Coleman writes, "There is virtually no reliable information about bookstore Buddhists, but it does seem safe to assume that they are literate and reasonably well educated" ([2], p. 192). The majority of convert Buddhists are "overwhelmingly white" ([2] p. 192). Though it has been speculated that Protestants would be most likely to convert, Jews in fact "are more likely to be attracted to Buddhism than any other Americans" and the term "Jewbus" has been coined to refer to convert Jews ([2], p. 192). While people of wide age groups can be found participating in Buddhist groups, the baby boom generation accounts for the greatest fraction of converts ([2], p. 193). Their appeal in Buddhism lies in "the relative lack of dogmatism and the willingness of many Buddhist leaders to submit their beliefs to the tests of reason and experience" ([2], p. 206). The amenable nature of Buddhist teachings "has particular appeal among intellectuals who are accustomed to the habit of critical thinking" ([2], p. 206). The disciplined self-control that is part of the Buddhist practice of right effort "is very much in harmony with the ideals of the middle and upper classes" ([2], p. 206). Consequently, many converts are highly educated and privileged. In fact, some Buddhist leaders and advocates are scholar-practitioners and university professors that provide both spiritual and intellectual guidance in their local communities.

In recent decades, there has been a surge in the growth of Vipassana or insight meditation groups among Euro-American converts. One of the reasons for this appeal is due to the considerable deemphasis of ritual and ceremony, in comparison to other Western groups ([2], p. 111). Metaphysical aspects such as rebirth and nirvana are also downplayed, while "a kind of down-to-earth psychological wisdom" is emphasized instead ([2], p. 110). Prominent Vipassana groups include the Insight Meditation Society founded by the Burmese monk Mahasi Sayadaw in 1975 and the Vipassana Meditation Centers established by S. N. Goenka (Satya Narayan).

Nonsectarian organizations account for the remainder of convert groups. Though these organizations typically have "fewer members than the other types of groups," they represent the fastest-growing organizations ([2], p. 114). Such groups typically do not have teachers or if there are, the teachers were previously trained in a single tradition and came to reject some tenets of that tradition ([2], p. 111). In regard to those groups without teachers, long-term members alternate in guiding less-experienced colleagues in meditation and Dharma study. An attractive feature about nonsectarian gatherings is "the idea of learning from all Buddhist (and even non-Buddhist) traditions" which is deemed "more attractive than following a single approach" ([2], p. 114). Since differences between schools are only a matter of accentuation, various traditions are frequently drawn upon to form a medley of practices and interpretations ([2], p. 121). While scholars such as Coleman have argued that the emergence of nonsectarian groups constitute a New Buddhism in the West, there is no consensus among the scholarly community. Prebish argues that Buddhism is still in its infancy, and since entirely new branches have taken centuries to develop within the history of the tradition, it is too premature to surmise that there is a new Buddhism [19].

Four main characteristics are applied to Euro-American convert communities within the academic literature. First, daily meditation and the practice of meditation retreats are regarded to be central practices that take precedence over ritual, making offerings or *dana*, and sutra chanting. There are exceptions to the case, especially in regard to converts of Tibetan Buddhism, which is a highly ritualized tradition in regard to the practice of intricate visualizations, the chanting of mantras, and their corresponding *mudras* or hand gestures. However, even within convert Tibetan Buddhist groups, small adjustments have been made by some communities to decrease the length of time allocated for the practice of rituals [22]. In regard to the second characteristic, there is less emphasis on devotion and reliance on Buddhas and bodhisattvas in their bliss forms or *sambhogakaya* bodies. Veneration to such deities which resemble god-like figures are often regarded as cultural adaptations that play little or no role in guiding beings toward inner realization. Hence, individuals are solely responsible for their spiritual accomplishments without any heavenly assistance. Third, Buddhism approaches a secularized form. For example, in the West, Buddhism is often emphasized as a way of life or psychology. Less emphasis is placed on Buddhism as a remedy for the cycle of birth and death, and more focus is placed on Buddhist teachings as a type of therapeutic tool to decrease worldly stress and to reach an inner calm. Though one of the main functions of Dharma is to remove unwholesome states of mind that obstruct inner realization, metaphysical aspects such as the six realms of reincarnation, including the hungry ghosts realm, and the appeasement of ancestors and spirits, are de-emphasized in convert groups. Fourth, the social distance between students and teachers is close. Hierarchical formalities have become more egalitarian. This is especially true within Vipassana meditation groups, where the role of teacher approaches a type of "spiritual friend rather than an authority figure or surrogate parent" ([2], p. 110). This, however, does not apply to all communities. In mixed-ethnic Vajrayana communities where the guru or teacher is revered as a living deity, the foreignness of the teacher has helped them to "maintain their charisma and the sense that they are something special and unique" ([2], p. 104).

Regardless of whether scholars agree that there is a wholly new form of Buddhism, the literature concurs that Buddhist groups, both ethnic-Asians and Euro-American converts, have acclimated their interpretations and practices as a response to the demands of the North American setting. For the Euro-American converts, there have been nuanced interpretations about the Buddhist cosmological view of the world that are more in line with the ideas of psychology and modern science. Furthermore, values of democracy, concerns about humanitarian issues, and ecological dilemmas are part of the global Buddhist concern that Asian Buddhist leaders and their disciples are involved in. In fact, Harding et al. clarify that "the changes in Buddhism that have been used to characterize 'American Buddhism' are in fact changes that were started in Asia by Asian Buddhists" ([5], p. 401). Thus, they proposed that the term "Post-Colonial Buddhism" would be a more accurate title to reflect new movements in Buddhism ([5], p. 402).

As the intricate and complex layers concerning the patterns of Buddhist development unfold, new findings question previous assumptions about how Buddhism is practiced in the West which, in turn, contribute toward a global definition. Like a vast ocean, Buddhism is a living tradition that will follow the ebbs and tides of the cultural concerns in each new shore it encounters. As time progresses, the tide will unearth new discoveries and juxtapositions.

Cross-References

- ▶ Buddhist History
- ▶ Mahāyāna
- ▶ Sociology (Buddhism)
- ▶ Syncretism (Buddhism)
- ▶ Theravāda
- ▶ Vajrayāna (Buddhism)

References

1. Beyer P (2010) Buddhism in Canada: a statistical overview from Canadian censuses, 1981–2001. In: Harding JS et al (eds) Wild geese: Buddhism in Canada. McGill-Queen's University Press, Montreal, pp 111–131
2. Coleman JW (2001) The New Buddhism. Oxford University Press, New York
3. Esposito JL (2009) Religions of Asia Today. Oxford University Press, New York
4. Fields R (1992) How the Swans Came to the Lake, 3rd edn. Shambhala Publications, Boston
5. Harding JS (ed) et al (2010) Conclusion. In: Harding JS et al (eds) Wild geese: Buddhism in Canada. McGill-Queen's University Press, Montreal, pp 400–406
6. Ho J (2010) The administrative processes of a modern Buddhist organization: changing roles of the Sangha in True Buddha school. Paper presented at the 2nd Buddhism in Canada Conference at the University of British Columbia, Vancouver, 15–17 Oct 2010
7. Hussain A, Amore RC (2010) Current issues. In: Oxtoby WG, Amore RC (eds) World religions – eastern traditions, 3rd edn. Oxford University Press, Don Mills, pp 366–381
8. Lopez DS (2002) The modern Buddhist Bible. Beacon, Boston
9. Lott DE (2004) All things are different appearances of the same emptiness: Buddhism and Jack Kerouac's nature writings. In: Skerl J (ed) Reconstructing the beats. Palgrave Macmillan, New York
10. Nattier J (1998) Who is a Buddhist? Charting the Landscape of Buddhist America. In: Prebish CS, Tanaka KK (eds) The faces of Buddhism in America. University of California Press, Berkeley, pp 183–195
11. Numrich P (2003) Two Buddhisms further considered. Contemp Buddhism 4(1):55–78
12. Matthews B (2006) Preface. In: Matthews B (ed) Buddhism in Canada. Routledge, Oxon, pp xvi–xxii
13. Metraux DA (2010) Global Soka Gakkai: SGI in Canada. Paper presented at the 2nd Buddhism in Canada conference at the University of British Columbia, Vancouver, 15–17 Oct 2010
14. Mitchell DW (2008) Buddhism – introducing the Buddhist experience, 2nd edn. Oxford University Press, New York
15. Mullins M (1989) Religious minorities in Canada: a sociological study of the Japanese experience. E. Mellen Press, Lewiston
16. Prebish CS (1979) American Buddhism. Duxbury Press, North Scituate
17. Prebish CS (1998) The faces of Buddhism in America. University of California Press, Berkeley
18. Prebish CS (1999) Luminous passage. University of California Press, Berkeley
19. Prebish CS (2010) The swans came to Canada too: looking backward and looking forward. Buddhism in Canada Conference, University of British Columbia, Vancouver
20. Skerl J (2004) Introduction. In: Skerl J (ed) Reconstructing the beats. Palgrave Macmillan, New York
21. Soucy A (2010) Asian reformers, global organizations: an exploration of the possibility of a Canadian Buddhism. In: Harding JS (ed) et al Wild geese: Buddhism in Canada. McGill-Queen's University Press, Montreal, pp 111–131
22. Statistics Canada (2001) Population by religion, by Province and Territory. In: 2001 Census. Statistics Canada, Ottawa. Database on-line. Available from http://www40.statcan.gc.ca/l01/cst01/demo30a-eng.htm
23. Sumegi A (2010) The play of meaning: reflections on a Canadian Buddhist death ritual. Paper presented at the 2nd Buddhism in Canada conference at the University of British Columbia, Vancouver, 15–17 Oct 2010
24. U.S. Census Bureau (2011) Self-described religious identification of adult population. 2011 statistical abstract. Database on-line. U.S. Census Bureau, Washington, DC. Available from http://www.census.gov/compendia/statab/cats/population/religion.html
25. Watada T (1996) Bukkyo Tozen. Toronto Buddhist Church, Toronto

What There Is

- ▶ Reality (Buddhism)
- ▶ Reality (Jainism)

Wheel of Life

- ▶ Rebirth (Buddhism)

Wisdom

- ▶ Knowledge (Buddhism)
- ▶ Paññā

Wisdom (Buddhism)

Angraj Chaudhary
Vipassana Research Institute, Dhammagiri, Igatpuri, Nashik, Maharashtra, India

Synonyms

Insight; Knowledge; Paññā; Understanding

Definition

Knowledge gained by a virtuous person at the experiential level is *paññā*, precisely called *bhāvanāmayā paññā*.

Knowledge gained at the experiential level is called wisdom (paññā). Living a virtuous life and practicing meditation are necessary conditions for gaining *paññā*.

Wisdom in Buddhism is knowledge gained at the experiential level. Of the three kinds of *paññā* [1], the Buddha gives great importance to *bhāvanāmayā paññā*, the other two being *sutamayā paññā* and *cintāmayā paññā*. Knowledge gained by listening to others is a secondhand knowledge. Knowledge gained by reading books and reflecting on it and even finding it logical may not be true knowledge because the tools that logic applies to verify whether the knowledge thus gained is true or not are not foolproof. Logic has its limitations.

One cannot have real understanding without his experiencing it. An example will make it clear. Suppose one speaks of the sweetness of different kinds of mangoes one has tasted. He knows what particular kind of sweetness a particular variety of mango has. There are degrees of sweetness. When he talks about different kinds of mangoes with different degrees of sweetness to others, he calls all of them sweet. But one who listens to him talking about various degrees of sweetness that he has relished cannot make a distinction between one variety of mango and the other. Unfortunately we do not have different words to denote the taste of different varieties of mango as the Arabs have different words for different kinds of horses. All sweet mangoes are sweet. But what is the degree of sweetness each variety of mango has can be understood only by personally tasting them. Nobody can taste it for others. Nobody can proxy for others.

By wisdom, therefore, the Buddha means full understanding, which is possible only when one knows it at the level of personal experience.

The Buddha says that real knowledge which is nothing but wisdom can be attained by knowing the impermanent nature of all objects we hanker after and annihilating cravings for them. This is possible by walking on the Noble Eightfold Path which consists of *śīla* (observation of five precepts), *samādhi* (concentration of mind), and *paññā* (wisdom).

Samādhi is of two kinds, *samatha* and vipassanā. By practicing *samādhi*, one attains concentration of mind, and vipassanā means seeing the nature of all objects of the world one hankers after and realizing their impermanent nature, knowing that they are suffering and nonsubstantial with concentrated mind again and again develop nonattachment toward them. In this way one destroys desires, drives out all defilements of the mind, breaks all fetters that bind him to the wheel of birth and death, and becomes liberated.

To have complete understanding of anything is to have wisdom. It is called *pariññā*, which has three stages. In the first stage called *ñāta pariññā*, one knows an object in terms of its characteristics, its function, its immediate cause, and its source from which it rises. In the second stage called *tīraṇa pariññā*, he knows at the experiential level that nothing is permanent, everything is in a constant state of flux, and in the third stage called *pahāna pariññā*, he, knowing the three characteristics (impermanent, suffering, and no soul) of all objects of the world, gives up craving for them and develops *nirveda* (nonattachment).

Wisdom thus developed can enable one to be free from suffering and attain nibbāna.

For more details on wisdom, see the entry on *paññā* in this encyclopedia.

W

Cross-References

- Bhāvanā
- Paññā
- Perfection of Understanding

References

1. Vis, 2.66 (Unless otherwise mentioned all books referred to here are published from Vipassana Research Institute, Dhammagiri in 1998)

Women (Buddhism)

K. T. S. Sarao
Department of Buddhist Studies, University of Delhi, Delhi, India

Definition

Indian Buddhist attitude toward women.

Introduction

Understanding of Indian Buddhist attitude toward women is largely based on the functioning of the Saṃgha and its members. Whereas the society could influence the decisions of the Buddhist saṃgha in many ways as the latter had to depend upon it for support, the saṃgha had very little or no control over the functioning of the society at large. In the absence of a towering personality such as the Buddha himself, the influence of the aggressively male-dominated ancient Indian society may have been inescapable. Personally, the Buddha treated women at par with men within the saṃgha. It appears that the antiwomen statements that one finds in the ancient Indian Buddhist literature are an interpolation into the original word of the Buddha (*buddhavacana*) by the monastic élite whose attitude toward women was shaped, at least partly, by the various historical developments (see [21], pp. 3–36). It may be pointed out that major portion of the Pāli *Tipiṭaka* appears to have been compiled at the Third Buddhist Council. In this and the earlier two councils, called to decide the *buddhavacana*, the dominant androcentric-patriarchal monks were able to carry through their own points of view. Thus, as a result of the repeated editing of the canon, one can find in it a multiplicity of opinions expressed regarding women. These opinions range from the unusually positive to downright condemnation and insult. In order to understand this kind of multiplicity of opinions, it is imperative to recognize the specific institutional or intellectual context out of which each of such opinions arose. One can often see such a diverse and sometimes even contradictory attitude within a single text. A quintessential example of such a paradox is the incident of the founding of the bhikkhunī-saṃgha, a story in which can be found Gotama, the Buddha, recognizing that women indeed are quite capable of attaining the highest goal of nibbāna, but adding at the same time that the formation of the bhikkhunī-saṃgha will tragically reduce the Dhamma's life by half ([15], Vol. iv, p. 278). It has been pointed out that Buddhist misogynistic attitude grew out of the fact that women's ordination was perceived as a serious and inescapable threat to the *dhamma* and Vinaya [5]. The Pāli *Vinaya* contains a meticulous transference of the authority of the Buddha onto the saṃgha as a corporate body, and if that authority is displayed as inherently masculine, then following that logic, women cannot be considered full members of the saṃgha (ibid). Women's presence in the saṃgha is depicted as a grave tragedy (compared to a house falling prey to robbers, a rice field stricken by disease, and sugarcane attacked by red rust). Blackstone perceives an important clue in it as to why women's ordination was seen as posing such a threat and how institutional subordination was used in the hope of averting it [5]. However, scholars who have tried to explain this can be divided into two diametrically opposite groups. One group explains this through an egalitarian attitude later modified by misogynistic editors (Horner ([11], p. 193); Barnes [3]; Church [6]; Gross ([9], pp. 34–38); and Bartholomeusz ([4], pp. 55–61)). The other group sees a bit-by-bit betterment from an inherently sexist, even misogynist attitude in Theravāda to the growth of sexual egalitarianism in Mahāyāna and Vajrayāna (Paul ([19], pp. 245–302); Lang ([13], p. 78); Willis ([27], pp. 59–85); Kabilsingh, [12]; Wijayaratna, ([26], pp. 158–163); Hhsken, ([10], pp. 151–170)).

Enlightenment and Nibbāna Were Not Available to Males Alone

Just as the goal set by the Buddha was not limited to those born in any particular social denomination, so it was not limited to those born as males. Both of these positions reflect an attempt to locate virtue and spiritual potential beyond conventional social and gender distortions. Many women were quick to take advantage of the opportunity provided by the Buddha. Some of the Buddha's most acclaimed benefactresses were women, indicating not only that there were a large number of women of independent means during this period but also that their support was instrumental in nursing the nascent saṃgha. Among the female followers of the Buddha, some remained lay followers and others gave up worldly pursuits to become nuns. In the role of nun or virgin, sexuality could be transcended as unimportant in the accomplishment of human potential. In the role of mother, sexuality is usually viewed as in a controlled state, a state of equilibrium. The Buddha viewed the masculine and the feminine as complementary aspects of a unified spirit, in the manner of compassion and wisdom. Undoubtedly, there were many women among Gotama's followers who were recognized as fully and equally enlightened, and the earliest strata of the Indian Buddhist literature agrees that women could and did become arahants, fully liberated individuals living free from the psychophysiological suffering that actualizes human existence. Sources within the *Tipiṭaka* offer many examples of arahants among the women who had renounced worldly life and even a few cases of women like Khemā, who, as chief consort to the king of Magadha, became fully enlightened even before giving up householder's life. Many among these well-known women followers like Pāṭācārā and Soṇā were known for their ability to teach the dhamma; others like Khemā were particularly held in high esteem by the Buddha himself for the depth of their knowledge. Some of the bhikkhunīs had their own following and were capable not just of introducing the dhamma but of bringing new aspirants to full liberation without the mediation of the Buddha or some other senior bhikkhu. In the *Tipiṭaka*, women most often are presented as teachers to other women, yet even the conservative editors of these texts preserved a few stories of women like Dhammadinnā, who, after becoming a bhikkhunī, had the opportunity to instruct her former husband, Visākha. In the *Cūḷavedallasutta* ([24], Vol. i, pp. 298–305), Dhammadinnā answers a long series of questions regarding aspects of the doctrine and practice put to her by Visākha, a prominent merchant and lay Buddhist teacher, who, the commentaries say, had a substantial following of his own. Visākha later reports Dhammadinnā's answers to the Buddha, who is greatly pleased, proclaiming that he would have answered in precisely the same way. There is enough evidence to suggest that women not only were conspicuously present in the earliest community but also seem to have held prominent and honored places both as practitioners and teachers. But as one moves to the post-Gotama period, though whereas women patrons and donors remain quite visible, the bhikkhunī-saṃgha does not appear to have enjoyed the prestige or creativity one might have expected of the successors of Khemā, Dhammadinnā, and the early arahant nuns ([21], p. 7). In Buddhism, not only is the path open to women, but it also is indeed the same path for both women and men. It is not that sex and gender differences do not exist, but they are rather "soteriologically insignificant" ([21], p. 9) that they amount at most to a diversion from the true goal of liberation. When 500 of King Udena's wives including Sāmāvatī perished in a fire, remarking on the tragic incidence, the Buddha said: "Monks, among these, some women disciples are stream-winners, some once-returners, some non-returners" ([22], Vol. vi, x). This clearly implies that women were considered quite capable of accomplishing the standard stages of the path of liberation by which one becomes an arahant.

Whatever limitations women might conventionally be held to have had, they were not to be kept out of any form of Buddhist practice nor from the ultimate goal, i.e., nibbāna ([8], Vol. i, pp. 5–6). Radical as this position was socially, it was quite consistent with the basic philosophical principles of the Buddha's teaching. It was a revolutionary breakthrough in the sense that women were explicitly included in the Buddhist quest for liberation. In other words, the Buddha clearly held the view that one's sex, like one's caste, presented no barrier to attaining the Buddhist goal of liberation from suffering. However, there may have been one negative side effect of the founding of the bhikkhunī-saṃgha. According to Altekar, the institution of nunnery in Jainism and Buddhism and the instances of several grown up maidens taking holy orders against their parents' wish and some of them later falling from high spiritual ideal must also have strengthened the view of those who favored marriage at an early age especially before puberty. It may, therefore, be concluded that after the establishment of the bhikkhunī-saṃgha, the marriageable age of girls was being constantly lowered ([1], pp. 54–55). Almost nonexistence of the bhikkhunī-saṃgha in the modern Theravāda countries also reflects this inherent bias of the South Asian society against women. However, as pointed out by Horner, it goes without saying that the Buddha "saw the potentially good, the potentially spiritual in them as he saw it in men" ([11], xxiv).

Buddhism Offered Better Opportunities to Women than Brāhmaṇical Hinduism

Buddhism offered better opportunities to women than did the surrounding Brāhmaṇism ([29], p. 16). Through the bhikkhunī-saṃgha, women did have an alternative to their family roles. In one form or another, this faith contained teachings about sexual equality and the ultimate irrelevance of gender. However, after the death of the Buddha, the saṃgha relied on popular, often non-Buddhist beliefs lifted from the surrounding Brāhmaṇical culture which believed that a woman should always be under the protective control of a male relative, whether father, husband, or son. Thus, it has been pointed out with some justification that though early Indian Buddhism had a strong ethical tradition, its tradition of social activism and criticism was not as strong. Buddhism has rather been censured for regarding the society at large as mulish and balky and, thus, for its lack of "the willingness and the courage to name oppression as *oppression*" ([19], p. 145).

If domesticity was oppressive (as, in fact, it was), then monasticism was liberating for women as far as Buddhism is concerned. Women's monasticism was most often women's closest approximation to the self-determination and prestige normally accorded to men. However, this was not without its problems as women's order fared far less well than men's monasticism. Women as nuns received less economic support and prestige and less access to ritual and study than was enjoyed by men. In Buddhism like many other religious traditions, men's celibacy and chastity were protected by isolating or restricting women to a delimited sphere. These institutions also have the power of limiting women's access to the highest quality teaching and practicing environment. Women, who could be cited as role models, were not very many as compared to their male counterparts. They are largely exceptions to the norm for their gender. They could be called tokens. More importantly, they were largely unsupported by the institutional fabric of their society and their religion.

The prosecution of Ānanda during the First Buddhist Council also hints at the hardening of attitudes among the monks after he was no longer there to guide or control them. Yet the subordination of women in the Buddhist community might not have been universal. While women were, indeed, reduced to lowliness by both precept and practice, history also offers examples to the contrary. Bartholomeusz has shown how the case of Saṃghamittā proves this point of view. She was the daughter of the powerful Indian king Asoka, who had sent her to establish bhikkhunī-saṃgha in Sri Lanka. This is an indication of the high position that a woman might attain in the Buddhist hierarchy and suggests that, at least in Asoka's time, nothing in Buddhist doctrine prevented women from being considered equal to men ([4], pp. 38–51). There are some references in the Pāli *Tipiṭaka* that accept and even appreciate the presence of women. For instance, Khemā was instructed by the Buddha in person. According to the legend, when he had finished, she attained arahantship together with a thorough grasp of the dhamma and its meaning. Thereafter, she became known for her great insight and was ranked high by the Buddha himself ([17], p. 61). Similarly, Sujātā, while returning from a festival, listened to the Buddha's discourse, and she attained arahantship, together with complete grasp of the dhamma in form and meaning ([17], p. 69). Kisā-Gotamī attained arahantship after understanding the dhamma preached by the Buddha ([17], p. 89). BhikkhunīSamā is said to have listened to the preachings of Ānanda and thereby attained arahantship ([17], p. 25). Cittā was ordained by Mahāpajāpati Gotamī and later won arahantship ([17], p. 36). Similarly, bhikkhunī Mettā claimed freedom not only from three crooked things, i.e., quern, mortar, and husband, but also from rebirth and death ([17], p. 11). All the above stated examples show that the Buddha respected women as equals and personally bestowed his teachings on many of them.

Society in General Was Not Very Sympathetic Toward Nuns

Considering that the bhikkhunī-saṃgha was founded 5 years later than the bhikkhu-saṃgha, during its early stages, bhikkhunīs may have learnt not only various forms of disciplinary acts but also different aspects of knowledge from bhikkhus. Here, it must be remembered that the social and spiritual opportunities offered by the Buddha to women being quite radical must have drawn many objections from men, including bhikkhus. As a result, he must have been well aware of the fact that his female disciples would be constantly harassed and humiliated. Moreover, apprehensions that bhikkhunīs would be susceptible to male violence were realistic and are proved by the various incidents of male violence against bhikkhunīs, as do regulations designed to prevent such violence. Thus, as pointed out by Rita Gross, these regulations usually restrict women from lonesome travel and practices, just as today one often counters male violence against women by advising them not to be at unsafe places at unusual hours ([9], p. 36). As a result of the establishment of the monasteries on the outskirts of human settlements, bhikkhunīs were exposed to the strong possibilities of laypeople finding faults with them, taking advantage of them or even sexually harassing them as single women. For instance, once several bhikkhunīs were going along a highroad to Sāvatthī through the country of Kosala. A certain bhikkhunī there, wanting to relieve herself, having stayed behind alone, went on afterward. People, having seen that bhikkhunī, seduced her ([14]. Vol. xii, p. 189). According to the Vinaya, laypeople and non-Buddhists were always free to criticize bad conduct of bhikkhunīs and bhikkhus. Incriminations and scandalmongering of people toward bhikkhunīs and bhikkhus abound in the Vinaya. It is worthy of notice that harsher opprobrium was directed toward bhikkhunīs than toward bhikkhus. Comparison of the criticisms of bhikkhunīs and bhikkhus suggests that people in ancient Indian society were more wrathful toward the wrongdoings of bhikkhunīs than those of bhikkhus. It also indicates that this provided a reason for the formulation of more rules for bhikkhunīs than bhikkhus in this category. People in the society were unwilling to permit women to fracture out from the household life. For women to regulate and protect themselves, even if consistent with the notion of parity, was nonetheless socially unthinkable. In the opinion of I.B. Horner, it is quite likely that they were in general considered as of poorer caliber than the monks and that, therefore, there had to be a severer testing in order to weed out those who had entered the saṃgha without having a real purpose ([14], xx.xiv).

The Buddha Granted a Religious Role to Nuns That Was Unique for Its Time

The Buddha treated women as individuals in their own right. Doctrinally also he considered them at par with men, though such a position appears limited to women's ability to attain nibbāna. Social rights of women within the society at large may not have drawn the attention of the Buddha as much as it deserved. Yet, it is important to remember that whenever opportunities came up, the Buddha did speak his mind. This is proved by his remark to Pasenadi, who became unhappy on hearing the news that his queen had given birth to a daughter rather than a son. The Buddha told him that a daughter may actually prove to be an even better offspring than a son as she may grow up to be wise and virtuous. Having once noted that women were quite capable of pursuing the religious life, the early Buddhist saṃgha had to decide as to what was to be done with regard to the interest that was generated by a view such as this. In the beginning, this does not appear to have posed any problem as the towering personality and charisma of the Buddha was enough to offset any worries regarding authority on the inside and acceptability at large on the outside. However, as the saṃgha developed during the post-Mahāparinibbāna period, it began to calibrate its character in relation to the society on the outside. With shift such as this, one can find increasing evidence of an attitude that meant that women indeed may pursue a full-time religious career, but only within a carefully regulated institutional structure that preserved and reinforced the conventionally accepted social standards of male dominance and female subordination.

It cannot be denied that with the founding of the bhikkhunī-saṃgha, the Buddha granted a religious role to women that for a long time to come remained virtually without parallel in the history of the world. However, after his death, some practical considerations appear to have formed the basis of an excuse to speculate about the limitations of the female nature. This kind of mentality became increasingly characteristic of Buddhism as the saṃgha became more institutionalized and male dominated in the first several centuries following the Buddha's death. In contrast to an attitude of parity, which focused on the capability of women to pursue the path, the focus, after the death of the Buddha, shifted from the women themselves, to a rather perceived danger to the integrity of the saṃgha, as it existed, within the broader social harmony. It was felt that women must be protected by some androcentric-patriarchal social structure like the family, and the bhikkhu-saṃgha was ill-suited to that task for the simple reason that monks, by definition, had simply given up such social responsibilities.

Contradictions of the Post-Buddha Period and Their Resolution

Various contradictions that appeared in the post-Mahāparinibbāna saṃgha were sought to be reconciled through the invention of the story of Gotamī Mahāpajāpatī as the first bhikkhunī and her acceptance of the eight restrictive rules. Interestingly, Mahāpajāpatī became bhikkhunī after her husband's death by which time the Buddha had converted many women. Due to her prestige, her name appears to have been included in the mythologized version. I.B. Horner feels that the whole prophecy of the decline of the dhamma after 500 years may have been an addition by monks ([11], p. 105). Now an increasing number of scholars find it difficult to believe that the Buddha whose teachings were based on universality and gender equality would have created rules such as these. The *Vinaya* redactors resolved this contradiction by reestablishing the (*proper*) hierarchy of bhikkhus over bhikkhunīs, thus separating the bhikkhu-saṃgha from the flood of contamination and allowing it to (re)gain its purity. By accepting the authority of the monks, at least nominally, the bhikkhunīs may have gained a more acceptable place in the eyes of the broader society. But long-term consequences of such an arrangement turned out to be disastrous for the bhikkhunī-saṃgha as it was subsequently relegated to a position of second-class status, a constraint that was certain to be reflected in the diminished prestige, educational opportunities, and financial support. Historically speaking, the bhikkhunī-saṃgha went into a steady decline in spite of having secured some degree of acceptability. Given the earlier precedent of accomplished women practitioners among the Buddhists, one might reasonably expect the bhikkhunīs to have maintained a creative religious life in the monasteries despite the increasing androcentric and patriarchal restrictions. Although that may have been the case at least for some centuries after the death of the Buddha, but in direct proportion to the increasing Brāhmaṇization and asceticization of Buddhism, life in the bhikkhunī-saṃgha appears to have become more and more marginalized and, finally, ceased to play any role in the official accounts of the tradition. By the third century C.E., the bhikkhunī-saṃgha in India appears to have virtually disappeared from the official records. The Chinese pilgrims in India, for example, reported that female monasteries existed well into the seventh century C.E. and beyond, yet there is no record of what these women achieved in their practice or what they contributed to the larger Buddhist community. All this would not have been possible without the overt support of the bhikkhu-saṃgha, which had much to lose and little to gain for asserting a place of parity for the bhikkhunīs. For all its adherence to gender parity at the doctrinal level, institutional Buddhism was not able to (or saw no reason to) challenge prevailing attitudes about gender roles in the society. Thus, the initial success of the bhikkhunī-saṃgha in ancient India was followed by decline because people supported bhikkhus more readily than they supported bhikkhunīs ([9], p. 83). There are unmistakable traces of the trends and the elements of lay mentality impressed in Saṃgha. The Saṃgha never aimed at completely isolating itself from the people as it was expected to work for the *bahujanahitāya*. In the *Milindapañha*, for instance, it has been pointed out that monks must make themselves accessible to laypeople and so live in monasteries ([23], p. 212). This monk-and-layman intercourse brought monkhood into such relationship with the life of the laity that it made inevitable the reflection of lay mentality on monk mind. Thus, it is actually quite surprising that the bhikkhunī-saṃgha managed to survive for as long as it did, however, marginally.

Ascetical Misogyny

Ascetical misogyny was the most hostile and negative tenor toward the feminine that one finds in the latest strata of Pāli *Tipiṭaka*. Such an attitude suggested that a woman could neither attain to the highest religious ideals such as nibbāna, arahanthood, bodhisattahood, or Buddhahood nor could she become a Sakka, Māra, or Brahmā ([15], Vol. i, p. 28; [24], Vol. ii, pp. 65–66). A bodhisatta is expected to abandon his female partner ([7], Vol. vi, p. 552). It is interesting to notice that none of the bodhisattas mentioned in the 547 *Jātakas* is a female. Now the feminine came to be perceived as base, closer to nature, conjurer, crackpot, crooked, deceitful, degraded, destructive, elusive, envious, fatuous, feeble-minded, foolish, greedy, imperfect, lustful, mundane, mysterious, prestidigitator, profligate, profane, ravaging, sensual, sinful, timid, treacherous, unbridled, ungrateful, untrustworthy, vile, vulnerable, weak in wisdom, and wicked ([7], Vol. i, pp. 111, 134, 285, 289, Vol. ii, pp. 474, 478, 527, Vol. iv, pp. 124–125, Vol. v, pp. 36, 435, 448, Vol. vi, pp. 17, 43, 339; [15], Vol. ii, p. 61). She came to be equated with a snake in five aspects, i.e., "angry, ill-tempered, deadly poisonous, forked-tongued and betrayer of friends" ([15], Vol. ii, pp. 260–261). The recurrent theme of post-Mahāparinibbāna Buddhism is that they are of easy virtue who end their lives unsatiated and unreplete with "intercourse, adornment, and childbearing" ([7], Vol. ii, p. 342). As a consequence of this kind of mind-set, it was given out that the female must be suppressed, controlled, and conquered by the male. Female sexuality began to be seen as a threat to culture, society, and religion which in turn was used as a rationale for relegating women to a marginal existence.

Rejection of household life by a religion with ascetic ideals basically meant rejection of woman and ancient Indian Buddhism of post-Mahāparinibbāna period came to perceive rejection of woman as an act of religious merit. The stories, images, and ideals frequently became vehicles of misogynist views as womanhood is invariably seen as "a snare of Māra" ([15], Vol. iii, p. 68). Like non-renunciants, transgressors, and novices, bhikkhunīs did not have the right to protest statements uttered during official proceedings or comment upon the behavior of the bhikkhus and, in fact, were completely subordinated to them ([15], Vol. iv, pp. 277–278; [18], Vol. v, p. 52). Women began to be ridiculed and condemned for their *typical womanish* characteristics and attitude ([7], Vol. i, pp. 126, 296, 433, Vol. ii, pp. 127, 329, Vol. iv, pp. 219, 472; [15], Vol. ii, p. 37, Vol. iv, pp. 57, 265; [16], Vol. iv, p. 197). It is not surprising that post-Mahāparinibbāna Buddhist ethos does not consider women as worthy of sitting in a court of justice, capable of embarking on business, good enough to reach the essence of things, mature enough to be good managers of households, or competent and desirable to be heads of social and political institutions ([7], Vol. i, pp. 43, 342, Vol. v, p. 152). This type of vehement, doctrinaire, terrifying logic painfully degraded women and obviously reduced them to a state of marginal existence.

Conclusion

Thus, in the post-Mahāparinibbāna Buddhism, only those women appear to have been accepted into the saṃgha who were either over and above the morality of the society like Emperor Asoka's daughter Saṃghamittā or those who were rootless and free and had already fractured out of the moral moorings of the society. But nevertheless, it offered a chance to some women in whatever condition or circumstance. In an androcentric-patriarchal society, it must have been indeed a tricky situation whereby on the one hand, the bhikkhus and the bhikkhunīs had to maintain sufficient distance from each other to avoid the question of impropriety, and on the other, the saṃgha had to deal with the social unacceptability (indeed unimaginability) of an autonomous group of women not under the direct regulation and control of some male authority. By being formally associated with the monks, the bhikkhunīs were able to enjoy the benefits of leaving the household life without incurring immediate harm. While it is understandable to abhor the attitude and behavior of the society toward women which necessitated such a protection, but it is misplaced to criticize the saṃgha for adopting this particular policy ([2], p. 208). Now women could improve their lot by taking their future into their own hands. It must be remembered that the worst enemies of a woman were and still are the family, marriage, and maternity – where she is exploited by man as a childbearing and child-rearing machine. The fact that Buddhism provided her with the opportunity of not only breaking free of such institutions but also of getting unionized is no mere achievement. It was only under such an environment that a unique text such as the *Therīgāthā* was produced, which should be mentioned whenever the issue of Buddhism and women is considered. This would balance the record. However, Rita M. Gross warns that though the stories of women related in the *Therīgāthā* are highly useful, their utility is also limited. These women are heroines, but they are also tokens in an androcentric and patriarchal past. One needs to know about and celebrate these heroines and role models, but on the other hand, it is important not to overcompensate by making more of them than is justified ([9], p. 118).

Cross-References

▶ Bhikkhunī
▶ Bodhisatta
▶ Dhamma
▶ Jātaka
▶ Khema-uyyāna
▶ Māra
▶ Theravāda
▶ Thera- and Therīgāthā
▶ Tipiṭaka

References

1. Altekar AS (1974) The Position of Women in Hindu Civilization, 3rd edn. Motilal Banarasidass, Delhi
2. Astley I (1992–1993) Book review of Buddhism after patriarchy: a feminist history, analysis, and reconstruction of Buddhism, in studies in Central and East Asian Religions, vol 5/6. Journal of the Seminar for Buddhist Studies, Copenhagen, p. 208
3. Barnes NS (1987) Buddhism. In: Sharma A, Young KK (eds) Women in religion. State University of New York, Albany, pp 105–133
4. Bartholomeusz T (1991) Women under the Bo tree. PhD Dissertation submitted to the University of Virginia
5. Blackstone K (1999) Damming the Dhamma: problems with Bhikkhunīs in the Pāli Vinaya. A paper presented at the Twelfth Conference of the International Association of Buddhist Studies, Lausanne, Switzerland, August 1999
6. Church CD (1975) Temptress, housewife, nun: women's role in early Buddhism. Anima 1:52–58
7. Fausböll V (ed) (1877–1897) The Jātakas, 7 vols. Trübner, London
8. Feer ML (ed) (1884–1898) The Saṃyutta Nikāya, 5 vols. Pali Text Society, London
9. Gross R (1992) Buddhism after patriarchy: a feminine history, analysis, and reconstruction of Buddhism. State University of New York, Albany
10. Hhsken U (1993) Die Legende von der Einrichtung des buddhistischenNonnenordensim Vinaya-Piṭaka der Theravādin. In: Grhnendahl R et al (eds) StudienzurIndologie und Buddhismuskunde. Indica et TibeticaVerlag, Bonn, pp 151–170
11. Horner IB (1930) Women under primitive Buddhism: laywomen and almswomen. Routledge, London
12. Kabilsingh C (1984) A Comparative Study of Bhikkhunī Pātimokkha. Chaukhambha Orientalia, Varanasi
13. Lang K (1986) Lord Death's Snare: gender-related Imagery in the Theragāthā and the Therīgāthā. J Fem Stud Relig 2(1986):63–79
14. Max Muller F (ed) (1966) Sacred Books of the Buddhists. Oxford University Press, Oxford
15. Morris R, Hardy E (trans) (1885–1900) The Aṅguttara Nikāya, 5 vols. Pali Text Society, London
16. Norman HC (ed) (1906) The Commentary on the Dhammapada, ed. H.C. Norman, 4 vols. Pali Text Society, London
17. Norman KR, Alsdorf L (eds) (1966) The Therīgāthā. Pali Text Society, London
18. Oldenberg H (ed) (1879–1883) The Vinaya Piṭakaṃ, 5 vols. Pali Text Society, London
19. Paul D (1979) Women in Buddhism: Images of the Feminine in the Mahāyāna Tradition. University of California Press, Berkeley
20. Rhys Davids TW, Carpenter JE (eds) (1890–1911) The Dīgha Nikāya, 3 vols. Pali Text Society, London
21. Sponberg A (1992) Attitudes toward women and the feminine in early Buddhism. In: Cabezon J (ed) Buddhism, sexuality, and gender. State University of New York Press, Albany, pp 3–36
22. Steinthal P (ed) (1885) The Udānaṃ. Pali Text Society, London
23. Trenckner V (ed) (1880) Milindapañha. Williams and Norgate, London
24. Trenckner V, Chalmers R (eds) (1888–1896) The Majjhima Nikāya, 3 vols. Pali Text Society, London
25. Walters J (1994) A voice from the silence: the Buddha's mother's story. Hist Religions 33/4, pp 358–379
26. Wijayaratna M (1990) Buddhist Monastic Life: According to the Texts of the Theravāda Tradition, tr. C. Grangier & S Collins, Cambridge University Press, London, pp. 158–163
27. Willis J (1985) Nuns and Benefactresses: The Role of Women in the Development of Buddhism. In: Haddad Y, Findly E (eds) Women, Religion, and Social Change. State University of New York Press, Albany, pp 59–85
28. Wilson L (1998) Women in the footsteps of the Buddha: struggle for liberation in the Therīgāthā. Curzon, London
29. Young KK (1987) Introduction. In: Sharma A, Young KK (eds) Women in World Religions. State University of New York, Albany, pp 1–16

World-Array of Flowers *Sūtra*

▶ Gaṇḍavyūha

X

Xuanzang (Hieun-Tsang)

Sau Lin Tong
Department of Cultural and Religious Studies, The Chinese University of Hong Kong, Hong Kong, China

Synonyms

Hieun-Tsang; Hsuan Chwang; Hsüan-Tsang; Hwen Thsang; Shuen Shang; Yuan Chwang; Yuen Chwang

Definition

Xuanzang (600?∼664 A.D.), a renowned Chinese pilgrim to India and the founder of the Faxiang school.

Xuanzang, whose name is written variously, for example, Hsüan-Tsang or Hieun-Tsang, was an eminent monk and a famous pilgrim to India. He was also one of the most prolific Chinese translators and most admired master of Buddhist teachings of his day. Owing to his encompassing mastery of Buddhist exegetical traditions, in China he was honored as *Sanzang Fashi* (Dharma Master of *Tripiṭaka*) ([1], p. 909). In India he received the titles of *Mahāyānadeva* and *Mokṣadeva*.

Xuanzang was born in Henan in 600 A.D. ([2], p. 1), whose surname was Chen and personal name Wei. It is said that he entered a monastery at 13 years of age and was extremely intelligent beyond his age. In 620 A.D. he was fully ordained in Chengdu. Under the guidance of his masters, Xuanzang distinguished himself first in the Vinaya canon, *Tattvasiddhi-śāstra* (in Chinese, *Chengshi Lun, Completion of Truth*), and *Mahāyāna-saṃparigraha-śāstra*, a collection of Mahāyāna *śāstra*s ascribed to Asaṅga. At the early Tang Dynasty in the seventh century, Xuanzang had become a famous figure for his comprehensive knowledge of all the principal Buddhist schools at that time. After having investigating these writings he once more thought of going to Changan, the capital, to inquire from the most celebrated masters concerning some difficulties he had met with in his studies. Subsequently in Changan he did visit the celebrated scholars all around. However, on verifying their doctrine, he discovered that the sacred texts differed much. Worse still, at that time China possessed only half of the Buddhist classics. Therefore, he resolved to travel to the West in order to obtain an authentic interpretation of the Yogācāra school, in particular, the *Yogācārya-bhūmi-śāstra* (in Chinese, *Yujiashidi Lun, The Stages of Yoga Practice*). He presented a petition to the royal court to ask permission of a journey westward, but there was an imperial rescript forbidding his pilgrimage; so in the autumn of 627 A.D. (the first year

K.T.S. Sarao, J.D. Long (eds.), *Buddhism and Jainism*, Encyclopedia of Indian Religions,
DOI 10.1007/978-94-024-0852-2

of Zhenguan or may be the third year of Zhenguan, i.e., 629 A.D., under the reign of Taizong), he resolved to travel alone. He was then 28 years of age.

Xuanzang secretly set out his epochal journey to the West from Changan. He went through Qinzhou (modern Tianshui in Gansu province), Lanzhou, and in the ninth month of 627 A.D. arrived in Liangzhou, or modern Wuwei, which was the last town of importance in the Gansu province. The pilgrim stayed in Liangzhou a month, preparing himself for his journey. While he was there, he preached to monks as well as to traders and merchants the Buddhist message. Nevertheless, the district governor of Liangzhou heard of the monk's journey and urged him to obey the emperor's edict and return to Changan. Fortunately, after Xuanzang's much traveling by night and hiding by day, and enduring many dangers, he was guided to Guazhou, not far from the oasis at Anxi, by two young disciples. From Guazhou he set forth to Hami, where he was invited to meet the king of Turfan, Qu Wentai, a powerful monarch of Chinese descent.

Since the king was a devout Buddhist, Xuanzang determined to see him in Turfan. Unexpectedly, the adamant king, though pious and hospitable, intended to detain the monk by force. Xuanzang stood firm and resisted by undertaking a hunger strike ([3], p. 29). In the end, Xuanzang promised to preach to his subjects in Turfan for a month. He also agreed to stop in Turfan for 3 years on his return journey to China. But this did not happen, for the king died in fright in 640 A.D. as he awaited the arrival of the Chinese armies ([4], p. 21).

After Xuanzang's month-long sojourn in Turfan, the king equipped him in a truly grand style for his pilgrimage, including 24 royal letters to be presented to the 24 different kingdoms on his itinerary, and most importantly, the king's claim to his formidable suzerain, Turkish Khan, for protection of the monk's pilgrimage. Since then, Xuanzang obtained official standing in his journey westward to the land of Buddha.

Xuanzang resumed his journey soon after he left Turfan. He went through Kucha, Aksu, crossed the Tian Shan Mountains, reached Suyab, Samarkand, Balhk, and Kapisa, a kingdom lying to the northwest of India. At long last, traversing the Hindu Kush Range, he arrived in Gandhāra on the western coast of Indus River. After visiting and studying in many parts of India such as Mathurā, Kuśinagara, and Bodhgaya, he reached his ultimate destination: the Nālandā monastery, located in the modern Indian state of Bihar, and a Buddhist center of learning from fifth to twelfth centuries. In or around 631 A.D., Xuanzang was escorted by several monks to the distinguished cloister to pay homage to Śīlabhadra, the head of Nālandā accredited with the title "Treasury of the Righteous Law." Not long afterward, Xuanzang became the venerable master's disciple. Over a period of 15 months, Śīlabhadra expounded on the *Yogācārya-bhūmi-śāstra* no fewer than three times. From him, Xuanzang was able to learn the pure Yogācāra tradition handed down from Asaṅga, Vasubandhu, Dignāga, to Dharmapāla. While at Nālandā, apart from Śīlabhadra's lectures, Xuanzang also attended various courses in Buddhist doctrines, such as the *Abhidharma-nyāyānusāra-śāstra*, and other lectures in grammar, logic, and Sanskrit. His preeminent linguistic skills in mastering the Indian language foreshadowed his later career as a translator of Sanskrit literature into Chinese.

After 5 years' studies at Nālandā, Xuanzang had read and fathomed all the sūtras and śāstras; yet he was not contented with his learning and believed that much still remained to be acquired. In search of the more profound knowledge of Buddhist doctrines, he took an extended tour to the whole continent of India that took several years. In 640 A.D., he returned to Nālandā. He was appointed by Śīlabhadra to give lectures on *Mahāyāna-sajparigraha-śāstra* and other idealist texts. In addition, Xuanzang wrote a 3,000-stanza treatise in Sanskrit to reconcile the divergence within the Yogācāra school. Besides, at Nālandā Xuanzang also became a triumphant critic of three major philosophical systems opposed to Buddhism: the Sāṃkhya, the Vaiśeṣika, and the materialism.

At age 41, Xuanzang had the experience of being sought out and quarreled over by the king of Assam and King Harṣa, the last great Buddhist potentate-patron before the triumph of Islam and

Hinduism. At last, the king of Assam complied. Xuanzang was saluted with royal welcomes and royal escorts to the court of King Harṣa. In one of the meetings at the palace, the king, having perused *The Destruction of Heresy* (in Chinese, *Zhiejian Lun*), a treatise Xuanzang composed at Nālandā, was so impressed that he proposed a grand tournament at Kanyākubja. In 641 A.D., the grand polemic, to which the disciples of all Brahmins, Jains, and heterodox Buddhists were invited, took place in the capital on the Ganges River. During the 18-day debate, in order to protect Xuanzang's life from being threatened by his vicious opponents, the king issued a proclamation that anyone daring to harm the monk would be beheaded and anyone insulting him would have his tongue cut out. As no one dared to refute Xuanzang's teaching during the 18-day period, the king declared him winner of the grand tournament ([4], p. 164).

As soon as the debate was over, Xuanzang was longing to begin his journey home. He sought permission to depart following King Harṣa's sixth Quinquennial Almsgiving. Finally, the king agreed to his departure, and Xuanzang was given a military escort to carry his books and images on horseback. In 644 A.D. he arrived in Khotan. There, he submitted a report to Emperor Taizong of Tang telling that he was now on the way back home. An imperial decree was issued welcoming his arrival by the emperor. In the year of 645 A.D., Xuanzang arrived at Changan and was received with highest honor. He presented his collections of a number of images and paintings, 150 pieces of relics, 520 scrolls of Buddhist sūtras, a total of 657 texts to the court of the Tang Empire ([5], p. 199).

Shortly after Xuanzang returned to Changan, he moved to the Hongfu Monastery and organized a translation workshop, where he devoted the rest of his life to the giant translation project of the Sanskrit works he brought back from the West. Since 645 A.D., with the assistance of over 60 luminary translators, he translated 74 texts in 1,335 volumes in 19 years, until he died in 664 A.D. His translations did not only outnumber his predecessors' works, but also surpassed them in terms of quality ([6], p. 103). Among these, his translations of Abhidharma, Mahayanist sūtras, Yogācāra, and hetuvidyā texts had won for him the greatest credit in dharma transmission. While the translation work was being carried on, Xuanzang lost no time in dictating his *Record of the Western Regions* (in Chinese, *Datang Xiyuji*), an account of his historical observation made during the journey. In 647 A.D., Xuanzang also translated the *Daode Jing* of Laozi into Sanskrit and sent it to India.

While being engaged in his translation project, Xuanzang was not oblivious of training disciples. He trained a number of adherents and taught them the Yogācāra doctrine so as to popularize his own theory on Buddhist studies and to lay the theoretical foundation of the Faxiang school. However, after the passing of Xuanzang and his successor Kuiji, the school swiftly declined.

Xuanzang reached China in 645 A.D., and till his death in 664 A.D., he was engrossed in producing the Chinese translations in all 74 texts. The translations included works like *Abhidharmajñānaprasthānaśāstra*, *Mahāvibhāṣāśāstra*, *Mahāprajñāpāramitāsūtra*, and *Vajrachedikāprajñāpāramitāsūtra*, which covered a wide variety of topics like Hīnayāna Abhidharma, Mahāyāna Vinaya and Abhidharma, Prajñāpāramitāsūtra, Hetuvidyā, Dhāraṇīs, the Yogācāra school, Pure Land series, and non-Buddhist works ([7], p. 279).

Xuanzang was no ordinary pilgrim who came to India to visit Buddhist shrines and return. As a matter of fact, he was a scholar-philosopher whose primary intention was to study the then popular school of Yogācāra or Vijñapti-mātratā and introduce the doctrine to the Chinese believers. He was keen on promoting the faithful transmission of the refined Yogācāra teachings from India and bridging the gap between the Mādhyamika and Yogācāra doctrines. For harmonizing of the disparity between these two schools, he once wrote a work called *On the Harmony of the Schools* (in Chinese, *Huizong Lun*). This writing was greatly appreciated by his teacher Śīlabhadra.

Due to Xuanzang's sophisticated exegesis, the development of Yogācāra thought in China entered a new phase. Xuanzang translated Vasubandhu's *Triṃśikā* and wrote a commentary on it. Furthermore, he summarized the teachings of ten other Yogācāra works in a writing known as *Cheng Weishi Lun* (*Vijñaptimātratāsiddhi*). It had then become a fundamental text of the Faxiang school, a new school of Buddhism propagated by Xuanzang on his return to China. The work is available in Chinese original and in French translation conducted by Poussin.

To the then Chinese Buddhist, there were quite many unusual Yogācāra ideas transmitted by Xuanzang's new school. Probably one of these was the notion of Five Lineages (*pañcagotrāṇi*), containing three categories of determinate *gotras*, namely, *śrāvakayānābhisamaya-gotra*, *pratyekabuddhayānābhi-gotra*, and *tathāgatayānābhi-gotra*, one indeterminate gotra (*aniyataikatara-gotra*), and *a-gotra*. The notion of the last gotra, *a-gotra* (also known as *icchantika*), was said not to possess the capacity to attain Buddhahood. It was this "subversive" idea advocated by the Faxiang school that had met with vehement oppositions from the contemporaries harboring the conventional belief that all sentient beings possess the Buddha-nature, and had ignited the subsequent debate over whether all sentient beings can attain Buddhahood. The debate came to a head when Fabao (c. 627–705 A.D.) launched a frontal attack on the Faxiang position and Huizhao (c. 650–714 A.D.), a leading Faxiang theorist, rose to defend Faxiang's doctrine with a rebuttal of Fabao's criticisms.

With its seemingly awkward theories to Xuanzang's contemporaries, the Faxiang school was too alien to be widely accepted in the Buddhist circle and, thus, speedily languished after Xuanzang and Kuiji's decease. In spite of its premature decline, the doctrine and writings of the Faxiang school were so seminal to the contemporary Buddhist theorists that they spread even abroad. In 653 A.D., a Japanese monk Dosho (629–700 A.D.) went to China to study under Xuanzang for 10 years. He was instructed in meditation by Xuanzang and requested to propagate the doctrine in the East. As expected by his Yogācāra master, Dosho was remembered for being the first transmitter of Hossō (in Chinese, *Faxiang*) teachings to Japan.

In India, Xuanzang is especially well known for his *Datang Xiyuji (Record of the Western Regions)*, where he described the India and Central Asia he saw during his visit, in the seventh century A.D. (around 630–640 A.D.). In this account of his travels, he provided information in all the aspects: geographical, social, religious, cultural, narrational, etc. Although he himself did not attach much importance to this account, it is, through the ages and even for the time being, regarded as the most comprehensive and precious memoir of the India and Central Asia of his time ([8], Foreword, p. xix). In Chinese folklore, the story of Xuanzang's legendary pilgrimage to India is almost a household word, and has become the prototype of the extremely popular Chinese novel *Xiyouji* (*Journey to the West*).

Cross-References

- Dignāga
- Faxian (337–422 C.E.)
- Idealism (Buddhism)
- Kumārajīva
- Mādhyamika
- Pilgrimage (Buddhism)
- Yijing
- Yogācāra

References

1. Buswell RE Jr (2004) Encyclopedia of Buddhism. Macmillan Reference USA/Thomson/Gale, New York
2. Yang T (1988) Xuanzang nian pu. Zhonghua shu ju, Beijing
3. Li, Shaman Hwui (1914) The life of Hiuen-Tsiang. Kegan Paul, Trench, Trübner, London
4. Wriggins SH (2004) The Silk Road journey with Xuanzang. Westview Press, Oxford
5. Fan J (2008) Sūtras translated by Xuanzang and Dunhuang wall paintings. In: Chandra L, Banerjee R (eds) Xuanzang and the Silk Road. Munshiram Manoharlal, New Delhi
6. Su Y, Song Y, Sun Y (2008) Xuanzang chuan san zhong. Shanghai ren min chu ban she, Shanghai
7. Shendge MJ (2008) Xuanzang's contribution to Chinese Buddhism. In: Chandra L, Banerjee R (eds) Xuanzang and the Silk Road. Munshiram Manoharlal, New Delhi
8. Devahuti D (ed) (2001) The unknown Hsüan-Tsang. Oxford University Press, New Delhi

Y

Yakṣa

Angraj Chaudhary
Vipassana Research Institute, Dhammagiri, Igatpuri, Nashik, Maharashtra, India

Synonyms

Demon; Jainism (Yakṣa)

Definition

Yakṣa is a class of non-human beings, some having wrathful temperament and some are benign if they are worshipped and respected.

Yakṣas, their Kinds and their Relationship with Human Beings

The Pali equivalent of Sanskrita Yakṣa is yakkha. Yakkha, according to Malalasekera is 'a class of non-human beings generally described as amanussa [1]. They are mentioned with Devas, Rakkhasas, Dānavas, Gandhabbas, Kinnaras and Mahoragas' [2]. According to Bhikkhu Bodhi, 'The Yakkhas are fierce spirits inhabiting remote areas such as forests, hills, and abandoned caves. They are depicted as of hideous mien and wrathful temperament, but when given offerings and shown respect they become benign and may protect people rather than harm them' ([3], pp. 85–86).

The word 'yaksa' is variously translated into English language. Some translate it as ghost, some as goblin, some as ogre, and some as spook. It is better to keep it as yaksa because a Yakṣa has some characteristics not found in other amanussas (non-humans).

Yakkhas are non-humans and as far as physical power is concerned they are swifter and more powerful than human beings. Therefore, generally human beings are afraid of them. But not all of them are harmful. Some of them do look dreadful but do not cause harm to human beings. Instead, some of them help them as said above. They are kind to men and are interested in their spiritual welfare. They are like angels, who save people from doing unwholesome actions. When people are about to go astray they guide them to be on the right path.

There are many yaksas who are protectors of Dhamma. In the Ambaṭṭha Sutta of the Dīgha Nikāya [4] Yakkha Vajirapaṇī with an iron hammer in his hand hovers in the sky when the dialogue between the Buddha and Ambaṭṭha goes on. When Ambaṭṭha hesitates to answer a question asked by the Buddha Yakkha Vajirapaṇī threatens to kill him if he does not answer his question. It is said in the Aṭṭhakathā by Buddhaghosa that that yakṣa was none other than Sakka himself (na yo vā so vā yakkho, Sakko devarājā ti veditabbo).

Yakkhas are not human beings but they are not gods either. Rhys Davids says that 'they range in

K.T.S. Sarao, J.D. Long (eds.), *Buddhism and Jainism*, Encyclopedia of Indian Religions,
DOI 10.1007/978-94-024-0852-2

appearance immediately above the petas... They correspond to our 'genii' or fairies of the fairy-tales and show all their qualities. In many respects they correspond to Vedic Piśācas, though different in many others and of different origin. Historically they are remnants of an ancient demonology and of considerable folkloristic interest, as in them old animistic beliefs are incorporated and as they represent creatures of the wilds and forests, some of them based on ethnological features' [2].

The word 'yakkha' like the word 'nāga,' is not derogatory. Both are used in good sense. Sakka and the Buddha are called Yakṣas. [5], Vol. I, p. 319; Vol. II, p. 55) Even gods like Kakudha are referred to as Yaksa ([6], Vol. I, p. 65). Four regent kings (Mahārājāno) viz. Kubera, Dhataraṭṭha, Virupakkha and Virūḷhaka are also called Yakṣas. Kubera is called Vessavaṇa. Yakkhas are the followers of Vessavaṇa.as he is their king. (Devo hi manussānaṃ ekaccānaṃ devānañca pūjanīyabhāvato 'yakkho' ti vuccati,. Apica Sakkopi cattāro mahārājānopi, vessavaṇapārisajjāpi purisopi 'yakkho'ti vuccati. VvA, p. 283) They are at his beck and call. Even Janavasabha (King Bimbisara after death was born as a yakṣa called Janavasabha) who is a sotāpanna among yakṣas runs errands for him. The *yakṣiṇīs* fetch water for him.

When it is said he works like a yakṣa and he looks like a yakṣa what is meant is that not only in physical appearance he looks strong and ferocious as his eyes are red but he has greater physical strength than man to work. Yakṣas have striking appearance as a result of former wholesome kammas. "All of them possess supernormal powers; they can transfer themselves at will, to any place, with their abodes, and work miracles, such as assuming any shape at will. An epithet frequently applied to them is *mahiddhika*" [1]. It is because of their supernormal power that they can create palaces in the air within a short time.

Like human beings they are also subject to the law of kamma and have to reap the fruits of past kammas. Because of their unwholesome kammas in the past lives most of them are shy and fear iron and palmyra leaf [1]. It means that if one has a piece of iron with him, yakṣas will not harm him. They will feel shy of going near him.

Vessavaṇa – the king of yakkhas (yakṣas) confesses to the Buddha in the Āṭānāṭiya Sutta where various kinds of yakkhas are mentioned that there are some powerful yakkhas and some others also who are not respectful towards the Buddha and his disciples. Most of the yakkhas do not have faith in him nor do they like his teachings such as abstention from killing, stealing, from sexual misconduct, from telling lies and from strong drink because most of them like to do these things. So when the Buddha's disciples meditate in the forests the Yakkhas disturb and terrify them. Vessavaṇa wanted the Buddha to learn the Āṭānātiya – a protective sutta from him so that his disciples might learn it from him (the Buddha) and protect themselves from their terrible looks and harms caused by the yakkhas.

It is also on record in Pali literature that although in the beginning yakṣas were not favourably inclined towards the Buddha and his teachings as is seen in the Āḷavaka Sutta [6] but after they hear him preach and answer their intelligent and difficult questions they are so changed that they become his devout followers and they devote themselves to the spreading of the teachings of the Buddha. For this purpose they go from one village to another and from one city to another as seen in the Āḷavaka Sutta [7].

'Their cult seems to originate' in the words of RhysDavids 'primarily from the woods and secondarily from the legends of sea-faring merchants' [2].

Yakkhas are called devatā ([8], p. 283; [9], 3.269) or devaputta ([2], p. 99). Māra is also called a yakṣa. (So dummano yakkho – [1], Vol. II, p. 426). An eminent person or a person of great worth is also called a yakkha ([10], p. 41).

All yakṣas are not celestial. Some of them live in the air and some of them live on land. Those living on the earth are either Rukkha devatā or Bhumma devatā because of their abodes in trees or on the land respectively. As a result, those trees are worshipped. Tree worship was very common in ancient India as proved by the anecdote of Sujātā, who offered kheer (rice boiled in milk) to the deity living there in the Banyan tree. E ven now they are worshipped. It is one of the most primitive religions.

Yakkhas, as said above, are both good and bad. Some help mankind, some want to harm them. It is recorded in the Tipitaka that one yaksa seeing Sariputta's shaven head wanted to hit him on his head. The other advised him not to do so. But when he hit him even though forbidden by his friend the earth opened and swallowed him ([11], p. 112).

But there must have been a large number of yaksas who helped people and so they were worshipped by them. In the Mahāparinibbāna Sutta it is recorded that a large number of cetiyas (shrines) were built in honour of different yakkhas in Vesāli where they were worshipped and offered food by the people. When the Buddha recited the Ratana Sutta to rid Vesāli of three dangers he asked all devas and yakkhas present there to have loving- kindness for suffering and troubled human beings as they offered them food day in and day out.

Yaksas have a city of their own. Its name is Āḷakamandā, which is inhabited and protected by yaksas.

In later literature for example in the Jātaka Aṭṭhakathā yaksas have been described as 'degraded to the state of red- eyed cannibal ogres.' Female yakkhinis are more fearful and evil-minded. They eat flesh and blood ([9], 3.444) devour men [9] and eat babies ([9], 4.446) as they are full of spite and vengeance ([12], Vol. I, p. 31).

A clue to the origin of Yakkhas and their functions is found from their names. They get their names from their physical appearance, from the places they live in, from the qualities of their character, from the weapon they keep in their hands and from embodiments of former persons. The name of a yakkha was Khara because he was rough-skinned ([13], Vol. II, p. 34). One was called Khara loma because his hair was rough, the other was called Kharadāthika because he had rough teeth. Sūciloma was called so because he had needle like hair ([13], Vol. I, p. 34), and Silesaloma was called so because he had sticky hair.

Some of them had their names after the place they lived. Āḷavaka got his name because he lived in a forest, Sātāgira was called so because he lived on a pleasant mountain, Kakudha was called so because he lived in a Kakudha tree, Serusaka because he lived in an Acacia tree.

Some yakkhas are named after the weapon they hold in their hands. VajirapaṇI was called so because he had a thunderbolt in his hand.

Some were called Adhamma because they lived unrighteous life and some were called Dhamma because they lived a righteous life.

Māra is called a Yakkha because he tempts. Janavasabha is called so because he is the lord of men [2].

In the Yakkha Saṃyutta of the Saṃyutta Nikāya it is recorded that some Yakkhas meet the Buddha and ask him questions of profound spiritual interest which the Buddha answers. It seems that the yakkhas do not like the Buddha. They are cross with him. When Āḷavaka hears the coming of the Buddha in his palace he is angry and says to the Buddha, 'I will ask you a question, ascetic. If you won't answer me I'll drive you insane or I'll split your heart or I'll grab you by the feet and hurl you across the Ganges' ([3], p. 306). The questions asked are

> What here is man's best treasure
> What practised well brings happiness
> What is really the sweetest of tastes
> How lives the one who they say lives the best.
> *The answers given by the Buddha are*
> Faith is here a man's best treasure
> Dhamma practised well brings happiness
> Truth is really the sweetest of tastes
> One living by wisdom they say lives best.

The Buddha knew how to tame such ferocious Yakkhas. First of all he obeyed Āḷavaka three times but then he showed that he also could be firm. And when the Buddha answered the questions of the Yakkha he (the yakkha) was fully satisfied. He became his disciple and devoted his time spreading the Dhamma.

> So ahaṃ vicarissāmi, gāmā gāmaṃ purā puraṃ/
> Namassamānā saṃbuddhaṃ, dhammassa ca sudhammataṃ//
> I myself will travel about
> From village to village, town to town
> Paying homage to the Enlightened One
> And to the excellence of the Dhamma. ([3], p. 316)

The Buddha tamed Sūciloma also by answering questions that he put to him. Sūciloma asked the Buddha the following question;

What is the source of lust and hatred?
Whence spring discontent, delight and terror?
Having arisen from what do the mind's thoughts
[Toss one around] as boys toss up a crow?
The Buddha gave the following answer:
Lust and hatred have their source here;
From this spring discontent, delight, and terror;
Having arisen from this, the mind's thoughts
[Toss one around] as boys toss up a crow.
Sprung from affection, arisen from oneself
Like the trunk-born shoots of the banyan tree;
Manifold, clinging to sensual pleasures
Like a *maluvā* creeper stretched across the woods.
Those who understand their source
They dispel it—listen,O Yakkha!—
They cross this flood so hard to cross

Uncrossed before, for no renewed existence. ([3], p. 307; [6] Yakkha Saṃyutta). In this Saṃyutta some yakkhinis like Piyankara's mother and Punabbasu's mother are seen hushing their children so that they could listen to the dhamma taught by the Buddha and his disciple Ven Anuruddha. They do not only want to understand a Dhamma-stanza but they want to practice it for their welfare. What does this show? This shows that even the yakkhinis and their children were interested in their welfare and they knew that their welfare is possible only by practicing the teachings of the Buddha.

Cross-References

- ▶ Demon
- ▶ Jainism (Yakṣa)

References

1. Malalasekera GP (1995) Dictionary of Pali Proper Names. Munshiram Manoharlal, New Delhi
2. RhysDavids TW, Stede W (eds) (1975) Pali English Dictionary. First Indian Edition, New Delhi
3. Bhikkhu Bodhi (Tr) (2000) The Connected Discourses of the Buddha. Wisdom Publications, Boston
4. Dīgha Nikāya (1998) (Unless otherwise mentioned all books referred to here are published by Vipassana Research Institute, Dhammagiri)
5. Majjhima Nikāya (Unless otherwise mentioned all books referred to here are published by Vipassana Research Institute, Dhammagiri)
6. Saṃyutta Nikāya (Unless otherwise mentioned all books referred to here are published by Vipassana Research Institute, Dhammagiri)
7. Suttanipāta (Unless otherwise mentioned all books referred to here are published by Vipassana Research Institute, Dhammagiri)
8. Vimānavatthu Aṭṭhakathā (Unless otherwise mentioned all books referred to here are published by Vipassana Research Institute, Dhammagiri)
9. Jātaka Aṭṭhakathā (Unless otherwise mentioned all books referred to here are published by Vipassana Research Institute, Dhammagiri)
10. Saddanītippakaraṇa Dhātumālā, Myānmāra (Unless otherwise mentioned all books referred to here are published by Vipassana Research Institute, Dhammagiri)
11. Udāna (Unless otherwise mentioned all books referred to here are published by Vipassana Research Institute, Dhammagiri)
12. Dhammapada Aṭṭhakathā (Unless otherwise mentioned all books referred to here are published by Vipassana Research Institute, Dhammagiri)
13. Suttanipāta Aṭṭhakathā (Unless otherwise mentioned all books referred to here are published by Vipassana Research Institute, Dhammagiri)
14. Petavatthu Aṭṭhakathā (Unless otherwise mentioned all books referred to here are published by Vipassana Research Institute, Dhammagiri)
15. Theragāthā Aṭṭhakathā (Unless otherwise mentioned all books referred to here are published by Vipassana Research Institute, Dhammagiri)

Yamaka

K. T. S. Sarao
Department of Buddhist Studies, University of Delhi, Delhi, India

Synonyms

The book of double questions; The Pairs-book; The Prakaraṇapada

Definition

It is the sixth book of the Abhidhamma Piṭaka.

The Yamaka is the sixth book of the Abhidhamma Piṭaka of the Theravāda Canon. This text which is very voluminous and extremely difficult to comprehend is meant to remove any misgivings that might still arise after the first five books of the Abhidhamma Piṭaka ([10], p. 166). It is subdivided into ten chapters (*yamaka*), namely, Mūla, Khandha, Āyatana, Dhātu, Sacca, Saṅkhārā, Anusaya, Citta, Dhamma, and Indriya. Each of these chapters deals with a particular topic of Buddhist doctrine. A very complicated method employed in the treatment of these chapters tends to be threefold (see [7], pp. xix–xx; [4]; [2], p. 74):

1. The *Paṇṇattivara (Paññattivāra)* or section delimitating the term and concept, divided into an *Uddesavāra* where only inquiries are stated, and a *Niddesavāra* in which the inquiries are repeated with their many answers
2. The *Pavattivāra* which refers not to procedure generally, but to living processes
3. The *Pariññāvāra* which deals with the extent to which a given individual (i.e., a class of beings) comprehends the category being considered

As the commentary of the Yamaka, the Yamakappakarṇaṭṭhakathā (included in the Pañcappakaraṇaṭṭhakathā), equates the word *yamaka* with *yugala* (a pair or twin), the title of the text may refer either to each of the ten categories so treated or to the entire work ([7], p. xv). The Yamakappakarṇaṭṭhakathā further points out that as to what each pair or twin consists of, this "constitutes a threefold basis: (1) the twin *attha* or double presentation of the matter, namely, by way of a proposition and its converse; (2) the twin textual method of the text, by way of positive and negative statements; and (3) the twin catechetical procedure by positive and negative questions" ([7], p. xv). But C.A.F. Rhys Davids feels that it may be more accurate to see the commentary's threefold basis as (1) reference to the pairs of terms strung together throughout the work, (2) reference to the mode of procedure by way of a proposition and its converse, or (3) reference to the fact that the questioning is so framed ([7], p. xv). According to Frauwallner, the original idea behind the title was that pairs are constituted by the origin of one thing, which conditions the origin of a second one ([1], p. 116). However, C.A.F. Rhys Davids feels that "the most impressive feature, likely to have formed the title to the work, is the dual grouping of question and converse" ([7], p. xvi).

All the *yamakas* are discussed at great length in the text, and possibly all imaginable combinations have been given which is "an excellent example of how the method of Abhidhamma can be expatiated insipidly" ([1], p. 117). B.C. Law ([3], p. 334) has summed up the subject matter of the ten chapters as follows: *The Mūla Yamaka* deals with the nature and roots of the *kusala* and *akusaladhammas*. *The Khandha Yamaka* deals with five *khandhas* (aggregates), e.g., *rūpa*, *vedanā*, *saññā*, *saṃkhāra*, and *viññāna*. *The Āyatana Yamaka* deals with 12 the 12 *āyatanas*, e.g., *cakkhu*, *sota*, *ghāna*, *jihvā*, *kāya*, and *rūpa*. *The Dhātu Yamaka* deals with the 18 *dhātus* or elements. *The Sacca Yamaka* treats of four noble truths. *The Saṃkhāra Yamaka* deals with three *saṃkhāras*. *The Anusaya Yamaka* treats of the *anusayas* (inclinations), e.g., *kāmarāga* (passion for sensual pleasures), *paṭigha* (hatred), *diṭṭhi* (false view), *vicikicchā* (doubt), *māna* (pride), *bhavarāga* (passion for existence), and *avijjā* (ignorance). According to Hinüber, this *yamaka* is possibly a later addition (see [2], p. 74). *The Citta Yamaka* deals with mind and mental states. *The Dhamma Yamaka* deals with kusaladhammā and akusaladhammā. *The Indriya Yamaka* deals with the 22 *indriyas*.

Though the scheme of the work lends itself well to condensation "without sacrifice of substance or of intelligibleness" ([7], p. ix), it is indeed a very lengthy work which even Buddhaghosa found "endless and immeasurable" (*anatam-aparimāṇaṃ*) when expanded or uncondensed, in its 2,000 sections for recitation ([5], p. 9).

It has been suggested that "When first compiled, the work was either orally and mentally registered only, for both teacher and pupil, or it may have been committed to writing only as a scheme of key-words with titles of procedure-*anulomaṃ*, *paṭilomaṃ*, etc. But even when it was committed in full to palm-leaf manuscript, probably only the teacher would refer to this. And for his graduate knowledge it would not matter if the theses were set down very concisely and in digest. Each term would be bodied out with more or less full intension in his mind, and this he could proceed to unfold" ([7], p. x–xi; see also [9], p. 290). According to C.A.F. Rhys Davids, this text "is no fit work for either reading or 'recitation' (*bhānavāra*). It is possible that Buddhaghosa used the word in its first intention, and that paragraphs were read out periodically in vihāras where Abhidhamma was regularly taught; and, indeed, the paragraphs lend themselves admirably to the intoning droning of regular mechanical routine of that kind. But to be an effective educational instrument the Yamaka's only chance is to be used (1) as a work of reference; (2) as a thesaurus of these, from which a teacher may select, and by which he may expound, like a preacher with his 'text'" ([7], p. x; see also [9], p. 290).

Cross-References

▶ Abhidhamma Piṭaka
▶ Avijjā
▶ Buddhaghosa
▶ Citta
▶ Dhamma
▶ Khandha

References

1. Frauwallner E (1971) Abhidbarma-Studien IV. Der Abhidharma der anderenSchulen. Wien Z KundeSüd- (und Ost)asiens 15:103–121
2. von Hinüber O (1996) A handbook of Pāli literature. Walter de Gruyter, Berlin
3. Law BC (1983) A history of Pali literature, reprint, vol 1. Indological Book House, Delhi
4. Malalasekera GP (1937–1938) Yamaka. In: Dictionary of Pāli proper names, 2 vols. Pali Txt Society, London
5. Müller E (ed) (1979) The Atthasālinī: Buddhaghosa's commentary on the Dhammasaṅgṇī, rev edn. Pali Text Society, London
6. Norman KR (1983) A history of Indian literature: Pāli literature, vol VII, Fasc. 2. Otto Harrassowitz, Wiesbaden
7. Rhys Davids CAF, Foly MC, Hunt M (1987) The Yamaka, 2 vols. Pali Text Society, London
8. Rhys Davids CAF (1912) Yamakappakarṇaṭṭhakathā from the Pañcappakarṇaṭṭhakathā. J Pali Text Soc VI:51–107 (1910–1912)
9. Warder AK (2000) Indian Buddhism, 3rd rev edn. Motilal Banarsidass, Delhi
10. Winternitz M (1983) History of Indian literature (trans: Sarma VS), rev edn, vol 2. Motilal Banarsidass, Delhi

Yānas

▶ Vehicles in Buddhism

Yati

▶ Śramaṇa

Yātrā

▶ Travel (Buddhism)

Yijing

Sau Lin Tong
Department of Cultural and Religious Studies, The Chinese University of Hong Kong, Hong Kong, China

Synonyms

I-ching

Definition

Yijing (635–713 A.D.), one of the most influential translators of Indian Buddhist Vinaya texts and an important Chinese pilgrim to travel to India.

Yijing is one of the great Buddhist pilgrims and translators of ancient China to sail a round-trip to India. Unlike another prestigious Chinese pilgrim Xuanzang, little is known of Yijing's family background and his early life, though there are some extant accounts in his own works *Nanhai jigui neifa zhuan* (*An Account of the Dharma Sent Back from the Southern Seas*) and *Datang xiyu qiufa gaoseng zhuan* (*Record of Eminent Monks Who [Traveled to] India in Search of the Dharma During the Tang*), as well as in *Song gaoseng zhuan* (*Records of Eminent Monks in the Song Dynasty*) and other scattered literature. As indicated in these records, Yijing came from a well-to-do family that had produced public officials for several generations. He was born in the ninth year of the Zhenguan era (635 A.D.) during Taizong's reign in Fanyang (modern Zhuoxian in Hebei province), according to his biography in *Song gaoseng zhuan*, or Qizhou (modern Jinan in Shandong province), as cited from his life story in *Kaiyuan shijiaolu* (*Record of the Śākya Teaching of the Kaiyuan Era*) ([1], p. 35). His family name was Zhang. At the age of 7, Yijing was sent to a monastery to the west of Qizhou to receive ordination. There, he not only learned Buddhist discipline and various *sūtras* under two monks, Shanyu and Huixi, but also received tender care from them in his novitiate.

In his 12th year, his beloved teacher Shanyu died. Thereafter Yijing decided to lay aside the study of secular texts and devote himself further to the sacred canon. Yijing recounted that he began to form the intention of traveling to India when he was 18. And it was not until his receiving of full ordination at age 21 that he chose to make the Vinaya his special field of study. Since then for 5 years he diligently occupied himself with research into the Rules of Discipline. He tried very hard to penetrate the meaning of the principal Chinese commentaries on the Vinaya.

At that time there was a milieu encouraging monks to pursue their scholarship by studying around. When Yijing was confident that he had mastered the Vinaya, at the suggestion of Huixi, he moved to Changan with a quest to learn about the Yogācāra school. In 664 A.D., the great Chinese pilgrim Xuanzang's funeral was held in Changan, and no doubt this made a deep impression on Yijing. That explained why he finally resolved to leave for India during his time in Changan. In November of 671 A.D., Yijing embarked on a Persian ship sailing from South China to Malay Islands. After 20 days at sea, he disembarked at Jaya, the capital of Śrīvijaya, on the vast island of Sumatra. The monasteries on Śrīvijaya were the then great centers of Buddhist studies in the seventh century. There Yijing spent almost half a year acquiring the elementary knowledge of Sanskrit.

In the second month of 673 A.D., Yijing eventually reached Tāmralipti (modern Tamluk in West Bengal). In the following year, in the company of his new acquaintance from China, Dachengdeng, and a large merchant caravan, Yijing set out on his pilgrimage to Magadha. They first paid visit to Nālandā, then ascended Mount Gṛdhrakūṭa, viewed the Buddhist relics in Bodhgaya, Kuśinagara, and Mṛgadāva at Varanasi, and mounted Kukkuṭapādagiri near Gaya. Although no definite record as to which other countries and places in India Yijing had journeyed to has been left to us, yet as revealed in the writings of Yijing himself, there were "more than thirty foreign countries" the heroic Chinese pilgrim had traveled across.

After venerating the Buddhist sites, Yijing returned to the Nālandā Monastery and spent 10 years (ca. 675–685 A.D.) living there. At Nālandā he became friends with several other Chinese monks staying in the same monastery, including Xuanzhao, Daolin, Wuxing, and Zhihong, whose biographies are embraced in *Datang xiyu qiufa gaoseng zhuan*. During his years at the celebrated Buddhist University, Yijing not only immersed himself in a copius volume of the Buddhist literature, but also collected an abundant quantity of Sanskrit texts, with an intention to bring them back to his homeland one day or another.

In 685 A.D., Yijing decided to return to his motherland. He took the same sea route by which he traveled westward the very first time to set sail for home. In ca. 687 A.D., Yijing returned to Śrīvijaya and for the last time dwelled in this Southeastern outpost of Buddhist culture. Six years later in 693 A.D., sailing from Śrīvijaya to

Guangzhou, he started off a voyage homeward. He reached Guangzhou in the summer of that year. In the midsummer of 695 A.D., he returned to Loyang. When he arrived, Empress Wu was waiting at the east gate of the city to welcome the famous pilgrim home. He received a grand procession formed by monks and nuns from all the temples in the city, the scale of which was said to exceed the one made to greet Xuanzang nearly half a century ago. By an imperial decree, Yijing was settled in the Foshouji Monastery in Loyang and then moved to the Dafuxian Monastery. Soon after that, at the Empress's summons, he devoted himself completely to the translation projects.

In collaboration with an eminent monk from Khotan, Śikṣānanda, and also two learned Buddhist leaders, Fuli and Fazang, Yijing completed the rendition of the *Avataṃsaka-sūtra* (the *Garland Sūtra*) in 699 A.D. Since 700 A.D., Yijing started to translate Buddhist *sūtras* on his own effort. From 700 to 703 A.D., he rendered 20 Buddhist works in 115 fascicles (*juan*), producing an average up to approximately 40 translated fascicles per year. When Yijing was not occupied with the translation labor, he took time to teach his followers and to lecture on the sacred texts, particularly the Vinaya piṭaka.

In 705 A.D., with the compelled abdication of Empress Wu (also known as *Zetian*, the Celestial Empress), the title of the reigning dynasty was restored to Tang. The Empress's son, Zhongzong, ascended the throne soon afterward. Like his mother, Zhongzong was a zealous patron of Buddhism and provided assistance and funds for the pilgrim's life and works. In 706 A.D., at the command of the new emperor, an official translation bureau which functioned as Yijing's workplace was established in the Dajianfu Monastery in Changan. Between 706 and 712 A.D., in the midst of a series of palace intrigues, Yijing continued his industrious translation and instruction work at the palace with his disciples and colleagues. In 713 A.D., he died at the age of 79 at the translation bureau of the Dajianfu Monastery in Changan. He was subsequently buried in a monastery of the national capital. Being a renowned pilgrim in his time, Yijing's outstanding achievements were reminisced now and then by later generations even after 40 years of his passing. For instance, in 758 A.D., to commemorate his translation of the *Suvarṇaprabhāsottama sūtra* (*The Sutra of Golden Light*), the then Emperor Suzong gave an order to build the Jinguangming Monastery in Changan.

A common goal of the then Chinese pilgrims was to bring back to their native land the Buddhist Sanskrit texts and also some relics. To Yijing, however, there was a more fundamental goal of his pilgrimage. Aiming to save the Chinese monks and nuns from the slackening monastic rules, his pilgrimage to India on a quest for the orthodox Vinaya texts was undertaken as a vital means to regulate and remedy the corrupted Buddhist discipline in China ([2], p. 133). Yijing's translation work in his afterlife attests to this original intention of his pilgrimage. According to the records in *Kaiyuan shijiaolu*, he is credited with translating altogether 56 works in 230 fascicles between years 700 and 711 A.D. Among these scriptures and treatises, 159 fascicles come under the category of the Vinaya texts, particularly of the Sarvāstivāda tradition. In addition, it is worth noting that according to the *Zhenyuan xindi shijiao mulu*, some extra works of 50 fascicles of the Sarvāstivāda Vinaya texts are also registered as Yijing's translations. Apart from the Vinaya texts, his translations of the Yogācāra sūtras and of esoteric Dhāraṇī are equally remarkable.

Yijing won an excellent reputation for being one of the only Chinese pilgrims who successfully visited India, and was devoted to spreading Buddhism by translating a variety of texts brought back from India. Added to this, he also expounded his knowledge of Sanskrit and his travel records in some exegetic works. He was the author of the earliest extant Sanskrit-Chinese Dictionary *Fanyu qianzi wen*. His two most important writings are *Nanhai jigui neifa zhuan* (*An Account of the Dharma Sent Back from the Southern Seas*) and (*Record of Eminent Monks Who [Traveled to] India in Search of the Dharma During the Tang*) ([3], p. 913). Both are precious observation reports made during his journey to India and the South seas.

Following the tradition and methodology as adopted by his predecessors like Hui Jiao, Yijing gave an account of the lives of eminent monks in *Da Tang siyu qiufa gaoseng zhuan*. In this writing, Yijing undertook a course of action to collect and compile the biographies of 56 monks whose contribution to the salvation of the individual and the promotion of universal enlightenment is considered to be indispensable and honorable. His main objective was not only to put down the biographies in praise of the self-sacrificing and adventurous spirit of these eminent monks, but also to establish the immortality of their wonderful accomplishment and brilliant scholarship. Yijing in the preface mentioned the immense hardship and perils the pilgrims encountered during their travel: "However, it was a great luck and fortune (to visit India), but it was extremely difficult and perilous undertaking. None of those who brought leaves, flowers and canopies (to offer), could produce any significant result, and a few of them could complete their mission… When I decided to leave China, I had 50 companions, but finally most of them stayed back" ([4], pp. 2, 3). No doubt Yijing's own experience was as arduous as that of the other Chinese pilgrims.

Yijing's another famous writing, *Nanhai jigui neifa chuan*, is an important document for Indian and Buddhist history. It illustrates the monastic regulations prevalent in India in the eighth century, most of which are based upon the disciplinary rules of the Mūla-Sarvāstivāda School, hence displaying quite a lot of similarities with the content of *Ten Recitations Vinaya*. Needless to say, Yijing had particular admiration for the monastic code observed by the Mūla-Sarvāstivāda School. His ardent impetus for promoting the monastic rules of this Hīnayāna school in China was driven by the commonly seen errors in observance of precepts by the majority of Chinese Buddhist practitioners. Worse still, the Chinese Buddhists were considerably confused by the multifarious explanations of the Vinaya texts. Commentaries on the disciplinary rules delivered by different schools sticked firmly only to his own argument, thus making the existing controversial issues even harder to be resolved. In order to popularize the proper disciplinary code, and salvage the Vinaya from endless arguments, Yijing believed that the sacred writings of the Vinaya originally imported from India had to be made available to the Buddhist population. People had to be given an opportunity to acquire correct knowledge of the monastic rules.

Nanhai jigui neifa chuan is a comprehensive illustration of the Mūla-Sarvāstivāda Vinaya which covers almost every aspect of the monastic rules, examples of which embrace regulations relating to Saṃgha's summer retreat, abstinence, monk's robe, ordination, ways of greeting guests and visitors, application of medicine, washing figures of the Buddha, tonsure, proper procedures of wearing kaṣāya, and so on. Apart from promoting the accurate knowledge of the discipline, Yijing in his work also clarified some misunderstandings spreading through the Buddhist community in China. In Chap. 4, Yijing pointed out the irreversible mistake caused by monks' self-immolation of body parts, whether fingers or genitals ([5], pp. 274–277). Also, a monk's suicide is conceived of as a guilty act only second to *pārājika*, the unpardonable sin that results in expulsion from the order. And as prescribed in the Vinaya canon, looking on or instigating someone to commit suicide or self-destruction constitutes the felonies of *pārājika* and *sthūlātyaya* ([5], pp. 278–281).

Yijing, a prolific translator of Buddhist canon, was during his lifetime honored with the title *sanzang fashi* (Master of the Tripiṭaka). As a pioneer among the then pilgrims, he was one of those to take up the sea voyage between China and India. In this regard, Yijing was rather ahead of time.

Cross-References

- ▶ Abhidharma (Theravāda)
- ▶ Faxian (337–422 C.E.)
- ▶ Kumārajīva
- ▶ Nālandā
- ▶ Pilgrimage (Buddhism)
- ▶ Vinaya
- ▶ Xuanzang (Hieun-Tsang)

References

1. Bangwei W (1996) Tang Gaoseng Yijing Shengping ji qi Zhuzuo Lunkao. Chongqing chubanshe, Chongqing
2. Boulton NE (1986) Early Chinese Buddhist travel records as a literary genre, vol I and II. University Microfilms International, Ann Arbor
3. Buswell RE Jr (2004) Encyclopedia of Buddhism. Macmillan Reference USA/Thomson/Gale, New York
4. I-Ching, Lahiri L (1995, trans and ed.) Chinese monks in India: biography of eminent monks who went to the Western world in search of the law during the great T'ang dynasty. Motilal Banarsidass, Delhi
5. Yijing, Tao H (1998) Nan hai ji gui nei fa zhuan. Fo guang Culture, Taipei

Yoga

▶ Ahiṃsā (Jainism)
▶ Āsavas (Āśravas)
▶ Karma (Jainism)
▶ Mysticism (Buddhism)
▶ Vajrayāna (Buddhism)

Yogācāra

C. D. Sebastian
Department of Humanities and Social Sciences, Indian Institute of Technology Bombay, Mumbai, India

Synonyms

Cittamātra, "consciousness only," and "mind-only"; Vijānavāda; Vijñaptimātra(tā); Yogācāra-Vijñānavāda

Definition

"Yogācāra" literally means the "practice of yoga." The Yogācāra is one of the two most important schools of Mahāyāna Buddhism (the other being the Mādhyamika).

Introduction

Yogācāra means "the practice of yoga" (*yoga* + *ācāra*). This school (founded by Maitreya, systematized by Asaṅga, and philosophically developed by Vasubandhu) emphasized mediation and practice of yoga as fundamental to the realization of *bodhi* (enlightenment). The Yogācāra school is so named, possibly because, this school held that meditation (*samādhi*) and wisdom (*prajñā*) were not widely divergent. Even though its name is Yogācāra ("practice of yoga"), the focal emphasis of the school is primarily philosophical. The Yogācāra is one of the most accepted and significant of the philosophical schools in India connected with Mahāyāna. The Yogācāra teaching is known as the Buddha's third and ultimate "turning of the wheel" (the technical term for Buddha's act of teaching is "turning of the wheel of the doctrine" – *Dharmacakrapravarttana*).

The Yogācāra system is also called Vijñānavada (or the Yogācāra-Vinjñānavāda), and according to this system, the only existent is *vijñāna* (consciousness). As philosophical Yogācāra school advocates the sole reality (only reality) of consciousness – *vijñaptimātratā*, some modern Buddhist scholars call this system as Buddhist "idealism" (contrasting it with the "realism" of early Buddhism and "criticism" of Mādhyamika (see ▶ Mādhyamika). Some of the Indian Buddhist scholars make a distinction between Yogācāra and Vijñānavāda: the school of pure idealism of Maitreya, Asaṅga, and Vasubandhu is called the Yogācāra, while the school of Dignāga and Dharmakīrti (the Buddhist logicians, because though they essentially accept the doctrine of *vijñaptimātratā*, and the unreality of the object, when they enter into logical discussions, they endorse the Sautrāntika standpoint of something being given in knowledge) is termed as Vijñānavāda [1].

The Yogācāra's *vijñaptimātratā*, with the notion of *ālayavijñāna* philosophy, mainly owes a great deal to the great three ācāryas, namely, Asaṅga, Vasubandhu, and their commentator Sthiramati. *Vijñaptimātratā* implies that no objects exist external to consciousness, and there is no phenomenon which is an entity different from the perceiving consciousness. *Ālayavijñāna* would imply a substratum which provides the preservation and activation of the latencies which determine the future of a sentient being.

Origin and Development

The origin of Yogācāra is shrouded with obscurity. Yogācāra, in all probability, emerged as a branch of the Mahāyāna tradition during the first/second century A.D. In Buddhist literature, the word "yogācāra" was probably used for the first time in the *Mahāvatsa Avadāna* which hypothetically dates back to second century B.C. However, in this text the term "yogācāra" carries a different connotation than that of Asaṅga and Vasubandhu. The Yogācāra school developed side by side with the Mādhyamika school. It reached its zenith during the time of Asaṅga and Vasubandhu (fourth century A.D.) who, in fact, developed the characteristic ideas of the Yogācāra school. They synthesized and systematized the Mahāyāna and Śravakayāna ideas. It could be hypothesized that in all probability Asaṅga's Mahīśāsaka upbringing which emphasized meditation must have led him to the practice of yoga which paved way for his Yogācāra school in which consciousness (*citta* or *vijñāna*) occupies the most important place. Asaṅga's writings were rooted mainly in practice while Vasubandhu was a theoretician *par excellence* who gave the Yogācāra its classical form [2].

The development of the philosophical system of Yogācāra could be seen as a complementary improvement of the Mādhyamika thought, and not as a reaction. The conception of *śūnyatā* (*śūnyatā* is translated as "emptiness," "nothingness," and this concept does not imply sheer nothingness, void, or nihilism, but it purports an implication that "nothing exists of its own, in its own right") which is one of the focal themes in the entire career of Buddhist thought, which Nāgārjuna (who lived some two centuries before Asaṅga) and his Mādhyamkika school critically explicated, was misinterpreted as a doctrine of rank nihilism and a "barren skepticism." This was an intellectually disturbed situation within the Buddhist community that Asaṅga inherited, and he, with his Yogācāra interpretation, sought to explain *śūnyatā* in a more positive manner [3]. And with Vasubandhu this system became an important philosophical school of Indian philosophy. The Yogācāra accepted the logic of the Mādhyamika, but disagreed with the Mādhyamika in the interpretation of subjectivity (for the Mādhyamika subjectivity creates unreality, and is itself unreal; whereas for the Yogācāra subjectivity, though basis of unreality, is real) [1]. Thus, Yogācāra advocated the doctrine of "sole reality of consciousness" or "only-consciousness" (*vijñapatimātrata*).

The Yogācāra system, after the formative years and its zenith with Asaṅga and Vasubandhu, nearly had a decline. It had a diversification with the scholastic tendencies of the time. During this period two groups could be traced in the Yogācāra system with different perspective on knowledge: a *sākāra* Yogācāra, claiming that knowledge has a content, or knowledge always has an image of its object, the object of the cognition; and a *nirākāra* Yogācāra, claiming the notion of the nonconceptual, imageless knowledge, following the tradition of Vasubandhu. The representatives of the *sākāra* Yogācāra were the great Buddhist logicians like Dignāga (sixth century A.D.), Dharmakīrti (seventh century A.D.), and Dharmapāla (sixth century A.D.). The *nirākāra Yogācāra* proponents after Vasubandhu were Sthiramati (fifth century A.D.), Kambala (fifth/sixth century A.D.), and Paramārtha (sixth century A.D.) [4].

Main Texts and Literature

The *Saṁdhinirmocana sūtra* might be the earliest *sūtra* of the Yogācāra tradition [5]. The other important *sūtra* is the *Laṅkāvatārasūtra*. The *Saṁdhinirmocana sūtra* speaks of the three *Dharmacakrapravartanas* (turning of the wheel of dharma), and states that the third one is the teaching of the Yogācāra, which is the definite and final teaching of the Buddha. The *Saṁdhinirmocana sūtra* and the *Lankāvatāra sūtra* became the foundational texts for the

Yogācāra school. Together with these works, the *Bodhisattvabhūmi* also gives evidence of Yogācāra's metaphysical speculation contemplated during meditative practice. The other texts of importance are the *Mahāyānasūtrālamkāra*, the *Madhyāntavibhāga*, the *Mahāyānasamgraha* of Asanga, the *Yogācārabhūmiśāstra*, and the two important works of Vasubandhu, namely, the *Trisvabhāvanirdeśa*, the *Vijñaptimātratāsiddhi* (i.e., the *Vimśatikā* and the *Trimśikā*) with the commentary by Sthiramati. In the *Trimśikā*, the concept of *vijñānapariṇāma* first appears denoting the evolution of the *ālayavijñāna* (store consciousness) into *manas* and six empirical senses. There are many other texts like the *Abhisamayālamkāra*, the *Dharmadharmatāvibhāga*, and the *Ratnagotravibhāgo Mahāyānottaratantraśāstra* (*Uttaratantra*) which come in the corpus of Yogācāra Buddhism. The literature of the Yogācāra is enormous and much of it has been preserved in Tibetan and Chinese versions and translations.

Main Doctrines

(a) **Theory of *Dharmas***: The Yogācāra accepted the phenomenology of early Buddhism, the dharma theory. *Dharmas*, in early Buddhism, are the ultimate realities/reality, those building blocks which cannot be reduced into further constituents. *Dharmas* (in plural: *dhammā* or *dharmāḥ*) is an Ābhidharmika technical term, used to denote experiential moments. According to the Yogācāra, there are 100 *dharmas*, and they are merely phenomenal reality. It means that the entire dharma theory in the Yogācāra is based on a pragmatic standpoint, and has nothing to do with a metaphysical status. There is no ontological status to the *dharmas*. Thus, like the Mādhyamika, the Yogācāra also advocated *dharmaśūnyatā*. The *dharmas* are divided into *samskṛta* and *asamskṛta dharmas*, the *dharmas* which are caused and conditioned, and the unconditioned respectively. The *samskṛta dharmas* are further divided into four categories: the *citta dharmas*, the *cetasikas* or *caittas, rūpa dharmas, cittaviprayukta-saṁskāra dharmas*.

(b) ***Vijñāna*(Consciousness)**: According to the Yogācāra, the sole existent is *vijñāna*. But the experience of an infinite phenomenal plurality is a fact. This plurality must be reflected in *vijñāna* itself, and to account for empirical distinctions Yogācāra accepts three kinds of *vijñānas*, namely, *Ālayavijñāna*, *Manovijñāna* (or *kliṣṭamanas*), and *Pravṛttivijñāna*. Though the evolutes of *vijñāna* are infinite, they are in these three stages of evolution. According to Vasubandhu's *Trimśikā* (*kārikā*: 2–8), *ālayavijñāna* is the storehouse from where all other *vijñānas* evolve, first *manovijñāna* (also called as *kliṣṭa-manas* or *kliṣṭa-manovijñāna*) and then *pravṛttivijñānas*. All these *pravṛttivijñānas* appear on the basis of an *ālaya* (storehouse or basis) which is called as *vipāka* (resultant or maturation). The conception of *ālayavijñāna* along with *manovijñāna* (whose primary task seems to be the ego function) and the six empirical consciousness, made up the eightfold consciousness of the Yogācāra [6].

(c) **Ālayavijñāna**: (See ► Ālaya-vijñāna).

(d) **Trisvabhāva**: The concept of *trisvabhāva* was central to the Yogācāra. "*Tri-svabhāva*" means "three natures." The purport of the notion of "*trisvabhāva*" is that the "neutral" reality, which is reduced to moments of causally branded *dhrama*, is the basis out of which all discursive thoughts come to pass. The three natures (*svabhāva*) of the reality are: *parikalpita, paratantra*, and *pariniṣpanna*. The empirical world of never-ending momentariness is called *paratantra-svabhāva* (dependent nature). An unenlightened person, due to his delusion of subject-object duality, sees the reality in an erroneous way, and remains in the bondage of *saṁsāra*. This deceptive and illusory perspective is called *parikalpita-svabhāva* (imagined nature). The cessation of the *parikalpita* is the realization of reality as it is, and it leads to *bodhi* or perfect enlightenment, and it is called *parinispanna-svabhāva* (consummated nature) [4].

The *trisvabhāva* doctrine of the Yogācāra speaks of the three natures of the reality: the utterly false or the erroneous which is imagined (*parikalpita*), the dependent or that which is dependent on causes and conditions (*paratantra*), and the *parinispana*. It is seen in Vasubandhu's *Trisvabhāvanirdeśa* and the *Trimśikā*. The Yogācāra thinkers realized the danger of misconstruing the *trisvabhāva* cognitions as metaphysical entities with ontological foundation. In order to avoid such misconception, the Yogācāra developed the doctrine of three *niḥsvabhāvatā* at a very early stage (*Trimśika*, verses 23–24). In contrast to the *trisvabhāva*, the three *niḥsvabhāvatā* were established on the basis of the teaching of *śūnyatā*.

The doctrine of *trisvabhāva* establishes the *niḥsvabhāvatā* (own nature less ness) of real ity. Vasubandhu states that there is no *svabhāva*, but only *niḥsvabhāvatā* or essence-less-ness (*Triśikā*: 24). For the Yogācāra, what appears is an illusory duality, the real is non-dual consciousness (*parinispanna*). According to the *trisvabhāva* doctrine, the object is unreal, and it is only imagined to exist (*parikalpita*). In the *paratantra svabhāva*, subject-object duality is imposed. It is dependent (*paratatatra*) as it is caused and conditioned. When *paratantra* (the subjective) is purified of the *parikalpita* (the imagined object), it becomes *parinispanna*. In other words, for the Yogācāra, the *parikalpita*, through the assumption of an independent object, leads to the assertion of an equally independent subject, and a thought process is arisen out of it, or dependent on it (*paratantra*), which makes conceptualization: There is a conceptualization of object (*grāhya*) and a metaphysical subject (*grāhaka*). When the conceptualization of the object is ceased, the conceptualization of the subject too falls apart, and what remains then is only the achievement or accomplishment in freedom, which is *parinispanna*, a subject-objectless consciousness. The subject-object dualism is denied at the end, and what remains is only consciousness (*Trimśika*: 26). There is experience of undifferentiated unity which transcends all knowledge, beyond the bifurcation of subject and object, a contentless objectless awareness (*Trimśika*: 28–29). This is the realization of *bodhi* or enlightenment (*Trimśika*: 27–28).

(e) **Āśrayaparāvṛtti**: The conception of *āśrayaparāvṛitti* or *āśrayaparivṛtti* in the Yogācāra texts stands for complete enlightenment. This is a transformation of the basis of ordinary existence into the full enlightenment of Buddha through yogic practice and realization. The impure state, which is the basis (*āśraya*), is transformed into the pure state of *Buddhatva* (Buddhahood) [7]. In *āśrayaparāvṛitti*, the usual flow of the *pravṛttivijñānas* stops, and the six sensory consciousnesses no longer present information. Having stopped discriminating "objects" in the flow of the six consciousnesses, *manas* refrains from all phenomenal data, and attains direct intuitive knowledge and realizes *ālayavijñāna* as its basis. In this realization, *ālayavijñāna* ceases to carry karmic "seeds." This intuition, thus, penetrates into the non-dual consciousness, the Dharma realm which is ultimate reality, so that everything is seen as "consciousness only" [2]. *Āśrayaparāvṛtti* is the disappearance of the unreal object, where there is no subject-object duality, and the realization of *Tathatā* which is nothing but liberation. *Saṁsāra* is nothing but an imagination of empirical forms by forgetting the essential nature of consciousness, the subject-object-lessness of its nature (*parinispanna*). When unreality of object is realized, the subject dimension also disappears and consciousness remains in consciousness itself. Consequently, when the imaginary phenomena are ceased, and realizing that all this is only imagination, one attains *bodhi* or enlightenment. The *Mahāyānasūtralamkāra* and its commentary describe Buddhahood as *āś rayaparāvṛtti*.

(f) **Trikāya doctrine**: The doctrine of *trikāya* (see ▶ Tri-kāya) is one of the most important doctrines in the entire Mahāyāna tradition [8], and the Yogācāra accepted the traditional doctrine. This doctrine explains the three bodies of Buddha, namely, *dharmakāya, sambhogakāya*, and *nirmānakāya*. From early times of Buddhism, there was a formulation of theories of two Buddha bodies: a body of form or maturation (*rūpakāya* and *vipākakāya*), referring to the body assumed by a Buddha in the phenomenal world and a body of Dharma (*dharmakāya*), the sum total of the Buddha's Dharma (doctrine). There was another interpretation of this body of Dharma as the supra-mundane state into which a Buddha goes after entering final *nirvāna* [9]. The Sarvāstivāda conception of the two bodies of Buddha was a more developed Buddhology: *rūpakāya* with 32 major and 80 minor marks and *dharmakāya* with 18 special powers and attributes (*āvennika dharmas*) [10]. This speculation of the early followers of Buddha paved way for the formulation of the *trikāyā* doctrine which the Yogācāra systematically theorized.

The *trikāya* doctrine presents the eternal nature of the Buddha, as he is revealed in a variety of ways according to the levels of individuals' spiritual development. This doctrine is a manifestation of an advanced Buddhology. The *trikāya* doctrine explains the three facets of the holy in Buddhism. *Dharmakāya* could be realized only by the Buddhas, *Sambhogakāya* by the great Bodhisattvas, and *Nirmāṇakāya* by all sentient beings. The *Saṁdhinirmocana sūtra* is, perhaps, the first Yogācāra text to explain *dharmakāya*, and the *Yogācārabhūmiśāstra* often quotes from the *Saṁdhinirmocana sūtra* while discussing the concept of *dharmakāya*. The *Mahāyānasūtrālankāra* perceives the three bodies as functions of the pure dharma realm (*dharmadhātu-viśuddha*), while the *Mahāyānasaṁgraha* regards that Buddhahood as a whole is *dharmakāya* which performs three functions relating to three categories of people.

The concept of Tathāgata (see ▶ Tathāgata) is constituted by different metaphysical principles, and this speculation is clearly seen in the *Trikāya* doctrine. The *Trikāya* doctrine explains the role of Tathāgata, who is not in the status of god as in other religions, as Tathāgata is the impersonation of truth itself who acts as an ordinary person in order to instill confidence in others to seek for enlightenment. There is a difference between these three *kāyas*, and hence, Asaṅga lists eight reasons for the existence of the *nirmāṇakāya* in his *Mahāyānasaṁgraha* and he gives six reasons why the Buddhas do not remain eternally in their *nirmāṇakāya* [11].

Yogācāra Practice

The Yogācāra literally is the practice of yoga. And the Yogācāra system has a spiritual discipline to follow. This spiritual discipline comprises of the six *pāramitās* (see ▶ Pāramitā) and ten *bhūmis* which a Bodhisattva practices in his career (see ▶ Bodhisattva). Various stages of practice have been discussed in the Yogācāra texts. The *Abhisamayālaṁkāra* and the *Mahāyānasūtrālaṁkāra* are some of the important texts which mention the details on spiritual practice [12].

Sambhāramārga: This is the first stage, which is called as the "path of accumulating merit." There are two kinds of obscurations (defilements) which one has to get rid off for a spiritual journey, namely, *kleśāvaraṇa* (moral defilements) and *jñeyāvaraṇa* (ignorance). These two obscurations could be removed by the accumulation of merit (*puṇya-saṁbhāra*) and the accumulation of wisdom (*jñāna-saṁbhāra*). In this initial stage, one strives to accumulate merit and wisdom.

Prayogamārga: The next stage is the "path of training" (*prayogamārga*) where a Bodhisattva, after accumulating merit and wisdom, is in a state to know the real nature of things. In this stage, a Bodhisattva undertakes intense cultivation of wisdom (*prajñā*), realizing the subject-object duality is unreal. Here even the reality of consciousness too ceases, and he achieves a higher state of *samādhi*.

Darśanamārga: *Darśanamārga* is the "path of vision" where a Bodhisattva has the intuition of the highest reality. Here he attains *āśrayaparāvṛtti* and *bodhi* and enters into the first *bhūmi* of Bodhisattva career.

Bhāvanāmārga: This is the last and final stage which is called as the "path of concentration." In this stage, a Bodhisattva enters into the rest of the *bhūmis* of the Bodhisattva career. This is the highest stage. In this stage, one attains complete *prājñā* and *bodhi*.

Yogācāra – Mādhyamika (or Yogācāra – Svātantrika)

In India, the period between the seventh to ninth centuries was a time of the Mādhyamika writers, and a slow decline of Yogācāra. Śāntarakṣita, Kamalaśīla, and Haribhadra criticized the Yogācāra by accepting the key conceptions of Yogācāra as useful intermediary understanding for gradual realization of the ultimate truth. For this reason, these scholars are classified by Tibetan scholars as Yogācāra-Mādhyamika. These Mādhyamika scholars appropriated Yogācāra standpoint of the conceptual construction of duality, the bodhisattva path, stages of meditation, and *trikāya* doctrine. Śāntarakṣita adopted the Yogācāra analysis of cognitive subject-object duality which is, according to the Yogācāra, is a mere conceptual construct. In his system, the Yogācāra theory of non-duality formed a valuable step to the realization of the *paramārtha satya* (ultimate truth) [13].

Yogācāra Mādhyamika is also known as Yogācāra Svātantrika. In Tibetan tradition, there are two main interpretations of the Mādhyamika (namely, Svātantrika by Bhāvaviveka and Prāsaṅgika by Buddhapālita and Candrakīrti). Bhāvaviveka's Svātantrika Mādhyamika is known as Sautrāntika-Svātantrika and a second branch of Svātantrika is known as Yogācāra-Svātantrika. Vimuktisena (c. 500 A.D.) and Śāntarakṣita (eighth century) are the main ācāryas of this tradition. The Yogācāra-Svātantrika asserts like the Yogācāra that there is a nonexistence of external objects, and there is a *nihsvabhāvatā* of phenomena. They do not hold the conception of *ālayavijñāna* and *kliṣṭamanas* [5].

Yogacāra and Mādhyamika

The Mādhyamika and the Yogācāra had their philosophical differences, but they both had *Buddhatva* (Buddhahood) as their goal. The Yogācāra is nothing but a continuation of the Mahāyāna tradition, initiated by the Mādhyamika. The Mādhyamika and the Yogācāra are not opposed to each other, for both the schools acknowledged the same fundamental tenets. There is no total rejection of the doctrine of *śūnyatā*, but only a modification of it. From the Mādhyamika, the Yogācāra adopted the theory of the relativity and consequent unreality (*śūnyatā-niḥsvabhāvatā*) of all individual existence, of all plurality, with the difference that they brought in different degrees of this unreality [14]. The basic ideas of the Mādhyamika were accepted by the Yogācāra, but there was a reaction against the extremism and unqualified negation of phenomena [15]. The Yogācāra sought to steer a middle course between the extremes reached by the Mādhyamika that "all is *śūnya*," and the Ābhidharmika who endowed the object with a reality of its own. The Yogācāra has got two contentions: firstly, *vijñāna* is real. It is not apparent and unreal. Secondly, *vijñāna* alone is real, and not the object. The first is against the Mādhyamika, for whom both the knowing consciousness and the object known are relative to each other, and therefore, nothing in themselves. They are *śūnya*. The second is against the realist like the Ābhidharmika, who accepts the object as real, on par with *vijñāna*. Both are extreme positions, and the Yogācāra maintains a middle position between them.

Mādhyamika and Yogācāra preserve the Middle Way. However, the Yogācāra criticized the Mādhyamika for their strong negativism of saying everything as *śūnya*, but the Mādhyamika criticized the Yogācāra as a form of substantialism by holding the *vijñaptimātratā* theory. The Mādhyamika was more analytical and dialectical in his approach and emphasized *prajñā*, while the Yogācāra emphasized *prajñā* in *samādhi* and the withdrawal of mind from sensory phenomena. For the Mādhyamika, the phenomena were empty, while for the Yogācāra the phenomena were mental constructions [2].

Yogācāra Idealism and Ontology

The classic Yogācāra texts (in India) suggest that Yogācāra had developed a transcendent approach without ontology. It was transcendent because the entire thinking process was to be discarded ultimately, and thereby an extraconceptual experience was reached beyond the notions of self and the other. Nothing existed outside consciousness and world was not created by mind, but only a projected mistaken identity. The conditions were cognitive, and not metaphysical, and correct cognition will remove the obstacles of perceiving it in the right manner. But Chinese schools of Yogācāra shifted toward ontology.

In the twentieth century, Yogācāra Buddhist scholarship had a metaphysical reading of Yogācāra. In modern India, we find an idealistic reading of the Yogācāra especially with scholars like A. K. Chateejee and P. T. Raju. Western scholars like Sylvian Lévi, Louis de la Vallée Poussin, Fyodor Ippolitovich Stcherbatsky, and others followed an idealist reading of the Yogācāra. The Chinese and the Japanese understanding was heavily influenced by the ontological reading which had prevailed in East Asia for a millennium. In modern times, Yogācāra was therefore understood mostly as a form of ontology. Since ontology was challenged in the West in modern times, in East Asia too there was a challenge in recent times to divest Yogācāra of the ontological reading. More recently some scholars have presented Yogācāra as similar to the Western thought of phenomenology.

According to the Yogācāra, individual ideas were unreal, since they were merged in the unique reality (*pariniṣpanna*) of the absolute. The appearance is unreal. The Yogācāra, thus, advocates the pure-consciousness (*vijñapti-mātratā*) that is devoid of duality (*dvayaśūnyatā*). The philosophical system of the Yogācāra is deeply oriented to idealistic and spiritualist notion regarding the view on a person's identity [16]. According to the idealistic interpreters, the Yogācāra is not only mere idealism, but it is also absolutism [1, 17]. They argue that absolutism is the logical culmination of idealism. The Absolute is a non-dual consciousness; it is *śūnya* – devoid of duality. It is nothing empirical, being free from all determinations. It is eternal, as it is beyond the succession of forms of consciousness (*Trimśikā*: 29–30). When these forms have all subsided, all change in the consciousness lapses, and what remains is only consciousness (*sarva-kālam tathābhāvāt saiva vijñaptimātratā* – *Trimśikā*: 25).

Cross-References

- ▶ Ālaya-vijñāna
- ▶ Asaṅga
- ▶ Mahāyāna
- ▶ Tri-kāya
- ▶ Vasubandhu
- ▶ Vijñāna
- ▶ Vijñānavāda

References

1. Chatterjee AK (1999) The Yogācāra idealism, new edn. Motilal Banarsidass, New Delhi
2. Harvey P (1990) An introduction to Buddhism: teaching, history and practices. Cambridge University Press, Cambridge
3. Willis JD (1979) The Yogācāra school of the Mahāyāna. In: Willis JD (tr) (ed) On knowing reality: the Tattvārtha chapter of Asaṅga's Bodhisattvabhūmi. Columbia University Press, New York
4. Boquist A (1993) Trisvabhāva: a study of the development of the three-nature-theory in Yogācāra Buddhism, vol 8, Lund Studies in African and Asian Religions. Department of History of Religions, University of Lund, Lund Sweden
5. Williams P (2009) Mahāyāna Buddhism: the doctrinal foundations, 2nd edn. Routledge, London/New York
6. Schmithausen L (2007) Ālayaviñāna: on the origin and the early development of a central concept of Yogācāra philosophy: reprint with Addenda and Corrigenda. International Institute for Buddhist Studies of the International College for Postgraduate Buddhist Studies, Tokyo
7. Makransky JJ (1997) Buddhahood embodied: sources of controversy in India and Tibet. State University of New York Press, Albany

8. Dutt N (1973) Mahāyāna Buddhism. Firma K. L. Mukhopadhyay, Calcutta, pp 143–177
9. Snellgrove D (2003) Indo-Tibetan Buddhism: Indian Buddhists and their Tibetan successors. Shambhala, Boston
10. Xing G (2005) The concept of Buddha: its evolution from early Buddhism to the trikāya theory. RoutledgeCurzon, London/New York
11. Griffiths P et al (1989) The realm of awakening: a translation and study of the tenth chapter of Asaṅga's Mahāyānasamgraha. Oxford University Press, New York, pp 251–263
12. Chatterjee AK (1999) The Yogācāra idealism, new edn. Motilal Banarsidass, New Delhi, pp 157–168
13. Makransky JJ (1997) Buddhahood embodied: sources of controversy in India and Tibet. State University of New York Press, Albany, pp 211–218
14. Stcherbatsky T (1996) The conception of Buddhist Nirvana, 2nd revised edn. Motilal Banarsidass, Delhi
15. Murti TRV (1998) The central philosophy of Buddhism. HarperCollins, New Delhi
16. Nagao GM (1992) Mādhyamika and Yogācāra: a study of Mahāyāna philosophies. Kawamura L S (ed and tr). Srisatuguru, Delhi
17. Dasgupta S (1962) Indian idealism. Cambridge University Press, London

Yogācāra-Vijñānavāda

► Vijñānavāda
► Yogācāra

Yuan Chwang

► Xuanzang (Hieun-Tsang)

Yuen Chwang

► Xuanzang (Hieun-Tsang)

Z

Zen

Chapla Verma
Department of Philosophy and Religion,
American Public University, Charles Town, WV,
USA

Definition

Zen is Japanese Buddhism, associated with the Mahayana school. It originated in China and was known as Ch'an. Meditation is an essential element of Zen Buddhism, it argues enlightenment does not depend on conventional knowledge.

Zen Buddhism is a school of Mahāyāna Buddhism originated in China and moved to Japan through Korea. This form of Buddhism is known as Ch'an in China, where it became influenced by Taoism, and Chinese people added their practical approach to Buddhism as well. These elements became integral part of Ch'an.

The first Zen teaching is accredited to Buddha. In front of a big assembly of people, Buddha was expected to give a lecture; he did not say even a word. Instead, he offered a flower to Mahākāśyapa, who understood the esoteric meaning of this gesture and accepted the flower with a smile [1]. Boddhidharma is considered the first patriarch of Ch'an Buddhism. He was the third son of a king from South India. He came to Southern China sometime after 500 C.E. The essence of Boddhidharma's teachings is expressed in this poem:

> Without relying on words and writings'
> A special transmission outside the scriptures;
> Pointing directly to the human mind,
> See your own nature and become Budhda [2].

He is mentioned as the first patriarch of Zen in Chinese Zen history known as "The Records of the Spread of the Lamp" written by Li-Tsun-hsü in 1029 and in the "The Accounts of the Orthodox Transmission of the Dharma" written by Ch'i-sung in 1064 [1]. After coming to China, Boddhidharma had an interesting encounter with emperor Wu of Liang. At that time, Buddhism was popular in China but the Ch'an form of Buddhism was neither known nor practiced. Emperor Wu invited Boddhidharma to his court and told him about his accomplishments. He had funded many temple constructions and copies of scriptures were made under his rule. He asked Boddhidharma what was his merit. To this Boddhidharma replied he had no merit at all. Boddhidharma's indication toward self-effort and cultivation of Buddhist understanding was not understood by the emperor.

Boddhidharma was asked to leave the palace and for the next 9 years he did meditation facing a wall in a cave [1]. This practice of doing meditation facing a wall still exists in Sōtō Zen school. It was after 200 years that Boddhidharma's

K.T.S. Sarao, J.D. Long (eds.), *Buddhism and Jainism*, Encyclopedia of Indian Religions,
DOI 10.1007/978-94-024-0852-2

philosophical thought came to be known as Ch'an Buddhism. The word Ch'an means "dhyāna" in Sanskrit or meditation.

After Boddhidharma, Hui-k'ê became the second patriarch (from 486 to 593) of Ch'an. The third patriarch was Sêng-ts'an (died 606), and the fourth patriarch in Ch'an Buddhism was Tao-hsin (580–651). Hung-jên (605–675) became the fifth patriarch. Hui-nêng (637–713) was the sixth patriarch [1]. Hui- nêng became famous for his profound understanding of dharma; he presented this understanding in a poem:

> Enlightenment is not a tree.
> The bright mirror has no stand;
> Originally there is no one thing-
> What place could there be for dust? [2]

Hui-nêng was either illiterate or at least not well educated in the conventional sense. Therefore, by this narrative, Ch'an Buddhism indicates enlightenment does not depend on conventional knowledge.

Meditation

Sitting meditation leads to enlightenment, also known as Satori. It is known as anuttara-samyaksaṁbodhi in Sanskrit [1]. In Ch'an Buddhism, it was believed that all human beings possess the Buddha nature or enlightened mind. Therefore, distinction of deluded mind and enlightened mind is itself an obstruction in progress [3].

Enlightenment is recognition of this mind which could not be expressed through words. It is called a breakthrough of consciousness from the world of dualism to absolute oneness. Zazen is an instrument which leads a person to such insight. In this state, mental dualism and all obstructions are removed from mind. Certain methods are used to help practitioners reach this state.

Koans are used in meditation practice; these are questions which have no logical answers and should be intuited upon. Some elementary koans are as follows: "What was your face before your parents were born?" "What is the sound of one hand clapping?" It is argued that by using koans one can look into their own nature. A state where consciousness is deprived of its habitual way of thinking and pure oneness is reached.

Sŏn (Korean Zen Buddhism)

Prior to Silla dynasty, the first attempt to bring Ch'an school of Buddhism was made. A Korean monk, Pŏmnang, studied under the fourth patriarch of Ch'an Tao-hsin. After his return from China, he tried to establish this school in Korea. Later in the tenth century, the Nine Mountains Sŏn School of Buddhism was founded. Seven schools out of these came from the lineage of the Chinese patriarch Ma-tzu [4].

Sŏn Buddhism was founded on the concept that for awakening one must move away from worldly concerns and focus on practice. Sŏn tradition emphasized on meditation and sudden awakening.

Zen Buddhism is a Japanese form of Buddhism and it has three major schools.

Rinzai Zen

At the time of prince Shōtoku, Zen Buddhism was first brought to Japan but it did not take roots then. In Kamakura period, Eisai who was a Tendai priest traveled to China twice. On his second visit to China in 1187, he studied Lin-chi school of Ch'an Buddhism; after receiving *inka* to teach Zen, he came back to Japan in 1191 and founded first Rinzai Zen temple Shōfuku-ji. This is considered the beginning of Rinzai Zen in Japan. Rinzai Zen believes in sudden enlightenment.

Another important teacher of this school is Enni Ben'en (1202–1280); he studied in China and on his return he founded Tofukuji in Kyoto. In this school, Zen meditation is practiced diligently and *koans* are used in the practice [4].

Sōtō Zen

In Kamakura period, Dōgen (1200–1253) founded the Sōtō school of Zen Buddhism in Japan. He was ordained at an early age; he was trained by Myōzen (1185–1225) and went to China and became a disciple of Ts'ao-tung. After coming back to Japan, he founded Eihei-ji temple in Fukui. Dōgen did recognize the value of koan practice, but he emphasized on *Shikan-taza*, just sitting. He wrote a famous text, Shōbōgenzō. Sōtō Zen believes in gradual enlightenment. The second important teacher is the fourth patriarch, Keizan

Jokin (1268–1325); he simplified Sōtō practice and Sōtō priests became involved in social issues. This attempt made Sōtō Zen popular among common people. Currently Sōtō Zen is the largest Buddhist organization in Japan [4].

Ōbaku Zen

Ōbaku Zen developed due to schism which arose within Rinzai Zen. This school includes Pure Land elements in Rinzai Zen practice. Yin-Yüan (1592–1673), who studied in China, came to Japan in 1654 and built Mampuku-ji; he also called this site Ōbaku-san after the region in China he belonged to. This became the third school of Zen. Yin-Yüan founded 24 Ōbaku monasteries. His successor, Mu-an, administered the physical growth of the sect. Ōbaku school is considered an independent school and now has about 500 affiliated temples. The first generation of monks who converted to Ōbaku Zen came from Myōshin-ji, a Rinzai Zen temple. It received patronage from Tokugawa shogunate. The earlier adherents of Ōbaku Zen consider this to be the "true lineage of Lin Chi Ch'an." It is designated an independent sect now; the practitioners acknowledge the historical and philosophical similarities with Rinzai [5].

Including these three schools, Japanese Zen Buddhism encountered major changes after early Meiji era. The changes added new financial burdens on priesthood. The change in monastic code resulted in acceptance of marriage among Buddhist priests. This brought major changes in the functioning of the temple system. Due to the married status of priests, a concern toward passing on temples from father to son became an important issue for priests, which previously did not exist.

Currently Zen in Japan is also known as Funeral Zen, due to its emphasis on performing funeral rites. Though this description is limiting in itself, still the funerals and memorial services play a very important role in a Zen Buddhist's life. The skillful means provided by Zen priest are looked at as important and practical ways for cross over [6].

Zen Buddhist ideas are reflected in tea ceremony, flower arrangement, etc. At one point in Japanese history, Samurai's training incorporated Zen ideas. Laṅkāvatāra Sūtra, Diamond Sūtra, Platform Sūtra, and Lotus Sūtra are some of the important Mahayana sūtras used in Zen Buddhism.

Zen Buddhism in the USA

Zen Buddhism came to Hawaii with Japanese laborers brought to work in sugar plantations. In order to provide Japanese national education to the children of Japanese immigrant who were in Hawaii on a temporary basis, the first Japanese schools were established in the 1890s. The Japanese parents wanted their children to get Buddhist teaching too. The Japanese language teachers in these schools were Buddhist priests. This is considered the beginning of Buddhism in Hawaii [7].

Currently both Rinzai and Sōtō school of Buddhism have representation in Hawaii, and they have celebrated their centennial year in Hawaii, though Hawaii became part of the Union in 1959.

The second major event in the history of Zen Buddhism is World Parliament of Religions in Chicago in 1893, which brought Zen Buddhist speakers to mainland USA. Soyen Shaku's talk at the parliament and later, DT. Suzuki's writings about Zen Buddhism made Zen accessible to American public. In 1905, Soyen Shaku moved to San Francisco to teach Zen in the USA [8].

Buddhism gradually became popular in the Bay area and temples cropped up first in rented accommodations and later bought their own temple land. After the attack on Pearl Harbor on December 7, 1941, all Japanese in the USA were under suspicion. In Hawaii, Japanese language teachers/priests were sent to internment camps. During this period, the priest families and the Japanese community took care of temples. Therefore, the development of Buddhism witnessed minor obstructions compared to the mainland USA. Here all people of Japanese origin were sent to internment camps. Zen temples became a place for storage of goods left behind by Japanese Americans. These temples were looted and property was damaged. This had its toll on development and spread of Zen Buddhism in mainland USA.

On May 23, 1959, with arrival of Shunryu Suzuki in the Bay area, another chapter of Zen Buddhism began. He came as a head priest in Soko-ji, a Sōtō Zen temple in the bay area. In a short span of 12 years of teaching life, he became a popular teacher of Zen Buddhism in the USA (he passed away in 1971) [9].

Soon Zen centers and temples of both Sōtō and Rinzai Zen were built. Among these, Green Gulch Farm Center, Tassajara Zen Mountain Center, and Mount Baldy Zen center are the most prominent ones. Zen in the USA has witnessed two major changes. In Japan Zen Buddhism is male dominated. Temples are inherited by the eldest son or by the son-in-law of the priest. The number of nuns is meager compared to monks. Women play a secondary role in decision-making roles in temple administration. Monasteries and nunneries are kept separate. In the USA, more than 50% of practitioners are women. They practice and are ordained in the same centers as their male counterparts. Many women have been abbesses of Zen centers, like Blanche Hartman, Linda Ruth Cutts, and Wendy Egyoku Nakao, to name a few.

Cross-References

▶ Bodhidharma
▶ Buddhist History
▶ Mahāyāna
▶ Prajñāpāramitā
▶ Śūnyatā

References

1. Suzuki DT (1927) Essays in Zen Buddhism, 1st series. Luzac, London
2. Addiss S, Lombardo S, Roitman J (eds) (2008) Zen source book: traditional documents from China, Korea, and Japan. Hackett, Indianapolis
3. Schlütter M (2008) How Zen became Zen: the dispute over enlightenment and formation of Chan Buddhism in Song–Dynasty China. Kuroda Institute, University of Hawaii, Honolulu
4. Mitchell DW (2002) Buddhism: introducing the Buddhist experience. Oxford University Press, New York
5. Baroni HJ (2000) Obaku Zen: the emergence of the third sect of Zen in Tokugawa Japan. University of Hawaii Press, Honolulu
6. Borup J (2008) Japanese Rinzai Zen Buddhism: Myōshinji, a living religion. Brill, Leiden
7. Williams DR, Moriya T (eds) (2010) Issei Buddhism in the Americas. University of Illinois Press, Urbana
8. Fields R (1992) How the swans came to the lake: a narrative history of Buddhism in America, 3rd edn. Shambhala, Boston
9. Chadwick D (1999) Crooked cucumber: the life and Zen teachings of Shunryu Suzuki. Broadway Books, New York

Zhenyan

▶ Vajrayāna (Buddhism)

Zhi ba lha

▶ Śāntideva

List of Entries

K.T.S. Sarao, J.D. Long (eds.), *Buddhism and Jainism*, Encyclopedia of Indian Religions,
DOI 10.1007/978-94-024-0852-2

Printed by Printforce, the Netherlands